FOURTH EDITION

LITERATURE
THE HUMAN EXPERIENCE

FOURTH EDITION

LITERATURE
THE HUMAN EXPERIENCE

RICHARD ABCARIAN AND MARVIN KLOTZ, EDITORS

California State University, Northridge

ST. MARTIN'S PRESS

New York

Library of Congress Catalog Card Number: 85-61241
Manufactured in the United States of America.

09876
fedcb

For information, write:
St. Martin's Press, Inc.
175 Fifth Avenue
New York, NY 10010

art research: June Lundborg

ISBN: 0-312-48799-1

ACKNOWLEDGMENTS

SAMUEL ALLEN: "A Moment Please" by Samuel Allen. © 1962 Samuel Allen. Reprinted by permission.

ATHENEUM: "For the Anniversary of My Death" from W. S. Merwin, *The Lice*. Copyright © 1967 by W. S. Merwin. (N.Y.: Atheneum, 1967). Reprinted with permission of Atheneum Publishers. "Grandmother Watching at Her Window" from W. S. Merwin, *The First Four Books of Poems*. Copyright © 1960, 1975 by W. S. Merwin (N.Y.: Atheneum, 1975). Reprinted by permission of Atheneum Publishers.

"The Dover Bitch" from *The Hard Hours* by Anthony E. Hecht. Copyright © 1967 Anthony E. Hecht. Reprinted with the permission of Atheneum Publishers, Inc.

ATV MUSIC GROUP: "Eleanor Rigby" by John Lennon & Paul McCartney. © 1966 Northern Songs Limited. All rights for the United States and Mexico controlled by Maclen Music, Inc., c/o ATV Music Corp. Used by permission. All Rights Reserved.

DONALD W. BAKER: "Formal Application" from *Selected Poems, 1960–1980* by Donald W. Baker, Barnwood Press, 1982. Reprinted with permission of the author.

VIRGINIA BARBER: "How I Met My Husband" from *Something I've Been Meaning to Tell You* by Alice Munro. Copyright © 1974 by Alice Munro. All rights reserved. Available in USA from NAL/Plume. Available in Canada from NAL. Reprinted by permission of the author.

BEACON PRESS: "A Poem About Intelligence for My Brothers and Sisters" from *Passion: New Poems, 1977–1980* by June Jordan. Copyright © 1980 by June Jordan. Reprinted by permission of Beacon Press.

EDWIN BROCK: "Five Ways to Kill a Man" by Edwin Brock. Reprinted by permission of the author.

JONATHAN CAPE LTD.: "Song" ("Come live with me and be my love . . ,") by C. Day Lewis from *Two Songs* from *Collected Poems 1954*, Hogarth Press. By permission of Jonathan Cape Ltd. on behalf of the Executors of the Estate of C. Day Lewis and by permission of A. D. Peters & Co. Ltd.

"Naming of Parts" from *A Map of Verona* by Henry Reed. Reprinted by permission of Jonathan Cape Ltd.

CARNEGIE-MELLON UNIVERSITY PRESS: "Gwen" first appeared in *Girlfriends and Wives*, by Robert Wallace, Carnegie-Mellon University Press.

CHATTO AND WINDUS LTD.: "On a Squirrel Crossing the Road in Autumn, in New England" from *Collected Poems 1930–1976* by Richard Eberhart. Reprinted by permission of Richard Eberhart and Chatto and Windus Ltd.

Acknowledgments and copyrights continue at the back of the book on pages 1390–1398, which constitute an extension of the copyright page.

PREFACE

The short stories, poems, and plays in this fourth edition of *Literature: The Human Experience* represent literary traditions ranging from 400 B.C. to the present and reflect widely diverse cultures. In choosing the selections, we have been governed by a belief that the first task of an introductory anthology of literature is to engage the reader's interest, to make the experience of literature immediate and exciting. A corollary of that belief is our conviction that a genuine interest in literary history or the formal analysis of literature arises out of the experience of being engaged by particular works. Thus, we have selected works not primarily because they illustrate critical definitions or lend themselves to a particular approach but because we find them exciting and believe that students will, too.

The arrangement of the works in four thematic groups provides opportunities to explore diverse attitudes toward the same powerful human tendencies and experiences and to contrast formal treatments as well. Each section is introduced by a short essay that examines some of the crucial issues embodied in the works that follow. These essays are deliberately polemical, and, no doubt, readers will sometimes take exception to them. This is all to the good, for we believe that our proper mission as editors is to provide the groundwork for discussion and debate, not to promulgate "truths" for the edification of students. Within each thematic section, the works are grouped by genre—fiction, poetry, drama—and arranged chronologically, according to the author's birthdate. (We also include a date for each individual work. Most of these indicate first appearance in a book, but dates enclosed in parentheses indicate date either of composition or of appearance in a publication other than a book. We have not attempted to date traditional ballads.)

We should perhaps say a word about the questions that we have placed after about half of the stories, most of the poems, and all of the plays and following each thematic section. We believe that too often students are prevented from responding to a work as fully as they might because they are immediately asked questions that require them to confront formal problems. But there are certain kinds of questions, our students have convinced us, that can be helpful by opening individual works that might otherwise prove difficult and by suggesting illuminating thematic connections among various works. The questions in this book are intended to serve this purpose.

In this edition, we have provided a number of writing topics following individual selections as well as each of the four thematic sections. In devising the writing topics, we have been guided by two considerations. First, we have tried to formulate topics that bear some relationship to the discussion questions that follow a work. Second, we have attempted to make the topics specific and con-

crete, so that even if students do not have the benefit of class discussion, they
will understand what they are being called upon to do. There is little virtue in
a writing assignment that forces students to spend great energy in understanding
the assignment itself.

Also new is the first of our appendices, "Poems About Poetry," which offers
some meditations by poets on what poetry is and why it is written. These ten
poems reveal how diverse the motives and aims of poets are as well as the difficulty even poets have in describing exactly what it is they do. The poems may
be profitably read in conjunction with the second appendix, "The Poet's Craft,"
which presents three poems in both early draft and published versions. Comparing the two versions of each poem will, we think, help students gain some
further insight into the ways in which poems are created.

Although the emphasis throughout this book is on the value of literature as
a means to enjoyment and to a better understanding of our own humanity, the
fullest appreciation of literary achievement requires a certain facility in formal
matters and some acquaintance with literary history as well. The essays "Reading Fiction," "Reading Poetry," and "Reading Drama" acquaint readers with
some formal concepts and historical considerations basic to the study of the major
genres of literary art. The essay on drama also includes a discussion of some of
the less obvious differences between live performance and film art.

In another essay, "Three Critical Approaches: Formalist, Sociological, Psychoanalytic," we develop, for one story and one poem, three critical readings
that emphasize different aspects of the works and reflect the diversity of response that may occur when readers bring different expectations and attitudes
to literature. Seeing that a variety of critical approaches may all illuminate a
work and complement one another helps to free students, we believe, from a
timid acquiescence to some "correct" received view and enables them to respond to literature more honestly and openly.

The final essay in the appendices, "Writing About Literature," has been significantly revised and expanded for this new edition. Our own experience and
that of many other instructors made us realize that students would be served
better if the essay were structured according to the major types of writing students are called on to produce rather than, as in the previous edition, according
to genre. Thus, we have completely restructured the essay around the three
major types of writing: explication, analysis, and comparison and contrast. Each
type is defined and discussed and then illustrated with a student essay.

The new structure, however, does not preclude attention to genre. In fact,
"Writing About Literature" contains extensive discussions—for each type of
writing—of poetry, fiction, and drama. These discussions provide suggested approaches and questions to help students write explication, analysis, and com-
parison-and-contrast essays for each of the three genres.

We have added, as well, sections on the journal and the summary report.
These discussions are intended to complement the sections on the formal essay,
illustrating other useful purposes student writing can serve. It is also worth noting that the section on manuscript mechanics now incorporates the most recent

revision of the MLA style sheet. And, finally, we have added to the end of "Writing About Literature" some eighty-five "Suggested Topics for Writing" that addresses all genres and types of writing. Concluding the text is a "Glossary of Literary Terms." Included here are brief excerpts to illustrate the definitions as well as specific references to selections in the anthology.

The main thing, of course, continues to be the literary works themselves. In the fourth edition, we have retained the stories, poems, and plays that we and our fellow teachers across the country have found most valuable; replaced a few selections that we discovered were seldom assigned and a number of others for which more exciting alternatives were suggested; and included some additional works in each genre for the sake of diversity or balance. Specifically, eight of the stories, eighteen of the poems, and five of the plays in this edition are new.

The five new plays represent the most substantial additions among the three genres, bringing the total number of plays to thirteen. Sean O'Casey's *The Shadow of a Gunman*, Arthur Miller's *Death of a Salesman*, Molière's *The Misanthrope*, August Strindberg's *The Stronger*, and Arthur Kopit's *End of the World* are all powerful plays that deal with issues likely to engage student interest. Among the other new selections are stories by Arna Bontemps, Ursula Le Guin, Thomas Mann, Bobbie Ann Mason, Alice Munro, Grace Paley, Luigi Pirandello, and Alice Walker, as well as poems by Donald W. Baker, Robert Conquest, Kathleen Cushman, Carlos Drummond De Andrade, Carolyn Forché, Mary Gordon, Molly Holden, Josephine Jacobson, Weldon Kees, David Kirby, Muriel Rukeyser, and Edward Thomas.

ACKNOWLEDGMENTS

A great many people have helped us, and among them we should like especially to acknowledge our colleagues: Philip Handler, John Hartzog, Charles Kaplan, Arthur Lane, Lewis Owens, and William Walsh. Our thanks too to Sean McClory who helped us with some of the Gaelic intricacies in O'Casey's play.

We gratefully and inadequately acknowledge our debt to Nancy Burns-McConnohie, whose bibliographer's sense and literary sensitivity saved us hours of work.

We are also grateful to the following colleagues across the country who have sent us helpful reactions and suggestions for this fourth edition: Ross Alexander, City College, CUNY; Raymond A. Anselment, University of Connecticut; Dora Jean Ashe, Lynchburg College; Thaddeo K. Babiiha, Xavier University of Louisiana; Beverly S. Baker, University of Richmond; Michelle A. Balee, St. Louis University; Stuart M. Bearup, College of Southern Idaho; Robert Benson, San Francisco State University; Louise C. Berry, University of Tennessee; R. Blakeslee, California State University at Northridge; Rocco Blase, Wilbur Wright College; Bryna Blustein, St. Louis University; Janice K. Boerner, Glendale Community College; Barbara Boyd, California State University at Northridge; Pearl Brandwein, Pace University; Kay Britton, Rose State College; James L. Brown, Kansas City Kansas Community College; Wayne A. Buchman, Rose State College; Linda Burton, University of Tennessee; Margaret N. Butler, Millersville University; Diane Tomchoff Callin, William Rainey Harper College; Mark A. Christiansen, University of Tennessee; G. B. Cohen, Columbia State Community College; Georgette Cok, Adelphi University; Richard Conway, Adelphi University; Dolores Cornacchione, Harford Community College/Dundalk Community College; Don Richard Cox, University of Tennessee; Richard A. Cox, Abilene Christian University; Nancy Dandrea, Lake Michigan College; Susan Declercq, University of Wyoming; Diane Dowdy, Texas A&M University; Patrick Ecker, Jefferson Community College; T. J. Eckstein, Wilbur Wright College; Karen Elias-Button, SUNY at Oswego; Walter Everett, Indiana State University at Evansville; Douglas A. Finn, Yavapai College; John Fulton, William Paterson College; Thomas J. Gasque, University of South Dakota; Larry Gentry, Middle Tennessee State University; Gwendolyn Gong, Texas A&M University; Charles F. Gray, Winston-Salem State University; Kenneth A. Halwas, Eastern Washington University; Duncan Harris, University of Wyoming; Grace Harris, Winston-Salem State University; Linda Hegarty, La Guardia Community College, CUNY; William Herman, City College, CUNY; Morgan Himelstein, Adelphi University; Robert Holkeboer, Eastern Michigan University; Dovie Horvitz, Harper Junior College; Barbara Horwitz, C. W. Post Center, Long Island University; Jane A. Hubbell, Monroe Community College; Abigail P. Israel, Montclair State College; Eric Johansson, Kansas City Kansas Community College; Patricia E. Johnson, University of Minnesota; Peggy Kraus-Kennedy, American River College; Les Keyser, College of Staten Island, CUNY; Suzanne F. Kistler, William Paterson College; Arlene Ladden, La Guardia Community College, CUNY; Richard Larschan, Southeastern Massachusetts University; Peter V. LePage, University of Cincinnati; A. B. MacLeod, Christopher Newport College; Robert Marshall, University of Pittsburgh; Forrest M. McCann, Abilene Christian University; Del McGinnis, Delgado Community College; Elisabeth McGregor, Boston University; Mary Meli, Fairfield University; David B. Merrell, Abilene Christian University; Alyce Miller, Montclair State College; Eberly Milles, St. Louis University; J. L. Milstead, Kansas City Kansas Community College; Michael Misbach, Jefferson Community College; Randy B. Monroe, Central Wyoming College; Joseph P. Moriarty, Holyoke Community College; Laurie P. Morrow, Louisiana State University at Shreveport; Gil Muller, La Guardia Community College, CUNY; Rebecca W. Nail, Winston-Salem State University; Jasper Neel, Francis Marion College; Patricia C. Nichols, San Jose State University; Rei R. Noguchi, California State University at Northridge; Sarah Palmer, University of Montevallo; Margaret Parish, University of North Carolina at Wilmington; Lee Pederson, Emory University; Dean Pettinger, College of Southern Idaho; John Phillipson, University of Akron; Kerry Powell, Miami University of Ohio; Edward Quinn, City College, CUNY; Richard Raleigh, St. Thomas College of Villanova University; Jere Real, Lynchburg College; Rosalind Reilly, University of Richmond; Marian Robinson, San Jose State University; Ben Rushin,

Delgado Community College; Margaret Scanlan, Indiana University at South Bend; Patricia M. Schmaus, Kansas City Kansas Community College; V. S. Schneider, Kansas City Kansas Community College; Caroline Schoon, University of South Dakota; William Sheidley, University of Connecticut; John Silva, La Guardia Community College, CUNY; Art Simpson, University of Wyoming; Robert Singer, Baruch College, CUNY; Carolyn H. Smith, University of Florida; Thomas N. Smith, University of Hartford; Betty Smither, Jefferson Community College; C. Spence, Southeastern Massachusetts University; Peter Stambler, University of Wisconsin at Green Bay; J. Stelboum, College of Staten Island, CUNY; Hazel Stewart, Santa Barbara City College; Laura Symons, Lynchburg College; Arnold Talentino, SUNY at Cortland; Retta Taney, Xavier University; Cynthia H. Taylor, University of Minnesota; Dora Tippens, McHenry County College; Craig Turner, Texas A&M University; D. Uhlman, Miami University of Ohio; Henry Van Slooten, California State University at Northridge; Rima Walker, Pace University; Wilma A. Washburn, Lynchburg College; Jacqueline Webber, American River College; Sylvia Welborn, University of North Carolina at Wilmington; Margaret Woodbridge, Millersville University; Lesta C. Wren, Monroe Community College; William H. Young, Lynchburg College; Eve Zarin, Lehman College, CUNY; Arthur Zeiger, City College, CUNY; and Allyn Zucker, C. W. Post Center, Long Island University.

Finally, we wish to thank the many people at St. Martin's Press for their good humor and the care they took in the preparation of this edition, particularly Nancy Perry, Patricia Mansfield, Mark Gallaher, Jane Dominik, Judy Rundel, and Darby Downey.

Richard Abcarian
Marvin Klotz

CONTENTS

Innocence and Experience   2

DRAMA

Conformity and Rebellion

FICTION

POETRY

DRAMA

Love and Hate   724

FICTION

POETRY

DRAMA

The Presence of Death 1018

FICTION

POETRY

DRAMA

Appendices

ALTERNATE TABLE OF CONTENTS
arranged by genre*

---

*Within each genre, authors are listed chronologically by date of birth.

POETRY

DRAMA

FOURTH EDITION

LITERATURE
THE HUMAN EXPERIENCE

Innocence and Experience

The Peaceable Kingdom, by Edward Hicks

Humans strive to give order and meaning to their lives, to reduce the mystery and unpredictability that constantly threaten them. Life is infinitely more complex and surprising than we imagine, and the categories we establish to give it order and meaning are, for the most part, "momentary stays against confusion." At any time, the equilibrium of our lives, the comfortable image of ourselves and the world around us, may be disrupted suddenly by something new, forcing us into painful reevaluation. These disruptions create pain, anxiety, and terror but also wisdom and awareness.

The works in this section deal generally with the movement of a central character from moral simplicities and certainties into a more complex and problematic world. Though these works frequently issue in awareness, even wisdom, their central figures rarely act decisively; the protagonist is more often a passive figure who learns the difference between the ideal world he or she imagines and the injurious real world. If the protagonist survives the ordeal (and he or she doesn't always, emotionally or physically), the protagonist will doubtless be a better human—better able to wrest some satisfaction from a bleak and threatening world. It is no accident that so many of the works here deal with the passage from childhood to adulthood, for childhood is a time of simplicities and certainties that must give way to the complexities and uncertainties of adult life.

Almost universally, innocence is associated with childhood and youth, as experience is with age. We teach the young about an ideal world, without explaining that it has not yet been and may never be achieved. As innocents, they are terribly vulnerable to falsehood, to intrusive sexuality, and to the machinations of the wicked, who, despite all the moral tales, often do triumph. We know, if we have not already forgotten what the innocence of childhood celebrates, that time and experience will disabuse them.

But the terms *innocence* and *experience* range widely in meaning, and that range is reflected here. Innocence may be defined almost biologically, as illustrated by the sexual innocence of the young boy in Sherwood Anderson's "I Want to Know Why." Innocence may be social—the innocence of Robin in Nathaniel Hawthorne's "My Kinsman, Major Molineux" or the young boy in Frank O'Connor's "My Oedipus Complex." Or innocence may be seen as the child's ignorance of his own mortality, as in Gerard Manley Hopkins's "Spring and Fall" and Dylan Thomas's "Fern Hill."

Innocence almost always reflects a foolishness based on ignorance; sometimes, as well, it is the occasion for arrogance. The narrator of Joseph Conrad's "The Secret Sharer," at the beginning of his account, asserts confidently that "the sea was not likely to keep any special surprises expressly for my discomfiture" and explains that he is attracted to the sea because of its "great security" and "the singleness of its purpose." The events of the story markedly change his attitudes about himself and the moral universe in which he operates. In such works as Sophocles's *Oedipus Rex* and Robert Browning's "My Last Duchess," one discovers the tragic and violent consequences of an innocence that is blind. And in Sean O'Casey's *The Shadow of a Gunman*, the life of the poetic and visionary Donal will be forever darkened by the experience that reveals the contrast between Millie's selfless courage and his own cowardice.

The contrast between what we thought in our youth and what we have come to know, painfully, as adults stands as an emblem of the passage from innocence to experience. Yet, all of us remain, to one degree or another, innocent throughout life, since we never, except with death, stop learning from experience. Looked at in this way, experience is the ceaseless assault life makes upon our innocence, moving us to a greater wisdom about ourselves and the world around us.

INNOCENCE
AND
EXPERIENCE

The Mistletoe Merchant, 1904 by Pablo Picasso

FICTION

My Kinsman, Major Molineux* 1832

NATHANIEL HAWTHORNE [1804–1864]

After the kings of Great Britain had assumed the right of appointing the colonial governors, the measures of the latter seldom met with the ready and generous approbation which had been paid to those of their predecessors, under the original charters. The people looked with most jealous scrutiny to the exercise of power which did not emanate from themselves, and they usually rewarded their rulers with slender gratitude for the compliances by which, in softening their instructions from beyond the sea, they had incurred the reprehension of those who gave them. The annals of Massachusetts Bay will inform us, that of six governors in the space of about forty years from the surrender of the old charter, under James II., two were imprisoned by a popular insurrection; a third, as Hutchinson inclines to believe, was driven from the province by the whizzing of a musket-ball; a fourth, in the opinion of the same historian, was hastened to his grave by continual bickerings with the House of Representatives; and the remaining two, as well as their successors, till the Revolution, were favored with few and brief intervals of peaceful sway. The inferior members of the court party, in times of high political excitement, led scarcely a more desirable life. These remarks may serve as a preface to the following adventures, which chanced upon a summer night, not far from a hundred years ago. The reader, in order to avoid a long and dry detail of colonial affairs, is requested to dispense with an account of the train of circumstances that had caused much temporary inflammation of the popular mind.

It was near nine o'clock of a moonlight evening, when a boat crossed the ferry with a single passenger, who had obtained his conveyance at that unusual hour by the promise of an extra fare. While he stood on the landing-place, searching in either pocket for the means of fulfilling his agreement, the ferryman lifted a lantern, by the aid of which, and the newly risen moon, he took a very accurate survey of the stranger's figure. He was a youth of barely eighteen years,

---

* This story is considered in detail in the essay "Three Critical Approaches: Formalist, Socio-logical, Psychoanalytic" at the end of the book.

evidently country-bred, and now, as it should seem, upon his first visit to town. He was clad in a coarse gray coat, well worn, but in excellent repair; his under garments were durably constructed of leather, and fitted tight to a pair of serviceable and well-shaped limbs; his stockings of blue yarn were the incontrovertible work of a mother or a sister; and on his head was a three-cornered hat, which in its better days had perhaps sheltered the graver brow of the lad's father. Under his left arm was a heavy cudgel formed of an oak sapling, and retaining a part of the hardened root; and his equipment was completed by a wallet, not so abundantly stocked as to incommode the vigorous shoulders on which it hung. Brown, curly hair, well-shaped features, and bright, cheerful eyes were nature's gifts, and worth all that art could have done for his adornment.

The youth, one of whose names was Robin, finally drew from his pocket the half of a little province bill of five shillings, which, in the depreciation in that sort of currency, did but satisfy the ferryman's demand, with the surplus of a sexangular piece of parchment, valued at three pence. He then walked forward into the town, with as light a step as if his day's journey had not already exceeded thirty miles, and with as eager an eye as if he were entering London city, instead of the little metropolis of a New England colony. Before Robin had proceeded far, however, it occurred to him that he knew not whither to direct his steps; so he paused, and looked up and down the narrow street, scrutinizing the small and mean wooden buildings that were scattered on either side.

"This low hovel cannot be my kinsman's dwelling," thought he, "nor yonder old house, where the moonlight enters at the broken casement; and truly I see none hereabouts that might be worthy of him. It would have been wise to inquire my way of the ferryman, and doubtless he would have gone with me, and earned a shilling from the Major for his pains. But the next man I meet will do as well."

He resumed his walk, and was glad to perceive that the street now became wider, and the houses more respectable in their appearance. He soon discerned a figure moving on moderately in advance, and hastened his steps to overtake it. As Robin drew nigh, he saw that the passenger was a man in years, with a full periwig of gray hair, a wide-skirted coat of dark cloth, and silk stockings rolled above his knees. He carried a long and polished cane, which he struck down perpendicularly before him at every step; and at regular intervals he uttered two successive hems, of a peculiarly solemn and sepulchral intonation. Having made these observations, Robin laid hold of the skirt of the old man's coat, just when the light from the open door and windows of a barber's shop fell upon both their figures.

"Good evening to you, honored sir," said he, making a low bow, and still retaining his hold of the skirt. "I pray you tell me whereabouts is the dwelling of my kinsman, Major Molineux."

The youth's question was uttered very loudly; and one of the barbers, whose razor was descending on a well-soaped chin, and another who was dressing a Ramillies wig, left their occupations, and came to the door. The citizen, in the mean time, turned a long-favored countenance upon Robin, and answered him in a tone of excessive anger and annoyance. His two sepulchral hems, however, broke into the very centre of his rebuke, with most singular effect, like a thought of the cold grave obtruding among wrathful passions.

"Let go my garment, fellow! I tell you, I know not the man you speak of. What! I have authority, I have—hem, hem—authority; and if this be the respect you show for your betters, your feet shall be brought acquainted with the stocks by daylight, tomorrow morning!"

Robin released the old man's skirt, and hastened away, pursued by an ill-mannered roar of laughter from the barber's shop. He was at first considerably surprised by the result of his question, but, being a shrewd youth, soon thought himself able to account for the mystery.

"This is some country representative," was his conclusion, "who has never seen the inside of my kinsman's door, and lacks the breeding to answer a stranger civilly. The man is old, or verily—I might be tempted to turn back and smite him on the nose. Ah, Robin, Robin! even the barber's boys laugh at you for choosing such a guide! You will be wiser in time, friend Robin."

He now became entangled in a succession of crooked and narrow streets, which crossed each other, and meandered at no great distance from the water-side. The smell of tar was obvious to his nostrils, the masts of vessels pierced the moonlight above the tops of the buildings, and the numerous signs, which Robin paused to read, informed him that he was near the centre of business. But the streets were empty, the shops were closed, and lights were visible only in the second stories of a few dwelling-houses. At length, on the corner of a narrow lane, through which he was passing, he beheld the broad countenance of a British hero swinging before the door of an inn, whence proceeded the voices of many guests. The casement of one of the lower windows was thrown back, and a very thin curtain permitted Robin to distinguish a party at supper, round a well-furnished table. The fragrance of the good cheer steamed forth into the outer air, and the youth could not fail to recollect that the last remnant of his travelling stock of provision had yielded to his morning appetite, and that noon had found and left him dinnerless.

"Oh, that a parchment three-penny might give me a right to sit down at yonder table!" said Robin, with a sigh. "But the Major will make me welcome to the best of his victuals; so I will even step boldly in, and inquire my way to his dwelling."

He entered the tavern, and was guided by the murmur of voices and the fumes of tobacco to the public-room. It was a long and low apartment, with oaken walls, grown dark in the continual smoke, and a floor which was thickly sanded, but of no immaculate purity. A number of persons—the larger part of whom appeared to be mariners, or in some way connected with the sea—occupied the wooden benches, or leather-bottomed chairs, conversing on various matters, and occasionally lending their attention to some topic of general interest. Three or four little groups were draining as many bowls of punch, which the West India trade had long since made a familiar drink in the colony. Others, who had the appearance of men who lived by regular and laborious handicraft, preferred the insulated bliss of an unshared potation, and became more taciturn under its influence. Nearly all, in short, evinced a predilection for the Good Creature in some of its various shapes, for this is a vice to which, as Fast Day sermons of a hundred years ago will testify, we have a long hereditary claim. The only guests to whom Robin's sympathies inclined him were two or three sheepish countrymen, who were using the inn somewhat after the fashion of a Turkish caravansary; they had gotten themselves into the darkest corner of the room, and heedless of the Nicotian atmosphere, were supping on the bread of their own ovens, and the bacon cured in their own chimney-smoke. But though Robin felt a sort of brotherhood with these strangers, his eyes were attracted from them to a person who stood near the door, holding whispered conversation with a group of ill-dressed associates. His features were separately striking almost to grotesqueness, and the whole face left a deep impression on the memory. The forehead bulged out into a double prominence, with a vale between; the nose came boldly forth in an irregular curve, and its bridge was of more than a finger's breadth; the eyebrows were deep and shaggy, and the eyes glowed beneath them like fire in a cave.

While Robin deliberated of whom to inquire respecting his kinsman's dwelling, he was accosted by the innkeeper, a little man in a stained white apron, who had come to pay his professional welcome to the stranger. Being in the second generation from a French Protestant, he seemed to have inherited the courtesy of his parent nation; but no variety of circumstances was ever known to change his voice from the one shrill note in which he now addressed Robin.

"From the country, I presume, sir?" said he, with a profound bow. "Beg leave to congratulate you on your arrival, and trust you intend a long stay with us. Fine town here, sir, beautiful buildings, and much that may interest a stranger. May I hope for the honor of your commands in respect to supper?"

"The man sees a family likeness! the rogue has guessed that I am related to the Major!" thought Robin, who had hitherto experienced little superfluous civility.

All eyes were now turned on the country lad, standing at the door, in his worn three-cornered hat, gray coat, leather breeches, and blue yarn stockings, leaning on an oaken cudgel, and bearing a wallet on his back.

Robin replied to the courteous innkeeper, with such an assumption of confidence as befitted the Major's relative. "My honest friend," he said, "I shall make it a point to patronize your house on some occasion, when"—here he could not help lowering his voice—"when I may have more than a parchment three-pence in my pocket. My present business," continued he, speaking with lofty confidence, "is merely to inquire my way to the dwelling of my kinsman, Major Molineux."

There was a sudden and general movement in the room, which Robin interpreted as expressing the eagerness of each individual to become his guide. But the innkeeper turned his eyes to a written paper on the wall, which he read, or seemed to read, with occasional recurrences to the young man's figure.

"What have we here?" said he, breaking his speech into little dry fragments.

"'Left the house of the subscriber, bounden servant, Hezekiah Mudge,—had on, when he went away, gray coat, leather breeches, master's third-best hat. One pound currency reward to whosoever shall lodge him in any jail of the providence.' Better trudge, boy; better trudge!"

Robin had begun to draw his hand towards the lighter end of the oak cudgel, but a strange hostility in every countenance induced him to relinquish his purpose of breaking the courteous innkeeper's head. As he turned to leave the room, he encountered a sneering glance from the bold-featured personage whom he had before noticed, and no sooner was he beyond the door, than he heard a general laugh, in which the innkeeper's voice might be distinguished, like the dropping of small stones into a kettle.

"Now, is it not strange," thought Robin, with his usual shrewdness,—"is it not strange that the confession of an empty pocket should outweigh the name of my kinsman, Major Molineux? Oh, if I had one of those grinning rascals in the woods, where I and my oak sapling grew up together, I would teach him that my arm is heavy though my purse be light!"

On turning the corner of the narrow lane, Robin found himself in a spacious street, with an unbroken line of lofty houses on each side, and a steepled building at the upper end, whence the ringing of a bell announced the hour of nine. The light of the moon, and the lamps from the numerous shop-windows, discovered people promenading on the pavement, and amongst them Robin had hoped to recognize his hitherto inscrutable relative. The result of his former inquiries made him unwilling to hazard another, in a scene of such publicity, and he determined to walk slowly and silently up the street, thrusting his face close to that of every elderly gentleman, in search of the Major's lineaments. In his progress, Robin encountered many gay and gallant figures. Embroidered garments of showy colors, enormous periwigs, gold-laced hats, and silver-hilted swords glided past him and dazzled his optics. Travelled youths, imitators of the European fine gentlemen of the period, trod jauntily along, half dancing to the fashionable tunes which they hummed, and making poor Robin ashamed of his quiet and natural gait. At length, after many pauses to examine the gorgeous display of goods in the shop-windows, and after suffering some rebukes for the impertinence of his scrutiny into people's faces, the Major's kinsman found himself near the steepled building, still unsuccessful in his search. As yet, however, he had seen only one side of the thronged street; so Robin crossed, and continued the same sort of inquisition down the opposite pavement, with stronger hopes than the philosopher seeking an honest man, but with no better fortune. He had arrived about midway towards the lower end, from which his course began, when he overheard the approach of some one who struck down a cane on the flag-stones at every step, uttering at regular intervals, two sepulchral hems.

"Mercy on us!" quoth Robin, recognizing the sound.

Turning a corner, which chanced to be close at his right hand, he hastened to pursue his researches in some other part of the town. His patience now was wearing low, and he seemed to feel more fatigue from his rambles since he crossed the ferry, than from his journey of several days on the other side. Hunger also pleaded loudly within him, and Robin began to balance the propriety of demanding, violently, and with lifted cudgel, the necessary guidance from the first solitary passenger whom he should meet. While a resolution to this effect was gaining strength, he entered a street of mean appearance, on either side of which a row of ill-built houses was straggling towards the harbor. The moonlight fell upon no passenger along the whole extent, but in the third domicile which Robin passed there was a half-opened door, and his keen glance detected a woman's garment within.

"My luck may be better here," said he to himself.

Accordingly, he approached the door, and beheld it shut closer as he did so; yet an open space remained, sufficing for the fair occupant to observe the stranger, without a corresponding display on her part. All that Robin could discern was a strip of scarlet petticoat, and the occasional sparkle of an eye, as if the moonbeams were trembling on some bright thing.

"Pretty mistress," for I may call her so with a good conscience, thought the shrewd youth, since I know nothing to the contrary,—"my sweet pretty mistress, will you be kind enough to tell me whereabouts I must seek the dwelling of my kinsman, Major Molineux?"

Robin's voice was plaintive and winning, and the female, seeing nothing to be shunned in the handsome country youth, thrust open the door, and came forth into the moonlight. She was a dainty little figure, with a white neck, round arms, and a slender waist, at the extremity of which her scarlet petticoat jutted out over a hoop, as if she were standing in a balloon. Moreover, her face was oval and pretty, her hair dark beneath the little cap, and her bright eyes possessed a sly freedom, which triumphed over those of Robin.

"Major Molineux dwells here," said this fair woman.

Now, her voice was the sweetest Robin had heard that night, yet he could not help doubting whether that sweet voice spoke Gospel truth. He looked up and down the mean street, and then surveyed the house before which they stood. It was a small, dark edifice of two stories, the second of which projected over the lower floor, and the front apartment had the aspect of a shop for petty commodities.

"Now, truly, I am in luck," replied Robin, cunningly, "and so indeed is my kinsman, the Major, in having so pretty a housekeeper. But I prithee trouble him to step to the door; I will deliver him a message from his friends in the country, and then go back to my lodgings at the inn."

"Nay, the Major has been abed this hour or more," said the lady of the scarlet petticoat; "and it would be to little purpose to disturb him to-night, seeing his evening draught was of the strongest. But he is a kind-hearted man, and it would be as much as my life's worth to let a kinsman of his turn away from the door. You are the good old gentleman's very picture, and I could swear that was his rainy-weather hat. Also he has garments very much resembling those leather small-clothes. But come in, I pray, for I bid you hearty welcome in his name."

So saying, the fair and hospitable dame took our hero by the hand; and the touch was light, and the force was gentleness, and though Robin read in her eyes what he did not hear in her words, yet the slender-waisted woman in the scarlet petticoat proved stronger than the athletic country youth. She had drawn his half-willing footsteps nearly to the threshold, when the opening of a door in the neighborhood startled the Major's housekeeper, and, leaving the Major's kinsman, she vanished speedily into her own domicile. A heavy yawn preceded the appearance of a man, who, like the Moonshine of Pyramus and Thisbe,[1] carried a lantern, needlessly aiding his sister luminary in the heavens. As he walked sleepily up the street, he turned his broad, dull face on Robin, and displayed a long staff, spiked at the end.

"Home, vagabond, home!" said the watchman, in accents that seemed to fall asleep as soon as they were uttered. "Home, or we'll set you in the stocks by peep of day!"

"This is the second hint of the kind," thought Robin. "I wish they would end my difficulties, by setting me there to-night."

Nevertheless, the youth felt an instinctive antipathy towards the guardian of midnight order, which at first prevented him from asking his usual question. But just when the man was about to vanish behind the corner, Robin resolved not to lose the opportunity, and shouted lustily after him,—

"I say, friend! will you guide me to the house of my kinsman, Major Molineux?"

The watchman made no reply, but turned the corner and was gone; yet Robin seemed to hear the sound of drowsy laughter stealing along the solitary street. At that moment, also, a pleasant titter saluted him from the open window above his head; he looked up, and caught the sparkle of a saucy eye; a round arm beckoned to him, and next he heard light footsteps descending the staircase within. But Robin, being of the household of a New England clergyman, was a good youth, as well as a shrewd one; so he resisted temptation, and fled away.

He now roamed desperately, and at random, through the town, almost ready to believe that a spell was on him, like that by which a wizard of his country had once kept three pursuers wandering, a whole winter night, within twenty paces of the cottage which they sought. The streets lay before him, strange and desolate, and the lights were extinguished in almost every house. Twice, however, little parties of men, among whom Robin distinguished individuals in outlandish attire, came hurrying along; but, though on both occasions, they paused to address him, such intercourse did not at all enlighten his perplexity. They did but utter a few words in some language of which Robin knew nothing, and perceiving his inability to answer, bestowed a curse upon him in plain English and hastened away. Finally, the lad determined to knock at the door of every mansion that might appear worthy to be occupied by his kinsman, trusting that perseverance would overcome the fatality that had hitherto thwarted him. Firm in this resolve, he was passing beneath the walls of a church, which

---

[1] In Shakespeare's A *Midsummer Night's Dream*, Act V, Scene 1, the moon is represented by a man carrying a lantern in the comic performance of the tragic love story of Pyramus and Thisbe.

formed the corner of two streets, when, as he turned into the shade of its steeple, he encountered a bulky stranger, muffled in a cloak. The man was proceeding with the speed of earnest business, but Robin planted himself full before him, holding the oak cudgel with both hands across his body as a bar to further passage.

"Halt, honest man, and answer me a question," said he, very resolutely. "Tell me, this instant, whereabouts is the dwelling of my kinsman, Major Molineux!"

"Keep your tongue between your teeth, fool, and let me pass!" said a deep, gruff voice, which Robin partly remembered. "Let me pass, or I'll strike you to the earth!"

"No, no, neighbor!" cried Robin, flourishing his cudgel, and then thrusting its larger end close to the man's muffled face. "No, no, I'm not the fool you take me for, nor do you pass till I have an answer to my question. Whereabouts is the dwelling of my kinsman, Major Molineux?"

The stranger, instead of attempting to force his passage, stepped back into the moonlight, unmuffled his face, and stared full into that of Robin.

"Watch here an hour, and Major Molineux will pass by," said he.

Robin gazed with dismay and astonishment on the unprecedented physiognomy of the speaker. The forehead with its double prominence, the broad hooked nose, the shaggy eyebrows, and fiery eyes were those which he had noticed at the inn, but the man's complexion had undergone a singular, or, more properly, a twofold change. One side of the face blazed an intense red, while the other was black as midnight, the division line being in the broad bridge of the nose; and a mouth which seemed to extend from ear to ear was black or red, in contrast to the color of the cheek. The effect was as if two individual devils, a fiend of fire and a fiend of darkness, had united themselves to form this infernal visage. The stranger grinned in Robin's face, muffled his party-colored features, and was out of sight in a moment.

"Strange things we travellers see!" ejaculated Robin.

He seated himself, however, upon the steps of the church-door, resolving to wait the appointed time for his kinsman. A few moments were consumed in philosophical speculations upon the species of man who had just left him; but having settled this point shrewdly, rationally, and satisfactorily, he was compelled to look elsewhere for his amusement. And first he threw his eyes along the street. It was of more respectable appearance than most of those into which he had wandered; and the moon, creating, like the imaginative power, a beautiful strangeness in familiar objects, gave something of romance to a scene that might not have possessed it in the light of day. The irregular and often quaint architecture of the houses, some of whose roofs were broken into numerous little peaks, while others ascended, steep and narrow, into a single point, and others again were square; the pure snow-white of some of their complexions, the aged darkness of others, and the thousand sparklings, reflected from bright substances in the walls of many; these matters engaged Robin's attention for a while, and then began to grow wearisome. Next he endeavored to define the

forms of distant objects, starting away, with almost ghostly indistinctness, just as his eye appeared to grasp them; and finally he took a minute survey of an edifice which stood on the opposite side of the street, directly in front of the church door, where he was stationed. It was a large, square mansion, distinguished from its neighbors by a balcony, which rested on tall pillars, and by an elaborate Gothic window, communicating therewith.

"Perhaps this is the very house I have been seeking," thought Robin.

Then he strove to speed away the time, by listening to a murmur which swept continually along the street, yet was scarcely audible, except to an unaccustomed ear like his; it was a low, dull, dreamy sound, compounded of many noises, each of which was at too great a distance to be separately heard. Robin marvelled at this snore of a sleeping town, and marvelled more whenever its continuity was broken by now and then a distant shout, apparently loud where it originated. But altogether it was a sleep-inspiring sound, and, to shake off its drowsy influence, Robin arose, and climbed a window-frame, that he might view the interior of the church. There the moonbeams came trembling in, and fell down upon the deserted pews, and extended along the quiet aisles. A fainter yet more awful radiance was hovering around the pulpit, and one solitary ray had dared to rest upon the open page of the great Bible. Had nature, in that deep hour, become a worshipper in the house which man had builded? Or was that heavenly light the visible sanctity of the place,—visible because no earthly and impure feet were within the walls? The scene made Robin's heart shiver with a sensation of loneliness stronger than he had ever felt in the remotest depths of his native woods; so he turned away and sat down again before the door. There were graves around the church, and now an uneasy thought obtruded into Robin's breast. What if the object of his search, which had been so often and so strangely thwarted, were all the time mouldering in his shroud? What if his kinsman should glide through yonder gate, and nod and smile to him in dimly passing by?

"Oh that any breathing thing were here with me!" said Robin.

Recalling his thoughts from this uncomfortable track, he sent them over forest, hill, and stream, and attempted to imagine how that evening of ambiguity and weariness had been spent by his father's household. He pictured them assembled at the door, beneath the tree, the great old tree, which had been spared for its huge twisted trunk and venerable shade, when a thousand leafy brethren fell. There, at the going down of the summer sun, it was his father's custom to perform domestic worship, that the neighbors might come and join with him like brothers of the family, and that the wayfaring man might pause to drink at that fountain, and keep his heart pure by freshening the memory of home. Robin distinguished the seat of every individual of the little audience; he saw the good man in the midst, holding the Scriptures in the golden light that fell from the western clouds; he beheld him close the book and all rise up to pray. He heard the old thanksgivings for daily mercies, the old supplications for their continuance, to which he had so often listened in weariness, but which were now among his dear remembrances. He perceived the slight inequality of

his father's voice when he came to speak of the absent one; he noted how his mother turned her face to the broad and knotted trunk; how his elder brother scorned, because the beard was rough upon his upper lip, to permit his features to be moved; how the younger sister drew down a low hanging branch before her eyes; and how the little one of all, whose sports had hitherto broken the decorum of the scene, understood the prayer for her playmate, and burst into clamorous grief. Then he saw them go in at the door; and when Robin would have entered also, the latch tinkled into its place, and he was excluded from his home.

"Am I here, or there?" cried Robin, starting; for all at once, when his thoughts had become visible and audible in a dream, the long, wide, solitary street shone out before him.

He aroused himself, and endeavored to fix his attention steadily upon the large edifice which he had surveyed before. But still his mind kept vibrating between fancy and reality; by turns, the pillars of the balcony lengthened into the tall, bare stems of pines, dwindled down to human figures, settled again into their true shape and size, and then commenced a new succession of changes. For a single moment, when he deemed himself awake, he could have sworn that a visage—one which he seemed to remember, yet could not absolutely name as his kinsman's—was looking towards him from the Gothic window. A deeper sleep wrestled with and nearly overcame him, but fled at the sound of footsteps along the opposite pavement. Robin rubbed his eyes, discerned a man passing at the foot of the balcony, and addressed him in a loud, peevish, and lamentable cry.

"Hallo, friend! must I wait here all night for my kinsman, Major Molineux?"

The sleeping echoes awoke, and answered the voice; and the passenger, barely able to discern a figure sitting in the oblique shade of the steeple, traversed the street to obtain a nearer view. He was himself a gentleman in his prime, of open, intelligent, cheerful, and altogether prepossessing countenance. Perceiving a country youth, apparently homeless and without friends, he accosted him in a tone of real kindness, which had become strange to Robin's ears.

"Well, my good lad, why are you sitting here?" inquired he. "Can I be of service to you in any way?"

"I am afraid not, sir," replied Robin, despondingly; "yet I shall take it kindly, if you'll answer me a single question. I've been searching, half the night, for one Major Molineux; now, sir, is there really such a person in these parts, or am I dreaming?"

"Major Molineux! The name is not altogether strange to me," said the gentleman, smiling. "Have you any objection to telling me the nature of your business with him?"

Then Robin briefly related that his father was a clergyman, settled on a small salary, at a long distance back in the country, and that he and Major Molineux were brothers' children. The Major, having inherited riches, and acquired civil and military rank, had visited his cousin, in great pomp, a year or two before; had manifested much interest in Robin and an elder brother, and, being child-

less himself, had thrown out hints respecting the future establishment of one of them in life. The elder brother was destined to succeed to the farm which his father cultivated in the interval of sacred duties; it was therefore determined that Robin should profit by his kinsman's generous intentions, especially as he seemed to be rather the favorite, and was thought to possess other necessary endowments.

"For I have the name of being a shrewd youth," observed Robin, in this part of his story.

"I doubt not you deserve it," replied his new friend, good-naturedly; "but pray proceed."

"Well, sir, being nearly eighteen years old, and well grown, as you see," continued Robin, drawing himself up to his full height, "I thought it high time to begin in the world. So my mother and sister put me in handsome trim, and my father gave me half the remnant of his last year's salary, and five days ago I started for this place, to pay the Major a visit. But, would you believe it, sir! I crossed the ferry a little after dark, and have yet found nobody that would show me the way to his dwelling; only, an hour or two since, I was told to wait here, and Major Molineux would pass by."

"Can you describe the man who told you this?" inquired the gentleman.

"Oh, he was a very ill-favored fellow, sir," replied Robin, "with two great bumps on his forehead, a hook nose, fiery eyes; and, what struck me as the strangest, his face was of two different colors. Do you happen to know such a man, sir?"

"Not intimately," answered the stranger, "but I chanced to meet him a little time previous to your stopping me. I believe you may trust his word, and that the Major will very shortly pass through this street. In the mean time, as I have a singular curiosity to witness your meeting, I will sit down here upon the steps and bear you company."

He seated himself accordingly, and soon engaged his companion in animated discourse. It was but of brief continuance, however, for a noise of shouting, which had long been remotely audible, drew so much nearer that Robin inquired its cause.

"What may be the meaning of this uproar?" asked he. "Truly, if your town be always as noisy, I shall find little sleep while I am an inhabitant."

"Why, indeed, friend Robin, there do appear to be three or four riotous fellows abroad to-night," replied the gentleman. "You must not expect all the stillness of your native woods here in our streets. But the watch will shortly be at the heels of these lads and"—

"Ay, and set them in the stocks by peep of day," interrupted Robin, recollecting his own encounter with the drowsy lantern-bearer. "But, dear sir, if I may trust my ears, an army of watchmen would never make head against such a multitude of rioters. There were at least a thousand voices went up to make that one shout."

"May not a man have several voices, Robin, as well as two complexions?" said his friend.

"Perhaps a man may; but Heaven forbid that a woman should!" responded the shrewd youth, thinking of the seductive tones of the Major's housekeeper.

The sounds of a trumpet in some neighboring street now became so evident and continual, that Robin's curiosity was strongly excited. In addition to the shouts, he heard frequent bursts from many instruments of discord, and a wild and confused laughter filled up the intervals. Robin rose from the steps, and looked wistfully towards a point whither people seemed to be hastening.

"Surely some prodigious merry-making is going on," exclaimed he. "I have laughed very little since I left home, sir, and should be sorry to lose an opportunity. Shall we step round the corner by that darkish house, and take our share of the fun?"

"Sit down again, sit down, good Robin," replied the gentleman, laying his hand on the skirt of the gray coat. "You forget that we must wait here for your kinsman; and there is reason to believe that he will pass by, in the course of a very few moments."

The near approach of the uproar had now disturbed the neighborhood; windows flew open on all sides; and many heads, in the attire of the pillow, and confused by sleep suddenly broken, were protruded to the gaze of whoever had leisure to observe them. Eager voices hailed each other from house to house, all demanding the explanation, which not a soul could give. Half-dressed men hurried towards the unknown commotion, stumbling as they went over the stone steps that thrust themselves into the narrow footwalk. The shouts, the laughter, and the tuneless bray, the antipodes of music, came onwards with increasing din, till scattered individuals, and then denser bodies, began to appear round a corner at the distance of a hundred yards.

"Will you recognize your kinsman, if he passes in this crowd?" inquired the gentleman.

"Indeed, I can't warrant it, sir; but I'll take my stand here, and keep a bright lookout," answered Robin, descending to the outer edge of the pavement.

A mighty stream of people now emptied into the street, and came rolling slowly towards the church. A single horseman wheeled the corner in the midst of them, and close behind him came a band of fearful wind-instruments, sending forth a fresher discord now that no intervening buildings kept it from the ear. Then a redder light disturbed the moonbeams, and a dense multitude of torches shone along the street, concealing, by their glare, whatever object they illuminated. The single horseman, clad in a military dress, and bearing a drawn sword, rode onward as the leader, and, by his fierce and variegated countenance, appeared like war personified; the red of one cheek was an emblem of fire and sword; the blackness of the other betokened the mourning that attends them. In his train were wild figures in the Indian dress, and many fantastic shapes without a model, giving the whole march a visionary air, as if a dream had broken forth from some feverish brain, and were sweeping visibly through the midnight streets. A mass of people, inactive, except as applauding spectators, hemmed the procession in; and several women ran along the sidewalk, piercing the confusion of heavier sounds with their shrill voices of mirth or terror.

"The double-faced fellow has his eye upon me," muttered Robin, with an indefinite but an uncomfortable idea that he was himself to bear a part in the pageantry.

The leader turned himself in the saddle, and fixed his glance full upon the country youth, as the steed went slowly by. When Robin had freed his eyes from those fiery ones, the musicians were passing before him, and the torches were close at hand; but the unsteady brightness of the latter formed a veil which he could not penetrate. The rattling of wheels over the stones sometimes found its way to his ear, and confused traces of a human form appeared at intervals, and then melted into the vivid light. A moment more, and the leader thundered a command to halt: the trumpets vomited a horrid breath, and then held their peace; the shouts and laughter of the people died away, and there remained only a universal hum, allied to silence. Right before Robin's eyes was an uncovered cart. There the torches blazed the brightest, there the moon shone out like day, and there, in tar-and-feathery dignity, sat his kinsman, Major Molineux!

He was an elderly man, of large and majestic person, and strong, square features betokening a steady soul; but steady as it was, his enemies had found means to shake it. His face was pale as death, and far more ghastly; the broad forehead was contracted in his agony, so that his eyebrows formed one grizzled line; his eyes were red and wild, and the foam hung white upon his quivering lip. His whole frame was agitated by a quick and continual tremor, which his pride strove to quell, even in those circumstances of overwhelming humiliation. But perhaps the bitterest pang of all was when his eyes met those of Robin; for he evidently knew him on the instant, as the youth stood witnessing the foul disgrace of a head grown gray in honor. They stared at each other in silence, and Robin's knees shook, and his hair bristled, with a mixture of pity and terror. Soon, however, a bewildering excitement began to seize upon his mind; the preceding adventures of the night, the unexpected appearance of the crowd, the torches, the confused din and the hush that followed, the spectre of his kinsman reviled by that great multitude,—all this, and, more than all, a perception of tremendous ridicule in the whole scene, affected him with a sort of mental inebriety. At that moment a voice of sluggish merriment saluted Robin's ears; he turned instinctively, and just behind the corner of the church stood the lantern-bearer, rubbing his eyes, and drowsily enjoying the lad's amazement. Then he heard a peal of laughter like the ringing of silvery bells; a woman twitched his arm, a saucy eye met his, and he saw the lady of the scarlet petticoat. A sharp, dry cachinnation appealed to his memory, and standing on tiptoe in the crowd, with his white apron over his head, he beheld the courteous little innkeeper. And lastly, there sailed over the heads of the multitude a great, broad laugh, broken in the midst by two sepulchral hems; thus, "Haw, haw, haw,—hem, hem,—haw, haw, haw, haw!"

The sound proceeded from the balcony of the opposite edifice, and thither Robin turned his eyes. In front of the Gothic window stood the old citizen, wrapped in a wide gown, his gray periwig exchanged for a nightcap, which was thrust back from his forehead, and his silk stockings hanging about his legs. He supported himself on his polished cane in a fit of convulsive merriment, which manifested itself on his solemn old features like a funny inscription on a tombstone. Then Robin seemed to hear the voices of the barbers, of the guests of the inn, and of all who had made sport of him that night. The contagion was spreading among the multitude, when all at once, it seized upon Robin, and he sent forth a shout of laughter that echoed through the street,—every man shook his sides, every man emptied his lungs, but Robin's shout was the loudest there. The cloud-spirits peeped from their silvery islands, as the congregated mirth went roaring up the sky! The Man in the Moon heard the far bellow. "Oho," quoth he, "the old earth is frolicsome to-night!"

When there was a momentary calm in that tempestuous sea of sound, the leader gave the sign, the procession resumed its march. On they went, like fiends that throng in mockery around some dead potentate, mighty no more, but majestic still in his agony. On they went, in counterfeited pomp, in senseless uproar, in frenzied merriment, trampling all on an old man's heart. On swept the tumult, and left a silent street behind.

"Well, Robin, are you dreaming?" inquired the gentleman, laying his hand on the youth's shoulder.

Robin started, and withdrew his arm from the stone post to which he had instinctively clung, as the living stream rolled by him. His cheek was somewhat pale, and his eye not quite as lively as in the earlier part of the evening.

"Will you be kind enough to show me the way to the ferry?" said he, after a moment's pause.

"You have, then, adopted a new subject of inquiry?" observed his companion, with a smile.

"Why, yes, sir," replied Robin, rather dryly. "Thanks to you, and to my other friends, I have at last met my kinsman, and he will scarce desire to see my face again. I begin to grow weary of a town life, sir. Will you show me the way to the ferry?"

"No, my good friend Robin,—not to-night, at least," said the gentleman. "Some few days hence, if you wish it, I will speed you on your journey. Or, if you prefer to remain with us, perhaps, as you are a shrewd youth, you may rise in the world without the help of your kinsman, Major Molineux."

QUESTIONS

1. Explain the function of the opening paragraph. 2. Does Robin change as a result of his experiences? 3. What evidence does the story provide to explain the hostility of the townspeople toward Major Molineux? 4. A few moments before Robin witnesses the procession that surges forward with his tarred and feathered kinsman, his thoughts turn to his family, and he tries to imagine how they have spent the same night. What function does this daydream serve? 5. Discuss Hawthorne's use of light and darkness.

The Secret Sharer

JOSEPH CONRAD [1857–1924]

I

On my right hand there were lines of fishing stakes resembling a mysterious system of half-submerged bamboo fences, incomprehensible in its division of the domain of tropical fishes, and crazy of aspect as if abandoned forever by some nomad tribe of fishermen now gone to the other end of the ocean; for there was no sign of human habitation as far as the eye could reach. To the left a group of barren islets, suggesting ruins of stone walls, towers, and blockhouses, had its foundations set in a blue sea that itself looked solid, so still and stable did it lie below my feet; even the track of light from the westering sun shone smoothly, without that animated glitter which tells of an imperceptible ripple. And when I turned my head to take a parting glance at the tug which had just left us anchored outside the bar, I saw the straight line of the flat shore joined to the stable sea, edge to edge, with a perfect and unmarked closeness, in one leveled floor half brown, half blue under the enormous dome of the sky. Corresponding in their insignificance to the islets of the sea, two small clumps of trees, one on each side of the only fault in the impeccable joint, marked the mouth of the river Meinam we had just left on the first preparatory stage of our homeward journey; and, far back on the inland level, a larger and loftier mass, the grove surrounding the great Paknam pagoda, was the only thing on which the eye could rest from the vain task of exploring the monotonous sweep of the horizon. Here and there gleams as of a few scattered pieces of silver marked the windings of the great river; and on the nearest of them, just within the bar, the tug steaming right into the land become lost to my sight, hull and funnel and masts, as though the impassive earth had swallowed her up without an effort, without a tremor. My eye followed the light cloud of her smoke, now here, now there, above the plain, according to the devious curves of the stream, but always fainter and farther away, till I lost it at last behind the miter-shaped hill of the great pagoda. And then I was left alone with my ship, anchored at the head of the Gulf of Siam.

She floated at the starting point of a long journey, very still in an immense stillness, the shadows of her spars flung far to the eastward by the setting sun. At that moment I was alone on her decks. There was not a sound in her—and around us nothing moved, nothing lived, not a canoe on the water, not a bird in the air, not a cloud in the sky. In this breathless pause at the threshold of a long passage we seemed to be measuring our fitness for a long and arduous enterprise, the appointed task of both our existences to be carried out, far from all human eyes, with only sky and sea for spectators and for judges.

There must have been some glare in the air to interfere with one's sight, because it was only just before the sun left us that my roaming eyes made out beyond the highest ridge of the principal islet of the group something which did away with the solemnity of perfect solitude. The tide of darkness flowed on swiftly; and with tropical suddenness a swarm of stars came out above the shadowy earth, while I lingered yet, my hand resting lightly on my ship's rail as if on the shoulder of a trusted friend. But, with all that multitude of celestial bodies staring down at one, the comfort of quiet communion with her was gone for good. And there were also disturbing sounds by this time—voices, footsteps forward; the steward flitted along the main deck, a busily ministering spirit; a hand bell tinkled urgently under the poop deck. . . .

I found my two officers waiting for me near the supper table, in the lighted cuddy. We sat down at once, and as I helped the chief mate, I said:

"Are you aware that there is a ship anchored inside the islands? I saw her mastheads above the ridge as the sun went down."

He raised sharply his simple face, overcharged by a terrible growth of whisker, and emitted his usual ejaculations: "Bless my soul, sir! You don't say so!"

My second mate was a round-cheeked, silent young man, grave beyond his years, I thought; but as our eyes happened to meet I detected a slight quiver on his lips. I looked down at once. It was not my part to encourage sneering on board my ship. It must be said, too, that I knew very little of my officers. In consequence of certain events of no particular significance, except to myself, I had been appointed to the command only a fortnight before. Neither did I know much of the hands forward. All these people had been together for eighteen months or so, and my position was that of the only stranger on board. I mention this because it has some bearing on what is to follow. But what I felt most was my being a stranger to the ship; and if truth must be told, I was somewhat of a stranger to myself. The youngest man on board (barring the second mate), and untried as yet by a position of the fullest responsibility, I was willing to take the adequacy of the others for granted. They had simply to be equal to their tasks: but I wondered how far I should turn out faithful to that ideal conception of one's own personality every man sets up for himself secretly.

Meantime the chief mate, with an almost visible effect of collaboration on the part of his round eyes and frightful whiskers, was trying to evolve a theory of the anchored ship. His dominant trait was to take all things into earnest consideration. He was of a painstaking turn of mind. As he used to say, he "liked to account to himself" for practically everything that came in his way, down to a miserable scorpion he had found in his cabin a week before. The why and the wherefore of that scorpion—how it got on board and came to select his room rather than the pantry (which was a dark place and more what a scorpion would be partial to), and how on earth it managed to drown itself in the inkwell of his writing desk—had exercised him infinitely. The ship within the islands was much more easily accounted for; and just as we were about to rise from the table he made his pronouncement. She was, he doubted not, a ship from home lately arrived. Probably she drew too much water to cross the bar except at the top of spring tides. Therefore she went into that natural harbor to wait for a few days in preference to remaining in an open roadstead.

"That's so," confirmed the second mate, suddenly, in his slightly hoarse voice. "She draws over twenty feet. She's the Liverpool ship *Sephora* with a cargo of coal. Hundred and twenty-three days from Cardiff."

We looked at him in surprise.

"The tugboat skipper told me when he came on board for your letters, sir," explained the young man. "He expects to take her up the river the day after tomorrow."

After thus overwhelming us with the extent of his information he slipped out of the cabin. The mate observed regretfully that he "could not account for that young fellow's whims." What prevented him telling us all about it at once, he wanted to know.

I detained him as he was making a move. For the last two days the crew had had plenty of hard work, and the night before they had very little sleep. I felt painfully that I—a stranger—was doing something unusual when I directed him to let all hands turn in without setting an anchor watch. I proposed to keep on deck myself till one o'clock or thereabouts. I would get the second mate to relieve me at that hour.

"He will turn out the cook and the steward at four," I concluded, "and then give you a call. Of course at the slightest sign of any sort of wind we'll have the hands up and make a start at once."

He concealed his astonishment. "Very well, sir." Outside the cuddy he put his head in the second mate's door to inform him of my unheard-of caprice to take a five hours' anchor watch on myself. I heard the other raise his voice incredulously: "What? The captain himself?" Then a few more murmurs, a door closed, then another. A few moments later I went on deck.

My strangeness, which had made me sleepless, had prompted that unconventional arrangement, as if I had expected in those solitary hours of the night to get on terms with the ship of which I knew nothing, manned by men of whom I knew very little more. Fast alongside a wharf, littered like any ship in port with a tangle of unrelated things, invaded by unrelated shore people, I had hardly seen her yet properly. Now, as she lay cleared for sea, the stretch of her main deck seemed to me very fine under the stars. Very fine, very roomy for her size, and very inviting. I descended the poop and paced the waist, my mind picturing to myself the coming passage through the Malay Archipelago, down the Indian Ocean, and up the Atlantic. All its phases were familiar enough to me, every characteristic, all the alternatives which were likely to face me on the high seas—everything! . . . except the novel responsibility of command. But I took heart from the reasonable thought that the ship was like other ships, the men like other men, and that the sea was not likely to keep any special surprises expressly for my discomfiture.

Arrived at that comforting conclusion, I bethought myself of a cigar and went below to get it. All was still down there. Everybody at the after end of the ship was sleeping profoundly. I came out again on the quarter-deck, agreeably at ease in my sleeping suit on that warm breathless night, barefooted, a glowing cigar in my teeth, and, going forward, I was met by the profound silence of the fore end of the ship. Only as I passed the door of the forecastle I heard a deep, quiet, trustful sigh of some sleeper inside. And suddenly I rejoiced in the great security of the sea as compared with the unrest of the land, in my choice of that untempted life presenting no disquieting problems, invested with an elementary moral beauty by the absolute straightforwardness of its appeal and by the singleness of its purpose.

The riding light in the fore-rigging burned with a clear, untroubled, as if symbolic, flame, confident and bright in the mysterious shades of the night. Passing on my way aft along the other side of the ship, I observed that the rope side ladder, put over, no doubt, for the master of the tug when he came to fetch away our letters, had not been hauled in as it should have been. I became annoyed at this, for exactitude in small matters is the very soul of discipline. Then I reflected that I had myself peremptorily dismissed my officers from duty, and by my own act had prevented the anchor watch being formally set and things properly attended to. I asked myself whether it was wise ever to interfere with the established routine of duties even from the kindest of motives. My action might have made me appear eccentric. Goodness only knew how that absurdly whiskered mate would "account" for my conduct, and what the whole ship thought of that informality of their new captain. I was vexed with myself.

Not from compunction certainly, but, as it were mechanically, I proceeded to get the ladder in myself. Now a side ladder of that sort is a light affair and comes in easily, yet my vigorous tug, which should have brought it flying on board, merely recoiled upon my body in a totally unexpected jerk. What the devil! . . . I was so astounded by the immovableness of that ladder that I remained stock-still, trying to account for it to myself like that imbecile mate of mine. In the end, of course, I put my head over the rail.

The side of the ship made an opaque belt of shadow on the darkling glassy shimmer of the sea. But I saw at once something elongated and pale floating very close to the ladder. Before I could form a guess a faint flash of phosphorescent light, which seemed to issue suddenly from the naked body of a man, flickered in the sleeping water with the elusive, silent play of summer lightning in a night sky. With a gasp I saw revealed to my stare a pair of feet, the long legs, a broad livid back immersed right up to the neck in a greenish cadaverous glow. One hand, awash, clutched the bottom rung of the ladder. He was complete but for the head. A headless corpse! The cigar dropped out of my gaping mouth with a tiny plop and a short hiss quite audible in the absolute stillness of all things under heaven. At that I suppose he raised up his face, a dimly pale oval in the shadow of the ship's side. But even then I could only barely make out down there the shape of his black-haired head. However, it was enough for the horrid, frost-bound sensation which had gripped me about the chest to pass off. The moment of vain exclamations was past, too. I only climbed on the spare spar and leaned over the rail as far as I could, to bring my eyes nearer to that mystery floating alongside.

As he hung by the ladder, like a resting swimmer, the sea lightning played about his limbs at every stir; and he appeared in it ghastly, silvery, fishlike. He remained as mute as a fish, too. He made no motion to get out of the water, either. It was inconceivable that he should not attempt to come on board, and strangely troubling to suspect that perhaps he did not want to. And my first words were prompted by just that troubled incertitude.

"What's the matter?" I asked in my ordinary tone, speaking down to the face upturned exactly under mine.

"Cramp," it answered, no louder. Then slightly anxious, "I say, no need to call anyone."

"I was not going to," I said.

"Are you alone on deck?"

"Yes."

I had somehow the impression that he was on the point of letting go the ladder to swim away beyond my ken—mysterious as he came. But, for the moment, this being appearing as if he had risen from the bottom of the sea (it was certainly the nearest land to the ship) wanted only to know the time. I told him. And he, down there, tentatively:

"I suppose your captain's turned in?"

"I am sure he isn't," I said.

He seemed to struggle with himself, for I heard something like the low, bitter murmur of doubt. "What's the good?" His next words came out with a hesitating effort.

"Look here, my man. Could you call him out quietly?"

I thought the time had come to declare myself.

"I am the captain."

I heard a "By Jove!" whispered at the level of the water. The phosphorescence flashed in the swirl of the water all about his limbs, his other hand seized the ladder.

"My name's Leggatt."

The voice was calm and resolute. A good voice. The self-possession of that man had somehow induced a corresponding state in myself. It was very quietly that I remarked:

"You must be a good swimmer."

"Yes. I've been in the water practically since nine o'clock. The question for me now is whether I am to let go this ladder and go on swimming till I sink from exhaustion, or—to come on board here."

I felt this was no mere formula of desperate speech, but a real alternative in the view of a strong soul. I should have gathered from this that he was young; indeed, it is only the young who are ever confronted by such clear issues. But at this time it was pure intuition on my part. A mysterious communication was established already between us two—in the face of that silent darkened tropical sea. I was young, too; young enough to make no comment. The man in the water began suddenly to climb up the ladder, and I hastened away from the rail to fetch some clothes.

Before entering the cabin I stood still, listening in the lobby at the foot of the stairs. A faint snore came through the closed door of the chief mate's room. The second mate's door was on the hook, but the darkness in there was absolutely soundless. He, too, was young and could sleep like a stone. Remained the steward, but he was not likely to wake up before he was called. I got a sleeping suit out of my room and, coming back on deck, saw the naked man from the sea sitting on the main hatch, glimmering white in the darkness, his elbows on his knees and his head in his hands. In a moment he had concealed his damp body in a sleeping suit of the same gray-stripe pattern as the one I was wearing and followed me like my double on the poop. Together we moved right aft, barefooted, silent.

"What is it?" I asked in a deadened voice, taking the lighted lamp out of the binnacle, and raising it to his face.

"An ugly business."

He had rather regular features; a good mouth; light eyes under somewhat heavy, dark eyebrows; a smooth, square forehead; no growth on his cheeks; a small, brown mustache, and a well-shaped, round chin. His expression was concentrated, meditative, under the inspecting light of the lamp I held up to his face; such as a man thinking hard in solitude might wear. My sleeping suit was just right for his size. A well-knit young fellow of twenty-five at most. He caught his lower lip with the edge of white, even teeth.

"Yes," I said, replacing the lamp in the binnacle. The warm, heavy tropical night closed upon his head again.

"There's a ship over there," he murmured.

"Yes, I know. The *Sephora*. Did you know of us?"

"Hadn't the slightest idea. I am the mate of her—" He paused and corrected himself. "I should say I *was*."

"Aha! Something wrong?"

"Yes. Very wrong indeed. I've killed a man."

"What do you mean? Just now?"

"No, on the passage. Weeks ago. Thirty-nine south. When I say a man—"

"Fit of temper," I suggested, confidently.

The shadowy, dark head, like mine, seemed to nod imperceptibly above the ghostly gray of my sleeping suit. It was, in the night, as though I had been faced by my own reflection in the depths of a somber and immense mirror.

"A pretty thing to have to own up to for a Conway boy," murmured my double, distinctly.

"You're a Conway boy?"

"I am," he said, as if startled. Then slowly . . . "Perhaps you too—"

It was so; but being a couple of years older I had left before he joined. After a quick interchange of dates a silence fell; and I thought suddenly of my absurd mate with his terrific whiskers and the "Bless my soul—you don't say so" type of intellect. My double gave me an inkling of his thoughts by saying:

"My father's a parson in Norfolk. Do you see me before a judge and jury on that charge? For myself I can't see the necessity. There are fellows that an angel from heaven—And I am not that. He was one of those creatures that are just simmering all the time with a silly sort of wickedness. Miserable devils that have no business to live at all. He wouldn't do his duty and wouldn't let anybody else do theirs. But what's the good of talking! You know well enough the sort of ill-conditioned snarling cur—"

He appealed to me as if our experiences had been as identical as our clothes. And I knew well enough the pestiferous danger of such a character where there are no means of legal repression. And I knew well enough also that my double there was no homicidal ruffian. I did not think of asking him for details, and he told me the story roughly in brusque, disconnected sentences. I needed no more. I saw it all going on as though I were myself inside that other sleeping suit.

"It happened while we were setting a reefed foresail, at dusk. Reefed foresail! You understand the sort of weather. The only sail we had left to keep the ship running; so you may guess what it had been like for days. Anxious sort of job, that. He gave me some of his cursed insolence at the sheet. I tell you I was overdone with this terrific weather that seemed to have no end to it. Terrific, I tell you—and a deep ship. I believe the fellow himself was half crazed with funk. It was no time for gentlemanly reproof, so I turned round and felled him like an ox. He up and at me. We closed just as an awful sea made for the ship. All hands saw it coming and took to the rigging, but I had him by the throat, and went on shaking him like a rat, the men above us yelling, 'Look out! look out!' Then a crash as if the sky had fallen on my head. They say that for over ten minutes hardly anything was to be seen of the ship—just the three masts and a bit of the forecastle head and of the poop all awash driving along in a smother of foam. It was a miracle that they found us, jammed together behind the forebits. It's clear that I meant business, because I was holding him by the throat still when they picked us up. He was black in the face. It was too much for them. It seems they rushed us aft together, gripped as we were, screaming 'Murder!' like a lot of lunatics, and broke into the cuddy. And the ship running for her life, touch and go all the time, any minute her last in a sea fit to turn your hair gray only a-looking at it. I understand that the skipper, too, started raving like the rest of them. The man had been deprived of sleep for more than a week, and to have this sprung on him at the height of a furious gale nearly drove him out of his mind. I wonder they didn't fling me overboard after getting the carcass of their precious shipmate out of my fingers. They had rather a job to separate us, I've been told. A sufficiently fierce story to make an old judge and a respectable jury sit up a bit. The first thing I heard when I came to myself was the maddening howling of that endless gale, and on that the voice of the old man. He was hanging on to my bunk, staring into my face out of his sou'wester.

" 'Mr. Leggatt, you have killed a man. You can act no longer as chief mate of this ship.' "

His care to subdue his voice made it sound monotonous. He rested a hand on the end of the skylight to steady himself with, and all that time did not stir a limb, so far as I could see. "Nice little tale for a quiet tea party," he concluded in the same tone.

One of my hands, too, rested on the end of the skylight; neither did I stir a limb, so far as I knew. We stood less than a foot from each other. It occurred to me that if old "Bless my soul—you don't say so" were to put his head up the companion and catch sight of us, he would think he was seeing double, or imagine himself come upon a scene of weird witchcraft; the strange captain having a quiet confabulation by the wheel with his own gray ghost. I became very much concerned to prevent anything of the sort. I heard the other's soothing undertone.

"My father's a parson in Norfolk," it said. Evidently he had forgotten he had told me this important fact before. Truly a nice little tale.

"You had better slip down into my stateroom now," I said, moving off stealthily. My double followed my movements; our bare feet made no sound; I let him in, closed the door with care, and, after giving a call to the second mate, returned on deck for my relief.

"Not much sign of any wind yet," I remarked when he approached.

"No, sir. Not much," he assented, sleepily, in his hoarse voice, with just enough deference, no more, and barely suppressing a yawn.

"Well, that's all you have to look out for. You have got your orders."

"Yes, sir."

I paced a turn or two on the poop and saw him take up his position face forward with his elbow in the rat-lines of the mizzen-rigging before I went below. The mate's faint snoring was still going on peacefully. The cuddy lamp was burning over the table on which stood a vase with flowers, a polite attention from the ships' provision merchant—the last flowers we should see for the next three months at the very least. Two bunches of bananas hung from the beam symmetrically, one on each side of the rudder casing. Everything was as before in the ship—except that two of her captain's sleeping suits were simultaneously in use, one motionless in the cuddy, the other keeping very still in the captain's stateroom.

It must be explained here that my cabin had the form of the capital letter L, the door being within the angle and opening into the short part of the letter. A couch was to the left, the bed-place to the right; my writing desk and the chronometers' table faced the door. But anyone opening it, unless he stepped right inside, had no view of what I call the long (or vertical) part of the letter. It contained some lockers surmounted by a bookcase; and a few clothes, a thick jacket or two, caps, oilskin coat, and such like, hung on the hooks. There was at the bottom of that part a door opening into my bathroom, which could be entered also directly from the saloon. But that way was never used.

The mysterious arrival had discovered the advantage of this particular shape. Entering my room, lighted strongly by a big bulkhead lamp swung on gimbals above my writing desk, I did not see him anywhere till he stepped out quietly from behind the coats hung in the recessed part.

"I heard somebody moving about, and went in there at once," he whispered.

I, too, spoke under my breath.

"Nobody is likely to come in here without knocking and getting permission."

He nodded. His face was thin and the sunburn faded, as though he had been ill. And no wonder. He had been, I heard presently, kept under arrest in his cabin for nearly seven weeks. But there was nothing sickly in his eyes or in his expression. He was not a bit like me, really; yet, as we stood leaning over my bed-place, whispering side by side, with our dark heads together and our backs to the door, anybody bold enough to open it stealthily would have been treated to the uncanny sight of a double captain busy talking in whispers with his other self.

"But all this doesn't tell me how you came to hang on to our side ladder," I inquired, in the hardly audible murmurs we used, after he had told me something more of the proceedings on board the *Sephora* once the bad weather was over.

"When we sighted Java Head I had had time to think all those matters out several times over. I had six weeks of doing nothing else, and with only an hour or so every evening for a tramp on the quarter-deck."

He whispered, his arms folded on the side of my bed-place, staring through the open port. And I could imagine perfectly the manner of this thinking out— a stubborn if not a steadfast operation; something of which I should have been perfectly incapable.

"I reckoned it would be dark before we closed with the land," he continued, so low that I had to strain my hearing, near as we were to each other, shoulder touching shoulder almost. "So I asked to speak to the old man. He always seemed very sick when he came to see me—as if he could not look me in the face. You know, that foresail saved the ship. She was too deep to have run long under bare poles. And it was I that managed to set it for him. Anyway, he came. When I had him in my cabin—he stood by the door looking at me as if I had the halter around my neck already—I asked him right away to leave my cabin door unlocked at night while the ship was going through Sunda Straits. There would be the Java coast within two or three miles, off Angier Point. I wanted nothing more. I've had a prize for swimming my second year in the Conway."

"I can believe it," I breathed out.

"God only knows why they locked me in every night. To see some of their faces you'd have thought they were afraid I'd go about at night strangling people. Am I a murdering brute? Do I look it? By Jove! if I had been he wouldn't have trusted himself like that into my room. You'll say I might have chucked him aside and bolted out, there and then—it was dark already. Well, no. And for the same reason I wouldn't think of trying to smash the door. There would have been a rush to stop me at the noise, and I did not mean to get into a confounded scrimmage. Somebody else might have got killed—for I would not have broken out only to get chucked back, and I did not want any more of that work. He refused, looking more sick than ever. He was afraid of the men, and also of that old second mate of his who had been sailing with him for years—a gray-headed old humbug; and his steward, too, had been with him devil knows how long—seventeen years or more—a dogmatic sort of loafer who hated me like poison, just because I was the chief mate. No chief mate ever made more than one voyage in the *Sephora,* you know. Those two old chaps ran the ship. Devil only knows what the skipper wasn't afraid of (all his nerve went to pieces altogether in that hellish spell of bad weather we had)—of what the law would do to him—of his wife, perhaps. Oh, yes! she's on board. Though I don't think she would have meddled. She would have been only too glad to have me out of the ship in any way. The 'brand of Cain' business, don't you see. That's all right. I was ready enough to go off wandering on the face of the earth—and that was price enough to pay for an Abel of that sort. Anyhow, he wouldn't listen to me. 'This thing must take its course. I represent the law here.' He was shaking like a leaf. 'So you won't?' 'No!' 'Then I hope you will be able to sleep on that,' I said, and turned my back on him. 'I wonder that *you* can,' cries he, and locks the door.

"Well, after that, I couldn't. Not very well. That was three weeks ago. We have had a slow passage through the Java Sea; drifted about Carimata for ten days. When we anchored here they thought, I suppose, it was all right. The nearest land (and that's five miles) is the ship's destination; the consul would soon set about catching me; and there would have been no object in bolting to these islets there. I don't suppose there's a drop of water on them. I don't know how it was, but tonight that steward, after bringing me my supper, went out to let me eat it, and left the door unlocked. And I ate it—all there was, too. After I had finished I strolled out on the quarter-deck. I don't know that I meant to do anything. A breath of fresh air was all I wanted, I believe. Then a sudden temptation came over me. I kicked off my slippers and was in the water before I had made up my mind fairly. Somebody heard the splash and they raised an awful hullabaloo. 'He's gone! Lower the boats! He's committed suicide! No, he's swimming.' Certainly I was swimming. It's not so easy for a swimmer like me to commit suicide by drowning. I landed on the nearest islet before the boat left the ship's side. I heard them pulling about in the dark, hailing, and so on, but after a bit they gave up. Everything quieted down and the anchorage became as still as death. I sat down on a stone and began to think. I felt certain they would start searching for me at daylight. There was no place to hide on those stony things—and if there had been, what would have been the good? But now I was clear of that ship, I was not going back. So after a while I took off all my clothes, tied them up in a bundle with a stone inside, and dropped them in the deep water on the outer side of the islet. That was suicide enough for me. Let them think what they liked, but I didn't mean to drown myself. I meant to swim till I sank—but that's not the same thing. I struck out for another of these little islands, and it was from that one that I first saw your riding light. Something to swim for. I went on easily, and on the way I came upon a flat rock a foot or two above water. In the daytime, I dare say, you might make it out with a glass from your poop. I scrambled up on it and rested myself for a bit. Then I made another start. That last spell must have been over a mile."

His whisper was getting fainter and fainter, and all the time he stared straight out through the porthole, in which there was not even a star to be seen. I had not interrupted him. There was something that made comment impossible in his narrative, or perhaps in himself; a sort of feeling, a quality, which I can't find a name for. And when he ceased, all I found was a futile whisper: "So you swam for our light?"

"Yes—straight for it. It was something to swim for. I couldn't see any stars low down because the coast was in the way, and I couldn't see the land, either. The water was like glass. One might have been swimming in a confounded thousand-feet deep cistern with no place for scrambling out anywhere; but what I didn't like was the notion of swimming round and round like a crazed bullock before I gave out; and as I didn't mean to go back . . . No. Do you see me being hauled back, stark naked, off one of these little islands by the scruff of the neck and fighting like a wild beast? Somebody would have got killed for certain, and I did not want any of that. So I went on. Then your ladder—"

"Why didn't you hail the ship?" I asked, a little louder.

He touched my shoulder lightly. Lazy footsteps came right over our heads and stopped. The second mate had crossed from the other side of the poop and might have been hanging over the rail, for all we knew.

"He couldn't hear us talking—could he?" My double breathed into my very ear, anxiously.

His anxiety was an answer, a sufficient answer, to the question I had put to him. An answer containing all the difficulty of that situation. I closed the porthole quietly, to make sure. A louder word might have been overheard.

"Who's that?" he whispered then.

"My second mate. But I don't know much more of the fellow than you do."

And I told him a little about myself. I had been appointed to take charge while I least expected anything of the sort, not quite a fortnight ago. I didn't know either the ship or the people. Hadn't had the time in port to look about me or size anybody up. And as to the crew, all they knew was that I was appointed to take the ship home. For the rest, I was almost as much of a stranger on board as himself, I said. And at the moment I felt it most acutely. I felt that it would take very little to make me a suspect person in the eyes of the ship's company.

He had turned about meantime; and we, the two strangers in the ship, faced each other in identical attitudes.

"Your ladder—" he murmured, after a silence. "Who'd have thought of finding a ladder hanging over at night in a ship anchored out here! I felt just then a very unpleasant faintness. After the life I've been leading for nine weeks, anybody would have got out of condition. I wasn't capable of swimming round as far as your rudder chains. And, lo and behold! there was a ladder to get hold of. After I gripped it I said to myself, 'What's the good?' When I saw a man's head looking over I thought I could swim away presently and leave him shout-ing—in whatever language it was. I didn't mind being looked at. I—I liked it. And then you speaking to me so quietly—as if you had expected me—made me hold on a little longer. It had been a confounded lonely time—I don't mean while swimming. I was glad to talk a little to somebody that didn't belong to the *Sephora*. As to asking for the captain, that was a mere impulse. It could have been no use, with all the ship knowing about me and the other people pretty certain to be round here in the morning. I don't know—I wanted to be seen, to talk with somebody, before I went on. I don't know what I would have said. . . . 'Fine night, isn't it?' or something of the sort."

"Do you think they will be round here presently?" I asked with some incre-dulity.

"Quite likely," he said, faintly.

He looked extremely haggard all of a sudden. His head rolled on his shoulders.

"H'm. We shall see then. Meantime get into that bed," I whispered. "Want help? There."

It was a rather high bed-place with a set of drawers underneath. This amazing swimmer really needed the lift I gave him by seizing his leg. He tumbled in, rolled over on his back, and flung one arm across his eyes. And then, with his face nearly hidden, he must have looked exactly as I used to look in that bed. I gazed upon my other self for a while before drawing across carefully the two green serge curtains which ran on a brass rod. I thought for a moment of pinning them together for greater safety, but I sat down on the couch, and once there I felt unwilling to rise and hunt for a pin. I would do it in a moment. I was extremely tired, in a peculiarly intimate way, by the strain of stealthiness, by the effort of whispering and the general secrecy of this excitement. It was three o'clock by now and I had been on my feet since nine, but I was not sleepy; I could not have gone to sleep. I sat there, fagged out, looking at the curtains, trying to clear my mind of the confused sensation of being in two places at once, and greatly bothered by an exasperating knocking in my head. It was a relief to discover suddenly that it was not in my head at all, but on the outside of the door. Before I could collect myself the words "Come in" were out of my mouth, and the steward entered with a tray, bringing in my morning coffee. I had slept, after all, and I was so frightened that I shouted, "This way! I am here, steward," as though he had been miles away. He put down the tray on the table next the couch and only then said, very quietly, "I can see you are here, sir." I felt him give me a keen look, but I dared not meet his eyes just then. He must have wondered why I had drawn the curtains of my bed before going to sleep on the couch. He went out, hooking the door open as usual.

I heard the crew washing decks above me. I knew I would have been told at once if there had been any wind. Calm, I thought, and I was doubly vexed. Indeed, I felt dual more than ever. The steward reappeared suddenly in the doorway. I jumped up from the couch so quickly that he gave a start.

"What do you want here?"

"Close your port, sir—they are washing decks."

"It is closed," I said, reddening.

"Very well, sir." But he did not move from the doorway and returned my stare in an extraordinary, equivocal manner for a time. Then his eyes wavered, all his expression changed, and in a voice unusually gentle, almost coaxingly:

"May I come in to take the empty cup away, sir?"

"Of course!" I turned my back on him while he popped in and out. Then I unhooked and closed the door and even pushed the bolt. This sort of thing could not go on very long. The cabin was as hot as an oven, too. I took a peep at my double, and discovered that he had not moved, his arm was still over his eyes; but his chest heaved; his hair was wet; his chin glistened with perspiration. I reached over him and opened the port.

"I must show myself on deck," I reflected.

Of course, theoretically, I could do what I liked, with no one to say nay to me within the whole circle of the horizon; but to lock my cabin door and take the key away I did not dare. Directly I put my head out of the companion I saw the group of my two officers, the second mate barefooted, the chief mate in long india-rubber boots, near the break of the poop, and the steward halfway down the poop ladder talking to them eagerly. He happened to catch sight of me and dived, the second ran down on the main deck shouting some order or other, and the chief mate came to meet me, touching his cap.

There was a sort of curiosity in his eye that I did not like. I don't know whether the steward had told them that I was "queer" only, or downright drunk, but I know the man meant to have a good look at me. I watched him coming with a smile which, as he got into point-blank range, took effect and froze his very whiskers. I did not give him time to open his lips.

"Square the yards by lifts and braces before the hands go to breakfast."

It was the first particular order I had given on board that ship; and I stayed on deck to see it executed, too. I had felt the need of asserting myself without loss of time. That sneering young cub got taken down a peg or two on that occasion, and I also seized the opportunity of having a good look at the face of every foremast man as they filed past me to go to the after braces. At breakfast time, eating nothing myself, I presided with such frigid dignity that the two mates were only too glad to escape from the cabin as soon as decency permitted; and all the time the dual working of my mind distracted me almost to the point of insanity. I was constantly watching myself, my secret self, as dependent on my actions as my own personality, sleeping in that bed, behind that door which faced me as I sat at the head of the table. It was very much like being mad, only it was worse because one was aware of it.

I had to shake him for a solid minute, but when at last he opened his eyes it was in the full possession of his senses, with an inquiring look.

"All's well so far," I whispered. "Now you must vanish into the bathroom."

He did so, as noiseless as a ghost, and I then rang for the steward, and facing him boldly, directed him to tidy up my stateroom while I was having my bath—"and be quick about it." As my tone admitted of no excuses, he said, "Yes, sir," and ran off to fetch his dustpan and brushes. I took a bath and did most of my dressing, splashing, and whistling softly for the steward's edification, while the secret sharer of my life stood drawn up bolt upright in that little space, his face looking very sunken in daylight, his eyelids lowered under the stern, dark line of his eyebrows drawn together by a slight frown.

When I left him there to go back to my room the steward was finished dusting. I sent for the mate and engaged him in some insignificant conversation. It was, as it were, trifling with the terrific character of whiskers; but my object was to give him an opportunity for a good look at my cabin. And then I could at last shut, with a clear conscience, the door of my stateroom and get my double back into the recessed part. There was nothing else for it. He had to sit still on a small folding stool, half smothered by the heavy coats hanging there. We listened to the steward going into the bathroom out of the saloon, filling the water bottles there, scrubbing the bath, setting things to rights, whisk, bang, clatter— out again into the saloon—turn the key—click. Such was my scheme for keeping my second self invisible. Nothing better could be contrived under the circumstances. And there we sat; I at my writing desk ready to appear busy with some papers, he behind me, out of sight of the door. It would not have been prudent to talk in daytime; and I could not have stood the excitement of that queer sense of whispering to myself. Now and then, glancing over my shoulder, I saw him far back there, sitting rigidly on the low stool, his bare feet close together, his arms folded, his head hanging on his breast—and perfectly still. Anybody would have taken him for me.

I was fascinated by it myself. Every moment I had to glance over my shoulder. I was looking at him when a voice outside the door said:

"Beg pardon, sir."

"Well!" . . . I kept my eyes on him, and so, when the voice outside the door announced, "There's a ship's boat coming our way, sir," I saw him give a start— the first movement he had made for hours. But he did not raise his bowed head.

"All right. Get the ladder over."

I hesitated. Should I whisper something to him? But what? His immobility seemed to have been never disturbed. What could I tell him he did not know already? . . . Finally I went on deck.

II

The skipper of the *Sephora* had a thin red whisker all round his face, and the sort of complexion that goes with hair of that color; also the particular, rather smeary shade of blue in the eyes. He was not exactly a showy figure; his shoulders were high, his stature but middling—one leg slightly more bandy than the other. He shook hands, looking vaguely around. A spiritless tenacity was his main characteristic, I judged. I behaved with a politeness which seemed to disconcert him. Perhaps he was shy. He mumbled to me as if he were ashamed of what he was saying; gave his name (it was something like Archbold—but at this distance of years I hardly am sure), his ship's name, and a few other particulars of that sort, in the manner of a criminal making a reluctant and doleful confession. He had had terrible weather on the passage out—terrible—terrible—wife aboard, too.

By this time we were seated in the cabin and the steward brought in a tray with a bottle and glasses. "Thanks! No." Never took liquor. Would have some water, though. He drank two tumblerfuls. Terrible thirsty work. Ever since daylight had been exploring the islands round his ship.

"What was that for—fun?" I asked, with an appearance of polite interest.

"No!" He sighed. "Painful duty."

As he persisted in his mumbling and I wanted my double to hear every word, I hit upon the notion of informing him that I regretted to say I was hard of hearing.

"Such a young man, too!" he nodded, keeping his smeary blue, unintelligent eyes fastened upon me. What was the cause of it—some disease? he inquired, without the least sympathy and as if he thought that, if so, I'd got no more than I deserved.

"Yes; disease," I admitted in a cheerful tone which seemed to shock him. But my point was gained, because he had to raise his voice to give me his tale. It is not worth while to record that version. It was just over two months since all this had happened, and he had thought so much about it that he seemed completely muddled as to its bearings, but still immensely impressed.

"What would you think of such a thing happening on board your own ship? I've had the *Sephora* for these fifteen years. I am a well-known shipmaster."

He was densely distressed—and perhaps I should have sympathized with him if I had been able to detach my mental vision from the unsuspected sharer of my cabin as though he were my second self. There he was on the other side of the bulkhead, four or five feet from us, no more, as we sat in the saloon. I looked politely at Captain Archbold (if that was his name), but it was the other I saw, in a gray sleeping suit, seated on a low stool, his bare feet close together, his arms folded, and every word said between us falling into the ears of his dark head bowed on his chest.

"I have been at sea now, man and boy, for seven-and-thirty years, and I've never heard of such a thing happening in an English ship. And that it should be my ship. Wife on board, too."

I was hardly listening to him.

"Don't you think," I said, "that the heavy sea which, you told me, came aboard just then might have killed the man? I have seen the sheer weight of a sea kill a man very neatly, by simply breaking his neck."

"Good God!" he uttered, impressively, fixing his smeary blue eyes on me. "The sea! No man killed by the sea ever looked like that." He seemed positively scandalized at my suggestion. And as I gazed at him, certainly not prepared for anything original on his part, he advanced his head close to mine and thrust his tongue out at me so suddenly that I couldn't help starting back.

After scoring over my calmness in this graphic way he nodded wisely. If I had seen the sight, he assured me, I would never forget it as long as I lived. The weather was too bad to give the corpse a proper sea burial. So next day at dawn they took it up on the poop, covering its face with a bit of bunting; he read a short prayer, and then, just as it was, in its oilskins and long boots, they launched it amongst those mountainous seas that seemed ready every moment to swallow up the ship herself and the terrified lives on board of her.

"That reefed foresail saved you," I threw in.

"Under God—it did," he exclaimed fervently. "It was by a special mercy, I firmly believe, that it stood some of those hurricane squalls."

"It was the setting of that sail which—" I began.

"God's own hand in it," he interrupted me. "Nothing less could have done it. I don't mind telling you that I hardly dared give the order. It seemed impossible that we could touch anything without losing it, and then our last hope would have been gone."

The terror of that gale was on him yet. I let him go on for a bit, then said, casually—as if returning to a minor subject:

"You were very anxious to give up your mate to the shore people, I believe?"

He was. To the law. His obscure tenacity on that point had in it something incomprehensible and a little awful; something, as it were, mystical, quite apart from his anxiety that he should not be suspected of "countenancing any doings of that sort." Seven-and-thirty virtuous years at sea, of which over twenty of immaculate command, and the last fifteen in the *Sephora*, seemed to have laid him under some pitiless obligation.

"And you know," he went on, groping shamefacedly amongst his feelings, "I did not engage that young fellow. His people had some interest with my owners. I was in a way forced to take him on. He looked very smart, very gentlemanly, and all that. But do you know—I never liked him, somehow. I am a plain man. You see, he wasn't exactly the sort for the chief mate of a ship like the *Sephora*."

I had become so connected in thoughts and impressions with the secret sharer of my cabin that I felt as if I, personally, were being given to understand that I, too, was not the sort that would have done for the chief mate of a ship like the *Sephora*. I had no doubt of it in my mind.

"Not at all the style of man. You understand," he insisted, superfluously, looking hard at me.

I smiled urbanely. He seemed at a loss for a while.

"I suppose I must report a suicide."

"Beg pardon?"

"Sui-cide! That's what I'll have to write to my owners directly I get in."

"Unless you manage to recover him before tomorrow," I assented, dispassionately. . . . "I mean, alive."

He mumbled something which I really did not catch, and I turned my ear to him in a puzzled manner. He fairly bawled:

"The land—I say, the mainland is at least seven miles off my anchorage."

"About that."

My lack of excitement, of curiosity, of surprise, of any sort of pronounced interest, began to arouse his distrust. But except for the felicitous pretense of deafness I had not tried to pretend anything. I had felt utterly incapable of playing the part of ignorance properly, and therefore was afraid to try. It is also certain that he had brought some ready-made suspicions with him, and that he viewed my politeness as a strange and unnatural phenomenon. And yet how else could I have received him? Not heartily! That was impossible for psychological reasons, which I need not state here. My only object was to keep off his inquiries. Surlily? Yes, but surliness might have provoked a point-blank question. From its novelty to him and from its nature, punctilious courtesy was the manner best calculated to restrain the man. But there was the danger of his breaking through my defense bluntly. I could not, I think, have met him by a direct lie, also for psychological (not moral) reasons. If he had only known how afraid I was of his putting my feeling of identity with the other to the test! But, strangely enough—(I thought of it only afterward)—I believe that he was not a little disconcerted by the reverse side of that weird situation, by something in me that reminded him of the man he was seeking—suggested a mysterious similitude to the young fellow he had distrusted and disliked from the first.

However that might have been, the silence was not very prolonged. He took another oblique step.

"I reckon I had no more than a two-mile pull to your ship. Not a bit more."

"And quite enough, too, in this awful heat," I said.

Another pause full of mistrust followed. Necessity, they say, is mother of invention, but fear, too, is not barren of ingenious suggestions. And I was afraid he would ask me point-blank for news of my other self.

"Nice little saloon, isn't it?" I remarked, as if noticing for the first time the way his eyes roamed from one closed door to the other. "And very well fitted out, too. Here, for instance," I continued reaching over the back of my seat negligently and flinging the door open, "is my bathroom."

He made an eager movement, but hardly gave it a glance. I got up, shut the door of the bathroom, and invited him to have a look round, as if I were very proud of my accommodation. He had to rise and be shown round, but he went through the business without any raptures whatever.

"And now we'll have a look at my stateroom," I declared, in a voice as loud as I dared to make it, crossing the cabin to the starboard side with purposely heavy steps.

He followed me in and gazed around. My intelligent double had vanished. I played my part.

"Very convenient—isn't it?"

"Very nice. Very comf . . ." He didn't finish, and went out brusquely as if to escape from some unrighteous wiles of mine. But it was not to be. I had been too frightened not to feel vengeful; I felt I had him on the run, and I meant to keep him on the run. My polite insistence must have had something menacing in it, because he gave in suddenly. And I did not let him off a single item; mate's room, pantry, storerooms, the very sail locker which was also under the poop—he had to look into them all. When at last I showed him out on the quarter-deck he drew a long, spiritless sigh, and mumbled dismally that he must really be going back to his ship now. I desired my mate, who had joined us, to see to the captain's boat.

The man of whiskers gave a blast on the whistle which he used to wear hanging round his neck, and yelled, "*Sephora* away!" My double down there in my cabin must have heard, and certainly could not feel more relieved than I. Four fellows came running out from somewhere forward and went over the side, while my own men, appearing on deck too, lined the rail. I escorted my visitor to the gangway ceremoniously, and nearly overdid it. He was a tenacious beast. On the very ladder he lingered, and in that unique, guiltily conscientious manner of sticking to the point:

"I say . . . you . . . you don't think that—"

I covered his voice loudly:

"Certainly not. . . . I am delighted. Good-by."

I had an idea of what he meant to say, and just saved myself by the privilege of defective hearing. He was too shaken generally to insist, but my mate, close witness of that parting, looked mystified and his face took on a thoughtful cast. As I did not want to appear as if I wished to avoid all communication with my officers, he had the opportunity to address me.

"Seems a very nice man. His boat's crew told our chaps a very extraordinary story, if what I am told by the steward is true. I suppose you had it from the captain, sir?"

"Yes. I had a story from the captain."

"A very horrible affair—isn't it, sir?"

"It is."

"Beats all these tales we hear about murders in Yankee ships."

"I don't think it beats them. I don't think it resembles them in the least."

"Bless my soul—you don't say so! But of course I've no acquaintance whatever with American ships, not I, so I couldn't go against your knowledge. It's horrible enough for me. . . . But the queerest part is that these fellows seemed to have some idea the man was hidden aboard here. They had really. Did you ever hear of such a thing?"

"Preposterous—isn't it?"

We were walking to and fro athwart the quarter-deck. No one of the crew forward could be seen (the day was Sunday), and the mate pursued:

"There was some little dispute about it. Our chaps took offense. 'As if we would harbor a thing like that,' they said. 'Wouldn't you like to look for him in our coal hole?' Quite a tiff. But they made it up in the end. I suppose he did drown himself. Don't you, sir?"

"I don't suppose anything."

"You have no doubt in the matter, sir?"

"None whatever."

I left him suddenly. I felt I was producing a bad impression, but with my double down there it was most trying to be on deck. And it was almost as trying to be below. Altogether a nerve-trying situation. But on the whole I felt less torn in two when I was with him. There was no one in the whole ship whom I dared take into my confidence. Since the hands had got to know his story, it would have been impossible to pass him off for anyone else, and an accidental discovery was to be dreaded now more than ever. . . . .

The steward being engaged in laying the table for dinner, we could talk only with our eyes when I first went down. Later in the afternoon we had a cautious try at whispering. The Sunday quietness of the ship was against us; the stillness of air and water around her was against us; the elements, the men were against us—everything was against us in our secret partnership; time itself—for this could not go on forever. The very trust in Providence was, I suppose, denied to his guilt. Shall I confess that this thought cast me down very much? And as to the chapter of accidents which counts for so much in the book of success, I could only hope that it was closed. For what favorable accident could be expected?

"Did you hear everything?" were my first words as soon as we took up our position side by side, leaning over my bed-place.

He had. And the proof of it was his earnest whisper, "The man told you he hardly dared to give the order."

I understood the reference to be to that saving foresail.

"Yes. He was afraid of it being lost in the setting."

"I assure you he never gave the order. He may think he did, but he never gave it. He stood there with me on the break of the poop after the maintopsail blew away, and whimpered about our last hope—positively whimpered about it and nothing else—and the night coming on! To hear one's skipper go on like that in such weather was enough to drive any fellow out of his mind. It worked me up into a sort of desperation. I just took it into my hands and went away from him, boiling, and—But what's the use telling you? *You* know! . . . Do you think that if I had not been pretty fierce with them I should have got the men to do anything? Not it! The bosun perhaps? Perhaps! It wasn't a heavy sea—it was a sea gone mad! I suppose the end of the world will be something like that; and a man may have the heart to see it coming once and be done with it—but to have to face it day after day—I don't blame anybody. I was precious little better than the rest. Only—I was an officer of that old coal-wagon, anyhow—"

"I quite understand," I conveyed that sincere assurance into his ear. He was out of breath with whispering; I could hear him pant slightly. It was all very simple. The same strung-up force which had given twenty-four men a chance, at least, for their lives, had, in a sort of recoil, crushed an unworthy mutinous existence.

But I had no leisure to weigh the merits of the matter—footsteps in the saloon, a heavy knock. "There's enough wind to get under way with, sir." Here was the call of a new claim upon my thoughts and even upon my feelings.

"Turn the hands up," I cried through the door. "I'll be on deck directly."

I was going out to make the acquaintance of my ship. Before I left the cabin our eyes met—the eyes of the only two strangers on board. I pointed to the recessed part where the little campstool awaited him and laid my finger on my lips. He made a gesture—somewhat vague—a little mysterious, accompanied by a faint smile, as if of regret.

This is not the place to enlarge upon the sensations of a man who feels for the first time a ship move under his feet to his own independent word. In my case they were not unalloyed. I was not wholly alone with my command; for there was that stranger in my cabin. Or rather, I was not completely and wholly with her. Part of me was absent. That mental feeling of being in two places at once affected me physically as if the mood of secrecy had penetrated my very soul. Before an hour had elapsed since the ship had begun to move, having occasion to ask the mate (he stood by my side) to take a compass bearing of the Pagoda, I caught myself reaching up to his ear in whispers. I say I caught myself, but enough had escaped to startle the man. I can't describe it otherwise than by saying that he shied. A grave, preoccupied manner, as though he were in possession of some perplexing intelligence, did not leave him henceforth. A little later I moved away from the rail to look at the compass with such a stealthy gait that the helmsman noticed it—and I could not help noticing the unusual roundness of his eyes. These are trifling instances, though it's to no commander's advantage to be suspected of ludicrous eccentricities. But I was also more seriously affected. There are to a seaman certain words, gestures, that should in given conditions come as naturally, as instinctively as the winking of a menaced eye. A certain order should spring on to his lips without thinking; a certain sign should get itself made, so to speak, without reflection. But all unconscious alertness had abandoned me. I had to make an effort of will to recall myself back (from the cabin) to the conditions of the moment. I felt that I was appearing an irresolute commander to those people who were watching me more or less critically.

And, besides, there were the scares. On the second day out, for instance, coming off the deck in the afternoon (I had straw slippers on my bare feet) I stopped at the open pantry door and spoke to the steward. He was doing something there with his back to me. At the sound of my voice he nearly jumped out of his skin, as the saying is, and incidentally broke a cup.

"What on earth's the matter with you?" I asked, astonished.

He was extremely confused. "Beg your pardon, sir. I made sure you were in your cabin."

"You see I wasn't."

"No, sir. I could have sworn I had heard you moving in there not a moment ago. It's most extraordinary . . . very sorry, sir."

I passed on with an inward shudder. I was so identified with my secret double that I did not even mention the fact in those scanty, fearful whispers we exchanged. I suppose he had made some slight noise of some kind or other. It would have been miraculous if he hadn't at one time or another. And yet, haggard as he appeared, he looked always perfectly self-controlled, more than calm—almost invulnerable. On my suggestion he remained almost entirely in the bathroom, which, upon the whole, was the safest place. There could be really no shadow of an excuse for anyone ever wanting to go in there, once the steward had done with it. It was a very tiny place. Sometimes he reclined on the floor, his legs bent, his head sustained on one elbow. At others I would find him on the campstool, sitting in his gray sleeping suit and with his cropped dark hair like a patient, unmoved convict. At night I would smuggle him into my bed-place, and we would whisper together, with the regular footfalls of the officer of the watch passing and repassing over our heads. It was an infinitely miserable time. It was lucky that some tins of fine preserves were stowed in a locker in my stateroom; hard bread I could always get hold of; and so he lived on stewed chicken, paté de foie gras, asparagus, cooked oysters, sardines—on all sorts of abominable sham delicacies out of tins. My early morning coffee he always drank; and it was all I dared do for him in that respect.

Every day there was the horrible maneuvering to go through so that my room and then the bathroom should be done in the usual way. I came to hate the sight of the steward, to abhor the voice of that harmless man. I felt that it was he who would bring on the disaster of discovery. It hung like a sword over our heads.

The fourth day out, I think (we were working down the east side of the Gulf of Siam, tack for tack, in light winds and smooth water)—the fourth day, I say, of this miserable juggling with the unavoidable, as we sat at our evening meal, that man, whose slightest movement I dreaded, after putting down the dishes ran up on deck busily. This could not be dangerous. Presently he came down again; and then it appeared that he had remembered a coat of mine which I had thrown over a rail to dry after having been wetted in a shower which had passed over the ship in the afternoon. Sitting stolidly at the head of the table I became terrified at the sight of the garment on his arm. Of course he made for my door. There was no time to lose.

"Steward," I thundered. My nerves were so shaken that I could not govern my voice and conceal my agitation. This was the sort of thing that made my terrifically whiskered mate tap his forehead with his forefinger. I had detected him using that gesture while talking on deck with a confidential air to the carpenter. It was too far to hear a word, but I had no doubt that this pantomime could only refer to the strange new captain.

"Yes, sir," the pale-faced steward turned resignedly to me. It was this maddening course of being shouted at, checked without rhyme or reason, arbitrarily chased out of my cabin, suddenly called into it, sent flying out of his pantry on incomprehensible errands, that accounted for the growing wretchedness of his expression.

"Where are you going with that coat?"

"To your room, sir."

"Is there another shower coming?"

"I'm sure I don't know, sir. Shall I go up again and see, sir?"

"No! never mind."

My object was attained, as of course my other self in there would have heard everything that passed. During this interlude my two officers never raised their eyes off their respective plates; but the lip of that confounded cub, the second mate, quivered visibly.

I expected the steward to hook my coat on and come out at once. He was very slow about it; but I dominated my nervousness sufficiently not to shout after him. Suddenly I became aware (it could be heard plainly enough) that the fellow for some reason or other was opening the door of the bathroom. It was the end. The place was literally not big enough to swing a cat in. My voice died in my throat and I went stony all over. I expected to hear a yell of surprise and terror, and made a movement, but had not the strength to get on my legs. Everything remained still. Had my second self taken the poor wretch by the throat? I don't know what I would have done next moment if I had not seen the steward come out of my room, close the door, and then stand quietly by the sideboard.

Saved, I thought. But, no! Lost! Gone! He was gone!

I laid my knife and fork down and leaned back in my chair. My head swam. After a while, when sufficiently recovered to speak in a steady voice, I instructed my mate to put the ship round at eight o'clock himself.

"I won't come on deck," I went on. "I think I'll turn in, and unless the wind shifts I don't want to be disturbed before midnight. I feel a bit seedy."

"You did look middling bad a little while ago," the chief mate remarked without showing any great concern.

They both went out, and I stared at the steward clearing the table. There was nothing to be read on that wretched man's face. But why did he avoid my eyes I asked myself. Then I thought I should like to hear the sound of his voice.

"Steward!"

"Sir!" Startled as usual.

"Where did you hang up that coat?"

"In the bathroom, sir." The usual anxious tone. "It's not quite dry yet, sir."

For some time longer I sat in the cuddy. Had my double vanished as he had come? But of his coming there was an explanation, whereas his disappearance would be inexplicable. . . . I went slowly into my dark room, shut the door, lighted the lamp, and for a time dared not turn round. When at last I did I saw him standing bolt upright in the narrow recessed part. It would not be true to say I had a shock, but an irresistible doubt of his bodily existence flitted through my mind. Can it be, I asked myself, that he is not visible to other eyes than mine? It was like being haunted. Motionless, with a grave face, he raised his hands slightly at me in a gesture which meant clearly, "Heavens! what a narrow escape!" Narrow indeed. I think I had come creeping quietly as near insanity as any man who has not actually gone over the border. That gesture restrained me, so to speak.

The mate with the terrific whiskers was now putting the ship on the other tack. In the moment of profound silence which follows upon the hands going to their stations I heard on the poop his raised voice: "Hard alee!" and the distant shout of the order repeated on the maindeck. The sails, in that light breeze, made but a faint fluttering noise. It ceased. The ship was coming round slowly; I held my breath in the renewed stillness of expectation; one wouldn't have thought that there was a single living soul on her decks. A sudden brisk shout, "Mainsail haul!" broke the spell, and in the noisy cries and rush overhead of the men running away with the main brace we two, down in my cabin, came together in our usual position by the bed-place.

He did not wait for my question. "I heard him fumbling here and just managed to squat myself down in the bath," he whispered to me. "The fellow only opened the door and put his arm in to hang the coat up. All the same—"

"I never thought of that," I whispered back, even more appalled than before at the closeness of the shave, and marveling at that something unyielding in his character which was carrying him through so finely. There was no agitation in his whisper. Whoever was being driven distracted, it was not he. He was sane. And the proof of his sanity was continued when he took up the whispering again.

"It would never do for me to come to life again."

It was something that a ghost might have said. But what he was alluding to was his old captain's reluctant admission of the theory of suicide. It would obviously serve his turn—if I had understood at all the view which seemed to govern the unalterable purpose of his action.

"You must maroon me as soon as ever you can get amongst these islands off the Cambodje shore," he went on.

"Maroon you! We are not living in a boy's adventure tale," I protested. His scornful whispering took me up.

"We aren't indeed! There's nothing of a boy's tale in this. But there's nothing else for it. I want no more. You don't suppose I am afraid of what can be done to me? Prison or gallows or whatever they may please. But you don't see me coming back to explain such things to an old fellow in a wig and twelve respectable tradesmen, do you? What can they know whether I am guilty or not— or of *what* I am guilty, either? That's my affair. What does the Bible say? 'Driven off the face of the earth.' Very well. I am off the face of the earth now. As I came at night so I shall go."

"Impossible!" I murmured. "You can't."

"Can't? . . . Not naked like a soul on the Day of Judgment. I shall freeze on to this sleeping suit. The Last Day is not yet—and . . . you have understood thoroughly. Didn't you?"

I felt suddenly ashamed of myself. I may say truly that I understood—and my hesitation in letting that man swim away from my ship's side had been a mere sham sentiment, a sort of cowardice.

"It can't be done now till next night," I breathed out. "The ship is on the offshore tack and the wind may fail us."

"As long as I know that you understand," he whispered. "But of course you do. It's a great satisfaction to have got somebody to understand. You seem to have been there on purpose." And in the same whisper, as if we two whenever we talked had to say things to each other which were not fit for the world to hear, he added, "It's very wonderful."

We remained side by side talking in our secret way—but sometimes silent or just exchanging a whispered word or two at long intervals. And as usual he stared through the port. A breath of wind came now and again into our faces. The ship might have been moored in dock, so gently and on an even keel she slipped through the water, that did not murmur even at our passage, shadowy and silent like a phantom sea.

At midnight I went on deck, and to my mate's great surprise put the ship round on the other tack. His terrible whiskers flitted round me in silent criticism. I certainly should not have done it if it had been only a question of getting out of that sleepy gulf as quickly as possible. I believe he told the second mate, who relieved him, that it was a great want of judgment. The other only yawned. That intolerable cub shuffled about so sleepily and lolled against the rails in such a slack, improper fashion that I came down on him sharply.

"Aren't you properly awake yet?"

"Yes, sir! I am awake."

"Well, then, be good enough to hold yourself as if you were. And keep a lookout. If there's any current we'll be closing with some islands before daylight."

The east side of the gulf is fringed with islands, some solitary, others in groups. On the blue background of the high coast they seem to float on silvery patches of calm water, arid and gray, or dark green and rounded like clumps of evergreen bushes, with the larger ones, a mile or two long, showing the outlines of ridges, ribs of gray rock under the dark mantle of matted leafage. Unknown to trade, to travel, almost to geography, the manner of life they harbor is an unsolved secret. There must be villages—settlements of fishermen at least—on the largest of them, and some communication with the world is probably kept up by native craft. But all forenoon, as we headed for them, fanned along by the faintest of breezes, I saw no sign of man or canoe in the field of the telescope I kept on pointing at the scattered group.

At noon I gave no orders for a change of course, and the mate's whiskers became much concerned and seemed to be offering themselves unduly to my notice. At last I said:

"I am going to stand right in. Quite in—as far as I can take her."

The stare of extreme surprise imparted an air of ferocity also to his eyes, and he looked truly terrific for a moment.

"We're not doing well in the middle of the gulf," I continued, casually. "I am going to look for the land breezes tonight."

"Bless my soul! Do you mean, sir, in the dark amongst the lot of all them islands and reefs and shoals?"

"Well—if there are any regular land breezes at all on this coast one must get close inshore to find them, mustn't one?"

"Bless my soul!" he exclaimed again under his breath. All that afternoon he wore a dreamy, contemplative appearance which in him was a mark of perplexity. After dinner I went into my stateroom as if I meant to take some rest. There we two bent our dark heads over a half-unrolled chart lying on my bed.

"There," I said. "It's got to be Koh-ring. I've been looking at it ever since sunrise. It has got two hills and a low point. It must be inhabited. And on the coast opposite there is what looks like the mouth of a biggish river—with some town, no doubt, not far up. It's the best chance for you that I can see."

"Anything. Koh-ring let it be."

He looked thoughtfully at the chart as if surveying chances and distances from a lofty height—and following with his eyes his own figure wandering on the blank land of Cochin China, and then passing off that piece of paper clean out of sight into uncharted regions. And it was as if the ship had two captains to plan her course for her. I had been so worried and restless running up and down that I had not had the patience to dress that day. I had remained in my sleeping suit, with straw slippers and a soft floppy hat. The closeness of the heat in the gulf had been most oppressive, and the crew were used to see me wandering in that airy attire.

"She will clear the south point as she heads now," I whispered into his ear. "Goodness only knows when, though, but certainly after dark. I'll edge her in to half a mile, as far as I may be able to judge in the dark—"

"Be careful," he murmured, warningly—and I realized suddenly that all my future, the only future for which I was fit, would perhaps go irretrievably to pieces in any mishap to my first command.

I could not stop a moment longer in the room. I motioned him to get out of sight and made my way on the poop. That unplayful cub had the watch. I walked up and down for a while thinking things out, then beckoned him over.

"Send a couple of hands to open the two quarter-deck ports," I said, mildly.

He actually had the impudence, or else so forgot himself in his wonder at such an incomprehensible order, as to repeat:

"Open the quarter-deck ports! What for, sir?"

"The only reason you need concern yourself about is because I tell you to do so. Have them open wide and fastened properly."

He reddened and went off, but I believe made some jeering remark to the carpenter as to the sensible practice of ventilating a ship's quarter-deck. I know he popped into the mate's cabin to impart the fact to him because the whiskers came on deck, as it were by chance, and stole glances at me from below—for signs of lunacy or drunkenness, I suppose.

A little before supper, feeling more restless than ever, I rejoined, for a moment, my second self. And to find him sitting so quietly was surprising, like something against nature, inhuman.

I developed my plan in a hurried whisper.

"I shall stand in as close as I dare and then put her round. I shall presently find means to smuggle you out of here into the sail locker, which communicates with the lobby. But there is an opening, a sort of square for hauling the sails out, which gives straight on the quarter-deck and which is never closed in fine weather, so as to give air to the sails. When the ship's way is deadened in stays and all the hands are aft at the main braces you shall have a clear road to slip out and get overboard through the open quarter-deck port. I've had them both fastened up. Use a rope's end to lower yourself into the water so as to avoid a splash—you know. It could be heard and cause some beastly complication."

He kept silent for a while, then whispered, "I understand."

"I won't be there to see you go," I began with an effort. "The rest . . . I only hope I have understood, too."

"You have. From first to last," and for the first time there seemed to be a faltering, something strained in his whisper. He caught hold of my arm, but the ringing of the supper bell made me start. He didn't, though; he only released his grip.

After supper I didn't come below again till well past eight o'clock. The faint, steady breeze was loaded with dew; and the wet, darkened sails held all there was of propelling power in it. The night, clear and starry, sparkled darkly, and the opaque, lightless patches shifting slowly against the low stars were the drifting islets. On the port bow there was a big one more distant and shadowily imposing by the great space of sky it eclipsed.

On opening the door I had a back view of my very own self looking at a chart. He had come out of the recess and was standing near the table.

"Quite dark enough," I whispered.

He stepped back and leaned against my bed with a level, quiet glance. I sat on the couch. We had nothing to say to each other. Over our heads the officer of the watch moved here and there. Then I heard him move quickly. I knew what that meant. He was making for the companion; and presently his voice was outside my door.

"We are drawing in pretty fast, sir. Land looks rather close."

"Very well," I answered. "I am coming on deck directly."

I waited till he was gone out of the cuddy, then rose. My double moved too. The time had come to exchange our last whispers, for neither of us was ever to hear each other's natural voice.

"Look here!" I opened a drawer and took out three sovereigns. "Take this, anyhow. I've got six and I'd give you the lot, only I must keep a little money to buy some fruit and vegetables for the crew from native boats as we go through Sunda Straits."

He shook his head.

"Take it," I urged him, whispering desperately. "No one can tell what—"

He smiled and slapped meaningly the only pocket of the sleeping jacket. It was not safe, certainly. But I produced a large old silk handkerchief of mine, and tying the three pieces of gold in a corner, pressed it on him. He was touched, I suppose, because he took it at last and tied it quickly round his waist under the jacket, on his bare skin.

Our eyes met; several seconds elapsed, till, our glances still mingled, I extended my hand and turned the lamp out. Then I passed through the cuddy, leaving the door of my room wide open. . . . "Steward!"

He was still lingering in the pantry in the greatness of his zeal, giving a rub-up to a plated cruet stand the last thing before going to bed. Being careful not to wake up the mate, whose room was opposite, I spoke in an undertone.

He looked round anxiously. "Sir!"

"Can you get me a little hot water from the galley?"

"I am afraid, sir, the galley fire's been out for some time now."

"Go and see."

He fled up the stairs.

"Now," I whispered, loudly, into the saloon—too loudly, perhaps, but I was afraid I couldn't make a sound. He was by my side in an instant—the double captain slipped past the stairs—through the tiny dark passage . . . a sliding door. We were in the sail locker, scrambling on our knees over the sails. A sudden thought struck me. I saw myself wandering barefooted, bareheaded, the sun beating on my dark poll. I snatched off my floppy hat and tried hurriedly in the dark to ram it on my other self. He dodged and fended off silently. I wonder what he thought had come to me before he understood and suddenly desisted. Our hands met gropingly, lingered united in a steady, motionless clasp for a second. . . . No word was breathed by either of us when they separated.

I was standing quietly by the pantry door when the steward returned.

"Sorry, sir. Kettle barely warm. Shall I light the spirit lamp?"

"Never mind."

I came out on deck slowly. It was now a matter of conscience to shave the land as close as possible—for now he must go overboard whenever the ship was put in stays. Must! There could be no going back for him. After a moment I walked over to leeward and my heart flew into my mouth at the nearness of the land on the bow. Under any other circumstances I would not have held on a minute longer. The second mate had followed me anxiously.

I looked on till I felt I could command my voice.

"She will weather," I said then in a quiet tone.

"Are you going to try that, sir?" he stammered out incredulously.

I took no notice of him and raised my tone just enough to be heard by the helmsman.

"Keep her good full."

"Good full, sir."

The wind fanned my cheek, the sails slept, the world was silent. The strain of watching the dark loom of the land grow bigger and denser was too much for me. I had shut my eyes—because the ship must go closer. She must! The stillness was intolerable. Were we standing still?

When I opened my eyes the second view started my heart with a thump. The black southern hill of Koh-ring seemed to hang right over the ship like a towering fragment of the everlasting night. On that enormous mass of blackness there was not a gleam to be seen, not a sound to be heard. It was gliding irresistibly toward us and yet seemed already within reach of the hand. I saw the vague figures of the watch grouped in the waist, gazing in awed silence.

"Are you going on, sir?" inquired an unsteady voice at my elbow.

I ignored it. I had to go on.

"Keep her full. Don't check her way. That won't do now," I said warningly.

"I can't see the sails very well," the helmsman answered me, in strange, quavering tones.

Was she close enough? Already she was, I won't say in the shadow of the land, but in the very blackness of it, already swallowed up as it were, gone too close to be recalled, gone from me altogether.

"Give the mate a call," I said to the young man who stood at my elbow still as death. "And turn all hands up."

My tone had a borrowed loudness reverberated from the height of the land. Several voices cried out together: "We are all on deck, sir."

Then stillness again, with the great shadow gliding closer, towering higher, without a light, without a sound. Such a hush had fallen on the ship that she might have been a bark of the dead floating in slowly under the very gate of Erebus.

"My God! Where are we?"

It was the mate moaning at my elbow. He was thunderstruck, and as it were deprived of the moral support of his whiskers. He clapped his hands and absolutely cried out, "Lost!"

"Be quiet," I said sternly.

He lowered his tone, but I saw the shadowy gesture of his despair. "What are we doing here?"

"Looking for the land wind."

He made as if to tear his hair, and addressed me recklessly.

"She will never get out. You have done it, sir. I knew it'd end in something like this. She will never weather, and you are too close now to stay. She'll drift ashore before she's round. O my God!"

I caught his arm as he was raising it to batter his poor devoted head, and shook it violently.

"She's ashore already," he wailed, trying to tear himself away.

"Is she? . . . Keep good full there!"

"Good full, sir," cried the helmsman in a frightened, thin, childlike voice.

I hadn't let go the mate's arm and went on shaking it. "Ready about, do you hear? You go forward"—shake—"and stop there"—shake—"and hold your noise"—shake—"and see these head sheets properly overhauled"—shake, shake—shake.

And all the time I dared not look toward the land lest my heart should fail me. I released my grip at last and he ran forward as if fleeing for dear life.

I wondered what my double there in the sail locker thought of this commotion. He was able to hear everything—and perhaps he was able to understand why, on my conscience, it had to be thus close—no less. My first order "Hard alee!" re-echoed ominously under the towering shadow of Koh-ring as if I had shouted in a mountain gorge. And then I watched the land intently. In that smooth water and light wind it was impossible to feel the ship coming-to. No!

I could not feel her. And my second self was making now ready to slip out and lower himself overboard. Perhaps he was gone already . . . ?

The great black mass brooding over our very mastheads began to pivot away from the ship's side silently. And now I forgot the secret stranger ready to depart, and remembered only that I was a total stranger to the ship. I did not know her. Would she do it? How was she to be handled?

I swung the mainyard and waited helplessly. She was perhaps stopped, and her very fate hung in the balance, with the black mass of Koh-ring like the gate of the everlasting night towering over her taffrail. What would she do now? Had she way on her yet? I stepped to the side swiftly, and on the shadowy water I could see nothing except a faint phosphorescent flash revealing the glassy smoothness of the sleeping surface. It was impossible to tell—and I had not learned yet the feel of my ship. Was she moving? What I needed was something easily seen, a piece of paper, which I could throw overboard and watch. I had nothing on me. To run down for it I didn't dare. There was no time. All at once my strained, yearning stare distinguished a white object floating within a yard of the ship's side. White on the black water. A phosphorescent flash passed under it. What was that thing? . . . I recognized my own floppy hat. It must have fallen off his head . . . and he didn't bother. Now I had what I wanted— the saving mark for my eyes. But I hardly thought of my other self, now gone from the ship, to be hidden forever from all friendly faces, to be a fugitive and a vagabond on the earth, with no brand of the curse on his sane forehead to stay a slaying hand . . . too proud to explain.

And I watched the hat—the expression of my sudden pity for his mere flesh. It had been meant to save his homeless head from the dangers of the sun. And now—behold—it was saving the ship, by serving me for a mark to help out the ignorance of my strangeness. Ha! It was drifting forward, warning me just in time that the ship had gathered sternway.

"Shift the helm," I said in a low voice to the seaman standing still like a statue.

The man's eyes glistened wildly in the binnacle light as he jumped round to the other side and spun round the wheel.

I walked to the break of the poop. On the overshadowed deck all hands stood by the forebraces waiting for my order. The stars ahead seemed to be gliding from right to left. And all was so still in the world that I heard the quiet remark "She's round," passed in a tone of intense relief between two seamen.

"Let go and haul."

The foreyards ran round with a great noise, amidst cheery cries. And now the frightful whiskers made themselves heard giving various orders. Already the ship was drawing ahead. And I was alone with her. Nothing! no one in the world should stand now between us, throwing a shadow on the way of silent knowledge and mute affection, the perfect communion of a seaman with his first command.

Walking to the taffrail, I was in time to make out, on the very edge of a darkness thrown by a towering black mass like the very gateway of Erebus—yes, I was in time to catch an evanescent glimpse of my white hat left behind to mark the spot where the secret sharer of my cabin and of my thoughts, as though he were my second self, had lowered himself into the water to take his punishment: a free man, a proud swimmer striking out for a new destiny.

QUESTIONS

1. "And suddenly I rejoiced in the great security of the sea as compared with the unrest of the land, in my choice of that untempted life presenting no disquieting problems, invested with an elementary moral beauty by the absolute straightforwardness of its appeal and by the singleness of its purpose" (p. 24). Do the events of the story justify these early musings of the captain? Explain. Who in the story might represent elementary morality? Can that elementary morality be described as "beautiful"? Why or why not?   **2.**   When the frightened mate cries out that the ship will founder, the captain catches his arm. "I hadn't let go the mate's arm and went on shaking it. 'Ready about, do you hear? You go forward'—shake—'and stop there'—shake—'and hold your noise'—shake—'and see these head sheets properly overhauled'—shake, shake—shake'" (p. 48). What is the significance of the captain's behavior?

WRITING TOPIC

If the captain is "innocent" at the outset, in what way is he "experienced" at the conclusion?

The Bride Comes to Yellow Sky

1898

STEPHEN CRANE [1871–1900]

I

The great Pullman was whirling onward with such dignity of motion that a glance from the window seemed simply to prove that the plains of Texas were pouring eastward. Vast flats of green grass, dull-hued space of mesquit and cactus, little groups of frame houses, woods of light and tender trees, all were sweeping into the east, sweeping over the horizon, a precipice.

A newly married pair had boarded this coach at San Antonio. The man's face was reddened from many days in the wind and sun, and a direct result of his new black clothes was that his brick-coloured hands were constantly performing in a most conscious fashion. From time to time he looked down respectfully at his attire. He sat with a hand on each knee, like a man waiting in a barber's shop. The glances he devoted to other passengers were furtive and shy.

The bride was not pretty, nor was she very young. She wore a dress of blue cashmere, with small reservations of velvet here and there, and with steel buttons abounding. She continually twisted her head to regard her puff sleeves, very stiff, straight, and high. They embarrassed her. It was quite apparent that she had cooked, and that she expected to cook, dutifully. The blushes caused by the careless scrutiny of some passengers as she had entered the car were strange to see upon this plain, under-class countenance, which was drawn in placid, almost emotionless lines.

They were evidently very happy. "Ever been in a parlour-car before?" he asked, smiling with delight.

"No," she answered; "I never was. It's fine, ain't it?"

"Great! And then after a while we'll go forward to the diner, and get a big lay-out. Finest meal in the world. Charge a dollar."

"Oh, do they?" cried the bride. "Charge a dollar? Why, that's too much—for us—ain't it, Jack?"

"Not this trip, anyhow," he answered bravely. "We're going to go the whole thing."

Later he explained to her about the trains. "You see, it's a thousand miles from one end of Texas to the other; and this train runs right across it, and never stops but four times." He had the pride of an owner. He pointed out to her the dazzling fittings of the coach; and in truth her eyes opened wider as she contemplated the sea-green figured velvet, the shining brass, silver, and glass, the wood that gleamed as darkly brilliant as the surface of a pool of oil. At one end

a bronze figure sturdily held a support for a separated chamber, and at convenient places on the ceiling were frescos in olive and silver.

To the minds of the pair, their surroundings reflected the glory of their
marriage that morning in San Antonio; this was the environment of their new
estate; and the man's face in particular beamed with an elation that made him
appear ridiculous to the negro porter. This individual at times surveyed them
from afar with an amused and superior grin. On other occasions he bullied
them with skill in ways that did not make it exactly plain to them that they were
being bullied. He subtly used all the manners of the most unconquerable kind
of snobbery. He oppressed them; but of this oppression they had small knowledge, and they speedily forgot that infrequently a number of travellers covered
them with stares of derisive enjoyment. Historically there was supposed to be
something infinitely humorous in their situation.

"We are due in Yellow Sky at 3:42," he said, looking tenderly into her eyes.

"Oh, are we?" she said, as if she had not been aware of it. To evince surprise
at her husband's statement was part of her wifely amiability. She took from a
pocket a little silver watch; and as she held it before her, and stared at it with
a frown of attention, the new husband's face shone.

"I bought it in San Anton' from a friend of mine," he told her gleefully.

"It's seventeen minutes past twelve," she said, looking up at him with a kind
of shy and clumsy coquetry. A passenger, noting this play, grew excessively
sardonic, and winked at himself in one of the numerous mirrors.

At last they went to the dining-car. Two rows of negro waiters, in glowing
white suits, surveyed their entrance with the interest, and also the equanimity,
of men who had been forewarned. The pair fell to the lot of a waiter who
happened to feel pleasure in steering them through their meal. He viewed them
with the manner of a fatherly pilot, his countenance radiant with benevolence.
The patronage, entwined with the ordinary deference, was not plain to them.
And yet, as they returned to their coach, they showed in their faces a sense of
escape.

To the left, miles down a long purple slope, was a little ribbon of mist where
moved the keening Rio Grande. The train was approaching it at an angle, and
the apex was Yellow Sky. Presently it was apparent that, as the distance from
Yellow Sky grew shorter, the husband became commensurately restless. His
brick-red hands were more insistent in their prominence. Occasionally he was
even rather absent-minded and far-away when the bride leaned forward and
addressed him.

As a matter of truth, Jack Potter was beginning to find the shadow of a deed
weigh upon him like a leaden slab. He, the town marshal of Yellow Sky, a man
known, liked, and feared in his corner, a prominent person, had gone to San
Antonio to meet a girl he believed he loved, and there, after the usual prayers,
had actually induced her to marry him, without consulting Yellow Sky for any
part of the transaction. He was now bringing his bride before an innocent and
unsuspecting community.

Of course people in Yellow Sky married as it pleased them, in accordance with a general custom; but such was Potter's thought of his duty to his friends, or of their idea of his duty, or of an unspoken form which does not control men in these matters, that he felt he was heinous. He had committed an extraordinary crime. Face to face with this girl in San Antonio, and spurred by his sharp impulse, he had gone headlong over all the social hedges. At San Antonio he was like a man hidden in the dark. A knife to sever any friendly duty, any form, was easy to his hand in that remote city. But the hour of Yellow Sky—the hour of daylight—was approaching.

He knew full well that his marriage was an important thing to his town. It could only be exceeded by the burning of the new hotel. His friends could not forgive him. Frequently he had reflected on the advisability of telling them by telegraph, but a new cowardice had been upon him. He feared to do it. And now the train was hurrying him toward a scene of amazement, glee, and reproach. He glanced out of the window at the line of haze swinging slowly in toward the train.

Yellow Sky had a kind of brass band, which played painfully, to the delight of the populace. He laughed without heart as he thought of it. If the citizens could dream of his prospective arrival with his bride, they would parade the band at the station and escort them, amid cheers and laughing congratulations, to his adobe home.

He resolved that he would use all the devices of speed and plainscraft in making the journey from the station to his house. Once within that safe citadel, he could issue some sort of vocal bulletin, and then not go among the citizens until they had time to wear off a little of their enthusiasm.

The bride looked anxiously at him. "What's worrying you, Jack?"

He laughed again. "I'm not worrying, girl; I'm only thinking of Yellow Sky."

She flushed in comprehension.

A sense of mutual guilt invaded their minds and developed a finer tenderness. They looked at each other with eyes softly aglow. But Potter often laughed the same nervous laugh; the flush upon the bride's face seemed quite permanent.

The traitor to the feelings of Yellow Sky narrowly watched the speeding landscape. "We're nearly there," he said.

Presently the porter came and announced the proximity of Potter's home. He held a brush in his hand, and, with all his airy superiority gone, he brushed Potter's new clothes as the latter slowly turned this way and that way. Potter fumbled out a coin and gave it to the porter, as he had seen others do. It was a heavy and muscle-bound business, as that of a man shoeing his first horse.

The porter took their bag, and as the train began to slow they moved forward to the hooded platform of the car. Presently the two engines and their string of coaches rushed into the station of Yellow Sky.

"They have to take water here," said Potter, from a constricted throat and in mournful cadence, as one announcing death. Before the train stopped his eye had swept the length of the platform, and he was glad and astonished to see there was none upon it but the station-agent, who, with a slightly hurried and anxious air, was walking toward the water-tanks. When the train had halted, the porter alighted first, and placed in position a little temporary step.

"Come on, girl," said Potter, hoarsely. As he helped her down they each laughed on a false note. He took the bag from the negro, and bade his wife cling to his arm. As they slunk rapidly away, his hang-dog glance perceived that they were unloading the two trunks, and also that the station-agent, far ahead near the baggage-car, had turned and was running toward him, making gestures. He laughed, and groaned as he laughed, when he noted the first effect of his marital bliss upon Yellow Sky. He gripped his wife's arm firmly to his side, and they fled. Behind them the porter stood, chuckling fatuously.

II

The California express on the Southern Railway was due at Yellow Sky in twenty-one minutes. There were six men at the bar of the Weary Gentleman saloon. One was a drummer who talked a great deal and rapidly; three were Texans who did not care to talk at that time; and two were Mexican sheep-herders, who did not talk as a general practice in the Weary Gentleman saloon. The barkeeper's dog lay on the board walk that crossed in front of the door. His head was on his paws, and he glanced drowsily here and there with the constant vigilance of a dog that is kicked on occasion. Across the sandy street were some vivid green grass-plots, so wonderful in appearance, amid the sands that burned near them in a blazing sun, that they caused a doubt in the mind. They exactly resembled the grass mats used to represent lawns on the stage. At the cooler end of the railway station, a man without a coat sat in a tilted chair and smoked his pipe. The fresh-cut bank of the Rio Grande circled near the town, and there could be seen beyond it a great plum-coloured plain of mesquit.

Save for the busy drummer and his companions in the saloon, Yellow Sky was dozing. The new-comer leaned gracefully upon the bar, and recited many tales with the confidence of a bard who has come upon a new field.

"—and at the moment that the old man fell downstairs with the bureau in his arms, the old woman was coming up with two scuttles of coal, and of course—"

The drummer's tale was interrupted by a young man who suddenly appeared in the open door. He cried· "Scratchy Wilson's drunk, and has turned loose with both hands." The two Mexicans at once set down their glasses and faded out of the rear entrance of the saloon.

The drummer, innocent and jocular, answered: "All right, old man. S'pose he has? Come in and have a drink, anyhow."

But the information had made such an obvious cleft in every skull in the room that the drummer was obliged to see its importance. All had become instantly solemn. "Say," said he, mystified, "what is this?" His three companions made the introductory gesture of eloquent speech; but the young man at the door forestalled them.

"It means, my friend," he answered, as he came into the saloon, "that for the next two hours this town won't be a health resort."

The barkeeper went to the door, and locked and barred it; reaching out of the window, he pulled in heavy wooden shutters, and barred them. Immediately a solemn chapel-like gloom was upon the place. The drummer was looking from one to another.

"But say," he cried, "what is this, anyhow? You don't mean there is going to be a gun-fight?"

"Don't know whether there'll be a fight or not," answered one man, grimly; "but there'll be some shootin'—some good shootin'."

The young man who had warned them waved his hand. "Oh, there'll be a fight fast enough, if any one wants it. Anybody can get a fight out there in the street. There's a fight just waiting."

The drummer seemed to be swayed between the interest of a foreigner and a perception of personal danger.

"What did you say his name was?" he asked.

"Scratchy Wilson," they answered in chorus.

"And will he kill anybody? What are you going to do? Does this happen often? Does he rampage around like this once a week or so? Can he break in that door?"

"No; he can't break down that door," replied the barkeeper. "He's tried it three times. But when he comes you'd better lay down on the floor, stranger. He's dead sure to shoot at it, and a bullet may come through."

Thereafter the drummer kept a strict eye upon the door. The time had not yet been called for him to hug the floor, but, as a minor precaution, he sidled near to the wall. "Will he kill anybody?" he said again.

The men laughed low and scornfully at the question.

"He's out to shoot, and he's out for trouble. Don't see any good in experimentin' with him."

"But what do you do in a case like this? What do you do?"

A man responded: "Why, he and Jack Potter—"

"But," in chorus the other men interrupted, "Jack Potter's in San Anton'."

"Well, who is he? What's he got to do with it?"

"Oh, he's the town marshal. He goes out and fights Scratchy when he gets on one of these tears."

"Wow!" said the drummer, mopping his brow. "Nice job he's got."

The voices had toned away to mere whisperings. The drummer wished to ask further questions, which were born of an increasing anxiety and bewilderment; but when he attempted them, the men merely looked at him in irritation and motioned him to remain silent. A tense waiting hush was upon them. In the deep shadows of the room their eyes shone as they listened for sounds from the street. One man made three gestures at the barkeeper; and the latter, moving like a ghost, handed him a glass and a bottle. The man poured a full glass of whisky, and set down the bottle noiselessly. He gulped the whisky in a swallow, and turned again toward the door in immovable silence. The drummer saw that the barkeeper, without a sound, had taken a Winchester from beneath the bar. Later he saw this individual beckoning to him, so he tiptoed across the room.

"You better come with me back of the bar."

"No, thanks," said the drummer, perspiring; "I'd rather be where I can make a break for the back door."

Whereupon the man of bottles made a kindly but peremptory gesture. The drummer obeyed it, and, finding himself seated on a box with his head below the level of the bar, balm was laid upon his soul at sight of various zinc and copper fittings that bore a resemblance to armour-plate. The barkeeper took a seat comfortably upon an adjacent box.

"You see," he whispered, "this here Scratchy Wilson is a wonder with a gun—a perfect wonder; and when he goes on the war-trail, we hunt our holes— naturally. He's about the last one of the old gang that used to hang out along the river here. He's a terror when he's drunk. When he's sober he's all right— kind of simple—wouldn't hurt a fly—nicest fellow in town. But when he's drunk—whoo!"

There were periods of stillness. "I wish Jack Potter was back from San Anton'," said the barkeeper. "He shot Wilson up once—in the leg—and he would sail in and pull out the kinks in this thing."

Presently they heard from a distance the sound of a shot, followed by three wild yowls. It instantly removed a bond from the men in the darkened saloon. There was a shuffling of feet. They looked at each other. "Here he comes," they said.

III

A man in a maroon-coloured flannel shirt, which had been purchased for purposes of decoration, and made principally by some Jewish women on the East Side of New York, rounded a corner and walked into the middle of the main street of Yellow Sky. In either hand the man held a long, heavy, blue-black revolver. Often he yelled, and these cries rang through a semblance of a deserted village, shrilly flying over the roofs in a volume that seemed to have no relation to the ordinary vocal strength of a man. It was as if the surrounding stillness formed the arch of a tomb over him. These cries of ferocious challenge rang against walls of silence. And his boots had red tops with gilded imprints, of the kind beloved in winter by little sledding boys on the hillsides of New England.

The man's face flamed in a rage begot of whisky. His eyes, rolling, and yet keen for ambush, hunted the still doorways and windows. He walked with the creeping movement of the midnight cat. As it occurred to him, he roared menacing information. The long revolvers in his hands were as easy as straws; they were moved with an electric swiftness. The little fingers of each hand played sometimes in a musician's way. Plain from the low collar of the shirt, the cords of his neck straightened and sank, straightened and sank, as passion moved him. The only sounds were his terrible invitations. The calm adobes preserved their demeanor at the passing of this small thing in the middle of the street.

There was no offer of fight—no offer of fight. The man called to the sky. There were no attractions. He bellowed and fumed and swayed his revolvers here and everywhere.

The dog of the barkeeper of the Weary Gentleman saloon had not appreciated the advance of events. He yet lay dozing in front of his master's door. At sight of the dog, the man paused and raised his revolver humorously. At sight of the man, the dog sprang up and walked diagonally away, with a sullen head, and growling. The man yelled, and the dog broke into a gallop. As it was about to enter an alley, there was a loud noise, a whistling, and something spat the ground directly before it. The dog screamed, and, wheeling in terror, galloped headlong in a new direction. Again there was a noise, a whistling, and sand was kicked viciously before it. Fear-stricken, the dog turned and flurried like an animal in a pen. The man stood laughing, his weapons at his hips.

Ultimately the man was attracted by the closed door of the Weary Gentleman saloon. He went to it and, hammering with a revolver, demanded drink.

The door remaining imperturbable, he picked a bit of paper from the walk, and nailed it to the framework with a knife. He then turned his back contemptuously upon this popular resort and, walking to the opposite side of the street and spinning there on his heel quickly and lithely, fired at the bit of paper. He missed it by a half-inch. He swore at himself, and went away. Later he comfortably fusilladed the windows of his most intimate friend. The man was playing with this town; it was a toy for him.

But still there was no offer of fight. The name of Jack Potter, his ancient antagonist, entered his mind, and he concluded that it would be a glad thing if he should go to Potter's house and by bombardment induce him to come out and fight. He moved in the direction of his desire, chanting Apache scalp-music.

When he arrived at it, Potter's house presented the same still front as had the other adobes. Taking up a strategic position, the man howled a challenge. But this house regarded him as might a great stone god. It gave no sign. After a decent wait, the man howled further challenges, mingling with them wonderful epithets.

Presently there came the spectacle of a man churning himself into deepest rage over the immobility of a house. He fumed at it as the winter wind attacks a prairie cabin in the North. To the distance there should have gone the sound of a tumult like the fighting of two hundred Mexicans. As necessity bade him, he paused for breath or to reload his revolvers.

IV

Potter and his bride walked sheepishly and with speed. Sometimes they laughed together shamefacedly and low.

"Next corner, dear," he said finally.

They put forth the efforts of a pair walking bowed against a strong wind. Potter was about to raise a finger to point the first appearance of the new home when, as they circled the corner, they came face to face with a man in a maroon-coloured shirt, who was feverishly pushing cartridges into a large revolver. Upon the instant the man dropped his revolver to the ground and, like lightning, whipped another from its holster. The second weapon was aimed at the bridegroom's chest.

There was a silence. Potter's mouth seemed to be merely a grave for his tongue. He exhibited an instinct to at once loosen his arm from the woman's grip, and he dropped the bag to the sand. As for the bride, her face had gone as yellow as old cloth. She was a slave to hideous rites, gazing at the apparitional snake.

The two men faced each other at a distance of three paces. He of the revolver smiled with a new and quiet ferocity.

"Tried to sneak up on me," he said. "Tried to sneak up on me!" His eyes grew more baleful. As Potter made a slight movement, the man thrust his revolver venomously forward. "No; don't you do it, Jack Potter. Don't you move a finger toward a gun just yet. Don't you move an eyelash. The time has come for me to settle with you, and I'm goin' to do it my own way, and loaf along with no interferin'. So if you don't want a gun bent on you, just mind what I tell you."

Potter looked at his enemy. "I ain't got a gun on me, Scratchy," he said. "Honest, I ain't." He was stiffening and steadying, but yet somewhere at the back of his mind a vision of the Pullman floated: the sea-green figured velvet, the shining brass, silver, and glass, the wood that gleamed as darkly brilliant as the surface of a pool of oil—all the glory of the marriage, the environment of the new estate. "You know I fight when it comes to fighting, Scratchy Wilson; but I ain't got a gun on me. You'll have to do all the shootin' yourself."

His enemy's face went livid. He stepped forward, and lashed his weapon to and fro before Potter's chest. "Don't you tell me you ain't got no gun on you, you whelp. Don't tell me no lie like that. There ain't a man in Texas ever seen you without no gun. Don't take me for no kid." His eyes blazed with light, and his throat worked like a pump.

"I ain't takin' you for no kid," answered Potter. His heels had not moved an inch backward. "I'm takin' you for a damn fool. I tell you I ain't got a gun, and I ain't. If you're goin' to shoot me up, you better begin now; you'll never get a chance like this again."

So much enforced reasoning had told on Wilson's rage; he was calmer. "If you ain't got a gun, why ain't you got a gun?" he sneered. "Been to Sunday-school?"

"I ain't got a gun because I've just come from San Anton' with my wife. I'm married," said Potter. "And if I'd thought there was going to be any galoots like you prowling around when I brought my wife home, I'd had a gun, and don't you forget it."

"Married!" said Scratchy, not at all comprehending.

"Yes, married. I'm married," said Potter, distinctly.

"Married?" said Scratchy. Seemingly for the first time, he saw the drooping, drowning woman at the other man's side. "No!" he said. He was like a creature allowed a glimpse of another world. He moved a pace backward, and his arm, with the revolver, dropped to his side. "Is this the lady?" he asked.

"Yes; this is the lady," answered Potter.

There was another period of silence.

"Well," said Wilson at last, slowly, "I s'pose it's all off now."

"It's all off if you say so, Scratchy. You know I didn't make the trouble." Potter lifted his valise.

"Well, I 'low it's off, Jack," said Wilson. He was looking at the ground. "Married!" He was not a student of chivalry; it was merely that in the presence of this foreign condition he was a simple child of the earlier plains. He picked up his starboard revolver, and, placing both weapons in their holsters, he went away. His feet made funnel-shaped tracks in the heavy sand.

QUESTIONS

1. Scratchy is described in the final paragraph as "a simple child of the earlier plains." What does this mean? Was Potter ever a simple child of the earlier plains? **2.** Early in the story we read that ". . . Jack Potter was beginning to find the shadow of a deed weigh upon him like a leaden slab. He, the town marshal of Yellow Sky, a man known, liked, and feared in his corner, a prominent person, had gone to San Antonio to meet a girl he believed he loved, and there, after the usual prayers, had actually induced her to marry him, without consulting Yellow Sky for any part of the transaction. He was now bringing his bride before an innocent and unsuspecting community." Jack Potter, like any man, has a right to marry. How do you account for his feelings as described in this passage? **3.** A "drummer" is a traveling salesman. What effect does his presence have on the "myth of the West"?

WRITING TOPICS

1. How would you characterize Scratchy's behavior? How does it relate to the "myth of the West" preserved in films and western novels? How does the description of Scratchy's shirt at the beginning of part III affect that view of the West? Why is Scratchy disconsolate at the end? **2.** Analyze Crane's metaphors and images. What function do they serve in the story?

I Want to Know Why   1921

SHERWOOD ANDERSON   [1876–1941]

We got up at four in the morning, that first day in the east. On the evening
before we had climbed off a freight train at the edge of town, and with the true
instinct of Kentucky boys had found our way across town and to the race track
and the stables at once. Then we knew we were all right. Hanley Turner right
away found a nigger we knew. It was Bildad Johnson who in the winter works
at Ed Becker's livery barn in our home town, Beckersville. Bildad is a good cook
as almost all our niggers are and of course he, like everyone in our part of
Kentucky who is anyone at all, likes the horses. In the spring Bildad begins to
scratch around. A nigger from our country can flatter and wheedle anyone into
letting him do most anything he wants. Bildad wheedles the stable men and the
trainers from the horse farms in our country around Lexington. The trainers
come into town in the evening to stand around and talk and maybe get into a
poker game. Bildad gets in with them. He is always doing little favors and telling
about things to eat, chicken browned in a pan, and how is the best way to cook
sweet potatoes and corn bread. It makes your mouth water to hear him.

When the racing season comes on and the horses go to the races and there
is all the talk on the streets in the evenings about the new colts, and everyone
says when they are going over to Lexington or to the spring meeting at Churchill
Downs or to Latonia, and the horsemen that have been down to New Orleans
or maybe at the winter meeting at Havana in Cuba come home to spend a week
before they start out again, at such a time when everything talked about in
Beckersville is just horses and nothing else and the outfits start out and horse
racing is in every breath of air you breathe, Bildad shows up with a job as cook
for some outfit. Often when I think about it, his always going all season to the
races and working in the livery barn in the winter where horses are and where
men like to come and talk about horses, I wish I was a nigger. It's a foolish
thing to say, but that's the way I am about being around horses, just crazy. I
can't help it.

Well, I must tell you about what we did and let you in on what I'm talking
about. Four of us boys from Beckersville, all whites and sons of men who live
in Beckersville regular, made up our minds we were going to the races, not just
to Lexington or Louisville, I don't mean, but to the big eastern track we were
always hearing our Beckersville men talk about, to Saratoga. We were all pretty
young then. I was just turned fifteen and I was the oldest of the four. It was my
scheme. I admit that and I talked the others into trying it. There was Hanley
Turner and Henry Rieback and Tom Tumberton and myself. I had thirty-seven
dollars I had earned during the winter working nights and Saturdays in Enoch
Myer's grocery. Henry Rieback had eleven dollars and the others, Hanley and

Tom, had only a dollar or two each. We fixed it all up and laid low until the Kentucky spring meetings were over and some of our men, the sportiest ones, the ones we envied the most, had cut out—then we cut out too.

I won't tell you the trouble we had beating our way on freights and all. We went through Cleveland and Buffalo and other cities and saw Niagara Falls. We bought things there, souvenirs and spoons and cards and shells with pictures of the falls on them for our sisters and mothers, but thought we had better not send any of the things home. We didn't want to put the folks on our trail and maybe be nabbed.

We got into Saratoga as I said at night and went to the track. Bildad fed us up. He showed us a place to sleep in hay over a shed and promised to keep still. Niggers are all right about things like that. They won't squeal on you. Often a white man you might meet, when you had run away from home like that, might appear to be all right and give you a quarter or a half-dollar or something, and then go right and give you away. White men will do that, but not a nigger. You can trust them. They are squarer with kids. I don't know why.

At the Saratoga meeting that year there were a lot of men from home. Dave Williams and Arthur Mulford and Jerry Myers and others. Then there was a lot from Louisville and Lexington Henry Rieback knew but I didn't. They were professional gamblers and Henry Rieback's father is one too. He is what is called a sheet writer and goes away most of the year to tracks. In the winter when he is home in Beckersville he don't stay there much but goes away to cities and deals faro. He is a nice man and generous, is always sending Henry presents, a bicycle and a gold watch and a boy scout suit of clothes and things like that.

My own father is a lawyer. He's all right, but don't make much money and can't buy me things and anyway I'm getting so old now I don't expect it. He never said nothing to me against Henry, but Hanley Turner and Tom Tumberton's fathers did. They said to their boys that money so come by is no good and they didn't want their boys brought up to hear gamblers' talk and be thinking about such things and maybe embrace them.

That's all right and I guess the men know what they are talking about, but I don't see what it's got to do with Henry or with horses either. That's what I'm writing this story about. I'm puzzled. I'm getting to be a man and want to think straight and be O.K., and there's something I saw at the race meeting at the eastern track I can't figure out.

I can't help it, I'm crazy about thoroughbred horses. I've always been that way. When I was ten years old and saw I was growing to be big and couldn't be a rider I was so sorry I nearly died. Harry Hellinfinger in Beckersville, whose father is Postmaster, is grown up and too lazy to work, but liked to stand around in the street and get up jokes on boys like sending them to a hardware store for a gimlet to bore square holes and other jokes like that. He played one on me. He told me that if I would eat a half a cigar I would be stunted and not grow any more and maybe could be a rider. I did it. When father wasn't looking I took a cigar out of his pocket and gagged it down some way. It made me awful sick and the doctor had to be sent for, and then it did no good. I kept right on growing. It was a joke. When I told what I had done and why most fathers would have whipped me but mine didn't.

Well, I didn't get stunted and didn't die. It serves Harry Hellinfinger right. Then I made up my mind I would like to be a stable boy, but had to give that up too. Mostly niggers do that work and I knew father wouldn't let me go into it. No use to ask him.

If you've never been crazy about thoroughbreds it's because you've never been around where they are much and don't know any better. They're beautiful. There isn't anything so lovely and clean and full of spunk and honest and everything as some race horses. On the big horse farms that are all around our town Beckersville there are tracks and the horses run in the early morning. More than a thousand times I've got out of bed before daylight and walked two or three miles to the tracks. Mother wouldn't of let me go but father always says, "Let him alone." So I got some bread out of the bread box and some butter and jam, gobbled it and lit out.

At the tracks you sit on the fence with men, whites and niggers, and they chew tobacco and talk, and then the colts are brought out. It's early and the grass is covered with shiny dew and in another field a man is plowing and they are frying things in a shed where the track niggers sleep, and you know how a nigger can giggle and laugh and say things that make you laugh. A white man can't do it and some niggers can't but a track nigger can every time.

And so the colts are brought out and some are just galloped by stable boys, but almost every morning on a big track owned by a rich man who lives maybe in New York, there are always, nearly every morning, a few colts and some of the old race horses and geldings and mares that are cut loose.

It brings a lump up into my throat when a horse runs. I don't mean all horses but some. I can pick them nearly every time. It's in my blood like in the blood of race track niggers and trainers. Even when they just go slob-jogging along with a little nigger on their backs I can tell a winner. If my throat hurts and it's hard for me to swallow, that's him. He'll run like Sam Hill when you let him out. If he don't win every time it'll be a wonder and because they've got him in a pocket behind another or he was pulled or got off bad at the post or something. If I wanted to be a gambler like Henry Rieback's father I could get rich. I know I could and Henry says so, too. All I would have to do is to wait 'til that hurt comes when I see a horse and then bet every cent. That's what I could do if I wanted to be a gambler, but I don't.

When you're at the tracks in the morning—not the race tracks but the training tracks around Beckersville—you don't see a horse the kind I've been talking about, very often, but it's nice anyway. Any thoroughbred, that is sired right and out of a good mare and trained by a man that knows how, can run. If he couldn't what would he be there for and not pulling a plow?

Well, out of the stables they come and the boys are on their backs and it's lovely to be there. You hunch down on top of the fence and itch inside you. Over in the sheds the niggers giggle and sing. Bacon is being fried and coffee made. Everything smells lovely. Nothing smells better than coffee and manure and horses and niggers and bacon frying and pipes being smoked out of doors on a morning like that. It just gets you, that's what it does.

But about Saratoga. We was there six days and not a soul from home seen us and everything came off just as we wanted it to, fine weather and horses and races and all. We beat our way home and Bildad gave us a basket with fried chicken and bread and other eatables in, and I had eighteen dollars when we got back to Beckersville. Mother jawed and cried but Pop didn't say much. I told everything we done except one thing. I did and saw that alone. That's what I'm writing about. It got me upset. I think about it at night. Here it is.

At Saratoga we laid up nights in the hay in the shed Bildad had showed us and ate with the niggers early and at night when the race people had all gone away. The men from home stayed mostly in the grandstand and betting field, and didn't come out around the places where the horses are kept except to the paddocks just before a race when the horses are saddled. At Saratoga they don't have paddocks under an open shed as at Lexington and Churchill Downs and other tracks down in our country, but saddle the horses right out in an open place under trees on a lawn as smooth and nice as Banker Bohon's front yard here in Beckersville. It's lovely. The horses are sweaty and nervous and shine and the men come out and smoke cigars and look at them and the trainers are there and the owners, and your heart thumps so you can hardly breathe.

Then the bugle blows for post and the boys that ride come running out with their silk clothes on and you run to get a place by the fence with the niggers.

I always am wanting to be a trainer or owner, and at the risk of being seen and caught and sent home I went to the paddocks before every race. The other boys didn't but I did.

We got to Saratoga on a Friday and on Wednesday the next week the big Mullford Handicap was to be run. Middlestride was in it and Sunstreak. The weather was fine and the track fast. I couldn't sleep the night before.

What had happened was that both these horses are the kind it makes my throat hurt to see. Middlestride is long and looks awkward and is a gelding. He belongs to Joe Thompson, a little owner from home who only has a half-dozen horses. The Mullford Handicap is for a mile and Middlestride can't untrack fast. He goes away slow and is always way back at the half, then he begins to run and if the race is a mile and a quarter he'll just eat up everything and get there.

Sunstreak is different. He is a stallion and nervous and belongs on the biggest farm we've got in our country, the Van Riddle place that belongs to Mr. Van Riddle of New York. Sunstreak is like a girl you think about sometimes but never see. He is hard all over and lovely too. When you look at his head you want to kiss him. He is trained by Jerry Tillford who knows me and has been good to me lots of times, lets me walk into a horse's stall to look at him close and other things. There isn't anything as sweet as that horse. He stands at the post quiet and not letting on, but he is just burning up inside. Then when the barrier goes up he is off like his name, Sunstreak. It makes you ache to see him.

It hurts you. He just lays down and runs like a bird dog. There can't anything I ever see run like him except Middlestride when he gets untracked and stretches himself.

Gee! I ached to see that race and those two horses run, ached and dreaded it too. I didn't want to see either of our horses beaten. We had never sent a pair like that to the races before. Old men in Beckersville said so and the niggers said so. It was a fact.

Before the race I went over to the paddocks to see. I looked a last look at Middlestride, who isn't such a much standing in a paddock that way, then I went to see Sunstreak.

It was his day. I knew when I see him. I forgot all about being seen myself and walked right up. All the men from Beckersville were there and no one noticed me except Jerry Tillford. He saw me and something happened. I'll tell you about that.

I was standing looking at that horse and aching. In some way, I can't tell how, I knew just how Sunstreak felt inside. He was quiet and letting the niggers rub his legs and Mr. Van Riddle himself put the saddle on, but he was just a raging torrent inside. He was like the water in the river at Niagara Falls just before it goes plunk down. That horse wasn't thinking about running. He don't have to think about that. He was just thinking about holding himself back 'til the time for the running came. I knew that. I could just in a way see right inside him. He was going to do some awful running and I knew it. He wasn't bragging or letting on much or prancing or making a fuss, but just waiting. I knew it and Jerry Tillford his trainer knew. I looked up and then that man and I looked into each other's eyes. Something happened to me. I guess I loved the man as much as I did the horse because he knew what I knew. Seemed to me there wasn't anything in the world but that man and the horse and me. I cried and Jerry Tillford had a shine in his eyes. Then I came away to the fence to wait for the race. The horse was better than me, more steadier, and now I know better than Jerry. He was the quietest and he had to do the running.

Sunstreak ran first of course and he busted the world's record for a mile. I've seen that if I never see anything more. Everything came out just as I expected. Middlestride got left at the post and was way back and closed up to be second, just as I knew he would. He'll get a world's record too some day. They can't skin the Beckersville country on horses.

I watched the race calm because I knew what would happen. I was sure. Hanley Turner and Henry Rieback and Tom Tumberton were all more excited than me.

A funny thing had happened to me. I was thinking about Jerry Tillford the trainer and how happy he was all through the race. I liked him that afternoon even more than I ever liked my own father. I almost forgot the horses thinking that way about him. It was because of what I had seen in his eyes as he stood in the paddocks beside Sunstreak before the race started. I knew he had been watching and working with Sunstreak since the horse was a baby colt, had taught him to run and be patient and when to let himself out and not to quit, never.

I knew that for him it was like a mother seeing her child do something brave or wonderful. It was the first time I ever felt for a man like that.

After the race that night I cut out from Tom and Hanley and Henry. I wanted to be by myself and I wanted to be near Jerry Tillford if I could work it. Here is what happened.

The track in Saratoga is near the edge of town. It is all polished up and trees around, the evergreen kind, and grass and everything painted and nice. If you go past the track you get to a hard road made of asphalt for automobiles, and if you go along this for a few miles there is a road turns off to a little rummy-looking farm house set in a yard.

That night after the race I went along that road because I had seen Jerry and some other men go that way in an automobile. I didn't expect to find them. I walked for a ways and then sat down by a fence to think. It was the direction they went in. I wanted to be as near Jerry as I could. I felt close to him. Pretty soon I went up the side road—I don't know why—and came to the rummy farm house. I was just lonesome to see Jerry, like wanting to see your father at night when you are a young kid. Just then an automobile came along and turned in. Jerry was in it and Henry Rieback's father, and Arthur Bedford from home, and Dave Williams and two other men I didn't know. They got out of the car and went into the house, all but Henry Rieback's father who quarreled with them and said he wouldn't go. It was only about nine o'clock, but they were all drunk and the rummy-looking farm house was a place for bad women to stay in. That's what it was. I crept up along a fence and looked through a window and saw.

It's what give me the fantods. I can't make it out. The women in the house were all ugly mean-looking women, not nice to look at or be near. They were homely too, except one who was tall and looked a little like the gelding Middle-stride, but not clean like him, but with a hard ugly mouth. She had red hair. I saw everything plain. I got up by an old rose bush by an open window and looked. The women had on loose dresses and sat around in chairs. The men came in and some sat on the women's laps. The place smelled rotten and there was rotten talk, the kind a kid hears around a livery stable in a town like Beckersville in the winter but don't ever expect to hear talked when there are women around. It was rotten. A nigger wouldn't go into such a place.

I looked at Jerry Tillford. I've told you how I had been feeling about him on account of his knowing what was going on inside of Sunstreak in the minute before he went to the post for the race in which he made a world's record.

Jerry bragged in that bad woman house as I know Sunstreak wouldn't never have bragged. He said that he made that horse, that it was him that won the race and made the record. He lied and bragged like a fool. I never heard such silly talk.

And then, what do you suppose he did! He looked at the woman in there, the one that was lean and hard-mouthed and looked a little like the gelding Middlestride, but not clean like him, and his eyes began to shine just as they did when he looked at me and at Sunstreak in the paddocks at the track in the afternoon. I stood there by the window—gee!—but I wished I hadn't gone away from the tracks, but had stayed with the boys and the niggers and the horses. The tall rotten-looking woman was between us just as Sunstreak was in the paddocks in the afternoon.

Then, all of a sudden, I began to hate that man. I wanted to scream and rush in the room and kill him. I never had such a feeling before. I was so mad clean through that I cried and my fists were doubled up so my finger nails cut my hands.

And Jerry's eyes kept shining and he waved back and forth, and then he went and kissed that woman and I crept away and went back to the tracks and to bed and didn't sleep hardly any, and then next day I got the other kids to start home with me and never told them anything I seen.

I been thinking about it ever since. I can't make it out. Spring has come again and I'm nearly sixteen and go to the tracks mornings same as always, and I see Sunstreak and Middlestride and a new colt named Strident I'll bet will lay them all out, but no one thinks so but me and two or three niggers.

But things are different. At the tracks the air don't taste as good or smell as good. It's because a man like Jerry Tillford, who knows what he does, could see a horse like Sunstreak run, and kiss a woman like that the same day. I can't make it out. Darn him, what did he want to do like that for? I keep thinking about it and it spoils looking at horses and smelling things and hearing niggers laugh and everything. Sometimes I'm so mad about it I want to fight someone. It gives me the fantods. What did he do it for? I want to know why.

Araby* 1914

JAMES JOYCE [1882–1941]

North Richmond Street, being blind, was a quiet street except at the hour when the Christian Brothers' School set the boys free. An uninhabited house of two storeys stood at the blind end, detached from its neighbours in a square ground. The other houses of the street, conscious of decent lives within them, gazed at one another with brown imperturbable faces.

The former tenant of our house, a priest, had died in the back drawing-room. Air, musty from having been long enclosed, hung in all the rooms, and the waste room behind the kitchen was littered with old useless papers. Among these I found a few paper-covered books, the pages of which were curled and damp: *The Abbot*, by Walter Scott, *The Devout Communicant* and *The Memoirs of Vidocq*. I liked the last best because its leaves were yellow. The wild garden behind the house contained a central apple-tree and a few straggling bushes under one of which I found the late tenant's rusty bicycle-pump. He had been a very charitable priest; in his will he had left all his money to institutions and the furniture of his house to his sister.

When the short days of winter came dusk fell before we had well eaten our dinners. When we met in the street the houses had grown sombre. The space of sky above us was the colour of ever-changing violet and towards it the lamps of the street lifted their feeble lanterns. The cold air stung us and we played till our bodies glowed. Our shouts echoed in the silent street. The career of our play brought us through the dark muddy lanes behind the houses where we ran the gauntlet of the rough tribes from the cottages, to the back doors of the dark dripping gardens where odours arose from the ashpits, to the dark odorous stables where a coachman smoothed and combed the horse or shook music from the buckled harness. When we returned to the street light from the kitchen windows had filled the areas. If my uncle was seen turning the corner we hid in the shadow until we had seen him safely housed. Or if Mangan's sister came out on the doorstep to call her brother in to his tea we watched her from our shadow peer up and down the street. We waited to see whether she would remain or go in and, if she remained, we left our shadow and walked up to Mangan's steps resignedly. She was waiting for us, her figure defined by the light from the half-opened door. Her brother always teased her before he obeyed and I stood by the railings looking at her. Her dress swung as she moved her body and the soft rope of her hair tossed from side to side.

Every morning I lay on the floor in the front parlour watching her door. The blind was pulled down to within an inch of the sash so that I could not be seen. When she came out on the doorstep my heart leaped. I ran to the hall, seized

---

* This story is considered in the essay "Reading Fiction" at the end of the book.

my books and followed her. I kept her brown figure always in my eye and, when we came near the point at which our ways diverged, I quickened my pace and passed her. This happened morning after morning. I had never spoken to her, except for a few casual words, and yet her name was like a summons to all my foolish blood.

Her image accompanied me even in places the most hostile to romance. On Saturday evenings when my aunt went marketing I had to go to carry some of the parcels. We walked through the flaring streets, jostled by drunken men and bargaining women, amid the curses of labourers, the shrill litanies of shop-boys who stood on guard by the barrels of pigs' cheeks, the nasal chanting of street-singers, who sang a *come-all-you*[1] about O'Donovan Rossa, or a ballad about the troubles in our native land. These noises converged in a single sensation of life for me: I imagined that I bore my chalice safely through a throng of foes. Her name sprang to my lips at moments in strange prayers and praises which I myself did not understand. My eyes were often full of tears (I could not tell why) and at times a flood from my heart seemed to pour itself out into my bosom. I thought little of the future. I did not know whether I would ever speak to her or not or, if I spoke to her, how I could tell her of my confused adoration. But my body was like a harp and her words and gestures were like fingers running upon the wires.

One evening I went into the back drawing-room in which the priest had died. It was a dark rainy evening and there was no sound in the house. Through one of the broken panes I heard the rain impinge upon the earth, the fine incessant needles of water playing in the sodden beds. Some distant lamp or lighted window gleamed below me. I was thankful that I could see so little. All my senses seemed to desire to veil themselves and, feeling that I was about to slip from them, I pressed the palms of my hands together until they trembled, murmuring: "*O love! O love!*" many times.

At last she spoke to me. When she addressed the first words to me I was so confused that I did not know what to answer. She asked me was I going to *Araby*. I forgot whether I answered yes or no. It would be a splendid bazaar, she said she would love to go.

"And why can't you?" I asked.

While she spoke she turned a silver bracelet round and round her wrist. She could not go, she said, because there would be a retreat that week in her convent. Her brother and two other boys were fighting for their caps and I was alone at the railings. She held one of the spikes, bowing her head towards me. The light from the lamp opposite our door caught the white curve of her neck, lit up her hair that rested there and, falling, lit up the hand upon the railing. It fell over one side of her dress and caught the white border of a petticoat, just visible as she stood at ease.

"It's well for you" she said.

---

[1] A street ballad beginning with these words. This one is about Jeremiah Donovan, a nineteenth-century Irish nationalist popularly known as O'Donovan Rossa.

"If I go," I said, "I will bring you something."

What innumerable follies laid waste my waking and sleeping thoughts after that evening! I wished to annihilate the tedious intervening days. I chafed against the work of school. At night in my bedroom and by day in the classroom her image came between me and the page I strove to read. The syllables of the word *Araby* were called to me through the silence in which my soul luxuriated and cast an Eastern enchantment over me. I asked for leave to go to the bazaar on Saturday night. My aunt was surprised and hoped it was not some Freemason affair. I answered few questions in class. I watched my master's face pass from amiability to sternness; he hoped I was not beginning to idle. I could not call my wandering thoughts together. I had hardly any patience with the serious work of life which, now that it stood between me and my desire, seemed to me child's play, ugly monotonous child's play.

On Saturday morning I reminded my uncle that I wished to go to the bazaar in the evening. He was fussing at the hallstand, looking for the hat-brush, and answered me curtly:

"Yes, boy, I know."

As he was in the hall I could not go into the front parlour and lie at the window. I left the house in bad humour and walked slowly towards the school. The air was pitilessly raw and already my heart misgave me.

When I came home to dinner my uncle had not yet been home. Still it was early. I sat staring at the clock for some time and, when its ticking began to irritate me, I left the room. I mounted the staircase and gained the upper part of the house. The high cold empty gloomy rooms liberated me and I went from room to room singing. From the front window I saw my companions playing below in the street. Their cries reached me weakened and indistinct and, leaning my forehead against the cool glass, I looked over at the dark house where she lived. I may have stood there for an hour, seeing nothing but the brown-clad figure cast by my imagination, touched discreetly by the lamplight at the curved neck, at the hand upon the railings and at the border below the dress.

When I came downstairs again I found Mrs. Mercer sitting at the fire. She was an old garrulous woman, a pawnbroker's widow, who collected used stamps for some pious purpose. I had to endure the gossip of the tea-table. The meal was prolonged beyond an hour and still my uncle did not come. Mrs. Mercer stood up to go: she was sorry she couldn't wait any longer, but it was after eight o'clock and she did not like to be out late, as the night air was bad for her. When she had gone I began to walk up and down the room, clenching my fists. My aunt said:

"I'm afraid you may put off your bazaar for this night of Our Lord."

At nine o'clock I heard my uncle's latchkey in the halldoor. I heard him talking to himself and heard the hallstand rocking when it had received the weight of his overcoat. I could interpret these signs. When he was midway through his dinner I asked him to give me the money to go to the bazaar. He had forgotten.

"The people are in bed and after their first sleep now," he said.

I did not smile. My aunt said to him energetically:

"Can't you give him the money and let him go? You've kept him late enough as it is."

My uncle said he was very sorry he had forgotten. He said he believed in the old saying: "All work and no play makes Jack a dull boy." He asked me where I was going and, when I had told him a second time he asked me did I know *The Arab's Farewell to his Steed*. When I left the kitchen he was about to recite the opening lines of the piece to my aunt.

I held a florin tightly in my hand as I strode down Buckingham Street towards the station. The sight of the streets thronged with buyers and glaring with gas recalled to me the purpose of my journey. I took my seat in a third-class carriage of a deserted train. After an intolerable delay the train moved out of the station slowly. It crept onward among ruinous houses and over the twinkling river. At Westland Row Station a crowd of people pressed to the carriage doors; but the porters moved them back, saying that it was a special train for the bazaar. I remained alone in the bare carriage. In a few minutes the train drew up beside an improvised wooden platform. I passed out on to the road and saw by the lighted dial of a clock that it was ten minutes to ten. In front of me was a large building which displayed the magical name.

I could not find any sixpenny entrance and, fearing that the bazaar would be closed, I passed in quickly through a turnstile, handing a shilling to a weary-looking man. I found myself in a big hall girdled at half its height by a gallery. Nearly all the stalls were closed and the greater part of the hall was in darkness. I recognised a silence like that which pervades a church after a service. I walked into the centre of the bazaar timidly. A few people were gathered about the stalls which were still open. Before a curtain, over which the words *Café Chantant* were written in coloured lamps, two men were counting money on a salver. I listened to the fall of the coins.

Remembering with difficulty why I had come I went over to one of the stalls and examined porcelain vases and flowered tea-sets. At the door of the stall a young lady was talking and laughing with two young gentlemen. I remarked their English accents and listened vaguely to their conversation.

"O, I never said such a thing!"

"O, but you did!"

"O, but I didn't!"

"Didn't she say that?"

"Yes. I heard her."

"O, there's a . . . fib!"

Observing me the young lady came over and asked me did I wish to buy anything. The tone of her voice was not encouraging; she seemed to have spoken to me out of a sense of duty. I looked humbly at the great jars that stood like eastern guards at either side of the dark entrance to the stall and murmured:

"No, thank you."

The young lady changed the position of one of the vases and went back to the two young men. They began to talk of the same subject. Once or twice the young lady glanced at me over her shoulder.

I lingered before her stall, though I knew my stay was useless, to make my interest in her wares seem the more real. Then I turned away slowly and walked down the middle of the bazaar. I allowed the two pennies to fall against the sixpence in my pocket. I heard a voice call from one end of the gallery that the light was out. The upper part of the hall was now completely dark.

Gazing up into the darkness I saw myself as a creature driven and derided by vanity; and my eyes burned with anguish and anger.

A Clean, Well-Lighted Place   1933

ERNEST HEMINGWAY [1898–1961]

It was late and everyone had left the café except an old man who sat in the shadow the leaves of the tree made against the electric light. In the day time the street was dusty, but at night the dew settled the dust and the old man liked to sit late because he was deaf and now at night it was quiet and he felt the difference. The two waiters inside the café knew that the old man was a little drunk, and while he was a good client they knew that if he became too drunk he would leave without paying, so they kept watch on him.

"Last week he tried to commit suicide," one waiter said.

"Why?"

"He was in despair."

"What about?"

"Nothing."

"How do you know it was nothing?"

"He has plenty of money."

They sat together at a table that was close against the wall near the door of the café and looked at the terrace where the tables were all empty except where the old man sat in the shadow of the leaves of the tree that moved slightly in the wind. A girl and a soldier went by in the street. The street light shone on the brass number on his collar. The girl wore no head covering and hurried beside him.

"The guard will pick him up," one waiter said.

"What does it matter if he gets what he's after?"

"He had better get off the street now. The guard will get him. They went by five minutes ago."

The old man sitting in the shadow rapped on his saucer with his glass. The younger waiter went over to him.

"What do you want?"

The old man looked at him. "Another brandy," he said.

"You'll be drunk," the waiter said. The old man looked at him. The waiter went away.

"He'll stay all night," he said to his colleague. "I'm sleepy now. I never get into bed before three o'clock. He should have killed himself last week."

The waiter took the brandy bottle and another saucer from the counter inside the café and marched out to the old man's table. He put down the saucer and poured the glass full of brandy.

"You should have killed yourself last week," he said to the deaf man. The old man motioned with his finger. "A little more," he said. The waiter poured on into the glass so that the brandy slopped over and ran down the stem into the top saucer of the pile. "Thank you," the old man said. The waiter took the bottle back inside the café. He sat down at the table with his colleague again.

"He's drunk now," he said.

"He's drunk every night."

"What did he want to kill himself for?"

"How should I know."

"How did he do it?"

"He hung himself with a rope."

"Who cut him down?"

"His niece."

"Why did they do it?"

"Fear for his soul."

"How much money has he got?"

"He's got plenty."

"He must be eighty years old."

"Anyway I should say he was eighty."

"I wish he would go home. I never get to bed before three o'clock. What kind of hour is that to go to bed?"

"He stays up because he likes it."

"He's lonely. I'm not lonely. I have a wife waiting in bed for me."

"He had a wife once too."

"A wife would be no good to him now."

"You can't tell. He might be better with a wife."

"His niece looks after him. You said she cut him down."

"I know."

"I wouldn't want to be that old. An old man is a nasty thing."

"Not always. This old man is clean. He drinks without spilling. Even now, drunk. Look at him."

"I don't want to look at him. I wish he would go home. He has no regard for those who must work."

The old man looked from his glass across the square, then over at the waiters.

"Another brandy," he said, pointing to his glass. The waiter who was in a hurry came over.

"Finished," he said, speaking with that omission of syntax stupid people employ when talking to drunken people or foreigners. "No more tonight. Close now."

"Another," said the old man.

"No. Finished." The waiter wiped the edge of the table with a towel and shook his head.

The old man stood up, slowly counted the saucers, took a leather coin purse from his pocket and paid for the drinks, leaving half a peseta tip.

The waiter watched him go down the street, a very old man walking unsteadily but with dignity.

"Why didn't you let him stay and drink?" the unhurried waiter asked. They were putting up the shutters. "It is not half-past two."

"I want to go home to bed."

"What is an hour?"

"More to me than to him."

"An hour is the same."

"You talk like an old man yourself. He can buy a bottle and drink at home."

"It's not the same."

"No, it is not," agreed the waiter with a wife. He did not wish to be unjust. He was only in a hurry.

"And you? You have no fear of going home before your usual hour?"

"Are you trying to insult me?"

"No, hombre, only to make a joke."

"No," the waiter who was in a hurry said, rising from pulling down the metal shutters. "I have confidence. I am all confidence."

"You have youth, confidence, and a job," the older waiter said. "You have everything."

"And what do you lack?"

"Everything but work."

"You have everything I have."

"No. I have never had confidence and I am not young."

"Come on. Stop talking nonsense and lock up."

"I am of those who like to stay late at the café," the older waiter said. "With all those who do not want to go to bed. With all those who need a light for the night."

"I want to go home and into bed."

"We are of two different kinds," the older waiter said. He was now dressed to go home. "It is not only a question of youth and confidence although those things are very beautiful. Each night I am reluctant to close up because there may be some one who needs the café."

"Hombre, there are bodegas open all night long."

"You do not understand. This is a clean and pleasant café. It is well lighted. The light is very good and also, now, there are shadows of the leaves."

"Good night," said the younger waiter.

"Good night," the other said. Turning off the electric light he continued the conversation with himself. It is the light of course but it is necessary that the place be clean and pleasant. You do not want music. Certainly you do not want music. Nor can you stand before a bar with dignity although that is all that is provided for these hours. What did he fear? It was not fear or dread. It was a nothing that he knew too well. It was all a nothing and a man was nothing too. It was only that and light was all it needed and a certain cleanness and order. Some lived in it and never felt it but he knew it was nada y pues nada y pues nada.[1] Our nada who art in nada, nada be thy name thy kingdom nada thy will be nada in nada as it is in nada. Give us this nada our daily nada and nada us our nada as we nada our nadas and nada us not into nada but deliver us from nada; pues nada. Hail nothing full of nothing, nothing is with thee. He smiled and stood before a bar with a shining steam pressure coffee machine.

"What's yours?" asked the barman.

---

[1] Nothing, and then nothing, and then nothing.

"Nada."

"Otro loco mas,"[2] said the barman and turned away.

"A little cup," said the waiter.

The barman poured it for him.

"The light is very bright and pleasant but the bar is unpolished," the waiter said.

The barman looked at him but did not answer. It was too late at night for conversation.

"You want another copita?" the barman asked.

"No, thank you," said the waiter and went out. He disliked bars and bodegas. A clean, well-lighted café was a very different thing. Now, without thinking further, he would go home to his room. He would lie in the bed and finally, with daylight, he would go to sleep. After all, he said to himself, it is probably only insomnia. Many must have it.

QUESTION
How do the two waiters differ in their attitudes toward the old man? What bearing does that difference have on the theme of the story?

---

[2] Another crazy one.

My Oedipus Complex

FRANK O'CONNOR [1903–1966]

Father was in the army all through the war—the first war, I mean—so, up to the age of five, I never saw much of him, and what I saw did not worry me. Sometimes I woke and there was a big figure in khaki peering down at me in the candlelight. Sometimes in the early morning I heard the slamming of the front door and the clatter of nailed boots down the cobbles of the lane. These were Father's entrances and exits. Like Santa Claus he came and went mysteriously.

In fact, I rather liked his visits, though it was an uncomfortable squeeze between Mother and him when I got into the big bed in the early morning. He smoked, which gave him a pleasant musty smell, and shaved, an operation of astounding interest. Each time he left a trail of souvenirs—model tanks and Gurkha knives with handles made of bullet cases, and German helmets and cap badges and button-sticks, and all sorts of military equipment—carefully stowed away in a long box on top of the wardrobe, in case they ever came in handy. There was a bit of the magpie about Father; he expected everything to come in handy. When his back was turned, Mother let me get a chair and rummage through his treasures. She didn't seem to think so highly of them as he did.

The war was the most peaceful period of my life. The window of my attic faced southeast. My mother had curtained it, but that had small effect. I always woke with the first light and, with all the responsibilities of the previous day melted, feeling myself rather like the sun, ready to illumine and rejoice. Life never seemed so simple and clear and full of possibilities as then. I put my feet out from under the clothes—I called them Mrs. Left and Mrs. Right—and invented dramatic situations for them in which they discussed the problems of the day. At least Mrs. Right did; she was very demonstrative, but I hadn't the same control of Mrs. Left, so she mostly contented herself with nodding agreement.

They discussed what Mother and I should do during the day, what Santa Claus should give a fellow for Christmas, and what steps should be taken to brighten the home. There was that little matter of the baby, for instance. Mother and I could never agree about that. Ours was the only house in the terrace without a new baby, and Mother said we couldn't afford one till Father came back from the war because they cost seventeen and six. That showed how simple she was. The Geneys up the road had a baby, and everyone knew they couldn't afford seventeen and six. It was probably a cheap baby, and Mother wanted something really good, but I felt she was too exclusive. The Geneys' baby would have done us fine.

Having settled my plans for the day, I got up, put a chair under the attic window, and lifted the frame high enough to stick out my head. The window overlooked the front gardens of the terrace behind ours, and beyond these it looked over a deep valley to the tall, red-brick houses terraced up the opposite hillside, which were all still in shadow, while those at our side of the valley were all lit up, though with long strange shadows that made them seem unfamiliar; rigid and painted.

After that I went into Mother's room and climbed into the big bed. She woke and I began to tell her of my schemes. By this time, though I never seem to have noticed it, I was petrified in my nightshirt, and I thawed as I talked until, the last frost melted, I fell asleep beside her and woke again only when I heard her below in the kitchen, making the breakfast.

After breakfast we went into town; heard Mass at St. Augustine's and said a prayer for Father, and did the shopping. If the afternoon was fine we either went for a walk in the country or a visit to Mother's great friend in the convent, Mother St. Dominic. Mother had them all praying for Father, and every night, going to bed, I asked God to send him back safe from the war to us. Little, indeed, did I know what I was praying for!

One morning, I got into the big bed, and there, sure enough, was Father in his usual Santa Claus manner, but later, instead of uniform, he put on his best blue suit, and Mother was as pleased as anything. I saw nothing to be pleased about, because, out of uniform, Father was altogether less interesting, but she only beamed, and explained that our prayers had been answered, and off we went to Mass to thank God for having brought Father safely home.

The irony of it! That very day when he came in to dinner he took off his boots and put on his slippers, donned the dirty old cap he wore about the house to save him from colds, crossed his legs, and began to talk gravely to Mother, who looked anxious. Naturally, I disliked her looking anxious, because it destroyed her good looks, so I interrupted him.

"Just a moment, Larry!" she said gently.

This was only what she said when we had boring visitors, so I attached no importance to it and went on talking.

"Do be quiet, Larry!" she said impatiently. "Don't you hear me talking to Daddy?"

This was the first time I had heard those ominous words, "talking to Daddy," and I couldn't help feeling that if this was how God answered prayers, he couldn't listen to them very attentively.

"Why are you talking to Daddy?" I asked with as great a show of indifference as I could muster.

"Because Daddy and I have business to discuss. Now, don't interrupt again!"

In the afternoon, at Mother's request, Father took me for a walk. This time we went into town instead of out to the country, and I thought at first, in my usual optimistic way, that it might be an improvement. It was nothing of the sort. Father and I had quite different notions of a walk in town. He had no proper interest in trams, ships, and horses, and the only thing that seemed to divert him was talking to fellows as old as himself. When I wanted to stop he simply went on, dragging me behind him by the hand; when he wanted to stop I had no alternative but to do the same. I noticed that it seemed to be a sign that he wanted to stop for a long time whenever he leaned against a wall. The second time I saw him do it I got wild. He seemed to be settling himself forever. I pulled him by the coat and trousers, but, unlike Mother who, if you were too persistent, got into a wax and said: "Larry, if you don't behave yourself, I'll give you a good slap," Father had an extraordinary capacity for amiable inattention. I sized him up and wondered would I cry, but he seemed to be too remote to be annoyed even by that. Really, it was like going for a walk with a mountain! He either ignored the wrenching and pummeling entirely, or else glanced down with a grin of amusement from his peak. I had never met anyone so absorbed in himself as he seemed.

At teatime, "talking to Daddy" began again, complicated this time by the fact that he had an evening paper, and every few minutes he put it down and told Mother something new out of it. I felt this was foul play. Man for man, I was prepared to compete with him any time for Mother's attention, but when he had it all made up for him by other people it left me no chance. Several times I tried to change the subject without success.

"You must be quiet while Daddy is reading, Larry," Mother said impatiently.

It was clear that she either genuinely liked talking to Father better than talking to me, or else that he had some terrible hold on her which made her afraid to admit the truth.

"Mummy," I said that night when she was tucking me up, "do you think if I prayed hard God would send Daddy back to the war?"

She seemed to think about that for a moment.

"No, dear," she said with a smile. "I don't think he would."

"Why wouldn't he, Mummy?"

"Because there isn't a war any longer, dear."

"But, Mummy, couldn't God make another war, if he liked?"

"He wouldn't like to, dear. It's not God who makes wars, but bad people."

"Oh!" I said.

I was disappointed about that. I began to think that God wasn't quite what he was cracked up to be.

Next morning I woke at my usual hour, feeling like a bottle of champagne. I put out my feet and invented a long conversation in which Mrs. Right talked of the trouble she had with her own father till she put him in the Home. I didn't quite know what the Home was but it sounded the right place for Father. Then I got my chair and stuck my head out of the attic window. Dawn was just breaking, with a guilty air that made me feel I had caught it in the act. My head bursting with stories and schemes, I stumbled in next door, and in the half-darkness scrambled into the big bed. There was no room at Mother's side so I had to get between her and Father. For the time being I had forgotten about him, and for several minutes I sat bolt upright, racking my brains to know what I could do with him. He was taking up more than his fair share of the bed, and I couldn't get comfortable, so I gave him several kicks that made him grunt and stretch. He made room all right, though. Mother waked and felt for me. I settled back comfortably in the warmth of the bed with my thumb in my mouth.

"Mummy!" I hummed, loudly and contentedly.

"Ssh! dear," she whispered. "Don't wake Daddy!"

This was a new development, which threatened to be even more serious than "talking to Daddy." Life without my early-morning conferences was unthinkable.

"Why?" I asked severely.

"Because poor Daddy is tired."

This seemed to me a quite inadequate reason, and I was sickened by the sentimentality of her "poor Daddy." I never liked that sort of gush; it always struck me as insincere.

"Oh!" I said lightly. Then in my most winning tone: "Do you know where I want to go with you today, Mummy?"

"No, dear," she sighed.

"I want to go down the Glen and fish for thornybacks with my new net, and then I want to go out to the Fox and Hounds, and—"

"Don't-wake-Daddy!" she hissed angrily, clapping her hand across my mouth.

But it was too late. He was awake, or nearly so. He grunted and reached for the matches. Then he stared incredulously at his watch.

"Like a cup of tea, dear?" asked Mother in a meek, hushed voice I had never heard her use before. It sounded almost as though she were afraid.

"Tea?" he exclaimed indignantly. "Do you know what the time is?"

"And after that I want to go up the Rathcooney Road," I said loudly, afraid I'd forget something in all those interruptions.

"Go to sleep at once, Larry!" she said sharply.

I began to snivel. I couldn't concentrate, the way that pair went on, and smothering my early-morning schemes was like burying a family from the cradle.

Father said nothing, but lit his pipe and sucked it, looking out into the shadows without minding Mother or me. I knew he was mad. Every time I made a remark Mother hushed me irritably. I was mortified. I felt it wasn't fair; there was even something sinister in it. Every time I had pointed out to her the waste of making two beds when we could both sleep in one, she had told me it was healthier like that, and now here was this man, this stranger, sleeping with her without the least regard for her health!

He got up early and made tea, but though he brought Mother a cup he brought none for me.

"Mummy," I shouted, "I want a cup of tea, too."

"Yes, dear," she said patiently. "You can drink from Mummy's saucer."

That settled it. Either Father or I would have to leave the house. I didn't want to drink from Mother's saucer; I wanted to be treated as an equal in my own home, so, just to spite her, I drank it all and left none for her. She took that quietly, too.

But that night when she was putting me to bed she said gently: "Larry, I want you to promise me something."

"What is it?" I asked.

"Not to come in and disturb poor Daddy in the morning. Promise?"

"Poor Daddy" again! I was becoming suspicious of everything involving that quite impossible man.

"Why?" I asked.

"Because poor Daddy is worried and tired and he doesn't sleep well."

"Why doesn't he, Mummy?"

"Well, you know, don't you, that while he was at the war Mummy got the pennies from the Post Office?"

"From Miss MacCarthy?"

"That's right. But now, you see, Miss MacCarthy hasn't any more pennies, so Daddy must go out and find us some. You know what would happen if he couldn't?"

"No," I said, "tell us."

"Well, I think we might have to go out and beg for them like the poor old woman on Fridays. We wouldn't like that, would we?"

"No," I agreed. "We wouldn't."

"So you'll promise not to come in and wake him?"

"Promise."

Mind you, I meant that. I knew pennies were a serious matter, and I was all against having to go out and beg like the old woman on Fridays. Mother laid out all my toys in a complete ring round the bed so that, whatever way I got out, I was bound to fall over one of them.

When I woke I remembered my promise all right. I got up and sat on the floor and played—for hours, it seemed to me. Then I got my chair and looked out the attic window for more hours. I wished it was time for Father to wake; I wished someone would make me a cup of tea. I didn't feel in the least like the sun; instead, I was bored and so very, very cold! I simply longed for the warmth and depth of the big featherbed.

At last I could stand it no longer. I went into the next room. As there was still no room at Mother's side I climbed over her and she woke with a start.

"Larry," she whispered, gripping my arm very tightly, "what did you promise?"

"But I did, Mummy," I wailed, caught in the very act. "I was quiet for ever so long."

"Oh, dear, and you're perished!" she said sadly, feeling me all over. "Now, if I let you stay will you promise not to talk?"

"But I want to talk, Mummy," I wailed.

"That has nothing to do with it," she said with a firmness that was new to me. "Daddy wants to sleep. Now, do you understand that?"

I understood it only too well. I wanted to talk, he wanted to sleep—whose house was it, anyway?

"Mummy," I said with equal firmness, "I think it would be healthier for Daddy to sleep in his own bed."

That seemed to stagger her, because she said nothing for a while.

"Now, once for all," she went on, "you're to be perfectly quiet or go back to your own bed. Which is it to be?"

The injustice of it got me down. I had convicted her out of her own mouth of inconsistency and unreasonableness, and she hadn't even attempted to reply. Full of spite, I gave Father a kick, which she didn't notice but which made him grunt and open his eyes in alarm.

"What time is it?" he asked in a panic-stricken voice, not looking at Mother but the door, as if he saw someone there.

"It's early yet," she replied soothingly. "It's only the child. Go to sleep again. . . . Now, Larry," she added, getting out of bed, "you've wakened Daddy and you must go back."

This time, for all her quiet air, I knew she meant it, and knew that my principal rights and privileges were as good as lost unless I asserted them at once. As she lifted me, I gave a screech, enough to wake the dead, not to mind Father. He groaned.

"That damn child! Doesn't he ever sleep?"

"It's only a habit, dear," she said quietly, though I could see she was vexed.

"Well, it's time he got out of it," shouted Father, beginning to heave in the bed. He suddenly gathered all the bedclothes about him, turned to the wall, and then looked back over his shoulder with nothing showing only two small, spiteful, dark eyes. The man looked very wicked.

To open the bedroom door, Mother had to let me down, and I broke free and dashed for the farthest corner, screeching. Father sat bolt upright in bed.

"Shut up, you little puppy!" he said in a choking voice.

I was so astonished that I stopped screeching. Never, never had anyone spoken to me in that tone before. I looked at him incredulously and saw his face convulsed with rage. It was only then that I fully realized how God had codded me, listening to my prayers for the safe return of this monster.

"Shut up, you!" I bawled, beside myself.

"What's that you said?" shouted Father, making a wild leap out of bed.

"Mick, Mick!" cried Mother. "Don't you see the child isn't used to you?"

"I see he's better fed than taught," snarled Father, waving his arms wildly. "He wants his bottom smacked."

All his previous shouting was as nothing to these obscene words referring to my person. They really made my blood boil.

"Smack your own!" I screamed hysterically. "Smack your own! Shut up! Shut up!"

At this he lost his patience and let fly at me. He did it with the lack of conviction you'd expect of a man under Mother's horrified eyes, and it ended up as a mere tap, but the sheer indignity of being struck at all by a stranger, a total stranger who had cajoled his way back from the war into our big bed as a result of my innocent intercession, made me completely dotty. I shrieked and shrieked, and danced in my bare feet, and Father, looking awkward and hairy in nothing but a short grey army shirt, glared down at me like a mountain out for murder. I think it must have been then that I realized he was jealous too. And there stood Mother in her nightdress, looking as if her heart was broken between us. I hoped she felt as she looked. It seemed to me that she deserved it all.

From that morning out my life was a hell. Father and I were enemies, open and avowed. We conducted a series of skirmishes against one another, he trying to steal my time with Mother and I his. When she was sitting on my bed, telling me a story, he took to looking for some pair of old boots which he alleged he had left behind him at the beginning of the war. While he talked to Mother I played loudly with my toys to show my total lack of concern. He created a terrible scene one evening when he came in from work and found me at his box, playing with his regimental badges, Gurkha knives and button-sticks. Mother got up and took the box from me.

"You mustn't play with Daddy's toys unless he lets you, Larry," she said severely. "Daddy doesn't play with yours."

For some reason Father looked at her as if she had struck him and then turned away with a scowl.

"Those are not toys," he growled, taking down the box again to see had I lifted anything. "Some of those curios are very rare and valuable."

But as time went on I saw more and more how he managed to alienate Mother and me. What made it worse was that I couldn't grasp his method or see what attraction he had for Mother. In every possible way he was less winning than I. He had a common accent and made noises at his tea. I thought for a while that it might be the newspapers she was interested in, so I made up bits of news of my own to read to her. Then I thought it might be the smoking, which I personally thought attractive, and took his pipes and went round the house dribbling into them till he caught me. I even made noises at my tea, but Mother only told me I was disgusting. It all seemed to hinge round that unhealthy habit of sleeping together, so I made a point of dropping into their bedroom and nosing round, talking to myself, so that they wouldn't know I was watching them, but they were never up to anything that I could see. In the end it beat me. It seemed to depend on being grownup and giving people rings, and I realized I'd have to wait.

But at the same time I wanted him to see that I was only waiting, not giving up the fight. One evening when he was being particularly obnoxious, chattering away well above my head, I let him have it.

"Mummy," I said, "do you know what I'm going to do when I grow up?"

"No, dear," she replied. "What?"

"I'm going to marry you," I said quietly.

Father gave a great guffaw out of him, but he didn't take me in. I knew it must only be pretense. And Mother, in spite of everything, was pleased. I felt she was probably relieved to know that one day Father's hold on her would be broken.

"Won't that be nice?" she said with a smile.

"It'll be very nice," I said confidently. "Because we're going to have lots and lots of babies."

"That's right, dear," she said placidly. "I think we'll have one soon, and then you'll have plenty of company."

I was no end pleased about that because it showed that in spite of the way she gave in to Father she still considered my wishes. Besides, it would put the Geneys in their place.

It didn't turn out like that, though. To begin with, she was very preoccupied—I supposed about where she would get the seventeen and six—and though Father took to staying out late in the evenings it did me no particular good. She stopped taking me for walks, became as touchy as blazes, and smacked me for nothing at all. Sometimes I wished I'd never mentioned the confounded baby—I seemed to have a genius for bringing calamity on myself.

And calamity it was! Sonny arrived in the most appalling hullabaloo—even that much he couldn't do without a fuss—and from the first moment I disliked him. He was a difficult child—so far as I was concerned he was always difficult—and demanded far too much attention. Mother was simply silly about him, and couldn't see when he was only showing off. As company he was worse than useless. He slept all day, and I had to go round the house on tiptoe to avoid waking him. It wasn't any longer a question of not waking Father. The slogan now was "Don't-wake-Sonny!" I couldn't understand why the child wouldn't sleep at the proper time, so whenever Mother's back was turned I woke him. Sometimes to keep him awake I pinched him as well. Mother caught me at it one day and gave me a most unmerciful flaking.

One evening, when Father was coming from work, I was playing trains in the front garden. I let on not to notice him; instead, I pretended to be talking to myself, and said in a loud voice: "If another bloody baby comes into this house, I'm going out."

Father stopped dead and looked at me over his shoulder.

"What's that you said?" he asked sternly.

"I was only talking to myself," I replied, trying to conceal my panic. "It's private."

He turned and went in without a word. Mind you, I intended it as a solemn warning, but its effect was quite different. Father started being quite nice to me. I could understand that, of course. Mother was quite sickening about Sonny. Even at mealtimes she'd get up and gawk at him in the cradle with an idiotic smile, and tell Father to do the same. He was always polite about it, but he looked so puzzled you could see he didn't know what she was talking about. He complained of the way Sonny cried at night, but she only got cross and said that Sonny never cried except when there was something up with him—which was a flaming lie, because Sonny never had anything up with him, and only cried for attention. It was really painful to see how simple-minded she was. Father wasn't attractive, but he had a fine intelligence. He saw through Sonny, and now he knew that I saw through him as well.

One night I woke with a start. There was someone beside me in the bed. For one wild moment I felt sure it must be Mother, having come to her senses and left Father for good, but then I heard Sonny in convulsions in the next room, and Mother saying: "There! There! There!" and I knew it wasn't she. It was Father. He was lying beside me, wide awake, breathing hard and apparently as mad as hell.

After a while it came to me what he was mad about. It was his turn now. After turning me out of the big bed, he had been turned out himself. Mother had no consideration now for anyone but that poisonous pup, Sonny. I couldn't help feeling sorry for Father. I had been through it all myself, and even at that age I was magnanimous. I began to stroke him down and say: "There! There!" He wasn't exactly responsive.

"Aren't you asleep either?" he snarled.

"Ah, come on and put your arm around us, can't you?" I said, and he did, in a sort of way. Gingerly, I suppose, is how you'd describe it. He was very bony but better than nothing.

At Christmas he went out of his way to buy me a really nice model railway.

QUESTIONS

1. Is the story narrated from the point of view of a young child or a mature man? **2.** Note that the narrator's most ardent wishes—for the return of his father and for a new baby in the house—are granted. What are the consequences for him? **3.** What specific details in the story contribute to the appropriateness of its title? **4.** With whom does the reader sympathize? How does the author control those sympathies?

WRITING TOPIC

Focusing on the ironies embodied in this story, describe the shifting relationships among the main characters.

A Conversation with My Father 1972

GRACE PALEY   [b.1922]

My father is eighty-six years old and in bed. His heart, that bloody motor, is equally old and will not do certain jobs any more. It still floods his head with brainy light. But it won't let his legs carry the weight of his body around the house. Despite my metaphors, this muscle failure is not due to his old heart, he says, but to a potassium shortage. Sitting on one pillow, leaning on three, he offers last-minute advice and makes a request.

"I would like you to write a simple story just once more," he says, "the kind de Maupassant wrote, or Chekhov,[1] the kind you used to write. Just recognizable people and then write down what happened to them next."

I say, "Yes, why not? That's possible." I want to please him, though I don't remember writing that way. I *would* like to try to tell such a story, if he means the kind that begins: "There was a woman . . ." followed by plot, the absolute line between two points which I've always despised. Not for literary reasons, but because it takes all hope away. Everyone, real or invented, deserves the open destiny of life.

Finally I thought of a story that had been happening for a couple of years right across the street. I wrote it down, then read it aloud. "Pa," I said, "how about this? Do you mean something like this?"

> Once in my time there was a woman and she had a son. They lived nicely, in a small apartment in Manhattan. This boy at about fifteen became a junkie, which is not unusual in our neighborhood. In order to maintain her close friendship with him, she became a junkie too. She said it was part of the youth culture, with which she felt very much at home. After a while, for a number of reasons, the boy gave it all up and left the city and his mother in disgust. Hopeless and alone, she grieved. We all visit her.

"O.K., Pa, that's it," I said, "an unadorned and miserable tale."

"But that's not what I mean," my father said. "You misunderstood me on purpose. You know there's a lot more to it. You know that. You left everything out. Turgenev[2] wouldn't do that. Chekhov wouldn't do that. There are in fact Russian writers you never heard of, you don't have an inkling of, as good as

---

[1] Guy de Maupassant (1850–1893) wrote stories that depended on ironic twists of plot for their effect. Anton Pavlovich Chekhov (1860–1904) wrote insistently realistic stories.
[2] Ivan Sergeyevich Turgenev (1818–1883), like Chekhov, wrote realistic fiction.

anyone, who can write a plain ordinary story, who would not leave out what you have left out. I object not to facts but to people sitting in trees talking senselessly, voices from who knows where. . . ."

"Forget that one, Pa, what have I left out now? In this one?"

"Her looks, for instance."

"Oh. Quite handsome, I think. Yes."

"Her hair?"

"Dark, with heavy braids, as though she were a girl or a foreigner."

"What were her parents like, her stock? That she became such a person. It's interesting, you know."

"From out of town. Professional people. The first to be divorced in their county. How's that? Enough?" I asked.

"With you, it's all a joke," he said. "What about the boy's father? Why didn't you mention him? Who was he? Or was the boy born out of wedlock?"

"Yes," I said. "He was born out of wedlock."

"For Godsakes, doesn't anyone in your stories get married? Doesn't anyone have the time to run down to City Hall before they jump into bed?"

"No," I said. "In real life, yes. But in my stories, no."

"Why do you answer me like that?"

"Oh, Pa, this is a simple story about a smart woman who came to N.Y.C. full of interest love trust excitement very up to date, and about her son, what a hard time she had in this world. Married or not, it's of small consequence."

"It is of great consequence," he said.

"O.K.," I said.

"O.K. O.K. yourself," he said, "but listen. I believe you that she's good-looking, but I don't think she was so smart."

"That's true," I said. "Actually that's the trouble with stories. People start out fantastic. You think they're extraordinary, but it turns out as the work goes along, they're just average with a good education. Sometimes the other way around, the person's a kind of dumb innocent, but he outwits you and you can't even think of an ending good enough."

"What do you do then?" he asked. He had been a doctor for a couple of decades and then an artist for a couple of decades and he's still interested in details, craft, technique.

"Well, you just have to let the story lie around till some agreement can be reached between you and the stubborn hero."

"Aren't you talking silly now?" he asked. "Start again," he said. "It so happens I'm not going out this evening. Tell the story again. See what you can do this time."

"O.K.," I said. "But it's not a five-minute job." Second attempt:

Once, across the street from us, there was a fine handsome woman, our neighbor. She had a son whom she loved because she'd known him since birth (in helpless chubby infancy, and in the wrestling, hugging ages, seven to ten, as well as earlier and later). This boy, when he fell into the fist of adolescence, became a junkie. He was not a hopeless one. He was in fact hopeful, an ideologue and successful converter. With his busy brilliance, he wrote persuasive articles for his high-school newspaper. Seeking a wider audience, using important connections, he drummed into Lower Manhattan newsstand distribution a periodical called *Oh! Golden Horse!*

In order to keep him from feeling guilty (because guilt is the stony heart of nine tenths of all clinically diagnosed cancers in America today, she said), and because she had always believed in giving bad habits room at home where one could keep an eye on them, she too became a junkie. Her kitchen was famous for a while—a center for intellectual addicts who knew what they were doing. A few felt artistic like Coleridge[3] and others were scientific and revolutionary like Leary.[4] Although she was often high herself, certain good mothering reflexes remained, and she saw to it that there was lots of orange juice around and honey and milk and vitamin pills. However, she never cooked anything but chili, and that no more than once a week. She explained, when we talked to her, seriously, with neighborly concern, that it was her part in the youth culture and she would rather be with the young, it was an honor, than with her own generation.

One week, while nodding through an Antonioni[5] film, this boy was severely jabbed by the elbow of a stern and proselytizing girl, sitting beside him. She offered immediate apricots and nuts for his sugar level, spoke to him sharply, and took him home.

She had heard of him and his work and she herself published, edited, and wrote a competitive journal called *Man Does Live by Bread Alone*. In the organic heat of her continuous presence he could not help but become interested once more in his muscles, his arteries, and nerve connections. In fact he began to love them, treasure them, praise them with funny little songs in *Man Does Live.* . . .

> the fingers of my flesh transcend
> my transcendental soul
> the tightness in my shoulders end
> my teeth have made me whole

To the mouth of his head (that glory of will and determination) he brought hard apples, nuts, wheat germ, and soybean oil. He said to his old friends, From now on, I guess I'll keep my wits about me. I'm going on the natch. He said he was about to begin a spiritual deep-breathing journey. How about you too, Mom? he asked kindly.

His conversion was so radiant, splendid, that neighborhood kids his age began to say that he had never been a real addict at all, only a journalist along for the smell of the story. The mother tried several times to give up what had become without her son and his friends a lonely habit. This effort only brought it to supportable levels. The boy and his girl took their electronic mimeograph and moved

---

[3] Samuel Taylor Coleridge (1772–1834), English poet who used opium.
[4] Timothy Leary (b. 1920), former professor of psychology at Harvard University, who promoted the use of psychedelic drugs.
[5] Michelangelo Antonioni (b. 1912), an Italian director of *avant-garde* films.

to the bushy edge of another borough. They were very strict. They said they would not see her again until she had been off drugs for sixty days.

At home alone in the evening, weeping, the mother read and reread the seven issues of *Oh! Golden Horse!* They seemed to her as truthful as ever. We often crossed the street to visit and console. But if we mentioned any of our children who were at college or in the hospital or dropouts at home, she would cry out, My baby! My baby! and burst into terrible, face-scarring, time-consuming tears. The End.

First my father was silent, then he said, "Number One: You have a nice sense of humor. Number Two: I see you can't tell a plain story. So don't waste time." Then he said sadly, "Number Three: I suppose that means she was alone, she was left like that, his mother. Alone: Probably sick?"

I said, "Yes."

"Poor woman. Poor girl, to be born in a time of fools, to live among fools. The end. The end. You were right to put that down. The end."

I didn't want to argue, but I had to say, "Well, it is not necessarily the end, Pa."

"Yes," he said, "what a tragedy. The end of a person."

"No, Pa," I begged him. "It doesn't have to be. She's only about forty. She could be a hundred different things in this world as time goes on. A teacher or a social worker. An ex-junkie! Sometimes it's better than having a master's in education."

"Jokes," he said. "As a writer that's your main trouble. You don't want to recognize it. Tragedy! Plain tragedy! Historical tragedy! No hope. The end."

"Oh, Pa," I said. "She could change."

"In your own life, too, you have to look it in the face." He took a couple of nitroglycerin. "Turn to five," he said, pointing to the dial on the oxygen tank. He inserted the tubes into his nostrils and breathed deep. He closed his eyes and said, "No."

I had promised the family to always let him have the last word when arguing, but in this case I had a different responsibility. That woman lives across the street. She's my knowledge and my invention. I'm sorry for her. I'm not going to leave her there in that house crying. (Actually neither would Life, which unlike me has no pity.)

Therefore: She did change. Of course her son never came home again. But right now, she's the receptionist in a storefront community clinic in the East Village. Most of the customers are young people, some old friends. The head doctor has said to her, "If we only had three people in this clinic with your experiences. . . ."

"The doctor said that?" My father took the oxygen tubes out of his nostrils and said, "Jokes. Jokes again."

"No, Pa, it could really happen that way, it's a funny world nowadays."

"No," he said. "Truth first. She will slide back. A person must have character. She does not."

"No, Pa," I said. "That's it. She's got a job. Forget it. She's in that storefront working."

"How long will it be?" he asked. "Tragedy! You too. When will you look it in the face?"

Good Country People   1955

FLANNERY O'CONNOR   [1925–1964]

Besides the neutral expression that she wore when she was alone, Mrs. Freeman had two others, forward and reverse, that she used for all her human dealings. Her forward expression was steady and driving like the advance of a heavy truck. Her eyes never swerved to left or right but turned as the story turned as if they followed a yellow line down the center of it. She seldom used the other expression because it was not often necessary for her to retract a statement, but when she did, her face came to a complete stop, there was an almost imperceptible movement of her black eyes, during which they seemed to be receding, and then the observer would see that Mrs. Freeman, though she might stand there as real as several grain sacks thrown on top of each other, was no longer there in spirit. As for getting anything across to her when this was the case, Mrs. Hopewell had given it up. She might talk her head off. Mrs. Freeman could never be brought to admit herself wrong on any point. She would stand there and if she could be brought to say anything, it was something like, "Well, I wouldn't of said it was and I wouldn't of said it wasn't," or letting her gaze range over the top kitchen shelf where there was an assortment of dusty bottles, she might remark, "I see you ain't ate many of them figs you put up last summer."

They carried on their most important business in the kitchen at breakfast. Every morning Mrs. Hopewell got up at seven o'clock and lit her gas heater and Joy's. Joy was her daughter, a large blonde girl who had an artificial leg. Mrs. Hopewell thought of her as a child though she was thirty-two years old and highly educated. Joy would get up while her mother was eating and lumber into the bathroom and slam the door, and before long, Mrs. Freeman would arrive at the back door. Joy would hear her mother call, "Come on in," and then they would talk for a while in low voices that were indistinguishable in the bathroom. By the time Joy came in, they had usually finished the weather report and were on one or the other of Mrs. Freeman's daughters, Glynese or Carramae. Joy called them Glycerin and Caramel. Glynese, a redhead, was eighteen and had many admirers; Carramae, a blonde, was only fifteen but already married and pregnant. She could not keep anything on her stomach. Every morning Mrs. Freeman told Mrs. Hopewell how many times she had vomited since the last report.

Mrs. Hopewell liked to tell people that Glynese and Carramae were two of the finest girls she knew and that Mrs. Freeman was a *lady* and that she was never ashamed to take her anywhere or introduce her to anybody they might meet. Then she would tell how she had happened to hire the Freemans in the first place and how they were a godsend to her and how she had had them four years. The reason for her keeping them so long was that they were not trash.

They were good country people. She had telephoned the man whose name they had given as a reference and he had told her that Mr. Freeman was a good farmer but that his wife was the nosiest woman ever to walk the earth. "She's got to be into everything," the man said. "If she don't get there before the dust settles, you can bet she's dead, that's all. She'll want to know all your business. I can stand him real good," he had said, "but me nor my wife neither could have stood that woman one more minute on this place." That had put Mrs. Hopewell off for a few days.

She had hired them in the end because there were no other applicants but she had made up her mind beforehand exactly how she would handle the woman. Since she was the type who had to be into everything, then, Mrs. Hopewell had decided, she would not only let her be into everything, she would *see to it* that she was into everything—she would give her the responsibility of everything, she would put her in charge. Mrs. Hopewell had no bad qualities of her own but she was able to use other people's in such a constructive way that she never felt the lack. She had hired the Freemans and she had kept them four years.

Nothing is, perfect. This was one of Mrs. Hopewell's favorite sayings. Another was: that is life! And still another, the most important, was: well, other people have their opinions too. She would make these statements, usually at the table, in a tone of gentle insistence as if no one held them but her, and the large hulking Joy, whose constant outrage had obliterated every expression from her face, would stare just a little to the side of her, her eyes icy blue, with the look of someone who has achieved blindness by an act of will and means to keep it.

When Mrs. Hopewell said to Mrs. Freeman that life was like that, Mrs. Freeman would say, "I always said so myself." Nothing had been arrived at by anyone that had not first been arrived at by her. She was quicker than Mr. Freeman. When Mrs. Hopewell said to her after they had been on the place a while, "You know, you're the wheel behind the wheel," and winked, Mrs. Freeman had said, "I know it. I've always been quick. It's some that are quicker than others."

"Everybody is different," Mrs. Hopewell said.

"Yes, most people is," Mrs. Freeman said.

"It takes all kinds to make the world."

"I always said it did myself."

The girl was used to this kind of dialogue for breakfast and more of it for dinner; sometimes they had it for supper too. When they had no guest they ate in the kitchen because that was easier. Mrs. Freeman always managed to arrive at some point during the meal and to watch them finish it. She would stand in the doorway if it were summer but in the winter she would stand with one elbow on top of the refrigerator and look down on them, or she would stand by the gas heater, lifting the back of her skirt slightly. Occasionally she would stand against the wall and roll her head from side to side. At no time was she in any hurry to leave. All this was very trying on Mrs. Hopewell but she was a woman of great patience. She realized that nothing is perfect and that in the Freemans she had good country people and that if, in this day and age, you get good country people, you had better hang onto them.

She had had plenty of experience with trash. Before the Freemans she had averaged one tenant family a year. The wives of these farmers were not the kind you would want to be around you for very long. Mrs. Hopewell, who had divorced her husband long ago, needed someone to walk over the fields with her; and when Joy had to be impressed for these services, her remarks were usually so ugly and her face so glum that Mrs. Hopewell would say, "If you can't come pleasantly, I don't want you at all," to which the girl, standing square and rigid-shouldered with her neck thrust slightly forward, would reply, "If you want me, here I am—LIKE I AM."

Mrs. Hopewell excused this attitude because of the leg (which had been shot off in a hunting accident when Joy was ten). It was hard for Mrs. Hopewell to realize that her child was thirty-two now and that for more than twenty years she had had only one leg. She thought of her still as a child because it tore her heart to think instead of the poor stout girl in her thirties who had never danced a step or had any *normal* good times. Her name was really Joy but as soon as she was twenty-one and away from home, she had had it legally changed. Mrs. Hopewell was certain that she had thought and thought until she had hit upon the ugliest name in any language. Then she had gone and had the beautiful name, Joy, changed without telling her mother until after she had done it. Her legal name was Hulga.

When Mrs. Hopewell thought the name, Hulga, she thought of the broad blank hull of a battleship. She would not use it. She continued to call her Joy to which the girl responded but in a purely mechanical way.

Hulga had learned to tolerate Mrs. Freeman, who saved her from taking walks with her mother. Even Glynese and Carramae were useful when they occupied attention that might otherwise have been directed at her. At first she had thought she could not stand Mrs. Freeman for she had found that it was not possible to be rude to her. Mrs. Freeman would take on strange resentments and for days together she would be sullen but the source of her displeasure was always obscure; a direct attack, a positive leer, blatant ugliness to her face—these never touched her. And without warning one day, she began calling her Hulga.

She did not call her that in front of Mrs. Hopewell who would have been incensed but when she and the girl happened to be out of the house together, she would say something and add the name Hulga to the end of it, and the big spectacled Joy-Hulga would scowl and redden as if her privacy had been intruded upon. She considered the name her personal affair. She had arrived at it first purely on the basis of its ugly sound and then the full genius of its fitness had struck her. She had a vision of the name working like the ugly sweating Vulcan who stayed in the furnace and to whom, presumably, the goddess had to come when called. She saw it as the name of her highest creative act. One of her major triumphs was that her mother had not been able to turn her dust into

Joy, but the greater one was that she had been able to turn it herself into Hulga. However, Mrs. Freeman's relish for using the name only irritated her. It was as if Mrs. Freeman's beady steel-pointed eyes had penetrated far enough behind her face to reach some secret fact. Something about her seemed to fascinate Mrs. Freeman and then one day Hulga realized that it was the artificial leg. Mrs. Freeman had a special fondness for the details of secret infections, hidden deformities, assaults upon children. Of diseases, she preferred the lingering or incurable. Hulga had heard Mrs. Hopewell give her the details of the hunting accident, how the leg had been literally blasted off, how she had never lost consciousness. Mrs. Freeman could listen to it any time as if it had happened an hour ago.

When Hulga stumped into the kitchen in the morning (she could walk without making the awful noise but she made it—Mrs. Hopewell was certain— because it was ugly-sounding), she glanced at them and did not speak. Mrs. Hopewell would be in her red kimono with her hair tied around her head in rags. She would be sitting at the table, finishing her breakfast and Mrs. Freeman would be hanging by her elbow outward from the refrigerator, looking down at the table. Hulga always put her eggs on the stove to boil and then stood over them with her arms folded, and Mrs. Hopewell would look at her—a kind of indirect gaze divided between her and Mrs. Freeman—and would think that if she would only keep herself up a little, she wouldn't be so bad looking. There was nothing wrong with her face that a pleasant expression wouldn't help. Mrs. Hopewell said that people who looked on the bright side of things would be beautiful even if they were not.

Whenever she looked at Joy this way, she could not help but feel that it would have been better if the child had not taken the Ph.D. It had certainly not brought her out any and now that she had it, there was no more excuse for her to go to school again. Mrs. Hopewell thought it was nice for girls to go to school to have a good time but Joy had "gone through." Anyhow, she would not have been strong enough to go again. The doctors had told Mrs. Hopewell that with the best of care, Joy might see forty-five. She had a weak heart. Joy had made it plain that if it had not been for this condition, she would be far from these red hills and good country people. She would be in a university lecturing to people who knew what she was talking about. And Mrs. Hopewell could very well picture her there, looking like a scarecrow and lecturing to more of the same. Here she went about all day in a six-year-old skirt and a yellow sweat shirt with a faded cowboy on a horse embossed on it. She thought this was funny; Mrs. Hopewell thought it was idiotic and showed simply that she was still a child. She was brilliant but she didn't have a grain of sense. It seemed to Mrs. Hopewell that every year she grew less like other people and more like herself—bloated, rude, and squint-eyed. And she said such strange things! To her own mother she had said—without warning, without excuse, standing up in the middle of a meal with her face purple and her mouth half full—"Woman! do you ever look inside? Do you ever look inside and see what you are *not*?

God!" she had cried sinking down again and staring at her plate, "Malebranche was right: we are not our own light. We are not our own light!" Mrs. Hopewell had no idea to this day what brought that on. She had only made the remark, hoping Joy would take it in, that a smile never hurt anyone.

The girl had taken the Ph.D. in philosophy and this left Mrs. Hopewell at a complete loss. You could say, "My daughter is a nurse," or "My daughter is a school teacher," or even, "My daughter is a chemical engineer." You could not say, "My daughter is a philosopher." That was something that had ended with the Greeks and Romans. All day Joy sat on her neck in a deep chair, reading. Sometimes she went for walks but she didn't like dogs or cats or birds or flowers or nature or nice young men. She looked at nice young men as if she could smell their stupidity.

One day Mrs. Hopewell had picked up one of the books the girl had just put down and opening it at random, she read, "Science, on the other hand, has to assert its soberness and seriousness afresh and declare that it is concerned solely with what-is. Nothing—how can it be for science anything but a horror and a phantasm? If science is right, then one thing stands firm: science wishes to know nothing of nothing. Such is after all the strictly scientific approach to Nothing. We know it by wishing to know nothing of Nothing." These words had been underlined with a blue pencil and they worked on Mrs. Hopewell like some evil incantation in gibberish. She shut the book quickly and went out of the room as if she were having a chill.

This morning when the girl came in, Mrs. Freeman was on Carramae. "She thrown up four times after supper," she said, "and was up twict in the night after three o'clock. Yesterday she didn't do nothing but ramble in the bureau drawer. All she did. Stand up there and see what she could run up on."

"She's got to eat," Mrs. Hopewell muttered, sipping her coffee, while she watched Joy's back at the stove. She was wondering what the child had said to the Bible salesman. She could not imagine what kind of a conversation she could possibly have had with him.

He was a tall gaunt hatless youth who had called yesterday to sell them a Bible. He had appeared at the door, carrying a large black suitcase that weighted him so heavily on one side that he had to brace himself against the door facing. He seemed on the point of collapse but he said in a cheerful voice, "Good morning, Mrs. Cedars!" and set the suitcase down on the mat. He was not a bad-looking young man though he had on a bright blue suit and yellow socks that were not pulled up far enough. He had prominent face bones and a streak of sticky-looking brown hair falling across his forehead.

"I'm Mrs. Hopewell," she said.

"Oh!" he said, pretending to look puzzled but with his eyes sparkling, "I saw it said 'The Cedars,' on the mailbox so I thought you was Mrs. Cedars!" and he burst out in a pleasant laugh. He picked up the satchel and under cover of a pant, he fell forward into her hall. It was rather as if the suitcase had moved first, jerking him after it. "Mrs. Hopewell!" he said and grabbed her hand. "I hope you are well!" and he laughed again and then all at once his face sobered completely. He paused and gave her a straight earnest look and said, "Lady, I've come to speak of serious things."

"Well, come in," she muttered, none too pleased because her dinner was almost ready. He came into the parlor and sat down on the edge of a straight chair and put the suitcase between his feet and glanced around the room as if he were sizing her up by it. Her silver gleamed on the two sideboards; she decided he had never been in a room as elegant as this.

"Mrs. Hopewell," he began, using her name in a way that sounded almost intimate, "I know you believe in Chrustian service."

"Well yes," she murmured.

"I know," he said and paused, looking very wise with his head cocked on one side, "that you're a good woman. Friends have told me."

Mrs. Hopewell never liked to be taken for a fool. "What are you selling?" she asked.

"Bibles," the young man said and his eye raced around the room before he added, "I see you have no family Bible in your parlor, I see that is the one lack you got!"

Mrs. Hopewell could not say, "My daughter is an atheist and won't let me keep the Bible in the parlor." She said, stiffening slightly, "I keep my Bible by my bedside." This was not the truth. It was in the attic somewhere.

"Lady," he said, "the word of God ought to be in the parlor."

"Well, I think that's a matter of taste," she began. "I think . . ."

"Lady," he said, "for a Chrustian, the word of God ought to be in every room in the house besides in his heart. I know you're a Chrustian because I can see it in every line of your face."

She stood up and said, "Well, young man, I don't want to buy a Bible and I smell my dinner burning."

He didn't get up. He began to twist his hands and looking down at them, he said softly, "Well lady, I'll tell you the truth—not many people want to buy one nowadays and besides, I know I'm real simple. I don't know how to say a thing but to say it. I'm just a country boy." He glanced up into her unfriendly face. "People like you don't like to fool with country people like me!"

"Why!" she cried, "good country people are the salt of the earth! Besides, we all have different ways of doing, it takes all kinds to make the world go 'round. That's life!"

"You said a mouthful," he said.

"Why, I think there aren't enough good country people in the world!" she said, stirred. "I think that's what's wrong with it!"

His face had brightened. "I didn't inraduce myself," he said. "I'm Manley Pointer from out in the country around Willohobie, not even from a place, just from near a place."

"You wait a minute," she said. "I have to see about my dinner." She went out to the kitchen and found Joy standing near the door where she had been listening.

"Get rid of the salt of the earth," she said, "and let's eat."

Mrs. Hopewell gave her a pained look and turned the heat down under the vegetables. "*I* can't be rude to anybody," she murmured and went back into the parlor.

He had opened the suitcase and was sitting with a Bible on each knee.

"You might as well put those up," she told him. "I don't want one."

"I appreciate your honesty," he said. "You don't see any more real honest people unless you go way out in the country."

"I know," she said, "real genuine folks!" Through the crack in the door she heard a groan.

"I guess a lot of boys come telling you they're working their way through college," he said, "but I'm not going to tell you that. Somehow," he said, "I don't want to go to college. I want to devote my life to Chrustian service. See," he said, lowering his voice, "I got this heart condition. I may not live long. When you know it's something wrong with you and you may not live long, well then, lady . . ." He paused, with his mouth open, and stared at her.

He and Joy had the same condition! She knew that her eyes were filling with tears but she collected herself quickly and murmured, "Won't you stay for dinner? We'd love to have you!" and was sorry the instant she heard herself say it.

"Yes mam," he said in an abashed voice, "I would sher love to do that!"

Joy had given him one look on being introduced to him and then throughout the meal had not glanced at him again. He had addressed several remarks to her, which she had pretended not to hear. Mrs. Hopewell could not understand deliberate rudeness, although she lived with it, and she felt she had always to overflow with hospitality to make up for Joy's lack of courtesy. She urged him to talk about himself and he did. He said he was the seventh child of twelve and that his father had been crushed under a tree when he himself was eight year old. He had been crushed very badly, in fact, almost cut in two and was practically not recognizable. His mother had got along the best she could by hard working and she had always seen that her children went to Sunday School and that they read the Bible every evening. He was now nineteen year old and he had been selling Bibles for four months. In that time he had sold seventy-seven Bibles and had the promise of two more sales. He wanted to become a missionary because he thought that was the way you could do most for people. "He who losest his life shall find it," he said simply and he was so sincere, so genuine and earnest that Mrs. Hopewell would not for the world have smiled. He prevented his peas from sliding onto the table by blocking them with a piece of bread which he later cleaned his plate with. She could see Joy observing sidewise how he handled his knife and fork and she saw too that every few minutes, the boy would dart a keen appraising glance at the girl as if he were trying to attract her attention.

After dinner Joy cleared the dishes off the table and disappeared and Mrs. Hopewell was left to talk with him. He told her again about his childhood and his father's accident and about various things that had happened to him. Every five minutes or so she would stifle a yawn. He sat for two hours until finally she told him she must go because she had an appointment in town. He packed his Bibles and thanked her and prepared to leave, but in the doorway he stopped and wrung her hand and said that not on any of his trips had he met a lady as nice as her and he asked if he could come again. She had said she would always be happy to see him.

Joy had been standing in the road, apparently looking at something in the distance, when he came down the steps toward her, bent to the side with his heavy valise. He stopped where she was standing and confronted her directly. Mrs. Hopewell could not hear what he said but she trembled to think what Joy would say to him. She could see that after a minute Joy said something and that then the boy began to speak again, making an excited gesture with his free hand. After a minute Joy said something else at which the boy began to speak once more. Then to her amazement, Mrs. Hopewell saw the two of them walk off together, toward the gate. Joy had walked all the way to the gate with him and Mrs. Hopewell could not imagine what they had said to each other, and she had not yet dared to ask.

Mrs. Freeman was insisting upon her attention. She had moved from the refrigerator to the heater so that Mrs. Hopewell had to turn and face her in order to seem to be listening. "Glynese gone out with Harvey Hill again last night," she said. "She had this sty."

"Hill," Mrs. Hopewell said absently, "is that the one who works in the garage?"

"Nome, he's the one that goes to chiropracter school," Mrs. Freeman said. "She had this sty. Been had it two days. So she says when he brought her in the other night he says, 'Lemme get rid of that sty for you,' and she says, 'How?' and he says, 'You just lay yourself down acrost the seat of that car and I'll show you.' So she done it and he popped her neck. Kept on a-popping it several times until she made him quit. This morning," Mrs. Freeman said, "she ain't got no sty. She ain't got no traces of a sty."

"I never heard of that before," Mrs. Hopewell said.

"He ast her to marry him before the Ordinary," Mrs. Freeman went on, "and she told him she wasn't going to be married in no *office*."

"Well, Glynese is a fine girl," Mrs. Hopewell said, "Glynese and Carramae are both fine girls."

"Carramae said when her and Lyman was married Lyman said it sure felt sacred to him. She said he said he wouldn't take five hundred dollars for being married by a preacher."

"How much would he take?" the girl asked from the stove.

"He said he wouldn't take five hundred dollars," Mrs. Freeman repeated.

"Well we all have work to do," Mrs. Hopewell said.

"Lyman said it just felt more sacred to him," Mrs. Freeman said. "The doctor wants Carramae to eat prunes. Says instead of medicine. Says them cramps is coming from pressure. You know where I think it is?"

"She'll be better in a few weeks," Mrs. Hopewell said.

"In the tube," Mrs. Freeman said. "Else she wouldn't be as sick as she is."

Hulga had cracked her two eggs into a saucer and was bringing them to the table along with a cup of coffee that she had filled too full. She sat down carefully and began to eat, meaning to keep Mrs. Freeman there by questions if for any reason she showed an inclination to leave. She could perceive her mother's eye on her. The first roundabout question would be about the Bible salesman and she did not wish to bring it on. "How did he pop her neck?" she asked.

Mrs. Freeman went into a description of how he had popped her neck. She said he owned a '55 Mercury but that Glynese said she would rather marry a man with only a '36 Plymouth who would be married by a preacher. The girl asked what if he had a '32 Plymouth and Mrs. Freeman said what Glynese had said was a '36 Plymouth.

Mrs. Hopewell said there were not many girls with Glynese's common sense. She said what she admired in those girls was their common sense. She said that reminded her that they had a nice visitor yesterday, a young man selling Bibles. "Lord," she said, "he bored me to death but he was so sincere and genuine I couldn't be rude to him. He was just good country people, you know," she said,"—just the salt of the earth."

"I seen him walk up," Mrs. Freeman said, "and then later—I seen him walk off," and Hulga could feel the slight shift in her voice, the slight insinuation, that he had not walked off alone, had he? Her face remained expressionless but the color rose into her neck and she seemed to swallow it down with the next spoonful of egg. Mrs. Freeman was looking at her as if they had a secret together.

"Well, it takes all kinds of people to make the world go 'round," Mrs. Hopewell said. "It's very good we aren't all alike."

"Some people are more alike than others," Mrs. Freeman said.

Hulga got up and stumped, with about twice the noise that was necessary, into her room and locked the door. She was to meet the Bible salesman at ten o'clock at the gate. She had thought about it half the night. She had started thinking of it as a great joke and then she had begun to see profound implications in it. She had lain in bed imagining dialogues for them that were insane on the surface but that reached below to depths that no Bible salesman would be aware of. Their conversation yesterday had been of this kind.

He had stopped in front of her and had simply stood there. His face was bony and sweaty and bright, with a little pointed nose in the center of it, and his look was different from what it had been at the dinner table. He was gazing at her with open curiosity, with fascination, like a child watching a new fantastic animal at the zoo, and he was breathing as if he had run a great distance to reach her. His gaze seemed somehow familiar but she could not think where she had been regarded with it before. For almost a minute he didn't say anything. Then on what seemed an insuck of breath, he whispered, "You ever ate a chicken that was two days old?"

The girl looked at him stonily. He might have just put this question up for consideration at the meeting of a philosophical association. "Yes," she presently replied as if she had considered it from all angles.

"It must have been mighty small!" he said triumphantly and shook all over with little nervous giggles, getting very red in the face, and subsiding finally into his gaze of complete admiration, while the girl's expression remained exactly the same.

"How old are you?" he asked softly.

She waited some time before she answered. Then in a flat voice she said, "Seventeen."

His smiles came in succession like waves breaking on the surface of a little lake. "I see you got a wooden leg," he said. "I think you're real brave. I think you're real sweet."

The girl stood blank and solid and silent.

"Walk to the gate with me," he said. "You're a brave sweet little thing and I liked you the minute I seen you walk in the door."

Hulga began to move forward.

"What's your name?" he asked, smiling down on the top of her head.

"Hulga," she said.

"Hulga," he murmured, "Hulga. Hulga. I never heard of anybody name Hulga before. You're shy, aren't you, Hulga?" he asked.

She nodded, watching his large red hand on the handle of the giant valise.

"I like girls that wear glasses," he said. "I think a lot. I'm not like these people that a serious thought don't ever enter their heads. It's because I may die."

"I may die too," she said suddenly and looked up at him. His eyes were very small and brown, glittering feverishly.

"Listen," he said, "don't you think some people was meant to meet on account of what all they got in common and all? Like they both think serious thoughts and all?" He shifted the valise to his other hand so that the hand nearest her was free. He caught hold of her elbow and shook it a little. "I don't work on Saturday," he said. "I like to walk in the woods and see what Mother Nature is wearing. O'er the hills and far away. Pic-nics and things. Couldn't we go on a pic-nic tomorrow? Say yes, Hulga," he said and gave her a dying look as if he felt his insides about to drop out of him. He had even seemed to sway slightly toward her.

During the night she had imagined that she seduced him. She imagined that the two of them walked on the place until they came to the storage barn beyond the two back fields and there, she imagined, that things came to such a pass that she very easily seduced him and that then, of course, she had to reckon with his remorse. True genius can get an idea across even to an inferior mind. She imagined that she took his remorse in hand and changed it into a deeper understanding of life. She took all his shame away and turned it into something useful.

She set off for the gate at exactly ten o'clock, escaping without drawing Mrs.

Hopewell's attention. She didn't take anything to eat, forgetting that food is usually taken on a picnic. She wore a pair of slacks and a dirty white shirt, and as an afterthought, she had put some Vapex on the collar of it since she did not own any perfume. When she reached the gate no one was there.

She looked up and down the empty highway and had the furious feeling that she had been tricked, that he had only meant to make her walk to the gate after the idea of him. Then suddenly he stood up, very tall, from behind a bush on the opposite embankment. Smiling, he lifted his hat which was new and wide-brimmed. He had not worn it yesterday and she wondered if he had bought it for the occasion. It was toast-colored with a red and white band around it and was slightly too large for him. He stepped from behind the bush still carrying the black valise. He had on the same suit and the same yellow socks sucked down in his shoes from walking. He crossed the highway and said, "I knew you'd come!"

The girl wondered acidly how he had known this. She pointed to the valise and asked, "Why did you bring your Bibles?"

He took her elbow, smiling down on her as if he could not stop. "You can never tell when you'll need the word of God, Hulga," he said. She had a moment in which she doubted that this was actually happening and then they began to climb the embankment. They went down into the pasture toward the woods. The boy walked lightly by her side, bouncing on his toes. The valise did not seem to be heavy today; he even swung it. They crossed half the pasture without saying anything and then, putting his hand easily on the small of her back, he asked softly, "Where does your wooden leg join on?"

She turned an ugly red and glared at him and for an instant the boy looked abashed. "I didn't mean you no harm," he said. "I only meant you're so brave and all. I guess God takes care of you."

"No," she said, looking forward and walking fast, "I don't even believe in God."

At this he stopped and whistled. "No!" he exclaimed as if he were too astonished to say anything else.

She walked on and in a second he was bouncing at her side, fanning with his hat. "That's very unusual for a girl," he remarked, watching her out of the corner of his eye. When they reached the edge of the wood, he put his hand on her back again and drew her against him without a word and kissed her heavily.

The kiss, which had more pressure than feeling behind it, produced that extra surge of adrenalin in the girl that enables one to carry a packed trunk out of a burning house, but in her, the power went at once to the brain. Even before he released her, her mind, clear and detached and ironic anyway, was regarding him from a great distance, with amusement but with pity. She had never been kissed before and she was pleased to discover that it was an unexceptional experience and all a matter of the mind's control. Some people might enjoy drain water if they were told it was vodka. When the boy, looking expectant but uncertain, pushed her gently away, she turned and walked on, saying nothing as if such business, for her, were common enough.

He came along panting at her side, trying to help her when he saw a root that she might trip over. He caught and held back the long swaying blades of thorn vine until she had passed beyond them. She led the way and he came breathing heavily behind her. Then they came out on a sunlit hillside, sloping softly into another one a little smaller. Beyond, they could see the rusted top of the old barn where the extra hay was stored.

The hill was sprinkled with small pink weeds. "Then you ain't saved?" he asked suddenly, stopping.

The girl smiled. It was the first time she had smiled at him at all. "In my economy," she said, "I'm saved and you are damned but I told you I didn't believe in God."

Nothing seemed to destroy the boy's look of admiration. He gazed at her now as if the fantastic animal at the zoo had put its paw through the bars and given him a loving poke. She thought he looked as if he wanted to kiss her again and she walked on before he had the chance.

"Ain't there somewheres we can sit down sometime?" he murmured, his voice softening toward the end of the sentence.

"In that barn," she said.

They made for it rapidly as if it might slide away like a train. It was a large two-story barn, cool and dark inside. The boy pointed up the ladder that led into the loft and said, "It's too bad we can't go up there."

"Why can't we?" she asked.

"Yer leg," he said reverently.

The girl gave him a contemptuous look and putting both hands on the ladder, she climbed it while he stood below, apparently awestruck. She pulled herself expertly through the opening and then looked down at him and said, "Well, come on if you're coming," and he began to climb the ladder, awkwardly bringing the suitcase with him.

"We won't need the Bible," she observed.

"You never can tell," he said, panting. After he had got into the loft, he was a few seconds catching his breath. She had sat down in a pile of straw. A wide sheath of sunlight, filled with dust particles, slanted over her. She lay back against a bale, her face turned away, looking out the front opening of the barn where hay was thrown from a wagon into the loft. The two pink-speckled hillsides lay back against a dark ridge of woods. The sky was cloudless and cold blue. The boy dropped down by her side and put one arm under her and the other over her and began methodically kissing her face, making little noises like a fish. He did not remove his hat but it was pushed far enough back not to interfere. When her glasses got in his way, he took them off of her and slipped them into his pocket.

The girl at first did not return any of the kisses but presently she began to and after she had put several on his cheek, she reached his lips and remained there, kissing him again and again as if she were trying to draw all the breath out of him. His breath was clear and sweet like a child's and the kisses were sticky like a child's. He mumbled about loving her and about knowing when he first seen her that he loved her, but the mumbling was like the sleepy fretting of a child being put to sleep by his mother. Her mind, throughout this, never stopped or lost itself for a second to her feelings. "You ain't said you love me none," he whispered finally, pulling back from her. "You got to say that."

She looked away from him off into the hollow sky and then down at a black ridge and then down farther into what appeared to be two green swelling lakes. She didn't realize he had taken her glasses but this landscape could not seem exceptional to her for she seldom paid any close attention to her surroundings.

"You got to say it," he repeated. "You got to say you love me."

She was always careful how she committed herself. "In a sense," she began, "if you use the word loosely, you might say that. But it's not a word I use. I don't have illusions. I'm one of those people who see *through* to nothing."

The boy was frowning. "You got to say it. I said it and you got to say it," he said.

The girl looked at him almost tenderly. "You poor baby," she murmured. "It's just as well you don't understand," and she pulled him by the neck, face-down, against her. "We are all damned," she said, "but some of us have taken off our blindfolds and see that there's nothing to see. It's a kind of salvation."

The boy's astonished eyes looked blankly through the ends of her hair. "Okay," he almost whined, "but do you love me or don'tcher?"

"Yes," she said and added, "in a sense. But I must tell you something. There mustn't be anything dishonest between us." She lifted his head and looked him in the eye. "I am thirty years old," she said. "I have a number of degrees."

The boy's look was irritated but dogged. "I don't care," he said. "I don't care a thing about what all you done. I just want to know if you love me or don'tcher?" and he caught her to him and wildly planted her face with kisses until she said, "Yes, yes."

"Okay then," he said, letting her go. "Prove it."

She smiled, looking dreamily out on the shifty landscape. She had seduced him without even making up her mind to try. "How?" she asked, feeling that he should be delayed a little.

He leaned over and put his lips to her ear. "Show me where your wooden leg joins on," he whispered.

The girl uttered a sharp little cry and her face instantly drained of color. The obscenity of the suggestion was not what shocked her. As a child she had sometimes been subject to feelings of shame but education had removed the last traces of that as a good surgeon scrapes for cancer; she would no more have felt it over what he was asking than she would have believed in his Bible. But she was as sensitive about the artificial leg as a peacock about his tail. No one ever touched it but her. She took care of it as someone else would his soul, in private and almost with her own eyes turned away. "No," she said.

"I known it," he muttered, sitting up. "You're just playing me for a sucker."

"Oh no no!" she cried. "It joins on at the knee. Only at the knee. Why do you want to see it?"

The boy gave her a long penetrating look. "Because," he said, "it's what makes you different. You ain't like anybody else."

She sat staring at him. There was nothing about her face or her round freezing-blue eyes to indicate that this had moved her; but she felt as if her heart had stopped and left her mind to pump her blood. She decided that for the first time in her life she was face to face with real innocence. This boy, with an instinct that came from beyond wisdom, had touched the truth about her. When after a minute, she said in a hoarse high voice, "All right," it was like surrendering to him completely. It was like losing her own life and finding it again, mirac-ulously, in his.

Very gently he began to roll the slack leg up. The artificial limb, in a white sock and brown flat shoe, was bound in a heavy material like canvas and ended in an ugly jointure where it was attached to the stump. The boy's face and his voice were entirely reverent as he uncovered it and said, "Now show me how to take it off and on."

She took it off for him and put it back on again and then he took it off himself, handling it as tenderly as if it were a real one. "See!" he said with a delighted child's face. "Now I can do it myself!"

"Put it back on," she said. She was thinking that she would run away with him and that every night he would take the leg off and every morning put it back on again. "Put it back on," she said.

"Not yet," he murmured, setting it on its foot out of her reach. "Leave it off for a while. You got me instead."

She gave a little cry of alarm but he pushed her down and began to kiss her again. Without the leg she felt entirely dependent on him. Her brain seemed to have stopped thinking altogether and to be about some other function that it was not very good at. Different expressions raced back and forth over her face. Every now and then the boy, his eyes like two steel spikes, would glance behind him where the leg stood. Finally she pushed him off and said, "Put it back on me now."

"Wait," he said. He leaned the other way and pulled the valise toward him and opened it. It had a pale blue spotted lining and there were only two Bibles in it. He took one of these out and opened the cover of it. It was hollow and contained a pocket flask of whiskey, a pack of cards, and a small blue box with printing on it. He laid these out in front of her one at a time in an evenly spaced row, like one presenting offerings at the shrine of a goddess. He put the blue box in her hand. THIS PRODUCT TO BE USED ONLY FOR THE PREVENTION OF DISEASE, she read, and dropped it. The boy was unscrewing the top of the flask. He stopped and pointed, with a smile, to the deck of cards. It was not an ordinary deck but one with an obscene picture on the back of each card. "Take a swig," he said, offering her the bottle first. He held it in front of her, but like one mesmerized, she did not move.

Her voice when she spoke had an almost pleading sound. "Aren't you," she murmured, "aren't you just good country people?"

The boy cocked his head. He looked as if he were just beginning to understand that she might be trying to insult him. "Yeah," he said, curling his lip slightly, "but it ain't held me back none. I'm as good as you any day in the week."

"Give me my leg," she said.

He pushed it farther away with his foot. "Come on now, let's begin to have us a good time," he said coaxingly. "We ain't got to know one another good yet."

"Give me my leg!" she screamed and tried to lunge for it but he pushed her down easily.

"What's the matter with you all of a sudden?" he asked, frowning as he screwed the top on the flask and put it quickly back inside the Bible. "You just a while ago said you didn't believe in nothing. I thought you was some girl!"

Her face was almost purple. "You're a Christian!" she hissed. "You're a fine Christian! You're just like them all—say one thing and do another. You're a perfect Christian, you're . . ."

The boy's mouth was set angrily. "I hope you don't think," he said in a lofty indignant tone, "that I believe in that crap! I may sell Bibles but I know which end is up and I wasn't born yesterday and I know where I'm going!"

"Give me my leg!" she screeched. He jumped up so quickly that she barely saw him sweep the cards and the blue box back into the Bible and throw the Bible into the valise. She saw him grab the leg and then she saw it for an instant slanted forlornly across the inside of the suitcase with a Bible at either side of its opposite ends. He slammed the lid shut and snatched up the valise and swung it down the hole and then stepped through himself.

When all of him had passed but his head, he turned and regarded her with a look that no longer had any admiration in it. "I've gotten a lot of interesting things," he said. "One time I got a woman's glass eye this way. And you needn't to think you'll catch me because Pointer ain't really my name. I use a different name at every house I call at and don't stay nowhere long. And I'll tell you another thing, Hulga," he said, using the name as if he didn't think much of it, "you ain't so smart. I been believing in nothing ever since I was born!" and then the toast-colored hat disappeared down the hole and the girl was left, sitting on the straw in the dusty sunlight. When she turned her churning face toward the opening, she saw his blue figure struggling successfully over the green speckled lake.

Mrs. Hopewell and Mrs. Freeman, who were in the back pasture, digging up onions, saw him emerge a little later from the woods and head across the meadow toward the highway. "Why, that looks like that nice dull young man that tried to sell me a Bible yesterday," Mrs. Hopewell said, squinting. "He must have been selling them to the Negroes back in there. He was so simple," she said, "but I guess the world would be better off if we were all that simple."

Mrs. Freeman's gaze drove forward and just touched him before he disappeared under the hill. Then she returned her attention to the evil-smelling onion shoot she was lifting from the ground. "Some can't be that simple," she said. "I know I never could."

QUESTIONS

1. Why does Joy feel that changing her name to Hulga is "her highest creative act"? **2.** In what ways do Mrs. Freeman's descriptions of her daughters Glynese and Carramae contribute to the theme of the story? **3.** Is the title ironic? Explain.

WRITING TOPICS

1. Does this story have any admirable characters or heroes in the conventional sense? Explain. **2.** Why does Hulga agree to meet with Manley Pointer? Does Hulga's experience with Manley Pointer confirm her cynical philosophy of "nothing"?

The Lesson

TONI CADE BAMBARA   [b. 1939]

Back in the days when everyone was old and stupid or young and foolish and me and Sugar were the only ones just right, this lady moved on our block with nappy hair and proper speech and no makeup. And quite naturally we laughed at her, laughed the way we did at the junk man who went about his business like he was some big-time president and his sorry-ass horse his secretary. And we kinda hated her too, hated the way we did the winos who cluttered up our parks and pissed on our handball walls and stank up our hallways and stairs so you couldn't halfway play hide-and-seek without a goddamn gas mask. Miss Moore was her name. The only woman on the block with no first name. And she was black as hell, cept for her feet, which were fish-white and spooky. And she was always planning these boring-ass things for us to do, us being my cousin, mostly, who lived on the block cause we all moved North the same time and to the same apartment then spread out gradual to breathe. And our parents would yank our heads into some kinda shape and crisp up our clothes so we'd be presentable for travel with Miss Moore, who always looked like she was going to church, though she never did. Which is just one of the things the grownups talked about when they talked behind her back like a dog. But when she came calling with some sachet she'd sewed up or some gingerbread she'd made or some book, why then they'd all be too embarrassed to turn her down and we'd get handed over all spruced up. She'd been to college and said it was only right that she should take responsibility for the young ones' education, and she not even related by marriage or blood. So they'd go for it. Specially Aunt Gretchen. She was the main gofer in the family. You got some old dumb shit foolishness you want somebody to go for, you send for Aunt Gretchen. She been screwed into the go-along for so long, it's a blood-deep natural thing with her. Which is how she got saddled with me and Sugar and Junior in the first place while our mothers were in a la-de-da apartment up the block having a good ole time.

So this one day Miss Moore rounds us all up at the mailbox and it's puredee hot and she's knockin herself out about arithmetic. And school suppose to let up in summer I heard, but she don't never let up. And the starch in my pinafore scratching the shit outta me and I'm really hating this nappy-head bitch and her goddamn college degree. I'd much rather go to the pool or to the show where it's cool. So me and Sugar leaning on the mailbox being surly, which is a Miss Moore word. And Flyboy checking out what everybody brought for lunch. And Fat Butt already wasting his peanut-butter-and-jelly sandwich like the pig he is. And Junebug punchin on Q.T.'s arm for potato chips. And Rosie Giraffe shifting from one hip to the other waiting for somebody to step on her foot or ask her if she from Georgia so she can kick ass, preferably Mercedes'. And Miss Moore asking us do we know what money is, like we a bunch of retards. I mean real money, she say, like it's only poker chips or monopoly papers we lay on the grocer. So right away I'm tired of this and say so. And would much rather snatch Sugar and go to the Sunset and terrorize the West Indian kids and take their hair ribbons and their money too. And Miss Moore files that remark away for next week's lesson on brotherhood, I can tell. And finally I say we oughta get to the subway cause it's cooler and besides we might meet some cute boys. Sugar done swiped her mama's lipstick, so we ready.

So we heading down the street and she's boring us silly about what things cost and what our parents make and how much goes for rent and how money ain't divided up right in this country. And then she gets to the part about we all poor and live in the slums, which I don't feature. And I'm ready to speak on that, but she steps out in the street and hails two cabs just like that. Then she hustles half the crew in with her and hands me a five-dollar bill and tells me to calculate 10 percent tip for the driver. And we're off. Me and Sugar and Junebug and Flyboy hangin out the window and hollering to everybody, putting lipstick on each other cause Flyboy a faggot anyway, and making farts with our sweaty armpits. But I'm mostly trying to figure how to spend this money. But they all fascinated with the meter ticking and Junebug starts laying bets as to how much it'll read when Flyboy can't hold his breath no more. Then Sugar lays bets as to how much it'll be when we get there. So I'm stuck. Don't nobody want to go for my plan, which is to jump out at the next light and run off to the first bar-b-que we can find. Then the driver tells us to get the hell out cause we there already. And the meter reads eighty-five cents. And I'm stalling to figure out the tip and Sugar say give him a dime. And I decide he don't need it bad as I do, so later for him. But then he tries to take off with Junebug foot still in the door so we talk about his mama something ferocious. Then we check out that we on Fifth Avenue and everybody dressed up in stockings. One lady in a fur coat, hot as it is. White folks crazy.

"This is the place," Miss Moore say, presenting it to us in the voice she uses at the museum. "Let's look in the windows before we go in."

"Can we steal?" Sugar asks very serious like she's getting the ground rules squared away before she plays. "I beg your pardon," say Miss Moore, and we fall out. So she leads us around the windows of the toy store and me and Sugar screamin, "This is mine, that's mine, I gotta have that, that was made for me, I was born for that," till Big Butt drowns us out.

"Hey, I'm goin to buy that there."

"That there? You don't even know what it is, stupid."

"I do so," he say punchin on Rosie Giraffe. "It's a microscope."

"Whatcha gonna do with a microscope, fool?"

"Look at things."

"Like what, Ronald?" ask Miss Moore. And Big Butt ain't got the first notion. So here go Miss Moore gabbing about the thousands of bacteria in a drop of water and the somethinorother in a speck of blood and the million and one living things in the air around us is invisible to the naked eye. And what she say that for? Junebug go to town on that "naked" and we rolling. Then Miss

Moore ask what it cost. So we all jam into the window smudgin it up and the price tag say $300. So then she ask how long'd take for Big Butt and Junebug to save up their allowances. "Too long," I say. "Yeh," adds Sugar, "outgrown it by that time." And Miss Moore say no, you never outgrow learning instruments. "Why, even medical students and interns and," blah, blah, blah. And we ready to choke Big Butt for bringing it up in the first damn place.

"This here costs four hundred eighty dollars," say Rosie Giraffe. So we pile up all over her to see what she pointin out. My eyes tell me it's a chunk of glass cracked with something heavy, and different-color inks dripped into the splits, then the whole thing put into a oven or something. But for $480 it don't make sense.

"That's a paperweight made of semi-precious stones fused together under tremendous pressure," she explains slowly, with her hands doing the mining and all the factory work.

"So what's a paperweight?" asks Rosie Giraffe.

"To weigh paper with, dumbbell," say Flyboy, the wise man from the East.

"Not exactly," say Miss Moore, which is what she say when you warm or way off too. "It's to weigh paper down so it won't scatter and make your desk untidy." So right away me and Sugar curtsy to each other and then to Mercedes who is more the tidy type.

"We don't keep paper on top of the desk in my class," say Junebug, figuring Miss Moore crazy or lyin one.

"At home, then," she say. "Don't you have a calendar and a pencil case and a blotter and a letter-opener on your desk at home where you do your homework?" And she know damn well what our homes look like cause she nosys around in them every chance she gets.

"I don't even have a desk," say Junebug. "Do we?"

"No. And I don't get no homework neither," says Big Butt.

"And I don't even have a home," say Flyboy like he do at school to keep the white folks off his back and sorry for him. Send this poor kid to camp posters, is his specialty.

"I do," says Mercedes. "I have a box of stationery on my desk and a picture of my cat. My godmother bought the stationery and the desk. There's a big rose on each sheet and the envelopes smell like roses."

"Who wants to know about your smelly-ass stationery," say Rosie Giraffe fore I can get my two cents in.

"It's important to have a work area all your own so that . . ."

"Will you look at this sailboat, please," say Flyboy, cuttin her off and pointin to the thing like it was his. So once again we tumble all over each other to gaze at this magnificent thing in the toy store which is just big enough to maybe sail two kittens across the pond if you strap them to the posts tight. We all start reciting the price tag like we in assembly. "Handcrafted sailboat of fiberglass at one thousand one hundred ninety-five dollars."

"Unbelievable," I hear myself say and am really stunned. I read it again for myself just in case the group recitation put me in a trance. Same thing. For some reason this pisses me off. We look at Miss Moore and she lookin at us, waiting for I dunno what.

"Who'd pay all that when you can buy a sailboat set for a quarter at Pop's, a tube of glue for a dime, and a ball of string for eight cents? It must have a motor and a whole lot else besides," I say. "My sailboat cost me about fifty cents."

"But will it take water?" say Mercedes with her smart ass.

"Took mine to Alley Pond Park once," say Flyboy. "String broke. Lost it. Pity."

"Sailed mine in Central Park and it keeled over and sank. Had to ask my father for another dollar."

"And you got the strap," laugh Big Butt. "The jerk didn't even have a string on it. My old man wailed on his behind."

Little Q.T. was staring hard at the sailboat and you could see he wanted it bad. But he too little and somebody'd just take it from him. So what the hell. "This boat for kids, Miss Moore?"

"Parents silly to buy something like that just to get all broke up," say Rosie Giraffe.

"That much money it should last forever," I figure.

"My father'd buy it for me if I wanted it."

"Your father, my ass," say Rosie Giraffe getting a chance to finally push Mercedes.

"Must be rich people shop here," say Q.T.

"You are a very bright boy," say Flyboy. "What was your first clue?" And he rap him on the head with the back of his knuckles, since Q.T. the only one he could get away with. Though Q.T. liable to come up behind you years later and get his licks in when you half expect it.

"What I want to know is," I says to Miss Moore though I never talk to her, I wouldn't give the bitch that satisfaction, "is how much a real boat costs? I figure a thousand'd get you a yacht any day."

"Why don't you check that out," she says, "and report back to the group?" Which really pains my ass. If you gonna mess up a perfectly good swim day least you could do is have some answers. "Let's go in," she say like she got something up her sleeve. Only she don't lead the way. So me and Sugar turn the corner to where the entrance is, but when we get there I kinda hang back. Not that I'm scared, what's there to be afraid of, just a toy store. But I feel funny, shame. But what I got to be shamed about? Got as much right to go in as anybody. But somehow I can't seem to get hold of the door, so I step away for Sugar to lead. But she hangs back too. And I look at her and she looks at me and this is ridiculous. I mean, damn, I have never ever been shy about doing nothing or going nowhere. But then Mercedes steps up and then Rosie Giraffe and Big Butt crowd in behind and shove, and next thing we all stuffed into the doorway with only Mercedes squeezing past us, smoothing out her jumper and walking right down the aisle. Then the rest of us tumble in like a glued-together jigsaw done all wrong. And people lookin at us. And it's like the time me and

Sugar crashed into the Catholic church on a dare. But once we got in there and everything so hushed and holy and the candles and the bowin and the handkerchiefs on all the drooping heads, I just couldn't go through with the plan. Which was for me to run up to the altar and do a tap dance while Sugar played the nose flute and messed around in the holy water. And Sugar kept givin me the elbow. Then later teased me so bad I tied her up in the shower and turned it on and locked her in. And she'd be there till this day if Aunt Gretchen hadn't finally figured I was lyin about the boarder takin a shower.

Same thing in the store. We all walkin on tiptoe and hardly touchin the games and puzzles and things. And I watched Miss Moore who is steady watchin us like she waitin for a sign. Like Mama Drewery watches the sky and sniffs the air and takes note of just how much slant is in the bird formation. Then me and Sugar bump smack into each other, so busy gazing at the toys, 'specially the sailboat. But we don't laugh and go into our fat-lady bump-stomach routine. We just stare at that price tag. Then Sugar run a finger over the whole boat. And I'm jealous and want to hit her. Maybe not her, but I sure want to punch somebody in the mouth.

"Watcha bring us here for, Miss Moore?"

"You sound angry, Sylvia. Are you mad about something?" Givin me one of them grins like she tellin a grown-up joke that never turns out to be funny. And she's lookin very closely at me like maybe she plannin to do my portrait from memory. I'm mad, but I won't give her that satisfaction. So I slouch around the store bein very bored and say, "Let's go."

Me and Sugar at the back of the train watchin the tracks whizzin by large then small then gettin gobbled up in the dark. I'm thinkin about this tricky toy I saw in the store. A clown that somersaults on a bar then does chin-ups just cause you yank lightly at his leg. Cost $35. I could see me askin my mother for a $35 birthday clown. "You wanna who that costs what?" she'd say, cocking her head to the side to get a better view of the hole in my head. Thirty-five dollars could buy new bunk beds for Junior and Gretchen's boy. Thirty-five dollars and the whole household could go visit Granddaddy Nelson in the country. Thirty-five dollars would pay for the rent and the piano bill too. Who are these people that spend that much for performing clowns and $1000 for toy sailboats? What kinda work they do and how they live and how come we ain't in on it? Where we are is who we are, Miss Moore always pointin out. But it don't necessarily have to be that way, she always adds then waits for somebody to say that poor people have to wake up and demand their share of the pie and don't none of us know what kind of pie she talkin about in the first damn place. But she ain't so smart cause I still got her four dollars from the taxi and she sure ain't gettin it. Messin up my day with this shit. Sugar nudges me in my pocket and winks.

Miss Moore lines us up in front of the mailbox where we started from, seem like years ago, and I got a headache for thinkin so hard. And we lean all over each other so we can hold up under the draggy-ass lecture she always finishes us off with at the end before we thank her for borin us to tears. But she just looks at us like she readin tea leaves. Finally she say, "Well, what did you think of F. A. O. Schwarz?"

Rosie Giraffe mumbles, "White folks crazy."

"I'd like to go there again when I get my birthday money," says Mercedes, and we shove her out the pack so she has to lean on the mailbox by herself.

"I'd like a shower. Tiring day," say Flyboy.

Then Sugar surprises me by sayin, "You know, Miss Moore, I don't think all of us here put together eat in a year what that sailboat costs." And Miss Moore lights up like somebody goosed her. "And?" she say, urging Sugar on. Only I'm standin on her foot so she don't continue.

"Imagine for a minute what kind of society it is in which some people can spend on a toy what it would cost to feed a family of six or seven. What do you think?"

"I think," say Sugar pushing me off her feet like she never done before, cause I whip her ass in a minute, "that this is not much of a democracy if you ask me. Equal chance to pursue happiness means an equal crack at the dough, don't it?" Miss Moore is besides herself and I am disgusted with Sugar's treachery. So I stand on her foot one more time to see if she'll shove me. She shuts up, and Miss Moore looks at me, sorrowfully I'm thinkin. And somethin weird is goin on, I can feel it in my chest.

"Anybody else learn anything today?" lookin dead at me. I walk away and Sugar has to run to catch up and don't even seem to notice when I shrug her arm off my shoulder.

"Well, we got four dollars anyway," she says.

"Uh hunh."

"We could go to Hascombs and get half a chocolate layer and then go to the Sunset and still have plenty money for potato chips and ice cream sodas."

"Uh hunh."

"Race you to Hascombs," she say.

We start down the block and she gets ahead which is O.K. by me cause I'm goin to the West End and then over to the Drive to think this day through. She can run if she want to and even run faster. But ain't nobody gonna beat me at nuthin.

QUESTIONS

1. Characterize the narrator of this story. **2.** How does the narrator describe her neighborhood? How does she feel when Miss Moore calls the neighborhood a slum? **3.** F. A. O. Schwarz is a famous toy store on Fifth Avenue in New York City, located about three miles south of Harlem where, doubtless, the children live. What lesson does Miss Moore convey by taking them there?

WRITING TOPIC

Is there any evidence at the end of the story that the narrator has been changed by the experience?

INNOCENCE
AND
EXPERIENCE

The Mysterious Rose Garden, by Aubrey Beardsley

POETRY

The Chimney Sweeper 1789

WILLIAM BLAKE [1757–1827]

When my mother died I was very young,
And my Father sold me while yet my tongue
Could scarcely cry " 'weep! 'weep! 'weep! 'weep!"
So your chimneys I sweep, and in soot I sleep.

There's little Tom Dacre, who cried when his head,
That curled like a lamb's back, was shaved: so I said,
"Hush, Tom! never mind it, for when your head's bare
You know that the soot cannot spoil your white hair."

And so he was quiet and that very night
As Tom was a-sleeping, he had such a sight!   10
That thousands of sweepers, Dick, Joe, Ned, and Jack,
Were all of them locked up in coffins of black.

And by came an Angel who had a bright key,
And he opened the coffins and set them all free;
Then down a green plain leaping, laughing, they run,
And wash in a river, and shine in the Sun.

Then naked and white, all their bags left behind,
They rise upon clouds and sport in the wind;
And the Angel told Tom, if he'd be a good boy,
He'd have God for his father, and never want joy.   20

And so Tom awoke; and we rose in the dark,
And got with our bags and our brushes to work.
Though the morning was cold, Tom was happy and warm;
So if all do their duty they need not fear harm.

The Tyger 1794

WILLIAM BLAKE [1757–1827]

Tyger! Tyger! burning bright
In the forests of the night,
What immortal hand or eye
Could frame thy fearful symmetry?

In what distant deeps or skies
Burnt the fire of thine eyes?
On what wings dare he aspire?
What the hand, dare seize the fire?

And what shoulder, & what art,
Could twist the sinews of thy heart? 10
And when thy heart began to beat,
What dread hand? & what dread feet?

What the hammer? what the chain?
In what furnace was thy brain?
What the anvil? what dread grasp
Dare its deadly terrors clasp?

When the stars threw down their spears,
And water'd heaven with their tears,
Did he smile his work to see?
Did he who made the Lamb make thee? 20

Tyger! Tyger! burning bright
In the forests of the night,
What immortal hand or eye
Dare frame thy fearful symmetry?

The Garden of Love 1793

WILLIAM BLAKE [1757–1827]

I went to the Garden of Love,
And saw what I never had seen:
A Chapel was built in the midst,
Where I used to play on the green.

And the gates of this Chapel were shut,
And "Thou shalt not" writ over the door;
So I turn'd to the Garden of Love,
That so many sweet flowers bore,

And I saw it was filled with graves,
And tomb-stones where flowers should be: 10
And Priests in black gowns were walking their rounds,
And binding with briars my joys & desires.

QUESTIONS
1.   What meanings does the word "love" have in this poem?   **2.**   What is Blake's
judgment on established religion?   **3.**   Explain the meaning of "Chapel" (l. 3) and
of "briars" (l. 12).

WRITING TOPIC
Read the definition of irony in the glossary of literary terms. Write an essay in
which you distinguish between the types of irony used in "The Chimney Sweeper" and "The Garden of Love."

To a Mouse   1786

ON TURNING HER UP IN HER NEST WITH THE PLOUGH, NOVEMBER, 1785

ROBERT BURNS   [1759–1796]

Wee, sleekit,° cow'rin, tim'rous beastie,   sleek
O, what a panic's in thy breastie!
Thou need na start awa sae hasty,
            Wi' bickering° brattle!°   hurried/scamper
I wad be laith to rin an' chase thee,
            Wi' murd'ring pattle!°   plowstaff

I'm truly sorry man's dominion
Has broken Nature's social union,
An' justifies that ill opinion
            Which makes thee startle   10

At me, thy poor earth-born companion,
      An' fellow-mortal!

I doubt na, whiles,° but thou may thieve;   sometimes
What then? poor beastie, thou maun° live!   must
A daimen° icker° in a thrave°   occasional/corn-ear/shock
      'S a sma' request:
I'll get a blessin wi' the lave,°   rest
      And never miss't!

Thy wee bit housie, too, in ruin!
Its silly wa's the win's are strewin!
An' naething, now, to big° a new ane,   20
      O' foggage° green!   build
An' bleak December's winds ensuin,   mosses
      Baith snell° an' keen!   bitter

Thou saw the fields laid bare and waste,
An' weary winter comin fast,
An' cozie here, beneath the blast,
      Thou thought to dwell,
Till crash! the cruel coulter° past   plowshare
      Out thro' thy cell.   30

That wee bit heap o' leaves an' stibble
Has cost thee mony a weary nibble!
Now thou's turned out, for a' thy trouble,
      But° house or hald,   without
To thole° the winter's sleety dribble,   endure
      An' cranreuch° cauld!   hoarfrost

But, Mousie, thou art no thy lane°   not alone
In proving foresight may be vain:
The best laid schemes o' mice an' men   39
      Gang° aft a-gley.°   go/awry
An' lea'e us nought but grief an' pain
      For promised joy.

Still thou art blest, compared wi' me!
The present only toucheth thee:
But och! I backward cast my e'e
      On prospects drear!
An' forward, tho' I canna see,
      I guess an' fear!

Lines[1]   1798

COMPOSED A FEW MILES ABOVE TINTERN ABBEY
ON REVISITING THE BANKS OF THE WYE
DURING A TOUR. JULY 13, 1798

WILLIAM WORDSWORTH   [1770–1850]

Five years have passed;[2] five summers, with the length
Of five long winters! and again I hear
These waters, rolling from their mountain-springs
With a soft inland murmur. Once again
Do I behold these steep and lofty cliffs,
That on a wild secluded scene impress
Thoughts of more deep seclusion; and connect
The landscape with the quiet of the sky.
The day is come when I again repose
Here, under this dark sycamore, and view   10
These plots of cottage ground, these orchard tufts,
Which at this season, with their unripe fruits,
Are clad in one green hue, and lose themselves
'Mid groves and copses. Once again I see
These hedgerows, hardly hedgerows, little lines
Of sportive wood run wild; these pastoral farms,
Green to the very door; and wreaths of smoke
Sent up, in silence, from among the trees!
With some uncertain notice, as might seem
Of vagrant dwellers in the houseless woods,   20
Or of some Hermit's cave, where by his fire
The Hermit sits alone.

        These beauteous forms,
Through a long absence, have not been to me
As is a landscape to a blind man's eye;
But oft, in lonely rooms, and 'mid the din
Of towns and cities, I have owed to them
In hours of weariness, sensations sweet,
Felt in the blood, and felt along the heart;
And passing even into my purer mind,
With tranquil restoration—feelings too   30
Of unremembered pleasure; such, perhaps,

Lines
  [1] Wordsworth wrote this poem during a four- or five-day walking tour through the Wye valley with his sister Dorothy.
  [2] The poet had visited the region on a solitary walking tour in August of 1793 when he was twenty-three years old.

As have no slight or trivial influence
On that best portion of a good man's life,
His little, nameless, unremembered, acts
Of kindness and of love. Nor less, I trust,
To them I may have owed another gift,
Of aspect more sublime; that blessed mood,
In which the burthen of the mystery,
In which the heavy and the weary weight
Of all this unintelligible world,   40
Is lightened—that serene and blessed mood,
In which the affections gently lead us on—
Until, the breath of this corporeal frame
And even the motion of our human blood
Almost suspended, we are laid asleep
In body, and become a living soul;
While with an eye made quiet by the power
Of harmony, and the deep power of joy,
We see into the life of things.

                If this
Be but a vain belief, yet, oh! how oft—   50
In darkness and amid the many shapes
Of joyless daylight; when the fretful stir
Unprofitable, and the fever of the world,
Have hung upon the beatings of my heart—
How oft, in spirit, have I turned to thee,
O sylvan Wye! thou wanderer through the woods,
How often has my spirit turned to thee!

   And now, with gleams of half-extinguished thought
With many recognitions dim and faint,
And somewhat of a sad perplexity,   60
The picture of the mind revives again;
While here I stand, not only with the sense
Of present pleasure, but with pleasing thoughts
That in this moment there is life and food
For future years. And so I dare to hope,
Though changed, no doubt, from what I was when first
I came among these hills; when like a roe
I bounded o'er the mountains, by the sides
Of the deep rivers, and the lonely streams,
Wherever nature led—more like a man   70
Flying from something that he dreads than one
Who sought the thing he loved. For nature then
(The coarser pleasures of my boyish days,
And their glad animal movements all gone by)

To me was all in all.—I cannot paint
What then I was. The sounding cataract
Haunted me like a passion; the tall rock,
The mountain, and the deep and gloomy wood,
Their colors and their forms, were then to me
An appetite; a feeling and a love,   80
That had no need of a remoter charm,
By thought supplied, nor any interest
Unborrowed from the eye.—That time is past,
And all its aching joys are now no more,
And all its dizzy raptures. Not for this
Faint[3] I, nor mourn nor murmur; other gifts
Have followed; for such loss, I would believe,
Abundant recompense. For I have learned
To look on nature, not as in the hour
Of thoughtless youth; but hearing oftentimes   90
The still, sad music of humanity,
Nor harsh nor grating, though of ample power
To chasten and subdue. And I have felt
A presence that disturbs me with the joy
Of elevated thoughts; a sense sublime
Of something far more deeply interfused,
Whose dwelling is the light of setting suns,
And the round ocean and the living air,
And the blue sky, and in the mind of man:
A motion and a spirit, that impels   100
All thinking things, all objects of all thought,
And rolls through all things. Therefore am I still
A lover of the meadows and the woods,
And mountains; and of all that we behold
From this green earth; of all the mighty world
Of eye, and ear—both what they half create,
And what perceive; well pleased to recognize
In nature and the language of the sense
The anchor of my purest thoughts, the nurse,
The guide, the guardian of my heart, and soul   110
Of all my moral being.

                              Nor perchance,
If I were not thus taught, should I the more
Suffer my genial spirits to decay:
For thou art with me here upon the banks
Of this fair river; thou my dearest Friend,[4]

---

[3] Lose heart.
[4] The poet addresses his sister Dorothy.

My dear, dear Friend; and in thy voice I catch
The language of my former heart, and read
My former pleasures in the shooting lights
Of thy wild eyes. Oh! yet a little while
May I behold in thee what I was once,   120
My dear, dear Sister! and this prayer I make,
Knowing that Nature never did betray
The heart that loved her; 'tis her privilege,
Through all the years of this our life, to lead
From joy to joy: for she can so inform
The mind that is within us, so impress
With quietness and beauty, and so feed
With lofty thoughts, that neither evil tongues,
Rash judgments, nor the sneers of selfish men,
Nor greetings where no kindness is, nor all   130
The dreary intercourse of daily life,
Shall e'er prevail against us, or disturb
Our cheerful faith, that all which we behold
Is full of blessings. Therefore let the moon
Shine on thee in they solitary walk;
And let the misty mountain winds be free
To blow against thee: and, in after years,
When these wild ecstasies shall be matured
Into a sober pleasure; when thy mind
Shall be a mansion for all lovely forms,   140
Thy memory be as a dwelling place
For all sweet sounds and harmonies; oh! then,
If solitude, or fear, or pain, or grief
Should be thy portion, with what healing thoughts
Of tender joy wilt thou remember me,
And these my exhortations! Nor, perchance—
If I should be where I no more can hear
Thy voice, nor catch from thy wild eyes these gleams
Of past existence[5]—wilt thou then forget
That on the banks of this delightful stream   150
We stood together; and that I, so long
A worshiper of Nature, hither came
Unwearied in that service; rather say
With warmer love—oh! with far deeper zeal
Of holier love. Nor wilt thou then forget,
That after many wanderings, many years
Of absence, these steep woods and lofty cliffs,
And this green pastoral landscape, were to me
More dear, both for themselves and for thy sake!

---

[5] I.e., the poet's past experience. Note lines 116–119.

QUESTIONS
1. In this poem the poet distinguishes between two important periods in his life: the first is described in lines 65–83, and the second is described in lines 83–111. How does he characterize these two periods? **2.** The poem describes a visit to a familiar scene of the poet's youth and includes a meditation upon the changes that have occurred. Are the changes in the poet, the scene itself, or both?

WRITING TOPIC
Discuss the ways in which the poet contrasts the city and the countryside.

It Is a Beauteous Evening   1807

WILLIAM WORDSWORTH   [1770–1850]

It is a beauteous evening, calm and free,
The holy time is quiet as a Nun
Breathless with adoration; the broad sun
Is sinking down in its tranquility;
The gentleness of heaven broods o'er the Sea:
Listen! the mighty Being is awake,
And doth with his eternal motion make
A sound like thunder—everlastingly.
Dear Child! Dear Girl! that walkest with me here,[1]
If thou appear untouched by solemn thought,   10
Thy nature is not therefore less divine:
Thou liest in Abraham's bosom[2] all the year;
And Worship'st at the Temple's inner shrine,[3]
God being with thee when we know it not.

QUESTION
Why does the poet excuse his "Dear Child's" lack of solemnity?

WRITING TOPIC
Compare this poem with McGinley's "Country Club Sunday."

It Is a Beauteous Evening
   [1] Wordsworth is walking with Caroline, his illegitimate daughter.
   [2] Close to God. See Luke 16:22.
   [3] The Temple's inner shrine is its holiest place. See 1 Kings 8:6.

On First Looking into Chapman's Homer[1]   1816

JOHN KEATS [1795–1821]

Much have I travelled in the realms of gold,
And many goodly states and kingdoms seen:
Round many western islands have I been
Which bards in fealty to Apollo[2] hold.
Oft of one wide expanse had I been told
That deep-browed Homer ruled as his demesne;°   realm
Yet did I never breathe its pure serene°   clear air
Till I heard Chapman speak out loud and bold:
Then felt I like some watcher of the skies
When a new planet swims into his ken;   10
Or like stout Cortez[3] when with eagle eyes
He stared at the Pacific—and all his men
Looked at each other with a wild surmise—
    Silent, upon a peak in Darien.

My Last Duchess   1842

ROBERT BROWNING [1812–1889]

FERRARA

That's my last Duchess painted on the wall,
Looking as if she were alive. I call
That piece a wonder, now: Frà Pandolf's[1] hands
Worked busily a day, and there she stands.

On First Looking into Chapman's Homer
   [1] George Chapman published translations of *The Iliad* (1611) and *The Odyssey* (1616).
   [2] The god of poetry.
   [3] Keats mistakenly attributes the discovery of the Pacific Ocean by Europeans to Hernando Cortez (1485–1547), the Spanish conqueror of Mexico. Vasco Nuñez de Balboa (1475–1517) first saw the Pacific from a mountain located in eastern Panama.

My Last Duchess
   [1] Frà Pandolf and Claus of Innsbruck (mentioned in the last line) are fictitious artists.

Will't please you sit and look at her? I said
"Frà Pandolf" by design, for never read
Strangers like you that pictured countenance,
The depth and passion of its earnest glance,
But to myself they turned (since none puts by
The curtain I have drawn for you, but I)   10
And seemed as they would ask me, if they durst,
How such a glance came there; so, not the first
Are you to turn and ask thus. Sir, 'twas not
Her husband's presence only, called that spot
Of joy into the Duchess' cheek: perhaps
Frà Pandolf chanced to say "Her mantle laps
"Over my lady's wrist too much," or "Paint
"Must never hope to reproduce the faint
"Half-flush that dies along her throat": such stuff
Was courtesy, she thought, and cause enough   20
For calling up that spot of joy. She had
A heart—how shall I say?—too soon made glad,
Too easily impressed; she liked whate'er
She looked on, and her looks went everywhere.
Sir, 'twas all one! My favor at her breast,
The dropping of the daylight in the West,
The bough of cherries some officious fool
Broke in the orchard for her, the white mule
She rode with round the terrace—all and each
Would draw from her alike the approving speech,   30
Or blush, at least. She thanked men—good! but thanked
Somehow—I know not how—as if she ranked
My gift of a nine-hundred-years-old name
With anybody's gift. Who'd stoop to blame
This sort of trifling? Even had you skill
In speech—which I have not—to make your will
Quite clear to such an one, and say, "Just this
"Or that in you disgusts me; here you miss,
"Or there exceed the mark"—and if she let
Herself be lessoned so, nor plainly set
Her wits to yours, forsooth, and made excuse,   40
—E'en then would be some stooping; and I choose
Never to stoop. Oh sir, she smiled, no doubt,
Whene'er I passed her; but who passed without
Much the same smile? This grew; I gave commands;
Then all smiles stopped together. There she stands
As if alive. Will't please you rise? We'll meet
The company below, then. I repeat,

The Count your master's known munificence
Is ample warrant that no just pretense   50
Of mine for dowry will be disallowed;
Though his fair daughter's self, as I avowed
At starting, is my object. Nay, we'll go
Together down, sir. Notice Neptune, though,
Taming a sea-horse, thought a rarity,
Which Claus of Innsbruck cast in bronze for me!

QUESTIONS

1. To whom is the Duke speaking and what is the occasion? **2.** Contrast the Duke's moral and aesthetic sensibility.

WRITING TOPIC

How is the reader supposed to respond to the Duke's judgment of his last Duchess? Explain.

Out of the Cradle Endlessly Rocking   1881

WALT WHITMAN [1819–1892]

Out of the cradle endlessly rocking,
Out of the mocking-bird's throat, the musical shuttle,
Out of the Ninth-month[1] midnight,
Over the sterile sands and the fields beyond, where the child leaving his
    bed wander'd alone, bareheaded, barefoot,
Down from the shower'd halo,
Up from the mystic play of shadows twining and twisting as if they were
    alive,
Out from the patches of briers and blackberries,
From the memories of the bird that chanted to me,
From your memories sad brother, from the fitful risings and fallings I
    heard,
From under that yellow half-moon late-risen and swollen as if with tears,   10
From those beginning notes of yearning and love there in the mist,
From the thousand responses of my heart never to cease,
From the myriad thence-arous'd words,

Out of the Cradle . . . .
    [1] Quaker designation for September.

From the word stronger and more delicious than any,
From such as now they start the scene revisiting,
As a flock, twittering, rising, or overhead passing,
Borne hither, ere all eludes me, hurriedly,
A man, yet by these tears a little boy again,
Throwing myself on the sand, confronting the waves,
I, chanter of pains and joys, uniter of here and hereafter,   20
Taking all hints to use them, but swiftly leaping beyond them,
A reminiscence sing.

Once Paumanok,²
When the lilac-scent was in the air and Fifth-month grass was growing,
Up this seashore in some briers,
Two feather'd guests from Alabama, two together,
And their nest, and four light-green eggs spotted with brown,
And every day the he-bird to and fro near at hand,
And every day the she-bird crouch'd on her nest, silent, with bright eyes,
And every day I, a curious boy, never too close, never disturbing them,   30
Cautiously peering, absorbing, translating.

Shine! shine! shine!
Pour down your warmth, great sun!
While we bask, we two together.

Two together!
Winds blow south, or winds blow north,
Day come white, or night come black,
Home, or rivers and mountains from home,
Singing all time, minding no time,
While we two keep together.   40

Till of a sudden,
May-be kill'd, unknown to her mate,
One forenoon the she-bird crouch'd not on the nest,
Nor return'd that afternoon, nor the next,
Nor ever appear'd again.

And thenceforward all summer in the sound of the sea,
And at night under the full of the moon in calmer weather,
Over the hoarse surging of the sea,
Or flitting from brier to brier by day,
I saw, I heard at intervals the remaining one, the he-bird,   50
The solitary guest from Alabama.

---

² Paumanok is the Indian name of Long Island, where the poet was born and grew up.

Blow! blow! blow!
Blow up sea-winds along Paumanok's shore;
I wait and I wait till you blow my mate to me.

Yes, when the stars glisten'd,
All night long on the prong of a moss-scallop'd stake,
Down almost amid the slapping waves,
Sat the lone singer wonderful causing tears.

He call'd on his mate,
He pour'd forth the meanings which I of all men know.   60

Yes my brother I know,
The rest might not, but I have treasur'd every note,
For more than once dimly down to the beach gliding,
Silent, avoiding the moonbeams, blending myself with the shadows,
Recalling now the obscure shapes, the echoes, the sounds and sights after
    their sorts,
The white arms out in the breakers tirelessly tossing,
I, with bare feet, a child, the wind wafting my hair,
Listen'd long and long.

Listen'd to keep, to sing, now translating the notes,
Following you my brother.   70

Soothe! soothe! soothe!
Close on its wave soothes the wave behind,
And again another behind embracing and lapping, every one close,
But my love soothes not me, not me.

Low hangs the moon, it rose late,
It is lagging—O I think it is heavy with love, with love.

O madly the sea pushes upon the land,
With love, with love.

O night! do I not see my love fluttering out among the breakers?
What is that little black thing I see there in the white?   80

Loud! loud! loud!
Loud I call to you, my love!

High and clear I shoot my voice over the waves,
Surely you must know who is here, is here,
You must know who I am, my love.

Low-hanging moon!
What is that dusky spot in your brown yellow?
O it is the shape, the shape of my mate!
O moon do not keep her from me any longer.

Land! land! O land!   90
Whichever way I turn, O I think you could give me my mate back again
    if you only would,
For I am almost sure I see her dimly whichever way I look.

O rising stars!
Perhaps the one I want so much will rise, will rise with some of you.

O throat! O trembling throat!
Sound clearer through the atmosphere!
Pierce the woods, the earth,
Somewhere listening to catch you must be the one I want.

Shake out carols!
Solitary here, the night's carols!   100
Carols of lonesome love! death's carols!
Carols under that lagging, yellow, waning moon!
O under that moon where she droops almost down into the sea!
O reckless despairing carols.

But soft! sink low!
Soft! let me just murmur,
And do you wait a moment you husky-nois'd sea,
For somewhere I believe I heard my mate responding to me,
So faint, I must be still, be still to listen,
But not altogether still, for then she might not come immediately to me. 110

Hither my love!
Here I am! here!
With this just-sustain'd note I announce myself to you,
This gentle call is for you my love, for you.

Do not be decoy'd elsewhere,
That is the whistle of the wind, it is not my voice,
That is the fluttering, the fluttering of the spray,
Those are the shadows of leaves.

O darkness! O in vain!
O I am very sick and sorrowful.   120

O brown halo in the sky near the moon, drooping upon the sea!
O troubled reflection in the sea!
O throat! O throbbing heart!
And I singing uselessly, uselessly all the night.

O past! O happy life! O songs of joy!
In the air, in the woods, over fields,
Loved! loved! loved! loved! loved!
But my mate no more, no more with me!
We two together no more.

The aria sinking,   130
All else continuing, the stars shining,
The winds blowing, the notes of the bird continuous echoing,
With angry moans the fierce old mother incessantly moaning,
On the sands of Paumanok's shore gray and rustling,
The yellow half-moon enlarged, sagging down, dropping, the face of the sea
    almost touching,
The boy ecstatic, with his bare feet the waves, with his hair the
    atmosphere dallying,
The love in the heart long pent, now loose, now at last tumultuously
    bursting,
The aria's meaning, the ears, the soul, swiftly depositing,
The strange tears down the cheeks coursing,
The colloquy there, the trio, each uttering,   140
The undertone, the savage old mother incessantly crying,
To the boy's soul's questions sullenly timing, some drown'd secret hissing,
To the outsetting bard.

Demon or bird! (said the boy's soul,)
Is it indeed toward your mate you sing? or is it really to me?
For I, that was a child, my tongue's use sleeping, now I have heard you,
Now in a moment I know what I am for, I awake,
And already a thousand singers, a thousand songs, clearer, louder and
    more sorrowful than yours,
A thousand warbling echoes have started to life within me, never to die.

O you singer solitary, singing by yourself, projecting me,   150
O solitary me listening, never more shall I cease perpetuating you,
Never more shall I escape, never more the reverberations,
Never more the cries of unsatisfied love be absent from me,
Never again leave me to be the peaceful child I was before what there in
    the night,
By the sea under the yellow and sagging moon,
The messenger there arous'd, the fire, the sweet hell within,
The unknown want, the destiny of me.

O give me the clew! (it lurks in the night here somewhere,)
O if I am to have so much, let me have more!

A word then, (for I will conquer it,)   160
The word final, superior to all,
Subtle, sent up—what is it?—I listen;
Are you whispering it, and have been all the time, you sea-waves?
Is that it from your liquid rims and wet sands?

Whereto answering, the sea,
Delaying not, hurrying not,
Whisper'd me through the night, and very plainly before daybreak,
Lisp'd to me the low and delicious word death,
And again death, death, death, death,
Hissing melodious, neither like the bird nor like my arous'd child's heart,   170
But edging near as privately for me rustling at my feet,
Creeping thence steadily up to my ears and laving me softly all over,
Death, death, death, death, death.

Which I do not forget,
But fuse the song of my dusky demon and brother,
That he sang to me in the moonlight on Paumanok's gray beach,
With the thousand responsive songs at random,
My own songs awaked from that hour,
And with them the key, the word up from the waves,
The word of the sweetest song and all songs,   180
That strong and delicious word which, creeping to my feet,
(Or like some old crone rocking the cradle, swathed in sweet garments,
    bending aside,)
The sea whisper'd me.

QUESTIONS
1. In this poem Whitman reminisces about an event that proved crucial to him. What was the event? What awareness did it generate in the young boy? **2.** In what way does the young boy emulate the bird? (See ll. 114–157.)

WRITING TOPIC
This poem employs neither rhyme nor metrical regularity. What poetic devices and patterns distinguish it from prose?

I Felt a Funeral, in My Brain   (1861)

EMILY DICKINSON   [1830–1886]

I felt a Funeral, in my Brain,
And Mourners to and fro

Kept treading—treading—till it seemed
That Sense was breaking through—

And when they all were seated,
A Service, like a Drum—
Kept beating—beating—till I thought
My Mind was going numb—

And then I heard them lift a Box
And creak across my Soul   10
With those same Boots of Lead, again,
Then Space—began to toll,

As all the Heavens were a Bell,
And Being, but an Ear,
And I, and Silence, some strange Race
Wrecked, solitary, here—

And then a Plank in Reason, broke,
And I dropped down, and down—
And hit a World, at every plunge,
And Finished knowing—then—   20

Hap   1898

THOMAS HARDY [1840–1928]

If but some vengeful god would call to me
From up the sky, and laugh: "Thou suffering thing,
Know that thy sorrow is my ecstasy,
That thy love's loss is my hate's profiting!"

Then would I bear it, clench myself, and die,
Steeled by the sense of ire unmerited;
Half-eased in that a Powerfuller than I
Had willed and meted me the tears I shed.

But not so. How arrives it joy lies slain,
And why unblooms the best hope ever sown?   10
—Crass Casualty° obstructs the sun and rain,   *chance*
And dicing Time for gladness casts a moan. . . .
These purblind Doomsters¹ had as readily strown
Blisses about my pilgrimage as pain.

Hap
¹ Those who decide one's fate.

The Ruined Maid   1902

THOMAS HARDY   [1840–1928]

"O Melia, my dear, this does everything crown!
Who could have supposed I should meet you in Town?
And whence such fair garments, such prosperi-ty?"
"O didn't you know I'd been ruined?" said she.

"You left us in tatters, without shoes or socks,
Tired of digging potatoes, and spudding up docks;°   digging herbs
And now you've gay bracelets and bright feathers three!"
"Yes: that's how we dress when we're ruined," said she.

"At home in the barton° you said 'thee' and 'thou,'   farmyard
And 'thik onn,' and 'theäs oon,' and 't'other; but now   10
Your talking quite fits 'ee for high compa-ny!"
"Some polish is gained with one's ruin," said she.

"Your hands were like paws then, your face blue and bleak
But now I'm bewitched by your delicate cheek,
And your little gloves fit as on any la-dy!"
"We never do work when we're ruined," said she.

"You used to call home-life a hag-ridden dream,
And you'd sigh, and you'd sock; but at present you seem
To know not of megrims° or melancho-ly!"   sick headaches
"True. One's pretty lively when ruined," said she.   20

"I wish I had feathers, a fine sweeping gown,
And a delicate face, and could strut about Town!"
"My dear—a raw country girl, such as you be,
Cannot quite expect that. You ain't ruined," said she.

Spring and Fall   (1880)

TO A YOUNG CHILD

GERARD MANLEY HOPKINS   [1844–1889]

Márgarét, áre you gríeving
Over Goldengrove unleaving?°   losing leaves
Leáves, líke the things of man, you
With your fresh thoughts care for, can you?
Áh! ás the heart grows older

It will come to such sights colder
By and by, nor spare a sigh
Though worlds of wanwood leafmeal[1] lie;
And yet you will weep and know why.
Now no matter, child, the name: 10
Sórrow's spríngs are the same.
Nor mouth had, no nor mind, expressed
What heart heard of, ghost° guessed: soul
It ís the blight man was born for,
It is Margaret you mourn for.

QUESTIONS
1. In this poem Margaret grieves over the passing of spring and the coming of fall.
What does the coming of fall symbolize? **2.** Why, when Margaret grows older,
will she not sigh over the coming of fall? **3.** What are "Sorrow's springs" (l. 11)?

When I Was
One-and-Twenty   1896

A. E. HOUSMAN [1859–1936]

When I was one-and-twenty
    I heard a wise man say,
"Give crowns and pounds and guineas
    But not your heart away;
Give pearls away and rubies
    But keep your fancy free."
But I was one-and-twenty,
    No use to talk to me.

When I was one-and-twenty
    I heard him say again,   10
"The heart out of the bosom
    Was never given in vain;
'Tis paid with sighs a plenty
    And sold for endless rue."
And I am two-and-twenty,
    And oh, 'tis true, 'tis true.

Spring and Fall
    [1] Pale woods littered with mouldering leaves.

Terence, This Is
Stupid Stuff[1]

1896

A. E. HOUSMAN [1859–1936]

"Terence, this is stupid stuff:
You eat your victuals fast enough;
There can't be much amiss, 'tis clear,
To see the rate you drink your beer.
But oh, good Lord, the verse you make,
It gives a chap the bellyache.
The cow, the old cow, she is dead;
It sleeps well, the hornéd head:
We poor lads, 'tis our turn now
To hear such tunes as killed the cow.   10
Pretty friendship 'tis to rhyme
Your friends to death before their time
Moping melancholy mad:
Come, pipe a tune to dance to, lad."

Why, if 'tis dancing you would be,
There's brisker pipes than poetry.
Say, for what were hopyards meant,
Or why was Burton built on Trent?[2]
Oh many a peer of England brews
Livelier liquor than the Muse,   20
And malt does more than Milton can
To justify God's ways to man.[3]
Ale, man, ale's the stuff to drink
For fellows whom it hurts to think:
Look into the pewter pot
To see the world as the world's not.
And faith, 'tis pleasant till 'tis past:
The mischief is that 'twill not last.
Oh I have been to Ludlow fair
And left my necktie God knows where,   30
And carried halfway home, or near,
Pints and quarts of Ludlow beer:
Then the world seemed none so bad,

Terence, This Is Stupid Stuff
    [1] Housman originally titled the volume in which this poem appeared *The Poems of Terence Hearsay.* Terence was a Roman satiric playwright.
    [2] The river Trent provides water for the town's brewing industry.
    [3] In the invocation to *Paradise Lost,* Milton declares that his epic will "justify the ways of God to men."

And I myself a sterling lad;
And down in lovely muck I've lain,
Happy till I woke again.
Then I saw the morning sky.
Heigho, the tale was all a lie;
The world, it was the old world yet,
I was I, my things were wet,   40
And nothing now remained to do
But begin the game anew.

      Therefore, since the world has still
Much good, but much less good than ill,
And while the sun and moon endure
Luck's a chance, but trouble's sure,
I'd face it as a wise man would,
And train for ill and not for good.
'Tis true the stuff I bring for sale
Is not so brisk a brew as ale: 50
Out of a stem that scored the hand
I wrung it in a weary land.
But take it: if the smack is sour,
The better for the embittered hour;
It should do good to heart and head
When your soul is in my soul's stead;
And I will friend you, if I may,
In the dark and cloudy day.

      There was a king reigned in the East:
There, when kings will sit to feast,
They get their fill before they think   60
With poisoned meat and poisoned drink.
He gathered all that springs to birth
From the many-venomed earth;
First a little, thence to more,
He sampled all her killing store;
And easy, smiling, seasoned sound,
Sate the king when healths went round.
They put arsenic in his meat
And stared aghast to watch him eat;   70
They poured strychnine in his cup
And shook to see him drink it up:
They shook, they stared as white's their shirt:
Them it was their poison hurt.
—I tell the tale that I heard told.
Mithridates, he died old.[4]

---

[4] Mithridates, the King of Pontus (in Asia Minor), reputedly immunized himself against poisons by administering to himself gradually increasing doses.

QUESTIONS
1. What does the speaker of the first fourteen lines object to in Terence's poetry? **2.** What is Terence's response to the criticism of his verse? What function of true poetry is implied by his comparison of bad poetry with liquor?

WRITING TOPIC
How does the story of Mithridates (lines 59–76) illustrate the theme of the poem?

Adam's Curse   1902

W. B. YEATS   [1865–1939]

We sat together at one summer's end,
That beautiful mild woman, your close friend,
And you and I, and talked of poetry.
I said, 'A line will take us hours maybe;
Yet if it does not seem a moment's thought,
Our stitching and unstitching has been naught.

Better go down upon your marrow-bones
And scrub a kitchen pavement, or break stones
Like an old pauper, in all kinds of weather;
For to articulate sweet sounds together   10
Is to work harder than all these, and yet
Be thought an idler by the noisy set
Of bankers, schoolmasters, and clergymen
The martyrs call the world.'

                    And thereupon
That beautiful mild woman for whose sake
There's many a one shall find out all heartache
On finding that her voice is sweet and low
Replied, 'To be born woman is to know—
Although they do not talk of it at school—   20
That we must labour to be beautiful.'

I said, 'It's certain there is no fine thing
Since Adam's fall but needs much labouring.
There have been lovers who thought love should be
So much compounded of high courtesy
That they would sigh and quote with learned looks
Precedents out of beautiful old books;
Yet now it seems an idle trade enough.'

We sat grown quiet at the name of love;
We saw the last embers of daylight die,

And in the trembling blue-green of the sky   30
A moon, worn as if it had been a shell
Washed by time's waters as they rose and fell
About the stars and broke in days and years.

I had a thought for no one's but your ears:
That you were beautiful, and that I strove
To love you in the old high way of love;
That it had all seemed happy, and yet we'd grown
As weary-hearted as that hollow moon.

Leda and the Swan[1]   1928

WILLIAM BUTLER YEATS [1865–1939]

A sudden blow: the great wings beating still
Above the staggering girl, her thighs caressed
By the dark webs, her nape caught in his bill;
He holds her helpless breast upon his breast.

How can those terrified vague fingers push
The feathered glory from her loosening thighs?
And how can body, laid in that white rush,
But feel the strange heart beating where it lies?

A shudder in the loins engenders there
The broken wall, the burning roof and tower   10
And Agamemnon dead.
                      Being so caught up,
So mastered by the brute blood of the air,
Did she put on his knowledge with his power
Before the indifferent beak could let her drop?

Birches   1916

ROBERT FROST [1874–1963]

When I see birches bend to left and right
Across the lines of straighter darker trees,

Leda and the Swan
    [1] In Greek myth, Zeus, in the form of a swan, rapes Leda. As a consequence, Helen and
Clytemnestra are born. Each sister marries the king of a city-state; Helen marries Menelaus and
Clytemnestra marries Agamemnon. Helen, the most beautiful woman on earth, elopes with Paris,
a prince of Troy, an act that precipitates the Trojan War in which Agamemnon commands the
combined Greek armies. The war ends with the destruction of Troy. Agamemnon, when he returns
to his home, is murdered by his unfaithful wife.

I like to think some boy's been swinging them.
But swinging doesn't bend them down to stay.
Ice-storms do that. Often you must have seen them
Loaded with ice a sunny winter morning
After a rain. They click upon themselves
As the breeze rises, and turn many-colored
As the stir cracks and crazes their enamel.
Soon the sun's warmth makes them shed crystal shells   10
Shattering and avalanching on the snow-crust—
Such heaps of broken glass to sweep away
You'd think the inner dome of heaven had fallen.
They are dragged to the withered bracken by the load,
And they seem not to break; though once they are bowed
So low for long, they never right themselves:
You may see their trunks arching in the woods
Years afterwards, trailing their leaves on the ground
Like girls on hands and knees that throw their hair
Before them over their heads to dry in the sun.   20
But I was going to say when Truth broke in
With all her matter-of-fact about the ice-storm
I should prefer to have some boy bend them
As he went out and in to fetch the cows—
Some boy too far from town to learn baseball,
Whose only play was what he found himself,
Summer or winter, and could play alone.
One by one he subdued his father's trees
By riding them down over and over again
Until he took the stiffness out of them,   30
And not one but hung limp, not one was left
For him to conquer. He learned all there was
To learn about not launching out too soon
And so not carrying the tree away
Clear to the ground. He always kept his poise
To the top branches, climbing carefully
With the same pains you use to fill a cup
Up to the brim, and even above the brim.
Then he flung outward, feet first, with a swish,
Kicking his way down through the air to the ground.   40
So was I once myself a swinger of birches.
And so I dream of going back to be.
It's when I'm weary of considerations,
And life is too much like a pathless wood
Where your face burns and tickles with the cobwebs
Broken across it, and one eye is weeping
From a twig's having lashed across it open.
I'd like to get away from earth awhile

And then come back to it and begin over.
May no fate willfully misunderstand me
And half grant what I wish and snatch me away   50
Not to return. Earth's the right place for love:
I don't know where it's likely to go better.
I'd like to go by climbing a birch tree,
And climb black branches up a snow-white trunk
Toward heaven, till the tree could bear no more,
But dipped its top and set me down again.
That would be good both going and coming back.
One could do worse than be a swinger of birches.

Provide, Provide   1936

ROBERT FROST   [1874–1963]

The witch that came (the withered hag)
To wash the steps with pail and rag,
Was once the beauty Abishag,[1]

The picture pride of Hollywood.
Too many fall from great and good
For you to doubt the likelihood.

Die early and avoid the fate.
Or if predestined to die late,
Make up your mind to die in state.

Make the whole stock exchange your own!   10
If need be occupy a throne,
Where nobody can call *you* crone.

Some have relied on what they knew;
Others on being simply true.
What worked for them might work for you.

No memory of having starred
Atones for later disregard,
Or keeps the end from being hard.

Provide, Provide
  [1] "Now King David was old and advanced in years; and although they covered him with clothes, he could not get warm. Therefore his servants said to him, 'Let a young maiden be sought for my lord the king, and let her wait upon the king, and be his nurse; let her lie in your bosom, that my lord the king may be warm.' So they sought for a beautiful maiden throughout all the territory of Israel, and found Abishag, the Shunammite, and brought her to the king. The maiden was very beautiful. . . ."—I Kings 1:1–4.

Better to go down dignified
With boughten friendship at your side   20
Than none at all. Provide, provide!

Peter Quince at the Clavier[1]   1923

WALLACE STEVENS   [1879–1955]

1

Just as my fingers on these keys
Make music, so the selfsame sounds
On my spirit make a music, too.

Music is feeling, then, not sound;
And thus it is that what I feel,
Here in this room, desiring you,

Thinking of your blue-shadowed silk,
Is music. It is like the strain
Waked in the elders by Susanna.[2]

Of a green evening, clear and warm,   10
She bathed in her still garden, while
The red-eyed elders watching, felt

The basses of their beings throb
In witching chords, and their thin blood
Pulse pizzicati of Hosanna.[3]

2

In the green water, clear and warm,
Susanna lay.

Peter Quince at the Clavier
   [1] A clavier is a keyboard instrument. The title is probably a whimsical reference to Peter Quince
of Shakespeare's *A Midsummer Night's Dream*, who directs the mechanics' production of the "most
cruel death of Pyramus and Thisby" to be performed at the king's wedding festival. One of the
actors, Bottom, advises the director, "First, good Peter Quince, say what the play treats on, then
read the names of the actors, and so grow on to a point." Peter Quince, here a musician, seems
to follow that advice.
   [2] The Old Testament Apocrypha includes the story of Susanna, who is saved by the wisdom of
Daniel from a death sentence for adultery based on the perjured testimony of the "elders."
   [3] Pizzicati notes are produced by plucking the strings rather than bowing. Hosanna is a cry of
acclamation and adoration.

She searched
The touch of springs,
And found   20
Concealed imaginings.
She sighed,
For so much melody.

Upon the bank, she stood
In the cool
Of spent emotions.
She felt, among the leaves,
The dew
Of old devotions.

She walked upon the grass,   30
Still quavering.
The winds were like her maids,
On timid feet,
Fetching her woven scarves,
Yet wavering.

A breath upon her hand
Muted the night.

She turned—
A cymbal crashed,
And roaring horns.   40

3

Soon, with a noise like tambourines,
Came her attendant Byzantines.[4]

They wondered why Susanna cried
Against the elders by her side;

And as they whispered, the refrain
Was like a willow swept by rain.

Anon, their lamps' uplifted flame
Revealed Susanna and her shame.

And then, the simpering Byzantines
Fled, with a noise like tambourines.   50

---

[4] From Byzantium (now Istanbul). The attendants are slaves.

4

Beauty is momentary in the mind—
The fitful tracing of a portal;
But in the flesh it is immortal.

The body dies; the body's beauty lives.
So evenings die, in their green going,
A wave, interminably flowing.
So gardens die, their meek breath scenting
The cowl of winter, done repenting.
So maidens die, to the auroral
Celebration of a maiden's choral.   60

Susanna's music touched the bawdy strings
Of those white elders; but, escaping,
Left only Death's ironic scraping.
Now, in its immortality, it plays
On the clear viol of her memory,
And makes a constant sacrament of praise.

QUESTIONS
1. What is the relationship of the narrative in lines 10–50 to lines 1–9 and to section 4? **2.** Is the statement contained in lines 51–54 a paradox? Explain.

WRITING TOPIC
This poem is famous for its sound patterns. What are the dominating consonant and vowel sounds in lines 1–11? What sounds dominate lines 12–15? Can you suggest how these sounds reinforce the sense of the poem?

Piano   1918

D. H. LAWRENCE   [1885–1930]

Softly, in the dusk, a woman is singing to me;
Taking me back down the vista of years, till I see
A child sitting under the piano, in the boom of the tingling strings
And pressing the small, poised feet of a mother who smiles as she sings.

In spite of myself, the insidious mastery of song
Betrays me back, till the heart of me weeps to belong
To the old Sunday evenings at home, with winter outside
And hymns in the cozy parlour, the tinkling piano our guide.

So now it is vain for the singer to burst into clamour
With the great black piano appassionato. The glamour   10
Of childish days is upon me, my manhood is cast
Down in the flood of remembrance, I weep like a child for the past.

Grown-up   1920

EDNA ST. VINCENT MILLAY   [1892–1950]

Was it for this I uttered prayers,
And sobbed and cursed and kicked the stairs,
That now, domestic as a plate,
I should retire at half-past eight?

To Carry the Child   1966

STEVIE SMITH   [1902–1971]

To carry the child into adult life
Is good? I say it is not,
To carry the child into adult life
Is to be handicapped.

The child in adult life is defenceless
And if he is grown-up, knows it,
And the grown-up looks at the childish part
And despises it.

The child, too, despises the clever grown-up,
The man-of-the-world, the frozen,   10
For the child has the tears alive on his cheek
And the man has none of them.

As the child has colours, and the man sees no
Colours or anything,
Being easy only in things of the mind,
The child is easy in feeling.

Easy in feeling, easily excessive
And in excess powerful,
For instance, if you do not speak to the child
He will make trouble.   20

You would say a man had the upper hand
Of the child, if a child survive,
But I say the child has fingers of strength
To strangle the man alive.

Oh! it is not happy, it is never happy,
To carry the child into adulthood,
Let the children lie down before full growth
And die in their infanthood
And be guilty of no man's blood.

But oh the poor child, the poor child, what can he do,   30
Trapped in a grown-up carapace,
But peer outside of his prison room
With the eye of an anarchist?

Incident   1925

COUNTEE CULLEN   [1903–1946]

Once riding in old Baltimore,
    Heart-filled, head-filled with glee,
I saw a Baltimorean
    Keep looking straight at me.

Now I was eight and very small,
    And he was no whit bigger,
And so I smiled, but he poked out
    His tongue and called me, "Nigger."

I saw the whole of Baltimore
    From May until December:
Of all the things that happened there   10
    That's all that I remember.

Country Club Sunday   1946

PHYLLIS McGINLEY   [1905–1978]

It is a beauteous morning, calm and free.
    The fairways sparkle. Gleam the shaven grasses.

Mirth fills the locker rooms and, hastily,
   Stewards fetch ice, fresh towels, and extra glasses.

On terraces the sandaled women freshen
   Their lipstick; gather to gossip, poised and cool;
And the shrill adolescent takes possession,
   Plunging and splashing, of the swimming pool.

It is a beauteous morn, opinion grants.
   Nothing remains of last night's Summer Formal   10
Save palms and streamers and the wifely glance,
   Directed with more watchfulness than normal,
At listless mate who tugs his necktie loose,
Moans, shuns the light, and gulps tomato juice.

QUESTION

1. Compare this poem with Wordsworth's "It Is a Beauteous Evening" (p. 121).
What is the author's purpose in parodying the opening line of the Wordsworth poem?

Tears   1981

JOSEPHINE JACOBSEN   [b. 1908]

Tears leave no mark on the soil
or pavement; certainly not in sand
or in any known rain forest.
Never a mark on stone.
You would think that no one in Persepolis
or Ur ever wept.[1]

You would assume that, like Alice,[2]
we would all be swimming, buffeted
in a tide of tears.
But they disappear. Their heat goes.   10
Yet the globe is salt
With that savor.

The animals want no part in this.
The hare both screams and weeps
at her death, one poet says.

Tears
   [1] Persepolis, the capital city of the Persian kings, was destroyed by Alexander the Great. Ur was
a principal city in Babylonia.
   [2] An allusion to Lewis Carroll's *Alice in Wonderland*.

The stag, at death, rolls round drops
down his muzzle; but he is in
Shakespeare's forest.[3]

These cases are mythically rare.
No, it is the human being who persistently   20
weeps; in some countries, openly, in others, not.
Children who, even when frightened, weep most hopefully;
women, licensed weepers;
men, in secret, or childishly; or nobly.

Could tears not make up a sea of their mass?
It could be salt and wild enough;
it could rouse storms and sink ships,
erode, erode its shores:
tears of rage, of love, of torture,
of loss. Of loss.   30

Must you see the future
in order to weep? Or the past?
Is that why the animals
refuse to shed tears?
But what of the present, the tears of the present?
The awful relief, like breath

after strangling? The generosity
in the verb *to shed*?
They are a classless possession
yet not to be found in the museum   40
of even our greatest city.
Sometimes what was human, turns
into an animal, dry-eyed.

QUESTIONS
1. Why would one think that no one in Persepolis or Ur ever wept? **2.** What
distinguishes real animals from mythical animals? What distinguishes human beings
from animals? What is the point of the last two lines?

Fern Hill   1946

DYLAN THOMAS [1914–1953]

Now as I was young and easy under the apple boughs
About the lilting house and happy as the grass was green,

---

[3] That is, an imaginary forest.

The night above the dingle° starry,   small wooded valley
    Time let me hail and climb
    Golden in the heydays of his eyes,
And honored among wagons I was prince of the apple towns
And once below a time I lordly had the trees and leaves
        Trail with daisies and barley
    Down the rivers of the windfall light.

And I was green and carefree, famous among the barns   10
About the happy yard and singing as the farm was home,
    In the sun that is young once only,
        Time let me play and be
    Golden in the mercy of his means,
And green and golden I was huntsman and herdsman, the calves
Sang to my horn, the foxes on the hills barked clear and cold,
        And the sabbath rang slowly
    In the pebbles of the holy streams.

All the sun long it was running, it was lovely, the hay
Fields high as the house, the tunes from the chimneys, it was air   20
    And playing, lovely and watery
    And fire green as grass.
    And nightly under the simple stars
As I rode to sleep the owls were bearing the farm away,
All the moon long I heard, blessed among stables, the nightjars[1]
        Flying with the ricks, and the horses
            Flashing into the dark.

And then to awake, and the farm, like a wanderer white
With the dew, come back, the cock on his shoulder: it was all
    Shining, it was Adam and maiden,   30
        The sky gathered again
    And the sun grew round that very day.
So it must have been after the birth of the simple light
In the first, spinning place, the spellbound horses walking warm
    Out of the whinnying green stable
        On to the fields of praise.

And honored among foxes and pheasants by the gay house
Under the new made clouds and happy as the heart was long,
    In the sun born over and over,
        I ran my heedless ways,   40

Fern Hill
[1] Nightjars are harsh-sounding nocturnal birds.

My wishes raced through the house high hay
And nothing I cared, at my sky blue trades, that time allows
In all his tuneful turning so few and such morning songs
    Before the children green and golden
        Follow him out of grace.

Nothing I cared, in the lamb white days, that time would take me
Up to the swallow thronged loft by the shadow of my hand,
    In the moon that is always rising,
        Nor that riding to sleep
I should hear him fly with the high fields   50
And wake to the farm forever fled from the childless land.
Oh as I was young and easy in the mercy of his means,
    Time held me green and dying
    Though I sang in my chains like the sea.

QUESTIONS

1. What emotional impact does the color imagery in the poem provide?   **2.** Trace the behavior of "time" in the poem.   **3.** Fairy tales often begin with the words "once upon a time." Why does Thomas alter that formula in line 7?   **4.** Explain the paradox in line 53.

WRITING TOPICS

1. Lines 17–18, 25, 45–46 incorporate religious language and biblical allusion. How do those allusions clarify the poet's vision of his childhood?   **2.** Compare this poem with Gerard Manley Hopkins's "Spring and Fall."

For My Daughter   1943

WELDON KEES [1914–1955?]

Looking into my daughter's eyes I read
Beneath the innocence of morning flesh
Concealed, hintings of death she does not heed.
Coldest of winds have blown this hair, and mesh
Of seaweed snarled these miniatures of hands:
The night's slow poison, tolerant and bland,
Has moved her blood. Parched years that I have seen
That may be hers appear: foul, lingering
Death in certain war, the slim legs green.
Or, fed on hate, she relishes the sting   10

Of others' agony; perhaps the cruel
Bride of a syphilitic or a fool.
These speculations sour in the sun.
I have no daughter. I desire none.

QUESTIONS
1. How would you characterize the several images the speaker associates with his "daughter"? Does he or does he not have a daughter?   **2.**   How does the poem justify the speaker's desire not to have a daughter?

A Moment Please   1962

SAMUEL ALLEN   [b. 1917]

When I gaze at the sun
    I walked to the subway booth
    for change for a dime.
and know that this great earth
    Two adolescent girls stood there
    alive with eagerness to know
is but a fragment from it thrown
    all in their new found world
    there was for them to know
in heat and flame a billion years ago,   10
    they looked at me and brightly asked
    "Are you Arabian?"
that when this world was lifeless
    I smiled and cautiously
    —for one grows cautious—
    shook my head.
as, a billion hence,
    "Egyptian?"
It shall again be,
    Again I smiled and shook my head   20
    and walked away.
what moment is it that I am betrayed,
    I've gone but seven paces now
oppressed, cast down,
    and from behind comes swift the sneer
or warm with love or triumph?
    "Or Nigger?"
    A moment, please

What is it that to fury I am roused?
    for still it takes a moment   30
What meaning for me
    and now
in this homeless clan
    I'll turn
the dupe of space
    and smile
the toy of time?
    and nod my head.

Curiosity   1959

ALASTAIR REID   [b. 1926]

may have killed the cat; more likely
the cat was just unlucky, or else curious
to see what death was like, having no cause
to go on licking paws, or fathering
litter on litter of kittens, predictably.

    Nevertheless, to be curious
is dangerous enough. To distrust
what is always said, what seems,
to ask odd questions, interfere in dreams,
leave home, smell rats, have hunches   10
does not endear him to those doggy circles
where well-smelt baskets, suitable wives, good lunches
are the order of things, and where prevails
much wagging of incurious heads and tails.

    Face it. Curiosity
will not cause him to die—
only lack of it will.
Never to want to see
the other side of the hill,
or that improbable country   20
where living is an idyll
(although a probable hell)
would kill us all.
Only the curious
have, if they live, a tale
worth telling at all.

Dogs say he loves too much, is irresponsible,
is changeable, marries too many wives,
deserts his children, chills all dinner tables
with tales of his nine lives.   30
Well, he is lucky. Let him be
nine-lived and contradictory,
curious enough to change, prepared to pay
the cat price, which is to die
and die again and again,
each time with no less pain.
A cat minority of one
is all that can be counted on
to tell the truth. And what he has to tell
on each return from hell   40
is this: that dying is what the living do,
that dying is what the loving do,
and that dead dogs are those who do not know
that hell is where, to live, they have to go.

April Inventory   1959

W. D. SNODGRASS [b. 1926]

The green catalpa tree has turned
All white; the cherry blooms once more.
In one whole year I haven't learned
A blessed thing they pay you for.
The blossoms snow down in my hair;
The trees and I will soon be bare.

The trees have more than I to spare.
The sleek, expensive girls I teach,
Younger and pinker every year,
Bloom gradually out of reach.
The pear tree lets its petals drop   10
Like dandruff on a tabletop.

The girls have grown so young by now
I have to nudge myself to stare.
This year they smile and mind me how
My teeth are falling with my hair.
In thirty years I may not get
Younger, shrewder, or out of debt.

The tenth time, just a year ago,
I made myself a little list
Of all the things I'd ought to know;   20
Then told my parents, analyst,
And everyone who's trusted me
I'd be substantial, presently.

I haven't read one book about
A book or memorized one plot.
Or found a mind I didn't doubt.
I learned one date. And then forgot.
And one by one the solid scholars
Get the degrees, the jobs, the dollars.   30

And smile above their starchy collars.
I taught my classes Whitehead's notions;
One lovely girl, a song of Mahler's.
Lacking a source-book or promotions,
I showed one child the colors of
A luna moth and how to love.

I taught myself to name my name,
To bark back, loosen love and crying;
To ease my woman so she came,
To ease an old man who was dying.   40
I have not learned how often I
Can win, can love, but choose to die.

I have not learned there is a lie
Love shall be blonder, slimmer, younger;
That my equivocating eye
Loves only by my body's hunger;
That I have poems, true to feel,
Or that the lovely world is real.

While scholars speak authority
And wear their ulcers on their sleeves,   50
My eyes in spectacles shall see
These trees procure and spend their leaves.
There is a value underneath
The gold and silver in my teeth.

Though trees turn bare and girls turn wives,
We shall afford our costly seasons;
There is a gentleness survives
That will outspeak and has its reasons.
There is a loveliness exists,
Preserves us. Not for specialists.   60

QUESTIONS

1. What do the words "I have not learned" (ll. 41, 43) mean in the context of the poem? **2.** In what way does the tone of the first four stanzas differ from the tone of the last two? **3.** What is the meaning of "specialists" in the last line? **4.** What is the speaker's conception of teaching?

WRITING TOPIC

Explicate the final stanza of this poem. Is it an appropriate conclusion? Explain.

Cinderella   1971

ANNE SEXTON   [1928–1974]

You always read about it:
the plumber with twelve children
who wins the Irish Sweepstakes.
From toilets to riches.
That story.

Or the nursemaid,
some luscious sweet from Denmark
who captures the oldest son's heart.
From diapers to Dior.
That story.   10

Or a milkman who serves the wealthy,
eggs, cream, butter, yogurt, milk,
the white truck like an ambulance
who goes into real estate
and makes a pile.
From homogenized to martinis at lunch.

Or the charwoman
who is on the bus when it cracks up
and collects enough from the insurance.
From mops to Bonwit Teller.   20
That story.

Once
the wife of a rich man was on her deathbed
and she said to her daughter Cinderella:
Be devout. Be good. Then I will smile
down from heaven in the seam of a cloud.
The man took another wife who had
two daughters, pretty enough
but with hearts like blackjacks.
Cinderella was their maid.   30
She slept on the sooty hearth each night
and walked around looking like Al Jolson.
Her father brought presents home from town,
jewels and gowns for the other women
but the twig of a tree for Cinderella.
She planted that twig on her mother's grave
and it grew to a tree where a white dove sat.
Whenever she wished for anything the dove
would drop it like an egg upon the ground.
The bird is important, my dears, so heed him.   40

Next came the ball, as you all know.
It was a marriage market.
The prince was looking for a wife.
All but Cinderella were preparing
and gussying up for the big event.
Cinderella begged to go too.
Her stepmother threw a dish of lentils
into the cinders and said: Pick them
up in an hour and you shall go.
The white dove brought all his friends;   50
all the warm wings of the fatherland came,
and picked up the lentils in a jiffy.
No, Cinderella, said the stepmother,
you have no clothes and cannot dance.
That's the way with stepmothers.

Cinderella went to the tree at the grave
and cried forth like a gospel singer:

Mama! Mama! My turtledove,
send me to the prince's ball!
The bird dropped down a golden dress   60
and delicate little gold slippers.
Rather a large package for a simple bird.
So she went. Which is no surprise.
Her stepmother and sisters didn't
recognize her without her cinder face
and the prince took her hand on the spot
and danced with no other the whole day.

As nightfall came she thought she'd better
get home. The prince walked her home
and she disappeared into the pigeon house   70
and although the prince took an axe and broke
it open she was gone. Back to her cinders.
These events repeated themselves for three days.
However on the third day the prince
covered the palace steps with cobbler's wax
and Cinderella's gold shoe stuck upon it.

Now he would find whom the shoe fit
and find his strange dancing girl for keeps.
He went to their house and the two sisters
were delighted because they had lovely feet.   80
The eldest went into a room to try the slipper on
but her big toe got in the way so she simply
sliced it off and put on the slipper.
The prince rode away with her until the white dove
told him to look at the blood pouring forth.
That is the way with amputations.
They don't just heal up like a wish.
The other sister cut off her heel
but the blood told as blood will.
The prince was getting tired.   90
He began to feel like a shoe salesman
but he gave it one last try.
This time Cinderella fit into the shoe
like a love letter into its envelope.

At the wedding ceremony
the two sisters came to curry favor
and the white dove pecked their eyes out.
Two hollow spots were left
like soup spoons.

Cinderella and the prince   100
lived, they say, happily ever after,
like two dolls in a museum case
never bothered by diapers or dust,
never arguing over the timing of an egg,
never telling the same story twice,
never getting a middle-aged spread,
their darling smiles pasted on for eternity.
Regular Bobbsey Twins.[1]
That story.

QUESTIONS
1. Where does one usually find the first four "stories" mentioned in the poem? Why do such stories interest readers? **2.** The story of Cinderella, of course, is well known. Do you remember your feelings at the success of Cinderella? How are those feelings modified by the last stanza?

WRITING TOPIC
Arguably, the language and formal structure of this poem are rather prosaic. Describe, by examining the image patterns and individual lines, the qualities that make the piece a poem.

First Confession   1961

X. J. KENNEDY   [b. 1929]

Blood thudded in my ears. I scuffed,
    Steps stubborn, to the telltale booth
Beyond whose curtained portal coughed
    The robed repositor of truth.

The slat shot back. The universe
    Bowed down his cratered dome to hear

Cinderella
    [1] The ever-cheerful central figures in a series of children's books.

Enumerated my each curse,
    The sip snitched from my old man's beer.

My sloth pride envy lechery,
    The dime held back from Peter's Pence   10
With which I'd bribed my girl to pee
    That I might spy her instruments.

Hovering scale-pans when I'd done
    Settled their balance slow as silt
While in the restless dark I burned
    Bright as a brimstone in my guilt

Until as one feeds birds he doled
    Seven Our Fathers and a Hail
Which I to double-scrub my soul
    Intoned twice at the altar rail   20

Where Sunday in seraphic light
    I knelt, as full of grace as most,
And stuck my tongue out at the priest:
    A fresh roost for the Holy Ghost.

The Middle-aged   1955

ADRIENNE RICH [b. 1929]

Their faces, safe as an interior
Of Holland tiles and Oriental carpet,
Where the fruit-bowl, always filled, stood in a light
Of placid afternoon—their voices' measure,
Their figures moving in the Sunday garden
To lay the tea outdoors or trim the borders,
Afflicted, haunted us. For to be young
Was always to live in other peoples' houses
Whose peace, if we sought it, had been made by others,
Was ours at second-hand and not for long.   10
The custom of the house, not ours, the sun

Fading the silver-blue Fortuny[1] curtains,
The reminiscence of a Christmas party
Of fourteen years ago—all memory,
Signs of possession and of being possessed,
We tasted, tense with envy. They were so kind,
Would have given us anything; the bowl of fruit
Was filled for us, there was a room upstairs
We must call ours: but twenty years of living
They could not give. Nor did they ever speak   20
Of the coarse stain on that polished balustrade,
The crack in the study window, or the letters
Locked in a drawer and the key destroyed.
All to be understood by us, returning
Late, in our own time—how that peace was made,
Upon what terms, with how much left unsaid.

Advice to My Son   1965

PETER MEINKE   [b. 1932]

The trick is, to live your days
as if each one may be your last
(for they go fast, and young men lose their lives
in strange and unimaginable ways)
but at the same time, plan long range
(for they go slow: if you survive
the shattered windshield and the bursting shell
you will arrive
at our approximation here below
of heaven or hell).   10

To be specific, between the peony and the rose
plant squash and spinach, turnips and tomatoes;
beauty is nectar
and nectar, in a desert, saves—
but the stomach craves stronger sustenance
than the honied vine.

The Middle-aged
   [1] Elegant fabric based on Moorish tile designs.

Therefore, marry a pretty girl
after seeing her mother;
speak truth to one man,
work with another;   20
and always serve bread with your wine.

But, son,
always serve wine.

QUESTIONS
1. Explain how the advice of lines 17–21 is logically related to the preceding
lines.   **2.**   What do the final two lines tell the reader about the speaker?

WRITING TOPIC
The advice of the first stanza seems contradictory. In what ways does the second
stanza attempt to resolve the contradiction or explain "The trick" (l. 1)? What do
the various plants and the bread and wine symbolize?

In a Spring Still Not Written Of 1965

ROBERT WALLACE   [b. 1932]

This morning
with a class of girls outdoors, I saw
how frail poems are
in a world burning up with flowers,
in which, overhead,
the great elms
—green, and tall—
stood carrying leaves in their arms.

The girls listened equally
to my drone, reading, and to the bees'   10
ricocheting
among them for the blossom on the bone,
or gazed off at a distant mower's
astronomies of green
and clover, flashing,
threshing in the new, untarnished sunlight.

And all the while, dwindling,
tinier, the voices—Yeats, Marvell, Donne—
sank drowning
in a spring still not written of,   20
as only the sky

clear above the brick bell-tower
—blue, and white—
was shifting toward the hour.

Calm, indifferent, cross-legged
or on elbows half-lying in the grass—
how should the great dead
tell them of dying?
They will come to time for poems at last,
when they have found they are no more   30
the beautiful and young
all poems are for.

QUESTIONS
1. What is the speaker's attitude toward the "class of girls" he is teaching? Toward his job as a teacher? **2.** Explain the meaning of the title. **3.** Explain the various meanings of "drone" (l. 10).

WRITING TOPIC
Explain the paradox developed in this poem.

My Mother   1970

ROBERT MEZEY [b. 1935]

My mother writes from Trenton,
a comedian to the bone
but underneath, serious
and all heart. "Honey," she says,
"be a mensch[1] and Mary too,
its no good to worry, you
are doing the best you can
your Dad and everyone
thinks you turned out very well
as long as you pay your bills   10
nobody can say a word
you can tell them to drop dead
so save a dollar it can't
hurt—remember Frank you went
to highschool with? he still lives
with his wife's mother, his wife

My Mother
    [1] Man, in the sense of "human being."

works while he writes his books and
did he ever sell a one
the four kids run around naked
36 and he's never had,   20
you'll forgive my expression
even a pot to piss in
or a window to throw it,
such a smart boy he couldn't
read the footprints on the wall
honey you think you know all
the answers you don't, please try
to put some money away
believe me it wouldn't hurt
artist shmartist life's too short   30
for that kind of, forgive me,
horseshit, I know what you want
better than you, all that counts
is to make a good living
and the best of everything,
as Sholem Aleichem said
he was a great writer did
you ever read his books dear,
you should make what he makes a year
anyway he says some place   40
Poverty is no disgrace
but its no honor either
that's what I say,
                    love,
                       Mother"

A Poem About Intelligence for My Brothers and Sisters   1980

JUNE JORDAN   [b. 1936]

A few year back and they told me Black
means a hole where other folks
got brain/it was like the cells in the heads
of Black children was out to every hour on the hour naps
Scientists called the phenomenon the Notorious

Jensen Lapse, remember?[1]
Anyway I was thinking
about how to devise
a test for the wise
like a Stanford-Binet   10
for the C. I. A.
you know?
Take Einstein
being the most the unquestionable the outstanding
the maximal mind of the century
right?
And I'm struggling against this lapse leftover
from my Black childhood to fathom why
anybody should say so:
$E = mc$ squared?   20
I try that on this old lady live on my block:
She sweeping away Saturday night from the stoop
and mad as can be because some absolute
jackass have left a kingsize mattress where
she have to sweep around it stains and all she
don't want to know nothing about in the first place
"Mrs. Johnson!" I say, leaning on the gate
between us: "What you think about somebody come up with an E equals
   $M C 2$?"
"How you doin," she answer me, sideways, like she don't   30
want to let on she know I ain
combed my hair yet and here it is
Sunday morning but still I have the nerve
to be bothering serious work with these crazy
questions about
"E equals what you say again, dear?"
Then I tell her, "Well
also this same guy? I think
he was undisputed Father of the Atom Bomb!"
"That right." She mumbles or grumbles, not too politely   40
"And dint remember to wear socks when he put on
his shoes!" I add on (getting desperate)
at which point Mrs. Johnson take herself and her broom
a very big step down the stoop away from me

A Poem About Intelligence . . .
   [1] An allusion to Arthur Robert Jensen (b. 1923), an educational psychologist whose long essay entitled "How Much Can We Boost IQ and Scholastic Achievement?" *Harvard Educational Review*, 39 (1969), was perceived by many as an argument that poor educational achievement was a function of inherited intellectual inferiority.

"And never did nothing for nobody in particular
lessen it was a committee
and
used to say, 'What time is it?'
and
you'd say, 'Six o'clock.'   50
and
he'd say, 'Day or night?'
and
and he never made nobody a cup of tea
in his whole brilliant life!"
"and
(my voice rises slightly)
and
he dint never boogie neither: never!"

"Well," say Mrs. Johnson, "Well, honey,   60
I do guess
that's genius for you."

The Last Song on the Jukebox   1983

DAVID KIRBY   [b. 1944]

It was a song about a man, a woman,
another man, and a car. The man
wanted to borrow the other man's car
but he didn't think it right
on account of his going out with
the woman, who was supposed to be the
other man's girlfriend, on the sly.
The woman didn't care. The man
cared, but not so much that he
didn't borrow it anyway. So they   10
went to a roadhouse. They had
several drinks, and the band played
rhythm and blues. Then they went
to a motel. Someone who knew the
other man told, but he got the
room number wrong. The other man
broke into the wrong room and
shot a preacher in the leg,
giving the man and the woman a

chance to escape. What could have   20
been tragic is now seen as comical,
at least with the passage of years.
Today the other man has suspicions
that cannot be verified. He has
sold the car, saying that he cannot
stand the sight of it. The man
no longer sees the woman on the
sly. The woman, who has since married
the other man, still doesn't care.
Neither does the preacher. He was   30
glad he got shot, he'll say from
time to time; he needed the pain.

INNOCENCE
AND
EXPERIENCE

The Red Armchair, 1931 by Pablo Picasso

DRAMA

Oedipus Rex*   (ca. 429 B.C.)

SOPHOCLES   [496?–406 B.C.]

PERSONS REPRESENTED

Oedipus	Messenger
A Priest	Shepherd of Laïos
Creon	Second Messenger
Teiresias	Chorus of Theban Elders
Iocastê	

SCENE

Before the palace of Oedipus, King of Thebes. A central door and two lateral doors open onto a platform which runs the length of the facade. On the platform, right and left, are altars; and three steps lead down into the "orchestra," or chorus-ground. At the beginning of the action these steps are crowded by suppliants who have brought branches and chaplets of olive leaves and who lie in various attitudes of despair. Oedipus enters.

Prologue

Oedipus.   My children, generations of the living
In the line of Kadmos,¹ nursed at his ancient hearth:
Why have you strewn yourselves before these altars
In supplication, with your boughs and garlands?
The breath of incense rises from the city
With a sound of prayer and lamentation.

---

* An English version by Dudley Fitts and Robert Fitzgerald.
¹ The legendary founder of Thebes.

                                        Children,
I would not have you speak through messengers,
And therefore I have come myself to hear you—
I, Oedipus, who bear the famous name.
[*To a Priest.*] You, there, since you are eldest in the company,   10
Speak for them all, tell me what preys upon you,
Whether you come in dread, or crave some blessing:
Tell me, and never doubt that I will help you
In every way I can; I should be heartless
Were I not moved to find you suppliant here.

Priest.   Great Oedipus, O powerful King of Thebes!
You see how all the ages of our people
Cling to your altar steps: here are boys
Who can barely stand alone, and here are priests
By weight of age, as I am a priest of God,   20
And young men chosen from those yet unmarried;
As for the others, all that multitude,
They wait with olive chaplets in the squares,
At the two shrines of Pallas,[2] and where Apollo[3]
Speaks in the glowing embers.
                                        Your own eyes
Must tell you: Thebes is in her extremity
And can not lift her head from the surge of death.
A rust consumes the buds and fruits of the earth;
The herds are sick; children die unborn,
And labor is vain. The god of plague and pyre   30
Raids like detestable lightning through the city,
And all the house of Kadmos is laid waste,
All emptied, and all darkened: Death alone
Battens upon the misery of Thebes.

You are not one of the immortal gods, we know;
Yet we have come to you to make our prayer
As to the man of all men best in adversity
And wisest in the ways of God. You saved us
From the Sphinx,[4] that flinty singer, and the tribute
We paid to her so long; yet you were never   40
Better informed than we, nor could we teach you:
It was some god breathed in you to set us free.

---

    [2] Athena, goddess of wisdom.
    [3] God of sunlight, medicine, and prophecy.
    [4] A winged monster, with a woman's head and breasts and a lion's body, that destroyed those
who failed to answer her riddle: "What walks on four feet in the morning, two at noon, and three
in the evening?" When the young Oedipus correctly answered, "Man" ("three" alluding to a cane
in old age), the Sphinx killed herself, and the plague ended.

Therefore, O mighty King, we turn to you:
Find us our safety, find us a remedy,
Whether by counsel of the gods or men.
A king of wisdom tested in the past
Can act in a time of troubles, and act well.
Noblest of men, restore
Life to your city! Think how all men call you
Liberator for your triumph long ago;   50
Ah, when your years of kingship are remembered,
Let them not say *We rose, but later fell*—
Keep the State from going down in the storm!
Once, years ago, with happy augury,
You brought us fortune; be the same again!
No man questions your power to rule the land:
But rule over men, not over a dead city!
Ships are only hulls, citadels are nothing,
When no life moves in the empty passageways.

Oedipus.   Poor children! You may be sure I know   60
All that you longed for in your coming here.
I know that you are deathly sick; and yet,
Sick as you are, not one is as sick as I.
Each of you suffers in himself alone
His anguish, not another's; but my spirit
Groans for the city, for myself, for you.

I was not sleeping, you are not waking me.
No, I have been in tears for a long while
And in my restless thought walked many ways.
In all my search, I found one helpful course,   70
And that I have taken: I have sent Creon,
Son of Menoikeus, brother of the Queen,
To Delphi, Apollo's place of revelation,
To learn there, if he can,
What act or pledge of mine may save the city.
I have counted the days, and now, this very day,
I am troubled, for he has overstayed his time.
What is he doing? He has been gone too long.
Yet whenever he comes back, I should do ill
To scant whatever hint the god may give.   80

Priest.   It is a timely promise. At this instant
They tell me Creon is here.

Oedipus.   O Lord Apollo!
May his news be fair as his face is radiant!

Priest.   It could not be otherwise: he is crowned with bay,
The chaplet is thick with berries.

Oedipus.   We shall soon know;
He is near enough to hear us now.

[*Enter Creon.*]

O Prince:
Brother: son of Menoikeus:
What answer do you bring us from the god?
Creon.   It is favorable. I can tell you, great afflictions
Will turn out well, if they are taken well.   90
Oedipus.   What was the oracle? These vague words
Leave me still hanging between hope and fear.
Creon.   Is it your pleasure to hear me with all these
Gathered around us? I am prepared to speak,
But should we not go in?
Oedipus.   Let them all hear it.
It is for them I suffer, more than for myself.
Creon.   Then I will tell you what I heard at Delphi.

In plain words
The god commands us to expel from the land of Thebes
An old defilement that it seems we shelter.   100
It is a deathly thing, beyond expiation.
We must not let it feed upon us longer.
Oedipus.   What defilement? How shall we rid ourselves of it?
Creon.   By exile or death, blood for blood. It was
Murder that brought the plague-wind on the city.
Oedipus.   Murder of whom? Surely the god has named him?
Creon.   My lord: long ago Laïos was our king,
Before you came to govern us.
Oedipus.   I know;
I learned of him from others; I never saw him.
Creon.   He was murdered; and Apollo commands us now   110
To take revenge upon whoever killed him.
Oedipus.   Upon whom? Where are they? Where shall we find a clue
To solve that crime, after so many years?
Creon.   Here in this land, he said.
If we make enquiry,
We may touch things that otherwise escape us.
Oedipus.   Tell me: Was Laïos murdered in his house,
Or in the fields, or in some foreign country?
Creon.   He said he planned to make a pilgrimage.
He did not come home again.
Oedipus.   And was there no one,
No witness, no companion, to tell what happened?   120

Creon.   They were all killed but one, and he got away
So frightened that he could remember one thing only.
Oedipus.   What was that one thing? One may be the key
To everything, if we resolve to use it.
Creon.   He said that a band of highwaymen attacked them,
Outnumbered them, and overwhelmed the King.
Oedipus.   Strange, that a highwayman should be so daring—
Unless some faction here bribed him to do it.
Creon.   We thought of that. But after Laïos' death
New troubles arose and we had no avenger.   130
Oedipus.   What troubles could prevent your hunting down the killers?
Creon.   The riddling Sphinx's song
Made us deaf to all mysteries but her own.
Oedipus.   Then once more I must bring what is dark to light.
It is most fitting that Apollo shows,
As you do, this compunction for the dead.
You shall see how I stand by you, as I should,
To avenge the city and the city's god,
And not as though it were for some distant friend,
But for my own sake, to be rid of evil.   140
Whoever killed King Laïos might—who knows?—
Decide at any moment to kill me as well.
By avenging the murdered king I protect myself.
Come, then, my children: leave the altar steps,
Lift up your olive boughs!
                                        One of you go
And summon the people of Kadmos to gather here.
I will do all that I can; you may tell them that.

[*Exit a page.*]

So, with the help of God,
We shall be saved—or else indeed we are lost.
Priest.   Let us rise, children. It was for this we came,   150
And now the King has promised it himself.
Phoibos[5] has sent us an oracle; may he descend
Himself to save us and drive out the plague.

[*Exeunt Oedipus and Creon into the palace by the central door. The Priest and
the suppliants disperse R and L. After a short pause the Chorus enters the
orchestra.*]

---

5 Phoebus Apollo, god of the sun.

Párodos[6]

Chorus.   What is God singing in his profound   [*Strophe 1*]
Delphi of gold and shadow?
What oracle for Thebes, the sunwhipped city?
Fear unjoints me, the roots of my heart tremble.
Now I remember, O Healer, your power, and wonder;
Will you send doom like a sudden cloud, or weave it
Like nightfall of the past?
Speak, speak to us, issue of holy sound:
Dearest to our expectancy: be tender!

Let me pray to Athenê, the immortal daughter of Zeus,   [*Antistrophe 1*]
And to Artemis her sister   11
Who keeps her famous throne in the market ring,
And to Apollo, bowman at the far butts of heaven—

O gods, descend! Like three streams leap against
The fires of our grief, the fires of darkness;
Be swift to bring us rest!

As in the old time from the brilliant house
Of air you stepped to save us, come again!

Now our afflictions have no end,   [*Strophe 2*]
Now all our stricken host lies down   20
And no man fights off death with his mind;

The noble plowland bears no grain,
And groaning mothers can not bear—

See, how our lives like birds take wing,
Like sparks that fly when a fire soars,
To the shore of the god of evening.

The plague burns on, it is pitiless,   [*Antistrophe 2*]
Though pallid children laden with death
Lie unwept in the stony ways,

And old gray women by every path   30
Flock to the strand about the altars

---

6 The *Párodos* is the ode sung by the Chorus as it entered the theater and moved down the aisles
to the playing area. The *strophe*, in Greek tragedy, is the unit of verse the Chorus chanted as it
moved to the left in a dance rhythm. The Chorus sang the *antistrophe* as it moved to the right and
the *epode* while standing still.

There to strike their breasts and cry
Worship of Phoibos in wailing prayers:
Be kind, God's golden child!

There are no swords in this attack by fire,   [*Strophe 3*]
No shields, but we are ringed with cries.
Send the besieger plunging from our homes
Into the vast sea-room of the Atlantic
Or into the waves that foam eastward of Thrace—
For the day ravages what the night spares—   40

Destroy our enemy, lord of the thunder!
Let him be riven by lightning from heaven!

Phoibus Apollo, stretch the sun's bowstring,   [*Antistrophe 3*]
That golden cord, until it sing for us,
Flashing arrows in heaven!
                    Artemis, Huntress
Race with flaring lights upon our mountains!

O scarlet god, O golden-banded brow,
O Theban Bacchos in a storm of Maenads,[7]

[*Enter Oedipus, C.*]

Whirl upon Death, that all the Undying hate!
Come with blinding cressets, come in joy!   50

Scene 1

Oedipus.   Is this your prayer? It may be answered. Come,
   Listen to me, act as the crisis demands,
   And you shall have relief from all these evils.

   Until now I was a stranger to this tale,
   As I had been a stranger to the crime.
   Could I track down the murderer without a clue?
   But now, friends,
   As one who became a citizen after the murder,
   I make this proclamation to all Thebans:
   If any man knows by whose hand Laïos, son of Labdakos,   10

---

[7] Bacchos is the god of wine and revelry, hence scarlet-faced. The Maenads were Bacchos'
female attendants.

Met his death, I direct that man to tell me everything,
No matter what he fears for having so long withheld it.
Let it stand as promised that no further trouble
Will come to him, but he may leave the land in safety.

Moreover: If anyone knows the murderer to be foreign,
Let him not keep silent: he shall have his reward from me.
However, if he does conceal it; if any man
Fearing for his friend or for himself disobeys this edict,
Hear what I propose to do:

I solemnly forbid the people of this country,   20
Where power and throne are mine, ever to receive that man
Or speak to him, no matter who he is, or let him
Join in sacrifice, lustration, or in prayer.
I decree that he be driven from every house,
Being, as he is, corruption itself to us: the Delphic
Voice of Zeus has pronounced this revelation.
Thus I associate myself with the oracle
And take the side of the murdered king.

As for the criminal, I pray to God—
Whether it be a lurking thief, or one of a number—   30
I pray that that man's life be consumed in evil and wretchedness.
And as for me, this curse applies no less
If it should turn out that the culprit is my guest here,
Sharing my hearth.
                    You have heard the penalty.
I lay it on you now to attend to this
For my sake, for Apollo's, for the sick
Sterile city that heaven has abandoned.
Suppose the oracle had given you no command:
Should this defilement go uncleansed for ever?
You should have found the murderer: your king,   40
A noble king, had been destroyed!
                    Now I,
Having the power that he held before me,
Having his bed, begetting children there
Upon his wife, as he would have, had he lived—
Their son would have been my children's brother,
If Laïos had had luck in fatherhood!
(But surely ill luck rushed upon his reign)—
I say I take the son's part, just as though
I were his son, to press the fight for him
And see it won! I'll find the hand that brought   50

Death to Labdakos' and Polydoros' child,
Heir of Kadmos's and Agenor's line.
And as for those who fail me,
May the gods deny them the fruit of the earth,
Fruit of the womb, and may they rot utterly!
Let them be wretched as we are wretched, and worse!

For you, for loyal Thebans, and for all
Who find my actions right, I pray the favor
Of justice, and of all the immortal gods.
Choragos.[8]   Since I am under oath, my lord, I swear   60
  I did not do the murder. I can not name
  The murderer. Might not the oracle
  That has ordained the search tell where to find him?
Oedipus.   An honest question. But no man in the world
  Can make the gods do more than the gods will.
Choragos.   There is one last expedient—
Oedipus.   Tell me what it is.
  Though it seem slight, you must not hold it back.
Choragos.   A lord clairvoyant to the lord Apollo,
  As we all know, is the skilled Teiresias.
  One might learn much about this from him, Oedipus.   70
Oedipus.   I am not wasting time:
  Creon spoke of this, and I have sent for him—
  Twice, in fact; it is strange that he is not here.
Choragos.   The other matter—that old report—seems useless.
Oedipus.   Tell me. I am interested in all reports.
Choragos.   The King was said to have been killed by highwaymen.
Oedipus.   I know. But we have no witnesses to that.
Choragos.   If the killer can feel a particle of dread,
  Your curse will bring him out of hiding!
Oedipus.   No.
  The man who dared that act will fear no curse.   80

[*Enter the blind seer Teiresias, led by a page.*]

Choragos.   But there is one man who may detect the criminal.
  This is Teiresias, this is the holy prophet
  In whom, alone of all men, truth was born.
Oedipus.   Teiresias: seer: student of mysteries,
  Of all that's taught and all that no man tells,
  Secrets of Heaven and secrets of the earth:
  Blind though you are, you know the city lies

---

[8] Choragos is the leader of the Chorus.

Sick with plague; and from this plague, my lord,
We find that you alone can guard or save us.

Possibly you did not hear the messengers?   90
Apollo, when we sent to him,
Sent us back word that this great pestilence
Would lift, but only if we established clearly
The identity of those who murdered Laïos.
They must be killed or exiled.
                          Can you use
Birdflight or any art of divination
To purify yourself, and Thebes, and me
From this contagion? We are in your hands.
There is no fairer duty
Than that of helping others in distress.   100
Teiresias. How dreadful knowledge of the truth can be
When there's no help in truth! I knew this well,
But did not act on it: else I should not have come.
Oedipus. What is troubling you? Why are your eyes so cold?
Teiresias. Let me go home. Bear your own fate, and I'll
Bear mine. It is better so: trust what I say.
Oedipus. What you say is ungracious and unhelpful
To your native country. Do not refuse to speak.
Teiresias. When it comes to speech, your own is neither temperate
Nor opportune. I wish to be more prudent.   110
Oedipus. In God's name, we all beg you—
Teiresias.   You are all ignorant.
No; I will never tell you what I know.
Now it is my misery; then, it would be yours.
Oedipus. What! You do know something, and will not tell us?
You would betray us all and wreck the State?
Teiresias. I do not intend to torture myself, or you.
Why persist in asking? You will not persuade me.
Oedipus. What a wicked old man you are! You'd try a stone's
Patience! Out with it! Have you no feeling at all?
Teiresias. You call me unfeeling. If you could only see   120
The nature of your own feelings . . .
Oedipus.   Why,
Who would not feel as I do? Who could endure
Your arrogance toward the city?
Teiresias.   What does it matter!
Whether I speak or not, it is bound to come.
Oedipus. Then, if "it" is bound to come, you are bound to tell me.
Teiresias. No, I will not go on. Rage as you please.

Oedipus.   Rage? Why not!
                                And I'll tell you what I think:
You planned it, you had it done, you all but
Killed him with your own hands: if you had eyes,
I'd say the crime was yours, and yours alone.   130
Teiresias.   So? I charge you, then,
Abide by the proclamation you have made:
From this day forth
Never speak again to these men or to me;
You yourself are the pollution of this country.
Oedipus.   You dare say that! Can you possibly think you have
Some way of going free, after such insolence?
Teiresias.   I have gone free. It is the truth sustains me.
Oedipus.   Who taught you shamelessness? It was not your craft.
Teiresias.   You did. You made me speak. I did not want to.   140
Oedipus.   Speak what? Let me hear it again more clearly.
Teiresias.   Was it not clear before? Are you tempting me?
Oedipus.   I did not understand it. Say it again.
Teiresias.   I say that you are the murderer whom you seek.
Oedipus.   Now twice you have spat out infamy! You'll pay for it!
Teiresias.   Would you care for more? Do you wish to be really angry?
Oedipus.   Say what you will. Whatever you say is worthless.
Teiresias.   I say you live in hideous shame with those
Most dear to you. You can not see the evil.
Oedipus.   It seems you can go on mouthing like this for ever.   150
Teiresias.   I can, if there is power in truth.
Oedipus.   There is:
But not for you, not for you,
You sightless, witless, senseless, mad old man!
Teiresias.   You are the madman. There is no one here
Who will not curse you soon, as you curse me.
Oedipus.   You child of endless night! You can not hurt me
Or any other man who sees the sun.
Teiresias.   True: it is not from me your fate will come.
That lies within Apollo's competence,
As it is his concern.
Oedipus.   Tell me: 160
Are you speaking for Creon or for yourself?
Teiresias.   Creon is no threat. You weave your own doom.
Oedipus.   Wealth, power, craft of statesmanship!
Kingly position, everywhere admired!
What savage envy is stored up against these,
If Creon, whom I trusted, Creon my friend,
For this great office which the city once

Put in my hands unsought—if for this power
Creon desires in secret to destroy me!

He has brought this decrepit fortune-teller, this   170
Collector of dirty pennies, this prophet fraud—
Why, he is no more clairvoyant than I am!
                                        Tell us:
Has your mystic mummery ever approached the truth?
When that hellcat the Sphinx was performing here,
What help were you to these people?
Her magic was not for the first man who came along:
It demanded a real exorcist. Your birds—
What good were they? or the gods, for the matter of that?
But I came by,
Oedipus, the simple man, who knows nothing—   180
I thought it out for myself, no birds helped me!
And this is the man you think you can destroy,
That you may be close to Creon when he's king!
Well, you and your friend Creon, it seems to me,
Will suffer most. If you were not an old man,
You would have paid already for your plot.
Choragos.   We can not see that his words or yours
Have been spoken except in anger, Oedipus,
And of anger we have no need. How can God's will
Be accomplished best? That is what most concerns us.   190
Teiresias.   You are a king. But where argument's concerned
I am your man, as much a king as you.
I am not your servant, but Apollo's.
I have no need of Creon to speak for me.

Listen to me. You mock my blindness, do you?
But I say that you, with both your eyes, are blind:
You can not see the wretchedness of your life,
Nor in whose house you live, no, nor with whom.
Who are your father and mother? Can you tell me?
You do not even know the blind wrongs   200
That you have done them, on earth and in the world below.
But the double lash of your parents' curse will whip you
Out of this land some day, with only night
Upon your precious eyes.
Your cries then—where will they not be heard?
What fastness of Kithairon[9] will not echo them?
And that bridal-descant of yours—you'll know it then,

---

[9] A mountain range near Thebes where the infant Oedipus was left to die.

The song they sang when you came here to Thebes
And found your misguided berthing.
All this, and more, that you can not guess at now,   210
Will bring you to yourself among your children.

Be angry, then. Curse Creon. Curse my words.
I tell you, no man that walks upon the earth
Shall be rooted out more horribly than you.
Oedipus.   Am I to bear this from him?—Damnation
Take you! Out of this place! Out of my sight!
Teiresias.   I would not have come at all if you had not asked me.
Oedipus.   Could I have told that you'd talk nonsense, that
You'd come here to make a fool of yourself, and of me?
Teiresias.   A fool? Your parents thought me sane enough.   220
Oedipus.   My parents again!—Wait: who were my parents?
Teiresias.   This day will give you a father, and break your heart.
Oedipus.   Your infantile riddles! Your damned abracadabra!
Teiresias.   You were a great man once at solving riddles.
Oedipus.   Mock me with that if you like; you will find it true.
Teiresias.   It was true enough. It brought about your ruin.
Oedipus.   But if it saved this town?
Teiresias [to the page].   Boy, give me your hand.
Oedipus.   Yes, boy; lead him away.
                                   —While you are here
We can do nothing. Go; leave us in peace.
Teiresias.   I will go when I have said what I have to say.   230
How can you hurt me? And I tell you again:
The man you have been looking for all this time,
The damned man, the murderer of Laïos,
That man is in Thebes. To your mind he is foreignborn,
But it will soon be shown that he is a Theban,
A revelation that will fail to please.
                                   A blind man,
Who has his eyes now; a penniless man, who is rich now;
And he will go tapping the strange earth with his staff;
To the children with whom he lives now he will be
Brother and father—the very same; to her   240
Who bore him, son and husband—the very same
Who came to his father's bed, wet with his father's blood.

Enough. Go think that over.
If later you find error in what I have said,
You may say that I have no skill in prophecy.

[Exit Teiresias, led by his page. Oedipus goes into the palace.]

Ode I

Chorus.   The Delphic stone of prophecies   [*Strophe 1*]
    Remembers ancient regicide
    And a still bloody hand.
    That killer's hour of flight has come.
    He must be stronger than riderless
    Coursers of untiring wind,
    For the son of Zeus[10] armed with his father's thunder
    Leaps in lightning after him;
    And the Furies follow him, the sad Furies.[11]

    Holy Parnassos' peak of snow   [*Antistrophe 1*]
    Flashes and blinds that secret man,   11
    That all shall hunt him down:
    Though he may roam the forest shade
    Like a bull gone wild from pasture
    To rage through glooms of stone.
    Doom comes down on him; flight will not avail him;
    For the world's heart calls him desolate,
    And the immortal Furies follow, for ever follow.

    But now a wilder thing is heard   [*Strophe 2*]
    From the old man skilled at hearing Fate in the wingbeat of a bird.   20
    Bewildered as a blown bird, my soul hovers and can not find
    Foothold in this debate, or any reason or rest of mind.
    But no man ever brought—none can bring
    Proof of strife between Thebes' royal house,
    Labdakos' line, and the son of Polybos;[12]
    And never until now has any man brought word
    Of Laïos' dark death staining Oedipus the King.

    Divine Zeus and Apollo hold   [*Antistrophe 2*]
    Perfect intelligence alone of all tales ever told;
    And well though this diviner works, he works in his own night;   30
    No man can judge that rough unknown or trust in second sight,
    For wisdom changes hands among the wise.
    Shall I believe my great lord criminal
    At a raging word that a blind old man let fall?
    I saw him, when the carrion woman faced him of old,
    Prove his heroic mind! These evil words are lies.

---

[10] I.e., Apollo (see note 3).
[11] The goddesses of divine vengeance.
[12] Labdakos was an early king of Thebes and an ancestor of Oedipus. Oedipus is mistakenly referred to as the son of Polybus.

Scene II

Creon.   Men of Thebes:
  I am told that heavy accusations
  Have been brought against me by King Oedipus.

  I am not the kind of man to bear this tamely.

  If in these present difficulties
  He holds me accountable for any harm to him
  Through anything I have said or done—why, then,
  I do not value life in this dishonor.
  It is not as though this rumor touched upon
  Some private indiscretion. The matter is grave.   10
  The fact is that I am being called disloyal
  To the State, to my fellow citizens, to my friends.
Choragos.   He may have spoken in anger, not from his mind.
Creon.   But did you not hear him say I was the one
  Who seduced the old prophet into lying?
Choragos.   The thing was said; I do not know how seriously.
Creon.   But you were watching him! Were his eyes steady?
  Did he look like a man in his right mind?
Choragos.   I do not know.
  I can not judge the behavior of great men.
  But here is the King himself.

[Enter Oedipus.]

Oedipus.   So you dared come back.   20
  Why? How brazen of you to come to my house,
  You murderer!
                    Do you think I do not know
  That you plotted to kill me, plotted to steal my throne?
  Tell me, in God's name: am I coward, a fool,
  That you should dream you could accomplish this?
  A fool who could not see your slippery game?
  A coward, not to fight back when I saw it?
  You are the fool, Creon, are you not? hoping
  Without support or friends to get a throne?
  Thrones may be won or bought: you could do neither.   30
Creon.   Now listen to me. You have talked; let me talk, too.
  You can not judge unless you know the facts.
Oedipus.   You speak well: there is one fact; but I find it hard
  To learn from the deadliest enemy I have.
Creon.   That above all I must dispute with you.
Oedipus.   That above all I will not hear you deny.

Creon.   If you think there is anything good in being stubborn
  Against all reason, then I say you are wrong.
Oedipus.   If you think a man can sin against his own kind
  And not be punished for it, I say you are mad.   40
Creon.   I agree. But tell me: what have I done to you?
Oedipus.   You advised me to send for that wizard, did you not?
Creon.   I did. I should do it again.
Oedipus.   Very well. Now tell me:
  How long has it been since Laïos—
Creon.   What of Laïos?
Oedipus.   Since he vanished in that onset by the road?
Creon.   It was long ago, a long time.
Oedipus.   And this prophet,
  Was he practicing here then?
Creon.   He was; and with honor, as now.
Oedipus.   Did he speak of me at that time?
Creon.   He never did;
  At least, not when I was present.
Oedipus.   But . . . . the enquiry?
  I suppose you held one?
Creon.   We did, but we learned nothing.   50
Oedipus.   Why did the prophet not speak against me then?
Creon.   I do not know; and I am the kind of man
  Who holds his tongue when he has no facts to go on.
Oedipus.   There's one fact that you know, and you could tell it.
Creon.   What fact is that? If I know it, you shall have it.
Oedipus.   If he were not involved with you, he could not say
  That it was I who murdered Laïos.
Creon.   If he says that, you are the one that knows it!—
  But now it is my turn to question you.
Oedipus.   Put your questions. I am no murderer.   60
Creon.   First then: You married my sister?
Oedipus.   I married your sister.
Creon.   And you rule the kingdom equally with her?
Oedipus.   Everything that she wants she has from me.
Creon.   And I am the third, equal to both of you?
Oedipus.   That is why I call you a bad friend.
Creon.   No. Reason it out, as I have done.
  Think of this first. Would any sane man prefer
  Power, with all a king's anxieties,
  To that same power and the grace of sleep?
  Certainly not I.   70
  I have never longed for the king's power—only his rights.
  Would any wise man differ from me in this?
  As matters stand, I have my way in everything

With your consent, and no responsibilities.
If I were king, I should be a slave to policy.

How could I desire a scepter more
Than what is now mine—untroubled influence?
No, I have not gone mad; I need no honors,
Except those with the perquisites I have now.
I am welcome everywhere; every man salutes me,   80
And those who want your favor seek my ear,
Since I know how to manage what they ask.
Should I exchange this ease for that anxiety?
Besides, no sober mind is treasonable.
I hate anarchy
And never would deal with any man who likes it.

Test what I have said. Go to the priestess
At Delphi, ask if I quoted her correctly.
And as for this other thing: if I am found
Guilty of treason with Teiresias,   90
Then sentence me to death! You have my word
It is a sentence I should cast my vote for—
But not without evidence!
                            You do wrong
When you take good men for bad, bad men for good.
A true friend thrown aside—why, life itself
Is not more precious!
                            In time you will know this well:
For time, and time alone, will show the just man,
Though scoundrels are discovered in a day.
Choragos.   This is well said, and a prudent man would ponder it.
Judgments too quickly formed are dangerous.   100
Oedipus.   But is he not quick in his duplicity?
And shall I not be quick to parry him?
Would you have me stand still, hold my peace, and let
This man win everything, through my inaction?
Creon.   And you want—what is it, then? To banish me?
Oedipus.   No, not exile. It is your death I want,
So that all the world may see what treason means.
Creon.   You will persist, then? You will not believe me?
Oedipus.   How can I believe you?
Creon.   Then you are a fool.
Oedipus.   To save myself?
Creon.   In justice, think of me.   110
Oedipus.   You are evil incarnate.
Creon.   But suppose that you are wrong?

Oedipus.   Still I must rule.
Creon.   But not if you rule badly.
Oedipus.   O city, city!
Creon.   It is my city, too!
Choragos.   Now, my lords, be still. I see the Queen,
    Iocastê, coming from her palace chambers;
    And it is time she came, for the sake of you both.
    This dreadful quarrel can be resolved through her.   120

[*Enter Iocastê.*]

Iocastê.   Poor foolish men, what wicked din is this?
    With Thebes sick to death, is it not shameful
    That you should rake some private quarrel up?
    [*To Oedipus.*] Come into the house.
                                    —And you, Creon, go now:
    Let us have no more of this tumult over nothing.
Creon.   Nothing? No, sister: what your husband plans for me
    Is one of two great evils: exile or death.
Oedipus.   He is right.
                          Why, woman I have caught him squarely
    Plotting against my life.
Creon.   No! Let me die
    Accurst if ever I have wished you harm!
Iocastê.   Ah, believe it, Oedipus!
    In the name of the gods, respect this oath of his
    For my sake, for the sake of these people here!   130

Choragos.   Open your mind to her my lord. Be ruled by her,   [*Strophe 1*]
    I beg you!
Oedipus.   What would you have me do?
Choragos.   Respect Creon's word. He has never spoken like a fool,
    And now he has sworn an oath.
Oedipus.   You know what you ask?
Choragos   I do.
Oedipus.   Speak on, then.
Choragos.   A friend so sworn should not be baited so,
    In blind malice, and without final proof.
Oedipus.   You are aware, I hope, that what you say
    Means death for me, or exile at the least.

Choragos.   No, I swear by Helios,[13] first in Heaven!   [*Strophe 2*]
    May I die friendless and accurst,   140

---

[13] The sun god.

The worst of deaths, if ever I meant that!
   It is the withering fields
     That hurt my sick heart:
   Must we bear all these ills,
    And now your bad blood as well?

Oedipus.   Then let him go. And let me die, if I must,
Or be driven by him in shame from the land of Thebes.
It is your unhappiness, and not his talk,
That touches me.
           As for him—
Wherever he is, I will hate him as long as I live.   150

Creon.   Ugly in yielding, as you were ugly in rage!
Natures like yours chiefly torment themselves.

Oedipus.   Can you not go? Can you not leave me?

Creon.   I can.
You do not know me; but the city knows me,
And in its eyes I am just, if not in yours.

[*Exit Creon.*]

Choragos.   Lady Iocastê, did you not ask the King to go   [*Antistrophe 1*]
to his chambers?

Iocastê.   First tell me what has happened.

Choragos.   There was suspicion without evidence; yet it rankled
As even false charges will.

Iocastê.   On both sides?

Choragos.   On both.

Iocastê.   But what was said?

Choragos.   Oh let it rest, let it be done with!   160
Have we not suffered enough?

Oedipus.   You see to what your decency has brought you:
You have made difficulties where my heart saw none.

Choragos.   Oedipus, it is not once only I have told you—   [*Antistrophe 2*]
You must know I should count myself unwise
To the point of madness, should I now forsake you—
   You, under whose hand,
     In the storm of another time,
   Our dear land sailed out free.
   But now stand fast at the helm!   170

Iocastê.   In God's name, Oedipus, inform your wife as well:
Why are you so set in this hard anger?

Oedipus.   I will tell you, for none of these men deserves
My confidence as you do. It is Creon's work,
His treachery, his plotting against me.

Iocastê.   Go on, if you can make this clear to me.

Oedipus.   He charges me with the murder of Laïos.

Iocastê.   Has he some knowledge? Or does he speak from hearsay?

Oedipus.   He would not commit himself to such a charge,
But he has brought in that damnable soothsayer   180
To tell his story.

Iocastê.   Set your mind at rest.
If it is a question of soothsayers, I tell you
That you will find no man whose craft gives knowledge
Of the unknowable.

                    Here is my proof:

An oracle was reported to Laïos once
(I will not say from Phoibos himself, but from
His appointed ministers, at any rate)
That his doom would be death at the hands of his own son—
His son, born of his flesh and of mine!

Now, you remember the story: Laïos was killed   190
By marauding strangers where three highways meet;
But his child had not been three days in this world
Before the King had pierced the baby's ankles
And left him to die on a lonely mountainside.

Thus, Apollo never caused that child
To kill his father, and it was not Laïos' fate
To die at the hands of his son, as he had feared.
This is what prophets and prophecies are worth!
Have no dread of them.

                    It is God himself
Who can show us what he wills, in his own way.   200

Oedipus.   How strange a shadowy memory crossed my mind,
Just now while you were speaking; it chilled my heart.

Iocastê.   What do you mean? What memory do you speak of?

Oedipus.   If I understand you, Laïos was killed
At a place where three roads meet.

Iocastê.   So it was said;
We have no later story.

Oedipus.   Where did it happen?

Iocastê.   Phokis, it is called: at a place where the Theban Way
Divides into the roads towards Delphi and Daulia.

Oedipus.   When?

Iocastê.   We had the news not long before you came
And proved the right to your succession here.   210

Oedipus.   Ah, what net has God been weaving for me?

Iocastê.   Oedipus! Why does this trouble you?

Oedipus.   Do not ask me yet.
First, tell me how Laïos looked, and tell me
How old he was.

Iocastê.   He was tall, his hair just touched
With white; his form was not unlike your own.

Oedipus.   I think that I myself may be accurst
By my own ignorant edict.

Iocastê.   You speak strangely.
It makes me tremble to look at you, my King.

Oedipus.   I am not sure that the blind man can not see.
But I should know better if you were to tell me—   220

Iocastê.   Anything—though I dread to hear you ask it.

Oedipus.   Was the King lightly escorted, or did he ride
With a large company, as a ruler should?

Iocastê.   There were five men with him in all: one was a herald;
And a single chariot, which he was driving.

Oedipus.   Alas, that makes it plain enough!
                                                          But who—
Who told you how it happened?

Iocastê.   A household servant,
The only one to escape.

Oedipus.   And is he still
A servant of ours?

Iocastê.   No; for when he came back at last
And found you enthroned in the place of the dead king,   230
He came to me, touched my hand with his, and begged
That I would send him away to the frontier district
Where only the shepherds go—
As far away from the city as I could send him.
I granted his prayer; for although the man was a slave,
He had earned more than this favor at my hands.

Oedipus.   Can he be called back quickly?

Iocastê.   Easily.
But why?

Oedipus.   I have taken too much upon myself
Without enquiry; therefore I wish to consult him.

Iocastê.   Then he shall come.
                                          But am I not one also   240
To whom you might confide these fears of yours?

Oedipus.   That is your right; it will not be denied you,
Now least of all; for I have reached a pitch
Of wild foreboding. Is there anyone
To whom I should sooner speak?
Polybos of Corinth is my father.

My mother is a Dorian: Meropê.
I grew up chief among the men of Corinth
Until a strange thing happened—
Not worth my passion, it may be, but strange.   250

At a feast, a drunken man maundering in his cups
Cries out that I am not my father's son!

I contained myself that night, though I felt anger
And a sinking heart. The next day I visited
My father and mother, and questioned them. They stormed,
Calling it all the slanderous rant of a fool;
And this relieved me. Yet the suspicion
Remained always aching in my mind;
I knew there was talk; I could not rest;
And finally, saying nothing to my parents,   260
I went to the shrine at Delphi.
The god dismissed my question without reply;
He spoke of other things.
                        Some were clear,
Full of wretchedness, dreadful, unbearable:
As, that I should lie with my own mother, breed
Children from whom all men would turn their eyes;
And that I should be my father's murderer.

I heard all this, and fled. And from that day
Corinth to me was only in the stars
Descending in that quarter of the sky,   270
As I wandered farther and farther on my way
To a land where I should never see the evil
Sung by the oracle. And I came to this country
Where, so you say, King Laïos was killed.

I will tell you all that happened there, my lady.

There were three highways
Coming together at a place I passed;
And there a herald came towards me, and a chariot
Drawn by horses, with a man such as you describe
Seated in it. The groom leading the horses   280
Forced me off the road at his lord's command;
But as this charioteer lurched over towards me
I struck him in my rage. The old man saw me
And brought his double goad down upon my head
As I came abreast.
                        He was paid back, and more!

Swinging my club in this right hand I knocked him
Out of his car, and he rolled on the ground.
                                                    I killed him.

I killed them all.
Now if that stranger and Laïos were—kin,
Where is a man more miserable than I?   290
More hated by the gods? Citizen and alien alike
Must never shelter me or speak to me—
I must be shunned by all.
                              And I myself
Pronounced this malediction upon myself!

Think of it: I have touched you with these hands,
These hands that killed your husband. What defilement!

Am I all evil, then? It must be so,
Since I must flee from Thebes, yet never again
See my own countrymen, my own country,
For fear of joining my mother in marriage   300
And killing Polybos, my father.
                              Ah,
If I was created so, born to this fate,
Who could deny the savagery of God?

O holy majesty of heavenly powers!
May I never see that day! Never!
Rather let me vanish from the race of men
Than know the abomination destined me!
Choragos.   We too, my lord, have felt dismay at this.
     But there is hope: you have yet to hear the shepherd.
Oedipus.   Indeed, I fear no other hope is left me.   310
Iocastê.   What do you hope from him when he comes?
Oedipus.   This much:
     If his account of the murder tallies with yours,
     Then I am cleared.
Iocastê.   What was it that I said
     Of such importance?
Oedipus.   Why, "marauders," you said,
     Killed the King, according to this man's story.
     If he maintains that still, if there were several,
     Clearly the guilt is not mine: I was alone.
     But if he says one man, singlehanded, did it,
     Then the evidence all points to me.
Iocastê.   You may be sure that he said there were several;   320
     And can he call back that story now? He can not.

The whole city heard it as plainly as I.
But suppose he alters some detail of it:
He can not ever show that Laïos' death
Fulfilled the oracle: for Apollo said
My child was doomed to kill him; and my child—
Poor baby!—it was my child that died first.

No. From now on, where oracles are concerned,
I would not waste a second thought on any.
Oedipus.   You may be right.

                           But come: let someone go   330
For the shepherd at once. This matter must be settled.
Iocastê.   I will send for him.
I would not wish to cross you in anything.
And surely not in this.— Let us go in.

[Exeunt into the palace.]

Ode II

Chorus.   Let me be reverent in the ways of right,   *[Strophe 1]*
  Lowly the paths I journey on;
  Let all my words and actions keep
  The laws of the pure universe
  From highest Heaven handed down.
  For Heaven is their bright nurse,
  Those generations of the realms of light;
  Ah, never of mortal kind were they begot,
  Nor are they slaves of memory, lost in sleep:
  Their Father is greater than Time, and ages not.   10

  The tyrant is a child of Pride   *[Antistrophe 1]*
  Who drinks from his great sickening cup
  Recklessness and vanity,
  Until from his high crest headlong
  He plummets to the dust of hope.
  That strong man is not strong.
  But let no fair ambition be denied;
  May God protect the wrestler for the State
  In government, in comely policy,
  Who will fear God, and on His ordinance wait.   20

  Haughtiness and the high hand of disdain   *[Strophe 2]*
  Tempt and outrage God's holy law;
  And any mortal who dares hold

No immortal Power in awe
Will be caught up in a net of pain:
The price for which his levity is sold.
Let each man take due earnings, then,
And keep his hands from holy things,
And from blasphemy stand apart—
Else the crackling blast of heaven   30
Blows on his head, and on his desperate heart;
Though fools will honor impious men,
In their cities no tragic poet sings.

Shall we lose faith in Delphi's obscurities,   [*Antistrophe* 2]
We who have heard the world's core
Discredited, and the sacred wood
Of Zeus at Elis praised no more?
The deeds and the strange prophecies
Must make a pattern yet to be understood.
Zeus, if indeed you are lord of all,   40
Throned in light over night and day,
Mirror this in your endless mind:
Our masters call the oracle
Words on the wind, and the Delphic vision blind!
Their hearts no longer know Apollo,
And reverence for the gods has died away.

Scene III

[*Enter Iocastê.*]

Iocastê.   Princes of Thebes, it has occurred to me
To visit the altars of the gods, bearing
These branches as a suppliant, and this incense.
Our King is not himself: his noble soul
Is overwrought with fantasies of dread,
Else he would consider
The new prophecies in the light of the old.
He will listen to any voice that speaks disaster,
And my advice goes for nothing.

[*She approaches the altar, R.*]

                                        To you, then, Apollo,
Lycean lord, since you are nearest, I turn in prayer.   10
Receive these offerings, and grant us deliverance
From defilement. Our hearts are heavy with fear

When we see our leader distracted, as helpless sailors
Are terrified by the confusion of their helmsman.

[*Enter Messenger.*]

Messenger.   Friends, no doubt you can direct me:
  Where shall I find the house of Oedipus,
  Or, better still, where is the King himself?
Choragos.   It is this very place, stranger; he is inside.
  This is his wife and mother of his children.
Messenger.   I wish her happiness in a happy house,   20
  Blest in all the fulfillment of her marriage.
Iocastê.   I wish as much for you: your courtesy
  Deserves a like good fortune. But now, tell me:
  Why have you come? What have you to say to us?
Messenger.   Good news, my lady, for your house and your husband.
Iocastê.   What news? Who sent you here?
Messenger.   I am from Corinth.
  The news I bring ought to mean joy for you,
  Though it may be you will find some grief in it.
Iocastê.   What is it? How can it touch us in both ways?
Messenger.   The people of Corinth, they say,   30
  Intend to call Oedipus to be their king.
Iocastê.   But old Polybos—is he not reigning still?
Messenger.   No. Death holds him in his sepulchre.
Iocastê.   What are you saying? Polybos is dead?
Messenger.   If I am not telling the truth, may I die myself.
Iocastê [*to a maidservant*].   Go in, go quickly; tell this to your master.
  O riddlers of God's will, where are you now!
  This was the man whom Oedipus, long ago,
  Feared so, fled so, in dread of destroying him—
  But it was another fate by which he died.   40

[*Enter Oedipus, C.*]

Oedipus.   Dearest Iocastê, why have you sent for me?
Iocastê.   Listen to what this man says, and then tell me
  What has become of the solemn prophecies.
Oedipus.   Who is this man? What is his news for me?
Iocastê.   He has come from Corinth to announce your father's death!
Oedipus.   Is it true, stranger? Tell me in your own words.
Messenger.   I can not say it more clearly: the King is dead.
Oedipus.   Was it by treason? Or by an attack of illness?
Messenger.   A little thing brings old men to their rest.
Oedipus.   It was sickness, then?
Messenger.   Yes, and his many years.   50

Oedipus. Ah!
Why should a man respect the Pythian hearth,[14] or
Give heed to the birds that jangle above his head?
They prophesied that I should kill Polybos,
Kill my own father; but he is dead and buried,
And I am here—I never touched him, never,
Unless he died of grief for my departure,
And thus, in a sense, through me. No. Polybos
Has packed the oracles off with him underground.
They are empty words.

Iocastê.   Had I not told you so?   60

Oedipus. You had; it was my faint heart that betrayed me.

Iocastê. From now on never think of those things again.

Oedipus. And yet—must I not fear my mother's bed?

Iocastê. Why should anyone in this world be afraid,
Since Fate rules us and nothing can be foreseen?
A man should live only for the present day.

Have no more fear of sleeping with your mother:
How many men, in dreams, have lain with their mothers!
No reasonable man is troubled by such things.

Oedipus. That is true; only—   70
If only my mother were not still alive!
But she is alive. I can not help my dread.

Iocastê. Yet this news of your father's death is wonderful.

Oedipus. Wonderful. But I fear the living woman.

Messenger. Tell me, who is this woman that you fear?

Oedipus. It is Meropê, man; the wife of King Polybos.

Messenger. Meropê? Why should you be afraid of her?

Oedipus. An oracle of the gods, a dreadful saying.

Messenger. Can you tell me about it or are you sworn to silence?

Oedipus. I can tell you, and I will.   80
Apollo said through his prophet that I was the man
Who should marry his own mother, shed his father's blood
With his own hands. And so, for all these years
I have kept clear of Corinth, and no harm has come—
Though it would have been sweet to see my parents again.

Messenger. And is this the fear that drove you out of Corinth?

Oedipus. Would you have me kill my father?

Messenger.   As for that
You must be reassured by the news I gave you.

Oedipus. If you could reassure me, I would reward you.

Messenger. I had that in mind, I will confess: I thought   90
I could count on you when you returned to Corinth.

---

[14] Delphi, where Apollo spoke through an oracle.

Oedipus.   No: I will never go near my parents again.

Messenger.   Ah, son, you still do not know what you are doing—

Oedipus.   What do you mean? In the name of God tell me!

Messenger.   —If these are your reasons for not going home.

Oedipus.   I tell you, I fear the oracle may come true.

Messenger.   And guilt may come upon you through your parents?

Oedipus.   That is the dread that is always in my heart.

Messenger.   Can you not see that all your fears are groundless?

Oedipus.   How can you say that? They are my parents, surely?   100

Messenger.   Polybos was not your father.

Oedipus.   Not my father?

Messenger.   No more your father than the man speaking to you.

Oedipus.   But you are nothing to me!

Messenger.   Neither was he.

Oedipus.   Then why did he call me son?

Messenger.   I will tell you:
  Long ago he had you from my hands, as a gift.

Oedipus.   Then how could he love me so, if I was not his?

Messenger.   He had no children, and his heart turned to you.

Oedipus.   What of you? Did you buy me? Did you find me by chance?

Messenger.   I came upon you in the crooked pass of Kithairon.

Oedipus.   And what were you doing there?

Messenger.   Tending my flocks   110

Oedipus.   A wandering shepherd?

Messenger.   But your savior, son, that day.

Oedipus.   From what did you save me?

Messenger.   Your ankles should tell you that.

Oedipus.   Ah, stranger, why do you speak of that childhood pain?

Messenger.   I cut the bonds that tied your ankles together.

Oedipus.   I have had the mark as long as I can remember.

Messenger.   That was why you were given the name you bear.[15]

Oedipus.   God! Was it my father or my mother who did it?
  Tell me!

Messenger.   I do not know. The man who gave you to me
  Can tell you better than I.   120

Oedipus.   It was not you that found me, but another?

Messenger.   It was another shepherd gave you to me.

Oedipus.   Who was he? Can you tell me who he was?

Messenger.   I think he was said to be one of Laïos' people.

Oedipus.   You mean the Laïos who was king here years ago?

Messenger.   Yes; King Laïos; and the man was one of his herdsmen.

Oedipus.   Is he still alive? Can I see him?

Messenger.   These men here
  Know best about such things.

---

[15] Oedipus literally means "swollen-foot."

Oedipus.   Does anyone here
   Know this shepherd that he is talking about?
   Have you seen him in the fields, or in the town?   130
   If you have, tell me. It is time things were made plain.
Choragos.   I think the man he means is that same shepherd
   You have already asked to see. Iocastê perhaps
   Could tell you something.
Oedipus.   Do you know anything
   About him, Lady? Is he the man we have summoned?
   Is that the man this shepherd means?
Iocastê.   Why think of him?
   Forget this herdsman. Forget it all.
   This talk is a waste of time.
Oedipus.   How can you say that?
   When the clues to my true birth are in my hands?
Iocastê.   For God's love, let us have no more questioning!   140
   Is your life nothing to you?
   My own is pain enough for me to bear.
Oedipus.   You need not worry. Suppose my mother a slave,
   And born of slaves: no baseness can touch you.
Iocastê.   Listen to me, I beg you: do not do this thing!
Oedipus.   I will not listen; the truth must be made known.
Iocastê.   Everything that I say is for your own good!
Oedipus.   My own good
   Snaps my patience, then; I want none of it.
Iocastê.   You are fatally wrong! May you never learn who you are!
Oedipus.   Go, one of you, and bring the shepherd here.   150
   Let us leave this woman to brag of her royal name.
Iocastê.   Ah, miserable!
   That is the only word I have for you now.
   That is the only word I can ever have.

[*Exit into the palace.*]

Choragos.   Why has she left us, Oedipus? Why has she gone
   In such a passion of sorrow? I fear this silence:
   Something dreadful may come of it.
Oedipus.   Let it come!
   However base my birth, I must know about it.
   The Queen, like a woman, is perhaps ashamed
   To think of my low origin. But I   160
   Am a child of Luck; I can not be dishonored.
   Luck is my mother; the passing months, my brothers,
   Have seen me rich and poor.
                          If this is so,

How could I wish that I were someone else?
How could I not be glad to know my birth?

Ode III

Chorus.   If ever the coming time were known   [*Strophe*]
To my heart's pondering,
Kithairon, now by Heaven I see the torches
At the festival of the next full moon,
And see the dance, and hear the choir sing
A grace to your gentle shade:
Mountain where Oedipus was found,
O mountain guard of a noble race!
May the god who heals us lend his aid,
And let that glory come to pass   10
For our king's cradling-ground.

Of the nymphs that flower beyond the years,   [*Antistrophe*]
Who bore you, royal child,
To Pan of the hills or the timberline Apollo,
Cold in delight where the upland clears,
Or Hermês for whom Kyllenê's heights are piled?[16]
Or flushed as evening cloud,
Great Dionysos, roamer of mountains,
He—was it he who found you there,
And caught you up in his own proud   20
Arms from the sweet god-ravisher
Who laughed by the Muses' fountains?

Scene IV

Oedipus.   Sirs: though I do not know the man,
I think I see him coming, this shepherd we want:
He is old, like our friend here, and the men
Bringing him seem to be servants of my house.
But you can tell, if you have ever seen him.

[*Enter Shepherd escorted by servants.*]

Choragos.   I know him, he was Laïos' man. You can trust him.
Oedipus.   Tell me first, you from Corinth: is this the shepherd
We were discussing?
Messenger.   This is the very man.

---

[16] Hermês, the herald of the Olympian gods, was born on the mountain of Kyllenê.

Oedipus [*to Shepherd*]. Come here. No, look at me. You must answer
  Everything I ask. You belonged to Laïos?   10
Shepherd.   Yes: born his slave, brought up in his house.
Oedipus.   Tell me what kind of work did you do for him?
Shepherd.   I was a shepherd of his, most of my life.
Oedipus.   Where mainly did you go for pasturage?
Shepherd.   Sometimes Kithairon, sometimes the hills near-by.
Oedipus.   Do you remember ever seeing this man out there?
Shepherd.   What would he be doing there? This man?
Oedipus.   This man standing here. Have you ever seen him before?
Shepherd.   No. At least, not to my recollection.
Messenger.   And that is not strange, my lord. But I'll refresh   20
  His memory: he must remember when we two
  Spent three whole seasons together, March to September,
  On Kithairon or thereabouts. He had two flocks;
  I had one. Each autumn I'd drive mine home
  And he would go back with his to Laïos' sheepfold.—
  Is this not true, just as I have described it?
Shepherd.   True, yes; but it was all so long ago.
Messenger.   Well, then: do you remember, back in those days
  That you gave me a baby boy to bring up as my own?
Shepherd.   What if I did? What are you trying to say?   30
Messenger.   King Oedipus was once that little child.
Shepherd.   Damn you, hold your tongue!
Oedipus.   No more of that!
  It is your tongue needs watching, not this man's.
Shepherd.   My King, my Master, what is it I have done wrong?
Oedipus.   You have not answered his question about the boy.
Shepherd.   He does not know . . . He is only making trouble . . .
Oedipus.   Come, speak plainly, or it will go hard with you.
Shepherd.   In God's name, do not torture an old man!
Oedipus.   Come here, one of you; bind his arms behind him.
Shepherd.   Unhappy king! What more do you wish to learn?   40
Oedipus.   Did you give this man the child he speaks of?
Shepherd.   I did.
  And I would to God I had died that very day.
Oedipus.   You will die now unless you speak the truth.
Shepherd.   Yet if I speak the truth, I am worse than dead.
Oedipus.   Very well; since you insist on delaying—
Shepherd.   No! I have told you already that I gave him the boy.
Oedipus.   Where did you get him? From your house? From somewhere
  else?
Shepherd.   Not from mine, no. A man gave him to me.
Oedipus.   Is that man here? Do you know whose slave he was?
Shepherd.   For God's love, my King, do not ask me any more!   50

Oedipus.   You are a dead man if I have to ask you again.
Shepherd.   Then . . . Then the child was from the palace of Laïos.
Oedipus.   A slave child? or a child of his own line?
Shepherd.   Ah, I am on the brink of dreadful speech!
Oedipus.   And I of dreadful hearing. Yet I must hear.
Shepherd.   If you must be told, then . . .

                           They said it was Laïos' child,
But it is your wife who can tell you about that.
Oedipus.   My wife!—Did she give it to you?
Shepherd.   My lord, she did.
Oedipus.   Do you know why?
Shepherd.   I was told to get rid of it.
Oedipus.   An unspeakable mother!
Shepherd.   There had been prophecies . . .   60
Oedipus.   Tell me.
Shepherd.   It was said that the boy would kill his own father.
Oedipus.   Then why did you give him over to this old man?
Shepherd.   I pitied the baby, my King,
And I thought that this man would take him far away
To his own country.

                 He saved him—but for what a fate!
For if you are what this man says you are,
No man living is more wretched than Oedipus.
Oedipus.   Ah God!
It was true!

        All the prophecies!

                 —Now,
O Light, may I look on you for the last time!   70
I, Oedipus,
Oedipus, damned in his birth, in his marriage damned,
Damned in the blood he shed with his own hand!

[*He rushes into the palace.*]

Ode IV

Chorus.   Alas for the seed of men.   [*Strophe 1*]

   What measure shall I give these generations
   That breathe on the void and are void
   And exist and do not exist?

   Who bears more weight of joy
   Than mass of sunlight shifting in images,
   Or who shall make his thought stay on
   That down time drifts away?

Your splendor is all fallen.

O naked brow of wrath and tears,   10
O change of Oedipus!
I who saw your days call no man blest—
Your great days like ghosts gone.

That mind was a strong bow.   [*Antistrophe 1*]

Deep, how deep you drew it then, hard archer,
At a dim fearful range,
And brought dear glory down!

You overcame the stranger—
The virgin with her hooking lion claws—
And though death sang, stood like a tower   20
To make pale Thebes take heart.

Fortress against our sorrow!

Divine king, giver of laws,
Majestic Oedipus!
No prince in Thebes had ever such renown,
No prince won such grace of power.

And now of all men ever known   [*Strophe 2*]
Most pitiful is this man's story:
His fortunes are most changed, his state
Fallen to a low slave's   30
Ground under bitter fate.

O Oedipus, most royal one!
The great door that expelled you to the light
Gave at night—ah, gave night to your glory:
As to the father, to the fathering son.

All understood too late.

How could that queen whom Laïos won,
The garden that he harrowed at his height,
Be silent when that act was done?

But all eyes fail before time's eye,   [*Antistrophe 2*]
All actions come to justice there   41
Though never willed, though far down the deep past,
Your bed, your dread sirings,
Are brought to book at last.

Child by Laïos doomed to die,
Then doomed to lose that fortunate little death,
Would God you never took breath in this air
That with my wailing lips I take to cry:

For I weep the world's outcast.

I was blind, and now I can tell why: 50
Asleep, for you had given ease of breath
To Thebes, while the false years went by.

Exodos

[*Enter, from the palace, Second Messenger.*]

Second Messenger.   Elders of Thebes, most honored in this land,
What horrors are yours to see and hear, what weight
Of sorrow to be endured, if, true to your birth,
You venerate the line of Labdakos!
I think neither Istros nor Phasis, those great rivers,
Could purify this place of the corruption
It shelters now, or soon must bring to light—
Evil not done unconsciously, but willed.

The greatest griefs are those we cause ourselves.
Choragos.   Surely, friend, we have grief enough already;   10
What new sorrow do you mean?
Second Messenger.   The Queen is dead.
Choragos.   Iocastê? Dead? But at whose hand?
Second Messenger.   Her own.
The full horror of what happened you can not know,
For you did not see it; but I, who did, will tell you
As clearly as I can how she met her death.

When she had left us,
In passionate silence, passing through the court,
She ran to her apartment in the house,
Her hair clutched by the fingers of both hands.

She closed the doors behind her; then, by that bed   20
Where long ago the fatal son was conceived—
The son who should bring about his father's death—
We heard her call upon Laïos, dead so many years,
And heard her wail for the double fruit of her marriage,
A husband by her husband, children by her child.

Exactly how she died I do not know:
For Oedipus burst in moaning and would not let us
Keep vigil to the end: it was by him
As he stormed about the room that our eyes were caught.
From one to another of us he went, begging a sword,   30
Cursing the wife who was not his wife, the mother
Whose womb had carried his own children and himself.
I do not know: it was none of us aided him,
But surely one of the gods was in control!
For with a dreadful cry
He hurled his weight, as though wrenched out of himself,
At the twin doors: the bolts gave, and he rushed in.
And there we saw her hanging, her body swaying
From the cruel cord she had noosed about her neck.
A great sob broke from him, heartbreaking to hear,   40
As he loosed the rope and lowered her to the ground.

I would blot out from my mind what happened next!
For the King ripped from her gown the golden brooches
That were her ornament, and raised them, and plunged them down
Straight into his own eyeballs, crying, "No more,
No more shall you look on the misery about me,
The horrors of my own doing! Too long have you known
The faces of those whom I should never have seen,
Too long been blind to those for whom I was searching!
From this hour, go in darkness!" And as he spoke,   50
He struck at his eyes—not once, but many times;
And the blood spattered his beard,
Bursting from his ruined sockets like red hail.

So from the unhappiness of two this evil has sprung,
A curse on the man and woman alike. The old
Happiness of the house of Labdakos
Was happiness enough: where is it today?
It is all wailing and ruin, disgrace, death—all
The misery of mankind that has a name—
And it is wholly and for ever theirs.   60
Choragos.   Is he in agony still? Is there no rest for him?
Second Messenger.   He is calling for someone to lead him to the gates
So that all the children of Kadmos may look upon
His father's murderer, his mother's—no,
I can not say it!
               And then he will leave Thebes,
Self-exiled, in order that the curse
Which he himself pronounced may depart from the house.
He is weak, and there is none to lead him,

So terrible is his suffering.
                                   But you will see:
Look, the doors are opening; in a moment   70
You will see a thing that would crush a heart of stone.

[The central door is opened; Oedipus, blinded, is led in.]

Choragos.   Dreadful indeed for men to see.
    Never have my own eyes
    Looked on a sight so full of fear.

    Oedipus!
    What madness came upon you, what daemon
    Leaped on your life with heavier
    Punishment than a mortal man can bear?
    No: I can not even
    Look at you, poor ruined one.   80
    And I would speak, question, ponder,
    If I were able. No.
    You make me shudder.
Oedipus.   God. God.
    Is there a sorrow greater?
    Where shall I find harbor in this world?
    My voice is hurled far on a dark wind.
    What has God done to me?
Choragos.   Too terrible to think of, or to see.

Oedipus.   O cloud of night,   *[Strophe 1]*
    Never to be turned away: night coming on,   91
    I can not tell how: night like a shroud!

    My fair winds brought me here.
                                   Oh God. Again
    The pain of the spikes where I had sight,
    The flooding pain
    Of memory, never to be gouged out.
Choragos.   This is not strange.
    You suffer it all twice over, remorse in pain,
    Pain in remorse.

Oedipus.   Ah dear friend   *[Antistrophe 1]*
    Are you faithful even yet, you alone?   101
    Are you still standing near me, will you stay here,
    Patient, to care for the blind?
                                   The blind man!

Yet even blind I know who it is attends me,
By the voice's tone—
Though my new darkness hide the comforter.
Choragos.   Oh fearful act!
What god was it drove you to rake black
Night across your eyes?

Oedipus.   Apollo. Apollo. Dear   [*Strophe 2*]
Children, the god was Apollo.   111
He brought my sick, sick fate upon me.
But the blinding hand was my own!
How could I bear to see
When all my sight was horror everywhere?
Choragos.   Everywhere; that is true.
Oedipus.   And now what is left?
Images? Love? A greeting even,
Sweet to the senses? Is there anything?
Ah no, friends: lead me away.   120
Lead me away from Thebes.
                          Lead the great wreck
And hell of Oedipus, whom the gods hate.
Choragos.   Your fate is clear, you are not blind to that.
Would God you had never found it out!

Oedipus.   Death take the man who unbound   [*Antistrophe 2*]
My feet on that hillside
And delivered me from death to life! What life?
If only I had died,
This weight of monstrous doom
Could not have dragged me and my darlings down.   130
Choragos.   I would have wished the same.
Oedipus.   Oh never to have come here
With my father's blood upon me! Never
To have been the man they call his mother's husband!
Oh accurst! Oh child of evil,
To have entered that wretched bed—
                          the selfsame one!
More primal than sin itself, this fell to me.
Choragos.   I do not know how I can answer you.
You were better dead than alive and blind.
Oedipus.   Do not counsel me any more. This punishment   140
That I have laid upon myself is just.
If I had eyes,
I do not know how I could bear the sight
Of my father, when I came to the house of Death,

Or my mother: for I have sinned against them both
So vilely that I could not make my peace
By strangling my own life.
              Or do you think my children,
Born as they were born, would be sweet to my eyes?
Ah never, never! Nor this town with its high walls,
Nor the holy images of the gods.
                  For I,   150
Thrice miserable!—Oedipus, noblest of all the line
Of Kadmos, have condemned myself to enjoy
These things no more, by my own malediction
Expelling that man whom the gods declared
To be a defilement in the house of Laïos.
After exposing the rankness of my own guilt,
How could I look men frankly in the eyes?
No, I swear it,
If I could have stifled my hearing at its source,
I would have done it and made all this body   160
A tight cell of misery, blank to light and sound:
So I should have been safe in a dark agony
Beyond all recollection.
                Ah Kithairon!
Why did you shelter me? When I was cast upon you,
Why did I not die? Then I should never
Have shown the world my execrable birth.

Ah Polybos! Corinth, city that I believed
The ancient seat of my ancestors: how fair
I seemed, your child! And all the while this evil
Was cancerous within me!
                For I am sick   170
In my daily life, sick in my origin.

O three roads, dark ravine, woodland and way
Where three roads met: you, drinking my father's blood,
My own blood, spilled by my own hand: can you remember
The unspeakable things I did there, and the things
I went on from there to do?
                O marriage, marriage!
The act that engendered me, and again the act
Performed by the son in the same bed—
                Ah, the net
Of incest, mingling fathers, brothers, sons,
With brides, wives, mothers; the last evil   180
That can be known by men: no tongue can say

How evil!

        No. For the love of God, conceal me
Somewhere far from Thebes; or kill me; or hurl me
Into the sea, away from men's eyes for ever.

Come, lead me. You need not fear to touch me.
Of all men, I alone can bear this guilt.

[*Enter Creon.*]

Choragos.   We are not the ones to decide; but Creon here
  May fitly judge of what you ask. He only
  Is left to protect the city in your place.
Oedipus.   Alas, how can I speak to him? What right have I   190
  To beg his courtesy whom I have deeply wronged?
Creon.   I have not come to mock you, Oedipus,
  Or to reproach you, either.
  [*To attendants.*]   —You, standing there:
  If you have lost all respect for man's dignity,
  At least respect the flame of Lord Helios:
  Do not allow this pollution to show itself
  Openly here, an affront to the earth
  And Heaven's rain and the light of day. No, take him
  Into the house as quickly as you can.
  For it is proper   200
  That only the close kindred see his grief.
Oedipus.   I pray you in God's name, since your courtesy
  Ignores my dark expectation, visiting
  With mercy this man of all men most execrable:
  Give me what I ask—for your good, not for mine.
Creon.   And what is it that you would have me do?
Oedipus.   Drive me out of this country as quickly as may be
  To a place where no human voice can ever greet me.
Creon.   I should have done that before now—only,
  God's will had not been wholly revealed to me.   210
Oedipus.   But his command is plain: the parricide
  Must be destroyed. I am that evil man.
Creon.   That is the sense of it, yes; but as things are,
  We had best discover clearly what is to be done.
Oedipus.   You would learn more about a man like me?
Creon.   You are ready now to listen to the god.
Oedipus.   I will listen. But it is to you
  That I must turn for help. I beg you, hear me.

The woman in there—
Give her whatever funeral you think proper: 220

She is your sister.
                —But let me go, Creon!
Let me purge my father's Thebes of the pollution
Of my living here, and go out to the wild hills,
To Kithairon, that has won such fame with me,
The tomb my mother and father appointed for me,
And let me die there, as they willed I should.
And yet I know
Death will not ever come to me through sickness
Or in any natural way: I have been preserved
For some unthinkable fate. But let that be.   230
As for my sons, you need not care for them.
They are men, they will find some way to live.
But my poor daughters, who have shared my table,
Who never before have been parted from their father—
Take care of them, Creon; do this for me.
And will you let me touch them with my hands
A last time, and let us weep together?
Be kind, my lord,
Great prince, be kind!
                     Could I but touch them,
They would be mine again, as when I had my eyes.   240

[*Enter Antigone and Ismene, attended.*]

Ah, God!
Is it my dearest children I hear weeping?
Has Creon pitied me and sent my daughters?
Creon.   Yes, Oedipus: I knew that they were dear to you
In the old days, and know you must love them still.
Oedipus.   May God bless you for this—and be a friendlier
Guardian to you than he has been to me!

Children, where are you?
Come quickly to my hands: they are your brother's—
Hands that have brought your father's once clear eyes   250
To this way of seeing—
                  Ah dearest ones,
I had neither sight nor knowledge then, your father
By the woman who was the source of his own life!
And I weep for you—having no strength to see you—,
I weep for you when I think of the bitterness
That men will visit upon you all your lives.
What homes, what festivals can you attend
Without being forced to depart again in tears?

And when you come to marriageable age,
Where is the man, my daughters, who would dare   260
Risk the bane that lies on all my children?
Is there any evil wanting? Your father killed
His father; sowed the womb of her who bore him;
Engendered you at the fount of his own existence!
That is what they will say of you.
                                        Then whom
Can you ever marry? There are no bridegrooms for you,
And your lives must wither away in sterile dreaming.
O Creon, son of Menoikeus!
You are the only father my daughters have,
Since we, their parents, are both of us gone for ever.   270
They are your own blood: you will not let them
Fall into beggary and loneliness;
You will keep them from the miseries that are mine!
Take pity on them; see, they are only children,
Friendless except for you. Promise me this,
Great Prince, and give me your hand in token of it.

[*Creon clasps his right hand.*]

Children:
I could say much, if you could understand me,
But as it is, I have only this prayer for you:
Live where you can, be as happy as you can—   280
Happier, please God, than God has made your father!
Creon.   Enough. You have wept enough. Now go within.
Oedipus.   I must; but it is hard.
Creon.   Time eases all things.
Oedipus.   But you must promise—
Creon.   Say what you desire.
Oedipus.   Send me from Thebes!
Creon.   God grant that I may!
Oedipus.   But since God hates me . . .
Creon.   No, he will grant your wish.
Oedipus.   You promise?
Creon.   I can not speak beyond my knowledge.
Oedipus.   Then lead me in.
Creon.   Come now, and leave your children.
Oedipus.   No! Do not take them from me!
Creon.   Think no longer
That you are in command here, but rather think   290
How, when you were, you served your own destruction.

[*Exeunt into the house all but the Chorus; the Choragos chants directly to the audience.*]

Choragos.   Men of Thebes: look upon Oedipus.

This is the king who solved the famous riddle
And towered up, most powerful of men.
No mortal eyes but looked on him with envy,
Yet in the end ruin swept over him.
Let every man in mankind's frailty
Consider his last day; and let none
Presume on his good fortune until he find
Life, at his death, a memory without pain.   300

QUESTIONS
1.   How does the Prologue establish the mood and theme of the play? What aspects of Oedipus's character are revealed there?   **2.**   Sophocles's audience knew the Oedipus story as you, for instance, know the story of the crucifixion. In the absence of suspense, what literary devices serve to hold the audience's attention?   **3.**   To what extent and in what ways does the chorus contribute to the dramatic development and tension of the play?

WRITING TOPICS
1.   Could Oedipus have avoided the tragic outcome of this drama? What characteristics of Sophocles's world view are suggested by your answer? Is our behavior in the world governed by free will or is our behavior determined? In view of your answers to the preceding questions, of what is Oedipus guilty?   **2.**   The play embodies a pattern of figurative and literal allusions to darkness and light, to vision and blindness. How does that figurative language function, and what relationship does it bear to Oedipus's self-inflicted punishment?

Pygmalion[1]   1913

BERNARD SHAW   [1856–1950]

Preface to Pygmalion

A Professor of Phonetics

As will be seen later on, Pygmalion needs, not a preface, but a sequel, which
I have supplied in its due place.

The English have no respect for their language, and will not teach their
children to speak it. They cannot spell it because they have nothing to spell it
with but an old foreign alphabet of which only the consonants—and not all of
them—have any agreed speech value. Consequently no man can teach himself
what it should sound like from reading it; and it is impossible for an Englishman
to open his mouth without making some other Englishman despise him. Most
European languages are now accessible in black and white to foreigners: English
and French are not thus accessible even to Englishmen and Frenchmen. The
reformer we need most today is an energetic enthusiast: that is why I have made
such a one the hero of a popular play.

There have been heroes of that kind crying in the wilderness for many years
past. When I became interested in the subject towards the end of the eighteen-
seventies, the illustrious Alexander Melville Bell, the inventor of Visible Speech,
had emigrated to Canada, where his son invented the telephone; but Alexander
J. Ellis was still a London Patriarch, with an impressive head always covered by
a velvet skull cap, for which he would apologize to public meetings in a very
courtly manner. He and Tito Pagliardini, another phonetic veteran, were men
whom it was impossible to dislike. Henry Sweet, then a young man, lacked
their sweetness of character: he was about as conciliatory to conventional mortals
as Ibsen or Samuel Butler. His great ability as a phonetician (he was, I think,
the best of them all at his job) would have entitled him to high official recognition, and perhaps enabled him to popularize his subject, but for his Satanic
contempt for all academic dignitaries and persons in general who thought more
of Greek than of phonetics. Once, in the days when the Imperial Institute rose

---

[1] In Greek mythology, Pygmalion sculpted a statue of the ideal woman and promptly fell in love
with it. Aphrodite, the goddess of love, was so moved by his devotion to the statue that she gave
it life as Galatea. Pygmalion then married Galatea, his own creation. Note that this play also
embodies aspects of the Cinderella story. The ending of the play, however, differs markedly from
those of the Greek myth and the fairy tale.

in South Kensington, and Joseph Chamberlain was booming the Empire, I induced the editor of a leading monthly review to commission an article from Sweet on the imperial importance of his subject. When it arrived, it contained nothing but a savagely derisive attack on a professor of language and literature whose chair Sweet regarded as proper to a phonetic expert only. The article, being libellous, had to be returned as impossible; and I had to renounce my dream of dragging its author into the limelight. When I met him afterwards, for the first time for many years, I found to my astonishment that he, who had been a quite tolerably presentable young man, had actually managed by sheer scorn to alter his personal appearance until he had become a sort of walking repudiation of Oxford and all its traditions. It must have been largely in his own despite that he was squeezed into something called a Readership of phonetics there. The future of phonetics rests probably with his pupils, who all swore by him; but nothing could bring the man himself into any sort of compliance with the university to which he nevertheless clung by divine right in an intensely Oxonian way. I daresay his papers, if he has left any, include some satires that may be published without too destructive results fifty years hence. He was, I believe, not in the least an ill-natured man: very much the opposite, I should say; but he would not suffer fools gladly; and to him all scholars who were not rabid phoneticians were fools.

Those who knew him will recognize in my third act the allusion to the Current Shorthand in which he used to write postcards. It may be acquired from a four and sixpenny manual published by the Clarendon Press. The postcards which Mrs. Higgins describes are such as I have received from Sweet. I would decipher a sound which a cockney would represent by *zerr*, and a Frenchman by *seu*, and then write demanding with some heat what on earth it meant. Sweet, with boundless contempt for my stupidity, would reply that it not only meant but obviously was the word Result, as no other word containing that sound, and capable of making sense with the context, existed in any language spoken on earth. That less expert mortals should require fuller indications was beyond Sweet's patience. Therefore, though the whole point of his Current Shorthand is that it can express every sound in the language perfectly, vowels as well as consonants, and that your hand has to make no stroke except the easy and current ones with which you write m, n, and u, l, p, and q, scribbling them at whatever angle comes easiest to you, his unfortunate determination to make this remarkable and quite legible script serve also as a shorthand reduced it in his own practice to the most inscrutable of cryptograms. His true objective was the provision of a full, accurate, legible script for our language; but he was led past that by his contempt for the popular Pitman system of shorthand, which he called the Pitfall system. The triumph of Pitman was a triumph of business organization: there was a weekly paper to persuade you to learn Pitman: there were cheap textbooks and exercise books and transcripts of speeches for you to copy, and schools where experienced teachers coached you up to the necessary proficiency. Sweet could not organize his market in that fashion. He might as well have been the Sybil who tore up the leaves of prophecy that nobody would attend to. The four and sixpenny manual, mostly in his lithographed hand-writing, that was never vulgarly advertized, may perhaps some day be taken up by a syndicate and pushed upon the public as The Times pushed the Ency-clopædia Britannica; but until then it will certainly not prevail against Pitman. I have bought three copies of it during my lifetime; and I am informed by the publishers that its cloistered existence is still a steady and healthy one. I actually learned the system two several times; and yet the shorthand in which I am writing these lines is Pitman's. And the reason is, that my secretary cannot transcribe Sweet, having been perforce taught in the schools of Pitman. In America I could use the commercially organized Gregg shorthand, which has taken a hint from Sweet by making its letters writable (current, Sweet would have called them) instead of having to be geometrically drawn like Pitman's; but all these systems, including Sweet's, are spoilt by making them available for verbatim reporting, in which complete and exact spelling and word division are impossible. A complete and exact phonetic script is neither practicable nor necessary for ordinary use; but if we enlarge our alphabet to the Russian size, and make our spelling as phonetic as Spanish, the advance will be prodigious.

Pygmalion Higgins is not a portrait of Sweet, to whom the adventure of Eliza Doolittle would have been impossible; still, as will be seen, there are touches of Sweet in the play. With Higgins's physique and temperament Sweet might have set the Thames on fire. As it was, he impressed himself professionally on Europe to an extent that made his comparative personal obscurity, and the failure of Oxford to do justice to his eminence, a puzzle to foreign specialists in his subject. I do not blame Oxford, because I think Oxford is quite right in demanding a certain social amenity from its nurslings (heaven knows it is not exorbitant in its requirement!); for although I well know how hard it is for a man of genius with a seriously underrated subject to maintain serene and kindly relations with the men who underrate it, and who keep all the best places for less important subjects which they profess without originality and sometimes without much capacity for them, still, if he overwhelms them with wrath and disdain, he cannot expect them to heap honors on him.

Of the later generations of phoneticians I know little. Among them towered Robert Bridges, to whom perhaps Higgins may owe his Miltonic sympathies, though here again I must disclaim all portraiture. But if the play makes the public aware that there are such people as phoneticians, and that they are among the most important people in England at present, it will serve its turn.

I wish to boast that Pygmalion has been an extremely successful play, both on stage and on screen, all over Europe and North America as well as at home. It is so intensely and deliberately didactic, and its subject is esteemed so dry, that I delight in throwing it at the heads of the wiseacres who repeat the parrot cry that art should never be didactic. It goes to prove my contention that great art can never be anything else.

Finally, and for the encouragement of people troubled with accents that cut them off from all high employment, I may add that the change wrought by Professor Higgins in the flower girl is neither impossible nor uncommon. The modern concierge's daughter who fulfills her ambition by playing the Queen of Spain in Ruy Blas at the Théâtre Français is only one of the many thousands of men and women who have sloughed off their native dialects and acquired a new tongue. Our West End shop assistants and domestic servants are bilingual. But the thing has to be done scientifically, or the last state of the aspirant may be worse than the first. An honest slum dialect is more tolerable than the attempts of phonetically untaught persons to imitate the plutocracy. Ambitious flower-girls who read this play must not imagine that they can pass themselves off as fine ladies by untutored imitation. They must learn their alphabet over again, and differently, from a phonetic expert. Imitation will only make them ridiculous.

Note for Technicians. A complete representation of the play as printed in this edition is technically possible only on the cinema screen or on stages furnished with exceptionally elaborate machinery. For ordinary theatrical use the scenes separated by rows of asterisks are to be omitted.

In the dialogue an e upside down indicates the indefinite vowel, sometimes called obscure or neutral, for which, though it is one of the commonest sounds in English speech, our wretched alphabet has no letter.

Act I

London at 11.15 P. M. *Torrents of heavy summer rain. Cab whistles blowing frantically in all directions. Pedestrians running for shelter into the portico of St. Paul's church (not Wren's cathedral but Inigo Jones's church in Covent Garden vegetable market), among them a lady and her daughter in evening dress. All are peering out gloomily at the rain, except one man with his back turned to the rest, wholly preoccupied with a notebook in which he is writing.*

The church clock strikes the first quarter.

The Daughter *(in the space between the central pillars, close to the one on her left)*.   I'm getting chilled to the bone. What can Freddy be doing all this time? He's been gone twenty minutes.

The Mother *(on her daughter's right)*.   Not so long. But he ought to have got us a cab by this.

A Bystander *(on the lady's right)*.   He wont get no cab not until half-past eleven, missus, when they come back after dropping their theatre fares.

The Mother.   But we must have a cab. We cant stand here until half-past eleven. It's too bad.

The Bystander.   Well, it aint my fault, missus.

The Daughter.   If Freddy had a bit of gumption, he would have got one at the theatre door.

The Mother.   What could he have done, poor boy?

The Daughter.   Other people got cabs. Why couldnt he?

Freddy rushes in out of the rain from the Southampton Street side, and comes between them closing a dripping umbrella. He is a young man of twenty, in evening dress, very wet round the ankles.

The Daughter.   Well, havnt you got a cab?

Freddy.   There's not one to be had for love or money.

The Mother.   Oh, Freddy, there must be one. You cant have tried.

The Daughter.   It's too tiresome. Do you expect us to go and get one ourselves?

Freddy.   I tell you theyre all engaged. The rain was so sudden: nobody was prepared; and everybody had to take a cab. Ive been to Charing Cross one way and nearly to Ludgate Circus the other; and they were all engaged.

The Mother.   Did you try Trafalgar Square?

Freddy.   There wasn't one at Trafalgar Square.

The Daughter.   Did you try?

Freddy.   I tried as far as Charing Cross Station. Did you expect me to walk to Hammersmith?

The Daughter.   You havnt tried at all.

The Mother.   You really are very helpless, Freddy. Go again; and dont come back until you have found a cab.

Freddy.   I shall simply get soaked for nothing.

The Daughter.   And what about us? Are we to stay here all night in this draught, with next to nothing on? You selfish pig—

Freddy.   Oh, very well: I'll go, I'll go. (*He opens his umbrella and dashes off Strandwards, but comes into collision with a flower girl who is hurrying in for shelter, knocking her basket out of her hands. A blinding flash of lightning, followed instantly by a rattling peal of thunder, orchestrates the incident.*)

The Flower Girl.   Nah then, Freddy: look wh' y' gowin, deah.

Freddy.   Sorry. (*He rushes off.*)

The Flower Girl (*picking up her scattered flowers and replacing them in the basket.*)   Theres menners f' yer! Tə-oo banches o voylets trod into the mad. (*She sits down on the plinth of the column, sorting her flowers, on the lady's right. She is not at all a romantic figure. She is perhaps eighteen, perhaps twenty, hardly older. She wears a little sailor hat of black straw that has long been exposed to the dust and soot of London and has seldom if ever been brushed. Her hair needs washing rather badly: its mousy color can hardly be natural. She wears a shoddy black coat that reaches nearly to her knees and is shaped to her waist. She has a brown skirt with a coarse apron. Her boots are much the worse for wear. She is no doubt as clean as she can afford to be; but compared to the ladies she is very dirty. Her features are no worse than* *theirs; but their condition leaves something to be desired; and she needs the services of a dentist.)*

The Mother.   How do you know that my son's name is Freddy, pray?

The Flower Girl.   Ow, eez yə-ooa san, is e? Wal, fewd dan y' də-ooty bawmz a mather should, eed now bettern to spawl, a pore gel's flahrzn than ran awy athaht pyin. Will ye-oo py me f'them? *(Here, with apologies, this desperate attempt to represent her dialect without a phonetic alphabet must be abandoned as unintelligible outside London.)*

The Daughter.   Do nothing of the sort, mother. The idea!

The Mother.   Please allow me, Clara. Have you any pennies?

The Daughter.   No, Ive nothing smaller than sixpence.

The Flower Girl *(hopefully)*.   I can give you change for a tanner, kind lady.

The Mother *(to Clara)*.   Give it to me. *(Clara parts reluctantly.)* Now *(to the girl)*. This is for your flowers.

The Flower Girl.   Thank you kindly, lady.

The Daughter.   Make her give you the change. These things are only a penny a bunch.

The Mother.   Do hold your tongue, Clara. *(To the girl.)* You can keep the change.

The Flower Girl.   Oh, thank you, lady.

The Mother.   Now tell me how you know that young gentleman's name.

The Flower.   I didnt.

The Mother.   I heard you call him by it. Dont try to deceive me.

The Flower Girl *(protesting)*.   Who's trying to deceive you? I called him Freddy or Charlie same as you might yourself if you was talking to a stranger and wished to be pleasant.

The Daughter.   Sixpence thrown away! Really, mamma, you might have spared Freddy that. *(She retreats in disgust behind the pillar.)*

An elderly gentleman of the amiable military type rushes into the shelter, and closes a dripping umbrella. He is in the same plight as Freddy, very wet about the ankles. He is in evening dress, with a light overcoat. He takes the place left vacant by the daughter.

The Gentleman.   Phew!

The Mother *(to the gentleman)*.   Oh, sir, is there any sign of its stopping?

The Gentleman.   I'm afraid not. It started worse than ever about two minutes ago.

(He goes to the plinth beside the flower girl; puts up his foot on it; and stoops to turn down his trouser ends.)

The Mother.   Oh dear! *(She retires sadly and joins her daughter.)*

The Flower Girl *(taking advantage of the military gentleman's proximity to establish friendly relations with him)*.   If it's worse, it's a sign it's nearly over. So cheer up, Captain; and buy a flower off a poor girl.

The Gentleman.   I'm sorry. I havnt any change.

The Flower Girl.   I can give you change, Captain.

The Gentleman.   For a sovereign? Ive nothing less.

The Flower Girl.   Garn! Oh do buy a flower off me, Captain. I can change half-a-crown. Take this for tuppence.

The Gentleman.   Now dont be troublesome: theres a good girl. (*Trying his pockets.*) I really havnt any change—Stop: heres three hapence, if thats any use to you. (*He retreats to the other pillar.*)

The Flower Girl. (*disappointed, but thinking three half-pence better than nothing*).   Thank you, sir.

The Bystander (*to the girl*).   You be careful: give him a flower for it. Theres a bloke here behind taking down every blessed word youre saying. (*All turn to the man who is taking notes.*)

The Flower Girl (*springing up terrified*).   I aint done nothing wrong by speaking to the gentleman. Ive a right to sell flowers if I keep off the kerb. (*Hysterically.*) I'm a respectable girl: so help me, I never spoke to him except to ask him to buy a flower off me.

General hubbub, mostly sympathetic to the flower girl, but deprecating her excessive sensibility. Cries of Dont start hollerin. Who's hurting you? Nobody's going to touch you. Whats the good of fussing? Steady on. Easy easy, etc., *come from the elderly staid spectators, who pat her comfortingly. Less patient ones bid her shut her head, or ask her roughly what is wrong with her. A remoter group, not knowing what the matter is, crowd in and increase the noise with question and answer:* Whats the row? What-she do? Where is he? A tec taking her down. What! him? Yes: him over there: Took money off the gentleman, etc.

The Flower Girl (*breaking through them to the gentleman, crying wildly*).   Oh, sir, dont let him charge me. You dunno what it means to me. Theyll take away my character and drive me on the streets for speaking to gentlemen. They—

The Note Taker (*coming forward on her right, the rest crowding after him*).   There! there! there! there! who's hurting you, you silly girl? What do you take me for?

The Bystander.   It's aw rawt: e's a gentleman: look at his bɜ-oots. (*Explaining to the note taker.*) She thought you was a copper's nark, sir.

The Note Taker (*with quick interest*).   Whats a copper's nark?

The Bystander (*inapt at definition*).   It's a—well, it's a copper's nark, as you might say. What else would you call it? A sort of informer.

The Flower Girl (*still hysterical*).   I take my Bible oath I never said a word—

The Note Taker (*overbearing but good-humored*).   Oh, shut up, shut up. Do I look like a policeman?

The Flower Girl (*far from reassured*).   Then what did you take down my words for? How do I know whether you took me down right? You just shew me what youve wrote about me. (*The note taker opens his book and holds it* steadily under her nose, though the pressure of the mob trying to read it over his shoulders would upset a weaker man.) Whats that? That aint proper writing. I cant read that.

The Note Taker.   I can. (Reads, reproducing her pronunciation exactly.) "Cheer ap, Keptin: n'baw ya flahr orf a pore gel."

The Flower Girl (much distressed).   It's because I called him Captain. I meant no harm. (To the gentleman.) Oh, sir, dont let him lay a charge agen me for a word like that. You—

The Gentleman.   Charge! I make no charge. (To the note taker.) Really, sir, if you are a detective, you need not begin protecting me against molestation by young women until I ask you. Anybody could see that the girl meant no harm.

The Bystanders Generally (demonstrating against police espionage).   Course they could. What business is it of yours? You mind your own affairs. He wants promotion, he does. Taking down people's words! Girl never said a word to him. What harm if she did? Nice thing a girl cant shelter from the rain without being insulted, etc., etc., etc. (She is conducted by the more sympathetic demonstrators back to her plinth, where she resumes her seat and struggles with her emotion.)

The Bystander.   He aint a tec. He's a blooming busybody: thats what he is. I tell you, look at his bɔ-oots.

The Note Taker (turning on him genially).   And how are all your people down at Selsey?

The Bystander (suspiciously).   Who told you my people come from Selsey?

The Note Taker.   Never you mind. They did. (To the girl.) How do you come to be up so far east? You were born in Lisson Grove.

The Flower Girl (appalled).   Oh, what harm is there in my leaving Lisson Grove? It wasnt fit for a pig to live in; and I had to pay four-and-six a week. (In tears.) Oh boo—hoo—oo—

The Note Taker.   Live where you like; but stop that noise.

The Gentleman (to the girl).   Come, come! he cant touch you: you have a right to live where you please.

A Sarcastic Bystander (thrusting himself between the note taker and the gentleman).   Park Lane, for instance. I'd like to go into the Housing Question with you, I would.

The Flower Girl (subsiding into a brooding melancholy over her basket, and talking very low-spiritedly to herself).   I'm a good girl, I am.

The Sarcastic Bystander (not attending to her).   Do you know where I come from?

The Note Taker (promptly).   Hoxton.

Titterings. Popular interest in the note taker's performance increases.

The Sarcastic One (amazed).   Well, who said I didnt? Bly me! You know everything you do.

The Flower Girl (*still nursing her sense of injury*).   Aint no call to meddle with me, he aint.

The Bystander (*to her*).   Of course he aint. Dont you stand it from him. (*To the note taker.*) See here: what call have you to know about people what never offered to meddle with you?

The Flower Girl.   Let him say what he likes. I dont want to have no truck with him.

The Bystander.   You take us for dirt under your feet, don't you? Catch you taking liberties with a gentleman!

The Sarcastic Bystander.   Yes: tell him where he come from if you want to go fortune-telling.

The Note Taker.   Cheltenham, Harrow, Cambridge, and India.

The Gentleman.   Quite right.

Great laughter. Reaction in the note taker's favor. Exclamations of He knows all about it. Told him proper. Hear him tell the toff where he come from? *etc.*

The Gentleman.   May I ask, sir, do you do this for your living at a music hall?

The Note Taker.   I've thought of that. Perhaps I shall some day.

The rain has stopped; and the persons on the outside of the crowd begin to drop off.

The Flower Girl (*resenting the reaction*).   He's no gentleman, he aint, to interfere with a poor girl.

The Daughter (*out of patience, pushing her way rudely to the front and displacing the gentleman, who politely retires to the other side of the pillar*).   What on earth is Freddy doing? I shall get pneumownia if I stay in this draught any longer.

The Note Taker (*to himself, hastily making a note of her pronunciation of* "monia").   Earlscourt.

The Daughter (*violently*).   Will you please keep your impertinent remarks to yourself.

The Note Taker.   Did I say that out loud? I didnt mean to. I beg your pardon. Your mother's Epsom, unmistakeably.

The Mother (*advancing between the daughter and the note taker*).   How very curious! I was brought up in Largelady Park, near Epsom.

The Note Taker (*uproariously amused*).   Ha! ha! What a devil of a name! Excuse me. (*To the daughter.*) You want a cab, do you?

The Daughter.   Dont dare speak to me.

The Mother.   Oh please, please, Clara. (*Her daughter repudiates her with an angry shrug and retires haughtily.*) We should be so grateful to you, sir, if you found us a cab. (*The note taker produces a whistle.*) Oh, thank you. (*She joins her daughter.*)

The note taker blows a piercing blast.

The Sarcastic Bystander.   There! I knowed he was a plainclothes copper.

The Bystander.   That aint a police whistle: thats a sporting whistle.

The Flower Girl (*still preoccupied with her wounded feelings*).   He's no right to take away my character. My character is the same to me as any lady's.

The Note Taker.   I dont know whether youve noticed it; but the rain stopped about two minutes ago.

The Bystander.   So it has. Why didn't you say so before? and us losing our time listening to your silliness! (*He walks off towards the Strand.*)

The Sarcastic Bystander.   I can tell where you come from. You come from Anwell. Go back there.

The Note Taker (*helpfully*).   Hanwell.

The Sarcastic Bystander (*affecting great distinction of speech*).   Thenk you, teacher. Haw haw! So long. (*He touches his hat with mock respect and strolls off.*)

The Flower Girl.   Frightening people like that! How would he like it himself?

The Mother.   It's quite fine now, Clara. We can walk to a motor bus. Come. (*She gathers her skirts above her ankles and hurries off towards the Strand.*)

The Daughter.   But the cab—(*Her mother is out of hearing.*) Oh, how tiresome! (*She follows angrily.*)

All the rest have gone except the note taker, the gentleman, and the flower girl, who sits arranging her basket, and still pitying herself in murmurs.

The Flower Girl.   Poor girl! Hard enough for her to live without being worrited and chivied.

The Gentleman (*returning to his former place on the note taker's left*).   How do you do it, if I may ask?

The Note Taker.   Simply phonetics. The science of speech. Thats my profession: also my hobby. Happy is the man who can make a living by his hobby! You can spot an Irishman or a Yorkshireman by his brogue. *I* can place any man within six miles. I can place him within two miles in London. Sometimes within two streets.

The Flower Girl.   Ought to be ashamed of himself, unmanly coward!

The Gentleman.   But is there a living in that?

The Note Taker.   Oh yes. Quite a fat one. This is an age of upstarts. Men begin in Kentish Town with £80 a year, and end in Park Lane with a hundred thousand. They want to drop Kentish Town; but they give themselves away every time they open their mouths. Now I can teach them—

The Flower Girl.   Let him mind his own business and leave a poor girl—

The Note Taker (*explosively*).   Woman: cease this detestable boohooing instantly; or else seek the shelter of some other place of worship.

The Flower Girl (*with feeble defiance*).   Ive a right to be here if I like, same as you.

The Note Taker.   A woman who utters such depressing and disgusting sounds has no right to be anywhere—no right to live. Remember that you are a human being with a soul and the divine gift of articulate speech: that your native language is the language of Shakespear and Milton and The Bible; and dont sit there crooning like a bilious pigeon.

The Flower Girl (*quite overwhelmed, looking up at him in mingled wonder and deprecation without daring to raise her head*).   Ah-ah-ah-ow-ow-ow-oo!

The Note Taker (*whipping out his book*).   Heavens! what a sound! (*He writes; then holds out the book and reads, reproducing her vowels exactly.*) Ah-ah-ah-ow-ow-ow-oo!

The Flower Girl (*tickled by the performance, and laughing in spite of herself*).   Garn!

The Note Taker.   You see this creature with her kerbstone English: the English that will keep her in the gutter to the end of her days. Well, sir, in three months I could pass that girl off as a duchess at an ambassador's garden party. I could even get her a place as a lady's maid or shop assistant, which requires better English.

The Flower Girl.   What's that you say?

The Note Taker.   Yes, you squashed cabbage leaf, you disgrace to the noble architecture of these columns, you incarnate insult to the English language: I could pass you off as the Queen of Sheba. (*To the Gentleman.*) Can you believe that?

The Gentleman.   Of course I can. I am myself a student of Indian dialects; and—

The Note Taker (*eagerly*).   Are you? Do you know Colonel Pickering, the author of Spoken Sanscrit?

The Gentleman.   I am Colonel Pickering. Who are you?

The Note Taker.   Henry Higgins, author of Higgins's Universal Alphabet.

Pickering (*with enthusiasm*).   I came from India to meet you.

Higgins.   I was going to India to meet you.

Pickering.   Where do you live?

Higgins.   27A Wimpole Street. Come and see me tomorrow.

Pickering.   I'm at the Carlton. Come with me now and lets have a jaw over some supper.

Higgins.   Right you are.

The Flower Girl (*to Pickering, as he passes her*).   Buy a flower, kind gentleman. I'm short for my lodging.

Pickering.   I really havnt any change. I'm sorry. (*He goes away.*)

Higgins (*shocked at the girl's mendacity*).   Liar. You said you could change half-a-crown.

The Flower Girl (*rising in desperation*).   You ought to be stuffed with nails, you ought. (*Flinging the basket at his feet.*) Take the whole blooming basket for sixpence.

The church clock strikes the second quarter.

Higgins (*hearing in it the voice of God, rebuking him for his Pharisaic want of charity to the poor girl*).   A reminder. (*He raises his hat solemnly; then throws a handful of money into the basket and follows Pickering.*)

The Flower Girl (*picking up a half-crown*).   Ah-ow-ooh! (*Picking up a couple of florins.*) Aaah-ow-ooh! (*Picking up several coins.*) Aaaaah-ow-ooh! (*Picking up a half-sovereign.*) Aaaaaaaaaaaah-ow-ooh!!!

Freddy (*springing out of a taxicab*).   Got one at last. Hallo! (*To the girl.*) Where are the two ladies that were here?

The Flower Girl.   They walked to the bus when the rain stopped.

Freddy.   And left me with a cab on my hands! Damnation!

The Flower Girl (*with grandeur*).   Never mind, young man. I'm going home in a taxi. (*She sails off to the cab. The driver puts his hand behind him and holds the door firmly shut against her. Quite understanding his mistrust, she shews him her handful of money.*) A taxi fare aint no object to me, Charlie. (*He grins and opens the door.*) Here. What about the basket?

The Taximan.   Give it here. Tuppence extra.

Liza.   No: I dont want nobody to see it. (*She crushes it into the cab and gets in, continuing the conversation through the window.*) Goodbye, Freddy.

Freddy (*dazedly raising his hat*).   Goodbye.

Taximan.   Where to?

Liza.   Bucknam Pellis [Buckingham Palace].

Taximan.   What d'ye mean—Bucknam Pellis?

Liza.   Dont you know where it is? In the Green Park, where the King lives. Goodbye, Freddy. Dont let me keep you standing there. Goodbye.

Freddy.   Goodbye. (*He goes.*)

Taximan.   Here? Whats this about Bucknam Pellis? What business have you at Bucknam Pellis?

Liza.   Of course I havnt none. But I wasn't going to let him know that. You drive me home.

Taximan.   And wheres home?

Liza.   Angel Court, Drury Lane, next Meiklejohn's oil shop.

Taximan.   That sounds more like it, Judy. (*He drives off.*)

*   *   *   *   *

Let us follow the taxi to the entrance to Angel Court, a narrow little archway between two shops, one of them Meiklejohn's oil shop. When it stops there, Eliza gets out, dragging her basket with her.

Liza.   How much?

Taximan (*indicating the taximeter*).   Cant you read? A shilling.

Liza.   A shilling for two minutes!!

Taximan.   Two minutes or ten: it's all the same.

Liza.   Well, I dont call it right.

Taximan.   Ever been in a taxi before?

Liza *(with dignity).*   Hundreds and thousands of times, young man.

Taximan *(laughing at her).*   Good for you, Judy. Keep the shilling, darling, with best love from all at home. Good luck! *(He drives off.)*

Liza *(humiliated).*   Impidence!

She picks up the basket and trudges up the alley with it to her lodging: a small room with very old wall paper hanging loose in the damp places. A broken pane in the window is mended with paper. A portrait of a popular actor and a fashion plate of ladies' dresses, all wildly beyond poor Eliza's means, both torn from newspapers, are pinned up on the wall. A birdcage hangs in the window; but its tenant died long ago: it remains as a memorial only.

These are the only visible luxuries: the rest is the irreducible minimum of poverty's needs: a wretched bed heaped with all sorts of coverings that have any warmth in them, a draped packing case with a basin and jug on it and a little looking glass over it, a chair and table, the refuse of some suburban kitchen, and an American alarum clock on the shelf above the unused fireplace: the whole lighted with a gas lamp with a penny in the slot meter. Rent: four shillings a week.

Here Eliza, chronically weary, but too excited to go to bed, sits, counting her new riches and dreaming and planning what to do with them, until the gas goes out, when she enjoys for the first time the sensation of being able to put in another penny without grudging it. This prodigal mood does not extinguish her gnawing sense of the need for economy sufficiently to prevent her from calculating that she can dream and plan in bed more cheaply and warmly than sitting up without a fire. So she takes off her shawl and skirt and adds them to the miscellaneous bedclothes. Then she kicks off her shoes and gets into bed without any further change.

Act II

Next day at 11 A.M.*, Higgins's laboratory in Wimpole Street. It is a room on the first floor, looking on the street, and was meant for the drawing room. The double doors are in the middle of the back wall; and persons entering find in the corner to their right two tall file cabinets at right angles to one another against the walls. In this corner stands a flat writing-table, on which are a phonograph, a laryngoscope, a row of tiny organ pipes with a bellows, a set of lamp chimneys for singing flames with burners attached to a gas plug in the wall by an india-rubber tube, several tuning-forks of different sizes, a life-size image of half a human head, shewing in section the vocal organs, and a box containing a supply of wax cylinders for the phonograph.*

Further down the room, on the same side, is a fireplace, with a comfortable leather-covered easy-chair at the side of the hearth nearest the door, and a coal-scuttle. There is a clock on the mantlepiece. Between the fireplace and the phonograph table is a stand for newspapers.

On the other side of the central door, to the left of the visitor, is a cabinet of shallow drawers. On it is a telephone and the telephone directory. The corner beyond, and most of the side wall, is occupied by a grand piano, with the keyboard at the end furthest from the door, and a bench for the players extending the full length of the keyboard. On the piano is a dessert dish heaped with fruit and sweets, mostly chocolates.

The middle of the room is clear. Besides the easy-chair, the piano bench, and two chairs at the phonograph table, there is one stray chair. It stands near the fireplace. On the walls, engravings: mostly Piranesis and mezzotint portraits. No paintings.

Pickering is seated at the table, putting down some cards and a tuning-fork which he has been using. Higgins is standing up near him, closing two or three file drawers which are hanging out. He appears in the morning light as a robust, vital, appetizing sort of man of forty or thereabouts, dressed in a professional-looking black frock-coat with a white linen collar and black silk tie. He is of energetic, scientific type, heartily, even violently interested in everything that can be studied as a scientific subject, and careless about himself and other people, including their feelings. He is, in fact, but for his years and size, rather like a very impetuous baby "taking notice" eagerly and loudly, and requiring almost as much watching to keep him out of unintended mischief. His manner varies from genial bullying when he is in a good humor to stormy petulance when anything goes wrong; but he is so entirely frank and void of malice that he remains likeable even in his least reasonable moments.

Higgins *(as he shuts the last drawer).*   Well, I think thats the whole show.

Pickering.   It's really amazing. I havnt taken half of it in, you know.

Higgins.   Would you like to go over any of it again?

Pickering *(rising and coming to the fireplace, where he plants himself with his back to the fire).*   No, thank you: not now. I'm quite done up for this morning.

Higgins *(following him, and standing beside him on his left).*   Tired of listening to sounds?

Pickering.   Yes. It's a fearful strain. I rather fancied myself because I can pronounce twenty-four distinct vowel sounds; but your hundred and thirty beat me. I cant hear a bit of difference between most of them.

Higgins *(chuckling, and going over to the piano to eat sweets).*   Oh, that comes with practice. You hear no difference at first; but you keep on listening, and presently you find theyre all as different as A from B. *(Mrs. Pearce looks in: she is Higgins's housekeeper.)* Whats the matter?

Mrs. Pearce *(hesitating, evidently perplexed).*   A young woman asks to see you, sir.

Higgins.   A young woman! What does she want?

should have sent her away, only I thought perhaps you wanted her to talk
into your machines. I hope Ive not done wrong; but really you see such queer
people sometimes—youll excuse me, I'm sure, sir—

Higgins. Oh, thats all right, Mrs. Pearce. Has she an interesting accent?

Mrs. Pearce. Oh, something dreadful, sir, really. I dont know how you can
take an interest in it.

Higgins *(to Pickering).* Lets have her up. Shew her up, Mrs. Pearce. *(He
rushes across to his working table and picks out a cylinder to use on the
phonograph).*

Mrs. Pearce *(only half resigned to it).* Very well, sir, It's for you to say. *(She
goes downstairs.)*

Higgins. This is rather a bit of luck. I'll shew you how I make records. We'll
set her talking; and I'll take it down first in Bell's Visible Speech; then in
broad Romic; and then we'll get her on the phonograph so that you can turn
her on as often as you like with the written transcript before you.

Mrs. Pearce *(returning).* This is the young woman, sir.

*The flower girl enters in state. She has a hat with three ostrich feathers, orange,
sky-blue, and red. She has a nearly clean apron, and the shoddy coat has been
tidied a little. The pathos of this deplorable figure, with its innocent vanity and
consequential air, touches Pickering, who has already straightened himself in the
presence of Mrs. Pearce. But as to Higgins, the only distinction he makes between
men and women is that when he is neither bullying nor exclaiming to the heavens
against some feather-weight cross, he coaxes women as a child coaxes its nurse
when it wants to get anything out of her.*

Higgins *(brusquely, recognizing her with unconcealed disappointment, and at
once, babylike, making an intolerable grievance of it).* Why, this is the girl
I jotted down last night. She's no use: I've got all the records I want of the
Lisson Grove lingo; and I'm not going to waste another cylinder on it. *(To
the girl.)* Be off with you: I dont want you.

The Flower Girl. Dont you be so saucy. You aint heard what I come for yet.
(To Mrs. Pearce, who is waiting at the door for further instructions.) Did you
tell him I come in a taxi?

Mrs. Pearce. Nonsense, girl! what do you think a gentleman like Mr. Higgins
cares what you came in?

The Flower Girl. Oh, we are so proud! He aint above giving lessons, not him:
I heard him say so. Well, I aint come here to ask for any compliment; and
if my money's not good enough I can go elsewhere.

Higgins. Good enough for what?

The Flower Girl. Good enough for yə-oo. Now you know, dont you? I've
come to have lessons, I am. And to pay for em tə-oo: make no mistake.

Higgins (*stupent*).   Well!!! (*Recovering his breath with a gasp.*) What do you expect me to say to you?

The Flower Girl.   Well, if you was a gentleman, you might ask me to sit down, I think. Dont I tell you I'm bringing you business?

Higgins.   Pickering: shall we ask this baggage to sit down, or shall we throw her out the window?

The Flower Girl (*running away in terror to the piano, where she turns at bay*).   Ah-ah-oh-ow-ow-ow-oo! (*Wounded and whimpering.*) I wont be called a baggage when Ive offered to pay like any lady.

Motionless, the two men stare at her from the other side of the room, amazed.

Pickering (*gently*).   But what is it you want?

The Flower Girl.   I want to be a lady in a flower shop stead of sellin at the corner of Tottenham Court Road. But they wont take me unless I can talk more genteel. He said he could teach me. Well, here I am ready to pay him—not asking any favor—and he treats me zif I was dirt.

Mrs. Pearce: How can you be such a foolish ignorant girl as to think you could afford to pay Mr. Higgins?

The Flower Girl.   Why shouldnt I? I know what lessons cost as well as you do; and I'm ready to pay.

Higgins.   How much?

The Flower Girl (*coming back to him, triumphant*).   Now youre talking! I thought youd come off it when you saw a chance of getting back a bit of what you chucked at me last night. (*Confidentially.*) Youd had a drop in, hadnt you?

Higgins (*peremptorily*).   Sit down.

The Flower Girl.   Oh, if youre going to make a compliment of it—

Higgins (*thundering at her*).   Sit down.

Mrs. Pearce (*severely*).   Sit down, girl. Do as youre told.

The Flower Girl.   Ah-ah-ah-ow-ow-oo! (*She stands, half rebellious, half bewildered.*)

Pickering (*very courteous*).   Wont you sit down? (*He places the stray chair near the hearthrug between himself and Higgins.*)

Liza (*coyly*).   Dont mind if I do. (*She sits down. Pickering returns to the hearth-rug.*)

Higgins.   Whats your name?

The Flower Girl.   Liza Doolittle.

Higgins (*declaiming gravely*).

> Eliza, Elizabeth, Betsy and Bess,
> They went to the woods to get a bird's nes':

Pickering.   They found a nest with four eggs in it:

Higgins.   They took one apiece, and left three in it.

They laugh heartily at their own fun.

Liza.   Oh, dont be silly.

Mrs. Pearce (*placing herself behind Eliza's chair*).   You mustnt speak to the gentleman like that.

Liza.   Well, why wont he speak sensible to me?

Higgins.   Come back to business. How much do you propose to pay me for the lessons?

Liza.   Oh, I know whats right. A lady friend of mine gets French lessons for eighteenpence an hour from a real French gentleman. Well, you wouldnt have the face to ask me the same for teaching me my own language as you would for French; so I wont give more than a shilling. Take it or leave it.

Higgins (*walking up and down the room, rattling his keys and his cash in his pockets*).   You know, Pickering, if you consider a shilling, not as a simple shilling, but as a percentage of this girl's income, it works out as fully equivalent to sixty or seventy guineas from a millionaire.

Pickering.   How so?

Higgins.   Figure it out. A millionaire has about £150 a day. She earns about half-a-crown.

Liza (*haughtily*).   Who told you I only—

Higgins (*continuing*).   She offers me two-fifths of her day's income for a lesson. Two-fifths of a millionaire's income for a day would be somewhere about £60. It's handsome. By George, it's enormous! it's the biggest offer I ever had.

Liza (*rising, terrified*).   Sixty pounds! What are you talking about? I never offered you sixty pounds. Where would I get—

Higgins.   Hold your tongue.

Liza (*weeping*).   But I aint got sixty pounds. Oh—

Mrs. Pearce.   Dont cry, you silly girl. Sit down. Nobody is going to touch your money.

Higgins.   Somebody is going to touch you, with a broomstick, if you dont stop snivelling. Sit down.

Liza (*obeying slowly*).   Ah-ah-ah-ow-oo-o! One would think you was my father.

Higgins.   If I decide to teach you. I'll be worse than two fathers to you. Here! (*He offers her his silk handkerchief.*)

Liza.   Whats this for?

Higgins.   To wipe your eyes. To wipe any part of your face that feels moist. Remember: thats your handkerchief; and thats your sleeve. Dont mistake the one for the other if you wish to become a lady in a shop.

Liza, utterly bewildered, stares helplessly at him.

Mrs. Pearce.   It's no use talking to her like that, Mr. Higgins: she doesnt understand you. Besides, youre quite wrong: she doesnt do it that way at all. (*She takes the handkerchief.*)

Liza (*snatching it*).   Here! You give me that handkerchief. He gev it to me, not to you.

Pickering *(laughing)*.   He did. I think it must be regarded as her property, Mrs. Pearce.

Mrs. Pearce *(resigning herself)*.   Serve you right, Mr. Higgins.

Pickering.   Higgins: I'm interested. What about the ambassador's garden party? I'll say youre the greatest teacher alive if you make that good. I'll bet you all the expenses of the experiment you cant do it. And I'll pay for the lessons.

Liza.   Oh, you are real good. Thank you, Captain.

Higgins *(tempted, looking at her)*.   It's almost irresistible. She's so deliciously low—so horribly dirty—

Liza *(protesting extremely)*.   Ah-ah-ah-ah-ow-ow-oo-oo!!! I aint dirty: I washed my face and hands afore I come, I did.

Pickering.   Youre certainly not going to turn her head with flattery, Higgins.

Mrs. Pearce *(uneasy)*.   Oh, dont say that, sir: theres more ways than one of turning a girl's head; nobody can do it better than Mr. Higgins, though he may not always mean it. I do hope, sir, you wont encourage him to do anything foolish.

Higgins *(becoming excited as the idea grows on him)*.   What is life but a series of inspired follies? The difficulty is to find them to do. Never lose a chance: it doesnt come every day. I shall make a duchess of this draggletailed gutter-snipe.

Liza *(strongly deprecating this view of her)*.   Ah-ah-ah-ow-ow-oo!

Higgins *(carried away)*.   Yes: in six months—in three if she has a good ear and a quick tongue—I'll take her anywhere and pass her off as anything. We'll start today: now! this moment! Take her away and clean her, Mrs. Pearce. Monkey Brand, if it wont come off any other way. Is there a good fire in the kitchen?

Mrs. Pearce *(protesting)*.   Yes; but—

Higgins *(storming on)*.   Take all her clothes off and burn them. Ring up Whitely or somebody for new ones. Wrap her up in brown paper til they come.

Liza.   Youre no gentleman, youre not, to talk of such things. I'm a good girl, I am; and I know what the like of you are, I do.

Higgins.   We want none of your Lisson Grove prudery here, young woman. Youve got to learn to behave like a duchess. Take her away, Mrs. Pearce. If she gives you any trouble, wallop her.

Liza *(springing up and running between Pickering and Mrs. Pearce for protection)*.   No! I'll call the police, I will.

Mrs. Pearce.   But Ive no place to put her.

Higgins.   Put her in the dustbin.

Liza.   Ah-ah-ah-ow-ow-oo!

Pickering.   Oh come, Higgins! be reasonable.

Mrs. Pearce *(resolutely)*.   You must be reasonable, Mr. Higgins: really you must. You cant walk over everybody like this.

Higgins, thus scolded, subsides. The hurricane is succeeded by a zephyr of amiable surprise.

Higgins (*with professional exquisiteness of modulation*).   I walk over everybody! My dear Mrs. Pearce, my dear Pickering, I never had the slightest intention of walking over anyone. All I propose is that we should be kind to this poor girl. We must help her to prepare and fit herself for her new station in life. If I did not express myself clearly it was because I did not wish to hurt her delicacy, or yours.

Liza, reassured, steals back to her chair.

Mrs. Pearce (*to Pickering*).   Well, did you ever hear anything like that, sir?

Pickering (*laughing heartily*).   Never, Mrs. Pearce: never.

Higgins (*patiently*).   Whats the matter?

Mrs. Pearce.   Well, the matter is, sir, that you cant take a girl up like that as if you were picking up a pebble on the beach.

Higgins.   Why not?

Mrs. Pearce.   Why not! But you dont know anything about her. What about her parents? She may be married.

Liza.   Garn!

Higgins.   There! As the girl very properly says, Garn! Married indeed! Dont you know that a woman of that class looks a worn out drudge of fifty a year after she's married?

Liza.   Whood marry me?

Higgins (*suddenly resorting to the most thrilling beautiful tones in his best elocutionary style*).   By George, Eliza, the streets will be strewn with the bodies of men shooting themselves for your sake before Ive done with you.

Mrs. Pearce.   Nonsense, sir. You mustnt talk like that to her.

Liza (*rising and squaring herself determinedly*).   I'm going away. He's off his chump, he is. I dont want no balmies teaching me.

Higgins (*wounded in his tenderest point by her insensibility to his elocution*).   Oh, indeed! I'm mad, am I? Very well, Mrs. Pearce: you neednt order the new clothes for her. Throw her out.

Liza (*whimpering*).   Nah-ow. You got no right to touch me.

Mrs. Pearce.   You see now what comes of being saucy. (*Indicating the door.*) This way, please.

Liza (*almost in tears*).   I didnt want no clothes. I wouldnt have taken them. (*She throws away the handkerchief.*) I can buy my own clothes.

Higgins (*deftly retrieving the handkerchief and intercepting her on her reluctant way to the door*).   Youre an ungrateful wicked girl. This is my return for offering to take you out of the gutter and dress you beautifully and make a lady of you.

Mrs. Pearce.   Stop, Mr. Higgins. I wont allow it. It's you that are wicked. Go home to your parents, girl; tell them to take better care of you.

Liza.   I aint got no parents. They told me I was big enough to earn my own living and turned me out.

Mrs. Pearce.   Wheres your mother?

Liza.   I aint got no mother. Her that turned me out was my sixth stepmother. But I done without them. And I'm a good girl, I am.

Higgins.   Very well, then, what on earth is all this fuss about? The girl doesnt belong to anybody—is no use to anybody but me. (*He goes to Mrs. Pearce and begins coaxing.*) You can adopt her, Mrs. Pearce: I'm sure a daughter would be a great amusement to you. Now dont make any more fuss. Take her downstairs; and—

Mrs. Pearce.   But whats to become of her? Is she to be paid anything? Do be sensible, sir.

Higgins.   Oh, pay her whatever is necessary: put it down in the housekeeping book. (*Impatiently*). What on earth will she want with money? She'll have her food and clothes. She'll only drink if you give her money.

Liza (*turning on him*).   Oh you are a brute, It's a lie: nobody ever saw the sign of liquor on me. (*To Pickering.*) Oh, sir: youre a gentleman: dont let him speak to me like that.

Pickering (*in good-humored remonstrance*).   Does it occur to you, Higgins, that the girl has some feelings?

Higgins (*looking critically at her*).   Oh no, I dont think so. Not any feelings that we need bother about. (*Cheerily.*) Have you, Eliza?

Liza.   I got my feelings same as anyone else.

Higgins (*to Pickering, reflectively*).   You see the difficulty?

Pickering.   Eh? What difficulty?

Higgins.   To get her to talk grammar. The mere pronunciation is easy enough.

Liza.   I dont want to talk grammar. I want to talk like a lady in a flower-shop.

Mrs. Pearce.   Will you please keep to the point, Mr. Higgins. I want to know on what terms the girl is to be here. Is she to have any wages? And what is to become of her when youve finished your teaching? You must look ahead a little.

Higgins (*impatiently*).   Whats to become of her if I leave her in the gutter? Tell me that, Mrs. Pearce.

Mrs. Pearce.   Thats her own business, not yours, Mr. Higgins.

Higgins.   Well, when Ive done with her, we can throw her back into the gutter; and then it will be her own business again; so thats all right.

Liza.   Oh, youve no feeling heart in you: you dont care for nothing but yourself (*She rises and takes the floor resolutely.*) Here! Ive had enough of this. I'm going. (*Making for the door.*) You ought to be ashamed of yourself, you ought.

Higgins (*snatching a chocolate cream from the piano, his eyes suddenly beginning to twinkle with mischief*).   Have some chocolates, Eliza.

Liza (*halting, tempted*).   How do I know what might be in them? Ive heard of girls being drugged by the like of you.

Higgins whips out his penknife; cuts a chocolate in two; puts one half into his mouth and bolts it; and offers her the other half.

Higgins.   Pledge of good faith, Eliza. I eat one half: you eat the other. *(Liza opens her mouth to retort: he pops the half chocolate into it.)* You shall have boxes of them, barrels of them, every day. You shall live on them. Eh?

Liza *(who has disposed of the chocolate after being nearly choked by it).*   I wouldnt have ate it, only I'm too ladylike to take it out of my mouth.

Higgins.   Listen, Eliza. I think you said you came in a taxi.

Liza.   Well, what if I did? Ive as good a right to take a taxi as anyone else.

Higgins.   You have, Eliza; and in future you shall have as many taxis as you want. You shall go up and down and round the town in a taxi every day. Think of that, Eliza.

Mrs. Pearce.   Mr. Higgins: youre tempting the girl. It's not right. She should think of the future.

Higgins.   At her age! Nonsense! Time enough to think of the future when you havnt any future to think of. No, Eliza: do as this lady does: think of other people's futures; but never think of your own. Think of chocolates, and taxis, and gold, and diamonds.

Liza.   No: I dont want no gold and no diamonds. I'm a good girl, I am. *(She sits down again, with an attempt at dignity.)*

Higgins.   You shall remain so, Eliza, under the care of Mrs. Pearce. And you shall marry an officer in the Guards, with a beautiful moustache: the son of a marquis, who will disinherit him for marrying you, but will relent when he sees your beauty and goodness—

Pickering.   Excuse me, Higgins; but I really must interfere. Mrs. Pearce is quite right. If this girl is to put herself in your hands for six months for an experiment in teaching, she must understand thoroughly what she's doing.

Higgins.   How can she? She's incapable of understanding anything. Besides, do any of us understand what we are doing? If we did, would we ever do it?

Pickering.   Very clever, Higgins; but not to the present point. *(To Eliza.)* Miss Doolittle—

Liza *(overwhelmed).*   Ah-ah-ow-oo!

Higgins.   There! Thats all youll get out of Eliza. Ah-ah-ow-oo! No use explaining. As a military man you ought to know that. Give her her orders: thats enough for her. Eliza: you are to live here for the next six months, learning how to speak beautifully, like a lady in a florist's shop. If youre good and do whatever youre told, you shall sleep in a proper bedroom, and have lots to eat, and money to buy chocolates and take rides in taxis. If youre naughty and idle you will sleep in the back kitchen among the black beetles, and be walloped by Mrs. Pearce with a broomstick. At the end of the six months you shall go to Buckingham Palace in a carriage, beautifully dressed. If the King finds out youre not a lady, you will be taken by the police to the Tower of London, where your head will be cut off as a warning to other presumptuous flower girls. If you are not found out, you shall have a present of seven-and-sixpence to start life with as lady in a shop. If you refuse this offer you will be a most ungrateful wicked girl; and the angels will weep for you. *(To Pickering.)* Now are you satisfied, Pickering? *(To Mrs. Pearce.)* Can I put it more plainly and fairly, Mrs. Pearce?

Mrs. Pearce *(patiently).*   I think youd better let me speak to the girl properly in private. I dont know that I can take charge of her or consent to the arrangement at all. Of course I know you dont mean her any harm; but when you get what you call interested in people's accents, you never think or care what may happen to them or you. Come with me, Eliza.

Higgins.   Thats all right. Thank you, Mrs. Pearce. Bundle her off to the bathroom.

Liza *(rising reluctantly and suspiciously).*   Youre a great bully, you are. I wont stay here if I dont like. I wont let nobody wallop me. I never asked to go to Bucknam Palace, I didnt. I was never in trouble with the police, not me. I'm a good girl—

Mrs. Pearce.   Dont answer back, girl. You dont understand the gentleman. Come with me. *(She leads the way to the door, and holds it open for Eliza.)*

Liza *(as she goes out).*   Well, what I say is right. I wont go near the King, not if I'm going to have my head cut off. If I'd known what I was letting myself in for, I wouldnt have come here. I always been a good girl; and I never offered to say a word to him; and I dont owe him nothing; and I dont care; and I wont be put upon; and I have my feelings the same as anyone else—

Mrs. Pearce shuts the door; and Eliza's plaints are no longer audible.

* * * * *

Eliza is taken upstairs to the third floor greatly to her surprise; for she expected to be taken down to the scullery. There Mrs. Pearce opens a door and takes her into a spare bedroom.

Mrs. Pearce.   I will have to put you here. This will be your bedroom.

Liza.   O-h, I couldn't sleep here, missus. It's too good for the likes of me. I should be afraid to touch anything. I aint a duchess yet, you know.

Mrs. Pearce.   You have got to make yourself as clean as the room: then you wont be afraid of it. And you must call me Mrs. Pearce, not missus. *(She throws open the door of the dressingroom, now modernized as a bathroom.)*

Liza.   Gawd! whats this? Is this where you wash clothes? Funny sort of copper I call it.

Mrs. Pearce.   It is not a copper. This is where we wash ourselves, Eliza, and where I am going to wash you.

Liza.   You expect me to get into that and wet myself all over! Not me. I should catch my death. I knew a woman did it every Saturday night, and she died of it.

Mrs. Pearce.   Mr. Higgins has the gentlemen's bathroom downstairs; and he has a bath every morning, in cold water.

Liza.   Ugh! He's made of iron, that man.

Mrs. Pearce.   If you are to sit with him and the Colonel and be taught you will have to do the same. They wont like the smell of you if you dont. But you can have the water as hot as you like. There are two taps: hot and cold.

Liza *(weeping)*.   I couldnt. I dursnt. Its not natural: it would kill me. Ive never had a bath in my life: not what youd call a proper one.

Mrs. Pearce.   Well, dont you want to be clean and sweet and decent, like a lady? You know you cant be a nice girl inside if youre a dirty slut outside.

Liza.   Boohoo!!!!

Mrs. Pearce.   Now stop crying and go back into your room and take off all your clothes. Then wrap yourself in this (*taking down a gown from its peg and handing it to her*) and come back to me. I will get the bath ready.

Liza *(all tears)*.   I cant. I wont. I'm not used to it. Ive never took off all my clothes before. It's not right: it's not decent.

Mrs. Pearce.   Nonsense, child. Dont you take off all your clothes every night when you go to bed?

Liza *(amazed)*:   No. Why should I? I should catch my death. Of course I take off my skirt.

Mrs. Pearce.   Do you mean that you sleep in the underclothes you wear in the daytime?

Liza.   What else have I to sleep in?

Mrs. Pearce.   You will never do that again as long as you live here. I will get you a proper nightdress.

Liza.   Do you mean change into cold things and lie awake shivering half the night? You want to kill me, you do.

Mrs. Pearce.   I want to change you from a frowzy slut to a clean respectable girl fit to sit with the gentlemen in the study. Are you going to trust me and do what I tell you or be thrown out and sent back to your flower basket?

Liza.   But you dont know what the cold is to me. You dont know how I dread it.

Mrs. Pearce.   Your bed won't be cold here: I will put a hot water bottle in it. (*Pushing her into the bedroom.*) Off with you and undress.

Liza.   Oh, if only I'd known what a dreadful thing it is to be clean I'd never have come. I didnt know when I was well off. I—(*Mrs. Pearce pushes her through the door, but leaves it partly open lest her prisoner should take to flight.*).

Mrs. Pearce puts on a pair of white rubber sleeves, and fills the bath, mixing hot and cold, and testing the result with the bath thermometer. She perfumes it with a handful of bath salts and adds a palmful of mustard. She then takes a formidable looking long handled scrubbing brush and soaps it profusely with a ball of scented soap.

Eliza comes back with nothing on but the bath gown huddled tightly round her, a piteous spectacle of abject terror.

Mrs. Pearce.   Now come along. Take that thing off.

Liza.   Oh I couldnt, Mrs. Pearce: I reely couldnt. I never done such a thing.

Mrs. Pearce.   Nonsense. Here: step in and tell me whether its hot enough for you.

Liza.   Ah-oo! Ah-oo! It's too hot.

Mrs. Pearce *(deftly snatching the gown away and throwing Eliza down on her back)*.   It wont hurt you. *(She sets to work with the scrubbing brush.)*

Eliza's screams are heartrending.

✳   ✳   ✳   ✳   ✳

Meanwhile the Colonel has been having it out with Higgins about Eliza. Pickering has come from the hearth to the chair and seated himself astride of it with his arms on the back to cross-examine him.

Pickering.   Excuse the straight question, Higgins. Are you a man of good character where women are concerned?

Higgins *(moodily)*.   Have you ever met a man of good character where women are concerned?

Pickering.   Yes: very frequently.

Higgins *(dogmatically, lifting himself on his hands to the level of the piano, and sitting on it with a bounce)*.   Well, I havnt. I find that the moment I let a woman make friends with me, she becomes jealous, exacting, suspicious, and a damned nuisance. I find that the moment I let myself make friends with a woman, I become selfish and tyrannical. Women upset everything. When you let them into your life, you find that the woman is driving at one thing and youre driving at another.

Pickering.   At what, for example?

Higgins *(coming off the piano restlessly)*.   Oh, Lord knows! I suppose the woman wants to live her own life; and the man wants to live his; and each tries to drag the other on to the wrong track. One wants to go north and the other south; and the result is that both have to go east, though they both hate the east wind. *(He sits down on the bench at the keyboard.)* So here I am, a confirmed old bachelor, and likely to remain so.

Pickering *(rising and standing over him gravely)*.   Come, Higgins! You know what I mean. If I'm to be in this business I shall feel responsible for that girl. I hope it's understood that no advantage is to be taken of her position.

Higgins.   What! That thing! Sacred, I assure you. *(Rising to explain.)* You see, she'll be a pupil; and teaching would be impossible unless pupils were sacred. Ive taught scores of American millionairesses how to speak English: the best looking women in the world. I'm seasoned. They might as well be a block of wood. It's—

Mrs. Pearce opens the door. She has Eliza's hat in her hand. Pickering retires to the easy-chair at the hearth and sits down.

Higgins *(eagerly)*.   Well, Mrs. Pearce: is it all right?

Mrs. Pearce *(at the door)*.   I just wish to trouble you with a word, if I may, Mr. Higgins.

Higgins.   Yes, certainly. Come in . *(She comes forward.)* Dont burn that, Mrs. Pearce. I'll keep it as a curiosity. *(He takes the hat.)*

Mrs. Pearce.   Handle it carefully, sir, please. I had to promise her not to burn it; but I had better put it in the oven for a while.

Higgins *(putting it down hastily on the piano)*.   Oh! thank you. Well, what have you to say to me?

Pickering.   Am I in the way?

Mrs. Pearce.   Not in the least, sir. Mr. Higgins: will you please be very particular what you say before the girl?

Higgins *(sternly)*.   Of course. I'm always particular about what I say. Why do you say this to me?

Mrs. Pearce *(unmoved)*.   No, sir: youre not at all particular when youve mislaid anything or when you get a little impatient. Now it doesnt matter before me: I'm used to it. But you really must not swear before the girl.

Higgins *(indignantly)*.   I swear! *(Most emphatically.)* I never swear. I detest the habit. What the devil do you mean?

Mrs. Pearce *(stolidly)*.   Thats what I mean, sir. You swear a great deal too much. I dont mind your damning and blasting, and what the devil and where the devil and who the devil—

Higgins.   Mrs. Pearce: this language from your lips! Really!

Mrs. Pearce *(not to be put off)*.   —but there is a certain word[2] I must ask you not to use. The girl used it herself when she began to enjoy the bath. It begins with the same letter as bath. She knows no better: she learnt it at her mother's knee. But she must not hear it from your lips.

Higgins *(loftily)*.   I cannot charge myself with having ever uttered it, Mrs. Pearce. *(She looks at him steadfastly. He adds, hiding an uneasy conscience with a judicial air.)* Except perhaps in a moment of extreme and justifiable excitement.

Mrs. Pearce.   Only this morning, sir, you applied it to your boots, to the butter, and to the brown bread.

Higgins.   Oh, that! Mere alliteration, Mrs. Pearce, natural to a poet.

Mrs. Pearce.   Well, sir, whatever you choose to call it, I beg you not to let the girl hear you repeat it.

Higgins.   Oh, very well, very well. Is that all?

Mrs. Pearce.   No, sir. We shall have to be very particular with this girl as to personal cleanliness.

Higgins.   Certainly. Quite right. Most important.

Mrs. Pearce.   I mean not to be slovenly about her dress or untidy in leaving things about.

---

[2] The word is *bloody*, a rather nasty oath in British English.

Higgins *(going to her solemnly)*.   Just so. I intended to call your attention to that. *(He passes on to Pickering, who is enjoying the conversation immensely.)* It is these little things that matter, Pickering. Take care of the pence and the pounds will take care of themselves is as true of personal habits as of money. *(He comes to anchor on the hearthrug, with the air of a man in an unassailable position.)*

Mrs. Pearce.   Yes, sir. Then might I ask you not to come down to breakfast in your dressing-gown, or at any rate not to use it as a napkin to the extent you do, sir. And if you would be so good as not to eat everything off the same plate, and to remember not to put the porridge saucepan out of your hand on the clean tablecloth, it would be a better example to the girl. You know you nearly choked yourself with a fishbone in a jam only last week.

Higgins *(routed from the hearthrug and drifting back to the piano)*.   I may do these things sometimes in absence of mind; but surely I dont do them habitually. *(Angrily.)* By the way: my dressing-gown smells most damnably of benzine.

Mrs. Pearce.   No doubt it does, Mr. Higgins. But if you will wipe your fingers—

Higgins *(yelling)*.   Oh very well, very well: I'll wipe them in my hair in the future.

Mrs. Pearce.   I hope youre not offended, Mr. Higgins.

Higgins *(shocked at finding himself thought capable of an unamiable sentiment)*.   Not at all, not at all. Youre quite right, Mrs. Pearce: I shall be particularly careful before the girl. Is that all?

Mrs. Pearce.   No, sir. Might she use some of those Japanese dresses you brought from abroad? I really cant put her back into her old things.

Higgins.   Certainly. Anything you like. Is that all?

Mrs. Pearce.   Thank you, sir. Thats all. *(She goes out.)*

Higgins.   You know, Pickering, that woman has the most extraordinary ideas about me. Here I am, a shy, diffident sort of man. Ive never been able to feel really grown-up and tremendous, like other chaps. And yet she's firmly persuaded that I'm an arbitrary overbearing bossing kind of person. I cant account for it.

Mrs. Pearce returns.

Mrs. Pearce.   If you please, sir, the trouble's beginning already. Theres a dustman downstairs, Alfred Doolittle, wants to see you. He says you have his daughter here.

Pickering *(rising)*.   Phew! I say!

Higgins *(promptly)*.   Send the blackguard up.

Mrs. Pearce.   Oh, very well, sir. *(She goes out.)*

Pickering.   He may not be a blackguard, Higgins.

Higgins.   Nonsense. Of course he's a blackguard.

Pickering.   Whether he is or not, I'm afraid we shall have some trouble with him.

Higgins *(confidently)*.   Oh, no: I think not. If theres any trouble he shall have it with me, not I with him. And we are sure to get something interesting out of him.

Pickering.   About the girl?

Higgins.   No. I mean his dialect.

Pickering.   Oh!

Mrs. Pearce *(at the door)*.   Doolittle, sir. *(She admits Doolittle and retires)*.

Alfred is an elderly but vigorous dustman,[3] *clad in the costume of his profession, including a hat with a back brim covering his neck and shoulders. He has well marked and rather interesting features, and seems equally free from fear and conscience. He has a remarkably expressive voice, the result of a habit of giving vent to his feelings without reserve. His present pose is that of wounded honor and stern resolution.*

Doolittle *(at the door, uncertain which of the two gentlemen is his man)*.   Professor Iggins?

Higgins.   Here. Good morning. Sit down.

Doolittle.   Morning, Governor. *(He sits down magisterially.)* I come about a very serious matter, Governor.

Higgins *(to Pickering)*.   Brought up in Hounslow. Mother Welsh, I should think. *(Doolittle opens his mouth, amazed. Higgins continues.)* What do you want, Doolittle?

Doolittle *(menacingly)*.   I want my daughter: thats what I want. See?

Higgins.   Of course you do. Youre her father, arnt you? You dont suppose anyone else wants her, do you? I'm glad to see you have some spark of family feeling left. She's upstairs. Take her away at once.

Doolittle *(rising, fearfully taken aback)*.   What?

Higgins.   Take her away. Do you suppose I'm going to keep your daughter for you?

Doolittle *(remonstrating)*.   Now, now, look here, Governor. Is this reasonable? Is it fairity to take advantage of a man like this? The girl belongs to me. You got her. Where do I come in? *(He sits down again.)*

Higgins.   Your daughter had the audacity to come to my house and ask me to teach her to speak properly so that she could get a place in a flower-shop. This gentleman and my housekeeper have been here all the time. *(Bullying him.)* How dare you come here and attempt to blackmail me? You sent her here on purpose.

Doolittle *(protesting)*.   No, Governor.

Higgins.   You must have. How else could you possibly know that she is here?

Doolittle.   Don't take a man up like that, Governor.

Higgins.   The police shall take you up. This is a plant—a plot to extort money by threats. I shall telephone for the police. *(He goes resolutely to the telephone and opens the directory.)*

---

[3] Garbage collector.

Doolittle.   Have I asked you for a brass farthing? I leave it to the gentleman here: have I said a word about money?

Higgins (*throwing the book aside and marching down on Doolittle with a poser*):   What else did you come for?

Doolittle (*sweetly*).   Well, what would a man come for? Be human, Governor.

Higgins (*disarmed*).   Alfred: did you put her up to it?

Doolittle.   So help me, Governor, I never did. I take my Bible oath I aint seen the girl these two months past.

Higgins.   Then how did you know she was here?

Doolittle (*"most musical, most melancholy"*).   I'll tell you, Governor, if youll only let me get a word in. I'm willing to tell you. I'm wanting to tell you. I'm waiting to tell you.

Higgins.   Pickering: this chap has a certain natural gift of rhetoric. Observe the rhythm of his native woodnotes wild. "I'm willing to tell you: I'm wanting to tell you: I'm waiting to tell you." Sentimental rhetoric! thats the Welsh strain in him. It also accounts for his mendacity and dishonesty.

Pickering.   Oh, please, Higgins: I'm west country myself. *(To Doolittle.)* How did you know the girl was here if you didnt send her?

Doolittle.   It was like this, Governor. The girl took a boy in the taxi to give him a jaunt. Son of her landlady, he is. He hung about on the chance of her giving him another ride home. Well, she sent him back for her luggage when she heard you was willing for her to stop here. I met the boy at the corner of Long Acre and Endell Street.

Higgins.   Public house. Yes.

Doolittle.   The poor man's club, Governor: why shouldnt I?

Pickering.   Do let him tell his story, Higgins.

Doolittle.   He told me what was up. And I ask you, what was my feelings and my duty as a father? I says to the boy, "You bring me the luggage,"

Pickering.   Why didnt you go for it yourself?

Doolittle.   Landlady wouldnt have trusted me with it, Governor. She's that kind of woman: you know. I had to give the boy a penny afore he trusted me with it, the little swine. I brought it to her just to oblige you like, and make myself agreeable. Thats all.

Higgins.   How much luggage?

Doolittle.   Musical instrument, Governor. A few pictures, a trifle of jewelry, and a bird-cage. She said she didnt want no clothes. What was I to think from that, Governor? I ask you as a parent what was I to think?

Higgins.   So you came to rescue her from worse than death, eh?

Doolittle (*appreciatively: relieved at being so well understood*).   Just so, Governor. Thats right.

Pickering.   But why did you bring her luggage if you intended to take her away?

Doolittle.   Have I said a word about taking her away? Have I now?

Higgins (*determinedly*).   You're going to take her away, double quick. *(He crosses to the hearth and rings the bell.)*

Doolittle *(rising)*.   No, Governor. Dont say that. I'm not the man to stand in my girl's light. Heres a career opening for her, as you might say; and—

Mrs. Pearce opens the door and awaits orders.

Higgins.   Mrs. Pearce: this is Eliza's father. He has come to take her away. Give her to him. *(He goes back to the piano, with an air of washing his hands of the whole affair.)*

Doolittle: No. This is a misunderstanding. Listen here—

Mrs. Pearce: He cant take her away, Mr. Higgins: how can he? You told me to burn her clothes.

Doolittle.   That's right. I cant carry the girl through the streets like a blooming monkey, can I? I put it to you.

Higgins.   You have put it to me that you want your daughter. Take your daughter. If she has no clothes go out and buy her some.

Doolittle *(desperate)*.   Wheres the clothes she come in? Did I burn them or did your missus here?

Mrs. Pearce.   I am the housekeeper, if you please. I have sent for some clothes for your girl. When they come you can take her away. You can wait in the kitchen. This way, please.

Doolittle, much troubled, accompanies her to the door; then hestitates; finally turns confidentially to Higgins.

Doolittle: Listen here, Governor. You and me is men of the world, aint we?

Higgins.   Oh! Men of the world, are we? Youd better go, Mrs. Pearce.

Mrs. Pearce.   I think so, indeed, sir. *(She goes, with dignity.)*

Pickering: The floor is yours, Mr. Doolittle.

Doolittle *(to Pickering)*.   I thank you, Governor. *(To Higgins, who takes refuge on the piano bench, a little overwhelmed by the proximity of his visitor; for Doolittle has a professional flavor of dust about him.)* Well, the truth is, I've taken a sort of fancy to you, Governor; and if you want the girl, I'm not so set on having her back home again but what I might be open to an arrangement. Regarded in the light of a young woman, she's a fine handsome girl. As a daughter she's not worth her keep; and so I tell you straight. All I ask is my rights as a father; and youre the last man alive to expect me to let her go for nothing; for I can see youre one of the straight sort, Governor. Well, whats a five-pound note to you? and whats Eliza to me? *(He returns to his chair and sits down judicially.)*

Pickering.   I think you ought to know, Doolittle, that Mr. Higgins's intentions are entirely honorable.

Doolittle.   Course they are, Governor. If I thought they wasn't, I'd ask fifty.

Higgins *(revolted)*.   Do you mean to say that you would sell your daughter for £50?

Doolittle: Not in a general way I would; but to oblige a gentleman like you I'd do a good deal, I do assure you.

Pickering.   Have you no morals, man?

Doolittle (*unabashed*).   Cant afford them, Governor. Neither could you if you was as poor as me. Not that I mean any harm, you know. But if Liza is going to have a bit out of this, why not me too?

Higgins (*troubled*).   I dont know what to do, Pickering. There can be no question that as a matter of morals it's a positive crime to give this chap a farthing. And yet I feel a sort of rough justice in his claim.

Doolittle.   Thats it, Governor. Thats all I say. A father's heart, as it were.

Pickering.   Well, I know the feeling; but, really it seems hardly right—

Doolittle.   Dont say that, Governor. Dont look at it that way. What am I, Governors both? I ask you, what am I? I'm one of the undeserving poor: thats what I am. Think of what that means to a man. It means that he's up agen middle class morality all the time. If theres anything going, and I put in for a bit of it, it's always the same story: "Youre undeserving; so you cant have it." But my needs is as great as the most deserving widow's that ever got money out of six different charities in one week for the death of the same husband. I dont need less than a deserving man: I need more. I dont eat less hearty than him; and I drink a lot more. I want a bit of amusement, cause I'm a thinking man. I want cheerfulness and a song and a band when I feel low. Well, they charge me just the same for everything as they charge the deserving. What is middle class morality? Just an excuse for never giving me anything. Therefore, I ask you, as two gentlemen, not to play that game on me. I'm playing straight with you. I aint pretending to be deserving. I'm undeserving; and I mean to go on being undeserving. I like it; and thats the truth. Will you take advantage of a man's nature to do him out of the price of his own daughter what he's brought up and fed and clothed by the sweat of his brow until she's growed big enough to be interesting to you two gentlemen? Is five pounds unreasonable? I put it to you; and I leave it to you.

Higgins (*rising, and going over to Pickering*).   Pickering: if we were to take this man in hand for three months, he could choose between a seat in the Cabinet and a popular pulpit in Wales.

Pickering.   What do you say to that, Doolittle?

Doolittle.   Not me, Governor, thank you kindly. Ive heard all the preachers and all the prime ministers—for I'm a thinking man and game for politics or religion or social reform same as all the other amusements—and I tell you it's a dog's life any way you look at it. Undeserving poverty is my line. Taking one station in society with another, it's—it's—well, it's the only one that has any ginger in it, to my taste.

Higgins.   I suppose we must give him a fiver.

Pickering.   He'll make a bad use of it, I'm afraid.

Doolittle.   Not me, Governor, so help me I wont. Dont you be afraid that I'll save it and spare it and live idle on it. There wont be a penny of it left by Monday: I'll have to go to work same as if I'd never had it. It wont pauperize me, you bet. Just one good spree for myself and the missus, giving pleasure to ourselves and employment to others, and satisfaction to you to think it's not been throwed away. You couldnt spend it better.

Higgins *(taking out his pocket book and coming between Doolittle and the piano.)*   This is irresistible. Lets give him ten. *(He offers two notes to the dustman.)*

Doolittle.   No, Governor. She wouldnt have the heart to spend ten; and perhaps I shouldnt neither. Ten pounds is a lot of money: it makes a man feel prudent like; and then goodbye to happiness. You give me what I ask you, Governor: not a penny more, and not a penny less.

Pickering.   Why dont you marry that missus of yours? I rather draw the line at encouraging that sort of immorality.

Doolittle.   Tell her so, Governor: tell her so. *I'm* willing. It's me that suffers by it. Ive no hold on her. I got to be agreeable to her. I got to give her presents. I got to buy her clothes something sinful. I'm a slave to that woman, Governor, just because I'm not her lawful husband. And she knows it too. Catch her marrying me! Take my advice, Governor: marry Eliza while she's young and dont know no better. If you dont you'll be sorry for it after. If you do, she'll be sorry for it after; but better her than you, because youre a man, and she's only a woman and dont know how to be happy anyhow.

Higgins.   Pickering: if we listen to this man another minute, we shall have no convictions left. *(To Doolittle.)* Five pounds I think you said.

Doolittle.   Thank you kindly, Governor.

Higgins.   Youre sure you wont take ten?

Doolittle.   Not now. Another time, Governor.

Higgins *(handing him a five-pound note)*.   Here you are.

Doolittle.   Thank you, Governor. Good morning. *(He hurries to the door, anxious to get away with his booty. When he opens it he is confronted with a dainty and exquisitely clean young Japanese lady in a simple blue cotton kimono printed cunningly with small white jasmine blossoms. Mrs. Pearce is with her. He gets out of her way deferentially and apologizes.)* Beg pardon, Miss.

The Japanese Lady: Garn! Dont you know your own daughter?

Doolittle	*exclaiming*	Bly me! it's Eliza!
Higgins	*simul-*	Whats that? This!
Pickering:	*taneously*	By Jove!

Liza.   Dont I look silly?

Higgins.   Silly?

Mrs. Pearce *(at the door)*.   Now, Mr. Higgins, please dont say anything to make the girl conceited about herself.

Higgins *(conscientiously)*.   Oh! Quite right, Mrs. Pearce. *(To Eliza.)* Yes: damned silly.

Mrs. Pearce.   Please, sir.

Higgins *(correcting himself)*.   I mean extremely silly.

Liza.   I should look all right with my hat on. *(She takes up her hat; puts it on; and walks across the room to the fireplace with a fashionable air.)*

Higgins.   A new fashion, by George! And it ought to look horrible!

Doolittle *(with fatherly pride)*.   Well, I never thought she'd clean up as good looking as that, Governor. She's a credit to me, aint she?

Lisa.   I tell you, it's easy to clean up here. Hot and cold water on tap, just as much as you like, there is. Woolly towels, there is; and a towel horse so hot, it burns your fingers. Soft brushes to scrub yourself, and a wooden bowl of soap smelling like primroses. Now I know why ladies is so clean. Washing's a treat for them. Wish they could see what it is for the like of me!

Higgins.   I'm glad the bathroom met with your approval.

Liza.   It didnt: not all of it; and I dont care who hears me say it. Mrs. Pearce knows.

Higgins.   What was wrong, Mrs. Pearce?

Mrs. Pearce *(blandly)*.   Oh, nothing, sir. It doesnt matter.

Liza.   I had a good mind to break it. I didnt know which way to look. But I hung a towel over it, I did.

Higgins.   Over what?

Mrs. Pearce.   Over the looking-glass, sir.

Higgins.   Doolittle: you have brought your daughter up too strictly.

Doolittle.   Me! I never brought her up at all, except to give her a lick of a strap now and again. Dont put it on me, Governor. She aint accustomed to it, you see: thats all. But she'll soon pick up your free-and-easy ways.

Liza.   I'm a good girl, I am; and I wont pick up no free-and-easy ways.

Higgins.   Eliza: if you say again that youre a good girl, your father shall take you home.

Liza.   Not him. You dont know my father. All he come here for was to touch you for some money to get drunk on.

Doolittle.   Well, what else would I want money for? To put into the plate in church, I suppose. *(She puts out her tongue at him. He is so incensed by this that Pickering presently finds it necessary to step between them.)* Dont you give me none of your lip; and dont let me hear you giving this gentleman any of it neither, or youll hear from me about it. See?

Higgins.   Have you any further advice to give her before you go, Doolittle? Your blessing, for instance.

Doolittle.   No, Governor: I aint such a mug as to put up my children to all I know myself. Hard enough to hold them in without that. If you want Eliza's mind improved, Governor, you do it yourself with a strap. So long, gentlemen. *(He turns to go.)*

Higgins *(impressively)*.   Stop. Youll come regularly to see your daughter. It's your duty, you know. My brother is a clergyman; and he could help you in your talks with her.

Doolittle *(evasively)*.   Certainly, I'll come, Governor. Not just this week, because I have a job at a distance. But later on you may depend on me. Afternoon, gentlemen. Afternoon, maam. *(He touches his hat to Mrs. Pearce, who disdains the salutation and goes out. He winks at Higgins, thinking him probably a fellow-sufferer from Mrs. Pearce's difficult disposition, and follows her.)*

Liza.   Dont you believe the old liar. He'd as soon you set a bulldog on him as a clergyman. You wont see him again in a hurry.

Higgins.   I dont want to, Eliza. Do you?

Liza.   Not me. I dont want never to see him again, I dont. He's a disgrace to me, he is, collecting dust, instead of working at his trade.

Pickering.   What is his trade, Eliza?

Liza.   Talking money out of other people's pockets into his own. His proper trade's a navvy; and he works at it sometimes too—for exercise—and earns good money at it. Aint you going to call me Miss Doolittle any more?

Pickering.   I beg your pardon, Miss Doolittle. It was a slip of the tongue.

Liza.   Oh, I dont mind; only it sounded so genteel. I should just like to take a taxi to the corner of Tottenham Court Road and get out there and tell it to wait for me, just to put the girls in their place a bit. I wouldnt speak to them, you know.

Pickering.   Better wait til we get you something really fashionable.

Higgins.   Besides, you shouldnt cut your old friends now that you have risen in the world. Thats what we call snobbery.

Liza.   You dont call the like of them my friends now, I should hope. Theyve took it out of me often enough with their ridicule when they had the chance; and now I mean to get a bit of my own back. But if I'm to have fashionable clothes, I'll wait. I should like to have some. Mrs. Pearce says youre going to give me some to wear in bed at night different to what I wear in the daytime; but it do seem a waste of money when you could get something to shew. Besides, I never could fancy changing into cold things on a winter night.

Mrs. Pearce (*coming back*).   Now, Eliza. The new things have come for you to try on.

Liza.   Ah-ow-oo-oooh! (*She rushes out.*)

Mrs. Pearce (*following her*).   Oh, dont rush about like that, girl. (*She shuts the door behind her.*)

Higgins.   Pickering: we have taken on a stiff job.

Pickering (*with conviction*).   Higgins: we have.

* * * * *

There seems to be some curiosity as to what Higgins's lessons to Eliza were like. Well, here is a sample: the first one..

Picture Eliza, in her new clothes, and feeling her inside put out of step by a lunch, dinner, and breakfast of a kind to which it is unaccustomed, seated with Higgins and the Colonel in the study, feeling like a hospital out-patient at a first encounter with the doctors.

Higgins, constitutionally unable to sit still, discomposes her still more by striding restlessly about. But for the reassuring presence and quietude of her friend the Colonel she would run for her life, even back to Drury Lane.

Higgins.   Say your alphabet.

Liza.   I know my alphabet. Do you think I know nothing? I dont need to be taught like a child.

Higgins (*thundering*).   Say your alphabet.

Pickering.   Say it, Miss Doolittle. You will understand presently. Do what he tells you; and let him teach you in his own way.

Liza.   Oh well, if you put it like that—Ahyee, bəyee, cəyee, dəyee—

Higgins *(with the roar of a wounded lion).*   Stop. Listen to this, Pickering. This is what we pay for as elementary education. This unfortunate animal has been locked up for nine years in school at our expense to teach her to speak and read the language of Shakespear and Milton. And the result is Ahyee, Bə-yee, Cə-yee, Dəyee. *(To Eliza.)* Say A, B, C, D.

Liza *(almost in tears).*   But I'm sayin it. Ahyee, Bəyee, Cəyee—

Higgins.   Stop. Say a cup of tea.

Liza.   A cappətə-ee.

Higgins.   Put your tongue forward until it squeezes against the top of your lower teeth. Now say cup.

Liza.   C-c-c—I cant. C-Cup.

Pickering.   Good. Splendid, Miss Doolittle.

Higgins.   By Jupiter, she's done it the first shot. Pickering: we shall make a duchess of her. *(To Eliza.)* Now do you think you could possibly say tea? Not tə-yee, mind: if you ever say bə-yee cə-yee də-yee again you shall be dragged round the room three times by the hair of your head. *(Fortissimo.)* T, T, T, T.

Liza *(weeping).*   I cant hear no difference cep that it sounds more genteel-like when you say it.

Higgins.   Well, if you can hear that difference, what the devil are you crying for? Pickering: give her a chocolate.

Pickering.   No, no. Never mind crying a little, Miss Doolittle: you are doing very well; and the lessons wont hurt. I promise you I wont let him drag you round the room by your hair.

Higgins.   Be off with you to Mrs. Pearce and tell her about it. Think about it. Try to do it by yourself: and keep your tongue well forward in your mouth instead of trying to roll it up and swallow it. Another lesson at half-past four this afternoon. Away with you.

Eliza, still sobbing, rushes from the room.

And that is the sort of ordeal poor Eliza has to go through for months before we meet her again on her first appearance in London society of the professional class.

Act III

It is Mrs. Higgins's at-home day. Nobody has yet arrived. Her drawing room, in a flat on Chelsea Embankment, has three windows looking on the river; and the ceiling is not so lofty as it would be in an older house of the same pretension.

The windows are open, giving access to a balcony, with flowers in pots. If you stand with your face to the windows, you have the fireplace on your left and the door in the righthand wall close to the corner nearest the windows.

Mrs. Higgins was brought up on Morris and Burne-Jones;[4] *and her room, which is very unlike her son's room in Wimpole Street, is not crowded with furniture and little tables and nicknacks. In the middle of the room there is a big ottoman; and this, with the carpet, the Morris wall-papers, and the Morris chintz window curtains and brocade covers of the ottoman and its cushions, supply all the ornament, and are much too handsome to be hidden by odds and ends of useless things. A few good oil-paintings from the exhibitions in the Grosvenor Gallery thirty years ago (the Burne-Jones, not the Whistler side of them) are on the walls. The only landscape is a Cecil Lawson on the scale of a Rubens. There is a portrait of Mrs. Higgins as she was when she defied the fashion in her youth in one of the beautiful Rossettian costumes which, when caricatured by people who did not understand, led to the absurdities of popular estheticism in the eighteen-seventies.*

In the corner diagonally opposite the door Mrs. Higgins, now over sixty and long past taking the trouble to dress out of the fashion, sits writing at an elegantly simple writing-table with a bell button within reach of her hand. There is a Chippendale chair further back in the room between her and the window nearest her side. At the other side of the room, further forward, is an Elizabethan chair roughly carved in the taste of Inigo Jones. On the same side a piano in a decorated case. The corner between the fireplace and the window is occupied by a divan cushioned in Morris chintz.

It is between four and five in the afternoon.

The door is opened violently; and Higgins enters with his hat on.

Mrs. Higgins (*dismayed*).   Henry! (*Scolding him.*) What are you doing here today? It is my at-home day: you promised not to come. (*As he bends to kiss her, she takes his hat off, and presents it to him.*)

Higgins.   Oh bother! (*He throws the hat down on the table.*)

Mrs. Higgins.   Go home at once.

Higgins (*kissing her*).   I know, mother. I came on purpose.

Mrs. Higgins.   But you mustnt. I'm serious, Henry. You offend all my friends: they stop coming whenever they meet you.

Higgins.   Nonsense! I know I have no small talk; but people dont mind. (*He sits on the settee.*)

Mrs. Higgins.   Oh! dont they? Small talk indeed! What about your large talk? Really, dear, you mustnt stay.

---

[4] William Morris (1834–1896), although he was a poet and an artist, is remembered principally as a furniture designer and interior decorator. Edward Burne-Jones (1833–1898) was a painter whose work somewhat reflects the influence of Dante Gabriel Rossetti (1828–1882), the founder of the Pre-Raphaelite Brotherhood. Rossetti's paintings, inspired by pre-Renaissance art, featured women in flowing gauzy gowns, the "Rossettian costumes" referred to later in this stage direction.

Higgins.   I must. Ive a job for you. A phonetic job.

Mrs. Higgins.   No use, dear. I'm sorry; but I cant get round your vowels; and though I like to get pretty postcards in your patent shorthand, I always have to read the copies in ordinary writing you so thoughtfully send me.

Higgins.   Well, this isnt a phonetic job.

Mrs. Higgins.   You said it was.

Higgins.   Not your part of it. Ive picked up a girl.

Mrs. Higgins.   Does that mean that some girl has picked you up?

Higgins.   Not at all. I dont mean a love affair.

Mrs. Higgins.   What a pity!

Higgins.   Why?

Mrs. Higgins.   Well, you never fall in love with anyone under forty-five. When will you discover that there are some rather nice-looking young women about?

Higgins.   Oh, I cant be bothered with young women. My idea of a lovable woman is somebody as like you as possible. I shall never get into the way of seriously liking young women: some habits lie too deep to be changed. *(Rising abruptly and walking about, jingling his money and his keys in his trouser pockets.)* Besides, theyre all idiots.

Mrs. Higgins.   Do you know what you would do if you really loved me, Henry?

Higgins.   Oh bother! What? Marry, I suppose.

Mrs. Higgins.   No. Stop fidgeting and take your hands out of your pockets. *(With a gesture of despair, he obeys and sits down again.)* Thats a good boy. Now tell me about the girl.

Higgins.   She's coming to see you.

Mrs. Higgins.   I dont remember asking her.

Higgins.   You didnt. *I* asked her. If youd known her you wouldnt have asked her.

Mrs. Higgins.   Indeed! Why?

Higgins.   Well, it's like this. She's a common flower girl. I picked her off the kerbstone.

Mrs. Higgins.   And invited her to my at-home!

Higgins *(rising and coming to her to coax her).*   Oh, thatll be all right. Ive taught her to speak properly; and she has strict orders as to her behavior. She's to keep to two subjects: the weather and everybody's health—Fine day and How do you do, you know—and not to let herself go on things in general. That will be safe.

Mrs. Higgins.   Safe! To talk about our health! about our insides! perhaps about our outsides! How could you be so silly, Henry?

Higgins *(impatiently).*   Well, she must talk about something. *(He controls himself and sits down again.)* Oh, she'll be all right: dont you fuss. Pickering is in it with me. Ive a sort of bet on that I'll pass her off as a duchess in six months. I started on her some months ago; and she's getting on like a house on fire. I shall win my bet. She has a quick ear; and she's easier to teach than my middle-class pupils because she's had to learn a complete new language. She talks English almost as you talk French.

Mrs. Higgins.   Thats satisfactory, at all events.

Higgins.   Well, it is and it isnt.

Mrs. Higgins.   What does that mean?

Higgins.   You see, Ive got her pronunciation all right; but you have to consider not only how a girl pronounces, but what she pronounces; and that's where—

They are interrupted by the parlor-maid, announcing guests.

The Parlor-Maid.   Mrs. and Miss Eynsford Hill. *(She withdraws.)*

Higgins.   Oh Lord! *(He rises; snatches his hat from the table; and makes for the door; but before he reaches it his mother introduces him.)*

Mrs. and Miss Eynsford Hill are the mother and daughter who sheltered from the rain in Covent Garden. The mother is well bred, quiet, and has the habitual anxiety of straitened means. The daughter has acquired a gay air of being very much at home in society: the bravado of genteel poverty.

Mrs. Eynsford Hill *(to Mrs. Higgins).*   How do you do? *(They shake hands.)*

Miss Eynsford Hill.   How d'you do? *(She shakes.)*

Mrs. Higgins *(introducing).*   My son Henry.

Mrs. Eynsford Hill: Your celebrated son! I have so longed to meet you, Professor Higgins.

Higgins *(glumly, making no movement in her direction).*   Delighted. *(He backs against the piano and bows brusquely.)*

Miss Eynsford Hill *(going to him with confident familiarity).*   How do you do?

Higgins *(staring at her).*   Ive seen you before somewhere. I havnt the ghost of a notion where; but Ive heard your voice. *(Drearily.)* It doesnt matter. Youd better sit down.

Mrs. Higgins.   I'm sorry to say that my celebrated son has no manners. You mustnt mind him.

Miss Eynsford Hill *(gaily).*   I don't. *(She sits in the Elizabethan chair.)*

Mrs. Eynsford Hill *(a little bewildered).*   Not at all. *(She sits on the ottoman between her daughter and Mrs. Higgins, who has turned her chair away from the writing-table.)*

Higgins.   Oh, have I been rude? I didnt mean to be.

He goes to the central window, through which, with his back to the company, he contemplates the river and the flowers in Battersea Park on the opposite bank as if they were a frozen desert.

   The parlor-maid returns, ushering in Pickering.

The Parlor-Maid.   Colonel Pickering. *(She withdraws.)*

Pickering.   How do you do, Mrs. Higgins?

Mrs. Higgins.   So glad youve come. Do you know Mrs. Eynsford Hill—Miss Eynsford Hill? *(Exchange of bows. The Colonel brings the Chippendale chair a little forward between Mrs. Hill and Mrs. Higgins, and sits down.)*

Pickering.   Has Henry told you what weve come for?

Higgins (*over his shoulder*).   We were interrupted: damn it!

Mrs. Higgins.   Oh Henry, Henry, really!

Mrs. Eynsford Hill (*half rising*).   Are we in the way?

Mrs. Higgins (*rising and making her sit down again*).   No, no. You couldnt have come more fortunately: we want you to meet a friend of ours.

Higgins (*turning hopefully*).   Yes, by George! We want two or three people. You'll do as well as anybody else.

The parlor-maid returns, ushering Freddy.

The Parlor-Maid.   Mr. Eynsford Hill.

Higgins (*almost audibly, past endurance*).   God of Heaven! another of them.

Freddy (*shaking hands with Mrs. Higgins*).   Ahdedo?

Mrs. Higgins.   Very good of you to come. (*Introducing.*) Colonel Pickering.

Freddy (*bowing*).   Ahdedo?

Mrs. Higgins.   I dont think you know my son, Professor Higgins.

Freddy (*going to Higgins*).   Ahdedo?

Higgins (*looking at him much as if he were a pickpocket*).   I'll take my oath Ive met you before somewhere. Where was it?

Freddy.   I dont think so.

Higgins (*resignedly*).   It dont matter, anyhow. Sit down.

He shakes Freddy's hand, and almost slings him on to the ottoman with his face to the window; then comes round to the other side of it.

Higgins.   Well, here we are, anyhow! (*He sits down on the ottoman next to Mrs. Eynsford Hill, on her left.*) And now, what the devil are we going to talk about until Eliza comes?

Mrs. Higgins.   Henry: you are the life and soul of the Royal Society's soirées; but really youre rather trying on more commonplace occasions.

Higgins.   Am I? Very sorry. (*Beaming suddenly.*) I suppose I am, you know. (*Uproariously.*) Ha, ha!

Miss Eynsford Hill (*who considers Higgins quite eligible matrimonially*).   I sympathize. *I* havnt any small talk. If people would only be frank and say what they really think!

Higgins (*relapsing into gloom*).   Lord forbid!

Mrs. Eynsford Hill (*taking up her daughter's cue*).   But why?

Higgins.   What they think they ought to think is bad enough, Lord knows; but what they really think would break up the whole show. Do you suppose it would be really agreeable if I were to come out now with what *I* really think?

Miss Eynsford Hill (*gaily*).   Is it so very cynical?

Higgins.   Cynical! Who the dickens said it was cynical? I mean it wouldnt be decent.

Mrs. Eynsford Hill (*seriously*).   Oh! I'm sure you dont mean that, Mr. Higgins.

Higgins.   You see, we're all savages, more or less. We're supposed to be civilized and cultured—to know all about poetry and philosophy and art and science, and so on; but how many of us know even the meanings of these names? *(To Miss Hill.)* What do you know of poetry? *(To Mrs. Hill.)* What do you know of science? *(Indicating Freddy.)* What does he know of art or science or anything else? What the devil do you imagine I know of philosophy?

Mrs. Higgins *(warningly).*   Or of manners, Henry?

The Parlor-Maid *(opening the door).*   Miss Doolittle. *(She withdraws.)*

Higgins *(rising hastily and running to Mrs. Higgins).*   Here she is, mother. *(He stands on tiptoe and makes signs over his mother's head at Eliza to indicate to her which lady is her hostess.)*

Eliza, who is exquisitely dressed, produces an impression of such remarkable distinction and beauty as she enters that they all rise, quite fluttered. Guided by Higgins's signals, she comes to Mrs. Higgins with studied grace.

Liza *(speaking with pedantic correctness of pronunciation and great beauty of tone).*   How do you do, Mrs. Higgins? *(She gasps slightly in making sure of the H in Higgins, but is quite successful.)* Mr. Higgins told me I might come.

Mrs. Higgins *(cordially).*   Quite right: I'm very glad indeed to see you.

Pickering.   How do you do, Miss Doolittle?

Liza *(shaking hands with him).*   Colonel Pickering, is it not?

Mrs. Eynsford Hill.   I feel sure we have met before, Miss Doolittle. I remember your eyes.

Liza.   How do you do? *(She sits down on the ottoman gracefully in the place just left vacant by Higgins.)*

Mrs. Eynsford Hill *(introducing).*   My daughter Clara.

Liza.   How do you do?

Clara *(impulsively).*   How do you do? *(She sits down on the ottoman beside Eliza, devouring her with her eyes.)*

Mrs. Eynsford Hill *(introducing).*   My son Freddy.

Liza.   How do you do?

Freddy bows and sits down in the Elizabethan chair, infatuated.

Higgins *(suddenly).*   By George, yes: it all comes back to me! *(They stare at him.)* Covent Garden! *(Lamentably.)* What a damned thing!

Mrs. Higgins.   Henry, please! *(He is about to sit on the edge of the table.)* Dont sit on my writing-table: youll break it.

Higgins *(sulkily).*   Sorry.

He goes to the divan, stumbling into the fender and over the fire-irons on his way; extricating himself with muttered imprecations; and finishing his disastrous

journey by throwing himself so impatiently on the divan that he almost breaks it. Mrs. Higgins looks at him, but controls herself and says nothing.
A long and painful pause ensues.

Mrs. Higgins *(at last, conversationally).*   Will it rain, do you think?

Liza.   The shallow depression in the west of these islands is likely to move slowly in an easterly direction. There are no indications of any great change in the barometrical situation.

Freddy.   Ha! ha! how awfully funny!

Liza.   What is wrong with that, young man? I bet I got it right.

Freddy.   Killing!

Mrs. Eynsford Hill.   I'm sure I hope it wont turn cold. Theres so much influenza about. It runs right through our whole family regularly every spring.

Liza *(darkly).*   My aunt died of influenza: so they said.

Mrs. Eynsford Hill *(clicks her tongue sympathetically).*   !!!

Liza *(in the same tragic tone).*   But it's my belief they done the old woman in.

Mrs. Higgins *(puzzled).*   Done her in?

Liza.   Y-e-e-e-es, Lord love you! Why should she die of influenza? She come through diphtheria right enough the year before. I saw her with my own eyes. Fairly blue with it, she was. They all thought she was dead; but my father he kept ladling gin down her throat til she came to so sudden that she bit the bowl off the spoon.

Mrs. Eynsford Hill *(startled).*   Dear me!

Liza *(piling up the indictment).*   What call would a woman with that strength in her have to die of influenza? What become of her new straw hat that should have come to me? Somebody pinched it; and what I say is, them as pinched it done her in.

Mrs. Eynsford Hill.   What does doing her in mean?

Higgins *(hastily).*   Oh, thats the new small talk. To do a person in means to kill them.

Mrs. Eynsford Hill *(to Eliza, horrified).*   You surely dont believe that your aunt was killed?

Liza.   Do I not! Them she lived with would have killed her for a hat-pin, let alone a hat.

Mrs. Eynsford Hill.   But it cant have been right for your father to pour spirits down her throat like that. It might have killed her.

Liza.   Not her. Gin was mother's milk to her. Besides, he'd poured so much down his own throat that he knew the good of it.

Mrs. Eynsford Hill.   Do you mean that he drank?

Liza.   Drank! My word! Something chronic.

Mrs. Eynsford Hill.   How dreadful for you!

Liza.   Not a bit. It never did him no harm what I could see. But then he did not keep it up regular. *(Cheerfully.)* On the burst, as you might say, from time to time. And always more agreeable when he had a drop in. When he was out of work, my mother used to give him fourpence and tell him to go out and not come back until he'd drunk himself cheerful and loving-like.

Theres lots of women has to make their husbands drunk to make them fit to live with. *(Now quite at her ease.)* You see, it's like this. If a man has a bit of conscience, it always takes him when he's sober; and then it makes him low-spirited. A drop of booze just takes that off and makes him happy. *(To Freddy, who is in convulsions of suppressed laughter.)* Here! what are you sniggering at?

Freddy.   The new small talk. You do it so awfully well.

Liza.   If I was doing it proper, what was you laughing at? *(To Higgins.)* Have I said anything I oughtnt?

Mrs. Higgins *(interposing)*.   Not at all, Miss Doolittle.

Liza.   Well, thats a mercy, anyhow. *(Expansively.)* What I always say is—

Higgins *(rising and looking at his watch)*.   Ahem!

Liza *(looking round at him; taking the hint; and rising)*.   Well: I must go. *(They all rise. Freddy goes to the door.)* So pleased to have met you. Goodbye. *(She shakes hands with Mrs. Higgins.)*

Mrs. Higgins.   Goodbye.

Liza.   Goodbye, Colonel Pickering.

Pickering.   Goodbye, Miss Doolittle. *(They shake hands.)*

Liza *(nodding to the others)*.   Goodbye, all.

Freddy *(opening the door for her)*.   Are you walking across the Park, Miss Doolittle? If so—

Liza *(with perfectly elegant diction)*.   Walk! Not bloody likely. *(Sensation.)* I am going in a taxi. *(She goes out.)*

Pickering gasps and sits down. Freddy goes out on the balcony to catch another glimpse of Eliza.

Mrs. Eynsford Hill *(suffering from shock)*.   Well, I really cant get used to the new ways.

Clara *(throwing herself discontentedly into the Elizabethan chair)*.   Oh, it's all right, mamma, quite right. People will think we never go anywhere or see anybody if you are so old-fashioned.

Mrs. Eynsford Hill.   I daresay I am very old-fashioned; but I do hope you wont begin using that expression, Clara. I have got accustomed to hear you talking about men as rotters, and calling everything filthy and beastly; though I do think it horrible and unlady like. But this last is really too much. Dont you think so, Colonel Pickering?

Pickering.   Dont ask me. Ive been away in India for several years; and manners have changed so much that I sometimes dont know whether I'm at a respectable dinnertable or in a ship's forecastle.

Clara.   It's all a matter of habit. Theres no right or wrong in it. Nobody means anything by it. And it's so quaint, and gives such a smart emphasis to things that are not in themselves very witty. I find the new small talk delightful and quite innocent.

Mrs. Eynsford Hill *(rising)*.   Well, after that, I think it's time for us to go.

Pickering and Higgins rise.

Clara *(rising).*   Oh yes: we have three at-homes to go to still. Goodbye, Mrs. Higgins. Goodbye, Colonel Pickering. Goodbye, Professor Higgins.

Higgins *(coming grimly at her from the divan, and accompanying her to the door).*   Goodbye. Be sure you try on that small talk at the three at-homes. Dont be nervous about it. Pitch it in strong.

Clara *(all smiles).*   I will. Goodbye. Such nonsense, all this early Victorian prudery!

Higgins *(tempting her).*   Such damned nonsense!

Clara.   Such bloody nonsense!

Mrs. Eynsford Hill *(convulsively).*   Clara!

Clara.   Ha! ha! *(She goes out radiant, conscious of being thoroughly up to date, and is heard descending the stairs in a stream of silvery laughter.)*

Freddy *(to the heavens at large).*   Well, I ask you—*(He gives it up, and comes to Mrs. Higgins.)* Goodbye.

Mrs. Higgins *(shaking hands).*   Goodbye. Would you like to meet Miss Doolittle again?

Freddy *(eagerly).*   Yes, I should, most awfully.

Mrs. Higgins.   Well, you know my days.

Freddy.   Yes. Thanks awfully. Goodbye. *(He goes out.)*

Mrs. Eynsford Hill.   Goodbye, Mr. Higgins.

Higgins.   Goodbye. Goodbye.

Mrs. Eynsford Hill *(to Pickering).*   It's no use. I shall never be able to bring myself to use that word.

Pickering.   Dont. It's not compulsory, you know. Youll get on quite well without it.

Mrs. Eynsford Hill.   Only, Clara is so down on me if I am not positively reeking with the latest slang. Goodbye.

Pickering.   Goodbye. *(They shake hands.)*

Mrs. Eynsford Hill *(to Mrs. Higgins).*   You mustnt mind Clara. *(Pickering, catching from her lowered tone that this is not meant for him to hear, discreetly joins Higgins at the window.)* We're so poor! and she gets so few parties, poor child! She doesnt quite know. *(Mrs. Higgins, seeing that her eyes are moist, takes her hand sympathetically and goes with her to the door.)* But the boy is nice. Dont you think so?

Mrs. Higgins.   Oh, quite nice. I shall always be delighted to see him.

Mrs. Eynsford Hill.   Thank you, dear. Goodbye. *(She goes out.)*

Higgins *(eagerly).*   Well? Is Eliza presentable? *(He swoops on his mother and drags her to the ottoman, where she sits down in Eliza's place with her son on her left.)*

Pickering returns to his chair on her right.

Mrs. Higgins.   You silly boy, of course she's not presentable. She's a triumph of your art and of her dressmaker's; but if you suppose for a moment that she doesn't give herself away in every sentence she utters, you must be perfectly cracked about her.

Pickering.   But dont you think something might be done? I mean something to eliminate the sanguinary element from her conversation.

Mrs. Higgins.   Not as long as she is in Henry's hands

Higgins *(aggrieved)*.   Do you mean that my language is improper?

Mrs. Higgins.   No, dearest: it would be quite proper—say on a canal barge; but it would not be proper for her at a garden party.

Higgins *(deeply injured)*.   Well I must say—

Pickering *(interrupting him)*.   Come, Higgins: you must learn to know yourself. I havent heard such language as yours since we used to review the volunteers in Hyde Park twenty years ago.

Higgins *(sulkily)*.   Oh, well, if you say so, I suppose I dont always talk like a bishop.

Mrs. Higgins *(quieting Henry with a touch)*.   Colonel Pickering: will you tell me what is the exact state of things in Wimpole Street?

Pickering *(cheerfully: as if this completely changed the subject)*.   Well, I have come to live there with Henry. We work together at my Indian Dialects; and we think it more convenient—

Mrs. Higgins.   Quite so. I know all about that: it's an excellent arrangement. But where does this girl live?

Higgins.   With us, of course. Where should she live?

Mrs. Higgins.   But on what terms? Is she a servant? If not, what is she?

Pickering *(slowly)*.   I think I know what you mean, Mrs. Higgins.

Higgins.   Well, dash me if *I* do! Ive had to work at the girl every day for months to get her to her present pitch. Besides, she's useful. She knows where my things are, and remembers my appointments and so forth.

Mrs. Higgins.   How does your housekeeper get on with her?

Higgins.   Mrs. Pearce? Oh, she's jolly glad to get so much taken off her hands; for before Eliza came, she used to have to find things and remind me of my appointments. But she's got some silly bee in her bonnet about Eliza. She keeps saying "You dont think, sir": doesnt she, Pick?

Pickering.   Yes, thats the formula. "You dont think, sir." Thats the end of every conversation about Eliza.

Higgins.   As if I ever stop thinking about the girl and her confounded vowels and consonants. I'm worn out, thinking about her, and watching her lips and her teeth and her tongue, not to mention her soul, which is the quaintest of the lot.

Mrs. Higgins.   You certainly are a pretty pair of babies, playing with your live doll.

Higgins.   Playing! The hardest job I ever tackled: make no mistake about that, mother. But you have no idea how frightfully interesting it is to take a human being and change her into a quite different human being by creating a new speech for her. It's filling up the deepest gulf that separates class from class and soul from soul.

Pickering *(drawing his chair closer to Mrs. Higgins and bending over to her eagerly)*.   Yes: it's enormously interesting. I assure you, Mrs. Higgins, we take Eliza very seriously. Every week—every day almost—there is some new change. (*Closer again.*) We keep records of every stage—dozens of gramophone disks and photographs—

Higgins (*assailing her at the other ear.*)   Yes, by George: it's the most absorbing experiment I ever tackled. She regularly fills our lives up: doesnt she, Pick?

Pickering.   We're always talking Eliza.

Higgins.   Teaching Eliza.

Pickering.   Dressing Eliza.

Mrs. Higgins.   What!

Higgins.   Inventing new Elizas.

Higgins.	*speaking together*	You know, she has the most extraordinary quickness of ear:
Pickering.		I assure you, my dear Mrs. Higgins, that girl
Higgins.		just like a parrot. Ive tried her with every
Pickering.		is a genius. She can play the piano quite beautifully.
Higgins.		possible sort of sound that a human being can make—
Pickering.		We have taken her to classical concerts and to music
Higgins.		Continental dialects, African dialects, Hottentot
Pickering.		halls; and it's all the same to her; she plays everything
Higgins.		clicks, things it took me years to get hold of; and
Pickering.		she hears right off when she comes home, whether it's
Higgins.		she picks them up like a shot, right away, as if she had
Pickering.		Beethoven and Brahms or Lehar and Lionel Monckton;
Higgins.		been at it all her life.
Pickering.		though six months ago, she'd never as much as touched a piano—

Mrs. Higgins (*putting her fingers in her ears, as they are by this time shouting one another down with an intolerable noise*).   Sh-sh-sh—sh! (*They stop.*)

Pickering.   I beg your pardon. (*He draws his chair back apologetically.*)

Higgins.   Sorry. When Pickering starts shouting nobody can get a word in edgeways.

Mrs. Higgins.   Be quiet, Henry. Colonel Pickering: dont you realize that when Eliza walked in Wimpole Street, something walked in with her?

Pickering.   Her father did. But Henry soon got rid of him.

Mrs. Higgins.   It would have been more to the point if her mother had. But as her mother didnt something else did.

Pickering.   But what?

Mrs. Higgins (*unconsciously dating herself by the word*).   A problem.

Pickering.   Oh, I see. The problem of how to pass her off as a lady.

Higgins.   I'll solve that problem. Ive half solved it already.

Mrs. Higgins.   No, you two infinitely stupid male creatures: the problem of what is to be done with her afterwards.

Higgins.   I dont see anything in that. She can go her own way, with all the advantages I have given her.

Mrs. Higgins.   The advantages of that poor woman who was here just now! The manners and habits that disqualify a fine lady from earning her own living without giving her a fine lady's income! Is that what you mean?

Pickering (*indulgently, being rather bored*).   Oh, that will be all right, Mrs. Higgins. (*He rises to go.*)

Higgins (*rising also*).   We'll find her some light employment.

Pickering.   She's happy enough. Dont you worry about her. Goodbye. (*He shakes hands as if he were consoling a frightened child, and makes for the door.*)

Higgins.   Anyhow, theres no good bothering now. The thing's done. Goodbye, mother. (*He kisses her, and follows Pickering.*)

Pickering (*turning for a final consolation*).   There are plenty of openings. We'll do whats right. Goodbye.

Higgins (*to Pickering as they go out together*).   Lets take her to the Shakespear exhibition at Earls Court.

Pickering.   Yes: lets. Her remarks will be delicious.

Higgins.   She'll mimic all the people for us when we get home.

Pickering.   Ripping. (*Both are heard laughing as they go downstairs.*)

Mrs. Higgins (*rises with an impatient bounce, and returns to her work at the writing-table. She sweeps a litter of disarranged papers out of the way; snatches a sheet of paper from her stationery case; and tries resolutely to write. At the third time she gives it up; flings down her pen; grips the table angrily and exclaims*): Oh, men! men!! men!!!

✻   ✻   ✻   ✻   ✻

Clearly Eliza will not pass as a duchess yet; and Higgins's bet remains unwon. But the six months are not yet exhausted and just in time Eliza does actually pass as a princess. For a glimpse of how she did it imagine an Embassy in London one summer evening after dark. The hall door has an awning and a carpet across the sidewalk to the kerb, because a grand reception is in progress. A small crowd is lined up to see the guests arrive.

A Rolls-Royce car drives up. Pickering, in evening dress, with medals and orders, alights, and hands out Eliza, in opera cloak, evening dress, diamonds, fan, flowers and all accessories. Higgins follows. The car drives off; and the three go up the steps and into the house, the door opening for them as they approach.

Inside the house they find themselves in a spacious hall from which the grand staircase rises. On the left are the arrangements for the gentlemen's cloaks. The male guests are depositing their hats and wraps there.

On the right is a door leading to the ladies' cloakroom. Ladies are going in cloaked and coming out in splendor. Pickering whispers to Eliza and points out the ladies' room. She goes into it. Higgins and Pickering take off their overcoats and take tickets for them from the attendant.

One of the guests, occupied in the same way, has his back turned. Having taken his ticket, he turns round and reveals himself as an important looking young man with an astonishingly hairy face. He has an enormous moustache, flowing out into luxuriant whiskers. Waves of hair cluster on his brow. His hair is cropped closely at the back, and glows with oil. Otherwise he is very smart. He wears several worthless orders. He is evidently a foreigner, guessable as a whiskered Pandour from Hungary; but in spite of the ferocity of his moustache he is amiable and genially voluble.

Recognizing Higgins, he flings his arms wide apart and approaches him enthusiastically.

Whiskers.   Maestro, maestro. *(He embraces Higgins and kisses him on both cheeks.)* You remember me?

Higgins.   No I dont. Who the devil are you?

Whiskers.   I am your pupil: your first pupil, your best and greatest pupil. I am little Nepommuck, the marvellous boy. I have made your name famous throughout Europe. You teach me phonetic. You cannot forget ME.

Higgins.   Why dont you shave?

Nepommuck.   I have not your imposing appearance, your chin, your brow. Nobody notice me when I shave. Now I am famous: they call me Hairy Faced Dick.

Higgins.   And what are you doing here among all these swells?

Nepommuck.   I am an interpreter. I speak 32 languages. I am indispensable at these international parties. You are great cockney specialist: you place a man anywhere in London the moment he opens his mouth. I place any man in Europe.

A footman hurries down the grand staircase and comes to Nepommuck.

Footman.   You are wanted upstairs. Her excellency cannot understand the Greek gentleman.

Nepommuck.   Thank you, yes, immediately.

The footman goes and is lost in the crowd.

Nepommuck *(to Higgins).*   This Greek diplomat pretends he cannot speak nor understand English. He cannot deceive me. He is the son of a Clerkenwell watchmaker. He speaks English so villainously that he dare not utter a word of it without betraying his origin. I help him to pretend; but I make him pay through the nose. I make them all pay. Ha ha! *(He hurries upstairs.)*

Pickering.   Is this fellow really an expert? Can he find out Eliza and blackmail her?

Higgins.   We shall see. If he finds her out I lose my bet.

Eliza comes from the cloakroom and joins them.

Pickering.   Well, Eliza, now for it. Are you ready?

Liza.   Are you nervous, Colonel?

Pickering.   Frightfully. I feel exactly as I felt before my first battle. It's the first time that frightens.

Liza.   It is not the first time for me, Colonel. I have done this fifty times—hundreds of times—in my little piggery in Angel Court in my daydreams. I am in a dream now. Promise me not to let Professor Higgins wake me; for if he does I shall forget everything and talk as I used to in Drury Lane.

Pickering.   Not a word, Higgins. *(To Eliza.)* Now, ready?

Liza.   Ready.

Pickering.   Go.

They mount the stairs, Higgins last. Pickering whispers to the footman on the first landing.

First Landing Footman.   Miss Doolittle, Colonel Pickering, Professor Higgins.

Second Landing Footman.   Miss Doolittle, Colonel Pickering, Professor Higgins.

At the top of the staircase the Ambassador and his wife, with Nepommuck at her elbow, are receiving.

Hostess *(taking Eliza's hand)*.   How d'ye do?

Host *(same play)*.   How d'ye do? How d'ye do, Pickering?

Liza *(with a beautiful gravity that awes her hostess)*.   How do you do? (She passes on to the drawingroom.)

Hostess.   Is that your adopted daughter, Colonel Pickering? She will make a sensation.

Pickering.   Most kind of you to invite her for me. *(He passes on.)*

Hostess *(to Nepommuck)*.   Find out all about her.

Nepommuck *(bowing)*.   Excellency—(He goes into the crowd.)

Host.   How d'ye do, Higgins? You have a rival here tonight. He introduced himself as your pupil. Is he any good?

Higgins.   He can learn a language in a fortnight—knows dozens of them. A sure mark of a fool. As a phonetician, no good whatever.

Hostess.   How d'ye do, Professor?

Higgins.   How do you do? Fearful bore for you this sort of thing. Forgive my part in it. *(He passes on.)*

In the drawing room and its suite of salons the reception is in full swing. Eliza passes through. She is so intent on her ordeal that she walks like a somnambulist in a desert instead of a debutante in a fashionable crowd. They stop talking to look at her, admiring her dress, her jewels, and her strangely attractive self. Some of the younger ones at the back stand on their chairs to see.

The Host and Hostess come in from the staircase and mingle with their guests. Higgins, gloomy and contemptuous of the whole business, comes into the group where they are chatting.

Hostess.   Ah, here is Professor Higgins: he will tell us. Tell us all about the wonderful young lady, Professor.

Higgins (*almost morosely*).   What wonderful young lady?

Hostess.   You know very well. They tell me there has been nothing like her in London since people stood on their chairs to look at Mrs. Langtry.

Nepommuck joins the group, full of news.

Hostess.   Ah, here you are at last, Nepommuck. Have you found out all about the Doolittle lady?

Nepommuck.   I have found out all about her. She is a fraud.

Hostess.   A fraud! Oh no.

Nepommuck.   YES, yes. She cannot deceive me. Her name cannot be Doolittle.

Higgins.   Why?

Nepommuck.   Because Doolittle is an English name. And she is not English.

Hostess.   Oh, nonsense! She speaks English perfectly.

Nepommuck.   Too perfectly. Can you shew me any English woman who speaks English as it should be spoken? Only foreigners who have been taught to speak it speak it well.

Hostess.   Certainly she terrified me by the way she said How d'ye do. I had a schoomistress who talked like that; and I was mortally afraid of her. But if she is not English what is she?

Nepommuck.   Hungarian.

All the Rest.   Hungarian!

Nepommuck.   Hungarian. And of royal blood. I am Hungarian. My blood is royal.

Higgins.   Did you speak to her in Hungarian?

Nepommuck.   I did. She was very clever. She said "Please speak to me in English: I do not understand French." French! She pretend not to know the difference between Hungarian and French. Impossible: she knows both.

Higgins.   And the blood royal? How did you find that out?

Nepommuck.   Instinct, maestro, instinct. Only the Magyar races can produce that air of the divine right, those resolute eyes. She is a princess.

Host.   What do you say, Professor?

Higgins.   I say an ordinary London girl out of the gutter and taught to speak by an expert. I place her in Drury Lane.

Nepommuck.   Ha ha ha! Oh, maestro, maestro, you are mad on the subject of cockney dialects. The London gutter is the whole world for you.

Higgins (*to the Hostess*).   What does your Excellency say?

Hostess.   Oh, of course I agree with Nepommuck. She must be a princess at least.

Host.   Not necessarily legitimate, of course. Morganatic perhaps. But that is undoubtedly her class.

Higgins.   I stick to my opinion.

Hostess.   Oh, you are incorrigible.

The group breaks up, leaving Higgins isolated. Pickering joins him.

Pickering.   Where is Eliza? We must keep an eye on her.

Eliza joins them.

Liza.   I dont think I can bear much more. The people all stare so at me. An old lady has just told me that I speak exactly like Queen Victoria. I am sorry if I have lost your bet. I have done my best; but nothing can make me the same as these people.

Pickering.   You have not lost it, my dear. You have won it ten times over.

Higgins.   Let us get out of this. I have had enough of chattering to these fools.

Pickering.   Eliza is tired; and I am hungry. Let us clear out and have supper somewhere.

Act IV

The Wimpole Street laboratory. Midnight. Nobody in the room. The clock on the mantelpiece strikes twelve. The fire is not alight: it is a summer night. Presently Higgins and Pickering are heard on the stairs.

Higgins *(calling down to Pickering)*.   I say, Pick: lock up, will you? I shant be going out again.

Pickering.   Right. Can Mrs. Pearce go to bed? We dont want anything more, do we?

Higgins.   Lord, no!

Eliza opens the door and is seen on the lighted landing in all the finery in which she has just won Higgins's bet for him. She comes to the hearth, and switches on the electric lights there. She is tired: her pallor contrasts strongly with her dark eyes and hair; and her expression is almost tragic. She takes off her cloak; puts her fan and gloves on the piano; and sits down on the bench, brooding and silent. Higgins, in evening dress, with overcoat and hat, comes in, carrying a smoking jacket which he has picked up downstairs. He takes off the hat and overcoat; throws them carelessly on the newspaper stand; disposes of his coat in the same way; puts on the smoking jacket; and throws himself wearily into the easy-chair at the hearth. Pickering, similarly attired, comes in. He also takes off his hat and overcoat, and is about to throw them on Higgins's when he hesitates.

Pickering.   I say: Mrs. Pearce will row if we leave these things lying about in the drawing room.

Higgins.   Oh, chuck them over the bannisters into the hall. She'll find them there in the morning and put them away all right. She'll think we were drunk.

Pickering.   We are, slightly. Are there any letters?

Higgins.   I didnt look. (*Pickering takes the overcoats and hats and goes downstairs. Higgins begins half singing half yawning an air from La Fanciulla del Golden West. Suddenly he stops and exclaims:*) I wonder where the devil my slippers are!

Eliza looks at him darkly; then rises suddenly and leaves the room. Higgins yawns again, and resumes his song. Pickering returns, with the contents of the letter-box in his hand.

Pickering.   Only circulars, and this coroneted billet-doux for you. (*He throws the circulars into the fender, and posts himself on the hearth-rug, with his back to the grate.*)

Higgins (*glancing at the billet-doux*).   Money-lender. (*He throws the letter after the circulars.*)

Eliza returns with a pair of large down-at-heel slippers. She places them on the carpet before Higgins, and sits as before without a word.

Higgins (*yawning again*).   Oh Lord! What an evening! What a crew! What a silly tomfoolery! (*He raises his shoe to unlace it, and catches sight of the slippers. He stops unlacing and looks at them as if they had appeared there of their own accord.*) Oh! theyre there, are they?

Pickering (*stretching himself*).   Well, I feel a bit tired. It's been a long day. The garden party, a dinner party, and the reception! Rather too much of a good thing. But youve won your bet, Higgins. Eliza did the trick, and something to spare, eh?

Higgins (*fervently*).   Thank God it's over!

Eliza flinches violently; but they take no notice of her; and she recovers herself and sits stonily as before.

Pickering.   Were you nervous at the garden party? *I* was. Eliza didnt seem a bit nervous.

Higgins.   Oh, she wasnt nervous. I knew she'd be all right. No: it's the strain of putting the job through all these months that has told on me. It was interesting enough at first, while we were at the phonetics; but after that I got deadly sick of it. If I hadnt backed myself to do it I should have chucked the whole thing up two months ago. It was a silly notion: the whole thing has been a bore.

Pickering.   Oh come! the garden party was frightfully exciting. My heart began beating like anything.

Higgins.   Yes, for the first three minutes. But when I saw we were going to win hands down, I felt like a bear in a cage, hanging about doing nothing. The dinner was worse: sitting gorging there for over an hour, with nobody but a damned fool of a fashionable woman to talk to! I tell you, Pickering, never again for me. No more artificial duchesses. The whole thing has been simple purgatory.

Pickering.   Youve never been broken in properly to the social routine. (*Strolling over to the piano.*) I rather enjoy dipping into it occasionally myself: it makes me feel young again. Anyhow, it was a great success: an immense success. I was quite frightened once or twice because Eliza was doing it so well. You see, lots of the real people cant do it at all: theyre such fools that they think style comes by nature to people in their position; and so they never learn. Theres always something professional about doing a thing superlatively well.

Higgins.   Yes: thats what drives me mad: the silly people dont know their own silly business. (*Rising.*) However, it's over and done with; and now I can go to bed at last without dreading tomorrow.

Eliza's beauty becomes murderous.

Pickering.   I think I shall turn in too. Still, it's been a great occasion: a triumph for you. Goodnight. (*He goes.*)

Higgins (*following him*).   Goodnight. (*Over his shoulder, at the door.*) Put out the lights, Eliza; and tell Mrs. Pearce not to make coffee for me in the morning: I'll take tea. (*He goes out.*)

Eliza tries to control herself and feel indifferent as she rises and walks across to the hearth to switch off the lights. By the time she gets there she is on the point of screaming. She sits down in Higgins's chair and holds on hard to the arms. Finally she gives way and flings herself furiously on the floor, raging.

Higgins (*in despairing wrath outside*).   What the devil have I done with my slippers? (*He appears at the door.*)

Liza (*snatching up the slippers, and hurling them at him one after the other with all her force*).   There are your slippers. And there. Take your slippers; and may you never have a day's luck with them!

Higgins (*astounded*).   What on earth—! (*He comes to her.*) Whats the matter? Get up. (*He pulls her up.*) Anything wrong?

Liza (*breathless*).   Nothing wrong—with you. Ive won your bet for you, havnt I? Thats enough for you. *I* dont matter, I suppose.

Higgins.   You won my bet! You! Presumptuous insect! *I* won it. What did you throw those slippers at me for?

Liza.   Because I wanted to smash your face. I'd like to kill you, you selfish brute. Why didnt you leave me where you picked me out of —in the gutter? You thank God it's all over, and that now you can throw me back again there, do you? (*She crisps her fingers frantically.*)

Higgins (*looking at her in cool wonder*).   The creature is nervous, after all.

Liza (*gives a suffocated scream of fury, and instinctively darts her nails at his face*).!!

Higgins (*catching her wrists*).   Ah! Would you? Claws in, you cat. How dare you shew your temper to me? Sit down and be quiet. (*He throws her roughly into the easy-chair.*)

Liza (*crushed by superior strength and weight*).   Whats to become of me? Whats to become of me?

Higgins.   How the devil do I know whats to become of you? What does it matter what becomes of you?

Liza.   You dont care. I know you dont care. You wouldnt care if I was dead. I'm nothing to you—not so much as them slippers.

Higgins (*thundering*).   Those slippers.

Liza (*with bitter submission*).   Those slippers. I didnt think it made any difference now.

A pause. Eliza hopeless and crushed. Higgins a little uneasy.

Higgins (*in his loftiest manner*).   Why have you begun going on like this? May I ask whether you complain of your treatment here?

Liza.   No.

Higgins.   Has anybody behaved badly to you? Colonel Pickering? Mrs. Pearce? Any of the servants?

Liza.   No.

Higgins.   I presume you dont pretend that *I* have treated you badly?

Liza.   No.

Higgins.   I am glad to hear it. (*He moderates his tone.*) Perhaps youre tired after the strain of the day. Will you have a glass of champagne? (*He moves towards the door.*)

Liza.   No. (*Recollecting her manners.*) Thank you.

Higgins (*good-humored again*).   This has been coming on you for some days. I suppose it was natural for you to be anxious about the garden party. But thats all over now. (*He pats her kindly on the shoulder. She writhes.*) Theres nothing more to worry about.

Liza.   No. Nothing more for you to worry about. (*She suddenly rises and gets away from him by going to the piano bench, where she sits and hides her face.*) Oh God! I wish I was dead.

Higgins (*staring after her in sincere surprise*).   Why? In heaven's name, why? (*Reasonably, going to her.*) Listen to me, Eliza. All this irritation is purely subjective.

Liza.   I dont understand. I'm too ignorant.

Higgins.   It's only imagination. Low spirits and nothing else. Nobody's hurting you. Nothing's wrong. You go to bed like a good girl and sleep it off. Have a little cry and say your prayers: that will make you comfortable.

Liza.   I heard your prayers. "Thank God it's all over!"

Higgins (*impatiently*).   Well, dont you thank God it's all over? Now you are free and can do what you like.

Liza *(pulling herself together in desperation).*   What am I fit for? What have you left me fit for? Where am I to go? What am I to do? Whats to become of me?

Higgins *(enlightened, but not at all impressed).*   Oh, thats whats worrying you, is it? *(He thrusts his hands into his pockets, and walks about in his usual manner, rattling the contents of his pockets, as if condescending to a trivial subject out of pure kindness.)* I shouldnt bother about it if I were you. I should imagine you wont have much difficulty in settling yourself somewhere or other, though I hadnt quite realized that you were going away. *(She looks quickly at him: he does not look at her, but examines the dessert stand on the piano and decides that he will eat an apple.)* You might marry, you know. *(He bites a large piece out of the apple and munches it noisily.)* You see, Eliza, all men are not confirmed old bachelors like me and the Colonel. Most men are the marrying sort (poor devils!); and youre not bad-looking: it's quite a pleasure to look at you sometimes—not now, of course, because youre crying and looking as ugly as the very devil; but when youre all right and quite yourself, youre what I should call attractive. That is, to the people in the marrying line, you understand. You go to bed and have a good nice rest; and then get up and look at yourself in the glass; and you wont feel so cheap.

Eliza again looks at him, speechless, and does not stir.
   The look is quite lost on him: he eats his apple with a dreamy expression of happiness, as it is quite a good one.

Higgins *(a genial afterthought occurring to him).*   I daresay my mother could find some chap or other who would do very well.

Liza.   We were above that at the corner of Tottenham Court Road.

Higgins *(waking up).*   What do you mean?

Liza.   I sold flowers. I didnt sell myself. Now youve made a lady of me I'm not fit to sell anything else. I wish youd left me where you found me.

Higgins *(slinging the core of the apple decisively into the grate).*   Tosh, Eliza. Dont you insult human relations by dragging all this cant about buying and selling into it. You neednt marry the fellow if you dont like him.

Liza.   What else am I to do?

Higgins.   Oh, lots of things. What about your old idea of a florist's shop? Pickering could set you up in one: he has lots of money. *(Chuckling.)* He'll have to pay for all those togs you have been wearing today; and that, with the hire of the jewelry, will make a big hole in two hundred pounds. Why, six months ago you would have thought it the millennium to have a flower shop of your own. Come! youll be all right. I must clear off to bed: I'm devilish sleepy. By the way, I came down for something: I forget what it was.

Liza.   Your slippers.

Higgins.   Oh yes, of course, You shied them at me. *(He picks them up, and is going out when she rises and speaks to him.)*

Liza.   Before you go, sir—

Higgins (*dropping the slippers in his surprise at her calling him Sir*).   Eh?

Liza.   Do my clothes belong to me or to Colonel Pickering?

Higgins (*coming back into the room as if her question were the very climax of unreason*).   What the devil use would they be to Pickering?

Liza.   He might want them for the next girl you pick up to experiment on.

Higgins (*shocked and hurt*).   Is that the way you feel towards us?

Liza.   I dont want to hear anything more about that. All I want to know is whether anything belongs to me. My own clothes were burnt.

Higgins.   But what does it matter? Why need you start bothering about that in the middle of the night?

Liza.   I want to know what I may take away with me. I dont want to be accused of stealing.

Higgins (*now deeply wounded*).   Stealing! You shouldnt have said that, Eliza. That shews a want of feeling.

Liza.   I'm sorry. I'm only a common ignorant girl; and in my station I have to be careful. There cant be any feelings between the like of you and the like of me. Please will you tell me what belongs to me and what doesnt?

Higgins (*very sulky*).   You may take the whole damned houseful if you like. Except the jewels. Theyre hired. Will that satisfy you? (*He turns on his heel and is about to go in extreme dudgeon.*)

Liza (*drinking in his emotion like nectar, and nagging him to provoke a further supply*).   Stop, please. (*She takes off her jewels.*) Will you take these to your room and keet them safe? I dont want to run the risk of their being missing.

Higgins (*furious*).   Hand them over. (*She puts them into his hands.*) If these belonged to me instead of to the jeweller, I'd ram them down your ungrateful throat. (*He perfunctorily thrusts them into his pockets, unconsciously decorating himself with the protruding ends of the chains.*)

Liza (*taking a ring off*).   This ring isnt the jeweller's: it's the one you bought me in Brighton. I dont want it now. (*Higgins dashes the ring violently into the fireplace, and turns on her so threateningly that she crouches over the piano with her hands over her face, and exclaims.*) Dont you hit me.

Higgins.   Hit you! You infamous creature, how dare you accuse me of such a thing? It is you who have hit me. You have wounded me to the heart.

Liza (*thrilling with hidden joy*).   I'm glad. Ive got a little of my own back, anyhow.

Higgins (*with dignity, in his finest professional style*).   You have caused me to lose my temper: a thing that has hardly ever happened to me before. I prefer to say nothing more tonight. I am going to bed.

Liza (*pertly*).   Youd better leave a note for Mrs. Pearce about the coffee; for she wont be told by me.

Higgins (*formally*).   Damn Mrs. Pearce; and damn the coffee; and damn you; and (*wildly*) damn my own folly in having lavished my hard-earned knowledge and the treasure of my regard and intimacy on a heartless guttersnipe. (*He goes out with impressive decorum, and spoils it by slamming the door savagely.*)

Eliza goes down on her knees on the heathrug to look for the ring. When she finds it she considers for a moment what to do with it. Finally she flings it down on the dessert stand and goes upstairs in a tearing rage.

*   *   *   *   *

The furniture of Eliza's room has been increased by a big wardrobe and a sumptuous dressing-table. She comes in and switches on the electric light. She goes to the wardrobe; opens it; and pulls out a walking dress, a hat, and a pair of shoes, which she throws on the bed. She takes off her evening dress and shoes; then takes a padded hanger from the wardrobe; adjusts it carefully in the evening dress; and hangs it in the wardrobe, which she shuts with a slam. She puts on her walking shoes, her walking dress, and hat. She takes her wrist watch from the dressing table and fastens it on. She pulls on her gloves; takes her vanity bag; and looks into it to see that her purse is there before hanging it on her wrist. She makes for the door. Every movement expresses her furious resolution.

She takes a last look at herself in the glass.

She suddenly puts out her tongue at herself; then leaves the room, switching off the electric light at the door.

Meanwhile, in the street outside, Freddy Eynsford Hill, lovelorn, is gazing up at the second floor, in which one of the windows is still lighted.

The light goes out.

Freddy.   Goodnight, darling, darling, darling.

Eliza comes out, giving the door a considerable bang behind her.

Liza.   Whatever are you doing here?

Freddy.   Nothing. I spend most of my nights here. It's the only place where I'm happy. Dont laugh at me, Miss Doolittle.

Liza.   Dont you call me Miss Doolittle, do you hear? Liza's good enough for me. (*She breaks down and grabs him by the shoulders.*) Freddy: you dont think I'm a heartless guttersnipe, do you?

Freddy.   Oh no, no, darling: how can you imagine such a thing? You are the loveliest, dearest—

He loses all self-control and smothers her with kisses. She, hungry for comfort, responds. They stand there in one another's arms.

An elderly police constable arrives.

Constable (*scandalized*).   Now then! Now then!! Now then!!!

They release one another hastily.

Freddy.   Sorry, constable. Weve only just become engaged.

They run away.

The constable shakes his head, reflecting on his own courtship and on the vanity of human hopes. He moves off in the opposite direction with slow professional steps.

The flight of the lovers takes them to Cavendish Square. There they halt to consider their next move.

Liza (*out of breath*).   He didnt half give me a fright, that copper. But you answered him proper.
Freddy.   I hope I havent taken you out of your way. Where were you going?
Liza.   To the river.
Freddy.   What for?
Liza.   To make a hole in it.
Freddy (*horrified*).   Eliza, darling. What do you mean? What's the matter?
Liza.   Never mind. It doesnt matter now. There's nobody in the world now but you and me, is there?
Freddy.   Not a soul.

They indulge in another embrace, and are again surprised by a much younger constable.

Second Constable.   Now then, you two! What's this? Where do you think you are? Move along here, double quick.
Freddy.   As you say, sir, double quick.

They run away again, and are in Hanover Square before they stop for another conference.

Freddy.   I had no idea the police were so devilishly prudish.
Liza.   It's their business to hunt girls off the streets.
Freddy.   We must go somewhere. We cant wander about the streets all night.
Liza.   Cant we? I think it'd be lovely to wander about for ever.
Freddy.   Oh, darling.

They embrace again, oblivious of the arrival of a crawling taxi. It stops.

Taximan.   Can I drive you and the lady anywhere, sir?

They start asunder.

Liza.   Oh, Freddy, a taxi. The very thing.
Freddy.   But, damn it, I've no money.
Liza.   I have plenty. The Colonel thinks you should never go out without ten pounds in your pocket. Listen. We'll drive about all night; and in the morning I'll call on old Mrs. Higgins and ask her what I ought to do. I'll tell you all about it in the cab. And the police wont touch us there.
Freddy.   Righto! Ripping. (*To the Taximan*). Wimbledon Common. (*They drive off.*)

Act V

Mrs. Higgins's drawing room. She is at her writing-table as before. The parlor-maid comes in.

The Parlor-Maid *(at the door)*.   Mr. Henry, maam, is downstairs with Colonel Pickering.

Mrs. Higgins.   Well, shew them up.

The Parlor-Maid.   Theyre using the telephone, maam. Telephoning to the police, I think.

Mrs. Higgins.   What!

The Parlor-Maid *(coming further in and lowering her voice)*.   Mr. Henry is in a state, maam. I thought I'd better tell you.

Mrs. Higgins.   If you had told me that Mr. Henry was not in a state it would have been more surprising. Tell them to come up when theyve finished with the police. I suppose he's lost something.

The Parlor-Maid.   Yes, maam. *(Going.)*

Mrs. Higgins.   Go upstairs and tell Miss Doolittle that Mr. Henry and the Colonel are here. Ask her not to come down til I send for her.

The Parlor-Maid.   Yes, maam.

Higgins bursts in. He is, as the parlor-maid has said, in a state.

Higgins.   Look here, mother: heres a confounded thing!

Mrs. Higgins.   Yes, dear. Good morning. *(He checks his impatience and kisses her, whilst the parlor-maid goes out.)* What is it?

Higgins.   Eliza's bolted.

Mrs. Higgins *(calmly continuing her writing)*.   You must have frightened her.

Higgins.   Frightened her! nonsense! She was left last night, as usual, to turn out the lights and all that; and instead of going to bed she changed her clothes and went right off: her bed wasnt slept in. She came in a cab for her things before seven this morning; and that fool Mrs. Pearce let her have them without telling me a word about it. What am I to do?

Mrs. Higgins.   Do without, I'm afraid, Henry. The girl has a perfect right to leave if she chooses.

Higgins *(wandering distractedly across the room)*.   But I cant find anything. I dont know what appointments Ive got. I'm— *(Pickering comes in. Mrs. Higgins puts down her pen and turns away from the writing-table.)*

Pickering *(shaking hands)*.   Good morning, Mrs. Higgins. Has Henry told you? *(He sits down on the ottoman.)*

Higgins.   What does that ass of an inspector say? Have you offered a reward?

Mrs. Higgins *(rising in indignant amazement)*.   You dont mean to say you have set the police after Eliza.

Higgins.   Of course. What are the police for? What else could we do? *(He sits in the Elizabethan chair.)*

Pickering.   The inspector made a lot of difficulties. I really think he suspected us of some improper purpose.

Mrs. Higgins.   Well, of course he did. What right have you to go to the police and give the girl's name as if she were a thief, or a lost umbrella, or something? Really! *(She sits down again, deeply vexed.)*

Higgins.   But we want to find her.

Pickering.   We cant let her go like this, you know, Mrs. Higgins. What were we to do?

Mrs. Higgins.   You have no more sense, either of you, than two children. Why—

The parlor-maid comes in and breaks off the conversation.

The Parlor-Maid.   Mr. Henry: a gentleman wants to see you very particular. He's been sent on from Wimpole Street.

Higgins.   Oh, bother! I cant see anyone now. Who is it?

The Parlor-Maid.   A Mr. Doolittle, sir.

Pickering.   Doolittle! Do you mean the dustman?

The Parlor-Maid.   Dustman! Oh no, sir: a gentleman.

Higgins *(springing up excitedly)*.   By George, Pick, it's some relative of hers that she's gone to. Somebody we know nothing about. *(To the parlor-maid.)* Send him up, quick.

The Parlor-Maid.   Yes, sir. *(She goes.)*

Higgins *(eagerly, going to his mother)*.   Genteel relatives! now we shall hear something. *(He sits down in the Chippendale chair.)*

Mrs. Higgins.   Do you know any of her people?

Pickering.   Only her father: the fellow we told you about.

The Parlor-Maid *(announcing)*.   Mr. Doolittle. *(She withdraws.)*

Doolittle enters. He is resplendently dressed as for a fashionable wedding, and might, in fact, be the bridegroom. A flower in his buttonhole, a dazzling silk hat, and patent leather shoes complete the effect. He is too concerned with the business he has come on to notice Mrs. Higgins. He walks straight to Higgins, and accosts him with vehement reproach.

Doolittle *(indicating his own person)*.   See here! Do you see this? You done this.

Higgins.   Done what, man?

Doolittle.   This, I tell you. Look at it. Look at this hat. Look at this coat.

Pickering.   Has Eliza been buying you clothes?

Doolittle.   Eliza! not she. Why would she buy me clothes?

Mrs. Higgins.   Good morning, Mr. Doolittle. Wont you sit down?

Doolittle *(taken aback as he becomes conscious that he has forgotten his hostess)*.   Asking your pardon, maam. *(He approaches her and shakes her proffered hand.)* Thank you. *(He sits down on the ottoman, on Pickering's right.)* I am that full of what has happened to me that I cant think of anything else.

Higgins.   What the dickens has happened to you?

Doolittle.   I shouldnt mind if it had only happened to me: anything might happen to anybody and nobody to blame but Providence, as you might say. But this is something that you done to me: yes, you, Enry Iggins.

Higgins.   Have you found Eliza?

Doolittle.   Have you lost her?

Higgins.   Yes.

Doolittle.   You have all the luck, you have. I aint found her; but she'll find me quick enough now after what you done to me.

Mrs. Higgins.   But what has my son done to you, Mr. Doolittle?

Doolittle.   Done to me! Ruined me. Destroyed my happiness. Tied me up and delivered me into the hands of middle class morality.

Higgins (*rising intolerantly and standing over Doolittle*).   Youre raving. Youre drunk. Youre mad. I gave you five pounds. After that I had two conversations with you, at half-a-crown an hour. Ive never seen you since.

Doolittle.   Oh! Drunk am I? Mad am I? Tell me this. Did you or did you not write a letter to an old blighter in America that was giving five millions to found Moral Reform Societies all over the world, and that wanted you to invent a universal language for him?

Higgins.   What! Ezra D. Wannafeller! He's dead. (*He sits down again carelessly.*)

Doolittle.   Yes: he's dead; and I'm done for. Now did you or did you not write a letter to him to say that the most original moralist at present in England, to the best of your knowledge, was Alfred Doolittle, a common dustman?

Higgins.   Oh, after your first visit I remember making some silly joke of the kind.

Doolittle.   Ah! you may well call it a silly joke. It put the lid on me right enough. Just give him the chance he wanted to shew that Americans is not like us: that they reckonize and respect merit in every class of life, however humble. Them words is in his blooming will, in which, Henry Higgins, thanks to your silly joking, he leaves me a share in his Pre-digested Cheese Trust worth three thousand a year on condition that I lecture for his Wannafeller Moral Reform World League as often as they ask me up to six times a year.

Higgins.   The devil he does! Whew! (*Brightening suddenly.*) What a lark!

Pickering.   A safe thing for you, Doolittle. They wont ask you twice.

Doolittle.   It aint the lecturing I mind. I'll lecture them blue in the face, I will, and not turn a hair. It's making a gentleman of me that I object to. Who asked him to make a gentleman of me? I was happy. I was free. I touched pretty nigh everybody for money when I wanted it, same as I touched you, Enry Iggins. Now I am worried; tied neck and heels; and everybody touches me for money. It's a fine thing for you, says my solicitor. Is it? says I. You mean it's a good thing for you, I says. When I was a poor man and had a solicitor once when they found a pram in the dust cart, he got me off, and got shut of me and got me shut of him as quick as he could. Same with the doctors: used to shove me out of the hospital before I could hardly stand on my legs, and nothing to pay. Now they finds out that I'm not a healthy man and cant live unless they looks after me twice a day. In the house I'm not let do a hand's turn for myself: somebody else must do it and touch me for it. A year ago I hadnt a relative in the world except for two or three that wouldnt speak to me. Now Ive fifty, and not a decent week's wages among the lot of them. I have to live for others and not for myself: thats middle class morality. You talk of losing Eliza. Dont you be anxious: I bet she's on my doorstep by this: she that could support herself easy by selling flowers if I wasnt respectable. And the next one to touch me will be you, Enry Iggins. I'll have to learn to speak middle class language from you, instead of speaking proper English. Thats where youll come in; and I daresay thats what you done it for.

Mrs. Higgins.   But, my dear Mr. Doolittle, you need not suffer all this if you are really in earnest. Nobody can force you to accept this bequest. You can repudiate it. Isnt that so, Colonel Pickering?

Pickering.   I believe so.

Doolittle *(softening his manner in deference to her sex)*.   Thats the tragedy of it, maam. It's easy to say chuck it; but I havnt the nerve. Which of us has? We're all intimidated. Intimidated, maam: thats what we are. What is there for me if I chuck it but the workhouse in my old age? I have to dye my hair already to keep my job as a dustman. If I was one of the deserving poor, and had put by a bit, I could chuck it; but then why should I, acause the deserving poor might as well be millionaires for all the happiness they ever has. They dont know what happiness is. But I, as one of the undeserving poor, have nothing between me and the pauper's uniform but this here blasted three thousand a year that shoves me into the middle class. (Excuse the expression, maam; youd use it yourself if you had my provocation.) Theyve got you every way you turn: it's a choice between the Skilly of the workhouse and the Char Bydis of the middle class;[5] and I havnt the nerve for the workhouse. Intimidated: thats what I am. Broke. Bought up. Happier men than me will call for my dust, and touch me for their tip; and I'll look on helpless, and envy them. And thats what your son brought me to. *(He is overcome by emotion.)*

Mrs. Higgins.   Well, I'm very glad youre not going to do anything foolish, Mr. Doolittle. For this solves the problem of Eliza's future. You can provide for her now.

Doolittle *(with melancholy resignation)*.   Yes, maam: I'm expected to provide for everyone now, out of three thousand a year.

Higgins *(jumping up)*.   Nonsense! he cant provide for her. He shant provide for her. She doesnt belong to him. I paid him five pounds for her. Doolittle: either youre an honest man or a rogue.

Doolittle *(tolerantly)*.   A little of both, Henry, like the rest of us: a little of both.

Higgins.   Well, you took money for the girl; and you have no right to take her as well.

---

[5] Doolittle's version of "between Scylla and Charybdis," an expression meaning "caught between two dangers," one of which cannot be avoided without encountering the other.

Mrs. Higgins.   Henry: dont be absurd. If you want to know where Eliza is, she is upstairs.

Higgins *(amazed)*.   Upstairs!!! Then I shall jolly soon fetch her downstairs. *(He makes resolutely for the door)*.

Mrs. Higgins *(rising and following him)*.   Be quiet, Henry. Sit down.

Higgins.   I—

Mrs. Higgins.   Sit down, dear; and listen to me.

Higgins.   Oh very well, very well, very well. *(He throws himself ungraciously on the ottoman, with his face towards the windows.)* But I think you might have told us this half an hour ago.

Mrs. Higgins.   Eliza came to me this morning. She told me of the brutal way you two treated her.

Higgins *(bounding up again.)*   What!

Pickering *(rising also)*.   My dear Mrs. Higgins, she's been telling you stories. We didnt treat her brutally. We hardly said a word to her; and we parted on particularly good terms. *(Turning on Higgins.)* Higgins: did you bully her after I went to bed?

Higgins.   Just the other way about. She threw my slippers in my face. She behaved in the most outrageous way. I never gave her the slightest provocation. The slippers came bang into my face the moment I entered the room— before I had uttered a word. And used perfectly awful language.

Pickering *(astonished)*.   But why? What did we do to her?

Mrs. Higgins.   I think I know pretty well what you did. The girl is naturally rather affectionate, I think. Isnt she, Mr. Doolittle?

Doolittle.   Very tender-hearted, maam. Takes after me.

Mrs. Higgins.   Just so. She had become attached to you both. She worked very hard for you, Henry. I dont think you quite realize what anything in the nature of brain work means to a girl of her class. Well, it seems that when the great day of trial came, and she did this wonderful thing for you without making a single mistake, you two sat there and never said a word to her, but talked together of how glad you were that it was all over and how you had been bored with the whole thing. And then you were surprised because she threw your slippers at you! I should have thrown the fire-irons at you.

Higgins.   We said nothing except that we were tired and wanted to go to bed. Did we, Pick?

Pickering *(shrugging his shoulders)*.   That was all.

Mrs. Higgins *(ironically)*.   Quite sure?

Pickering.   Absolutely. Really, that was all.

Mrs. Higgins.   You didnt thank her, or pet her, or admire her, or tell her how splendid she'd been.

Higgins *(impatiently)*.   But she knew all about that. We didnt make speeches to her, if thats what you mean.

Pickering *(conscience striken)*.   Perhaps we were a little inconsiderate. Is she very angry?

Mrs. Higgins *(returning to her place at the writing-table)*.   Well, I'm afraid she wont go back to Wimpole Street, especially now that Mr. Doolittle is able to keep up the position you have thrust on her; but she says she is quite willing to meet you on friendly terms and let bygones be bygones.

Higgins (*furious*).   Is she, by George? Ho!

Mrs. Higgins.   If you promise to behave yourself, Henry, I'll ask her to come down. If not, go home; for you have taken up quite enough of my time.

Higgins.   Oh, all right. Very well. Pick: you behave yourself. Let us put on our best Sunday manners for this creature that we picked out of the mud.

(*He flings himself sulkily into the Elizabethan chair.*)

Doolittle (*remonstrating.*)   Now, now, Enry Iggins! Have some consideration for my feelings as a middle class man.

Mrs. Higgins.   Remember your promise, Henry. (*She presses the bell-button on the writing-table.*) Mr. Doolittle: will you be so good as to step out on the balcony for a moment. I dont want Eliza to have the shock of your news until she has made it up with these two gentlemen. Would you mind?

Doolittle.   As you wish, lady. Anything to help Henry to keep her off my hands.

(*He disappears through the window.*)

The parlor-maid answers the bell. Pickering sits down in Doolittle's place.

Mrs. Higgins.   Ask Miss Doolittle to come down, please.

The Parlor-Maid.   Yes, maam. (*She goes out.*)

Mrs. Higgins.   Now, Henry: be good.

Higgins.   I am behaving myself perfectly.

Pickering.   He is doing his best, Mrs. Higgins.

A pause. Higgins throws back his head; stretches out his legs; and begins to whistle.

Mrs. Higgins.   Henry, dearest, you dont look at all nice in that attitude.

Higgins (*pulling himself together*).   I was not trying to look nice, mother.

Mrs. Higgins.   It doesn't matter, dear. I only wanted to make you speak.

Higgins.   Why?

Mrs. Higgins.   Because you cant speak and whistle at the same time.

Higgins groans. Another very trying pause.

Higgins (*springing up, out of patience*).   Where the devil is that girl? Are we to wait here all day?

Eliza enters, sunny, self-possessed, and giving a staggeringly convincing exhibition of ease of manner. She carries a little workbasket, and is very much at home. Pickering is too much taken aback to rise.

Liza.   How do you do, Professor Higgins? Are you quite well?

Higgins (*choking*).   Am I—(*He can say no more.*)

Liza.   But of course you are: you are never ill. So glad to see you again, Colonel Pickering. (*He rises hastily; and they shake hands.*) Quite chilly this morning, isnt it? (*She sits down on his left. He sits beside her.*)

Higgins.   Dont you dare try this game on me. I taught it to you; and it doesnt take me in. Get up and come home; and dont be a fool.

Eliza takes a piece of needlework from her basket, and begins to stitch at it, without the least notice of this outburst.

Mrs. Higgins.   Very nicely put, indeed, Henry. No woman could resist such an invitation.

Higgins.   You let her alone, mother. Let her speak for herself. You will jolly soon see whether she has an idea that I havnt put into her head or a word that I havent put into her mouth. I tell you I have created this thing out of the squashed cabbage leaves of Covent Garden; and now she pretends to play the fine lady with me.

Mrs. Higgins (*placidly*).   Yes, dear; but youll sit down, wont you?

Higgins sits down again, savagely.

Liza (*to Pickering, taking no apparent notice of Higgins, and working away deftly*).   Will you drop me altogether now that the experiment is over, Colonel Pickering?

Pickering.   Oh dont. You mustnt think of it as an experiment. It shocks me, somehow.

Liza.   Oh, I'm only a squashed cabbage leaf—

Pickering (*impulsively*).   No.

Liza (*continuing quietly*).   —but I owe so much to you that I should be very unhappy if you forgot me.

Pickering.   It's very kind of you to say so, Miss Doolittle.

Liza.   It's not because you paid for my dresses. I know you are generous to everybody with money. But it was from you that I learnt really nice manners; and that is what makes one a lady, isnt it? You see it was so very difficult for me with the example of Professor Higgins always before me. I was brought up to be just like him, unable to control myself, and using bad language on the slightest provocation. And I should never have known that ladies and gentlemen didnt behave like that if you hadnt been there.

Higgins.   Well!!

Pickering.   Oh, thats only his way, you know. He doesnt mean it.

Liza.   Oh, *I* didnt mean it either, when I was a flower girl. It was only my way. But you see I did it; and thats what makes the difference after all.

Pickering.   No doubt. Still, he taught you to speak, and I couldnt have done that, you know.

Liza (*trivially*).   Of course: that is his profession.

Higgins.   Damnation!

Liza *(continuing).*   It was just like learning to dance in the fashionable way: there was nothing more than that in it. But do you know what began my real education?

Pickering.   What?

Liza *(stopping her work for a moment).*   Your calling me Miss Doolittle that day when I first came to Wimpole Street. That was the beginning of self-respect for me. *(She resumes her stitching.)* And there were a hundred little things you never noticed, because they came naturally to you. Things about standing up and taking off your hat and opening doors—

Pickering.   Oh, that was nothing.

Liza.   Yes: things that shewed you thought and felt about me as if I were something better than a scullery-maid; though of course I know you would have been just the same to a scullery-maid if she had been let into the drawing room. You never took off your boots in the dining room when I was there.

Pickering.   You mustnt mind that. Higgins takes off his boots all over the place.

Liza.   I know. I am not blaming him. It is his way, isnt it? But it made such a difference to me that you didnt do it. You see, really and truly, apart from the things anyone can pick up (the dressing and the proper way of speaking, and so on), the difference between a lady and a flower girl is not how she behaves, but how she's treated. I shall always be a flower girl to Professor Higgins, because he always treats me as a flower girl, and always will; but I know I can be a lady to you, because you always treat me as a lady, and always will.

Mrs. Higgins.   Please dont grind your teeth, Henry.

Pickering.   Well, this is really very nice of you, Miss Doolittle.

Liza.   I should like you to call me Eliza, now, if you would.

Pickering.   Thank you. Eliza, of course.

Liza.   And I should like Professor Higgins to call me Miss Doolittle.

Higgins.   I'll see you damned first.

Mrs. Higgins.   Henry! Henry!

Pickering *(laughing).*   Why dont you slang back at him? Dont stand it. It would do him a lot of good.

Liza.   I cant. I could have done it once; but now I cant go back to it. You told me, you know, that when a child is brought to a foreign country, it picks up the language in a few weeks, and forgets its own. Well, I am a child in your country. I have forgotten my own language, and can speak nothing but yours. Thats the real break-off with the corner of Tottenham Court Road. Leaving Wimpole Street finishes it.

Pickering *(much alarmed).*   Oh! but youre coming back to Wimpole Street, arnt you? Youll forgive Higgins?

Higgins *(rising).*   Forgive! Will she, by George! Let her go. Let her find out how she can get on without us. She will relapse into the gutter in three weeks without me at her elbow.

Doolittle appears at the centre window. With a look of dignified reproach at Higgins, he comes slowly and silently to his daughter, who, with her back to the window, is unconscious of his approach.

Pickering.   He's incorrigible, Eliza. You wont relapse, will you?

Liza.   No: not now. Never again. I have learnt my lesson. I dont believe I could utter one of the old sounds if I tried. *(Doolittle touches her on the left shoulder. She drops her work, losing her self-possession utterly at the spectacle of her father's spendor.)* A-a-a-a-ah-ow-ooh!

Higgins *(with a crow of triumph).*   Aha! Just so. A-a-a-a-ahowooh! A-a-a-a-ahowooh! A-a-a-a-ahowooh! Victory! Victory! *(He throws himself on the divan, foling his arms, and spraddling arrogantly.)*

Doolittle.   Can you blame the girl? Dont look at me like that, Eliza. It aint my fault. Ive come into some money.

Liza.   You must have touched a millionaire this time, dad.

Doolittle.   I have. But I'm dressed something special today. I'm going to St. George's, Hanover Square. Your stepmother is going to marry me.

Liza *(angrily).*   Youre going to let yourself down to marry that low common woman!

Pickering *(quietly).*   He ought to, Eliza. *(To Doolittle.)* Why has she changed her mind?

Doolittle *(sadly).*   Intimidated, Governor. Intimidated. Middle class morality claims its victim. Wont you put on your hat, Liza, and come and see me turned off?

Liza.   If the Colonel says I must, I—I'll *(almost sobbing)* I'll demean myself. And get insulted for my pains, like enough.

Doolittle.   Dont be afraid: she never comes to words with anyone now, poor woman! respectability has broke all the spirit out of her.

Pickering *(squeezing Eliza's elbow gently).*   Be kind to them, Eliza. Make the best of it.

Liza *(forcing a little smile for him through her vexation).*   Oh well, just to shew theres no ill feeling. I'll be back in a moment. *(She goes out.)*

Doolittle *(sitting down beside Pickering).*   I feel uncommon nervous about the ceremony, Colonel. I wish youd come and see me through it.

Pickering.   But youve been through it before, man. You were married to Eliza's mother.

Doolittle.   Who told you that, Colonel?

Pickering.   Well, nobody told me. But I concluded—naturally—

Doolittle.   No: that aint the natural way, Colonel: it's only the middle class way. My way was always the undeserving way. But dont say nothing to Eliza. She dont know: I always had a delicacy about telling her.

Pickering.   Quite right. We'll leave it so, if you dont mind.

Doolittle.   And youll come to the church, Colonel, and put me through straight?

Pickering.   With pleasure. As far as a bachelor can.

Mrs. Higgins.   May I come, Mr. Doolittle? I should be very sorry to miss your wedding.

Doolittle.   I should indeed be honored by your condescension, maam; and my poor old woman would take it as a tremendous compliment. She's been very low, thinking of the happy days that are no more.

Mrs. Higgins *(rising.)*   I'll order the carriage and get ready. *(The men rise, except Higgins.)* I shant be more than fifteen minutes. *(As she goes to the door Eliza comes in, hatted and buttoning her gloves.)* I'm going to the church to see your father married, Eliza. You had better come in the brougham with me. Colonel Pickering can go on with the bridegroom.

Mrs. Higgins goes out. Eliza comes to the middle of the room between the centre window and the ottoman. Pickering joins her.

Doolittle.   Bridegroom. What a word! It makes a man realize his position, somehow. *(He takes up his hat and goes towards the door.)*

Pickering.   Before I go, Eliza, do forgive Higgins and come back to us.

Liza.   I dont think dad would allow me. Would you, dad?

Doolittle *(sad but magnanimous).*   They played you off very cunning, Eliza, them two sportsmen. If it had been only one of them, you could have nailed him. But you see, there was two; and one of them chaperoned the other, as you might say. *(To Pickering.)* It was artful of you, Colonel; but I bear no malice: I should have done the same myself. I been the victim of one woman after another all my life, and I dont grudge you two getting the better of Liza. I shant interfere. It's time for us to go, Colonel. So long, Henry. See you in St. George's, Eliza. *(He goes out.)*

Pickering *(coaxing).*   Do stay with us, Eliza. *(He follows Doolittle.)*

Eliza goes out on the balcony to avoid being alone with Higgins. He rises and joins her there. She immediately comes back into the room and makes for the door; but he goes along the balcony and gets his back to the door before she reaches it.

Higgins.   Well, Eliza, youve had a bit of your own back, as you call it. Have you had enough? and are you going to be reasonable? Or do you want any more?

Liza.   You want me back only to pick up your slippers and put up with your tempers and fetch and carry for you.

Higgins.   I havnt said I wanted you back at all.

Liza.   Oh, indeed. Then what are we talking about?

Higgins.   About you, not about me. If you come back I shall treat you just as I have always treated you. I cant change my nature; and I dont intend to change my manners. My manners are exactly the same as Colonel Pickering's.

Liza.   Thats not true. He treats a flower girl as if she was a duchess.

Higgins.   And I treat a duchess as if she was a flower girl.

Liza.   I see. *(She turns away composedly, and sits on the ottoman, facing the window.)* The same to everybody.

Higgins.   Just so.

Liza.   Like father.

Higgins *(grinning, a little taken down).*   Without accepting the comparison at all points, Eliza, it's quite true that your father is not a snob, and that he will be quite at home in any station of life to which his eccentric destiny may call him. *(Seriously.)* The great secret, Eliza, is not having bad manners or good manners or any other particular sort of manners, but having the same manner for all human souls: in short, behaving as if you were in Heaven, where there are no third-class carriages, and one soul is as good as another.

Liza.   Amen. You are a born preacher.

Higgins *(irritated).*   The question is not whether I treat you rudely, but whether you ever heard me treat anyone else better.

Liza *(with sudden sincerity).*   I dont care how you treat me. I dont mind your swearing at me. I shouldnt mind a black eye: Ive had one before this. But *(standing up and facing him)* I wont be passed over.

Higgins.   Then get out of my way; for I wont stop for you. You talk about me as if I were a motor bus.

Liza.   So you are a motor bus: all bounce and go, and no consideration for anyone. But I can do without you: dont think I cant.

Higgins.   I know you can. I told you you could.

Liza *(wounded, getting away from him to the other side of the ottoman with her face to the hearth).*   I know you did, you brute. You wanted to get rid of me.

Higgins.   Liar.

Liza.   Thank you. *(She sits down with dignity.)*

Higgins.   You never asked yourself, I suppose, whether I could do without you.

Liza *(earnestly).*   Dont you try to get round me. Youll have to do without me.

Higgins *(arrogant).*   I can do without anybody. I have my own soul: my own spark of divine fire. But *(with sudden humility)* I shall miss you, Eliza. *(He sits down near her on the ottoman.)* I have learnt something from your idiotic notions: I confess that humbly and gratefully. And I have grown accustomed to your voice and appearance. I like them, rather.

Liza.   Well, you have both of them on your gramophone and in your book of photographs. When you feel lonely without me, you can turn the machine on. It's got no feelings to hurt.

Higgins.   I cant turn your soul on. Leave me those feelings; and you can take away the voice and the face. They are not you.

Liza.   Oh, you are a devil. You can twist the heart in a girl as easy as some could twist her arms to hurt her. Mrs. Pearce warned me. Time and again she has wanted to leave you; and you always got round her at the last minute. And you dont care a bit for her. And you dont care a bit for me.

Higgins.   I care for life, for humanity; and you are a part of it that has come my way and been built into my house. What more can you or anyone ask?

Liza.   I wont care for anybody that doesnt care for me.

Higgins.   Commercial principles, Eliza. Like *(reproducing her Covent Garden pronunciation with professional exactness)* s'yollin voylets [selling violets], isnt it?

Liza.   Dont sneer at me. It's mean to sneer at me.

Higgins.   I have never sneered in my life. Sneering doesnt become either the human face or the human soul. I am expressing my righteous contempt for Commercialism. I dont and wont trade in affection. You call me a brute because you couldnt buy a claim on me by fetching my slippers and finding my spectacles. You were a fool: I think a woman fetching a man's slippers is a disgusting sight: did I ever fetch your slippers? I think a good deal more of you for throwing them in my face. No use slaving for me and then saying you want to be cared for: who cares for a slave? If you come back come back for the sake of good fellowship; for youll get nothing else. Youve had a thousand times as much out of me as I have out of you; and if you dare to set up your little dog's tricks of fetching and carrying slippers against my creation of a Duchess Eliza, I'll slam the door in your silly face.

Liza.   What did you do it for if you didnt care for me?

Higgins *(heartily)*.   Why, because it was my job.

Liza.   You never thought of the trouble it would make for me.

Higgins.   Would the world ever have been made if its maker had been afraid of making trouble? Making life means making trouble. Theres only one way of escaping trouble; and thats killing things. Cowards, you notice, are always shrieking to have troublesome people killed.

Liza.   I'm no preacher: I dont notice things like that. I notice that you dont notice me.

Higgins *(jumping up and walking about intolerantly)*.   Eliza: youre an idiot. I waste the treasures of my Miltonic mind by spreading them before you. Once for all, understand that I go my way and do my work without caring twopence what happens to either of us. I am not intimidated, like your father and stepmother. So you can come back or go to the devil: which you please.

Liza.   What am I to come back for?

Higgins *(bouncing up on his knees on the ottoman and leaning over it to her)*.   For the fun of it. Thats why I took you on.

Liza *(with averted face)*.   And you may throw me out tomorrow if I dont do everything you want me to?

Higgins.   Yes; and you may walk out tomorrow if I dont do everything you want me to.

Liza.   And live with my stepmother?

Higgins.   Yes, or sell flowers.

Liza.   Oh! if I only could go back to my flower basket! I should be independent of both you and father and all the world! Why did you take my independence from me? Why did I give it up? I'm a slave now, for all my fine clothes.

Higgins.   Not a bit. I'll adopt you as my daughter and settle money on you if you like. Or would you rather marry Pickering?

Liza (*looking fiercely round at him*).   I wouldnt marry you if you asked me; and youre nearer my age than what he is.

Higgins (*gently*).   Than he is: not "than what he is."

Liza (*losing her temper and rising*).   I'll talk as I like. Youre not my teacher now.

Higgins (*reflectively*).   I dont suppose Pickering would, though. He's as confirmed an old bachelor as I am.

Liza.   Thats not what I want; and dont you think it. I've always had chaps enough wanting me that way. Freddy Hill writes to me twice and three times a day, sheets and sheets.

Higgins (*disagreeably surprised*).   Damn his impudence! (*He recoils and finds himself sitting on his heels.*)

Liza.   He has a right to if he likes, poor lad. And he does love me.

Higgins (*getting off the ottoman*).   You have no right to encourage him.

Liza.   Every girl has a right to be loved.

Higgins.   What! By fools like that?

Liza.   Freddy's not a fool. And if he's weak and poor and wants me, may be he'd make me happier than my betters that bully me and dont want me.

Higgins.   Can he make anything of you? That's the point.

Liza.   Perhaps I could make something of him. But I never thought of us making anything of one another; and you never think of anything else. I only want to be natural.

Higgins.   In short, you want me to be as infatuated about you as Freddy? Is that it?

Liza.   No I dont. Thats not the sort of feeling I want from you. And dont you be too sure of yourself or of me. I could have been a bad girl if I'd liked. Ive seen more of some things than you, for all your learning. Girls like me can drag gentlemen down to make love to them easy enough. And they wish each other dead the next minute.

Higgins.   Of course they do. Then what in thunder are we quarrelling about?

Liza (*much troubled*).   I want a little kindness. I know I'm a common ignorant girl, and you a book-learned gentleman; but I'm not dirt under your feet. What I done (*correcting herself*) what I did was not for the dresses and the taxis: I did it because we were pleasant together and I come—came—to care for you; not to want you to make love to me, and not forgetting the difference between us, but more friendly like.

Higgins.   Well, of course. Thats just how I feel. And how Pickering feels. Eliza: youre a fool.

Liza.   Thats not a proper answer to give me. (*She sinks on the chair at the writing-table in tears.*)

Higgins.   It's all youll get until you stop being a common idiot. If youre going to be a lady, youll have to give up feeling neglected if the men you know dont spend half their time snivelling over you and the other half giving you black eyes. If you cant stand the coldness of my sort of life, and the strain of it, go back to the gutter. Work till youre more a brute than a human being; and then cuddle and squabble and drink till you fall asleep. Oh, it's a fine life, the life of the gutter. It's real: it's warm: it's violent: you can feel it through the thickest skin: you can taste it and smell it without any training or any work. Not like Science and Literature and Classical Music and Philosophy and Art. You find me cold, unfeeling, selfish, dont you? Very well: be off with you to the sort of people you like. Marry some sentimental hog or other with lots of money, and a thick pair of lips to kiss you with and a thick pair of boots to kick you with. If you cant appreciate what youve got, youd better get what you can appreciate.

Liza (desperate).   Oh, you are a cruel tyrant. I cant talk to you: you turn everything against me: I'm always in the wrong. But you know very well all the time that youre nothing but a bully. You know I cant go back to the gutter, as you call it, and that I have no real friends in the world but you and the Colonel. You know well I couldnt bear to live with a low common man after you two; and it's wicked and cruel of you to insult me by pretending I could. You think I must go back to Wimpole Street because I have nowhere else to go but father's. But dont you be too sure that you have me under your feet to be trampled on and talked down. I'll marry Freddy, I will, as soon as I'm able to support him.

Higgins (thunderstruck).   Freddy!!! that young fool! That poor devil who couldnt get a job as an errand boy even if he had the guts to try for it! Woman: do you not understand that I have made you a consort for a king?

Liza.   Freddy loves me: that makes him king enough for me. I dont want him to work: he wasnt brought up to it as I was. I'll go and be a teacher.

Higgins.   Whatll you teach, in heaven's name?

Liza.   What you taught me. I'll teach phonetics.

Higgins.   Ha! ha! ha!

Liza.   I'll offer myself as an assistant to that hairyfaced Hungarian.

Higgins (rising in a fury).   What! That imposter! that humbug! that toadying ignoramus! Teach him my methods! my discoveries! You take one step in his direction and I'll wring your neck. (He lays hands on her.) Do you hear?

Liza (defiantly non-resistant).   Wring away. What do I care? I knew youd strike me some day. (He lets her go, stamping with rage at having forgotten himself, and recoils so hastily that he stumbles back into his seat on the ottoman.) Aha! Now I know how to deal with you. What a fool I was not to think of it before! You cant take away the knowledge you gave me. You said I had a finer ear than you. And I can be civil and kind to people, which is more than you can. Aha! (Purposely dropping her aitches to annoy him.) Thats done you, Enry Iggins, it az. Now I dont care that (snapping her fingers) for your bullying and your big talk. I'll advertize it in the papers that your duchess is only a flower girl that you taught, and that she'll teach anybody to be a duchess just the same in six months for a thousand guineas. Oh, when I think of myself crawling under your feet and being trampled on and called names, when all the time I had only to lift up my finger to be as good as you, I could just kick myself.

Higgins (*wondering at her*).   You damned impudent slut, you! But it's better than snivelling; better than fetching slippers and finding spectacles, isn't it? (*Rising.*) By George, Eliza, I said I'd make a woman of you; and I have. I like you like this.

Liza.   Yes: you turn round and make up to me now that I'm not afraid of you, and can do without you.

Higgins.   Of course I do, you little fool. Five minutes ago you were like a millstone round my neck. Now youre a tower of strength: a consort battleship. You and I and Pickering will be three old bachelors instead of only two men and a silly girl.

Mrs. Higgins returns, dressed for the wedding. Eliza instantly becomes cool and elegant.

Mrs. Higgins.   The carriage is waiting, Eliza. Are you ready?

Liza.   Quite. Is the Professor coming?

Mrs. Higgins.   Certainly not. He cant behave himself in church. He makes remarks out loud all the time on the clergyman's pronunciation.

Liza.   Then I shall not see you again, Professor. Goodbye. (*She goes to the door.*)

Mrs. Higgins (*coming to Higgins*).   Goodbye, dear.

Higgins.   Goodbye, mother. (*He is about to kiss her, when he recollects something.*) Oh, by the way, Eliza, order a ham and a Stilton cheese, will you? And buy me a pair of reindeer gloves, number eights, and a tie to match that new suit of mine. You can choose the color. (*His cheerful, careless, vigorous voice shews that he is incorrigible.*)

Liza (*disdainfully*).   Number eights are too small for you if you want them lined with lamb's wool. You have three new ties that you have forgotten in the drawer of your washstand. Colonel Pickering prefers double Gloucester to Stilton; and you dont notice the difference. I telephoned Mrs. Pearce this morning not to forget the ham. What you are to do without me I cannot imagine. (*She sweeps out.*)

Mrs. Higgins.   I'm afraid youve spoilt that girl, Henry. I should be uneasy about you and her if she were less fond of Colonel Pickering.

Higgins.   Pickering! Nonsense: she's going to marry Freddy. Ha ha! Freddy! Freddy!! Ha ha ha ha ha!!!!! (*He roars with laughter as the play ends.*)

The rest of the story need not be shown in action, and indeed, would hardly need telling if our imaginations were not so enfeebled by their lazy dependence on the ready-mades and reach-me-downs of the ragshop in which Romance keeps its stock of "happy endings" to misfit all stories. Now, the history of Eliza Doolittle, though called a romance because the transfiguration it records seems exceedingly improbable, is common enough. Such transfigurations have been achieved by hundreds of resolutely ambitious young women since Nell Gwynne set them the example by playing queens and fascinating kings in the theatre in which she began by selling oranges. Nevertheless, people in all directions have assumed, for no other reason than that she became the heroine of a romance, that she must have married the hero of it. This is unbearable, not only because her little drama, if acted on such a thoughtless assumption, must be spoiled, but because the true sequel is patent to anyone with a sense of human nature in general, and of feminine instinct in particular.

Eliza, in telling Higgins she would not marry him if he asked her, was not coquetting: she was announcing a well-considered decision. When a bachelor interests, and dominates, and teaches, and becomes important to a spinster, as Higgins with Eliza, she always, if she has character enough to be capable of it, considers very seriously indeed whether she will play for becoming that bachelor's wife, especially if he is so little interested in marriage that a determined and devoted woman might capture him if she set herself resolutely to do it. Her decision will depend a good deal on whether she is really free to choose; and that, again, will depend on her age and income. If she is at the end of her youth, and has no security for her livelihood, she will marry him because she must marry anybody who will provide for her. But at Eliza's age a good-looking girl does not feel that pressure: she feels free to pick and choose. She is therefore guided by her instinct in the matter. Eliza's instinct tells her not to marry Higgins. It does not tell her to give him up. It is not in the slightest doubt as to his remaining one of the strongest personal interests in her life. It would be very sorely strained if there was another woman likely to supplant her with him. But as she feels sure of him on that last point, she has no doubt at all as to her course, and would not have any, even if the difference of twenty years in age, which seems so great to youth, did not exist between them.

As our own instincts are not appealed to by her conclusion, let us see whether we cannot discover some reason in it. When Higgins excused his indifference to young women on the ground that they had an irresistible rival in his mother, he gave the clue to his inveterate old-bachelordom. The case is uncommon only to the extent that remarkable mothers are uncommon. If an imaginative boy has a sufficiently rich mother who has intelligence, personal grace, dignity of character without harshness, and a cultivated sense of the best art of her time to enable her to make her house beautiful, she sets a standard for him against which very few women can struggle, besides effecting for him a disengagement of his affections, his sense of beauty, and his idealism from his specifically sexual impulses. This makes him a standing puzzle to the huge number of uncultivated people who have been brought up in tasteless homes by commonplace or disagreeable parents, and to whom, consequently, literature, painting, sculpture, music, and affectionate personal relations come as modes of sex if they come at all. The word passion means nothing else to them; and that Higgins could have a passion for phonetics and idealize his mother instead of Eliza, would seem to them absurd and unnatural. Nevertheless, when we look round and see that hardly anyone is too ugly or disagreeable to find a wife or a husband if he or she wants one, whilst many old maids and bachelors are above the average in quality and culture, we cannot help suspecting that the disentanglement of sex from the associations with which it is so commonly confused, a disentanglement which persons of genius achieve by sheer intellectual analysis, is sometimes produced or aided by parental fascination.

Now, though Eliza was incapable of thus explaining to herself Higgin's formidable powers of resistance to the charm that prostrated Freddy at the first glance, she was instinctively aware that she could never obtain a complete grip of him, or come between him and his mother (the first necessity of the married woman). To put it shortly, she knew that for some mysterious reason he had not the makings of a married man in him, according to her conception of a husband as one to whom she would be his nearest and fondest and warmest interest. Even had there been no mother-rival, she would still have refused to accept an interest in herself that was secondary to philosophic interests. Had Mrs. Higgins died, there would still have been Milton and the Universal Alphabet. Landor's remark that to those who have the greatest power of loving, love is a secondary affair, would not have recommended Landor to Eliza. Put that along with her resentment of Higgins's domineering superiority, and her mistrust of his coaxing cleverness in getting round her and evading her wrath when he had gone too far with his impetuous bullying, and you will see that Eliza's instinct had good grounds for warning her not to marry her Pygmalion.

And now, whom did Eliza marry? For if Higgins was a predestinate old bachelor, she was most certainly not a predestinate old maid. Well, that can be told very shortly to those who have not guessed it from the indications she has herself given them.

Almost immediately after Eliza is stung into proclaiming her considered determination not to marry Higgins, she mentions the fact that young Mr. Frederick Eynsford Hill is pouring out his love for her daily through the post. Now Freddy is young, practically twenty years younger than Higgins: he is a gentleman (or, as Eliza would qualify him, a toff), and speaks like one. He is nicely dressed, is treated by the Colonel as an equal, loves her unaffectedly, and is not her master, not ever likely to dominate her in spite of his advantage of social standing. Eliza has no use for the foolish romantic tradition that all women love to be mastered, if not actually bullied and beaten. "When you go to women," says Nietzsche, "take your whip with you." Sensible despots have never confined that precaution to women: they have taken their whips with them when they have dealt with men, and been slavishly idealized by the men over whom they have flourished the whip much more than by women. No doubt there are slavish women as well as slavish men; and women, like men, admire those that are stronger than themselves. But to admire a strong person and to live under that strong person's thumb are two different things. The weak may not be admired and hero-worshipped; but they are by no means disliked or shunned; and they never seem to have the least difficulty in marrying people who are too good for them. They may fail in emergencies; but life is not one long emergency: it is mostly a string of situations for which no exceptional strength is needed, and with which even rather weak people can cope if they have a stronger partner to help them out. Accordingly, it is a truth everywhere in evidence that strong people, masculine or feminine, not only do not marry stronger people, but do not show any preference for them in selecting their friends. When a lion meets another with a louder roar "the first lion thinks the last a bore." The man or woman who feels strong enough for two, seeks for every other quality in a partner than strength.

The converse is also true. Weak people want to marry strong people who do not frighten them too much; and this often leads them to make the mistake we describe metaphorically as "biting off more than they can chew." They want too much for too little; and when the bargain is unreasonable beyond all bearing, the union becomes impossible: it ends in the weaker party being either discarded or borne as a cross, which is worse. People who are not only weak, but silly or obtuse as well, are often in these difficulties.

This being the state of human affairs, what is Eliza fairly sure to do when she is placed between Freddy and Higgins? Will she look forward to a lifetime of fetching Higgins's slippers or to a lifetime of Freddy fetching hers? There can be no doubt about the answer. Unless Freddy is biologically repulsive to her, and Higgins biologically attractive to a degree that overwhelms all her other instincts, she will, if she marries either of them, marry Freddy.

And that is just what Eliza did.

Complications ensued; but they were economic, not romantic. Freddy had no money and no occupation. His mother's jointure, a last relic of the opulence of Largelady Park, had enabled her to struggle along in Earlscourt with an air of gentility, but not to procure any serious secondary education for her children, much less give the boy a profession. A clerkship at thirty shillings a week was beneath Freddy's dignity, and extremely distasteful to him besides. His prospects consisted of a hope that if he kept up appearances somebody would do something for him. The something appeared vaguely to his imagination as a private secretaryship or a sinecure of some sort. To his mother it perhaps appeared as a marriage to some lady of means who could not resist her boy's niceness. Fancy her feelings when he married a flower girl who had become disclassed under extraordinary circumstances which were now notorious!

It is true that Eliza's situation did not seem wholly ineligible. Her father, though formerly a dustman, and now fantastically disclassed, had become extremely popular in the smartest society by a social talent which triumphed over every prejudice and every disadvantage. Rejected by the middle class, which be loathed, he had shot up at once into the highest circles by his wit, his dustmanship (which he carried like a banner), and his Nietzschean transcendence of good and evil. At intimate ducal dinners he sat on the right hand of the Duchess; and in country houses he smoked in the pantry and was made much of by the butler when he was not feeding in the dining room and being consulted by cabinet ministers. But he found it almost as hard to do all this on four thousand a year as Mrs. Eynsford Hill to live in Earlscourt on an income so pitiably smaller that I have not the heart to disclose its exact figure. He absolutely refused to add the last straw to his burden by contributing to Eliza's support.

Thus Freddy and Eliza, now Mr. and Mrs. Eynsford Hill, would have spent a penniless honeymoon but for a wedding present of £500 from the Colonel to Eliza. It lasted a long time because Freddy did not know how to spend money, never having had any to spend, and Eliza, socially trained by a pair of old bachelors, wore her clothes as long as they held together and looked pretty, without the least regard to their being many months out of fashion. Still, £500 will not last two young people for ever; and they both knew, and Eliza felt as well, that they must shift for themselves in the end. She could quarter herself on Wimpole Street because it had come to be her home; but she was quite aware that she ought not to quarter Freddy there, and that it would not be good for his character if she did.

Not that the Wimpole Street bachelors objected. When she consulted them, Higgins declined to be bothered about her housing problem when that solution was so simple. Eliza's desire to have Freddy in the house with her seemed of no more importance than if she had wanted an extra piece of bedroom furniture. Pleas as to Freddy's character, and the moral obligation on him to earn his own living, were lost on Higgins. He denied that Freddy had any character, and declared that if he tried to do any useful work some competent person would have the trouble of undoing it; a procedure involving a net loss to the community, and great unhappiness to Freddy himself, who was obviously intended by Nature for such light work as amusing Eliza, which Higgins declared, was a much more useful and honorable occupation than working in the city. When Eliza referred again to her project of teaching phonetics, Higgins abated not a jot of his violent opposition to it. He said she was not within ten years of being qualified to meddle with his pet subject; and as it was evident that the Colonel agreed with him, she felt she could not go against them in this grave matter, and that she had no right, without Higgins's consent, to exploit the knowledge he had given her; for his knowledge seemed to her much his private property as his watch: Eliza was no communist. Besides, she was superstitiously devoted to them both, more entirely and frankly after her marriage than before it.

It was the Colonel who finally solved the problem, which had cost him much perplexed cogitation. He one day asked Eliza, rather shyly, whether she had quite given up her notion of keeping a flower shop. She replied that she had thought of it, but had put it out of her head, because the Colonel had said, that day at Mrs. Higgins's, that it would never do. The Colonel confessed that when he said that, he had not quite recovered from the dazzling impression of the day before. They broke the matter to Higgins that evening. The sole comment vouchsafed by him very nearly led to a serious quarrel with Eliza. It was to the effect that she would have in Freddy an ideal errand boy.

Freddy himself was next sounded on the subject. He said he had been thinking of a shop himself; though it had presented itself to his pennilessness as a small place in which Eliza should sell tobacco at one counter whilst he sold newspapers at the opposite one. But he agreed that it would be extraordinarily jolly to go early every morning with Eliza to Covent Garden and buy flowers on the scene of their first meeting: a sentiment which earned him many kisses from his wife. He added that he had always been afraid to propose anything of the sort, because Clara would make an awful row about a step that must damage her matrimonial chances, and his mother could not be expected to like it after clinging for so many years to that step of the social ladder on which retail trade is impossible.

This difficulty was removed by an event highly unexpected by Freddy's mother. Clara, in the course of her incursions into those artistic circles which were the highest within her reach, discovered that her conversational qualifi- cations were expected to include a grounding in the novels of Mr. H. G. Wells. She borrowed them in various directions so energetically that she swallowed them all within two months. The result was a conversion of a kind quite com- mon today. A modern Acts of the Apostles would fill fifty whole Bibles if anyone were capable of writing it.

Poor Clara, who appeared to Higgins and his mother as a disagreeable and ridiculous person, and to her own mother as in some inexplicable way a social failure, had never seen herself in either light; for, though to some extent ridi- culed and mimicked in West Kensington like everybody else there, she was accepted as a rational and normal—or shall we say inevitable?—sort of human being. At worst they called her The Pusher; but to them no more than to herself had it ever occurred that she was pushing the air, and pushing it in a wrong direction. Still, she was not happy. She was growing desperate. Her one asset, the fact that her mother was what the Epsom greengrocer called a carriage lady, had no exchange value, apparently. It had prevented her from getting educated, because the only education she could have afforded was education with the Earlscourt greengrocer's daughter. It had led her to seek the society of her mother's class; and that class simply would not have her, because she was much poorer than the greengrocer, and, far from being able to afford a maid, could not afford even a housemaid, and had to scrape along at home with an illiberally treated general servant. Under such circumstances nothing could give her an air of being a genuine product of Largelady Park. And yet its tradition made her regard marriage with anyone within her reach as an unbearable humiliation. Commercial people and professional people in a small way were odious to her. She ran after painters and novelists; but she did not charm them; and her bold attempts to pick up and practise artistic and literary talk irritated them. She was, in short, an utter failure, an ignorant, incompetent, pretentious, unwelcome, penniless, useless little snob; and though she did not admit these qualifications (for nobody ever faces unpleasant truths of this kind until the possibility of a way out dawns on them) she felt their effects too keenly to be satisfied with her position.

Clara had a startling eyeopener when, on being suddenly wakened to enthu- siasm by a girl of her own age who dazzled her and produced in her a gushing desire to take her for a model, and gain her friendship, she discovered that this exquisite apparition had graduated from the gutter in a few months time. It shook her so violently, that when Mr. H. G. Wells lifted her on the point of his puissant pen, and placed her at the angle of view from which the life she was leading and the society to which she clung appeared in its true relation to real human needs and worthy social structure, he effected a conversion and a conviction of sin comparable to the most sensational feats of General Booth or Gypsy Smith. Clara's snobbery went bang. Life suddenly began to move with her. Without knowing how or why, she began to make friends and enemies. Some of the acquaintances to whom she had been a tedious or indifferent or ridiculous affliction, dropped her: others became cordial. To her amazement she found that some "quite nice" people were saturated with Wells, and that this accessibility to ideas was the secret of their niceness. People she had thought deeply religious, and had tried to conciliate on that tack with disastrous results, suddenly took an interest in her, and revealed a hostility to conventional religion which she had never conceived possible except among the most desperate characters. They made her read Galsworthy; and Galsworthy exposed the vanity of Largelady Park and finished her. It exasperated her to think that the dungeon in which she had languished for so many unhappy years had been unlocked all the time, and that the impulses she had so carefully struggled with and stifled for the sake of keeping well with society, were precisely those by which alone she could have come into any sort of sincere human contact. In the radiance of these discoveries, and the tumult of their reaction, she made a fool of herself as freely and conspicuously as when she so rashly adopted Eliza's expletive in Mrs. Higgins's drawing room; for the new-born Wellsian had to find her bearings almost as ridiculously as a baby; but nobody hates a baby for its ineptitudes, or thinks the worse of it for trying to eat the matches; and Clara lost no friends by her follies. They laughed at her to her face this time; and she had to defend herself and fight it out as best she could.

When Freddy paid a visit to Earlscourt (which he never did when he could possibly help it) to make the desolating announcement that he and his Eliza were thinking of blackening the Largelady scutcheon by opening a shop, he found the little household already convulsed by a prior announcement from Clara that she also was going to work in an old furniture shop in Dover Street, which had been started by a fellow Wellsian. This appointment Clara owed, after all, to her old social accomplishment of Push. She had made up her mind that, cost what it might, she would see Mr. Wells in the flesh; and she had achieved her end at a garden party. She had better luck than so rash an enterprise deserved. Mr. Wells came up to her expectations. Age had not withered him, nor could custom stale his infinite variety in half an hour. His pleasant neatness and compactness, his small hands and feet, his teeming ready brain, his unaffected accessibility, and a certain fine apprehensiveness which stamped him as susceptible from his topmost hair to his tipmost toe, proved irresistible. Clara talked of nothing else for weeks and weeks afterwards. And as she happened to talk to the lady of the furniture shop, and that lady also desired above all things to know Mr. Wells and sell pretty things to him, she offered Clara a job on the chance of achieving that end through her.

And so it came about that Eliza's luck held, and the expected opposition to the flower shop melted away. The shop is in the arcade of a railway station not very far from the Victoria and Albert Museum; and if you live in that neighborhood you may go there any day and buy a buttonhole from Eliza.

Now here is a last opportunity for romance. Would you not like to be assured that the shop was an immense success, thanks to Eliza's charms and her early business experience in Covent Garden? Alas! the truth is the truth: the shop did not pay for a long time, simply because Eliza and her Freddy did not know how to keep it. True, Eliza had not to begin at the very beginning: she knew the names and prices of the cheaper flowers; and her elation was unbounded when she found that Freddy, like all youths educated at cheap, pretentious, and thoroughly inefficient schools, knew a little Latin. It was very little, but enough to make him appear to her a Porson or Bentley, and to put him at his ease with botanical nomenclature. Unfortunately he knew nothing else; and Eliza, though she could count money up to eighteen shillings or so, and had acquired a certain familiarity with the language of Milton from her struggles to qualify herself for winning Higgins's bet, could not write out a bill without utterly disgracing the establishment. Freddy's power of stating in Latin that Balbus built a wall and that Gaul was divided into three parts did not carry with it the slightest knowledge of accounts or business: Colonel Pickering had to explain to him what a cheque book and a bank account meant. And the pair were by no means easily teachable. Freddy backed up Eliza in her obstinate refusal to believe that they could save money by engaging a bookkeeper with some knowledge of the business. How, they argued, could you possibly save money by going to extra expense when you already could not make both ends meet? But the Colonel, after making the ends meet over and over again, at last gently insisted; and Eliza, humbled to the dust by having to beg from him so often, and stung by the uproarious derision of Higgins, to whom the notion of Freddy succeeding at anything was a joke that never palled, grasped the fact that business, like phonetics, has to be learned.

On the piteous spectacle of the pair spending their evenings in shorthand schools and polytechnic classes, learning bookkeeping and typewriting with incipient junior clerks, male and female, from the elementary schools, let me not dwell. There were even classes at the London School of Economics, and a humble personal appeal to the director of that institution to recommend a course bearing on the flower business. He, being a humorist, explained to them the method of the celebrated Dickensian essay on Chinese Metaphysics by the gentleman who read an article on China and an article on Metaphysics and combined the information. He suggested that they should combine the London School with Kew Gardens. Eliza, to whom the procedure of the Dickensian gentleman seemed perfectly correct (as in fact it was) and not in the least funny (which was only her ignorance), took the advice with entire gravity. But the effort that cost her the deepest humiliation was a request to Higgins, whose pet artistic fancy, next to Milton's verse, was caligraphy, and who himself wrote a most beautiful Italian hand, that he would teach her to write. He declared that she was congenitally incapable of forming a single letter worthy of the least of Milton's words; but she persisted; and again he suddenly threw himself into the task of teaching her with a combination of stormy intensity, concentrated patience, and occasional bursts of interesting disquisition on the beauty and nobility, the august mission and destiny, of human handwriting. Eliza ended by acquiring an extremely uncommercial script which was a positive extension of her personal beauty, and spending three times as much on stationery as anyone else because certain qualities and shapes on paper became indispensable to her. She could not even address an envelope in the usual way because it made the margins all wrong.

Their commercial schooldays were a period of disgrace and despair for the young couple. They seemed to be learning nothing about flower shops. At last they gave it up as hopeless, and shook the dust of the shorthand schools, and the polytechnics, and the London School of Economics from their feet for ever. Besides, the business was in some mysterious way beginning to take care of itself. They had somehow forgotten their objections to employing other people. They came to the conclusion that their own way was the best, and that they had really a remarkable talent for business. The Colonel, who had been compelled for some years to keep a sufficient sum on current account at his bankers to make up their deficits, found that the provision was unnecessary: the young people were prospering. It is true that there was not quite fair play between them and their competitors in trade. Their weekends in the country cost them nothing, and saved them the price of their Sunday dinners; for the motor car was the Colonel's; and he and Higgins paid the hotel bills. Mr. F. Hill, florist and greengrocer (they soon discovered that there was money in asparagus; and asparagus led to other vegetables), had an air which stamped the business as classy; and in private life he was still Frederick Eynsford Hill, Esquire. Not that there was any swank about him; nobody but Eliza knew that he had been christened Frederick Challoner. Eliza herself swanked like anything.

That is all. That is how it has turned out. It is astonishing how much Eliza still manages to meddle in the housekeeping at Wimpole Street in spite of the shop and her own family. And it is notable that though she never nags her husband, and frankly loves the Colonel as if she were his favorite daughter, she has never got out of the habit of nagging Higgins that was established on the fatal night when she won his bet for him. She snaps his head off on the faintest provocation, or on none. He no longer dares to tease her by assuming an abysmal inferiority of Freddy's mind to his own. He storms and bullies and derides; but she stands up to him so ruthlessly that the Colonel has to ask her from time to time to be kinder to Higgins; and it is the only request of his that brings a mulish expression into her face. Nothing but some emergency or calamity great enough to break down all likes and dislikes, and throw them both back on their common humanity—and may they be spared any such trial!—will ever alter this. She knows that Higgins does not need her, just as her father did not need her. The very scrupulousness with which he told her that day that he had become used to having her there, and dependent on her for all sorts of little services, and he should miss her if she went away (it would never have occurred to Freddy or the Colonel to say anything of the sort) deepens her inner certainty that she is "no more to him than them slippers"; yet she has a sense, too, that his indifference is deeper than the infatuation of commoner souls. She is immensely interested in him. She has even secret mischievous moments in which she wishes she could get him alone, on a desert island, away from all ties and with nobody else in the world to consider, and just drag him off his pedestal and see him making love like any common man. We all have private imaginations of that sort. But when it comes to business, to the life that she really leads as distinguished from the life of dreams and fancies, she likes Freddy and she likes the Colonel; and she does not like Higgins and Mr. Doolittle. Galatea never does quite like Pygmalion: his relation to her is too godlike to be altogether agreeable.

QUESTIONS

1. Does this play have a hero? What, finally, are your feelings about Henry Higgins? Eliza Doolittle? **2.** Are you disappointed that Eliza does not marry Higgins? What would such a marriage be like? Do you believe that Eliza will marry Freddy, as Shaw indicates in the afterword to the play? What will that marriage be like? **3.** Why does Higgins name Alfred Doolittle as the most original moralist in England in a letter to the philanthropist Ezra D. Wannafeller? What effect does that casual reference have on Alfred's life? Do you accept Alfred's judgment of his new position? Explain. **4.** How do you account for those passages among the stage directions that do not lend themselves to dramatic interpretation—the passage at the end of Act I, for instance? **5.** This play addresses a central issue: the consequences of meddling with the social and economic ecology through godlike interference. Certainly the fortunes of the Doolittle family are improved by that meddling—but are they the better for it? Explain. Are the issues raised in the play relevant only to a rigid society in which social caste is determined mainly by birth, or do they apply to societies, such as ours, that allow for greater social mobility? Explain.

WRITING TOPICS

1. This play embodies an implicit criticism of English social mores. What is that criticism? Do contemporary social mores lend themselves to the same criticism? **2.** What function do the several minor characters—Pickering, Mrs. Higgins, Mrs. Pearce, the Eysnford Hill family—serve in the play?

The Shadow of a Gunman   1923

A TRAGEDY IN TWO ACTS

SEAN O'CASEY   [1880–1964]

CHARACTERS IN THE PLAY

Donal Davoren
Seumas Shields, a pedlar
Tommy Owens   Residents in
Adolphus Grigson   the Tenement
Mrs. Grigson
Minnie Powell
Mr. Mulligan, the landlord
Mr. Maguire, soldier of the I.R.A.
Mrs. Henderson } Residents of an
Mr. Gallogher } adjoining Tenement
An Auxiliary

SCENE   *A room in a tenement in Hilljoy Square, Dublin.*
Some hours elapse between the two acts. The period of the Play is May 1920.

Act I

A *Return Room*[1] *in a tenement house in Hilljoy Square. At the back two large windows looking out into the yard; they occupy practically the whole of the back wall space. Between the windows is a cupboard, on the top of which is a pile of books. The doors are open, and on these are hanging a number of collars and ties. Running parallel with the windows is a stretcher bed; another runs at right angles along the wall at right. At the head of this bed is a door leading to the rest of the house. The wall on the left runs diagonally, so that the fireplace—which is in the centre—is plainly visible. On the mantelshelf to the right is a statue of the Virgin, to the left a statue of the Sacred Heart, and in the centre a crucifix. Around the fireplace are a few common cooking utensils. In the centre of the room is a table, on which are a typewriter, a candle and candlestick, a bunch of wild flowers in a vase, writing materials and a number of books. There are two chairs, one near the fireplace and one at the table. The aspect of the*

---

[1]These tenements were often converted mansions. A Return Room was a small storage room, here converted to a bedroom.

*place is one of absolute untidiness, engendered on the one hand by the congen-
ital slovenliness of Seumas Shields, and on the other by the temperament of Donal
Davoren, making it appear impossible to effect an improvement in such a place.*

*Davoren is sitting at the table typing. He is about thirty. There is in his face
an expression that seems to indicate an eternal war between weakness and strength;
there is in the lines of the brow and chin an indication of a desire for activity,
while in his eyes there is visible an unquenchable tendency towards rest. His
struggle through life has been a hard one, and his efforts have been handicapped
by an inherited and self-developed devotion to "the might of design, the mystery
of colour, and the belief in the redemption of all things by beauty everlasting."
His life would drive him mad were it not for the fact that he never knew any
other. He bears upon his body the marks of the struggle for existence and the
efforts towards self-expression.*

*Seumas Shields, who is in the bed next the wall to the right, is a heavily built
man of thirty-five; he is dark-haired and sallow-complexioned. In him is frequently manifested the superstition, the fear and the malignity of primitive man.*

Davoren [*lilting an air as he composes*]:

> Or when sweet Summer's ardent arms outspread,
> Entwined with flowers,
> Enfold us, like two lovers newly wed,
> Thro' ravish'd hours—
> Then sorrow, woe and pain lose all their powers,
> For each is dead, and life is only ours.

[*A woman's figure appears at the window and taps loudly on one of the panes;
at the same moment there is loud knocking at the door.*

Voice of Woman at Window.   Are you awake, Mr. Shields—Mr. Shields, are
you awake? Are you goin' to get up to-day at all, at all?

Voice at the Door.   Mr. Shields, is there any use of callin' you at all? This is
a nice nine o'clock: do you know what time it is, Mr. Shields?

Seumas [*loudly*].   Yus!

Voice at the Door. Why don't you get up, then, an' not have the house turned
into a bedlam tryin' to waken you?

Seumas [*shouting*].   All right, all right, all right! The way these oul' ones bawl
at a body! Upon my soul! I'm beginnin' to believe that the Irish People are
still in the stone age. If they could they'd throw a bomb at you.

Davoren.   A land mine exploding under the bed is the only thing that would
lift you out of it.

Seumas [*stretching himself*].   Oh-h-h. I was fast in the arms of Morpheus[2]—
he was one of the infernal deities, son of Somnus, wasn't he?

---

[2] Morpheus was one of the sons of Somnus, the god of sleep. Morpheus called up human shapes
in dreams.

Davoren.   I think so.

Seumas.   The poppy was his emblem, wasn't it?

Davoren.   Ah, I don't know.

Seumas.   It's a bit cold this morning, I think, isn't it?

Davoren.   It's quite plain I'm not going to get much quietness in this house.

Seumas [*after a pause*].   I wonder what time is it?

Davoren.   The Angelus[3] went some time ago.

Seumas [*sitting up in bed suddenly*].   The Angelus! It couldn't be that late, could it? I asked them to call me at nine so that I could get Mass before I went on my rounds. Why didn't you give us a rap?

Davoren.   Give you a rap! Why, man, they've been thundering at the door and hammering at the window for the past two hours, till the house shook to its very foundations, but you took less notice of the infernal din than I would take of the strumming of a grasshopper.

Seumas.   There's no fear of you thinking of any one else when you're at your poetry. The land of Saints and Scholars 'ill shortly be a land of bloody poets. [*Anxiously*] I suppose Maguire has come and gone?

Davoren.   Maguire? No, he hasn't been here—why, did you expect him?

Seumas [*in a burst of indignation*].   He said he'd be here at nine. "Before the last chime has struck," says he, "I'll be coming in on the door," and it must be—what time is it now?

Davoren.   Oh, it must be half-past twelve.

Seumas.   Did anybody ever see the like of the Irish People? Is there any use of tryin' to do anything in this country? Have everything packed and ready, have everything packed and ready, have . . .

Davoren.   And have you everything packed and ready?

Seumas.   What's the use of having anything packed and ready when he didn't come? [*He rises and dresses himself.*] No wonder this unfortunate country is as it is, for you can't depend upon the word of a single individual in it. I suppose he was too damn lazy to get up; he wanted the streets to be well aired first.—Oh, Kathleen ni Houlihan,[4] your way's a thorny way.

Davoren.   Ah me! alas, pain, pain ever, for ever!

Seumas.   That's from Shelley's *Prometheus Unbound*. I could never agree with Shelley, not that there's anything to be said against him as a poet—as a poet—but . . .

Davoren.   He flung a few stones through stained-glass windows.

Seumas.   He wasn't the first nor he won't be the last to do that, but the stained-glass windows—more than ever of them—are here still, and Shelley is doing a jazz dance down below.

---

[3] The Angelus is a Roman Catholic devotion in memory of the Annunciation, the announcement to the Virgin Mary that she would be the mother of Jesus Christ. It is recited three times daily, when the Angelus bell is rung at 6 A.M., noon, and 6 P.M.

[4] Because they were forbidden by the English to write nationalistic prose and poetry, Irish writers often created names that stood for Ireland. Kathleen ni Houlihan is one of these names.

[*He gives a snarling laugh of pleasure.*

Davoren [*shocked*].   And you actually rejoice and are exceedingly glad that, as you believe, Shelley, the sensitive, high-minded, noble-hearted Shelley, is suffering the tortures of the damned.

Seumas.   I rejoice in the vindication of the Church and Truth.

Davoren.   Bah. You know as little about truth as anybody else, and you care as little about the Church as the least of those that profess her faith; your religion is simply the state of being afraid that God will torture your soul in the next world as you are afraid the Black and Tans[5] will torture your body in this.

Seumas.   Go on, me boy; I'll have a right laugh at you when both of us are dead.

Davoren.   You're welcome to laugh as much as you like at me when both of us are dead.

Seumas [*as he is about to put on his collar and tie*].   I don't think I need to wash meself this morning; do I look all right?

Davoren.   Oh, you're all right; it's too late now to start washing yourself. Didn't you wash yourself yesterday morning?

Seumas.   I gave meself a great rub yesterday. [*He proceeds to pack various articles into an attaché case—spoons, forks, laces, thread, etc.*] I think I'll bring out a few of the braces too; damn it, they're well worth sixpence each; there's great stuff in them—did you see them?

Davoren.   Yes, you showed them to me before.

Seumas.   They're great value; I only hope I'll be able to get enough o' them. I'm wearing a pair of them meself—they'd do Cuchullian,[6] they're so strong. [*Counting the spoons*] There's a dozen in each of these parcels—three, six, nine—damn it, there's only eleven in this one. I better try another. Three, six, nine—my God, there's only eleven in this one too, and one of them bent! Now I suppose I'll have to go through the whole bloody lot of them, for I'd never be easy in me mind thinkin' there'd be more than a dozen in some o' them. And still we're looking for freedom—ye gods, it's a glorious country! [*He lets one fall, which he stoops to pick up.*] Oh, my God, there's the braces after breakin'.

Davoren.   That doesn't look as if they were strong enough for Cuchullian.

Seumas.   I put a heavy strain on them too sudden. There's that fellow Maguire never turned up, either; he's almost too lazy to wash himself. [*As he is struggling with the braces the door is hastily shoved in and Maguire rushes in with a handbag.*] This is a nice nine o'clock. What's the use of you coming at this hour o' the day? Do you think we're going to work be moonlight? If

---

[5] A particularly hated militia formed by the British to defend British rule in Ireland. These irregular troops were frequently recruited from prisons, and their uniforms were an amalgam of black tunics and tan trousers.

[6] Also spelled *Cuchulainn*. A mythical Irish warrior hero, the central figure in a cycle of Irish legends.

you weren't goin' to come at nine couldn't you say you weren't. . . .

Maguire.   Keep your hair on; I just blew in to tell you that I couldn't go to-day at all. I have to go to Knocksedan.

Seumas.   Knocksedan! An' what, in the name o' God, is bringin' you to Knocksedan?

Maguire.   Business, business. I'm going out to catch butterflies.

Seumas.   If you want to make a cod of anybody, make a cod of somebody else, an' don't be tryin' to make a cod o' me. Here I've had everything packed an' ready for hours; you were to be here at nine, an' you wait till just one o'clock to come rushin' in like a mad bull to say you've got to go to Knocksedan! Can't you leave Knocksedan till to-morrow?

Maguire.   Can't be did, can't be did, Seumas; if I waited till to-morrow all the butterflies might be dead. I'll leave this bag here till this evening. [*He puts the bag in a corner of the room.*] Good-bye . . . ee.

[*He is gone before Seumas is aware of it.*

Seumas [*with a gesture of despair*].   Oh, this is a hopeless country! There's a fellow that thinks that the four cardinal virtues are not to be found outside an Irish Republic. I don't want to boast about myself—I don't want to boast about myself, and I suppose I could call meself as good a Gael as some of those that are knocking about now—knocking about now—as good a Gael as some that are knocking about now,—but I remember the time when I taught Irish six nights a week, when in the Irish Republic Brotherhood I paid me rifle levy like a man, an' when the Church refused to have anything to do with James Stephens,[7] I tarred a prayer for the repose of his soul on the steps of the Pro-Cathedral. Now, after all me work for Dark Rosaleen,[8] the only answer you can get from a roarin' Republican to a simple question is "good-bye . . . ee." What, in the name o' God, can be bringin' him to Knocksedan?

Davoren.   Hadn't you better run out and ask him?

Seumas.   That's right, that's right—make a joke about it! That's the Irish People all over—they treat a joke as a serious thing and a serious thing as a joke. Upon me soul, I'm beginning to believe that the Irish People aren't, never were, an' never will be fit for self-government. They've made Balor of the Evil Eye[9] King of Ireland, an' so signs on it there's neither conscience nor honesty from one end of the country to the other. Well, I hope he'll have a happy day in Knocksedan. [*A knock at the door.*] Who's that?

[*Another knock.*

---

[7]An Irish novelist and poet actively connected with the Irish nationalist movement.
[8]Another name for Ireland, taken from the work of James Clarence Mangan (1803–1840).
[9]In Irish mythology, a notorious villain.

Seumas [*irritably*].   Who's that; who's there?

Davoren [*more irritably*].   Halt and give the countersign—damn it, man, can't you go and see?

[*Seumas goes over and opens the door. A man of about sixty is revealed, dressed in a faded blue serge suit; a half tall hat is on his head. It is evident that he has no love for Seumas, who denies him the deference he believes is due from a tenant to a landlord. He carries some papers in his hand.*

The Landlord [*ironically*].   Good-day, Mr. Shields; it's meself that hopes you're feelin' well—you're lookin' well, anyhow—though you can't always go be looks nowadays.

Seumas.   It doesn't matter whether I'm lookin' well or feelin' well; I'm all right, thanks be to God.

The Landlord.   I'm very glad to hear it.

Seumas.   It doesn't matter whether you're glad to hear it or not, Mr. Mulligan.

The Landlord.   You're not inclined to be very civil, Mr. Shields.

Seumas.   Look here, Mr. Mulligan, if you come here to raise an argument, I've something to do—let me tell you that.

The Landlord.   I don't come here to raise no argument; a person ud have small gains argufyin' with you—let me tell you that.

Seumas.   I've no time to be standin' here gostherin' with you—let me shut the door, Mr. Mulligan.

The Landlord.   You'll not shut no door till you've heard what I've got to say.

Seumas.   Well, say it then, an' go about your business.

The Landlord.   You're very high an' mighty, but take care you're not goin' to get a drop. What a baby you are not to know what brings me here! Maybe you thought I was goin' to ask you to come to tea.

Davoren.   Ah me! alas, pain, pain ever, for ever!

Seumas.   Are you goin' to let me shut the door, Mr. Mulligan?

The Landlord.   I'm here for me rent; you don't like the idea of bein' asked to pay your just an' lawful debts.

Seumas.   You'll get your rent when you learn to keep your rent-book in a proper way.

The Landlord.   I'm not goin' to take any lessons from you, anyhow.

Seumas.   I want to have no more talk with you, Mr. Mulligan.

The Landlord.   Talk or no talk, you owe me eleven weeks' rent, an' it's marked down again' you in black an' white.

Seumas.   I don't care a damn if it was marked down in green, white, an' yellow.

The Landlord.   You're a terribly independent fellow, an' it ud be fitter for you to be less funny an' stop tryin' to be billickin' honest an' respectable people.

Seumas.   Just you be careful what you're sayin', Mr. Mulligan. There's law in the land still.

The Landlord.   Be me sowl there is, an' you're goin' to get a little of it now. [*He offers the papers to Seumas*] Them's for you.

Seumas [*hesitating to take them*].   I want to have nothing to do with you, Mr. Mulligan.

The Landlord [*throwing the papers in the centre of the room*].   What am I better? It was the sorry day I ever let you come into this house. Maybe them notices to quit will stop your writin' letters to the papers about me an' me house.

Davoren.   For goodness' sake, bring the man in, and don't be discussing the situation like a pair of primitive troglodytes.

Seumas [*taking no notice*].   Writing letters to the papers is my business, an' I'll write as often as I like, when I like, an' how I like.

The Landlord.   You'll not write about this house at all events. You can blow about the state of the yard, but you took care to say nothin' about payin' rent: oh no, that's not in your line. But since you're not satisfied with the house, you can pack up an' go to another.

Seumas.   I'll go, Mr. Mulligan, when I think fit, an' no sooner.

The Landlord.   Not content with keeping the rent, you're startin' to bring in lodgers—[*to Davoren*] not that I'm sayin' anythin' again' you, sir. Bringin' in lodgers without as much as be your leave—what's the world comin' to at all that a man's house isn't his own? But I'll soon put a stop to your gallop, for on the twenty-eight of the next month out you go, an' there'll be few sorry to see your back.

Seumas.   I'll go when I like.

The Landlord.   I'll let you see whether you own the house or no.

Seumas.   I'll go when I like!

The Landlord.   We'll see about that.

Seumas.   We'll see.

The Landlord.   Ay, we'll see.

[*The Landlord goes out and Seumas shuts the door.*

The Landlord [*outside*].   Mind you, I'm in earnest; you'll not stop in this house a minute longer than the twenty-eight.

Seumas [*with a roar*].   Ah, go to hell!

Davoren [*pacing the room as far as the space will permit*].   What in the name of God persuaded me to come to such a house as this?

Seumas.   It's nothing when you're used to it; you're too thin-skinned altogether. The oul' sod's got the wind up about you, that's all.

Davoren.   Got the wind up about me!

Seumas.   He thinks you're on the run. He's afraid of a raid, and that his lovely property'll be destroyed.

Davoren.   But why, in the name of all that's sensible, should he think that I'm on the run?

Seumas.   Sure they all think you're on the run. Mrs. Henderson thinks it,

Tommy Owens thinks it, Mrs. an' Mr. Grigson think it, an' Minnie Powell thinks it too. [*Picking up his attaché case*] I'd better be off if I'm goin' to do anything to-day.

Davoren.   What are we going to do with these notices to quit?

Seumas.   Oh, shove them up on the mantelpiece behind one of the statues.

Davoren.   Oh, I mean what action shall we take?

Seumas.   I haven't time to stop now. We'll talk about them when I come back. . . . I'll get me own back on that oul' Mulligan yet. I wish to God they would come an' smash his rookery to pieces, for it's all he thinks of, and, mind you, oul' Mulligan would call himself a descendant of the true Gaels of Banba[10]—[*as he goes out*]:

> Oh, proud were the chieftains of famed Inisfail.
> Is truagh gan oidher 'na Vfarradh.[11]
> The stars of our sky an' the salt of our soil—

Oh, Kathleen ni Houlihan, your way's a thorny way!

[*He goes out.*

Davoren [*returning to the table and sitting down at the typewriter*].   Oh, Donal Og O'Davoren, your way's a thorny way. Your last state is worse than your first. Ah me, alas! Pain, pain ever, for ever. Like thee, Prometheus, no change, no pause, no hope. Ah, life, life, life! [*There is a gentle knock at the door.*] Another Fury come to plague me now! [*Another knock, a little louder.*

Davoren.   You can knock till you're tired.

[*The door opens and Minnie Powell enters with an easy confidence one would not expect her to possess from her gentle way of knocking. She is a girl of twenty-three, but the fact of being forced to earn her living, and to take care of herself, on account of her parents' early death, has given her a force and an assurance beyond her years. She has lost the sense of fear (she does not know this), and, consequently, she is at ease in all places and before all persons, even those of a superior education, so long as she meets them in the atmosphere that surrounds the members of her own class. Her hair is brown, neither light nor dark, but partaking of both tints according to the light or shade she may happen to be in. Her well-shaped figure—a rare thing in a city girl—is charmingly dressed in a brown tailor-made costume, her stockings and shoes are a darker brown tint than the costume, and all are crowned by a silk tam-o'-shanter of a rich blue tint.*

Minnie.   Are you in, Mr. Shields?

Davoren [*rapidly*].   No, he's not, Minnie; he's just gone out—if you run out quickly you're sure to catch him.

Minnie.   Oh, it's all right, Mr. Davoren, you'll do just as well; I just come in

---

[10] *Banba* is another name for Ireland.
[11] It's a pity they have no heirs.

for a drop o' milk for a cup o' tea; I shouldn't be troublin' you this way, but I'm sure you don't mind.

Davoren [*dubiously*].   No trouble in the world; delighted, I'm sure. [*Giving her the milk*] There, will you have enough?

Minnie.   Plenty, lashins,[12] thanks. Do you be all alone all the day, Mr. Davoren?

Davoren.   No, indeed; I wish to God I was.

Minnie.   It's not good for you then. I don't know how you like to be by yourself—I couldn't stick it long.

Davoren [*wearily*].   No?

Minnie.   No, indeed; [*with rapture*] there's nothin' I'm more fond of than a Hooley.[13] I was at one last Sunday—I danced rings round me! Tommy Owens was there—you know Tommy Owens, don't you?

Davoren.   I can't say I do.

Minnie.   D'ye not? The little fellow that lives with his mother in the two-pair back—[*ecstatically*] he's a gorgeous melodeon player!

Davoren.   A gifted son of Orpheus, eh?[14]

Minnie [*who never heard of Orpheus*].   You've said it, Mr. Davoren: the son of poor oul' Battie Owens, a weeshy, dawny, bit of a man that was never sober an' was always talkin' politics. Poor man, it killed him in the long run.

Davoren.   A man should always be drunk, Minnie, when he talks politics—it's the only way in which to make them important.

Minnie.   Tommy takes after the oul' fellow, too; he'd talk from morning till night when he has a few jars in him. [*Suddenly; for like all of her class, Minnie is not able to converse very long on the one subject, and her thoughts spring from one thing to another*] Poetry is a grand thing, Mr. Davoren, I'd love to be able to write a poem—a lovely poem on Ireland an' the men o' '98.[15]

Davoren.   Oh, we've had enough of poems, Minnie, about '98, and of Ireland, too.

Minnie.   Oh, there's a thing for a Republican to say! But I know what you mean: it's time to give up the writing an' take to the gun. [*Her roving eye catches sight of the flowers in the vase*] What's Mr. Shields doin' with the oul' weeds?

Davoren.   Those aren't Shields', they're mine. Wild flowers is a kindlier name for them, Minnie, than weeds. These are wild violets, this is an *Arum maculatum*, or Wake Robin, and these are Celandines, a very beautiful flower related to the buttercups. [*He quotes*]:

> One day, when Morn's half-open'd eyes
> Were bright with Spring sunshine—

---

[12] Another way of saying "plenty."

[13] A party with drinking and dancing.

[14] In Greek myth, Orpheus was a musician of such skill that he charmed not only humans, but beasts and even trees and rivers with his music.

[15] A fierce, but futile uprising occurred in 1798.

> My hand was clasp'd in yours, dear love,
> And yours was clasp'd in mine—
> We bow'd as worshippers before
> The Golden Celandine.

Minnie.   Oh, aren't they lovely, an' isn't the poem lovely, too! I wonder, now, who she was.

Davoren [*puzzled*].   She, who?

Minnie.   Why, the . . . [*roguishly*] Oh, be the way you don't know.

Davoren.   Know! I'm sure I don't know.

Minnie.   It doesn't matter, anyhow—that's your own business; I suppose I don't know her.

Davoren.   Know her—know whom?

Minnie [*shyly*].   Her whose hand was clasped in yours, an' yours was clasped in hers.

Davoren.   Oh, that—that was simply a poem I quoted about the Celandine, that might apply to any girl—to you, for instance.

Minnie [*greatly relieved, coming over and sitting beside Davoren*].   But you have a sweetheart, all the same, Mr. Davoren, haven't you?

Davoren.   I? No, not one, Minnie.

Minnie.   Oh, now, you can tell that to some one else; aren't you a poet an' aren't all the girls fond o' poets?

Davoren.   That may be, but all the poets aren't fond of girls.

Minnie.   They are in the story-books, ay, and fond of more than one, too. [*With a questioning look*] Are you fond of them, Mr. Davoren?

Davoren.   Of course I like girls, Minnie, especially girls who can add to their charms by the way in which they dress, like you, for instance.

Minnie.   Oh, now, you're on for coddin' me, Mr. Davoren.

Davoren.   No, really, Minnie, I'm not; you are a very charming little girl indeed.

Minnie.   Then if I'm a charmin' little girl, you ought to be able to write a poem about me.

Davoren [*who has become susceptible to the attractiveness of Minnie, catching her hand*].   And so I will, so I will, Minnie; I have written them about girls not half so pretty as yourself.

Minnie.   Ah, I knew you had one, I knew you had one now.

Davoren.   Nonsense. Every girl a poet writes about isn't his sweetheart; Annie Laurie wasn't the sweetheart of Bobbie Burns.[16]

Minnie.   You needn't tell me she wasn't; "An' for bonnie Annie Laurie I'd lay me down an' die." No man ud lay down an' die for any but a sweetheart, not even for a wife.

Davoren.   No man, Minnie, willingly dies for anything.

---

[16] Robert Burns (1759–1796) was a Scot poet; Annie Laurie is the subject of one of his poems.

Minnie.   Except for his country, like Robert Emmet.[17]

Davoren.   Even he would have lived on if he could; he died not to deliver Ireland. The British Government killed him to save the British nation.

Minnie.   You're only jokin' now; you'd die for your country.

Davoren.   I don't know so much about that.

Minnie.   You would, you would, you would—I know what you are.

Davoren.   What am I?

Minnie [*in a whisper*].   A gunman on the run!

Davoren [*too pleased to deny it*].   Maybe I am, and maybe I'm not.

Minnie.   Oh, I know, I know, I know. Do you never be afraid?

Davoren.   Afraid! Afraid of what?

Minnie.   Why, the ambushes of course; *I'm* all of a tremble when I hear a shot go off, an' what must it be in the middle of the firin'?

Davoren [*delighted at Minnie's obvious admiration; leaning back in his chair, and lighting a cigarette with placid affectation*].   I'll admit one does be a little nervous at first, but a fellow gets used to it after a bit, till, at last, a gunman throws a bomb as carelessly as a schoolboy throws a snowball.

Minnie [*fervently*].   I wish it was all over, all the same. [*Suddenly, with a tremor in her voice*] You'll take care of yourself, won't you, won't you, Donal— I mean, Mr. Davoren?

Davoren [*earnestly*].   Call me Donal, Minnie; we're friends, great friends now— [*putting his arm around her*] go on, Minnie, call me Donal, let me hear you say Donal.

Minnie.   The place badly needs a tidyin' up . . . Donal—there now, are you satisfied? [*Rapidly, half afraid of Davoren's excited emotions*] But it really does, it's in an awful state. To-morrow's a half-day, an' I'll run in an' straighten it up a bit.

Davoren [*frightened at the suggestion*].   No, no, Minnie, you're too pretty for that sort of work; besides, the people of the house would be sure to start talking about you.

Minnie.   An' do you think Minnie Powell cares whether they'll talk or no? She's had to push her way through life up to this without help from any one, an' she's not goin' to ask their leave, now, to do what she wants to do.

Davoren [*forgetting his timidity in the honest joy of appreciating the independent courage of Minnie*].   My soul within art thou, Minnie! A pioneer in action as I am a pioneer in thought. The two powers that shall "grasp this sorry scheme of things entire, and mould life nearer to the heart's desire." Lovely little Minnie, and brave as well; brave little Minnie, and lovely as well!

---

[17] Robert Emmet (1778–1803) was an Irish patriot who was involved in a number of violent encounters with the authorities. He was captured and convicted of treason. After delivering a moving speech, he was hanged.

[*His disengaged hand lifts up her bent head, and he looks earnestly at her; he is stooping to kiss her, when Tommy Owens appears at the door, which Minnie has left partially open. Tommy is about twenty-five years of age. He is small and thin; his words are uttered in a nasal drawl; his voice is husky, due to frequent drinks and perpetual cigarette-smoking. He tries to get rid of the huskiness by an occasional cough. Tommy is a hero-worshipper, and, like many others, he is anxious to be on familiar terms with those who he thinks are braver than he is himself, and whose approbation he tries to win by an assumption equal to their own. He talks in a staccato manner. He has a few drinks taken—it is too early to be drunk—that make him talkative. He is dressed in a suit of dungarees, and gives a gentle cough to draw attention to his presence.*]

Tommy.   I seen nothin'—honest—thought you was learnin' to typewrite—Mr. Davoren teachin' you. I seen nothin' else—s'help me God!

Minnie.   We'd be hard put to it if we minded what you seen, Tommy Owens.

Tommy.   Right, Minnie, Tommy Owens has a heart—Evenin', Mr. Davoren—don't mind me comin' in—I'm Tommy Owens—live up in the two-pair back, workin' in Ross an' Walpole's—Mr. Shields knows me well; you needn't be afraid o' me, Mr. Davoren.

Davoren.   Why should I be afraid of you, Mr. Owens, or of anybody else?

Tommy.   Why should you, indeed? We're all friends here—Mr. Shields knows me well—all you've got to say is, "Do you know Tommy Owens?" an' he'll tell you the sort of a man Tommy Owens is. There's no flies on Tommy—got me?

Minnie.   For goodness' sake, Tommy, leave Mr. Davoren alone—he's got enough burgeons[18] on him already.

Tommy.   Not a word, Minnie, not a word—Mr. Davoren understands me well, as man to man. It's "Up the Republic" all the time—eh, Mr. Davoren?

Davoren.   I know nothing about the Republic; I have no connection with the politics of the day, and I don't want to have any connection.

Tommy.   You needn't say no more—a nod's as good as a wink to a blind horse—you've no meddlin' or makin' with it, good, bad, or indifferent, pro nor con; I know it an' Minnie knows it—give me your hand. [*He catches Davoren's hand*] Two firm hands clasped together will all the power outbrave of the heartless English tyrant, the Saxon coward an' knave. That's Tommy Owens' hand, Mr. Davoren, the hand of a man, a man—Mr. Shields knows me well.

[*He breaks into song.*

High upon the gallows tree stood the noble-hearted three,
By the vengeful tyrant stricken in their bloom;

---

[18] Burdens.

But they met him face to face with the spirit of their race,
And they went with souls undaunted to their doom!

Minnie [*in an effort to quell his fervour*].   Tommy Owens, for goodness'
sake . . .
Tommy [*overwhelming her with a shout*]:

God save Ireland ses the hayros, God save Ireland ses we all,
Whether on the scaffold high or the battle-field we die,
Oh, what matter when for Ayryinn dear we fall!

[*Tearfully*] Mr. Davoren, I'd die for Ireland!
Davoren.   I know you would, I know you would, Tommy.
Tommy.   I never got a chance—they never gave me a chance—but all the
same I'd be there if I was called on—Mr. Shields knows that—ask Mr. Shields,
Mr. Davoren.
Davoren.   There's no necessity, Tommy; I know you're the right stuff if you
got the chance, but remember that "he also serves who only stands and waits."
Tommy [*fiercely*].   I'm bloody well tired o' waitin'—we're all tired o' waitin'.
Why isn't every man in Ireland out with the I.R.A.?[19] Up with the barri-
cades, up with the barricades; it's now or never, now an' for ever, as Sarsfield
said at the battle o' Vinegar Hill. Up with the barricades—that's Tommy
Owens—an' a penny buys a whistle. Let them as thinks different say different—what do you say, Mr. Davoren?
Davoren.   I say, Tommy, you ought to go up and get your dinner, for if you
wait much longer it won't be worth eating.
Tommy.   Oh, damn the dinner; who'd think o' dinner an' Ireland fightin' to
be free?—not Tommy Owens, anyhow. It's only the Englishman who's always thinkin' of his belly.
Minnie.   Tommy Owens!
Tommy.   Excuse me, Miss Powell, in the ardure ov me anger I disremem-
bered there was a lady present.

[*Voices are heard outside, and presently Mrs. Henderson comes into the room,
followed by Mr. Gallogher, who, however, lingers at the door, too timid to come
any farther. Mrs. Henderson is a massive woman in every way; massive head,
arms, and body; massive voice, and a massive amount of self-confidence. She is
a mountain of good nature, and during the interview she behaves towards Davoren with deferential self-assurance. She dominates the room, and seems to occupy the whole of it. She is dressed poorly but tidily, wearing a white apron and
a large shawl. Mr. Gallogher, on the other hand, is a spare little man with a
spare little grey beard and a thin, nervous voice. He is dressed as well as a faded
suit of blue will allow him to be. He is obviously ill at ease during his interview*

---

[19] The illegal Irish Republican Army.

with Davoren. He carries a hard hat, much the worse for wear, under his left arm, and a letter in his right hand.

Mrs. Henderson [*entering the room*].   Come along in, Mr. Gallicker, Mr. Davoren won't mind; it's him as can put you in the way o' havin' your wrongs righted; come on in, man, an' don't be so shy—Mr. Davoren is wan ov ourselves that stands for govermint ov the people with the people by the people. You'll find you'll be as welcome as the flowers in May. Good evenin', Mr. Davoren, an' God an' His holy angels be between you an' all harm.

Tommy [*effusively*].   Come on, Mr. Gallicker, an' don't be a stranger—we're all friends here—anything special to be done or particular advice asked, here's your man here.

Davoren [*subconsciously pleased, but a little timid of the belief that he is connected with the gunmen*].   I'm very busy just now, Mrs. Henderson, and really . . .

Mrs. Henderson [*mistaking the reason of his embarrassment*].   Don't be put out, Mr. Davoren, we won't keep you more nor a few minutes. It's not in me or in Mr. Gallicker to spoil sport. Him an' me was young once, an' knows what it is to be strolling at night in the pale moonlight, with arms round one another. An' I wouldn't take much an' say there's game in Mr. Gallicker still, for I seen, sometimes, a dangerous cock in his eye. But we won't keep you an' Minnie long asunder; he's the letter an' all written. You must know, Mr. Davoren—excuse me for not introducin' him sooner—this is Mr. Gallicker, that lives in the front drawin'-room ov number fifty-five, as decent an' honest an' quiet a man as you'd meet in a day's walk. An' so signs on it, it's them as 'ill be imposed upon—read the letter, Mr. Gallicker.

Tommy.   Read away, Mr. Gallicker, it will be attended to, never fear; we know our own know, eh, Mr. Davoren?

Minnie.   Hurry up, Mr. Gallicker, an' don't be keeping Mr. Davoren.

Mrs. Henderson.   Give him time, Minnie Powell. Give him time. You must know in all fairity, Mr. Davoren, that the family livin' in the next room to Mr. Gallicker—the back drawin'-room, to be particular—am I right or am I wrong, Mr. Gallicker?

Mr. Gallogher.   You're right, Mrs. Henderson, perfectly right, indeed—that's the very identical room.

Mrs. Henderson.   Well, Mr. Davoren, the people in the back drawin'-room, or, to be more particular, the residents—that's the word that's writ in the letter—am I right or am I wrong, Mr. Gallicker?

Mr. Gallogher.   You're right, Mrs. Henderson, perfectly accurate—that's the very identical word.

Mrs. Henderson.   Well, Mr. Davoren, the residents in the back drawin'-room, as I aforesaid, is nothin' but a gang o' tramps that oughtn't to be allowed to associate with honest, decent, quiet, respectable people. Mr. Gallicker has tried to reason with them, and make them behave themselves—which in my opinion they never will—however, that's only an opinion, an' not legal—ever since they have made Mr. Gallicker's life a HELL! Mr. Gallicker, am I right or am I wrong?

Mr. Gallogher.   I'm sorry to say you're right, Mrs. Henderson, perfectly right—not a word of exaggeration.

Mrs. Henderson.   Well, now, Mr. Gallicker, seein' as I have given Mr. Davoren a fair account ov how you're situated, an' ov these tramps' cleverality, I'll ask you to read the letter, which I'll say, not because you're there, or that you're a friend o' mine, is as good a letter as was decomposed by a scholar. Now, Mr. Gallicker, an' don't forget the top sayin'.

[*Mr. Gallogher prepares to read; Minnie leans forward to listen; Tommy takes out a well-worn note-book and a pencil stump, and assumes a very important attitude.*

Tommy.   One second. Mr. Gallicker, is this the twenty-first or twenty-second?

Mr. Gallogher.   The twenty-first, sir.

Tommy.   Thanks; proceed, Mr. Gallicker.

Mr. Gallogher [*with a few preliminary tremors, reads the letter. Reading*]:
"To ALL TO WHOM THESE PRESENTS COME,
GREETING

"Gentlemen of the Irish Republican Army . . ."

Mrs. Henderson.   There's a beginnin' for you, Mr. Davoren.

Minnie.   That's some swank.

Tommy.   There's a lot in that sayin', mind you; it's a hard wallop at the British Empire.

Mrs. Henderson [*proudly*].   Go on, Mr. Gallicker.

Mr. Gallogher [*reading*]:

"I wish to call your attention to the persecution me and my family has to put up with in respect of and appertaining to the residents of the back drawing-room of the house known as fifty-five, Saint Teresa Street, situate in the Parish of St. Thomas, in the Borough and City of Dublin. This persecution started eighteen months ago—or to be precise—on the tenth day of the sixth month, in the year nineteen hundred and twenty."

Mrs. Henderson.   That's the word I was trying to think ov—precise—it cuts the ground from under their feet—so to speak.

Mr. Gallogher [*reading*]:
"We, the complainants, resident on the ground floor, deeming it disrespectable . . ."

Mrs. Henderson [*with an emphatic nod*].   Which it was.

Mr. Gallogher [*reading*]:

"Deeming it disrespectable to have an open hall door, and to have the hall turned

into a playground, made a solemn protest, and, in consequence, we the complainants aforesaid has had no peace ever since. Owing to the persecution, as aforesaid
specified, we had to take out a summons again them some time ago as there was
no Republican Courts then; but we did not proceed again them as me and my
wife—to wit, James and Winifred Gallogher—has a strong objection to foreign Courts
as such. We had peace for some time after that, but now things have gone from
bad to worse. The name calling and the language is something abominable . . ."

Mrs. Henderson [*holding out her hand as a constable would extend his to stop
a car that another may pass*]. Excuse me, Mr. Gallicker, but I think the
word "shockin' " should be put in there after abominable; for the language
used be these tramps has two ways o' bein' looked at—for it's abominable to
the childer an' shockin' to your wife—am I right or am I wrong, Mr. Davoren?

Tommy [*judicially*]. Shockin' is a right good word, with a great deal o' meanin',
an' . . .

Mrs. Henderson [*with a deprecating gesture that extinguishes Tommy*]. Tommy,
let Mr. Davoren speak; whatever Mr. Davoren ses, Julia Henderson'll abide
be.

Davoren [*afraid to say anything else*]. I think the word might certainly be introduced with advantage.

Mrs. Henderson. Go over there, Mr. Gallicker, an' put in the word shockin',
as aforesaid.

[*Gallogher goes over to the table, and with a great deal of difficulty enters the
word.*

Tommy [*to Mr. Gallogher as he writes*]. Ey, there's two k's in shockin'!
Mr. Gallogher [*reading*]:

"The language is something abominable and shocking. My wife has often to
lock the door of the room to keep them from assaulting her. If you would be so
kind as to send some of your army or police down to see for themselves we would
give them full particulars. I have to be always from home all day, as I work with
Mr. Hennessy, the harness maker of the Coombe, who will furnish all particulars
as to my unvarnished respectability, also my neighbours. The name of the resi-
dent-tenant who is giving all this trouble and who, pursuant to the facts of the case
aforesaid, mentioned, will be the defendant, is Dwyer. The husband of the aforesaid Mrs. Dwyer, or the aforesaid defendant, as the case may be, is a seaman, who
is coming home shortly, and we beg The Irish Republican Army to note that the
said Mrs. Dwyer says he will settle us when he comes home. While leaving it
entirely in the hands of the gentlemen of The Republican Army, the defendant,
that is to say, James Gallogher of fifty-five St. Teresa Street, ventures to say that
he thinks he has made out a Primmy Fashy[20] Case against Mrs. Dwyer and all her
heirs, male and female as aforesaid mentioned in the above written schedule.

---

[20] He means *prima facie*, legalistic Latin for "at first view."

"N.B.—If you send up any of your men, please tell them to bring their guns. I beg to remain the humble servant and devoted admirer of the Gentlemen of the Irish Republican Army.

"Witness my hand this tenth day of the fifth month of the year nineteen hundred and twenty.

"JAMES GALLOGHER."

Mr. Gallogher [*with a modest cough*]. Ahem.

Mrs. Henderson.   There's a letter for you, Mr. Davoren!

Tommy.   It's the most powerfullest letter I ever heard read.

Minnie.   It wasn't you, really, that writ it, Mr. Gallicker?

Mrs. Henderson.   Sinn Fein Amhain:[21] him an' him only, Minnie. I seen him with me own two eyes when me an' Winnie—Mrs. Gallicker, Mr. Davoren, aforesaid as appears in the letter—was havin' a chat be the fire.

Minnie.   You'd never think it was in him to do it.

Mrs. Henderson.   An' to think that the likes ov such a man is to have the sowl-case worried out ov him by a gang o' tramps; but it's in good hands now, an' instead ov them settlin' yous, Mr. Gallicker, it's yous 'ill settle them. Give the letter to Mr. Davoren, an' we'll be goin'.

[*Gallogher gives the letter to Davoren.*]

Mrs. Henderson [*moving towards the door*]. I hope you an' Mr. Shields is gettin' on all right together, Mr. Davoren.

Davoren.   Fairly well, thanks, Mrs. Henderson. We don't see much of each other. He's out during the day, and I'm usually out during the evening.

Mrs. Henderson.   I'm afraid he'll never make a fortune out ov what he's sellin'. He'll talk above an hour over a pennorth o' pins. Every time he comes to our place I buy a package o' hairpins from him to give him a little encouragement. I 'clare to God I have as many pins now as ud make a wire mattress for a double bed. All the young divils about the place are beginnin' to make a jeer ov him, too; I gave one ov them a mallavogin'[22] the other day for callin' him oul' hairpins!

Mr. Gallogher [*venturing an opinion*].   Mr. Shields is a man of exceptional mental capacity, and is worthy of a more dignified position.

Mrs. Henderson.   Them words is true, Mr. Gallicker, and they aren't. For to be wise is to be a fool, an' to be a fool is to be wise.

Mr. Gallogher [*with deprecating tolerance*].   Oh, Mrs. Henderson, that's a parrotox.[23]

---

[21] *Sinn Fein* means "ourselves alone." Irish nationalists formed a political party with this name when it became apparent that they could not depend on the efforts of English politicians to bring about Irish home rule.

[22] Tongue-lashing.

[23] He means *paradox*.

Mrs. Henderson.   It may be what a parrot talks, or a blackbird, or, for the matter of that, a lark—but it's what Julia Henderson thinks, any . . . whisht, is that a *Stop Press?*

[*Outside is heard the shriek of a newsboy calling "Stop Press."*

Mrs. Henderson.   Run out, Tommy, an' get it till we see what it is.

Tommy.   I haven't got a make.

Mrs. Henderson.   I never seen you any other way, an' you'll be always the same if you keep follyin' your Spearmints, an' your Bumble Bees an' your Night Patrols. [*Shouting to someone outside*] Is that a *Stop Press*, Mrs. Grigson?

Voice outside.   Yis; an ambush out near Knocksedan.

Mrs. Henderson.   That's the stuff to give them. [*Loudly*] Was there anybody hurted?

Voice outside.   One poor man killed—some chap named Maguire, the paper says.

Davoren [*agitated*].   What name did she say?

Minnie.   Maguire; did you know him, Mr. Davoren?

Davoren.   Yes—no, no; I didn't know him, no, I didn't know him, Minnie.

Minnie.   I wonder is it the Maguire that does be with Mr. Shields?

Davoren.   Oh no, not at all, it couldn't be.

Mrs. Henderson.   Knocksedan? That's in the County Sligo, now, or I'm greatly mistaken—am I right, Mr. Gallicker, or am I wrong?

Mr. Gallogher [*who knows perfectly well that it is in the County Dublin, but dare not correct Mrs. Henderson*].   That's where it is—Knocksedan, that's the very identical county.

Mrs. Henderson.   Well, I think we better be makin' a move, Mr. Gallicker; we've kep' Mr. Davoren long enough, an' you'll find the letter'll be in good hans.

[*Mr. Gallogher and Mrs. Henderson move towards the door, which when he reaches it Mr. Gallogher grips, hesitates, buttons his coat, and turns to Davoren.*

Mr. Gallogher.   Mr. Davoren, sir, on behalf ov meself, James Gallicker, an' Winifred, Mrs. Gallicker, wife ov the said James, I beg to offer, extend an' furnish our humble an' hearty thanks for your benevolent goodness in interferin' in the matter specified, particularated an' expanded upon in the letter, mandamus or schedule, as the case may be. An' let me interpretate to you on behalf ov meself an' Winifred Gallicker, that whenever you visit us you will be supernally positive ov a hundred thousand welcomes—ahem.

Mrs. Henderson [*beaming with pride for the genius of her friend*].   There's a man for you, Mr. Davoren! You forgot to mention Biddy and Shaun, Mr.

Gallicker—[*to Davoren*] his two children—it's himself has them trained well. It ud make your heart thrill like an alarm clock to hear them singin' "Faith ov Our Fathers" an' "Wrap the Green Flag Roun' Me."

Mr. Gallogher [*half apologetically and half proudly*].   Faith an' Fatherland, Mrs. Henderson, Faith and Fatherland.

Mrs. Henderson.   Well, good-day, Mr. Davoren, an' God keep you an' strengthen all the men that are fightin' for Ireland's freedom.

[*She and Gallogher go out.*

Tommy.   I must be off too; so-long, Mr. Davoren, an' remember that Tommy Owens only waits the call.

[*He goes out too.*

Davoren.   Well, Minnie, we're by ourselves once more.

Minnie.   Wouldn't that Tommy Owens give you the sick—only waitin' to hear the call! Ah, then it'll take all the brass bands in the country to blow the call before Tommy Owens ud hear it. [*She looks at her wristlet watch.*] Sacred Heart, I've only ten minutes to get back to work! I'll have to fly! Quick, Mr. Davoren, write me name in typewritin' before I go—just "Minnie."

[*Davoren types the name.*

Minnie [*shyly but determinedly*].   Now yours underneath—just "Donal." [*Davoren does so.*] Minnie, Donal; Donal, Minnie; good-bye now.

Davoren.   Here, what about your milk?

Minnie.   I haven't time to take it now. [*Slyly*] I'll come for it this evening.

[*They both go towards the door.*

Davoren.   Minnie, the kiss I didn't get.

Minnie.   What kiss?

Davoren.   When we were interrupted; you know, you little rogue, come, just one.

Minnie.   Quick, then.

[*Davoren kisses her and she runs out. Davoren returns thoughtfully to the table.*

Davoren.   Minnie, Donal; Donal, Minnie. Very pretty, but very ignorant. A gunman on the run! Be careful, be careful, Donal Davoren. But Minnie is attracted to the idea, and I am attracted to Minnie. And what danger can there be in being the shadow of a gunman?

Act II

The same as in Act I. But it is now night. Seumas is in the bed that runs along the wall at back. Davoren is seated near the fire, to which he has drawn the table. He has a fountain-pen in his hand, and is attracted in thought towards the moon, which is shining in through the windows. An open writing-pad is on the table at Davoren's elbow. The bag left by Maguire is still in the same place.

Davoren:

> The cold chaste moon, the Queen of Heaven's bright isles,
> Who makes all beautiful on which she smiles;
> That wandering shrine of soft yet icy flame,
> Which ever is transformed yet still the same.

Ah, Shelley, Shelley, you yourself were a lovely human orb shining through clouds of whirling human dust. "She makes all beautiful on which she smiles." Ah, Shelley, she couldn't make this thrice accursed room beautiful. Her beams of beauty only make its horrors more full of horrors still. There is an ugliness that can be made beautiful, and there is an ugliness that can only be destroyed, and this is part of that ugliness. Donal, Donal, I fear your last state is worse than your first.

[*He lilts a verse, which he writes on the pad before him.*

> When night advances through the sky with slow
>   And solemn tread,
> The queenly moon looks down on life below,
>   As if she read
> Man's soul, and in her scornful silence said:
>   All beautiful and happiest things are dead.

Seumas [*sleepily*].   Donal, Donal, are you awake? [*A pause.*] Donal, Donal, are you asleep?

Davoren.   I'm neither awake nor asleep: I'm thinking.

Seumas.   I was just thinkin', too—I was just thinkin', too, that Maguire is sorry now that he didn't come with me instead of going to Knocksedan. He caught something besides butterflies—two of them he got, one through each lung.

Davoren.   The Irish people are very fond of turning a serious thing into a joke; that was a serious affair—for poor Maguire.

Seumas [*defensively*].   Why didn't he do what he arranged to do? Did he think of me when he was goin' to Knocksedan? How can he expect me to have any sympathy with him now?

Davoren.   He can hardly expect that now that he's dead.

Seumas.   The Republicans 'll do a lot for him, now. How am I goin' to get back the things he has belongin' to me, either? There's some of them in that bag over there, but that's not quarter of what he had; an' I don't know where he was stoppin', for he left his old digs a week or so ago—I suppose there's nothing to be said about my loss; I'm to sing dumb.

Davoren.   I hope there's nothing else in the bag, besides thread and hairpins.

Seumas.   What else ud be in it? . . . I can't sleep properly ever since they put on this damned curfew. A minute ago I thought I heard some of the oul' ones standin' at the door; they won't be satisfied till they bring a raid on the house; an' they never begin to stand at the door till after curfew. . . . Are you gone to bed, Donal?

Davoren.   No; I'm trying to finish this poem.

Seumas [*sitting up in bed*].   If I was you I'd give that game up; it doesn't pay a working-man to write poetry. I don't profess to know much about poetry— I don't profess to know much about poetry—about poetry—I don't know much about the pearly glint of the morning dew, or the damask sweetness of the rare wild rose, or the subtle greenness of the serpent's eye—but I think a poet's claim to greatness depends upon his power to put passion in the common people.

Davoren.   Ay, passion to howl for his destruction. The People! Damn the people! They live in the abyss, the poet lives on the mountain-top; to the people there is no mystery of colour: it is simply the scarlet coat of the soldier; the purple vestments of a priest; the green banner of a party; the brown or blue overalls of industry. To them the might of design is a three-roomed house or a capacious bed. To them beauty is for sale in a butcher's shop. To the people the end of life is the life created for them; to the poet the end of life is the life that he creates for himself; life has a stifling grip upon the people's throat—it is the poet's musician. The poet ever strives to save the people; the people ever strive to destroy the poet. The people view life through creeds, through customs, and through necessities; the poet views creeds, customs, and necessities through life. The people . . .

Seumas [*suddenly, and with a note of anxiety in his voice*].   Whisht! What's that? Is that the tappin' again?

Davoren.   Tappin'. What tappin'?

Seumas [*in an awed whisper*].   This is the second night I heard that tappin'! I believe it bodes no good to me. There, do you hear it again—a quiet, steady, mysterious tappin' on the wall.

Davoren.   I hear no tappin'.

Seumas.   It ud be better for me if you did. It's a sure sign of death when nobody hears it but meself.

Davoren.   Death! What the devil are you talking about, man?

Seumas.   I don't like it at all; there's always something like that heard when one of our family dies.

Davoren.   I don't know about that; but I know there's a hell of a lot of things heard when one of your family lives.

Seumas.   God between us an' all harm! Thank God I'm where I ought to be— in bed. . . . It's always best to be in your proper place when such things happen—Sacred Heart! There it is again; do you not hear it now?

Davoren. Ah, for God's sake go asleep.

Seumas. Do you believe in nothing?

Davoren. I don't believe in tappin'.

Seumas. Whisht, it's stopped again; I'll try to go asleep for fear it ud begin again.

Davoren. Ay, do; and if it starts again I'll be sure to waken you up.

[*A pause.*

Seumas. It's very cold to-night. Do you feel cold?

Davoren. I thought you were goin' asleep?

Seumas. The bloody cold won't let me. . . . You'd want a pair of pyjamas on you. [*A pause.*] Did you ever wear pyjamas, Donal?

Davoren. No, no, no.

Seumas. What kind of stuff is in them?

Davoren [*angrily*]. Oh, it depends on the climate; in India, silk; in Italy, satin; and the Eskimo wears them made from the skin of the Polar bear.

Seumas [*emphatically*]. If you take my advice you'll get into bed—that poem is beginnin' to get on your nerves.

Davoren [*extinguishing the candle with a vicious blow*].   Right; I'm going to bed now, so you can shut up.

[*Visibility is still maintained from the light of the moon.*

Seumas. I was goin' to say something when you put out the light—what's this it was?—um, um, oh, ay: when I was comin' in this evenin' I saw Minnie Powell goin' out. If I was you I wouldn't have that one comin' in here.

Davoren. She comes in; I don't bring her in, do I?

Seumas. The oul' ones'll be talkin', an' once they start you don't know how it'll end. Surely a man that has read Shelley couldn't be interested in an ignorant little bitch that thinks of nothin' but jazz dances, fox-trots, picture theatres an' dress.

Davoren.   Right glad I am that she thinks of dress, for she thinks of it in the right way, and makes herself a pleasant picture to the eye. Education has been wasted on many persons, teaching them to talk only, but leaving them with all their primitive instincts. Had poor Minnie received an education she would have been an artist. She is certainly a pretty girl. I'm sure she is a good girl, and I believe she is a brave girl.

Seumas.   A Helen of Troy[24] come to live in a tenement! You think a lot about her simply because she thinks a lot about you, an' she thinks a lot about you because she looks upon you as a hero—a kind o' Paris . . . she'd give the

---

[24] In legend, the most beautiful woman of ancient Greece. She eloped with Paris, a prince of Troy—this event precipitated the Trojan War.

world an' all to be gaddin' about with a gunman. An' what ecstasy it ud give her if after a bit you were shot or hanged; she'd be able to go about then— like a good many more—singin', "I do not mourn me darlin' lost, for he fell in his Jacket Green." An' then, for a year an' a day, all round her hat she'd wear the Tri-coloured Ribbon O, till she'd pick up an' marry someone else— possibly a British Tommy with a Mons Star.[25] An' as for bein' brave, it's easy to be that when you've no cause for cowardice; I wouldn't care to have me life dependin' on brave little Minnie Powell—she wouldn't sacrifice a jazz dance to save it.

Davoren [*sitting on the bed and taking off his coat and vest, preparatory to going to bed*].   There; that's enough about Minnie Powell. I'm afraid I'll soon have to be on the run out of this house, too; it is becoming painfully obvious that there is no peace to be found here.

Seumas.   Oh, this house is all right; barrin' the children, it does be quiet enough. Wasn't there children in the last place you were in too?

Davoren.   Ay, ten; [*viciously*] and they were all over forty.

[*A pause as Davoren is removing his collar and tie.*

Seumas.   Everything is very quiet now; I wonder what time is it?

Davoren.   The village cock hath thrice done salutation to the morn.

Seumas.   Shakespeare, Richard the III, Act Five, Scene III. It was Ratcliffe said that to Richard just before the battle of Bosworth. . . . How peaceful the heavens look now with the moon in the middle; you'd never think there were men prowlin' about tryin' to shoot each other. I don't know how a man who has shot any one can sleep in peace at night.

Davoren.   There's plenty of men can't sleep in peace at night now unless they know that they have shot somebody.

Seumas.   I wish to God it was all over. The country is gone mad. Instead of counting their beads now they're countin' bullets; their Hail Marys and paternosters are burstin' bombs—burstin' bombs, an' the rattle of machine-guns; petrol is their holy water; their Mass is a burnin' buildin'; their De Profundis is "The Soldiers' Song," an' their creed is, I believe in the gun almighty, maker of heaven an' earth—an' it's all for "the glory o' God an' the honour o' Ireland."

Davoren.   I remember the time when you yourself believed in nothing but the gun.

Seumas.   Ay, when there wasn't a gun in the country; I've a different opinion now when there's nothin' but guns in the country. . . . An' you daren't open your mouth, for Kathleen ni Houlihan is very different now to the woman who used to play the harp an' sing "Weep on, weep on, your hour is past," for she's a ragin' divil now, an' if you only look crooked at her you're sure

---

[25] Mons is a city in Belgium. The first battle involving the British Expeditionary Force in World War I occurred at Mons, and the Mons Star would be a campaign ribbon.

of a punch in th' eye. But this is the way I look at it—I look at it this way: You're not goin'—you're not goin' to beat the British Empire—the British Empire, by shootin' an occasional Tommy at the corner of an occasional street. Besides, when the Tommies have the wind up—when the Tommies have the wind up they let bang at everything they see—they don't give a God's curse who they plug.

Davoren.   Maybe they ought to get down off the lorry and run to the Records Office to find out a man's pedigree before they plug him.

Seumas.   It's the civilians that suffer; when there's an ambush they don't know where to run. Shot in the back to save the British Empire, an' shot in the breast to save the soul of Ireland. I'm a Nationalist meself, right enough—a Nationalist right enough, but all the same—I'm a Nationalist right enough; I believe in the freedom of Ireland, an' that England has no right to be here, but I draw the line when I hear the gunmen blowin' about dyin' for the people, when it's the people that are dyin for the gunmen! With all due respect to the gunmen, I don't want them to die for me.

Davoren   Not likely; you object to any one of them deliberately dying for you for fear that one of these days you might accidentally die for one of them.

Seumas.   You're one of the brave fellows that doesn't fear death.

Davoren.   Why should I be afraid of it? It's all the same to me how it comes, where it comes, or when it comes. I leave fear of death to the people that are always praying for eternal life; "Death is here and death is there, death is busy everywhere."

Seumas.   Ay, in Ireland. Thanks be to God I'm a daily communicant. There's a great comfort in religion; it makes a man strong in time of trouble an' brave in time of danger. No man need be afraid with a crowd of angels round him; thanks to God for His Holy religion!

Davoren.   You're welcome to your angels; philosophy is mine; philosophy that makes the coward brave; the sufferer defiant; the weak strong; the . . .

[A *volley of shots is heard in a lane that runs parallel with the wall of the back-yard. Religion and philosophy are forgotten in the violent fear of a nervous equality.*

Seumas.   Jesus, Mary, an' Joseph, what's that?

Davoren.   My God, that's very close.

Seumas.   Is there no Christianity at all left in the country?

Davoren.   Are we ever again going to know what peace and security are?

Seumas.   If this continues much longer I'll be nothing but a galvanic battery o' shocks.

Davoren.   It's dangerous to be in and it's equally dangerous to be out.

Seumas.   This is a dangerous spot to be in with them windows; you couldn't tell the minute a bullet ud come in through one of them—through one of them, an' hit the—hit the—an' hit the . . .

Davoren [*irritably*].   Hit the what, man?

Seumas.   The wall.

Davoren.   Couldn't you say that at first without making a song about it?

Seumas [*suddenly*].   I don't believe there's horses in the stable at all.

Davoren.   Stable! What stable are you talking about?

Seumas.   There's a stable at the back of the house with an entrance from the yard; it's used as a carpenter's shop. Didn't you often hear the peculiar noises at night? They give out that it's the horses shakin' their chains.

Davoren.   And what is it?

Seumas.   Oh, there I'll leave you!

Davoren.   Surely you don't mean . . .

Seumas.   But I do mean it.

Davoren.   You do mean what?

Seumas.   I wouldn't—I wouldn't be surprised—wouldn't be surprised—surprised . . .

Davoren.   Yes, yes, surprised—go on.

Seumas.   I wouldn't be surprised if they were manufacturin' bombs there.

Davoren.   My God, that's a pleasant contemplation! The sooner I'm on the run out of this house the better. How is it you never said anything about this before?

Seumas.   Well—well, I didn't want—I didn't want to—to . . .

Davoren.   You didn't want to what?

Seumas.   I didn't want to frighten you.

Davoren [*sarcastically*].   You're bloody kind!

[*A knock at the door; the voice of Mrs. Grigson heard.*

Mrs. Grigson.   Are you asleep, Mr. Shields?

Seumas.   What the devil can she want at this hour of the night? [*To Mrs. Grigson*] No, Mrs. Grigson, what is it?

Mrs. Grigson [*Opening the door and standing at the threshold. She is a woman about forty, but looks much older. She is one of the cave-dwellers of Dublin, living as she does in a tenement kitchen, to which only an occasional sickly beam of sunlight filters through a grating in the yard; the consequent general dimness of her abode has given her a habit of peering through half-closed eyes. She is slovenly dressed in an old skirt and bodice; her face is grimy, not because her habits are dirty—for, although she is untidy, she is a clean woman— but because of the smoky atmosphere of her room. Her hair is constantly falling over her face, which she is as frequently removing by rapid movements of her right hand*].   He hasn't turned up yet, an' I'm stiff with the cold waitin' for him.

Seumas.   Mr. Grigson, is it?

Mrs. Grigson.   Adolphus, Mr. Shields, after takin' his tea at six o'clock—no, I'm tellin' a lie—it was before six, for I remember the Angelus was ringin' out an' we sittin' at the table—after takin' his tea he went out for a breath o' fresh air, an' I haven't seen sign or light of him since. 'Clare to God me heart is up in me mouth, thinkin' he might be shot be the Black an' Tans.

Seumas.   Aw, he'll be all right, Mrs. Grigson. You ought to go to bed an' rest yourself; it's always the worst that comes into a body's mind; go to bed, Mrs. Grigson, or you'll catch your death of cold.

Mrs. Grigson.   I'm afraid to go to bed, Mr. Shields, for I'm always in dread that some night or another, when he has a sup taken, he'll fall down the kitchen stairs an' break his neck. Not that I'd be any the worse if anything did happen to him, for you know the sort he is, Mr. Shields; sure he has me heart broke.

Seumas.   Don't be downhearted, Mrs. Grigson; he may take a thought one of these days an' turn over a new leaf.

Mrs. Grigson.   Sorra leaf Adolphus'll ever turn over, he's too far gone in the horns for that now. Sure no one ud mind him takin' a pint or two, if he'd stop at that, but he won't; nothin' could fill him with beer, an' no matter how much he may have taken, when he's taken more he'll always say, "Here's the first to-day."

Davoren [*to Seumas*].   Christ! Is she going to stop talking there all the night?

Seumas.   'Sh, she'll hear you; right enough, the man has the poor woman's heart broke.

Davoren.   And because he has her heart broken, she's to have the privilege of breaking everybody else's.

Mrs. Grigson.   Mr. Shields.

Seumas.   Yes?

Mrs. Grigson.   Do the insurance companies pay if a man is shot after curfew?

Seumas.   Well, now, that's a thing I couldn't say, Mrs. Grigson.

Mrs. Grigson [*plaintively*].   Isn't he a terrible man to be takin' such risks, an' not knowin' what'll happen to him. He knows them Societies only want an excuse to do people out of their money—is it after one, now, Mr. Shields?

Seumas.   Aw, it must be after one, Mrs. Grigson.

Mrs. Grigson [*emphatically*].   Ah, then, if I was a young girl again I'd think twice before gettin' married. Whisht! There's somebody now—it's him, I know be the way he's fumblin'.

[*She goes out a little way. Stumbling steps are heard in the hall.*

Mrs. Grigson [*outside*].   Is that you, Dolphie, dear?

[*After a few moments Adolphus, with Mrs. Grigson holding his arm, stumbles into the room.*

Mrs. Grigson.   Dolphie, dear, mind yourself.

Adolphus [*he is a man of forty-five, but looks, relatively, much younger than Mrs. Grigson. His occupation is that of a solicitor's clerk. He has all the appearance of being well fed; and, in fact, he gets most of the nourishment, Mrs. Grigson getting just enough to give her strength to do the necessary work of the household. On account of living most of his life out of the kitchen, his* complexion is fresh, and his movements, even when sober, are livelier than those of his wife. He is comfortably dressed; heavy top-coat, soft trilby hat, a fancy coloured scarf about his neck, and he carries an umbrella]. I'm all right; do you see anything wrong with me?

Mrs. Grigson.   Of course you're all right, dear; there's no one mindin' you.

Adolphus Grigson.   Mindin' me, is it, mindin' me? He'd want to be a good thing that ud mind me. There's a man here—a man, mind you, afraid av nothin'—not in this bloody house anyway.

Mrs. Grigson [*imploringly*].   Come on downstairs, Dolphie, dear; sure there's not one in the house ud say a word to you.

Adolphus Grigson.   Say a word to me, is it? He'd want to be a good thing that ud say anything to Dolphus Grigson. [*Loudly*] Is there anyone wants to say anything to Dolphus Grigson? If there is, he's here—a man, too—there's no blottin' it out—a man.

Mrs. Grigson.   You'll wake everybody in the house; can't you speak quiet.

Adolphus Grigson [*more loudly still*].   What do I care for anybody in the house? Are they keepin' me; are they givin' me anything? When they're keepin' Grigson it'll be time enough for them to talk. [*With a shout*] I can tell them Adolphus Grigson wasn't born in a bottle!

Mrs. Grigson [*tearfully*].   Why do you talk like that, dear? We all know you weren't born in a bottle.

Adolphus Grigson.   There's some of them in this house think that Grigson was born in a bottle.

Davoren [*to Seumas*].   A most appropriate place for him to be born in.

Mrs. Grigson.   Come on down to bed, now, an' you can talk about them in the mornin'.

Grigson.   I'll talk about them, now; do you think I'm afraid of them? Dolphus Grigson's afraid av nothin', creepin' or walkin',—if there's any one in the house thinks he's fit to take a fall out av Adolphus Grigson, he's here—a man; they'll find that Grigson's no soft thing.

Davoren.   Ah me, alas! Pain, pain ever, for ever.

Mrs. Grigson.   Dolphie, dear, poor Mr. Davoren wants to go to bed.

Davoren.   Oh, she's terribly anxious about poor Mr. Davoren, all of a sudden.

Grigson [*stumbling towards Davoren, and holding out his hand*].   Davoren! He's a man. Leave it there, mate. You needn't be afraid av Dolphus Grigson; there never was a drop av informer's blood in the whole family av Grigson. I don't know what you are or what you think, but you're a man, an' not like some of the goughers in this house, that ud hang you. Not referrin' to you, Mr. Shields.

Mrs. Grigson.   Oh, you're not deludin' to Mr. Shields.

Seumas.   I know that, Mr. Grigson; go on down, now, with Mrs. Grigson, an' have a sleep.

Grigson.   I tie meself to no woman's apron strings, Mr. Shields; I know how to keep Mrs. Grigson in her place; I have the authority of the Bible for that.

I know the Bible from cover to cover, Mr. Davoren, an' that's more than some in this house could say. And what does the Holy Scripture say about woman? It says, "The woman shall be subject to her husband," an' I'll see that Mrs. Grigson keeps the teachin' av the Holy Book in the letter an' in the spirit. If you're ever in trouble, Mr. Davoren, an' Grigson can help— I'm your man—have you me?

Davoren.   I have you, Mr. Grigson, I have you.

Grigson.   Right; I'm an Orangeman,[26] an' I'm not ashamed av it, an' I'm not afraid av it, but I can feel for a true man, all the same—have *you* got me, Mr. Shields?

Seumas.   Oh, we know you well, Mr. Grigson; many a true Irishman was a Protestant—Tone, Emmet an' Parnell.[27]

Grigson.   Mind you, I'm not sayin' as I agree with them you've mentioned, Mr. Shields, for the Bible forbids it, an' Adolphus Grigson 'll always abide be the Bible. Fear God an' honour the King—that's written in Holy Scripture, an' there's no blottin' it out. [*Pulling a bottle out of his pocket*] But here, Mr. Davoren, have a drink, just to show there's no coolness.

Davoren.   No, no, Mr. Grigson, it's too late now to take anything. Go on down with Mrs. Grigson, and we can have a chat in the morning.

Grigson.   Sure you won't have a drink?

Davoren.   Quite sure—thanks all the same.

Grigson [*drinking*].   Here's the first to-day! To all true men, even if they were born in a bottle. Here's to King William, to the battle av the Boyne; to the Hobah Black Chapter—that's my Lodge, Mr. Davoren; an' to The Orange Lily O.[28]

[*Singing in a loud shout:*

An' dud ya go to see the show, each rose an' pinkadilly O,
To feast your eyes an' view the prize won be the Orange
    Lily O.
The Vic'roy there, so debonair, just like a daffadilly O,
With Lady Clarke, blithe as a lark, approached the Orange
    Lily O.
            Heigh Ho the Lily O,
            The Royal, Loyal Lily O,

---

[26]That is, a Protestant. William of Orange defeated a Catholic force consisting of Irish and French troops striving to restore James II to the throne. Protestants, particularly in Northern Ireland, celebrate July 12 as an anniversary of the Protestant victory and wear orange to commemorate William's military feat.

[27]Theobald Wolfe Tone (1763–1798), Robert Emmet, and Charles Stewart Parnell (1846–1891) were Irish patriots. Tone was captured during a naval engagement during the rebellion of 1798 and sentenced to hang. The day before his scheduled execution, he cut his throat with a penknife and died of the wound eight days later. For Emmet, see note 17. Parnell was an important political leader in the struggle for Irish home rule. His power was damaged beyond recovery when he was named as correspondent in a scandalous divorce case.

[28]See note 26.

Beneath the sky what flower can vie with Erin's Orange
   Lily O!

Davoren. Holy God, isn't this terrible!
Grigson [*singing*]:

The elated Muse, to hear the news, jumped like a Connaught
   filly O,
As gossip Fame did loud proclaim the triumph av the
   Lily O.
The Lowland field may roses yield, gay heaths the High-
   lands hilly O;
But high or low no flower can show like Erin's Orange
   Lily O.
        Heigh Ho the Lily O,
        The Royal, Loyal Lily O,
Beneath the sky what flower can vie with Erin's Or . . .

[*While Grigson has been singing, the sound of a rapidly moving motor is heard,
faintly at first, but growing rapidly louder, till it apparently stops suddenly
somewhere very near the house, bringing Grigson's song to an abrupt conclusion. They are all startled, and listen attentively to the throbbing of the engines,
which can be plainly heard. Grigson is considerably sobered, and anxiously keeps
his eyes on the door. Seumas sits up in bed and listens anxiously. Davoren, with
a shaking hand, lights the candle, and begins to search hurriedly among the
books and papers on the table.*]

Grigson [*with a tremor in his voice*]. There's no need to be afraid, they couldn't
be comin' here.
Mrs. Grigson. God forbid! It ud be terrible if they came at this hour ov the
night.
Seumas. You never know now, Mrs. Grigson; they'd rush in on you when
you'd be least expectin' them. What, in the name o' God, is goin' to come
out of it all? Nobody now cares a traneen about the orders of the Ten Com-
mandments; the only order that anybody minds now is, "Put your hands up."
Oh, it's a hopeless country.
Grigson. Whisht; do you hear them talking outside at the door? You're sure
of your life nowhere now; it's just as safe to go everywhere as it is to anywhere. An' they don't give a damn whether you're a loyal man or not. If
you're a Republican they make you sing "God save the King," an' if you're
loyal they'll make you sing the "Soldiers' Song." The singin' ud be all right
if they didn't make you dance afterwards.
Mrs. Grigson. They'd hardly come here unless they heard something about
Mr. Davoren.
Davoren. About me! What could they hear about me?
Grigson. You'll never get some people to keep their mouths shut. I was in

the Blue Lion this evening, an' who do you think was there, blowin' out av him, but that little blower, Tommy Owens; there he was tellin' everybody that *he* knew where there was bombs; that *he* had a friend that was a General in the I.R.A.; that *he* could tell them what the Staff was thinkin' av doin'; that *he* could lay his hand on tons av revolvers; that they wasn't a mile from where he was livin', but that *he* knew his own know, an' would keep it to himself.

Seumas.   Well, God blast the little blower, anyway; it's the like ov him that deserves to be plugged! [*To Davoren*] What are you lookin' for among the books, Donal?

Davoren.   A letter that I got to-day from Mr. Gallogher and Mrs. Henderson; I'm blessed if I know where I put it.

Seumas [*peevishly*].   Can't you look for it in the mornin'?

Davoren.   It's addressed to the Irish Republican Army, and, considering the possibility of a raid, it would be safer to get rid of it.

[*Shots again heard out in the lane, followed by loud shouts of Halt, halt, halt!*

Grigson.   I think we had better be gettin' to bed, Debby; it's not right to be keepin' Mr. Davoren an' Mr. Shields awake.

Seumas.   An' what made them give you such a letter as that; don't they know the state the country is in? An' you were worse to take it. Have you got it?

Davoren.   I can't find it anywhere; isn't this terrible!

Grigson.   Good-night, Mr. Davoren; good-night, Mr. Shields.

Mrs. Grigson.   Good-night, Mr. Shields; good-night, Mr. Davoren.

[*They go out. Seumas and Davoren are too much concerned about the letter to respond to their good-nights.*

Seumas.   What were you thinkin' of when you took such a letter as that? Ye gods, has nobody any brains at all, at all? Oh, this is a hopeless country. Did you try in your pockets?

Davoren [*searching in his pockets*].   Oh, thanks be to God, here it is.

Seumas.   Burn it now, an', for God's sake, don't take any letters like that again. . . . There's the motor goin' away; we can sleep in peace now for the rest of the night. Just to make sure of everything now, have a look in that bag o' Maguire's: not that there can be anything in it.

Davoren.   If there's nothing in it, what's the good of looking?

Seumas.   It won't kill you to look, will it?

[*Davoren goes over to the bag, puts it on the table, opens it, and jumps back, his face pale and his limbs trembling.*

Davoren.   My God, it's full of bombs, Mills bombs!

Seumas.   Holy Mother of God, you're jokin'!

Davoren. If the Tans come you'll find whether I'm jokin' or no.

Seumas. Isn't this a nice pickle to be in? St. Anthony, look down on us!

Davoren. There's no use of blaming St. Anthony; why did you let Maguire leave the bag here?

Seumas. Why did I let him leave the bag here; why did I let him leave the bag here! How did I know what was in it? Didn't I think there was nothin' in it but spoons an' hairpins? What'll we do now; what'll we do now? Mother o' God, grant there'll be no raid to-night. I knew things ud go wrong when I missed Mass this mornin'.

Davoren. Give over your praying and let us try to think of what is best to be done. There's one thing certain: as soon as morning comes I'm on the run out of this house.

Seumas. Thinkin' of yourself, like the rest of them. Leavin' me to bear the brunt of it.

Davoren. And why shouldn't you bear the brunt of it? Maguire was no friend of mine; besides, it's your fault; you knew the sort of a man he was, and you should have been on your guard.

Seumas. Did I know he was a gunman; did I know he was a gunman; did I know he was a gunman? Did . . .

Davoren. Do you mean to tell me that . . .

Seumas. Just a moment . . .

Davoren. You didn't know . . .

Seumas. Just a moment . . .

Davoren. That Maguire was connected with . . .

Seumas. [*loudly*]. Just a moment; can't . . .

Davoren. The Republican Movement? What's the use of trying to tell damn lies!

[*Minnie Powell rushes into the room. She is only partly dressed, and has thrown a shawl over her shoulders. She is in a state of intense excitement.*]

Minnie. Mr. Davoren, Donal, they're all round the house; they must be goin' to raid the place; I was lookin' out of the window an' I seen them; I do be on the watch every night; have you anything? If you have . . .

[*There is heard at street door a violent and continuous knocking, followed by the crash of glass and the beating of the door with rifle butts.*]

Minnie. There they are, there they are, there they are!

[*Davoren reclines almost fainting on the bed; Seumas sits up in an attitude of agonized prayerfulness; Minnie alone retains her presence of mind. When she sees their panic she becomes calm, though her words are rapidly spoken, and her actions are performed with decisive celerity.*]

Minnie.   What is it; what have you got; where are they?

Davoren.   Bombs, bombs, bombs; my God! in the bag on the table there; we're done, we're done!

Seumas.   Hail, Mary, full of grace—pray for us miserable sinners—Holy St. Anthony, do you hear them batterin' at the door—now an' at the hour of our death—say an act of contrition, Donal—there's the glass gone!

Minnie.   I'll take them to my room; maybe they won't search it; if they do aself, they won't harm a girl. Good-bye . . . Donal.

[*She glances lovingly at Donal—who is only semi-conscious—as she rushes out with the bag.*

Seumas.   If we come through this I'll never miss a Mass again! If it's the Tommies it won't be so bad, but if it's the Tans, we're goin' to have a terrible time.

[*The street door is broken open and heavy steps are heard in the hall, punctuated with shouts of "'Old the light 'ere," "Put 'em up," etc. An Auxiliary opens the door of the room and enters, revolver in one hand and electric torch in the other. His uniform is black, and he wears a black beret.*

The Auxiliary.   'Oo's 'ere?

Seumas [*as if he didn't know*].   Who—who's that?

The Auxiliary [*peremptorily*].   'Oo's 'ere?

Seumas.   Only two men, mister; me an' me mate in t'other bed.

The Auxiliary.   Why didn't you open the door?

Seumas.   We didn't hear you knockin', sir.

The Auxiliary.   You must be a little awd of 'earing, ay?

Seumas.   I had rheumatic fever a few years ago, an' ever since I do be a —I do be a little deaf sometimes.

The Auxiliary [*to Davoren*].   'Ow is it you're not in bed?

Davoren.   I was in bed; when I heard the knockin' I got up to open the door.

The Auxiliary.   You're a koind blowke, you are. Deloighted, like, to have a visit from us, ay? Ay? [*Threatening to strike him*] Why down't you answer?

Davoren.   Yes, sir.

The Auxiliary.   What's your name?

Davoren.   Davoren, Dan[29] Davoren, sir.

The Auxiliary.   You're not an Irishman, are you?

Davoren.   I-I-I was born in Ireland.

The Auxiliary.   Ow, you were, were you; Irish han' proud of it, ay? [*To Seumas*] What's *your* name?

Seumas.   Seuma . . . Oh no; Jimmie Shields, sir.

The Auxiliary.   Ow, you're a selt [*he means a Celt*], one of the seltic race that speaks a lingo of its ahn, and that's going to overthrow the British Empire—

---

[29] Note that Donal assumes an English name, as does Seumas in his next speech.

I don't think! 'Ere, where's your gun?

Seumas.   I never had a gun in me hand in me life.

The Auxiliary.   Now; you wouldn't know what a gun is if you sawr one, I suppowse. [*Displaying his revolver in a careless way*] 'Ere, what's that?

Seumas.   Oh, be careful, please, be careful.

The Auxiliary.   Why, what 'ave I got to be careful abaht?

Seumas.   The gun; it-it-it might go off.

The Auxiliary.   An' what prawse if it did; it can easily be relowded. Any ammunition 'ere? What's in that press?

[*He searches and scatters contents of press.*

Seumas.   Only a little bit o' grub; you'll get nothin' here, sir; no one in the house has any connection with politics.

The Auxiliary.   Now? I've never met a man yet that didn't say that, but we're a little bit too ikey now to be kidded with that sort of talk.

Seumas.   May I go an' get a drink o' water?

The Auxiliary.   You'll want a barrel of watah before you're done with us. [*The Auxiliary goes about the room examining places*] 'Ello, what's 'ere? A statue o' Christ! An' a Crucifix! You'd think you was in a bloomin' monastery.

[*Mrs. Grigson enters, dressed disorderly and her hair awry.*

Mrs. Grigson.   They're turning the place upside-down. Upstairs an' downstairs they're makin' a litter of everything! I declare to God, it's awful what law-abidin' people have to put up with. An' they found a pint bottle of whisky under Dolphie's pillow, an' they're drinkin' every drop of it—an' Dolphie'll be like a devil in the mornin' when he finds he has no curer.

The Auxiliary [*all attention when he hears the word whisky*].   A bottle of whisky, ay? 'Ere, where do you live—quick, where do you live?

Mrs. Grigson.   Down in the kitchen—an' when you go down will you ask them not to drink—oh, he's gone without listenin' to me.

[*While Mrs. Grigson is speaking the Auxiliary rushes out.*

Seumas [*anxiously to Mrs. Grigson*].   Are they searchin' the whole house, Mrs. Grigson?

Mrs. Grigson.   They didn't leave a thing in the kitchen that they didn't flitter about the floor; the things in the cupboard, all the little odds an' ends that I keep in the big box, an . . .

Seumas.   Oh, they're a terrible gang of blaguards—did they go upstairs?—they'd hardly search Minnie Powell's room—do you think would they, Mrs. Grigson?

Mrs. Grigson.   Just to show them the sort of a man he was, before they come in, Dolphie put the big Bible on the table, open at the First Gospel of St.

Peter, second chapter, an' marked the thirteenth to the seventeenth verse in red ink—you know the passages, Mr. Shields—[*quoting*]:

> "Submit yourselves to every ordinance of man for the Lord's sake: whether it be to the king, as supreme; or unto governors, as unto them that are sent by him for the punishment of evildoers, an' for the praise of them that do well. . . . Love the brotherhood. Fear God. Honour the King."

An' what do you think they did, Mr. Shields? They caught a hold of the Bible an' flung it on the floor—imagine that, Mr. Shields—flingin' the Bible on the floor! Then one of them says to another—"Jack," says he, "have you seen the light; is your soul saved?" An' then they grabbed hold of poor Dolphie, callin' him Mr. Moody an' Mr. Sankey, an' wanted him to offer up a prayer for the Irish Republic! An' when they were puttin' me out, there they had the poor man sittin' up in bed, his hands crossed on his breast, his eyes lookin' up at the ceilin', an' he singin' a hymn—"We shall meet in the Sweet Bye an' Bye"—an' all the time, Mr. Shields, there they were drinkin' his whisky; there's torture for you, an' they all laughin' at poor Dolphie's terrible sufferins.

Davoren.   In the name of all that's sensible, what did he want to bring whisky home with him for? They're bad enough sober, what'll they be like when they're drunk?

Mrs. Grigson [*plaintively*].   He always brings a drop home with him—he calls it his medicine.

Seumas [*still anxious*].   They'll hardly search all the house; do you think they will, Mrs. Grigson?

Mrs. Grigson.   An' we have a picture over the mantelpiece of King William crossing the Boyne, an' do you know what they wanted to make out, Mr. Shields, that it was Robert Emmet, an' the picture of a sacret society!

Seumas.   She's not listenin' to a word I'm sayin'! Oh, the country is hopeless an' the people is hopeless.

Davoren.   For God's sake tell her to go to hell out of this—she's worse than the Auxsie.[30]

Seumas [*thoughtfully*].   Let her stay where she is; it's safer to have a woman in the room. If they come across the bombs I hope to God Minnie 'll say nothin'.

Davoren.   We're a pair of pitiable cowards to let poor Minnie suffer when we know that we and not she are to blame.

Seumas.   What else can we do, man? Do you want us to be done in? If you're anxious to be riddled, I'm not. Besides, they won't harm her, she's only a girl, an' so long as she keeps her mouth shut it'll be all right.

Davoren.   I wish I could be sure of that.

Seumas.   D'ye think are they goin', Mrs. Grigson? What are they doin' now?

---

[30] Auxiliaries, a military support group under the control of the Black and Tans.

Mrs. Grigson [*who is standing at the door, looking out into the hall*].   There's not a bit of me that's not shakin' like a jelly!

Seumas.   Are they gone upstairs, Mrs. Grigson? Do you think, Mrs. Grigson, will they soon be goin'?

Mrs. Grigson.   When they were makin' poor Dolphie sit up in the bed, I 'clare to God I thought every minute I'd hear their guns goin' off, an' see poor Dolphie stretched out dead in the bed—whisht, God bless us, I think I hear him moanin'!

Seumas.   You might as well be talking to a stone! They're all hopeless, hopeless, hopeless, hopeless! She thinks she hears him moanin'! It's bloody near time somebody made him moan!

Davoren [*with a sickly attempt at humour*].   He's moaning for the loss of his whisky.

[*During the foregoing dialogue the various sounds of a raid—orders, the tramping of heavy feet, the pulling about of furniture, etc., are heard. Now a more definite and sustained commotion is apparent. Loud and angry commands of "Go on," "Get out and get into the lorry," are heard, mingled with a girl's voice— it is Minnie's—shouting bravely, but a little hysterically, "Up the Republic."*]

Mrs. Grigson [*from the door*].   God save us, they're takin' Minnie, they're takin' Minnie Powell! [*Running out*] What in the name of God can have happened?

Seumas.   Holy Saint Anthony grant that she'll keep her mouth shut.

Davoren [*sitting down on the bed and covering his face with his hands*].   We'll never again be able to lift up our heads if anything happens to Minnie.

Seumas.   For God's sake keep quiet or somebody'll hear you; nothin'll happen to her, nothin' at all—it'll be all right if she only keeps her mouth shut.

Mrs. Grigson [*running in*].   They're after gettin' a whole lot of stuff in Minnie's room! Enough to blow up the whole street, a Tan says! God to-night, who'd have ever thought that of Minnie Powell!

Seumas.   Did she say anything, is she sayin' anything, what's she sayin', Mrs. Grigson?

Mrs. Grigson.   She's shoutin' "Up the Republic" at the top of her voice. An' big Mrs. Henderson is fightin' with the soldiers—she's after nearly knockin' one of them down, an' they're puttin' her into the lorry too.

Seumas.   God blast her! Can she not mind her own business? What does she want here—didn't she know there was a raid on? Is the whole damn country goin' mad? They'll open fire in a minute an' innocent people'll be shot!

Davoren.   What way are they using Minnie, Mrs. Grigson; are they rough with her?

Mrs. Grigson.   They couldn't be half rough enough; the little hussy, to be so deceitful; she might as well have had the house blew up! God to-night, who'd think it was in Minnie Powell!

Seumas.   Oh, grant she won't say anything!

Mrs. Grigson.   There they're goin' away now; ah, then I hope they'll give that Minnie Powell a coolin'.

Seumas.   God grant she won't say anything! Are they gone, Mrs. Grigson?

Mrs. Grigson.   With her fancy stockins, an' her pompoms, an' her crêpe de chine blouses! I knew she'd come to no good!

Seumas.   God grant she'll keep her mouth shut! Are they gone, Mrs Grigson?

Mrs. Grigson.   They're gone, Mr. Shields, an' here's poor Dolphie an' not a feather astray on him. Oh, Dolphie, dear, you're all right, thanks to God; I thought you'd never see the mornin'.

Grigson [*entering without coat or vest*].   Of course I'm all right; what ud put a bother on Dolphie Grigson?—not the Tans anyway!

Mrs. Grigson.   When I seen you stretched out on the bed, an' you . . . singin' a hymn . . .

Grigson [*fearful of possible humiliation*].   Who was singin' a hymn? D'ye hear me talkin' to you—where did you hear me singin' a hymn?

Mrs. Grigson.   I was only jokin', Dolphie, dear; I . . .

Grigson.   Your place is below, an' not gosterin' here to men; down with you quick!

[*Mrs. Grigson hurriedly leaves the room.*

Grigson [*nonchalantly taking out his pipe, filling it, lighting it, and beginning to smoke*].   Excitin' few moments, Mr. Davoren; Mrs. G. lost her head completely—panic-stricken. But that's only natural, all women is very nervous. The only thing to do is to show them that they can't put the wind up you; show the least sign of fright an' they'd walk on you, simply walk on you. Two of them come down—"Put them up," revolvers under your nose—you know, the usual way. "What's all the bother about?" says I, quite calm. "No bother at all," says one of them, "only this gun might go off an' hit somebody—have you me?" says he. "What if it does," says I, "a man can only die once, an' you'll find Grigson won't squeal." "God, you're a cool one," says the other, "there's no blottin' it out."

Seumas.   That's the best way to take them; it only makes things worse to show that you've got the wind up. "Any ammunition here?" says the fellow that come in here. "I don't think so," says I, "but you better have a look." "No back talk," says he, "or you might get plugged." "I don't know of any clause," says I, "in the British Constitution that makes it a crime for a man to speak in his own room,"—with that, he just had a look round, an' off he went.

Grigson.   If a man keeps a stiff upper front—Merciful God, there's an ambush!

[*Explosions of two bursting bombs are heard on the street outside the house, followed by fierce and rapid revolver and rifle fire. People are heard rushing into the hall, and there is general clamour and confusion. Seumas and Davoren cower down in the room; Grigson, after a few moments' hesitation, frankly rushes out of the room to what he conceives to be the safer asylum of the kitchen. A lull follows, punctuated by an odd rifle-shot; then comes a peculiar and ominous stillness, broken in a few moments by the sounds of voices and movement. Questions are heard being asked:* "Who was it was killed?" "Where was she shot?" *which are answered by:* "Minnie Powell"; "She went to jump off the lorry an' she was shot"; "She's not dead, is she?"; "They say she's dead—shot through the buzzom!"

Davoren [*in a tone of horror-stricken doubt*].   D'ye hear what they're sayin', Shields, d'ye hear what they're sayin'?—Minnie Powell is shot.

Seumas.   For God's sake speak easy, an' don't bring them in here on top of us again.

Davoren.   Is that all you're thinking of? Do you realize that she has been shot to save us?

Seumas.   Is it my fault; am I to blame?

Davoren.   It is your fault and mine, both; oh, we're a pair of dastardly cowards to have let her do what she did.

Seumas.   She did it off her own bat—we didn't ask her to do it.

[*Mrs. Grigson enters. She is excited and semi-hysterical, and sincerely affected by the tragic occurrence.*

Mrs. Grigson [*falling down in a sitting posture on one of the beds*].   What's goin' to happen next! Oh, Mr. Davoren, isn't it terrible, isn't it terrible! Minnie Powell, poor little Minnie Powell's been shot dead! They were raidin' a house a few doors down, an' had just got up in their lorries to go away, when they was ambushed. You never heard such shootin'! An' in the thick of it, poor Minnie went to jump off the lorry she was on, an' she was shot through the buzzom. Oh, it was horrible to see the blood pourin' out, an' Minnie moanin'. They found some paper in her breast, with "Minnie" written on it, an' some other name they couldn't make out with the blood; the officer kep' it. The ambulance is bringin' her to the hospital, but what good's that when she's dead! Poor little Minnie, poor little Minnie Powell, to think of you full of life a few minutes ago, an' now she's dead!

Davoren.   Ah me, alas! Pain, pain, pain ever, for ever! It's terrible to think that little Minnie is dead, but it's still more terrible to think that Davoren and Shields are alive! Oh, Donal Davoren, shame is your portion now till the silver cord is loosened and the golden bowl be broken.[31] Oh, Davoren, Donal Davoren, poet and poltroon, poltroon and poet!

Seumas [*solemnly*].   I knew something ud come of the tappin' on the wall!

---

[31] That is, until death. See Ecclesiastes 12:6.

QUESTIONS

1. Aside from the soldiers who raid the tenement, does the play have a villain? What is the central conflict? **2.** Donal Davoren, a poet who constantly quotes English romantic poetry, is seen by his neighbors and by Minnie as an Irish nationalist gunman. Why does he not correct their mistaken impression? What are the consequences of his pretense? **3.** The Grigsons are Protestants. What function do they serve in the play? Why does Mr. Gallogher give his letter to Donal? What are the consequences of that letter? What function does Maguire serve in the play? **4.** Seumas Shields professes a pious Catholicism, and religion played a significant role in Ireland's struggle for independence. Is Seumas's religiosity a positive or negative feature of his character? Explain.

WRITING TOPICS

1. Does the play have a hero? What, finally, are your feelings about Donal Davoren, Seumas Shields, and Minnie Powell? **2.** The play is set against the political turmoil of Ireland's struggle for independence from Great Britain during the early 1920s. Would you characterize the play as political? Explain.

The Glass Menagerie   1945

TENNESSEE WILLIAMS   [1911–1983]

CHARACTERS

Amanda Wingfield, the mother. A little woman of great but confused vitality
clinging frantically to another time and place. Her characterization must be
carefully created, not copied from type. She is not paranoiac, but her life is
paranoia. There is much to admire in Amanda, and as much to love and
pity as there is to laugh at. Certainly she has endurance and a kind of
heroism, and though her foolishness makes her unwittingly cruel at times,
there is tenderness in her slight person.

Laura Wingfield, her daughter. Amanda, having failed to establish contact with
reality, continues to live vitally in her illusions, but Laura's situation is even
graver. A childhood illness has left her crippled, one leg slightly shorter than
the other, and held in a brace. This defect need not be more than suggested
on the stage. Stemming from this, Laura's separation increases till she is like
a piece of her own glass collection, too exquisitely fragile to move from the
shelf.

Tom Wingfield, her son. And the narrator of the play. A poet with a job in a
warehouse. His nature is not remorseless, but to escape from a trap he has
to act without pity.

Jim O'Connor, the gentleman caller. A nice, ordinary, young man.

SCENE. *An alley in St. Louis.*

TIME. *Now and the Past.*

Scene I

*The Wingfield apartment is in the rear of the building, one of those vast hivelike
conglomerations of cellular living-units that flower as warty growths in over-
crowded urban centers of lower middle-class population and are symptomatic of
the impulse of this largest and fundamentally enslaved section of American society
to avoid fluidity and differentiation and to exist and function as one interfused
mass of automatism.*

*The apartment faces an alley and is entered by a fire-escape, a structure whose
name is a touch of accidental poetic truth, for all these huge buildings are always
burning with the slow and implacable fires of human desperation. The fire-escape
is included in the set—that is, the landing of it and steps descending from it.*

*The scene is memory and is therefore nonrealistic. Memory takes a lot of poetic
license. It omits some details; others are exaggerated, according to the emotional*

325

value of the articles it touches, for memory is seated predominantly in the heart. The interior is therefore rather dim and poetic.

At the rise of the curtain, the audience is faced with the dark, grim rear wall of the Wingfield tenement. This building, which runs parallel to the footlights, is flanked on both sides by dark, narrow alleys which run into murky canyons of tangled clotheslines, garbage cans and the sinister latticework of neighboring fire-escapes. It is up and down these side alleys that exterior entrances and exits are made, during the play. At the end of Tom's opening commentary, the dark tenement wall slowly reveals (by means of a transparency) the interior of the ground floor Wingfield apartment.

Downstage is the living room, which also serves as a sleeping room for Laura, the sofa unfolding to make her bed. Upstage, center, and divided by a wide arch or second proscenium with transparent faded portieres (or second curtain), is the dining room. In an old-fashioned what-not in the living room are seen scores of transparent glass animals. A blown-up photograph of the father hangs on the wall of the living room, facing the audience, to the left of the archway. It is the face of a very handsome young man in a doughboy's First World War cap. He is gallantly smiling, ineluctably smiling, as if to say, "I will be smiling forever."

The audience hears and sees the opening scene in the dining room through both the transparent fourth wall of the building and the transparent gauze portieres of the dining-room arch. It is during this revealing scene that the fourth wall slowly ascends, out of sight. This transparent exterior wall is not brought down again until the very end of the play, during Tom's final speech.

The narrator is an undisguised convention of the play. He takes whatever license with dramatic convention as is convenient to his purposes.

Tom enters dressed as a merchant sailor from alley, stage left, and strolls across the front of the stage to the fire-escape. There he stops and lights a cigarette. He addresses the audience.

Tom.   Yes, I have tricks in my pocket, I have things up my sleeve. But I am the opposite of a stage magician. He gives you illusion that has the appearance of truth. I give you truth in the pleasant disguise of illusion. To begin with, I turn back time. I reverse it to that quaint period, the thirties, when the huge middle class of America was matriculating in a school for the blind. Their eyes had failed them, or they had failed their eyes, and so they were having their fingers pressed forcibly down on the fiery Braille alphabet of a dissolving economy. In Spain there was revolution. Here there was only shouting and confusion. In Spain there was Guernica. Here there were disturbances of labor, sometimes pretty violent, in otherwise peaceful cities such as Chicago, Cleveland, Saint Louis. . . . This is the social background of the play.

Music.

The play is memory. Being a memory play, it is dimly lighted, it is sentimental, it is not realistic. In memory everything seems to happen to music.

That explains the fiddle in the wings. I am the narrator of the play, and also a character in it. The other characters are my mother, Amanda, my sister, Laura, and a gentleman caller who appears in the final scenes. He is the most realistic character in the play, being an emissary from a world of reality that we were somehow set apart from. But since I have a poet's weakness for symbols, I am using this character also as a symbol; he is the long delayed but always expected something that we live for. There is a fifth character in the play who doesn't appear except in this larger-than-life photograph over the mantel. This is our father who left us a long time ago. He was a telephone man who fell in love with long distances; he gave up his job with the telephone company and skipped the light fantastic out of town. . . . The last we heard of him was a picture post-card from Mazatlán, on the Pacific coast of Mexico, containing a message of two words—"Hello—Good-bye!" and no address. I think the rest of the play will explain itself. . . .

Amanda's voice becomes audible through the portieres.

(Legend on Screen: "Où Sont Les Neiges.")

He divides the portieres and enters the upstage area.
Amanda and Laura are seated at a drop-leaf table. Eating is indicated by gestures without food or utensils. Amanda faces the audience. Tom and Laura are seated in profile.
The interior has lit up softly and through the scrim we see Amanda and Laura seated at the table in the upstage area.

Amanda *(calling)*.   Tom?
Tom.   Yes, Mother.
Amanda.   We can't say grace until you come to the table!
Tom.   Coming, Mother.

(He bows slightly and withdraws, reappearing a few moments later in his place at the table.)

Amanda *(to her son)*.   Honey, don't *push* with your *fingers*. If you have to push with something, the thing to push with is a crust of bread. And chew—chew! Animals have sections in their stomachs which enable them to digest food without mastication, but human beings are supposed to chew their food before they swallow it down. Eat food leisurely, son, and really enjoy it. A well-cooked meal has lots of delicate flavors that have to be held in the mouth for appreciation. So chew your food and give your salivary glands a chance to function!

Tom deliberately lays his imaginary fork down and pushes his chair back from the table.

Tom.   I haven't enjoyed one bite of this dinner because of your constant directions on how to eat it. It's you that makes me rush through meals with your hawk-like attention to every bite I take. Sickening—spoils my appetite— all this discussion of animals' secretion—salivary glands—mastication!

Amanda *(lightly).*   Temperament like a Metropolitan star! *(He rises and crosses downstage.)* You're not excused from the table.

Tom.   I am getting a cigarette.

Amanda.   You smoke too much.

Laura rises.

Laura.   I'll bring in the blanc mange.

He remains standing with his cigarette by the portieres during the following.

Amanda *(rising).*   No, sister, no, sister—you be the lady this time and I'll be the darky.

Laura.   I'm already up.

Amanda.   Resume your seat, little sister—I want you to stay fresh and pretty— for gentlemen callers!

Laura.   I'm not expecting any gentlemen callers.

Amanda *(crossing out to kitchenette. Airily).*   Sometimes they come when they are least expected! Why, I remember one Sunday afternoon in Blue Mountain—*(Enters kitchenette.)*

Tom.   I know what's coming!

Laura.   Yes. But let her tell it.

Tom.   Again?

Laura.   She loves to tell it.

Amanda returns with bowl of dessert.

Amanda.   One Sunday afternoon in Blue Mountain—your mother received— seventeen!—gentlemen callers! Why, sometimes there weren't chairs enough to accommodate them all. We had to send the nigger over to bring in folding chairs from the parish house.

Tom *(remaining at portieres).*   How did you entertain those gentlemen callers?

Amanda.   I understood the art of conversation!

Tom.   I bet you could talk.

Amanda.   Girls in those days *knew* how to talk, I can tell you.

Tom.   Yes?

(Image on Screen: Amanda As A Girl On A Porch Greeting Callers.)

Amanda.   They knew how to entertain their gentlemen callers. It wasn't enough for a girl to be possessed of a pretty face and a graceful figure—

although I wasn't slighted in either respect. She also needed to have a nimble wit and a tongue to meet all occasions.

Tom.   What did you talk about?

Amanda.   Things of importance going on in the world! Never anything coarse or common or vulgar. *(She addresses Tom as though he were seated in the vacant chair at the table though he remains by portieres. He plays this scene as though he held the book.)* My callers were gentlemen—all! Among my callers were some of the most prominent young planters of the Mississippi Delta—planters and sons of planters!

Tom motions for music and a spot of light on Amanda. Her eyes lift, her face glows, her voice becomes rich and elegiac.

(Legend on Screen: "Où Sont Les Neiges.")

There was young Champ Laughlin who later became vice-president of the Delta Planters Bank. Hadley Stevenson who was drowned in Moon Lake and left his widow one hundred and fifty thousand in Government bonds. There were the Cutrere brothers, Wesley and Bates. Bates was one of my bright particular beaux! He got in a quarrel with that wild Wainright boy. They shot it out on the floor of Moon Lake Casino. Bates was shot through the stomach. Died in the ambulance on his way to Memphis. His widow was also well-provided for, came into eight or ten thousand acres, that's all. She married him on the rebound—never loved her—carried my picture on him the night he died! And there was that boy that every girl in the Delta had set her cap for! That beautiful, brilliant young Fitzhugh boy from Green County!

Tom.   What did he leave his widow?

Amanda.   He never married! Gracious, you talk as though all of my old admirers had turned up their toes to the daisies!

Tom.   Isn't this the first you mentioned that still survives?

Amanda.   That Fitzhugh boy went North and made a fortune—came to be known as the Wolf of Wall Street! He had the Midas touch, whatever he touched turned to gold! And I could have been Mrs. Duncan J. Fitzhugh, mind you! But—I picked your *father!*

Laura *(rising).*   Mother, let me clear the table.

Amanda.   No dear, you go in front and study your typewriter chart. Or practice your shorthand a little. Stay fresh and pretty!—It's almost time for our gentlemen callers to start arriving. *(She flounces girlishly toward the kitchenette.)* How many do you suppose we're going to entertain this afternoon?

Tom throws down the paper and jumps up with a groan.

Laura *(alone in the dining room).*   I don't believe we're going to receive any, Mother.

Amanda *(reappearing, airily).*   What? No one—not one? You must be joking! *(Laura nervously echoes her laugh. She slips in a fugitive manner through the half-open portieres and draws them gently behind her. A shaft of very clear light is thrown on her face against the faded tapestry of the curtains.) (Music: "The Glass Menagerie" under faintly.) (Lightly.)* Not one gentleman caller? It can't be true! There must be a flood, there must have been a tornado!

Laura.   It isn't a flood, it's not a tornado, Mother. I'm just not popular like you were in Blue Mountain. . . . *(Tom utters another groan. Laura glances at him with a faint, apologetic smile. Her voice catching a little).* Mother's afraid I'm going to be an old maid.

The scene dims out with "Glass Menagerie" music.

Scene II

"Laura, Haven't You Ever Liked Some Boy?"

On the dark stage the screen is lighted with the image of blue roses.
   Gradually Laura's figure becomes apparent and the screen goes out.
   The music subsides.
   Laura is seated in the delicate ivory chair at the small clawfoot table.
   She wears a dress of soft violet material for a kimono—her hair tied back from her forehead with a ribbon.
   She is washing and polishing her collection of glass.
   Amanda appears on the fire-escape steps. At the sound of her ascent, Laura catches her breath, thrusts the bowl of ornaments away and seats herself stiffly before the diagram of the typewriter keyboard as though it held her spellbound. Something has happened to Amanda. It is written in her face as she climbs to the landing: a look that is grim and hopeless and a little absurd.
   She has on one of those cheap or imitation velvety-looking cloth coats with imitation fur collar. Her hat is five or six years old, one of those dreadful cloche hats that were worn in the late twenties, and she is clasping an enormous black patent-leather pocketbook with nickel clasp and initials. This is her full-dress outfit, the one she usually wears to the D.A.R.
   Before entering she looks through the door.
   She purses her lips, opens her eyes wide, rolls them upward and shakes her head.
   Then she slowly lets herself in the door. Seeing her mother's expression Laura touches her lips with a nervous gesture.

Laura.   Hello, Mother, I was—*(She makes a nervous gesture toward the chart on the wall. Amanda leans against the shut door and stares at Laura with a martyred look.)*

Amanda.   Deception? Deception? *(She slowly removes her hat and gloves, continuing the swift suffering stare. She lets the hat and gloves fall on the floor—a bit of acting.)*

Laura *(shakily)*.   How was the D.A.R. meeting? *(Amanda slowly opens her purse and removes a dainty white handkerchief which she shakes out delicately and delicately touches to her lips and nostrils.)* Didn't you go to the D.A.R. meeting, Mother?

Amanda *(faintly, almost inaudibly)*.   —No.—No. *(Then more forcibly.)* I did not have the strength—to go to the D.A.R. In fact, I did not have the courage! I wanted to find a hole in the ground and hide myself in it forever! *(She crosses slowly to the wall and removes the diagram of the typewriter keyboard. She holds it in front of her for a second, staring at it sweetly and sorrowfully—then bites her lips and tears it in two pieces.)*

Laura *(faintly)*.   Why did you do that, Mother? *(Amanda repeats the same procedure with the chart of the Gregg Alphabet.)* Why are you—

Amanda.   Why? Why? How old are you, Laura?

Laura.   Mother, you know my age.

Amanda.   I thought that you were an adult; it seems that I was mistaken. *(She crosses slowly to the sofa and sinks down and stares at Laura.)*

Laura.   Please don't stare at me, Mother.

Amanda closes her eyes and lowers her head. Count ten.

Amanda.   What are we going to do, what is going to become of us, what is the future?

Count ten.

Laura.   Has something happened, Mother? *(Amanda draws a long breath and takes out the handkerchief again. Dabbing process.)* Mother, has—something happened?

Amanda.   I'll be all right in a minute. I'm just bewildered—*(count five)*—by life. . . .

Laura.   Mother, I wish that you would tell me what's happened.

Amanda.   As you know, I was supposed to be inducted into my office at the D.A.R. this afternoon. **(Image on Screen: A Swarm of Typewriters.)** But I stopped off at Rubicam's Business College to speak to your teachers about your having a cold and ask them what progress they thought you were making down there.

Laura.   Oh. . . .

Amanda.   I went to the typing instructor and introduced myself as your mother. She didn't know who you were. Wingfield, she said. We don't have any such student enrolled at the school! I assured her she did, that you had been going to classes since early in January. "I wonder," she said, "if you could be talking about that terribly shy little girl who dropped out of school after only a few days' attendance?" "No," I said, "Laura, my daughter, has been going to school every day for the past six weeks!" "Excuse me," she said. She took the attendance book out and there was your name, unmistakably printed, and all the dates you were absent until they decided that you had dropped out of school. I still said, "No, there must have been some mistake! There must have been some mix-up in the records!" And she said, "No—I remember her perfectly now. Her hand shook so that she couldn't hit the right keys! The first time we gave a speed-test, she broke down completely—was sick at the stomach and almost had to be carried into the wash-room! After that morning she never showed up any more. We phoned the house but never got any answer"—while I was working at Famous and Barr, I suppose, demonstrating those—Oh! I felt so weak I could barely keep on my feet. I had to sit down while they got me a glass of water! Fifty dollars' tuition, all of our plans—my hopes and ambitions for you—just gone up the spout, just gone up the spout like that. *(Laura draws a long breath and gets awkwardly to her feet. She crosses to the victrola and winds it up.)* What are you doing?

Laura. Oh! *(She releases the handle and returns to her seat.)*

Amanda. Laura, where have you been going when you've gone out pretending that you were going to business college?

Laura. I've just been going out walking.

Amanda. That's not true.

Laura. It is. I just went walking.

Amanda. Walking? Walking? In winter? Deliberately courting pneumonia in that light coat? Where did you walk to, Laura?

Laura. It was the lesser of two evils, Mother. **(Image on Screen: Winter Scene In Park.)** I couldn't go back up. I—threw up—on the floor!

Amanda. From half past seven till after five every day you mean to tell me you walked around in the park, because you wanted to make me think that you were still going to Rubicam's Business College?

Laura. It wasn't as bad as it sounds. I went inside places to get warmed up.

Amanda. Inside where?

Laura. I went in the art museum and the bird-houses at the Zoo. I visited the penguins every day! Sometimes I did without lunch and went to the movies. Lately I've been spending most of my afternoons in the Jewel-box, that big glass house where they raise the tropical flowers.

Amanda. You did all this to deceive me, just for the deception? *(Laura looks down.)* Why?

Laura. Mother, when you're disappointed, you get that awful suffering look on your face, like the picture of Jesus' mother in the museum!

Amanda. Hush!

Laura. I couldn't face it.

Pause. A whisper of strings.

(Legend on Screen: "The Crust of Humility.")

Amanda *(hopelessly fingering the huge pocketbook).*   So what are we going to do the rest of our lives? Stay home and watch the parades go by? Amuse ourselves with the glass menagerie, darling? Eternally play those worn-out phonograph records your father left as a painful reminder of him? We won't have a business career—we've given that up because it gave us nervous indigestion! *(Laughs wearily.)* What is there left but dependency all our lives? I know so well what becomes of unmarried women who aren't prepared to occupy a position. I've seen such pitiful cases in the South—barely tolerated spinsters living upon the grudging patronage of sister's husband or brother's wife!—stuck away in some little mouse-trap of a room—encouraged by one in-law to visit another—little birdlike women without any nest—eating the crust of humility all their life! Is that the future that we've mapped out for ourselves? I swear it's the only alternative I can think of! It isn't a very pleasant alternative, is it? Of course—some girls *do marry.* *(Laura twists her hands nervously.)* Haven't you ever liked some boy?

Laura.   Yes. I liked one once. *(Rises.)* I came across his picture a while ago.

Amanda *(with some interest).*   He gave you his picture?

Laura.   No, it's in the year-book.

Amanda *(disappointed).*   Oh—a high-school boy.

(Image on Screen: Jim As A High-School Hero Bearing A Silver Cup.)

Laura.   Yes. His name was Jim. *(Laura lifts the heavy annual from the clawfoot table.)* Here he is in *The Pirates of Penzance.*

Amanda *(absently).*   The what?

Laura.   The operetta the senior class put on. He had a wonderful voice and we sat across the aisle from each other Mondays, Wednesdays and Fridays in the Aud. Here he is with the silver cup for debating! See his grin?

Amanda *(absently).*   He must have had a jolly disposition.

Laura.   He used to call me—Blue Roses.

(Image on Screen: Blue Roses.)

Amanda.   Why did he call you such a name as that?

Laura.   When I had the attack of pleurosis—he asked me what was the matter when I came back. I said pleurosis—he thought that I said Blue Roses! So that's what he always called me after that. Whenever he saw me, he'd holler, "Hello, Blue Roses!" I didn't care for the girl that he went out with. Emily Meisenbach. Emily was the best-dressed girl at Soldan. She never struck me, though, as being sincere . . . It says in the Personal Section—they're engaged. That's—six years ago! They must be married by now.

Amanda.   Girls that aren't cut out for business careers usually wind up married to some nice man. *(Gets up with a spark of revival.)* Sister, that's what you'll do!

Laura utters a startled, doubtful laugh. She reaches quickly for a piece of glass.

Laura.   But, Mother—
Amanda.   Yes? *(Crossing to photograph.)*
Laura *(in a tone of frightened apology).*   I'm—crippled!
Amanda.   Nonsense! Laura, I've told you never, never to use that word. Why, you're not crippled, you just have a little defect—hardly noticeable, even! When people have some slight disadvantage like that, they cultivate other things to make up for it—develop charm—and vivacity—and—*charm!* That's all you have to do! *(She turns again to the photograph.)* One thing your father had *plenty of—was charm!*

Tom motions to the fiddle in the wings. The scene fades out with music.

Scene III

(Legend on Screen: "After the Fiasco—")

Tom speaks from the fire-escape landing.

Tom.   After the fiasco at Rubicam's Business College, the idea of getting a gentleman caller for Laura began to play a more important part in Mother's calculations. It became an obsession. Like some archetype of the universal unconscious, the image of the gentleman caller haunted our small apartment. . . . **(Image on Screen: Young Man At Door With Flowers.)** An evening at home rarely passed without some allusion to this image, this spectre, this hope. . . . Even when he wasn't mentioned, his presence hung in Mother's preoccupied look and in my sister's frightened, apologetic manner— hung like a sentence passed upon the Wingfields! Mother was a woman of action as well as words. She began to take logical steps in the planned direction. Late that winter and in the early spring—realizing that extra money would be needed to properly feather the nest and plume the bird—she conducted a vigorous campaign on the telephone, roping in subscribers to one of those magazines for matrons called *The Home-maker's Companion*, the type of journal that features the serialized sublimations of ladies of letters who think in terms of delicate cup-like breasts, slim, tapering waists, rich, creamy thighs, eyes like wood-smoke in autumn, fingers that soothe and caress like strains of music, bodies as powerful as Etruscan sculpture.

(Image on Screen: Glamor Magazine Cover.)

Amanda enters with phone on long extension cord. She is spotted in the dim stage.

Amanda.   Ida Scott? This is Amanda Wingfield! We *missed* you at the D.A.R. last Monday! I said to myself: She's probably suffering with that sinus condition! How is that sinus condition? Horrors! Heaven have mercy!—You're a Christian martyr, yes, that's what you are, a Christian martyr! Well, I just now happened to notice that your subscription to the *Companion's* about to expire! Yes, it expires with the next issue, honey!—just when that wonderful new serial by Bessie Mae Hopper is getting off to such an exciting start. Oh, honey, it's something that you can't miss! You remember how *Gone With the Wind* took everybody by storm? You simply couldn't go out if you hadn't read it. All everybody *talked* was Scarlett O'Hara. Well, this is a book that critics already compare to *Gone With the Wind*. It's the *Gone With the Wind* of the post-World War generation!—What?—Burning?—Oh, honey, don't let them burn, go take a look in the oven and I'll hold the wire! Heavens— I think she's hung up!

Dim out.

(Legend on Screen: "You Think I'm In Love With Continental Shoemakers?")

Before the stage is lighted, the violent voices of Tom and Amanda are heard. They are quarreling behind the portieres. In front of them stands Laura with clenched hands and panicky expression.
    A clear pool of light on her figure throughout this scene.

Tom.   What in Christ's name am I—
Amanda *(shrilly)*.   Don't you use that—
Tom.   Supposed to do!
Amanda.   Expression! Not in my—
Tom.   Ohhh!
Amanda.   Presence! Have you gone out of your senses?
Tom.   I have, that's true, *driven* out!
Amanda.   What is the matter with you, you—big—big—IDIOT!
Tom.   Look—I've got *no thing*, no single thing—
Amanda.   Lower your voice!
Tom.   In my life here that I can call my OWN! Everything is—
Amanda.   Stop that shouting!
Tom.   Yesterday you confiscated my books! You had the nerve to—
Amanda.   I took that horrible novel back to the library—yes! That hideous book by that insane Mr. Lawrence. *(Tom laughs wildly.)* I cannot control the output of diseased minds or people who cater to them—*(Tom laughs still*

more wildly.) BUT I WON'T ALLOW SUCH FILTH BROUGHT INTO MY HOUSE! No, no, no, no, no!

Tom.   House, house! Who pays rent on it, who makes a slave of himself to—

Amanda *(fairly screeching).*   Don't you DARE to—

Tom.   No, no, I mustn't say things! *I've* got to just—

Amanda.   Let me tell you—

Tom.   I don't want to hear any more! *(He tears the portieres open. The upstage area is lit with a turgid smoky red glow.)*

Amanda's hair is in metal curlers and she wears a very old bathrobe, much too large for her slight figure, a relic of the faithless Mr. Wingfield.

An upright typewriter and a wild disarray of manuscripts are on the drop-leaf table. The quarrel was probably precipitated by Amanda's interruption of his creative labor. A chair lying overthrown on the floor.

Their gesticulating shadows are cast on the ceiling by the fiery glow.

Amanda.   You *will* hear more, you—

Tom.   No, I won't hear more, I'm going out!

Amanda.   You come right back in—

Tom.   Out, out, out! Because I'm—

Amanda.   Come back here, Tom Wingfield! I'm not through talking to you!

Tom.   Oh, go—

Laura *(desperately).*   Tom!

Amanda.   You're going to listen, and no more insolence from you! I'm at the end of my patience! *(He comes back toward her.)*

Tom.   What do you think I'm at? Aren't I supposed to have any patience to reach the end of, Mother? I know, I know. It seems unimportant to you, what I'm *doing*—what I *want* to do—having a little *difference* between them! You don't think that—

Amanda.   I think you've been doing things that you're ashamed of. That's why you act like this. I don't believe that you go every night to the movies. Nobody goes to the movies night after night. Nobody in their right minds goes to the movies as often as you pretend to. People don't go to the movies at nearly midnight, and movies don't let out at two A.M. Come in stumbling. Muttering to yourself like a maniac! You get three hours sleep and then go to work. Oh, I can picture the way you're doing down there. Moping, doping, because you're in no condition.

Tom *(wildly).*   No, I'm in no condition!

Amanda.   What right have you got to jeopardize your job? Jeopardize the security of us all? How do you think we'd manage if you were—

Tom.   Listen! You think I'm crazy *about* the *warehouse?* *(He bends fiercely toward her slight figure.)* You think I'm in love with the Continental Shoe-makers? You think I want to spend fifty-five years down there in that—*celotex interior!* with—*fluorescent—tubes!* Look! I'd rather somebody picked up a crowbar and battered out my brains—than go back mornings! I *go!* Every time you come in yelling that God damn *"Rise and Shine!" "Rise and Shine!"*

I say to myself "How *lucky dead* people are!" But I get up. I *go!* For sixty-five dollars a month I give up all that I dream of doing and being *ever!* And you say self—*self's* all I ever think of. Why, listen, if self is what I thought of, Mother, I'd be where he is—GONE! *(Pointing to father's picture.)* As far as the system of transportation reaches! *(He starts past her. She grabs his arm.)* Don't grab at me, Mother!

Amanda. Where are you going?

Tom. I'm going to the *movies!*

Amanda. I don't believe that lie!

Tom *(crouching toward her, overtowering her tiny figure. She backs away, gasping).* I'm going to opium dens! Yes, opium dens, dens of vice and criminals' hang-outs, Mother. I've joined the Hogan gang, I'm a hired assassin, I carry a tommy-gun in a violin case! I run a string of cat-houses in the Valley! They call me Killer, Killer Wingfield, I'm leading a double-life, a simple, honest warehouse worker by day, by night a dynamic *czar* of the *underworld*, Mother. I go to gambling casinos, I spin away fortunes on the roulette table! I wear a patch over one eye and a false mustache, sometimes I put on green whiskers. On those occasions they call me—*El Diablo!* Oh, I could tell you things to make you sleepless! My enemies plan to dynamite this place. They're going to blow us all sky-high some night! I'll be glad, very happy, and so will you! You'll go up, up on a broomstick over Blue Mountain with seventeen gentlemen callers! You ugly—babbling old—*witch*. . . . *((He goes through a series of violent, clumsy movements, seizing his overcoat, lunging to the door, pulling it fiercely open. The women watch him, aghast. His arm catches in the sleeve of the coat as he struggles to pull it on. For a moment he is pinioned by the bulky garment. With an outraged groan he tears the coat off again, splitting the shoulders of it, and hurls it across the room. It strikes against the shelf of Laura's glass collection, there is a tinkle of shattering glass. Laura cries out as if wounded.)*

Music: "The Glass Menagerie."

Laura *(shrilly).* My glass!—menagerie. . . . *(She covers her face and turns away.)*

But Amanda is still stunned and stupefied by the "ugly witch" so that she barely notices this occurrence. Now she recovers her speech.

Amanda *(in an awful voice).* I won't speak to you—until you apologize! *(She crosses through portieres and draws them together behind her. Tom is left with Laura. Laura clings weakly to the mantel with her face averted. Tom stares at her stupidly for a moment. Then he crosses to shelf. Drops awkwardly to his knees to collect the fallen glass, glancing at Laura as if he would speak but couldn't.)*

"The Glass Menagerie" music steals in as the scene dims out.

Scene IV

The interior is dark. Faint light in the alley.

A deep-voiced bell in a church is tolling the hour of five as the scene commences.

Tom appears at the top of the alley. After each solemn boom of the bell in the tower, he shakes a little noise-maker or rattle as if to express the tiny spasm of man in contrast to the sustained power and dignity of the Almighty. This and the unsteadiness of his advance make it evident that he has been drinking.

As he climbs the few steps to the fire-escape landing light steals up inside. Laura appears in night-dress, observing Tom's empty bed in the front room.

Tom fishes in his pockets for the door-key, removing a motley assortment of articles in the search, including a perfect shower of movie-ticket stubs and an empty bottle. At last he finds the key, but just as he is about to insert it, it slips from his fingers. He strikes a match and crouches below the door.

Tom *(bitterly).* One crack—and it falls through!

Laura opens the door.

Laura.   Tom! Tom, what are you doing?

Tom.   Looking for a door-key.

Laura.   Where have you been all this time?

Tom.   I have been to the movies.

Laura.   All this time at the movies?

Tom.   There was a very long program. There was a Garbo picture and a Mickey Mouse and a travelogue and a newsreel and a preview of coming attractions. And there was an organ solo and a collection for the milk-fund— simultaneously—which ended up in a terrible fight between a fat lady and an usher!

Laura *(innocently).*   Did you have to stay through everything?

Tom.   Of course! And, oh, I forgot! There was a big stage show! The headliner on this stage show was Malvolio the Magician. He performed wonderful tricks, many of them, such as pouring water back and forth between pitchers. First it turned to wine and then it turned to beer and then it turned to whiskey. I know it was whiskey it finally turned into because he needed somebody to come up out of the audience to help him, and I came up—both shows! It was Kentucky Straight Bourbon. A very generous fellow, he gave souvenirs. *(He pulls from his back pocket a shimmering rainbow-colored scarf.)* He gave me this. This is his magic scarf. You can have it, Laura. You wave it over a canary cage and you get a bowl of gold-fish. You wave it over the gold-fish bowl and they fly away canaries. . . . But the wonderfullest trick of all was the coffin trick. We nailed him into a coffin and he got out of the coffin without removing one nail. *(He has come inside.)* There is a trick that would come in handy for me—get me out of this 2 by 4 situation! *(Flops onto bed and starts removing shoes.)*

Laura.   Tom—Shhh!

Tom.   What're you shushing me for?

Laura.   You'll wake up Mother.

Tom.   Goody, goody! Pay'er back for all those "Rise an' Shines." *(Lies down, groaning.)* You know it don't take much intelligence to get yourself into a nailed-up coffin, Laura. But who in hell ever got himself out of one without removing one nail?

As if in answer, the father's grinning photograph lights up. Scene dims out.
  Immediately following: The church bell is heard striking six. At the sixth stroke the alarm clock goes off in Amanda's room, and after a few moments we hear her calling: "Rise and Shine! Rise and Shine! Laura, go tell your brother to rise and shine!"

Tom *(sitting up slowly)*.   I'll rise—but I won't shine.

The light increases.

Amanda.   Laura, tell your brother his coffee is ready.

Laura slips into front room.

Laura.   Tom! it's nearly seven. Don't make Mother nervous. *(He stares at her stupidly. Beseechingly.)* Tom, speak to Mother this morning. Make up with her, apologize, speak to her!

Tom.   She won't to me. It's her that started not speaking.

Laura.   If you just say you're sorry she'll start speaking.

Tom.   Her not speaking—is that such a tragedy?

Laura.   Please—please!

Amanda *(calling from kitchenette)*.   Laura, are you going to do what I asked you to do, or do I have to get dressed and go out myself?

Laura.   Going, going—soon as I get on my coat! *(She pulls on a shapeless felt hat with nervous, jerky movement, pleadingly glancing at Tom. Rushes awkwardly for coat. The coat is one of Amanda's, inaccurately made-over, the sleeves too short for Laura.)* Butter and what else?

Amanda *(entering upstage)*.   Just butter. Tell them to charge it.

Laura.   Mother, they make faces when I do that.

Amanda.   Sticks and stones may break our bones, but the expression on Mr. Garfinkel's face won't harm us! Tell your brother his coffee is getting cold.

Laura *(at door)*.   Do what I asked you, will you, will you, Tom?

He looks sullenly away.

Amanda.   Laura, go now or just don't go at all!

Laura (*rushing out*).   Going—going! (*A second later she cries out. Tom springs up and crosses to the door. Amanda rushes anxiously in. Tom opens the door.*)

Tom.   Laura?

Laura.   I'm all right. I slipped, but I'm all right.

Amanda (*peering anxiously after her*).   If anyone breaks a leg on those fire-escape steps, the landlord ought to be sued for every cent he possesses! (*She shuts door. Remembers she isn't speaking and returns to other room.*)

As Tom enters listlessly for his coffee, she turns her back to him and stands rigidly facing the window on the gloomy gray vault of the areaway. Its light on her face with its aged but childish features is cruelly sharp, satirical as a Daumier print.

Music under: "Ave Maria."

Tom glances sheepishly but sullenly at her averted figure and slumps at the table. The coffee is scalding hot; he sips it and gasps and spits it back in the cup. At his gasp, Amanda catches her breath and half turns. Then catches herself and turns back to window.

Tom blows on his coffee, glancing sidewise at his mother. She clears her throat. Tom clears his. He starts to rise. Sinks back down again, scratches his head, clears his throat again. Amanda coughs. Tom raises his cup in both hands to blow on it, his eyes staring over the rim of it at his mother for several moments. Then he slowly sets the cup down and awkwardly and hesitantly rises from the chair.

Tom (*hoarsely*).   Mother. I—I apologize. Mother. (*Amanda draws a quick, shuddering breath. Her face works grotesquely. She breaks into childlike tears.*) I'm sorry for what I said, for everything that I said, I didn't mean it.

Amanda (*sobbingly*).   My devotion has made me a witch and so I make myself hateful to my children!

Tom.   No, you *don't*.

Amanda.   I worry so much, don't sleep, it makes me nervous!

Tom (*gently*).   I understand that.

Amanda.   I've had to put up a solitary battle all these years. But you're my right-hand bower! Don't fall down, don't fail!

Tom (*gently*).   I try, Mother.

Amanda (*with great enthusiasm*).   Try and you will SUCCEED! (*The notion makes her breathless.*) Why, you—you're just *full* of natural endowments! Both of my children—they're *unusual* children! Don't you think I know it? I'm so—*proud*! Happy and—feel I've—so much to be thankful for but— Promise me one thing, son!

Tom.   What, Mother?

Amanda.   Promise, son, you'll—never be a drunkard!

Tom (*turns to her grinning*).   I will never be a drunkard, Mother.

Amanda.   That's what frightened me so, that you'd be drinking! Eat a bowl of Purina!

Tom.   Just coffee, Mother.

Amanda.   Shredded wheat biscuit?

Tom.   No. No, Mother, just coffee.

Amanda.   You can't put in a day's work on an empty stomach. You've got ten minutes—don't gulp! Drinking too-hot liquids makes cancer of the stomach. . . . Put cream in.

Tom.   No, thank you.

Amanda.   To cool it.

Tom.   No! No, thank you, I want it black.

Amanda.   I know, but it's not good for you. We have to do all that we can to build ourselves up. In these trying times we live in, all that we have to cling to is—each other. . . . That's why it's so important to — Tom, I — I sent out your sister so I could discuss something with you. If you hadn't spoken I would have spoken to you. *(Sits down.)*

Tom *(gently).*   What is it, Mother, that you want to discuss?

Amanda.   Laura!

Tom puts his cup down slowly.

(Legend on Screen: "Laura.")

Music: "The Glass Menagerie."

Tom.   —Oh.—Laura . . .

Amanda *(touching his sleeve).*   You know how Laura is. So quiet but—still water runs deep! She notices things and I think she—broods about them. *(Tom looks up.)* A few days ago I came in and she was crying.

Tom.   What about?

Amanda.   You.

Tom.   Me?

Amanda.   She has an idea that you're not happy here.

Tom.   What gave her that idea?

Amanda.   What gives her any idea? However, you do act strangely. I—I'm not criticizing, understand *that!* I know your ambitions do not lie in the warehouse, that like everybody in the whole wide world—you've had to—make sacrifices, but—Tom—Tom—life's not easy, it calls for—Spartan endurance! There's so many things in my heart that I cannot describe to you! I've never told you but I—*loved* your father. . . .

Tom *(gently).*   I know that, Mother.

Amanda.   And you—when I see you taking after his ways! Staying out late— and—well, you *had* been drinking the night you were in that—terrifying condition! Laura says that you hate the apartment and that you go out nights to get away from it! Is that true, Tom?

Tom. No. You say there's so much in your heart that you can't describe to me. That's true of me, too. There's so much in my heart that I can't describe to *you!* So let's respect each other's—

Amanda. But, why—*why*, Tom—are you always so *restless*? Where do you go to, nights?

Tom. I—go to the movies.

Amanda. Why do you go to the movies so much, Tom?

Tom. I go to the movies because—I like adventure. Adventure is something I don't have much of at work, so I go to the movies.

Amanda. But, Tom, you go to the movies *entirely* too *much!*

Tom. I like a lot of adventure.

Amanda looks baffled, then hurt. As the familiar inquisition resumes he becomes hard and impatient again. Amanda slips back into her querulous attitude toward him.

(Image on Screen: Sailing Vessel With Jolly Roger.)

Amanda. Most young men find adventure in their careers.

Tom. Then most young men are not employed in a warehouse.

Amanda. The world is full of young men employed in warehouses and offices and factories.

Tom. Do all of them find adventure in their careers?

Amanda. They do or they do without it! Not everybody has a craze for adventure.

Tom. Man is by instinct a lover, a hunter, a fighter, and none of those instincts are given much play at the warehouse!

Amanda. Man is by instinct! Don't quote instinct to me! Instinct is something that people have got away from! It belongs to animals! Christian adults don't want it!

Tom. What do Christian adults want, then, Mother?

Amanda. Superior things! Things of the mind and the spirit! Only animals have to satisfy instincts! Surely your aims are somewhat higher than theirs! Than monkeys—pigs—

Tom. I reckon they're not.

Amanda. You're joking. However, that isn't what I wanted to discuss.

Tom *(rising).* I haven't much time.

Amanda *(pushing his shoulders).* Sit down.

Tom. You want me to punch in red at the warehouse, Mother?

Amanda. You have five minutes. I want to talk about Laura.

(Legend on Screen: "Plans And Provisions.")

Tom. All right! What about Laura?

Amanda. We have to be making plans and provisions for her. She's older than you, two years, and nothing has happened. She just drifts along doing nothing. It frightens me terribly how she just drifts along.

Tom.   I guess she's the type that people call home girls.

Amanda.   There's no such type, and if there is, it's a pity! That is unless the home is hers, with a husband!

Tom.   What?

Amanda.   Oh, I can see the handwriting on the wall as plain as I see the nose in front of my face! It's terrifying! More and more you remind me of your father! He was out all hours without explanation—Then *left! Goodbye!* And me with the bag to hold. I saw that letter you got from the Merchant Marine. I know what you're dreaming of. I'm not standing here blindfolded. Very well, then. Then *do* it! But not till there's somebody to take your place.

Tom.   What do you mean?

Amanda.   I mean that as soon as Laura has got somebody to take care of her, married, a home of her own, independent—why, then you'll be free to go wherever you please, on land, on sea, whichever way the wind blows! But until that time you've got to look out for your sister. I don't say me because I'm old and don't matter! I say for your sister because she's young and dependent. I put her in business college—a dismal failure! Frightened her so it made her sick to her stomach. I took her over to the Young People's League at the church. Another fiasco. She spoke to nobody, nobody spoke to her. Now all she does is fool with those pieces of glass and play those worn-out records. What kind of a life is that for a girl to lead!

Tom.   What can I do about it?

Amanda.   Overcome selfishness! Self, self, self is all that you ever think of! (*Tom springs up and crosses to get his coat. It is ugly and bulky. He pulls on a cap with earmuffs.*) Where is your muffler? Put your wool muffler on! (*He snatches it angrily from the closet and tosses it around his neck and pulls both ends tight.*) Tom! I haven't said what I had in mind to ask you.

Tom.   I'm too late to—

Amanda (*catching his arms—very importunately. Then shyly*).   Down at the warehouse, aren't there some—nice young men?

Tom.   No!

Amanda.   There *must* be—*some* . . .

Tom.   Mother—(*Gesture.*)

Amanda.   Find out one that's clean-living—doesn't drink and—ask him out for sister!

Tom.   What?

Amanda.   For *sister!* To *meet!* Get *acquainted!*

Tom (*stamping to door*).   Oh, my go-osh!

Amanda.   Will you? (*He opens door. Imploringly.*) Will you? (*He starts down.*) Will you? *Will* you, dear?

Tom (*calling back*).   YES!

Amanda closes the door hesitantly and with a troubled but faintly hopeful expression.

(Image on Screen: Glamor Magazine Cover.)

Spot Amanda at phone.

Amanda.   Ella Cartwright? This is Amanda Wingfield! How are you, honey? How is that kidney condition! *(Count five.)* Horrors! *(Count five.)* You're a Christian martyr, yes, honey, that's what you are, a Christian martyr! Well, I just happened to notice in my little red book that your subscription to the *Companion* has just run out! I knew that you wouldn't want to miss out on the wonderful serial starting in this new issue. It's by Bessie Mae Hopper, the first thing she's written since *Honeymoon for Three.* Wasn't that a strange and interesting story? Well, this one is even lovelier, I believe. It has a sophisticated society background. It's all about the horsey set on Long Island!

Fade out.

Scene V

(Legend on Screen: "Annunciation.") *Fade with music.*

It is early dusk of a spring evening. Supper has just been finished in the Wingfield apartment. Amanda and Laura in light-colored dresses are removing dishes from the table, in the upstage area, which is shadowy, their movements formalized almost as a dance or ritual, their moving forms as pale and silent as moths.

Tom, in white shirt and trousers, rises from the table and crosses toward the fire-escape.

Amanda *(as he passes her).*   Son, will you do me a favor?
Tom.   What?
Amanda.   Comb your hair! You look so pretty when your hair is combed! *(Tom slouches on sofa with evening paper. Enormous caption "Franco Triumphs.")* There is only one respect in which I would like you to emulate your father.
Tom.   What respect is that?
Amanda.   The care he always took of his appearance. He never allowed himself to look untidy. *(He throws down the paper and crosses to fire-escape.)* Where are you going?
Tom.   I'm going out to smoke.
Amanda.   You smoke too much. A pack a day at fifteen cents a pack. How much would that amount to in a month? Thirty times fifteen is how much, Tom? Figure it out and you will be astounded at what you could save. Enough to give you a night-school course in accounting at Washington U! Just think what a wonderful thing that would be for you, son!

Tom is unmoved by the thought.

Tom.   I'd rather smoke. *(He steps out on landing, letting the screen door slam.)*
Amanda *(sharply)*.   I know! That's the tragedy of it. . . . *(Alone, she turns to look at her husband's picture.)*

Dance music: "All the World Is Waiting for the Sunrise!"

Tom *(to the audience)*.   Across the alley from us was the Paradise Dance Hall. On evenings in spring the windows and doors were open and the music came outdoors. Sometimes the lights were turned out except for a large glass sphere that hung from the ceiling. It would turn slowly about and filter the dusk with delicate rainbow colors. Then the orchestra played a waltz or a tango, something that had a slow and sensuous rhythm. Couples would come outside, to the relative privacy of the alley. You could see them kissing behind ash-pits and telephone poles. This was the compensation for lives that passed like mine, without any change or adventure. Adventure and change were imminent in this year. They were waiting around the corner for all these kids. Suspended in the mist over Berchtesgaden, caught in the folds of Chamberlain's umbrella—In Spain there was Guernica! But here there was only hot swing music and liquor, dance halls, bars, and movies, and sex that hung in the gloom like a chandelier and flooded the world with brief, deceptive rainbows. . . . All the world was waiting for bombardments!

Amanda turns from the picture and comes outside.

Amanda *(sighing)*.   A fire-escape landing's a poor excuse for a porch. *(She spreads a newspaper on a step and sits down, gracefully and demurely as if she were settling into a swing on a Mississippi veranda.)* What are you looking at?
Tom.   The moon.
Amanda.   Is there a moon this evening?
Tom.   It's rising over Garfinkel's Delicatessen.
Amanda.   So it is! A little silver slipper of a moon. Have you made a wish on it yet?
Tom.   Um-hum.
Amanda.   What did you wish for?
Tom.   That's a secret.
Amanda.   A secret, huh? Well, I won't tell mine either. I will be just as mysterious as you.
Tom.   I bet I can guess what yours is.
Amanda.   Is my head so transparent?
Tom.   You're not a sphinx.
Amanda.   No, I don't have secrets. I'll tell you what I wished for on the moon. Success and happiness for my precious children! I wish for that whenever there's a moon, and when there isn't a moon, I wish for it, too.
Tom.   I thought perhaps you wished for a gentleman caller.

Amanda.   Why do you say that?

Tom.   Don't you remember asking me to fetch one?

Amanda.   I remember suggesting that it would be nice for your sister if you brought home some nice young man from the warehouse. I think I've made that suggestion more than once.

Tom.   Yes, you have made it repeatedly.

Amanda.   Well?

Tom.   We are going to have one.

Amanda.   *What?*

Tom.   A gentleman caller!

The annunciation is celebrated with music. Amanda rises.

(Image on Screen: Caller With Bouquet.)

Amanda.   You mean you have asked some nice young man to come over?

Tom.   Yep. I've asked him to dinner.

Amanda.   You really did?

Tom.   I did!

Amanda.   You did, and did he—*accept?*

Tom.   He did!

Amanda.   Well, well—well, well! That's—lovely!

Tom.   I thought that you would be pleased.

Amanda.   It's definite, then?

Tom.   Very definite.

Amanda.   Soon?

Tom.   Very soon.

Amanda.   For heaven's sake, stop putting on and tell me some things, will you?

Tom.   What things do you want me to tell you?

Amanda.   *Naturally* I would like to know when he's *coming!*

Tom.   He's coming tomorrow.

Amanda.   *Tomorrow?*

Tom.   Yep. Tomorrow.

Amanda.   But, Tom!

Tom.   Yes, Mother?

Amanda.   Tomorrow gives me no time!

Tom.   Time for what?

Amanda.   Preparations! Why didn't you phone me at once, as soon as you asked him, the minute that he accepted? Then, don't you see, I could have been getting ready!

Tom.   You don't have to make any fuss.

Amanda.   Oh, Tom, Tom, Tom, of course I have to make a fuss! I want things nice, not sloppy! Not thrown together. I'll certainly have to do some fast thinking, won't I?

Tom. I don't see why you have to think at all.

Amanda. You just don't know. We can't have a gentleman caller in a pig-sty! All my wedding silver has to be polished, the monogrammed table linen ought to be laundered! The windows have to be washed and fresh curtains put up. And how about clothes? We have to *wear* something, don't we?

Tom. Mother, this boy is no one to make a fuss over!

Amanda. Do you realize he's the first young man we've introduced to your sister? It's terrible, dreadful, disgraceful that poor little sister has never received a single gentleman caller! Tom, come inside! *(She opens the screen door.)*

Tom. What for?

Amanda. I want to ask you some things.

Tom. If you're going to make such a fuss, I'll call it off, I'll tell him not to come.

Amanda. You certainly won't do anything of the kind. Nothing offends people worse than broken engagements. It simply means I'll have to work like a Turk! We won't be brilliant, but we'll pass inspection. Come on inside. *(Tom follows, groaning.)* Sit down.

Tom. Any particular place you would like me to sit?

Amanda. Thank heavens I've got that new sofa! I'm also making payments on a floor lamp I'll have sent out! And put the chintz covers on, they'll brighten things up! Of course I'd hoped to have these walls re-papered. . . . What is the young man's name?

Tom. His name is O'Connor.

Amanda. That, of course, means fish—tomorrow is Friday! I'll have that salmon loaf—with Durkee's dressing! What does he do? He works at the warehouse?

Tom. Of course! How else would I—

Amanda. Tom, he—doesn't drink?

Tom. Why do you ask me that?

Amanda. Your father *did!*

Tom. Don't get started on that!

Amanda. He *does* drink, then?

Tom. Not that I know of!

Amanda. Make sure, be certain! The last thing I want for my daughter's a boy who drinks!

Tom. Aren't you being a little premature? Mr. O'Connor has not yet appeared on the scene!

Amanda. But will tomorrow. To meet your sister, and what do I know about his character? Nothing! Old maids are better off than wives of drunkards!

Tom. Oh, my God!

Amanda. Be still!

Tom *(leaning forward to whisper).* Lots of fellows meet girls whom they don't marry!

Amanda. Oh, talk sensibly, Tom—and don't be sarcastic! *(She has gotten a hairbrush.)*

Tom.   What are you doing?

Amanda.   I'm brushing that cow-lick down! What is this young man's position at the warehouse?

Tom (*submitting grimly to the brush and the interrogation*).   This young man's position is that of a shipping clerk, Mother.

Amanda.   Sounds to me like a fairly responsible job, the sort of a job *you* would be in if you just had more *get-up*. What is his salary? Have you got any idea?

Tom.   I would judge it to be approximately eighty-five dollars a month.

Amanda.   Well—not princely, but—

Tom.   Twenty more than I make.

Amanda.   Yes, how well I know! But for a family man, eighty-five dollars a month is not much more than you can just get by on. . . .

Tom.   Yes, but Mr. O'Connor is not a family man.

Amanda.   He might be, mightn't he? Some time in the future?

Tom.   I see. Plans and provisions.

Amanda.   You are the only young man that I know of who ignores the fact that the future becomes the present, the present the past, and the past turns into everlasting regret if you don't plan for it!

Tom.   I will think that over and see what I can make of it.

Amanda.   Don't be supercilious with your mother! Tell me some more about this—what do you call him?

Tom.   James D. O'Connor. The D. is for Delaney.

Amanda.   Irish on *both* sides! *Gracious!* And doesn't drink?

Tom.   Shall I call him up and ask him right this minute?

Amanda.   The only way to find out about those things is to make discreet inquiries at the proper moment. When I was a girl in Blue Mountain and it was suspected that a young man drank, the girl whose attentions he had been receiving, if any girl *was*, would sometimes speak to the minister of his church, or rather her father would if her father was living, and sort of feel him out on the young man's character. That is the way such things are discreetly handled to keep a young woman from making a tragic mistake!

Tom.   Then how did you happen to make a tragic mistake?

Amanda.   That innocent look of your father's had everyone fooled! He smiled—the world was *enchanted*! No girl can do worse than put herself at the mercy of a handsome appearance! I hope that Mr. O'Connor is not too good-looking.

Tom.   No, he's not too good-looking. He's covered with freckles and hasn't too much of a nose.

Amanda.   He's not right-down homely, though?

Tom.   Not right-down homely. Just medium homely, I'd say.

Amanda.   Character's what to look for in a man.

Tom.   That's what I've always said, Mother.

Amanda.   You've never said anything of the kind and I suspect you would never give it a thought.

Tom.   Don't be suspicious of me.

Amanda.   At least I hope he's the type that's up and coming.

Tom.   I think he really goes in for self-improvement.

Amanda.   What reason have you to think so?

Tom.   He goes to night school.

Amanda (beaming).   Splendid! What does he do, I mean study?

Tom.   Radio engineering and public speaking!

Amanda.   Then he has visions of being advanced in the world! Any young man who studies public speaking is aiming to have an executive job some day! And radio engineering? A thing for the future! Both of these facts are very illuminating. Those are the sort of things that a mother should know concerning any young man who comes to call on her daughter. Seriously or—not.

Tom.   One little warning. He doesn't know about Laura. I didn't let on that we had dark ulterior motives. I just said, why don't you come have dinner with us? He said okay and that was the whole conversation.

Amanda.   I bet it was! You're eloquent as an oyster. However, he'll know about Laura when he gets here. When he sees how lovely and sweet and pretty she is, he'll thank his lucky stars he was asked to dinner.

Tom.   Mother, you mustn't expect too much of Laura.

Amanda.   What do you mean?

Tom.   Laura seems all those things to you and me because she's ours and we love her. We don't even notice she's crippled any more.

Amanda.   Don't say crippled! You know that I never allow that word to be used!

Tom.   But face facts, Mother. She is and—that's not all—

Amanda.   What do you mean "not all"?

Tom.   Laura is very different from other girls.

Amanda.   I think the difference is all to her advantage.

Tom.   Not quite all—in the eyes of others—strangers—she's terribly shy and lives in a world of her own and those things make her seem a little peculiar to people outside the house.

Amanda.   Don't say peculiar.

Tom.   Face the facts. She is.

The dance-hall music changes to a tango that has a minor and somewhat ominous tone.

Amanda.   In what way is she peculiar—may I ask?

Tom (gently).   She lives in a world of her own—a world of—little glass ornaments, Mother. . . . (Gets up. Amanda remains holding brush, looking at him, troubled.) She plays old phonograph records and—that's about all—(He glances at himself in the mirror and crosses to door.)

Amanda (sharply).   Where are you going?

Tom.   I'm going to the movies. (Out screen door.)

Amanda.   Not to the movies, every night to the movies! *(Follows quickly to screen door.)* I don't believe you always go to the movies! *(He is gone. Amanda looks worriedly after him for a moment. Then vitality and optimism return and she turns from the door. Crossing to portieres.)* Laura! Laura! *(Laura answers from the kitchenette.)*

Laura.   Yes, Mother.

Amanda.   Let those dishes go and come in front! *(Laura appears with dish towel. Gaily.)* Laura, come here and make a wish on the moon!

Laura *(entering)*.   Moon—moon?

Amanda.   A little silver slipper of a moon. Look over your left shoulder, Laura, and make a wish! *(Laura looks faintly puzzled as if called out of sleep. Amanda seizes her shoulders and turns her at an angle by the door.)* Now! Now, darling, *wish!*

(Image on Screen: The Moon.)

Laura.   What shall I wish for, Mother?

Amanda *(her voice trembling and her eyes suddenly filling with tears)*.   Happiness! Good Fortune!

The violin rises and the stage dims out.

Scene VI

(Image on Screen: High School Hero.)

Tom.   And so the following evening I brought Jim home to dinner. I had known Jim slightly in high school. In high school Jim was a hero. He had tremendous Irish good nature and vitality with the scrubbed and polished look of white chinaware. He seemed to move in a continual spotlight. He was a star in basketball, captain of the debating club, president of the senior class and the glee club and he sang the male lead in the annual light operas. He was always running or bounding, never just walking. He seemed always at the point of defeating the law of gravity. He was shooting with such velocity through his adolescence that you would logically expect him to arrive at nothing short of the White House by the time he was thirty. But Jim apparently ran into more interference after his graduation from Soldan. His speed had definitely slowed. Six years after he left high school he was holding a job that wasn't much better than mine.

(Image on Screen: Clerk.)

He was the only one at the warehouse with whom I was on friendly terms. I was valuable to him as someone who could remember his former glory, who had seen him win basketball games and the silver cup in debating. He knew of my secret practice of retiring to a cabinet of the washroom to work on poems when business was slack in the warehouse. He called me Shakespeare. And while the other boys in the warehouse regarded me with suspicious hostility, Jim took a humorous attitude toward me. Gradually his attitude affected the others, their hostility wore off and they also began to smile at me as people smile at an oddly fashioned dog who trots across their path at some distance.

I knew that Jim and Laura had known each other at Soldan, and I had heard Laura speak admiringly of his voice. I didn't know if Jim remembered her or not. In high school Laura had been as unobtrusive as Jim had been astonishing. If he did remember Laura, it was not as my sister, for when I asked him to dinner, he grinned and said, "You know, Shakespeare, I never thought of you as having folks!"

He was about to discover that I did. . . .

Light up stage.

(Legend on Screen: "The Accent Of A Coming Foot.")

Friday evening. It is about five o'clock of a late spring evening which comes "scattering poems in the sky."

A delicate lemony light is in the Wingfield apartment.

Amanda has worked like a Turk in preparation for the gentleman caller. The results are astonishing. The new floor lamp with its rose-silk shade is in place, a colored paper lantern conceals the broken light fixture in the ceiling, new billowing white curtains are at the windows, chintz covers are on chairs and sofa, a pair of new sofa pillows make their initial appearance.

Open boxes and tissue paper are scattered on the floor.

Laura stands in the middle with lifted arms while Amanda crouches before her, adjusting the hem of the new dress, devout and ritualistic. The dress is colored and designed by memory. The arrangement of Laura's hair is changed; it is softer and more becoming. A fragile, unearthly prettiness has come out in Laura: she is like a piece of translucent glass touched by light, given a momentary radiance, not actual, not lasting.

Amanda *(impatiently).*   Why are you trembling?

Laura.   Mother, you've made me so nervous!

Amanda.   How have I made you nervous?

Laura.   By all this fuss! You make it seem so important!

Amanda.   I don't understand you, Laura. You couldn't be satisfied with just sitting home, and yet whenever I try to arrange something for you, you seem to resist it. *(She gets up.)* Now take a look at yourself. No, wait! Wait just a moment—I have an idea!

Laura.   What is it now?

Amanda produces two powder puffs which she wraps in handkerchiefs and stuffs in Laura's bosom.

Laura.   Mother, what are you doing?
Amanda.   They call them "Gay Deceivers"!
Laura.   I won't wear them!
Amanda.   You will!
Laura.   Why should I?
Amanda.   Because, to be painfully honest, your chest is flat.
Laura.   You make it seem like we were setting a trap.
Amanda.   All pretty girls are a trap, a pretty trap, and men expect them to be.
(**Legend on Screen: "A Pretty Trap."**) Now look at yourself, young lady.
This is the prettiest you will ever be! I've got to fix myself now! You're going
to be surprised by your mother's appearance! *(She crosses through portieres,
humming gaily.)*

Laura moves slowly to the long mirror and stares solemnly at herself.
  *A wind blows the white curtains inward in a slow, graceful motion and with
a faint, sorrowful sighing.*

Amanda *(off stage).*   It isn't dark enough yet. *(She turns slowly before the
mirror with a troubled look.)*

(**Legend on Screen: "This Is My Sister: Celebrate Her With Strings!"**)

Music.

Amanda *(laughing, off).*   I'm going to show you something. I'm going to make
a spectacular appearance!
Laura.   What is it, mother?
Amanda.   Possess your soul in patience—you will see! Something I've resur-
rected from that old trunk! Styles haven't changed so terribly much after
all. . . . *(She parts the portieres.)* Now just look at your mother! *(She wears
a girlish frock of yellowed voile with a blue silk sash. She carries a bunch of
jonquils—the legend of her youth is nearly revived. Feverishly.)* This is the
dress in which I led the cotillion. Won the cakewalk twice at Sunset Hill,
wore one spring to the Governor's ball in Jackson! See how I sashayed around
the ballroom, Laura? *(She raises her skirt and does a mincing step around the
room.)* I wore it on Sundays for my gentlemen callers! I had it on the day I
met your father—I had malaria fever all that spring. The change of climate
from East Tennessee to the Delta—weakened resistance—I had a little temperature all the time—not enough to be serious—just enough to make me
restless and giddy! Invitations poured in—parties all over the Delta!—"Stay
in bed," said Mother, "you have fever!"—but I just wouldn't.—I took quinine
but kept on going, going!—Evenings, dances!—Afternoons, long, long rides!

Picnics—lovely!—So lovely, that country in May.—All lacy with dogwood, literally flooded with jonquils!—That was the spring I had the craze for jonquils. Jonquils became an absolute obsession. Mother said, "Honey, there's no more room for jonquils." And still I kept bringing in more jonquils. Whenever, wherever I saw them, I'd say "Stop! Stop! I see jonquils!" I made the young men help me gather the jonquils! It was a joke, Amanda and her jonquils! Finally there were no more vases to hold them, every available space was filled with jonquils. No vases to hold them? All right, I'll hold them myself! And then I—*(She stops in front of the picture. Music plays.)* met your father! Malaria fever and jonquils and then—this—boy. . . . *(She switches on the rose-colored lamp.)* I hope they get here before it starts to rain. *(She crosses upstage and places the jonquils in bowl on table.)* I gave your brother a little extra change so he and Mr. O'Connor could take the service car home.

Laura *(with altered look).*   What did you say his name was?
Amanda.   O'Connor.
Laura.   What is his first name?
Amanda.   I don't remember. Oh, yes, I do. It was—Jim!

Laura sways slightly and catches hold of a chair.

(Legend on Screen: "Not Jim!")

Laura *(faintly).*   Not—Jim!
Amanda.   Yes, that was it, it was Jim! I've never known a Jim that wasn't nice!

Music: ominous.

Laura.   Are you sure his name is Jim O'Connor?
Amanda.   Yes. Why?
Laura.   Is he the one that Tom used to know in high school?
Amanda.   He didn't say so. I think he just got to know him at the warehouse.
Laura.   There was a Jim O'Connor we both knew in high school—*(Then, with effort.)* If that is the one that Tom is bringing to dinner—you'll have to excuse me, I won't come to the table.
Amanda.   What sort of nonsense is this?
Laura.   You asked me once if I'd ever liked a boy. Don't you remember I showed you this boy's picture?
Amanda.   You mean the boy you showed me in the year book?
Laura.   Yes, that boy.
Amanda.   Laura, Laura, were you in love with that boy?
Laura.   I don't know, Mother. All I know is I couldn't sit at the table if it was him!
Amanda.   It won't be him! It isn't the least bit likely. But whether it is or not, you will come to the table. You will not be excused.

Laura.   I'll have to be, Mother.

Amanda.   I don't intend to humor your silliness, Laura. I've had too much from you and your brother, both! So just sit down and compose yourself till they come. Tom has forgotten his key so you'll have to let them in, when they arrive.

Laura *(panicky)*.   Oh, Mother—*you* answer the door!

Amanda *(lightly)*.   I'll be in the kitchen—busy!

Laura.   Oh, Mother, please answer the door, don't make me do it!

Amanda *(crossing into kitchenette)*.   I've got to fix the dressing for the salmon. Fuss, fuss—silliness!—over a gentleman caller!

Door swings shut. Laura is left alone.

(Legend on Screen: "Terror!")

She utters a low moan and turns off the lamp—sits stiffly on the edge of the sofa, knotting her fingers together.

(Legend on Screen: "The Opening Of A Door!")

Tom and Jim appear on the fire-escape steps and climb to landing. Hearing their approach, Laura rises with a panicky gesture. She retreats to the portieres.
The doorbell. Laura catches her breath and touches her throat. Low drums.

Amanda *(calling)*.   Laura, sweetheart! The door!

Laura stares at it without moving.

Jim.   I think we just beat the rain.

Tom.   Uh-huh. *(He rings again, nervously. Jim whistles and fishes for a cigarette.)*

Amanda *(very, very gaily)*.   Laura, that is your brother and Mr. O'Connor! Will you let them in, darling?

Laura crosses toward kitchenette door.

Laura *(breathlessly)*.   Mother—you go to the door!

Amanda steps out of kitchenette and stares furiously at Laura. She points imperiously at the door.

Laura.   Please, please!

Amanda *(in a fierce whisper)*.   What is the matter with you, you silly thing?

Laura *(desperately)*.   Please, you answer it, *please!*

Amanda.   I told you I wasn't going to humor you, Laura. Why have you chosen this moment to lose your mind?

Laura.   Please, please, please, you go!

Amanda.   You'll have to go to the door because I can't!

Laura *(despairingly)*.   I can't either!

Amanda.   Why?

Laura.   I'm *sick!*

Amanda.   I'm sick, too—of your nonsense! Why can't you and your brother be normal people? Fantastic whims and behavior! *(Tom gives a long ring.)* Preposterous goings on! Can you give me one reason—*(Calls out lyrically.)* COMING! JUST ONE SECOND!—why should you be afraid to open a door? Now you answer it, Laura!

Laura.   Oh, oh, oh . . . *(She returns through the portieres. Darts to the victrola and winds it frantically and turns it on.)*

Amanda.   Laura Wingfield, you march right to that door!

Laura.   Yes—yes, Mother!

A faraway, scratchy rendition of "Dardanella" softens the air and gives her strength to move through it. She slips to the door and draws it cautiously open. Tom enters with the caller, Jim O'Connor.

Tom.   Laura, this is Jim. Jim this is my sister, Laura.

Jim *(stepping inside)*.   I didn't know that Shakespeare had a sister!

Laura *(retreating stiff and trembling from the door)*.   How—how do you do?

Jim *(heartily extending his hand)*.   Okay!

Laura touches it hesitantly with hers.

Jim.   Your hand's *cold*, Laura!

Laura.   Yes, well—I've been playing the victrola. . . .

Jim.   Must have been playing classical music on it! You ought to play a little hot swing music to warm you up!

Laura.   Excuse me—I haven't finished playing the victrola. . . .

She turns awkwardly and hurries into the front room. She pauses a second by the victrola. Then catches her breath and darts through the portieres like a frightened deer.

Jim *(grinning)*.   What was the matter?

Tom.   Oh—with Laura? Laura is—terribly shy.

Jim.   Shy, huh? It's unusual to meet a shy girl nowadays. I don't believe you ever mentioned you had a sister.

Tom.   Well, now you know. I have one. Here is the *Post Dispatch*. You want a piece of it?

Jim. Uh-huh.

Tom. What piece? The comics?

Jim. Sports! *(Glances at it.)* Ole Dizzy Dean is on his bad behavior.

Tom *(uninterested)*. Yeah? *(Lights cigarette and crosses back to fire-escape door.)*

Jim. Where are *you* going?

Tom. I'm going out on the terrace.

Jim *(goes after him)*. You know, Shakespeare—I'm going to sell you a bill of goods!

Tom. What goods?

Jim. A course I'm taking.

Tom. Huh?

Jim. In public speaking! You and me, we're not the warehouse type.

Tom. Thanks—that's good news. But what has public speaking got to do with it?

Jim. It fits you for—executive positions!

Tom. Awww.

Jim. I tell you it's done a helluva lot for me.

(Image on Screen: Executive At Desk.)

Tom. In what respect?

Jim. In every! Ask yourself what is the difference between you an' me and men in the office down front? Brains?—No!—Ability?—No! Then what? Just one little thing—

Tom. What is that one little thing?

Jim. Primarily it amounts to—social poise! Being able to square up to people and hold your own on any social level!

Amanda *(off stage)*. Tom?

Tom. Yes, Mother?

Amanda. Is that you and Mr. O'Connor?

Tom. Yes, Mother.

Amanda. Well, you just make yourselves comfortable in there.

Tom. Yes, Mother.

Amanda. Ask Mr. O'Connor if he would like to wash his hands.

Jim. Aw—no—no—thank you— I took care of that at the warehouse. Tom—

Tom. Yes?

Jim. Mr. Mendoza was speaking to me about you.

Tom. Favorably?

Jim. What do you think?

Tom. Well—

Jim. You're going to be out of a job if you don't wake up.

Tom. I am waking up—

Jim. You show no signs.

Tom. The signs are interior.

(Image on Screen: The Sailing Vessel With Jolly Roger Again.)

Tom. I'm planning to change. *(He leans over the rail speaking with quiet exhilaration. The incandescent marquees and signs of the first-run movie houses light his face from across the alley. He looks like a voyager.)* I'm right at the point of committing myself to a future that doesn't include the warehouse and Mr. Mendoza or even a night-school course in public speaking.

Jim. What are you gassing about?

Tom. I'm tired of the movies.

Jim. Movies!

Tom. Yes, movies! Look at them—*(A wave toward the marvels of Grand Avenue.)* All of those glamorous people—having adventures—hogging it all, gobbling the whole thing up! You know what happens? People go to the *movies* instead of *moving!* Hollywood characters are supposed to have all the adventures for everybody in America, while everybody in America sits in a dark room and watches them have them! Yes, until there's a war. That's when adventure becomes available to the masses! *Everyone's* dish, not only Gable's! Then the people in the dark room come out of the dark room to have some adventures themselves—Goody, goody—It's our turn now, to go to the South Sea Island—to make a safari—to be exotic, far-off—But I'm not patient. I don't want to wait till then. I'm tired of the *movies* and I am *about* to *move!*

Jim *(incredulously).* Move?

Tom. Yes.

Jim. When?

Tom. Soon!

Jim. Where? Where?

Theme three: Music seems to answer the question, while Tom thinks it over. He searches among his pockets.

Tom. I'm starting to boil inside. I know I seem dreamy, but inside—well, I'm boiling! Whenever I pick up a shoe, I shudder a little thinking how short life is and what I am doing!—Whatever that means. I know it doesn't mean shoes—except as something to wear on a traveler's feet! *(Finds paper.)* Look—

Jim. What?

Tom. I'm a member.

Jim *(reading).* The Union of Merchant Seamen.

Tom. I paid my dues this month, instead of the light bill.

Jim. You will regret it when they turn the lights off.

Tom. I won't be here.

Jim. How about your mother?

Tom. I'm like my father. The bastard son of a bastard! See how he grins? And he's been absent going on sixteen years!

Jim.   You're just talking, you drip. How does your mother feel about it?

Tom.   Shhh—Here comes Mother! Mother is not acquainted with my plans!

Amanda (*enters portieres*).   Where are you all?

Tom.   On the terrace, Mother.

They start inside. She advances to them. Tom is distinctly shocked at her ap-
pearance. Even Jim blinks a little. He is making his first contact with girlish
Southern vivacity and in spite of the night-school course in public speaking is
somewhat thrown off the beam by the unexpected outlay of social charm.

Certain responses are attempted by Jim but are swept aside by Amanda's gay
laughter and chatter. Tom is embarrassed but after the first shock Jim reacts very
warmly. Grins and chuckles, is altogether won over.

(Image on Screen: Amanda As A Girl.)

Amanda (*coyly smiling, shaking her girlish ringlets*).   Well, well, well, so this
is Mr. O'Connor. Introductions entirely unnecessary. I've heard so much
about you from my boy. I finally said to him, Tom—good gracious!—why
don't you bring this paragon to supper? I'd like to meet this nice young man
at the warehouse!—Instead of just hearing him sing your praises so much! I
don't know why my son is so stand-offish—that's not Southern behavior! Let's
sit down and—I think we could stand a little more air in here! Tom, leave
the door open. I felt a nice fresh breeze a moment ago. Where has it gone?
Mmm, so warm already! And not quite summer, even. We're going to burn
up when summer really gets started. However, we're having—we're having
a very light supper. I think light things are better fo' this time of year. The
same as light clothes are. Light clothes an' light food are what warm weather
calls fo'. You know our blood gets so thick during th' winter—it takes a while
fo' us to *adjust* ou'selves!—when the season changes . . . It's come so quick
this year. I wasn't prepared. All of a sudden—heavens! Already summer!—I
ran to the trunk an' pulled out this light dress—Terribly old! Historical almost!
But feels so good—so good an' co-ol, y'know. . . .

Tom.   Mother—

Amanda.   Yes, honey?

Tom.   How about—supper?

Amanda.   Honey, you go ask Sister if supper is ready! You know that Sister is
in full charge of supper! Tell her you hungry boys are waiting for it. (*To Jim.*)
Have you met Laura?

Jim.   She—

Amanda.   Let you in? Oh, good, you've met already! It's rare for a girl as sweet
an' pretty as Laura to be domestic! But Laura is, thank heavens, not only
pretty but also very domestic. I'm not at all. I never was a bit. I never could
make a thing but angel-food cake. Well, in the South we had so many
servants. Gone, gone, gone. All vestiges of gracious living! Gone completely!

I wasn't prepared for what the future brought me. All of my gentlemen callers were sons of planters and so of course I assumed that I would be married to one and raise my family on a large piece of land with plenty of servants. But man proposes—and woman accepts the proposal!—To vary that old, old saying a little bit—I married no planter! I married a man who worked for the telephone company!—that gallantly smiling gentleman over there! *(Points to the picture.)* A telephone man who—fell in love with long-distance!—Now he travels and I don't even know where!—But what am I going on for about my—tribulations? Tell me yours—I hope you don't have any! Tom?

Tom *(returning).*   Yes, Mother?

Amanda.   Is supper nearly ready?

Tom.   It looks to me like supper is on the table.

Amanda.   Let me look—*(She rises prettily and looks through portieres.)* Oh, lovely—But where is Sister?

Tom.   Laura is not feeling well and she says that she thinks she'd better not come to the table.

Amanda.   What?—Nonsense!—Laura? Oh, Laura!

Laura *(off stage, faintly).*   Yes, Mother.

Amanda.   You really must come to the table. We won't be seated until you come to the table! Come in, Mr. O'Connor. You sit over there and I'll— Laura? Laura Wingfield! You're keeping us waiting, honey! We can't say grace until you come to the table!

The back door is pushed weakly open and Laura comes in. She is obviously quite faint, her lips trembling, her eyes wide and staring. She moves unsteadily toward the table.

(Legend on Screen: "Terror!")

Outside a summer storm is coming on abruptly. The white curtains billow inward at the windows and there is a sorrowful murmur and deep blue dusk.
Laura suddenly stumbles—She catches at a chair with a faint moan.

Tom.   Laura!

Amanda.   Laura! *(There is a clap of thunder.)* **(Legend on Screen: "Ah!")** *(Despairingly.)* Why, Laura you *are* sick, darling! Tom, help your sister into the living room, dear! Sit in the living room, Laura—rest on the sofa. Well! *(To the gentleman caller.)* Standing over the hot stove made her ill!—I told her that it was just too warm this evening, but—*(Tom comes back in. Laura is on the sofa.)* Is Laura all right now?

Tom.   Yes.

Amanda.   What *is* that? Rain? A nice cool rain has come up! *(She gives the gentleman caller a frightened look.)* I think we may—have grace—now . . . *(Tom looks at her stupidly.)* Tom, honey—you say grace!

Tom.   Oh . . . "For these and all thy mercies—" *(They bow their heads, Amanda stealing a nervous glance at Jim. In the living room Laura, stretched on the sofa, clenches her hand to her lips, to hold back a shuddering sob.)* God's Holy Name be praised—

The scene dims out.

Scene VII

(A SOUVENIR.)

Half an hour later. Dinner is just being finished in the upstage area which is concealed by the drawn portieres.

As the curtain rises Laura is still huddled upon the sofa, her feet drawn under her, her head resting on a pale blue pillow, her eyes wide and mysteriously watchful. The new floor lamp with its shade of rose-colored silk gives a soft, becoming light to her face, bringing out the fragile, unearthly prettiness which usually escapes attention. There is a steady murmur of rain, but it is slackening and stops soon after the scene begins; the air outside becomes pale and luminous as the moon breaks out.

A moment after the curtain rises, the lights in both rooms flicker and go out.

Jim.   Hey, there, Mr. Light Bulb!

Amanda laughs nervously.

(Legend on Screen: "Suspension Of A Public Service.")

Amanda.   Where was Moses when the lights went out? Ha-ha. Do you know the answer to that one, Mr. O'Connor?
Jim.   No, Ma'am, what's the answer?
Amanda.   In the dark! *(Jim laughs appreciatively.)* Everybody sit still. I'll light the candles. Isn't it lucky we have them on the table? Where's a match? Which of you gentlemen can provide a match?
Jim.   Here.
Amanda.   Thank you, sir.
Jim.   Not at all, Ma'am!
Amanda.   I guess the fuse has burnt out. Mr. O'Connor, can you tell a burnt-out fuse? I know I can't and Tom is a total loss when it comes to mechanics. *(Sound: getting up: voices recede a little to kitchenette.)* Oh, be careful you don't bump into something. We don't want our gentleman caller to break his neck. Now wouldn't that be a fine howdy-do?

Jim.   Ha-ha! Where is the fuse-box?

Amanda.   Right here next to the stove. Can you see anything?

Jim.   Just a minute.

Amanda.   Isn't electricity a mysterious thing? Wasn't it Benjamin Franklin who tied a key to a kite? We live in such a mysterious universe, don't we? Some people say that science clears up all the mysteries for us. In my opinion it only creates more! Have you found it yet?

Jim.   No, Ma'am. All these fuses look okay to me.

Amanda.   Tom!

Tom.   Yes, Mother?

Amanda.   That light bill I gave you several days ago. The one I told you we got the notices about?

Tom.   Oh.—Yeah.

(Legend on Screen: "Ha!")

Amanda.   You didn't neglect to pay it by any chance?

Tom.   Why, I—

Amanda.   Didn't! I might have known it!

Jim.   Shakespeare probably wrote a poem on that light bill, Mrs. Wingfield.

Amanda.   I might have known better than to trust him with it! There's such a high price for negligence in this world!

Jim.   Maybe the poem will win a ten-dollar prize.

Amanda.   We'll just have to spend the remainder of the evening in the nineteenth century, before Mr. Edison made the Mazda lamp!

Jim.   Candlelight is my favorite kind of light.

Amanda.   That shows you're romantic! But that's no excuse for Tom. Well, we got through dinner. Very considerate of them to let us get through dinner before they plunged us into everlasting darkness, wasn't it, Mr. O'Connor?

Jim.   Ha-ha!

Amanda.   Tom, as a penalty for your carelessness you can help me with the dishes.

Jim.   Let me give you a hand.

Amanda.   Indeed you will not!

Jim.   I ought to be good for something.

Amanda.   Good for something? (*Her tone is rhapsodic.*) You? Why, Mr. O'Connor, nobody, *nobody's* given me this much entertainment in years— as you have!

Jim.   Aw, now, Mrs. Wingfield!

Amanda.   I'm not exaggerating, not one bit! But Sister is all by her lonesome. You go keep her company in the parlor! I'll give you this lovely old candelabrum that used to be on the altar at the church of the Heavenly Rest. It was melted a little out of shape when the church burnt down. Lightning struck it one spring. Gypsy Jones was holding a revival at the time and he intimated that the church was destroyed because the Episcopalians gave card parties.

Jim. Ha-ha.

Amanda. And how about coaxing Sister to drink a little wine? I think it would be good for her! Can you carry both at once?

Jim. Sure. I'm Superman!

Amanda. Now, Thomas, get into this apron!

The door of kitchenette swings closed on Amanda's gay laughter; the flickering light approaches the portieres.

Laura sits up nervously as he enters. Her speech at first is low and breathless from the almost intolerable strain of being alone with a stranger.

(Legend on Screen: "I Don't Suppose You Remember Me At All!")

In her first speeches in this scene, before Jim's warmth overcomes her paralyzing shyness, Laura's voice is thin and breathless as though she has run up a steep flight of stairs.

Jim's attitude is gently humorous. In playing this scene it should be stressed that while the incident is apparently unimportant, it is to Laura the climax of her secret life.

Jim. Hello, there, Laura.

Laura *(faintly).* Hello. *(She clears her throat.)*

Jim. How are you feeling now? Better?

Laura. Yes. Yes, thank you.

Jim. This is for you. A little dandelion wine. *(He extends it toward her with extravagant gallantry.)*

Laura. Thank you.

Jim. Drink it—but don't get drunk! *(He laughs heartily. Laura takes the glass uncertainly; laughs shyly.)* Where shall I set the candles?

Laura. Oh—oh, anywhere . . .

Jim. How about here on the floor? Any objections?

Laura. No.

Jim. I'll spread a newspaper under to catch the drippings. I like to sit on the floor. Mind if I do?

Laura. Oh, no.

Jim. Give me a pillow?

Laura. What?

Jim. A pillow!

Laura. Oh . . . *(Hands him one quickly.)*

Jim. How about you? Don't you like to sit on the floor?

Laura. Oh—yes.

Jim. Why don't you, then?

Laura. I—will.

Jim. Take a pillow! *(Laura does. Sits on the other side of the candelabrum.*

Jim crosses his legs and smiles engagingly at her.) I can't hardly see you sitting way over there.

Laura. I can—see you.

Jim. I know, but that's not fair, I'm in the limelight. *(Laura moves her pillow closer.)* Good! Now I can see you! Comfortable?

Laura. Yes.

Jim. So am I. Comfortable as a cow. Will you have some gum?

Laura. No, thank you.

Jim. I think that I will indulge, with your permission. *(Musingly unwraps it and holds it up.)* Think of the fortune made by the guy that invented the first piece of chewing gum. Amazing, huh? The Wrigley Building is one of the sights of Chicago—I saw it summer before last when I went up to the Century of Progress. Did you take in the Century of Progress?

Laura. No, I didn't.

Jim. Well, it was quite a wonderful exposition. What impressed me most was the Hall of Science. Gives you an idea of what the future will be in America, even more wonderful than the present time is! *(Pause. Smiling at her.)* Your brother tells me you're shy. Is that right, Laura?

Laura. I—don't know.

Jim. I judge you to be an old-fashioned type of girl. Well, I think that's a pretty good type to be. Hope you don't think I'm being too personal—do you?

Laura *(hastily, out of embarrassment).* I believe I *will* take a piece of gum, if you—don't mind. *(Clearing her throat.)* Mr. O'Connor, have you—kept up with your singing?

Jim. Singing? Me?

Laura. Yes. I remember what a beautiful voice you had.

Jim. When did you hear me sing?

Voice offstage in the pause.

Voice *(offstage).*
> O blow, ye winds, heigh-ho,
> A-roving I will go!
> I'm off to my love
> With a boxing glove—
> Ten thousand miles away!

Jim. You say you've heard me sing?

Laura. Oh, yes! Yes, very often . . . I—don't suppose you remember me—at all?

Jim *(smiling doubtfully).* You know I have an idea I've seen you before. I had that idea soon as you opened the door. It seemed almost like I was about to remember your name. But the name that I started to call you—wasn't a name! And so I stopped myself before I said it.

Laura. Wasn't it—Blue Roses?

Jim *(springs up, grinning).* Blue Roses! My gosh, yes—Blue Roses! That's what I had on my tongue when you opened the door! Isn't it funny what tricks your memory plays? I didn't connect you with the high school somehow or other. But that's where it was; it was high school. I didn't even know you were Shakespeare's sister! Gosh, I'm sorry.

Laura.   I didn't expect you to. You—barely knew me!

Jim.   But we did have a speaking acquaintance, huh?

Laura.   Yes, we—spoke to each other.

Jim.   When did you recognize me?

Laura.   Oh, right away!

Jim.   Soon as I came in the door?

Laura.   When I heard your name I thought it was probably you. I knew that Tom used to know you a little in high school. So when you came in the door—Well, then I was—sure.

Jim.   Why didn't you *say* something, then?

Laura *(breathlessly)*.   I didn't know what to say, I was—too surprised!

Jim.   For goodness' sakes! You know, this sure is funny!

Laura.   Yes! Yes, isn't it, though . . .

Jim.   Didn't we have a class in something together?

Laura.   Yes, we did.

Jim.   What class was that?

Laura.   It was—singing—Chorus!

Jim.   Aw!

Laura.   I sat across the aisle from you in the Aud.

Jim.   Aw.

Laura.   Mondays, Wednesdays and Fridays.

Jim.   Now I remember—you always came in late.

Laura.   Yes, it was so hard for me, getting upstairs. I had that brace on my leg—it clumped so loud!

Jim.   I never heard any clumping.

Laura *(wincing at the recollection)*.   To me it sounded like—thunder!

Jim.   Well, well, well. I never even noticed.

Laura.   And everybody was seated before I came in. I had to walk in front of all those people. My seat was in the back row. I had to go clumping all the way up the aisle with everyone watching!

Jim.   You shouldn't have been self-conscious.

Laura.   I know, but I was. It was always such a relief when the singing started.

Jim.   Aw, yes, I've placed you now! I used to call you Blue Roses. How was it that I got started calling you that?

Laura.   I was out of school a little while with pleurosis. When I came back you asked me what was the matter. I said I had pleurosis—you thought I said Blue Roses. That's what you always called me after that!

Jim.   I hope you didn't mind.

Laura.   Oh, no—I liked it. You see, I wasn't acquainted with many—people. . . .

Jim.   As I remember you sort of stuck by yourself.

Laura.   I—I—never had much luck at—making friends.

Jim. I don't see why you wouldn't.

Laura. Well, I—started out badly.

Jim. You mean being—

Laura. Yes, it sort of—stood between me—

Jim. You shouldn't have let it!

Laura. I know, but it did, and—

Jim. You were shy with people!

Laura. I tried not to be but never could—

Jim. Overcome it?

Laura. No, I—I never could!

Jim. I guess being shy is something you have to work out of kind of gradually.

Laura *(sorrowfully).*   Yes—I guess it—

Jim. Takes time!

Laura. Yes—

Jim. People are not so dreadful when you know them. That's what you have to remember! And everybody has problems, not just you, but practically everybody has got some problems. You think of yourself as having the only problems, as being the only one who is disappointed. But just look around you and you will see lots of people as disappointed as you are. For instance, I hoped when I was going to high school that I would be further along at this time, six years later, than I am now—You remember that wonderful write-up I had in *The Torch?*

Laura. Yes! *(She rises and crosses to table.)*

Jim. It said I was bound to succeed in anything I went into! *(Laura returns with the annual.)* Holy Jeez! *The Torch!* *(He accepts it reverently. They smile across it with mutual wonder. Laura crouches beside him and they begin to turn through it. Laura's shyness is dissolving in his warmth.)*

Laura. Here you are in *Pirates of Penzance!*

Jim *(wistfully).*   I sang the baritone lead in that operetta.

Laura. *(rapidly).*   So—*beautifully!*

Jim *(protesting).*   Aw—

Laura. Yes, yes—beautifully—beautifully!

Jim. You heard me?

Laura. All three times!

Jim. No!

Laura. Yes!

Jim. All three performances?

Laura *(looking down).*   Yes.

Jim. Why?

Laura. I—wanted to ask you to—autograph my program.

Jim. Why didn't you ask me to?

Laura. You were always surrounded by your own friends so much that I never had a chance to.

Jim. You should have just—

Laura. Well, I—thought you might think I was—

Jim. Thought I might think you was—what?

Laura. Oh—

Jim *(with reflective relish).* I was beleaguered by females in those days.

Laura. You were terribly popular!

Jim. Yeah—

Laura. You had such a—friendly way—

Jim. I was spoiled in high school.

Laura. Everybody—liked you!

Jim. Including you?

Laura. I—yes, I—I did, too—*(She gently closes the book in her lap.)*

Jim. Well, well, well!—Give me that program, Laura. *(She hands it to him. He signs it with a flourish.)* There you are—better late than never!

Laura. Oh, I—what a—surprise!

Jim. My signature isn't worth very much right now. But some day—maybe— it will increase in value! Being disappointed is one thing and being discouraged is something else. I am disappointed but I'm not discouraged. I'm twenty-three years old. How old are you?

Laura. I'll be twenty-four in June.

Jim. That's not old age!

Laura. No, but—

Jim. You finished with high school?

Laura *(with difficulty).* I didn't go back.

Jim. You mean you dropped out?

Laura. I made bad grades in my final examinations. *(She rises and replaces the book and the program. Her voice strained.)* How is—Emily Meisenbach getting along?

Jim. Oh, that kraut-head!

Laura. Why do you call her that?

Jim. That's what she was.

Laura. You're not still—going with her?

Jim. I never see her.

Laura. It said in the Personal Section that you were—engaged!

Jim. I know, but I wasn't impressed by that—propaganda!

Laura. It wasn't—the truth?

Jim. Only in Emily's optimistic opinion!

Laura. Oh—

(Legend on Screen: "What Have You Done Since High School?")

Jim lights a cigarette and leans indolently back on his elbows smiling at Laura with a warmth and charm which light her inwardly with altar candles. She remains by the table and turns in her hands a piece of glass to cover her tumult.

Jim *(after several reflective puffs on a cigarette).* What have you done since high school? *(She seems not to hear him.)* Huh? *(Laura looks up.)* I said what have you done since high school, Laura?

Laura.   Nothing much.

Jim.   You must have been doing something these six long years.

Laura.   Yes.

Jim.   Well, then, such as what?

Laura.   I took a business course at business college—

Jim.   How did that work out?

Laura.   Well, not very—well—I had to drop out, it gave me—indigestion—

Jim laughs gently.

Jim.   What are you doing now?

Laura.   I don't do anything—much. Oh, please don't think I sit around doing nothing! My glass collection takes up a good deal of my time. Glass is something you have to take good care of.

Jim.   What did you say—about glass?

Laura.   Collection I said—I have one—*(She clears her throat and turns away again, acutely shy.)*

Jim *(abruptly).*   You know what I judge to be the trouble with you? Inferiority complex! Know what that is? That's what they call it when someone lowrates himself! I understand it because I had it, too. Although my case was not so aggravated as yours seems to be. I had it until I took up public speaking, developed my voice, and learned that I had an aptitude for science. Before that time I never thought of myself as being outstanding in any way whatsoever! Now I've never made a regular study of it, but I have a friend who says I can analyze people better than doctors that make a profession of it. I don't claim that to be necessarily true, but I can sure guess a person's psychology, Laura! *(Takes out his gum.)* Excuse me, Laura. I always take it out when the flavor is gone. I'll use this scrap of paper to wrap it in. I know how it is to get it stuck on a shoe. Yep—that's what I judge to be your principal trouble. A lack of confidence in yourself as a person. You don't have the proper amount of faith in yourself. I'm basing that fact on a number of your remarks and also on certain observations I've made. For instance that clumping you thought was so awful in high school. You say that you even dreaded to walk into class. You see what you did? You dropped out of school, you gave up an education because of a clump, which as far as I know was practically non-existent! A little physical defect is what you have. Hardly noticeable even! Magnified thousands of times by imagination! You know what my strong advice to you is? Think of yourself as *superior* in some way!

Laura.   In what way would I think?

Jim.   Why, man alive, Laura! Just look about you a little. What do you see? A world full of common people! All of 'em born and all of 'em going to die! Which of them has one-tenth of your good points! Or mine! Or anyone else's, as far as that goes—Gosh! Everybody excels in some one thing. Some in many! *(Unconsciously glances at himself in the mirror.)* All you've got to do is discover in *what!* Take me, for instance. *(He adjusts his tie at the mirror.)*

My interest happens to lie in electro-dynamics. I'm taking a course in radio engineering at night school, Laura, on top of a fairly responsible job at the warehouse. I'm taking that course and studying public speaking.

Laura.   Ohhhh.

Jim.   Because I believe in the future of television! *(Turning back to her.)* I wish to be ready to go up right along with it. Therefore I'm planning to get in on the ground floor. In fact, I've already made the right connections and all that remains is for the industry itself to get under way! Full steam—*(His eyes are starry.)* Knowledge—*Zzzzzp!* Money—*Zzzzzzp!*—Power! That's the cycle democracy is built on! *(His attitude is convincingly dynamic. Laura stares at him, even her shyness eclipsed in her absolute wonder. He suddenly grins.)* I guess you think I think a lot of myself!

Laura.   No—o-o-o, I—

Jim.   Now how about you? Isn't there something you take more interest in than anything else?

Laura.   Well, I do—as I said—have my—glass collection—

A peal of girlish laughter from the kitchen.

Jim.   I'm not right sure I know what you're talking about. What kind of glass is it?

Laura.   Little articles of it, they're ornaments mostly! Most of them are little animals made out of glass, the tiniest little animals in the world. Mother calls them a glass menagerie! Here's an example of one, if you'd like to see it! This one is one of the oldest. It's nearly thirteen. *(He stretches out his hand.)* *(Music: "The Glass Menagerie.")* Oh, be careful—if you breathe, it breaks!

Jim.   I'd better not take it. I'm pretty clumsy with things.

Laura.   Go on, I trust you with him! *(Places it in his palm.)* There now— you're holding him gently! Hold him over the light, he loves the light! You see how the light shines through him?

Jim.   It sure does shine!

Laura.   I shouldn't be partial, but he is my favorite one.

Jim.   What kind of a thing is this one supposed to be?

Laura.   Haven't you noticed the single horn on his forehead?

Jim.   A unicorn, huh?

Laura.   Mmm-hmmm!

Jim.   Unicorns, aren't they extinct in the modern world?

Laura.   I know!

Jim.   Poor little fellow, he must feel sort of lonesome.

Laura *(smiling).*   Well, if he does he doesn't complain about it. He stays on a shelf with some horses that don't have horns and all of them seem to get along nicely together.

Jim.   How do you know?

Laura *(lightly).*   I haven't heard any arguments among them!

Jim *(grinning).*   No arguments, huh? Well, that's a pretty good sign! Where shall I set him?

Laura. Put him on the table. They all like a change of scenery once in a while!

Jim *(stretching).* Well, well, well, well—Look how big my shadow is when I stretch!

Laura. Oh, oh, yes—it stretches across the ceiling!

Jim *(crossing to door).* I think it's stopped raining. *(Opens fire-escape door.)* Where does the music come from?

Laura. From the Paradise Dance Hall across the alley.

Jim. How about cutting the rug a little, Miss Wingfield?

Laura. Oh, I—

Jim. Or is your program filled up? Let me have a look at it. *(Grasps imaginary card.)* Why, every dance is taken! I'll just have to scratch some out. *(Waltz music: "La Golondrina.")* Ahhh, a waltz! *(He executes some sweeping turns by himself, then holds his arms toward Laura.)*

Laura *(breathlessly).* I—can't dance!

Jim. There you go, that inferiority stuff!

Laura. I've never danced in my life!

Jim. Come on, try!

Laura. Oh, but I'd step on you!

Jim. I'm not made out of glass.

Laura. How—how—how do we start?

Jim. Just leave it to me. You hold your arms out a little.

Laura. Like this?

Jim. A little bit higher. Right. Now don't tighten up, that's the main thing about it—relax.

Laura *(laughing breathlessly).* It's hard not to.

Jim. Okay.

Laura. I'm afraid you can't budge me.

Jim. What do you bet I can't? *(He swings her into motion.)*

Laura. Goodness, yes, you can!

Jim. Let yourself go, now, Laura, just let yourself go.

Laura. I'm—

Jim. Come on!

Laura. Trying!

Jim. Not so stiff—Easy does it!

Laura. I know but I'm—

Jim. Loosen th' backbone! There now, that's a lot better.

Laura. Am I?

Jim. Lots, lots better! *(He moves her about the room in a clumsy waltz.)*

Laura. Oh, my!

Jim. Ha-ha!

Laura. Oh, my goodness!

Jim. Ha-ha-ha! *(They suddenly bump into the table. Jim stops.)* What did we hit on?

Laura. Table.

Jim. Did something fall off it? I think—

Laura.   Yes.

Jim.   I hope that it wasn't the little glass horse with the horn!

Laura.   Yes.

Jim.   Aw, aw, aw. Is it broken?

Laura.   Now it is just like all the other horses.

Jim.   It's lost its—

Laura.   Horn! It doesn't matter. Maybe it's a blessing in disguise.

Jim.   You'll never forgive me. I bet that that was your favorite piece of glass.

Laura.   I don't have favorites much. It's no tragedy, Freckles. Glass breaks so easily. No matter how careful you are. The traffic jars the shelves and things fall off them.

Jim.   Still I'm awfully sorry that I was the cause.

Laura *(smiling)*.   I'll just imagine he had an operation. The horn was removed to make him feel less—freakish! *(They both laugh.)* Now he will feel more at home with the other horses, the ones that don't have horns . . .

Jim.   Ha-ha, that's very funny! *(Suddenly serious.)* I'm glad to see that you have a sense of humor. You know—you're—well—very different! Surprisingly different from anyone else I know! *(His voice becomes soft and hesitant with a genuine feeling.)* Do you mind me telling you that? *(Laura is abashed beyond speech.)* You make me feel sort of—I don't know how to put it! I'm usually pretty good at expressing things, but—This is something that I don't know how to say! *(Laura touches her throat and clears it—turns the broken unicorn in her hands.)* *(Even softer.)* Has anyone ever told you that you were pretty? *(Pause: music.)* *(Laura looks up slowly, with wonder, and shakes her head.)* Well, you are! In a very different way from anyone else. And all the nicer, because of the difference, too. *(His voice becomes low and husky. Laura turns away, nearly faint with the novelty of her emotions.)* I wish that you were my sister. I'd teach you to have some confidence in yourself. The different people are not like other people, but being different is nothing to be ashamed of. Because other people are not such wonderful people. They're one hundred times one thousand. You're one times one! They walk all over the earth. You just stay here. They're common as—weeds, but—you—well, you're—*Blue Roses!*

(Image on Screen: Blue Roses.)

Music changes.

Laura.   But blue is wrong—for roses . . .

Jim.   It's right for you—You're—pretty!

Laura.   In what respect am I pretty?

Jim.   In all respects—believe me! Your eyes—your hair—are pretty! Your hands are pretty! *(He catches hold of her hand.)* You think I'm making this up because I'm invited to dinner and have to be nice. Oh, I could do that! I could put on an act for you, Laura, and say lots of things without being very sincere. But this time I am. I'm talking to you sincerely. I happened to notice you had this inferiority complex that keeps you from feeling comfortable with people. Somebody needs to build your confidence up and make you proud instead of shy and turning away and—blushing—Somebody ought to—Ought to—*kiss* you, Laura! *(His hand slips slowly up her arm to her shoulder.) (Music swells tumultuously.) (He suddenly turns her about and kisses her on the lips. When he releases her Laura sinks on the sofa with a bright, dazed look. Jim backs away and fishes in his pocket for a cigarette.)* **(Legend on Screen: "Souvenir.")** Stumble-john! *(He lights the cigarette, avoiding her look. There is a peal of girlish laughter from Amanda in the kitchen. Laura slowly raises and opens her hand. It still contains the little broken glass animal. She looks at it with a tender, bewildered expression.)* Stumble-john! I shouldn't have done that—That was way off the beam. You don't smoke, do you? *(She looks up, smiling, not hearing the question. He sits beside her a little gingerly. She looks at him speechlessly—waiting. He coughs decorously and moves a little farther aside as he considers the situation and senses her feelings, dimly, with perturbation. Gently.)* Would you—care for a—mint? *(She doesn't seem to hear him but her look grows brighter even.)* Peppermint—Life Saver? My pocket's a regular drug store—wherever I go . . . *(He pops a mint in his mouth. Then gulps and decides to make a clean breast of it. He speaks slowly and gingerly.)* Laura, you know, if I had a sister like you, I'd do the same thing as Tom. I'd bring out fellows—introduce her to them. The right type of boys of a type to—appreciate her. Only—well—he made a mistake about me. Maybe I've got no call to be saying this. That may not have been the idea in having me over. But what if it was? There's nothing wrong about that. The only trouble is that in my case—I'm not in a situation to—do the right thing. I can't take down your number and say I'll phone. I can't call up next week and—ask for a date. I thought I had better explain the situation in case you misunderstood it and—I hurt your feelings. . . . *(Pause. Slowly, very slowly, Laura's look changes, her eyes returning slowly from his to the ornament in her palm.)*

Amanda utters another gay laugh in the kitchen.

Laura *(faintly)*.   You—won't—call again?

Jim.   No, Laura, I can't. *(He rises from the sofa.)* As I was just explaining, I've—got strings on me, Laura, I've—been going steady! I go out all the time with a girl named Betty. She's a home-girl like you, and Catholic, and Irish, and in a great many ways we—get along fine. I met her last summer on a moonlight boat trip up the river to Alton, on the *Majestic*. Well—right away from the start it was—love! **(Legend on Screen: Love!)** *(Laura sways slightly forward and grips the arm of the sofa. He fails to notice, now enrapt in his own comfortable being.)* Being in love has made a new man of me! *(Leaning stiffly forward, clutching the arm of the sofa, Laura struggles visibly with her storm. But Jim is oblivious, she is a long way off.)* The power of love is really pretty tremendous! Love is something that—changes the whole world, Laura! *(The storm abates a little and Laura leans back. He notices her again.)* It happened that Betty's aunt took sick, she got a wire and had to go to Centralia. So Tom—when he asked me to dinner—I naturally just accepted the invitation, not knowing that you—that he—that I—*(He stops awkwardly.)* Huh— I'm a stumble-john! *(He flops back on the sofa. The holy candles in the altar of Laura's face have been snuffed out! There is a look of almost infinite desolation. Jim glances at her uneasily.)* I wish that you would—say something. *(She bites her lip which was trembling and then bravely smiles. She opens her hand again on the broken glass ornament. Then she gently takes his hand and raises it level with her own. She carefully places the unicorn in the palm of his hand, then pushes his fingers closed upon it.)* What are you—doing that for? You want me to have him?—Laura? *(She nods.)* What for?

Laura.   A—souvenir . . .

She rises unsteadily and crouches beside the victrola to wind it up.

(Legend on Screen: "Things Have A Way Of Turning Out So Badly.")

(Or Image: "Gentleman Caller Waving Good-bye!—Gaily.")

At this moment Amanda rushes brightly back in the front room. She bears a pitcher of fruit punch in an old-fashioned cut-glass pitcher and a plate of macaroons. The plate has a gold border and poppies painted on it.

Amanda.   Well, well, well! Isn't the air delightful after the shower? I've made you children a little liquid refreshment. *(Turns gaily to the gentleman caller.)* Jim, do you know that song about lemonade?

"Lemonade, lemonade
Made in the shade and stirred with a spade—
Good enough for any old maid!"

Jim *(uneasily).*   Ha-ha! No—I never heard it.
Amanda.   Why, Laura! You look so serious!
Jim.   We were having a serious conversation.
Amanda.   Good! Now you're better acquainted!
Jim *(uncertainly).*   Ha-ha! Yes.
Amanda.   You modern young people are much more serious-minded than my generation. I was so gay as a girl!
Jim.   You haven't changed, Mrs. Wingfield.
Amanda.   Tonight I'm rejuvenated! The gaiety of the occasion, Mr. O'Connor! *(She tosses her head with a peal of laughter. Spills lemonade.)* Oooo! I'm baptizing myself!

Jim. Here—let me—

Amanda *(setting the pitcher down).* There now. I discovered we had some maraschino cherries. I dumped them in, juice and all!

Jim. You shouldn't have gone to that trouble, Mrs. Wingfield.

Amanda. Trouble, trouble? Why it was loads of fun! Didn't you hear me cutting up in the kitchen? I bet your ears were burning! I told Tom how outdone with him I was for keeping you to himself so long a time! He should have brought you over much, much sooner! Well, now that you've found your way, I want you to be a very frequent caller! Not just occasional but all the time. Oh, we're going to have a lot of gay times together! I see them coming! Mmm, just breathe that air! So fresh, and the moon's so pretty! I'll skip back out—I know where my place is when young folks are having a— serious conversation!

Jim. Oh, don't go out. Mrs. Wingfield. The fact of the matter is I've got to be going.

Amanda. Going, now? You're joking! Why, it's only the shank of the evening, Mr. O'Connor!

Jim. Well, you know how it is.

Amanda. You mean you're a young workingman and have to keep working-men's hours. We'll let you off early tonight. But only on the condition that next time you stay later. What's the best night for you? Isn't Saturday night the best night for you workingmen?

Jim. I have a couple of time-clocks to punch, Mrs. Wingfield. One at morn-ing, another one at night!

Amanda. My, but you *are* ambitious! You work at night, too?

Jim. No, Ma'am, not work but—Betty! *(He crosses deliberately to pick up his hat. The band at the Paradise Dance Hall goes into a tender waltz.)*

Amanda. Betty? Betty? Who's—Betty! *(There is an ominous cracking sound in the sky.)*

Jim. Oh, just a girl. The girl I go steady with! *(He smiles charmingly. The sky falls.)*

(Legend on Screen: "The Sky Falls.")

Amanda *(a long-drawn exhalation).* Ohhhh . . . Is it a serious romance, Mr. O'Connor?

Jim. We're going to be married the second Sunday in June.

Amanda. Ohhhh—how nice! Tom didn't mention that you were engaged to be married.

Jim. The cat's not out of the bag at the warehouse yet. You know how they are. They call you Romeo and stuff like that. *(He stops at the oval mirror to put on his hat. He carefully shapes the brim and the crown to give a discreetly dashing effect.)* It's been a wonderful evening, Mrs. Wingfield. I guess this is what they mean by Southern hospitality.

Amanda.   It really wasn't anything at all.

Jim.   I hope it don't seem like I'm rushing off. But I promised Betty I'd pick her up at the Wabash depot, an' by the time I get my jalopy down there her train'll be in. Some women are pretty upset if you keep 'em waiting.

Amanda.   Yes, I know—The tyranny of women! *(Extends her hand.)* Goodbye, Mr. O'Connor. I wish you luck—and happiness—and success! All three of them, and so does Laura!—Don't you, Laura?

Laura.   Yes!

Jim *(taking her hand).*   Goodbye, Laura. I'm certainly going to treasure that souvenir. And don't you forget the good advice I gave you. *(Raises his voice to a cheery shout.)* So long, Shakespeare! Thanks again, ladies—Good night!

He grins and ducks jauntily out.

   Still bravely grimacing, Amanda closes the door on the gentleman caller. Then she turns back to the room with a puzzled expression. She and Laura don't dare to face each other. Laura crouches beside the victrola to wind it.

Amanda *(faintly).*   Things have a way of turning out so badly. I don't believe that I would play the victrola. Well, well—well—Our gentleman caller was engaged to be married! Tom!

Tom *(from back).*   Yes, Mother?

Amanda.   Come in here a minute. I want to tell you something awfully funny.

Tom *(enters with macaroon and a glass of the lemonade).*   Has the gentleman caller gotten away already?

Amanda.   The gentleman caller has made an early departure. What a wonderful joke you played on us!

Tom.   How do you mean?

Amanda.   You didn't mention that he was engaged to be married.

Tom.   Jim? Engaged?

Amanda.   That's what he just informed us.

Tom.   I'll be jiggered! I didn't know about that.

Amanda.   That seems very peculiar.

Tom.   What's peculiar about it?

Amanda.   Didn't you call him your best friend down at the warehouse?

Tom.   He is, but how did I know?

Amanda.   It seems extremely peculiar that you wouldn't know your best friend was going to be married!

Tom.   The warehouse is where I work, not where I know things about people!

Amanda.   You don't know things anywhere! You live in a dream; you manufacture illusions! *(He crosses to door.)* Where are you going?

Tom.   I'm going to the movies.

Amanda.   That's right, now that you've had us make such fools of ourselves. The effort, the preparations, all the expense! The new floor lamp, the rug, the clothes for Laura! All for what? To entertain some other girl's fiancé! Go to the movies, go! Don't think about us, a mother deserted, an unmarried sister who's crippled and has no job! Don't let anything interfere with your selfish pleasure! Just go, go, go—to the movies!

Tom.   All right, I will! The more you shout about my selfishness to me the quicker I'll go, and I won't go to the movies!

Amanda.   Go, then! Then go to the moon—you selfish dreamer!

Tom smashes his glass on the floor. He plunges out on the fire-escape, slamming the door. Laura screams.

Dance-hall music up. Tom goes to the rail and grips it desperately, lifting his face in the chill white moonlight penetrating the narrow abyss of the alley.

(Legend on Screen: "And So Good-bye . . .")

Tom's closing speech is timed with the interior pantomime. The interior scene is played as though viewed through soundproof glass. Amanda appears to be making a comforting speech to Laura who is huddled upon the sofa. Now that we cannot hear the mother's speech, her silliness is gone and she has dignity and tragic beauty. Laura's dark hair hides her face until at the end of the speech she lifts it to smile at her mother. Amanda's gestures are slow and graceful, almost dancelike, as she comforts her daughter. At the end of her speech she glances a moment at the father's picture—then withdraws through the portieres. At close of Tom's speech, Laura blows out the candles, ending the play.

Tom.   I didn't go to the moon, I went much further—for time is the longest distance between two places—Not long after that I was fired for writing a poem on the lid of a shoe-box. I left Saint Louis. I descended the steps of this fire-escape for a last time and followed, from then on, in my father's footsteps, attempting to find in motion what was lost in space—I traveled around a great deal. The cities swept about me like dead leaves, leaves that were brightly colored but torn away from the branches. I would have stopped, but I was pursued by· something. It always came upon me unawares, taking me altogether by surprise. Perhaps it was a familiar bit of music. Perhaps it was only a piece of transparent glass—Perhaps I am walking along a street at night, in some strange city, before I have found companions. I pass the lighted window of a shop where perfume is sold. The window is filled with pieces of colored glass, tiny transparent bottles in delicate colors, like bits of a shattered rainbow. Then all at once my sister touches my shoulder. I turn around and look into her eyes . . . Oh, Laura, Laura, I tried to leave you behind me, but I am more faithful than I intended to be! I reach for a cigarette, I cross the street, I run into the movies or a bar, I buy a drink, I speak to the nearest stranger—anything that can blow your candles out! *(Laura bends over the candles.)*—for nowadays the world is lit by lightning! Blow out your candles, Laura—and so goodbye . . .

She blows the candles out. The scene dissolves.

PRODUCTION NOTES

Being a "memory play," *The Glass Menagerie* can be presented with unusual freedom of convention. Because of its considerably delicate or tenuous material, atmospheric touches and subtleties of direction play a particularly important part. Expressionism and all other unconventional techniques in drama have only one valid aim, and that is a closer approach to truth. When a play employs unconventional techniques, it is not, or certainly shouldn't be, trying to escape its responsibility of dealing with reality, or interpreting experience, but is actually or should be attempting to find a closer approach, a more penetrating and vivid expression of things as they are. The straight realistic play with its genuine frigidaire and authentic ice-cubes, its characters that speak exactly as its audience speaks, corresponds to the academic landscape and has the same virtue of a photographic likeness. Everyone should know nowadays the unimportance of the photographic in art: that truth, life, or reality is an organic thing which the poetic imagination can represent or suggest, in essence, only through transformation, through changing into other forms than those which were merely present in appearance.

These remarks are not meant as comments only on this particular play. They have to do with a conception of a new, plastic theater which must take the place of the exhausted theater of realistic conventions if the theater is to resume vitality as a part of our culture.

The Screen Device

There is *only one important difference between the original and acting version of the play* and that is the *omission* in the latter of the device which I tentatively included in my *original* script. This device was the use of a screen on which were projected magic-lantern slides bearing images or titles. I do not regret the omission of this device from the . . . Broadway production. The extraordinary power of Miss Taylor's performance made it suitable to have the utmost simplicity in the physical production. But I think it may be interesting to some readers to see how this device was conceived. So I am putting it into the published manuscript. These images and legends, projected from behind, were cast on a section of wall between the front-room and dining-room areas, which should be indistinguishable from the rest when not in use.

The purpose of this will probably be apparent. It is to give accent to certain values in each scene. Each scene contains a particular point (or several) which is structurally the most important. In an episodic play, such as this, the basic structure or narrative line may be obscured from the audience; the effect may seem fragmentary rather than architectural. This may not be the fault of the play so much as a lack of attention in the audience. The legend or image upon the screen will strengthen the effect of what is merely allusion in the writing and allow the primary point to be made more simply and lightly than if the entire responsibility were on the spoken lines. Aside from this structural value, I think the screen will have a definite emotional appeal, less definable but just as important. An imaginative producer or director may invent many other uses for this device than those indicated in the present script. In fact the possibilities of the device seem much larger to me than the instance of this play can possibly utilize.

The Music

Another extra-literary accent in this play is provided by the use of music. A single recurring tune, "The Glass Menagerie," is used to give emotional emphasis to suitable passages. This tune is like circus music, not when you are on the grounds or in the immediate vicinity of the parade, but when you are at some distance and very likely thinking of something else. It seems under those circumstances to continue almost interminably and it weaves in and out of your preoccupied consciousness; then it is the lightest, most delicate music in the world and perhaps the saddest. It expresses the surface vivacity of life with the underlying strain of immutable and inexpressible sorrow. When you look at a piece of delicately spun glass you think of two things: how beautiful it is and how easily it can be broken. Both of those ideas should be woven into the recurring tune, which dips in and out of the play as if it were carried on a wind that changes. It serves as a thread of connection and allusion between the narrator with his separate point in time and space and the subject of his story. Between each episode it returns as reference to the emotion, nostalgia, which is the first condition of the play. It is primarily Laura's music and therefore comes out most clearly when the play focuses upon her and the lovely fragility of glass which is her image.

The Lighting

The lighting in the play is not realistic. In keeping with the atmosphere of memory, the stage is dim. Shafts of light are focused on selected areas or actors, sometimes in contradistinction to what is the apparent center. For instance, in the quarrel scene between Tom and Amanda, in which Laura has no active part, the clearest pool of light is on her figure. This is also true of the supper scene. The light upon Laura should be distinct from the others, having a peculiar pristine clarity such as light used in early religious portraits of female saints or madonnas. A certain correspondence to light in religious paintings, such as El Greco's, where the figures are radiant in atmosphere that is relatively dusky, could be effectively used throughout the play. (It will also permit a more effective use of the screen.) A free, imaginative use of light can be of enormous value in giving a mobile, plastic quality to plays of a more or less static nature.

QUESTIONS

1. Who is the central character in the play?   **2.** What does the glass menagerie symbolize? Specifically, what does the unicorn symbolize? Why does Laura give the unicorn, after its horn has broken off, to Jim?   **3.** In his address to the audience that begins the play, Tom tells the audience that Jim "is the most realistic character in the play . . . an emissary from a world of reality that we were somehow set apart from." What is the world of reality Jim represents? **4.** Although she has refused to accept the characterization from Tom, in her final words Amanda refers to Laura as "crippled." Why? **5.** In his opening address, Tom sketches in "the social background of the play." Why? **6.** Is Tom's escape as complete as his father's seems to have been? Explain. **7.** Are the magic lantern slides an effective device? Explain.

WRITING TOPIC

Are we meant to admire Amanda for holding together her family under very difficult circumstances or to condemn her for her destructive illusions? In this connection, explain the statement in the final stage direction: "Now that we cannot hear the mother's speech, her silliness is gone and she has dignity and tragic beauty."

Innocence and Experience

QUESTIONS AND WRITING TOPICS

1. What support do the works in this section provide for Thomas Gray's well-known observation that "where ignorance is bliss,/ 'Tis folly to be wise"? **Writing Topic:** Use Gray's observation as the basis for an analysis of either Frank O'Connor's "My Oedipus Complex" or Flannery O'Connor's "Good Country People."

2. In such poems as William Blake's "The Garden of Love," William Wordsworth's "Lines Composed a Few Miles Above Tintern Abbey," Robert Frost's "Birches," and Stevie Smith's "To Carry the Child," growing up is seen as a growing away from a kind of truth and reality; in other poems, such as Walt Whitman's "Out of the Cradle Endlessly Rocking," Gerard Manley Hopkins's "Spring and Fall," Dylan Thomas's "Fern Hill," and Robert Wallace's "In a Spring Still Not Written of," growing up is seen as growing into truth and reality. Do these two groups of poems embody contradictory and mutually exclusive conceptions of childhood? Explain. **Writing Topic:** Select one poem from each of these two groups and contrast the conception of childhood embodied in each.

3. An eighteenth-century novelist wrote: "Oh Innocence, how glorious and happy a portion art thou to the breast that possesses thee! Thou fearest neither the eyes nor the tongues of men. Truth, the most powerful of all things, is thy strongest friend; and the brighter the light is in which thou art displayed, the more it discovers thy transcendent beauties." Which works in this section support this assessment of innocence? Which works contradict it? How would you characterize the relationship between "truth" and "innocence" in the fiction and the drama presented here? **Writing Topic:** Use this observation as the basis for an analysis of *Oedipus Rex*.

4. A certain arrogance is associated with the innocence of Oedipus in Sophocles's *Oedipus Rex*, Robin in Hawthorne's "My Kinsman, Major Molineux," the captain in Conrad's "The Secret Sharer," and Hulga in Flannery O'Connor's "Good Country People." On what is their arrogance based, and how is it modified? **Writing Topic:** Select two of these three works and contrast the nature and the consequences of the central characters' arrogance.

5. Sherwood Anderson's "I Want to Know Why," James Joyce's "Araby," Frank O'Connor's "My Oedipus Complex," and Flannery O'Connor's "Good Country People" all deal with some aspect of sexuality as a force that moves the protagonist from innocence toward experience. How does the recognition of sexuality function in each of the stories? **Writing Topic:** Choose two of these stories, and discuss the relationship between sexuality and innocence.

6. Which poems in this section depend largely on irony for their force? Can you suggest why irony is a particularly useful device in literature that portrays innocence and experience? **Writing Topic:** Write an analysis of the function of irony in Blake's "The Garden of Love" and Hardy's "The Ruined Maid."

7. Compare Oedipus in *Oedipus Rex* with Donal in O'Casey's *The Shadow of a Gunman*. In your opinion, which character is more admirable? Explain. **Writing Topic:** Contrast the sources of the "tragedy" that marks the life of each character.

8. Is the passage from innocence to experience a loss or a gain or both? Explain. **Writing Topic:** Compare the passage from innocence to experience in O'Casey's *The Shadow of a Gunman* and Shaw's *Pygmalion*.

Conformity
and
Rebellion

The Uprising, © 1860 by Honoré Daumier

Although the works in this section, like those in "Innocence and Experience," may also feature a violation of innocence, the events are usually based on the clash between the two well-articulated positions; the rebel, on principle, confronts and struggles with established authority. Central in these works is the sense of tremendous external forces—the state, the church, tradition—which can be obeyed only at the expense of conscience and humanity. At the most general level, these works confront a dilemma older than Antigonê's. Thebes: the very organizations men and women establish to protect and nurture the individual demand—on pain of economic ruin, social ostracism, even spiritual or physical death—that they violate their most deeply cherished beliefs. When individuals refuse such a demand, they translate their awareness of a hostile social order into action against it and precipitate a crisis. In *Antigonê*, the issue is drawn with utter clarity: Antigonê must obey either the state (Creon) or the gods. In *A Doll's House*, Nora Helmer finally realizes that dehumanization is too high a price to pay for social stability. On a different note, in "Bartleby the Scrivener," Bartleby's "preference" not to conform to the established structures of Wall Street results in a crisis of passive resistance.

Many of the works in this section, particularly the poems, do not treat the theme of conformity and rebellion quite so explicitly and dramatically. Some, like "Eleanor Rigby," describe a world devoid of human communion and community without directly accounting for it; others, like W. H. Auden's "The Unknown Citizen," tell us that the price exacted for total conformity to the industrial superstate is spiritual death. In "Easter 1916," William Butler Yeats meditates upon the awesome meaning of the lives and deaths of political revolutionaries, and in "Harlem," Langston Hughes warns that an inflexible and constricting social order will generate explosion.

Two basic modes, then, inform the literary treatment of conformity and rebellion. While in many of the works, the individual is caught up in a crisis that forces him or her into rebellion, in other works, especially the poems, the focus may be on the individual's failure to move from awareness into action, as in Amy Lowell's "Patterns." Indeed, the portrait of Auden's unknown citizen and of E. E. Cummings's "Cambridge ladies" affirm the necessity for rebellion by rendering so effectively the hollow life of mindless conformity.

However diverse in treatment and technique, all the works in this section are about individuals trapped by complex sets of external forces that regulate and define their lives. Social beings—men and women—sometimes submit to these forces, but it is always an uneasy submission, for the purpose of these forces is to curb and control people. Individuals may recognize that they must be controlled for some larger good; yet they are aware that established social power is often abusive. The tendency of power, at its best, is to act as a conserving force that brakes the disruptive impulse to abandon and destroy old ways and ideas. At its worst, power is self-serving. The individual must constantly judge which tendency power is enhancing. And because the power of the individual is negligible beside that of frequently abusive social forces, it is not surprising that many artists since the advent of the great nation-states have found a fundamental human dignity in the resistance of the individual to organized society. One of humanity's ancient and profound recognitions, after all, is that the impulse of a Creon is always to make unknown citizens of us all.

CONFORMITY
AND
REBELLION

Epoch, 1950 by Ben Shahn.

FICTION

Bartleby the Scrivener   1853
A STORY OF WALL STREET

HERMAN MELVILLE   [1819–1891]

I am a rather elderly man. The nature of my avocations, for the last thirty years, has brought me into more than ordinary contact with what would seem an interesting and somewhat singular set of men, of whom, as yet, nothing, that I know of, has ever been written—I mean, the law-copyists, or scriveners. I have known very many of them, professionally and privately, and, if I pleased, could relate divers histories, at which good-natured gentlemen might smile, and sentimental souls might weep. But I waive the biographies of all other scriveners, for a few passages in the life of Bartleby, who was a scrivener, the strangest I ever saw, or heard of. While, of other law-copyists, I might write the complete life, of Bartleby nothing of that sort can be done. I believe that no materials exist for a full and satisfactory biography of this man. It is an irreparable loss to literature. Bartleby was one of those beings of whom nothing is ascertainable, except from the original sources, and, in his case, those are very small. What my own astonished eyes saw of Bartleby, *that* is all I know of him, except, indeed, one vague report, which will appear in the sequel.

Ere introducing the scrivener, as he first appeared to me, it is fit I make some mention of myself, my employees, my business, my chambers, and general surroundings; because some such description is indispensable to an adequate understanding of the chief character about to be presented. Imprimis: I am a man who, from his youth upwards, has been filled with a profound conviction that the easiest way of life is the best. Hence, though I belong to a profession proverbially energetic and nervous, even to turbulence, at times, yet nothing of that sort have I ever suffered to invade my peace. I am one of those unambitious lawyers who never addresses a jury, or in any way draws down public applause; but, in the cool tranquillity of a snug retreat, do a snug business among rich men's bonds, and mortgages, and title-deeds. All who know me, consider me an eminently *safe* man. The late John Jacob Astor,[1] a personage little given to

---

[1] A poor immigrant who rose to become one of the great business tycoons of the nineteenth century.

poetic enthusiasm, had no hesitation in pronouncing my first grand point to be prudence; my next, method. I do not speak it in vanity, but simply record the fact, that I was not unemployed in my profession by the late John Jacob Astor; a name which, I admit, I love to repeat; for it hath a rounded and orbicular sound to it, and rings like unto bullion. I will freely add, that I was not insensible to the late John Jacob Astor's good opinion.

Some time prior to the period at which this little history begins, my avocations had been largely increased. The good old office, now extinct in the State of New York, of a Master in Chancery,[2] had been conferred upon me. It was not a very arduous office, but very pleasantly remunerative. I seldom lose my temper; much more seldom indulge in dangerous indignation at wrongs and outrages; but, I must be permitted to be rash here, and declare that I consider the sudden and violent abrogation of the office of Master in Chancery, by the new Constitution, as a—premature act; inasmuch as I had counted upon a life-lease of the profits, whereas I only received those of a few short years. But this is by the way.

My chambers were up stairs, at No. —— Wall Street. At one end, they looked upon the white wall of the interior of a spacious sky-light shaft, penetrating the building from top to bottom.

This view might have been considered rather tame than otherwise, deficient in what landscape painters call "life." But, if so, the view from the other end of my chambers offered, at least, a contrast, if nothing more. In that direction, my windows commanded an unobstructed view of a lofty brick wall, black by age and everlasting shade; which wall required no spyglass to bring out its lurking beauties, but, for the benefit of all near-sighted spectators, was pushed up to within ten feet of my window panes. Owing to the great height of the surrounding buildings, and my chambers being on the second floor, the interval between this wall and mine not a little resembled a huge square cistern.

At the period just preceding the advent of Bartleby, I had two persons as copyists in my employment, and a promising lad as an office-boy. First, Turkey; second, Nippers; third, Ginger Nut. These may seem names, the like of which are not usually found in the Directory. In truth, they were nicknames, mutually conferred upon each other by my three clerks, and were deemed expressive of their respective persons or characters. Turkey was a short, pursy Englishman, of about my own age—that is, somewhere not far from sixty. In the morning, one might say, his face was of a fine florid hue, but after twelve o'clock, meridian—his dinner hour—it blazed like a grate full of Christmas coals; and continued blazing—but, as it were, with a gradual wane—till six o'clock P.M., or thereabouts; after which, I saw no more of the proprietor of the face, which, gaining its meridian with the sun, seemed to set with it, to rise, culminate, and decline the following day, with the like regularity and undiminished glory. There are many singular coincidences I have known in the course of my life, not the least among which was the fact, that, exactly when Turkey displayed

---

[2] Courts of Chancery often adjudicated business disputes.

his fullest beams from his red and radiant countenance, just then, too, at that critical moment, began the daily period when I considered his business capacities as seriously disturbed for the remainder of the twenty-four hours. Not that he was absolutely idle, or averse to business, then; far from it. The difficulty was, he was apt to be altogether too energetic. There was a strange, inflamed, flurried, flighty recklessness of activity about him. He would be incautious in dipping his pen into his inkstand. All his blots upon my documents were dropped there after twelve o'clock meridian. Indeed, not only would he be reckless, and sadly given to making blots in the afternoon, but, some days, he went further, and was rather noisy. At such times, too, his face flamed with augmented blazonry, as if cannel coal had been heaped on anthracite. He made an unpleasant racket with his chair; spilled his sand-box; in mending his pens, impatiently split them all to pieces, and threw them on the floor in a sudden passion; stood up, and leaned over his table, boxing his papers about in a most indecorous manner, very sad to behold in an elderly man like him. Nevertheless, as he was in many ways a most valuable person to me, and all the time before twelve o'clock meridian, was the quickest, steadiest creature, too, accomplishing a great deal of work in a style not easily to be matched—for these reasons, I was willing to overlook his eccentricities, though, indeed, occasionally, I remonstrated with him. I did this very gently, however, because, though the civilest, nay, the blandest and most reverential of men in the morning, yet, in the afternoon, he was disposed, upon provocation, to be slightly rash with his tongue—in fact, insolent. Now, valuing his morning services as I did, and resolved not to lose them—yet, at the same time, made uncomfortable by his inflamed ways after twelve o'clock—and being a man of peace, unwilling by my admonitions to call forth unseemly retorts from him, I took upon me, one Saturday noon (he was always worse on Saturdays) to hint to him, very kindly, that, perhaps, now that he was growing old, it might be well to abridge his labors; in short, he need not come to my chambers after twelve o'clock, but, dinner over, had best go home to his lodgings, and rest himself till tea-time. But no; he insisted upon his afternoon devotions. His countenance became intolerably fervid, as he oratorically assured me—gesticulating with a long ruler at the other end of the room—that if his services in the morning were useful, how indispensable, then, in the afternoon?

"With submission, sir," said Turkey, on this occasion, "I consider myself your right-hand man. In the morning I but marshal and deploy my columns; but in the afternoon I put myself at their head, and gallantly charge the foe, thus"—and he made a violent thrust with the ruler.

"But the blots, Turkey," intimated I.

"True; but, with submission, sir, behold these hairs! I am getting old. Surely, sir, a blot or two of a warm afternoon is not to be severely urged against gray hairs. Old age—even if it blot the page—is honorable. With submission, sir, we *both* are getting old."

This appeal to my fellow-feeling was hardly to be resisted. At all events, I saw that go he would not. So, I made up my mind to let him stay, resolving, nevertheless, to see to it that, during the afternoon, he had to do with my less important papers.

Nippers, the second on my list, was a whiskered, sallow, and upon the whole, rather piratical-looking young man, of about five and twenty. I always deemed him the victim of two evil powers—ambition and indigestion. The ambition was evinced by a certain impatience of the duties of a mere copyist, an unwarrantable usurpation of strictly professional affairs, such as the original drawing up of legal documents. The indigestion seemed betokened in an occasional nervous testiness and grinning irritability, causing the teeth to audibly grind together over mistakes committed in copying; unnecessary maledictions, hissed, rather than spoken, in the heat of business; and especially by a continual discontent with the height of the table where he worked. Though of a very ingenious, mechanical turn, Nippers could never get this table to suit him. He put chips under it, blocks of various sorts, bits of pasteboard, and at last went so far as to attempt an exquisite adjustment, by final pieces of folded blotting-paper. But no invention would answer. If, for the sake of easing his back, he brought the table lid at a sharp angle well up towards his chin, and wrote there like a man using the steep roof of a Dutch house for his desk, then he declared that it stopped the circulation in his arms. If now he lowered the table to his waistbands, and stooped over it in writing, then there was a sore aching in his back. In short, the truth of the matter was, Nippers knew not what he wanted. Or, if he wanted anything, if was to be rid of a scrivener's table altogether. Among the manifestations of his diseased ambition was a fondness he had for receiving visits from certain ambiguous-looking fellows in seedy coats, whom he called his clients. Indeed, I was aware that not only was he, at times, considerable of a ward-politician, but he occasionally did a little business at the Justices' courts, and was not unknown on the steps of the Tombs.[3] I have good reason to believe, however, that one individual who called upon him at my chambers, and who, with a grand air, he insisted was his client, was no other than a dun, and the alleged title-deed, a bill. But, with all his failings, and the annoyances he caused me, Nippers, like his compatriot Turkey, was a very useful man to me; wrote a neat, swift hand; and, when he chose, was not deficient in a gentlemanly sort of deportment. Added to this, he always dressed in a gentlemanly sort of way; and so, incidentally, reflected credit upon my chambers. Whereas, with respect to Turkey, I had much ado to keep him from being a reproach to me. His clothes were apt to look oily, and smell of eating-houses. He wore his pantaloons very loose and baggy in summer. His coats were execrable; his hat not to be handled. But while the hat was a thing of indifference to me, inasmuch as his natural civility and deference, as a dependent Englishman, always led him to doff it the moment he entered the room, yet his coat was another matter. Concerning his coats, I reasoned with him; but with no effect. The truth was, I suppose, that a man with so small an income could not afford to sport such a lustrous face and a lustrous coat at one and the same time. As Nippers once

---

[3] A prison in New York City.

observed, Turkey's money went chiefly for red ink. One winter day, I presented Turkey with a highly respectable-looking coat of my own—a padded gray coat, of a most comfortable warmth, and which buttoned straight up from the knee to the neck. I thought Turkey would appreciate the favor, and abate his rashness and obstreperousness of afternoons. But no; I verily believe that buttoning himself up in so downy and blanket-like a coat had a pernicious effect upon him— upon the same principle that too much oats are bad for horses. In fact, precisely as a rash, restive horse is said to feel his oats, so Turkey felt his coat. It made him insolent. He was a man whom prosperity harmed.

Though, concerning the self-indulgent habits of Turkey, I had my own private surmises, yet, touching Nippers, I was well persuaded that, whatever might be his faults in other respects, he was, at least, a temperate young man. But, indeed, nature herself seemed to have been his vintner, and, at his birth, charged him so thoroughly with an irritable, brandy-like disposition, that all subsequent potations were needless. When I consider how, amid the stillness of my chambers, Nippers would sometimes impatiently rise from his seat, and stopping over his table, spread his arms wide apart, seize the whole desk, and move it, and jerk it, with a grim, grinding motion on the floor, as if the table were a perverse voluntary agent and vexing him, I plainly perceive that, for Nippers, brandy-and-water were altogether superfluous.

It was fortunate for me that, owing to its peculiar cause—indigestion—the irritability and consequent nervousness of Nippers were mainly observable in the morning, while in the afternoon he was comparatively mild. So that, Turkey's paroxysms only coming on about twelve o'clock, I never had to do with their eccentricities at one time. Their fits relieved each other, like guards. When Nippers's was on, Turkey's was off; and *vice versa.* This was a good natural arrangement, under the circumstances.

Ginger Nut, the third on my list, was a lad, some twelve years old. His father was a car-man, ambitious of seeing his son on the bench instead of a cart, before he died. So he sent him to my office, as student at law, errand-boy, cleaner and sweeper, at the rate of one dollar a week. He had a little desk to himself; but he did not use it much. Upon inspection, the drawer exhibited a great array of shells of various sorts of nuts. Indeed, to this quick-witted youth, the whole noble science of the law was contained in a nutshell. Not the least among the employments of Ginger Nut, as well as one which he discharged with the most alacrity, was his duty as cake and apple purveyor for Turkey and Nippers. Copying law-papers being proverbially a dry, husky sort of business, my two scriveners were fain to moisten their mouths very often with Spitzenbergs, [4] to be had at the numerous stalls nigh the Custom House and Post Office. Also, they sent Ginger Nut very frequently for that peculiar cake—small, flat, round, and very spicy—after which he had been named by them. Of a cold morning, when business was but dull, Turkey would gobble up scores of these cakes, as if they were mere wafers—indeed, they sell them at the rate of six or

---

[4] A variety of apple.

eight for a penny—the scrape of his pen blending with the crunching of the crisp particles in his mouth. Rashest of all the fiery afternoon blunders and flurried rashnesses of Turkey, was his once moistening a ginger-cake between his lips, and clapping it on to a mortgage, for a seal. I came within an ace of dismissing him then. But he mollified me by making an oriental bow, and saying—

"With submission, sir, it was generous of me to find you in stationery on my own account."

Now my original business—that of a conveyancer and title hunter, and drawer-up of recondite documents of all sorts—was considerably increased by receiving the master's office. There was now great work for scriveners. Not only must I push the clerks already with me, but I must have additional help.

In answer to my advertisement, a motionless young man one morning stood upon my office threshold, the door being open, for it was summer. I can see that figure now—pallidly neat, pitiably respectable, incurably forlorn! It was Bartleby.

After a few words touching his qualifications, I engaged him, glad to have among my corps of copyists a man of so singularly sedate an aspect, which I thought might operate beneficially upon the flighty temper of Turkey, and the fiery one of Nippers.

I should have stated before that ground glass folding-doors divided my premises into two parts, one of which was occupied by my scriveners, the other by myself. According to my humor, I threw open these doors, or closed them. I resolved to assign Bartleby a corner by the folding-doors, but on my side of them, so as to have this quiet man within easy call, in case any trifling thing was to be done. I placed his desk close up to a small side-window in that part of the room, a window which originally had afforded a lateral view of certain grimy backyards and bricks, but which, owing to subsequent erections, commanded at present no view at all, though it gave some light. Within three feet of the panes was a wall, and the light came down from far above, between two lofty buildings, as from a very small opening in a dome. Still further to a satisfactory arrangement, I procured a high green folding screen, which might entirely isolate Bartleby from my sight, though not remove him from my voice. And thus, in a manner, privacy and society were conjoined.

At first, Bartleby did an extraordinary quantity of writing. As if long famishing for something to copy, he seemed to gorge himself on my documents. There was no pause for digestion. He ran a day and night line, copying by sun-light and by candle-light. I should have been quite delighted with his application, had he been cheerfully industrious. But he wrote on silently, palely, mechanically.

It is, of course, an indispensable part of a scrivener's business to verify the accuracy of his copy, word by word. Where there are two or more scriveners in an office, they assist each other in this examination, one reading from the copy, the other holding the original. It is a very dull, wearisome, and lethargic affair. I can readily imagine that, to some sanguine temperaments, it would be altogether intolerable. For example, I cannot credit that the mettlesome poet, Byron, would have contentedly sat down with Bartleby to examine a law document of, say five hundred pages, closely written in a crimpy hand.

Now and then, in the haste of business, it had been my habit to assist in comparing some brief document myself, calling Turkey or Nippers for this purpose. One object I had, in placing Bartleby so handy to me behind the screen, was to avail myself of his services on such trivial occasions. It was on the third day, I think, of his being with me, and before any necessity had arisen for having his own writing examined, that, being much hurried to complete a small affair I had in hand, I abruptly called to Bartleby. In my haste and natural expectancy of instant compliance, I sat with my head bent over the original on my desk, and my right hand sideways, and somewhat nervously extended with the copy, so that, immediately upon emerging from his retreat, Bartleby might snatch it and proceed to business without the least delay.

In this very attitude did I sit when I called to him, rapidly stating what it was I wanted him to do—namely, to examine a small paper with me. Imagine my surprise, nay, my consternation, when, without moving from his privacy, Bartleby, in a singularly mild, firm voice, replied, "I would prefer not to."

I sat awhile in perfect silence, rallying my stunned faculties. Immediately it occurred to me that my ears had deceived me, or Bartleby had entirely misunderstood my meaning. I repeated my request in the clearest tone I could assume; but in quite as clear a one came the previous reply, "I would prefer not to."

"Prefer not to," echoed I, rising in high excitement, and crossing the room with a stride. "What do you mean? Are you moon-struck? I want you to help me compare this sheet here—take it," and I thrust it towards him.

"I would prefer not to," said he.

I looked at him steadfastly. His face was leanly composed; his gray eye dimly calm. Not a wrinkle of agitation rippled him. Had there been the least uneasiness, anger, impatience, or impertinence in his manner; in other words, had there been any thing ordinarily human about him, doubtless I should have violently dismissed him from the premises. But as it was, I should have as soon thought of turning my pale plaster-of-paris bust of Cicero out of doors. I stood gazing at him awhile, as he went on with his own writing, and then reseated myself at my desk. This is very strange, thought I. What had one best do? But my business hurried me. I concluded to forget the matter for the present, reserving it for my future leisure. So calling Nippers from the other room, the paper was speedily examined.

A few days after this, Bartleby concluded four lengthy documents, being quadruplicates of a week's testimony taken before me in my High Court of Chancery. It became necessary to examine them. It was an important suit, and great accuracy was imperative. Having all things arranged, I called Turkey, Nippers, and Ginger Nut from the next room, meaning to place the four copies in the hands of my four clerks, while I should read from the original. Accordingly, Turkey, Nippers, and Ginger Nut had taken their seats in a row, each with his document in his hand, when I called to Bartleby to join this interesting group.

"Bartleby! quick, I am waiting."

I heard a slow scrape of his chair legs on the uncarpeted floor, and soon he appeared standing at the entrance of his hermitage.

"What is wanted?" said he, mildly.

"The copies, the copies," said I, hurriedly. "We are going to examine them. There—" and I held towards him the fourth quadruplicate.

"I would prefer not to," he said, and gently disappeared behind the screen.

For a few moments I was turned into a pillar of salt, standing at the head of my seated column of clerks. Recovering myself, I advanced towards the screen, and demanded the reason for such extraordinary conduct.

"*Why* do you refuse?"

"I would prefer not to."

With any other man I should have flown outright into a dreadful passion, scorned all further words, and thrust him ignominiously from my presence. But there was something about Bartleby that not only strangely disarmed me, but in a wonderful manner, touched and disconcerted me. I began to reason with him.

"These are your own copies we are about to examine. It is labor saving to you, because one examination will answer for your four papers. It is common usage. Every copyist is bound to help examine his copy. Is it not so? Will you not speak? Answer!"

"I prefer not to," he replied in a flutelike tone. It seemed to me that, while I had been addressing him, he carefully revolved every statement that I made; fully comprehended the meaning; could not gainsay the irresistible conclusion; but, at the same time, some paramount consideration prevailed with him to reply as he did.

"You are decided, then, not to comply with my request—a request made according to common usage and common sense?"

He briefly gave me to understand, that on that point my judgment was sound. Yes: his decision was irreversible.

It is not seldom the case that, when a man is browbeaten in some unprecedented and violently unreasonable way, he begins to stagger in his own plainest faith. He begins, as it were, vaguely to surmise that, wonderful as it may be, all the justice and all the reason is on the other side. Accordingly, if any disinterested persons are present, he turns to them for some reinforcement of his own faltering mind.

"Turkey," said I, "what do you think of this? Am I not right?"

"With submission, sir," said Turkey, in his blandest tone, "I think that you are."

"Nippers," said I, "what do *you* think of it?"

"I think I should kick him out of the office."

(The reader, of nice perceptions, will here perceive that, it being morning, Turkey's answer is couched in polite and tranquil terms, but Nippers replies in ill-tempered ones. Or, to repeat a previous sentence, Nippers's ugly mood was on duty, and Turkey's off.)

"Ginger Nut," said I, willing to enlist the smallest suffrage in my behalf, "what do *you* think of it?"

"I think, sir, he's a little *luny*," replied Ginger Nut, with a grin.

"You hear what they say," said I, turning towards the screen, "come forth and do your duty."

But he vouchsafed no reply. I pondered a moment in sore perplexity. But once more business hurried me. I determined again to postpone the consideration of this dilemma to my future leisure. With a little trouble we made out to examine the papers without Bartleby, though at every page or two Turkey deferentially dropped his opinion, that this proceeding was quite out of the common; while Nippers, twitching in his chair with a dyspeptic nervousness, ground out, between his set teeth, occasional hissing maledictions against the stubborn oaf behind the screen. And for his (Nippers's) part, this was the first and the last time he would do another man's business without pay.

Meanwhile Bartleby sat in his hermitage, oblivious to everything but his own peculiar business there.

Some days passed, the scrivener being employed upon another lengthy work. His late remarkable conduct led me to regard his ways narrowly. I observed that he never went to dinner; indeed, that he never went anywhere. As yet I had never, of my personal knowledge, known him to be outside of my office. He was a perpetual sentry in the corner. At about eleven o'clock though, in the morning, I noticed that Ginger Nut would advance toward the opening in Bartleby's screen, as if silently beckoned thither by a gesture invisible to me where I sat. The boy would then leave the office, jingling a few pence, and reappear with a handful of ginger-nuts, which he delivered in the hermitage, receiving two of the cakes for his trouble.

He lives, then, on ginger-nuts, thought I; never eats a dinner, properly speaking; he must be a vegetarian, then; but no; he never eats even vegetables; he eats nothing but ginger-nuts. My mind then ran on in reveries concerning the probable effects upon the human consitution of living entirely on ginger-nuts. Ginger-nuts are so called, because they contain ginger as one of their peculiar constituents, and the final flavoring one. Now, what was ginger? A hot, spicy thing. Was Bartleby hot and spicy? Not at all. Ginger, then, had no effect upon Bartleby. Probably he preferred it should have none.

Nothing so aggravates an earnest person as a passive resistance. If the individual so resisted be of a not inhumane temper, and the resisting one perfectly harmless in his passivity, then, in the better moods of the former, he will endeavor charitably to construe to his imagination what proves impossible to be solved by his judgement. Even so, for the most part, I regarded Bartleby and his ways. Poor fellow! thought I, he means no mischief; it is plain he intends no insolence; his aspect sufficiently evinces that his eccentricities are involuntary. He is useful to me. I can get along with him. If I turn him away, the chances are he will fall in with some less-indulgent employer, and then he will be rudely treated, and perhaps driven forth miserably to starve. Yes. Here I can cheaply purchase a delicious self-approval. To befriend Bartleby; to humor him in his strange willfulness, will cost me little or nothing, while I lay up in my soul what will eventually prove a sweet morsel for my conscience. But this mood was not invariable with me. The passiveness of Bartleby sometimes irritated me. I felt strangely goaded on to encounter him in new opposition—to elicit some angry spark from him answerable to my own. But, indeed, I might as well have essayed to strike fire with my knuckles against a bit of Windsor soap. But one afternoon the evil impulse in me mastered me, and the following little scene ensued:

"Bartleby," said I, "when those papers are all copied, I will compare them with you."

"I would prefer not to."

"How? Surely you do not mean to persist in that mulish vagary?"

No answer.

I threw open the folding-doors near by, and, turning upon Turkey and Nippers, exclaimed:

"Bartleby a second time says, he won't examine his papers. What do you think of it, Turkey?"

It was afternoon, be it remembered. Turkey sat glowing like a brass boiler; his bald head steaming; his hands reeling among his blotted papers.

"Think of it?" roared Turkey; "I think I'll just step behind his screen, and black his eyes for him!"

So saying, Turkey rose to his feet and threw his arms into a pugilistic position. He was hurrying away to make good his promise, when I detained him, alarmed at the effect of incautiously rousing Turkey's combativeness after dinner.

"Sit down, Turkey," said I, "and hear what Nippers has to say. What do you think of it, Nippers? Would I not be justified in immediately dismissing Bartleby?"

"Excuse me, that is for you to decide, sir. I think his conduct quite unusual, and, indeed, unjust, as regards Turkey and myself. But it may only be a passing whim."

"Ah," exclaimed I, "you have strangely changed your mind, then—you speak very gently of him now."

"All beer," cried Turkey; "gentleness is effects of beer—Nippers and I dined together to-day. You see how gentle *I* am, sir. Shall I go and black his eyes?"

"You refer to Bartleby, I suppose. No, not to-day, Turkey," I replied; "pray, put up your fists."

I closed the doors, and again advanced towards Bartleby. I felt additional incentives tempting me to my fate. I burned to be rebelled against again. I remembered that Bartleby never left the office.

"Bartleby," said I, "Ginger Nut is away; just step around to the Post Office, won't you? (it was but a three minutes' walk), and see if there is anything for me."

"I would prefer not to."

"You *will* not?"

"I *prefer* not."

I staggered to my desk, and sat there in a deep study. My blind inveteracy returned. Was there any other thing in which I could procure myself to be ignominiously repulsed by this lean, penniless wight?—my hired clerk? What added thing is there, perfectly reasonable, that he will be sure to refuse to do? "Bartleby!"

No answer.

"Bartleby," in a louder tone.

No answer.

"Bartleby," I roared.

Like a very ghost, agreeably to the laws of magical invocation, at the third summons, he appeared at the entrance of his hermitage.

"Go to the next room, and tell Nippers to come to me."

"I prefer not to," he respectfully and slowly said and mildly disappeared.

"Very good, Bartleby," said I, in a quiet sort of serenely-severe, self-possessed tone, intimating the unalterable purpose of some terrible retribution very close at hand. At the moment I half intended something of the kind. But upon the whole, as it was drawing towards my dinner-hour, I thought it best to put on my hat and walk home for the day, suffering much from perplexity and distress of mind.

Shall I acknowledge it? The conclusion of this whole business was, that it soon became a fixed fact of my chambers, that a pale young scrivener, by the name of Bartleby, had a desk there; that he copied for me at the usual rate of four cents a folio (one hundred words); but he was permanently exempt from examining the work done by him, that duty being transferred to Turkey and Nippers, out of compliment, doubtless, to their superior acuteness; moreover, said Bartleby was never, on any account, to be dispatched on the most trivial errand of any sort; and that even if entreated to take upon him such a matter, it was generally understood that he would "prefer not to"—in other words, he would refuse point blank.

As days passed on, I became considerably reconciled to Bartleby. His steadiness, his freedom from all dissipation, his incessant industry (except when he chose to throw himself into a standing revery behind his screen), his great stillness, his unalterableness of demeanor under all circumstances, made him a valuable acquisition. One prime thing was this—*he was always there*—first in the morning, continually through the day, and the last at night. I had a singular confidence in his honesty. I felt my most precious papers perfectly safe in his hands. Sometimes, to be sure, I could not, for the very soul of me, avoid falling into sudden spasmodic passions with him. For it was exceeding difficult to bear in mind all the time those strange peculiarities, privileges, and unheard of exemptions, forming the tacit stipulations on Bartleby's part under which he remained in my office. Now and then, in the eagerness of dispatching pressing business, I would inadvertently summon Bartleby, in a short, rapid tone, to put his finger, say, on the incipient tie of a bit of red tape with which I was about compressing some papers. Of course, from behind the screen the usual answer, "I prefer not to," was sure to come; and then, how could a human creature, with the common infirmities of our nature, refrain from bitterly exclaiming upon such perverseness—such unreasonableness. However, every added repulse of this sort which I received only tended to lessen the probability of my repeating the inadvertence.

Here it must be said, that according to the custom of most legal gentlemen occupying chambers in densely-populated law buildings, there were several keys to my door. One was kept by a woman residing in the attic, which person weekly scrubbed and daily swept and dusted my apartments. Another was kept by Turkey for convenience sake. The third I sometimes carried in my own pocket. The fourth I knew not who had.

Now, one Sunday morning I happened to go to Trinity Church, to hear a celebrated preacher, and finding myself rather early on the ground I thought I would walk around to my chambers for a while. Luckily I had my key with me; but upon applying it to the lock, I found it resisted by something inserted from the inside. Quite surprised, I called out; when to my consternation a key was turned from within; and thrusting his lean visage at me, and holding the door ajar, the apparition of Bartleby appeared, in his shirt sleeves, and otherwise in a strangely tattered *déshabillé,* saying quietly that he was sorry, but he was deeply engaged just then, and—preferred not admitting me at present. In a brief word or two, he moreover added, that perhaps I had better walk around the block two or three times, and by that time he would probably have concluded his affairs.

Now, the utterly unsurmised appearance of Bartleby, tenanting my law-chambers of a Sunday morning, with his cadaverously gentlemanly *nonchalance,* yet withal firm and self-possessed, had such a strange effect upon me, that incontinently I slunk away from my own door, and did as desired. But not without sundry twinges of impotent rebellion against the mild effrontery of this unaccountable scrivener. Indeed, it was his wonderful mildness chiefly, which not only disarmed me, but unmanned me as it were. For I consider that one, for the time, is somehow unmanned when he tranquilly permits his hired clerk to dictate to him, and order him away from his own premises. Furthermore, I was full of uneasiness as to what Bartleby could possibly be doing in my office in his shirt sleeves, and in an otherwise dismantled condition of a Sunday morning. Was anything amiss going on? Nay, that was out of the question. It was not to be thought of for a moment that Bartleby was an immoral person. But what could he be doing there?—copying? Nay again, whatever might be his eccentricities, Bartleby was an eminently decorous person. He would be the last man to sit down to his desk in any state approaching to nudity. Besides, it was Sunday; and there was something about Bartleby that forbade the supposition that he would by any secular occupation violate the proprieties of the day.

Nevertheless, my mind was not pacified; and full of a restless curiosity, at last I returned to the door. Without hindrance I inserted my key, opened it, and entered. Bartleby was not to be seen. I looked round anxiously, peeped behind his screen; but it was very plain that he was gone. Upon more closely examining the place, I surmised that for an indefinite period Bartleby must have eaten, dressed, and slept in my office, and that, too, without plate, mirror, or bed. The cushioned seat of a rickety old sofa in one corner bore the faint impress of a lean, reclining form. Rolled away under his desk, I found a blanket; under the empty grate, a blacking box and brush; on a chair, a tin basin, with soap and a ragged towel; in a newspaper a few crumbs of ginger-nuts and a morsel of cheese. Yes, thought I, it is evident enough that Bartleby has been making his home here, keeping bachelor's hall all by himself. Immediately then the thought came sweeping across me, what miserable friendlessness and loneliness are here revealed! His poverty is great; but his solitude, how horrible! Think of it. Of a Sunday, Wall Street is deserted as Petra[5]; and every night of every day it is an emptiness. This building, too, which of week-days hums with industry and life, at nightfall echoes with sheer vacancy, and all through Sunday is forlorn. And here Bartleby makes his home; sole spectator of a solitude which he has seen all populous—a sort of innocent and transformed Marius brooding among the ruins of Carthage![6]

For the first time in my life a feeling of over-powering stinging melancholy seized me. Before, I had never experienced aught but a not unpleasing sadness. The bond of a common humanity now drew me irresistibly to gloom. A fraternal melancholy! for both I and Bartleby were sons of Adam. I remembered the bright silks and sparkling faces I had seen that day, in gala trim, swan-like sailing down the Mississippi of Broadway; and I contrasted them with the pallid copyist, and thought to myself, Ah, happiness courts the light, so we deem the world is gay; but misery hides aloof, so we deem that misery there is none. These sad fancyings—chimeras, doubtless, of a sick and silly brain—led on to other and more special thoughts, concerning the eccentricities of Bartleby. Presentiments of strange discoveries hovered round me. The scrivener's pale form appeared to me laid out, among uncaring strangers, in its shivering winding sheet.

Suddenly I was attracted by Bartleby's closed desk, the key in open sight left in the lock.

I mean no mischief, seek the gratification of no heartless curiosity, thought I; besides, the desk is mine, and its contents, too, so I will make bold to look within. Everything was methodically arranged, the papers smoothly placed. The pigeon holes were deep, and removing the files of documents, I groped into their recesses. Presently I felt something there, and dragged it out. It was an old bandanna handkerchief, heavy and knotted. I opened it, and saw it was a savings bank.

I now recalled all the quiet mysteries which I had noted in the man. I remembered that he never spoke but to answer; that, though at intervals he had

---

[5] A city in Palestine found by explorers in 1812. It had been deserted and lost for centuries.
[6] Caius Marius (155–86 B.C.), a plebeian general who was forced to flee from Rome. Nineteenth-century democratic literature sometimes pictured him old and alone among the ruins of Carthage.

considerable time to himself, yet I had never seen him reading—no, not even a newspaper; that for long periods he would stand looking out, at his pale window behind the screen, upon the dead brick wall; I was quite sure he never visited any refectory or eating house; while his pale face clearly indicated that he never drank beer like Turkey, or tea and coffee even, like other men; that he never went anywhere in particular that I could learn; never went out for a walk, unless, indeed, that was the case at present; that he had declined telling who he was, or whence he came, or whether he had any relatives in the world; that though so thin and pale, he never complained of ill health. And more than all, I remembered a certain unconscious air of pallid—how shall I call it?—of pallid haughtiness, say, or rather an austere reserve about him, which had positively awed me into my tame compliance with his eccentricities, when I had feared to ask him to do the slightest incidental thing for me, even though I might know, from his long-continued motionlessness, that behind his screen he must be standing in one of those dead-wall reveries of his.

Revolving all these things, and coupling them with the recently discovered fact, that he made my office his constant abiding place and home, and not forgetful of his morbid moodiness; revolving all these things, a prudential feeling began to steal over me. My first emotions had been those of pure melancholy and sincerest pity; but just in proportion as the forlornness of Bartleby grew and grew to my imagination, did that same melancholy merge into fear, that pity into repulsion. So true it is, and so terrible, too, that up to a certain point the thought or sight of misery enlists our best affections; but, in certain special cases, beyond that point it does not. They err who would assert that invariably this is owing to the inherent selfishness of the human heart. It rather proceeds from a certain hopelessness of remedying excessive and organic ill. To a sensitive being, pity is not seldom pain. And when at last it is perceived that such pity cannot lead to effectual succor, common sense bids the soul be rid of it. What I saw that morning persuaded me that the scrivener was the victim of innate and incurable disorder. I might give alms to his body; but his body did not pain him; it was his soul that suffered, and his soul I could not reach.

I did not accomplish the purpose of going to Trinity Church that morning. Somehow, the things I had seen disqualified me for the time from churchgoing. I walked homeward, thinking what I would do with Bartleby. Finally, I resolved upon this—I would put certain calm questions to him the next morning, touching his history, etc., and if he declined to answer them openly and unreservedly (and I supposed he would prefer not), then to give him a twenty dollar bill over and above whatever I might owe him, and tell him his services were no longer required; but that if in any other way I could assist him, I would be happy to do so, especially if he desired to return to his native place, wherever that might be, I would willingly help to defray the expenses. Moreover, if, after reaching home, he found himself at any time in want of aid, a letter from him would be sure of a reply.

The next morning came.

"Bartleby," said I, gently calling to him behind his screen.

No reply.

"Bartleby," said I, in a still gentler tone, "come here; I am not going to ask you to do anything you would prefer not to do—I simply wish to speak to you."

Upon this he noiselessly slid into view.

"Will you tell me, Bartleby, where you were born?"

"I would prefer not to."

"Will you tell me *anything* about yourself?"

"I would prefer not to."

"But what reasonable objection can you have to speak to me? I feel friendly towards you."

He did not look at me while I spoke, but kept his glance fixed upon my bust of Cicero, which, as I then sat, was directly behind me, some six inches above my head.

"What is your answer, Bartleby," said I, after waiting a considerable time for a reply, during which his countenance remained immovable, only there was the faintest conceivable tremor of the white attenuated mouth.

"At present I prefer to give no answer," he said, and retired into his hermitage.

It was rather weak in me I confess, but his manner, on this occasion, nettled me. Not only did there seem to lurk in it a certain calm disdain, but his perverseness seemed ungrateful, considering the undeniable good usage and indulgence he had received from me.

Again I sat ruminating what I should do. Mortified as I was at his behavior, and resolved as I had been to dismiss him when I entered my office, nevertheless I strangely felt something superstitious knocking at my heart, and forbidding me to carry out my purpose, and denouncing me for a villain if I dared to breathe one bitter word against this forlornest of mankind. At last, familiarly drawing my chair behind his screen, I sat down and said: "Bartleby, never mind, then, about revealing your history; but let me entreat you, as a friend, to comply as far as may be with the usages of this office. Say now, you will help to examine papers to-morrow or next day: in short, say now, that in a day or two you will begin to be a little reasonable:—say so, Bartleby."

"At present I would prefer not to be a little reasonable," was his mildly cadaverous reply.

Just then the folding-doors opened, and Nippers approached. He seemed suffering from an unusually bad night's rest, induced by severer indigestion than common. He overheard those final words of Bartleby.

"*Prefer not*, eh?" gritted Nippers—"I'd *prefer* him, if I were you, sir," addressing me—"I'd *prefer* him; I'd give him preferences, the stubborn mule! What is it, sir, pray, that he *prefers* not to do now?"

Bartleby moved not a limb.

"Mr. Nippers," said I, "I'd prefer that you would withdraw for the present."

Somehow, of late, I had got into the way of involuntarily using this word "prefer" upon all sorts of not exactly suitable occasions. And I trembled to think that my contact with the scrivener had already and seriously affected me in a mental way. And what further and deeper aberration might it not yet produce? This apprehension had not been without efficacy in determining me to summary measures.

As Nippers, looking very sour and sulky, was departing, Turkey blandly and deferentially approached.

"With submission, sir," said he, "yesterday I was thinking about Bartleby here, and I think that if he would but prefer to take a quart of good ale every day, it would do much towards mending him, and enabling him to assist in examining his papers."

"So you have got the word, too," said I, slightly excited.

"With submission, what word, sir," asked Turkey, respectfully crowding himself into the contracted space behind the screen, and by so doing, making me jostle the scrivener. "What word, sir?"

"I would prefer to be left alone here," said Bartleby, as if offended at being mobbed in his privacy.

"That's the word, Turkey," said I—*"that's* it."

"Oh, *prefer?* oh yes—queer word. I never use it myself. But, sir, as I was saying, if he would but prefer—"

"Turkey," interrupted I, "you will please withdraw."

"Oh certainly, sir, if you prefer that I should."

As he opened the folding-door to retire, Nippers at his desk caught a glimpse of me, and asked whether I would prefer to have a certain paper copied on blue paper or white. He did not in the least roguishly accent the word prefer. It was plain that it involuntarily rolled from his tongue. I thought to myself, surely I must get rid of a demented man, who already has in some degree turned the tongues, if not the heads of myself and clerks. But I thought it prudent not to break the dismission at once.

The next day I noticed that Bartleby did nothing but stand at his window in his dead-wall revery. Upon asking him why he did not write, he said that he had decided upon doing no more writing."

"Why, how now? What next?" exclaimed I, "do no more writing?"

"No more."

"And what is the reason?"

"Do you not see the reason for yourself," he indifferently replied.

I looked steadfastly at him, and perceived that his eyes looked dull and glazed. Instantly it occurred to me, that his unexampled diligence in copying by his dim window for the first few weeks of his stay with me might have temporarily impaired his vision.

I was touched. I said something in condolence with him. I hinted that of course he did wisely in abstaining from writing for a while; and urged him to embrace that opportunity of taking wholesome exercise in the open air. This, however, he did not do. A few days after this, my other clerks being absent, and being in a great hurry to dispatch certain letters by the mail, I thought that, having nothing else earthly to do, Bartleby would surely be less inflexible than usual, and carry these letters to the post-office. But he blankly declined. So, much to my inconvenience, I went myself.

Still added days went by. Whether Bartleby's eyes improved or not, I could not say. To all appearance I thought they did. But when I asked him if they did, he vouchsafed no answer. At all events, he would do no copying. At last, in reply to my urgings, he informed me that he had permanently given up copying.

"What!" exclaimed I; "suppose your eyes should get entirely well—better than ever before—would you not copy then?"

"I have given up copying," he answered, and slid aside.

He remained as ever, a fixture in my chamber. Nay—if that were possible—he became still more of a fixture than before. What was to be done? He would do nothing in the office; why should he stay there? In plain fact, he had now become a millstone to me, not only useless as a necklace, but afflictive to bear. Yet I was sorry for him. I speak less than truth when I say that, on his own account, he occasioned me uneasiness. If he would but have named a single relative or friend, I would instantly have written, and urged their taking the poor fellow away to some convenient retreat. But he seemed alone, absolutely alone in the universe. A bit of wreck in the mid Atlantic. At length, necessities connected with my business tyrannized over all other considerations. Decently as I could, I told Bartleby that in six days time he must unconditionally leave the office. I warned him to take measures, in the interval, for procuring some other abode. I offered to assist him in his endeavor, if he himself would but take the first step towards a removal. "And when you finally quit me, Bartleby," added I, "I shall see that you go not away entirely unprovided. Six days from this hour, remember."

At the expiration of that period, I peeped behind the screen, and lo! Bartleby was there.

I buttoned up my coat, balanced myself; advanced slowly towards him, touched his shoulder, and said, "The time has come; you must quit this place; I am sorry for you; here is money; but you must go."

"I would prefer not" he replied, with his back still towards me.

"You *must*."

He remained silent.

Now I had an unbounded confidence in this man's common honesty. He had frequently restored to me sixpences and shillings carelessly dropped upon the floor, for I am apt to be very reckless in such shirt-button affairs. The proceeding, then, which followed will not be deemed extraordinary.

"Bartleby," said I, "I owe you twelve dollars on account; here are thirty-two; the odd twenty are yours—Will you take it?" and I handed the bills towards him.

But he made no motion.

"I will leave them here, then," putting them under a weight on the table. Then taking my hat and cane and going to the door, I tranquilly turned and added—"After you have removed your things from these offices, Bartleby, you will of course lock the door—since every one is now gone for the day but you—and if you please, slip your key underneath the mat, so that I may have it in the morning. I shall not see you again; so good-by to you. If, hereafter, in your new place of abode, I can be of any service to you, do not fail to advise me by letter. Good-by, Bartleby, and fare you well.

But he answered not a word; like the last column of some ruined temple, he remained standing mute and solitary in the middle of the otherwise deserted room.

As I walked home in a pensive mood, my vanity got the better of my pity. I could not but highly plume myself on my masterly management in getting rid of Bartleby. Masterly I call it, and such it must appear to any dispassionate thinker. The beauty of my procedure seemed to consist in its perfect quietness. There was no vulgar bullying, no bravado of any sort, no choleric hectoring, and striding to and fro across the apartment, jerking out vehement commands for Bartleby to bundle himself off with his beggarly traps. Nothing of the kind. Without loudly bidding Bartleby depart—as an inferior genius might have done—I *assumed* the ground that depart he must; and upon that assumption built all I had to say. The more I thought over my procedure, the more I was charmed with it. Nevertheless, next morning, upon awakening, I had my doubts—I had somehow slept off the fumes of vanity. One of the coolest and wisest hours a man has, is just after he awakes in the morning. My procedure seemed as sagacious as ever—but only in theory. How it would prove in practice—there was the rub. It was truly a beautiful thought to have assumed Bartleby's departure; but, after all, that assumption was simply my own, and none of Bartleby's. The great point was, not whether I had assumed that he would quit me, but whether he would prefer so to do. He was more a man of preferences than assumptions.

After breakfast, I walked down town, arguing the probabilities *pro* and *con*. One moment I thought it would prove a miserable failure, and Bartleby would be found all alive at my office as usual; the next moment it seemed certain that I should find his chair empty. And so I kept veering about. At the corner of Broadway and Canal Street, I saw quite an excited group of people standing in earnest conversation.

"I'll take odds he doesn't," said a voice as I passed.

"Doesn't go?—done!" said I; "put up your money."

I was instinctively putting my hand in my pocket to produce my own, when I remembered that this was an election day. The words I had overheard bore no reference to Bartleby, but to the success or non-success of some candidate for the mayoralty. In my intent frame of mind, I had, as it were, imagined that all Broadway shared in my excitement, and were debating the same question with me. I passed on, very thankful that the uproar of the street screened my momentary absent-mindedness.

As I had intended, I was earlier than usual at my office door. I stood listening for a moment. All was still. He must be gone. I tried the knob. The door was locked. Yes, my procedure had worked to a charm; he indeed must be vanished. Yet a certain melancholy mixed with this: I was almost sorry for my brilliant success. I was fumbling under the door mat for the key, which Bartleby was to have left there for me, when accidentally my knee knocked against a panel, producing a summoning sound, and in response a voice came to me from within—"Not yet; I am occupied."

It was Bartleby.

I was thunderstruck. For an instant I stood like the man who, pipe in mouth, was killed one cloudless afternoon long ago in Virginia, by summer lightning; at his own warm open window he was killed, and remained leaning out there upon the dreamy afternoon, till some one touched him, when he fell.

"Not gone!" I murmured at last. But again obeying that wondrous ascendancy which the inscrutable scrivener had over me, and from which ascendancy, for all my chafing, I could not completely escape, I slowly went down stairs and out into the street, and while walking round the block, considered what I should next do in this unheard-of perplexity. Turn the man out by an actual thrusting I could not; to drive him away by calling him hard names would not do; calling in the police was an unpleasant idea; and yet, permit him to enjoy his cadaverous triumph over me—this, too, I could not think of. What was to be done? or, if nothing could be done, was there anything further that I could *assume* in the matter? Yes, as before I had prospectively assumed that Bartleby would depart, so now I might retrospectively assume that departed he was. In the legitimate carrying out of this assumption, I might enter my office in a great hurry, and pretending not to see Bartleby at all, walk straight against him as if he were air. Such a proceeding would in a singular degree have the appearance of a home-thrust. It was hardly possible that Bartleby could withstand such an application of the doctrine of assumptions. But upon second thoughts the success of the plan seemed rather dubious. I resolved to argue the matter over with him again.

"Bartleby," said I, entering the office, with a quietly severe expression, "I am seriously displeased. I am pained, Bartleby. I had thought better of you. I had imagined you of such a gentlemanly organization, that in any delicate dilemma a slight hint would suffice—in short, an assumption. But it appears I am deceived. Why," I added, unaffectedly starting, "you have not even touched that money yet," pointing to it, just where I had left it the evening previous.

He answered nothing.

"Will you, or will you not, quit me?" I now demanded in a sudden passion, advancing close to him.

"I would prefer *not* to quit you," he replied, gently emphasizing the *not*.

"What earthly right have you to stay here? Do you pay any rent? Do you pay my taxes? Or is this property yours?"

He answered nothing.

"Are you ready to go on and write now? Are your eyes recovered? Could you copy a small paper for me this morning? or help examine a few lines? or step round to the post-office? In a word, will you do anything at all, to give a coloring to your refusal to depart the premises?"

He silently retired into his hermitage.

I was now in such a state of nervous resentment that I thought it but prudent to check myself at present from further demonstrations. Bartleby and I were alone. I remembered the tragedy of the unfortunate Adams and the still more unfortunate Colt in the solitary office of the latter; and how poor Colt, being dreadfully incensed by Adams, and imprudently permitting himself to get wildly excited, was at unawares hurried into his fatal act—an act which certainly no man could possibly deplore more than the actor himself.[7] Often it had occurred to me in my ponderings upon the subject, that had that altercation taken place in the public street, or at a private residence, it would not have terminated as it did. It was the circumstance of being alone in a solitary office, up stairs, of a building entirely unhallowed by humanizing domestic associations—an un-carpeted office, doubtless, of a dusty, haggard sort of appearance—this it must have been, which greatly helped to enhance the irritable desperation of the hapless Colt.

But when this old Adam of resentment rose in me and tempted me concerning Bartleby, I grappled him and threw him. How? Why, simply by recalling the divine injunction: "A new commandment give I unto you, that ye love one another." Yes, this it was that saved me. Aside from higher considerations, charity often operates as a vastly wise and prudent principle—a great safeguard to its possessor. Men have committed murder for jealousy's sake, and anger's sake, and hatred's sake, and selfishness' sake, and spiritual pride's sake; but no man that ever I heard of, ever committed a diabolical murder for sweet charity's sake. Mere self-interest, then, if no better motive can be enlisted, should, es-pecially with high-tempered men, prompt all beings to charity and philanthropy. At any rate, upon the occasion in question, I strove to drown my exasperated feelings towards the scrivener by benevolently construing his conduct. Poor fellow, poor fellow! thought I, he don't mean anything; and besides, he has seen hard times, and ought to be indulged.

I endeavored, also, immediately to occupy myself, and at the same time to comfort my despondency. I tried to fancy, that in the course of the morning, at such time as might prove agreeable to him, Bartleby, of his own free accord, would emerge from his hermitage and take up some decided line of march in the direction of the door. But no. Half-past twelve o'clock came; Turkey began to glow in the face, overturn his inkstand, and become generally obstreperous; Nippers abated down into quietude and courtesy; Ginger Nut munched his noon apple; and Bartleby remained standing at his window in one of his pro-foundest dead-wall reveries. Will it be credited? Ought I to acknowledge it? That afternoon I left the office without saying one further word to him.

Some days now passed, during which, at leisure intervals I looked a little into "Edwards on the Will," and "Priestley on Necessity."[8] Under the circumstances, those books induced a salutary feeling. Gradually I slid into the persuasion that these troubles of mine, touching the scrivener, had been all predestinated from eternity, and Bartleby was billeted upon me for some mysterious purpose of an all-wise Providence, which it was not for a mere mortal like me to fathom. Yes, Bartleby, stay there behind your screen, thought I; I shall persecute you no more; you are harmless and noiseless as any of these old chairs; in short, I never feel so private as when I know you are here. At last I see it, I feel it; I penetrate

---

[7] A sensational homicide case in which Colt murdered Adams in a fit of passion.

[8] Jonathan Edwards (1703–1758), American theologian, and Joseph Priestley (1733–1804), Eng-lish clergyman and chemist, both held that man's life was predetermined.

to the predestinated purpose of my life. I am content. Others may have loftier parts to enact; but my mission in this world, Bartleby, is to furnish you with office-room for such period as you may see fit to remain.

I believe that this wise and blessed frame of mind would have continued with me, had it not been for the unsolicited and uncharitable remarks obtruded upon me by my professional friends who visited the rooms. But thus it often is, that the constant friction of illiberal minds wears out at last the best resolves of the more generous. Though to be sure, when I reflected upon it, it was not strange that people entering my office should be struck by the peculiar aspect of the unaccountable Bartleby, and so be tempted to throw out some sinister observations concerning him. Sometimes an attorney, having business with me, and calling at my office, and finding no one but the scrivener there, would undertake to obtain some sort of precise information from him touching my whereabouts; but without heeding his idle talk, Bartleby would remain standing immovable in the middle of the room. So after contemplating him in that position for a time, the attorney would depart, no wiser than he came.

Also, when a reference was going on, and the room full of lawyers and witnesses, and business driving fast, some deeply-occupied legal gentleman present, seeing Bartleby wholly unemployed, would request him to run round to his (the legal gentleman's) office and fetch some papers for him. Thereupon, Bartleby would tranquilly decline, and yet remain idle as before. Then the lawyer would give a great stare, and turn to me. And what could I say? At last I was made aware that all through the circle of my professional acquaintance, a whisper of wonder was running round, having reference to the strange creature I kept at my office. This worried me very much. And as the idea came upon me of his possibly turning out a long-lived man, and keep occupying my chambers, and denying my authority; and perplexing my visitors; and scandalizing my professional reputation; and casting a general gloom over the premises; keeping soul and body together to the last upon his savings (for doubtless he spent but half a dime a day), and in the end perhaps outlive me, and claim possession of my office by right of his perpetual occupancy: as all these dark anticipations crowded upon me more and more, and my friends continually intruded their relentless remarks upon the apparition in my room; a great change was wrought in me. I resolved to gather all my faculties together, and forever rid me of this intolerable incubus.

Ere revolving any complicated project, however, adapted to this end, I first simply suggested to Bartleby the propriety of his permanent departure. In a calm and serious tone, I commended the idea to his careful and mature consideration. But, having taken three days to meditate upon it, he apprised me, that his original determination remained the same; in short, that he still preferred to abide with me.

What shall I do? I now said to myself, buttoning up my coat to the last button. What shall I do? what ought I to do? what does conscience say I *should* do with this man, or, rather, ghost. Rid myself of him, I must; go, he shall. But how? You will not thrust him, the poor, pale, passive mortal—you will not thrust such a helpless creature out of your door? you will not dishonor yourself by such cruelty? No, I will not, I cannot do that. Rather would I let him live and die here, and then mason up his remains in the wall. What, then, will you do? For all your coaxing, he will not budge. Bribes he leaves under your own paper-weight on your table; in short, it is quite plain that he prefers to cling to you.

Then something severe, something unusual must be done, What! surely you will not have him collared by a constable, and commit his innocent pallor to the common jail? And upon what ground could you procure such a thing to be done?—a vagrant, is he? What! he a vagrant, a wanderer, who refuses to budge? It is because he will *not* be a vagrant, then, that you seek to count him *as a* vagrant. This is too absurd. No visible means of support: there I have him. Wrong again: for indubitably he *does* support himself, and that is the only unanswerable proof that any man can show of his possessing the means so to do. No more, then. Since he will not quit me, I must quit him. I will change my offices; I will move elsewhere, and give him fair notice, that if I find him on my new premises I will then proceed against him as a common trespasser.

Acting accordingly, next day I thus addressed him: "I find these chambers too far from the City Hall; the air is unwholesome. In a word, I propose to remove my offices next week, and shall no longer require your services. I tell you this now, in order that you may seek another place."

He made no reply; and nothing more was said.

On the appointed day I engaged carts and men, proceeded to my chambers, and, having but little furniture, everything was removed in a few hours. Throughout, the scrivener remained standing behind the screen, which I directed to be removed the last thing. It was withdrawn; and, being folded up like a huge folio, left him the motionless occupant of a naked room. I stood in the entry watching him a moment, while something from within me upbraided me.

I re-entered, with my hand in my pocket—and—and my heart in my mouth.

"Good-by, Bartleby; I am going—good-by, and God some way bless you; and take that," slipping something in his hand. But it dropped upon the floor, and then—strange to say—I tore myself from him whom I had so longed to be rid of.

Established in my new quarters, for a day or two I kept the door locked, and started at every footfall in the passages. When I returned to my rooms, after any little absence, I would pause at the threshold for an instant, and attentively listen, ere applying my key. But these fears were needless. Bartleby never came nigh me.

I thought all was going well, when a perturbed-looking stranger visited me, inquiring whether I was the person who had recently occupied rooms at No. —— Wall Street.

Full of forebodings, I replied that I was.

"Then, sir," said the stranger, who proved a lawyer, "you are responsible for the man you left there. He refuses to do any copying; he refuses to do anything; he says he prefers not to; and he refuses to quit the premises."

"I am very sorry, sir," said I, with assumed tranquillity, but an inward tremor, "but, really, the man you allude to is nothing to me—he is no relation or apprentice of mine, that you should hold me responsible for him."

"In mercy's name, who is he?"

"I certainly cannot inform you. I know nothing about him. Formerly I employed him as a copyist; but he has done nothing for me now for some time past."

"I shall settle him, then—good morning, sir."

Several days passed, and I heard nothing more; and, though I often felt a charitable prompting to call at the place and see poor Bartleby, yet a certain squeamishness, of I know not what, withheld me.

All is over with him, by this time, thought I, at last, when, through another week, no further intelligence reached me. But, coming to my room the day after, I found several persons waiting at my door in a high state of nervous excitement.

"That's the man—here he comes," cried the foremost one, whom I recognized as the lawyer who had previously called upon me alone.

"You must take him away, sir, at once," cried a portly person among them, advancing upon me, and whom I knew to be the landlord of No. —— Wall Street. "These gentlemen, my tenants, cannot stand it any longer; Mr. B—," pointing to the lawyer, "has turned him out of his room, and he now persists in haunting the building generally, sitting upon the banisters of the stairs by day, and sleeping in the entry by night. Everybody is concerned; clients are leaving the offices; some fears are entertained of a mob; something you must do, and that without delay."

Aghast at this torrent, I fell back before it, and would fain have locked myself in my new quarters. In vain I persisted that Bartleby was nothing to me—no more than to any one else. In vain—I was the last person known to have anything to do with him, and they held me to the terrible account. Fearful, then, of being exposed in the papers (as one person present obscurely threatened), I considered the matter, and, at length, said, that if the lawyer would give me a confidential interview with the scrivener, in his (the lawyer's) own room, I would, that afternoon, strive my best to rid them of the nuisance they complained of.

Going up stairs to my old haunt, there was Bartleby silently sitting upon the banister at the landing.

"What are you doing here, Bartleby?" said I.

"Sitting upon the banister," he mildly replied.

I motioned him into the lawyer's room, who then left us.

"Bartleby," said I, "are you aware that you are the cause of great tribulation to me, by persisting in occupying the entry after being dismissed from the office?"

No answer.

"Now one of two things must take place. Either you must do something, or something must be done to you. Now what sort of business would you like to engage in? Would you like to re-engage in copying for some one?"

"No; I would prefer not to make any change."

"Would you like a clerkship in a dry-goods store?"

"There is too much confinement about that. No, I would not like a clerkship; but I am not particular."

"Too much confinement," I cried, "why you keep yourself confined all the time!"

"I would prefer not to take a clerkship," he rejoined, as if to settle that little item at once.

"How would a bar-tender's business suit you? There is no trying of the eyesight in that."

"I would not like it at all; though, as I said before, I am not particular."

His unwonted wordiness inspirited me. I returned to the charge.

"Well, then, would you like to travel through the country collecting bills for the merchants? That would improve your health."

"No, I would prefer to be doing something else."

"How, then, would going as a companion to Europe, to entertain some young gentleman with your conversation—how would that suit you?"

"Not at all. It does not strike me that there is anything definite about that. I like to be stationary. But I am not particular."

"Stationary you shall be, then," I cried, now losing all patience, and, for the first time in all my exasperating connection with him, fairly flying into a passion. "If you do not go away from these premises before night, I shall feel bound— indeed, I *am* bound—to—to—to quit the premises myself!" I rather absurdly concluded, knowing not with what possible threat to try to frighten his immobility into compliance. Despairing of all further efforts, I was precipitately leaving him, when a final thought occurred to me—one which had not been wholly unindulged before.

"Bartleby," said I, in the kindest tone I could assume under such exciting circumstances, "will you go home with me now—not to my office, but my dwelling—and remain there till we can conclude upon some convenient arrangement for you at our leisure? Come, let us start now, right away."

"No: at present I would prefer not to make any change at all."

I answered nothing; but, effectually dodging every one by the suddenness and rapidity of my flight, rushed from the building, ran up Wall Street towards Broadway, and, jumping into the first omnibus, was soon removed from pursuit. As soon as tranquillity returned, I distinctly perceived that I had now done all that I possibly could, both in respect to the demands of the landlord and his tenants, and with regard to my own desire and sense of duty, to benefit Bartleby, and shield him from rude persecution. I now strove to be entirely care-free and quiescent; and my conscience justified me in the attempt; though, indeed, it was not so successful as I could have wished. So fearful was I of being again hunted out by the incensed landlord and his exasperated tenants, that, surrendering my business to Nippers, for a few days, I drove about the upper part of the town and through the suburbs, in my rockaway; crossed over to Jersey City and Hoboken, and paid fugitive visits to Manhattanville and Astoria. In fact, I almost lived in my rockaway for the time.

When again I entered my office, lo, a note from the landlord lay upon the desk. I opened it with trembling hands. It informed me that the writer had sent to the police, and had Bartleby removed to the Tombs as a vagrant. Moreover, since I knew more about him than any one else, he wished me to appear at that place, and make a suitable statement of the facts. These tidings had a conflicting effect upon me. At first I was indignant; but, at last, almost approved. The landlord's energetic, summary disposition, had led him to adopt a procedure which I do not think I would have decided upon myself; and yet, as a last resort, under such peculiar circumstances, it seemed the only plan.

As I afterwards learned, the poor scrivener, when told that he must be conducted to the Tombs, offered not the slightest obstacle, but, in his pale, unmoving way, silently acquiesced.

Some of the compassionate and curious bystanders joined the party; and headed by one of the constables arm in arm with Bartleby, the silent procession filed its way through all the noise, and heat, and joy of the roaring thoroughfares at noon.

The same day I received the note, I went to the Tombs, or, to speak more properly, the Halls of Justice. Seeking the right officer, I stated the purpose of my call, and was informed that the individual I described was, indeed, within. I then assured the functionary that Bartleby was a perfectly honest man, and greatly to be compassionated, however unaccountably eccentric. I narrated all I knew, and closed by suggesting the idea of letting him remain in as indulgent confinement as possible, till something less harsh might be done—though, indeed, I hardly knew what. At all events, if nothing else could be decided upon, the alms-house must receive him. I then begged to have an interview.

Being under no disgraceful charge, and quite serene and harmless in all his ways, they had permitted him freely to wander about the prison, and, especially, in the inclosed grass-platted yards thereof. And so I found him there, standing all alone in the quietest of the yards, his face towards a high wall, while all around, from the narrow slits of the jail windows, I thought I saw peering out upon him the eyes of murderers and thieves.

"Bartleby!"

"I know you," he said, without looking round—"and I want nothing to say to you."

"It was not I that brought you here, Bartleby," said I, keenly pained at his implied suspicion. "And to you, this should not be so vile a place. Nothing reproachful attaches to you by being here. And see, it is not so sad a place as one might think. Look, there is the sky, and here is the grass."

"I know where I am," he replied, but would say nothing more, and so I left him.

As I entered the corridor again, a broad meat-like man, in an apron, accosted me, and, jerking his thumb over his shoulder, said—"Is that your friend?"

"Yes."

"Does he want to starve? If he does, let him live on the prison fare, that's all."

"Who are you?" asked I, not knowing what to make of such an unofficially speaking person in such a place.

"I am the grub-man. Such gentlemen as have friends here, hire me to provide them with something good to eat."

"Is this so?" said I, turning to the turnkey.

He said it was.

"Well, then," said I, slipping some silver into the grub-man's hands (for so they called him), "I want you to give particular attention to my friend there; let him have the best dinner you can get. And you must be as polite to him as possible."

"Introduce me, will you?" said the grub-man, looking at me with an expression which seemed to say he was all impatience for an opportunity to give a specimen of his breeding.

Thinking it would prove of benefit to the scrivener, I acquiesced; and, asking the grub-man his name, went up with him to Bartleby.

"Bartleby, this is a friend; you will find him very useful to you."

"Your sarvant, sir, your sarvant," said the grub-man, making a low salutation behind his apron. "Hope you find it pleasant here, sir; nice grounds—cool apartments—hope you'll stay with us sometime—try to make it agreeable. What will you have for dinner to-day?"

"I prefer not to dine to-day," said Bartleby, turning away. "It would disagree with me; I am unused to dinners." So saying, he slowly moved to the other side of the inclosure, and took up a position fronting the dead-wall.

"How's this?" said the grub-man, addressing me with a stare of astonishment. "He's odd, ain't he?"

"I think he is a little deranged," said I, sadly.

"Deranged? deranged is it? Well, now, upon my word, I thought that friend of yourn was a gentleman forger; they are always pale and genteel-like, them forgers. I can't help pity 'em—can't help it, sir. Did you know Monroe Edwards?" he added, touchingly, and paused. Then, laying his hand piteously on my shoulder, sighed, "he died of consumption at Sing-Sing.[9] So you weren't acquainted with Monroe?"

"No, I was never socially acquainted with any forgers. But I cannot stop longer. Look to my friend yonder. You will not lose by it. I will see you again."

Some few days after this, I again obtained admission to the Tombs, and went through the corridors in quest of Bartleby; but without finding him.

"I saw him coming from his cell not long ago," said a turnkey, "may be he's gone to loiter in the yards."

So I went in that direction.

"Are you looking for the silent man?" said another turnkey, passing me. "Yonder he lies—sleeping in the yard there. 'Tis not twenty minutes since I saw him lie down."

The yard was entirely quiet. It was not accessible to the common prisoners.

---

[9] The state prison near Ossining, New York.

The surrounding walls of amazing thickness, kept off all sounds behind them. The Egyptian character of the masonry weighed upon me with its gloom. But a soft imprisoned turf grew under foot. The heart of the eternal pyramids, it seemed, wherein, by some strange magic, through the clefts, grass-seed, dropped by birds, had sprung.

Strangely huddled at the base of the wall, his knees drawn up, and lying on his side, his head touching the cold stones, I saw the wasted Bartleby. But nothing stirred. I paused; then went close up to him; stooped over, and saw that his dim eyes were open; otherwise he seemed profoundly sleeping. Something prompted me to touch him. I felt his hand, when a tingling shiver ran up my arm and down my spine to my feet.

The round face of the grub-man peered upon me now. "His dinner is ready. Won't he dine to-day, either? Or does he live without dining?"

"Lives without dining," said I, and closed the eyes.

"Eh!—He's asleep, ain't he?"

"With kings and counselors," murmured I.

There would seem little need for proceeding further in this history. Imagination will readily supply the meagre recital of poor Bartleby's interment. But, ere parting with the reader, let me say, that if this little narrative has sufficiently interested him, to awaken curiosity as to who Bartleby was, and what manner of life he led prior to the present narrator's making his acquaintance, I can only reply, that in such curiosity I fully share, but am wholly unable to gratify it. Yet here I hardly know whether I should divulge one little item of rumor, which came to my ear a few months after the scrivener's decease. Upon what basis it rested, I could never ascertain; and hence, how true it is I cannot now tell. But, inasmuch as this vague report has not been without a certain suggestive interest to me, however said, it may prove the same with some others; and so I will briefly mention it. The report was this: that Bartleby had been a subordinate clerk in the Dead Letter Office at Washington, from which he had been suddenly removed by a change in the administration. When I think over this rumor, hardly can I express the emotions which seize me. Dead letters! does it not sound like dead men? Conceive a man by nature and misfortune prone to a pallid hopelessness, can any business seem more fitted to heighten it than that of continually handling these dead letters, and assorting them for the flames? For by the cart-load they are annually burned. Some times from out the folded paper the pale clerk takes a ring—the finger it was meant for, perhaps, moulders in the grave; a bank-note sent in swiftest charity—he whom it would relieve, nor eats nor hungers any more; pardon for those who died despairing; hope for those who died unhoping; good tidings for those who died stifled by unrelieved calamities. On errands of life, these letters speed to death.

Ah, Bartleby! Ah, humanity!

QUESTIONS

1. What is it about Bartleby that so intrigues and fascinates the narrator? Why does the narrator continue to feel a moral obligation to an employee who refuses to work and curtly rejects kindly offers of help?   **2.** With his final utterance, "Ah, Bartleby! Ah, humanity!" the narrator apparently penetrates the mystery of Bartleby. The comments seem to suggest that for the narrator Bartleby is a representative of humanity. In what sense might the narrator come to see Bartleby in this light?   **3.** What functions do Turkey and Nippers serve?   **4.** Would it be fair to describe Bartleby as a rebel without a cause, as a young man who refuses to participate in a comfortable and well-ordered business world but fails to offer any alternative way of life? Justify your answer.

WRITING TOPICS

1. Readers differ as to whether this is the story of Bartleby or the story of the lawyer-narrator. What is your view?   **2.** Why does Melville allow the narrator (and the reader) to discover so little about Bartleby and the causes of his behavior? All we learn of Bartleby's past is contained in the next-to-last paragraph. What, if anything, in this paragraph establishes a link between Bartleby and the narrator?

War *

LUIGI PIRANDELLO [1867–1936]   1918

The passengers who had left Rome by the night express had had to stop until dawn at the small station of Fabriano in order to continue their journey by the small old-fashioned "local" joining the main line with Sulmona.

At dawn, in a stuffy and smoky second-class carriage in which five people had already spent the night, a bulky woman in deep mourning, was hoisted in—almost like a shapeless bundle. Behind her—puffing and moaning, followed her husband—a tiny man, thin and weakly, his face death-white, his eyes small and bright and looking shy and uneasy.

Having at last taken a seat he politely thanked the passengers who had helped his wife and who had made room for her; then he turned round to the woman trying to pull down the collar of her coat and politely enquired:

"Are you all right, dear?"

The wife, instead of answering, pulled up her collar again to her eyes, so as to hide her face.

"Nasty world," muttered the husband with a sad smile.

And he felt it his duty to explain to his travelling companions that the poor woman was to be pitied for the war was taking away from her her only son, a boy of twenty to whom both had devoted their entire life, even breaking up their home at Sulmona to follow him to Rome where he had to go as a student, then allowing him to volunteer for war with an assurance, however, that at least for six months he would not be sent to the front and now, all of a sudden, receiving a wire saying that he was due to leave in three days' time and asking them to go and see him off.

The woman under the big coat was twisting and wriggling, at times growling like a wild animal, feeling certain that all those explanations would not have aroused even a shadow of sympathy from those people who—most likely—were in the same plight as herself. One of them, who had been listening with particular attention, said:

"You should thank God that your son is only leaving now for the front. Mine has been sent there the first day of the war. He has already come back twice wounded and been sent back again to the front."

"What about me? I have two sons and three nephews at the front," said another passenger.

"Maybe, but in our case it is our *only* son," ventured the husband.

"What difference can it make? You may spoil your only son with excessive attentions, but you cannot love him more than you would all your other children if you had any. Paternal love is not like bread that can be broken into

* Translated by Michele Pettinati.

413

pieces and split amongst the children in equal shares. A father gives *all* his love to each one of his children without discrimination, whether it be one or ten, and if I am suffering now for my two sons, I am not suffering half for each of them but double. . . ."

"True . . . true . . ." sighed the embarrassed husband, "but suppose (of course we all hope it will never be your case) a father has two sons at the front and he loses one of them, there is still one left to console him . . . while . . ."

"Yes," answered the other, getting cross, "a son left to console him but also a son left for whom he must survive, while in the case of the father of an only son if the son dies the father can die too and put an end to his distress. Which of the two positions is the worse? Don't you see how my case would be worse than yours?"

"Nonsense," interrupted another traveller, a fat, red-faced man with blood-shot eyes of the palest grey.

He was panting. From his bulging eyes seemed to spurt inner violence of an uncontrolled vitality which his weakened body could hardly contain.

"Nonsense," he repeated, trying to cover his mouth with his hand so as to hide the two missing front teeth. "Nonsense. Do we give life to our children for our own benefit?"

The other travellers stared at him in distress. The one who had had his son at the front since the first day of the war sighed: "You are right. Our children do not belong to us, they belong to the Country. . . ."

"Bosh," retorted the fat traveller. "Do we think of the Country when we give life to our children? Our sons are born because . . . well, because they must be born and when they come to life they take our own life with them. This is the truth. We belong to them but they never belong to us. And when they reach twenty they are exactly what we were at their age. We too had a father and mother, but there were so many other things as well . . . girls, cigarettes, illusions, new ties . . . and the Country, of course, whose call we would have answered—when we were twenty—even if father and mother had said no. Now, at our age, the love of our Country is still great, of course, but stronger than it is the love for our children. Is there any one of us here who wouldn't gladly take his son's place at the front if he could?"

There was a silence all round, everybody nodding as to approve.

"Why then," continued the fat man, "shouldn't we consider the feelings of our children when they are twenty? Isn't it *natural* that at their age they should consider the love for their Country (I am speaking of decent boys, of course) even greater than the love for us? Isn't it *natural* that it should be so, as after all they must look upon us as upon old boys who cannot move any more and must stay at home? If Country exists, if Country is a natural necessity like bread, of which each of us must eat in order not to die of hunger, somebody must go to defend it. And our sons go, when they are twenty, and they don't want tears, because if they die, they die inflamed and happy (I am speaking, of course, of decent boys). Now, if one dies young and happy, without having the ugly sides of life, the boredom of it, the pettiness, the bitterness of disillusion . . . what more can we ask for him? Everyone should stop crying: everyone should laugh, as I do . . . or at least thank God—as I do—because my son, before dying, sent me a message saying that he was dying satisfied at having ended his life in the best way he could have wished. That is why, as you see, I do not even wear mourning. . . ."

He shook his light fawn coat as to show it; his livid lip over his missing teeth was trembling, his eyes were watery and motionless and soon after he ended with a shrill laugh which might well have been a sob.

"Quite so . . . quite so . . ." agreed the others.

The woman who, bundled in a corner under her coat, had been sitting and listening had—for the last three months—tried to find in the words of her husband and her friends something to console her in her deep sorrow, something that might show her how a mother should resign herself to send her son not even to death but to a probable danger of life. Yet not a word had she found amongst the many which had been said . . . and her grief had been greater in seeing that nobody—as she thought—could share her feelings.

But now the words of the traveller amazed and almost stunned her. She suddenly realized that it wasn't the others who were wrong and could not understand her but herself who could not rise up to the same height of those fathers and mothers willing to resign themselves, without crying, not only to the departure of their sons but even to their death.

She lifted her head, she bent over from her corner trying to listen with great attention to the details which the fat man was giving to his companions about the way his son had fallen as a hero, for his King and his Country, happy and without regrets. It seemed to her that she had stumbled into a world she had never dreamt of, a world so far unknown to her and she was so pleased to hear everyone joining in congratulating that brave father who could so stoically speak of his child's death.

Then suddenly, just as if she had heard nothing of what had been said and almost as if waking up from a dream, she turned to the old man, asking him:

"Then . . . is your son really dead?"

Everybody stared at her. The old man, too, turned to look at her, fixing his great, bulging, horribly watery light grey eyes, deep in her face. For some little time he tried to answer, but words failed him. He looked and looked at her, almost as if only then—at that silly, incongruous question—he had suddenly realized at last that his son was really dead . . . gone for ever . . . for ever. His face contracted, became horribly distorted, then he snatched in haste a handkerchief from his pocket and, to the amazement of everyone, broke into harrowing, heart-rending, uncontrollable sobs.

Gladius Dei *

1902

THOMAS MANN   [1875–1955]

Munich was radiant. Above the gay squares and white columned temples, the classicistic monuments and the baroque churches, the leaping fountains, the palaces and parks of the Residence there stretched a sky of luminous blue silk. Well-arranged leafy vistas laced with sun and shade lay basking in the sunshine of a beautiful day in early June.

There was a twittering of birds and a blithe holiday spirit in all the little streets. And in the squares and past the rows of villas there swelled, rolled, and hummed the leisurely, entertaining traffic of that easy-going, charming town. Travellers of all nationalities drove about in the slow little droshkies, looking right and left in aimless curiosity at the house-fronts; they mounted and descended museum stairs. Many windows stood open and music was heard from within: practising on piano, cello, or violin—earnest and well-meant amateur efforts; while from the Odeon came the sound of serious work on several grand pianos.

Young people, the kind that can whistle the Nothung motif,[1] who fill the pit of the Schauspielhaus every evening, wandered in and out of the University and Library with literary magazines in their coat pockets. A court carriage stood before the Academy, the home of the plastic arts, which spreads its white wings between the Türkenstrasse and the Siegestor. And colourful groups of models, picturesque old men, women and children in Albanian costume, stood or lounged at the top of the balustrade.

Indolent, unhurried sauntering was the mode in all the long streets of the northern quarter. There life is lived for pleasanter ends than the driving greed of gain. Young artists with little round hats on the backs of their heads, flowing cravats and no canes—carefree bachelors who paid for their lodgings with colour-sketches—were strolling up and down to let the clear blue morning play upon their mood, also to look at the little girls, the pretty, rather plump type, with the brunette bandeaux, the too large feet, and the unobjectionable morals. Every fifth house had studio windows blinking in the sun. Sometimes a fine piece of architecture stood out from a middle-class row, the work of some imaginative young architect; a wide front with shallow bays and decorations in a bizarre style very expressive and full of invention. Or the door to some monotonous façade would be framed in a bold improvisation of flowing lines and sunny colours, with bacchantes, naiads,[2] and rosy-skinned nudes.

---

*Translated by H. T. Lowe-Porter. *Gladius Dei* means "sword of God."

[1] *Nothung* means "sword." The Nothung motif is a musical passage from Richard Wagner's opera *Siegfried*. *Schauspielhaus* means "theater."

[2] Bacchantes are female followers of Bacchus, the god of wine; naiads are water nymphs.

It was always a joy to linger before the windows of the cabinet-makers and the shops for modern articles *de luxe*. What a sense for luxurious nothings and amusing, significant line was displayed in the shape of everything! Little shops that sold picture frames, sculptures, and antiques there were in endless number; in their windows you might see those busts of Florentine women of the Renaissance, so full of noble poise and poignant charm. And the owners of the smallest and meanest of these shops spoke of Mino da Fiesole[3] and Donatello as though he had received the rights of reproduction from them personally.

But on the Odeonsplatz, in view of the mighty loggia with the spacious mosaic pavement before it, diagonally opposite to the Regent's palace, people were crowding round the large windows and glass show-cases of the big art-shop owned by M. Blüthenzweig. What a glorious display! There were reproductions of the masterpieces of all the galleries in the world, in costly decorated and tinted frames, the good taste of which was precious in its very simplicity. There were copies of modern paintings, works of a joyously sensuous fantasy, in which the antiques seemed born again in humorous and realistic guise; bronze nudes and fragile ornamental glassware; tall, thin earthenware vases with an iridescent glaze produced by a bath in metal steam; *éditions de luxe* which were triumphs of modern binding and presswork, containing the works of the most modish poets, set out with every possible advantage of sumptuous elegance. Cheek by jowl with these, the portraits of artists, musicians, philosophers, actors, writers, displayed to gratify the public taste for personalities.—In the first window, next the book-shop, a large picture stood on an easel, with a crowd of people in front of it, a fine sepia photograph in a wide old-gold frame, a very striking reproduction of the sensation at this year's great international exhibition, to which public attention is always invited by means of effective and artistic posters stuck up everywhere on hoardings among concert programmes and clever advertisements of toilet preparations.

If you looked into the windows of the book-shop your eye met such titles as *Interior Decoration Since the Renaissance, The Renaissance in Modern Decorative Art, The Book as Work of Art, The Decorative Arts, Hunger for Art,* and many more. And you would remember that these thought-provoking pamphlets were sold and read by the thousand and that discussions on these subjects were the preoccupation of all the salons.

You might be lucky enough to meet in person one of the famous fair ones whom less fortunate folk know only through the medium of art; one of those rich and beautiful women whose Titian-blond colouring Nature's most sweet and cunning hand did *not* lay on, but whose diamond parures and beguiling charms had received immortality from the hand of some portrait-painter of genius and whose love-affairs were the talk of the town. These were the queens of the artist balls at carnival-time. They were a little painted, a little made up, full of haughty caprices, worthy of adoration, avid of praise. You might see a

[3] Mino da Fiesole and Donatello were fourteenth-century Italian artists.

carriage rolling up the Ludwigstrasse, with such a great painter and his mistress inside. People would be pointing out the sight, standing still to gaze after the pair. Some of them would curtsy. A little more and the very policemen would stand at attention.

Art flourished, art swayed the destinies of the town, art stretched above it her rose-bound sceptre and smiled. On every hand obsequious interest was displayed in her prosperity, on every hand she was served with industry and devotion. There was a downright cult of line, decoration, form, significance, beauty. Munich was radiant.

A youth was coming down the Schellingstrasse. With the bells of cyclists ringing about him he strode across the wooden pavement towards the broad façade of the Ludwigskirche. Looking at him it was as though a shadow passed across the sky, or cast over the spirit some memory of melancholy hours. Did he not love the sun which bathed the lovely city in its festal light? Why did he walk wrapped in his own thoughts, his eyes directed on the ground?

No one in that tolerant and variety-loving town would have taken offence at his wearing no hat; but why need the hood of his ample black cloak have been drawn over his head, shadowing his low, prominent, and peaked forehead, covering his ears and framing his haggard cheeks? What pangs of conscience, what scruples and self-tortures had so availed to hollow out these cheeks? It is frightful, on such a sunny day, to see care sitting in the hollows of the human face. His dark brows thickened at the narrow base of his hooked and prominent nose. His lips were unpleasantly full, his eyes brown and close-lying. When he lifted them, diagonal folds appeared on the peaked brow. His gaze expressed knowledge, limitation, and suffering. Seen in profile his face was strikingly like an old painting preserved at Florence in a narrow cloister cell whence once a frightful and shattering protest issued against life and her triumphs.

Hieronymus walked along the Schellingstrasse with a slow, firm stride, holding his wide cloak together with both hands from inside. Two little girls, two of those pretty, plump little creatures with the bandeaux, the big feet, and the unobjectionable morals, strolled towards him arm in arm, on pleasure bent. They poked each other and laughed, they bent double with laughter, they even broke into a run and ran away still laughing, at his hood and his face. But he paid them no heed. With bent head, looking neither to the right nor to the left, he crossed the Ludwigstrasse and mounted the church steps.

The great wings of the middle portal stood wide open. From somewhere within the consecrated twilight, cool, dank, incense-laden, there came a pale red glow. An old woman with inflamed eyes rose from a prayer-stool and slipped on crutches through the columns. Otherwise the church was empty.

Hieronymus sprinkled brow and breast at the stoup, bent the knee before the high altar, and then paused in the centre nave. Here in the church his stature seemed to have grown. He stood upright and immovable; his head was flung up and his great hooked nose jutted domineeringly above the thick lips. His eyes no longer sought the ground, but looked straight and boldly into the distance, at the crucifix on the high altar. Thus he stood awhile, then retreating he bent the knee again and left the church.

He strode up the Ludwigstrasse, slowly, firmly, with bent head, in the centre of the wide unpaved road, towards the mighty loggia with its statues. But arrived at the Odeonsplatz, he looked up, so that the folds came out on his peaked forehead, and checked his step, his attention being called to the crowd at the windows of the big art-shop of M. Blüthenzweig.

People moved from window to window, pointing out to each other the treasures displayed and exchanging views as they looked over one another's shoulders. Hieronymus mingled among them and did as they did, taking in all these things with his eyes, one by one.

He saw the reproductions of masterpieces from all the galleries in the world, the priceless frames so precious in their simplicity, the Renaissance sculpture, the bronze nudes, the exquisitely bound volumes, the iridescent vases, the portraits of artists, musicians, philosophers, actors, writers; he looked at everything and turned a moment of his scrutiny· upon each object. Holding his mantle closely together with both hands from inside, he moved his hood-covered head in short turns from one thing to the next, gazing at each awhile with a dull, inimical, and remotely surprised air, lifting the dark brows which grew so thick at the base of the nose. At length he stood in front of the last window, which contained the startling picture. For a while he looked over the shoulders of people before him and then in his turn reached a position directly in front of the window.

The large red-brown photograph in the choice old-gold frame stood on an easel in the centre. It was a Madonna, but an utterly unconventional one, a work of entirely modern feeling. The figure of the Holy Mother was revealed as enchantingly feminine and beautiful. Her great smouldering eyes were rimmed with darkness, and her delicate and strangely smiling lips were half-parted. Her slender fingers held in a somewhat nervous grasp the hips of a Child, a nude boy of pronounced, almost primitive leanness. He was playing with her breast and glancing aside at the beholder with a wise look in his eyes.

Two other youths stood near Hieronymus, talking about the picture. They were two young men with books under their arms, which they had fetched from the Library or were taking thither. Humanistically educated people, that is, equipped with science and with art.

"The little chap is in luck, devil take me!" said one.

"He seems to be trying to make one envious," replied the other. "A bewildering female!"

"A female to drive a man crazy! Gives you funny ideas about the Immaculate Conception."

"No, she doesn't look exactly immaculate. Have you seen the original?"

"Of course; I was quite bowled over. She makes an even more aphrodisiac impression in colour. Especially the eyes."

"The likeness is pretty plain."

"How so?"

"Don't you know the model? Of course he used his little dressmaker. It is almost a portrait, only with a lot more emphasis on the corruptible. The girl is more innocent."

"I hope so. Life would be altogether too much of a strain if there were many like this *mater amata*."[4]

"The Pinakothek has bought it."

"Really? Well, well! They knew what they were about, anyhow. The treatment of the flesh and the flow of the linen garment are really first-class."

"Yes, an incredibly gifted chap."

"Do you know him?"

"A little. He will have a career, that is certain. He has been invited twice by the Prince Regent."

This last was said as they were taking leave of each other.

"Shall I see you this evening at the theatre?" asked the first. "The Dramatic Club is giving Machiavelli's *Mandragola*."[5]

"Oh, bravo! That will be great, of course. I had meant to go to the Variété, but I shall probably choose our stout Niccolò after all. Good-bye."

They parted, going off to right and left. New people took their places and looked at the famous picture. But Hieronymus stood where he was, motionless, with his head thrust out; his hands clutched convulsively at the mantle as they held it together from inside. His brows were no longer lifted with that cool and unpleasantly surprised expression; they were drawn and darkened; his cheeks, half-shrouded in the black hood, seemed more sunken than ever and his thick lips had gone pale. Slowly his head dropped lower and lower, so that finally his eyes stared upwards at the work of art, while the nostrils of his great nose dilated.

Thus he remained for perhaps a quarter of an hour. The crowd about him melted away, but he did not stir from the spot. At last he turned slowly on the balls of his feet and went hence.

But the picture of the Madonna went with him. Always and ever, whether in his hard and narrow little room or kneeling in the cool church, it stood before his outraged soul, with its smouldering, dark-rimmed eyes, its riddlingly smiling lips—stark and beautiful. And no prayer availed to exorcize it.

But the third night it happened that a command and summons from on high came to Hieronymus, to intercede and lift his voice against the frivolity, blasphemy, and arrogance of beauty. In vain like Moses he protested that he had not the gift of tongues. God's will remained unshaken; in a loud voice He demanded that the faint-hearted Hieronymus go forth to sacrifice amid the jeers of the foe.

---

[4]Beloved mother. The Pinakothek is a municipal art gallery.
[5]Niccolò Machiavelli (1469–1527) was a playwright as well as a political philosopher. His play, *Mandragola*, is a sex comedy.

And since God would have it so, he set forth one morning and wended his way to the great art-shop of M. Blüthenzweig. He wore his hood over his head and held his mantle together in front from inside with both hands as he went.

The air had grown heavy, the sky was livid and thunder threatened. Once more crowds were besieging the show-cases at the art-shop and especially the window where the photograph of the Madonna stood. Hieronymus cast one brief glance thither; then he pushed up the latch of the glass door hung with placards and art magazines. "As God wills," said he, and entered the shop.

A young girl was somewhere at a desk writing in a big book. She was a pretty brunette thing with bandeaux of hair and big feet. She came up to him and asked pleasantly what he would like.

"Thank you," said Hieronymus in a low voice and looked her earnestly in the face, with diagonal wrinkles in his peaked brow. "I would speak not to you but to the owner of this shop, Herr Blüthenzweig."

She hesitated a little, turned away, and took up her work once more. He stood there in the middle of the shop.

Instead of the single specimens in the show-windows there was here a riot and a heaping-up of luxury, a fullness of colour, line, form, style, invention, good taste, and beauty. Hieronymus looked slowly round him, drawing his mantle close with both hands.

There were several people in the shop besides him. At one of the broad tables running across the room sat a man in a yellow suit, with a black goat's-beard, looking at a portfolio of French drawings, over which he now and then emitted a bleating laugh. He was being waited on by an undernourished and vegetarian young man, who kept on dragging up fresh portfolios. Diagonally opposite the bleating man sat an elegant old dame, examining art embroideries with a pattern of fabulous flowers in pale tones standing together on tall perpendicular stalks. An attendant hovered about her too. A leisurely Englishman in a travelling-cap, with his pipe in his mouth, sat at another table. Cold and smooth-shaven, of indefinite age, in his good English clothes, he sat examining bronzes brought to him by M. Blüthenzweig in person. He was holding up by the head the dainty figure of a nude young girl, immature and delicately articulated, her hands crossed in coquettish innocence upon her breast. He studied her thoroughly, turning her slowly about. M. Blüthenzweig, a man with a short, heavy brown beard and bright brown eyes of exactly the same colour, moved in a semicircle round him, rubbing his hands, praising the statuette with all the terms his vocabulary possessed.

"A hundred and fifty marks, sir," he said in English. "Munich art—very charming, in fact. Simply full of charm, you know. Grace itself. Really extremely pretty, good, admirable, in fact." Then he thought of some more and went on: "Highly attractive, fascinating." Then he began again from the beginning.

His nose lay a little flat on his upper lip, so that he breathed constantly with a slight sniff into his moustache. Sometimes he did this as he approached a

customer, stooping over as though he were smelling at him. When Hieronymus entered, M. Blüthenzweig had examined him cursorily in this way, then
devoted himself again to his Englishman.

The elegant old dame made her selection and left the shop. A man entered.
M. Blüthenzweig sniffed briefly at him as though to scent out his capacity to
buy and left him to the young bookkeeper. The man purchased a faience bust
of young Piero de' Medici, son of Lorenzo, and went out again. The Englishman began to depart. He had acquired the statuette of the young girl and left
amid bowings from M. Blüthenzweig. Then the art-dealer turned to Hieronymus and came forward.

"You wanted something?" he said, without any particular courtesy.

Hieronymus held his cloak together with both hands and looked the other in
the face almost without winking an eyelash. He parted his big lips slowly and
said:

"I have come to you on account of the picture in the window there, the big
photograph, the Madonna." His voice was thick and without modulation.

"Yes, quite right," said M. Blüthenzweig briskly and began rubbing his hands.
"Seventy marks in the frame. It is unfadable—a first-class reproduction. Highly
attractive and full of charm."

Hieronymus was silent. He nodded his head in the hood and shrank a little
into himself as the dealer spoke. Then he drew himself up again and said:

"I would remark to you first of all that I am not in the position to purchase
anything, nor have I the desire. I am sorry to have to disappoint your expectations. I regret if it upsets you. But in the first place I am poor and in the
second I do not love the things you sell. No, I cannot buy anything."

"No? Well, then?" asked M. Blüthenzweig, sniffing a good deal. "Then may
I ask—"

"I suppose," Hieronymus went on, "that being what you are you look down
on me because I am not in a position to buy."

"Oh—er—not at all," said M. Blüthenzweig. "Not at all. Only—"

"And yet I beg you to hear me and give some consideration to my words."

"Consideration to your words. H'm—may I ask—"

"You may ask," said Hieronymus, "and I will answer you. I have come to
beg you to remove that picture, the big photograph, the Madonna, out of your
window and never display it again."

M. Blüthenzweig looked awhile dumbly into Hieronymus's face—as though
he expected him to be abashed at the words he had just uttered. But as this did
not happen he gave a violent sniff and spoke himself:

"Will you be so good as to tell me whether you are here in any official capacity which authorizes you to dictate to me, or what does bring you here?"

"Oh, no," replied Hieronymus, "I have neither office nor dignity from the
state. I have no power on my side, sir. What brings me hither is my conscience
alone."

M. Blüthenzweig, searching for words, snorted violently into his moustache.
At length he said:

"Your conscience . . . well, you will kindly understand that I take not the faintest interest in your conscience." With which he turned round and moved quickly to his desk at the back of the shop, where he began to write. Both attendants laughed heartily. The pretty Fräulein giggled over her account-book. As for the yellow gentleman with the goat's beard, he was evidently a foreigner, for he gave no sign of comprehension but went on studying the French drawings and emitting from time to time his bleating laugh.

"Just get rid of the man for me," said M. Blüthenzweig shortly over his shoulder to his assistant. He went on writing. The poorly paid young vegetarian approached Hieronymus, smothering his laughter, and the other salesman came up too.

"May we be of service to you in any other way?" the first asked mildly. Hieronymus fixed him with his glazed and suffering eyes.

"No," he said, "you cannot. I beg you to take the Madonna picture out of the window, at once and forever."

"But—why?"

"It is the Holy Mother of God," said Hieronymus in a subdued voice.

"Quite. But you have heard that Herr Blüthenzweig is not inclined to accede to your request."

"We must bear in mind that it is the Holy Mother of God," said Hieronymus again and his head trembled on his neck.

"So we must. But should we not be allowed to exhibit any Madonnas—or paint any?"

"It is not that," said Hieronymus, almost whispering. He drew himself up and shook his head energetically several times. His peaked brow under the hood was entirely furrowed with long, deep cross-folds. "You know very well that it is vice itself that is painted there—naked sensuality. I was standing near two simple young people and overheard with my own ears that it led them astray upon the doctrine of the Immaculate Conception."

"Oh, permit me—that is not the point," said the young salesman, smiling. In his leisure hours he was writing a brochure on the modern movement in art and was well qualified to conduct a cultured conversation. "The picture is a work of art," he went on, "and one must measure it by the appropriate standards as such. It has been very highly praised on all hands. The state has purchased it."

"I know that the state has purchased it," said Hieronymus. "I also know that the artist has twice dined with the Prince Regent. It is common talk—and God knows how people interpret the fact that a man can become famous by such work as this. What does such a fact bear witness to? To the blindness of the world, a blindness inconceivable, if not indeed shamelessly hypocritical. This picture has its origin in sensual lust and is enjoyed in the same—is that true or not? Answer me! And you too answer me, Herr Blüthenzweig!"

A pause ensued. Hieronymus seemed in all seriousness to demand an answer to his question, looking by turns at the staring attendants and the round back M. Blüthenzweig turned upon him, with his own piercing and anguishing brown eyes. Silence reigned. Only the yellow man with the goat's beard, bending over the French drawings, broke it with his bleating laugh.

"It is true," Hieronymus went on in a hoarse voice that shook with his profound indignation. "You do not dare deny it. How then can honour be done to its creator, as though he had endowed mankind with a new ideal possession? How can one stand before it and surrender unthinkingly to the base enjoyment which it purveys, persuading oneself in all seriousness that one is yielding to a noble and elevated sentiment, highly creditable to the human race? Is this reckless ignorance or abandoned hypocrisy? My understanding falters, it is completely at a loss when confronted by the absurd fact that a man can achieve renown on this earth by the stupid and shameless exploitation of the animal instincts. Beauty? What is beauty? What forces are they which use beauty as their tool today—and upon what does it work? No one can fail to know this, Herr Blüthenzweig. But who, understanding it clearly, can fail to feel disgust and pain? It is criminal to play upon the ignorance of the immature, the lewd, the brazen, and the unscrupulous by elevating beauty into an idol to be worshipped, to give it even more power over those who know not affliction and have no knowledge of redemption. You are unknown to me, and you look at me with black looks—yet answer me! Knowledge, I tell you, is the profoundest torture in the world; but it is the purgatory without whose purifying pangs no soul can reach salvation. It is not infantile, blasphemous shallowness that can save us, Herr Blüthenzweig; only knowledge can avail, knowledge in which the passions of our loathsome flesh die away and are quenched."

Silence.—The yellow man with the goat's beard gave a sudden little bleat.

"I think you really must go now," said the underpaid assistant mildly.

But Hieronymus made no move to do so. Drawn up in his hooded cape, he stood with blazing eyes in the centre of the shop and his thick lips poured out condemnation in a voice that was harsh and rusty and clanking.

"Art, you cry; enjoyment, beauty! Enfold the world in beauty and endow all things with the noble grace of style!—Profligate, away! Do you think to wash over with lurid colours the misery of the world? Do you think with the sounds of feasting and music to drown out the voice of the tortured earth? Shameless one, you err! God lets not Himself be mocked, and your impudent deification of the glistering surface of things is an abomination in His eyes. You tell me that I blaspheme art. I say to you that you lie. I do not blaspheme art. Art is no conscienceless delusion, lending itself to reinforce the allurements of the fleshly. Art is the holy torch which turns its light upon all the frightful depths, all the shameful and woeful abysses of life; art is the godly fire laid to the world that, being redeemed by pity, it may flame up and dissolve altogether with its shames and torments.—Take it out, Herr Blüthenzweig, take away the work of that famous painter out of your window—you would do well to burn it with a hot fire and strew its ashes to the four winds—yes, to all the four winds—"

His harsh voice broke off. He had taken a violent backwards step, snatched one arm from his black wrappings, and stretched it passionately forth, gesturing towards the window with a hand that shook as though palsied. And in this commanding attitude he paused. His great hooked nose seemed to jut more than ever, his dark brows were gathered so thick and high that folds crowded upon the peaked forehead shaded by the hood; a hectic flush mantled his hollow cheeks.

But at this point M. Blüthenzweig turned round. Perhaps he was outraged by the idea of burning his seventy-mark reproduction; perhaps Hieronymus's speech had completely exhausted his patience. In any case he was a picture of stern and righteous anger. He pointed with his pen to the door of the shop, gave several short, excited snorts into his moustache, struggled for words, and uttered with the maximum of energy those which he found:

"My fine fellow, if you don't get out at once I will have my packer help you—do you understand?"

"Oh, you cannot intimidate me, you cannot drive me away, you cannot silence my voice!" cried Hieronymus as he clutched his cloak over his chest with his fists and shook his head doughtily. "I know that I am single-handed and powerless, but yet I will not cease until you hear me, Herr Blüthenzweig! Take the picture out of your window and burn it even today! Ah, burn not it alone! Burn all these statues and busts, the sight of which plunges the beholder into sin! Burn these vases and ornaments, these shameless revivals of paganism, these elegantly bound volumes of erotic verse! Burn everything in your shop, Herr Blüthenzweig, for it is a filthiness in God's sight. Burn it, burn it!" he shrieked, beside himself, describing a wild, all-embracing circle with his arm. "The harvest is ripe for the reaper, the measure of the age's shamelessness is full—but I say unto you—"

"Krauthuber!" Herr Blüthenzweig raised his voice and shouted towards a door at the back of the shop. "Come in here at once!"

And in answer to the summons there appeared upon the scene a massive overpowering presence, a vast and awe-inspiring, swollen human bulk, whose limbs merged into each other like links of sausage—a gigantic son of the people, malt-nourished and immoderate, who weighed in, with puffings, bursting with energy, from the packing-room. His appearance in the upper reaches of his form was notable for a fringe of walrus beard; a hide apron fouled with paste covered his body from the waist down, and his yellow shirt-sleeves were rolled back from his heroic arms.

"Will you open the door for this gentleman, Krauthuber?" said M. Blüthenzweig; "and if he should not find the way to it, just help him into the street."

"Huh," said the man, looking from his enraged employer to Hieronymus and back with his little elephant eyes. It was a heavy monosyllable, suggesting reserve force restrained with difficulty. The floor shook with his tread as he went to the door and opened it.

Hieronymus had grown very pale. "Burn—" he shouted once more. He was about to go on when he felt himself turned round by an irresistible power, by a physical preponderance to which no resistance was even thinkable. Slowly and inexorably he was propelled towards the door.

"I am weak," he managed to ejaculate. "My flesh cannot bear the force . . . it cannot hold its ground, no . . . but what does that prove? Burn—"

He stopped. He found himself outside the art-shop. M. Blüthenzweig's giant packer had let him go with one final shove, which set him down on the stone threshold of the shop, supporting himself with one hand. Behind him the door closed with a rattle of glass.

He picked himself up. He stood erect, breathing heavily, and pulled his cloak together with one fist over his breast, letting the other hang down inside. His hollow cheeks had a grey pallor; the nostrils of his great hooked nose opened and closed; his ugly lips were writhen in an expression of hatred and despair and his red-rimmed eyes wandered over the beautiful square like those of a man in a frenzy.

He did not see that people were looking at him with amusement and curiosity. For what he beheld upon the mosaic pavement before the great loggia were all the vanities of this world: the masked costumes of the artist balls, the decorations, vases and art objects, the nude statues, the female busts, the picturesque rebirths of the pagan age, the portraits of famous beauties by the hands of masters, the elegantly bound erotic verse, the art brochures—all these he saw heaped in a pyramid and going up in crackling flames amid loud exultations from the people enthralled by his own frightful words. A yellow background of cloud had drawn up over the Theatinerstrasse, and from it issued wild rumblings; but what he saw was a burning fiery sword, towering in sulphurous light above the joyous city.

"*Gladius Dei super terram . . .*" his thick lips whispered; and drawing himself still higher in his hooded cloak while the hand hanging down inside it twitched convulsively, he murmured, quaking: "*cito et velociter!*"[6]

QUESTIONS

1. How would you characterize Munich as it is described in the first six paragraphs? Does it sound attractive? 2. What effect does the conversation between the two youths (pp. 419–420) have on the reader? On Hieronymus?

WRITING TOPIC

What finally does the story say about the relationship between art, religion, and morality?

---

[6]*Gladius Dei super terram* means "sword of God over the earth"; *cito et velociter* means "swiftly and quickly."

A Hunger Artist*   1924

FRANZ KAFKA   [1883–1924]

During these last decades the interest in professional fasting has markedly diminished. It used to pay very well to stage such great performances under one's own management, but today that is quite impossible. We live in a different world now. At one time the whole town took a lively interest in the hunger artist; from day to day of his fast the excitement mounted; everybody wanted to see him at least once a day; there were people who bought season tickets for the last few days and sat from morning till night in front of his small barred cage; even in the nighttime there were visiting hours, when the whole effect was heightened by torch flares; on fine days the cage was set out in the open air, and then it was the children's special treat to see the hunger artist; for their elders he was often just a joke that happened to be in fashion, but the children stood open-mouthed, holding each other's hands for greater security, marveling at him as he sat there pallid in black tights, with his ribs sticking out so prominently, not even on a seat but down among straw on the ground, sometimes giving a courteous nod, answering questions with a constrained smile, or perhaps stretching an arm through the bars so that one might feel how thin it was, and then again withdrawing deep into himself, paying no attention to anyone or anything, not even to the all-important striking of the clock that was the only piece of furniture in his cage, but merely staring into vacancy with half shut eyes, now and then taking a sip from a tiny glass of water to moisten his lips.

Beside casual onlookers there were also relays of permanent watchers selected by the public, usually butchers, strangely enough, and it was their task to watch the hunger artist day and night, three of them at a time, in case he should have some secret recourse to nourishment. This was nothing but a formality, instituted to reassure the masses, for the initiates knew well enough that during his fast the artist would never in any circumstances, not even under forcible compulsion, swallow the smallest morsel of food; the honor of his profession forbade it. Not every watcher, of course, was capable of understanding this; there were often groups of night watchers who were very lax in carrying out their duties and deliberately huddled together in a retired corner to play cards with great absorption, obviously intending to give the hunger artist the chance of a little refreshment, which they supposed he could draw from some private hoard. Nothing annoyed the artist more than such watchers; they made him miserable; they made his fast seem unendurable; sometimes he mastered his feebleness sufficiently to sing during their watch for as long as he could keep going, to show them how unjust their suspicions were. But that was of little use; they only wondered at his cleverness in being able to fill his mouth even while

---

* Translated by Edwin and Willa Muir.

singing. Much more to his taste were the watchers who sat close up to the bars, who were not content with the dim night lighting of the hall but focused him in the full glare of the electric pocket torch given them by the impresario. The harsh light did not trouble him at all, in any case he could never sleep properly, and he could always drowse a little, whatever the light, at any hour, even when the hall was thronged with noisy onlookers. He was quite happy at the prospect of spending a sleepless night with such watchers; he was ready to exchange jokes with them, to tell them stories out of his nomadic life, anything at all to keep them awake and demonstrate to them again that he had no eatables in his cage and that he was fasting as not one of them could fast. But his happiest moment was when the morning came and an enormous breakfast was brought them, at his expense, on which they flung themselves with the keen appetite of healthy men after a weary night of wakefulness. Of course there were people who argued that this breakfast was an unfair attempt to bribe the watchers, but that was going rather too far, and when they were invited to take on a night's vigil without a breakfast, merely for the sake of the cause, they made themselves scarce, although they stuck stubbornly to their suspicions.

Such suspicions, anyhow, were a necessary accompaniment to the profession of fasting. No one could possibly watch the hunger artist continuously, day and night, and so no one could produce first-hand evidence that the fast had really been rigorous and continuous; only the artist himself could know that, he was therefore bound to be the sole completely satisfied spectator of his own fast. Yet for other reasons he was never satisfied; it was not perhaps mere fasting that had brought him to such skeleton thinness that many people had regretfully to keep away from his exhibitions, because the sight of him was too much for them, perhaps it was dissatisfaction with himself that had worn him down. For he alone knew, what no other initiate knew, how easy it was to fast. It was the easiest thing in the world. He made no secret of this, yet people did not believe him, at the best they set him down as modest; most of them, however, thought he was out for publicity or else was some kind of cheat who found it easy to fast because he had discovered a way of making it easy, and then had the impudence to admit the fact, more or less. He had to put up with all that, and in the course of time had got used to it, but his inner dissatisfaction always rankled, and never yet, after any term of fasting—this must be granted to his credit—had he left the cage of his own free will. The longest period of fasting was fixed by his impresario at forty days, beyond that term he was not allowed to go, not even in great cities, and there was good reason for it, too. Experience had proved that for about forty days the interest of the public could be stimulated by a steadily increasing pressure of advertisement, but after that the town began to lose interest, sympathetic support began notably to fall off; there were of course local variations as between one town and another or one country and another, but as a general rule forty days marked the limit. So on the fortieth day the flower bedecked cage was opened, enthusiastic spectators filled the hall, a military band played, two doctors entered the cage to measure the results of the fast, which were announced through a megaphone, and finally two young ladies appeared, blissful at having been selected for the honor, to help the hunger artist down the few steps leading to a small table on which was spread a carefully chosen invalid repast. And at this very moment the artist always turned stubborn. True, he would entrust his bony arms to the outstretched helping hands of the ladies bending over him, but stand up he would not. Why stop fasting at this particular moment, after forty days of it? He had held out for a long time, an illimitably long time; why stop now, when he was in his best fasting form, or rather, not yet quite in his best fasting form? Why should he be cheated of the fame he would get for fasting longer, for being not only the record hunger artist of all time, which presumably he was already, but for beating his own record by a performance beyond human imagination, since he felt that there were no limits to his capacity for fasting? His public pretended to admire him so much, why should it have so little patience with him; if he could endure fasting longer, why shouldn't the public endure it? Besides, he was tired, he was comfortable sitting in the straw, and now he was supposed to lift himself to his full height and go down to a meal the very thought of which gave him a nausea that only the presence of the ladies kept him from betraying, and even that with an effort. And he looked up into the eyes of the ladies who were apparently so friendly and in reality so cruel, and shook his head, which felt too heavy on its strengthless neck. But then there happened yet again what always happened. The impresario came forward, without a word—for the band made speech impossible—lifted his arms in the air above the artist, as if inviting Heaven to look down upon its creature here in the straw, this suffering martyr, which indeed he was, although in quite another sense; grasped him round the emaciated waist, with exaggerated caution, so that the frail condition he was in might be appreciated; and committed him to the care of the blenching ladies, not without secretly giving him a shaking so that his legs and body tottered and swayed. The artist now submitted completely; his head lolled on his breast as if it had landed there by chance; his body was hollowed out; his legs in a spasm of self-preservation clung close to each other at the knees, yet scraped on the ground as if it were not really solid ground, as if they were only trying to find solid ground; and the whole weight of his body, a feather-weight after all, relapsed onto one of the ladies, who, looking round for help and panting a little—this post of honor was not at all what she had expected it to be—first stretched her neck as far as she could to keep her face at least free from contact with the artist, when finding this impossible, and her more fortunate companion not coming to her aid but merely holding extended on her own trembling hand the little bunch of knuckle-bones that was the artist's, to the great delight of the spectators burst into tears and had to be replaced by an attendant who had long been stationed in readiness. Then came the food, a little of which the impresario managed to get between the artist's lips, while he sat in a kind of half-fainting trance, to the accompaniment of cheerful patter designed to distract the public's attention from the artist's condition; after that, a toast was drunk to the public, supposedly prompted by a whisper from the artist in the impresario's ear; the band confirmed it with a mighty flourish, the spectators melted away, and no one had any cause to be dissatisfied with the proceedings, no one except the hunger artist himself, he only, as always.

So he lived for many years, with small regular intervals of recuperation, in visible glory, honored by the world, yet in spite of that troubled in spirit, and all the more troubled because no one would take his trouble seriously. What comfort could he possibly need? What more could he possibly wish for? And if some good-natured person, feeling sorry for him, tried to console him by pointing out that his melancholy was probably caused by fasting; it could happen, especially when he had been fasting for some time, that he reacted with an outburst of fury and to the general alarm began to shake the bars of his cage like a wild animal. Yet the impresario had a way of punishing these outbreaks which he rather enjoyed putting into operation. He would apologize publicly for the artist's behavior, which was only to be excused, he admitted, because of the irritability caused by fasting; a condition hardly to be understood by well-fed people; then by natural transition he went on to mention the artist's equally incomprehensible boast that he could fast for much longer than he was doing; he praised the high ambition, the good will, the great self-denial undoubtedly implicit in such a statement; and then quite simply countered it by bringing out photographs, which were also on sale to the public, showing the artist on the fortieth day of a fast lying in bed almost dead from exhaustion. This perversion of the truth, familiar to the artist though it was, always unnerved him afresh and proved too much for him. What was a consequence of the premature ending of his fast was here presented as the cause of it! To fight against this lack of understanding, against a whole world of non-understanding, was impossible. Time and again in good faith he stood by the bars listening to the impresario, but as soon as the photographs appeared he always let go and sank with a groan back on to his straw, and the reassured public could once more come close and gaze at him.

A few years later when the witnesses of such scenes called them to mind, they often failed to understand themselves at all. For meanwhile the aforementioned change in public interest had set in; it seemed to happen almost overnight; there may have been profound causes for it, but who was going to bother about that; at any rate the pampered hunger artist suddenly found himself deserted one fine day by the amusement seekers, who went streaming past him to other more favored attractions. For the last time the impresario hurried him over half Europe to discover whether the old interest might still survive here and there; all in vain; everywhere, as if by secret agreement, a positive revulsion from professional fasting was in evidence. Of course it could not really have sprung up so suddenly as all that, and many premonitory symptoms which had not been sufficiently remarked or suppressed during the rush and glitter of success now came retrospectively to mind, but it was now too late to take any countermeasures. Fasting would surely come into fashion again at some future date, yet that was no comfort for those living in the present. What, then, was the hunger artist to do? He had been applauded by thousands in his time and could hardly come down to showing himself in a street booth at village fairs, and as for adopting another profession, he was not only too old for that but too frantically devoted to fasting. So he took leave of the impresario, his partner in an unparalleled career, and hired himself to a large circus; in order to spare his own feelings he avoided reading the conditions of his contract.

A large circus with its enormous traffic in replacing and recruiting men, animals and apparatus can always find a use for people at any time, even for a hunger artist, provided of course that he does not ask too much, and in this particular case anyhow it was not only the artist who was taken on but his famous and long-known name as well, indeed considering the peculiar nature of his performance, which was not impaired by advancing age, it could not be objected that there was an artist past his prime, no longer at the height of his professional skill, seeking a refuge in some quiet corner of a circus; on the contrary, the hunger artist averred that he could fast as well as ever, which was entirely credible; he even alleged that if he were allowed to fast as he liked, and this was at once promised him without more ado, he could astound the world by establishing a record never yet achieved, a statement which certainly provoked a smile among the other professionals, since it left out of account the change in public opinion, which the hunger artist in his zeal conveniently forgot.

He had not, however, actually lost his sense of the real situation and took it as a matter of course that he and his cage should be stationed, not in the middle of the ring as a main attraction, but outside, near the animal cages, on a site that was after all easily accessible. Large and gaily painted placards made a frame for the cage and announced what was to be seen inside it. When the public came thronging out in the intervals to see the animals, they could hardly avoid passing the hunger artist's cage and stopping there for a moment; perhaps they might even have stayed longer had not those pressing behind them in the narrow gangway, who did not understand why they should be held up on their way toward the excitements of the menagerie, made it impossible for anyone to stand gazing quietly for any length of time. And that was the reason why the hunger artist, who had of course been looking forward to these visiting hours as the main achievement of his life, began instead to shrink from them. At first he could hardly wait for the intervals; it was exhilarating to watch the crowds come streaming his way, until only too soon—not even the most obstinate self-deception, clung to almost consciously, could hold out against the fact—the conviction was borne in upon him that these people, most of them, to judge from their actions, again and again, without exception, were all on their way to the menagerie. And the first sight of them from the distance remained the best. For when they reached his cage he was at once deafened by the storm of shouting and abuse that arose from the two contending factions, which renewed themselves continuously, of those who wanted to stop and stare at him—he soon began to dislike them more than the others—not out of real interest but only out of obstinate self-assertiveness, and those who wanted to go straight on to the animals. When the first great rush was past, the stragglers came along, and these, whom nothing could have prevented from stopping to look at him as long as they had breath, raced past with long strides, hardly even glancing at him, in their haste to get to the menagerie in time. And all too rarely did it happen that he had a stroke of luck, when some father of a family fetched up before him with his children, pointed a finger at the hunger artist and explained at length what the phenomenon meant, telling stories of earlier years when he himself had watched similar but much more thrilling performances, and the children, still rather uncomprehending, since neither inside nor outside school had they been sufficiently prepared for this lesson—what did they care about fasting?—yet showed by the brightness of their intent eyes that new and better times might be coming. Perhaps, said the hunger artist to himself many a time, things would be a little better if his cage were set not quite so near the menagerie. That made it too easy for people to make their choice, to say nothing of what he suffered from the stench of the menagerie, the animals' restlessness by night, the carrying past of raw lumps of flesh for the beasts of prey, the roaring at feeding times, which depressed him continually. But he did not dare to lodge a complaint with the management; after all, he had the animals to thank for the troops of people who passed his cage, among whom there might always be one here and there to take an interest in him, and who could tell where they might seclude him if he called attention to his existence and thereby to the fact that, strictly speaking, he was only an impediment on the way to the menagerie.

A small impediment, to be sure, one that grew steadily less. People grew familiar with the strange idea that they could be expected, in times like these, to take an interest in a hunger artist, and with this familiarity the verdict went out against him. He might fast as much as he could, and he did so; but nothing could save him now, people passed him by. Just try to explain to anyone the art of fasting! Anyone who has no feeling for it cannot be made to understand it. The fine placards grew dirty and illegible, they were torn down; the little notice board telling the number of fast days achieved, which at first was changed carefully every day, had long stayed at the same figure, for after the first few weeks even this small task seemed pointless to the staff; and so the artist simply fasted on and on, as he had once dreamed of doing, and it was no trouble to him, just as he had always foretold, but no one counted the days, no one, not even the artist himself, knew what records he was already breaking, and his heart grew heavy. And when once in a time some leisurely passer-by stopped, made merry over the old figure on the board and spoke of swindling, that was in its way the stupidest lie ever invented by indifference and inborn malice, since it was not the hunger artist who was cheating; he was working honestly, but the world was cheating him of his reward.

Many more days went by, however, and that too came to an end. An overseer's eye fell on the cage one day and asked the attendants why this perfectly good cage should be left standing there unused with dirty straw inside it; nobody knew, until one man, helped out by the notice board, remembered about the hunger artist. They poked into the straw with sticks and found him in it. "Are you still fasting?" asked the overseer. "When on earth do you mean to stop?" "Forgive me, everybody," whispered the hunger artist; only the overseer, who had his ear to the bars, understood him. "Of course," said the overseer, and tapped his forehead with a finger to let the attendants know what state the man was in, "we forgive you." "I always wanted you to admire my fasting," said the hunger artist. "We do admire it," said the overseer, affably. "But you shouldn't admire it," said the hunger artist. "Well, then we don't admire it," said the overseer, "but why shouldn't we admire it?" "Because I have to fast, I can't help it," said the hunger artist. "What a fellow you are," said the overseer, "and why can't you help it?" "Because," said the hunger artist, lifting his head a little and speaking, with his lips pursed, as if for a kiss, right into the overseer's ear, so that no syllable might be lost, "because I couldn't find the food I liked. If I had found it, believe me, I should have made no fuss and stuffed myself like you or anyone else." These were his last words, but in his dimming eyes remained the firm though no longer proud persuasion that he was still continuing to fast.

"Well, clear this out now!" said the overseer, and they buried the hunger artist, straw and all. Into the cage they put a young panther. Even the most insensitive felt it refreshing to see this wild creature leaping around the cage that had so long been dreary. The panther was all right. The food he liked was brought him without hesitation by the attendants; he seemed not even to miss his freedom; his noble body, furnished almost to the bursting point with all that it needed, seemed to carry freedom around with it too; somewhere in his jaws it seemed to lurk; and the joy of life streamed with such ardent passion from his throat that for the onlookers it was not easy to stand the shock of it. But they braced themselves, crowded round the cage, and did not want ever to move away.

QUESTIONS

1. What is the hunger artist's relationship to his audiences? Even though his greatest achievements involve a deep inwardness and withdrawal, why does he nevertheless seem to need the audiences? **2.** How does Kafka manage to achieve such a bizarre and dreamlike effect with dry and factual prose?

WRITING TOPICS

1. Many readers interpret this story as a parable of the artist in the modern world, while others see it as a religious parable. What evidence do you find in the story to support either reading? Why would Kafka select an expert in fasting rather than someone (say a singer or a priest) whose profession would make the theme clearer? **2.** Should the hunger artist be admired for his passionate and single-minded devotion to his art or condemned for his withdrawal from humanity and his sickness of will? Why? In this connection, what is the significance of the panther put in the cage after the artist's death?

The Greatest Man in the World 1935

JAMES THURBER [1894–1961]

Looking back on it now, from the vantage point of 1950, one can only marvel that it hadn't happened long before it did. The United States of America had been, ever since Kitty Hawk, blindly constructing the elaborate petard by which, sooner or later, it must be hoist. It was inevitable that some day there would come roaring out of the skies a national hero of insufficient intelligence, background, and character successfully to endure the mounting orgies of glory prepared for aviators who stayed up a long time or flew a great distance. Both Lindbergh and Byrd, fortunately for national decorum and international amity, had been gentlemen; so had our other famous aviators. They wore their laurels gracefully, withstood the awful weather of publicity, married excellent women, usually of fine family, and quietly retired to private life and the enjoyment of their varying fortunes. No untoward incidents, on a worldwide scale, marred the perfection of their conduct on the perilous heights of fame. The exception to the rule was, however, bound to occur and it did, in July, 1937, when Jack ("Pal") Smurch, erstwhile mechanics' helper in a small garage in Westfield, Iowa, flew a second-hand, single-motored Bresthaven Dragon-Fly III monoplane all the way around the world, without stopping.

Never before in the history of aviation had such a flight as Smurch's ever been dreamed of. No one had even taken seriously the weird floating auxiliary gas tanks, invention of the mad New Hampshire professor of astronomy, Dr. Charles Lewis Gresham, upon which Smurch placed full reliance. When the garage worker, a slightly built, surly, unprepossessing young man of twenty-two appeared at Roosevelt Field in early July, 1937, slowly chewing a great quid of scrap tobacco, and announced "Nobody ain't seen no flyin' yet," the newspapers touched briefly and satirically upon his projected twenty-five-thousand-mile flight. Aeronautical and automotive experts dismissed the idea curtly, implying that it was a hoax, a publicity stunt. The rusty, battered, second-hand plane wouldn't go. The Gresham auxiliary tanks wouldn't work. It was simply a cheap joke.

Smurch, however, after calling on a girl in Brooklyn who worked in the flap-folding department of a large paper-box factory, a girl whom he later described as his "sweet patootie," climbed nonchalantly into his ridiculous plane at dawn of the memorable seventh of July, 1937, spat a curve of tobacco juice into the still air, and took off, carrying with him only a gallon of bootleg gin and six pounds of salami.

When the garage boy thundered out over the ocean the papers were forced to record, in all seriousness, that a mad, unknown young man—his name was variously misspelled—had actually set out upon a preposterous attempt to span the world in a rickety, one-engined contraption, trusting to the long-distance

434

refueling device of a crazy schoolmaster. When, nine days later, without having stopped once, the tiny plane appeared above San Francisco Bay, headed for New York, spluttering and choking, to be sure, but still magnificently and miraculously aloft, the headlines, which long since had crowded everything else off the front page—even the shooting of the Governor of Illinois by the Vileti gang—swelled to unprecedented size, and the news stories began to run to twenty-five and thirty columns. It was noticeable, however, that the accounts of the epoch-making flight touched rather lightly upon the aviator himself. This was not because facts about the hero as a man were too meagre, but because they were too complete.

Reporters, who had been rushed out to Iowa when Smurch's plane was first sighted over the little French coast town of Serly-le-Mar, to dig up the story of the great man's life, had promptly discovered that the story of his life could not be printed. His mother, a sullen short-order cook in a shack restaurant on the edge of a tourists' camping ground near Westfield, met all enquiries as to her son with an angry, "Ah, the hell with him; I hope he drowns." His father appeared to be in jail somewhere for stealing spotlights and laprobes from tourists' automobiles; his younger brother, a weak-minded lad, had but recently escaped from the Preston, Iowa Reformatory and was already wanted in several Western towns for the theft of money-order blanks from post offices. These alarming discoveries were still piling up at the very time that Pal Smurch, the greatest hero of the twentieth century, blear-eyed, dead for sleep, half-starved, was piloting his crazy junk-heap high above the region in which the lamentable story of his private life was being unearthed, headed for New York under greater glory than any man of his time had ever known.

The necessity for printing some account in the papers of the young man's career and personality had led to a remarkable predicament. It was of course impossible to reveal the facts, for a tremendous popular feeling in favor of the young hero had sprung up, like a grass fire, when he was halfway across Europe on his flight around the globe. He was, therefore, described as a modest chap, taciturn, blond, popular with his friends, popular with girls. The only available snapshot of Smurch, taken at the wheel of a phony automobile in a cheap photo studio at an amusement park, was touched up so that the little vulgarian looked quite handsome. His twisted leer was smoothed into a pleasant smile. The truth was, in this way, kept from the youth's ecstatic compatriots; they did not dream that the Smurch family was despised and feared by its neighbors in the obscure Iowa town, nor that the hero himself, because of numerous unsavory exploits, had come to be regarded in Westfield as a nuisance and a menace. He had, the reporters discovered, once knifed the principal of his high school—not mortally, to be sure, but he had knifed him; and on another occasion, surprised in the act of stealing an altar-cloth from a church, he had bashed the sacristan over the head with a pot of Easter lilies; for each of these offences he had served a sentence in the reformatory.

Inwardly, the authorities, both in New York and in Washington, prayed that an understanding Providence might, however awful such a thing seemed, bring disaster to the rusty, battered plane and its illustrious pilot, whose unheard-of flight had aroused the civilized world to hosannas of hysterical praise. The authorities were convinced that the character of the renowned aviator was such that the limelight of adulation was bound to reveal him to all the world, as a congenital hooligan mentally and morally unequipped to cope with his own prodigious fame. "I trust," said the Secretary of State, at one of many secret Cabinet meetings called to consider the national dilemma, "I trust that his mother's prayer will be answered," by which he referred to Mrs. Emma Smurch's wish that her son might be drowned. It was, however, too late for that—Smurch had leaped the Atlantic and then the Pacific as if they were millponds. At three minutes after two o'clock in the afternoon of 17 July, 1937, the garage boy brought his idiotic plane into Roosevelt Field for a perfect three-point landing.

It had, of course, been out of the question to arrange a modest little reception for the greatest flier in the history of the world. He was received at Roosevelt Field with such elaborate and pretentious ceremonies as rocked the world. Fortunately, however, the worn and spent hero promptly swooned, had to be removed bodily from his plane, and was spirited from the field without having opened his mouth once. Thus he did not jeopardize the dignity of this first reception, a reception illumined by the presence of the Secretaries of War and the Navy, Mayor Michael J. Moriarity of New York, the Premier of Canada, Governors Fanniman, Groves, McFeely, and Critchfield, and a brillant array of European diplomats. Smurch did not, in fact, come to in time to take part in the gigantic hullabaloo arranged at City Hall for the next day. He was rushed to a secluded nursing home and confined to bed. It was nine days before he was able to get up, or to be more exact, before he was permitted to get up. Meanwhile the greatest minds in the country, in solemn assembly, had arranged a secret conference of city, state and government officials, which Smurch was to attend for the purpose of being instructed in the ethics and behavior of heroism.

On the day that the little mechanic was finally allowed to get up and dress and, for the first time in two weeks, took a great chew of tobacco, he was permitted to receive the newspapermen—this by way of testing him out. Smurch did not wait for questions. "Youse guys," he said—and the *Times* man winced— "youse guys can tell the cock-eyed world dat I put it over on Lindbergh, see? Yeh—an' made an ass o' them two frogs." The "two frogs" was a reference to a pair of gallant French fliers who, in attempting a flight only halfway round the world, had, two weeks before, unhappily been lost at sea. The *Times* man was bold enough, at this point, to sketch out for Smurch the accepted formula for interviews in cases of this kind; he explained that there should be no arrogant statements belittling the achievements of other heroes, particularly heroes of foreign nations. "Ah, the hell with that," said Smurch. "I did it, see? I did it, an' I'm talkin' about it." And he did talk about it.

None of this extraordinary interview was, of course, printed. On the contrary, the newspapers, already under the disciplined direction of a secret directorate created for the occasion and composed of statesmen and editors, gave out to a panting and restless world that "Jacky," as he had been arbitrarily nicknamed, would consent to say only that he was very happy and that anyone could have done what he did. "My achievement has been, I fear, slightly exaggerated," the *Times* man's article had him protest, with a modest smile. These newspaper stories were kept from the hero, a restriction which did not serve to abate the rising malevolence of his temper. The situation was, indeed, extremely grave, for Pal Smurch was, as he kept insisting, "rarin' to go." He could not much longer be kept from a nation clamorous to lionize him. It was the most desperate crisis the United States of America had faced since the sinking of the *Lusitania*.

On the afternoon of the twenty-seventh of July, Smurch was spirited away to a conference-room in which were gathered mayors, governors, government officials, behaviorist psychologists, and editors. He gave them each a limp, moist paw and a brief unlovely grin. "Hah ya?" he said. When Smurch was seated, the Mayor of New York arose and, with obvious pessimism, attempted to explain what he must say and how he must act when presented to the world, ending his talk with a high tribute to the hero's courage and integrity. The Mayor was followed by Governor Fanniman of New York, who, after a touching declaration of faith, introduced Cameron Spottiswood, Second Secretary of the American Embassy in Paris, the gentlemen selected to coach Smurch in the amenities of public ceremonies. Sitting in a chair, with a soiled yellow tie in his hand and his shirt open at the throat, unshaved, smoking a rolled cigarette, Jack Smurch listened with a leer on his lips. "I get ya, I get ya," he cut in nastily. "Ya want me to ack like a softy, huh? Ya want me to ack like that—baby-faced Lindbergh, huh? Well, nuts to that, see?" Everyone took in his breath sharply; it was a sigh and a hiss. "Mr. Lindbergh," began a United States Senator, purple with rage, "and Mr. Byrd—" Smurch, who was paring his nails with a jackknife, cut in again, "Byrd!" he exclaimed. "Aw fa God's sake, dat big—" Somebody shut off his blasphemies with a sharp word. A newcomer had entered the room. Everyone stood up, except Smurch, who, still busy with his nails, did not even glance up. "Mr. Smurch," said someone sternly, "the President of the United States!" It had been thought that the presence of the Chief Executive might have a chastening effect upon the young hero, and the former had been, thanks to the remarkable co-operation of the press, secretly brought to the obscure conference-room.

A great, painful silence fell. Smurch looked up, waved a hand at the President. "How ya comin'?" he asked, and began rolling a fresh cigarette. The silence deepened. Someone coughed in a strained way. "Geez, it's hot, ain't it?" said Smurch. He loosened two more shirt buttons, revealing a hairy chest and the tattooed word "Sadie" enclosed in a stenciled heart. The great and important men in the room, faced by the most serious crisis in recent American history, exchanged worried frowns. Nobody seemed to know how to proceed. "Come awn, come awn," said Smurch. "Let's get the hell out of here! When do I start cuttin' in on de parties, huh? And what's they goin' to be *in* it?" He rubbed a thumb and a forefinger together meaningly. "Money!" exclaimed a state senator, shocked, pale. "Yeh, money," said Pal, flipping his cigarette out of a window, "an' big money." He began rolling a fresh cigarette. "Big money," he repeated, frowning over the rice paper. He tilted back in his chair, and leered at each gentleman, separately, the leer of an animal that knows its power, the leer of a leopard loose in a bird-and-dog shop. "Aw, fa God's sake, let's get some place where it's cooler," he said. "I been cooped up plenty for three weeks!"

Smurch stood up and walked over to an open window, where he stood staring down into the street, nine floors below. The faint shouting of newsboys floated up to him. He made out his name. "Hot dog!" he cried, grinning, ecstatic. He leaned out over the sill. "You tell 'em, babies!" he shouted down. "Hot diggity dog!" In the tense little knot of men standing behind him, a quick, mad impulse flared up. An unspoken word of appeal, of command, seemed to ring through the room. Yet it was deadly silent. Charles K. L. Brand, secretary to the Mayor of New York City, happened to be standing nearest Smurch; he looked inquiringly at the President of the United States. The President, pale, grim, nodded shortly. Brand, a tall, powerfully built man, once a tackle at Rutgers, stepped forward, seized the greatest man in the world by his left shoulder and the seat of his pants, and pushed him out of the window.

"My God, he's fallen out the window!" cried a quick-witted editor.

"Get me out of here!" cried the President. Several men sprang to his side and he was hurriedly escorted out of a door toward a side-entrance of the building. The editor of the Associated Press took charge, being used to such things. Crisply he ordered certain men to leave, others to stay; quickly he outlined a story which all the papers were to agree on, sent two men to the street to handle that end of the tragedy, commanded a Senator to sob and two Congressmen to go to pieces nervously. In a word, he skillfully set the stage for the gigantic task that was to follow, the task of breaking to a grief-stricken world the sad story of the untimely, accidental death of its most illustrious and spectacular figure.

The funeral was, as you know, the most elaborate, the finest, the solemnest, and the saddest ever held in the United States of America. The monument in Arlington Cemetery, with its clean white shaft of marble and the simple device of a tiny plane carved on its base, is a place for pilgrims, in deep reverence, to visit. The nations of the world paid lofty tributes to little Jacky Smurch, America's greatest hero. At a given hour there were two minutes of silence throughout the nation. Even the inhabitants of the small, bewildered town of Westfield, Iowa, observed this touching ceremony; agents of the Department of Justice saw to that. One of them was especially assigned to stand grimly in the doorway of a little shack restaurant on the edge of the tourists' camping ground just outside the town. There, under his stern scrutiny, Mrs. Emma Smurch bowed her head above two hamburger steaks sizzling on her grill—bowed her head and turned away, so that the Secret Service man could not see the twisted, strangely familiar, leer on her lips.

The Second Tree
From the Corner
(1947)

E. B. WHITE [1899–1985]

"Ever have any bizarre thoughts?" asked the doctor.

Mr. Trexler failed to catch the word. "What kind?" he said.

"Bizarre," repeated the doctor, his voice steady. He watched his patient for any slight change of expression, any wince. It seemed to Trexler that the doctor was not only watching him closely but was creeping slowly toward him, like a lizard toward a bug. Trexler shoved his chair back an inch and gathered himself for a reply. He was about to say "Yes" when he realized that if he said yes the next question would be unanswerable. Bizarre thoughts, bizarre thoughts? Ever have any bizarre thoughts? What kind of thoughts *except* bizarre had he had since the age of two?

Trexler felt the time passing, the necessity for an answer. These psychiatrists were busy men, overloaded, not to be kept waiting. The next patient was probably already perched out there in the waiting room, lonely, worried, shifting around on the sofa, his mind stuffed with bizarre thoughts and amorphous fears. Poor bastard, thought Trexler. Out there all alone in that misshapen antechamber, staring at the filing cabinet and wondering whether to tell the doctor about that day on the Madison Avenue bus.

Let's see, bizarre thoughts. Trexler dodged back along the dreadful corridor of the years to see what he could find. He felt the doctor's eyes upon him and knew that time was running out. Don't be so conscientious, he said to himself. If a bizarre thought is indicated here, just reach into the bag and pick anything at all. A man as well supplied with bizarre thoughts as you are should have no difficulty producing one for the record. Trexler darted into the bag, hung for a moment before one of his thoughts, as a hummingbird pauses in the delphinium. No, he said, not that one. He darted to another (the one about the rhesus monkey), paused, considered. No, he said, not that.

Trexler knew he must hurry. He had already used up pretty nearly four seconds since the question had been put. But it was an impossible situation—just one more lousy, impossible situation such as he was always getting himself into. When, he asked himself, are you going to quit maneuvering yourself into a pocket? He made one more effort. This time he stopped at the asylum, only the bars were lucite—fluted, retractable. Not here, he said. Not this one.

He looked straight at the doctor. "No," he said quietly. "I never have any bizarre thoughts."

The doctor sucked in on his pipe, blew a plume of smoke toward the rows of medical books. Trexler's gaze followed the smoke. He managed to make out one of the titles, "The Genito-Urinary System." A bright wave of fear swept cleanly over him, and he winced under the first pain of kidney stones. He remembered when he was a child, the first time he ever entered a doctor's office, sneaking a look at the titles of the books—and the flush of fear, the shirt wet under the arms, the book on t.b., the sudden knowledge that he was in the advanced stages of consumption, the quick vision of the hemorrhage. Trexler sighed wearily. Forty years, he thought, and I still get thrown by the title of a medical book. Forty years and I still can't stay on life's little bucky horse. No wonder I'm sitting here in this dreary joint at the end of this woebegone afternoon, lying about my bizarre thoughts to a doctor who looks, come to think of it, rather tired.

The session dragged on. After about twenty minutes, the doctor rose and knocked his pipe out. Trexler got up, knocked the ashes out of his brain, and waited. The doctor smiled warmly and stuck out his hand. "There's nothing the matter with you—you're just scared. Want to know how I know you're scared?"

"How?" asked Trexler.

"Look at the chair you've been sitting in! See how it has moved back away from my desk? You kept inching away from me while I asked you questions. That means you're scared."

"Does it?" said Trexler, faking a grin. "Yeah, I suppose it does."

They finished shaking hands. Trexler turned and walked out uncertainly along the passage, then into the waiting room and out past the next patient, a ruddy pin-striped man who was seated on the sofa twirling his hat nervously and staring straight ahead at the files. Poor, frightened guy, thought Trexler, he's probably read in the *Times* that one American male out of every two is going to die of heart disease by twelve o'clock next Thursday. It says that in the paper almost every morning. And he's also probably thinking about that day on the Madison Avenue bus.

A week later, Trexler was back in the patient's chair. And for several weeks thereafter he continued to visit the doctor, always toward the end of the afternoon, when the vapors hung thick above the pool of the mind and darkened the whole region of the East Seventies.[1] He felt no better as time went on, and he found it impossible to work. He discovered that the visits were becoming routine and that although the routine was one to which he certainly did not look forward, at least he could accept it with cool resignation, as once, years ago, he had accepted a long spell with a dentist who had settled down to a steady fooling with a couple of dead teeth. The visits, moreover, were now assuming a pattern recognizable to the patient.

Each session would begin with a résumé of symptoms—the dizziness in the streets, the constricting pain in the back of the neck, the apprehensions, the tightness of the scalp, the inability to concentrate, the despondency and the melancholy times, the feeling of pressure and tension, the anger at not being able to work, the anxiety over work not done, the gas on the stomach. Dullest set of neurotic symptoms in the world, Trexler would think, as he obediently

---

[1] The East Seventies is a neighborhood, much of it elegant and expensive, in Manhattan.

trudged back over them for the doctor's benefit. And then, having listened attentively to the recital, the doctor would spring his question: "Have you ever found anything that gives you relief?" And Trexler would answer, "Yes. A drink." And the doctor would nod his head knowingly.

As he became familiar with the pattern Trexler found that he increasingly tended to identify himself with the doctor, transferring himself into the doctor's seat—probably (he thought) some rather slick form of escapism. At any rate, it was nothing new for Trexler to identify himself with other people. Whenever he got into a cab, he instantly became the driver, saw everything from the hackman's angle (and the reaching over with the right hand, the nudging of the flag, the pushing it down, all the way down along the side of the meter), saw everything—traffic, fare, everything—through the eyes of Anthony Rocco, or Isidore Freedman, or Matthew Scott. In a barbershop, Trexler was the barber, his fingers curled around the comb, his hand on the tonic. Perfectly natural, then, that Trexler should soon be occupying the doctor's chair, asking the questions, waiting for the answers. He got quite interested in the doctor, in this way. He liked him, and he found him a not too difficult patient.

It was on the fifth visit, about halfway through, that the doctor turned to Trexler and said, suddenly, "What do you want?" He gave the word "want" special emphasis.

"I d'know," replied Trexler uneasily. "I guess nobody knows the answer to that one."

"Sure they do," replied the doctor.

"Do *you* know what *you* want?" asked Trexler narrowly.

"Certainly," said the doctor. Trexler noticed that at this point the doctor's chair slid slightly backward, away from him. Trexler stifled a small, internal smile. Scared as a rabbit, he said to himself. Look at him scoot!

"What *do* you want?" continued Trexler, pressing his advantage, pressing it hard.

The doctor glided back another inch away from his inquisitor. "I want a wing on the small house I own in Westport. I want more money, and more leisure to do the things I want to do."

Trexler was just about to say, "And what are those things you want to do, Doctor?" when he caught himself. Better not go too far, he mused. Better not lose possession of the ball. And besides, he thought, what the hell goes on here, anyway—me paying fifteen bucks a throw for these séances and then doing the work myself, asking the questions, weighing the answers. So he wants a new wing! There's a fine piece of theatrical gauze for you! A new wing.

Trexler settled down again and resumed the role of patient for the rest of the visit. It ended on a kindly, friendly note. The doctor reassured him that his fears were the cause of his sickness, and that his fears were unsubstantial. They shook hands, smiling.

Trexler walked dizzily through the empty waiting room and the doctor followed along to let him out. It was late; the secretary had shut up shop and gone home. Another day over the dam. "Goodbye," said Trexler. He stepped into the street, turned west toward Madison, and thought of the doctor all alone there, after hours, in that desolate hole—a man who worked longer hours than his secretary. Poor, scared, overworked bastard, thought Trexler. And that new wing!

It was an evening of clearing weather, the Park showing green and desirable in the distance, the last daylight applying a high lacquer to the brick and brownstone walls and giving the street scene a luminous and intoxicating splendor. Trexler meditated, as he walked, on what he wanted. "What do you want?" he heard again. Trexler knew what he wanted, and what, in general, all men wanted; and he was glad, in a way, that it was both inexpressible and unattainable, and that it wasn't a wing. He was satisfied to remember that it was deep, formless, enduring, and impossible of fulfillment, and that it made men sick, and that when you sauntered along Third Avenue and looked through the doorways into the dim saloons, you could sometimes pick out from the unregenerate ranks the ones who had not forgotten, gazing steadily into the bottoms of the glasses on the long chance that they could get another little peek at it. Trexler found himself renewed by the remembrance that what he wanted was at once great and microscopic, and that although it borrowed from the nature of large deeds and of youthful love and of old songs and early intimations, it was not any one of these things, and that it had not been isolated or pinned down, and that a man who attempted to define it in the privacy of a doctor's office would fall flat on his face.

Trexler felt invigorated. Suddenly his sickness seemed health, his dizziness stability. A small tree, rising between him and the light, stood there saturated with the evening, each gilt-edged leaf perfectly drunk with excellence and delicacy. Trexler's spine registered an ever so slight tremor as it picked up this natural disturbance in the lovely scene. "I want the second tree from the corner, just as it stands," he said, answering an imaginary question from an imaginary physician. And he felt a slow pride in realizing that what he wanted none could bestow, and that what he had none could take away. He felt content to be sick, unembarrassed at being afraid; and in the jungle of his fear he glimpsed (as he had so often glimpsed them before) the flashy tail feathers of the bird courage.

Then he thought once again of the doctor, and of his being left there all alone, tired, frightened. (The poor, scared guy, thought Trexler.) Trexler began humming "Moonshine Lullaby," his spirit reacting instantly to the hypodermic of Merman's[2] healthy voice. He crossed Madison, boarded a downtown bus, and rode all the way to Fifty-second Street before he had a thought that could rightly have been called bizarre.

QUESTIONS

1. At the beginning of the story, the doctor asks Mr. Trexler if he ever had any bizarre thoughts. What is Trexler's reply? Why does he give that reply? Can you

---

[2] Ethel Merman (b. 1909), a musical comedy star with a strong voice.

imagine, from Trexler's ruminations, what sort of bizarre thoughts he might have had? Would it be more effective if White indicated precisely what Trexler's thoughts had been? Explain.   **2.**   The seminal question in this story is put by the doctor to Trexler: "What do you want?" What is Trexler's answer? What is the doctor's response? What do *you* want?   **3.**   Trexler, we are told, knew what he wanted and was glad "that it was both inexpressible and unattainable." In what sense is Trexler's desire inexpressible and unattainable?   **4.**   In what sense might this be a story about the difference between being afraid and unafraid?

WRITING TOPIC
How does Trexler's recognition that he wants "the second tree from the corner, just as it stands" result in his feeling "content to be sick"?

The Man Who Lived Underground

RICHARD WRIGHT [1908–1960]

1944

I've got to hide, he told himself. His chest heaved as he waited, crouching in a dark corner of the vestibule. He was tired of running and dodging. Either he had to find a place to hide, or he had to surrender. A police car swished by through the rain, its siren rising sharply. They're looking for me all over . . . He crept to the door and squinted through the fogged plate glass. He stiffened as the siren rose and died in the distance. Yes, he had to hide, but where? He gritted his teeth. Then a sudden movement in the street caught his attention. A throng of tiny columns of water snaked into the air from the perforations of a manhole cover. The columns stopped abruptly, as though the perforations had become clogged; a gray spout of sewer water jutted up from underground and lifted the circular metal cover, juggled it for a moment, then let it fall with a clang.

He hatched a tentative plan: he would wait until the siren sounded far off, then he would go out. He smoked and waited, tense. At last the siren gave him his signal; it wailed, dying, going away from him. He stepped to the sidewalk, then paused and looked curiously at the open manhole, half expecting the cover to leap up again. He went to the center of the street and stooped and peered into the hole, but could see nothing. Water rustled in the black depths.

He started with terror; the siren sounded so near that he had the idea that he had been dreaming and had awakened to find the car upon him. He dropped instinctively to his knees and his hands grasped the rim of the manhole. The siren seemed to hoot directly above him and with a wild gasp of exertion he snatched the cover far enough off to admit his body. He swung his legs over the opening and lowered himself into watery darkness. He hung for an eternal moment to the rim by his finger tips, then he felt rough metal prongs and at once, he knew that sewer workmen used these ridges to lower themselves into manholes. Fist over fist, he let his body sink until he could feel no more prongs. He swayed in dank space; the siren seemed to howl at the very rim of the manhole. He dropped and was washed violently into an ocean of warm, leaping water. His head was battered against a wall and he wondered if this were death. Frenziedly his fingers clawed and sank into a crevice. He steadied himself and measured the strength of the current with his own muscular tension. He stood slowly in water that dashed past his knees with fearful velocity.

He heard a prolonged scream of brakes and the siren broke off. Oh, God! They had found him! Looming above his head in the rain a white face hovered over the hole. "How did this damn thing get off?" he heard a policeman ask. He saw the steel cover move slowly until the hole looked like a quarter moon turned black. "Give me a hand here," someone called. The cover clanged into place, muffling the sights and sounds of the upper world. Knee-deep in the pulsing current, he breathed with aching chest, filling his lungs with the hot stench of yeasty rot.

From the perforations of the manhole cover, delicate lances of hazy violet sifted down and wove a mottled pattern upon the surface of the streaking current. His lips parted as a car swept past along the wet pavement overhead, its heavy rumble soon dying out, like the hum of a plane speeding through a dense cloud. He had never thought that cars could sound like that; everything seemed strange and unreal under here. He stood in darkness for a long time, knee-deep in rustling water, musing.

The odor of rot had become so general that he no longer smelled it. He got his cigarettes, but discovered that his matches were wet. He searched and found a dry folder in the pocket of his shirt and managed to strike one; it flared weirdly in the wet gloom, glowing greenishly, turning red, orange, then yellow. He lit a crumpled cigarette; then, by the flickering light of the match, he looked for support so that he would not have to keep his muscles flexed against the pouring water. His pupils narrowed and he saw to either side of him two steaming walls that rose and curved inward some six feet above his head to form a dripping, mouse-colored dome. The bottom of the sewer was a sloping V-trough. To the left, the sewer vanished in ashen fog. To the right was a steep down-curve into which water plunged.

He saw now that had he not regained his feet in time, he would have been swept to death, or had he entered any other manhole he would have probably drowned. Above the rush of the current he heard sharper juttings of water; tiny streams were spewing into the sewer from smaller conduits. The match died; he struck another and saw a mass of debris sweep past him and clog the throat of the down-curve. At once the water began rising rapidly. Could he climb out before he drowned? A long hiss sounded and the debris was sucked from sight; the current lowered. He understood now what had made the water toss the manhole cover; the down-curve had become temporarily obstructed and the perforations had become clogged.

He was in danger; he might slide into a down-curve; he might wander with a lighted match into a pocket of gas and blow himself up; or he might contract some horrible disease . . . Though he wanted to leave, an irrational impulse held him rooted. To the left, the convex ceiling swooped to a height of less than five feet. With cigarette slanting from pursed lips, he waded with taut muscles, his feet sloshing over the slimy bottom, his shoes sinking into spongy slop, the slate-colored water cracking in creamy foam against his knees. Pressing flat his left palm against the lowered ceiling, he struck another match and saw a metal pole nestling in a niche of the wall. Yes, some sewer workman had left it. He reached for it, then jerked his head away as a whisper of scurrying life whisked past and was still. He held the match close and saw a huge rat, wet with slime, blinking beady eyes and baring tiny fangs. The light blinded the rat and the frizzled head moved aimlessly. He grabbed the pole and let it fly against the rat's soft body; there was shrill piping and the grizzly body splashed into the dun-colored water and was snatched out of sight, spinning in the scuttling stream.

He swallowed and pushed on, following the curve of the misty cavern, sounding the water with the pole. By the faint light of another manhole cover he saw, amid loose wet brick, a hole with walls of damp earth leading into blackness. Gingerly he poked the pole into it; it was hollow and went beyond the length of the pole. He shoved the pole before him, hoisted himself upward, got to his hands and knees, and crawled. After a few yards he paused, struck to wonderment by the silence; it seemed that he had traveled a million miles away from the world. As he inched forward again he could sense the bottom of the dirt tunnel becoming dry and lowering slightly. Slowly he rose and to his astonishment he stood erect. He could not hear the rustling of the water now and he felt confoundingly alone, yet lured by the darkness and silence.

He crept a long way, then stopped, curious, afraid. He put his right foot forward and it dangled in space; he drew back in fear. He thrust the pole outward and it swung in emptiness. He trembled, imagining the earth crumbling and burying him alive. He scratched a match and saw that the dirt floor sheered away steeply and widened into a sort of cave some five feet below him. An old sewer, he muttered. He cocked his head, hearing a feathery cadence which he could not identify. The match ceased to burn.

Using the pole as a kind of ladder, he slid down and stood in darkness. The air was a little fresher and he could still hear vague noises. Where was he? He felt suddenly that someone was standing near him and he turned sharply, but there was only darkness. He poked cautiously and felt a brick wall; he followed it and the strange sounds grew louder. He ought to get out of here. This was crazy. He could not remain here for any length of time; there was no food and no place to sleep. But the faint sounds tantalized him; they were strange but familiar. Was it a motor? A baby crying? Music? A siren? He groped on, and the sounds came so clearly that he could feel the pitch and timbre of human voices. Yes, singing! That was it! He listened with open mouth. It was a church service. Enchanted, he groped toward the waves of melody.

> Jesus, take me to your home above
> And fold me in the bosom of Thy love . . .

The singing was on the other side of the brick wall. Excited, he wanted to watch the service without being seen. Whose church was it? He knew most of the churches in this area above ground, but the singing sounded too strange and detached for him to guess. He looked to the left, to the right, down to the black dirt, then upward and was startled to see a bright sliver of light slicing the darkness like the blade of a razor. He struck one of his two remaining matches and saw rusty pipes running along an old concrete ceiling. Photographically he located the exact position of the pipes in his mind. The match flame sank and he sprang upward; his hands clutched a pipe. He swung his legs and tossed his body onto the bed of pipes and they creaked, swaying up and down; he thought that the tier was about to crash, but nothing happened. He edged to the crevice and saw a segment of black men and women, dressed in white robes, singing, holding tattered songbooks in their black palms. His first impulse was to laugh, but he checked himself.

What was he doing? He was crushed with a sense of guilt. Would God strike him dead for that? The singing swept on and he shook his head, disagreeing in spite of himself. They oughtn't to do that, he thought. But he could think of no reason *why* they should not do it. Just singing with the air of the sewer blowing in on them . . . He felt that he was gazing upon something abysmally obscene, yet he could not bring himself to leave.

After a long time he grew numb and dropped to the dirt. Pain throbbed in his legs and a deeper pain, induced by the sight of those black people groveling and begging for something they could never get, churned in him. A vague conviction made him feel that those people should stand unrepentant and yield no quarter in singing and praying, yet *he* had run away from the police, had pleaded with them to believe in *his* innocence. He shook his head, bewildered.

How long had he been down here? He did not know. This was a new kind of living for him; the intensity of feelings he had experienced when looking at the church people sing made him certain that he had been down here a long time, but his mind told him that the time must have been short. In this darkness the only notion he had of time was when a match flared and measured time by its fleeting light. He groped back through the hole toward the sewer and the waves of song subsided and finally he could not hear them at all. He came to where the earth hole ended and he heard the noise of the current and time lived again for him, measuring the moments by the wash of the water.

The rain must have slackened, for the flow of water had lessened and came only to his ankles. Ought he to go up into the streets and take his chances on hiding somewhere else? But they would surely catch him. The mere thought of dodging and running again from the police made him tense. No, he would stay and plot how to elude them. But what could he do down here? He walked forward into the sewer and came to another manhole cover; he stood beneath it, debating. Fine pencils of gold spilled suddenly from the little circles in the manhole cover and trembled on the surface of the current. Yes, street lamps . . . It must be night . . .

He went forward for about a quarter of an hour, wading aimlessly, poking the pole carefully before him. Then he stopped, his eyes fixed and intent. What's that? A strangely familiar image attracted and repelled him. Lit by the yellow stems from another manhole cover was a tiny nude body of a baby snagged by debris and half-submerged in water. Thinking that the baby was alive, he moved impulsively to save it, but his roused feelings told him that it was dead, cold, nothing, the same nothingness he had felt while watching the men and women singing in the church. Water blossomed about the tiny legs, the tiny arms, the tiny head, and rushed onward. The eyes were closed, as though in sleep; the fists were clenched, as though in protest; and the mouth gaped black in a soundless cry.

He straightened and drew in his breath, feeling that he had been staring for all eternity at the ripples of veined water skimming impersonally over the shriveled limbs. He felt as condemned as when the policemen had accused him. Involuntarily he lifted his hand to brush the vision away, but his arm fell listlessly to his side. Then he acted; he closed his eyes and reached forward slowly with the soggy shoe of his right foot and shoved the dead baby from where it had been lodged. He kept his eyes closed, seeing the little body twisting in the current as it floated from sight. He opened his eyes, shivered, placed his knuckles in the sockets, hearing the water speed in the somber shadows.

He tramped on, sensing at times a sudden quickening in the current as he passed some conduit whose waters were swelling the stream that slid by his feet. A few minutes later he was standing under another manhole cover, listening to the faint rumble of noises above ground. Streetcars and trucks, he mused. He looked down and saw a stagnant pool of gray-green sludge; at intervals a balloon pocket rose from the scum, glistening a bluish-purple, and burst. Then another. He turned, shook his head, and tramped back to the dirt cave by the church, his lips quivering.

Back in the cave, he sat and leaned his back against a dirt wall. His body was trembling slightly. Finally his senses quieted and he slept. When he awakened he felt stiff and cold. He had to leave this foul place, but leaving meant facing those policemen who had wrongly accused him. No, he could not go back aboveground. He remembered the beating they had given him and how he had signed his name to a confession, a confession which he had not even read. He had been too tired when they had shouted at him, demanding that he sign his name; he had signed it to end his pain.

He stood and groped about in the darkness. The church singing had stopped. How long had he slept? He did not know. But he felt refreshed and hungry. He doubled his fist nervously, realizing that he could not make a decision. As he walked about he stumbled over an old rusty iron pipe. He picked it up and felt a jagged edge. Yes, there was a brick wall and he could dig into it. What would he find? Smiling, he groped to the brick wall, sat, and began digging idly into damp cement. I can't make any noise, he cautioned himself. As time passed he grew thirsty, but there was no water. He had to kill time or go aboveground. The cement came out of the wall easily; he extracted four bricks and felt a soft draft blowing into his face. He stopped, afraid. What was beyond? He waited a long time and nothing happened; then he began digging again, soundlessly, slowly; he enlarged the hole and crawled through into a dark room and collided with another wall. He felt his way to the right; the wall ended and his fingers toyed in space, like the antennae of an insect.

He fumbled on and his feet struck something hollow, like wood. What's this? He felt with his fingers. Steps . . . He stooped and pulled off his shoes and mounted the stairs and saw a yellow chink of light shining and heard a low voice speaking. He placed his eye to a keyhole and saw the nude waxen figure of a man stretched out upon a white table. The voice, low-pitched and vibrant, mumbled indistinguishable words, neither rising nor falling. He craned his neck and squinted to see the man who was talking, but he could not locate him. Above the naked figure was suspended a huge glass container filled with a blood-red liquid from which a white rubber tube dangled. He crouched closer to the door and saw the tip end of a black object lined with pink satin. A coffin, he breathed. This is an undertaker's establishment . . . A fine-spun lace of ice covered his body and he shuddered. A throaty chuckle sounded in the depths of the yellow room.

He turned to leave. Three steps down it occurred to him that a light switch should be nearby; he felt along the wall, found an electric button, pressed it, and a blinding glare smote his pupils so hard that he was sightless, defenseless. His pupils contracted and he wrinkled his nostrils at a peculiar odor. At once he knew that he had been dimly aware of this odor in the darkness, but the light had brought it sharply to his attention. Some kind of stuff they use to embalm, he thought. He went down the steps and saw piles of lumber, coffins, and a long workbench. In one corner was a tool chest. Yes, he could use tools, could tunnel through walls with them. He lifted the lid of the chest and saw nails, a hammer, a crowbar, a screwdriver, a light bulb, and a long length of electric wire. Good! He would lug these back to his cave.

He was about to hoist the chest to his shoulders when he discovered a door behind the furnace. Where did it lead? He tried to open it and found it securely bolted. Using the crowbar so as to make no sound, he pried the door open; it swung on creaking hinges, outward. Fresh air came to his face and he caught the faint roar of faraway sound. Easy now, he told himself. He widened the door and a lump of coal rattled toward him. A coalbin . . . Evidently the door led into another basement. The roaring noise was louder, but he could not identify it. Where was he? He groped slowly over the coal pile, then ranged in darkness over a gritty floor. The roaring noise seemed to come from above him, then below. His fingers followed a wall until he touched a wooden ridge. A door, he breathed.

The noise died to a low pitch; he felt his skin prickle. It seemed that he was playing a game with an unseen person whose intelligence outstripped his. He put his ear to the flat surface of the door. Yes, voices . . . Was this a prize fight stadium? The sound of the voices came near and sharp, but he could not tell if they were joyous or despairing. He twisted the knob until he heard a soft click and felt the springy weight of the door swinging toward him. He was afraid to open it, yet captured by curiosity and wonder. He jerked the door wide and saw on the far side of the basement a furnace glowing red. Ten feet away was still another door, half ajar. He crossed and peered through the door into an empty, high-ceilinged corridor that terminated in a dark complex of shadow. The belling voices rolled about him and his eagerness mounted. He stepped into the corridor and the voices swelled louder. He crept on and came to a narrow stairway leading circularly upward; there was no question but that he was going to ascend those stairs.

Mounting the spiraled staircase, he heard the voices roll in a steady wave, then leap to crescendo, only to die away, but always remaining audible. Ahead of him glowed red letters: E—X—I—T. At the top of the steps he paused in front of a black curtain that fluttered uncertainly. He parted the folds and looked into a convex depth that gleamed with clusters of shimmering lights. Sprawled below him was a stretch of human faces, tilted upward, chanting, whistling, screaming, laughing. Dangling before the faces, high upon a screen of silver, were jerking shadows. A movie, he said with slow laughter breaking from his lips.

He stood in a box in the reserved section of a movie house and the impulse he had had to tell the people in the church to stop their singing seized him. These people were laughing at their lives, he thought with amazement. They were shouting and yelling at the animated shadows of themselves. His compassion fired his imagination and he stepped out of the box, walked out upon thin air, walked on down to the audience; and, hovering in the air just above them, he stretched out his hand to touch them . . . His tension snapped and he found himself back in the box, looking down into the sea of faces. No; it could not be done; he could not awaken them. He sighed. Yes, these people were children, sleeping in their living, awake in their dying.

He turned away, parted the black curtain, and looked out. He saw no one. He started down the white stone steps and when he reached the bottom he saw a man in trim blue uniform coming toward him. So used had he become to being underground that he thought that he could walk past the man, as though he were a ghost. But the man stopped. And he stopped.

"Looking for the men's room, sir?" the man asked, and without waiting for an answer, he turned and pointed. "This way, sir. The first door to your right."

He watched the man turn and walk up the steps and go out of sight. Then he laughed. What a funny fellow! He went back to the basement and stood in the red darkness, watching the glowing embers in the furnace. He went to the sink and turned the faucet and the water flowed in a smooth silent stream that looked like a spout of blood. He brushed the mad image from his mind and began to wash his hands leisurely, looking about for the usual bar of soap. He found one and rubbed it in his palms until a rich lather bloomed in his cupped fingers, like a scarlet sponge. He scrubbed and rinsed his hands meticulously, then hunted for a towel; there was none. He shut off the water, pulled off his shirt, dried his hands on it; when he put it on again he was grateful for the cool dampness that came to his skin.

Yes, he was thirsty; he turned on the faucet again, bowled his fingers and when the water bubbled over the brim of his cupped palms, he drank in long, slow swallows. His bladder grew tight; he shut off the water, faced the wall, bent his head, and watched a red stream strike the floor. His nostrils wrinkled against acrid wisps of vapor; though he had tramped in the waters of the sewer; he stepped back from the wall so that his shoes, wet with sewer slime, would not touch his urine.

He heard footsteps and crawled quickly into the coalbin. Lumps rattled noisily. The footsteps came into the basement and stopped. Who was it? Had someone heard him and come down to investigate? He waited, crouching, sweating. For a long time there was silence, then he heard the clang of metal and a brighter glow lit the room. Somebody's tending the furnace, he thought. Footsteps came closer and he stiffened. Looming before him was a white face lined with coal dust, the face of an old man with watery blue eyes. Highlights spotted his gaunt cheekbones, and he held a huge shovel. There was a screechy scrape of metal against stone, and the old man lifted a shovelful of coal and went from sight.

The room dimmed momentarily, then a yellow glare came as coal flared at the furnace door. Six times the old man came to the bin and went to the furnace with shovels of coal, but not once did he lift his eyes. Finally he dropped the shovel, mopped his face with a dirty handkerchief, and sighed: "Wheeew!" He turned slowly and trudged out of the basement, his footsteps dying away.

He stood, and lumps of coal clattered down the pile. He stepped from the bin and was startled to see the shadowy outline of an electric bulb hanging above his head. Why had not the old man turned it on? Oh, yes . . . He understood. The old man had worked here for so long that he had no need for light; he had learned a way of seeing in his dark world, like those sightless worms that inch along underground by a sense of touch.

His eyes fell upon a lunch pail and he was afraid to hope that it was full. He picked it up; it was heavy. He opened it. *Sandwiches!* He looked guiltily around; he was alone. He searched farther and found a folder of matches and a half-empty tin of tobacco; he put them eagerly into his pocket and clicked off the light. With the lunch pail under his arm, he went through the door, groped over the pile of coal, and stood again in the lighted basement of the undertaking establishment. I've got to get those tools, he told himself. And turn off that light. He tiptoed back up the steps and switched off the light; the invisible voice still droned on behind the door. He crept down and, seeing with his fingers, opened the lunch pail and tore off a piece of paper bag and brought out the tin and spilled grains of tobacco into the makeshift concave. He rolled it and wet it with spittle, then inserted one end into his mouth and lit it: he sucked smoke that bit his lungs. The nicotine reached his brain, went out along his arms to his finger tips, down to his stomach, and over all the tired nerves of his body.

He carted the tools to the hole he had made in the wall. Would the noise of the falling chest betray him? But he would have to take a chance; he had to have those tools. He lifted the chest and shoved it; it hit the dirt on the other side of the wall with a loud clatter. He waited, listening; nothing happened. Head first, he slithered through and stood in the cave. He grinned, filled with a cunning idea. Yes, he would now go back into the basement of the undertaking establishment and crouch behind the coal pile and dig another hole. Sure! Fumbling, he opened the tool chest and extracted a crowbar, a screwdriver, and a hammer; he fastened them securely about his person.

With another lumpish cigarette in his flexed lips, he crawled back through the hole and over the coal pile and sat, facing the brick wall. He jabbed with the crowbar and the cement sheered away; quicker than he thought, a brick came loose. He worked an hour; the other bricks did not come easily. He sighed, weak from effort. I ought to rest a little, he thought. I'm hungry. He felt his way back to the cave and stumbled along the wall till he came to the tool chest. He sat upon it, opened the lunch pail, and took out two thick sandwiches. He smelled them. Pork chops . . . His mouth watered. He closed his eyes and devoured a sandwich, savoring the smooth rye bread and juicy meat. He ate rapidly, gulping down lumpy mouthfuls that made him long for water. He ate the other sandwich and found an apple and gobbled that up too, sucking the core till the last trace of flavor was drained from it. Then, like a dog, he ground the meat bones with his teeth, enjoying the salty, tangy marrow. He finished and stretched out full length on the ground and went to sleep. . . .

 . . . His body was washed by cold water that gradually turned warm and he was buoyed upon a stream and swept out to sea where waves rolled gently and suddenly he found himself walking upon the water how strange and delightful to walk upon the water and he came upon a nude woman holding a nude baby in her arms and the woman was sinking into the water holding the baby above her head and screaming *help* and he ran over the water to the woman and he reached her just before she went down and he took the baby from her hands and stood watching the breaking bubbles where the woman sank and he called *lady* and still no answer yes dive down there and rescue that woman but he could not take this baby with him and he stooped and laid the baby tenderly upon the surface of the water expecting it to sink but it floated and he leaped into the water and held his breath and strained his eyes to see through the gloomy volume of water but there was no woman and he opened his mouth and called *lady* and the water bubbled and his chest ached and his arms were tired but he could not see the woman and he called again *lady lady* and his feet touched sand at the bottom of the sea and his chest felt as though it would burst and he bent his knees and propelled himself upward and water rushed past him and his head bobbed out and he breathed deeply and looked around where was the baby the baby was gone and he rushed over the water looking for the baby calling *where is it* and the empty sky and sea threw back his voice *where is it* and he began to doubt that he could stand upon the water and then he was sinking and as he struggled the water rushed him downward spinning dizzily and he opened his mouth to call for help and water surged into his lungs and he choked . . .

He groaned and leaped erect in the dark, his eyes wide. The images of terror that thronged his brain would not let him sleep. He rose, made sure that the tools were hitched to his belt, and groped his way to the coal pile and found the rectangular gap from which he had taken the bricks. He took out the crowbar and hacked. Then dread paralyzed him. How long had he slept? Was it day or night now? He had to be careful. Someone might hear him if it were day. He hewed softly for hours at the cement, working silently. Faintly quivering in the air above him was the dim sound of yelling voices. Crazy people, he muttered. They're still there in that movie . . .

Having rested, he found the digging much easier. He soon had a dozen bricks out. His spirits rose. He took out another brick and his fingers fluttered in space. Good! What lay ahead of him? Another basement? He made the hole larger, climbed through, walked over an uneven floor and felt a metal surface. He lighted a match and saw that he was standing behind a furnace in a basement; before him, on the far side of the room, was a door. He crossed and opened it; it was full of odds and ends. Daylight spilled from a window above his head.

Then he was aware of a soft, continuous tapping. What was it? A clock? No, it was louder than a clock and more irregular. He placed an old empty box beneath the window, stood upon it, and looked into an areaway. He eased the window up and crawled through; the sound of the tapping came clearly now. He glanced about; he was alone. Then he looked upward at a series of window ledges. The tapping identified itself. That's a typewriter, he said to himself. It seemed to be coming from just above. He grasped the ridges of a rain pipe and lifted himself upward; through a half-inch opening of window he saw a doorknob about three feet away. No, it was not a doorknob; it was a small circular disk made of stainless steel with many fine markings upon it. He held his breath; an eerie white hand, seemingly detached from its arm, touched the metal knob and whirled it, first to the left, then to the right. It's a safe! . . . Suddenly he could see the dial no more; a huge metal door swung slowly toward him and he was looking into a safe filled with green wads of paper money, rows of coins wrapped in brown paper, and glass jars and boxes of various sizes. His heart quickened. Good Lord! The white hand went in and out of the safe, taking wads of bills and cylinders of coins. The hand vanished and he heard the muffled click of the big door as it closed. Only the steel dial was visible now. The typewriter still tapped in his ears, but he could not see it. He blinked, wondering if what he had seen was real. There was more money in that safe than he had seen in all his life.

As he clung to the rain pipe, a daring idea came to him and he pulled the screwdriver from his belt. If the white hand twirled that dial again, he would be able to see how far to left and right it spun and he would have the combination! His blood tingled. I can scratch the numbers right here, he thought. Holding the pipe with one hand, he made the sharp edge of the screwdriver bite into the brick wall. Yes, he could do it. Now, he was set. Now, he had a reason for staying here in the underground. He waited for a long time, but the white hand did not return. Goddamn! Had he been more alert, he could have counted the twirls and he would have had the combination. He got down and stood in the areaway, sunk in reflection.

How could he get into that room? He climbed back into the basement and saw wooden steps leading upward. Was that the room where the safe stood? Fearing that the dial was now being twirled, he clambered through the window, hoisted himself up the rain pipe, and peered; he saw only the naked gleam of the steel dial. He got down and doubled his fists. Well, he would explore the basement. He returned to the basement room and mounted the steps to the door and squinted through the keyhole; all was dark, but the tapping was still somewhere near, still faint and directionless. He pushed the door in; along one wall of a room was a table piled with radios and electrical equipment. A radio shop, he muttered.

Well, he could rig up a radio in his cave. He found a sack, slid the radio into it, and slung it across his back. Closing the door, he went down the steps and stood again in the basement, disappointed. He had not solved the problem of the steel dial and he was irked. He set the radio on the floor and again hoisted himself through the window and up the rain pipe and squinted; the metal door was swinging shut. Goddamn! He's worked the combination again. If I had been patient, I'd have had it! How could he get into that room? He *had* to get into it. He could jimmy the window, but it would be much better if he could get in without any traces. To the right of him, he calculated, should be the basement of the building that held the safe; therefore, if he dug a hole right *here,* he ought to reach his goal.

He began a quiet scraping; it was hard work, for the bricks were not damp. He eventually got one out and lowered it softly to the floor. He had to be careful; perhaps people were beyond this wall. He extracted a second layer of brick and found still another. He gritted his teeth, ready to quit. I'll dig one more, he resolved. When the next brick came out he felt air blowing into his face. He waited to be challenged, but nothing happened.

He enlarged the hole and pulled himself through and stood in quiet darkness. He scratched a match to flame and saw steps; he mounted and peered through a keyhole; Darkness . . . He strained to hear the typewriter, but there was only silence. Maybe the office had closed? He twisted the knob and swung the door in; a frigid blast made him shiver. In the shadows before him were halves and quarters of hogs and lambs and steers hanging from metal hooks on the low ceiling, red meat encased in folds of cold white fat. Fronting him was frost-coated glass from behind which came indistinguishable sounds. The odor of fresh raw meat sickened him and he backed away. A meat market, he whispered.

He ducked his head, suddenly blinded by light. He narrowed his eyes; the red-white rows of meat were drenched in yellow glare. A man wearing a crimson spotted jacket came in and took down a bloody meat cleaver. He eased the door to, holding it ajar just enough to watch the man, hoping that the darkness in which he stood would keep him from being seen. The man took down a hunk of steer and placed it upon a bloody wooden block and bent forward and whacked with the cleaver. The man's face was hard, square, grim; a jet of mustache smudged his upper lip and a glistening cowlick of hair fell over his left eye. Each time he lifted the cleaver and brought it down upon the meat, he let out a short, deep-chested grunt. After he had cut the meat, he wiped blood off the wooden block with a sticky wad of gunny sack and hung the cleaver upon a hook. His face was proud as he placed the chunk of meat in the crook of his elbow and left.

The door slammed and the light went off; once more he stood in shadow. His tension ebbed. From behind the frosted glass he heard the man's voice: "Forty-eight cents a pound, ma'am." He shuddered, feeling that there was something he had to do. But what? He stared fixedly at the cleaver, then he sneezed and was terrified for fear that the man had heard him. But the door did not open. He took down the cleaver and examined the sharp edge smeared with cold blood. Behind the ice-coated glass a cash register rang with a vibrating, musical tinkle.

Absent-mindedly holding the meat cleaver, he rubbed the glass with his thumb and cleared a spot that enabled him to see into the front of the store. The shop was empty, save for the man who was now putting on his hat and coat. Beyond the front window a wan sun shone in the streets; people passed and now and then a fragment of laughter or the whir of a speeding auto came to him. He peered closer and saw on the right counter of the shop a mosquito netting covering pears, grapes, lemons, oranges, bananas, peaches, and plums. His stomach contracted.

The man clicked out the light and he gritted this teeth, muttering, Don't lock the icebox door . . . The man went through the door of the shop and locked it from the outside. Thank God! Now, he would eat some more! He waited, trembling. The sun died and its rays lingered on in the sky, turning the streets to dusk. He opened the door and stepped inside the shop. In reverse letters across the front window was: NICK'S FRUITS AND MEATS. He laughed, picked up a soft ripe yellow pear and bit into it; juice squirted; his mouth ached as his saliva glands reacted to the acid of the fruit. He ate three pears, gobbled six bananas, and made away with several oranges, taking a bite out of their tops and holding them to his lips and squeezing them as he hungrily sucked the juice.

He found a faucet, turned it on, laid the cleaver aside, pursed his lips under the stream until his stomach felt about to burst. He straightened and belched, feeling satisfied for the first time since he had been underground. He sat upon the floor, rolled and lit a cigarette, his bloodshot eyes squinting against the film of drifting smoke. He watched a patch of sky turn red, then purple; night fell and he lit another cigarette, brooding. Some part of him was trying to remember the world he had left, and another part of him did not want to remember it. Sprawling before him in his mind was his wife, Mrs. Wooten for whom he worked, the three policemen who had picked him up . . . He possessed them now more completely than he had ever possessed them when he had lived aboveground. How this had come about he could not say, but he had no desire to go back to them. He laughed, crushed the cigarette, and stood up.

He went to the front door and gazed out. Emotionally he hovered between the world aboveground and the world underground. He longed to go out, but sober judgment urged him to remain here. Then impulsively he pried the lock loose with one swift twist of the crowbar; the door swung outward. Through the twilight he saw a white man and a white woman coming toward him. He held himself tense, waiting for them to pass; but they came directly to the door and confronted him.

"I want to buy a pound of grapes," the woman said.

Terrified, he stepped back into the store. The white man stood to one side and the woman entered.

"Give me a pound of dark ones," the woman said.

The white man came slowly forward, blinking his eyes.

"Where's Nick?" the man asked.

"Were you just closing?" the woman asked.

"Yes, ma'am," he mumbled. For a second he did not breathe, then he mumbled again: "Yes, ma'am."

"I'm sorry," the woman said.

The street lamps came on, lighting the store somewhat. Ought he run? But that would raise an alarm. He moved slowly, dreamily, to a counter and lifted up a bunch of grapes and showed them to the woman.

"Fine," the woman said. "But isn't that more than a pound?"

He did not answer. The man was staring at him intently.

"Put them in a bag for me," the woman said, fumbling with her purse.

"Yes, ma'am."

He saw a pile of paper bags under a narrow ledge; he opened one and put the grapes in.

"Thanks," the woman said, taking the bag and placing a dime in his dark palm.

"Where's Nick?" the man asked again. "At supper?"

"Sir? Yes, sir," he breathed.

They left the store and he stood trembling in the doorway. When they were out of sight, he burst out laughing and crying. A trolley car rolled noisily past and he controlled himself quickly. He flung the dime to the pavement with a gesture of contempt and stepped into the warm night air. A few shy stars trembled above him. The look of things was beautiful, yet he felt a lurking threat. He went to an unattended newsstand and looked at a stack of papers. He saw a headline: HUNT NEGRO FOR MURDER.

He felt that someone had slipped up on him from behind and was stripping off his clothes; he looked about wildly, went quickly back into the store, picked up the meat cleaver where he had left it near the sink, then made his way through the icebox to the basement. He stood for a long time, breathing heavily. They know I didn't do anything, he muttered. But how could he prove it? He had signed a confession. Though innocent, he felt guilty, condemned. He struck a match and held it near the steel blade, fascinated and repelled by the dried blotches of blood. Then his fingers gripped the handle of the cleaver with all the strength of his body, he wanted to fling the cleaver from him, but he could not. The match flame wavered and fled; he struggled through the hole and put the cleaver in the sack with the radio. He was determined to keep it for what purpose he did not know.

He was about to leave when he remembered the safe. Where was it? He wanted to give up, but felt that he ought to make one more try. Opposite the last hole he had dug, he tunneled again, plying the crowbar. Once he was so exhausted that he lay on the concrete floor and panted. Finally he made another hole. He wriggled through and his nostrils filled with the fresh smell of coal. He struck a match; yes, the usual steps led upward. He tiptoed to a door and eased it open. A fair-haired white girl stood in front of a steel cabinet, her blue eyes wide upon him. She turned chalky and gave a high-pitched scream. He bounded down the steps and raced to his hole and clambered through, replacing the bricks with nervous haste. He paused, hearing loud voices.

"What's the matter, Alice?"

"A man . . ."

"What man? Where?"

"A man was at that door . . ."

"Oh, nonsense!"

"He was looking at me through the door!"

"Aw, you're dreaming."

"I *did* see a man!"

The girl was crying now.

"There's nobody here."

Another man's voice sounded.

"What is it, Bob?"

"Alice says she saw a man in here, in that door!"

"Let's take a look."

He waited, poised for flight. Footsteps descended the stairs.

"There's nobody down here."

"The window's locked."

"And there's no door."

"You ought to fire that dame."

"Oh, I don't know. Women are that way."

"She's too hysterical."

The men laughed. Footsteps sounded again on the stairs. A door slammed. He sighed, relieved that he had escaped. But he had not done what he had set out to do; his glimpse of the room had been too brief to determine if the safe was there. He had to know. Boldly he groped through the hole once more; he reached the steps and pulled off his shoes and tip-toed up and peered through the keyhole. His head accidentally touched the door and it swung silently in a fraction of an inch; he saw the girl bent over the cabinet, her back to him. Beyond her was the safe. He crept back down the steps, thinking exultingly: I found it!

Now he had to get the combination. Even if the window in the areaway was locked and bolted, he could gain entrance when the office closed. He scoured through the holes he had dug and stood again in the basement where he had left the radio and the cleaver. Again he crawled out of the window and lifted himself up the rain pipe and peered. The steel dial showed lonely and bright, reflecting the yellow glow of an unseen light. Resigned to a long wait, he sat and leaned against the wall. From far off came the faint sounds of life above-ground; once he looked with a baffled expression at the dark sky. Frequently he rose and climbed the pipe to see the white hand spin the dial, but nothing happened. He bit his lip with impatience. It was not the money that was luring him, but the mere fact that he could get it with impunity. Was the hand now twirling the dial? He rose and looked, but the white hand was not in sight.

Perhaps it would be better to watch continuously? Yes; he clung to the pipe and watched the dial until his eyes thickened with tears. Exhausted, he stood again in the areaway. He heard a door being shut and he clawed up the pipe and looked. He jerked tense as a vague figure passed in front of him. He stared unblinkingly, hugging the pipe with one hand and holding the screwdriver with the other, ready to etch the combination upon the wall. His ears caught: *Dong . . . Dong . . . Dong . . . Dong . . . Dong . . . Dong . . . Dong. . . .* Seven o'clock, he whispered. Maybe they were closing now? What kind of a store would be open as late as this? he wondered. Did anyone live in the rear? Was there a night watchman? Perhaps the safe was *already* locked for the night! Goddamn! While he had been eating in that shop, they had locked up everything . . . Then, just as he was about to give up, the white hand touched the dial and turned it once to the right and stopped at six. With quivering fingers, he etched 1—R—6 upon the brick wall with the tip of the screwdriver. The hand twisted the dial twice to the left and stopped at two, and he engraved 2—L—2 upon the wall. The dial was spun four times to the right and stopped at six again: he wrote 4—R—6. The dial rotated three times to the left and was centered straight up and down; he wrote 3—L—0. The door swung open and again he saw the piles of green money and the rows of wrapped coins. I got it, he said grimly.

Then he was stone still, astonished. There were two hands now. A right hand lifted a wad of green bills and deftly slipped it up the sleeve of the left arm. The hands trembled; again the right hand slipped a packet of bills up the left sleeve. He's stealing he said to himself. He grew indignant, as if the money belonged to him. Though *he* had planned to steal the money, he despised and pitied the man. He felt that his stealing the money and the man's stealing were two entirely different things. He wanted to steal the money merely for the sensation involved in getting it, and he had no intention whatever of spending a penny of it; but he knew that the man who was now stealing it was going to spend it, perhaps for pleasure. The huge steel door closed with a soft click.

Though angry, he was somewhat satisfied. The office would close soon. I'll clean the place out, he mused. He imagined the entire office staff cringing with fear; the police would question everyone for a crime they had not committed, just as they had questioned him. And they would have no idea of how the money had been stolen until they discovered the holes he had tunneled in the walls of the basements. He lowered himself and laughed mischievously, with the abandoned glee of an adolescent.

He flattened himself against the wall as the window above him closed with a rasping sound. He looked; somebody was bolting the window securely with a metal screen. That won't help you, he snickered to himself. He clung to the rain pipe until the yellow light in the office went out. He went back into the basement, picked up the sack containing the radio and cleaver, and crawled through the two holes he had dug and groped his way into the basement of the building that held the safe. He moved in slow motion, breathing softly. Be careful now, he told himself. There might be a night watchman . . . In his memory was the combination written in bold white characters as upon a blackboard. Eel-like he squeezed through the last hole and crept up the steps and put his hand on the knob and pushed the door in about three inches. Then his courage ebbed; his imagination wove dangers for him.

Perhaps the night watchman was waiting in there, ready to shoot. He dangled his cap on a forefinger and poked it past the jamb of the door. If anyone fired, they would hit his cap; but nothing happened. He widened the door, holding the crowbar high above his head, ready to beat off an assailant. He stood like that for five minutes; the rumble of a streetcar brought him to himself. He entered the room. Moonlight floated in from a side window. He confronted the safe, then checked himself. Better take a look around first . . . . He stepped about and found a closed door. Was the night watchman in there? He opened it and saw a washbowl, a faucet, and a commode. To the left was still another door that opened into a huge dark room that seemed empty; on the far side of that room he made out the shadow of still another door. Nobody's here, he told himself.

He turned back to the safe and fingered the dial; it spun with ease. He laughed and twirled it just for fun. Get to work, he told himself. He turned the dial to the figures he saw on the blackboard of his memory; it was so easy that he felt that the safe had not been locked at all. The heavy door eased loose and he caught hold of the handle and pulled hard, but the door swung open with a slow momentum of its own. Breathless, he gaped at wads of green bills, rows of wrapped coins, curious glass jars full of white pellets, and many oblong green metal boxes. He glanced guiltily over his shoulder; it seemed impossible that someone should not call to him to stop.

They'll be surprised in the morning, he thought. He opened the top of the sack and lifted a wad of compactly tied bills; the money was crisp and new. He admired the smooth, cleancut edges. The fellows in Washington sure know how to make this stuff, he mused. He rubbed the money with his fingers, as though expecting it to reveal hidden qualities. He lifted the wad to his nose and smelled the fresh odor of ink. Just like any other paper, he mumbled. He dropped the wad into the sack and picked up another. Holding the bag, he thought and laughed.

There was in him no sense of possessiveness; he was intrigued with the form and color of the money, with the manifold reactions which he knew that men aboveground held toward it. The sack was one-third full when it occurred to him to examine the denominations of the bills; without realizing it, he had put many wads of one-dollar bills into the sack. Aw, nuts, he said in disgust. Take the big ones . . . He dumped the one-dollar bills onto the floor and swept all the hundred-dollar bills he could find into the sack, then he raked in rolls of coins with crooked fingers.

He walked to a desk upon which sat a typewriter, the same machine which the blond girl had used. He was fascinated by it; never in his life had he used one of them. It was a queer instrument of business, something beyond the rim of his life. Whenever he had been in an office where a girl was typing, he had almost always spoken in whispers. Remembering vaguely what he had seen others do, he inserted a sheet of paper into the machine; it went in lopsided and he did not know how to straighten it. Spelling in a soft diffident voice, he pecked out his name on the keys: *freddaniels*. He looked at it and laughed. He would learn to type correctly one of these days.

Yes, he would take the typewriter too. He lifted the machine and placed it atop the bulk of money in the sack. He did not feel that he was stealing, for the cleaver, the radio, the money, and the typewriter were all on the same level of value, all meant the same thing to him. They were the serious toys of the men who lived in the dead world of sunshine and rain he had left, the world that had condemned him, branded him guilty.

But what kind of a place is this? He wondered. What was in that dark room to his rear? He felt for his matches and found that he had only one left. He leaned the sack against the safe and groped forward into the room, encountering smooth, metallic objects that felt like machines. Baffled, he touched a wall and tried vainly to locate an electric switch. Well, he *had* to strike his last match. He knelt and struck it, cupping the flame near the floor with his palms. The place seemed to be a factory, with benches and tables. There were bulbs with green shades spaced about the tables; he turned on a light and twisted it low so that the glare was limited. He saw a half-filled packet of cigarettes and appropriated it. There were stools at the benches and he concluded that men worked here at some trade. He wandered and found a few half-used folders of matches. If only he could find more cigarettes! But there were none.

But what kind of a place was this? On a bench he saw a pad of paper captioned: PEER'S—MANUFACTURING JEWELERS. His lips formed an "O," then he snapped off the light and ran back to the safe and lifted one of the glass jars and stared at the tiny white pellets. Gingerly he picked up one and found that it was wrapped in tissue paper. He peeled the paper and saw a glittering stone that looked like glass, glinting white and blue sparks. Diamonds, he breathed.

Roughly he tore the paper from the pellets and soon his palm quivered with precious fire. Trembling, he took all four glass jars from the safe and put them into the sack. He grabbed one of the metal boxes, shook it, and heard a tinny rattle. He pried off the lid with the screwdriver. Rings! Hundreds of them . . . Were they worth anything? He scooped up a handful and jets of fire shot fitfully from the stones. These are diamonds too, he said. He pried open another box. Watches! A chorus of soft, metallic ticking filled his ears. For a moment he could not move, then he dumped all the boxes into the sack.

He shut the safe door, then stood looking around, anxious not to overlook anything. Oh! He had seen a door in the room where the machines were. What was in there? More valuables? He re-entered the room, crossed the floor, and stood undecided before the door. He finally caught hold of the knob and pushed the door in; the room beyond was dark. He advanced cautiously inside and ran his fingers along the wall for the usual switch, then he was stark still. *Something had moved in the room!* What was it? Ought he to creep out, taking the rings and diamonds and money? Why risk what he already had? He waited and the ensuing silence gave him confidence to explore further. Dare he strike a match?

Would not a match flame make him a good target? He tensed again as he heard a faint sigh; he was now convinced that there was something alive near him, something that lived and breathed. On tiptoe he felt slowly along the wall, hoping that he would not collide with anything. Luck was with him; he found the light switch.

No; don't turn the light on . . . Then suddenly he realized that he did not know in what direction the door was. Goddamn! He had to turn the light on or strike a match. He fingered the switch for a long time, then thought of an idea. He knelt upon the floor, reached his arm up to the switch and flicked the button, hoping that if anyone shot, the bullet would go above his head. The moment the light came on he narrowed his eyes to see quickly. He sucked in his breath and his body gave a violent twitch and was still. In front of him, so close that it made him want to bound up and scream, was a human face.

He was afraid to move lest he touch the man. If the man had opened his eyes at that moment, there was no telling what he might have done. The man— long and rawboned—was stretched out on his back upon a little cot, sleeping in his clothes, his head cushioned by a dirty pillow; his face, clouded by a dark stubble of beard, looked straight up to the ceiling. The man sighed, and he grew tense to defend himself; the man mumbled and turned his face away from the light. I've got to turn off that light, he thought. Just as he was about to rise, he saw a gun and cartridge belt on the floor at the man's side. Yes, he would take the gun and cartridge belt, not to use them, but just to keep them, as one takes a memento from a country fair. He picked them up and was about to click off the light when his eyes fell upon a photograph perched upon a chair near the man's head; it was the picture of a woman, smiling, shown against a background of open fields; at the woman's side were two young children, a boy and a girl. He smiled indulgently; he could send a bullet into that man's brain and time would be over for him. . . .

He clicked off the light and crept silently back into the room where the safe stood; he fastened the cartridge belt about him and adjusted the holster at his right hip. He strutted about the room on tiptoe, lolling his head nonchalantly, then paused, abruptly pulled the gun, and pointed it with grim face toward an imaginary foe. "Boom!" he whispered fiercely. Then he bent forward with silent laughter. That's just like they do it in the movies, he said.

He contemplated his loot for a long time, then got a towel from the washroom and tied the sack securely. When he looked up he was momentarily frightened by his shadow looming on the wall before him. He lifted the sack, dragged it down the basement steps, lugged it across the basement, gasping for breath. After he had struggled through the hole, he clumsily replaced the bricks, then tussled with the sack until he got it to the cave. He stood in the dark, wet with sweat, brooding about the diamonds, the rings, the watches, the money; he remembered the singing in the church, the people yelling in the movie, the dead baby, the nude man stretched out upon the white table . . . He saw these items hovering before his eyes and felt that some dim meaning linked them together, that some magical relationship made them kin. He stared with vacant eyes, convinced that all of these images, with their tongueless reality, were striving to tell him something . . .

Later, seeing with his fingers, he untied the sack and set each item neatly upon the dirt floor. Exploring, he took the bulb, the socket, and the wire out of the tool chest; he was elated to find a double socket at one end of the wire. He crammed the stuff into his pockets and hoisted himself upon the rusty pipes and squinted into the church; it was dim and empty. Somewhere in this wall were live electric wires; but where? He lowered himself, groped and tapped the wall with the butt of the screwdriver, listening vainly for hollow sounds. I'll just take a chance and dig, he said.

For an hour he tried to dislodge a brick, and when he struck a match, he found that he had dug a depth of only an inch! No use in digging here, he sighed. By the flickering light of a match, he looked upward, then lowered his eyes, only to glance up again, startled. Directly above his head, beyond the pipes, was a wealth of electric wiring. I'll be damned, he snickered.

He got an old dull knife from the chest and, seeing again with his fingers, separated the two strands of wire and cut away the insulation. Twice he received a slight shock. He scraped the wiring clean and managed to join the two twin ends, then screwed in the bulb. The sudden illumination blinded him and he shut his lids to kill the pain in his eyeballs. I've got that much done, he thought jubilantly.

He placed the bulb on the dirt floor and the light cast a blatant glare on the bleak clay walls. Next he plugged one end of the wire that dangled from the radio into the light socket and bent down and switched on the button; almost at once there was the harsh sound of static, but no words or music. Why won't it work? he wondered. Had he damaged the mechanism in any way? Maybe it needed grounding? Yes . . . He rummaged in the tool chest and found another length of wire, fastened it to the ground of the radio, and then tied the opposite end to a pipe. Rising and growing distinct, a slow strain of music entranced him with its measured sound. He sat upon the chest, deliriously happy.

Later he searched again in the chest and found a half-gallon can of glue; he opened it and smelled a sharp odor. Then he recalled that he had not even looked at the money. He took a wad of green bills and weighed it in his palm, then broke the seal and held one of the bills up to the light and studied it closely. *The United States of America will pay to the bearer on demand one hundred dollars,* he read in slow speech; then: *This note is legal tender for all debts, public and private* . . . He broke into a musing laugh, feeling that he was reading of the doings of people who lived on some far-off planet. He turned the bill over and saw on the other side of it a delicately beautiful building gleaming with paint and set amidst green grass. He had no desire whatever to count the money; it was what it stood for—the various currents of life swirling aboveground—that captivated him. Next he opened the rolls of coins and let them slide from their paper wrappings to the ground; the bright, new gleaming pennies and nickels and dimes piled high at his feet, a glowing mound of shimmering copper and silver. He sifted them through his fingers, listening to their tinkle as they struck the conical heap.

Oh, yes! He had forgotten. He would now write his name on the typewriter. He inserted a piece of paper and poised his fingers to write. But what was his name? He stared, trying to remember. He stood and glared about the dirt cave, his name on the tip of his lips. But it would not come to him. Why was he here? Yes, he had been running away from the police. But why? His mind was blank. He bit his lips and sat again, feeling a vague terror. But why worry? He laughed, then pecked slowly: *itwasalonghotday*. He was determined to type the sentence without making any mistakes. How did one make capital letters? He experimented and luckily discovered how to lock the machine for capital letters and then shift it back to lower case. Next he discovered how to make spaces, then he wrote neatly and correctly: *It was a long hot day.* Just why he selected that sentence he did not know; it was merely the ritual of performing the thing that appealed to him. He took the sheet out of the machine and looked around with stiff neck and hard eyes and spoke to an imaginary person:

"Yes, I'll have the contracts ready tomorrow."

He laughed. That's just the way they talk, he said. He grew weary of the game and pushed the machine aside. His eyes fell upon the can of glue, and a mischievous idea bloomed in him, filling him with nervous eagerness. He leaped up and opened the can of glue, then broke the seals on all the wads of money. I'm going to have some wallpaper, he said with a luxurious, physical laugh that made him bend at the knees. He took the towel with which he had tied the sack and balled it into a swab and dipped it into the can of glue and dabbed glue onto the wall; then he pasted one green bill by the side of another. He stepped back and cocked his head. Jesus! That's funny . . . He slapped his thighs and guffawed. He had triumphed over the world aboveground! He was free! If only people could see this! He wanted to run from this cave and yell his discovery to the world.

He swabbed all the dirt walls of the cave and pasted them with green bills; when he had finished the walls blazed with a yellow-green fire. Yes, this room would be his hide-out; between him and the world that had branded him guilty would stand this mocking symbol. He had not stolen the money; he had simply picked it up, just as a man would pick up firewood in a forest. And that was how the world aboveground now seemed to him, a wild forest filled with death.

The walls of money finally palled on him and he looked about for new interests to feed his emotions. The cleaver! He drove a nail into the wall and hung the bloody cleaver upon it. Still another idea welled up. He pried open the metal boxes and lined them side by side on the dirt floor. He grinned at the gold and fire. From one box he lifted up a fistful of ticking gold watches and dangled them by their gleaming chains. He stared with an idle smile, then began to wind them up; he did not attempt to set them at any given hour, for there was no time for him now. He took a fistful of nails and drove them into the papered walls and hung the watches upon them, letting them swing down by their glittering chains, trembling and ticking busily against the backdrop of green with the lemon sheen of the electric light shining upon the metal watch casings, converting the golden disks into blobs of liquid yellow. Hardly had he hung up the last watch than the idea extended itself; he took more nails from the chest and drove them into the green paper and took the boxes of rings and went from nail to nail and hung up the golden bands. The blue and white sparks from the stones filled the cave with brittle laughter, as though enjoying his hilarious secret. People certainly can do some funny things, he said to himself.

He sat upon the tool chest, alternately laughing and shaking his head soberly. Hours later he became conscious of the gun sagging at his hip and he pulled it from the holster. He had seen men fire guns in movies, but somehow his life had never led him into contact with firearms. A desire to feel the sensation others felt in firing came over him. But someone might hear . . . Well, what if they did? They would not know where the shot had come from. Not in their wildest notions would they think that it had come from under the streets! He tightened his fingers on the trigger; there was a deafening report and it seemed that the entire underground had caved in upon his eardrums; and in the same instant there flashed an orange-blue spurt of flame that died quickly but lingered on as a vivid after-image. He smelled the acrid stench of burnt powder filling his lungs and he dropped the gun abruptly.

The intensity of his feelings died and he hung the gun and cartridge belt upon the wall. Next he lifted the jars of diamonds and turned them bottom upward, dumping the white pellets upon the ground. One by one he picked them up and peeled the tissue paper from them and piled them in a neat heap. He wiped his sweaty hands on his trousers, lit a cigarette, and commenced playing another game. He imagined that he was a rich man who lived above-ground in the obscene sunshine and he was strolling through a park of a summer morning, smiling, nodding to his neighbors, sucking an after-breakfast cigar. Many times he crossed the floor of the cave, avoiding the diamonds with his feet, yet subtly gauging his footsteps so that his shoes, wet with sewer slime, would strike the diamonds at some undetermined moment. After twenty minutes of sauntering, his right foot smashed into the heap and diamonds lay scattered in all directions, glinting with a million tiny chuckles of icy laughter. Oh, shucks, he mumbled in mock regret, intrigued by the damage he had wrought. He continued walking, ignoring the brittle fire. He felt that he had a glorious victory locked in his heart.

He stooped and flung the diamonds more evenly over the floor and they showered rich sparks, collaborating with him. He went over the floor and trampled the stones just deeply enough for them to be faintly visible, as though they were set deliberately in the prongs of a thousand rings. A ghostly light bathed the cave. He sat on the chest and frowned. Maybe *any*thing's right, he mumbled. Yes, if the world as men had made it was right, then anything else was right, any act a man took to satisfy himself, murder, theft, torture.

He straightened with a start. What was happening to him? He was drawn to these crazy thoughts, yet they made him feel vaguely guilty. He would stretch out upon the ground, then get up; he would want to crawl again through the holes he had dug, but would restrain himself; he would think of going up into the streets, but fear would hold him still. He stood in the middle of the cave, surrounded by green walls and a laughing floor, trembling. He was going to do something, but what? Yes, he was afraid of himself, afraid of doing some nameless thing.

To control himself, he turned on the radio. A melancholy piece of music rose. Brooding over the diamonds on the floor was like looking up into a sky full of restless stars; then the illusion turned into its opposite: he was high up in the air looking down at the twinkling lights of a sprawling city. The music ended and a man recited news events. In the same attitude in which he had contemplated the city, so now, as he heard the cultivated tone, he looked down upon land and sea as men fought, as cities were razed, as planes scattered death upon open towns, as long lines of trenches wavered and broke. He heard the names of generals and the names of mountains and the names of countries and the names and numbers of divisions that were in action on different battle fronts. He saw black smoke billowing from the stacks of warships as they neared each other over wastes of water and he heard their huge thunder as red-hot shells screamed across the surface of night seas. He saw hundreds of planes wheeling and droning in the sky and heard the clatter of machine guns as they fought each other and he saw planes falling in plumes of smoke and and blaze of fire. He saw steel tanks rumbling across fields of ripe wheat to meet other tanks and there was a loud clang of steel as numberless tanks collided. He saw troops with fixed bayonets charging in waves against other troops who held fixed bayonets and men groaned as steel ripped into their bodies and they went down to die . . . The voice of the radio faded and he was staring at the diamonds on the floor at his feet.

He shut off the radio, fighting an irrational compulsion to act. He walked aimlessly about the cave, touching the walls with his finger tips. Suddenly he stood still. *What was the matter with him?* Yes, he knew . . . It was these walls; these crazy walls were filling him with a wild urge to climb out into the dark sunshine aboveground. Quickly he doused the light to banish the shouting walls, then sat again upon the tool chest. Yes, he was trapped. His muscles were flexed taut and sweat ran down his face. He knew now that he could not stay here and he could not go out. He lit a cigarette with shaking fingers; the match flame revealed the green-papered walls with militant distinctness; the purple on the gun barrel glinted like a threat; the meat cleaver brooded with its eloquent splotches of blood; the mound of silver and copper smoldered angrily; the diamonds winked at him from the floor, and the gold watches ticked and trembled, crowning time the king of consciousness, defining the limits of living . . . The match blaze died and he bolted from where he stood and collided brutally with the nails upon the walls. The spell was broken. He shuddered, feeling that, in spite of his fear, sooner or later he would go up into that dead sunshine and somehow say something to somebody about all this.

He sat again upon the tool chest. Fatigue weighed upon his forehead and eyes. Minutes passed and he relaxed. He dozed, but his imagination was alert. He saw himself rising, wading again in the sweeping water of the sewer; he came to a manhole and climbed out and was amazed to discover that he hoisted himself into a room filled with armed policemen who were watching him intently. He jumped awake in the dark; he had not moved. He sighed, closed his eyes, and slept again; this time his imagination designed a scheme of protection for him. His dreaming made him feel that he was standing in a room watching over his own nude body lying stiff and cold upon a white table. At the far end of the room he saw a crowd of people huddled in a corner, afraid of his body. Though lying dead upon the table, he was standing in some mysterious way at his side, warding off the people, guarding his body, and laughing to himself as he observed the situation. They're scared of me, he thought.

He awakened with a start, leaped to his feet, and stood in the center of the black cave. It was a full minute before he moved again. He hovered between sleeping and waking, unprotected, a prey of wild fears. He could neither see nor hear. One part of him was asleep; his blood coursed slowly and his flesh was numb. On the other hand he was roused to a strange, high pitch of tension. He lifted his fingers to his face, as though about to weep. Gradually his hands lowered and he struck a match, looking about, expecting to see a door through which he could walk to safety; but there was no door, only the green walls and the moving floor. The match flame died and it was dark again.

Five minutes later he was still standing when the thought came to him that he had been asleep. Yes . . . But he was not yet fully awake; he was still queerly blind and deaf. How long had he slept? Where was he? Then suddenly he recalled the green-papered walls of the cave and in the same instant he heard loud singing coming from the church beyond the wall. Yes, they woke me up, he muttered. He hoisted himself and lay atop the bed of pipes and brought his face to the narrow slit. Men and women stood here and there between pews. A song ended and a young black girl tossed back her head and closed her eyes and broke plaintively into another hymn:

> *Glad, glad, glad, oh, so glad*
> *I got Jesus in my soul . . .*

Those few words were all she sang, but what her words did not say, her emotions said as she repeated the lines, varying the mood and tempo, making her tone express meanings which her conscious mind did not know. Another woman melted her voice with the girl's, and then an old man's voice merged with that of the two women. Soon the entire congregation was singing:

> *Glad, glad, glad, oh, so glad*
> *I got Jesus in my soul . . .*

They're wrong, he whispered in the lyric darkness. He felt that their search for a happiness they could never find made them feel that they had committed some dreadful offense which they could not remember or understand. He was now in possession of the feeling that had gripped him when he had first come into the underground. It came to him in a series of questions: Why was this sense of guilt so seemingly innate, so easy to come by, to think, to feel, so verily physical? It seemed that when one felt this guilt one was retracing in one's feelings a faint pattern designed long before; it seemed that one was always trying to remember a gigantic shock that had left a haunting impression upon one's body which one could not forget or shake off, but which had been forgotten by the conscious mind, creating in one's life a state of eternal anxiety.

He had to tear himself away from this; he got down from the pipes. His nerves were so taut that he seemed to feel his brain pushing through his skull. He felt that he had to do something, but he could not figure out what it was. Yet he knew that if he stood here until he made up his mind, he would never move. He crawled through the hole he had made in the brick wall and the exertion afforded him respite from tension. When he entered the basement of the radio store, he stopped in fear, hearing loud voices.

"Come on, boy! Tell us what you did with the radio!"

"Mister, I didn't steal the radio! I swear!"

He heard a dull thumping sound and he imagined a boy being struck violently.

"Please, mister!"

"Did you take it to a pawn shop?"

"No, sir! I didn't steal the radio! I got a radio at home," the boy's voice pleaded hysterically. "Go to my home and look!"

There came to his ears the sound of another blow. It was so funny that he had to clap his hand over his mouth to keep from laughing out loud. They're beating some poor boy, he whispered to himself, shaking his head. He felt a sort of distant pity for the boy and wondered if he ought to bring back the radio and leave it in the basement. No. Perhaps it was a good thing that they were beating the boy; perhaps the beating would bring to the boy's attention, for the first time in his life, the secret of his existence, the guilt that he could never get rid of.

Smiling, he scampered over a coal pile and stood again in the basement of the building where he had stolen the money and jewelry. He lifted himself into the areaway, climbed the rain pipe, and squinted through a two-inch opening of window. The guilty familiarity of what he saw made his muscles tighten. Framed before him in a bright tableau of daylight was the night watchman sitting upon the edge of a chair, stripped to the waist, his head sagging forward, his eyes red and puffy. The watchman's face and shoulders were stippled with red and black welts. Back of the watchman stood the safe, the steel door wide open showing the empty vault. Yes, they think he did it, he mused.

Footsteps sounded in the room and a man in a blue suit passed in front of him, then another, then still another. Policeman, he breathed. Yes, they were trying to make the watchman confess, just as they had once made him confess to a crime he had not done. He stared into the room, trying to recall something. Oh . . . Those were the same policemen who had beaten him, had made him sign that paper when he had been too tired and sick to care. Now, they were doing the same thing to the watchman. His heart pounded as he saw one of the policeman shake a finger into the watchman's face.

"Why don't you admit it's an inside job, Thompson?" the policeman said.

"I've told you all I know," the watchman mumbled through swollen lips.

"But nobody was here but you!" the policeman shouted.

"I was sleeping," the watchman said. "It was wrong, but I was sleeping all that night!"

"Stop telling us that lie!"

"It's the truth!"

"When did you get the combination?"

"I don't know how to open the safe," the watchman said.

He clung to the rain pipe, tense; he wanted to laugh, but he controlled himself. He felt a great sense of power; yes, he could go back to the cave, rip the money off the walls, pick up the diamonds and rings, and bring them here and write a note, telling them where to look for their foolish toys. No . . . . What good would that do? It was not worth the effort. The watchman was guilty; although he was not guilty of the crime of which he had been accused, he was guilty, had always been guilty. The only thing that worried him was that the man who had been really stealing was not being accused. But he consoled himself: they'll catch him sometime during his life.

He saw one of the policeman slap the watchman across the mouth.

"Come clean, you bastard!"

"I've told you all I know," the watchman mumbled like a child.

One of the police went to the rear of the watchman's chair and jerked it from under him; the watchman pitched forward upon his face.

"Get up!" a policeman said.

Trembling, the watchman pulled himself up and sat limply again in the chair.

"Now, are you going to talk?"

"I've told you all I know," the watchman gasped.

"Where did you hide the stuff?"

"I didn't take it!"

"Thompson, your brains are in your feet," one of the policemen said. "We're going to string you up and get them back into your skull."

He watched the policemen clamp handcuffs on the watchman's wrists and ankles; then they lifted the watchman and swung him upside-down and hoisted his feet to the edge of a door. The watchman hung, head down, his eyes bulging. They're crazy, he whispered to himself as he clung to the ridges of the pipe.

"You going to talk?" a policeman shouted into the watchman's ear.

He heard the watchman groan.

"We'll let you hang there till you talk, see?"

He saw the watchman close his eyes.

"Let's take 'im down. He passed out," a policeman said.

He grinned as he watched them take the body down and dump it carelessly upon the floor. The policeman took off the handcuffs.

"Let 'im come to. Let's get a smoke," a policeman said.

The three policemen left the scope of his vision. A door slammed. He had an impulse to yell to the watchman that he could escape through the hole in the basement and live with him in the cave. But he wouldn't understand, he told himself. After a moment he saw the watchman rise and stand, swaying from weakness. He stumbled across the room to a desk, opened a drawer, and took out a gun. He's going to kill himself, he thought, intent, eager, detached, yearning to see the end of the man's actions. As the watchman stared vaguely about he lifted the gun to his temple; he stood like that for some minutes, biting his lips until a line of blood etched its way down a corner of his chin. No, he oughtn't do that, he said to himself in a mood of pity.

"Don't!" he half whispered and half yelled.

The watchman looked wildly about; he had heard him. But it did not help; there was a loud report and the watchman's head jerked violently and he fell like a log and lay prone, the gun clattering over the floor.

The three policemen came running into the room with drawn guns. One of the policemen knelt and rolled the watchman's body over and stared at a ragged, scarlet hole in the temple.

"Our hunch was right," the kneeling policeman said. "He was guilty, all right."

"Well, this ends the case," another policeman said.

"He knew he was licked," the third one said with grim satisfaction.

He eased down the rain pipe, crawled back through the holes he had made, and went back into his cave. A fever burned in his bones. He had to act, yet he was afraid. His eyes stared in the darkness as though propped open by invisible hands, as though they had become lidless. His muscles were rigid and he stood for what seemed to him a thousand years.

When he moved again his actions were informed with precision, his muscular system reinforced from a reservoir of energy. He crawled through the hole of earth, dropped into the gray sewer current, and sloshed ahead. When his right foot went forward at a street intersection, he fell backward and shot down into water. In a spasm of terror his right hand grabbed the concrete ledge of a down-curve and he felt the streaking water tugging violently at his body. The current reached his neck and for a moment he was still. He knew if he moved clumsily he would be sucked under. He held onto the ledge with both hands and slowly pulled himself up. He sighed, standing once more in the sweeping water, thankful that he had missed death.

He waded on through sludge, moving with care, until he came to a web of light sifting down from a manhole cover. He saw steel hooks running up the side of the sewer wall; he caught hold and lifted himself and put his shoulder to the cover and moved it an inch. A crash of sound came to him as he looked into a hot glare of sunshine through which blurred shapes moved. Fear scalded him and he dropped back into the pallid current and stood paralyzed in the shadows. A heavy car rumbled past overhead, jarring the pavement, warning him to stay in his world of dark light, knocking the cover back into place with an imperious clang.

He did not know how much fear he felt, for fear claimed him completely; yet it was not a fear of the police or of people, but a cold dread at the thought of the actions he knew he would perform if he went out into that cruel sunshine. His mind said no; his body said yes; and his mind could not understand his feelings. A low whine broke from him and he was in the act of uncoiling. He climbed upward and heard the faint honking of auto horns. Like a frantic cat clutching a rag, he clung to the steel prongs and heaved his shoulder against the cover and pushed it off halfway. For a split second his eyes were drowned in the terror of yellow light and he was in a deeper darkness than he had ever known in the underground.

Partly out of the hole, he blinked, regaining enough sight to make out mean-ingful forms. An odd thing was happening: No one was rushing forward to challenge him. He had imagined the moment of his emergence as a desperate tussle with men who wanted to cart him off to be killed; instead, life froze about him as the traffic stopped. He pushed the cover aside, stood, swaying in a world so fragile that he expected it to collapse and drop him into some deep void. But nobody seemed to pay him heed. The cars were now swerving to shun him and the gaping hole.

"Why in hell don't you put up a red light, dummy?" a raucous voice yelled.

He understood; they thought that he was a sewer workman. He walked toward the sidewalk, weaving unsteadily through the moving traffic.

"Look where you're going, nigger!"

"That's right! Stay there and get killed!"

"You blind, you bastard?"

"Go home and sleep your drunk off!"

A policeman stood at the curb, looking in the opposite direction. When he passed the policeman, he feared that he would be grabbed, but nothing hap-pened. Where was he? Was this real? He wanted to look about to get his bearings, but felt that something awful would happen to him if he did. He wandered into a spacious doorway of a store that sold men's clothing and saw his reflection in a long mirror: his cheekbones protruded from a hairy black face; his greasy cap was perched askew upon his head and his eyes were red and glassy. His shirt and trousers were caked with mud and hung loosely. His hands were gummed with a black stickiness. He threw back his head and laughed so loudly that passers-by stopped and stared.

He ambled on down the sidewalk, not having the merest notion of where he was going. Yet, sleeping within him, was the drive to go somewhere and say something to somebody. Half an hour later his ears caught the sound of spirited singing.

> The Lamb, the Lamb, the Lamb
>   I hear thy voice a-calling
> The Lamb, the Lamb, the Lamb
>   I feel thy grace a-falling

A church! He exclaimed. He broke into a run and came to brick steps leading downward to a subbasement. This is it! The church into which he had peered.

Yes, he was going in and tell them. What? He did not know; but, once face to face with them, he would think of what to say. Must be Sunday, he mused. He ran down the steps and jerked the door open; the church was crowded and a deluge of song swept over him.

> The Lamb, the Lamb, the Lamb
> > Tell me again your story
> The Lamb, the Lamb, the Lamb
> > Flood my soul with your glory

He stared at the singing faces with a trembling smile.
"Say!" he shouted.
Many turned to look at him, but the song rolled on. His arm was jerked violently.
"I'm sorry, Brother, but you can't do that in here," a man said.
"But, mister!"
"You can't act rowdy in God's house," the man said.
"He's filthy," another man said.
"But I want to tell 'em," he said loudly.
"He stinks," someone muttered.
The song had stopped, but at once another one began.

> Oh, wondrous sight upon the cross
> > Vision sweet and divine
> Oh, wondrous sight upon the cross
> > Full of such love sublime

He attempted to twist away, but other hands grabbed him and rushed him into the doorway.
"Let me alone!" he screamed, struggling.
"Get out!"
"He's drunk," somebody said. "He ought to be ashamed!"
"He acts crazy!"
He felt that he was failing and he grew frantic.
"But, mister, let me tell—"
"Get away from this door, or I'll call the police!"
He stared, his trembling smile fading in a sense of wonderment.
"The police," he repeated vacantly.
"Now, get!"
He was pushed toward the brick steps and the door banged shut. The waves of song came.

> Oh, wondrous sight, wondrous sight
> > Lift my heavy heart above
> Oh, wondrous sight, wondrous sight
> > Fill my weary soul with love

He was smiling again now. Yes, the police . . . That was it! Why had he not thought of it before? The idea had been deep down in him, and only now did it assume supreme importance. He looked up and saw a street sign: COURT STREET—HARTSDALE AVENUE. He turned and walked northward, his mind filled with the image of the police station. Yes, that was where they had beaten him, accused him, and had made him sign a confession of his guilt. He would go there and clear up everything, make a statement. What statement? He did not know. He was the statement, and since it was all so clear to him, surely he would be able to make it clear to others.

He came to the corner of Hartsdale Avenue and turned westward. Yeah, there's the station . . . A policeman came down the steps and walked past him without a glance. He mounted the stone steps and went through the door, paused; he was in a hallway where several policemen were standing, talking, smoking. One turned to him.

"What do you want, boy?"

He looked at the policeman and laughed.

"What in hell are you laughing about?" the policeman asked.

He stopped laughing and stared. His whole being was full of what he wanted to say to them, but he could not say it.

"Are you looking for the Desk Sergeant?"

"Yes, sir," he said quickly; then: "Oh, no, sir."

"Well, make up your mind, now."

Four policemen grouped themselves around him.

"I'm looking for the men," he said.

"What men?"

Peculiarly, at that moment he could not remember the names of the policemen; he recalled their beating him, the confession he had signed, and how he had run away from them. He saw the cave next to the church, the money on the walls, the gun, the rings, the cleaver, the watches, and the diamonds on the floor.

"They brought me here," he began.

"When?"

His mind flew back over the blur of the time lived in the underground blackness. He had no idea of how much time had elapsed, but the intensity of what had happened to him told him that it could not have transpired in a short space of time, yet his mind told him that time must have been brief.

"It was a long time ago." He spoke like a child relating a dimly remembered dream. "It was a long time," he repeated, following the promptings of his emotions. "They beat me . . . I was scared . . . I ran away."

A policeman raised a finger to his temple and made a derisive circle.

"Nuts," the policeman said.

"Do you know what place this is, boy?"

"Yes, sir. The police station," he answered sturdily, almost proudly.

"Well, who do you want to see?"

"The men," he said again, feeling that surely they knew the men. "You know the men," he said in a hurt tone.

"What's your name?"

He opened his lips to answer and no words came. He had forgotten. But what did it matter if he had? It was not important.

"Where do you live?"

Where did he live? It had been so long ago since he had lived up here in this strange world that he felt it was foolish even to try to remember. Then for a a moment the old mood that had dominated him in the underground surged back. He leaned forward and spoke eagerly.

"They said I killed the woman."

"What woman?" a policeman asked.

"And I signed a paper that said I was guilty," he went on, ignoring their questions. "Then I ran off . . ."

"Did you run off from an institution?"

"No, sir," he said, blinking and shaking his head. "I came from under the ground. I pushed off the manhole cover and climbed out . . ."

"All right, now," a policeman said, placing an arm about his shoulder. "We'll send you to the psycho and you'll be taken care of."

"Maybe he's a Fifth Columnist!" a policeman shouted.

There was laughter and, despite his anxiety, he joined in. But the laughter lasted so long that it irked him.

"I got to find those men," he protested mildly.

"Say, boy, what have you been drinking?"

"Water," he said. "I got some water in a basement."

"Were the men you ran away from dressed in white, boy?"

"No, sir," he said brightly. "They were men like you."

An elderly policeman caught hold of his arm.

"Try and think hard. Where did they pick you up?"

He knotted his brows in an effort to remember, but he was blank inside. The policeman stood before him demanding logical answers and he could no longer think with his mind; he thought with his feelings and no words came.

"I was guilty," he said. "Oh, no, sir. I wasn't then, I mean, mister!"

"Aw, talk sense. Now, where did they pick you up?"

He felt challenged and his mind began reconstructing events in reverse; his feelings ranged back over the long hours and he saw the cave, the sewer, the bloody room where it was said that a woman had been killed.

"Oh, yes, sir," he said, smiling. "I was coming from Mrs. Wooten's."

"Who is she?"

"I work for her."

"Where does she live?"

"Next door to Mrs. Peabody, the woman who was killed."

The policemen were very quiet now, looking at him intently.

"What do you know about Mrs. Peabody's death, boy?"

"Nothing, sir. But they said I killed her. But it doesn't make any difference, I'm guilty!"

"What are you talking about, boy?"

His smile faded and he was possessed with memories of the underground; he saw the cave next to the church and his lips moved to speak. But how could he say it? The distance between what he felt and what these men meant was vast. Something told him, as he stood there looking into their faces, that he would never be able to tell them, that they would never believe him even if he told them.

"All the people I saw was guilty," he began slowly.

"Aw, nuts," a policeman muttered.

"Say," another policeman said, "that Peabody woman was killed over on Winewood. That's Number Ten's beat."

"Where's Number Ten?" a policeman asked.

"Upstairs in the swing room," someone answered.

"Take this boy up, Sam," a policeman ordered.

"O.K. Come along, boy."

An elderly policeman caught hold of his arm and led him up a flight of wooden stairs, down a long hall, and to a door.

"Squad Ten!" the policeman called through the door.

"What?" a gruff voice answered.

"Someone to see you!"

"About what?"

The old policeman pushed the door in and then shoved him into the room.

He stared, his lips open, his heart barely beating. Before him were the three policemen who had picked him up and had beaten him to extract the confession. They were seated about a small table, playing cards. The air was blue with smoke and sunshine poured through a high window, lighting up fantastic smoke shapes. He saw one of the policemen look up; the policeman's face was tired and a cigarette drooped limply from one corner of his mouth and both of his fat, puffy eyes were squinting and his hands gripped his cards.

"Lawson!" the man exclaimed.

The moment the man's name sounded he remembered the names of all of them: Lawson, Murphy, and Johnson. How simple it was. He waited, smiling, wondering how they would react when they knew that he had come back.

"Looking for me?" the man who had been called Lawson mumbled, sorting his cards. "For what?"

So far only Murphy, the red-headed one, had recognized him.

"Don't you-all remember me?" he blurted, running to the table.

All three of the policemen were looking at him now. Lawson, who seemed the leader, jumped to his feet.

"Where in hell have you been?"

"Do you know 'im, Lawson?" the old policeman asked.

"Huh?" Lawson frowned. "Oh, yes. I'll handle 'im." The old policeman left the room and Lawson crossed to the door and turned the key in the lock "Come here, boy," he ordered in a cold tone.

He did not move; he looked from face to face. Yes, he would tell them about his cave.

"He looks batty to me," Johnson said, the one who had not spoken before.

"Why in hell did you come back here?" Lawson said.

"I—I just didn't want to run away no more," he said. "I'm all right, now." He paused; the men's attitude puzzled him.

"You've been hiding, huh?" Lawson asked in a tone that denoted that he had not heard his previous words. "You told us you were sick, and when we left you in the room, you jumped out of the window and ran away."

Panic filled him. Yes, they were indifferent to what he would say! They were waiting for him to speak and they would laugh at him. He had to rescue himself from this bog; he had to force the reality of himself upon them.

"Mister, I took a sackful of money and pasted it on the walls . . ." he began.

"I'll be damned," Lawson said.

"Listen," said Murphy, "let me tell you something for your own good. We don't want you, see? You're free, free as air. Now go home and forget it. It was all a mistake. We caught the guy who did the Peabody job. He wasn't colored at all. He was an Eyetalian."

"Shut up!" Lawson yelled. "Have you no sense!"

"But I want to tell 'im," Murphy said.

"We can't let this crazy fool go," Lawson exploded. "He acts nuts, but this may be a stunt . . ."

"I was down in the basement," he began in a childlike tone, as though repeating a lesson learned by heart; "and I went into a movie . . ." His voice failed. He was getting ahead of his story. First, he ought to tell them about the singing in the church, but what words could he use? He looked at them appealingly. "I went into a shop and took a sackful of money and diamonds and watches and rings . . . I didn't steal 'em, I'll give 'em all back. I just took 'em to play with . . ." He paused, stunned by their disbelieving eyes.

Lawson lit a cigarette and looked at him coldly.

"What did you do with the money?" he asked in a quiet, waiting voice.

"I pasted the hundred-dollar bills on the walls."

"What walls?" Lawson asked.

"The walls of the dirt room," he said, smiling, "the room next to the church. I hung up the rings and the watches and I stamped the diamonds into the dirt . . ." He saw that they were not understanding what he was saying. He grew frantic to make them believe, his voice tumbled on eagerly. "I saw a dead baby and a dead man . . ."

"Aw, you're nuts," Lawson snarled, shoving him into a chair.

"But mister . . ."

"Johnson, where's the paper he signed?" Lawson asked.

"What paper?"

"The confession, fool!"

Johnson pulled out his billfold and extracted a crumpled piece of paper.

"Yes, sir, mister," he said, stretching forth his hand. "That's the paper I signed . . ."

Lawson slapped him and he would have toppled had his chair not struck a wall behind him. Lawson scratched a match and held the paper over the flame; the confession burned down to Lawson's finger-tips.

He stared, thunderstruck; the sun of the underground was fleeting and the terrible darkness of the day stood before him. They did not believe him, but he *had* to make them believe him!

"But mister . . ."

"It's going to be all right, boy," Lawson said with a quiet, soothing laugh. "I've burned your confession, see? You didn't sign anything." Lawson came close to him with the black ashes in his palm. "You don't remember a thing about this, do you?"

"Don't you-all be scared of me," he pleaded, sensing their uneasiness. "I'll sign another paper, if you want me to. I'll show you the cave."

"What's your game, boy?" Lawson asked suddenly.

"What are you trying to find out?" Johnson asked.

"Who sent you here?" Murphy demanded.

"Nobody sent me, mister," he said. "I just want to show you the room . . ."

"Aw, he's plumb bats," Murphy said. "Let's ship 'im to the psycho."

"No," Lawson said. "He's playing a game and I wish to God I knew what it was."

There flashed through his mind a definite way to make them believe him; he rose from the chair with nervous excitement.

"Mister, I saw the night watchman blow his brains out because you accused him of stealing," he told them. "But he didn't steal the money and diamonds. I took 'em."

Tigerishly Lawson grabbed his collar and lifted him bodily.

"Who told you about that?"

"Don't get excited, Lawson," Johnson said. "He read about it in the papers."

Lawson flung him away.

"He couldn't have," Lawson said, pulling papers from his pocket. "I haven't turned in the reports yet."

"Then how *did* he find out?" Murphy asked.

"Let's get out of here," Lawson said with quick resolution. "Listen, boy, we're going to take you to a nice, quiet place, see?"

"Yes, sir," he said. "And I'll show you the underground."

"Goddamn," Lawson muttered, fastening the gun at his hip. He narrowed his eyes at Johnson and Murphy. "Listen," he spoke just above a whisper, "say nothing about this, you hear?"

"O.K.," Johnson said.

"Sure," Murphy said.

Lawson unlocked the door and Johnson and Murphy led him down the stairs. The hallway was crowded with policemen.

"What have you got there, Lawson?"

"What did he do, Lawson?"

"He's psycho, ain't he, Lawson?"

Lawson did not answer; Johnson and Murphy led him to the car parked at the curb, pushed him into the back seat. Lawson got behind the steering wheel and the car rolled forward.

"What's up, Lawson?" Murphy asked.

"Listen," Lawson began slowly, "we tell the papers that he spilled about the Peabody job, then he escapes. The Wop is caught and we tell the papers that we steered them wrong to trap the real guy, see? Now this dope shows up and acts nuts. If we let him go, he'll squeal that we framed him, see?"

"I'm all right, mister," he said, feeling Murphy's and Johnson's arms locked rigidly into his. "I'm guilty . . . I'll show you everything in the underground. I laughed and laughed . . ."

"Shut that fool up!" Lawson ordered.

Johnson tapped him across the head with a blackjack and he fell back against the seat cushion, dazed.

"Yes, sir," he mumbled. "I'm all right."

The car sped along Hartsdale Avenue, then swung onto Pine Street and rolled to State Street, then turned south. It slowed to a stop, turned in the middle of a block, and headed north again.

"You're going around in circles, Lawson," Murphy said.

Lawson did not answer; he was hunched over the steering wheel. Finally he pulled the car to a stop at a curb.

"Say, boy, tell us the truth," Lawson asked quietly. "Where did you hide?"

"I didn't hide, mister."

The three policemen were staring at him now; he felt that for the first time they were willing to understand him.

"Then what happened?"

"Mister, when I looked through all of those holes and saw how people were living, I loved 'em . . ."

"Cut out that crazy talk!" Lawson snapped. "Who sent you back here?"

"Nobody, mister."

"Maybe he's talking straight," Johnson ventured.

"All right," Lawson said. "Nobody hid you. Now, tell us where you hid."

"I went underground . . ."

"What goddamn underground do you keep talking about?"

"I just went . . ." He paused and looked into the street, then pointed to a manhole cover. "I went down in there and stayed."

"In the sewer?"

"Yes, sir."

The policemen burst into a sudden laugh and ended quickly. Lawson swung the car around and drove to Woodside Avenue; he brought the car to a stop in front of a tall apartment building.

"What're we going to do, Lawson?" Murphy asked.

"I'm taking him up to my place," Lawson said. "We've got to wait until night. There's nothing we can do now."

They took him out of the car and led him into a vestibule.

"Take the steps," Lawson muttered.

They led him up four flights of stairs and into the living room of a small apartment. Johnson and Murphy let go of his arms and he stood uncertainly in the middle of the room.

"Now, listen, boy," Lawson began, "forget those wild lies you've been telling us. Where did you hide?"

"I just went underground, like I told you."

The room rocked with laughter. Lawson went to a cabinet and got a bottle of whiskey; he placed glasses for Johnson and Murphy. The three of them drank.

He felt that he could not explain himself to them. He tried to muster all the sprawling images that floated in him; the images stood out sharply in his mind, but he could not make them have the meaning for others that they had for him. He felt so helpless that he began to cry.

"He's nuts, all right," Johnson said. "All nuts cry like that."

Murphy crossed the room and slapped him.

"Stop that raving!"

A sense of excitement flooded him; he ran to Murphy and grabbed his arm.

"Let me show you the cave," he said. "Come on, and you'll see!"

Before he knew it a sharp blow had clipped him on the chin; darkness covered his eyes. He dimly felt himself being lifted and laid out on the sofa. He heard low voices and struggled to rise, but hard hands held him down. His brain was clearing now. He pulled to a sitting posture and stared with glazed eyes. It had grown dark. How long had he been out?

"Say, boy," Lawson said soothingly, "will you show us the underground?"

His eyes shone and his heart swelled with gratitude. Lawson believed him! He rose, glad; he grabbed Lawson's arm, making the policeman spill whiskey from the glass to his shirt.

"Take it easy, goddammit," Lawson said.

"Yes, sir."

"O.K. We'll take you down. But you'd better be telling us the truth, you hear?"

He clapped his hands in wild joy.

"I'll show you everything!"

He had triumphed at last! He would now do what he had felt was compelling him all along. At last he would be free of his burden.

"Take 'im down," Lawson ordered.

They led him down to the vestibule; when he reached the side-walk he saw that it was night and a fine rain was falling.

"It's just like when I went down," he told them.

"What?" Lawson asked.

"The rain," he said, sweeping his arm in a wide arc. "It was raining when I went down. The rain made the water rise and lift the cover off."

"Cut it out," Lawson snapped.

They did not believe him now, but they would. A mood of high selflessness throbbed in him. He could barely contain his rising spirits. They would see what he had seen; they would feel what he had felt. He would lead them through all the holes he had dug and . . . . He wanted to make a hymn, prance about in physical ecstasy, throw his arm about the policemen in fellowship.

"Get into the car," Lawson ordered.

He climbed in and Johnson and Murphy sat at either side of him; Lawson slid behind the steering wheel and started the motor.

"Now, tell us where to go," Lawson said.

"It's right around the corner from where the lady was killed," he said.

The car rolled slowly and he closed his eyes, remembering the song he had heard in the church, the song that had wrought him to such a high pitch of terror and pity. He sang softly, lolling his head:

> Glad, glad, glad, oh, so glad
> I got Jesus in my soul . . .

"Mister," he said, stopping his song, "you ought to see how funny the rings look on the wall." He giggled. "I fired a pistol, too. Just once, to see how it felt."

"What do you suppose he's suffering from?" Johnson asked.

"Delusions of grandeur, maybe," Murphy said.

"Maybe it's because he lives in a white man's world," Lawson said.

"Say, boy, what did you eat down there?" Murphy asked, prodding Johnson anticipatorily with his elbow.

"Pears, oranges, bananas, and pork chops," he said.

The car filled with laughter.

"You didn't eat any watermelon?" Lawson asked, smiling.

"No, sir," he answered calmly. "I didn't see any."

The three policemen roared harder and louder.

"Boy, you're sure some case," Murphy said, shaking his head in wonder.

The car pulled to a curb.

"All right, boy," Lawson said. "Tell us where to go."

He peered through the rain and saw where he had gone down. The streets, save for a few dim lamps glowing softly through the rain, were dark and empty.

"Right there, mister," he said, pointing.

"Come on; let's take a look," Lawson said.

"Well, suppose he did hide down there," Johnson said, "what is that supposed to prove?"

"I don't believe he hid down there," Murphy said.

"It won't hurt to look," Lawson said. "Leave things to me."

Lawson got out of the car and looked up and down the street.

He was eager to show them the cave now. If he could show them what he had seen, then they would feel what he had felt and they in turn would show it to others and those others would feel as they had felt, and soon everybody would be governed by the same impulse of pity.

"Take 'im out," Lawson ordered.

Johnson and Murphy opened the door and pushed him out; he stood trembling in the rain, smiling. Again Lawson looked up and down the street; no one was in sight. The rain came down hard, slanting like black wires across the wind-swept air.

"All right," Lawson said. "Show us."

He walked to the center of the street, stopped and inserted a finger in one of the tiny holes of the cover and tugged, but he was too weak to budge it.

"Did you really go down in there, boy?" Lawson asked; there was a doubt in his voice.

"Yes, sir. Just a minute. I'll show you."

"Help 'im get that damn thing off," Lawson said.

Johnson stepped forward and lifted the cover; it clanged against the wet pavement. The hole gaped round and black.

"I went down in there," he announced with pride.

Lawson gazed at him for a long time without speaking, then he reached his right hand to his holster and drew his gun.

"Mister, I got a gun just like that down there," he said, laughing, and looking into Lawson's face. "I fired it once then hung it on the wall. I'll show you."

"Show us how you went down," Lawson said quietly.

"I'll go down first, mister, and then you-all can come after me, hear?" he spoke like a little boy playing a game.

"Sure, sure," Lawson said soothingly. "Go ahead. We'll come."

He looked brightly at the policemen; he was bursting with happiness. He bent down and placed his hands on the rim of the hole and sat on the edge, his feet dangling into watery darkness. He heard the familiar drone of the gray current. He lowered his body and hung for a moment by his fingers, then he went downward on the steel prongs, hand over hand, until he reached the last rung. He dropped and his feet hit the water and he felt the stiff current trying to suck him away. He balanced himself quickly and looked back upward at the policemen.

"Come on, you-all!" he yelled, casting his voice above the rustling at his feet.

The vague forms that towered above him in the rain did not move. He laughed, feeling that they doubted him. But, once they saw the things he had done, they would never doubt again.

"Come on! The cave isn't far!" he yelled. "But be careful when your feet hit the water, because the current's pretty rough down here!"

Lawson still held the gun. Murphy and Johnson looked at Lawson quizzically.

"What are we going to do, Lawson?" Murphy asked.

"We are not going to follow that crazy nigger down into that sewer, are we?" Johnson asked.

"Come on, you-all!" he begged in a shout.

He saw Lawson raise the gun and point it directly at him. Lawson's face twitched, as though he were hesitating.

Then there was a thunderous report and a streak of fire ripped through his chest. He was hurled into the water, flat on his back. He looked in amazement at the blurred white faces above him. They shot me, he said to himself. The water flowed past him, blossoming in foam about his arms, his legs, and his head. His jaw sagged and his mouth gaped soundless. A vast pain gripped his head and gradually squeezed out consciousness. As from a great distance he heard hollow voices.

"What did you shoot him for, Lawson?"

"I had to."

"Why?"

"You've got to shoot his kind. They'd wreck things."

As though in a deep dream, he heard a metallic clank; they had replaced the manhole cover, shutting out forever the sound of wind and rain. From overhead came the muffled roar of a powerful motor and the swish of a speeding car. He felt the strong tide pushing him slowly into the middle of the sewer, turning him about. For a split second there hovered before his eyes the glittering cave, the shouting walls, and the laughing floor . . . Then his mouth was full of thick, bitter water. The current spun him around. He sighed and closed his eyes, a whirling object rushing alone in the darkness, veering, tossing, lost in the heart of the earth.

QUESTIONS

1. The police officer who kills Daniels sees him as a dangerous rebel, as the kind who'd "wreck things." In what sense could Daniels be seen as a rebel? **2.** What is the significance of Fred Daniels's pecking out his own name on the typewriter? **3.** What significance do you see in the fact that Daniels tries to communicate his joyous feelings at a church and a police station? What is it that he wants to communicate?

WRITING TOPICS

1. Fred Daniels goes underground to escape punishment for a crime he did not commit. He is a black man, and the underground is an appropriate metaphor for the position white America has accorded blacks. The underground is more than a place of escape for him, however; it is a place where he comes to understand what the society he lives in, black and white, is about. How do various episodes—the discovery of the dead baby, the funeral parlor, the movie house, the meat market, the black church—contribute to this understanding? **2.** What significance do Fred Daniels's two dreams have in this story?

The Lottery

1948

SHIRLEY JACKSON [1919–1965]

The morning of June 27th was clear and sunny, with the fresh warmth of a full-summer day; the flowers were blossoming profusely and the grass was richly green. The people of the village began to gather in the square, between the post office and the bank, around ten o'clock; in some towns there were so many people that the lottery took two days and had to be started on June 26th, but in this village, where there were only about three hundred people, the whole lottery took less than two hours, so it could begin at ten o'clock in the morning and still be through in time to allow the villagers to get home for noon dinner.

The children assembled first, of course. School was recently over for the summer, and the feeling of liberty sat uneasily on most of them; they tended to gather together quietly for a while before they broke into boisterous play, and their talk was still of the classroom and the teacher, of books and reprimands. Bobby Martin had already stuffed his pockets full of stones, and the other boys soon followed his example, selecting the smoothest and roundest stones; Bobby and Harry Jones and Dickie Delacroix—the villagers pronounced his name "Dellacroy"—eventually made a great pile of stones in one corner of the square and guarded it against the raids of the other boys. The girls stood aside, talking among themselves, looking over their shoulders at the boys, and the very small children rolled in the dust or clung to the hands of their older brothers or sisters.

Soon the men began to gather, surveying their own children, speaking of planting and rain, tractors and taxes. They stood together, away from the pile of stones in the corner, and their jokes were quiet and they smiled rather than laughed. The women, wearing faded house dresses and sweaters, came shortly after their menfolk. They greeted one another and exchanged bits of gossip as they went to join their husbands. Soon the women, standing by their husbands, began to call to their children, and the children came reluctantly, having to be called four or five times. Bobby Martin ducked under his mother's grasping hand and ran, laughing, back to the pile of stones. His father spoke up sharply, and Bobby came quickly and took his place between his father and his oldest brother.

The lottery was conducted—as were the square dances, the teen-age club, the Halloween program—by Mr. Summers, who had time and energy to devote to civic activities. He was a round-faced, jovial man and he ran the coal business, and people were sorry for him, because he had no children and his wife was a scold. When he arrived in the square, carrying the black wooden box, there was a murmur of conversation among the villagers, and he waved and called, "Little late today, folks." The postmaster, Mr. Graves, followed him, carrying a three-legged stool, and the stool was put in the center of the square and Mr. Summers set the black box down on it. The villagers kept their distance, leaving a space between themselves and the stool, and when Mr. Summers said, "Some of you fellows want to give me a hand?" there was a hesitation before two men, Mr. Martin and his oldest son, Baxter, came forward to hold the box steady on the stool while Mr. Summers stirred up the papers inside it.

The original paraphernalia for the lottery had been lost long ago, and the black box now resting on the stool had been put into use even before Old Man Warner, the oldest man in town, was born. Mr. Summers spoke frequently to the villagers about making a new box, but no one liked to upset even as much tradition as was represented by the black box. There was a story that the present box had been made with some pieces of the box that had preceded it, the one that had been constructed when the first people settled down to make a village here. Every year, after the lottery, Mr. Summers began talking again about a new box, but every year the subject was allowed to fade off without anything's being done. The black box grew shabbier each year; by now it was no longer completely black but splintered badly along one side to show the original wood color, and in some places faded or stained.

Mr. Martin and his oldest son, Baxter, held the black box securely on the stool until Mr. Summers had stirred the papers thoroughly with his hand. Because so much of the ritual had been forgotten or discarded, Mr. Summers had been successful in having slips of paper substituted for the chips of wood that had been used for generations. Chips of wood, Mr. Summers had argued, had been all very well when the village was tiny, but now that the population was more than three hundred and likely to keep on growing, it was necessary to use something that would fit more easily into the black box. The night before the lottery, Mr. Summers and Mr. Graves made up the slips of paper and put them in the box, and it was then taken to the safe of Mr. Summers' coal company and locked up until Mr. Summers was ready to take it to the square next morning. The rest of the year, the box was put away, sometimes one place, sometimes another; it had spent one year in Mr. Graves' barn and another year underfoot in the post office, and sometimes it was set on a shelf in the Martin grocery and left there.

There was a great deal of fussing to be done before Mr. Summers declared the lottery open. There were the lists to make up—of heads of families, heads of households in each family, members of each household in each family. There was the proper swearing-in of Mr. Summers by the postmaster, as the official of the lottery; at one time, some people remembered, there had been a recital of some sort, performed by the official of the lottery, a perfunctory, tuneless chant that had been rattled off duly each year; some people believed that the official of the lottery used to stand just so when he said or sang it, others believed that he was supposed to walk among the people, but years and years ago this part of the ritual had been allowed to lapse. There had been, also, a ritual salute, which the official of the lottery had had to use in addressing each person who came up to draw from the box, but this also had changed with time, until now it was felt necessary only for the official to speak to each person approaching. Mr. Summers was very good at all this; in his clean white shirt and blue jeans, with one hand resting carelessly on the black box, he seemed very proper and important as he talked interminably to Mr. Graves and the Martins.

Just as Mr. Summers finally left off talking and turned to the assembled villagers, Mrs. Hutchinson came hurriedly along the path to the square, her sweater thrown over her shoulders, and slid into place in the back of the crowd. "Clean forgot what day it was," she said to Mrs. Delacroix, who stood next to her, and they both laughed softly. "Thought my old man was out back stacking wood," Mrs. Hutchinson went on, "and then I looked out the window and the kids were gone, and then I remembered it was the twenty-seventh and came a-running." She dried her hands on her apron, and Mrs. Delacroix said, "You're in time, though. They're still talking away up there."

Mrs. Hutchinson craned her neck to see through the crowd and found her husband and children standing near the front. She tapped Mrs. Delacroix on the arm as a farewell and began to make her way through the crowd. The people separated good-humoredly to let her through; two or three people said, in voices just loud enough to be heard across the crowd, "Here comes your Missus, Hutchinson," and "Bill, she made it after all." Mrs. Hutchinson reached her husband, and Mr. Summers, who had been waiting, said cheerfully, "Thought we were going to have to get on without you, Tessie." Mrs. Hutchinson said, grinning, "Wouldn't have me leave m'dishes in the sink, now, would you, Joe?," and soft laughter ran through the crowd as the people stirred back into position after Mrs. Hutchinson's arrival.

"Well, now," Mr. Summers said soberly, "guess we better get started, get this over with, so's we can go back to work. Anybody ain't here?"

"Dunbar," several people said. "Dunbar, Dunbar."

Mr. Summers consulted his list. "Clyde Dunbar," he said. "That's right. He's broke his leg, hasn't he? Who's drawing for him?"

"Me, I guess," a woman said, and Mr. Summers turned to look at her. "Wife draws for her husband," Mr. Summers said. "Don't you have a grown boy to do it for you, Janey?" Although Mr. Summers and everyone else in the village knew the answer perfectly well, it was the business of the official of the lottery to ask such questions formally. Mr. Summers waited with an expression of polite interest while Mrs. Dunbar answered.

"Horace's not but sixteen yet," Mrs. Dunbar said regretfully. "Guess I gotta fill in for the old man this year."

"Right," Mr. Summers said. He made a note on the list he was holding. Then he asked, "Watson boy drawing this year?"

A tall boy in the crowd raised his hand. "Here," he said. "I'm drawing for m'mother and me." He blinked his eyes nervously and ducked his head as several voices in the crowd said things like "Good fellow, Jack," and "Glad to see your mother's got a man to do it."

"Well," Mr. Summers said, "guess that's everyone. Old Man Warner make it?"

"Here," a voice said, and Mr. Summers nodded.

A sudden hush fell on the crowd as Mr. Summers cleared his throat and looked at the list. "All ready?" he called. "Now, I'll read the names—heads of families first—and the men come up and take a paper out of the box. Keep the paper folded in your hand without looking at it until everyone has had a turn. Everything clear?"

The people had done it so many times that they only half listened to the directions; most of them were quiet, wetting their lips, not looking around. Then Mr. Summers raised one hand high and said, "Adams." A man disengaged himself from the crowd and came forward. "Hi, Steve," Mr. Summers said, and Mr. Adams said, "Hi, Joe." They grinned at one another humorlessly and nervously. Then Mr. Adams reached into the black box and took out a folded paper. He held it firmly by one corner as he turned and went hastily back to his place in the crowd, where he stood a little apart from his family, not looking down at his hand.

"Allen." Mr. Summers said. "Anderson. . . . Bentham."

"Seems like there's no time at all between lotteries any more," Mrs. Delacroix said to Mrs. Graves in the back row. "Seems like we got through with the last one only last week."

"Time sure goes fast," Mrs. Graves said.

"Clark. . . . Delacroix."

"There goes my old man," Mrs. Delacroix said. She held her breath while her husband went forward.

"Dunbar," Mr. Summers said, and Mrs. Dunbar went steadily to the box while one of the women said, "Go on, Janey," and another said, "There she goes."

"We're next," Mrs. Graves said. She watched while Mr. Graves came around from the side of the box, greeted Mr. Summers gravely, and selected a slip of paper from the box. By now, all through the crowd there were men holding the small folded papers in their large hands, turning them over and over nervously. Mrs. Dunbar and her two sons stood together, Mrs. Dunbar holding the slip of paper.

"Harburt. . . . Hutchinson."

"Get up there, Bill," Mrs. Hutchinson said, and the people near her laughed.

"Jones."

"They do say," Mr. Adams said to Old Man Warner, who stood next to him, "that over in the north village they're talking of giving up the lottery."

Old Man Warner snorted. "Pack of crazy fools," he said. "Listening to the young folks, nothing's good enough for *them*. Next thing you know, they'll be wanting to go back to living in caves, nobody work any more, live *that* way for a while. Used to be a saying about 'Lottery in June, corn be heavy soon.' First thing you know, we'd all be eating stewed chickweed and acorns. There's *always* been a lottery," he added petulantly. "Bad enough to see young Joe Summers up there joking with everybody."

"Some places have already quit lotteries," Mrs. Adams said.

"Nothing but trouble in *that*," Old Man Warner said stoutly. "Pack of young fools."

"Martin." And Bobby Martin watched his father go forward. "Overdyke. . . . Percy."

"I wish they'd hurry," Mrs. Dunbar said to her older son. "I wish they'd hurry."

"They're almost through," her son said.

"You get ready to run tell Dad," Mrs. Dunbar said.

Mr. Summers called his own name and then stepped forward precisely and selected a slip from the box. Then he called, "Warner."

"Seventy-seventh year I been in the lottery," Old Man Warner said as he went through the crowd. "Seventy-seventh time."

"Watson." The tall boy came awkwardly through the crowd. Someone said, "Don't be nervous, Jack," and Mr. Summers said, "Take your time, son."

"Zanini."

After that, there was a long pause, a breathless pause, until Mr. Summers, holding his slip of paper in the air, said, "All right, fellows." For a minute, no one moved, and then all the slips of paper were opened. Suddenly, all the women began to speak at once, saying, "Who is it," "Who's got it?," "Is it the Dunbars?," "Is it the Watsons?" Then the voices began to say, "It's Hutchinson. It's Bill," "Bill Hutchinson's got it."

"Go tell your father," Mrs. Dunbar said to her older son.

People began to look around to see the Hutchinsons. Bill Hutchinson was standing quiet, staring down at the paper in his hand. Suddenly, Tessie Hutchinson shouted to Mr. Summers, "You didn't give him time enough to take any paper he wanted. I saw you. It wasn't fair!"

"Be a good sport, Tessie," Mrs. Delacroix called, and Mrs. Graves said, "All of us took the same chance."

"Shut up, Tessie," Bill Hutchinson said.

"Well, everyone," Mr. Summers said, "that was done pretty fast, and now we've got to be hurrying a little more to get it done in time." He consulted his next list. "Bill," he said, "you draw for the Hutchinson family. You got any other households in the Hutchinsons?"

"There's Don and Eva," Mrs. Hutchinson yelled. "Make *them* take their chance!"

"Daughters draw with their husbands' families, Tessie," Mr. Summers said gently. "You know that as well as anyone else."

"It wasn't *fair*," Tessie said.

"I guess not, Joe," Bill Hutchinson said regretfully. "My daughter draws with her husband's family, that's only fair. And I've got no other family except the kids."

"Then, as far as drawing for families is concerned, it's you," Mr. Summers said in explanation, "and as far as drawing for households is concerned, that's you, too. Right?"

"Right," Bill Hutchinson said.

"How many kids, Bill?" Mr. Summers asked formally.

"Three," Bill Hutchinson said. "There's Bill, Jr., and Nancy, and little Dave. And Tessie and me."

"All right, then," Mr. Summers said. "Harry, you got their tickets back?"

Mr. Graves nodded and held up the slips of paper. "Put them in the box, then," Mr. Summers directed. "Take Bill's and put it in."

"I think we ought to start over," Mrs. Hutchinson said, as quietly as she could. "I tell you it wasn't *fair*. You didn't give him time enough to choose. *Every*body saw that."

Mr. Graves had selected the five slips and put them in the box, and he dropped all the papers but those onto the ground, where the breeze caught them and lifted them off.

"Listen, everybody," Mrs. Hutchinson was saying to the people around her.

"Ready, Bill?" Mr. Summers asked, and Bill Hutchinson, with one quick glance around at his wife and children, nodded.

"Remember," Mr. Summers said, "take the slips and keep them folded until each person has taken one. Harry, you help little Dave." Mr. Graves took the hand of the little boy, who came willingly with him up to the box. "Take a paper out of the box, Davy," Mr. Summers said. Davy put his hand into the box and laughed. "Take just *one* paper," Mr. Summers said. "Harry, you hold it for him." Mr. Graves took the child's hand and removed the folded paper from the tight fist and held it while little Dave stood next to him and looked up at him wonderingly.

"Nancy next," Mr. Summers said. Nancy was twelve, and her school friends breathed heavily as she went forward, switching her skirt, and took a slip daintily from the box. "Bill, Jr.," Mr. Summers said, and Billy, his face red and his feet over-large, nearly knocked the box over as he got a paper out. "Tessie," Mr. Summers said. She hesitated for a minute, looking around defiantly, and then set her lips and went up to the box. She snatched a paper out and held it behind her.

"Bill," Mr. Summers said, and Bill Hutchinson reached into the box and felt around, bringing his hand out at last with the slip of paper in it.

The crowd was quiet. A girl whispered, "I hope it's not Nancy," and the sound of the whisper reached the edges of the crowd.

"It's not the way it used to be," Old Man Warner said clearly. "People ain't the way they used to be."

"All right," Mr. Summers said. "Open the papers. Harry, you open little Dave's."

Mr. Graves opened the slip of paper and there was a general sigh through the crowd as he held it up and everyone could see that it was blank. Nancy and Bill, Jr., opened theirs at the same time, and both beamed and laughed, turning around to the crowd and holding their slips of paper above their heads.

"Tessie," Mr. Summers said. There was a pause, and then Mr. Summers looked at Bill Hutchinson, and Bill unfolded his paper and showed it. It was blank.

"It's Tessie," Mr. Summers said, and his voice was hushed. "Show us her paper, Bill."

Bill Hutchinson went over to his wife and forced the slip of paper out of her hand. It had a black spot on it, the black spot Mr. Summers had made the night before with the heavy pencil in the coal-company office. Bill Hutchinson held it up, and there was a stir in the crowd.

"All right, folks," Mr. Summers said. "Let's finish quickly."

Although the villagers had forgotten the ritual and lost the original black box, they still remembered to use stones. The pile of stones the boys had made earlier was ready; there were stones on the ground with the blowing scraps of paper that had come out of the box. Mrs. Delacroix selected a stone so large she had to pick it up with both hands and turned to Mrs. Dunbar. "Come on," she said. "Hurry up."

Mrs. Dunbar had small stones in both hands, and she said, gasping for breath, "I can't run at all. You'll have to go ahead and I'll catch up with you."

The children had stones already, and someone gave little Davy Hutchinson a few pebbles.

Tessie Hutchinson was in the center of a cleared space by now, and she held her hands out desperately as the villagers moved in on her. "It isn't fair," she said. A stone hit her on the side of the head.

Old Man Warner was saying, "Come on, come on, everyone." Steve Adams was in the front of the crowd of villagers, with Mrs. Graves beside him.

"It isn't fair, it isn't right," Mrs. Hutchinson screamed, and then they were upon her.

QUESTIONS
1. What evidence in the story suggests that the lottery is a ritualistic ceremony?
2. What set of beliefs underlie the old saying "Lottery in June, corn be heavy soon?" 3. Might this story be a comment on religious orthodoxy? Explain.

The Ones Who Walk Away from Omelas

1974

URSULA K. LE GUIN   [b. 1929]

With a clamor of bells that set the swallows soaring, the Festival of Summer came to the city Omelas, bright-towered by the sea. The rigging of the boats in harbor sparkled with flags. In the streets between houses with red roofs and painted walls, between old moss-grown gardens and under avenues of trees, past great parks and public buildings, processions moved. Some were decorous: old people in long stiff robes of mauve and grey, grave master workmen, quiet, merry women carrying their babies and chatting as they walked. In other streets the music beat faster, a shimmering of gong and tambourine, and the people went dancing, the procession was a dance. Children dodged in and out, their high calls rising like the swallows' crossing flights over the music and the singing. All the processions wound towards the north side of the city, where on the great water-meadow called the Green Fields boys and girls, naked in the bright air, with mud-stained feet and ankles and long, lithe arms, exercised their restive horses before the race. The horses wore no gear at all but a halter without bit. Their manes were braided with streamers of silver, gold, and green. They flared their nostrils and pranced and boasted to one another; they were vastly excited, the horse being the only animal who has adopted our ceremonies as his own. Far off to the north and west the mountains stood up half encircling Omelas on her bay. The air of morning was so clear that the snow still crowning the Eighteen Peaks burned with white-gold fire across the miles of sunlit air, under the dark blue of the sky. There was just enough wind to make the banners that marked the racecourse snap and flutter now and then. In the silence of the broad green meadows one could hear the music winding through the city streets, farther and nearer and ever approaching, a cheerful faint sweetness of the air that from time to time trembled and gathered together and broke out into the great joyous clanging of the bells.

Joyous! How is one to tell about joy? How describe the citizens of Omelas?

They were not simple folk, you see, though they were happy. But we do not say the words of cheer much any more. All smiles have become archaic. Given a description such as this one tends to make certain assumptions. Given a description such as this one tends to look next for the King, mounted on a splendid stallion and surrounded by his noble knights, or perhaps in a golden litter borne by great-muscled slaves. But there was no king. They did not use swords, or keep slaves. They were not barbarians. I do not know the rules and laws of their society, but I suspect that they were singularly few. As they did without monarchy and slavery, so they also go on without the stock exchange, the advertisement, the secret police, and the bomb. Yet I repeat that these were not

489

simple folk, not dulcet shepherds, noble savages, bland utopians. They were not less complex than us. The trouble is that we have a bad habit, encouraged by pedants and sophisticates, of considering happiness as something rather stupid. Only pain is intellectual, only evil interesting. This is the treason of the artist: a refusal to admit the banality of evil and the terrible boredom of pain. If you can't lick 'em, join 'em. If it hurts, repeat it. But to praise despair is to condemn delight, to embrace violence is to lose hold of everything else. We have almost lost hold; we can no longer describe a happy man, nor make any celebration of joy. How can I tell you about the people of Omelas? They were not naïve and happy children—though their children were, in fact, happy. They were mature, intelligent, passionate adults whose lives were not wretched. O miracle! but I wish I could describe it better. I wish I could convince you. Omelas sounds in my words like a city in a fairy tale, long ago and far away, once upon a time. Perhaps it would be best if you imagined it as your own fancy bids, assuming it will rise to the occasion, for certainly I cannot suit you all. For instance, how about technology? I think that there would be no cars or helicopters in and above the streets; this follows from the fact that the people of Omelas are happy people. Happiness is based on a just discrimination of what is necessary, what is neither necessary nor destructive, and what is destructive. In the middle category, however—that of the unnecessary but undestructive, that of comfort, luxury, exuberance, etc.—they could perfectly well have central heating, subway trains, washing machines, and all kinds of marvelous devices not yet invented here, floating light-sources, fuelless power, a cure for the common cold. Or they could have none of that: it doesn't matter. As you like it. I incline to think that people from towns up and down the coast have been coming in to Omelas during the last days before the Festival on very fast little trains and double-decker trams, and that the train station of Omelas is actually the handsomest building in town, though plainer than the magnificent Farmers' Market. But even granted trains, I fear that Omelas so far strikes some of you as goody-goody. Smiles, bells, parades, horses, bleh. If so, please add an orgy. If an orgy would help, don't hesitate. Let us not, however, have temples from which issue beautiful nude priests and priestesses already half in ecstasy and ready to copulate with any man or woman, lover or stranger, who desires union with the deep godhead of the blood, although that was my first idea. But really it would be better not to have any temples in Omelas—at least, not manned temples. Religion yes, clergy no. Surely the beautiful nudes can just wander about, offering themselves like divine soufflés to the hunger of the needy and the rapture of the flesh. Let them join the processions. Let tambourines be struck above the copulations, and the glory of desire be proclaimed upon the gongs, and (a not unimportant point) let the offspring of these delightful rituals be beloved and looked after by all. One thing I know there is none of in Omelas is guilt. But what else should there be? I thought at first there were no drugs, but that is puritanical. For those who like it, the faint insistent sweetness of *drooz* may perfume the ways of the city, *drooz* which first brings a great lightness and brilliance to the mind and limbs, and then after some hours a dreamy languor, and wonderful visions at last of the very arcana and inmost secrets of the Universe, as well as exciting the pleasure of sex beyond all belief; and it is not habit-forming. For more modest tastes I think there ought to be beer. What else, what else belongs in the joyous city? The sense of victory, surely, the celebration of courage. But as we did without clergy, let us do without soldiers. The joy built upon successful slaughter is not the right kind of joy; it will not do; it is fearful and it is trivial. A boundless and generous contentment, a magnanimous triumph felt not against some outer enemy but in communion with the finest and fairest in the souls of all men everywhere and the splendor of the world's summer: this is what swells the hearts of the people of Omelas, and the victory they celebrate is that of life. I really don't think many of them need to take *drooz*.

Most of the processions have reached the Green Fields by now. A marvelous smell of cooking goes forth from the red and blue tents of the provisioners. The faces of small children are amiably sticky; in the benign grey beard of a man a couple of crumbs of rich pastry are entangled. The youths and girls have mounted their horses and are beginning to group around the starting line of the course. An old woman, small, fat, and laughing, is passing out flowers from a basket, and tall young men wear her flowers in their shining hair. A child of nine or ten sits at the edge of the crowd, alone, playing on a wooden flute. People pause to listen, and they smile, but they do not speak to him, for he never ceases playing and never sees them, his dark eyes wholly rapt in the sweet, thin magic of the tune.

He finishes, and slowly lowers his hands holding the wooden flute.

As if that little private silence were the signal, all at once a trumpet sounds from the pavilion near the starting line: imperious, melancholy, piercing. The horses rear on their slender legs, and some of them neigh in answer. Soberfaced, the young riders stroke the horses' necks and soothe them, whispering, "Quiet, quiet, there my beauty, my hope. . . ." They begin to form in rank along the starting line. The crowds along the racecourse are like a field of grass and flowers in the wind. The Festival of Summer has begun.

Do you believe? Do you accept the festival, the city, the joy? No? Then let me describe one more thing.

In a basement under one of the beautiful public buildings of Omelas, or perhaps in the cellar of one of its spacious private homes, there is a room. It has one locked door, and no window. A little light seeps in dustily between cracks in the boards, secondhand from a cobwebbed window somewhere across the cellar. In one corner of the little room a couple of mops, with stiff, clotted, foul-smelling heads, stand near a rusty bucket. The floor is dirt, a little damp to the touch, as cellar dirt usually is. The room is about three paces long and two wide: a mere broom closet or disused tool room. In the room a child is sitting. It could be a boy or a girl. It looks about six, but actually is nearly ten. It is feeble-minded. Perhaps it was born defective, or perhaps it has become imbecile through fear, malnutrition, and neglect. It picks its nose and occasionally fumbles vaguely with its toes or genitals, as it sits hunched in the corner farthest from the bucket and the two mops. It is afraid of the mops. It finds them horrible. It shuts its eyes, but it knows the mops are still standing there; and the door is locked; and nobody will come. The door is always locked; and nobody ever comes, except that sometimes—the child has no understanding of time or interval—sometimes the door rattles terribly and opens, and a person, or several people, are there. One of them may come in and kick the child to make it stand up. The others never come close, but peer in at it with frightened, disgusted eyes. The food bowl and the water jug are hastily filled, the door is locked, the eyes disappear. The people at the door never say anything, but the child, who has not always lived in the tool room, and can remember sunlight and its mother's voice, sometimes speaks. "I will be good," it says. "Please let me out. I will be good!" They never answer. The child used to scream for help at night, and cry a good deal, but now it only makes a kind of whining, "eh-haa, eh-haa," and it speaks less and less often. It is so thin there are no calves to its legs; its belly protrudes; it lives on a half-bowl of corn meal and grease a day. It is naked. Its buttocks and thighs are a mass of festered sores, as it sits in its own excrement continually.

They all know it is there, all the people of Omelas. Some of them have come to see it, others are content merely to know it is there. They all know that it has to be there. Some of them understand why, and some do not, but all understand that their happiness, the beauty of their city, the tenderness of their friendships, the health of their children, the wisdom of their scholars, the skill of their makers, even the abundance of their harvest and the kindly weathers of their skies, depend wholly on this child's abominable misery.

This is usually explained to children when they are between eight and twelve, whenever they seem capable of understanding; and most of those who come to see the child are young people, though often enough an adult comes, or comes back, to see the child. No matter how well the matter has been explained to them, these young spectators are always shocked and sickened at the sight. They feel disgust, which they had thought themselves superior to. They feel anger, outrage, impotence, despite all the explanations. They would like to do something for the child. But there is nothing they can do. If the child were brought up into the sunlight out of that vile place, if it were cleaned and fed and comforted, that would be a good thing, indeed; but if it were done, in that day and hour all the prosperity and beauty and delight of Omelas would wither and be destroyed. Those are the terms. To exchange all the goodness and grace of every life in Omelas for that single, small improvement: to throw away the happiness of thousands for the chance of the happiness of one: that would be to let guilt within the walls indeed.

The terms are strict and absolute; there may not even be a kind word spoken to the child.

Often the young people go home in tears, or in a tearless rage, when they have seen the child and faced this terrible paradox. They may brood over it for weeks or years. But as time goes on they begin to realize that even if the child could be released, it would not get much good of its freedom: a little vague pleasure of warmth and food, no doubt, but little more. It is too degraded and imbecile to know any real joy. It has been afraid too long ever to be free of fear. Its habits are too uncouth for it to respond to humane treatment. Indeed, after so long it would probably be wretched without walls about it to protect it, and darkness for its eyes, and its own excrement to sit in. Their tears at the bitter injustice dry when they begin to perceive the terrible justice of reality, and to accept it. Yet it is their tears and anger, the trying of their generosity and the acceptance of their helplessness, which are perhaps the true source of the splendor of their lives. Theirs is no vapid, irresponsible happiness. They know that they, like the child, are not free. They know compassion. It is the existence of the child, and their knowledge of its existence, that makes possible the nobility of their architecture, the poignancy of their music, the profundity of their science. It is because of the child that they are so gentle with children. They know that if the wretched one were not there snivelling in the dark, the other one, the flute-player, could make no joyful music as the young riders line up in their beauty for the race in the sunlight of the first morning of summer.

Now do you believe in them? Are they not more credible? But there is one more thing to tell, and this is quite incredible.

At times one of the adolescent girls or boys who go to see the child does not go home to weep or rage, does not, in fact, go home at all. Sometimes also a man or woman much older falls silent for a day or two, and then leaves home. These people go out into the street, and walk down the street alone. They keep walking, and walk straight out of the city of Omelas, through the beautiful gates. They keep walking across the farmlands of Omelas. Each one goes alone, youth or girl, man or woman. Night falls; the traveler must pass down village streets, between the houses with yellow-lit windows, and on out into the darkness of the fields. Each alone, they go west or north, towards the mountains. They go on. They leave Omelas, they walk ahead into the darkness, and they do not come back. The place they go towards is a place even less imaginable to most of us than the city of happiness. I cannot describe it at all. It is possible that it does not exist. But they seem to know where they are going, the ones who walk away from Omelas.

The Sandman

DONALD BARTHELME [b. 1931]

Dear Dr. Hodder, I realize that it is probably wrong to write a letter to one's
girl friend's shrink but there are several things going on here that I think ought
to be pointed out to you. I thought of making a personal visit but the situation
then, as I'm sure you understand, would be completely untenable—I would be
visiting a psychiatrist. I also understand that in writing to you I am in some
sense interfering with the process but you don't have to discuss with Susan what
I have said. Please consider this an "eyes only" letter. Please think of it as
personal and confidential.

You must be aware, first, that because Susan is my girl friend pretty much
everything she discusses with you she also discusses with me. She tells me what
she said and what you said. We have been seeing each other for about six
months now and I am pretty familiar with her story, or stories. Similarly, with
your responses, or at least the general pattern. I know, for example, that my
habit of referring to you as "the sandman" annoys you but let me assure you
that I mean nothing unpleasant by it. It is simply a nickname. The reference
is to the old rhyme: "Sea-sand does the sandman bring/Sleep to end the day/
He dusts the children's eyes with sand/And steals their dreams away." (This is
a variant; there are other versions, but this is the one I prefer.) I also understand
that you are a little bit shaky because the prestige of analysis is now, as I'm sure
you know far better than I, at a nadir. This must tend to make you nervous and
who can blame you? One always tends to get a little bit shook when one's
methodology is in question. Of course! (By the bye, let me say that I am very
pleased that you are one of the ones that talk, instead of just sitting there. I
think that's a good thing, an excellent thing, I congratulate you.)

To the point. I fully understand that Susan's wish to terminate with you and
buy a piano instead has disturbed you. You have every right to be disturbed and
to say that she is not electing the proper course, that what she says conceals
something else, that she is evading reality, etc., etc. Go ahead. But there is one
possibility here that you might be, just might be, missing. Which is that she
means it.

Susan says: "I want to buy a piano."

You think: She wishes to terminate the analysis and escape into the piano.

Or: Yes, it is true that her father wanted her to be a concert pianist and that
she studied for twelve years with Goetzmann. But she does not really want to
reopen that can of maggots. She wants me to disapprove.

Or: Having failed to achieve a career as a concert pianist, she wishes to fail
again. She is now too old to achieve the original objective. The spontaneous
organization of defeat!

Or: She is flirting again.

Or:

494

Or:

Or:

Or:

The one thing you cannot consider, by the nature of your training and of the discipline itself, is that she really might want to terminate the analysis and buy a piano. That the piano might be more necessary and valuable to her than the analysis.[1]

What we really have to consider here is the locus of hope. Does hope reside in the analysis or rather in the piano? As a shrink rather than a piano salesman you would naturally tend to opt for the analysis. But there are differences. The piano salesman can stand behind his product; you, unfortunately, cannot. A Steinway is a known quantity, whereas an analysis can succeed or fail. I don't reproach you for this, I simply note it. (An interesting question: Why do laymen feel such a desire to, in plain language, fuck over shrinks? As I am doing here, in a sense? I don't mean hostility in the psychoanalytic encounter, I mean in general. This is an interesting phenomenon and should be investigated by somebody.)

It might be useful if I gave you a little taste of my own experience of analysis. I only went five or six times. Dr. Behring was a tall thin man who never said anything much. If you could get a "What comes to mind?" out of him you were doing splendidly. There was a little incident that is, perhaps, illustrative. I went for my hour one day and told him about something I was worried about. (I was then working for a newspaper down in Texas.) There was a story that four black teenagers had come across a little white boy, about ten, in a vacant lot, sodomized him repeatedly and then put him inside a refrigerator and closed the door (this was before they had that requirement that abandoned refrigerators had to have their doors removed) and he suffocated. I don't know to this day what actually happened, but the cops had picked up *some* black kids and were reportedly beating the shit out of them in an effort to make them confess. I was not on the police run at that time but one of the police reporters told me about it and I told Dr. Behring. A good liberal, he grew white with anger and said what was I doing about it? It was the first time he had talked. So I was shaken— it hadn't occurred to me that I was required to do something about it, he was right—and after I left I called my then sister-in-law, who was at that time secretary to a City Councilman. As you can imagine, such a position is a very powerful one—the councilmen are mostly off making business deals and the executive secretaries run the office—and she got on to the chief of police with an inquiry as to what was going on and if there was any police brutality involved and if so, how much. The case was a very sensational one, you see; *Ebony* had a writer down there trying to cover it but he couldn't get in to see the boys and the cops had roughed him up some, they couldn't understand at that time that

---

[1] For an admirable discussion of this sort of communication failure and many other matters of interest see Percy, "Toward a Triadic Theory of Meaning," *Psychiatry*, Vol. 35 (February 1972), pp. 6–14 *et seq.* [Editors' note: This and all subsequent footnotes to this story are part of the text.]

there could be such a thing as a black reporter. They understood that they had to be a little careful with the white reporters, but a black reporter was beyond them. But my sister-in-law threw her weight (her Councilman's weight) around a bit and suggested to the chief that if there was a serious amount of brutality going on the cops had better stop it, because there was too much outside interest in the case and it would be extremely bad PR if the brutality stuff got out. I also called a guy I knew pretty high up in the sheriff's department and suggested that *he* suggest to his colleagues that they cool it. I hinted at unspeakable political urgencies and he picked it up. The sheriff's department was separate from the police department but they both operated out of the Courthouse Building and they interacted quite a bit, in the normal course. So the long and short of it was that the cops decided to show the four black kids at a press conference to demonstrate that they weren't really beat all to rags, and that took place at four in the afternoon. I went and the kids looked O.K., except for one whose teeth were out and who the cops said had fallen down the stairs. Well, we all know the falling-down-the-stairs story but the point was the *degree* of mishandling and it was clear that the kids had not been half-killed by the cops, as the rumor stated. They were walking and talking naturally, although scared to death, as who would not be? There weren't any TV pictures because the newspaper people always pulled out the plugs of the TV people, at important moments, in those days—it was a standard thing. Now while I admit it sounds callous to be talking about the degree of brutality being minimal, let me tell you that it was no small matter, in that time and place, to force the cops to show the kids to the press at all. It was an achievement, of sorts. So about eight o'clock I called Dr. Behring at home, I hope interrupting his supper, and told him that the kids were O.K., relatively, and he said that was fine, he was glad to hear it. They were later no-billed and I stopped seeing him. That was my experience of analysis and that it may have left me a little sour, I freely grant. Allow for this bias.

To continue. I take exception to your remark that Susan's "openness" is a form of voyeurism. This remark interested me for a while, until I thought about it. Voyeurism I take to be an eroticized expression of curiosity whose chief phenomenological characteristic is the distance maintained between the voyeur and the object. The tension between the desire to draw near the object and the necessity to maintain the distance becomes a libidinous energy nondischarge, which is what the voyeur seeks.[2] The tension. But your remark indicates, in my opinion, a radical misreading of the problem. Susan's "openness"—a willingness of the heart, if you will allow such a term—is not at all comparable to the activities of the voyeur. Susan draws near. Distance is not her thing—not by a long chalk. Frequently, as you know, she gets burned, but she always tries again. What is operating here, I suggest, is an attempt on your part to "stabilize" Susan's behavior in reference to a state-of-affairs that you feel should obtain. Susan gets married and lives happily ever after. Or: There is within Susan a

---

[2] See, for example, Straus, "Shame As a Historiological Problem," in *Phenomenological Psychology.* (New York: Basic Books, 1966), p. 219.

certain amount of creativity which should be liberated and actualized. Susan becomes an artist and lives happily ever after.

But your norms are, I suggest, skewing your view of the problem, and very badly.

Let us take the first case. You reason: If Susan is happy or at least functioning in the present state of affairs (that is, moving from man to man as a silver dollar moves from hand to hand), then why is she seeing a shrink? Something is wrong. New behavior is indicated. Susan is to get married and live happily ever after. May I offer another view? That is, that "seeing a shrink" might be precisely a maneuver in a situation in which Susan *does not want* to get married and live happily ever after? That getting married and living happily ever after might be, for Susan, the worst of fates, and that in order to validate her nonacceptance of this norm she defines herself to herself as shrink-needing? That you are actually certifying the behavior which you seek to change? (When she says to you that she's not shrinkable, you should listen.)

Perhaps, Dr. Hodder, my logic is feeble, perhaps my intuitions are frail. It is, God knows, a complex and difficult question. Your perception that Susan is an artist of some kind *in potentia* is, I think, an acute one. But the proposition "Susan becomes an artist and lives happily ever after" is ridiculous. (I realize that I am couching the proposition in such terms—"happily ever after"—that it is ridiculous on the face of it, but there is ridiculousness piled upon ridiculousness.) Let me point out, if it has escaped your notice, that what an artist does, is fail. Any reading of the literature[3] (I mean the theory of artistic creation), however summary, will persuade you instantly that the paradigmatic artistic experience is that of failure. The actualization fails to meet, equal, the intuition. There is something "out there" which cannot be brought "here." This is standard. I don't mean bad artists, I mean good artists. There is no such thing as a "successful artist" (except, of course, in worldly terms). The proposition should read, "Susan becomes an artist and lives unhappily ever after." This is the case. Don't be deceived.

What I am saying is, that the therapy of choice is not clear. I deeply sympathize. You have a dilemma.

I ask you to note, by the way, that Susan's is not a seeking after instant gratification as dealt out by so-called encounter or sensitivity groups, nude marathons, or dope. None of this is what is going down. "Joy" is not Susan's bag. I praise her for seeking out you rather than getting involved with any of this other idiocy. Her forte, I would suggest, is mind, and if there are games being played they are being conducted with taste, decorum, and some amount of intellectual rigor. Not-bad games. When I take Susan out to dinner she does not order chocolate-covered ants, even if they are on the menu. (Have you, by the way, tried Alfredo's, at the corner of Bank and Hudson streets? It's wonderful.) (Parenthetically, the problem of analysts sleeping with their patients is well known and I understand that Susan has been routinely seducing you—a

---

[3] Especially, perhaps, Ehrenzweig, *The Hidden Order of Art* (University of California Press, 1966), pp. 234–9.

reflex, she can't help it—throughout the analysis. I understand that there is a new splinter group of therapists, behaviorists of some kind, who take this to be some kind of ethic? Is this true? Does this mean that they do it only when they want to, or whether they want to or not? At a dinner party the other evening a lady analyst was saying that three cases of this kind had recently come to her attention and she seemed to think that this was rather a lot. The problem of maintaining mentorship is, as we know, not easy. I think you have done very well in this regard, and God knows it must have been difficult, given those skirts Susan wears that unbutton up to the crotch and which she routinely leaves unbuttoned to the third button.)

Am I wandering too much for you? Bear with me. The world is waiting for the sunrise.

We are left, I submit, with the problem of her depressions. They are, I agree, terrible. Your idea that I am not "supportive" enough is, I think, wrong. I have found, as a practical matter, that the best thing to do is to just do ordinary things, read the newspaper for example, or watch basketball, or wash the dishes. That seems to allow her to come out of it better than any amount of so-called "support." (About the *chasmus hystericus* or hysterical yawning I don't worry any more. It is masking behavior, of course, but after all, you must allow us our tics. The world is waiting for the sunrise.) What do you do with a patient who finds the world unsatisfactory? The world *is* unsatisfactory; only a fool would deny it. I know that your own ongoing psychic structuralization is still going on—you are thirty-seven and I am forty-one—but you must be old enough by now to realize that shit is shit. Susan's perception that America has somehow got hold of the greed ethic and that the greed ethic has turned America into a tidy little hell is not, I think, wrong. What do you do with such a perception? Apply Band-Aids, I suppose. About her depressions, I wouldn't do anything. I'd leave them alone. Put on a record.[4]

Let me tell you a story.

One night we were at her place, about three a.m., and this man called, another lover, quite a well-known musician who is very good, very fast—a good man. He asked Susan "Is he there?," meaning me, and she said "Yes," and he said, "What are you doing?," and she said, "What do you think?," and he said, "When will you be finished?," and she said, "Never." Are you, Doctor dear, in a position to appreciate the beauty of this reply, in this context?

What I am saying is that Susan is wonderful. *As is.* There are not so many things around to which that word can be accurately applied. Therefore I must view your efforts to improve her with, let us say, a certain amount of ambivalence. If this makes me a negative factor in the analysis, so be it. I will be a negative factor until the cows come home, and cheerfully. I can't help it, Doctor, I am voting for the piano.

With best wishes,

---

[4] For example, Harrison, "Wah Wah," Apple Records, STCH 639, Side One, Track 3.

"Repent, Harlequin!" Said the Ticktockman (1965)

HARLAN ELLISON [b. 1934]

There are always those who ask, what is it all about? For those who need to ask, for those who need points sharply made, who need to know "where it's at," this:

> *"The mass of men serve the state thus, not as men mainly, but as machines, with their bodies. They are the standing army, and the militia, jailors, constables, posse comitatus, etc. In most cases there is no free exercise whatever of the judgment or of the moral sense; but they put themselves on a level with wood and earth and stones; and wooden men can perhaps be manufactured that will serve the purpose as well. Such command no more respect than men of straw or a lump of dirt. They have the same sort of worth only as horses and dogs. Yet such as these even are commonly esteemed good citizens. Others—as most legislators, politicians, lawyers, ministers, and officeholders—serve the state chiefly with their heads; and, as they rarely make any moral distinctions, they are as likely to serve the Devil, without intending it, as God. A very few, as heroes, patriots, martyrs, reformers in the great sense, and men, serve the state with their consciences also, and so necessarily resist it for the most part; and they are commonly treated as enemies by it."*
>
> *Henry David Thoreau,*
> CIVIL DISOBEDIENCE

That is the heart of it. Now begin in the middle, and later learn the beginning; the end will take care of itself.

But because it was the very world it was, the very world they had allowed it to *become*, for months his activities did not come to the alarmed attention of The Ones Who Kept The Machine Functioning Smoothly, the ones who poured the very best butter over the cams and mainsprings of the culture. Not until it had become obvious that somehow, someway, he had become a notoriety, a celebrity, perhaps even a hero for (what Officialdom inescapably tagged) "an emotionally disturbed segment of the populace," did they turn it over to the Ticktockman and his legal machinery. But by then, because it was the very world it was, and they had no way to predict he would happen—possibly a strain of disease long-defunct, now, suddenly, reborn in a system where immunity had been forgotten, had lapsed—he had been allowed to become too real. Now he had form and substance.

He had become a *personality*, something they had filtered out of the system many decades before. But there it was, and there *he* was, a very definitely imposing personality. In certain circles—middle-class circles—it was thought disgusting. Vulgar ostentation. Anarchistic. Shameful. In others, there was only sniggering: those strata where thought is subjugated to form and ritual, niceties, proprieties. But down below, ah, down below, where the people always needed their saints and sinners, their bread and circuses, their heroes and villains, he was considered a Bolivar; a Napoleon; a Robin Hood; a Dick Bong (Ace of Aces); a Jesus; a Jomo Kenyatta.

And at the top—where, like socially-attuned Shipwreck Kellys, every tremor and vibration threatens to dislodge the wealthy, powerful and titled from their flagpoles—he was considered a menace; a heretic; a rebel; a disgrace; a peril. He was known down the line, to the very heart-meat core, but the important reactions were high above and far below. At the very top, at the very bottom.

So his file was turned over, along with his time-card and his cardioplate, to the office of the Ticktockman.

The Ticktockman: very much over six feet tall, often silent, a soft purring man when things went timewise. The Ticktockman.

Even in the cubicles of the hierarchy, where fear was generated, seldom suffered, he was called the Ticktockman. But no one called him that to his mask.

You don't call a man a hated name, not when that man, behind his mask, is capable of revoking the minutes, the hours, the days and nights, the years of your life. He was called the Master Timekeeper to his mask. It was safer that way.

"This is *what* he is," said the Ticktockman with genuine softness, "but not *who* he is. This time-card I'm holding in my left hand has a name on it, but it is the name of *what* he is, not *who* he is. The cardioplate here in my right hand is also named, but not *whom* named, merely *what* named. Before I can exercise proper revocation, I have to know *who* this *what* is."

To his staff, all the ferrets, all the loggers, all the finks, all the commex, even the mineez, he said, "Who is this Harlequin?"

He was not purring smoothly. Timewise, it was jangle.

However, it *was* the longest speech they had ever heard him utter at one time, the staff, the ferrets, the loggers, the finks, the commex, but not the mineez, who usually weren't around to know, in any case. But even they scurried to find out.

Who is the Harlequin?

High above the third level of the city, he crouched on the humming aluminum-frame platform of the air-boat (foof! air-boat, indeed! swizzleskid is what it was, with a tow-rack jerry-rigged) and he stared down at the neat Mondrian arrangement of the buildings.

Somewhere nearby, he could hear the metronomic left-right-left of the 2:47 P.M. shift, entering the Timkin roller-bearing plant in their sneakers. A minute later, precisely, he heard the softer right-left-right of the 5:00 A.M. formation, going home.

An elfin grin spread across his tanned features, and his dimples appeared for a moment. Then, scratching at his thatch of auburn hair, he shrugged within his motley, as though girding himself for what came next, and threw the joystick forward, and bent into the wind as the air-boat dropped. He skimmed over a slidewalk, purposely dropping a few feet to crease the tassels of the ladies of fashion, and—inserting thumbs in large ears—he stuck out his tongue, rolled his eyes and went wugga-wugga-wugga. It was a minor diversion. One pedestrian skittered and tumbled, sending parcels everywhichway, another wet herself, a third keeled slantwise and the walk was stopped automatically by the servitors till she could be resuscitated. It was a minor diversion.

Then he swirled away on a vagrant breeze, and was gone. Hi-ho.

As he rounded the cornice of the Time-Motion Study Building, he saw the shift, just boarding the slidewalk. With practiced motion and an absolute conservation of movement, they sidestepped up onto the slow-strip and (in a chorus line reminiscent of a Busby Berkeley film of the antediluvian 1930s) advanced across the strips ostrich-walking till they were lined up on the expresstrip.

Once more, in anticipation, the elfin grin spread, and there was a tooth missing back there on the left side. He dipped, skimmed, and swooped over them; and then, scrunching about on the air-boat, he released the holding pins that fastened shut the ends of the home-made pouring troughs that kept his cargo from dumping prematurely. And as he pulled the trough-pins, the air-boat slid over the factory workers and one hundred and fifty thousand dollars' worth of jelly beans cascaded down on the expresstrip.

Jelly beans! Millions and billions of purples and yellows and greens and licorice and grape and raspberry and mint and round and smooth and crunchy outside and soft-mealy inside and sugary and bouncing jouncing tumbling clittering clattering skittering fell on the heads and shoulders and hardhats and carapaces of the Timkin workers, tinkling on the slidewalk and bouncing away and rolling about underfoot and filling the sky on their way down with all the colors of joy and childhood and holidays, coming down in a steady rain, a solid wash, a torrent of color and sweetness out of the sky from above, and entering a universe of sanity and metronomic order with quite-mad coocoo newness. Jelly beans!

The shift workers howled and laughed and were pelted, and broke ranks, and the jelly beans managed to work their way into the mechanism of the slidewalks after which there was a hideous scraping as the sound of a million fingernails rasped down a quarter of a million blackboards, followed by a coughing and a sputtering, and then the slidewalks all stopped and everyone was dumped thisawayandthataway in a jackstraw tumble, still laughing and popping little jelly bean eggs of childish color into their mouths. It was a holiday, and a jollity, an absolute insanity, a giggle. But . . .

The shift was delayed seven minutes.

They did not get home for seven minutes.

The master schedule was thrown off by seven minutes.

Quotas were delayed by inoperative slidewalks for seven minutes.

He had tapped the first domino in the line, and one after another, like chik chik chik, the others had fallen.

The System had been seven minutes' worth of disrupted. It was a tiny matter, one hardly worthy of note, but in a society where the single driving force was order and unity and equality and promptness and clocklike precision and attention to the clock, reverence of the gods of the passage of time, it was a disaster of major importance.

So he was ordered to appear before the Ticktockman. It was broadcast across every channel of the communications web. He was ordered to be *there* at 7:00 dammit on time. And they waited, and they waited, but he didn't show up till almost ten-thirty, at which time he merely sang a little song about moonlight in a place no one had ever heard of, called Vermont, and vanished again. But they had all been waiting since seven, and it wrecked *hell* with their schedules. So the question remained: Who is the Harlequin?

But the *unasked* question (more important of the two) was: how did we get *into* this position, where a laughing, irresponsible japer of jabberwocky and jive could disrupt our entire economic and cultural life with a hundred and fifty thousand dollars' worth of jelly beans. . . .

Jelly for God's sake *beans*. This is madness! Where did he get the money to buy a hundred and fifty thousand dollars' worth of jelly beans? (They knew it would have cost that much, because they had a team of Situation Analysts pulled off another assignment, and rushed to the slidewalk scene to sweep up and count the candies, and produce findings, which disrupted *their* schedules and threw their entire branch at least a day behind.) Jelly beans! Jelly . . . *beans?* Now wait a second—a second accounted for—no one has manufactured jelly beans for over a hundred years. Where did he get jelly beans?

That's another good question. More than likely it will never be answered to your complete satisfaction. But then, how many questions ever are?

The middle you know. Here is the beginning. How it starts:

A desk pad. Day for day, and turn each day. 9:00—open the mail. 9:45—appointment with planning commission board. 10:30—discuss installation progress charts with J. L. 11:45—pray for rain. 12:00—lunch. *And so it goes.*

"I'm sorry, Miss Grant, but the time for interviews was set at 2:30, and it's almost five now. I'm sorry you're late, but those are the rules. You'll have to wait till next year to submit application for this college again." *And so it goes.*

The 10:10 local stops at Cresthaven, Galesville, Tonawanda Junction, Selby and Farnhurst, but not at Indiana City, Lucasville and Colton, except on Sunday. The 10:35 express stops at Galesville, Selby and Indiana City, except on Sundays & Holidays, at which time it stops at . . . *and so it goes.*

"I couldn't wait, Fred. I had to be at Pierre Cartain's by 3:00, and you said you'd meet me under the clock in the terminal at 2:45, and you weren't there, so I had to go on. You're always late, Fred. If you'd been there, we could have sewed it up together, but as it was, well, I took the order alone . . ." *And so it goes.*

Dear Mr. and Mrs. Atterley: In reference to your son Gerold's constant tardiness, I am afraid we will have to suspend him from school unless some more reliable method can be instituted guaranteeing he will arrive at his classes on time. Granted he is an exemplary student, and his marks are high, his constant flouting of the schedules of this school makes it impractical to maintain him in a system where the other children seem capable of getting where they are supposed to be on time *and so it goes*.

YOU CANNOT VOTE UNLESS YOU APPEAR AT 8:45 A.M.

"I don't care if the script is *good*, I need it Thursday!"

CHECK-OUT TIME IS 2:00 P.M.

"You got here late. The job's taken. Sorry."

YOUR SALARY HAS BEEN DOCKED FOR TWENTY MINUTES TIME LOST.

"God, what time is it, I've gotta run!"

And so it goes. And so it goes. And so it goes. And so it goes goes goes goes goes tick tock tick tock tick tock and one day we no longer let time serve us, we serve time and we are slaves of the schedule, worshippers of the sun's passing; bound into a life predicated on restrictions because the system will not function if we don't keep the schedule tight.

Until it becomes more than a minor inconvenience to be late. It becomes a sin. Then a crime. Then a crime punishable by this:

EFFECTIVE 15 JULY 2389 12:00:00 midnight, the office of the Master Timekeeper will require all citizens to submit their time-cards and cardioplates for processing. In accordance with Statute 555-7-SGH-999 governing the revocation of time per capita, all cardioplates will be keyed to the individual holder and—

What they had done, was to devise a method of curtailing the amount of life a person could have. If he was ten minutes late, he lost ten minutes of his life. An hour was proportionately worth more revocation. If someone was consistently tardy, he might find himself, on a Sunday night, receiving a communique from the Master Timekeeper that his time had run out, and he would be "turned off" at high noon on Monday, please straighten your affairs, sir, madame or bisex.

And so, by this simple scientific expedient (utilizing a scientific process held dearly secret by the Ticktockman's office) the System was maintained. It was the only expedient thing to do. It was, after all, patriotic. The schedules had to be met. After all, there *was* a war on!

But, wasn't there always?

"Now that is really disgusting," the Harlequin said, when Pretty Alice showed him the wanted poster. "Disgusting and *highly* improbable. After all, this isn't the Day of the Desperado. A *wanted* poster!"

"You know," Pretty Alice noted, "you speak with a great deal of inflection."

"I'm sorry," said the Harlequin, humbly.

"No need to be sorry. You're always saying 'I'm sorry.' You have such massive guilt, Everett, it's really very sad."

"I'm sorry," he said again, then pursed his lips so the dimples appeared momentarily. He hadn't wanted to say that at all. "I have to go out again. I have to *do* something."

Pretty Alice slammed her coffee-bulb down on the counter. "Oh for God's *sake*, Everett, can't you stay home just *one* night! Must you always be out in that ghastly clown suit, running around an*noy*ing people?"

"I'm—" He stopped, and clapped the jester's hat onto his auburn thatch with a tiny tingling of bells. He rose, rinsed out his coffee-bulb at the spray, and put it into the drier for a moment. "I have to go."

She didn't answer. The faxbox was purring, and she pulled a sheet out, read it, threw it toward him on the counter. "It's about you. Of course. You're ridiculous."

He read it quickly. It said the Ticktockman was trying to locate him. He didn't care, he was going out to be late again. At the door, dredging for an exit line, he hurled back petulantly, "Well, *you* speak with inflection, *too!*"

Pretty Alice rolled her pretty eyes heavenward. "You're ridiculous." The Harlequin stalked out, slamming the door, which sighed shut softly, and locked itself.

There was a gentle knock, and Pretty Alice got up with an exhalation of exasperated breath, and opened the door. He stood there. "I'll be back about ten-thirty, okay?"

She pulled a rueful face. "Why do you tell me that? Why? You *know* you'll be late! You *know it!* You're *always* late, so why do you tell me these dumb things?" She closed the door.

On the other side, the Harlequin nodded to himself. *She's right. She's always right. I'll be late. I'm always late. Why do I tell her these dumb things?*

He shrugged again, and went off to be late once more.

He had fired off the firecracker rockets that said: I will attend the 115th annual International Medical Association Invocation at 8:00 P.M. precisely. I do hope you will all be able to join me.

The words had burned in the sky, and of course the authorities were there, lying in wait for him. They assumed, naturally, that he would be late. He arrived twenty minutes early, while they were setting up the spiderwebs to trap and hold him. Blowing a large bullhorn, he frightened and unnerved them so, their own moisturized encirclement webs sucked closed, and they were hauled up, kicking and shrieking, high above the amphitheater's floor. The Harlequin laughed and laughed, and apologized profusely. The physicians, gathered in solemn conclave, roared with laughter, and accepted the Harlequin's apologies with exaggerated bowing and posturing, and a merry time was had by all, who thought the Harlequin was a regular foofaraw in fancy pants; all, that is, but the authorities, who had been sent out by the office of the Ticktockman; they hung there like so much dockside cargo, hauled up above the floor of the amphitheater in a most unseemly fashion.

(In another part of the same city where the Harlequin carried on his "activities," totally unrelated in every way to what concerns us here, save that it illustrates the Ticktockman's power and import, a man named Marshall Delahanty received his turn-off notice from the Ticktockman's office. His wife received the notification from the gray-suited minee who delivered it, with the traditional "look of sorrow" plastered hideously across his face. She knew what it was, even without unsealing it. It was a billet-doux of immediate recognition to everyone these days. She gasped, and held it as though it were a glass slide tinged with botulism, and prayed it was not for her. Let it be for Marsh, she thought, brutally, realistically, or one of the kids, but not for me, please dear God, not for me. And then she opened it, and it *was* for Marsh, and she was at one and the same time horrified and relieved. The next trooper in the line had caught the bullet. "Marshall," she screamed, "Marshall! Termination, Marshall! OhmiGod, Marshall, whattl we do, whattl we do, Marshall omigod-marshall . . ." and in their home that night was the sound of tearing paper and fear, and the stink of madness went up the flue and there was nothing, absolutely nothing they could do about it.

(But Marshall Delahanty tried to run. And early the next day, when turn-off time came, he was deep in the Canadian forest two hundred miles away, and the office of the Ticktockman blanked his cardioplate, and Marshall Delahanty keeled over, running, and his heart stopped, and the blood dried up on its way to his brain, and he was dead that's all. One light went out on the sector map in the office of the Master Timekeeper, while notification was entered for fax reproduction, and Georgette Delahanty's name was entered on the dole roles till she could remarry. Which is the end of the footnote, and all the point that need be made, except don't laugh, because that is what would happen to the Harlequin if ever the Ticktockman found out his real name. It isn't funny.)

The shopping level of the city was thronged with the Thursday-colors of the buyers. Women in canary yellow chitons and men in pseudo-Tyrolean outfits that were jade and leather and fit very tightly, save for the balloon pants.

When the Harlequin appeared on the still-being-constructed shell of the new Efficiency Shopping Center, his bullhorn to his elfishly-laughing lips, everyone pointed and stared, and he berated them:

"Why let them order you about? Why let them tell you to hurry and scurry like ants or maggots? Take your time! Saunter a while! Enjoy the sunshine, enjoy the breeze, let life carry you at your own pace! Don't be slaves of time, it's a helluva way to die, slowly, by degrees . . . down with the Ticktockman!"

Who's the nut? Most of the shoppers wanted to know. Who's the nut oh wow I'm gonna be late I gotta run . . .

And the construction gang on the Shopping Center received an urgent order from the office of the Master Timekeeper that the dangerous criminal known as the Harlequin was atop their spire, and their aid was urgently needed in apprehending him. The work crew said no, they would lose time on their construction schedule, but the Ticktockman managed to pull the proper threads of governmental webbing, and they were told to cease work and catch that nitwit up there on the spire; up there with the bullhorn. So a dozen and more burly workers began climbing into their construction platforms, releasing the a-grav plates, and rising toward the Harlequin.

After the debacle (in which, through the Harlequin's attention to personal safety, no one was seriously injured), the workers tried to reassemble, and assault him again, but it was too late. He had vanished. It had attracted quite a crowd, however, and the shopping cycle was thrown off by hours, simply hours. The purchasing needs of the system were therefore falling behind, and so measures were taken to accelerate the cycle for the rest of the day, but it got bogged down and speeded up and they sold too many float-valves and not nearly enough wegglers, which meant that the popli ratio was off, which made it necessary to rush cases and cases of spoiling Smash-O to stores that usually needed a case only every three or four hours. The shipments were bollixed, the transshipments were misrouted, and in the end, even the swizzleskid industries felt it.

"Don't come back till you have him!" the Ticktockman said, very quietly, very sincerely, extremely dangerously.

They used dogs. They used probes. They used cardioplate crossoffs. They used teepers. They used bribery. They used stiktytes. They used intimidation. They used torment. They used torture. They used finks. They used cops. They used search&seizure. They used fallaron. They used betterment incentive. They used fingerprints. They used the Bertillon system. They used cunning. They used guile. They used treachery. They used Raoul Mitgong, but he didn't help much. They used applied physics. They used techniques of criminology.

And what the hell: they caught him.

After all, his name was Everett C. Marm, and he wasn't much to begin with, except a man who had no sense of time.

"Repent, Harlequin!" said the Ticktockman.

"Get stuffed!" the Harlequin replied, sneering.

"You've been late a total of sixty-three years, five months, three weeks, two days, twelve hours, forty-one minutes, fifty-nine seconds, point oh three six one one one microseconds. You've used up everything you can, and more. I'm going to turn you off."

"Scare someone else. I'd rather be dead than live in a dumb world with a bogeyman like you."

"It's my job."

"You're full of it. You're a tyrant. You have no right to order people around and kill them if they show up late."

"You can't adjust. You can't fit in."

"Unstrap me, and I'll fit my fist into your mouth."

"You're a non-conformist."

"That didn't used to be a felony."

"It is now. Live in the world around you."

"I hate it. It's a terrible world."

"Not everyone thinks so. Most people enjoy order."

"I don't, and most of the people I know don't."

"That's not true. How do you think we caught you?"

"I'm not interested."

"A girl named Pretty Alice told us who you were."

"That's a lie."

"It's true. You unnerve her. She wants to belong; she wants to conform; I'm going to turn you off."

"Then do it already, and stop arguing with me."

"I'm not going to turn you off."

"You're an idiot!"

"Repent, Harlequin!" said the Ticktockman.

"Get stuffed."

So they sent him to Coventry. And in Coventry they worked him over. It was just like what they did to Winston Smith in *Nineteen Eigthy-four*, which was a book none of them knew about, but the techniques are really quite ancient, and so they did it to Everett C. Marm; and one day, quite a long time later, the Harlequin appeared on the communications web, appearing elfin and dimpled and bright-eyed, and not at all brainwashed, and he said he had been wrong, that it was a good, a very good thing indeed, to belong, to be right on time hip-ho and away we go, and everyone stared up at him on the public screens that covered an entire city block, and they said to themselves, well, you see, he was just a nut after all, and if that's the way the system is run, then let's do it that way, because it doesn't pay to fight city hall, or in this case, the Ticktockman. So Everett C. Marm was destroyed, which was a loss, because of what Thoreau said earlier, but you can't make an omelet without breaking a few eggs, and in every revolution a few die who shouldn't, but they have to, because that's the way it happens, and if you make only a little change, then it seems to be worthwhile. Or, to make the point lucidly:

"Uh, excuse me, sir, I, uh, don't know how to uh, to uh, tell you this, but you were three minutes late. The schedule is a little, uh, bit off."

He grinned sheepishly.

"That's ridiculous!" murmured the Ticktockman behind his mask. "Check your watch." And then he went into his office, going *mrmee, mrmee, mrmee, mrmee.*

Everyday Use   1973

FOR YOUR GRANDMAMA

ALICE WALKER   [b. 1944]

I will wait for her in the yard that Maggie and I made so clean and wavy yesterday afternoon. A yard like this is more comfortable than most people know. It is not just a yard. It is like an extended living room. When the hard clay is swept clean as a floor and the fine sand around the edges lined with tiny, irregular grooves anyone can come and sit and look up into the elm tree and wait for the breezes that never come inside the house.

Maggie will be nervous until after her sister goes: she will stand hopelessly in corners homely and ashamed of the burn scars down her arms and legs, eyeing her sister with a mixture of envy and awe. She thinks her sister has held life always in the palm of one hand, that "no" is a word the world never learned to say to her.

You've no doubt seen those TV shows where the child who has "made it" is confronted, as a surprise, by her own mother and father, tottering in weakly from backstage. (A pleasant surprise, of course: What would they do if parent and child came on the show only to curse out and insult each other?) On TV mother and child embrace and smile into each other's faces. Sometimes the mother and father weep, the child wraps them in her arms and leans across the table to tell how she would not have made it without their help. I have seen these programs.

Sometimes I dream a dream in which Dee and I are suddenly brought together on a TV program of this sort. Out of a dark and soft-seated limousine I am ushered into a bright room filled with many people. There I meet a smiling, gray, sporty man like Johnny Carson who shakes my hand and tells me what a fine girl I have. Then we are on the stage and Dee is embracing me with tears in her eyes. She pins on my dress a large orchid, even though she has told me once that she thinks orchids are tacky flowers.

In real life I am a large, big-boned woman with rough, man-working hands. In the winter I wear flannel nightgowns to bed and overalls during the day. I can kill and clean a hog as mercilessly as a man. My fat keeps me hot in zero weather. I can work all day, breaking ice to get water for washing. I can eat pork liver cooked over the open fire minutes after it comes steaming from the hog. One winter I knocked a bull calf straight in the brain between the eyes with a sledge hammer and had the meat hung up to chill before nightfall. But of course all this does not show on television. I am the way my daughter would want me to be: a hundred pounds lighter, my skin like an uncooked barley pancake. My hair glistens in the hot bright lights. Johnny Carson has much to do to keep up with my quick and witty tongue.

But that is a mistake. I know even before I wake up. Who ever knew a Johnson with a quick tongue? Who can even imagine me looking a strange white man in the eye? It seems to me I have talked to them always with one foot raised in flight, with my head turned in whichever way is farthest from them. Dee, though. She would always look anyone in the eye. Hesitation was no part of her nature.

"How do I look, Mama?" Maggie says, showing just enough of her thin body enveloped in pink skirt and red blouse for me to know she's there, almost hidden by the door.

"Come out into the yard," I say.

Have you ever seen a lame animal, perhaps a dog run over by some careless person rich enough to own a car, sidle up to someone who is ignorant enough to be kind to him? That is the way my Maggie walks. She has been like this, chin on chest, eyes on ground, feet in shuffle, ever since the fire that burned the other house to the ground.

Dee is lighter than Maggie, with nicer hair and a fuller figure. She's a woman now, though sometimes I forget. How long ago was it that the other house burned? Ten, twelve years? Sometimes I can still hear the flames and feel Maggie's arm sticking to me, her hair smoking and her dress falling off her in little black papery flakes. Her eyes seemed stretched open, blazed open by the flames reflected in them. And Dee. I see her standing off under the sweet gum tree she used to dig gum out of; a look of concentration on her face as she watched the last dingy gray board of the house fall in toward the red-hot brick chimney. Why don't you do a dance around the ashes? I'd wanted to ask her. She had hated the house that much.

I used to think she hated Maggie, too. But that was before we raised the money, the church and me, to send her to Augusta to school. She used to read to us without pity; forcing words, lies, other folks' habits, whole lives upon us two, sitting trapped and ignorant underneath her voice. She washed us in a river of make-believe, burned us with a lot of knowledge we didn't necessarily need to know. Pressed us to her with the serious way she read, to shove us away at just the moment, like dimwits, we seemed about to understand.

Dee wanted nice things. A yellow organdy dress to wear to her graduation from high school; black pumps to match a green suit she'd made from an old suit somebody gave me. She was determined to stare down any disaster in her efforts. Her eyelids would not flicker for minutes at a time. Often I fought off the temptation to shake her. At sixteen she had a style of her own: and knew what style was.

I never had an education myself. After second grade the school was closed down. Don't ask me why: in 1927 colored asked fewer questions than they do now. Sometimes Maggie reads to me. She stumbles along good-naturedly but can't see well. She knows she is not bright. Like good looks and money, quickness passed her by. She will marry John Thomas (who has mossy teeth in an earnest face) and then I'll be free to sit here and I guess just sing church songs to myself. Although I never was a good singer. Never could carry a tune. I was always better at a man's job. I used to love to milk till I was hoofed in the side in '49. Cows are soothing and slow and don't bother you, unless you try to milk them the wrong way.

I have deliberately turned my back on the house. It is three rooms, just like the one that burned, except the roof is tin; they don't make shingle roofs any more. There are no real windows, just some holes cut in the sides, like the portholes in a ship, but not round and not square, with rawhide holding the shutters up on the outside. This house is in a pasture, too, like the other one. No doubt when Dee sees it she will want to tear it down. She wrote me once that no matter where we "choose" to live, she will manage to come see us. But she will never bring her friends. Maggie and I thought about this and Maggie asked me, "Mama, when did Dee ever *have* any friends?"

She had a few. Furtive boys in pink shirts hanging about on washday after school. Nervous girls who never laughed. Impressed with her they worshiped the well-turned phrase, the cute shape, the scalding humor that erupted like bubbles in lye. She read to them.

When she was courting Jimmy T she didn't have much time to pay to us, but turned all her faultfinding power on him. He *flew* to marry a cheap gal from a family of ignorant flashy people. She hardly had time to recompose herself.

When she comes I will meet—but there they are!

Maggie attempts to make a dash for the house, in her shuffling way, but I stay her with my hand. "Come back here," I say. And she stops and tries to dig a well in the sand with her toe.

It is hard to see them clearly through the strong sun. But even the first glimpse of leg out of the car tells me it is Dee. Her feet were always neat-looking, as if God himself had shaped them with a certain style. From the other side of the car comes a short, stocky man. Hair is all over his head a foot long and hanging from his chin like a kinky mule tail. I hear Maggie suck in her breath. "Uhnnnh," is what it sounds like. Like when you see the wriggling end of a snake just in front of your foot on the road. "Uhnnnh."

Dee next. A dress down to the ground, in this hot weather. A dress so loud it hurts my eyes. There are yellows and oranges enough to throw back the light of the sun. I feel my whole face warming from the heat waves it throws out. Earrings, too, gold and hanging down to her shoulders. Bracelets dangling and making noises when she moves her arm up to shake the folds of the dress out of her armpits. The dress is loose and flows, and as she walks closer, I like it. I hear Maggie go "Uhnnnh" again. It is her sister's hair. It stands straight up like the wool on a sheep. It is black as night and around the edges are two long pigtails that rope about like small lizards disappearing behind her ears.

"Wa-su-zo-Tean-o!" she says, coming on in that gliding way the dress makes her move. The short stocky fellow with the hair to his navel is all grinning and he follows up with "Asalamalakim, my mother and sister!" He moves to hug

Maggie but she falls back, right up against the back of my chair. I feel her trembling there and when I look up I see the perspiration falling off her chin.

"Don't get up," says Dee. Since I am stout it takes something of a push. You can see me trying to move a second or two before I make it. She turns, showing white heels through her sandals, and goes back to the car. Out she peeks next with a Polaroid. She stoops down quickly and lines up picture after picture of me sitting there in front of the house with Maggie cowering behind me. She never takes a shot without making sure the house is included. When a cow comes nibbling around the edge of the yard she snaps it and me and Maggie *and* the house. Then she puts the Polaroid in the back seat of the car, and comes up and kisses me on the forehead.

Meanwhile Asalamalakim is going through the motions with Maggie's hand. Maggie's hand is as limp as a fish, and probably as cold, despite the sweat, and she keeps trying to pull it back. It looks like Asalamalakim wants to shake hands but wants to do it fancy. Or maybe he don't know how people shake hands. Anyhow, he soon gives up on Maggie.

"Well," I say. "Dee."

"No, Mama," she says. "Not 'Dee,' Wangero Leewanika Kemanjo!"

"What happened to 'Dee'?" I wanted to know.

"She's dead," Wangero said. "I couldn't bear it any longer being named after the people who oppress me."

"You know as well as me you was named after your aunt Dicie," I said. Dicie is my sister. She named Dee. We called her "Big Dee" after Dee was born.

"But who was *she* named after?" asked Wangero.

"I guess after Grandma Dee," I said.

"And who was she named after?" asked Wangero.

"Her mother," I said, and saw Wangero was getting tired. "That's about as far back as I can trace it," I said. Though, in fact, I probably could have carried it back beyond the Civil War through the branches.

"Well," said Asalamalakim, "there you are."

"Uhnnnh," I heard Maggie say.

"There I was not," I said, "before 'Dicie' cropped up in our family, so why should I try to trace it that far back?"

He just stood there grinning, looking down on me like somebody inspecting a Model A car. Every once in a while he and Wangero sent eye signals over my head.

"How do you pronounce this name?" I asked.

"You don't have to call me by it if you don't want to," said Wangero.

"Why shouln' I?" I asked. "If that's what you want us to call you, we'll call you."

"I know it might sound awkward at first," said Wangero.

"I'll get used to it," I said. "Ream it out again."

Well, soon we got the name out of the way. Asalamalakim had a name twice as long and three times as hard. After I tripped over it two or three times he told me to just call him Hakim-a-barber. I wanted to ask him was he a barber, but I didn't really think he was, so I didn't ask.

"You must belong to those beef-cattle peoples down the road," I said. They said "Asalamalakim" when they met you, too, but they didn't shake hands. Always too busy: feeding the cattle, fixing the fences, putting up salt-lick shelters, throwing down hay. When the white folks poisoned some of the herd the men stayed up all night with rifles in their hands. I walked a mile and a half just to see the sight.

Hakim-a-barber said, "I accept some of their doctrines, but farming and raising cattle is not my style." (They didn't tell me, and I didn't ask, whether Wangero [Dee] had really gone and married him.)

We sat down to eat and right away he said he didn't eat collards and pork was unclean. Wangero, though, went on through the chitlins and corn bread, the greens and everything else. She talked a blue streak over the sweet potatoes. Everything delighted her. Even the fact that we still used the benches her daddy made for the table when we couldn't afford to buy chairs.

"Oh, Mama!" she cried. Then turned to Hakim-a-barber. "I never knew how lovely these benches are. You can feel the rump prints," she said, running her hands underneath her and along the bench. Then she gave a sigh and her hand closed over Grandma Dee's butter dish. "That's it!" she said. "I knew there was something I wanted to ask you if I could have." She jumped up from the table and went over in the corner where the churn stood, the milk in its clabber by now. She looked at the churn and looked at it.

"This churn top is what I need," she said. "Didn't Uncle Buddy whittle it out of a tree you all used to have?"

"Yes," I said.

"Uh huh," she said happily. "And I want the dasher, too."

"Uncle Buddy whittle that, too?" asked the barber.

Dee (Wangero) looked up at me.

"Aunt Dee's first husband whittled the dash," said Maggie so low you almost couldn't hear her. "His name was Henry, but they called him Stash."

"Maggie's brain is like an elephant's," Wangero said, laughing. "I can use the churn top as a centerpiece for the alcove table," she said, sliding a plate over the churn, "and I'll think of something artistic to do with the dasher."

When she finished wrapping the dasher the handle stuck out. I took it for a moment in my hands. You didn't even have to look close to see where hands pushing the dasher up and down to make butter had left a kind of sink in the wood. In fact, there were a lot of small sinks; you could see where thumbs and fingers had sunk into the wood. It was beautiful light yellow wood, from a tree that grew in the yard where Big Dee and Stash had lived.

After dinner Dee (Wangero) went to the trunk at the foot of my bed and started rifling through it. Maggie hung back in the kitchen over the dishpan. Out came Wangero with two quilts. They had been pieced by Grandma Dee and then Big Dee and me had hung them on the quilt frames on the front porch and quilted them. One was in the Lone Star pattern. The other was Walk Around the Mountain. In both of them were scraps of dresses Grandma Dee had worn fifty and more years ago. Bits and pieces of Grandpa Jarrell's Paisley shirts. And one teeny faded blue piece, about the size of a penny matchbox, that was from Great Grandpa Ezra's uniform that he wore in the Civil War.

"Mama," Wangero said sweet as a bird. "Can I have these old quilts?"

I heard something fall in the kitchen, and a minute later the kitchen door slammed.

"Why don't you take one or two of the others?" I asked "These old things was just done by me and Big Dee from some tops your grandma pieced before she died."

"No," said Wangero. "I don't want those. They are stitched around the borders by machine."

"That's make them last better," I said.

"That's not the point," said Wangero. "These are all pieces of dresses Grandma used to wear. She did all this stitching by hand. Imagine!" She held the quilts securely in her arms, stroking them.

"Some of the pieces, like those lavender ones, come from old clothes her mother handed down to her," I said, moving up to touch the quilts. Dee (Wangero) moved back just enough so that I couldn't reach the quilts. They already belonged to her.

"Imagine!" she breathed again, clutching them closely to her bosom.

"The truth is," I said, "I promised to give them quilts to Maggie, for when she marries John Thomas."

She gasped like a bee had stung her.

"Maggie can't appreciate these quilts!" she said. "She'd probably be backward enough to put them to everyday use."

"I reckon she would," I said. "God knows I been saving 'em for long enough with nobody using 'em. I hope she will!" I didn't want to bring up how I had offered Dee (Wangero) a quilt when she went away to college. Then she had told me they were old-fashioned, out of style.

"But they're *priceless!*" she was saying now, furiously; for she has a temper. "Maggie would put them on the bed and in five years they'd be in rags. Less than that!"

"She can always make some more," I said. "Maggie knows how to quilt."

Dee (Wangero) looked at me with hatred. "You just will not understand. The point is these quilts, *these* quilts!"

"Well," I said, stumped. "What would *you* do with them?"

"Hang them," she said. As if that was the only thing you *could* do with quilts.

Maggie by now was standing in the door. I could almost hear the sound her feet made as they scraped over each other.

"She can have them, Mama," she said, like somebody used to never winning anything, or having anything reserved for her. "I can 'member Grandma Dee without the quilts."

I looked at her hard. She had filled her bottom lip with checkerberry snuff and it gave her face a kind of dopey, hangdog look. It was Grandma Dee and Big Dee who taught her how to quilt herself. She stood there with her scarred hands hidden in the folds of her skirt. She looked at her sister with something like fear but she wasn't mad at her. This was Maggie's portion. This was the way she knew God to work.

When I looked at her like that something hit me in the top of my head and ran down to the soles of my feet. Just like when I'm in church and the spirit of God touches me and I get happy and shout. I did something I never had done before: hugged Maggie to me, then dragged her on into the room, snatched the quilts out of Miss Wangero's hands and dumped them into Maggie's lap. Maggie just sat there on my bed with her mouth open.

"Take one or two of the others," I said to Dee.

But she turned without a word and went out to Hakim-a-barber.

"You just don't understand," she said, as Maggie and I came out to the car.

"What don't I understand?" I wanted to know.

"Your heritage," she said. And then she turned to Maggie, kissed her, and said, "You ought to try to make something of yourself, too, Maggie. It's really a new day for us. But from the way you and Mama still live you'd never know it."

She put on some sunglasses that hid everything above the tip of her nose and her chin.

Maggie smiled; maybe at the sunglasses. But a real smile, not scared. After we watched the car dust settle I asked Maggie to bring me a dip of snuff. And then the two of us sat there just enjoying, until it was time to go in the house and go to bed.

CONFORMITY
AND
REBELLION

Au Moulin Rouge. Le Depart du Quadrille, 1892 after a painting by Henri de Toulouse-Lautrec,

POETRY

Sonnet XVII   (1655)

JOHN MILTON [1608–1674]

When I consider how my light is spent,[1]
    Ere half my days, in this dark world and wide,
    And that one talent[2] which is death to hide
    Lodged with me useless, though my soul more bent
To serve therewith my maker, and present
    My true account, lest he, returning, chide.
    'Doth God exact day-labour, light denied?'
    I fondly° ask; but Patience, to prevent   *foolishly*
That murmur, soon replies: 'God doth not need
    Either man's work or his own gifts; who best   10
    Bear his mild yoke, they serve him best; his state
Is kingly—thousands at his bidding speed
    And post o'er land and ocean without rest:
    They also serve who only stand and wait.'

from

Paradise Lost[1]   1667

JOHN MILTON [1608–1674]

    "Is this the region, this the soil, the clime,"
Said then the lost archangel, "this the seat
That we must change for Heaven? this mournful gloom

Sonnet XVII
    [1] Milton was blind when he wrote this sonnet.
    [2] The parable of the Master who gave his servants "talents" (literally, coins of precious metal) occurs in Matthew 25:14–30.

Paradise Lost
    [1] The first part of *Paradise Lost*, a poem on the expulsion of Adam and Eve from the Garden of Eden, tells the story of Satan's rebellion against God, his defeat and expulsion from heaven. In this passage, Satan surveys the infernal region to which God has banished him.

For that celestial light? Be it so, since he
Who now is sovereign can dispose and bid
What shall be right: farthest from him is best,
Whom reason hath equaled, force hath made supreme
Above his equals. Farewell, happy fields,
Where joy forever dwells! Hail, horrors! hail,
Infernal world! and thou, profoundest Hell,   10
Receive thy new possessor, one who brings
A mind not to be changed by place or time.
The mind is its own place, and in itself
Can make a Heaven of Hell, a Hell of Heaven.
What matter where, if I be still the same,
And what I should be, all but° less than he   only
Whom thunder hath made greater? Here at least
We shall be free; th' Almighty hath not built
Here for his envy, will not drive us hence:
Here we may reign secure; and, in my choice,   20
To reign is worth ambition, though in Hell:
Better to reign in Hell than serve in Heaven.
But wherefore let we then our faithful friends,
Th' associates and copartners of our loss,
Lie thus astonished on th' oblivious pool,
And call them not to share with us their part
In this unhappy mansion, or once more
With rallied arms to try what may be yet
Regained in Heaven, or what more lost in Hell?"

QUESTIONS

1. Is the statement in line 22 a logical extension of the statement in lines 13–14? Explain. **2.** Is the rebellious Satan heroic or ignoble? Defend your answer. **3.** What are the political implications of Satan's analysis of power (ll. 4–8)?

from

An Essay on Man   1733

ALEXANDER POPE [1688–1744]

Cease then, nor ORDER imperfection name:
Our proper bliss depends on what we blame.
Know thy own point: this kind, this due degree
Of blindness, weakness, Heaven bestows on thee.
Submit—In this, or any other sphere,
Secure to be as blest as thou canst bear:
Safe in the hand of one disposing Power,
Or in the natal, or the mortal hour.
All Nature is but art, unknown to thee;

All chance, direction, which thou canst not see;   10
All discord, harmony not understood;
All partial evil, universal good:
And, spite of pride, in erring reason's spite,
One truth is clear: Whatever IS, is RIGHT.

The World Is
Too Much with Us   1807

WILLIAM WORDSWORTH   [1770–1850]

The world is too much with us; late and soon,
Getting and spending, we lay waste our powers;
Little we see in Nature that is ours;
We have given our hearts away, a sordid boon!
This Sea that bares her bosom to the moon,
The winds that will be howling at all hours,
And are up-gathered now like sleeping flowers,
For this, for everything, we are out of tune;
It moves us not.—Great God! I'd rather be
A Pagan suckled in a creed outworn;   10
So might I, standing on this pleasant lea,
Have glimpses that would make me less forlorn;
Have sight of Proteus rising from the sea;
Or hear Old Triton blow his wreathèd horn.¹

QUESTIONS
1.   What does "world" mean in line 1?   **2.**   What does Wordsworth complain of
in the first four lines?   **3.**   In lines 4–8 Wordsworth tells us what we have lost; in
the concluding lines he suggests a remedy. What is that remedy? What do Proteus
and Triton symbolize?

WRITING TOPIC
In what ways does Wordsworth's use of images both define what we have lost
and suggest a remedy for this loss?

Sonnet: To Science   (1829)

EDGAR ALLAN POE   [1809–1849]

Science! true daughter of Old Time thou art!
Who alterest all things with thy peering eyes.

The World . . .
  ¹ Proteus and Triton are both figures from Greek mythology. Proteus had the power to assume
different forms; Triton was often represented as blowing on a conch shell.

Why preyest thou thus upon the poet's heart,
Vulture, whose wings are dull realities?
How should he love thee? or how deem thee wise,
Who wouldst not leave him in his wandering
To seek for treasure in the jewelled skies,
Albeit he soared with an undaunted wing?
Hast thou not dragged Diana[1] from her car?
And driven the Hamadryad[2] from the wood   10
To seek a shelter in some happier star?
Hast thou not torn the Naiad from her flood,
The Elfin from the green grass, and from me
The summer dream beneath the tamarind tree?

QUESTIONS
1. How does Poe characterize science? How does he characterize the poet?
2. Why does Poe allude to Diana, the Hamadryad, and the Naiad? What impact upon the imagination has scientific inquiry?

Ulysses[1]   (1833)

ALFRED, LORD TENNYSON [1809–1892]

It little profits that an idle king,
By this still hearth, among these barren crags,
Matched with an aged wife, I mete and dole
Unequal laws unto a savage race,
That hoard, and sleep, and feed, and know not me.

I cannot rest from travel; I will drink
Life to the lees. All times I have enjoyed
Greatly, have suffered greatly, both with those
That loved me, and alone; on shore, and when
Through scudding drifts the rainy Hyades[2]   10
Vexed the dim sea. I am become a name;
For always roaming with a hungry heart

Sonnet: To Science
    [1] Diana is a Roman goddess and her car is the moon.
    [2] The Hamadryad and Naiad (line 12) are nymphs associated, in classical mythology, with woods and fountains.

Ulysses
    [1] Ulysses, according to Greek legend, was the king of Ithaca and a hero of the Trojan War. Tennyson represents him as eager to resume the life of travel and adventure.
    [2] A group of stars in the constellation Taurus. According to Greek mythology, the rising of these stars with the sun foretold rain.

Much have I seen and known—cities of men
And manners, climates, councils, governments,
Myself not least, but honored of them all—
And drunk delight of battle with my peers,
Far on the ringing plains of windy Troy.
I am a part of all that I have met;
Yet all experience is an arch wherethrough
Gleams that untraveled world whose margin fades   20
Forever and forever when I move.
How dull it is to pause, to make an end,
To rust unburnished, not to shine in use!
As though to breathe were life! Life piled on life
Were all too little, and of one to me
Little remains; but every hour is saved
From that eternal silence, something more,
A bringer of new things; and vile it were
For some three suns to store and hoard myself,
And this gray spirit yearning in desire   30
To follow knowledge like a sinking star,
Beyond the utmost bound of human thought.

   This is my son, mine own Telemachus,
To whom I leave the scepter and the isle—
Well-loved of me, discerning to fulfill
This labor, by slow prudence to make mild
A rugged people, and through soft degrees
Subdue them to the useful and the good.
Most blameless is he, centered in the sphere
Of common duties, decent not to fail   40
In offices of tenderness, and pay
Meet° adoration to my household gods,   proper
When I am gone. He works his work, I mine.

   There lies the port; the vessel puffs her sail;
There gloom the dark, broad seas. My mariners,
Souls that have toiled, and wrought, and thought with me—
That ever with a frolic welcome took
The thunder and the sunshine, and opposed
Free hearts, free foreheads—you and I are old;
Old age hath yet his honor and his toil.   50
Death closes all; but something ere the end,
Some work of noble note, may yet be done,
Not unbecoming men that strove with Gods.
The lights begin to twinkle from the rocks;
The long day wanes; the slow moon climbs; the deep

Moans round with many voices. Come, my friends,
'Tis not too late to seek a newer world.
Push off, and sitting well in order smite
The sounding furrows; for my purpose holds
To sail beyond the sunset, and the baths   60
Of all the western stars, until I die.
It may be that the gulfs will wash us down;
It may be we shall touch the Happy Isles,[3]
And see the great Achilles, whom we knew.
Though much is taken, much abides; and though
We are not now that strength which in old days
Moved earth and heaven, that which we are, we are—
One equal temper of heroic hearts,
Made weak by time and fate, but strong in will
To strive, to seek, to find, and not to yield.   70

QUESTIONS
1. Is Ulysses' desire to abdicate his duties as king irresponsible? Defend your answer. **2.** Contrast Ulysses with his son Telemachus as the latter is described in lines 33–43. Is Telemachus admirable? Explain.

WRITING TOPIC
At the conclusion of the poem Ulysses is determined not to yield. Yield to what?

I'm Nobody! Who Are You? (ca. 1861)

EMILY DICKINSON   [1830–1886]

I'm nobody! Who are you?
Are you nobody, too?
Then there's a pair of us—don't tell!
They'd banish us, you know.

How dreary to be somebody!
How public, like a frog

---

   [3] The Islands of the Blessed (also Elysium), thought to be in the far western oceans, where those favored by the gods, such as Achilles, enjoyed life after death.

To tell your name the livelong June
To an admiring bog!

Much Madness
Is Divinest Sense   (1862)

EMILY DICKINSON   [1830–1886]

Much Madness is divinest Sense—
To a discerning Eye—
Much Sense—the starkest Madness—
'Tis the Majority
In this, as All, prevail—
Assent—and you are sane—
Demur—you're straightway dangerous—
And handled with a Chain—

What Soft—
Cherubic Creatures   (ca. 1862)

EMILY DICKINSON   [1830–1886]

What Soft—Cherubic Creatures—
These Gentlewomen are—
One would as soon assault a Plush—
Or violate a Star—

Such Dimity Convictions—
A Horror so refined
Of freckled Human Nature—
Of Deity—ashamed—

It's such a common-Glory—
A Fisherman's—Degree—
Redemption—Brittle Lady—
Be so—ashamed of Thee—

Thou Art Indeed Just, Lord   (1889)

GERARD MANLEY HOPKINS   [1844–1889]

> *Justus quidem tu es, Domine, si disputem tecum: verumtamen*
> *justa loquar ad te: Quare via impiorum prosperatur? & c.*[1]

Thou art indeed just, Lord, if I contend
With thee; but, sir, so what I plead is just.
Why do sinners' ways prosper? and why must
Disappointment all I endeavour end?
   Wert thou my enemy, O thou my friend,
How wouldst thou worse, I wonder, than thou dost
Defeat, thwart me? Oh, the sots and thralls of lust
Do in spare hours more thrive than I that spend,
Sir, life upon thy cause. See, banks and brakes
Now, leavèd how thick! lacèd they are again   10
With fretty chervil,° look, and fresh wind shakes   parsley
Them; birds build—but not I build; no, but strain,
Time's eunuch, and not breed one work that wakes.
Mine, O thou lord of life, send my roots rain.

QUESTIONS
1.   How is the nature imagery used to indicate the speaker's plight?   **2.**   How
would you characterize the poet's attitude toward God?

WRITING TOPIC
Summarize the debate in this poem. What implications about divine justice emerge
from the poet's questions in lines 3 and 4?

Easter 1916[1]   (1916)

WILLIAM BUTLER YEATS   [1865–1939]

I have met them at close of day
Coming with vivid faces
From counter or desk among grey

Thou Art Indeed . . .
   [1] The first three lines of the poem translate the Latin epigraph.
Easter 1916
   [1] On Easter Sunday of 1916, a group of Irish nationalists seized key points in Ireland, including
the Dublin Post Office, from which they proclaimed an independent Irish Republic. At first, most
Irishmen were indifferent to the nationalists' futile and heroic gesture, but as the rebellion was
crushed and the leaders executed, they became heroes in their countrymen's eyes. Some of those
leaders are alluded to in the second stanza and are named in lines 75 and 76.

Eighteenth-century houses.
I have passed with a nod of the head
Or polite meaningless words,
Or have lingered awhile and said
Polite meaningless words,
And thought before I had done
Of a mocking tale or a gibe   10
To please a companion
Around the fire at the club,
Being certain that they and I
But lived where motley is worn:
All changed, changed utterly:
A terrible beauty is born.

That woman's days were spent
In ignorant good-will,
Her nights in argument
Until her voice grew shrill.   20
What voice more sweet than hers
When, young and beautiful,
She rode to harriers?
This man had kept a school
And rode our winged horse;[2]
This other his helper and friend
Was coming into his force;
He might have won fame in the end,
So sensitive his nature seemed,
So daring and sweet his thought.   30
This other man I had dreamed
A drunken, vainglorious lout.
He had done most bitter wrong
To some who are near my heart,
Yet I number him in the song;
He, too, has resigned his part
In the casual comedy;
He, too, has been changed in his turn,
Transformed utterly:
A terrible beauty is born.   40

Hearts with one purpose alone
Through summer and winter seem
Enchanted to a stone
To trouble the living stream.
The horse that comes from the road,

---

[2] In Greek mythology, a winged horse is associated with poetic inspiration.

The rider, the birds that range
From cloud to tumbling cloud,
Minute by minute they change;
A shadow of cloud on the stream
Changes minute by minute;   50
A horse-hoof slides on the brim,
And a horse plashes within it;
The long-legged moor-hens dive,
And hens to moor-cocks call;
Minute by minute they live:
The stone's in the midst of all.

Too long a sacrifice
Can make a stone of the heart.
O when may it suffice?
That is Heaven's part, our part   60
To murmur name upon name,
As a mother names her child
When sleep at last has come
On limbs that had run wild.
What is it but nightfall?
No, no, not night but death;
Was it needless death after all?
For England may keep faith
For all that is done and said.
We know their dream; enough   70
To know they dreamed and are dead;
And what if excess of love
Bewildered them till they died?
I write it out in a verse—
MacDonagh and MacBride
And Connolly and Pearse
Now and in time to be,
Wherever green is worn,
Are changed, changed utterly:
A terrible beauty is born.   80

QUESTIONS

1. What is "changed utterly," and in what sense can beauty be "terrible"? **2.** What does "they" in line 55 refer to? What does the "stone" in lines 43 and 56 symbolize? What is Yeats contrasting? **3.** How does the poet answer the question he asks in line 67?

WRITING TOPIC

In the first stanza the attitude of the poet toward the people he is describing is indifferent, even contemptuous. How is that attitude modified in the rest of the poem?

Miniver Cheevy   1910

EDWIN ARLINGTON ROBINSON   [1869–1935]

Miniver Cheevy, child of scorn,
    Grew lean while he assailed the seasons;
He wept that he was ever born,
    And he had reasons.

Miniver loved the days of old
    When swords were bright and steeds were prancing;
The vision of a warrior bold
    Would set him dancing.

Miniver sighed for what was not,
    And dreamed, and rested from his labors;   10
He dreamed of Thebes and Camelot,
    And Priam's neighbors.[1]

Miniver mourned the ripe renown
    That made so many a name so fragrant;
He mourned Romance, now on the town,
    And Art, a vagrant.

Miniver loved the Medici,[2]
    Albeit he had never seen one;
He would have sinned incessantly
    Could he have been one.   20

Miniver cursed the commonplace
    And eyed a khaki suit with loathing;
He missed the medieval grace
    Of iron clothing.

Miniver scorned the gold he sought,
    But sore annoyed was he without it;
Miniver thought, and thought, and thought,
    And thought about it.

Miniver Cheevy
    [1] Thebes was an ancient Greek city, famous in history and legend; Camelot was the site of the legendary King Arthur's court; Priam was king of Troy during the Trojan War.
    [2] A family of bankers and statesmen, notorious for their cruelty, who ruled Florence for nearly two centuries during the Italian Renaissance.

Miniver Cheevy, born too late,
    Scratched his head and kept on thinking;   30
Miniver coughed, and called it fate,
    And kept on drinking.

We Wear the Mask   1896

PAUL LAURENCE DUNBAR   [1872–1906]

We wear the mask that grins and lies,
It hides our cheeks and shades our eyes—
This debt we pay to human guile;
With torn and bleeding hearts we smile,
And mouth with myriad subtleties.

Why should the world be over-wise,
In counting all our tears and sighs?
Nay, let them only see us, while
    We wear the mask.

We smile, but, O great Christ, our cries   10
To thee from tortured souls arise.
We sing, but oh the clay is vile
Beneath our feet, and long the mile;
But let the world dream otherwise,
    We wear the mask!

Patterns   1916

AMY LOWELL   [1874–1925]

I walk down the garden-paths,
And all the daffodils
Are blowing, and the bright blue squills.
I walk down the patterned garden-paths
In my stiff, brocaded gown.
With my powdered hair and jeweled fan,
I too am a rare
Pattern. As I wander down
The garden-paths.

My dress is richly figured,   10
And the train
Makes a pink and silver stain
On the gravel, and the thrift
Of the borders.
Just a plate of current fashion,
Tripping by in high-heeled, ribboned shoes.
Not a softness anywhere about me,
Only whalebone and brocade.
And I sink on a seat in the shade
Of a lime tree. For my passion   20
Wars against the stiff brocade.
The daffodils and squills
Flutter in the breeze
As they please.
And I weep;
For the lime-tree is in blossom
And one small flower has dropped upon my bosom.

And the plashing of waterdrops
In the marble fountain
Comes down the garden-paths.   30
The dripping never stops.
Underneath my stiffened gown
Is the softness of a woman bathing in a marble basin,
A basin in the midst of hedges grown
So thick, she cannot see her lover hiding,
But she guesses he is near,
And the sliding of the water
Seems the stroking of a dear
Hand upon her.
What is Summer in a fine brocaded gown!   40
I should like to see it lying in a heap upon the ground.
All the pink and silver crumpled up on the ground.

I would be the pink and silver as I ran along the paths,
And he would stumble after,
Bewildered by my laughter.
I should see the sun flashing from his sword-hilt and the buckles on his
    shoes.
I would choose
To lead him in a maze along the patterned paths,
A bright and laughing maze for my heavy-booted lover.
Till he caught me in the shade,   50
And the buttons of his waistcoat bruised my body as he clasped me,
Aching, melting, unafraid.

With the shadows of the leaves and the sundrops,
And the plopping of the waterdrops,
All about us in the open afternoon—
I am very like to swoon
With the weight of this brocade,
For the sun sifts through the shade.

Underneath the fallen blossom
In my bosom
Is a letter I have hid.   60
It was brought to me this morning by a rider from the Duke.
"Madam, we regret to inform you that Lord Hartwell
Died in action Thursday se'nnight."
As I read it in the white, morning sunlight,
The letters squirmed like snakes.
"Any answer, Madam," said my footman.
"No," I told him.
"See that the messenger takes some refreshment.
No, no answer."   70
And I walked into the garden,
Up and down the patterned paths,
In my stiff, correct brocade.
The blue and yellow flowers stood up proudly in the sun,
Each one.
I stood upright too,
Held rigid to the pattern
By the stiffness of my gown;
Up and down I walked,
Up and down.   80

In a month he would have been my husband.
In a month, here, underneath this lime,
We would have broke the pattern;
He for me, and I for him,
He as Colonel, I as Lady,
On this shady seat.
He had a whim
That sunlight carried blessing.
And I answered, "It shall be as you have said."
Now he is dead.   90

In Summer and in Winter I shall walk
Up and down
The patterned garden-paths
In my stiff, brocaded gown.
The squills and daffodils

Will give place to pillared roses, and to asters, and to snow.
I shall go
Up and down
In my gown.
Gorgeously arrayed,   100
Boned and stayed.
And the softness of my body will be guarded from embrace
By each button, hook, and lace.
For the man who should loose me is dead,
Fighting with the Duke in Flanders,
In a pattern called a war.
Christ! What are patterns for?

Departmental   1936

ROBERT FROST   [1874–1963]

An ant on the table cloth
Ran into a dormant moth
Of many times his size.
He showed not the least surprise.
His business wasn't with such.
He gave it scarcely a touch,
And was off on his duty run.
Yet if he encountered one
Of the hive's enquiry squad
Whose work is to find out God   10
And the nature of time and space,
He would put him onto the case.
Ants are a curious race;
One crossing with hurried tread
The body of one of their dead
Isn't given a moment's arrest—
Seems not even impressed.
But he no doubt reports to any
With whom he crosses antennae,
And they no doubt report   20
To the higher up at court.
Then word goes forth in Formic:
"Death's come to Jerry McCormic,
Our selfless forager Jerry.
Will the special Janizary
Whose office it is to bury
The dead of the commissary
Go bring him home to his people.

Lay him in state on a sepal.
Wrap him for shroud in a petal.   30
Embalm him with ichor of nettle.
This is the word of your Queen."
And presently on the scene
Appears a solemn mortician;
And taking formal position
With feelers calmly atwiddle,
Seizes the dead by the middle,
And heaving him high in air,
Carries him out of there.
No one stands round to stare.   40
It is nobody else's affair.
It couldn't be called ungentle.
But how thoroughly departmental.

QUESTIONS
1. What comment does this poem make on human society? Is ant society a
good metaphor for human society? Explain. **2.** How do the diction and rhyme
help establish the tone?

WRITING TOPIC
How does the diction in this poem convey the speaker's attitude toward the
social order he describes?

Sunday Morning   1923

WALLACE STEVENS [1879–1955]

I

Complacencies of the peignoir, and late
Coffee and oranges in a sunny chair,
And the green freedom of a cockatoo
Upon a rug mingle to dissipate
The holy hush of ancient sacrifice.
She dreams a little, and she feels the dark
Encroachment of that old catastrophe,
As a calm darkens among water-lights.
The pungent oranges and bright, green wings
Seem things in some procession of the dead,   10
Winding across wide water, without sound.
The day is like wide water, without sound,

Stilled for the passing of her dreaming feet
Over the seas, to silent Palestine,
Dominion of the blood and sepulchre.

II

Why should she give her bounty to the dead?
What is divinity if it can come
Only in silent shadows and in dreams?
Shall she not find in comforts of the sun,
In pungent fruit and bright, green wings, or else   20
In any balm or beauty of the earth,
Things to be cherished like the thought of heaven?
Divinity must live within herself:
Passions of rain, or moods in falling snow;
Grievings in loneliness, or unsubdued
Elations when the forest blooms; gusty
Emotions on wet roads on autumn nights;
All pleasures and all pains, remembering
The bough of summer and the winter branch.
These are the measures destined for her soul.   30

III

Jove in the clouds had his inhuman birth.[1]
No mother suckled him, no sweet land gave
Large-mannered motions to his mythy mind
He moved among us, as a muttering king,
Magnificent, would move among his hinds,°   farm servants
Until our blood, commingling, virginal,
With heaven, brought such requital to desire
The very hinds discerned it, in a star.
Shall our blood fail? Or shall it come to be
The blood of paradise? And shall the earth   40
Seem all of paradise that we shall know?
The sky will be much friendlier then than now,
A part of labor and a part of pain,
And next in glory to enduring love,
Not this dividing and indifferent blue.

IV

She says, "I am content when wakened birds,
Before they fly, test the reality

Sunday Morning
   [1] Jove is Jupiter, the principal god of the Romans, who, unlike Jesus, had an "inhuman birth."

Of misty fields, by their sweet questionings;
But when the birds are gone, and their warm fields
Return no more, where, then, is paradise?"   50
There is not any haunt of prophecy,
Nor any old chimera[2] of the grave,
Neither the golden underground, nor isle
Melodious, where spirits gat them home,
Nor visionary south, nor cloudy palm
Remote on heaven's hill, that has endured
As April's green endures; or will endure
Like her remembrance of awakened birds,
Or her desire for June and evening, tipped
By the consummation of the swallow's wings.   60

V

She says, "But in contentment I still feel
The need of some imperishable bliss."
Death is the mother of beauty; hence from her,
Alone, shall come fulfilment to our dreams
And our desires. Although she strews the leaves
Of sure obliteration on our paths,
The path sick sorrow took, the many paths
Where triumph rang its brassy phrase, or love
Whispered a little out of tenderness,
She makes the willow shiver in the sun   70
For maidens who were wont to sit and gaze
Upon the grass, relinquished to their feet.
She causes boys to pile new plums and pears
On disregarded plate. The maidens taste
And stray impassioned in the littering leaves.

VI

Is there no change of death in paradise?
Does ripe fruit never fall? Or do the boughs
Hang always heavy in that perfect sky,
Unchanging, yet so like our perishing earth,
With rivers like our own that seek for seas   80
They never find, the same receding shores
That never touch with inarticulate pang?

---

[2] A monster with a lion's head, a goat's body, and a serpent's tail. Here an emblem for the belief
in other worlds described in the following lines.

Why set the pear upon those river-banks
Or spice the shores with odors of the plum?
Alas, that they should wear our colors there,
The silken weavings of our afternoons,
And pick the strings of our insipid lutes!
Death is the mother of beauty, mystical,
Within whose burning bosom we devise
Our earthly mothers waiting, sleeplessly.   90

VII

Supple and turbulent, a ring of men
Shall chant in orgy on a summer morn
Their boisterous devotion to the sun,
Not as a god, but as a god might be,
Naked among them, like a savage source.
Their chant shall be a chant of paradise,
Out of their blood, returning to the sky;
And in their chant shall enter, voice by voice,
The windy lake wherein their lord delights,
The trees, like serafin, and echoing hills,   100
That choir among themselves long afterward.
They shall know well the heavenly fellowship
Of men that perish and of summer morn.
And whence they came and whither they shall go
The dew upon their feet shall manifest.

VIII

She hears, upon that water without sound,
A voice that cries, "The tomb in Palestine
Is not the porch of spirits lingering.
It is the grave of Jesus, where he lay."
We live in an old chaos of the sun,   110
Or old dependency of day and night,
Or island solitude, unsponsored, free,
Of that wide water, inescapable.
Deer walk upon our mountains, and the quail
Whistle about us their spontaneous cries;
Sweet berries ripen in the wilderness;
And, in the isolation of the sky,
At evening, casual flocks of pigeons make
Ambiguous undulations as they sink,
Downward to darkness, on extended wings.   120

QUESTIONS
1. In the opening stanza, the woman's enjoyment of a late Sunday morning breakfast in a relaxed and sensuous atmosphere is troubled by thoughts of what Sunday morning should mean to her. What are the thoughts that disturb her complacency? **2.** What does the speaker mean when he says, "Death is the mother of beauty" (ll. 63 and 88)? **3.** In stanza VI, what is the speaker's attitude toward the conventional Christian conception of paradise? **4.** Stanza VII presents the speaker's vision of an alternative religion. How does it differ from the paradise of stanza VI? **5.** In what ways does the cry of the voice in the final stanza (ll. 107–110) state the woman's dilemma? How do the lines about the pigeons at the end of the poem sum up the speaker's belief?

WRITING TOPIC
This poem is, in a sense, a commentary by the speaker on the woman's desire for truth and certainty more enduring than the physical world can provide. Is the speaker sympathetic to her quest? Explain.

If We Must Die   1922

CLAUDE McKAY [1890–1948]

If we must die, let it not be like hogs
Hunted and penned in an inglorious spot,
While round us bark the mad and hungry dogs,
Making their mock at our accursèd lot.
If we must die, O let us nobly die,
So that our precious blood may not be shed
In vain; then even the monsters we defy
Shall be constrained to honor us though dead!
O kinsmen! we must meet the common foe!
Though far outnumbered let us show us brave,   10
And for their thousand blows deal one deathblow!
What though before us lies the open grave?
Like men we'll face the murderous, cowardly pack,
Pressed to the wall, dying, but fighting back!

the Cambridge ladies
who live in furnished souls   1923

E. E. CUMMINGS [1894–1962]

the Cambridge ladies who live in furnished souls
are unbeautiful and have comfortable minds

(also, with the church's protestant blessings
daughters, unscented shapeless spirited)
they believe in Christ and Longfellow, both dead,
are invariably interested in so many things—
at the present writing one still finds
delighted fingers knitting for the is it Poles?
perhaps. While permanent faces coyly bandy
scandal of Mrs. N and Professor D   10
. . . . the Cambridge ladies do not care, above
Cambridge if sometimes in its box of
sky lavender and cornerless, the
moon rattles like a fragment of angry candy

QUESTIONS
1. What images does the poet use to describe "the Cambridge ladies"? What do the images suggest? **2.** What is the effect of the interruption "is it" in line 8? **3.** In the final lines, the moon seems to protest against the superficiality of these women. What is the effect of comparing the moon to a fragment of candy?

WRITING TOPIC
Compare this poem with Emily Dickinson's "What Soft—Cherubic Creatures."

Harlem   1951

LANGSTON HUGHES   [1902–1967]

What happens to a dream deferred?

   Does it dry up
   like a raisin in the sun?
   Or fester like a sore—
   And then run?
   Does it stink like rotten meat?
   Or crust and sugar over—
   like a syrupy sweet?

   Maybe it just sags
   like a heavy load.   10

   Or does it explode?

Same in Blues

1951

LANGSTON HUGHES   [1902–1967]

I said to my baby,
Baby take it slow.
I can't, she said, I can't!
I got to go!

> *There's a certain*
> *amount of traveling*
> *in a dream deferred.*

Lulu said to Leonard,
I want a diamond ring.
Leonard said to Lulu,   10
You won't get a goddam thing!

> *A certain*
> *amount of nothing*
> *in a dream deferred.*

Daddy, daddy, daddy,
All I want is you.
You can have me, baby—
but my lovin' days is through.

> *A certain*
> *amount of impotence*   20
> *in a dream deferred.*

Three parties
On my party line—
But that third party,
Lord, ain't mine!

> *There's liable*
> *to be confusion*
> *in a dream deferred.*

From river to river
Uptown and down,   30
There's liable to be confusion
when a dream gets kicked around.

The Unknown Citizen   1940

*(To JS/07/M/378 This Marble Monument Is Erected
by the State)*

W. H. AUDEN   [1907–1973]

He was found by the Bureau of Statistics to be
One against whom there was no official complaint,
And all the reports on his conduct agree
That, in the modern sense of an old-fashioned word, he was a saint,
For in everything he did he served the Greater Community.
Except for the War till the day he retired
He worked in a factory and never got fired,
But satisfied his employers, Fudge Motors Inc.
Yet he wasn't a scab or odd in his views,
For his Union reports that he paid his dues,   10
(Our report on his Union shows it was sound)
And our Social Psychology workers found
That he was popular with his mates and liked a drink.
The Press are convinced that he bought a paper every day
And that his reactions to advertisements were normal in every way.
Policies taken out in his name prove that he was fully insured,
And his Health-card shows he was once in hospital but left it cured.
Both Producers Research and High-Grade Living declare
He was fully sensible to the advantages of the Installment Plan
And had everything necessary to the Modern Man,   20
A phonograph, a radio, a car and a frigidaire.
Our researchers into Public Opinion are content
That he held the proper opinions for the time of year;
When there was peace, he was for peace; when there was war, he went.
He was married and added five children to the population,
Which our Eugenist says was the right number for a parent of his generation,
And our teachers report that he never interfered with their education.
Was he free? Was he happy? The question is absurd:
Had anything been wrong, we should certainly have heard.

Dolor   (1943)

THEODORE ROETHKE   [1908–1963]

I have known the inexorable sadness of pencils,
Neat in their boxes, dolor of pad and paper-weight,

All the misery of manilla folders and mucilage,
Desolation in immaculate public places,
Lonely reception room, lavatory, switchboard,
The unalterable pathos of basin and pitcher,
Ritual of multigraph, paper-clip, comma,
Endless duplication of lives and objects.
And I have seen dust from the walls of institutions,
Finer than flour, alive, more dangerous than silica,   10
Sift, almost invisible, through long afternoons of tedium,
Dropping a fine film on nails and delicate eyebrows,
Glazing the pale hair, the duplicate grey standard faces.

From a Correct Address in a Suburb of a Major City   1971

HELEN SORRELLS   [b. 1908]

She wears her middle age like a cowled
gown, sleeved in it, folded high
at the breast,

charming, proper at cocktails
but the inner one raging
and how to hide her,

how to keep her leashed, contain
the heat of her, the soaring cry
never yet loosed,

demanding a chance before the years devour her,   10
before the marrow of her fine long legs
congeals and she

settles forever for this street, this house,
her face set to the world
sweet, sweet

above the shocked, astonished
hunger.

Myth   1973

MURIEL RUKEYSER   [1913–1980]

Long afterward, Oedipus, old and blinded, walked the
roads.[1]   He smelled a familiar smell.   It was
the Sphinx.   Oedipus said, "I want to ask one question.
Why didn't I recognize my mother?"   "You gave the
wrong answer," said the Sphinx.   "But that was what
made everything possible," said Oedipus.   "No," she said.
"When I asked, What walks on four legs in the morning,
two at noon, and three in the evening, you answered,
Man.   You didn't say anything about woman."
"When you say Man," said Oedipus, "you include women   10
too. Everyone knows that."   She said, "That's what
you think."

The Conscientious Objector   1947

KARL SHAPIRO   [b. 1913]

The gates clanged and they walked you into jail
More tense than felons but relieved to find
The hostile world shut out, flags that dripped
From every mother's windowpane, obscene
The bloodlust sweating from the public heart,
The dog authority slavering at your throat.
A sense of quiet, of pulling down the blind
Possessed you. Punishment you felt was clean.

The decks, the catwalks, and the narrow light
Composed a ship. This was a mutinous crew   10
Troubling the captains for plain decencies,
A *Mayflower* brim with pilgrims headed out
To establish new theocracies to west,
A Noah's ark coasting the topmost seas
Ten miles above the sodomites and fish.
These inmates loved the only living doves.

Myth

[1]Oedipus became King of Thebes when he solved the riddle of the Sphinx quoted in the poem.
He blinded himself when he discovered that he had married his own mother.

Like all men hunted from the world you made
A good community, voyaging the storm
To no safe Plymouth or green Ararat;
Trouble or calm, the men with Bibles prayed,   20
The gaunt politicals construed our hate.
The opposite of all armies, you were best
Opposing uniformity and yourselves;
Prison and personality were your fate.

You suffered not so physically but knew
Maltreatment, hunger, ennui of the mind.
Well might the soldier kissing the hot beach
Erupting in his face damn all your kind.
Yet you who saved neither yourselves nor us
Are equally with those who shed the blood   30
The heroes of our cause. Your conscience is
What we come back to in the armistice.

QUESTIONS
1. Who is the speaker of this poem, and what are his assumptions about "good
citizenship"? **2.** Why does the conscientious objector feel that punishment is
clean (l. 8)? **3.** The prison is compared to the Mayflower and Noah's ark. Do you
find the allusive comparisons between the prisoners and the occupants of the Mayflower and the ark effective? Explain. **4.** What, finally, are the differences between
the man described here and Auden's unknown citizen? Is the conscientious objector
"free"? "Happy"? Is he an unknown citizen?

Naming of Parts   1946

HENRY REED   [b. 1914]

Today we have naming of parts. Yesterday,
We had daily cleaning. And tomorrow morning
We shall have what to do after firing. But today,
Today we have naming of parts. Japonica
Glistens like coral in all of the neighboring gardens,
        And today we have naming of parts.

This is the lower sling swivel. And this
Is the upper sling swivel, whose use you will see,
When you are given your slings. And this is the piling swivel,
Which in your case you have not got. The branches   10

Hold in the gardens their silent, eloquent gestures,
    Which in our case we have not got.

This is the safety-catch, which is always released
With an easy flick of the thumb. And please do not let me
See anyone using his finger. You can do it quite easy
If you have any strength in your thumb. The blossoms
Are fragile and motionless, never letting anyone see
    Any of them using their finger.

And this you can see is the bolt. The purpose of this
Is to open the breech, as you see. We can slide it   20
Rapidly backwards and forwards: we call this
Easing the spring. And rapidly backwards and forwards
The early bees are assaulting and fumbling the flowers:
    They call it easing the Spring.

They call it easing the Spring: it is perfectly easy
If you have any strength in your thumb: like the bolt,
And the breech, and the cocking-piece, and the point of balance,
Which in our case we have not got; and the almond-blossom
Silent in all of the gardens and the bees going backwards and forwards,
    For today we have naming of parts.   30

QUESTIONS

1. The poem has two speakers. Identify their speeches, and characterize the speakers. **2.** The last line of each stanza repeats a phrase from within the stanza. What is the effect of the repetition?

WRITING TOPIC

This poem incorporates a subtle underlying sexuality. Trace the language that generates it. What function does that sexuality serve in the poem?

The Sundays of Satin-Legs Smith   (1945)

GWENDOLYN BROOKS [b. 1917]

Inamoratas, with an approbation,
Bestowed his title. Blessed his inclination.
He wakes, unwinds, elaborately: a cat

Tawny, reluctant, royal. He is fat
And fine this morning. Definite. Reimbursed.

He waits a moment, he designs his reign,
That no performance may be plain or vain.
Then rises in a clear delirium.

He sheds, with his pajamas, shabby days.
And his desertedness, his intricate fear, the   10
Postponed resentments and the prim precautions.

Now, at his bath, would you deny him lavender
Or take away the power of his pine?
What smelly substitute, heady as wine,
Would you provide? life must be aromatic.
There must be scent, somehow there must be some.
Would you have flowers in his life? suggest
Asters? a Really Good geranium?
A white carnation? would you prescribe a Show
With the cold lilies, formal chrysanthemum   20
Magnificence, poinsettias, and emphatic
Red of prize roses? might his happiest
Alternative (you muse) be, after all,
A bit of gentle garden in the best
Of taste and straight tradition? Maybe so.
But you forget, or did you ever know,
His heritage of cabbage and pigtails,
Old intimacy with alleys, garbage pails,
Down in the deep (but always beautiful) South
Where roses blush their blithest (it is said)   30
And sweet magnolias put Chanel to shame.

No! He has not a flower to his name.
Except a feather one, for his lapel.
Apart from that, if he should think of flowers
It is in terms of dandelions or death.
Ah, there is little hope. You might as well—
Unless you care to set the world a-boil
And do a lot of equalizing things,
Remove a little ermine, say, from kings,
Shake hands with paupers and appoint them men,   40
For instance—certainly you might as well
Leave him his lotion, lavender and oil.

Let us proceed. Let us inspect, together
With his meticulous and serious love,

The innards of this closet. Which is a vault
Whose glory is not diamonds, not pearls,
Not silver plate with just enough dull shine.
But wonder-suits in yellow and in wine,
Sarcastic green and zebra-striped cobalt.
With shoulder padding that is wide   50
And cocky and determined as his pride;
Ballooning pants that taper off to ends
Scheduled to choke precisely.
                              Here are hats
Like bright umbrellas; and hysterical ties
Like narrow banners for some gathering war.

People are so in need, in need of help.
People want so much that they do not know.

Below the tinkling trade of little coins
The gold impulse not possible to show   60
Or spend. Promise piled over and betrayed.

These kneaded limbs receive the kiss of silk.
Then they receive the brave and beautiful
Embrace of some of that equivocal wool.
He looks into his mirror, loves himself—
The near curve here; the angularity
That is appropriate at just its place;
The technique of a variegated grace.

Here is all his sculpture and his art
And all his architectural design.   70
Perhaps you would prefer to this a fine
Value of marble, complicated stone.
Would have him think with horror of baroque,
Rococo. You forget and you forget.

He dances down the hotel steps that keep
Remnants of last night's high life and distress.
As spat-out purchased kisses and spilled beer.
He swallows sunshine with a secret yelp.
Passes to coffee and a roll or two.
Has breakfasted.
                      Out. Sounds about him smear,   80
Become a unit. He hears and does not hear
The alarm clock meddling in somebody's sleep;
Children's governed Sunday happiness;
The dry tone of a plane; a woman's oath;

Consumption's spiritless expectoration;
An indignant robin's resolute donation
Pinching a track through apathy and din;
Restaurant vendors weeping; and the L°   elevated train
That comes on like a slightly horrible thought.   90

Pictures, too, as usual, are blurred.
He sees and does not see the broken windows
Hiding their shame with newsprint; little girl
With ribbons decking wornness, little boy
Wearing the trousers with the decentest patch,
To honor Sunday; women on their way
From "service," temperate holiness arranged
Ably on asking faces; men estranged
From music and from wonder and from joy
But far familiar with the guiding awe   100
Of foodlessness.
              He loiters.
                       Restaurant vendors
Weep, or out of them rolls a restless glee.
The Lonesome Blues, the Long-lost Blues, I Want A
Big Fat Mama. Down these sore avenues
Comes no Saint-Saëns, no piquant elusive Grieg,
And not Tschaikovsky's wayward eloquence
And not the shapely tender drift of Brahms.
But could he love them? Since a man must bring   110
To music what his mother spanked him for
When he was two: bits of forgotten hate,
Devotion: whether or not his mattress hurts:
The little dream his father humored: the thing
His sister did for money: what he ate
For breakfast—and for dinner twenty years
Ago last autumn: all his skipped desserts.

The pasts of his ancestors lean against
Him. Crowd him. Fog out his identity.
Hundreds of hungers mingle with his own,   120
Hundreds of voices advise so dexterously
He quite considers his reactions his,
Judges he walks most powerfully alone,
That everything is—simply what it is.

But movie-time approaches, time to boo
The hero's kiss, and boo the heroine
Whose ivory and yellow it is sin

For his eye to eat of. The Mickey Mouse,
However, is for everyone in the house.
Squires his lady to dinner at Joe's Eats.   130
His lady alters as to leg and eye,
Thickness and heights, such minor points as these,
From Sunday to Sunday. But no matter what
Her name or body positively she's
In Queen Lace stockings with ambitious heels
That strain to kiss the calves, and vivid shoes
Frontless and backless, Chinese fingernails,
Earrings, three layers of lipstick, intense hat
Dripping with the most voluble of veils.
Her affable extremes are like sweet bombs   140
About him, whom no middle grace or good
Could gratify. He had no education
In quiet arts of compromise. He would
Not understand your counsels on control, nor
Thank you for your late trouble.
                                        At Joe's Eats
You get your fish or chicken on meat platters.
With coleslaw, macaroni, candied sweets,
Coffee and apple pie. You go out full.
(The end is—isn't it?—all that really matters.)   150

          And even and intrepid come
          The tender boots of night to home.

          Her body is like new brown bread
          Under the Woolworth mignonette.
          Her body is a honey bowl
          Whose waiting honey is deep and hot.
          Her body is like summer earth,
          Receptive, soft, and absolute . . .

QUESTIONS
1. Who are the "you" of the poem? Why do they disapprove of Satin-Legs? 2. What does the description of Satin-Legs's wardrobe (ll. 43–56) tell us about him? 3. What is Satin-Legs's "heritage of cabbage and pigtails" (l. 27)? With what is that heritage contrasted?

WRITING TOPIC
Is this poem a tribute to Satin-Legs or a criticism of him?

from

The Children of the Poor   (1949)

GWENDOLYN BROOKS   [b. 1917]

4

First fight. Then fiddle. Ply the slipping string
With feathery sorcery; muzzle the note
With hurting love, the music that they wrote
Bewitch, bewilder. Qualify to sing
Threadwise. Devise no salt, no hempen thing
For the dear instrument to bear. Devote
The bow to silks and honey. Be remote
A while from malice and from murdering.
But first to arms, to armor. Carry hate
In front of you and harmony behind.   10
Be deaf to music and to beauty blind.
Win war. Rise bloody, maybe not too late
For having first to civilize a space
Wherein to play your violin with grace.

11

Life for my child is simple, and is good.
He knows his wish. Yes, but that is not all.
Because I know mine too.
And we both want joy of undeep and unabiding things,
Like kicking over a chair or throwing blocks out of a window
Or tipping over an icebox pan
Or snatching down curtains or fingering an electric outlet
Or a journey or a friend or an illegal kiss.
No. There is more to it than that.
It is that he has never been afraid.   10
Rather, he reaches out and lo the chair falls with a beautiful crash,
And the blocks fall, down on the people's heads,
And the water comes slooshing sloppily out across the floor.
And so forth.
Not that success, for him, is sure, infallible.
But never has he been afraid to reach.
His lesions are legion.
But reaching is his rule.

QUESTIONS

1. In sonnet 4, the poet advises the children: "First fight, Then fiddle." The meaning of "fight" is clear. What does "fiddle" symbolize?   **2.** Why does the poet advocate violence?   **3.**   Is the child described in poem 11 different from the children addressed in sonnet 4?   **4.**   Explain the meaning of line 4 in poem 11.   **5.**   What does "reaching" in the last line mean?

In Goya's Greatest Scenes   1958

LAWRENCE FERLINGHETTI   [b. 1919]

In Goya's greatest scenes[1] we seem to see
                        the people of the world
        exactly at the moment when
                they first attained the title of
                                'suffering humanity'
            They writhe upon the page
                        in a veritable rage
                                of adversity
        Heaped up
                groaning with babies and bayonets   10
                            under cement skies
        in an abstract landscape of blasted trees
            bent statues bats wings and beaks
                        slippery gibbets
            cadavers and carnivorous cocks
        and all the final hollering monsters
            of the
                'imagination of disaster'
        they are so bloody real
                    it is as if they really still existed   20

    And they do

        Only the landscape is changed

They still are ranged along the roads
    plagued by legionaires
                    false windmills and demented roosters
They are the same people
                    only further from home
    on freeways fifty lanes wide
                on a concrete continent
                    spaced with bland billboards   30
        illustrating imbecile illusions of happiness

In Goya's Greatest Scenes
    [1] Francisco Jose de Goya (1764–1828), famous Spanish artist, celebrated for his representations of "suffering humanity."

    The scene shows fewer tumbrils[2]
          but more maimed citizens
                in painted cars
  and they have strange license plates
  and engines
        that devour America

QUESTIONS

1. To whom does the word "they" refer in line 26? **2.** What is responsible for the "suffering" of modern American "humanity"?

Women   1970

MAY SWENSON   [b. 1919]

Women	Or they
should be	should be
pedestals	little horses
moving	those wooden
pedestals	sweet
moving	oldfashioned
to the	painted
motions	rocking
of men	horses

    the gladdest things in the toyroom

The	feelingly
pegs	and then
of their	unfeelingly
ears	To be
so familiar	joyfully
and dear	ridden
to the trusting	rockingly
fists	ridden until
To be chafed	the restored

egos dismount and the legs stride away

immobile	willing
sweetlipped	to be set
sturdy	into motion
and smiling	Women
women	should be
should always	pedestals
be waiting	to men

---

[2] Carts in which prisoners were conducted to the place of execution.

Poetry of Departures   1955

PHILIP LARKIN   [1922–1985]

Sometimes you hear, fifth-hand,
As epitaph:
He chucked up everything
And just cleared off,
And always the voice will sound
Certain you approve
This audacious, purifying,
Elemental move.

And they are right, I think.
We all hate home   10
And having to be there:
I detest my room,
Its specially-chosen junk,
The good books, the good bed,
And my life, in perfect order:
So to hear it said

He walked out on the whole crowd
Leaves me flushed and stirred,
Like *Then she undid her dress*
Or *Take that you bastard;*   20
Surely I can, if he did?
And that helps me stay
Sober and industrious.
But I'd go today,

Yes, swagger the nut-strewn roads,
Crouch in the fo'c'sle
Stubbly with goodness, if
It weren't so artificial,
Such a deliberate step backwards
To create an object: 30
Books; china; a life
Reprehensibly perfect.

QUESTIONS

1. What motivates the kind of person who "chucked up everything and just cleared off"? Why might such an action be characterized as "purifying" and "elemental"?
2. In what sense is the simile of lines 16–20 appropriate? What function does it serve?   **3.** Why does the poet conclude that departing is "artificial" (l.28) and that perfection is "reprehensible" (l.32)?

Formal Application   (1963)

DONALD W. BAKER   [b. 1923]

"The poets apparently want to rejoin the human race."   TIME

I shall begin by learning to throw
the knife, first at trees, until it sticks
in the trunk and quivers every time;

next from a chair, using only wrist
and fingers, at a thing on the ground,
a fresh ant hill or a fallen leaf;

then at a moving object, perhaps
a pieplate swinging on twine, until
I pot it at least twice in three tries.

Meanwhile, I shall be teaching the birds   10
that the skinny fellow in sneakers
is a source of suet and bread crumbs,

first putting them on a shingle nailed
to a pine tree, next scattering them
on the needles, closer and closer

to my seat, until the proper bird,
a towhee, I think, in black and rust
and gray, takes tossed crumbs six feet away.

Finally, I shall coordinate
conditioned reflex and functional   20
form and qualify as Modern Man.

You see the splash of blood and feathers
and the blade pinning it to the tree?
It's called an "Audubon Crucifix."

The phrase has pleasing (even pious)
connotations, like *Arbeit Macht Frei*,
"Molotov Cocktail," and *Enola Gay*.[1]

Formal Application

   [1] *Arbeit Macht Frei*, the motto of the German Nazi party, means "labor liberates." A Molotov cocktail is a homemade hand grenade named after Vyacheslav M. Molotov, the foreign minister of Russia during the reign of Joseph Stalin. *Enola Gay* was the name of the United States plane that dropped the atomic bomb on Hiroshima in 1945.

QUESTIONS

1. What did *Time* mean by the line Baker uses as an epigraph to this poem? How, for example, are poets not members of the human race? What does the title of the poem mean? **2.** In what sense does "Audubon Crucifix" have "pleasing (even pious) connotations"? What are the pleasing connotations of the expressions in the last two lines? According to this poem, what are the attributes necessary to join the human race?

Hard Rock Returns to Prison from the Hospital for the Criminal Insane   1968

ETHERIDGE KNIGHT   [b. 1933]

Hard Rock was "known not to take no shit
From nobody," and he had the scars to prove it:
Split purple lips, lumped ears, welts above
His yellow eyes, and one long scar that cut
Across his temple and plowed through a thick
Canopy of kinky hair.

The WORD was that Hard Rock wasn't a mean nigger
Anymore, that the doctors had bored a hole in his head,
Cut out part of his brain, and shot electricity
Through the rest. When they brought Hard Rock back,   10
Handcuffed and chained, he was turned loose,
Like a freshly gelded stallion, to try his new status.
And we all waited and watched, like Indians at a corral,
To see if the WORD was true.

As we waited we wrapped ourselves in the cloak
Of his exploits: "Man, the last time, it took eight
Screws to put him in the Hole." "Yeah, remember when he
Smacked the captain with his dinner tray?" "He set
The record for time in the Hole—67 straight days!"
"Ol Hard Rock! man, that's one crazy nigger."   20
And then the jewel of a myth that Hard Rock had once bit
A screw on the thumb and poisoned him with syphilitic spit.

The testing came, to see if Hard Rock was really tame.
A hillbilly called him a black son of a bitch
And didn't lose his teeth, a screw who knew Hard Rock
From before shook him down and barked in his face.

And Hard Rock did *nothing*. Just grinned and looked silly,
His eyes empty like knot holes in a fence.

And even after we discovered that it took Hard Rock
Exactly 3 minutes to tell you his first name,   30
We told ourselves that he had just wised up,
Was being cool; but we could not fool ourselves for long,
And we turned away, our eyes on the ground. Crushed.

He had been our Destroyer, the doer of things
We dreamed of doing but could not bring ourselves to do,
The fears of years, like a biting whip,
Had cut grooves too deeply across our backs.

Confession to Settle a Curse   1972

ROSMARIE WALDROP   [b. 1935]

You don't
know
who I am
because
you don't know
my mother
she's always been an exemplary mother
told me so herself
there were reasons she
had to lock   10
everything that could be locked
there's much can be
locked
in a good German household crowded
with wardrobes dressers sideboards
bookcases cupboards chests bureaus
desks trunks caskets coffers all with lock
and key
and locked
it was lots of trouble   20
for her
just carry that enormous key ring
be bothered all the time
I wanted scissors stationery
my winter coat and she had to unlock

the drawer get it out and lock
all up again
me she reproached for lacking
confidence not being open
I have a mother I can tell everything   30
she told me so
I've
been bound
made fast
locked
by the key witch
but a small
winner
I'm not
in turn locking   40
a child
in my arms.

Eleanor Rigby   1966

JOHN LENNON [1940–1980] **and PAUL McCARTNEY** [b. 1942]

Ah, look at all the lonely people!
Ah, look at all the lonely people!
Eleanor Rigby picks up the rice
    in the church
Where a wedding has been.
Lives in a dream.
Waits at the window, wearing the face
    that she keeps in a jar by the door.
Who is it for?

All the lonely people,   10
    where do they all come from?
All the lonely people,
    where do they all belong?

Father McKenzie writing the words
    of a sermon that no one will hear—
No one comes near. Look at him
    working, darning his socks in the night
    when there's nobody there.
What does he care?

All the lonely people,   20
   where do they all come from?
All the lonely people.
   where do they all belong?

Ah, look at all the lonely people!
Ah, look at all the lonely people!
Eleanor Rigby died in the church and
   was buried along with her name.
Nobody came.
Father McKenzie wiping the dirt from
   his hands as he walks from the grave.   30
No one was saved.

All the lonely people,
   where do they all come from?
All the lonely people,
   where do they all belong?

QUESTIONS
1.   How does the first stanza establish Eleanor Rigby's character? What is the meaning of lines 7–8?   **2.**   What does the portrait of Father McKenzie contribute to our understanding of the theme of the lyric?   **3.**   What significance has the juxtaposition of Father McKenzie's writing "a sermon that no one will hear" and "darning his socks in the night" (stanza 3)?   **4.**   What is the significance of Eleanor Rigby's dying in the church? Why was "No one saved" (l.31)?   **5.**   What answers, if any, does the poem suggest to the questions in the last stanza?

Dreams   1968

NIKKI GIOVANNI   [b. 1943]

i used to dream militant
dreams of taking
over america to show
these white folks how it should be
done
i used to dream radical dreams
of blowing everyone away with my perceptive powers
of correct analysis
i even used to think i'd be the one
to stop the riot and negotiate the peace   10
then i awoke and dug
that if i dreamed natural

dreams of being a natural
woman doing what a woman
does when she's natural
i would have a revolution

The Colonel   1981

CAROLYN FORCHÉ   [b. 1950]

What you have heard is true. I was in his house. His wife carried a tray of coffee and sugar. His daughter filed her nails, his son went out for the night. There were daily papers, pet dogs, a pistol on the cushion beside him. The moon swung bare on its black cord over the house. On the television was a cop show. It was in English. Broken bottles were embedded in the walls round the house to scoop the kneecaps from a man's legs or cut his hands to lace. On the windows there were gratings like those in liquor stores. We had dinner, rack of lamb, good wine, a gold bell was on the table for calling the maid. The maid brought green mangoes, salt, a type of bread. I was asked how I enjoyed the country. There was a brief commercial in Spanish. His wife took everything away. There was some talk then of how difficult it had become to govern. The parrot said hello on the terrace. The colonel told it to shut up, and pushed himself from the table. My friend said to me with his eyes: say nothing. The colonel returned with a sack used to bring groceries home. He spilled many human ears on the table. They were like dried peach halves. There is no other way to say this. He took one of them in his hands, shook it in our faces, dropped it into a water glass. It came alive there. I am tired of fooling around he said. As for the rights of anyone, tell your people they can go fuck themselves. He swept the ears to the floor with his arm and held the last of his wine in the air. Something for your poetry, no? he said. Some of the ears on the floor caught this scrap of his voice. Some of the ears on the floor were pressed to the ground.

QUESTIONS
1.   What is the occasion of this poem? Where is it set? How would you characterize the colonel's family?   2.   "There was some talk of how difficult it had become to govern." Can you suggest why it had become difficult to govern? How does the colonel respond to these difficulties?   3.   What does the last sentence suggest?

WRITING TOPIC
This piece is printed as if it were prose. Does it have any of the formal characteristics of a poem?

CONFORMITY
AND
REBELLION

The Accused, 1886 by Odilon Redon

DRAMA

Antigone* (ca. 441 B.C.)

SOPHOCLES [496?–406 B.C.]

CHARACTERS

Antigonê	Teiresias
Ismenê	A Sentry
Eurydicê	A Messenger
Creon	Chorus
Haimon	

SCENE

Before the Palace of Creon, King of Thebes. A central double door, and two lateral doors. A platform extends the length of the façade, and from this platform three steps lead down into the "orchestra," or chorus-ground.

TIME

Dawn of the day after the repulse of the Argive army from the assault on Thebes.

Prologue

[Antigonê and Ismenê enter from the central door of the Palace.]

Antigonê. Ismenê, dear sister,
You would think that we had already suffered enough
For the curse on Oedipus[1]:

---

* An English version by Dudley Fitts and Robert Fitzgerald.
[1] Oedipus, a former King of Thebes, unwittingly killed his father and married his own mother, Iocastê. By her he had four children, the sisters Antigonê and Ismenê and the brothers Polyneicês and Eteoclês. When Oedipus realized what he had done, he blinded himself and left Thebes. Eteoclês drove Polyneicês out of Thebes after a quarrel, but Polyneicês returned with an army and laid siege to Thebes. In the ensuing struggle, the brothers killed each other. Creon became king and, as a punishment, decreed that Polyneicês be denied the rites of burial.

I cannot imagine any grief
That you and I have not gone through. And now—
Have they told you of the new decree of our King Creon?
Ismenê.   I have heard nothing: I know
That two sisters lost two brothers, a double death
In a single hour; and I know that the Argive army
Fled in the night; but beyond this, nothing.   10
Antigonê.   I thought so. And that is why I wanted you
To come out here with me. There is something we must do.
Ismenê.   Why do you speak so strangely?
Antigonê.   Listen, Ismenê:
Creon buried our brother Eteoclês
With military honors, gave him a soldier's funeral,
And it was right that he should; but Polyneicês,
Who fought as bravely and died as miserably,—
They say that Creon has sworn
No one shall bury him, no one mourn for him,   20
But his body must lie in the fields, a sweet treasure
For carrion birds to find as they search for food.
That is what they say, and our good Creon is coming here
To announce it publicly; and the penalty—
Stoning to death in the public square!
                                                    There it is,
And now you can prove what you are:
A true sister, or a traitor to your family.
Ismenê.   Antigonê, you are mad! What could I possibly do?
Antigonê.   You must decide whether you will help me or not.
Ismenê.   I do not understand you. Help you in what?   30
Antigonê.   Ismenê, I am going to bury him. Will you come?
Ismenê.   Bury him! You have just said the new law forbids it.
Antigonê.   He is my brother. And he is your brother, too.
Ismenê.   But think of the danger! Think what Creon will do!
Antigonê.   Creon is not strong enough to stand in my way.
Ismenê.   Ah sister!
Oedipus died, everyone hating him
For what his own search brought to light, his eyes
Ripped out by his own hand; and Iocastê died,
His mother and wife at once: she twisted the cords   40
That strangled her life; and our two brothers died,
Each killed by the other's sword. And we are left:
But oh, Antigonê,
Think how much more terrible than these
Our own death would be if we should go against Creon
And do what he has forbidden! We are only women,
We cannot fight with men, Antigonê!

The law is strong, we must give in to the law
In this thing, and in worse. I beg the Dead
To forgive me, but I am helpless: I must yield   50
To those in authority. And I think it is dangerous business
To be always meddling.
Antigonê.   If that is what you think,
I should not want you, even if you asked to come.
You have made your choice, you can be what you want to be.
But I will bury him; and if I must die,
I say that this crime is holy: I shall lie down
With him in death, and I shall be as dear
To him as he to me.
                     It is the dead,
Not the living, who make the longest demands:
We die for ever . . .
                     You may do as you like,   60
Since apparently the laws of the gods mean nothing to you.
Ismenê.   They mean a great deal to me; but I have no strength
To break laws that were made for the public good.
Antigonê.   That must be your excuse, I suppose. But as for me,
I will bury the brother I love.
Ismenê.   Antigonê,
I am so afraid for you!
Antigonê.   You need not be:
You have yourself to consider, after all.
Ismenê.   But no one must hear of this, you must tell no one!
I will keep it a secret, I promise!
Antigonê.   Oh tell it! Tell everyone!
Think how they'll hate you when it all comes out   70
If they learn that you knew about it all the time!
Ismenê.   So fiery! You should be cold with fear.
Antigonê.   Perhaps. But I am doing only what I must.
Ismenê.   But can you do it? I say that you cannot.
Antigonê.   Very well: when my strength gives out, I shall do no more.
Ismenê.   Impossible things should not be tried at all.
Antigonê.   Go away, Ismenê:
I shall be hating you soon, and the dead will too,
For your words are hateful. Leave me my foolish plan:
I am not afraid of the danger; if it means death,   80
It will not be the worst of deaths—death without honor.
Ismenê.   Go then, if you feel that you must.
You are unwise,
But a loyal friend indeed to those who love you.

[*Exit into the Palace. Antigonê goes off, L. Enter the Chorus.*]

Párodos²

Chorus.   Now the long blade of the sun, lying   [*Strophe 1*]
    Level east to west, touches with glory
    Thebes of the Seven Gates. Open, unlidded
    Eye of golden day! O marching light
    Across the eddy and rush of Dircê's stream,³
    Striking the white shields of the enemy
    Thrown headlong backward from the blaze of morning!
Choragos.⁴   Polyneicês their commander
    Roused them with windy phrases,
    He the wild eagle screaming   10
    Insults above our land,
    His wings their shields of snow,
    His crest their marshalled helms.

Chorus.   Against our seven gates in a yawning ring   [*Antistrophe 1*]
    The famished spears came onward in the night;
    But before his jaws were sated with our blood,
    Or pinefire took the garland of our towers,
    He was thrown back; and as he turned, great Thebes—
    No tender victim for his noisy power—
    Rose like a dragon behind him, shouting war.   20
Choragos.   For God hates utterly
    The bray of bragging tongues;
    And when he beheld their smiling,
    Their swagger of golden helms,
    The frown of his thunder blasted
    Their first man from our walls.

Chrous.   We heard his shout of triumph high in the air   [*Strophe 2*]
    Turn to a scream; far out in a flaming arc
    He fell with his windy torch, and the earth struck him.
    And others storming in fury no less than his   30
    Found shock of death in the dusty joy of battle.
Choragos.   Seven captains at seven gates
    Yielded their clanging arms to the god
    That bends the battle-line and breaks it.
    These two only, brothers in blood,
    Face to face in matchless rage,

---

² The *Párodos* is the ode sung by the Chorus as it entered the theater and moved down the aisles to the playing area. The *strophe*, in Greek tragedy, is the unit of verse the Chorus chanted as it moved to the left in a dance rhythm. The Chorus sang the *antistrophe* as it moved to the right, and the *epode* while standing still.
³ A stream near Thebes.
⁴ Choragos is the leader of the Chorus.

Mirroring each the other's death,
Clashed in long combat.

Chorus.   But now in the beautiful morning of victory   [*Antistrophe* 2]
Let Thebes of the many chariots sing for joy!   40
With hearts for dancing we'll take leave of war:
Our temples shall be sweet with hymns of praise,
And the long night shall echo with our chorus.

Scene I

Choragos.   But now at last our new King is coming:
Creon of Thebes, Menoikeus' son.
In this auspicious dawn of his reign
What are the new complexities
That shifting Fate has woven for him?
What is his counsel? Why has he summoned
The old men to hear him?

[*Enter Creon from the Palace, C. He addresses the Chorus from the top step.*]

Creon.   Gentlemen: I have the honor to inform you that our Ship of State,
which recent storms have threatened to destroy, has come safely to harbor at
last, guided by the merciful wisdom of Heaven. I have summoned you here
this morning because I know that I can depend upon you: your devotion to
King Laïos was absolute; you never hesitated in your duty to our late ruler
Oedipus; and when Oedipus died, your loyalty was transferred to his children.
Unfortunately, as you know, his two sons, the princes Eteoclês and Polyneicês, have killed each other in battle; and I, as the next in blood, have
succeeded to the full power of the throne.
    I am aware, of course, that no Ruler can expect complete loyalty from his
subjects until he has been tested in office. Nevertheless, I say to you at the
very outset that I have nothing but contempt for the kind of Governor who
is afraid, for whatever reason, to follow the course that he knows is best for
the State; and as for the man who sets private friendship above the public
welfare,—I have no use for him, either. I call God to witness that if I saw
my country headed for ruin, I should not be afraid to speak out plainly; and
I need hardly remind you that I would never have any dealings with an enemy
of the people. No one values friendship more highly than I; but we must
remember that friends made at the risk of wrecking our Ship are not real
friends at all.
    These are my principles, at any rate, and that is why I have made the
following decision concerning the sons of Oedipus: Eteoclês, who died as a
man should die, fighting for his country, is to be buried with full military
honors, with all the ceremony that is usual when the greatest heroes die; but

his brother Polyneicês, who broke his exile to come back with fire and sword against his native city and the shrines of his fathers' gods, whose one idea was to spill the blood of his blood and sell his own people into slavery—Polyneicês, I say, is to have no burial: no man is to touch him or say the least prayer for him; he shall lie on the plain, unburied; and the birds and the scavenging dogs can do with him whatever they like.

This is my command, and you can see the wisdom behind it. As long as I am King, no traitor is going to be honored with the loyal man. But whoever shows by word and deed that he is on the side of the State,—he shall have my respect while he is living and my reverence when he is dead.

Choragos.   If that is your will, Creon son of Menoikeus,
   You have the right to enforce it: we are yours.
Creon.   That is my will. Take care that you do your part.
Choragos.   We are old men: let the younger ones carry it out.
Creon.   I do not mean that: the sentries have been appointed.
Choragos.   Then what is it that you would have us do?
Creon.   You will give no support to whoever breaks this law.
Choragos.   Only a crazy man is in love with death!
Creon.   And death it is; yet money talks, and the wisest
   Have sometimes been known to count a few coins too many.

[*Enter Sentry from L.*]

Sentry.   I'll not say that I'm out of breath from running, King, because every
   time I stopped to think about what I have to tell you, I felt like going back.
   And all the time a voice kept saying, "You fool, don't you know you're
   walking straight into trouble?"; and then another voice: "Yes, but if you let
   somebody else get the news to Creon first, it will be even worse than that for
   you!" But good sense won out, at least I hope it was good sense, and here I
   am with a story that makes no sense at all; but I'll tell it anyhow, because,
   as they say, what's going to happen's going to happen, and—
Creon.   Come to the point. What have you to say?
Sentry.   I did not do it. I did not see who did it. You must not punish me for
   what someone else has done.
Creon.   A comprehensive defense! More effective, perhaps,
   If I knew its purpose. Come: what is it?
Sentry.   A dreadful thing . . . I don't know how to put it—
Creon.   Out with it!
Sentry.   Well, then;
   The dead man—
                    Polyneicês—

[*Pause. The Sentry is overcome, fumbles for words. Creon waits impassively.*]

                         out there—
                              someone,—
   New dust on the slimy flesh!

[*Pause. No sign from Creon.*]

Someone has given it burial that way, and
Gone . . .

[*Long pause. Creon finally speaks with deadly control.*]

Creon.   And the man who dared do this?
Sentry.   I swear I
Do not know! You must believe me!
                                              Listen:
The ground was dry, not a sign of digging, no,
Not a wheeltrack in the dust, no trace of anyone.
It was when they relieved us this morning: and one of them,
The corporal, pointed to it.
                              There it was,
The strangest—
              Look:
The body, just mounded over with light dust: you see?
Not buried really, but as if they'd covered it
Just enough for the ghost's peace. And no sign
Of dogs or any wild animal that had been there.

And then what a scene there was! Every man of us
Accusing the other: we all proved the other man did it,
We all had proof that we could not have done it.
We were ready to take hot iron in our hands,
Walk through fire, swear by all the gods,
It was not I!
I do not know who it was, but it was not I!

[*Creon's rage has been mounting steadily, but the Sentry is too intent upon his story to notice it.*]

And then, when this came to nothing, someone said
A thing that silenced us and made us stare
Down at the ground: you had to be told the news,
And one of us had to do it! We threw the dice,
And the bad luck fell to me. So here I am,
No happier to be here than you are to have me:
Nobody likes the man who brings bad news.
Choragos.   I have been wondering, King: can it be that the gods have done
    this?
Creon [*furiously*].   Stop!
Must you doddering wrecks
Go out of your heads entirely? "The gods!"
Intolerable!

The gods favor this corpse? Why? How had he served them?
Tried to loot their temples, burn their images,
Yes, and the whole State, and its laws with it!
Is it your senile opinion that the gods love to honor bad men?
A pious thought!—
                              No, from the very beginning
There have been those who have whispered together,
Stiff-necked anarchists, putting their heads together,
Scheming against me in alleys. These are the men,
And they have bribed my own guard to do this thing.
[*Sententiously.*] Money!
There's nothing in the world so demoralizing as money.
Down go your cities,
Homes gone, men gone, honest hearts corrupted,
Crookedness of all kinds, and all for money!
[*To Sentry.*]   But you—!
I swear by God and by the throne of God,
The man who has done this thing shall pay for it!
Find that man, bring him here to me, or your death
Will be the least of your problems: I'll string you up
Alive, and there will be certain ways to make you
Discover your employer before you die;
And the process may teach you a lesson you seem to have missed:
The dearest profit is sometimes all too dear:
That depends on the source. Do you understand me?
A fortune won is often misfortune.

Sentry.   King, may I speak?
Creon.   Your very voice distresses me.
Sentry.   Are you sure that it is my voice, and not your conscience?
Creon.   By God, he wants to analyze me now!
Sentry.   It is not what I say, but what has been done, that hurts you.
Creon.   You talk too much.
Sentry.   Maybe; but I've done nothing.
Creon.   Sold your soul for some silver: that's all you've done.
Sentry.   How dreadful it is when the right judge judges wrong!
Creon.   Your figures of speech
    May entertain you now; but unless you bring me the man,
    You will get little profit from them in the end.

[*Exit Creon into the Palace.*]

Sentry.   "Bring me the man"—!
    I'd like nothing better than bringing him the man!
    But bring him or not, you have seen the last of me here.
    At any rate, I am safe!

[*Exit Sentry.*]

inery.

Ode I

Chorus. Numberless are the world's wonders, but none   [*Strophe 1*]
   More wonderful than man; the stormgray sea
   Yields to his prows, the huge crests bear him high;
   Earth, holy and inexhaustible, is graven
   With shining furrows where his plows have gone
   Year after year, the timeless labor of stallions.

   The lightboned birds and beasts that cling to cover,   [*Antistrophe 1*]
   The lithe fish lighting their reaches of dim water,
   All are taken, tamed in the net of his mind;
   The lion on the hill, the wild horse windy-maned,   10
   Resign to him; and his blunt yoke has broken
   The sultry shoulders of the mountain bull.

   Words also, and thought as rapid as air,   [*Strophe 2*]
   He fashions to his good use; statecraft is his,
   And his the skill that deflects the arrows of snow,
   The spears of winter rain: from every wind
   He has made himself secure—from all but one:
   In the late wind of death he cannot stand.

   O clear intelligence, force beyond all measure!   [*Antistrophe 2*]
   O fate of man, working both good and evil!   20
   When the laws are kept, how proudly his city stands!
   When the laws are broken, what of his city then?
   Never may the anarchic man find rest at my hearth,
   Never be it said that my thoughts are his thoughts.

Scene II

[*Re-enter Sentry leading Antigonê.*]

Choragos. What does this mean? Surely this captive woman
   Is the Princess, Antigonê. Why should she be taken?
Sentry. Here is the one who did it! We caught her
   In the very act of burying him.—Where is Creon?
Choragos. Just coming from the house.

[*Enter Creon, C.*]

Creon.   What has happened?
   Why have you come back so soon?

Sentry [*expansively*].   O King,
  A man should never be too sure of anything:
  I would have sworn
  That you'd not see me here again: your anger
  Frightened me so, and the things you threatened me with;   10
  But how could I tell then
  That I'd be able to solve the case so soon?
  No dice-throwing this time: I was only too glad to come!

  Here is this woman. She is the guilty one:
  We found her trying to bury him.
  Take her, then; question her; judge her as you will.
  I am through with the whole thing now, and glad of it.
Creon.   But this is Antigonê! Why have you brought her here?
Sentry.   She was burying him, I tell you!
Creon [*severely*].   Is this the truth?
Sentry.   I saw her with my own eyes. Can I say more?   20
Creon.   The details: come, tell me quickly!
Sentry.   It was like this:
  After those terrible threats of yours, King,
  We went back and brushed the dust away from the body.
  The flesh was soft by now, and stinking,
  So we sat on a hill to windward and kept guard.
  No napping this time! We kept each other awake.
  But nothing happened until the white round sun
  Whirled in the center of the round sky over us:
  Then, suddenly,
  A storm of dust roared up from the earth, and the sky   30
  Went out, the plain vanished with all its trees
  In the stinging dark. We closed our eyes and endured it.
  The whirlwind lasted a long time, but it passed;
  And then we looked, and there was Antigonê!
  I have seen
  A mother bird come back to a stripped nest, heard
  Her crying bitterly a broken note or two
  For the young ones stolen. Just so, when this girl
  Found the bare corpse, and all her love's work wasted,
  She wept, and cried on heaven to damn the hands   40
  That had done this thing.
                     And then she brought more dust
  And sprinkled wine three times for her brother's ghost.
  We ran and took her at once. She was not afraid,
  Not even when we charged her with what she had done.
  She denied nothing.
                 And this was a comfort to me,
  And some uneasiness: for it is a good thing

To escape from death, but it is no great pleasure
To bring death to a friend.
                              Yet I always say
There is nothing so comfortable as your own safe skin!
Creon [*slowly, dangerously*].   And you, Antigonê,   50
    You with your head hanging,—do you confess this thing?
Antigonê.   I do. I deny nothing.
Creon [*to Sentry*].   You may go.

[*Exit Sentry.*]

[*To Antigonê.*] Tell me, tell me briefly:
Had you heard my proclamation touching this matter?
Antigonê.   It was public. Could I help hearing it?
Creon.   And yet you dared defy the law.
Antigonê.   I dared.
    It was not God's proclamation. That final Justice
    That rules the world below makes no such laws.

    Your edict, King, was strong,
    But all your strength is weakness itself against   60
    The immortal unrecorded laws of God.
    They are not merely now: they were, and shall be,
    Operative for ever, beyond man utterly.

    I knew I must die, even without your decree:
    I am only mortal. And if I must die
    Now, before it is my time to die,
    Surely this is no hardship: can anyone
    Living, as I live, with evil all about me,
    Think Death less than a friend? This death of mine
    Is of no importance; but if I had left my brother   70
    Lying in death unburied, I should have suffered.
    Now I do not.
                    You smile at me. Ah Creon,
    Think me a fool, if you like; but it may well be
    That a fool convicts me of folly.
Choragos.   Like father, like daughter: both headstrong, deaf to reason!
    She has never learned to yield.
Creon.   She has much to learn.
    The inflexible heart breaks first, the toughest iron
    Cracks first, and the wildest horses bend their necks
    At the pull of the smallest curb.
                            Pride? In a slave?
    This girl is guilty of a double insolence,   80
    Breaking the given laws and boasting of it.

Who is the man here,
She or I, if this crime goes unpunished?
Sister's child, or more than sister's child,
Or closer yet in blood—she and her sister
Win bitter death for this!
[*To servants.*]   Go, some of you,
Arrest Ismenê. I accuse her equally.
Bring her: you will find her sniffling in the house there.

Her mind's a traitor: crimes kept in the dark
Cry for light, and the guardian brain shudders;   90
But how much worse than this
Is brazen boasting of barefaced anarchy!
Antigonê.   Creon, what more do you want than my death?
Creon.   Nothing.
That gives me everything.
Antigonê.   Then I beg you: kill me.
This talking is a great weariness: your words
Are distasteful to me, and I am sure that mine
Seem so to you. And yet they should not seem so:
I should have praise and honor for what I have done.
All these men here would praise me
Were their lips not frozen shut with fear of you.   100
[*Bitterly.*] Ah the good fortune of kings,
Licensed to say and do whatever they please!
Creon.   You are alone here in that opinion.
Antigonê.   No, they are with me. But they keep their tongues in leash.
Creon.   Maybe. But you are guilty, and they are not.
Antigonê.   There is no guilt in reverence for the dead.
Creon.   But Eteoclês—was he not your brother too?
Antigonê.   My brother too.
Creon.   And you insult his memory?
Antigonê [*softly*].   The dead man would not say that I insult it.
Creon.   He would: for you honor a traitor as much as him.   110
Antigonê.   His own brother, traitor or not, and equal in blood.
Creon.   He made war on his country. Eteoclês defended it.
Antigonê.   Nevertheless, there are honors due all the dead.
Creon.   But not the same for the wicked as for the just.
Antigonê.   Ah Creon, Creon,
Which of us can say what the gods hold wicked?
Creon.   An enemy is an enemy, even dead.
Antigonê.   It is my nature to join in love, not hate.
Creon [*finally losing patience*].   Go join them, then; if you must have your
    love,
Find it in hell!   120
Choragos.   But see, Ismenê comes:

[Enter Ismenê, guarded.]

Those tears are sisterly, the cloud
That shadows her eyes rains down gentle sorrow.
Creon.   You too, Ismenê,
Snake in my ordered house, sucking my blood
Stealthily—and all the time I never knew
That these two sisters were aiming at my throne!
                                                    Ismenê,
Do you confess your share in this crime, or deny it?
Answer me.
Ismenê.   Yes, if she will let me say so. I am guilty.   130
Antigonê [*coldly*].   No, Ismenê. You have no right to say so.
You would not help me, and I will not have you help me.
Ismenê.   But now I know what you meant; and I am here
To join you, to take my share of punishment.
Antigonê.   The dead man and the gods who rule the dead
Know whose act this was. Words are not friends.
Ismenê.   Do you refuse me, Antigonê? I want to die with you:
I too have a duty that I must discharge to the dead.
Antigonê.   You shall not lessen my death by sharing it.
Ismenê.   What do I care for life when you are dead?   140
Antigonê.   Ask Creon. You're always hanging on his opinions.
Ismenê.   You are laughing at me. Why, Antigonê?
Antigonê.   It's a joyless laughter, Ismenê.
Ismenê.   But can I do nothing?
Antigonê.   Yes. Save yourself. I shall not envy you.
There are those who will praise you; I shall have honor, too.
Ismenê.   But we are equally guilty!
Antigonê.   No more, Ismenê.
You are alive, but I belong to Death.
Creon [*to the Chrous*].   Gentlemen, I beg you to observe these girls:
One has just now lost her mind; the other,
It seems, has never had a mind at all.   150
Ismenê.   Grief teaches the steadiest minds to waver, King.
Creon.   Yours certainly did, when you assumed guilt with the guilty!
Ismenê.   But how could I go on living without her?
Creon.   You are.
She is already dead.
Ismenê.   But your own son's bride!
Creon.   There are places enough for him to push his plow.
I want no wicked women for my sons!
Ismenê.   O dearest Haimon, how your father wrongs you!
Creon.   I've had enough of your childish talk of marriage!
Choragos.   Do you really intend to steal this girl from your son?
Creon.   No; Death will do that for me.

Choragos.   Then she must die?   160
Creon [*ironically*].   You dazzle me.
                              —But enough of this talk!
  [*To Guards.*] You there, take them away and guard them well:
  For they are but women, and even brave men run
  When they see Death coming.

[*Exeunt Ismenê, Antigonê, and Guards.*]

Ode II

Chorus.   Fortunate is the man who has never tasted   [*Strophe 1*]
        God's vengeance!
  Where once the anger of heaven has struck, that house is shaken
  For ever: damnation rises behind each child
  Like a wave cresting out of the black northeast,
  When the long darkness under sea roars up
  And bursts drumming death upon the windwhipped sand.

  I have seen this gathering sorrow from time long past   [*Antistrophe 1*]
  Loom upon Oedipus' children: generation from generation
  Takes the compulsive rage of the enemy god.
  So lately this last flower of Oedipus' line   10
  Drank the sunlight! but now a passionate word
  And a handful of dust have closed up all its beauty.

        What mortal arrogance   [*Strophe 2*]
        Transcends the wrath of Zeus?
  Sleep cannot lull him, nor the effortless long months
  Of the timeless gods: but he is young for ever,
  And his house is the shining day of high Olympos.
        All that is and shall be,
        And all the past, is his.
  No pride on earth is free of the curse of heaven.   20

        The straying dreams of men   [*Antistrophe 2*]
        May bring them ghosts of joy:
  But as they drowse, the waking embers burn them;
  Or they walk with fixed eyes, as blind men walk.
  But the ancient wisdom speaks for our own time:
        Fate works most for woe
        With Folly's fairest show.
  Man's little pleasure is the spring of sorrow.

Scene III

Choragos.   But here is Haimon, King, the last of all your sons.
Is it grief for Antigonê that brings him here,
And bitterness at being robbed of his bride?

[*Enter Haimon.*]

Creon.   We shall soon see, and no need of diviners.
                                                —Son,
You have heard my final judgment on that girl:
Have you come here hating me, or have you come
With deference and with love, whatever I do?
Haimon.   I am your son, father. You are my guide.
You make things clear for me, and I obey you.
No marriage means more to me than your continuing wisdom.   10
Creon.   Good. That is the way to behave: subordinate
Everything else, my son, to your father's will.
This is what a man prays for, that he may get
Sons attentive and dutiful in his house,
Each one hating his father's enemies,
Honoring his father's friends. But if his sons
Fail him, if they turn out unprofitably,
What has he fathered but trouble for himself
And amusement for the malicious?
                                        So you are right
Not to lose your head over this woman.   20
Your pleasure with her would soon grow cold, Haimon,
And then you'd have a hellcat in bed and elsewhere.
Let her find her husband in Hell!
Of all the people in this city, only she
Has had contempt for my law and broken it.

Do you want me to show myself weak before the people?
Or to break my sworn word? No, and I will not.
The woman dies.
I suppose she'll plead "family ties." Well, let her.
If I permit my own family to rebel,   30
How shall I earn the world's obedience?
Show me the man who keeps his house in hand,
He's fit for public authority.
                            I'll have no dealings
With law-breakers, critics of the government:
Whoever is chosen to govern should be obeyed—
Must be obeyed, in all things, great and small,

Just and unjust! O Haimon,
The man who knows how to obey, and that man only,
Knows how to give commands when the time comes.
You can depend on him, no matter how fast   40
The spears come: he's a good soldier, he'll stick it out.

Anarchy, anarchy! Show me a greater evil!
This is why cities tumble and the great houses rain down,
This is what scatters armies!

No, no: good lives are made so by discipline.
We keep the laws then, and the lawmakers,
And no woman shall seduce us. If we must lose,
Let's lose to a man, at least! Is a woman stronger than we?
Choragos.   Unless time has rusted my wits,
What you say, King, is said with point and dignity.   50
Haimon [*boyishly earnest*].   Father:
Reason is God's crowning gift to man, and you are right
To warn me against losing mine. I cannot say—
I hope that I shall never want to say!—that you
Have reasoned badly. Yet there are other men
Who can reason, too; and their opinions might be helpful.
You are not in a position to know everything
That people say or do, or what they feel:
Your temper terrifies them—everyone
Will tell you only what you like to hear.   60
But I, at any rate, can listen; and I have heard them
Muttering and whispering in the dark about this girl.
They say no woman has ever, so unreasonably,
Died so shameful a death for a generous act:
"She covered her brother's body. Is this indecent?
She kept him from dogs and vultures. Is this a crime?
Death?—She should have all the honor that we can give her!"

This is the way they talk out there in the city.

You must believe me:
Nothing is closer to me than your happiness.   70
What could be closer? Must not any son
Value his father's fortune as his father does his?
I beg you, do not be unchangeable:
Do not believe that you alone can be right.
The man who thinks that,
The man who maintains that only he has the power
To reason correctly, the gift to speak, the soul—
A man like that, when you know him, turns out empty.

It is not reason never to yield to reason!

In flood time you can see how some trees bend   80
And because they bend, even their twigs are safe,
While stubborn trees are torn up, roots and all.
And the same thing happens in sailing:
Make your sheet fast, never slacken,—and over you go,
Head over heels and under: and there's your voyage.
Forget you are angry! Let yourself be moved!
I know I am young; but please let me say this:
The ideal condition
Would be, I admit, that men should be right by instinct;
But since we are all too likely to go astray,   90
The reasonable thing is to learn from those who can teach.

Choragos.   You will do well to listen to him, King,
If what he says is sensible. And you, Haimon,
Must listen to your father.—Both speak well.

Creon.   You consider it right for a man of my years and experience
To go to school to a boy?

Haimon.   It is not right
If I am wrong. But if I am young, and right,
What does my age matter?

Creon.   You think it right to stand up for an anarchist?

Haimon.   Not at all. I pay no respect to criminals.   100

Creon.   Then she is not a criminal?

Haimon.   The City would deny it, to a man.

Creon.   And the City proposes to teach me how to rule?

Haimon.   Ah. Who is it that's talking like a boy now?

Creon.   My voice is the one voice giving orders in this City!

Haimon.   It is no City if it takes orders from one voice.

Creon.   The State is the King!

Haimon.   Yes, if the State is a desert.

[*Pause.*]

Creon.   This boy, it seems, has sold out to a woman.

Haimon.   If you are a woman: my concern is only for you.

Creon.   So? Your "concern"! In a public brawl with your father!   110

Haimon.   How about you, in a public brawl with justice?

Creon.   With justice, when all that I do is within my rights?

Haimon.   You have no right to trample on God's right.

Creon [*completely out of control*].   Fool, adolescent fool! Taken in by a
    woman!

Haimon.   You'll never see me taken in by anything vile.

Creon.   Every word you say is for her!

Haimon [*quietly, darkly*].   And for you.
  And for me. And for the gods under the earth.
Creon.   You'll never marry her while she lives.
Haimon.   Then she must die.—But her death will cause another.
Creon.   Another?   120
  Have you lost your senses? Is this an open threat?
Haimon.   There is no threat in speaking to emptiness.
Creon.   I swear you'll regret this superior tone of yours!
  You are the empty one!
Haimon.   If you were not my father,
  I'd say you were perverse.
Creon.   You girlstruck fool, don't play at words with me!
Haimon.   I am sorry. You prefer silence.
Creon.   Now, by God—!
  I swear, by all the gods in heaven above us,
  You'll watch it, I swear you shall!
  [*To the servants.*]   Bring her out!
  Bring the woman out! Let her die before his eyes!   130
  Here, this instant, with her bridegroom beside her!
Haimon.   Not here, no; she will not die here, King.
  And you will never see my face again.
  Go on raving as long as you've a friend to endure you.

[*Exit Haimon.*]

Choragos.   Gone, gone.
  Creon, a young man in a rage is dangerous!
Creon.   Let him do, or dream to do, more than a man can.
  He shall not save these girls from death.
Choragos.   These girls?
  You have sentenced them both?
Creon.   No, you are right.
  I will not kill the one whose hands are clean.   140
Choragos.   But Antigonê?
Creon [*somberly*].   I will carry her far away
  Out there in the wilderness, and lock her
  Living in a vault of stone. She shall have food,
  As the custom is, to absolve the State of her death.
  And there let her pray to the gods of hell:
  They are her only gods:
  Perhaps they will show her an escape from death,
  Or she may learn,
                  though late,
  That piety shown the dead is pity in vain.

[*Exit Creon.*]

Ode III

Chorus.   Love, unconquerable   [Strophe]
    Waster of rich men, keeper
    Of warm lights and all-night vigil
    In the soft face of a girl:
    Sea-wanderer, forest-visitor!
    Even the pure Immortals cannot escape you,
    And mortal man, in his one day's dusk,
    Trembles before your glory.

    Surely you swerve upon ruin   [Antistrophe]
    The just man's consenting heart,   10
    As here you have made bright anger
    Strike between father and son—
    And none had conquered but Love!
    A girl's glance working the will of heaven:
    Pleasure to her alone who mocks us,
    Merciless Aphroditê.[5]

Scene IV

Choragos [as Antigonê enters guarded].   But I can no longer stand in awe of
        this,
    Nor, seeing what I see, keep back my tears.
    Here is Antigonê, passing to that chamber
    Where all find sleep at last.

Antigonê.   Look upon me, friends, and pity me   [Strophe 1]
    Turning back at the night's edge to say
    Good-by to the sun that shines for me no longer;
    Now sleepy Death
    Summons me down to Acheron,[6] that cold shore:
    There is no bridesong there, nor any music.   10
Chorus.   Yet not unpraised, not without a kind of honor,
    You walk at last into the underworld;
    Untouched by sickness, broken by no sword.
    What woman has ever found your way to death?

Antigonê.   How often I have heard the story of Niobê,[7]   [Antistrophe 1]
    Tantalos' wretched daughter, how the stone

---

    [5] Aphroditê is the goddess of love.
    [6] A river of Hades.
    [7] Niobê married an ancestor of Oedipus named Amphion. Her fourteen children were killed by Apollo and Artemis after Niobê boasted to their mother, Leto, that her children were superior to them. She wept incessantly and was finally transformed into a rock on Mt. Sipylos, whose streams are her tears.

Clung fast about her, ivy-close: and they say
The rain falls endlessly
And sifting soft snow; her tears are never done.
I feel the loneliness of her death in mine.   20
Chorus.   But she was born of heaven, and you
Are woman, woman-born. If her death is yours,
A mortal woman's, is this not for you
Glory in our world and in the world beyond?

Antigonê.   You laugh at me. Ah, friends, friends,   [*Strophe 2*]
Can you not wait until I am dead? O Thebes,
O men many-charioted, in love with Fortune,
Dear springs of Dircê, sacred Theban grove,
Be witnesses for me, denied all pity,
Unjustly judged! and think a word of love   30
For her whose path turns
Under dark earth, where there are no more tears.
Chorus.   You have passed beyond human daring and come at last
Into a place of stone where Justice sits.
I cannot tell
What shape of your father's guilt appears in this.

Antigonê.   You have touched it at last: that bridal bed   [*Antistrophe 2*]
Unspeakable, horror of son and mother mingling:
Their crime, infection of all our family!
O Oedipus, father and brother!   40
Your marriage strikes from the grave to murder mine.
I have been a stranger here in my own land:
All my life
The blasphemy of my birth has followed me.
Chorus.   Reverence is a virtue, but strength
Lives in established law: that must prevail.
You have made your choice,
Your death is the doing of your conscious hand.

Antigonê.   Then let me go, since all your words are bitter,   [*Epode*]
And the very light of the sun is cold to me.   50
Lead me to my vigil, where I must have
Neither love nor lamentation; no song, but silence.

[*Creon interrupts impatiently.*]

Creon.   If dirges and planned lamentations could put off death,
Men would be singing for ever.
[*To the servants.*]   Take her, go!
You know your orders: take her to the vault

And leave her alone there. And if she lives or dies,
That's her affair, not ours: our hands are clean.

Antigonê.   O tomb, vaulted bride-bed in eternal rock,
Soon I shall be with my own again
Where Persephonê[8] welcomes the thin ghosts underground: 60
And I shall see my father again, and you, mother,
And dearest Polyneicês—
                                         dearest indeed
To me, since it was my hand
That washed him clean and poured the ritual wine:
And my reward is death before my time!

And yet, as men's hearts know, I have done no wrong,
I have not sinned before God. Or if I have,
I shall know the truth in death. But if the guilt
Lies upon Creon who judged me, then, I pray,
May his punishment equal my own.
Choragos.   O passionate heart,   70
Unyielding, tormented still by the same winds!
Creon.   Her guards shall have good cause to regret their delaying.
Antigonê.   Ah! That voice is like the voice of death!
Creon.   I can give you no reason to think you are mistaken.
Antigonê.   Thebes, and you my fathers' gods,
And rulers of Thebes, you see me now, the last
Unhappy daughter of a line of kings,
Your kings, led away to death. You will remember
What things I suffer, and at what men's hands,
Because I would not transgress the laws of heaven.   80
[*To the guards, simply.*] Come: let us wait no longer.

[*Exit Antigonê, L., guarded.*]

Ode IV

Chorus.   All Danaê's[9] beauty was locked away   [*Strophe 1*]
In a brazen cell where the sunlight could not come:
A small room, still as any grave, enclosed her.
Yet she was a princess too,
And Zeus in a rain of gold poured love upon her.
O child, child,

---

   [8] Queen of Hades.
   [9] Though Danaê, a beautiful princess of Aῖgos, was confined by her father, Zeus visited her in
the form of a shower of gold, and she gave birth to Perseus as a result.

No power in wealth or war
Or tough sea-blackened ships
Can prevail against untiring Destiny!

And Dryas' son[10] also, that furious king,   [*Antistrophe 1*]
Bore the god's prisoning anger for his pride: 11
Sealed up by Dionysos in deaf stone,
His madness died among echoes.
So at the last he learned what dreadful power
His tongue had mocked:
For he had profaned the revels,
And fired the wrath of the nine
Implacable Sisters[11] that love the sound of the flute.

And old men tell a half-remembered tale   [*Strophe 2*]
Of horror where a dark ledge splits the sea   20
And a double surf beats on the gray shores:
How a king's new woman,[12] sick
With hatred for the queen he had imprisoned,
Ripped out his two sons' eyes with her bloody hands
While grinning Arês[13] watched the shuttle plunge
Four times: four blind wounds crying for revenge,

Crying, tears and blood mingled.—Piteously born,   [*Antistrophe 2*]
Those sons whose mother was of heavenly birth!
Her father was the god of the North Wind
And she was cradled by gales,   30
She raced with young colts on the glittering hills
And walked untrammeled in the open light:
But in her marriage deathless Fate found means
To build a tomb like yours for all her joy.

Scene V

[*Enter blind Teiresias, led by a boy. The opening speeches of Teiresias should be in singsong contrast to the realistic lines of Creon.*]

Teiresias.   This is the way the blind man comes, Princes, Princes,
Lock-step, two heads lit by the eyes of one.

---

[10] Lycurgus, King of Thrace, who was driven mad by Dionysos, the god of wine.
[11] The Muses.
[12] The ode alludes to a story indicating the uselessness of high birth against implacable fate. The king's new woman is Eidothea, the second wife of King Phineus. Though Cleopatra, his first wife, was the daughter of Boreas, the north wind, and Phineus was descended from kings, yet Eidothea, out of hatred for Cleopatra, blinded her two sons.
[13] The god of war.

Creon.   What new thing have you to tell us, old Teiresias?
Teiresias.   I have much to tell you: listen to the prophet, Creon.
Creon.   I am not aware that I have ever failed to listen.
Teiresias.   Then you have done wisely, King, and ruled well.
Creon.   I admit my debt to you. But what have you to say?
Teiresias.   This, Creon: you stand once more on the edge of fate.
Creon.   What do you mean? Your words are a kind of dread.
Teiresias.   Listen, Creon: 10
  I was sitting in my chair of augury, at the place
  Where the birds gather about me. They were all a-chatter,
  As is their habit, when suddenly I heard
  A strange note in their jangling, a scream, a
  Whirring fury; I knew that they were fighting,
  Tearing each other, dying
  In a whirlwind of wings clashing. And I was afraid.
  I began the rites of burnt-offering at the altar,
  But Hephaistos[14] failed me: instead of bright flame,
  There was only the sputtering slime of the fat thigh-flesh   20
  Melting: the entrails dissolved in gray smoke;
  The bare bone burst from the welter. And no blaze!

  This was a sign from heaven. My boy described it,
  Seeing for me as I see for others.

  I tell you, Creon, you yourself have brought
  This new calamity upon us. Our hearths and altars
  Are stained with the corruption of dogs and carrion birds
  That glut themselves on the corpse of Oedipus' son.
  The gods are deaf when we pray to them, their fire
  Recoils from our offering, their birds of omen   30
  Have no cry of comfort, for they are gorged
  With the thick blood of the dead.
                                      O my son,
  These are no trifles! Think: all men make mistakes,
  But a good man yields when he knows his course is wrong,
  And repairs the evil. The only crime is pride.

  Give in to the dead man, then: do not fight with a corpse—
  What glory is it to kill a man who is dead?
  Think, I beg you:
  It is for your own good that I speak as I do.
  You should be able to yield for your own good.   40
Creon.   It seems that prophets have made me their especial province.
  All my life long

---

[14] The god of fire.

I have been a kind of butt for the dull arrows
Of doddering fortune-tellers!
                              No, Teiresias:
If your birds—if the great eagles of God himself
Should carry him stinking bit by bit to heaven,
I would not yield. I am not afraid of pollution:
No man can defile the gods.
                              Do what you will,
Go into business, make money, speculate
In India gold or that synthetic gold from Sardis,   50
Get rich otherwise than by my consent to bury him.
Teiresias, it is a sorry thing when a wise man
Sells his wisdom, lets out his words for hire!
Teiresias.   Ah Creon! Is there no man left in the world—
Creon.   To do what?—Come, let's have the aphorism!
Teiresias.   No man who knows that wisdom outweighs any wealth?
Creon.   As surely as bribes are baser than any baseness.
Teiresias.   You are sick, Creon! You are deathly sick!
Creon.   As you say: it is not my place to challenge a prophet.
Teiresias.   Yet you have said my prophecy is for sale.   60
Creon.   The generation of prophets has always loved gold.
Teiresias.   The generation of kings has always loved brass.
Creon.   You forget yourself! You are speaking to your King.
Teiresias.   I know it. You are a king because of me.
Creon.   You have a certain skill; but you have sold out.
Teiresias.   King, you will drive me to words that—
Creon.   Say them, say them!
   Only remember: I will not pay you for them.
Teiresias.   No, you will find them too costly.
Creon.   No doubt. Speak:
   Whatever you say, you will not change my will.
Teiresias.   Then take this, and take it to heart!   70
   The time is not far off when you shall pay back
   Corpse for corpse, flesh of your own flesh.
   You have thrust the child of this world into living night,
   You have kept from the gods below the child that is theirs:
   The one in a grave before her death, the other,
   Dead, denied the grave. This is your crime:
   And the Furies and the dark gods of Hell
   Are swift with terrible punishment for you.

   Do you want to buy me now, Creon?
                              Not many days,
   And your house will be full of men and women weeping,   80
   And curses will be hurled at you from far
   Cities grieving for sons unburied, left to rot
   Before the walls of Thebes.

These are my arrows, Creon: they are all for you.

[*To boy.*] But come, child: lead me home.
Let him waste his fine anger upon younger men.
Maybe he will learn at last
To control a wiser tongue in a better head.

[*Exit Teiresias.*]

Choragos.   The old man has gone, King, but his words
Remain to plague us. I am old, too,   90
But I cannot remember that he was ever false.
Creon.   That is true. . . . It troubles me.
Oh it is hard to give in! but it is worse
To risk everything for stubborn pride.
Choragos.   Creon: take my advice.
Creon.   What shall I do?
Choragos.   Go quickly: free Antigonê from her vault
And build a tomb for the body of Polyneicês.
Creon.   You would have me do this?
Choragos.   Creon, yes!
And it must be done at once: God moves
Swiftly to cancel the folly of stubborn men.   100
Creon.   It is hard to deny the heart! But I
Will do it: I will not fight with destiny.
Choragos.   You must go yourself, you cannot leave it to others.
Creon.   I will go.
                    —Bring axes, servants:
Come with me to the tomb. I buried her, I
Will set her free.
                    Oh quickly!
My mind misgives—
The laws of the gods are mighty, and a man must serve them
To the last days of his life!

[*Exit Creon.*]

Paean[15]

Choragos.   God of many names   [*Strophe 1*]
Chorus.   O Iacchos[16]
                                        son

of Kadmeian Sémelê
                    O born of the Thunder!

---

[15] A hymn.
[16] Iacchos is a name for Dionysos. His mother was Sémelê, daughter of Kadmos, the founder
of Thebes. His father was Zeus. The Maenads were priestesses of Dionysos who cry "evohé evohé."

Guardian of the West
                        Regent
of Eleusis's plain
                        O Prince of maenad Thebes
and the Dragon Field by rippling Ismenos:[17]

Choragos.   God of many names   [*Antistrophe 1*]
Chorus.   the flame of torches
flares on our hills
                        the nymphs of Iacchos
dance at the spring of Castalia:[18]
from the vine-close mountain
                                come ah come in ivy:
Evohé evohé! sings through the streets of Thebes   10

Choragos.   God of many names   [*Strophe 2*]
Chorus.   Iacchos of Thebes
heavenly Child
                        of Sémelê bride of the Thunderer!
The shadow of plague is upon us:
                                come
with clement feet
                        oh come from Parnasos
down the long slopes
                        across the lamenting water

Choragos.   Iô Fire! Chorister of the throbbing stars!   [*Antistrophe 2*]
O purest among the voices of the night!
Thou son of God, blaze for us!
Chorus.   Come with choric rapture of circling Maenads
Who cry *Iô Iacche!*
                        God of many names!   20

Exodos

[*Enter Messenger, L.*]

Messenger.   Men of the line of Kadmos, you who live
Near Amphion's[19] citadel:
                        I cannot say

---

[17] A river of Thebes, sacred to Apollo. Dragon Field refers to the legend that the ancestors of Thebes sprang from the dragon's teeth sown by Kadmus.

[18] A spring on Mt. Parnasos.

[19] A child of Zeus and Antiope. He is noted for building the walls of Thebes by charming the stones into place with a lyre.

Of any condition of human life "This is fixed,
This is clearly good, or bad." Fate raises up,
And Fate casts down the happy and unhappy alike:
No man can foretell his Fate.
                              Take the case of Creon:
Creon was happy once, as I count happiness:
Victorious in battle, sole governor of the land,
Fortunate father of children nobly born.
And now it has all gone from him! Who can say   10
That a man is still alive when his life's joy fails?
He is a walking dead man. Grant him rich,
Let him live like a king in his great house:
If his pleasure is gone, I would not give
So much as the shadow of smoke for all he owns.

Choragos.   Your words hint at sorrow: what is your news for us?
Messenger.   They are dead. The living are guilty of their death.
Choragos.   Who is guilty? Who is dead? Speak!
Messenger.   Haimon.
  Haimon is dead; and the hand that killed him
  Is his own hand.
Choragos.   His father's? or his own?   20
Messenger.   His own, driven mad by the murder his father had done.
Choragos.   Teiresias, Teiresias, how clearly you saw it all!
Messenger.   This is my news: you must draw what conclusions you can from
                  it.
Choragos.   But look: Eurydicê, our Queen:
  Has she overheard us?

[*Enter Eurydicê from the Palace, C.*]

Eurydicê.   I have heard something, friends:
  As I was unlocking the gate of Pallas'[20] shrine,
  For I needed her help today, I heard a voice
  Telling of some new sorrow. And I fainted
  There at the temple with all my maidens about me.   30
  But speak again: whatever it is, I can bear it:
  Grief and I are no strangers.
Messenger.   Dearest Lady,
  I will tell you plainly all that I have seen.
  I shall not try to comfort you: what is the use,
  Since comfort could lie only in what is not true?
  The truth is always best.
                            I went with Creon
  To the outer plain where Polyneicês was lying,

---

[20] Pallas Athene, goddess of wisdom.

No friend to pity him, his body shredded by dogs.
We made our prayers in that place to Hecatê[21]
And Pluto,[22] that they would be merciful. And we bathed   40
The corpse with holy water, and we brought
Fresh-broken branches to burn what was left of it,
And upon the urn we heaped up a towering barrow
Of the earth of his own land.
                  When we were done, we ran
To the vault where Antigonê lay on her couch of stone.
One of the servants had gone ahead,
And while he was yet far off he heard a voice
Grieving within the chamber, and he came back
And told Creon. And as the King went closer,
The air was full of wailing, the words lost,   50
And he begged us to make all haste. "Am I a prophet?"
He said, weeping, "And must I walk this road,
The saddest of all that I have gone before?
My son's voice calls me on. Oh quickly, quickly!
Look through the crevice there, and tell me
If it is Haimon, or some deception of the gods!"

We obeyed; and in the cavern's farthest corner
We saw her lying:
She had made a noose of her fine linen veil
And hanged herself. Haimon lay beside her,   60
His arms about her waist, lamenting her,
His love lost under ground, crying out
That his father had stolen her away from him.

When Creon saw him the tears rushed to his eyes
And he called to him: "What have you done, child? Speak to me.
What are you thinking that makes your eyes so strange?
O my son, my son, I come to you on my knees!"
But Haimon spat in his face. He said not a word,
Staring—
           And suddenly drew his sword
And lunged. Creon shrank back, the blade missed; and the boy,   70
Desperate against himself, drove it half its length
Into his own side, and fell. And as he died
He gathered Antigonê close in his arms again,
Choking, his blood bright red on her white cheek.

---

[21] Hecatê is often identified with Persephone, a goddess of Hades; generally Hecatê is a goddess of sorcery and witchcraft.

[22] King of Hades and brother of Zeus and Poseidon.

And now he lies dead with the dead, and she is his
At last, his bride in the houses of the dead.

[*Exit Eurydicê into the Palace.*]

Choragos.   She has left us without a word. What can this mean?
Messenger.   It troubles me, too; yet she knows what is best,
Her grief is too great for public lamentation,
And doubtless she has gone to her chamber to weep   80
For her dead son, leading her maidens in his dirge.
Choragos.   It may be so: but I fear this deep silence.

[*Pause.*]

Messenger.   I will see what she is doing. I will go in.

[*Exit Messenger into the Palace.*]
[*Enter Creon with attendants, bearing Haimon's body.*]

Choragos.   But here is the King himself: oh look at him,
Bearing his own damnation in his arms.
Creon.   Nothing you say can touch me any more.
My own blind heart has brought me
From darkness to final darkness. Here you see
The father murdering, the murdered son—
And all my civic wisdom!   90
Haimon my son, so young to die,
I was the fool, not you; and you died for me.
Choragos.   That is the truth; but you were late in learning it.
Creon.   This truth is hard to bear. Surely a god
Has crushed me beneath the hugest weight of heaven,
And driven me headlong a barbaric way
To trample out the thing I held most dear.

The pains that men will take to come to pain!

[*Enter Messenger from the Palace.*]

Messenger.   The burden you carry in your hands is heavy,
But it is not all: you will find more in your house.   100
Creon.   What burden worse than this shall I find there?
Messenger.   The Queen is dead.
Creon.   O port of death, deaf world,
Is there no pity for me? And you, Angel of evil,
I was dead, and your words are death again.

Is it true, boy? Can it be true?
Is my wife dead? Has death bred death?
Messenger.   You can see for yourself.

[*The doors are opened, and the body of Eurydicê is disclosed within.*]

Creon.   Oh pity!
All true, all true, and more than I can bear!   110
O my wife, my son!
Messenger.   She stood before the altar, and her heart
Welcomed the knife her own hand guided,
And a great cry burst from her lips for Megareus[23] dead,
And for Haimon dead, her sons; and her last breath
Was a curse for their father, the murderer of her sons,
And she fell, and the dark flowed in through her closing eyes.
Creon.   O God, I am sick with fear.
Are there no swords here? Has no one a blow for me?
Messenger.   Her curse is upon you for the deaths of both.   120
Creon.   It is right that it should be. I alone am guilty.
I know it, and I say it. Lead me in,
Quickly, friends.
I have neither life nor substance. Lead me in.
Choragos.   You are right, if there can be right in so much wrong.
The briefest way is best in a world of sorrow.
Creon.   Let it come,
Let death come quickly, and be kind to me.
I would not ever see the sun again.
Choragos.   All that will come when it will; but we, meanwhile,   130
Have much to do. Leave the future to itself.
Creon.   All my heart was in that prayer!
Choragos.   Then do not pray any more: the sky is deaf.
Creon.   Lead me away. I have been rash and foolish.
I have killed my son and my wife.
I look for comfort; my comfort lies here dead.
Whatever my hands have touched has come to nothing.
Fate has brought all my pride to a thought of dust.

[*As Creon is being led into the house, the Choragos advances and speaks directly to the audience.*]

Choragos.   There is no happiness where there is no wisdom;
No wisdom but in submission to the gods.   140
Big words are always punished,
And proud men in old age learn to be wise.

---

[23] Son of Creon who was killed in the attack on Thebes.

QUESTIONS

1. Critics have traditionally divided over the question of whether Antigonê or Creon is the protagonist in the play. How does the answer to this question affect one's interpretation of the play? **2.** How does the Prologue establish the mood and theme of the play? **3.** Does the character of Antigonê change during the course of the play? **4.** Does the action of the play prepare us for the change in Creon—that is, for his realization that he has been wrong? **5.** Is there any justification for Antigonê's cold refusal to allow Ismenê to share her martyrdom? Explain.

WRITING TOPICS

1. Can *Antigonê* be read as a justification for civil disobedience? Explain. **2.** To what extent and in what ways does the Chorus contribute to the dramatic development and tension of the play?

A Doll's House[*] (1879)

HENRIK IBSEN [1828–1906]

CHARACTERS

Torvald Helmer, a lawyer
Nora, his wife
Dr. Rank
Mrs. Linde
Krogstad

The Helmers' three small children
Anne-Marie, the children's nurse
A Housemaid
A Porter

SCENE. *The Helmers' living room.*

Act I

A pleasant, tastefully but not expensively furnished, living room. A door on the rear wall, right, leads to the front hall, another door, left, to Helmer's study. Between the two doors a piano. A third door in the middle of the left wall; further front a window. Near the window a round table and a small couch. Towards the rear of the right wall a fourth door; further front a tile stove with a rocking chair and a couple of armchairs in front of it. Between the stove and the door a small table. Copperplate etchings on the walls. A whatnot with porcelain figurines and other small objects. A small bookcase with de luxe editions. A rug on the floor; fire in the stove. Winter day.

The doorbell rings, then the sound of the front door opening. Nora, dressed for outdoors, enters, humming cheerfully. She carries several packages, which she puts down on the table, right. She leaves the door to the front hall open; there a Porter is seen holding a Christmas tree and a basket. He gives them to the Maid who has let them in.

Nora.   Be sure to hide the Christmas tree, Helene. The children mustn't see it before tonight when we've trimmed it. (*Opens her purse; to the Porter.*) How much?
Porter.   Fifty øre.
Nora.   Here's a crown. No, keep the change. (*The Porter thanks her, leaves. Nora closes the door. She keeps laughing quietly to herself as she takes off her coat, etc. She takes a bag of macaroons from her pocket and eats a couple. She walks cautiously over to the door to the study and listens.*) Yes, he's home. (*Resumes her humming, walks over to the table, right.*)
Helmer (*in his study*).   Is that my little lark twittering out there?
Nora (*opening some packages*).   That's right.

---

[*] A new translation by Otto Reinert.

Helmer.   My squirrel bustling about?

Nora.   Yes.

Helmer.   When did squirrel come home?

Nora.   Just now. *(Puts the bag of macaroons back in her pocket, wipes her mouth.)* Come out here, Torvald. I want to show you what I've bought.

Helmer.   I'm busy! *(After a little while he opens the door and looks in, pen in hand.)* Bought, eh? All that? So little wastrel has been throwing money around again?

Nora.   Oh but Torvald, this Christmas we can be a little extravagant, can't we? It's the first Christmas we don't have to scrimp.

Helmer.   I don't know about that. We certainly don't have money to waste.

Nora.   Yes, Torvald, we do. A little, anyway. Just a tiny little bit? Now that you're going to get that big salary and make lots and lots of money.

Helmer.   Starting at New Year's, yes. But payday isn't till the end of the quarter.

Nora.   That doesn't matter. We can always borrow.

Helmer.   Nora! *(Goes over to her and playfully pulls her ear.)* There you go being irresponsible again. Suppose I borrowed a thousand crowns today and you spent it all for Christmas and on New Year's Eve a tile hit me in the head and laid me out cold.

Nora *(putting her hand over his mouth).*   I won't have you say such horrid things.

Helmer.   But suppose it happened. Then what?

Nora.   If it did, I wouldn't care whether we owed money or not.

Helmer.   But what about the people I had borrowed from?

Nora.   Who cares about them! They are strangers.

Helmer.   Nora, Nora, you *are* a woman! No, really! You know how I feel about that. No debts! A home in debt isn't a free home, and if it isn't free it isn't beautiful. We've managed nicely so far, you and I, and that's the way we'll go on. It won't be for much longer.

Nora *(walks over toward the stove).*   All right, Torvald. Whatever you say.

Helmer *(follows her).*   Come, come, my little songbird mustn't droop her wings. What's this? Can't have a pouty squirrel in the house, you know. *(Takes out his wallet.)* Nora, what do you think I have here?

Nora *(turns around quickly).*   Money!

Helmer.   Here. *(Gives her some bills.)* Don't you think I know Christmas is expensive?

Nora *(counting).*   Ten—twenty—thirty—forty. Thank you, thank you, Torvald. This helps a lot.

Helmer.   I certainly hope so.

Nora.   It does, it does. But I want to show you what I got. It was cheap, too. Look. New clothes for Ivar. And a sword. And a horse and trumpet for Bob. And a doll and a little bed for Emmy. It isn't any good, but it wouldn't last, anyway. And here's some dress material and scarves for the maids. I feel bad about old Anne-Marie, though. She really should be getting much more.

Helmer.   And what's in here?

Nora *(cries).* Not till tonight!

Helmer. I see. But now what does my little prodigal have in mind for herself?

Nora. Oh, nothing. I really don't care.

Helmer. Of course you do. Tell me what you'd like. Within reason.

Nora. Oh, I don't know. Really, I don't. The only thing—

Helmer. Well?

Nora *(fiddling with his buttons, without looking at him).* If you really want to give me something, you might—you could—

Helmer. All right, let's have it.

Nora *(quickly).* Some money, Torvald. Just as much as you think you can spare. Then I'll buy myself something one of these days.

Helmer. No, really Nora—

Nora. Oh yes, please, Torvald. Please? I'll wrap the money in pretty gold paper and hang it on the tree. Won't that be nice?

Helmer. What's the name for little birds that are always spending money?

Nora. Wastrels, I know. But please let's do it my way, Torvald. Then I'll have time to decide what I need most. Now that's sensible, isn't it?

Helmer *(smiling).* Oh, very sensible. That is, if you really bought yourself something you could use. But it all disappears in the household expenses or you buy things you don't need. And then you come back to me for more.

Nora. Oh, but Torvald—

Helmer. That's the truth, dear little Nora, and you know it. *(Puts his arm around her.)* My wastrel is a little sweetheart, but she *does* go through an awful lot of money awfully fast. You've no idea how expensive it is for a man to keep a wastrel.

Nora. That's not fair, Torvald. I really save all I can.

Helmer *(laughs).* Oh, I believe that. All you can. Meaning, exactly nothing!

Nora *(hums, smiles mysteriously).* You don't know all the things we songbirds and squirrels need money for, Torvald.

Helmer. You know, you're funny. Just like your father. You're always looking for ways to get money, but as soon as you do it runs through your fingers and you can never say what you spent it for. Well, I guess I'll just have to take you the way you are. It's in your blood. Yes, that sort of thing is hereditary, Nora.

Nora. In that case, I wish I had inherited many of Daddy's qualities.

Helmer. And I don't want you any different from just what you are—my own sweet little songbird. Hey!—I think I just noticed something. Aren't you looking—what's the word?—a little—sly—?

Nora. I am?

Helmer. You definitely are. Look at me.

Nora *(looks at him).* Well?

Helmer *(wagging a finger).* Little sweet-tooth hasn't by any chance been on a rampage today, has she?

Nora. Of course not. Whatever makes you think that?

Helmer. A little detour by the pastryshop maybe?

Nora.   No, I assure you, Torvald—

Helmer.   Nibbled a little jam?

Nora.   Certainly not!

Helmer.   Munched a macaroon or two?

Nora.   No, really, Torvald, I honestly—

Helmer.   All right. Of course I was only joking.

Nora *(walks toward the table, right)*.   You know I wouldn't do anything to displease you.

Helmer.   I know. And I have your promise. *(Over to her.)* All right, keep your little Christmas secrets to yourself, Nora darling. They'll all come out tonight, I suppose, when we light the tree.

Nora.   Did you remember to invite Rank?

Helmer.   No, but there's no need to. He knows he'll have dinner with us. Anyway, I'll see him later this morning. I'll ask him then. I did order some good wine. Oh Nora, you've no idea how much I'm looking forward to tonight!

Nora.   Me, too. And the children Torvald! They'll have such a good time!

Helmer.   You know, it *is* nice to have a good, safe job and a comfortable income. Feels good just thinking about it. Don't you agree?

Nora.   Oh, it's wonderful!

Helmer.   Remember last Christmas? For three whole weeks you shut yourself up every evening till long after midnight making ornaments for the Christmas tree and I don't know what else. Some big surprise for all of us, anyway. I'll be damned if I've ever been so bored in my whole life!

Nora.   I wasn't bored at all!

Helmer *(smiling)*.   But you've got to admit you didn't have much to show for it in the end.

Nora.   Oh, don't tease me again about that! Could I help it that the cat got in and tore up everything?

Helmer.   Of course you couldn't, my poor little Nora. You just wanted to please the rest of us, and that's the important thing. But I *am* glad the hard times are behind us. Aren't you?

Nora.   Oh yes. I think it's just wonderful.

Helmer.   This year, I won't be bored and lonely. And you won't have to strain your dear eyes and your delicate little hands—

Nora *(claps her hands)*.   No I won't, will I Torvald? Oh, how wonderful, how lovely, to hear you say that! *(Puts her arm under his.)* Let me tell you how I think we should arrange things, Torvald. Soon as Christmas is over—*(The doorbell rings.)* Someone's at the door. *(Straightens things up a bit.)* A caller, I suppose. Bother!

Helmer.   Remember, I'm not home for visitors.

The Maid *(in the door to the front hall)*.   Ma'am, there's a lady here—

Nora.   All right. Ask her to come in.

The Maid *(to Helmer)*.   And the Doctor just arrived.

Helmer.   Is he in the study?

The Maid.   Yes, sir.

Helmer exits into his study. The Maid shows Mrs. Linde in and closes the door behind her as she leaves. Mrs. Linde is in travel dress.

Mrs. Linde *(timid and a little hesitant)*.   Good morning, Nora.

Nora *(uncertainly)*.   Good morning.

Mrs. Linde.   I don't believe you know who I am.

Nora.   No—I'm not sure—Though I know I should—Of course! Kristine! It's you!

Mrs. Linde.   Yes, it's me.

Nora.   And I didn't even recognize you! I had no idea! *(In a lower voice.)* You've changed, Kristine.

Mrs. Linde.   I'm sure I have. It's been nine or ten long years.

Nora.   Has it really been that long? Yes, you're right. I've been so happy these last eight years. And now you're here. Such a long trip in the middle of winter. How brave!

Mrs. Linde.   I got in on the steamer this morning.

Nora.   To have some fun over the holidays, of course. That's lovely. For we are going to have fun. But take off your coat! You aren't cold, are you? *(Helps her.)* There, now! Let's sit down here by the fire and just relax and talk. No, you sit there. I want the rocking chair. *(Takes her hands.)* And now you've got your old face back. It was just for a minute, right at first—Though you are a little more pale, Kristine. And maybe a little thinner.

Mrs. Linde.   And much, much older, Nora.

Nora.   Maybe a little older. Just a teeny-weeny bit, not much. *(Interrupts herself, serious.)* Oh, but how thoughtless of me, chatting away like this! Sweet, good Kristine, can you forgive me?

Mrs. Linde.   Forgive you what, Nora?

Nora *(in a low voice)*.   You poor dear, you lost your husband, didn't you?

Mrs. Linde.   Three years ago, yes.

Nora.   I know. I saw it in the paper. Oh please believe me, Kristine. I really meant to write you, but I never got around to it. Something was always coming up.

Mrs. Linde.   Of course, Nora. I understand.

Nora.   No, that wasn't very nice of me. You poor thing, all you must have been through. And he didn't leave you much, either, did he?

Mrs. Linde.   No.

Nora.   And no children?

Mrs. Linde.   No.

Nora.   Nothing at all, in other words?

Mrs. Linde.   Not so much as a sense of loss—a grief to live on—

Nora *(incredulous)*.   But Kristine, how can that *be?*

Mrs. Linde *(with a sad smile, strokes Nora's hair)*.   That's the way it sometimes is, Nora.

Nora.   All alone. How awful for you. I have three darling children. You can't see them right now, though; they're out with their nurse. But now you must tell me everything—

Mrs. Linde.   No, no; I'd rather listen to you.

Nora.   No, you begin. Today I won't be selfish. Today I'll think only of you. Except there's one thing I've just got to tell you first. Something marvelous that's happened to us just these last few days. You haven't heard, have you?

Mrs. Linde.   No; tell me.

Nora.   Just think. My husband's been made manager of the Mutual Bank.

Mrs. Linde.   Your husband—! Oh, I'm so glad!

Nora.   Yes, isn't that great? You see, private law practice is so uncertain, especially when you won't have anything to do with cases that aren't—you know—quite nice. And of course Torvald won't do that and I quite agree with him. Oh, you've no idea how delighted we are! He takes over at New Year's, and he'll be getting a big salary and all sorts of extras. From now on we'll be able to live in quite a different way—exactly as we like. Oh, Kristine! I feel so carefree and happy! It's lovely to have lots and lots of money and not have to worry about a thing! Don't you agree?

Mrs. Linde.   It would be nice to have enough at any rate.

Nora.   No, I don't mean just enough. I mean lots and lots!

Mrs. Linde (*smiles*).   Nora, Nora, when are you going to be sensible? In school you spent a great deal of money.

Nora (*quietly laughing*).   Yes, and Torvald says I still do. (*Raises her finger at Mrs. Linde.*) But "Nora, Nora" isn't so crazy as you all think. Believe me, we've had nothing to be extravagant with. We've both had to work.

Mrs. Linde.   You too?

Nora.   Yes. Oh, it's been little things, mostly—sewing, crocheting, embroidery—that sort of thing. (*Casually.*) And other things too. You know, of course, that Torvald left government service when we got married? There was no chance of promotion in his department, and of course he had to make more money than he had been making. So for the first few years he worked altogether too hard. He had to take jobs on the side and work night and day. It turned out to be too much for him. He became seriously ill. The doctors told him he needed to go south.

Mrs. Linde.   That's right; you spent a year in Italy, didn't you?

Nora.   Yes, we did. But you won't believe how hard it was to get away. Ivar had just been born. But of course we had to go. Oh, it was a wonderful trip. And it saved Torvald's life. But it took a lot of money, Kristine.

Mrs. Linde.   I'm sure it did.

Nora.   Twelve hundred specie dollars. Four thousand eight hundred crowns. That's a lot of money.

Mrs. Linde.   Yes. So it's lucky you have it when something like that happens.

Nora.   Well, actually we got the money from Daddy.

Mrs. Linde.   I see. That was about the time your father died, I believe.

Nora.   Yes, just about then. And I couldn't even go and take care of him. I was expecting little Ivar any day. And I had poor Torvald to look after, desperately sick and all. My dear, good Daddy! I never saw him again, Kristine. That's the saddest thing that's happened to me since I got married.

Mrs. Linde.   I know you were very fond of him. But then you went to Italy?

Nora. Yes, for now we had the money, and the doctors urged us to go. So we left about a month later.

Mrs. Linde. And when you came back your husband was well again?

Nora. Healthy as a horse!

Mrs. Linde. But—the doctor?

Nora. What do you mean?

Mrs. Linde. I thought the maid said it was the doctor, that gentleman who came the same time I did.

Nora. Oh, that's Dr. Rank. He doesn't come as a doctor. He's our closest friend. He looks in at least once every day. No, Torvald hasn't been sick once since then. And the children are strong and healthy, too, and so am I. *(Jumps up and claps her hands.)* Oh God, Kristine! Isn't it wonderful to be alive and happy! Isn't it just lovely!—But now I'm being mean again, talking only about myself and my things. *(Sits down on a footstool close to Mrs. Linde and puts her arms on her lap.)* Please don't be angry with me! Tell me, is it really true that you didn't care for your husband? Then why did you marry him?

Mrs. Linde. Mother was still alive then, but she was bedridden and helpless. And I had my two younger brothers to look after. I didn't think I had the right to turn him down.

Nora. No, I suppose not. So he had money then?

Mrs. Linde. He was quite well off, I think. But it was an uncertain business, Nora. When he died, the whole thing collapsed and there was nothing left.

Nora. And then—?

Mrs. Linde. Well, I had to manage as best I could. With a little store and a little school and anything else I could think of. The last three years have been one long work day for me, Nora, without any rest. But now it's over. My poor mother doesn't need me any more. She's passed away. And the boys are on their own too. They've both got jobs and support themselves.

Nora. What a relief for you—

Mrs. Linde. No, not relief. Just a great emptiness. Nobody to live for any more. *(Gets up restlessly.)* That's why I couldn't stand it any longer in that little hole. Here in town it has to be easier to find something to keep me busy and occupy my thoughts. With a little luck I should be able to find a permanent job, something in an office—

Nora. Oh but Kristine, that's exhausting work, and you look worn out already. It would be much better for you to go to a resort.

Mrs. Linde *(walks over to the window)*. I don't have a Daddy who can give me the money, Nora.

Nora *(getting up)*. Oh, don't be angry with me.

Mrs. Linde *(over to her)*. Dear Nora, don't *you* be angry with *me*. That's the worst thing about my kind of situation: you become so bitter. You've nobody to work for, and yet you have to look out for yourself, somehow. You've got to keep on living, and so you become selfish. Do you know—when you told me about your husband's new position I was delighted not so much for your sake as for my own.

Nora.   Why was that? Oh, I see. You think maybe Torvald can give you a job?

Mrs. Linde.   That's what I had in mind.

Nora.   And he will too, Kristine. Just leave it to me. I'll be ever so subtle about it. I'll think of something nice to tell him, something he'll like. Oh I so much want to help you.

Mrs. Linde.   That's very good of you, Nora—making an effort like that for me. Especially since you've known so little trouble and hardship in your own life.

Nora.   I—?—have known so little—?

Mrs. Linde (*smiling*).   Oh well, a little sewing or whatever it was. You're still a child, Nora.

Nora (*with a toss of her head, walks away*).   You shouldn't sound so superior.

Mrs. Linde.   I shouldn't?

Nora.   You're just like all the others. None of you think I'm good for anything really serious.

Mrs. Linde.   Well, now—

Nora.   That I've never been through anything difficult.

Mrs. Linde.   But Nora! You just told me all your troubles!

Nora.   That's nothing! (*Lowers her voice.*) I haven't told you about *it.*

Mrs. Linde.   It? What's that? What do you mean?

Nora.   You patronize me, Kristine, and that's not fair. You're proud that you worked so long and so hard for your mother.

Mrs. Linde.   I don't think I patronize anyone. But it *is* true that I'm both proud and happy that I could make mother's last years comparatively easy.

Nora.   And you're proud of all you did for your brothers.

Mrs. Linde.   I think I have the right to be.

Nora.   And so do I. But now I want to tell you something, Kristine. I have something to be proud and happy about too.

Mrs. Linde.   I don't doubt that for a moment. But what exactly do you mean?

Nora.   Not so loud! Torvald mustn't hear—not for anything in the world. Nobody must know about this, Kristine. Nobody but you.

Mrs. Linde.   But what is it?

Nora.   Come here. (*Pulls her down on the couch beside her.*) You see, I *do* have something to be proud and happy about. I've saved Torvald's life.

Mrs. Linde.   Saved—? How do you mean—"saved"?

Nora.   I told you about our trip to Italy. Torvald would have died if he hadn't gone.

Mrs. Linde.   I understand that. And so your father gave you the money you needed.

Nora (*smiles*).   Yes, that's what Torvald and all the others think. But—

Mrs. Linde.   But what?

Nora.   Daddy didn't give us a penny. *I* raised that money.

Mrs. Linde.   *You* did? That whole big amount?

Nora.   Twelve hundred specie dollars. Four thousand eight hundred crowns. *Now* what do you say?

Mrs. Linde.   But Nora, how could you? Did you win in the state lottery?

Nora *(contemptuously).*   State lottery! *(Snorts.)* What is so great about that?

Mrs. Linde.   Where did it come from then?

Nora *(humming and smiling, enjoying her secret).*   Hmmm. Tra-la-la-la-la!

Mrs. Linde.   You certainly couldn't have borrowed it.

Nora.   Oh? And why not?

Mrs. Linde.   A wife can't borrow money without her husband's consent.

Nora *(with a toss of her head).*   Oh, I don't know—take a wife with a little bit
of a head for business—a wife who knows how to manage things—

Mrs. Linde.   But Nora, I don't understand at all—

Nora.   You don't have to. I didn't say I borrowed the money, did I? I could
have gotten it some other way. *(Leans back.)* An admirer may have given it
to me. When you're as tolerably goodlooking as I am—

Mrs. Linde.   Oh, you're crazy.

Nora.   I think you're dying from curiosity, Kristine.

Mrs. Linde.   I'm beginning to think you've done something very foolish, Nora.

Nora *(sits up).*   Is it foolish to save your husband's life?

Mrs. Linde.   I say it's foolish to act behind his back.

Nora.   But don't you see: he couldn't be told! You're missing the whole point,
Kristine. We couldn't even let him know how seriously ill he was. The doctors
came to *me* and told me his life was in danger, that nothing could save him
but a stay in the south. Don't you think I tried to work on him? I told him
how lovely it would be if I could go abroad like other young wives. I cried
and begged. I said he'd better remember what condition I was in, that he had
to be nice to me and do what I wanted. I even hinted he could borrow the
money. But that almost made him angry with me. He told me I was being
irresponsible and that it was his duty as my husband not to give in to my
moods and whims—I think that's what he called it. All right, I said to myself,
you've got to be saved somehow, and so I found a way—

Mrs. Linde.   And your husband never learned from your father that the money
didn't come from him?

Nora.   Never. Daddy died that same week. I thought of telling him all about
it and ask him not to say anything. But since he was so sick—It turned out
I didn't have to—

Mrs. Linde.   And you've never told your husband?

Nora.   Of course not! Good heavens, how could I? He, with his strict principles! Besides, you know how men are. Torvald would find it embarrassing
and humiliating to learn that he owed me anything. It would upset our whole
relationship. Our happy, beautiful home would no longer be what it is.

Mrs. Linde.   Aren't you ever going to tell him?

Nora *(reflectively, half smiling).*   Yes—one day, maybe. Many, many years
from now, when I'm no longer young and pretty. Don't laugh! I mean when
Torvald no longer feels about me the way he does now, when he no longer
thinks it's fun when I dance for him and put on costumes and recite for him.
Then it will be good to have something in reserve—*(Interrupts herself.)* Oh,

I'm just being silly! That day will never come.—Well, now, Kristine, what do you think of my great secret? Don't you think I'm good for something too?—By the way, you wouldn't believe all the worry I've had because of it. It's been very hard to meet my obligations on schedule. You see, in business there's something called quarterly interest and something called installments on the principal, and those are terribly hard to come up with. I've had to save a little here and a little there, whenever I could. I couldn't use much of the housekeeping money, for Torvald has to eat well. And I couldn't use what I got for clothes for the children. They have to look nice, and I didn't think it would be right to spend less than I got—the sweet little things!

Mrs. Linde.   Poor Nora! So you had to take it from your own allowance!

Nora.   Yes, of course. After all, it was my affair. Every time Torvald gave me money for a new dress and things like that, I never used more than half of it. I always bought the cheapest, simplest things for myself. Thank God, everything looks good on me, so Torvald never noticed. But it was hard many times, Kristine, for it's fun to have pretty clothes. Don't you think?

Mrs. Linde.   Certainly.

Nora.   Anyway, I had other ways of making money too. Last winter I was lucky enough to get some copying work. So I locked the door and sat up writing every night till quite late. God! I often got so tired—! But it was great fun, too, working and making money. It was almost like being a man.

Mrs. Linde.   But how much have you been able to pay off this way?

Nora.   I couldn't tell you exactly. You see, it's very difficult to keep track of business like that. All I know is I have been paying off as much as I've been able to scrape together. Many times I just didn't know what to do. (*Smiles.*) Then I used to imagine a rich old gentleman had fallen in love with me—

Mrs. Linde.   What! What old gentleman?

Nora.   Phooey! And now he was dead and they were reading his will, and there it said in big letters, "All my money is to be paid in cash immediately to the charming Mrs. Nora Helmer."

Mrs. Linde.   But dearest Nora—who *was* this old gentleman?

Nora.   For heaven's sake, Kristine, don't you see? There *was* no old gentleman. He was just somebody I made up when I couldn't think of any way to raise the money. But never mind him. The old bore can be anyone he likes to for all I care. I have no use for him or his last will, for now I don't have a single worry in the world. (*Jumps up.*) Dear God, what a lovely thought this is! To be able to play and have fun with the children, to have everything nice and pretty in the house, just the way Torvald likes it! Not a care! And soon spring will be here, and the air will be blue and high. Maybe we can travel again. Maybe I'll see the ocean again! Oh, yes, yes!—it's wonderful to be alive and happy!

The doorbell rings.

Mrs. Linde (*getting up*).   There's the doorbell. Maybe I better be going.

Nora.   No, please stay. I'm sure it's just someone for Torvald—

The Maid (*in the hall door*).   Excuse me, ma'am. There's a gentleman here who'd like to see Mr. Helmer.

Nora.   You mean the bank manager.

The Maid.   Sorry, ma'am; the bank manager. But I didn't know—since the Doctor is with him—

Nora.   Who is the gentleman?

Krogstad (*appearing in the door*).   It's just me, Mrs. Helmer.

Mrs. Linde starts, looks, turns away toward the window.

Nora (*takes a step toward him, tense, in a low voice*).   You? What do you want? What do you want with my husband?

Krogstad.   Bank business—in a way. I have a small job in the Mutual, and I understand your husband is going to be our new boss—

Nora.   So it's just—

Krogstad.   Just routine business, ma'am. Nothing else.

Nora.   All right. In that case, why don't you go through the door to the office.

Dismisses him casually as she closes the door. Walks over to the stove and tends the fire.

Mrs. Linde.   Nora—who was that man?

Nora.   His name's Krogstad. He's a lawyer.

Mrs. Linde.   So it *was* him.

Nora.   Do you know him?

Mrs. Linde.   I used to—many years ago. For a while he clerked in our part of the country.

Nora.   Right. He did.

Mrs. Linde.   He has changed a great deal.

Nora.   I believe he had a very unhappy marriage.

Mrs. Linde.   And now he's a widower, isn't he?

Nora.   With many children. There now; it's burning nicely again. (*Closes the stove and moves the rocking chair a little to the side.*)

Mrs. Linde.   They say he's into all sorts of business.

Nora.   Really? Maybe so. I wouldn't know. But let's not think about business. It's such a bore.

Dr. Rank (*appears in the door to Helmer's study*).   No, I don't want to be in the way. I'd rather talk to your wife a bit. (*Closes the door and notices Mrs. Linde.*) Oh, I beg your pardon. I believe I'm in the way here too.

Nora.   No, not at all. (*Introduces them.*) Dr. Rank. Mrs. Linde.

Rank.   Aha. A name often heard in this house. I believe I passed you on the stairs coming up.

Mrs. Linde.   Yes. I'm afraid I climb stairs very slowly. They aren't good for me.

Rank.   I see. A slight case of inner decay, perhaps?

Mrs. Linde.   Overwork, rather.

Rank.   Oh, is that all? And now you've come to town to relax at all the parties?

Mrs. Linde.   I have come to look for a job.

Rank.   A proven cure for overwork, I take it?

Mrs. Linde.   One has to live, Doctor.

Rank.   Yes, that seems to be the common opinion.

Nora.   Come on, Dr. Rank—you want to live just as much as the rest of us.

Rank.   Of course I do. Miserable as I am, I prefer to go on being tortured as long as possible. All my patients feel the same way. And that's true of the moral invalids too. Helmer is talking with a specimen right this minute.

Mrs. Linde (*in a low voice*).   Ah!

Nora.   What do you mean?

Rank.   Oh, this lawyer, Krogstad. You don't know him. The roots of his character are decayed. But even he began by saying something about having *to live*—as if it were a matter of the highest importance.

Nora.   Oh? What did he want with Torvald?

Rank.   I don't really know. All I heard was something about the bank.

Nora.   I didn't know that Krog—that this Krogstad had anything to do with the Mutual Bank.

Rank.   Yes, he seems to have some kind of job there. (*To Mrs. Linde.*) I don't know if you are familiar in your part of the country with the kind of person who is always running around trying to sniff out cases of moral decrepitude and as soon as he finds one puts the individual under observation in some excellent position or other. All the healthy ones are left out in the cold.

Mrs. Linde.   I should think it's the sick who need looking after the most.

Rank (*shrugs his shoulders*).   There we are. That's the attitude that turns society into a hospital.

Nora, absorbed in her own thoughts, suddenly starts giggling and clapping her hands.

Rank.   What's so funny about that? Do you even know what society is?

Nora.   What do I care about your stupid society! I laughed at something entirely different—something terribly amusing. Tell me, Dr. Rank—all the employees in the Mutual Bank, from now on they'll all be dependent on Torvald, right?

Rank.   Is that what you find so enormously amusing?

Nora (*smiles and hums*).   That's my business, that's my business! (*Walks around.*) Yes, I do think it's fun that we—that Torvald is going to have so much influence on so many people's lives. (*Brings out the bag of macaroons.*) Have a macaroon, Dr. Rank.

Rank.   Well, well—macaroons. I thought they were banned around here.

Nora.   Yes, but these were some that Kristine gave me.

Mrs. Linde.   What! I?

Nora.   That's all right. Don't look so scared. You couldn't know that Torvald

won't let me have them. He's afraid they'll ruin my teeth. But who cares!
Just once in a while—! Right, Dr. Rank? Have one! *(Puts a macaroon into
his mouth.)* You too, Kristine. And one for me. A very small one. Or at most
two. *(Walks around again.)* Yes, I really feel very, very happy. Now there's
just one thing I'm dying to do.

Rank.   Oh? And what's that?

Nora.   Something I'm dying to say so Torvald could hear.

Rank.   And why can't you?

Nora.   I don't dare to, for it's not nice.

Mrs. Linde.   Not nice?

Rank.   In that case, I guess you'd better not. But surely to the two of us—?
What is it you'd like to say for Helmer to hear?

Nora.   I want to say, "Goddammit!"

Rank.   Are you out of your mind!

Mrs. Linde.   For heaven's sake, Nora!

Rank.   Say it. Here he comes.

Nora *(hiding the macaroons)*.   Shhh!

Helmer enters from his study, carrying his hat and overcoat.

Nora *(going to him)*.   Well, dear, did you get rid of him?

Helmer.   Yes, he just left.

Nora.   Torvald, I want you to meet Kristine. She's just come to town.

Helmer.   Kristine—? I'm sorry; I don't think—

Nora.   Mrs. Linde, Torvald dear. Mrs. Kristine Linde.

Helmer.   Ah, yes. A childhood friend of my wife's, I suppose.

Mrs. Linde.   Yes, we've known each other for a long time.

Nora.   Just think; she has come all this way just to see you.

Helmer.   I'm not sure I understand—

Mrs. Linde.   Well, not really—

Nora.   You see, Kristine is an absolutely fantastic secretary, and she would so
much like to work for a competent executive and learn more than she knows
already—

Helmer.   Very sensible, I'm sure, Mrs. Linde.

Nora.   So when she heard about your appointment—there was a wire—she
came here as fast as she could. How about it, Torvald? Couldn't you do
something for Kristine? For my sake. Please?

Helmer.   Quite possibly. I take it you're a widow, Mrs. Linde?

Mrs. Linde.   Yes.

Helmer.   And you've had office experience?

Mrs. Linde.   Some—yes.

Helmer.   In that case I think it's quite likely that I'll be able to find you a
position.

Nora *(claps her hands)*.   I knew it! I knew it!

Helmer.   You've arrived at a most opportune time, Mrs. Linde.

Mrs. Linde.   Oh, how can I ever thank you—

Helmer.   Not at all, not at all. *(Puts his coat on.)* But today you'll have to excuse me—

Rank.   Wait a minute; I'll come with you. *(Gets his fur coat from the front hall, warms it by the stove.)*

Nora.   Don't be long, Torvald.

Helmer.   An hour or so; no more.

Nora.   Are you leaving, too, Kristine?

Mrs. Linde *(putting on her things).*   Yes, I'd better go and find a place to stay.

Helmer.   Good. Then we'll be going the same way.

Nora *(helping her).*   I'm sorry this place is so small, but I don't think we very well could—

Mrs. Linde.   Of course! Don't be silly, Nora. Goodbye, and thank you for everything.

Nora.   Goodbye. We'll see you soon. You'll be back this evening, of course. And you too, Dr. Rank; right? If you feel well enough? Of course you will. Just wrap yourself up.

General small talk as all exit into the hall. Children's voices are heard on the stairs.

Nora.   There they are! There they are! *(She runs and opens the door. The nurse Anne-Marie enters with the children.)*

Nora.   Come in! Come in! *(Bends over and kisses them.)* Oh, you sweet, sweet darlings! Look at them, Kristine! Aren't they beautiful?

Rank.   No standing around in the draft!

Helmer.   Come along, Mrs. Linde. This place isn't fit for anyone but mothers right now.

Dr. Rank, Helmer, and Mrs. Linde go down the stairs. The Nurse enters the living room with the children. Nora follows, closing the door behind her.

Nora.   My, how nice you all look! Such red cheeks! Like apples and roses. *(The children all talk at the same time.)* You've had so much fun? I bet you have. Oh, isn't that nice! You pulled both Emmy and Bob on your sleigh? Both at the same time? That's very good, Ivar. Oh, let me hold her for a minute, Anne-Marie. My sweet little doll baby! *(Takes the smallest of the children from the Nurse and dances with her.)* Yes, yes, of course; Mama'll dance with you too, Bob. What? You threw snowballs? Oh, I wish I'd been there! No, no; I want to take their clothes off, Anne-Marie. Please let me; I think it's so much fun. You go on in. You look frozen. There's hot coffee on the stove.

The Nurse exits into the room to the left. Nora takes the children's wraps off and throws them all around. They all keep telling her things at the same time.

Nora.   Oh, really? A big dog ran after you? But it didn't bite you. Of course not. Dogs don't bite sweet little doll babies. Don't peek at the packages, Ivar! What's in them? Wouldn't you like to know! No, no; that's something terrible! Play? You want to play? What do you want to play? Okay, let's play hide-and-seek. Bob hides first. You want *me* to? All right. I'll go first.

Laughing and shouting, Nora and the children play in the living room and in the adjacent room, right. Finally, Nora hides herself under the table; the children rush in, look for her, can't find her. They hear her low giggle, run to the table, lift the rug that covers it, see her. General hilarity. She crawls out, pretends to scare them. New delight. In the meantime there has been a knock on the door between the living room and the front hall, but nobody has noticed. Now the door is opened halfway; Krogstad appears. He waits a little. The play goes on.

Krogstad.   Pardon me, Mrs. Helmer—

Nora *(with a muted cry turns around, jumps up)*.   Ah! What do you want?

Krogstad.   I'm sorry. The front door was open. Somebody must have forgotten to close it—

Nora *(standing up)*.   My husband isn't here, Mr. Krogstad.

Krogstad.   I know.

Nora.   So what do you want?

Krogstad.   I'd like a word with you.

Nora.   With—? *(To the children.)* Go in to Anne-Marie. What? No, the strange man won't do anything bad to Mama. When he's gone we'll play some more.

She takes the children into the room to the left and closes the door.

Nora *(tense, troubled)*.   You want to speak with me?

Krogstad.   Yes I do.

Nora.   Today—? It isn't the first of the month yet.

Krogstad.   No, it's Christmas Eve. It's up to you what kind of holiday you'll have.

Nora.   What do you want? I can't possibly—

Krogstad.   Let's not talk about that just yet. There's something else. You do have a few minutes, don't you?

Nora.   Yes. Yes, of course. That is,—

Krogstad.   Good. I was sitting in Olsen's restaurant when I saw your husband go by.

Nora.   Yes—?

Krogstad.   —with a lady.

Nora.   What of it?

Krogstad.   May I be so free as to ask: wasn't that lady Mrs. Linde?

Nora.   Yes.

Krogstad.   Just arrived in town?

Nora.   Yes, today.

Krogstad.   She's a good friend of yours, I understand?

Nora.   Yes, she is. But I fail to see—

Krogstad.   I used to know her myself.

Nora.   I know that.

Krogstad.   So you know about that. I thought as much. In that case, let me ask you a simple question. Is Mrs. Linde going to be employed in the bank?

Nora.   What makes you think you have the right to cross-examine me like this, Mr. Krogstad—you, one of my husband's employees? But since you ask, I'll tell you. Yes, Mrs. Linde is going to be working in the bank. And it was I who recommended her, Mr. Krogstad. Now you know.

Krogstad.   So I was right.

Nora (*walks up and down*).   After all, one does have a little influence, you know. Just because you're a woman, it doesn't mean that—Really, Mr. Krogstad, people in a subordinate position should be careful not to offend someone who—oh well—

Krogstad.   —has influence?

Nora.   Exactly.

Krogstad (*changing his tone*).   Mrs. Helmer, I must ask you to be good enough to use your influence on my behalf.

Nora.   What do you mean?

Krogstad.   I want you to make sure that I am going to keep my subordinate position in the bank.

Nora.   I don't understand. Who is going to take your position away from you?

Krogstad.   There's no point in playing ignorant with me, Mrs. Helmer. I can very well appreciate that your friend would find it unpleasant to run into me. So now I know who I can thank for my dismissal.

Nora.   But I assure you—

Krogstad.   Never mind. Just want to say you still have time. I advise you to use your influence to prevent it.

Nora.   But Mr. Krogstad, I don't have any influence—none at all.

Krogstad.   No? I thought you just said—

Nora.   Of course I didn't mean it that way. I! Whatever makes you think that I have any influence of that kind on my husband?

Krogstad.   I went to law school with your husband. I have no reason to think that the bank manager is less susceptible than other husbands.

Nora.   If you're going to insult my husband, I'll ask you to leave.

Krogstad.   You're brave, Mrs. Helmer.

Nora.   I'm not afraid of you any more. After New Year's I'll be out of this thing with you.

Krogstad (*more controlled*).   Listen, Mrs. Helmer. If necessary I'll fight as for my life to keep my little job in the bank.

Nora.   So it seems.

Krogstad.   It isn't just the money; that's really the smallest part of it. There is something else—Well, I guess I might as well tell you. It's like this. I'm sure you know, like everybody else, that some years ago I committed—an impropriety.

Nora. I believe I've heard it mentioned.

Krogstad. The case never came to court, but from that moment all doors were closed to me. So I took up the kind of business you know about. I had to do something, and I think I can say about myself that I have not been among the worst. But now I want to get out of all that. My sons are growing up. For their sake I must get back as much of my good name as I can. This job in the bank was like the first rung on the ladder. And now your husband wants to kick me down and leave me back in the mud again.

Nora. But I swear to you, Mr. Krogstad; it's not at all in my power to help you.

Krogstad. That's because you don't want to. But I have the means to force you.

Nora. You don't mean you're going to tell my husband I owe you money?

Krogstad. And if I did?

Nora. That would be a mean thing to do. (*Almost crying.*) That secret, which is my joy and my pride—for him to learn about it in such a coarse and ugly manner—to learn it from *you*—! It would be terribly unpleasant for me.

Krogstad. Just unpleasant?

Nora (*heatedly*). But go ahead! Do it! It will be worse for you than for me. When my husband realizes what a bad person you are, you'll be sure to lose your job.

Krogstad. I asked you if it was just domestic unpleasantness you were afraid of?

Nora. When my husband finds out, of course he'll pay off the loan, and then we won't have anything more to do with you.

Krogstad (*stepping closer*). Listen, Mrs. Helmer—either you have a very bad memory, or you don't know much about business. I think I had better straighten you out on a few things.

Nora. What do you mean?

Krogstad. When your husband was ill, you came to me to borrow twelve hundred dollars.

Nora. I knew nobody else.

Krogstad. I promised to get you the money—

Nora. And you did.

Krogstad. I promised to get you the money on certain conditions. At the time you were so anxious about your husband's health and so set on getting him away that I doubt very much that you paid much attention to the details of our transaction. That's why I remind you of them now. Anyway, I promised to get you the money if you would sign an I.O.U., which I drafted.

Nora. And which I signed.

Krogstad. Good. But below your signature I added a few lines, making your father security for the loan. Your father was supposed to put his signature to those lines.

Nora. Supposed to—? He did.

Krogstad.   I had left the date blank. That is, your father was to date his own signature. You recall that, don't you, Mrs. Helmer?

Nora.   I guess so—

Krogstad.   I gave the note to you. You were to mail it to your father. Am I correct?

Nora.   Yes.

Krogstad.   And of course you did so right away, for no more than five or six days later you brought the paper back to me, signed by your father. Then I paid you the money.

Nora.   Well? And haven't I been keeping up with the payments?

Krogstad.   Fairly well, yes. But to get back to what we were talking about— those were difficult days for you, weren't they, Mrs. Helmer?

Nora.   Yes, they were.

Krogstad.   Your father was quite ill, I believe.

Nora.   He was dying.

Krogstad.   And died shortly afterwards?

Nora.   That's right.

Krogstad.   Tell me, Mrs. Helmer; do you happen to remember the date of your father's death? I mean the exact day of the month?

Nora.   Daddy died on September 29.

Krogstad.   Quite correct. I have ascertained that fact. That's why there is something peculiar about this *(takes out a piece of paper)*, which I can't account for.

Nora.   Peculiar? How? I don't understand—

Krogstad.   It seems very peculiar, Mrs. Helmer, that your father signed this promissory note three days after his death.

Nora.   How so? I don't see what—

Krogstad.   Your father died on September 29. Now look. He has dated his signature October 2. Isn't that odd?

Nora remains silent.

Krogstad.   Can you explain it?

Nora is still silent.

Krogstad.   I also find it striking that the date and the month and the year are not in your father's handwriting but in a hand I think I recognize. Well, that might be explained. Your father may have forgotten to date his signature and somebody else may have done it here, guessing at the date before he had learned of your father's death. That's all right. It's only the signature itself that matters. And that is genuine, isn't it, Mrs. Helmer? Your father *did* put his name to this note?

Nora *(after a brief silence tosses her head back and looks defiantly at him).*   No, he didn't. *I* wrote Daddy's name.

Krogstad. Mrs. Helmer—do you realize what a dangerous admission you just made?

Nora. Why? You'll get your money soon.

Krogstad. Let me ask you something. Why didn't you mail this note to your father?

Nora. Because it was impossible. Daddy was sick—you know that. If I had asked him to sign it, I would have had to tell him what the money was for. But I couldn't tell him, as sick as he was, that my husband's life was in danger. That was impossible. Surely you can see that.

Krogstad. Then it would have been better for you if you had given up your trip abroad.

Nora. No, that was impossible! That trip was to save my husband's life. I couldn't give it up.

Krogstad. But didn't you realize that what you did amounted to fraud against me?

Nora. I couldn't let that make any difference. I didn't care about you at all. I hated the way you made all those difficulties for me, even though you knew the danger my husband was in. I thought you were cold and unfeeling.

Krogstad. Mrs. Helmer, obviously you have no clear idea of what you have done. Let me tell you that what I did that time was no more and no worse. And it ruined my name and reputation.

Nora. You! Are you trying to tell me that you did something brave once in order to save your wife's life?

Krogstad. The law doesn't ask about motives.

Nora. Then it's a bad law.

Krogstad. Bad or not—if I produce this note in court you'll be judged according to the law.

Nora. I refuse to believe you. A daughter shouldn't have the right to spare her dying old father worry and anxiety? A wife shouldn't have the right to save her husband's life? I don't know the laws very well, but I'm sure that somewhere they make allowance for cases like that. And you, a lawyer, don't know that? I think you must be a bad lawyer, Mr. Krogstad.

Krogstad. That may be. But business—the kind of business you and I have with one another—don't you think I know something about that? Very well. Do what you like. But let me tell you this: if I'm going to be kicked out again, you'll keep me company. *(He bows and exits through the front hall.)*

Nora *(pauses thoughtfully; then, with a defiant toss of her head).* Oh, nonsense! Trying to scare me like that! I'm not all that silly. *(Starts picking up the children's clothes; soon stops.)* But—? No! That's impossible! I did it for love!

The Children *(in the door to the left).* Mama, the strange man just left. We saw him.

Nora. Yes, yes; I know. But don't tell anybody about the strange man. Do you hear? Not even Daddy.

The Children. We won't. But now you'll play with us again, won't you, Mama?

Nora.   No, not right now.

The Children.   But Mama—you promised.

Nora.   I know, but I can't just now. Go to your own room. I've so much to do. Be nice now, my little darlings. Do as I say. *(She nudges them gently into the other room and closes the door. She sits down on the couch, picks up a piece of embroidery, makes a few stitches, then stops.)* No! *(Throws the embroidery down, goes to the hall door and calls out.)* Helene! Bring the Christmas tree in here, please! *(Goes to the table, left, opens the drawer, halts.)* No—that's impossible!

The Maid *(with the Christmas tree).*   Where do you want it, ma'am?

Nora.   There. The middle of the floor.

The Maid.   You want anything else?

Nora.   No, thanks. I have everything I need. *(The Maid goes out. Nora starts trimming the tree.)* I want candles—and flowers—That awful man! Oh, nonsense! There's nothing wrong. This will be a lovely tree. I'll do everything you want me to, Torvald. I'll sing for you—dance for you—

Helmer, a bundle of papers under his arm, enters from outside.

Nora.   Ah—you're back already?

Helmer.   Yes. Has anybody been here?

Nora.   Here? No.

Helmer.   That's funny. I saw Krogstad leaving just now.

Nora.   Oh? Oh yes, that's right. Krogstad was here for just a moment.

Helmer.   I can tell from your face that he came to ask you to put in a word for him.

Nora.   Yes.

Helmer.   And it was supposed to be your own idea, wasn't it? You were not to tell me he'd been here. He asked you that too, didn't he?

Nora.   Yes, Torvald, but—

Helmer.   Nora, Nora, how could you! Talk to a man like that and make him promises! And lying to me about it afterwards—!

Nora.   Lying—?

Helmer.   Didn't you say nobody had been here? *(Shakes his finger at her.)* My little songbird must never do that again. Songbirds are supposed to have clean beaks to chirp with—no false notes. *(Puts his arm around her waist.)* Isn't that so? Of course it is. *(Lets her go.)* And that's enough about that. *(Sits down in front of the fireplace.)* Ah, it's nice and warm in here. *(Begins to leaf through his papers.)*

Nora *(busy with the tree; after a brief pause).*   Torvald.

Helmer.   Yes.

Nora.   I'm looking forward so much to the Stenborgs' costume party day after tomorrow.

Helmer.   And I can't wait to find out what you're going to surprise me with.

Nora.   Oh, that silly idea!

Helmer.   Oh?

Nora.   I can't think of anything. It all seems so foolish and pointless.

Helmer.   Ah, my little Nora admits that?

Nora *(behind his chair, her arms on the back of the chair)*.   Are you very busy, Torvald?

Helmer.   Well—

Nora.   What are all those papers?

Helmer.   Bank business.

Nora.   Already?

Helmer.   I've asked the board to give me the authority to make certain changes in organization and personnel. That's what I'll be doing over the holidays. I want it all settled before New Year's.

Nora.   So that's why this poor Krogstad—

Helmer.   Hm.

Nora *(leisurely playing with the hair on his neck)*.   If you weren't so busy, Torvald, I'd ask you for a great big favor.

Helmer.   Let's hear it, anyway.

Nora.   I don't know anyone with better taste than you, and I want so much to look nice at the party. Couldn't you sort of take charge of me, Torvald, and decide what I'll wear—Help me with my costume?

Helmer.   Aha! Little Lady Obstinate is looking for someone to rescue her?

Nora.   Yes, Torvald. I won't get anywhere without your help.

Helmer.   All right. I'll think about it. We'll come up with something.

Nora.   Oh, you *are* nice! *(Goes back to the Christmas tree. A pause.)* Those red flowers look so pretty.—Tell me, was it really all that bad what this Krogstad fellow did?

Helmer.   He forged signatures. Do you have any idea what that means?

Nora.   Couldn't it have been because he felt he had to?

Helmer.   Yes, or like so many others he may simply have been thoughtless. I'm not so heartless as to condemn a man absolutely because of a single imprudent act.

Nora.   Of course not, Torvald!

Helmer.   People like him can redeem themselves morally by openly confessing their crime and taking their punishment.

Nora.   Punishment—?

Helmer.   But that was not the way Krogstad chose. He got out of it with tricks and evasions. That's what has corrupted him.

Nora.   So you think that if—?

Helmer.   Can't you imagine how a guilty person like that has to lie and fake and dissemble wherever he goes—putting on a mask before everybody he's close to, even his own wife and children. It's this thing with the children that's the worst part of it, Nora.

Nora.   Why is that?

Helmer.   Because when a man lives inside such a circle of stinking lies he brings infection into his own home and contaminates his whole family. With every breath of air his children inhale the germs of something ugly.

Nora *(moving closer behind him).*   Are you so sure of that?

Helmer.   Of course I am. I have seen enough examples of that in my work. Nearly all young criminals have had mothers who lied.

Nora.   Why mothers—particularly?

Helmer.   Most often mothers. But of course fathers tend to have the same influence. Every lawyer knows that. And yet, for years this Krogstad has been poisoning his own children in an atmosphere of lies and deceit. That's why I call him a lost soul morally. *(Reaches out for her hands.)* And that's why my sweet little Nora must promise me never to take his side again. Let's shake on that.—What? What's this? Give me your hand. There! Now that's settled. I assure you, I would find it impossible to work in the same room with that man. I feel literally sick when I'm around people like that.

Nora *(withdraws her hand and goes to the other side of the Christmas tree).*   It's so hot in here. And I have so much to do.

Helmer *(gets up and collects his papers).*   Yes, and I really should try to get some of this reading done before dinner. I must think about your costume too. And maybe just possibly I'll have something to wrap in gilt paper and hang on the Christmas tree. *(Puts his hand on her head.)* Oh my adorable little songbird! *(Enters his study and closes the door.)*

Nora *(after a pause, in a low voice).*   It's all a lot of nonsense. It's not that way at all. It's impossible. It has to be impossible.

The Nurse *(in the door, left).*   The little ones are asking ever so nicely if they can't come in and be with their mama.

Nora.   No, no, no! Don't let them in here! You stay with them, Anne-Marie.

The Nurse.   If you say so, ma'am. *(Closes the door.)*

Nora *(pale with terror).*   Corrupt my little children—! Poison my home—? *(Brief pause; she lifts her head.)* That's not true. Never. Never in a million years.

Act II

The same room. The Christmas tree is in the corner by the piano, stripped shabby-looking, with burnt-down candles. Nora's outside clothes are on the couch. Nora is alone. She walks around restlessly. She stops by the couch and picks up her coat.

Nora *(drops the coat again).*   There's somebody now! *(Goes to the door, listens.)* No. Nobody. Of course not—not on Christmas. And not tomorrow either.[1]—But perhaps—*(Opens the door and looks.)* No, nothing in the mailbox. All empty. *(Comes forward.)* How silly I am! Of course he isn't serious. Nothing like that could happen. After all, I have three small children.

---

[1] In Norway both December 25 and 26 are legal holidays.

The Nurse enters from the room, left, carrying a big carton.

The Nurse.   Well, at last I found it—the box with your costume.

Nora.   Thanks. Just put it on the table.

Nurse *(does so)*.   But it's all a big mess, I'm afraid.

Nora.   Oh, I wish I could tear the whole thing to little pieces!

Nurse.   Heavens! It's not as bad as all that. It can be fixed all right. All it takes is a little patience.

Nora.   I'll go over and get Mrs. Linde to help me.

Nurse.   Going out again? In this awful weather? You'll catch a cold.

Nora.   That might not be such a bad thing. How are the children?

Nurse.   The poor little dears are playing with their presents, but—

Nora.   Do they keep asking for me?

Nurse.   Well, you know, they're used to being with their mamma.

Nora.   I know. But Anne-Marie, from now on I can't be with them as much as before.

Nurse.   Oh well. Little children get used to everything.

Nora.   You think so? Do you think they'll forget their mamma if I were gone altogether?

Nurse.   Goodness me—gone altogether?

Nora.   Listen, Anne-Marie—something I've wondered about. How could you bring yourself to leave your child with strangers?

Nurse.   But I had to, if I were to nurse you.

Nora.   Yes, but how could you *want* to?

Nurse.   When I could get such a nice place? When something like that happens to a poor young girl, she'd better be grateful for whatever she gets. For *he* didn't do a thing for me—the louse!

Nora.   But your daughter has forgotten all about you, hasn't she?

Nurse.   Oh no! Not at all! She wrote to me both when she was confirmed and when she got married.

Nora *(putting her arms around her neck)*.   You dear old thing—you were a good mother to me when I was little.

Nurse.   Poor little Nora had no one else, you know.

Nora.   And if my little ones didn't, I know you'd—oh, I'm being silly! *(Opens the carton.)* Go in to them, please. I really should—. Tomorrow you'll see how pretty I'll be.

Nurse.   I know. There won't be anybody at that party half as pretty as you, ma'am. *(Goes out, left.)*

Nora *(begins to take clothes out of the carton; in a moment she throws it all down)*.   If only I dared to go out. If only I knew nobody would come. That nothing would happen while I was gone.—How silly! Nobody'll come. Just don't think about it. Brush the muff. Beautiful gloves. Beautiful gloves. Forget it. Forget it. One, two, three, four, five, six—*(Cries out.)* There they are! *(Moves toward the door, stops irresolutely.)*

Mrs. Linde enters from the hall. She has already taken off her coat.

Nora. Oh, it's you, Kristine. There's no one else out there, is there? I'm so glad you're here.

Mrs. Linde. They told me you'd asked for me.

Nora. I just happened to walk by. I need your help with something—badly. Let's sit here on the couch. Look. Torvald and I are going to a costume party tomorrow night—at Consul Stenborg's upstairs—and Torvald wants me to go as a Neapolitan fisher girl and dance the tarantella. I learned it when we were on Capri.

Mrs. Linde. Well, well! So you'll be putting on a whole show?

Nora. Yes. Torvald thinks I should. Look, here's the costume. Torvald had it made for me while we were there. But it's all so torn and everything. I just don't know—

Mrs. Linde. Oh, that can be fixed. It's not that much. The trimmings have come loose in a few places. Do you have needle and thread? Ah, here we are. All set.

Nora. I really appreciate it, Kristine.

Mrs. Linde (sewing). So you'll be in disguise tomorrow night, eh? You know—I may come by for just a moment, just to look at you.—Oh dear. I haven't even thanked you for the nice evening last night.

Nora (gets up, moves around). Oh, I don't know. I don't think last night was as nice as it usually is.—You should have come to town a little earlier, Kristine.—Yes, Torvald knows how to make it nice and pretty around here.

Mrs. Linde. You too, I should think. After all, you're your father's daughter. By the way, is Dr. Rank always as depressed as he was last night?

Nora. No, last night was unusual. He's a very sick man, you know—very sick. Poor Rank, his spine is rotting away. Tuberculosis, I think. You see, his father was a nasty old man with mistresses and all that sort of thing. Rank has been sickly ever since he was a little boy.

Mrs. Linde (dropping her sewing to her lap). But dearest Nora, where have you learned about things like that?

Nora (still walking about). Oh, you know—with three children you sometimes get to talk with—other wives. Some of them know quite a bit about medicine. So you pick up a few things.

Mrs. Linde (resumes her sewing; after a brief pause). Does Dr. Rank come here every day?

Nora. Every single day. He's Torvald's oldest and best friend, after all. And my friend too, for that matter. He's part of the family, almost.

Mrs. Linde. But tell me, is he quite sincere? I mean, isn't he the kind of man who likes to say nice things to people?

Nora. No, not at all. Rather the opposite, in fact. What makes you say that?

Mrs. Linde. When you introduced us yesterday, he told me he'd often heard my name mentioned in this house. But later on it was quite obvious that your husband really had no idea who I was. So how could Dr. Rank—?

Nora. You're right, Kristine, but I can explain that. You see, Torvald loves me so very much that he wants me all to himself. That's what he says. When we were first married he got almost jealous when I as much as mentioned anybody from back home that I was fond of. So of course I soon stopped doing that. But with Dr. Rank I often talk about home. You see, he likes to listen to me.

Mrs. Linde.   Look here, Nora. In many ways you're still a child. After all, I'm quite a bit older than you and have had more experience. I want to give you a piece of advice. I think you should get out of this thing with Dr. Rank.

Nora.   Get out of what thing?

Mrs. Linde.   Several things in fact, if you want my opinion. Yesterday you said something about a rich admirer who was going to give you money—

Nora.   One who doesn't exist, unfortunately. What of it?

Mrs. Linde.   Does Dr. Rank have money?

Nora.   Yes, he does.

Mrs. Linde.   And no dependents?

Nora.   No. But—?

Mrs. Linde.   And he comes here every day?

Nora.   Yes, I told you that already.

Mrs. Linde.   But how can that sensitive man be so tactless?

Nora.   I haven't the slightest idea what you're talking about.

Mrs. Linde.   Don't play games with me, Nora. Don't you think I know who you borrowed the twelve hundred dollars from?

Nora.   Are you out of your mind! The very idea—! A friend of both of us who sees us every day—! What a dreadfully uncomfortable position that would be!

Mrs. Linde.   So it really isn't Dr. Rank?

Nora.   Most certainly not! I would never have dreamed of asking him—not for a moment. Anyway, he didn't have any money then. He inherited it afterwards.

Mrs. Linde.   Well, I still think it may have been lucky for you, Nora dear.

Nora.   The idea! It would never have occurred to me to ask Dr. Rank—. Though I'm sure that if I *did* ask him—

Mrs. Linde.   But of course you wouldn't.

Nora.   Of course not. I can't imagine that that would ever be necessary. But I am quite sure that if I told Dr. Rank—

Mrs. Linde.   Behind your husband's back?

Nora.   I must get out of—this other thing. That's also behind his back. I *must* get out of it.

Mrs. Linde.   That's what I told you yesterday. But—

Nora (*walking up and down*).   A man manages these things so much better than a woman—

Mrs. Linde.   One's husband, yes.

Nora.   Silly, silly! (*Stops.*) When you've paid off all you owe, you get your I.O.U. back; right?

Mrs. Linde.   Yes, of course.

Nora.   And you can tear it into a hundred thousand little pieces and burn it— that dirty, filthy, paper!

Mrs. Linde (*looks hard at her, puts down her sewing, rises slowly*).   Nora— you're hiding something from me.

Nora.   Can you tell?

Mrs. Linde.   Something's happened to you, Nora, since yesterday morning.
What is it?

Nora *(going to her)*.   Kristine! *(Listens.)* Shhh. Torvald just came back. Listen.
Why don't you go in to the children for a while. Torvald can't stand having
sewing around. Get Anne-Marie to help you.

Mrs. Linde *(gathers some of the sewing things together)*.   All right, but I'm not
leaving here till you and I have talked.

She goes out left, just as Helmer enters from the front hall.

Nora *(towards him)*.   I have been waiting and waiting for you, Torvald.

Helmer.   Was that the dressmaker?

Nora.   No, it was Kristine. She's helping me with my costume. Oh Torvald,
just wait till you see how nice I'll look!

Helmer.   I told you. Pretty good idea I had, wasn't it?

Nora.   Lovely! And wasn't it nice of me to go along with it?

Helmer *(his hand under her chin)*.   Nice? To do what your husband tells you?
All right, you little rascal; I know you didn't mean it that way. But don't let
me interrupt you. I suppose you want to try it on.

Nora.   And you'll be working?

Helmer.   Yes. *(Shows her a pile of papers.)* Look. I've been down to the bank.
(Is about to enter his study.)

Nora.   Torvald.

Helmer *(halts)*.   Yes?

Nora.   What if your little squirrel asked you ever so nicely—

Helmer.   For what?

Nora.   Would you do it?

Helmer.   Depends on what it is.

Nora.   Squirrel would run around and do all sorts of fun tricks if you'd be nice
and agreeable.

Helmer.   All right. What is it?

Nora.   Lark would chirp and twitter in all the rooms, up and down—

Helmer.   So what? Lark does that anyway.

Nora.   I'll be your elfmaid and dance for you in the moonlight, Torvald.

Helmer.   Nora, don't tell me it's the same thing you mentioned this morning?

Nora *(closer to him)*.   Yes, Torvald. I beg you!

Helmer.   You really have the nerve to bring that up again?

Nora.   Yes. You've just got to do as I say. You *must* let Krogstad keep his job.

Helmer.   My dear Nora. It's his job I intend to give to Mrs. Linde.

Nora.   I know. And that's ever so nice of you. But can't you just fire somebody
else?

Helmer.   This is incredible! You just don't give up do you? Because you make
some foolish promise, *I* am supposed to—!

Nora.   That's not the reason, Torvald. It's for your own sake. That man writes
for the worst newspapers. You've said so yourself. There's no telling what he
may do to you. I'm scared to death of him.

Helmer. Ah, I understand. You're afraid because of what happened before.

Nora. What do you mean?

Helmer. You're thinking of your father, of course.

Nora. Yes. Yes, you're right. Remember the awful things they wrote about Daddy in the newspapers. I really think they might have forced him to resign if the ministry hadn't sent you to look into the charges and if you hadn't been so helpful and understanding.

Helmer. My dear little Nora, there is a world of difference between your father and me. Your father's official conduct was not above reproach. Mine is, and I intend for it to remain that way as long as I hold my position.

Nora. Oh, but you don't know what vicious people like that may think of. Oh, Torvald! Now all of us could be so happy together here in our own home, peaceful and carefree. Such a good life, Torvald, for you and me and the children! That's why I implore you—

Helmer. And it's exactly because you plead for him that you make it impossible for me to keep him. It's already common knowledge in the bank that I intend to let Krogstad go. If it gets out that the new manager has changed his mind because of his wife—

Nora. Yes? What then?

Helmer. No, of course, that wouldn't matter at all as long as little Mrs. Pighead here got her way! Do you want me to make myself look ridiculous before my whole staff—make people think I can be swayed by just anybody—by outsiders? Believe me, I would soon enough find out what the consequences would be! Besides, there's another thing that makes it absolutely impossible for Krogstad to stay on in the bank now that I'm in charge.

Nora. What's that?

Helmer. I suppose in a pinch I could overlook his moral shortcomings—

Nora. Yes, you could; couldn't you, Torvald?

Helmer. And I understand he's quite a good worker, too. But we've known each other for a long time. It's one of those imprudent relationships you get into when you're young that embarrass you for the rest of your life. I guess I might as well be frank with you: he and I are on a first name basis. And that tactless fellow never hides the fact even when other people are around. Rather, he seems to think it entitles him to be familiar with me. Every chance he gets he comes out with his damn "Torvald, Torvald." I'm telling you, I find it most awkward. He would make my position in the bank intolerable.

Nora. You don't really mean any of this, Torvald.

Helmer. Oh? I don't? And why not?

Nora. No, for it's all so petty.

Helmer. What! Petty? You think I'm being petty!

Nora. No, I *don't* think you are petty, Torvald dear. That's exactly why I—

Helmer. Never mind. You think my reasons are petty, so it follows that I must be petty too. Petty! Indeed! By God, I'll put an end to this right now! (*Opens the door to the front hall and calls out.*) Helene!

Nora. What are you doing?

Helmer *(searching among his papers).*   Making a decision. *(The Maid enters.)* Here. Take this letter. Go out with it right away. Find somebody to deliver it. But quick. The address is on the envelope. Wait. Here's money.

The Maid.   Very good sir. *(She takes the letter and goes out.)*

Helmer *(collecting his papers).*   There now, little Mrs. Obstinate!

Nora *(breathless).*   Torvald—what was that letter?

Helmer.   Krogstad's dismissal.

Nora.   Call it back, Torvald! There's still time! Oh Torvald, please—call it back! For my sake, for your own sake, for the sake of the children! Listen to me, Torvald! Do it! You don't know what you're doing to all of us!

Helmer.   Too late.

Nora.   Yes. Too late.

Helmer.   Dear Nora, I forgive you this fear you're in, although it really is an insult to me. Yes, it is! It's an insult to think that I am scared of a shabby scrivener's revenge. But I forgive you, for it's such a beautiful proof how much you love me. *(Takes her in his arms.)* And that's the way it should be, my sweet darling. Whatever happens, you'll see that when things get really rough I have both strength and courage. You'll find out that I am man enough to shoulder the whole burden.

Nora *(terrified).*   What do you mean by that?

Helmer.   All of it, I tell you—

Nora *(composed).*   You'll never have to do that.

Helmer.   Good. Then we'll share the burden, Nora—like husband and wife, the way it ought to be. *(Caresses her.)* Now are you satisfied? There, there there. Not that look in your eyes—like a frightened dove. It's all your own foolish imagination.—Why don't you practice the tarantella—and your tambourine, too. I'll be in the inner office and close both doors, so I won't hear you. You can make as much noise as you like. *(Turning in the doorway.)* And when Rank comes, tell him where to find me. *(He nods to her, enters his study carrying his papers, and closes the door.)*

Nora *(transfixed by terror, whispers).*   He would do it. He'll do it. He'll do it in spite of the whole world.—No, this mustn't happen. Anything rather than that! There must be a way—! *(The doorbell rings.)* Dr. Rank! Anything rather than that! Anything—anything at all!

She passes her hand over her face, pulls herself together, and opens the door to the hall. Dr. Rank is out there, hanging up his coat. Darkness begins to fall during the following scene.

Nora.   Hello there, Dr. Rank. I recognized your ringing. Don't go in to Torvald yet. I think he's busy.

Rank.   And you?

Nora *(as he enters and she closes the door behind him).*   You know I always have time for you.

Rank.   Thanks. I'll make use of that as long as I can.

Nora.   What do you mean by that—As long as you can?

Rank.   Does that frighten you?

Nora.   Well, it's a funny expression. As if something was going to happen.

Rank.   Something is going to happen that I've long been expecting. But I admit I hadn't thought it would come quite so soon.

Nora (*seizes his arm*).   What is it you've found out? Dr. Rank—tell me!

Rank (*sits down by the stove*).   I'm going downhill fast. There's nothing to do about that.

Nora (*with audible relief*).   So it's *you*—

Rank.   Who else? No point in lying to myself. I'm in worse shape than any of my other patients, Mrs. Helmer. These last few days I've been making up my inner status. Bankrupt. Chances are that within a month I'll be rotting up in the cemetery.

Nora.   Shame on you! Talking that horrid way!

Rank.   The thing itself is horrid—damn horrid. The worst of it, though, is all that other horror that comes first. There is only one more test I need to make. After that I'll have a pretty good idea when I'll start coming apart. There is something I want to say to you. Helmer's refined nature can't stand anything hideous. I don't want him in my sick room.

Nora.   Oh, but Dr. Rank—

Rank.   I don't want him there. Under no circumstance. I'll close my door to him. As soon as I have full certainty that the worst is about to begin I'll give you my card with a black cross on it. Then you'll know the last horror of destruction has started.

Nora.   Today you're really quite impossible. And I had hoped you'd be in a particularly good mood.

Rank.   With death on my hands? Paying for someone else's sins? Is there justice in that? And yet there isn't a single family that isn't ruled by the same law of ruthless retribution, in one way or another.

Nora (*puts her hands over her ears*).   Poppycock! Be fun! Be fun!

Rank.   Well, yes. You may just as well laugh at the whole thing. My poor, innocent spine is suffering from my father's frolics as a young lieutenant.

Nora (*over by the table, left*).   Right. He was addicted to asparagus and goose liver paté, wasn't he?

Rank.   And truffles.

Nora.   Of course. Truffles. And oysters too, I think.

Rank.   And oysters. Obviously.

Nora.   And all the port and champagne that go with it. It's really too bad that goodies like that ruin your backbone.

Rank.   Particularly an unfortunate backbone that never enjoyed any of it.

Nora.   Ah yes, that's the saddest part of it all.

Rank (*looks searchingly at her*).   Hm—

Nora (*after a brief pause*).   Why did you smile just then?

Rank.   No, it was you that laughed.

Nora.   No, it was you that smiled, Dr. Rank!

Rank *(gets up).*   You're more of a mischief-maker than I thought.

Nora.   I feel in the mood for mischief today.

Rank.   So it seems.

Nora *(with both her hands on his shoulders).*   Dear, dear Dr. Rank, don't you go and die and leave Torvald and me.

Rank.   Oh, you won't miss me for very long. Those who go away are soon forgotten.

Nora *(with an anxious look).*   Do you believe that?

Rank.   You'll make new friends, and then—

Nora.   Who'll make new friends?

Rank.   Both you and Helmer, once I'm gone. You yourself seem to have made a good start already. What was this Mrs. Linde doing here last night?

Nora.   Aha—Don't tell me you're jealous of poor Kristine?

Rank.   Yes, I am. She'll be my successor in this house. As soon as I have made my excuses, that woman is likely to—

Nora.   Shh—not so loud. She's in there.

Rank.   Today too? There you are!

Nora.   She's mending my costume. My God, you really *are* unreasonable. *(Sits down on the couch).* Now be nice, Dr. Rank. Tomorrow you'll see how beautifully I'll dance, and then you are to pretend I'm dancing just for you— and for Torvald too, of course. *(Takes several items out of the carton.)* Sit down, Dr. Rank; I want to show you something.

Rank *(sitting down).*   What?

Nora.   Look.

Rank.   Silk stockings.

Nora.   Flesh-colored. Aren't they lovely? Now it's getting dark in here, but tomorrow—No, no. You only get to see the foot. Oh well, you might as well see all of it.

Rank.   Hmm.

Nora.   Why do you look so critical? Don't you think they'll fit?

Rank.   That's something I can't possibly have a reasoned opinion about.

Nora *(looks at him for a moment).*   Shame on you. *(Slaps his ear lightly with the stocking.)* That's what you get. *(Puts the things back in the carton.)*

Rank.   And what other treasures are you going to show me?

Nora.   Nothing at all, because you're naughty. *(She hums a little and rummages in the carton.)*

Rank *(after a brief silence).*   When I sit here like this, talking confidently with you, I can't imagine—I can't possibly imagine what would have become of me if I hadn't had you and Helmer.

Nora *(smiles).*   Well, yes—I do believe you like being with us.

Rank *(in a lower voice, lost in thought).*   And then to have to go away from it all—

Nora.   Nonsense. You are not going anywhere.

Rank *(as before)*.   —and not to leave behind as much as a poor little token of gratitude, hardly a brief memory of someone missed, nothing but a vacant place that anyone can fill.

Nora.   And what if I were to ask you—? No—

Rank.   Ask me what?

Nora.   For a great proof of your friendship—

Rank.   Yes, yes—?

Nora.   No, I mean—for an enormous favor—

Rank.   Would you really for once make me as happy as all that?

Nora.   But you don't even know what it is.

Rank.   Well, then; tell me.

Nora.   Oh, but I can't, Dr. Rank. It's altogether too much to ask—It's advice and help and a favor—

Rank.   So much the better. I can't even begin to guess what it is you have in mind. So for heaven's sake tell me! Don't you trust me?

Nora.   Yes, I trust you more than anyone else I know. You are my best and most faithful friend. I know that. So I will tell you. All right, Dr. Rank. There is something you can help me prevent. You know how much Torvald loves me—beyond all words. Never for a moment would he hesitate to give his life for me.

Rank *(leaning over to her)*.   Nora—do you really think he's the only one—?

Nora *(with a slight start)*.   Who—?

Rank.   —would gladly give his life for you.

Nora *(heavily)*.   I see.

Rank.   I have sworn an oath to myself to tell you before I go. I'll never find a better occasion.—All right, Nora; now you know. And now you also know that you can confide in me more than in anyone else.

Nora *(gets up; in a calm, steady voice)*.   Let me get by.

Rank *(makes room for her but remains seated)*.   Nora—

Nora *(in the door to the front hall)*.   Helene, bring the lamp in here, please. *(Walks over to the stove.)* Oh, dear Dr. Rank. That really wasn't very nice of you.

Rank *(gets up)*.   That I have loved you as much as anybody—was that not nice?

Nora.   No; not that. But that you told me. There was no need for that.

Rank.   What do you mean? Have you known—?

The Maid enters with the lamp, puts it on the table, and goes out.

Rank.   Nora—Mrs. Helmer—I'm asking you: did you know?

Nora.   Oh, how can I tell what I knew and didn't know! I really can't say— But that you could be so awkward, Dr. Rank! Just when everything was so comfortable.

Rank.   Well, anyway, now you know that I'm at your service with my life and soul. And now you must speak.

Nora *(looks at him).*   After what just happened?

Rank.   I beg of you—let me know what it is.

Nora.   There is nothing I can tell you now.

Rank.   Yes, yes. You mustn't punish me this way. Please let me do for you whatever anyone *can* do.

Nora.   Now there is nothing you can do. Besides, I don't think I really need any help, anyway. It's probably just my imagination. Of course that's all it is. I'm sure of it! *(Sits down in the rocking chair, looks at him, smiles.)* Well, well, well, Dr. Rank! What a fine gentleman you turned out to be! Aren't you ashamed of yourself, now that we have light?

Rank.   No, not really. But perhaps I ought to leave—and not come back?

Nora.   Don't be silly; of course not! You'll come here exactly as you have been doing. You know perfectly well that Torvald can't do without you.

Rank.   Yes, but what about you?

Nora.   Oh, I always think it's perfectly delightful when you come.

Rank.   That's the very thing that misled me. You are a riddle to me. It has often seemed to me that you'd just as soon be with me as with Helmer.

Nora.   Well, you see, there are people you love, and then there are other people you'd almost rather be with.

Rank.   Yes, there is something in that.

Nora.   When I lived at home with Daddy, of course I loved him most. But I always thought it was so much fun to sneak off down to the maids' room, for they never gave me good advice and they always talked about such fun things.

Rank.   Aha! So it's *their* place I have taken.

Nora *(jumps up and goes over to him).*   Oh dear, kind Dr. Rank, you know very well I didn't mean it that way. Can't you see that with Torvald it is the way it used to be with Daddy?

The Maid enters from the front hall.

The Maid.   Ma'am! *(Whispers to her and gives her a caller's card.)*

Nora *(glances at the card).*   Ah! *(Puts it in her pocket.)*

Rank.   Anything wrong?

Nora.   No, no; not at all. It's nothing—just my new costume—

Rank.   But your costume is lying right there!

Nora.   Oh yes, that one. But this is another one. I ordered it. Torvald mustn't know—

Rank.   Aha. So that's the great secret.

Nora.   That's it. Why don't you go in to him, please. He's in the inner office. And keep him there for a while—

Rank.   Don't worry. He won't get away. *(Enters Helmer's study.)*

Nora *(to the Maid).*   You say he's waiting in the kitchen?

The Maid.   Yes. He came up the back stairs.

Nora.   But didn't you tell him there was somebody with me?

The Maid.   Yes, but he wouldn't listen.

Nora.   He won't leave?

The Maid.   No, not till he's had a word with you, ma'am.

Nora.   All right. But try not to make any noise. And, Helene—don't tell anyone he's here. It's supposed to be a surprise for my husband.

The Maid.   I understand, ma'am—*(She leaves.)*

Nora.   The terrible is happening. It's happening, after all. No, no, no. It can't
happen. It won't happen. *(She bolts the study door.)*

*The maid opens the front hall door for Krogstad and closes the door behind him.
He wears a fur coat for traveling, boots, and a fur hat.*

Nora *(toward him).*   Keep your voice down. My husband's home.

Krogstad.   That's all right.

Nora.   What do you want?

Krogstad.   To find out something.

Nora.   Be quick, then. What is it?

Krogstad.   I expect you know I've been fired.

Nora.   I couldn't prevent it, Mr. Krogstad. I fought for you as long and as hard
as I could but it didn't do any good.

Krogstad.   Your husband doesn't love you any more than that? He knows what
I can do to you, and yet he runs the risk—

Nora.   Surely you didn't think I'd tell him?

Krogstad.   No, I really didn't. It wouldn't be like Torvald Helmer to show that
kind of guts—

Nora.   Mr. Krogstad, I insist that you show respect for my husband.

Krogstad.   By all means. All due respect. But since you're so anxious to keep
this a secret, may I assume that you are a little better informed than yesterday
about exactly what you have done?

Nora.   Better than *you* could ever teach me.

Krogstad.   Of course. Such a bad lawyer as I am—

Nora.   What do you want of me?

Krogstad.   I just wanted to find out how you are, Mrs. Helmer. I've been
thinking about you all day. You see, even a bill collector, a pen pusher, a—
anyway, someone like me—even he has a little of what they call a heart.

Nora.   Then show it. Think of my little children.

Krogstad.   Have you and your husband thought of mine? Never mind. All I
want to tell you is that you don't need to take this business too seriously. I
have no intention of bringing charges right away.

Nora.   Oh no, you wouldn't; would you? I knew you wouldn't.

Krogstad.   The whole thing can be settled quite amiably. Nobody else needs
to know anything. It will be between the three of us.

Nora.   My husband must never find out about this.

Krogstad.   How are you going to prevent that? Maybe you can pay me the
balance on the loan?

Nora. No, not right now.

Krogstad. Or do you have a way of raising the money one of these next few days?

Nora. None I intend to make use of.

Krogstad. It wouldn't do you any good, anyway. Even if you had the cash in your hand right this minute, I wouldn't give you your note back. It wouldn't make any difference *how* much money you offered me.

Nora. Then you'll have to tell me what you plan to use the note *for*.

Krogstad. Just keep it; that's all. Have it on hand, so to speak. I won't say a word to anybody else. So if you've been thinking about doing something desperate—

Nora. I have.

Krogstad. —like leaving house and home—

Nora. I have!

Krogstad. —or even something worse—

Nora. How did you know?

Krogstad. —then: don't.

Nora. How did you know I was thinking of *that*?

Krogstad. Most of us do, right at first. I did, too, but when it came down to it I didn't have the courage—

Nora (*tonelessly*). Nor do I.

Krogstad (*relieved*). See what I mean? I thought so. You don't either.

Nora. I don't. I don't.

Krogstad. Besides, it would be very silly of you. Once that first domestic blow-up is behind you—. Here in my pocket is a letter for your husband.

Nora. Telling him everything?

Krogstad. As delicately as possible.

Nora (*quickly*). He mustn't get that letter. Tear it up. I'll get you the money somehow.

Krogstad. Excuse me, Mrs. Helmer, I thought I just told you—

Nora. I'm not talking about the money I owe you. Just let me know how much money you want from my husband, and I'll get it for you.

Krogstad. I want no money from your husband.

Nora. Then, what *do* you want?

Krogstad. I'll tell you, Mrs. Helmer. I want to rehabilitate myself; I want to get up in the world; and your husband is going to help me. For a year and a half I haven't done anything disreputable. All that time I have been struggling with the most miserable circumstances. I was content to work my way up step by step. Now I've been kicked out, and I'm no longer satisfied just getting my old job back. I want more than that; I want to get to the top. I'm being quite serious. I want the bank to take me back but in a higher position. I want your husband to create a new job for me—

Nora. He'll never do that!

Krogstad. He will. I know him. He won't dare not to. And once I'm back inside and he and I are working together, you'll see! Within a year I'll be the manager's right hand. It will be Nils Krogstad and not Torvald Helmer who'll be running the Mutual Bank!

Nora. You'll never see that happen!

Krogstad. Are you thinking of—?

Nora. Now I *do* have the courage.

Krogstad. You can't scare me. A fine, spoiled lady like you—

Nora. You'll see, you'll see!

Krogstad. Under the ice, perhaps? Down into that cold, black water? Then spring comes, and you float up again—hideous, can't be identified, hair all gone—

Nora. You don't frighten me.

Krogstad. Nor you me. One doesn't do that sort of thing, Mrs. Helmer. Besides, what good would it do? He'd still be in my power.

Nora. Afterwards? When I'm no longer—?

Krogstad. Aren't you forgetting that your reputation would be in my hands?

Nora stares at him, speechless.

Krogstad. All right; now I've told you what to expect. So don't do anything foolish. When Helmer gets my letter I expect to hear from him. And don't you forget that it's your husband himself who forces me to use such means again. That I'll never forgive him. Goodbye, Mrs. Helmer. *(Goes out through the hall.)*

Nora *(at the door, opens it a little, listens).* He's going. And no letter. Of course not! That would be impossible! *(Opens the door more.)* What's he doing? He's still there. Doesn't go down. Having second thoughts—? Will he—?

The sound of a letter dropping into the mailbox. Then Krogstad's steps are heard going down the stairs, gradually dying away.

Nora *(with a muted cry runs forward to the table by the couch; brief pause).* In the mailbox. *(Tiptoes back to the door to the front hall.)* There it is. Torvald, Torvald—now we're lost!

Mrs. Linde *(enters from the left, carrying Nora's Capri costume).* There now. I think it's all fixed. Why don't we try it on you—

Nora *(in a low, hoarse voice).* Kristine, come here.

Mrs. Linde. What's wrong with you? You look quite beside yourself.

Nora. Come over here. Do you see that letter? There, look—through the glass in the mailbox.

Mrs. Linde. Yes, yes; I see it.

Nora. That letter is from Krogstad.

Mrs. Linde. Nora—it was Krogstad who lent you the money!

Nora. Yes, and now Torvald will find out about it.

Mrs. Linde.   Oh believe me, Nora. That's the best thing for both of you.

Nora.   There's more to it than you know. I forged a signature—

Mrs. Linde.   Oh my God—!

Nora.   I just want to tell you this, Kristine, that you must be my witness.

Mrs. Linde.   Witness? How? Witness to what?

Nora.   If I lose my mind—and that could very well happen—

Mrs. Linde.   Nora!

Nora.   —or if something were to happen to me—something that made it impossible for me to be here—

Mrs. Linde.   Nora, Nora! You're not yourself!

Nora.   —and if someone were to take all the blame, assume the whole responsibility—Do you understand—?

Mrs. Linde.   Yes, yes; but how can you think—!

Nora.   Then you are to witness that that's not so, Kristine. I am not beside myself. I am perfectly rational, and what I'm telling you is that nobody else has known about this. I've done it all by myself, the whole thing. Just remember that.

Mrs. Linde.   I will. But I don't understand any of it.

Nora.   Oh, how could you! For it's the wonderful that's about to happen.

Mrs. Linde.   The wonderful?

Nora.   Yes, the wonderful. But it's so terrible, Kristine. It mustn't happen for anything in the whole world!

Mrs. Linde.   I'm going over to talk to Krogstad right now.

Nora.   No, don't. Don't go to him. He'll do something bad to you.

Mrs. Linde.   There was a time when he would have done anything for me.

Nora.   He!

Mrs. Linde.   Where does he live?

Nora.   Oh, I don't know—Yes, wait a minute—*(Reaches into her pocket.)* here's his card.—But the letter, the letter—!

Helmer *(in his study, knocks on the door).*   Nora!

Nora *(cries out in fear).*   Oh, what is it? What do you want?

Helmer.   That's all right. Nothing to be scared about. We're not coming in. For one thing, you've bolted the door, you know. Are you modeling your costume?

Nora.   Yes, yes; I am. I'm going to be so pretty, Torvald.

Mrs. Linde *(having looked at the card).*   He lives just around the corner.

Nora.   Yes, but it's no use. Nothing can save us now. The letter is in the mailbox.

Mrs. Linde.   And your husband has the key?

Nora.   Yes. He always keeps it with him.

Mrs. Linde.   Krogstad must ask for his letter back, unread. He's got to think up some pretext or other—

Nora.   But this is just the time of day when Torvald—

Mrs. Linde.   Delay him. Go in to him. I'll be back as soon as I can. *(She hurries out through the hall door.)*

Nora *(walks over to Helmer's door, opens it, and peeks in)*.   Torvald

Helmer *(still offstage)*.   Well, well! So now one's allowed in one's own living room again. Come on, Rank. Now we'll see—*(In the doorway.)* But what's this?

Nora.   What, Torvald dear?

Helmer.   Rank prepared me for a splendid metamorphosis.

Rank *(in the doorway)*.   That's how I understood it. Evidently I was mistaken.

Nora.   Nobody gets to admire me in my costume before tomorrow.

Helmer.   But, dearest Nora—you look all done in. Have you been practicing too hard?

Nora.   No, I haven't practiced at all.

Helmer.   But you'll have to, you know.

Nora.   I know it, Torvald. I simply must. But I can't do a thing unless you help me. I have forgotten everything.

Helmer.   Oh it will all come back. We'll work on it.

Nora.   Oh yes, please, Torvald. You just have to help me. Promise? I am so nervous. That big party—. You mustn't do anything else tonight. Not a bit of business. Don't even touch a pen. Will you promise, Torvald?

Helmer.   I promise. Tonight I'll be entirely at your service—you helpless little thing.—Just a moment, though. First I want to—*(Goes to the door to the front hall.)*

Nora.   What are you doing out there?

Helmer.   Just looking to see if there's any mail.

Nora.   No, no! Don't, Torvald!

Helmer.   Why not?

Nora.   Torvald, I beg you. There is no mail.

Helmer.   Let me just look, anyway. *(Is about to go out.)*

Nora by the piano, plays the first bars of the tarantella dance.

Helmer *(halts at the door)*.   Aha!

Nora.   I won't be able to dance tomorrow if I don't get to practice with you.

Helmer *(goes to her)*.   Are you really all that scared, Nora dear?

Nora.   Yes, so terribly scared. Let's try it right now. There's still time before we eat. Oh please, sit down and play for me, Torvald. Teach me, coach me, the way you always do.

Helmer.   Of course I will, my darling, if that's what you want. *(Sits down at the piano.)*

Nora takes the tambourine out of the carton, as well as a long, many-colored shawl. She quickly drapes the shawl around herself, then leaps into the middle of the floor.

Nora.   Play for me! I want to dance!

Helmer plays and Nora dances. Dr. Rank stands by the piano behind Helmer and watches.

Helmer *(playing)*.   Slow down, slow down!
Nora.   Can't!
Helmer.   Not so violent, Nora!
Nora.   It has to be this way.
Helmer *(stops playing)*.   No, no. This won't do at all.
Nora *(laughing, swinging her tambourine)*.   What did I tell you?
Rank.   Why don't you let me play?
Helmer *(getting up)*.   Good idea. Then I can direct her better.

Rank sits down at the piano and starts playing. Nora dances more and more wildly. Helmer stands over by the stove, repeatedly correcting her. She doesn't seem to hear. Her hair comes loose and falls down over her shoulders. She doesn't notice but keeps on dancing. Mrs. Linde enters.

Mrs. Linde *(stops by the door, dumbfounded)*.   Ah—!
Nora *(dancing)*.   We're having such fun, Kristine!
Helmer.   My dearest Nora, you're dancing as if it were a matter of life and death!
Nora.   It is! It is!
Helmer.   Rank, stop. This is sheer madness. Stop, I say!

Rank stops playing; Nora suddenly stops dancing.

Helmer *(goes over to her)*.   If I hadn't seen it I wouldn't have believed it. You've forgotten every single thing I ever taught you.
Nora *(tosses away the tambourine)*.   See? I told you.
Helmer.   Well! You certainly need coaching.
Nora.   Didn't I tell you I did? Now you've seen for yourself. I'll need your help till the very minute we're leaving for the party. Will you promise, Torvald?
Helmer.   You can count on it.
Nora.   You're not to think of anything except me—not tonight and not tomorrow. You're not to read any letters—not to look in the mailbox—
Helmer.   Ah, I see. You're still afraid of that man.
Nora.   Yes—yes, that too.
Helmer.   Nora, I can tell from looking at you. There's a letter from him out there.
Nora.   I don't know. I think so. But you're not to read it now. I don't want anything ugly to come between us before it's all over.
Rank *(to Helmer in a low voice)*.   Better not argue with her.
Helmer *(throws his arm around her)*.   The child shall have her way. But tomorrow night, when you've done your dance—
Nora.   Then you'll be free.
The Maid *(in the door, right)*.   Dinner can be served any time, ma'am.
Nora.   We want champagne, Helene.
The Maid.   Very good, ma'am. *(Goes out.)*
Helmer.   Aha! Having a party, eh?

Nora.   Champagne from now till sunrise! *(Calls out.)* And some macaroons, Helene. Lots!—just this once.

Helmer *(taking her hands)*.   There, there—I don't like this wild—frenzy—Be my own sweet little lark again, the way you always are.

Nora.   Oh, I will. But you go on in. You too, Dr. Rank. Kristine, please help me put up my hair.

Rank *(in a low voice to Helmer as they go out)*.   You don't think she is—you know—expecting—?

Helmer.   Oh no. Nothing like that. It's just this childish fear I was telling you about. *(They go out, right.)*

Nora.   Well?

Mrs. Linde.   Left town.

Nora.   I saw it in your face.

Mrs. Linde.   He'll be back tomorrow night. I left him a note.

Nora.   You shouldn't have. I don't want you to try to stop anything. You see, it's a kind of ecstasy, too, this waiting for the wonderful.

Mrs. Linde.   But what is it you're waiting *for*?

Nora.   You wouldn't understand. Why don't you go in to the others. I'll be there in a minute.

Mrs. Linde enters the dining room, right.

Nora. *(stands still for a little while, as if collecting herself; she looks at her watch)*.   Five o'clock. Seven hours till midnight. Twenty-four more hours till next midnight. Then the tarantella is over. Twenty-four plus seven— thirty-one more hours to live.

Helmer *(in the door, right)*.   What's happening to my little lark?

Nora *(to him, with open arms)*.   Here's your lark!

Act III

The same room. The table by the couch and the chairs around it have been moved to the middle of the floor. A lighted lamp is on the table. The door to the front hall is open. Dance music is heard from upstairs.

Mrs. Linde is seated by the table, idly leafing through the pages of a book. She tries to read but seems unable to concentrate. Once or twice she turns her head in the direction of the door, anxiously listening.

Mrs. Linde *(looks at her watch)*.   Not yet. It's almost too late. If only he hasn't—(Listens again.) Ah! There he is. *(She goes to the hall and opens the front door carefully. Quiet footsteps on the stairs. She whispers.)* Come in. There's nobody here.

Krogstad *(in the door)*.   I found your note when I got home. What's this all about?

Mrs. Linde.   I've got to talk to you.

Krogstad.   Oh? And it has to be here?

Mrs. Linde.   It couldn't be at my place. My room doesn't have a separate entrance. Come in. We're quite alone. The maid is asleep and the Helmers are at a party upstairs.

Krogstad *(entering)*.   Really? The Helmers are dancing tonight, are they?

Mrs. Linde.   And why not?

Krogstad.   You're right. Why not, indeed.

Mrs. Linde.   All right, Krogstad. Let's talk, you and I.

Krogstad.   I didn't know we had anything to talk about.

Mrs. Linde.   We have much to talk about.

Krogstad.   I didn't think so.

Mrs. Linde.   No, because you've never really understood me.

Krogstad.   What was there to understand? What happened was perfectly commonplace. A heartless woman jilts a man when she gets a more attractive offer.

Mrs. Linde.   Do you think I'm all that heartless? And do you think it was easy for me to break with you?

Krogstad.   No?

Mrs. Linde.   You really thought it was?

Krogstad.   If it wasn't, why did you write the way you did that time?

Mrs. Linde.   What else could I do? If I had to make a break, I also had the duty to destroy whatever feelings you had for me.

Krogstad *(clenching his hands)*.   So that's the way it was. And you did—*that*—just for money!

Mrs. Linde.   Don't forget I had a helpless mother and two small brothers. We couldn't wait for you, Krogstad. You know yourself how uncertain your prospects were then.

Krogstad.   All right. But you still didn't have the right to throw me over for somebody else.

Mrs. Linde.   I don't know. I have asked myself that question many times. Did I have that right?

Krogstad *(in a lower voice)*.   When I lost you I lost my footing. Look at me now. A shipwrecked man on a raft.

Mrs. Linde.   Rescue may be near.

Krogstad.   It *was* near. Then you came between.

Mrs. Linde.   I didn't know that, Krogstad. Only today did I find out it's your job I'm taking over in the bank.

Krogstad.   I believe you when you say so. But now that you *do* know, aren't you going to step aside?

Mrs. Linde.   No, for it wouldn't do you any good.

Krogstad.   Whether it would or not—*I* would do it.

Mrs. Linde.   I have learned common sense. Life and hard necessity have taught me that.

Krogstad.   And life has taught me not to believe in pretty speeches.

Mrs. Linde. Then life has taught you a very sensible thing. But you do believe in actions, don't you?

Krogstad. How do you mean?

Mrs. Linde. You referred to yourself just now as a shipwrecked man.

Krogstad. It seems to me I had every reason to do so.

Mrs. Linde. And I am a shipwrecked woman. No one to grieve for, no one to care for.

Krogstad. You made your choice.

Mrs. Linde. I had no other choice that time.

Krogstad. Let's say you didn't. What then?

Mrs. Linde. Krogstad, how would it be if we two shipwrecked people got together?

Krogstad. What's this!

Mrs. Linde. Two on one wreck are better off than each on his own.

Krogstad. Kristine!

Mrs. Linde. Why do you think I came to town?

Krogstad. Surely not because of me?

Mrs. Linde. If I'm going to live at all I must work. All my life, for as long as I can remember, I have worked. That's been my one and only pleasure. But now that I'm all alone in the world I feel nothing but this terrible emptiness and desolation. There is no joy in working just for yourself. Krogstad—give me someone and something to work for.

Krogstad. I don't believe this. Only hysterical females go in for that kind of high-minded self-sacrifice.

Mrs. Linde. Did you ever know me to be hysterical?

Krogstad. You really could do this? Listen—do you know about my past? All of it?

Mrs. Linde. Yes, I do.

Krogstad. Do you also know what people think of me around here?

Mrs. Linde. A little while ago you sounded as if you thought that together with me you might have become a different person.

Krogstad. I'm sure of it.

Mrs. Linde. Couldn't that still be?

Krogstad. Kristine—do you know what you are doing? Yes, I see you do. And you think you have the courage—?

Mrs. Linde. I need someone to be a mother to, and your children need a mother. You and I need one another. Nils, I believe in you—in the real you. Together with you I dare to do anything.

Krogstad (*seizes her hands*). Thanks, thanks, Kristine—now I know I'll raise myself in the eyes of others—Ah, but I forget—!

Mrs. Linde (*listening*). Shh!—There's the tarantella. You must go; hurry!

Krogstad. Why? What is it?

Mrs. Linde. Do you hear what they're playing up there? When that dance is over they'll be down.

Krogstad. All right. I'm leaving. The whole thing is pointless, anyway. Of course you don't know what I'm doing to the Helmers.

Mrs. Linde.   Yes, Krogstad; I do know.

Krogstad.   Still, you're brave enough—?

Mrs. Linde.   I very well understand to what extremes despair can drive a man like you.

Krogstad.   If only it could be undone!

Mrs. Linde.   It could, for your letter is still out there in the mailbox.

Krogstad.   Are you sure?

Mrs. Linde.   Quite sure. But—

Krogstad (*looks searchingly at her*).   Maybe I'm beginning to understand. You want to save your friend at any cost. Be honest with me. That's it, isn't it?

Mrs. Linde.   Krogstad, you may sell yourself once for somebody else's sake, but you don't do it twice.

Krogstad.   I'll demand my letter back.

Mrs. Linde.   No, no.

Krogstad.   Yes, of course. I'll wait here till Helmer comes down. Then I'll ask him for my letter. I'll tell him it's just about my dismissal—that he shouldn't read it.

Mrs. Linde.   No, Krogstad. You are not to ask for that letter back.

Krogstad.   But tell me—wasn't that the real reason you wanted to meet me here?

Mrs. Linde.   At first it was, because I was so frightened. But that was yesterday. Since then I have seen the most incredible things going on in this house. Helmer must learn the whole truth. This miserable secret must come out in the open; those two must come to a full understanding. They simply can't continue with all this concealment and evasion.

Krogstad.   All right; if you want to take that chance. But there is one thing I *can* do, and I'll do that right now.

Mrs. Linde (*listening*).   But hurry! Go! The dance is over. We aren't safe another minute.

Krogstad.   I'll be waiting for you downstairs.

Mrs. Linde.   Yes, do. You must see me home.

Krogstad.   I've never been so happy in my whole life. (*He leaves through the front door. The door between the living room and the front hall remains open.*)

Mrs. Linde (*straightens up the room a little and gets her things ready*).   What a change! Oh yes!—what a change! People to work for—to live for—a home to bring happiness to. I can't wait to get to work—! If only they'd come soon—(*Listens.*) Ah, there they are. Get my coat on—(*Puts on her coat and hat.*)

Helmer's and Nora's voices are heard outside. A key is turned in the lock, and Helmer almost forces Nora into the hall. She is dressed in her Italian costume, with a big black shawl over her shoulders. He is in evening dress under an open black cloak.

Nora (*in the door, still resisting*).   No, no, no! I don't want to! I want to go back upstairs. I don't want to leave so early.

Helmer.   But dearest Nora—

Nora.   Oh please, Torvald—please! I'm asking you as nicely as I can—just another hour!

Helmer.   Not another minute, sweet. You know we agreed. There now. Get inside. You'll catch a cold out here. (*She still resists, but he guides her gently into the room.*)

Mrs. Linde.   Good evening.

Nora.   Kristine!

Helmer.   Ah, Mrs. Linde. Still here?

Mrs. Linde.   I know. I really should apologize, but I so much wanted to see Nora in her costume.

Nora.   You've been waiting up for me?

Mrs. Linde.   Yes, unfortunately I didn't get here in time. You were already upstairs, but I just didn't feel like leaving till I had seen you.

Helmer (*removing Nora's shawl*).   Yes, do take a good look at her, Mrs. Linde. I think I may say she's worth looking at. Isn't she lovely?

Mrs. Linde.   She certainly is—

Helmer.   Isn't she a miracle of loveliness, though? That was the general opinion at the party, too. But dreadfully obstinate—that she is, the sweet little thing. What can we do about that? Will you believe it—I practically had to use force to get her away.

Nora.   Oh Torvald, you're going to be sorry you didn't give me even half an hour more.

Helmer.   See what I mean, Mrs. Linde? She dances the tarantella—she is a tremendous success—quite deservedly so, though perhaps her performance was a little too natural—I mean, more than could be reconciled with the rules of art. But all right! The point is: she's a success, a tremendous success. So should I let her stay after that? Weaken the effect? Of course not. So I take my lovely little Capri girl—I might say, my capricious little Capri girl—under my arm—a quick turn around the room—a graceful bow in all directions, and—as they say in the novels—the beautiful apparition is gone. A finale should always be done for effect, Mrs. Linde, but there doesn't seem to be any way of getting that into Nora's head. Poooh—! It's hot in here. (*Throws his cloak down on a chair and opens the door to his room.*) Why, it's dark in here! Of course. Excuse me—(*Goes inside and lights a couple of candles.*)

Nora (*in a hurried, breathless whisper*).   Well?

Mrs. Linde (*in a low voice*).   I have talked to him.

Nora.   And—?

Mrs. Linde.   Nora—you've got to tell your husband everything.

Nora (*no expression in her voice*).   I knew it.

Mrs. Linde.   You have nothing to fear from Krogstad. But you must speak.

Nora.   I'll say nothing.

Mrs. Linde.   Then the letter will.

Nora.   Thank you, Kristine. Now I know what I have to do. Shh!

Helmer (*returning*).   Well, Mrs. Linde, have you looked your fill?

Mrs. Linde.   Yes. And now I'll say goodnight.

Helmer.   So soon? Is that your knitting?

Mrs. Linde *(takes it)*.   Yes, thank you. I almost forgot.

Helmer.   So you knit, do you?

Mrs. Linde.   Oh yes.

Helmer.   You know—you ought to take up embroidery instead.

Mrs. Linde.   Oh? Why?

Helmer.   Because it's so much more beautiful. Look. You hold the embroidery so—in your left hand. Then with your right you move the needle—like this—in an easy, elongated arc—you see?

Mrs. Linde.   Maybe you're right—

Helmer.   Knitting, on the other hand, can never be anything but ugly. Look here: arms pressed close to the sides—the needles going up and down—there's something Chinese about it somehow—. That really was an excellent champagne they served us tonight.

Mrs. Linde.   Well, goodnight, Nora. And don't be obstinate any more.

Helmer.   Well said, Mrs. Linde!

Mrs. Linde.   Goodnight, sir.

Helmer *(sees her to the front door)*.   Goodnight, goodnight. I hope you'll get home all right? I'd be very glad to—but of course you don't have far to walk, do you? Goodnight, goodnight. *(She leaves. He closes the door behind her and returns to the living room.)* There! At last we got rid of her. She really is an incredible bore, that woman.

Nora.   Aren't you very tired, Torvald?

Helmer.   No, not in the least.

Nora.   Not sleepy either?

Helmer.   Not at all. Quite the opposite. I feel enormously—animated. How about you? Yes, you do look tired and sleepy.

Nora.   Yes, I am very tired. Soon I'll be asleep.

Helmer.   What did I tell you? I was right, wasn't I? Good thing I didn't let you stay any longer.

Nora.   Everything you do is right.

Helmer *(kissing her forehead)*.   Now my little lark is talking like a human being. But did you notice what splended spirits Rank was in tonight?

Nora.   Was he? I didn't notice. I didn't get to talk with him.

Helmer.   Nor did I—hardly. But I haven't seen him in such a good mood for a long time. *(Looks at her, comes closer to her.)* Ah! It does feel good to be back in our own home again, to be quite alone with you—my young, lovely, ravishing woman!

Nora.   Don't look at me like that, Torvald!

Helmer.   Am I not to look at my most precious possession? All that loveliness that is mine, nobody's but mine, all of it mine.

Nora *(walks to the other side of the table)*.   I won't have you talk to me like that tonight.

Helmer *(follows her)*.   The tarantella is still in your blood. I can tell. That only makes you all the more alluring. Listen! The guests are beginning to leave. *(Softly.)* Nora—soon the whole house will be quiet.

Nora.   Yes, I hope so.

Helmer.   Yes, don't you, my darling? Do you know—when I'm at a party with you, like tonight—do you know why I hardly ever talk to you, why I keep away from you, only look at you once in a while—a few stolen glances—do you know why I do that? It's because I pretend that you are my secret love, my young, secret bride-to-be, and nobody has the slightest suspicion that there is anything between us.

Nora.   Yes, I know. All your thoughts are with me.

Helmer.   Then when we're leaving and I lay your shawl around your delicate young shoulders—around that wonderful curve of your neck—then I imagine you're my young bride, that we're coming away from the wedding, that I am taking you to my home for the first time—that I am alone with you for the first time—quite alone with you, you young, trembling beauty! I have desired you all evening—there hasn't been a longing in me that hasn't been for you. When you were dancing the tarantella, chasing, inviting—my blood was on fire; I couldn't stand it any longer—that's why I brought you down so early—

Nora.   Leave me now, Torvald. Please! I don't want all this.

Helmer.   What do you mean? You're only playing your little teasing bird game with me; aren't you, Nora? Don't want to? I'm your husband, aren't I?

There is a knock on the front door.

Nora *(with a start)*.   Did you hear that—?

Helmer *(on his way to the hall)*.   Who is it?

Rank *(outside)*.   It's me. May I come in for a moment?

Helmer *(in a low voice, annoyed)*.   Oh, what does he want now? *(Aloud.)* Just a minute. *(Opens the door.)* Well! How good of you not to pass by our door.

Rank.   I thought I heard your voice, so I felt like saying hello. *(Looks around.)* Ah yes—this dear, familiar room. What a cozy, comfortable place you have here, you two.

Helmer.   Looked to me as if you were quite comfortable upstairs too.

Rank.   I certainly was. Why not? Why not enjoy all you can in this world? As much as you can for as long as you can, anyway. Excellent wine.

Helmer.   The champagne, particularly.

Rank.   You noticed that too? Incredible how much I managed to put away.

Nora.   Torvald drank a lot of champagne tonight, too.

Rank.   Did he?

Nora.   Yes, he did, and then he's always so much fun afterwards.

Rank.   Well, why not have some fun in the evening after a well spent day?

Helmer.   Well spent? I'm afraid I can't claim that.

Rank *(slapping him lightly on the shoulder)*.   But you see, I can!

Nora.   Dr. Rank, I believe you must have been conducting a scientific test today.

Rank.   Exactly.

Helmer.   What do you know—little Nora talking about scientific tests!

Nora.   May I congratulate you on the result?

Rank.   You may indeed.

Nora.   It was a good one?

Rank.   The best possible for both doctor and patient—certainty.

Nora (*a quick query*).   Certainty?

Rank.   Absolute certainty. So why shouldn't I have myself an enjoyable evening afterwards?

Nora.   I quite agree with you, Dr. Rank. You should.

Helmer.   And so do I. If only you don't pay for it tomorrow.

Rank.   Oh well—you get nothing for nothing in this world.

Nora.   Dr. Rank—you are fond of costume parties, aren't you?

Rank.   Yes, particularly when there is a reasonable number of amusing disguises.

Nora.   Listen—what are the two of us going to be the next time?

Helmer.   You frivolous little thing! Already thinking about the next party!

Rank.   You and I? That's easy. You'll be Fortune's Child.

Helmer.   Yes, but what is a fitting costume for that?

Rank.   Let your wife appear just the way she always is.

Helmer.   Beautiful. Very good indeed. But how about yourself? Don't you know what you'll go as?

Rank.   Yes, my friend. I know precisely what I'll be.

Helmer.   Yes?

Rank.   At the next masquerade I'll be invisible.

Helmer.   That's a funny idea.

Rank.   There's a certain black hat—you've heard about the hat that makes you invisible, haven't you? You put that on, and nobody can see you.

Helmer (*suppressing a smile*).   I guess that's right.

Rank.   But I'm forgetting what I came for. Helmer, give me a cigar—one of your dark Havanas.

Helmer.   With the greatest pleasure. (*Offers him his case.*)

Rank (*takes one and cuts off the tip*).   Thanks.

Nora (*striking a match*).   Let me give you a light.

Rank.   Thanks. (*She holds the match; he lights his cigar.*) And now goodbye!

Helmer.   Goodbye, goodbye, my friend.

Nora.   Sleep well, Dr. Rank.

Rank.   I thank you.

Nora.   Wish me the same.

Rank.   You? Well, if you really want me to—. Sleep well. And thanks for the light. (*He nods to both of them and goes out.*)

Helmer (*in a low voice*).   He had had quite a bit to drink.

Nora (*absently*).   Maybe so.

Helmer takes out his keys and goes out into the hall.

Nora.   Torvald—what are you doing out there?

Helmer.   Emptying the mailbox. It is quite full. There wouldn't be room for the newspapers in the morning—

Nora.   Are you going to work tonight?

Helmer.   You know very well I won't.—Say! What's this? Somebody's been at the lock.

Nora.   The lock—?

Helmer.   Yes. Why, I wonder. I hate to think that any of the maids—. Here's a broken hairpin. It's one of yours. Nora.

Nora (*quickly*).   Then it must be one of the children.

Helmer.   You better make damn sure they stop that. Hm, hm.—There! I got it open, finally. (*Gathers up the mail, calls out to the kitchen.*) Helene?— Oh Helene—turn out the light here in the hall, will you? (*He comes back into the living room and closes the door.*) Look how it's been piling up. (*Shows her the bundle of letters. Starts leafing through it.*) What's this?

Nora (*by the window*).   The letter! Oh no, no, Torvald!

Helmer.   Two calling cards—from Rank.

Nora.   From Dr. Rank?

Helmer (*looking at them*).   "Doctor medicinae Rank." They were on top. He must have put them there when he left just now.

Nora.   Anything written on them?

Helmer.   A black cross above the name. What a macabre idea. Like announcing his own death.

Nora.   That's what it is.

Helmer.   Hm? You know about this? Has he said anything to you?

Nora.   That card means he has said goodbye to us. He'll lock himself up to die.

Helmer.   My poor friend. I knew of course he wouldn't be with me very long. But so soon—. And hiding himself away like a wounded animal—

Nora.   When it has to be, it's better it happens without words. Don't you think so, Torvald?

Helmer (*walking up and down*).   He'd grown so close to us. I find it hard to think of him as gone. With his suffering and loneliness he was like a clouded background for our happy sunshine. Well, it may be better this way. For him, at any rate. (*Stops.*) And perhaps for us, too, Nora. For now we have nobody but each other. (*Embraces her.*) Oh you—my beloved wife! I feel I just can't hold you close enough. Do you know, Nora—many times I have wished some great danger threatened you, so I could risk my life and blood and everything—everything, for your sake.

Nora (*frees herself and says in a strong and firm voice*).   I think you should go and read your letters now, Torvald.

Helmer.   No, no—not tonight. I want to be with you, my darling.

Nora.   With the thought of your dying friend—?

Helmer.   You are right. This has shaken both of us. Something not beautiful has come between us. Thoughts of death and dissolution. We must try to get over it—out of it. Till then—we'll each go to our own room.

Nora (*her arms around his neck*).   Torvald—goodnight! Goodnight!

Helmer (*kisses her forehead*).   Goodnight, my little songbird. Sleep well, Nora. Now I'll read my letters. (*He goes into his room, carrying the mail. Closes the door.*)

Nora (*her eyes desperate, her hands groping, finds Helmer's black cloak and throws it around her; she whispers, quickly, brokenly, hoarsely*).   Never see him again. Never. Never. Never. (*Puts her shawl over her head.*) And never see the children again, either. Never; never.—The black, icy water— fathomless—this—! If only it was all over.—Now he has it. Now he's reading it. No, no; not yet. Torvald—goodbye—you—the children—

She is about to hurry through the hall, when Helmer flings open the door to his room and stands there with an open letter in his hand.

Helmer.   Nora!

Nora (*cries out*).   Ah—!

Helmer.   What is it? You know what's in this letter?

Nora.   Yes, I do! Let me go! Let me out!

Helmer (*holds her back*).   Where do you think you're going?

Nora (*trying to tear herself loose from him*).   I won't let you save me, Torvald!

Helmer (*tumbles back*).   True! Is it true what he writes? Oh my God! No, no—this can't possibly be true.

Nora.   It is true. I have loved you more than anything else in the whole world.

Helmer.   Oh, don't give me any silly excuses.

Nora (*taking a step towards him*).   Torvald—!

Helmer.   You wretch! What have you done!

Nora.   Let me go. You are not to sacrifice yourself for me. You are not to take the blame.

Helmer.   No more playacting. (*Locks the door to the front hall.*) You'll stay here and answer me. Do you understand what you have done? Answer me! Do you understand?

Nora (*gazes steadily at him with an increasingly frozen expression*).   Yes. Now I'm beginning to understand.

Helmer (*walking up and down*).   What a dreadful awakening. All these years— all these eight years—she, my pride and my joy—a hypocrite, a liar—oh worse! worse!—a criminal! Oh, the bottomless ugliness in all this! Damn! Damn! Damn!

Nora, silent, keeps gazing at him.

Helmer (*stops in front of her*).   I ought to have guessed that something like this would happen. I should have expected it. All your father's loose principles—Silence! You have inherited every one of your father's loose principles. No religion, no morals, no sense of duty—. Now I am being punished for my leniency with him. I did it for your sake, and this is how you pay me back.

Nora.   Yes. This is how.

Helmer.   You have ruined all my happiness. My whole future—that's what you have destroyed. Oh, it's terrible to think about. I am at the mercy of an unscrupulous man. He can do with me whatever he likes, demand anything of me, command me and dispose of me just as he pleases—I dare not say a word! To go down so miserably, to be destroyed—all because of an irresponsible woman!

Nora.   When I am gone from the world, you'll be free.

Helmer.   No noble gestures, please. Your father was always full of such phrases too. What good would it do me if you were gone from the world, as you put it? Not the slightest good at all. He could still make the whole thing public, and if he did, people would be likely to think I had been your accomplice. They might even think it was my idea—that it was I who urged you to do it! And for all this I have you to thank—you, whom I've borne on my hands through all the years of our marriage. Now do you understand what you've done to me?

Nora *(with cold calm)*.   Yes.

Helmer.   I just can't get it into my head that this is happening; it's all so incredible. But we have to come to terms with it somehow. Take your shawl off. Take it off, I say! I have to satisfy him one way or another. The whole affair must be kept quiet at whatever cost.—And as far as you and I are concerned, nothing must seem to have changed. I'm talking about appearances, of course. You'll go on living here; that goes without saying. But I won't let you bring up the children; I dare not trust you with them. —Oh! Having to say this to one I have loved so much, and whom I still—! But all that is past. It's not a question of happiness any more but of hanging on to what can be salvaged—pieces, appearances—*(The doorbell rings.)*

Helmer *(jumps)*.   What's that? So late. Is the worst—? Has he—! Hide, Nora! Say you're sick.

Nora doesn't move. Helmer opens the door to the hall.

The Maid *(half dressed, out in the hall)*.   A letter for your wife, sir.

Helmer.   Give it to me. *(Takes the letter and closes the door.)* Yes, it's from him. But I won't let you have it. I'll read it myself.

Nora.   Yes—you read it.

Helmer *(by the lamp)*.   I hardly dare. Perhaps we're lost, both you and I. No; I've got to know. *(Tears the letter open, glances through it, looks at an enclosure; a cry of joy.)* Nora!

Nora looks at him with a question in her eyes.

Helmer.   Nora!—No, I must read it again.—Yes, yes; it is so! I'm saved! Nora,
I'm saved!

Nora.   And I?

Helmer.   You too, of course; we're both saved, both you and I. Look! He's
returning your note. He writes that he's sorry, he regrets, a happy turn in his
life—oh, it doesn't matter what he writes. We're saved, Nora! Nobody can
do anything to you now. Oh Nora, Nora—. No, I want to get rid of this
disgusting thing first. Let me see—*(Looks at the signature.)* No, I don't want
to see it. I don't want it to be more than a bad dream, the whole thing. *(Tears
up the note and both letters, throws the pieces in the stove, and watches them
burn.)* There! Now it's gone.—He wrote that ever since Christmas Eve—.
Good God, Nora, these must have been three terrible days for you.

Nora.   I have fought a hard fight these last three days.

Helmer.   And been in agony and seen no other way out than—. No, we won't
think of all that ugliness. We'll just rejoice and tell ourselves it's over, it's all
over! Oh, listen to me, Nora. You don't seem to understand. It's over. What
is it? Why do you look like that—that frozen expression on your face? Oh
my poor little Nora, don't you think I know what it is? You can't make
yourself believe that I have forgiven you. But I have, Nora; I swear to you,
I have forgiven you for everything. Of course I know that what you did was
for love of me.

Nora.   That is true.

Helmer.   You have loved me the way a wife ought to love her husband. You
just didn't have the wisdom to judge the means. But do you think I love you
any less because you don't know how to act on your own? Of course not. Just
lean on me. I'll advise you; I'll guide you. I wouldn't be a man if I didn't
find you twice as attractive because of your womanly helplessness. You
mustn't pay any attention to the hard words I said to you right at first. It was
just that first shock when I thought everything was collapsing all around me.
I have forgiven you, Nora. I swear to you—I really have forgiven you.

Nora.   I thank you for your forgiveness. *(She goes out through the door, right.)*

Helmer.   No, stay—*(Looks into the room she entered.)* What are you doing in
there?

Nora *(within).*   Getting out of my costume.

Helmer *(by the open door).*   Good, good. Try to calm down and compose
yourself, my poor little frightened songbird. Rest safely; I have broad wings to
cover you with. *(Walks around near the door.)* What a nice and cozy home
we have, Nora. Here's shelter for you. Here I'll keep you safe like a hunted
dove I have rescued from the hawk's talons. Believe me: I'll know how to
quiet your beating heart. It will happen by and by, Nora; you'll see. Why,
tomorrow you'll look at all this in quite a different light. And soon everything
will be just the way it was before. I won't need to keep reassuring you that
I have forgiven you; you'll feel it yourself. Did you really think I could have
abandoned you, or even reproached you? Oh, you don't know a real man's
heart, Nora. There is something unspeakably sweet and satisfactory for a man

to know deep in himself that he has forgiven his wife—forgiven her in all the fullness of his honest heart. You see, that way she becomes his very own all over again—in a double sense, you might say. He has, so to speak, given her a second birth; it is as if she had become his wife and his child, both. From now on that's what you'll be to me, you lost and helpless creature. Don't worry about a thing, Nora. Only be frank with me, and I'll be your will and your conscience.—What's this? You're not in bed? You've changed your dress—!

Nora (*in an everyday dress*). Yes, Torvald. I have changed my dress.

Helmer. But why—now—this late—?

Nora. I'm not going to sleep tonight.

Helmer. But my dear Nora—

Nora (*looks at her watch*). It isn't all that late. Sit down here with me, Torvald. You and I have much to talk about. (*Sits down at the table.*)

Helmer. Nora—what is this all about? That rigid face—

Nora. Sit down. This will take a while. I have much to say to you.

Helmer (*sits down, facing her across the table*). You worry me, Nora. I don't understand you.

Nora. No, that's just it. You don't understand me. And I have never understood you—not till tonight. No, don't interrupt me. Just listen to what I have to say.—This is a settling of accounts, Torvald.

Helmer. What do you mean by that?

Nora (*after a brief silence*). Doesn't one thing strike you, now that we are sitting together like this?

Helmer. What would that be?

Nora. We have been married for eight years. Doesn't it occur to you that this is the first time that you and I, husband and wife, are having a serious talk?

Helmer. Well—serious—. What do you mean by that?

Nora. For eight whole years—longer, in fact—ever since we first met, we have never talked seriously to each other about a single serious thing.

Helmer. You mean I should forever have been telling you about worries you couldn't have helped me with anyway?

Nora. I am not talking about worries. I'm saying we have never tried seriously to get to the bottom of anything together.

Helmer. But dearest Nora, I hardly think that would have been something *you*—

Nora. That's the whole point. You have never understood me. Great wrong has been done to me, Torvald. First by Daddy and then by you.

Helmer. What! By us two? We who have loved you more deeply than anyone else?

Nora (*shakes her head*). You never loved me—neither Daddy nor you. You only thought it was fun to be in love with me.

Helmer But, Nora—what an expression to use!

Nora. That's the way it has been, Torvald. When I was home with Daddy, he told me all his opinions, and so they became my opinions too. If I disagreed with him I kept it to myself, for he wouldn't have liked that. He called me his little doll baby, and he played with me the way I played with my dolls. Then I came to your house—

Helmer.   What a way to talk about our marriage!

Nora *(imperturbably).*   I mean that I passed from Daddy's hands into yours. You arranged everything according to your taste, and so I came to share it—or I pretended to; I'm not sure which. I think it was a little of both, now one and now the other. When I look back on it now, it seems to me I've been living here like a pauper—just a hand-to-mouth kind of existence. I have earned my keep by doing tricks for you, Torvald. But that's the way you wanted it. You have great sins against me to answer for, Daddy and you. It's your fault that nothing has become of me.

Helmer.   Nora, you're being both unreasonable and ungrateful. Haven't you been happy here?

Nora.   No, never. I thought I was, but I wasn't.

Helmer.   Not—not happy!

Nora.   No; just having fun. And you have always been very good to me. But our home has never been more than a playroom. I have been your doll wife here, just the way I used to be Daddy's doll child. And the children have been my dolls. I thought it was fun when you played with me, just as they thought it was fun when I played with them. That's been our marriage, Torvald.

Helmer.   There is something in what you are saying—exaggerated and hysterical though it is. But from now on things will be different. Playtime is over; it's time for growing up.

Nora.   Whose growing up—mine or the children's?

Helmer.   Both yours and the children's, Nora darling.

Nora.   Oh Torvald, you're not the man to bring me up to be the right kind of wife for you.

Helmer.   How can you say that?

Nora.   And I—? What qualifications do I have for bringing up the children?

Helmer.   Nora!

Nora.   You said so yourself a minute ago—that you didn't dare to trust me with them.

Helmer.   In the first flush of anger, yes. Surely, you're not going to count that.

Nora.   But you were quite right. I am *not* qualified. Something else has to come first. Somehow I have to grow up myself. And you are not the man to help me do that. That's a job I have to do by myself. And that's why I'm leaving you.

Helmer *(jumps up).*   What did you say!

Nora.   I have to be by myself if I am to find out about myself and about all the other things too. So I can't stay here with you any longer.

Helmer.   Nora, Nora!

Nora.   I'm leaving now. I'm sure Kristine will put me up for tonight.

Helmer.   You're out of your mind! I won't let you! I forbid you!

Nora.   You can't forbid me anything any more; it won't do any good. I'm taking my own things with me. I won't accept anything from you, either now or later.

Helmer.   But this is madness!

Nora.   Tomorrow I'm going home—I mean back to my old home town. It will be easier for me to find some kind of job there.

Helmer.   Oh, you blind, inexperienced creature—!

Nora.   I must see to it that I get experience, Torvald.

Helmer.   Leaving your home, your husband, your children! Not a thought of what people will say!

Nora.   I can't worry about that. All I know is that I have to leave.

Helmer.   Oh, this is shocking! Betraying your most sacred duties like this!

Nora.   And what do you consider my most sacred duties?

Helmer.   Do I need to tell you that? They are your duties to your husband and your children.

Nora.   I have other duties equally sacred.

Helmer.   You do not. What duties would they be?

Nora.   My duties to myself.

Helmer.   You are a wife and a mother before you are anything else.

Nora.   I don't believe that any more. I believe I am first of all a human being, just as much as you—or at any rate that I must try to become one. Oh, I know very well that most people agree with you, Torvald, and that it says something like that in all the books. But what people say and what the books say is no longer enough for me. I have to think about these things myself and see if I can't find the answers.

Helmer.   You mean to tell me you don't know what your proper place in your own home is? Don't you have a reliable guide in such matters? Don't you have religion?

Nora.   Oh but Torvald—I don't really know what religion is.

Helmer.   What are you saying!

Nora.   All I know is what the Reverend Hansen told me when he prepared me for confirmation. He said that religion was *this* and it was *that*. When I get by myself, away from here, I'll have to look into that, too. I have to decide if what the Reverend Hansen said was right, or anyway if it is right for *me*.

Helmer.   Oh, this is unheard of in a young woman! If religion can't guide you, let me appeal to your conscience. For surely you have moral feelings? Or—answer me—maybe you don't?

Nora.   Well, you see, Torvald, I don't really know what to say. I just don't know. I am confused about these things. All I know is that my ideas are quite different from yours. I have just found out that the laws are different from what I thought they were, but in no way can I get it into my head that those laws are right. A woman shouldn't have the right to spare her dying old father or save her husband's life! I just can't believe that.

Helmer.   You speak like a child. You don't understand the society you live in.

Nora.   No, I don't. But I want to find out about it. I have to make up my mind who is right, society or I.

Helmer.   You are sick, Nora; you have a fever. I really don't think you are in your right mind.

Nora.   I have never felt so clearheaded and sure of myself as I do tonight.

Helmer.   And clearheaded and sure of yourself you're leaving your husband and children?

Nora.   Yes.

Helmer.   Then there is only one possible explanation.

Nora.   What?

Helmer.   You don't love me any more.

Nora   No, that's just it.

Helmer.   Nora! Can you say that?

Nora.   I am sorry, Torvald, for you have always been so good to me. But I can't help it. I don't love you any more.

Helmer *(with forced composure)*.   And this too is a clear and sure conviction?

Nora.   Completely clear and sure. That's why I don't want to stay here any more.

Helmer.   And are you ready to explain to me how I came to forfeit your love?

Nora.   Certainly I am. It was tonight, when the wonderful didn't happen. That was when I realized you were not the man I thought you were.

Helmer.   You have to explain. I don't understand.

Nora.   I have waited patiently for eight years, for I wasn't such a fool that I thought the wonderful is something that happens any old day. Then this—thing—came crashing in on me, and then there wasn't a doubt in my mind that now—now comes the wonderful. When Krogstad's letter was in that mailbox, never for a moment did it even occur to me that you would submit to his conditions. I was so absolutely certain that you would say to him: make the whole thing public—tell everybody. And when that had happened—

Helmer.   Yes, then what? When I had surrendered my wife to shame and disgrace—!

Nora.   When that had happened, I was absolutely certain that you would stand up and take the blame and say, "I'm the guilty one."

Helmer.   Nora!

Nora.   You mean I never would have accepted such a sacrifice from you? Of course not. But what would my protests have counted against yours? *That* was the wonderful I was hoping for in terror. And to prevent that I was going to kill myself.

Helmer.   I'd gladly work nights and days for you, Nora—endure sorrow and want for your sake. But nobody sacrifices his *honor* for his love.

Nora.   A hundred thousand women have done so.

Helmer.   Oh, you think and talk like a silly child.

Nora.   All right. But you don't think and talk like the man I can live with. When you had gotten over your fright—not because of what threatened *me* but because of the risk to *you*—and the whole danger was past, then you acted as if nothing at all had happened. Once again I was your little songbird, your doll, just as before, only now you had to handle her even more carefully, because she was so frail and weak. *(Rises.)* Torvald—that moment I realized that I had been living here for eight years with a stranger and had borne him three children—Oh, I can't stand thinking about it! I feel like tearing myself to pieces!

Helmer *(heavily).*   I see it, I see it. An abyss has opened up between us.—Oh but Nora—surely it can be filled?

Nora.   The way I am now I am no wife for you.

Helmer.   I have it in me to change.

Nora.   Perhaps—if your doll is taken from you.

Helmer.   To part—to part from you! No, no, Nora! I can't grasp that thought!

Nora *(goes out, right).*   All the more reason why it has to be. *(She returns with her outdoor clothes and a small bag, which she sets down on the chair by the table.)*

Helmer.   Nora, Nora! Not now! Wait till tomorrow.

Nora *(putting on her coat).*   I can't spend the night in a stranger's rooms.

Helmer.   But couldn't we live here together like brother and sister—?

Nora *(tying on her hat).*   You know very well that wouldn't last long—. *(Wraps her shawl around her.)* Goodbye, Torvald. I don't want to see the children. I know I leave them in better hands than mine. The way I am now I can't be anything to them.

Helmer.   But some day, Nora—some day—?

Nora.   How can I tell? I have no idea what's going to become of me.

Helmer.   But you're still my wife, both as you are now and as you will be.

Nora.   Listen, Torvald—when a wife leaves her husband's house, the way I am doing now, I have heard he has no more legal responsibilities for her. At any rate, I now release you from all responsibility. You are not to feel yourself obliged to me for anything, and I have no obligations to you. There has to be full freedom on both sides. Here is your ring back. Now give me mine.

Helmer.   Even this?

Nora.   Even this.

Helmer.   Here it is.

Nora.   There. So now it's over. I'm putting the keys here. The maids know everything about the house—better than I. Tomorrow, after I'm gone, Kristine will come over and pack my things from home. I want them sent after me.

Helmer.   Over! It's all over! Nora, will you never think of me?

Nora.   I'm sure I'll often think of you and the children and this house.

Helmer.   May I write to you, Nora?

Nora.   No—never. I won't have that.

Helmer.   But send you things—? You must let me

Nora.   Nothing, nothing.

Helmer.   —help you, when you need help—

Nora.   I told you, no; I won't have it. I'll accept nothing from strangers.

Helmer.   Nora—can I never again be more to you than a stranger?

Nora *(picks up her bag).*   Oh Torvald—then the most wonderful of all would have to happen—

Helmer. Tell me what that would be—!

Nora. For that to happen, both you and I would have to change so that—Oh Torvald, I no longer believe in the wonderful.

Helmer. But I *will* believe. Tell me! Change, so that—?

Nora. So that our living together would become a true marriage. Goodbye. *(She goes out through the hall.)*

Helmer *(sinks down on a chair near the door and covers his face with his hands).* Nora! Nora! *(Looks around him and gets up.)* All empty. She's gone. *(With sudden hope.)* The most wonderful—?!

From downstairs comes the sound of a heavy door slamming shut.

QUESTIONS

1. What evidence does the play provide that *A Doll's House* is about not only Nora's marriage but the institution of marriage itself? **2.** On a number of occasions Nora recalls her father. What relevance do these recollections have to the development of the theme? **3.** Is Krogstad presented as a stock villain, or are we meant to sympathize with him? **4.** What function does Dr. Rank serve in the play?

WRITING TOPICS

1. Does the fact that Nora abandons her children undermine her otherwise heroic decision to walk out on a hollow marriage? For an 1880 German production of the play, Ibsen—in response to public demand—provided an alternate ending in which Nora, after struggling with her conscience, decides that she cannot abandon her children. Is this ending better than the original ending? Explain. **2.** How does the subplot involving Mrs. Linde and Krogstad add force to the main plot of *A Doll's House*?

Death of a Salesman 1949

CERTAIN PRIVATE CONVERSATIONS IN TWO ACTS AND A REQUIEM

ARTHUR MILLER [b. 1915]

CHARACTERS

Willy Loman
Linda, his wife
Biff ⎫ his sons
Happy ⎭
Uncle Ben, his older brother
Howard Wagner, his employer
The Woman

Charley, a neighbor
Bernard, Charley's son
Jenny, Charley's secretary
Stanley, a waiter
Miss Forsythe ⎫ young women
Letta ⎭

The action takes place in Willy Loman's house and yard and in various places he visits in the New York and Boston of today.

Act I

A melody is heard, played upon a flute. It is small and fine, telling of grass and trees and the horizon. The curtain rises.

Before us is the Salesman's house. We are aware of towering, angular shapes behind it, surrounding it on all sides. Only the blue light of the sky falls upon the house and forestage; the surrounding area shows an angry glow of orange. As more light appears, we see a solid vault of apartment houses around the small, fragile-seeming home. An air of the dream clings to the place, a dream rising out of reality. The kitchen at center seems actual enough, for there is a kitchen table with three chairs, and a refrigerator. But no other fixtures are seen. At the back of the kitchen there is a draped entrance, which leads to the living-room. To the right of the kitchen, on a level raised two feet, is a bedroom furnished only with a brass bedstead and a straight chair. On a shelf over the bed a silver athletic trophy stands. A window opens onto the apartment house at the side.

Behind the kitchen, on a level raised six and a half feet, is the boys' bedroom, at present barely visible. Two beds are dimly seen, and at the back of the room a dormer window. (This bedroom is above the unseen living-room.) At the left a stairway curves up to it from the kitchen.

646

The entire setting is wholly, or, in some places, partially transparent. The roof-line of the house is one-dimensional; under and over it we see the apartment buildings. Before the house lies an apron, curving beyond the forestage into the orchestra. This forward area serves as the back yard as well as the locale of all Willy's imaginings and of his city scenes. Whenever the action is in the present the actors observe the imaginary wall-lines, entering the house only through its door at the left. But in the scenes of the past these boundaries are broken, and characters enter or leave a room by stepping "through" a wall onto the forestage.

From the right, Willy Loman, the Salesman, enters, carrying two large sample cases. The flute plays on. He hears but is not aware of it. He is past sixty years of age, dressed quietly. Even as he crosses the stage to the doorway of the house his exhaustion is apparent. He unlocks the door, comes into the kitchen, and thankfully lets his burden down, feeling the soreness of his palms. A word-sigh escapes his lips—it might be "Oh, boy, oh, boy." He closes the door, then carries his cases out into the living-room, through the draped kitchen doorway.

Linda, his wife, has stirred in her bed at the right. She gets out and puts on a robe, listening. Most often jovial, she has developed an iron repression of her exceptions to Willy's behavior—she more than loves him, she admires him, as though his mercurial nature, his temper, his massive dreams and little cruelties, served her only as sharp reminders of the turbulent longings within him, longings which she shares but lacks the temperament to utter and follow to their end.

Linda, *hearing Willy outside the bedroom, calls with some trepidation.*   Willy!
Willy.   It's all right. I came back.
Linda.   Why? What happened? *Slight pause.* Did something happen, Willy?
Willy.   No, nothing happened.
Linda.   You didn't smash the car, did you?
Willy, *with casual irritation.*   I said nothing happened. Didn't you hear me?
Linda.   Don't you feel well?
Willy.   I'm tired to the death. *The flute has faded away. He sits on the bed beside her, a little numb.* I couldn't make it. I just couldn't make it, Linda.
Linda, *very carefully, delicately.*   Where were you all day? You look terrible.
Willy.   I got as far as a little above Yonkers. I stopped for a cup of coffee. Maybe it was the coffee.
Linda.   What?
Willy, *after a pause.*   I suddenly couldn't drive any more. The car kept going off onto the shoulder, y'know?
Linda, *helpfully.*   Oh. Maybe it was the steering again. I don't think Angelo knows the Studebaker.
Willy.   No, it's me, it's me. Suddenly I realize I'm goin' sixty miles an hour and I don't remember the last five minutes. I'm—I can't seem to—keep my mind to it.
Linda.   Maybe it's your glasses. You never went for your new glasses.
Willy.   No, I see everything. I came back ten miles an hour. It took me nearly four hours from Yonkers.

Linda, *resigned.*   Well, you'll just have to take a rest, Willy, you can't continue this way.

Willy.   I just got back from Florida.

Linda.   But you didn't rest your mind. Your mind is overactive, and the mind is what counts, dear.

Willy.   I'll start out in the morning. Maybe I'll feel better in the morning. *She is taking off his shoes.* These goddam arch supports are killing me.

Linda.   Take an aspirin. Should I get you an aspirin? It'll soothe you.

Willy, *with wonder.*   I was driving along, you understand? And I was fine. I was even observing the scenery. You can imagine, me looking at scenery, on the road every week of my life. But it's so beautiful up there, Linda, the trees are so thick, and the sun is warm. I opened the windshield and just let the warm air bathe over me. And then all of a sudden I'm goin' off the road! I'm tellin' ya, I absolutely forgot I was driving. If I'd've gone the other way over the white line I might've killed somebody. So I went on again—and five minutes later I'm dreamin' again, and I nearly—*He presses two fingers against his eyes.* I have such thoughts, I have such strange thoughts.

Linda.   Willy, dear. Talk to them again. There's no reason why you can't work in New York.

Willy.   They don't need me in New York. I'm the New England man. I'm vital in New England.

Linda.   But you're sixty years old. They can't expect you to keep traveling every week.

Willy.   I'll have to send a wire to Portland. I'm supposed to see Brown and Morrison tomorrow morning at ten o'clock to show the line. Goddammit, I could sell them! *He starts putting on his jacket.*

Linda, *taking the jacket from him.*   Why don't you go down to the place tomorrow and tell Howard you've simply got to work in New York? You're too accommodating, dear.

Willy.   If old man Wagner was alive I'd a been in charge of New York now! That man was a prince, he was a masterful man. But that boy of his, that Howard, he don't appreciate. When I went north the first time, the Wagner Company didn't know where New England was!

Linda.   Why don't you tell those things to Howard, dear?

Willy, *encouraged.*   I will, I definitely will. Is there any cheese?

Linda.   I'll make you a sandwich.

Willy.   No, go to sleep. I'll take some milk. I'll be up right away. The boys in?

Linda.   They're sleeping. Happy took Biff on a date tonight.

Willy, *interested.*   That so?

Linda.   It was so nice to see them shaving together, one behind the other, in the bathroom. And going out together. You notice? The whole house smells of shaving lotion.

Willy.   Figure it out. Work a lifetime to pay off a house. You finally own it, and there's nobody to live in it.

Linda.   Well, dear, life is a casting off. It's always that way.

Willy.   No, no, some people—some people accomplish something. Did Biff say anything after I went this morning?

Linda.   You shouldn't have criticized him, Willy, especially after he just got off the train. You mustn't lose your temper with him.

Willy.   When the hell did I lose my temper? I simply asked him if he was making any money. Is that a criticism?

Linda.   But, dear, how could he make any money?

Willy, *worried and angered.*   There's such an undercurrent in him. He became a moody man. Did he apologize when I left this morning?

Linda.   He was crestfallen, Willy. You know how he admires you. I think if he finds himself, then you'll both be happier and not fight any more.

Willy.   How can he find himself on a farm? Is that a life? A farmhand? In the beginning, when he was young, I thought, well, a young man, it's good for him to tramp around, take a lot of different jobs. But it's more than ten years now and he has yet to make thirty-five dollars a week!

Linda.   He's finding himself, Willy.

Willy.   Not finding yourself at the age of thirty-four is a disgrace!

Linda.   Shh!

Willy.   The trouble is he's lazy, goddammit!

Linda.   Willy, please!

Willy.   Biff is a lazy bum!

Linda.   They're sleeping. Get something to eat. Go on down.

Willy.   Why did he come home? I would like to know what brought him home.

Linda.   I don't know. I think he's still lost, Willy. I think he's very lost.

Willy.   Biff Loman is lost. In the greatest country in the world a young man with such—personal attractiveness, gets lost. And such a hard worker. There's one thing about Biff—he's not lazy.

Linda.   Never.

Willy, *with pity and resolve.*   I'll see him in the morning; I'll have a nice talk with him. I'll get him a job selling. He could be big in no time. My God! Remember how they used to follow him around in high school? When he smiled at one of them their faces lit up. When he walked down the street . . . *He loses himself in reminiscences.*

Linda, *trying to bring him out of it.*   Willy, dear, I got a new kind of American-type cheese today. It's whipped.

Willy.   Why do you get American when I like Swiss?

Linda.   I just thought you'd like a change—

Willy.   I don't want a change! I want Swiss cheese. Why am I always being contradicted?

Linda, *with a covering laugh.*   I thought it would be a surprise.

Willy.   Why don't you open a window in here, for God's sake?

Linda, *with infinite patience.*   They're all open, dear.

Willy.   The way they boxed us in here. Bricks and windows, windows and bricks.

Linda.   We should've bought the land next door.

Willy.   The street is lined with cars. There's not a breath of fresh air in the neighborhood. The grass don't grow any more, you can't raise a carrot in the back yard. They should've had a law against apartment houses. Remember those two beautiful elm trees out there? When I and Biff hung the swing between them?

Linda.   Yeah, like being a million miles from the city.

Willy.   They should've arrested the builder for cutting those down. They massacred the neighborhood. *Lost:* More and more I think of those days, Linda. This time of year it was lilac and wisteria. And then the peonies would come out, and the daffodils. What fragrance in this room!

Linda.   Well, after all, people had to move somewhere.

Willy.   No, there's more people now.

Linda.   I don't think there's more people. I think—

Willy.   There's more people! That's what's ruining this country! Population is getting out of control. The competition is maddening! Smell the stink from that apartment house! And another one on the other side . . . . How can they whip cheese?

On Willy's last line, Biff and Happy raise themselves up in their beds, listening.

Linda.   Go down, try it. And be quiet.

Willy, *turning to Linda, guiltily.*   You're not worried about me, are you, sweetheart?

Biff.   What's the matter?

Happy.   Listen!

Linda.   You've got too much on the ball to worry about.

Willy.   You're my foundation and my support, Linda.

Linda.   Just try to relax, dear. You make mountains out of molehills.

Willy.   I won't fight with him any more. If he wants to go back to Texas, let him go.

Linda.   He'll find his way.

Willy.   Sure. Certain men just don't get started till later in life. Like Thomas Edison, I think. Or B. F. Goodrich. One of them was deaf. *He starts for the bedroom doorway.* I'll put my money on Biff.

Linda.   And Willy—if it's warm Sunday we'll drive in the country. And we'll open the windshield, and take lunch.

Willy.   No, the windshields don't open on the new cars.

Linda.   But you opened it today.

Willy.   Me? I didn't. *He stops.* Now isn't that peculiar! Isn't that a remarkable—*He breaks off in amazement and fright as the flute is heard distantly.*

Linda.   What, darling?

Willy.   That is the most remarkable thing.

Linda.   What, dear?

Willy.   I was thinking of the Chevvy. *Slight pause.* Nineteen twenty-eight . . . . when I had that red Chevvy—*Breaks off.* That funny? I coulda sworn I was driving that Chevvy today.

Linda.   Well, that's nothing. Something must've reminded you.

Willy.   Remarkable. Ts. Remember those days? The way Biff used to simon-
ize that car? The dealer refused to believe there was eighty thousand miles
on it. *He shakes his head.* Heh! *To Linda.*   Close your eyes, I'll be right up.
He walks out of the bedroom.

Happy, *to Biff.*   Jesus, maybe he smashed up the car again!

Linda, *calling after Willy.*   Be careful on the stairs, dear! The cheese is on
the middle shelf! *She turns, goes over to the bed, takes his jacket, and goes
out of the bedroom.*

*Light has risen on the boys' room. Unseen, Willy is heard talking to himself,
"Eighty thousand miles," and a little laugh. Biff gets out of bed, comes downstage a bit, and stands attentively. Biff is two years older than his brother Happy,
well built, but in these days bears a worn air and seems less self-assured. He has
succeeded less, and his dreams are stronger and less acceptable than Happy's.
Happy is tall, powerfully made. Sexuality is like a visible color on him, or a
scent that many women have discovered. He, like his brother, is lost, but in a
different way, for he has never allowed himself to turn his face toward defeat
and is thus more confused and hard-skinned, although seemingly more content.*

Happy, *getting out of bed.*   He's going to get his license taken away if he keeps
that up. I'm getting nervous about him, y'know, Biff?

Biff.   His eyes are going.

Happy.   No, I've driven with him. He sees all right. He just doesn't keep his
mind on it. I drove into the city with him last week. He stops at a green
light and then it turns red and he goes. *He laughs.*

Biff.   Maybe he's color-blind.

Happy.   Pop? Why he's got the finest eye for color in the business. You know
that.

Biff, *sitting down on his bed.*   I'm going to sleep.

Happy.   You're not still sour on Dad, are you, Biff?

Biff.   He's all right, I guess.

Willy, *underneath them, in the living-room.*   Yes, sir, eighty thousand miles—
eighty-two thousand!

Biff.   You smoking?

Happy, *holding out a pack of cigarettes.*   Want one?

Biff, *taking a cigarette.*   I can never sleep when I smell it.

Happy, *with deep sentiment.*   Funny, Biff, y'know? Us sleeping in here again?
The old beds. *He pats his bed affectionately.* All the talk that went across
those two beds, huh? Our whole lives.

Biff.   Yeah. Lotta dreams and plans.

Happy, *with a deep and masculine laugh.*   About five hundred women would
like to know what was said in this room.

They share a soft laugh.

Biff.   Remember that big Betsy something—what the hell was her name—over on Bushwick Avenue?

Happy, *combing his hair.*   With the collie dog!

Biff.   That's the one. I got you in there, remember?

Happy.   Yeah, that was my first time—I think. Boy there was a pig! *They laugh, almost crudely.* You taught me everything I know about women. Don't forget that.

Biff.   I bet you forgot how bashful you used to be. Especially with girls.

Happy.   Oh, I still am, Biff.

Biff.   Oh, go on.

Happy.   I just control it, that's all. I think I got less bashful and you got more so. What happened, Biff? Where's the old humor, the old confidence? *He shakes Biff's knee. Biff gets up and moves restlessly about the room.* What's the matter?

Biff.   Why does Dad mock me all the time?

Happy.   He's not mocking you, he—

Biff.   Everything I say there's a twist of mockery on his face. I can't get near him.

Happy.   He just wants you to make good, that's all. I wanted to talk to you about Dad for a long time, Biff. Something's—happening to him. He—talks to himself.

Biff.   I noticed that this morning. But he always mumbled.

Happy.   But not so noticeable. It got so embarrassing I sent him to Florida. And you know something? Most of the time he's talking to you.

Biff.   What's he say about me?

Happy.   I can't make it out.

Biff.   What's he say about me?

Happy.   I think the fact that you're not settled, that you're still kind of up in the air . . .

Biff.   There's one or two other things depressing him, Happy.

Happy.   What do you mean?

Biff.   Never mind. Just don't lay it all to me.

Happy.   But I think if you just got started—I mean—is there any future for you out there?

Biff.   I tell ya, Hap, I don't know what the future is. I don't know—what I'm supposed to want.

Happy.   What do you mean?

Biff.   Well, I spent six or seven years after high school trying to work myself up. Shipping clerk, salesman, business of one kind or another. And it's a measly manner of existence. To get on that subway on the hot mornings in summer. To devote your whole life to keeping stock, or making phone calls, or selling or buying. To suffer fifty weeks of the year for the sake of a two-week vacation, when all you really desire is to be outdoors, with your shirt off. And always to have to get ahead of the next fella. And still—that's how you build a future.

Happy. Well, you really enjoy it on a farm? Are you content out there?

Biff, *with rising agitation.* Hap, I've had twenty or thirty different kinds of jobs since I left home before the war, and it always turns out the same. I just realized it lately. In Nebraska when I herded cattle, and the Dakotas, and Arizona, and now in Texas. It's why I came home now, I guess, because I realized it. This farm I work on, it's spring there now, see? And they've got about fifteen new colts. There's nothing more inspiring or—beautiful than the sight of a mare and a new colt. And it's cool there now, see? Texas is cool now, and it's spring. And whenever spring comes to where I am, I suddenly get the feeling, my God, I'm not gettin' anywhere! What the hell am I doing, playing around with horses, twenty-eight dollars a week! I'm thirty-four years old, I oughta be makin' my future. That's when I come running home. And now, I get here, and I don't know what to do with myself. *After a pause:* I've always made a point of not wasting my life, and everytime I come back here I know that all I've done is to waste my life.

Happy. You're a poet, you know that, Biff? You're a—you're an idealist!

Biff. No, I'm mixed up very bad. Maybe I oughta get married. Maybe I oughta get stuck into something. Maybe that's my trouble. I'm like a boy. I'm not married, I'm not in business, I just—I'm like a boy. Are you content, Hap? You're a success, aren't you? Are you content?

Happy. Hell, no!

Biff. Why? You're making money, aren't you?

Happy, *moving about with energy, expressiveness.* All I can do now is wait for the merchandise manager to die. And suppose I get to be merchandise manager? He's a good friend of mine, and he just built a terrific estate on Long Island. And he lived there about two months and sold it, and now he's building another one. He can't enjoy it once it's finished. And I know that's just what I would do. I don't know what the hell I'm workin' for. Sometimes I sit in my apartment—all alone. And I think of the rent I'm paying. And it's crazy. But then, it's what I always wanted. My own apartment, a car, and plenty of women. And still, goddammit, I'm lonely.

Biff, *with enthusiasm.* Listen, why don't you come out West with me?

Happy. You and I, heh?

Biff. Sure, maybe we could buy a ranch. Raise cattle, use our muscles. Men built like we are should be working out in the open.

Happy, *avidly.* The Loman Brothers, heh?

Biff, *with vast affection.* Sure, we'd be known all over the counties!

Happy, *enthralled.* That's what I dream about, Biff. Sometimes I want to just rip my clothes off in the middle of the store and outbox that goddam merchandise manager. I mean I can outbox, outrun, and outlift anybody in that store, and I have to take orders from those common, petty sons-of-bitches till I can't stand it any more.

Biff. I'm tellin' you, kid, if you were with me I'd be happy out there.

Happy, *enthused.* See, Biff, everybody around me is so false that I'm constantly lowering my ideals . . .

Biff. Baby, together we'd stand up for one another, we'd have someone to trust.

Happy. If I were around you—

Biff. Hap, the trouble is we weren't brought up to grub for money. I don't know how to do it.

Happy. Neither can I!

Biff. Then let's go!

Happy. The only thing is—what can you make out there?

Biff. But look at your friend. Builds an estate and then hasn't the peace of mind to live in it.

Happy. Yeah, but when he walks into the store the waves part in front of him. That's fifty-two thousand dollars a year coming through the revolving door, and I got more in my pinky finger than he's got in his head.

Biff. Yeah, but you just said—

Happy. I gotta show some of those pompous, self-important executives over there that Hap Loman can make the grade. I want to walk into the store the way he walks in. Then I'll go with you, Biff. We'll be together yet, I swear. But take those two we had tonight. Now weren't they gorgeous creatures?

Biff. Yeah, yeah, most gorgeous I've had in years.

Happy. I get that any time I want, Biff. Whenever I feel disgusted. The only trouble is, it gets like bowling or something. I just keep knockin' them over and it doesn't mean anything. You still run around a lot?

Biff. Naa. I'd like to find a girl—steady, somebody with substance.

Happy. That's what I long for.

Biff. Go on! You'd never come home.

Happy. I would! Somebody with character, with resistance! Like Mom, y'know? You're gonna call me a bastard when I tell you this. That girl Charlotte I was with tonight is engaged to be married in five weeks. *He tries on his new hat.*

Biff. No kiddin'!

Happy. Sure, the guy's in line for the vice-presidency of the store. I don't know what gets into me, maybe I just have an overdeveloped sense of competition or something, but I went and ruined her, and furthermore I can't get rid of her. And he's the third executive I've done that to. Isn't that a crummy characteristic? And to top it all, I go to their weddings! *Indignantly, but laughing.* Like I'm not supposed to take bribes. Manufacturers offer me a hundred-dollar bill now and then to throw an order their way. You know how honest I am, but it's like this girl, see. I hate myself for it. Because I don't want the girl, and, still, I take it and—I love it!

Biff. Let's go to sleep.

Happy. I guess we didn't settle anything, heh?

Biff: I just got one idea that I think I'm going to try.

Happy. What's that?

Biff. Remember Bill Oliver?

Happy. Sure, Oliver is very big now. You want to work for him again?

Biff. No, but when I quit he said something to me. He put his arm on my shoulder, and he said, "Biff, if you ever need anything, come to me."

Happy. I remember that. That sounds good.

Biff. I think I'll go to see him. If I could get ten thousand or even seven or eight thousand dollars I could buy a beautiful ranch.

Happy. I bet he'd back you. 'Cause he thought highly of you, Biff. I mean, they all do. You're well liked, Biff. That's why I say to come back here, and we both have the apartment. And I'm tellin' you, Biff, any babe you want . . .

Biff. No, with a ranch I could do the work I like and still be something. I just wonder though. I wonder if Oliver still thinks I stole that carton of basketballs.

Happy. Oh, he probably forgot that long ago. It's almost ten years. You're too sensitive. Anyway, he didn't really fire you.

Biff. Well, I think he was going to. I think that's why I quit. I was never sure whether he knew or not. I know he thought the world of me, though. I was the only one he'd let lock up the place.

Willy, *below.* You gonna wash the engine, Biff?

Happy. Shh!

Biff looks at Happy, who is gazing down, listening. Willy is mumbling in the parlor.

Happy. You hear that?

They listen. Willy laughs warmly.

Biff, *growing angry.* Doesn't he know Mom can hear that?

Willy. Don't get your sweater dirty, Biff!

A look of pain crosses Biff's face.

Happy. Isn't that terrible? Don't leave again, will you? You'll find a job here. You gotta stick around. I don't know what to do about him, it's getting embarrassing.

Willy. What a simonizing job!

Biff. Mom's hearing that!

Willy. No kiddin', Biff, you got a date? Wonderful!

Happy. Go on to sleep. But talk to him in the morning, will you?

Biff, *reluctantly getting into bed.* With her in the house. Brother!

Happy, *getting into bed.* I wish you'd have a good talk with him.

The light on their room begins to fade.

Biff, *to himself in bed.* That selfish, stupid . . .

Happy. Sh . . . Sleep, Biff.

Their light is out. Well before they have finished speaking, Willy's form is dimly seen below in the darkened kitchen. He opens the refrigerator, searches in there, and takes out a bottle of milk. The apartment houses are fading out, and the entire house and surroundings become covered with leaves. Music insinuates itself as the leaves appear.

Willy.   Just wanna be careful with those girls, Biff, that's all. Don't make any promises. No promises of any kind. Because a girl, y'know, they always believe what you tell 'em, and you're very young, Biff, you're too young to be talking seriously to girls.

Light rises on the kitchen. Willy, talking, shuts the refrigerator door and comes downstage to the kitchen table. He pours milk into a glass. He is totally immersed in himself, smiling faintly.

Willy.   Too young entirely, Biff. You want to watch your schooling first. Then when you're all set, there'll be plenty of girls for a boy like you. *He smiles broadly at a kitchen chair.* That so? The girls pay for you? *He laughs.* Boy, you must really be makin' a hit.

Willy is gradually addressing—physically—a point offstage, speaking through the wall of the kitchen, and his voice has been rising in volume to that of a normal conversation.

Willy.   I been wondering why you polish the car so careful. Ha! Don't leave the hubcaps, boys. Get the chamois to the hubcaps. Happy, use newspaper on the windows, it's the easiest thing. Show him how to do it, Biff! You see, Happy? Pad it up, use it like a pad. That's it, that's it, good work. You're doin' all right, Hap. *He pauses, then nods in approbation for a few seconds, then looks upward.* Biff, first thing we gotta do when we get time is clip that big branch over the house. Afraid it's gonna fall in a storm and hit the roof. Tell you what. We get a rope and sling her around, and then we climb up there with a couple of saws and take her down. Soon as you finish the car, boys, I wanna see ya. I got a surprise for you, boys.
Biff, *offstage.*   Whatta ya got, Dad?
Willy.   No, you finish first. Never leave a job till you're finished—remember that. *Looking toward the "big trees":*   Biff, up in Albany I saw a beautiful hammock. I think I'll buy it next trip, and we'll hang it right between those two elms. Wouldn't that be something? Just swingin' there under those branches. Boy, that would be . . .

Young Biff and Young Happy appear from the direction Willy was addressing. Happy carries rags and a pail of water. Biff, wearing a sweater with a block "S," carries a football.

Biff, *pointing in the direction of the car offstage.*   How's that, Pop, professional?

Willy.   Terrific. Terrific job, boys. Good work, Biff.

Happy.   Where's the surprise, Pop?

Willy.   In the back seat of the car.

Happy.   Boy! *He runs off.*

Biff.   What is it, Dad? Tell me, what'd you buy?

Willy, *laughing, cuffs him.*   Never mind, something I want you to have.

Biff, *turns and starts off.*   What is it, Hap?

Happy, *offstage.*   It's a punching bag!

Biff.   Oh, Pop!

Willy.   It's got Gene Tunney's signature on it!

Happy runs onstage with a punching bag.

Biff.   Gee, how'd you know we wanted a punching bag?

Willy.   Well, it's the finest thing for the timing.

Happy, *lies down on his back and pedals with his feet.*   I'm losing weight, you notice, Pop?

Willy, *to Happy.*   Jumping rope is good too.

Biff.   Did you see the new football I got?

Willy, *examining the ball.*   Where'd you get a new ball?

Biff.   The coach told me to practice my passing.

Willy.   That so? And he gave you the ball, heh?

Biff.   Well, I borrowed it from the locker room. *He laughs confidentially.*

Willy, *laughing with him at the theft.*   I want you to return that.

Happy.   I told you he wouldn't like it!

Biff, *angrily.*   Well, I'm bringing it back!

Willy, *stopping the incipient argument, to Happy.*   Sure, he's gotta practice with a regulation ball, doesn't he? *To Biff.*   Coach'll probably congratulate you on your initiative!

Biff.   Oh, he keeps congratulating my initiative all the time, Pop.

Willy.   That's because he likes you. If somebody else took that ball there'd be an uproar. So what's the report, boys, what's the report?

Biff.   Where'd you go this time, Dad? Gee we were lonesome for you.

Willy, *pleased, puts an arm around each boy and they come down to the apron.*   Lonesome, heh?

Biff.   Missed you every minute.

Willy.   Don't say? Tell you a secret, boys. Don't breathe it to a soul. Someday I'll have my own business, and I'll never have to leave home any more.

Happy.   Like Uncle Charley, heh?

Willy.   Bigger than Uncle Charley! Because Charley is not—liked. He's liked, but he's not—well liked.

Biff.   Where'd you go this time, Dad?

Willy.   Well, I got on the road, and I went north to Providence. Met the Mayor.

Biff.   The Mayor of Providence!

Willy.   He was sitting in the hotel lobby.

Biff.   What'd he say?

Willy.   He said, "Morning!" And I said, "You got a fine city here, Mayor." And then he had coffee with me. And then I went to Waterbury. Waterbury is a fine city. Big clock city, the famous Waterbury clock. Sold a nice bill there. And then Boston—Boston is the cradle of the Revolution. A fine city. And a couple of other towns in Mass., and on to Portland and Bangor and straight home!

Biff.   Gee, I'd love to go with you sometime, Dad.

Willy.   Soon as summer comes.

Happy.   Promise?

Willy.   You and Hap and I, and I'll show you all the towns. America is full of beautiful towns and fine, upstanding people. And they know me, boys, they know me up and down New England. The finest people. And when I bring you fellas up, there'll be open sesame for all of us, 'cause one thing, boys: I have friends. I can park my car in any street in New England, and the cops protect it like their own. This summer, heh?

Biff and Happy, *together:*   Yeah! You bet!

Willy.   We'll take our bathing suits.

Happy.   We'll carry your bags, Pop!

Willy.   Oh, won't that be something! Me comin' into the Boston stores with you boys carryin' my bags. What a sensation!

Biff is prancing around, practicing passing the ball.

Willy.   You nervous, Biff, about the game?

Biff.   Not if you're gonna be there.

Willy.   What do they say about you in school, now that they made you captain?

Happy.   There's a crowd of girls behind him everytime the classes change.

Biff, *taking Willy's hand.*   This Saturday, Pop, this Saturday—just for you, I'm going to break through for a touchdown.

Happy.   You're supposed to pass.

Biff.   I'm takin' one play for Pop. You watch me, Pop, and when I take off my helmet, that means I'm breakin' out. Then you watch me crash through that line!

Willy, *kisses Biff.*   Oh, wait'll I tell this in Boston!

Bernard enters in knickers. He is younger than Biff, earnest and loyal, a worried boy.

Bernard.   Biff, where are you? You're supposed to study with me today.

Willy.   Hey, looka Bernard. What're you lookin' so anemic about, Bernard?

Bernard.   He's gotta study, Uncle Willy. He's got Regents next week.

Happy, *tauntingly, spinning Bernard around.*   Let's box, Bernard!

Bernard.   Biff! *He gets away from Happy.* Listen, Biff, I heard Mr. Birnbaum say that if you don't start studyin' math he's gonna flunk you, and you won't graduate. I heard him!

Willy.   You better study with him, Biff. Go ahead now.

Bernard.   I heard him!

Biff.   Oh, Pop, you didn't see my sneakers!   *He holds up a foot for Willy to look at.*

Willy.   Hey, that's a beautiful job of printing!

Bernard, *wiping his glasses.*   Just because he printed University of Virginia on his sneakers doesn't mean they've got to graduate him, Uncle Willy!

Willy, *angrily.*   What're you talking about? With scholarships to three universities they're gonna flunk him?

Bernard.   But I heard Mr. Birnbaum say—

Willy.   Don't be a pest, Bernard! *To his boys.*   What an anemic!

Bernard.   Okay, I'm waiting for you in my house, Biff.

Bernard goes off. The Lomans laugh.

Willy.   Bernard is not well liked, is he?

Biff.   He's liked, but he's not well liked.

Happy.   That's right, Pop.

Willy.   That's just what I mean. Bernard can get the best marks in school, y'understand, but when he gets out in the business world, y'understand, you are going to be five times ahead of hm. That's why I thank Almighty God you're both built like Adonises. Because the man who makes an appearance in the business world, the man who creates personal interest, is the man who gets ahead. Be liked and you will never want. You take me, for instance. I never have to wait in line to see a buyer. "Willy Loman is here!" That's all they have to know, and I go right through.

Biff.   Did you knock them dead, Pop?

Willy.   Knocked 'em cold in Providence, slaughtered 'em in Boston.

Happy, *on his back, pedaling again.*   I'm losing weight, you notice, Pop?

Linda enters, as of old, a ribbon in her hair, carrying a basket of washing.

Linda, *with youthful energy.*   Hello, dear!

Willy.   Sweetheart!

Linda.   How'd the Chevvy run?

Willy.   Chevrolet, Linda, is the greatest car ever built. *To the boys:*   Since when do you let your mother carry wash up the stairs?

Biff.   Grab hold there, boy!

Happy.   Where to, Mom?

Linda.   Hang them up on the line. And you better go down to your friends,

Biff. The cellar is full of boys. They don't know what to do with themselves.

Biff. Ah, when Pop comes home they can wait!

Willy, *laughs appreciatively.* You better go down and tell them what to do, Biff.

Biff. I think I'll have them sweep out the furnace room.

Willy. Good work, Biff.

Biff, *goes through wall-line of kitchen to doorway at back and calls down:* Fellas! Everybody sweep out the furnace room! I'll be right down!

Voices. All right! Okay, Biff.

Biff. George and Sam and Frank, come out back! We're hangin' up the wash! Come on, Hap, on the double! *He and Happy carry out the basket.*

Linda. The way they obey him!

Willy. Well, that's training, the training. I'm tellin' you, I was sellin' thousands and thousands, but I had to come home.

Linda. Oh, the whole block'll be at that game. Did you sell anything?

Willy. I did five hundred gross in Providence and seven hundred gross in Boston.

Linda. No! Wait a minute, I've got a pencil. *She pulls pencil and paper out of her apron pocket.* That makes your commission . . . Two hundred—my God! Two hundred and twelve dollars!

Willy. Well, I didn't figure it yet, but . . .

Linda. How much did you do?

Willy. Well, I—I did—about a hundred and eighty gross in Providence. Well, no—it came to—roughly two hundred gross on the whole trip.

Linda, *without hesitation:* Two hundred gross. That's . . . *She figures.*

Willy. The trouble was that three of the stores were half closed for inventory in Boston. Otherwise I woulda broke records.

Linda. Well, it makes seventy dollars and some pennies. That's very good.

Willy. What do we owe?

Linda. Well, on the first there's sixteen dollars on the refrigerator—

Willy. Why sixteen?

Linda. Well, the fan belt broke, so it was a dollar eighty.

Willy. But it's brand new.

Linda. Well, the man said that's the way it is. Till they work themselves in, y'know.

They move through the wall-line into the kitchen.

Willy. I hope we didn't get stuck on that machine.

Linda. They got the biggest ads of any of them!

Willy. I know, it's a fine machine. What else?

Linda. Well, there's nine-sixty for the washing machine. And for the vacuum cleaner there's three and a half due on the fifteenth. Then the roof, you got twenty-one dollars remaining.

Willy. It don't leak, does it?

Linda.   No, they did a wonderful job. Then you owe Frank for the carbu-
  retor.
Willy.   I'm not going to pay that man! That goddam Chevrolet, they ought to
  prohibit the manufacture of that car!
Linda.   Well, you owe him three and a half. And odds and ends, comes to
  around a hundred and twenty dollars by the fifteenth.
Willy.   A hundred and twenty dollars! My God, if business don't pick up I
  don't know what I'm gonna do!
Linda.   Well, next week you'll do better.
Willy.   Oh, I'll knock 'em dead next week. I'll go to Hartford. I'm very well
  liked in Hartford. You know, the trouble is, Linda, people don't seem to take
  to me.

They move onto the forestage.

Linda.   Oh, don't be foolish.
Willy.   I know it when I walk in. They seem to laugh at me.
Linda.   Why? Why would they laugh at you? Don't talk that way, Willy.

*Willy moves to the edge of the stage. Linda goes into the kitchen and starts to
darn stockings.*

Willy.   I don't know the reason for it, but they just pass me by. I'm not noticed.
Linda.   But you're doing wonderful, dear. You're making seventy to a hundred
  dollars a week.
Willy.   But I gotta be at it ten, twelve hours a day. Other men—I don't know—
  they do it easier. I don't know why—I can't stop myself—I talk too much. A
  man oughta come in with a few words. One thing about Charley. He's a
  man of few words, and they respect him.
Linda.   You don't talk too much, you're just lively.
Willy, *smiling.*   Well, I figure, what the hell, life is short, a couple of jokes.
  To himself. I joke too much! *The smile goes.*
Linda.   Why? You're—
Willy.   I'm fat. I'm very—foolish to look at, Linda. I didn't tell you, but
  Christmas time I happened to be calling on F. H. Stewarts, and a salesman
  I know, as I was going in to see the buyer I heard him say something about—
  walrus. And I—I cracked him right across the face. I won't take that. I sim-
  ply will not take that. But they do laugh at me. I know that.
Linda.   Darling . . .
Willy.   I gotta overcome it. I know I gotta overcome it. I'm not dressing to
  advantage, maybe.
Linda.   Willy, darling, you're the handsomest man in the world—
Willy.   Oh, no, Linda.
Linda.   To me you are. *Slight pause.* The handsomest.

From the darkness is heard the laughter of a woman. Willy doesn't turn to it, but it continues through Linda's lines.

Linda.   And the boys, Willy. Few men are idolized by their children the way you are.

Music is heard as behind a scrim, to the left of the house, The Woman, dimly seen, is dressing.

Willy, *with great feeling.*   You're the best there is, Linda, you're a pal, you know that? On the road—on the road I want to grab you sometimes and just kiss the life outa you.

The laughter is loud now, and he moves into a brightening area at the left, where The Woman has come from behind the scrim and is standing, putting on her hat, looking into a "mirror" and laughing.

Willy.   'Cause I get so lonely—especially when business is bad and there's nobody to talk to. I get the feeling that I'll never sell anything again, that I won't make a living for you, or a business, a business for the boys. *He talks through The Woman's subsiding laughter; The Woman primps at the "mirror."* There's so much I want to make for—
The Woman.   Me? You didn't make me, Willy. I picked you.
Willy, *pleased.*   You picked me?
The Woman, *who is quite proper-looking, Willy's age.*   I did. I've been sitting at that desk watching all the salesmen go by, day in, day out. But you've got such a sense of humor, and we do have such a good time together, don't we?
Willy.   Sure, sure. *He takes her in his arms.* Why do you have to go now?
The Woman.   It's two o'clock . . .
Willy.   No, come on in! *He pulls her.*
The Woman.   . . . my sisters'll be scandalized. When'll you be back?
Willy.   Oh, two weeks about. Will you come up again?
The Woman.   Sure thing. You do make me laugh. It's good for me. *She squeezes his arm, kisses him.* And I think you're a wonderful man.
Willy.   You picked me, heh?
The Woman.   Sure. Because you're so sweet. And such a kidder.
Willy.   Well, I'll see you next time I'm in Boston.
The Woman.   I'll put you right through to the buyers.
Willy, *slapping her bottom.*   Right. Well, bottoms up!
The Woman, *slaps him gently and laughs.*   You just kill me, Willy. *He suddenly grabs her and kisses her roughly.* You kill me. And thanks for the stockings. I love a lot of stockings. Well, good night.
Willy.   Good night. And keep your pores open!
The Woman.   Oh, Willy!

The Woman bursts out laughing, and Linda's laughter blends in. The Woman disappears into the dark. Now the area at the kitchen table brightens. Linda is sitting where she was at the kitchen table, but now is mending a pair of her silk stockings.

Linda.   You are, Willy. The handsomest man. You've got no reason to feel that—

Willy, *coming out of The Woman's dimming area and going over to Linda.*   I'll make it all up to you, Linda, I'll—

Linda.   There's nothing to make up, dear. You're doing fine, better than—

Willy, *noticing her mending.*   What's that?

Linda.   Just mending my stockings. They're so expensive—

Willy, *angrily, taking them from her.*   I won't have you mending stockings in this house! Now throw them out!

Linda puts the stockings in her pocket.

Bernard, *entering on the run.*   Where is he? If he doesn't study!

Willy, *moving to the forestage, with great agitation.*   You'll give him the answers!

Bernard.   I do, but I can't on a Regents! That's a state exam! They're liable to arrest me!

Willy.   Where is he? I'll whip him, I'll whip him!

Linda.   And he'd better give back that football, Willy, it's not nice.

Willy.   Biff! Where is he? Why is he taking everything?

Linda.   He's too rough with the girls, Willy. All the mothers are afraid of him!

Willy.   I'll whip him!

Bernard.   He's driving the car without a license!

The Woman's laugh is heard.

Willy: Shut up!

Linda.   All the mothers—

Willy.   Shut up!

Bernard, *backing quietly away and out.*   Mr. Birnbaum says he's stuck up.

Willy.   Get outa here!

Bernard.   If he doesn't buckle down he'll flunk math! *He goes off.*

Linda.   He's right, Willy, you've gotta—

Willy, *exploding at her.*   There's nothing the matter with him! You want him to be a worm like Bernard? He's got spirit, personality . . .

As he speaks, Linda, almost in tears, exits into the living-room. Willy is alone in the kitchen, wilting and staring. The leaves are gone. It is night again, and the apartment houses look down from behind.

Willy.   Loaded with it. Loaded! What is he stealing? He's giving it back, isn't he? Why is he stealing? What did I tell him? I never in my life told him anything but decent things.

Happy in pajamas has come down the stairs; Willy suddenly becomes aware of Happy's presence.

Happy.   Let's go now, come on.
Willy, *sitting down at the kitchen table.*   Huh! Why did she have to wax the floors herself? Everytime she waxes the floors she keels over. She knows that!
Happy.   Shh! Take it easy. What brought you back tonight?
Willy.   I got an awful scare. Nearly hit a kid in Yonkers. God! Why didn't I go to Alaska with my brother Ben that time! Ben! That man was a genius, that man was success incarnate! What a mistake! He begged me to go.
Happy.   Well, there's no use in—
Willy.   You guys! There was a man started with the clothes on his back and ended up with diamond mines!
Happy.   Boy, someday I'd like to know how he did it.
Willy.   What's the mystery? The man knew what he wanted and went out and got it! Walked into a jungle, and comes out, the age of twenty-one, and he's rich! The world is an oyster, but you don't crack it open on a mattress!
Happy.   Pop, I told you I'm gonna retire you for life.
Willy.   You'll retire me for life on seventy goddam dollars a week? And your women and your car and your apartment, and you'll retire me for life! Christ's sake, I couldn't get past Yonkers today! Where are you guys, where are you? The woods are burning! I can't drive a car!

Charley has appeared in the doorway. He is a large man, slow of speech, laconic, immovable. In all he says, despite what he says, there is pity, and, now, trepidation. He has a robe over pajamas, slippers on his feet. He enters the kitchen.

Charley.   Everything all right?
Happy.   Yeah, Charley, everything's . . .
Willy.   What's the matter?
Charley.   I heard some noise. I thought something happened. Can't we do something about the walls? You sneeze in here, and in my house hats blow off.
Happy.   Let's go to bed, Dad. Come on.

Charley signals to Happy to go.

Willy.   You go ahead, I'm not tired at the moment.
Happy, *to Willy.*   Take it easy, huh? *He exits.*
Willy.   What're you doin' up?
Charley, *sitting down at the kitchen table opposite Willy.*   Couldn't sleep good. I had a heartburn.

Willy.   Well, you don't know how to eat.

Charley.   I eat with my mouth.

Willy: No, you're ignorant. You gotta know about vitamins and things like that.

Charley.   Come on, let's shoot. Tire you out a little.

Willy, *hesitantly.*   All right. You got cards?

Charley, *taking a deck from his pocket.*   Yeah, I got them. Someplace. What is it with those vitamins?

Willy, *dealing.*   They build up your bones. Chemistry.

Charley.   Yeah, but there's no bones in a heartburn.

Willy.   What are you talkin' about? Do you know the first thing about it?

Charley.   Don't get insulted.

Willy.   Don't talk about something you don't know anything about.

They are playing. Pause.

Charley.   What're you doin' home?

Willy.   A little trouble with the car.

Charley.   Oh. *Pause.* I'd like to take a trip to California.

Willy.   Don't say.

Charley.   You want a job?

Willy.   I got a job, I told you that. *After a slight pause:* What the hell are you offering me a job for?

Charley.   Don't get insulted.

Willy.   Don't insult me.

Charley.   I don't see no sense in it. You don't have to go on this way.

Willy.   I got a good job. *Slight pause.* What do you keep comin' in here for?

Charley.   You want me to go?

Willy, *after a pause, withering.*   I can't understand it. He's going back to Texas again. What the hell is that?

Charley.   Let him go.

Willy.   I got nothin' to give him, Charley, I'm clean, I'm clean.

Charley.   He won't starve. None a them starve. Forget about him.

Willy.   Then what have I got to remember?

Charley.   You take it too hard. To hell with it. When a deposit bottle is broken you don't get your nickel back.

Willy.   That's easy enough for you to say.

Charley.   That ain't easy for me to say.

Willy.   Did you see the ceiling I put up in the living-room?

Charley.   Yeah, that's a piece of work. To put up a ceiling is a mystery to me. How did you do it?

Willy.   What's the difference?

Charley.   Well, talk about it.

Willy.   You gonna put up a ceiling?

Charley.   How could I put up a ceiling?

Willy.   Then what the hell are you bothering me for?

Charley.   You're insulted again.

Willy.   A man who can't handle tools is not a man. You're disgusting.

Charley.   Don't call me disgusting, Willy.

Uncle Ben, carrying a valise and an umbrella, enters the forestage from around the right corner of the house. He is a stolid man, in his sixties, with a mustache and an authoritative air. He is utterly certain of his destiny, and there is an aura of far places about him. He enters exactly as Willy speaks.

Willy.   I'm getting awfully tired, Ben.

Ben's music is heard. Ben looks around at everything.

Charley.   Good, keep playing; you'll sleep better. Did you call me Ben?

Ben looks at his watch.

Willy.   That's funny. For a second there you reminded me of my brother Ben.

Ben.   I only have a few minutes. *He strolls, inspecting the place. Willy and Charley continue playing.*

Charley.   You never heard from him again, heh? Since that time?

Willy.   Didn't Linda tell you? Couple of weeks ago we got a letter from his wife in Africa. He died.

Charley.   That so.

Ben, *chuckling.*   So this is Brooklyn, eh?

Charley.   Maybe you're in for some of his money.

Willy.   Naa, he had seven sons. There's just one opportunity I had with that man . . .

Ben.   I must make a train, William. There are several properties I'm looking at in Alaska.

Willy.   Sure, sure! If I'd gone with him to Alaska that time, everything would've been totally different.

Charley.   Go on, you'd froze to death up there.

Willy.   What're you talking about?

Ben.   Opportunity is tremendous in Alaska, William. Surprised you're not up there.

Willy.   Sure, tremendous.

Charley.   Heh?

Willy.   There was the only man I ever met who knew the answers.

Charley.   Who?

Ben.   How are you all?

Willy, *taking a pot, smiling.*   Fine, fine.

Charley.   Pretty sharp tonight.

Ben.   Is Mother living with you?

Willy.   No, she died a long time ago.

Charley.   Who?

Ben.   That's too bad. Fine specimen of a lady, Mother.

Willy, *to Charley.*   Heh?

Ben.   I'd hoped to see the old girl.

Charley.   Who died?

Ben.   Heard anything from Father, have you?

Willie, *unnerved.*   What do you mean, who died?

Charley, *taking a pot.*   What're you talkin' about?

Ben, *looking at his watch.*   William, it's half-past eight!

Willy, *as though to dispel his confusion he angrily stops Charley's hand.*   That's my build!

Charley.   I put the ace—

Willy.   If you don't know how to play the game I'm not gonna throw my money away on you!

Charley, *rising.*   It was my ace, for God's sake!

Willy.   I'm through, I'm through!

Ben.   When did Mother die?

Willy.   Long ago. Since the beginning you never knew how to play cards.

Charley, *picks up the cards and goes to the door.*   All right! Next time I'll bring a deck with five aces.

Willy.   I don't play that kind of game!

Charley, *turning to him.*   You ought to be ashamed of yourself!

Willy.   Yeah?

Charley.   Yeah! *He goes out.*

Willy, *slamming the door after him.*   Ignoramus!

Ben, *as Willy comes toward him through the wall-line of the kitchen.*   So you're William.

Willy, *shaking Ben's hand.*   Ben! I've been waiting for you so long! What's the answer? How did you do it?

Ben.   Oh, there's a story in that.

Linda enters the forestage, as of old, carrying the wash basket.

Linda.   Is this Ben?

Ben, *gallantly.*   How do you do, my dear.

Linda.   Where've you been all these years? Willy's always wondered why you—

Willy, *pulling Ben away from her impatiently.*   Where is Dad? Didn't you follow him? How did you get started?

Ben.   Well, I don't know how much you remember.

Willy.   Well, I was just a baby, of course, only three or four years old—

Ben.   Three years and eleven months.

Willy.   What a memory, Ben!

Ben.   I have many enterprises, William, and I have never kept books.

Willy.   I remember I was sitting under the wagon in—was it Nebraska?

Ben.   It was South Dakota, and I gave you a bunch of wild flowers.

Willy. I remember you walking away down some open road.

Ben, *laughing.* I was going to find Father in Alaska.

Willy. Where is he?

Ben. At that age I had a very faulty view of geography, William. I discovered after a few days that I was heading due south, so instead of Alaska, I ended up in Africa.

Linda. Africa!

Willy. The Gold Coast!

Ben. Principally diamond mines.

Linda. Diamond mines!

Ben. Yes, my dear. But I've only a few minutes—

Willy. No! Boys! Boys! *Young Biff and Happy appear.* Listen to this. This is your Uncle Ben, a great man! Tell my boys, Ben!

Ben. Why, boys, when I was seventeen I walked into the jungle, and when I was twenty-one I walked out. *He laughs.* And by God I was rich.

Willy, *to the boys.* You see what I been talking about? The greatest things can happen!

Ben, *glancing at his watch.* I have an appointment in Ketchikan Tuesday week.

Willy. No, Ben! Please tell about Dad. I want my boys to hear. I want them to know the kind of stock they spring from. All I remember is a man with a big beard, and I was in Mamma's lap, sitting around a fire, and some kind of high music.

Ben. His flute. He played the flute.

Willy. Sure, the flute, that's right!

New music is heard, a high, rollicking tune.

Ben. Father was a very great and a very wild-hearted man. We would start in Boston, and he'd toss the whole family into the wagon, and then he'd drive the team right across the country; through Ohio, and Indiana, Michigan, Illinois, and all the Western states. And we'd stop in the towns and sell the flutes that he'd made on the way. Great inventor, Father. With one gadget he made more in a week than a man like you could make in a lifetime.

Willy. That's just the way I'm bringing them up, Ben—rugged, well liked, all-around.

Ben. Yeah? *To Biff.* Hit that, boy—hard as you can. *He pounds his stomach.*

Biff. Oh, no, sir!

Ben, *taking boxing stance.* Come on, get to me! *He laughs.*

Willy. Go to it, Biff! Go ahead, show him!

Biff. Okay! *He cocks his fists and starts in.*

Linda, *to Willy.* Why must he fight, dear?

Ben, *sparring with Biff.* Good boy! Good boy!

Willy. How's that, Ben, heh?

Happy. Give him the left, Biff!

Linda. Why are you fighting?

Ben.   Good boy! *Suddenly comes in, trips Biff, and stands over him, the point of his umbrella poised over Biff's eye.*

Linda.   Look out, Biff!

Biff.   Gee!

Ben, *patting Biff's knee.*   Never fight fair with a stranger, boy. You'll never get out of the jungle that way. *Taking Linda's hand and bowing.* It was an honor and a pleasure to meet you, Linda.

Linda, *withdrawing her hand coldly, frightened.*   Have a nice—trip.

Ben, *to Willy.*   And good luck with your—what do you do?

Willy.   Selling.

Ben.   Yes. Well . . . *He raises his hand in farewell to all.*

Willy.   No, Ben, I don't want you to think . . . *He takes Ben's arm to show him.* It's Brooklyn, I know, but we hunt too.

Ben.   Really, now.

Willy.   Oh, sure, there's snakes and rabbits and—that's why I moved out here. Why, Biff can fell any one of these trees in no time! Boys! Go right over to where they're building the apartment house and get some sand. We're gonna rebuild the entire front stoop right now! Watch this, Ben!

Biff.   Yes, sir! On the double, Hap!

Happy, *as he and Biff run off.*   I lost weight, Pop, you notice?

Charley enters in knickers, even before the boys are gone.

Charley.   Listen, if they steal any more from that building the watchman'll put the cops on them!

Linda, *to Willy.*   Don't let Biff . . .

Ben laughs lustily.

Willy.   You shoulda seen the lumber they brought home last week. At least a dozen six-by-tens worth all kinds a money.

Charley.   Listen, if that watchman—

Willy.   I gave them hell, understand. But I got a couple of fearless characters there.

Charley.   Willy, the jails are full of fearless characters.

Ben, *clapping Willy on the back, with a laugh at Charley.*   And the stock exchange, friend!

Willy, *joining in Ben's laughter.*   Where are the rest of your pants?

Charley.   My wife bought them.

Willy.   Now all you need is a golf club and you can go upstairs and go to sleep. *To Ben.* Great athlete! Between him and his son Bernard they can't hammer a nail!

Bernard, *rushing in.*   The watchman's chasing Biff!

Willy, *angrily.*   Shut up! He's not stealing anything!

Linda, *alarmed, hurrying off left.*   Where is he? Biff, dear! *She exits.*

Willy, *moving toward the left, away from Ben.*   There's nothing wrong. What's the matter with you?

Ben.   Nervy boy. Good!

Willy, *laughing.*   Oh, nerves of iron, that Biff!

Charley.   Don't know what it is. My New England man comes back and he's bleedin', they murdered him up there.

Willy.   It's contacts, Charley, I got important contacts!

Charley, *sarcastically.*   Glad to hear it, Willy. Come in later, we'll shoot a little casino. I'll take some of your Portland money. *He laughs at Willy and exits.*

Willy, *turning to Ben.*   Business is bad, it's murderous. But not for me, of course.

Ben.   I'll stop by on my way back to Africa.

Willy, *longingly.*   Can't you stay a few days? You're just what I need, Ben, because I—I have a fine position here, but I—well, Dad left when I was such a baby and I never had a chance to talk to him and I still feel—kind of temporary about myself.

Ben.   I'll be late for my train.

They are at opposite ends of the stage.

Willy.   Ben, my boys—can't we talk? They'd go into the jaws of hell for me, see, but I—

Ben.   William, you're being first-rate with your boys. Outstanding, manly chaps!

Willy, *hanging on to his words.*   Oh, Ben, that's good to hear! Because sometimes I'm afraid that I'm not teaching them the right kind of—Ben, how should I teach them?

Ben, *giving great weight to each word, and with a certain vicious audacity.*   William, when I walked into the jungle, I was seventeen. When I walked out I was twenty-one. And, by God, I was rich! *He goes off into the darkness around the right corner of the house.*

Willy.   . . . was rich! That's just the spirit I want to imbue them with! To walk into a jungle! I was right! I was right! I was right!

Ben is gone, but Willy is still speaking to him as Linda, in nightgown and robe, enters the kitchen, glances around for Willy, then goes to the door of the house, looks out and sees him. Comes down to his left. He looks at her.

Linda.   Willy, dear? Willy?

Willy.   I was right!

Linda.   Did you have some cheese? *He can't answer.* It's very late, darling. Come to bed, heh?

Willy, *looking straight up.*   Gotta break your neck to see a star in this yard.

Linda.   You coming in?

Willy.   Whatever happened to that diamond watch fob? Remember? When

Ben came from Africa that time? Didn't he give me a watch fob with a diamond in it?

Linda.   You pawned it, dear. Twelve, thirteen years ago. For Biff's radio correspondence course.

Willy.   Gee, that was a beautiful thing. I'll take a walk.

Linda.   But you're in slippers.

Willy, *starting to go around the house at the left.*   I was right! I was! *Half to
Linda, as he goes, shaking his head.* What a man! There was a man worth
talking to. I was right!

Linda, *calling after Willy.*   But in your slippers, Willy!

*Willy is almost gone when Biff, in his pajamas, comes down the stairs and en-
ters the kitchen.*

Biff.   What is he doing out there?

Linda.   Sh!

Biff.   God Almighty, Mom, how long has he been doing this?

Linda.   Don't, he'll hear you.

Biff.   What the hell is the matter with him?

Linda.   It'll pass by morning.

Biff.   Shouldn't we do anything?

Linda.   Oh, my dear, you should do a lot of things, but there's nothing to do,
so go to sleep.

Happy comes down the stair and sits on the steps.

Happy.   I never heard him so loud, Mom.

Linda.   Well, come around more often; you'll hear him. *She sits down at the
table and mends the lining of Willy's jacket.*

Biff.   Why didn't you ever write me about this, Mom?

Linda.   How would I write to you? For over three months you had no address.

Biff.   I was on the move. But you know I thought of you all the time. You
know that, don't you, pal?

Linda.   I know, dear, I know. But he likes to have a letter. Just to know that
there's still a possibility for better things.

Biff.   He's not like this all the time, is he?

Linda.   It's when you come home he's always the worst.

Biff.   When I come home?

Linda.   When you write you're coming, he's all smiles, and talks about the
future, and—he's just wonderful. And then the closer you seem to come,
the more shaky he gets, and then, by the time you get here, he's arguing,
and he seems angry at you. I think it's just that maybe he can't bring himself
to—to open up to you. Why are you so hateful to each other? Why is that?

Biff, *evasively.*   I'm not hateful, Mom.

Linda. But you no sooner come in the door than you're fighting!

Biff. I don't know why. I mean to change. I'm tryin', Mom, you understand?

Linda. Are you home to stay now?

Biff. I don't know. I want to look around, see what's doin'.

Linda. Biff, you can't look around all your life, can you?

Biff. I just can't take hold, Mom. I can't take hold of some kind of a life.

Linda. Biff, a man is not a bird, to come and go with the springtime.

Biff. Your hair . . . *He touches her hair.* Your hair got so gray.

Linda. Oh, it's been gray since you were in high school. I just stopped dyeing it, that's all.

Biff. Dye it again, will ya? I don't want my pal looking old. *He smiles.*

Linda. You're such a boy! You think you can go away for a year and . . . You've got to get it into your head now that one day you'll knock on this door and there'll be strange people here—

Biff. What are you talking about? You're not even sixty, Mom.

Linda. But what about your father?

Biff, *lamely.* Well, I meant him too.

Happy. He admires Pop.

Linda. Biff, dear, if you don't have any feeling for him, then you can't have any feeling for me.

Biff. Sure I can, Mom.

Linda. No. You can't just come to see me, because I love him. *With a threat, but only a threat, of tears.* He's the dearest man in the world to me, and I won't have anyone making him feel unwanted and low and blue. You've got to make up your mind now, darling, there's no leeway any more. Either he's your father and you pay him that respect, or else you're not to come here. I know he's not easy to get along with—nobody knows that better than me— but . . .

Willy, *from the left, with a laugh.* Hey, hey, Biffo!

Biff, *starting to go out after Willy.* What the hell is the matter with him? *Happy stops him.*

Linda. Don't—don't go near him!

Biff. Stop making excuses for him! He always, always wiped the floor with you. Never had an ounce of respect for you.

Happy. He's always had respect for—

Biff. What the hell do you know about it?

Happy, *surlily.* Just don't call him crazy!

Biff. He's got no character—Charley wouldn't do this. Not in his own house— spewing out that vomit from his mind.

Happy. Charley never had to cope with what he's got to.

Biff. People are worse off than Willy Loman. Believe me, I've seen them!

Linda. Then make Charley your father, Biff. You can't do that, can you? I don't say he's a great man. Willy Loman never made a lot of money. His name was never in the paper. He's not the finest character that ever lived. But he's a human being, and a terrible thing is happening to him. So attention must be paid. He's not to be allowed to fall into his grave like an old dog. Attention, attention must be finally paid to such a person. You called him crazy—

Biff. I didn't mean—

Linda. No, a lot of people think he's lost his—balance. But you don't have to be very smart to know what his trouble is. The man is exhausted.

Happy. Sure!

Linda. A small man can be just as exhausted as a great man. He works for a company thirty-six years this March, opens up unheard-of territories to their trademark, and now in his old age they take his salary away.

Happy, *indignantly.* I didn't know that, Mom.

Linda. You never asked, my dear! Now that you get your spending money someplace else you don't trouble your mind with him.

Happy. But I gave you money last—

Linda. Christmas time, fifty dollars! To fix the hot water it cost ninety-seven fifty! For five weeks he's been on straight commission, like a beginner, an unknown!

Biff. Those ungrateful bastards!

Linda. Are they any worse than his sons? When he brought them business, when he was young, they were glad to see him. But now his old friends, the old buyers that loved him so and always found some order to hand him in a pinch—they're all dead, retired. He used to be able to make six, seven calls a day in Boston. Now he takes his valises out of the car and puts them back and takes them out again and he's exhausted. Instead of walking he talks now. He drives seven hundred miles, and when he gets there no one knows him any more, no one welcomes him. And what goes through a man's mind, driving seven hundred miles home without having earned a cent? Why shouldn't he talk to himself? Why? When he has to go to Charley and borrow fifty dollars a week and pretend to me that it's his pay? How long can that go on? How long? You see what I'm sitting here and waiting for? And you tell me he has no character? The man who never worked a day but for your benefit? When does he get the medal for that? Is this his reward—to turn around at the age of sixty-three and find his sons, who he loved better than his life, one a philandering bum—

Happy. Mom!

Linda. That's all you are, my baby! *To Biff.* And you! What happened to the love you had for him? You were such pals! How you used to talk to him on the phone every night! How lonely he was till he could come home to you!

Biff. All right, Mom. I'll live here in my room, and I'll get a job. I'll keep away from him, that's all.

Linda. No, Biff. You can't stay here and fight all the time.

Biff. He threw me out of this house, remember that.

Linda. Why did he do that? I never knew why.

Biff. Because I know he's a fake and he doesn't like anybody around who knows!

Linda. Why a fake? In what way? What do you mean?

Biff.   Just don't lay it all at my feet. It's between me and him—that's all I have to say. I'll chip in from now on. He'll settle for half my pay check. He'll be all right. I'm going to bed. *He starts for the stairs.*

Linda.   He won't be all right.

Biff, *turning on the stairs, furiously.*   I hate this city and I'll stay here. Now what do you want?

Linda.   He's dying, Biff.

Happy turns quickly to her, shocked.

Biff, *after a pause.*   Why is he dying?

Linda.   He's been trying to kill himself.

Biff, *with great horror.*   How?

Linda.   I live from day to day.

Biff.   What're you talking about?

Linda.   Remember I wrote you that he smashed up the car again? In February?

Biff.   Well?

Linda.   The insurance inspector came. He said that they have evidence. That all these accidents in the last year—weren't—weren't—accidents.

Happy.   How can you tell that? That's a lie.

Linda.   It seems there's a woman . . . *She takes a breath as*

{ **Biff,** *sharply but contained.*   What woman?

{ **Linda,** *simultaneously.* . . . . and this woman . . .

Linda.   What?

Biff.   Nothing. Go ahead.

Linda.   What did you say?

Biff.   Nothing. I just said what woman?

Happy.   What about her?

Linda.   Well, it seems she was walking down the road and saw his car. She says that he wasn't driving fast at all, and that he didn't skid. She says he came to that little bridge, and then deliberately smashed into the railing, and it was only the shallowness of the water that saved him.

Biff.   Oh, no, he probably just fell asleep again.

Linda.   I don't think he fell asleep.

Biff.   Why not?

Linda.   Last month . . . *With great difficulty.* Oh, boys, it's so hard to say a thing like this! He's just a big stupid man to you, but I tell you there's more good in him than in many other people. *She chokes, wipes her eyes.* I was looking for a fuse. The lights blew out, and I went down the cellar. And behind the fuse box—it happened to fall out—was a length of rubber pipe— just short.

Happy.   No kidding?

Linda.   There's a little attachment on the end of it. I knew right away. And sure enough, on the bottom of the water heater there's a new little nipple on the gas pipe.

Happy, *angrily.*   That—jerk.

Biff.   Did you have it taken off?

Linda.   I'm—I'm ashamed to. How can I mention it to him? Every day I go down and take away that little rubber pipe. But, when he comes home, I put it back where it was. How can I insult him that way? I don't know what to do. I live from day to day, boys. I tell you, I know every thought in his mind. It sounds so old-fashioned and silly, but I tell you he put his whole life into you and you've turned your backs on him. *She is bent over in the chair, weeping, her face in her hands.* Biff, I swear to God! Biff, his life is in your hands!

Happy, *to Biff.*   How do you like that damned fool!

Biff, *kissing her.*   All right, pal, all right. It's all settled now. I've been remiss. I know that, Mom. But now I'll stay, and I swear to you, I'll apply myself. *Kneeling in front of her, in a fever of self-reproach.* It's just—you see, Mom, I don't fit in business. Not that I won't try. I'll try, and I'll make good.

Happy.   Sure you will. The trouble with you in business was you never tried to please people.

Biff.   I know, I—

Happy.   Like when you worked for Harrison's. Bob Harrison said you were tops, and then you go and do some damn fool thing like whistling whole songs in the elevator like a comedian.

Biff, *against Happy.*   So what? I like to whistle sometimes.

Happy.   You don't raise a guy to a responsible job who whistles in the elevator!

Linda.   Well, don't argue about it now.

Happy.   Like when you'd go off and swim in the middle of the day instead of taking the line around.

Biff, *his resentment rising.*   Well, don't you run off? You take off sometimes, don't you? On a nice summer day?

Happy.   Yeah, but I cover myself!

Linda.   Boys!

Happy.   If I'm going to take a fade the boss can call any number where I'm supposed to be and they'll swear to him that I just left. I'll tell you something that I hate to say, Biff, but in the business world some of them think you're crazy.

Biff, *angered.*   Screw the business world!

Happy.   All right, screw it! Great, but cover yourself!

Linda.   Hap, Hap!

Biff.   I don't care what they think! They've laughed at Dad for years, and you know why? Because we don't belong in this nuthouse of a city! We should be mixing cement on some open plain, or—or carpenters. A carpenter is allowed to whistle!

Willy walks in from the entrance of the house, at left.

Willy.   Even your grandfather was better than a carpenter. *Pause. They watch*

him. You never grew up. Bernard does not whistle in the elevator, I assure
   you.

Biff, *as though to laugh Willy out of it.*   Yeah, but you do, Pop.

Willy.   I never in my life whistled in an elevator! And who in the business
   world thinks I'm crazy?

Biff.   I didn't mean it like that, Pop. Now don't make a whole thing out of it,
   will ya?

Willy.   Go back to the West! Be a carpenter, a cowboy, enjoy yourself!

Linda.   Willy, he was just saying—

Willy.   I heard what he said!

Happy, *trying to quiet Willy.*   Hey, Pop, come on now . . .

Willy, *continuing over Happy's line.*   They laugh at me, heh? Go to Filene's,
   go to the Hub, go to Slattery's, Boston. Call out the name Willy Loman and
   see what happens! Big shot!

Biff.   All right, Pop.

Willy.   Big!

Biff.   All right!

Willy.   Why do you always insult me?

Biff.   I didn't say a word. *To Linda.* Did I say a word?

Linda.   He didn't say anything, Willy.

Willy, *going to the doorway of the living-room.*   All right, good night, good
   night.

Linda.   Willy, dear, he just decided . . .

Willy, *to Biff.*   If you get tired hanging around tomorrow, paint the ceiling I
   put up in the living-room.

Biff.   I'm leaving early tomorrow.

Happy.   He's going to see Bill Oliver, Pop.

Willy, *interestedly.*   Oliver? For what?

Biff, *with reserve, but trying, trying.*   He always said he'd stake me. I'd like to
   go into business, so maybe I can take him up on it.

Linda.   Isn't that wonderful?

Willy.   Don't interrupt. What's wonderful about it? There's fifty men in the
   City of New York who'd stake him. *To Biff.* Sporting goods?

Biff.   I guess so. I know something about it and—

Willy.   He knows something about it! You know sporting goods better than
   Spalding, for God's sake! How much is he giving you?

Biff.   I don't know, I didn't even see him yet, but—

Willy.   Then what're you talkin' about?

Biff, *getting angry.*   Well, all I said was I'm gonna see him, that's all!

Willy, *turning away.*   Ah, you're counting your chickens again.

Biff, *starting left for the stairs.*   Oh, Jesus, I'm going to sleep!

Willy, *calling after him.*   Don't curse in this house!

Biff, *turning.*   Since when did you get so clean?

Happy, *trying to stop them.*   Wait a . . .

Willy.   Don't use that language to me! I won't have it!

Happy, *grabbing Biff, shouts.*   Wait a minute! I got an idea. I got a feasible idea. Come here, Biff, let's talk this over now, let's talk some sense here. When I was down in Florida last time, I thought of a great idea to sell sporting goods. It just came back to me. You and I, Biff—we have a line, the Loman Line. We train a couple of weeks, and put on a couple of exhibitions, see?

Willy.   That's an idea!

Happy.   Wait! We form two basketball teams, see? Two water-polo teams. We play each other. It's a million dollars' worth of publicity. Two brothers, see? The Loman Brothers. Displays in the Royal Palms—all the hotels. And banners over the ring and the basketball court: "Loman Brothers." Baby, we could sell sporting goods!

Willy.   That is a one-million-dollar idea!

Linda.   Marvelous!

Biff.   I'm in great shape as far as that's concerned.

Happy.   And the beauty of it is, Biff, it wouldn't be like a business. We'd be out playin' ball again . . .

Biff, *enthused.*   Yeah, that's . . .

Willy.   Million-dollar . . .

Happy.   And you wouldn't get fed up with it, Biff. It'd be the family again. There'd be the old honor, and comradeship, and if you wanted to go off for a swim or somethin'—well, you'd do it! Without some smart cooky gettin' up ahead of you!

Willy.   Lick the world! You guys together could absolutely lick the civilized world.

Biff.   I'll see Oliver tomorrow. Hap, if we could work that out . . .

Linda.   Maybe things are beginning to—

Willy, *wildly enthused, to Linda.*   Stop interrupting! *To Biff.* But don't wear sport jacket and slacks when you see Oliver.

Biff.   No, I'll—

Willy.   A business suit, and talk as little as possible, and don't crack any jokes.

Biff.   He did like me. Always liked me.

Linda.   He loved you!

Willy, *to Linda.*   Will you stop! *To Biff.* Walk in very serious. You are not applying for a boy's job. Money is to pass. Be quiet, fine, and serious. Everybody likes a kidder, but nobody lends him money.

Happy.   I'll try to get some myself, Biff. I'm sure I can.

Willy.   I see great things for you kids, I think your troubles are over. But remember, start big and you'll end big. Ask for fifteen. How much you gonna ask for?

Biff.   Gee, I don't know—

Willy.   And don't say "Gee." "Gee" is a boy's word. A man walking in for fifteen thousand dollars does not say "Gee!"

Biff.   Ten, I think, would be top though.

Willy.   Don't be so modest. You always started too low. Walk in with a big laugh. Don't look worried. Start off with a couple of your good stories to lighten things up. It's not what you say, it's how you say it—because personality always wins the day.

Linda.   Oliver always thought the highest of him—

Willy.   Will you let me talk?

Biff.   Don't yell at her, Pop, will ya?

Willy, *angrily.*   I was talking, wasn't I?

Biff.   I don't like you yelling at her all the time, and I'm tellin' you, that's all.

Willy.   What're you, takin' over this house?

Linda.   Willy—

Willy, *turning on her.*   Don't take his side all the time, goddammit!

Biff, *furiously.*   Stop yelling at her!

Willy, *suddenly pulling on his cheek, beaten down, guilt ridden.*   Give my best to Bill Oliver—he may remember me. *He exits through the living-room doorway.*

Linda, *her voice subdued.*   What'd you have to start that for? *Biff turns away.* You see how sweet he was as soon as you talked hopefully? *She goes over to Biff.* Come up and say good night to him. Don't let him go to bed that way.

Happy.   Come on, Biff, let's buck him up.

Linda.   Please, dear. Just say good night. It takes so little to make him happy. Come. *She goes through the living-room doorway, calling upstairs from within the living-room.* Your pajamas are hanging in the bathroom, Willy!

Happy, *looking toward where Linda went out.*   What a woman! They broke the mold when they made her. You know that, Biff?

Biff.   He's off salary. My God, working on commission!

Happy.   Well, let's face it: he's no hot-shot selling man. Except that sometimes, you have to admit, he's a sweet personality.

Biff, *deciding.*   Lend me ten bucks, will ya? I want to buy some new ties.

Happy.   I'll take you to a place I know. Beautiful stuff. Wear one of my striped shirts tomorrow.

Biff.   She got gray. Mom got awful old. Gee, I'm gonna go in to Oliver tomorrow and knock him for a—

Happy.   Come on up. Tell that to Dad. Let's give him a whirl. Come on.

Biff, *steamed up.*   You know, with ten thousand bucks, boy!

Happy, *as they go into the living-room.*   That's the talk, Biff, that's the first time I've heard the old confidence out of you! *From within the living-room, fading off.* You're gonna live with me, kid, and any babe you want just say the word . . . *The last lines are hardly heard. They are mounting the stairs to their parents' bedroom.*

Linda, *entering her bedroom and addressing Willy, who is in the bathroom. She is straightening the bed for him.*   Can you do anything about the shower? It drips.

Willy, *from the bathroom.*   All of a sudden everything falls to pieces! Goddam plumbing, oughta be sued, those people. I hardly finished putting it in and the thing . . . *His words rumble off.*

Linda.   I'm just wondering if Oliver will remember him. You think he might?

Willy, *coming out of the bathroom in his pajamas.*   Remember him? What's the matter with you, you crazy? If he'd've stayed with Oliver he'd be on top by now! Wait'll Oliver gets a look at him. You don't know the average caliber any more. The average young man today—*he is getting into bed*—is got a caliber of zero. Greatest thing in the world for him was to bum around.

Biff and Happy enter the bedroom. Slight pause.

Willy, *stops short, looking at Biff.*   Glad to hear it, boy.

Happy.   He wanted to say good night to you, sport.

Willy, *to Biff.*   Yeah. Knock him dead, boy. What'd you want to tell me?

Biff.   Just take it easy, Pop. Good night. *He turns to go.*

Willy, *unable to resist.*   And if anything falls off the desk while you're talking to him—like a package or something—don't you pick it up. They have office boys for that.

Linda.   I'll make a big breakfast—

Willy.   Will you let me finish? *To Biff.* Tell him you were in the business in the West. Not farm work.

Biff.   All right, Dad.

Linda.   I think everything—

Willy, *going right through her speech.*   And don't undersell yourself. No less than fifteen thousand dollars.

Biff, *unable to bear him.*   Okay. Good night, Mom. *He starts moving.*

Willy.   Because you got a greatness in you, Biff, remember that. You got all kinds a greatness . . . *He lies back, exhausted. Biff walks out.*

Linda, *calling after Biff.*   Sleep well, darling!

Happy.   I'm gonna get married, Mom. I wanted to tell you.

Linda.   Go to sleep, dear.

Happy, *going.*   I just wanted to tell you.

Willy.   Keep up the good work. *Happy exits.* God . . . remember that Ebbets Field game? The championship of the city?

Linda.   Just rest. Should I sing to you?

Willy.   Yeah. Sing to me. *Linda hums a soft lullaby.* When that team came out—he was the tallest, remember?

Linda.   Oh, yes. And in gold.

Biff enters the darkened kitchen, takes a cigarette, and leaves the house. He comes downstage into a golden pool of light. He smokes, staring at the night.

Willy.   Like a young god. Hercules—something like that. And the sun, the sun all around him. Remember how he waved to me? Right up from the field, with the representatives of three colleges standing by? And the buyers I brought, and the cheers when he came out—Loman, Loman, Loman! God

Almighty, he'll be great yet. A star like that, magnificent, can never really fade away!

The light on Willy is fading. The gas heater begins to glow through the kitchen wall, near the stairs, a blue flame beneath red coils.

Linda, *timidly.*   Willy dear, what has he got against you?
Willy.   I'm so tired. Don't talk any more.

Biff slowly returns to the kitchen. He stops, stares toward the heater.

Linda.   Will you ask Howard to let you work in New York?
Willy.   First thing in the morning. Everything'll be all right.

Biff reaches behind the heater and draws out a length of rubber tubing. He is horrified and turns his head toward Willy's room, still dimly lit, from which the strains of Linda's desperate but monotonous humming rise.

Willy, *staring through the window into the moonlight.*   Gee, look at the moon moving between the buildings!

Biff wraps the tubing around his hand and quickly goes up the stairs.

Act II

Music is heard, gay and bright. The curtain rises as the music fades away. Willy, in shirt sleeves, is sitting at the kitchen table, sipping coffee, his hat in his lap. Linda is filling his cup when she can.

Willy.   Wonderful coffee. Meal in itself.
Linda.   Can I make you some eggs?
Willy.   No. Take a breath.
Linda.   You look so rested, dear.
Willy.   I slept like a dead one. First time in months. Imagine, sleeping till ten on a Tuesday morning. Boys left nice and early, heh?
Linda.   They were out of here by eight o'clock.
Willy.   Good work!
Linda.   It was so thrilling to see them leaving together. I can't get over the shaving lotion in this house!
Willy, *smiling.*   Mmm—
Linda.   Biff was very changed this morning. His whole attitude seemed to be hopeful. He couldn't wait to get downtown to see Oliver.

Willy. He's heading for a change. There's no question, there simply are certain men that take longer to get—solidified. How did he dress?

Linda. His blue suit. He's so handsome in that suit. He could be a—anything in that suit!

Willy gets up from the table. Linda holds his jacket for him.

Willy. There's no question, no question at all. Gee, on the way home tonight I'd like to buy some seeds.

Linda, *laughing.* That'd be wonderful. But not enough sun gets back there. Nothing'll grow any more.

Willy. You wait, kid, before it's all over we're gonna get a little place out in the country, and I'll raise some vegetables, a couple of chickens . . .

Linda. You'll do it yet, dear.

Willy walks out of his jacket. Linda follows him.

Willy. And they'll get married, and come for a weekend. I'd build a little guest house. 'Cause I got so many fine tools, all I'd need would be a little lumber and some peace of mind.

Linda, *joyfully.* I sewed the lining . . .

Willy. I could build two guest houses, so they'd both come. Did he decide how much he's going to ask Oliver for?

Linda, *getting him into the jacket.* He didn't mention it, but I imagine ten or fifteen thousand. You going to talk to Howard today?

Willy. Yeah. I'll put it to him straight and simple. He'll just have to take me off the road

Linda. And Willy, don't forget to ask for a little advance, because we've got the insurance premium. It's the grace period now.

Willy. That's a hundred . . . ?

Linda. A hundred and eight, sixty-eight. Because we're a little short again.

Willy. Why are we short?

Linda. Well, you had the motor job on the car . . .

Willy. That goddam Studebaker!

Linda. And you got one more payment on the refrigerator . . .

Willy. But it just broke again!

Linda. Well, it's old, dear.

Willy. I told you we should've bought a well-advertised machine. Charley bought a General Electric and it's twenty years old and it's still good, that son-of-a-bitch.

Linda. But, Willy—

Willy. Whoever heard of a Hastings refrigerator? Once in my life I would like to own something outright before it's broken! I'm always in a race with the junkyard! I just finished paying for the car and it's on its last legs. The refrigerator consumes belts like a goddam maniac. They time those things. They time them so when you finally paid for them, they're used up.

Linda, *buttoning up his jacket as he unbuttons it.*   All told, about two hundred dollars would carry us, dear. But that includes the last payment on the mortgage. After this payment, Willy, the house belongs to us.

Willy.   It's twenty-five years!

Linda.   Biff was nine years old when we bought it.

Willy.   Well, that's a great thing. To weather a twenty-five year mortgage is—

Linda.   It's an accomplishment.

Willy.   All the cement, the lumber, the reconstruction I put in this house! There ain't a crack to be found in it any more.

Linda.   Well, it served its purpose.

Willy.   What purpose? Some stranger'll come along, move in, and that's that. If only Biff would take this house, and raise a family . . . *He starts to go.* Good-by, I'm late.

Linda, *suddenly remembering.*   Oh, I forgot! You're supposed to meet them for dinner.

Willy.   Me?

Linda.   At Frank's Chop House on Forty-eighth near Sixth Avenue.

Willy.   Is that so! How about you?

Linda.   No, just the three of you. They're gonna blow you to a big meal!

Willy.   Don't say! Who thought of that?

Linda.   Biff came to me this morning, Willy, and he said, "Tell Dad, we want to blow him to a big meal." Be there six o'clock. You and your two boys are going to have dinner.

Willy.   Gee whiz! That's really somethin'. I'm gonna knock Howard for a loop, kid. I'll get an advance, and I'll come home with a New York job. Goddammit, now I'm gonna do it!

Linda.   Oh, that's the spirit, Willy!

Willy.   I will never get behind a wheel the rest of my life!

Linda.   It's changing, Willy, I can feel it changing!

Willy.   Beyond a question. G'by, I'm late. *He starts to go again.*

Linda, *calling after him as she runs to the kitchen table for a handkerchief.*   You got your glasses?

Willy, *feels for them, then comes back in.*   Yeah, yeah, got my glasses.

Linda, *giving him the handkerchief.*   And a handkerchief.

Willy.   Yeah, handkerchief.

Linda.   And your saccharine?

Willy.   Yeah, my saccharine.

Linda.   Be careful on the subway stairs.

She kisses him, and a silk stocking is seen hanging from her hand. Willy notices it.

Willy.   Will you stop mending stockings? At least while I'm in the house. It gets me nervous. I can't tell you. Please.

Linda hides the stocking in her hand as she follows Willy across the forestage in front of the house.

Linda.   Remember, Frank's Chop House.
Willy, *passing the apron.*   Maybe beets would grow out there.
Linda, *laughing.*   But you tried so many times.
Willy.   Yeah. Well, don't work hard today. *He disappears around the right corner of the house.*
Linda.   Be careful!

As Willy vanishes, Linda waves to him. Suddenly the phone rings. She runs across the stage and into the kitchen and lifts it.

Linda.   Hello? Oh, Biff! I'm so glad you called, I just . . . Yes, sure, I just told him. Yes, he'll be there for dinner at six o'clock, I didn't forget. Listen, I was just dying to tell you. You know that little rubber pipe I told you about? That he connected to the gas heater? I finally decided to go down the cellar this morning and take it away and destroy it. But it's gone! Imagine? He took it away himself, it isn't there! *She listens.* When? Oh, then you took it. Oh—nothing, it's just that I'd hoped he'd taken it away himself. Oh, I'm not worried, darling, because this morning he left in such high spirits, it was like the old days! I'm not afraid any more. Did Mr. Oliver see you? . . . Well, you wait there then. And make a nice impression on him, darling. Just don't perspire too much before you see him. And have a nice time with Dad. He may have big news too! . . . That's right, a New York job. And be sweet to him tonight, dear. Be loving to him. Because he's only a little boat looking for a harbor. *She is trembling with sorrow and joy.* Oh, that's wonderful, Biff, you'll save his life. Thanks, darling. Just put your arm around him when he comes into the restaurant. Give him a smile. That's the boy . . . Good-by, dear. . . . You got your comb? . . . That's fine. Good-by, Biff dear.

In the middle of her speech, Howard Wagner, thirty-six, wheels on a small type-writer table on which is a wire-recording machine and proceeds to plug it in. This is on the left forestage. Light slowly fades on Linda as it rises on Howard. Howard is intent on threading the machine and only glances over his shoulder as Willy appears.

Willy.   Pst! Pst!
Howard.   Hello, Willy, come in.
Willy.   Like to have a little talk with you, Howard.
Howard.   Sorry to keep you waiting. I'll be with you in a minute.
Willy.   What's that, Howard?
Howard.   Didn't you ever see one of these? Wire recorder.

Willy.   Oh. Can we talk a minute?

Howard.   Records things. Just got delivery yesterday. Been driving me crazy, the most terrific machine I ever saw in my life. I was up all night with it.

Willy.   What do you do with it?

Howard.   I bought it for dictation, but you can do anything with it. Listen to this. I had it home last night. Listen to what I picked up. The first one is my daughter. Get this. *He flicks the switch and "Roll out the Barrel" is heard being whistled.* Listen to that kid whistle.

Willy.   That is lifelike, isn't it?

Howard.   Seven years old. Get that tone.

Willy.   Ts, ts. Like to ask a little favor if you . . .

The whistling breaks off, and the voice of Howard's daughter is heard.

His Daughter.   "Now you, Daddy."

Howard.   She's crazy for me! *Again the same song is whistled.* That's me! Ha! *He winks.*

Willy.   You're very good!

The whistling breaks off again. The machine runs silent for a moment.

Howard.   Sh! Get this now, this is my son.

His Son.   "The capital of Alabama is Montgomery; the capital of Arizona is Phoenix; the capital of Arkansas is Little Rock; the capital of California is Sacramento . . ." *and so on, and on.*

Howard, *holding up five fingers.*   Five years old, Willy!

Willy.   He'll make an announcer some day!

His son, *continuing.*   "The capital . . ."

Howard.   Get that—alphabetical order! *The machine breaks off suddenly.* Wait a minute. The maid kicked the plug out.

Willy.   It certainly is a—

Howard.   Sh, for God's sake!

His Son.   "It's nine o'clock, Bulova watch time. So I have to go to sleep."

Willy.   That really is—

Howard.   Wait a minute! The next is my wife.

They wait.

Howard's Voice.   "Go on, say something." *Pause.* "Well, you gonna talk?"

His Wife.   "I can't think of anything."

Howard's Voice.   "Well, talk—it's turning."

His Wife, *shyly, beaten.*   "Hello." *Silence.* "Oh, Howard, I can't talk into this . . ."

Howard, *snapping the machine off.*   That was my wife.

Willy.   That is a wonderful machine. Can we—

Howard.   I tell you, Willy, I'm gonna take my camera, and my bandsaw, and all my hobbies, and out they go. This is the most fascinating relaxation I ever found.

Willy.   I think I'll get one myself.

Howard.   Sure, they're only a hundred and a half. You can't do without it. Supposing you wanna hear Jack Benny, see? But you can't be at home at that hour. So you tell the maid to turn the radio on when Jack Benny comes on, and this automatically goes on with the radio . . .

Willy.   And when you come home you . . .

Howard.   You can come home twelve o'clock, one o'clock, any time you like, and you get yourself a Coke and sit yourself down, throw the switch, and there's Jack Benny's program in the middle of the night!

Willy.   I'm definitely going to get one. Because lots of time I'm on the road, and I think to myself, what I must be missing on the radio!

Howard.   Don't you have a radio in the car?

Willy.   Well, yeah, but who ever thinks of turning it on?

Howard.   Say, aren't you supposed to be in Boston?

Willy.   That's what I want to talk to you about, Howard. You got a minute? *He draws a chair in from the wing.*

Howard.   What happened? What're you doing here?

Willy.   Well . . .

Howard.   You didn't crack up again, did you?

Willy.   Oh, no. No . . .

Howard.   Geez, you had me worried there for a minute. What's the trouble?

Willy.   Well, tell you the truth, Howard. I've come to the decision that I'd rather not travel any more.

Howard.   Not travel! Well, what'll you do?

Willy.   Remember, Christmas time, when you had the party here? You said you'd try to think of some spot for me here in town.

Howard.   With us?

Willy.   Well, sure.

Howard.   Oh, yeah, yeah. I remember. Well, I couldn't think of anything for you, Willy.

Willy.   I tell ya, Howard. The kids are all grown up, y'know. I don't need much any more. If I could take home—well, sixty-five dollars a week, I could swing it.

Howard.   Yeah, but Willy, see I—

Willy.   I tell ya why, Howard. Speaking frankly and between the two of us, y'know—I'm just a little tired.

Howard.   Oh, I could understand that, Willy. But you're a road man, Willy, and we do a road business. We've only got a half-dozen salesmen on the floor here.

Willy.   God knows, Howard, I never asked a favor of any man. But I was with the firm when your father used to carry you in here in his arms.

Howard.   I know that, Willy, but—

Willy.   Your father came to me the day you were born and asked me what I thought of the name of Howard, may he rest in peace.

Howard.   I appreciate that, Willy, but there just is no spot here for you. If I had a spot I'd slam you right in, but I just don't have a single solitary spot.

He looks for his lighter. Willy has picked it up and gives it to him. Pause.

Willy, *with increasing anger.*   Howard, all I need to set my table is fifty dollars a week.

Howard.   But where am I going to put you, kid?

Willy.   Look, it isn't a question of whether I can sell merchandise, is it?

Howard.   No, but it's a business, kid, and everybody's gotta pull his own weight.

Willy, *desperately.*   Just let me tell you a story, Howard—

Howard.   'Cause you gotta admit, business is business.

Willy, *angrily.*   Business is definitely business, but just listen for a minute. You don't understand this. When I was a boy—eighteen, nineteen—I was already on the road. And there was a question in my mind as to whether selling had a future for me. Because in those days I had a yearning to go to Alaska. See, there were three gold strikes in one month in Alaska, and I felt like going out. Just for the ride, you might say.

Howard, *barely interested.*   Don't say.

Willy.   Oh, yeah, my father lived many years in Alaska. He was an adventurous man. We've got quite a little streak of self-reliance in our family. I thought I'd go out with my older brother and try to locate him, and maybe settle in the North with the old man. And I was almost decided to go, when I met a salesman in the Parker House. His name was Dave Singleman. And he was eighty-four years old, and he'd drummed merchandise in thirty-one states. And old Dave, he'd go up to his room, y'understand, put on his green velvet slippers—I'll never forget—and pick up his phone and call the buyers, and without ever leaving his room, at the age of eighty-four, he made his living. And when I saw that, I realized that selling was the greatest career a man could want. 'Cause what could be more satisfying than to be able to go, at the age of eighty-four, into twenty or thirty different cities, and pick up a phone, and be remembered and loved and helped by so many different people? Do you know? when he died—and by the way he died the death of a salesman, in his green velvet slippers in the smoker of the New York, New Haven and Hartford, going into Boston—when he died, hundreds of salesmen and buyers were at his funeral. Things were sad on a lotta trains for months after that. *He stands up. Howard has not looked at him.* In those days there was personality in it, Howard. There was respect, and comradeship, and gratitude in it. Today, it's all cut and dried, and there's no chance for bringing friendship to bear—or personality. You see what I mean? They don't know me any more.

Howard, *moving away, to the right.*   That's just the thing, Willy.

Willy.   If I had forty dollars a week—that's all I'd need. Forty dollars, Howard.

Howard.   Kid, I can't take blood from a stone, I—

Willy, *desperation is on him now.*   Howard, the year Al Smith was nominated, your father came to me and—

Howard, *starting to go off.*   I've got to see some people, kid.

Willy, *stopping him.*   I'm talking about your father! There were promises made across this desk! You mustn't tell me you've got people to see—I put thirty-four years into this firm, Howard, and now I can't pay my insurance! You can't eat the orange and throw the peel away—a man is not a piece of fruit! *After a pause.* Now pay attention. Your father—in 1928 I had a big year. I averaged a hundred and seventy dollars a week in commissions.

Howard, *impatiently.*   Now, Willy, you never averaged—

Willy, *banging his hand on the desk.*   I averaged a hundred and seventy dollars a week in the year of 1928! And your father came to me—or rather, I was in the office here—it was right over this desk—and he put his hand on my shoulder—

Howard, *getting up.*   You'll have to excuse me, Willy, I gotta see some people. Pull yourself together. *Going out.* I'll be back in a little while.

On Howard's exit, the light on his chair grows very bright and strange.

Willy.   Pull myself together! What the hell did I say to him? My God, I was yelling at him! How could I! *Willy breaks off, staring at the light, which occupies the chair, animating it. He approaches this chair, standing across the desk from it.* Frank, Frank, don't you remember what you told me that time? How you put your hand on my shoulder, and Frank . . . *He leans on the desk and as he speaks the dead man's name he accidentally switches on the recorder, and instantly*

Howard's Son.   ". . . of New York is Albany. The capital of Ohio is Cincinnati, the capital of Rhode Island is . . ." *The recitation continues.*

Willy, *leaping away with fright, shouting.*   Ha! Howard! Howard! Howard!

Howard, *rushing in.*   What happened?

Willy, *pointing at the machine, which continues nasally, childishly, with the capital cities.*   Shut it off! Shut it off!

Howard, *pulling the plug out.*   Look, Willy . . .

Willy, *pressing his hands to his eyes.*   I gotta get myself some coffee. I'll get some coffee. . .

Willy starts to walk out. Howard stops him.

Howard, *rolling up the cord.*   Willy, look . . .

Willy.   I'll go to Boston.

Howard.   Willy, you can't go to Boston for us.

Willy.   Why can't I go?

Howard.   I don't want you to represent us. I've been meaning to tell you for a long time now.

Willy.   Howard, are you firing me?

Howard.   I think you need a good long rest, Willy.

Willy.   Howard—

Howard.   And when you feel better, come back, and we'll see if we can work something out.

Willy.   But I gotta earn money, Howard. I'm in no position to—

Howard.   Where are your sons? Why don't your sons give you a hand?

Willy.   They're working on a very big deal.

Howard.   This is no time for false pride, Willy. You go to your sons and tell them that you're tired. You've got two great boys, haven't you?

Willy.   Oh, no question, no question, but in the meantime . . .

Howard.   Then that's that, heh?

Willy.   All right, I'll go to Boston tomorrow.

Howard.   No, no.

Willy.   I can't throw myself on my sons. I'm not a cripple!

Howard.   Look, kid, I'm busy this morning.

Willy, *grasping Howard's arm.*   Howard, you've got to let me go to Boston!

Howard, *hard, keeping himself under control.*   I've got a line of people to see this morning. Sit down, take five minutes, and pull yourself together, and then go home, will ya? I need the office, Willy. *He starts to go, turns, remembering the recorder, starts to push off the table holding the recorder.* Oh, yeah. Whenever you can this week, stop by and drop off the samples. You'll feel better, Willy, and then come back and we'll talk. Pull yourself together, kid, there's people outside.

Howard exits, pushing the table off left. Willy stares into space, exhausted. Now the music is heard—Ben's music—first distantly, then closer, closer. As Willy speaks, Ben enters from the right. He carries valise and umbrella.

Willy.   Oh, Ben, how did you do it? What is the answer? Did you wind up the Alaska deal already?

Ben.   Doesn't take much time if you know what you're doing. Just a short business trip. Boarding ship in an hour. Wanted to say good-by.

Willy.   Ben, I've got to talk to you.

Ben, *glancing at his watch.*   Haven't the time, William.

Willy, *crossing the apron to Ben.*   Ben, nothing's working out. I don't know what to do.

Ben.   Now, look here, William. I've bought timberland in Alaska and I need a man to look after things for me.

Willy.   God, timberland! Me and my boys in those grand outdoors!

Ben.   You've a new continent at your doorstep, William. Get out of these cities, they're full of talk and time payments and courts of law. Screw on your fists and you can fight for a fortune up there.

Willy.   Yes, yes! Linda, Linda!

Linda enters as of old, with the wash.

Linda.   Oh, you're back?

Ben.   I haven't much time.

Willy.   No, wait! Linda, he's got a proposition for me in Alaska.

Linda.   But you've got—*To Ben.*   He's got a beautiful job here.

Willy.   But in Alaska, kid, I could—

Linda.   You're doing well enough, Willy!

Ben, *to Linda.*   Enough for what, my dear?

Linda, *frightened of Ben and angry at him.*   Don't say those things to him! Enough to be happy right here, right now. *To Willy, while Ben laughs.* Why must everybody conquer the world? You're well liked, and the boys love you, and someday—*to Ben*—why, old man Wagner told him just the other day that if he keeps it up he'll be a member of the firm, didn't he, Willy?

Willy.   Sure, sure. I am building something with this firm, Ben, and if a man is building something he must be on the right track, mustn't he?

Ben.   What are you building? Lay your hand on it. Where is it?

Willy, *hesitantly.*   That's true, Linda, there's nothing.

Linda.   Why? *To Ben.* There's a man eighty-four years old—

Willy.   That's right, Ben, that's right. When I look at that man I say, what is there to worry about?

Ben.   Bah!

Willy.   It's true, Ben. All he has to do is go into any city, pick up the phone, and he's making his living and you know why?

Ben, *picking up his valise.*   I've got to go.

Willy, *holding Ben back.*   Look at this boy!

Biff, in his high school sweater, enters carrying suitcase. Happy carries Biff's shoulder guards, gold helmet, and football pants.

Willy.   Without a penny to his name, three great universities are begging for him, and from there the sky's the limit, because it's not what you do, Ben. It's who you know and the smile on your face! It's contacts, Ben, contacts! The whole wealth of Alaska passes over the lunch table at the Commodore Hotel, and that's the wonder, the wonder of this country, that a man can end with diamonds here on the basis of being liked! *He turns to Biff.* And that's why when you get out on that field today it's important. Because thousands of people will be rooting for you and loving you. *To Ben, who has again begun to leave.* And Ben! when he walks into a business office his name will sound out like a bell and all the doors will open to him! I've seen it, Ben, I've seen it a thousand times! You can't feel it with your hand like timber, but it's there!

Ben.   Good-by, William.

Willy.   Ben, am I right? Don't you think I'm right? I value your advice.

Ben.   There's a new continent at your doorstep, William. You could walk out rich. Rich. *He is gone.*

Willy.   We'll do it here, Ben! You hear me? We're gonna do it here!

Young Bernard rushes in. The gay music of the Boys is heard.

Bernard. Oh, gee, I was afraid you left already!

Willy. Why? What time is it?

Bernard. It's half-past one!

Willy. Well, come on, everybody! Ebbets Field next stop! Where's the pennants? *He rushes through the wall-line of the kitchen and out into the living-room.*

Linda, *to Biff.* Did you pack fresh underwear?

Biff, *who has been limbering up.* I want to go!

Bernard. Biff, I'm carrying your helmet, ain't I?

Happy. No, I'm carrying the helmet.

Bernard. Oh, Biff, you promised me.

Happy. I'm carrying the helmet.

Bernard. How am I going to get in the locker room?

Linda. Let him carry the shoulder guards. *She puts her coat and hat on in the kitchen.*

Bernard. Can I, Biff? 'Cause I told everybody I'm going to be in the locker room.

Happy. In Ebbets Field it's the clubhouse.

Bernard. I meant the clubhouse. Biff!

Happy. Biff!

Biff, *grandly, after a slight pause.* Let him carry the shoulder guards.

Happy, *as he gives Bernard the shoulder guards.* Stay close to us now.

Willy rushes in with the pennants.

Willy, *handing them out.* Everybody wave when Biff comes out on the field. *Happy and Bernard run off.* You set now, boy?

The music has died away.

Biff. Ready to go, Pop. Every muscle is ready.

Willy, *at the edge of the apron.* You realize what this means?

Biff. That's right, Pop.

Willy, *feeling Biff's muscles.* You're comin' home this afternoon captain of the All-Scholastic Championship Team of the City of New York.

Biff. I got it, Pop. And remember, pal, when I take off my helmet, that touchdown is for you.

Willy. Let's go! *He is starting out, with his arm around Biff, when Charley enters, as of old, in knickers.* I got no room for you, Charley.

Charley. Room? For what?

Willy. In the car.

Charley. You goin' for a ride? I wanted to shoot some casino.

Willy, *furiously.* Casino! *Incredulously.* Don't you realize what today is?

Linda. Oh, he knows, Willy. He's just kidding you.

Willy. That's nothing to kid about!

Charley. No. Linda, what's goin' on?

Linda.   He's playing in Ebbets Field.

Charley.   Baseball in this weather?

Willy.   Don't talk to him. Come on, come on! *He is pushing them out.*

Charley.   Wait a minute, didn't you hear the news?

Willy.   What?

Charley.   Don't you listen to the radio? Ebbets Field just blew up.

Willy.   You go to hell! *Charley laughs. Pushing them out.* Come on, come on! We're late.

Charley, *as they go.*   Knock a homer, Biff, knock a homer!

Willy, *the last to leave, turning to Charley.*   I don't think that was funny, Charley. This is the greatest day of his life.

Charley.   Willy, when are you going to grow up?

Willy.   Yeah, heh? When this game is over, Charley, you'll be laughing out of the other side of your face. They'll be calling him another Red Grange. Twenty-five thousand a year.

Charley, *kidding.*   Is that so?

Willy.   Yeah, that's so.

Charley.   Well, then, I'm sorry, Willy. But tell me something.

Willy.   What?

Charley.   Who is Red Grange?

Willy.   Put up your hands. Goddam you, put up your hands!

Charley, chuckling, shakes his head and walks away, around the left corner of the stage. Willy follows him. The music rises to a mocking frenzy.

Willy.   Who the hell do you think you are, better than everybody else? You don't know everything, you big, ignorant, stupid . . . Put up your hands!

Light rises, on the right side of the forestage, on a small table in the reception room of Charley's office. Traffic sounds are heard. Bernard, now mature, sits whistling to himself. A pair of tennis rackets and an overnight bag are on the floor beside him.

Willy, *offstage.*   What are you walking away for? Don't walk away! If you're going to say something say it to my face! I know you laugh at me behind my back. You'll laugh out of the other side of your goddam face after this game. Touchdown! Touchdown! Eighty thousand people! Touchdown! Right between the goal posts.

Bernard is a quiet, earnest, but self-assured young man. Willy's voice is coming from right upstage now. Bernard lowers his feet off the table and listens. Jenny, his father's secretary, enters.

Jenny, *distressed.*   Say, Bernard, will you go out in the hall?

Bernard.   What is that noise? Who is it?

Jenny.   Mr. Loman. He just got off the elevator.

Bernard, *getting up.*   Who's he arguing with?

Jenny.   Nobody. There's nobody with him. I can't deal with him any more, and your father gets all upset everytime he comes. I've got a lot of typing to do, and your father's waiting to sign it. Will you see him?

Willy, *entering.*   Touchdown! Touch—*He sees Jenny.* Jenny, Jenny, good to see you. How're ya? Workin'? Or still honest?

Jenny.   Fine. How've you been feeling?

Willy.   Not much any more, Jenny. Ha, ha! *He is surprised to see the rackets.*

Bernard.   Hello, Uncle Willy.

Willy, *almost shocked.*   Bernard! Well, look who's here! *He comes quickly, guiltily, to Bernard and warmly shakes his hand.*

Bernard.   How are you? Good to see you.

Willy.   What are you doing here?

Bernard.   Oh, just stopped by to see Pop. Get off my feet till my train leaves. I'm going to Washington in a few minutes.

Willy.   Is he in?

Bernard.   Yes, he's in his office with the accountant. Sit down.

Willy, *sitting down.*   What're you going to do in Washington?

Bernard.   Oh, just a case I've got there, Willy.

Willy.   That so? *Indicating the rackets.* You going to play tennis there?

Bernard.   I'm staying with a friend who's got a court.

Willy.   Don't say. His own tennis court. Must be fine people, I bet.

Bernard.   They are, very nice. Dad tells me Biff's in town.

Willy, *with a big smile.*   Yeah, Biff's in. Working on a very big deal, Bernard.

Bernard.   What's Biff doing?

Willy.   Well, he's been doing very big things in the West. But he decided to establish himself here. Very big. We're having dinner. Did I hear your wife had a boy?

Bernard.   That's right. Our second.

Willy.   Two boys! What do you know!

Bernard.   What kind of a deal has Biff got?

Willy.   Well, Bill Oliver—very big sporting-goods man—he wants Biff very badly. Called him in from the West. Long distance, carte blanche, special deliveries. Your friends have their own private tennis court?

Bernard.   You still with the old firm, Willy?

Willy, *after a pause.*   I'm—I'm overjoyed to see how you made the grade, Bernard, overjoyed. It's an encouraging thing to see a young man really—really—Looks very good for Biff—very—*He breaks off, then.* Bernard—*He is so full of emotion, he breaks off again.*

Bernard.   What is it, Willy?

Willy, *small and alone.*   What—what's the secret?

Bernard.   What secret?

Willy.   How—how did you? Why didn't he ever catch on?

Bernard.   I wouldn't know that, Willy.

Willy, *confidentially, desperately.*   You were his friend, his boyhood friend. There's something I don't understand about it. His life ended after that Ebbets Field game. From the age of seventeen nothing good ever happened to him.

Bernard.   He never trained himself for anything.

Willy.   But he did, he did. After high school he took so many correspondence courses. Radio mechanics; television; God knows what, and never made the slightest mark.

Bernard, *taking off his glasses.*   Willy, do you want to talk candidly?

Willy, *rising, faces Bernard.*   I regard you as a very brilliant man, Bernard. I value your advice.

Bernard.   Oh. the hell with the advice, Willy. I couldn't advise you. There's just one thing I've always wanted to ask you. When he was supposed to graduate, and the math teacher flunked him—

Willy.   Oh, that son-of-a-bitch ruined his life.

Bernard.   Yeah, but, Willy, all he had to do was go to summer school and make up that subject.

Willy.   That's right, that's right.

Bernard.   Did you tell him not to go to summer school?

Willy.   Me? I begged him to go. I ordered him to go!

Bernard.   Then why wouldn't he go?

Willy.   Why? Why! Bernard, that question has been trailing me like a ghost for the last fifteen years. He flunked the subject, and laid down and died like a hammer hit him!

Bernard.   Take it easy, kid.

Willy.   Let me talk to you—I got nobody to talk to. Bernard, Bernard, was it my fault? Y'see? It keeps going around in my mind, maybe I did something to him. I got nothing to give him.

Bernard.   Don't take it so hard.

Willy.   Why did he lay down? What is the story there? You were his friend!

Bernard.   Willy, I remember, it was June, and our grades came out. And he'd flunked math.

Willy.   That son-of-a-bitch!

Bernard.   No, it wasn't right then. Biff just got very angry, I remember, and he was ready to enroll in summer school.

Willy, *surprised.*   He was?

Bernard.   He wasn't beaten by it at all. But then, Willy, he disappeared from the block for almost a month. And I got the idea that he'd gone up to New England to see you. Did he have a talk with you then?

Willy stares in silence.

Bernard.   Willy?

Willy, *with a strong edge of resentment in his voice.*   Yeah, he came to Boston. What about it?

Bernard.   Well, just that when he came back—I'll never forget this, it always mystifies me. Because I'd thought so well of Biff, even though he'd always taken advantage of me. I loved him, Willy, y'know? And he came back after that month and took his sneakers—remember those sneakers with "University of Virginia" printed on them? He was so proud of those, wore them every day. And he took them down in the cellar, and burned them up in the furnace. We had a fist fight. It lasted at least half an hour. Just the two of us, punching each other down the cellar, and crying right through it. I've often thought of how strange it was that I knew he'd given up his life. What happened in Boston, Willy?

Willy looks at him as at an intruder.

Bernard.   I just bring it up because you asked me.
Willy, *angrily.*   Nothing. What do you mean, "What happened?" What's that got to do with anything?
Bernard.   Well, don't get sore.
Willy.   What are you trying to do, blame it on me? If a boy lays down is that my fault?
Bernard.   Now, Willy, don't get—
Willy.   Well, don't—don't talk to me that way! What does that mean, "What happened?"

Charley enters. He is in his vest, and he carries a bottle of bourbon.

Charley.   Hey, you're going to miss that train. *He waves the bottle.*
Bernard.   Yeah, I'm going. *He takes the bottle.* Thanks, Pop. *He picks up his rackets and bag.* Good-by, Willy, and don't worry about it. You know, "If at first you don't succeed . . ."
Willy.   Yes, I believe in that.
Bernard.   But sometimes, Willy, it's better for a man just to walk away.
Willy.   Walk away?
Bernard.   That's right.
Willy.   But if you can't walk away?
Bernard, *after a slight pause.*   I guess that's when it's tough. *Extending his hand.* Good-by, Willy.
Willy, *shaking Bernard's hand.*   Good-by, boy.
Charley, *an arm on Bernard's shoulder.*   How do you like this kid? Gonna argue a case in front of the Supreme Court.
Bernard, *protesting.*   Pop!
Willy, *genuinely shocked, pained, and happy.*   No! The Supreme Court!
Bernard.   I gotta run. 'By, Dad!
Charley.   Knock 'em dead, Bernard!

Bernard goes off.

Willy, *as Charley takes out his wallet.*   The Supreme Court! And he didn't even mention it!
Charley, *counting out money on the desk.*   He don't have to—he's gonna do it.

Willy.   And you never told him what to do, did you? You never took any interest in him.

Charley.   My salvation is that I never took any interest in anything. There's some money—fifty dollars. I got an accountant inside.

Willy.   Charley, look . . . *With difficulty.* I got my insurance to pay. If you can manage it—I need a hundred and ten dollars.

Charley doesn't reply for a moment; merely stops moving.

Willy.   I'd draw it from my bank but Linda would know, and I . . .

Charley.   Sit down, Willy.

Willy, *moving toward the chair.*   I'm keeping an account of everything, remember. I'll pay every penny back. *He sits.*

Charley.   Now listen to me, Willy.

Willy.   I want you to know I appreciate . . .

Charley, *sitting down on the table.*   Willy, what're you doin'? What the hell is goin' on in your head?

Willy.   Why? I'm simply . . .

Charley.   I offered you a job. You can make fifty dollars a week. And I won't send you on the road.

Willy.   I've got a job.

Charley.   Without pay? What kind of a job is a job without pay? *He rises.* Now, look, kid, enough is enough. I'm no genius but I know when I'm being insulted.

Willy.   Insulted!

Charley.   Why don't you want to work for me?

Willy.   What's the matter with you? I've got a job.

Charley.   Then what're you walkin' in here every week for?

Willy, *getting up.*   Well, if you don't want me to walk in here—

Charley.   I am offering you a job.

Willy.   I don't want your goddam job!

Charley.   When the hell are you going to grow up?

Willy, *furiously.*   You big ignoramus, if you say that to me again I'll rap you one! I don't care how big you are! *He's ready to fight.*

Pause.

Charley, *kindly, going to him.*   How much do you need, Willy?

Willy.   Charley, I'm strapped, I'm strapped. I don't know what to do. I was just fired.

Charley.   Howard fired you?

Willy.   That snotnose. Imagine that? I named him. I named him Howard.

Charley.   Willy, when're you gonna realize that them things don't mean anything? You named him Howard, but you can't sell that. The only thing you got in this world is what you can sell. And the funny thing is that you're a salesman, and you don't know that.

Willy.   I've always tried to think otherwise, I guess. I always felt that if a man was impressive, and well liked, that nothing—

Charley.   Why must everybody like you? Who liked J. P. Morgan? Was he impressive? In a Turkish bath he'd look like a butcher. But with his pockets on he was very well liked. Now listen, Willy, I know you don't like me, and nobody can say I'm in love with you, but I'll give you a job because—just for the hell of it, put it that way. Now what do you say?

Willy.   I—I just can't work for you, Charley.

Charley.   What're you, jealous of me?

Willy.   I can't work for you, that's all, don't ask me why.

Charley, *angered, takes out more bills.*   You been jealous of me all your life, you damned fool! Here, pay your insurance. *He puts the money in Willy's hand.*

Willy.   I'm keeping strict accounts.

Charley.   I've got some work to do. Take care of yourself. And pay your insurance.

Willy, *moving to the right.*   Funny, y'know? After all the highways, and the trains, and the appointments, and the years, you end up worth more dead than alive.

Charley.   Willy, nobody's worth nothin' dead. *After a slight pause.* Did you hear what I said?

Willy stands still, dreaming.

Charley.   Willy!

Willy.   Apologize to Bernard for me when you see him. I didn't mean to argue with him. He's a fine boy. They're all fine boys, and they'll end up big— all of them. Someday they'll all play tennis together. Wish me luck, Charley. He saw Bill Oliver today.

Charley.   Good luck.

Willy, *on the verge of tears.*   Charley, you're the only friend I got. Isn't that a remarkable thing? *He goes out.*

Charley.   Jesus!

Charley stares after him a moment and follows. All light blacks out. Suddenly raucous music is heard, and a red glow rises behind the screen at right. Stanley, a young waiter, appears, carrying a table, followed by Happy, who is carrying two chairs.

Stanley, *putting the table down.*   That's all right, Mr. Loman, I can handle it myself. *He turns and takes the chairs from Happy and places them at the table.*

Happy, *glancing around.*   Oh, this is better.

Stanley.   Sure, in the front there you're in the middle of all kinds a noise. Whenever you got a party, Mr. Loman, you just tell me and I'll put you back here. Y'know, there's a lotta people they don't like it private, because when they go out they like to see a lotta action around them because they're sick and tired to stay in the house by theirself. But I know you, you ain't from Hackensack. You know what I mean?

Happy, *sitting down.*   So how's it coming, Stanley?

Stanley.   Ah, it's a dog's life. I only wish during the war they'd a took me in the Army. I coulda been dead by now.

Happy.   My brother's back, Stanley.

Stanley.   Oh, he come back, heh? From the Far West.

Happy.   Yeah, big cattle man, my brother, so treat him right. And my father's coming too.

Stanley.   Oh, your father too!

Happy.   You got a couple of nice lobsters?

Stanley.   Hundred per cent, big.

Happy.   I want them with the claws.

Stanley.   Don't worry, I don't give you no mice. *Happy laughs.* How about some wine? It'll put a head on the meal.

Happy.   No. You remember, Stanley, that recipe I brought you from overseas? With the champagne in it?

Stanley.   Oh, yeah, sure. I still got it tacked up yet in the kitchen. But that'll have to cost a buck apiece anyways.

Happy.   That's all right.

Stanley.   What'd you, hit a number or somethin'?

Happy.   No, it's a little celebration. My brother is—I think he pulled off a big deal today. I think we're going into business together.

Stanley.   Great! That's the best for you. Because a family business, you know what I mean?—that's the best.

Happy.   That's what I think.

Stanley.   'Cause what's the difference? Somebody steals? It's in the family. Know what I mean? *Sotto voce.* Like this bartender here. The boss is goin' crazy what kinda leak he's got in the cash register. You put it in but it don't come out.

Happy, *raising his head.*   Sh!

Stanley.   What?

Happy.   You notice I wasn't lookin' right or left, was I?

Stanley.   No.

Happy.   And my eyes are closed.

Stanley.   So what's the—?

Happy.   Strudel's comin'.

Stanley, *catching on, looks around.*   Ah, no, there's no—

He breaks off as a furred, lavishly dressed girl enters and sits at the next table. Both follow her with their eyes.

Stanley.   Geez, how'd ya know?

Happy.   I got radar or something. *Staring directly at her profile.* Oooooooooo . . . Stanley.

Stanley.   I think that's for you, Mr. Loman.

Happy.   Look at that mouth. Oh, God. And the binoculars.

Stanley.   Geez, you got a life, Mr. Loman.

Happy.   Wait on her.

Stanley, *going to the girl's table.*   Would you like a menu, ma'am?

Girl.   I'm expecting someone, but I'd like a—

Happy.   Why don't you bring her—excuse me, miss, do you mind? I sell champagne, and I'd like you to try my brand. Bring her a champagne, Stanley.

Girl.   That's awfully nice of you.

Happy.   Don't mention it. It's all company money. *He laughs.*

Girl.   That's a charming product to be selling, isn't it?

Happy.   Oh, gets to be like everything else. Selling is selling, y'know?

Girl.   I suppose.

Happy.   You don't happen to sell, do you?

Girl.   No, I don't sell.

Happy.   Would you object to a compliment from a stranger? You ought to be on a magazine cover.

Girl, *looking at him a little archly.*   I have been.

Stanley comes in with a glass of champagne.

Happy.   What'd I say before, Stanley? You see? She's a cover girl.

Stanley.   Oh, I could see, I could see.

Happy, *to the Girl.*   What magazine?

Girl.   Oh, a lot of them. *She takes the drink.* Thank you.

Happy.   You know what they say in France, don't you? "Champagne is the drink of the complexion"—Hya, Biff!

Biff has entered and sits with Happy.

Biff.   Hello, kid. Sorry I'm late.

Happy.   I just got here. Uh, Miss—?

Girl.   Forsythe.

Happy.   Miss Forsythe, this is my brother.

Biff.   Is Dad here?

Happy.   His name is Biff. You might've heard of him. Great football player.

Girl.   Really? What team?

Happy.   Are you familiar with football?

Girl.   No, I'm afraid I'm not.

Happy.   Biff is quarterback with the New York Giants.

Girl.   Well, that is nice, isn't it? *She drinks.*

Happy.   Good health.

Girl.   I'm happy to meet you.

Happy.   That's my name. Hap. It's really Harold, but at West Point they called me Happy.

Girl, *now really impressed.*   Oh, I see. How do you do? *She turns her profile.*

Biff.   Isn't Dad coming?
Happy.   You want her?
Biff.   Oh, I could never make that.
Happy.   I remember the time that idea would never come into your head. Where's the old confidence, Biff?
Biff.   I just saw Oliver—
Happy.   Wait a minute. I've got to see that old confidence again. Do you want her? She's on call.
Biff.   Oh, no. *He turns to look at the Girl.*
Happy.   I'm telling you. Watch this. *Turning to the Girl.* Honey? *She turns to him.* Are you busy?
Girl.   Well, I am . . . but I could make a phone call.
Happy.   Do that, will you, honey? And see if you can get a friend. We'll be here for a while. Biff is one of the greatest football players in the country.
Girl, *standing up.*   Well, I'm certainly happy to meet you.
Happy.   Come back soon.
Girl.   I'll try.
Happy.   Don't try, honey, try hard.

The Girl exits. Stanley follows, shaking his head in bewildered admiration.

Happy.   Isn't that a shame now? A beautiful girl like that? That's why I can't get married. There's not a good woman in a thousand. New York is loaded with them, kid!
Biff.   Hap, look—
Happy.   I told you she was on call!
Biff, *strangely unnerved.*   Cut it out, will ya? I want to say something to you.
Happy.   Did you see Oliver?
Biff.   I saw him all right. Now look, I want to tell Dad a couple of things and I want you to help me.
Happy.   What? Is he going to back you?
Biff.   Are you crazy? You're out of your goddam head, you know that?
Happy.   Why? What happened?
Biff, *breathlessly.*   I did a terrible thing today, Hap. It's been the strangest day I ever went through. I'm all numb, I swear.
Happy.   You mean he wouldn't see you?
Biff.   Well, I waited six hours for him, see? All day. Kept sending my name in. Even tried to date his secretary so she'd get me to him, but no soap.
Happy.   Because you're not showin' the old confidence, Biff. He remembered you, didn't he?
Biff, *stopping Happy with a gesture.*   Finally, about five o'clock, he comes out. Didn't remember who I was or anything. I felt like such an idiot, Hap.
Happy.   Did you tell him my Florida idea?
Biff.   He walked away. I saw him for one minute. I got so mad I could've torn

the walls down! How the hell did I ever get the idea I was a salesman there? I even believed myself that I'd been a salesman for him! And then he gave me one look and—I realized what a ridiculous lie my whole life has been! We've been talking in a dream for fifteen years. I was a shipping clerk.

Happy. What'd you do?

Biff, *with great tension and wonder.* Well, he left, see. And the secretary went out. I was all alone in the waiting-room. I don't know what came over me, Hap. The next thing I know I'm in his office—paneled walls, everything. I can't explain it. I—Hap, I took his fountain pen.

Happy. Geez, did he catch you?

Biff. I ran out. I ran down all eleven flights. I ran and ran and ran.

Happy. That was an awful dumb—what'd you do that for?

Biff, *agonized.* I don't know, I just—wanted to take something, I don't know. You gotta help me, Hap, I'm gonna tell Pop.

Happy. You crazy? What for?

Biff. Hap, he's got to understand that I'm not the man somebody lends that kind of money to. He thinks I've been spiting him all these years and it's eating him up.

Happy. That's just it. You tell him something nice.

Biff. I can't.

Happy. Say you got a lunch date with Oliver tomorrow.

Biff. So what do I do tomorrow?

Happy. You leave the house tomorrow and come back at night and say Oliver is thinking it over. And he thinks it over for a couple of weeks, and gradually it fades away and nobody's the worse.

Biff. But it'll go on forever!

Happy. Dad is never so happy as when he's looking forward to something!

Willy enters.

Happy. Hello, scout!

Willy. Gee, I haven't been here in years!

Stanley has followed Willy in and sets a chair for him. Stanley starts off but Happy stops him.

Happy. Stanley!

Stanley stands by, waiting for an order.

Biff, *going to Willy with guilt, as to an invalid.* Sit down, Pop. You want a drink?

Willy. Sure, I don't mind.

Biff. Let's get a load on.

Willy. You look worried.

Biff. N-no. *To Stanley.* Scotch all around. Make it doubles.

Stanley.   Doubles, right. *He goes.*

Willy.   You had a couple already, didn't you.

Biff.   Just a couple, yeah.

Willy.   Well, what happened, boy? *Nodding affirmatively, with a smile.* Everything go all right?

Biff, *takes a breath, then reaches out and grasps Willy's hand.*   Pal . . . *He is smiling bravely, and Willy is smiling too.* I had an experience today.

Happy.   Terrific, Pop.

Willy.   That so? What happened?

Biff, *high, slightly alcoholic, above the earth.*   I'm going to tell you everything from first to last. It's been a strange day. *Silence. He looks around, composes himself as best he can, but his breath keeps breaking the rhythm of his voice.* I had to wait quite a while for him, and—

Willy.   Oliver?

Biff.   Yeah, Oliver. All day, as a matter of cold fact. And a lot of—in-stances—facts, Pop, facts about my life came back to me. Who was it, Pop? Who ever said I was a salesman with Oliver?

Willy.   Well, you were.

Biff.   No, Dad, I was a shipping clerk.

Willy.   But you were practically—

Biff, *with determination.*   Dad, I don't know who said it first, but I was never a salesman for Bill Oliver.

Willy.   What're you talking about?

Biff.   Let's hold on to the facts tonight, Pop. We're not going to get anywhere bullin' around. I was a shipping clerk.

Willy, *angrily.*   All right, now listen to me—

Biff.   Why don't you let me finish?

Willy.   I'm not interested in stories about the past or any crap of that kind because the woods are burning, boys, you understand? There's a big blaze going on all around. I was fired today.

Biff, *shocked.*   How could you be?

Willy.   I was fired, and I'm looking for a little good news to tell your mother, because the woman has waited and the woman has suffered. The gist of it is that I haven't got a story left in my head, Biff. So don't give me a lecture about facts and aspects. I am not interested. Now what've you got to say to me?

Stanley enters with three drinks. They wait until he leaves.

Willy.   Did you see Oliver?

Biff.   Jesus, Dad!

Willy.   You mean you didn't go up there?

Happy.   Sure he went up there.

Biff.   I did. I—saw him. How could they fire you?

Willy, *on the edge of his chair.*   What kind of a welcome did he give you?

Biff.   He won't even let you work on commission?

Willy. I'm out! *Driving.* So tell me, he gave you a warm welcome?

Happy. Sure, Pop, sure!

Biff, *driven.* Well, it was kind of—

Willy. I was wondering if he'd remember you. *To Happy.* Imagine, man doesn't see him for ten, twelve years and gives him that kind of a welcome!

Happy. Damn right!

Biff, *trying to return to the offensive.* Pop, look—

Willy. You know why he remembered you, don't you? Because you impressed him in those days.

Biff. Let's talk quietly and get this down to the facts, huh?

Willy, *as though Biff had been interrupting.* Well, what happened? It's great news, Biff. Did he take you into his office or'd you talk in the waiting-room?

Biff. Well, he came in, see, and—

Willy, *with a big smile.* What'd he say? Betcha he threw his arm around you.

Biff. Well, he kinda—

Willy. He's a fine man. *To Happy.* Very hard man to see, y'know.

Happy, *agreeing.* Oh, I know.

Willy, *to Biff.* Is that where you had the drinks?

Biff. Yeah, he gave me a couple of—no, no!

Happy, *cutting in.* He told him of my Florida idea.

Willy. Don't interrupt. *To Biff.* How'd he react to the Florida idea?

Biff. Dad, will you give me a minute to explain?

Willy. I've been waiting for you to explain since I sat down here! What happened? He took you into his office and what?

Biff. Well—I talked. And—and he listened, see.

Willy. Famous for the way he listens, y'know. What was his answer?

Biff. His answer was—*He breaks off, suddenly angry.* Dad, you're not letting me tell you what I want to tell you!

Willy, *accusing, angered.* You didn't see him, did you?

Biff. I did see him!

Willy. What'd you insult him or something? You insulted him, didn't you?

Biff. Listen, will you let me out of it, will you just let me out of it!

Happy. What the hell!

Willy. Tell me what happened!

Biff, *to Happy.* I can't talk to him!

A single trumpet note jars the ear. The light of green leaves stains the house, which holds the air of night and a dream. Young Bernard enters and knocks on the door of the house.

Young Bernard, *frantically.* Mrs. Loman, Mrs. Loman!

Happy. Tell him what happened!

Biff, *to Happy.* Shut up and leave me alone!

Willy. No, no! You had to go and flunk math!

Biff. What math? What're you talking about?

Young Bernard. Mrs. Loman, Mrs. Loman!

Linda appears in the house, as of old.

Willy, *wildly.*   Math, math, math!

Biff.   Take it easy, Pop!

Young Bernard.   Mrs. Loman!

Willy, *furiously.*   If you hadn't flunked you'd've been set by now!

Biff.   Now, look, I'm gonna tell you what happened, and you're going to listen to me.

Young Bernard.   Mrs. Loman!

Biff.   I waited six hours—

Happy.   What the hell are you saying?

Biff.   I kept sending in my name but he wouldn't see me. So finally he . . .
    He continues unheard as light fades low on the restaurant.

Young Bernard.   Biff flunked math!

Linda.   No!

Young Bernard.   Birnbaum flunked him! They won't graduate him!

Linda.   But they have to. He's gotta go to the university. Where is he? Biff! Biff!

Young Bernard.   No, he left. He went to Grand Central.

Linda.   Grand—You mean he went to Boston!

Young Bernard.   Is Uncle Willy in Boston?

Linda.   Oh, maybe Willy can talk to the teacher. Oh, the poor, poor boy!

Light on house area snaps out.

Biff, *at the table, now audible, holding up a gold fountain pen. . . .* so I'm washed up with Oliver, you understand? Are you listening to me?

Willy, *at a loss.*   Yeah, sure. If you hadn't flunked—

Biff.   Flunked what? What're you talking about?

Willy.   Don't blame everything on me! I didn't flunk math—you did! What pen?

Happy.   That was awful dumb, Biff, a pen like that is worth—

Willy, *seeing the pen for the first time.*   You took Oliver's pen?

Biff, *weakening.*   Dad, I just explained it to you.

Willy.   You stole Bill Oliver's fountain pen!

Biff.   I didn't exactly steal it! That's just what I've been explaining to you!

Happy.   He had it in his hand and just then Oliver walked in, so he got nervous and stuck it in his pocket!

Willy.   My God, Biff!

Biff.   I never intended to do it, Dad!

Operator's Voice.   Standish Arms, good evening!

Willy, *shouting.*   I'm not in my room!

Biff, *frightened.*   Dad, what's the matter? *He and Happy stand up.*

Operator.   Ringing Mr. Loman for you!

Willy.   I'm not there, stop it!

Biff, *horrified, gets down on one knee before Willy.*   Dad, I'll make good, I'll make good. *Willy tries to get to his feet. Biff holds him down.* Sit down now.

Willy.   No, you're no good, you're no good for anything.

Biff.   I am, Dad, I'll find something else, you understand? Now don't worry about anything. *He holds up Willy's face.* Talk to me, Dad.

Operator.   Mr. Loman does not answer. Shall I page him?

Willy, *attempting to stand, as though to rush and silence the Operator.*   No, no, no!

Happy.   He'll strike something, Pop.

Willy.   No, no . . .

Biff, *desperately, standing over Willy.*   Pop, listen! Listen to me! I'm telling you something good. Oliver talked to his partner about the Florida idea. You listening? He—he talked to his partner, and he came to me . . . I'm going to be all right, you hear? Dad, listen to me, he said it was just a question of the amount!

Willy.   Then you . . . got it?

Happy.   He's gonna be terrific, Pop!

Willy, *trying to stand.*   Then you got it, haven't you? You got it! You got it!

Biff, *agonized, holds Willy down.*   No, no. Look, Pop. I'm supposed to have lunch with them tomorrow. I'm just telling you this so you'll know that I can still make an impression, Pop. And I'll make good somewhere, but I can't go tomorrow, see?

Willy.   Why not? You simply—

Biff.   But the pen, Pop!

Willy.   You give it to him and tell him it was an oversight!

Happy.   Sure, have lunch tomorrow!

Biff.   I can't say that—

Willy.   You were doing a crossword puzzle and accidentally used his pen!

Biff.   Listen, kid, I took those balls years ago, now I walk in with his fountain pen? That clinches it, don't you see? I can't face him like that! I'll try elsewhere.

Page's Voice.   Paging Mr. Loman!

Willy.   Don't you want to be anything?

Biff.   Pop, how can I go back?

Willy.   You don't want to be anything, is that what's behind it?

Biff, *now angry at Willy for not crediting his sympathy.*   Don't take it that way! You think it was easy walking into that office after what I'd done to him? A team of horses couldn't have dragged me back to Bill Oliver!

Willy.   Then why'd you go?

Biff.   Why did I go? Why did I go! Look at you! Look at what's become of you!

Off left, The Woman laughs.

Willy.   Biff, you're going to go to that lunch tomorrow, or—

Biff.   I can't go. I've got no appointment!

Happy.   Biff, for . . . !

Willy.   Are you spiting me?

Biff.   Don't take it that way! Goddammit!

Willy, *strikes Biff and falters away from the table.*   You rotten little louse! Are you spiting me?

The Woman.   Someone's at the door, Willy!

Biff.   I'm no good, can't you see what I am?

Happy, *separating them.*   Hey, you're in a restaurant! Now cut it out, both of you! *The girls enter.* Hello, girls, sit down.

The Woman laughs, off left.

Miss Forsythe.   I guess we might as well. This is Letta.

The Woman.   Willy, are you going to wake up?

Biff, *ignoring Willy.*   How're ya, miss, sit down. What do you drink?

Miss Forsythe.   Letta might not be able to stay long.

Letta.   I gotta get up very early tomorrow. I got jury duty. I'm so excited! Were you fellows ever on a jury?

Biff.   No, but I been in front of them! *The girls laugh.* This is my father.

Letta.   Isn't he cute? Sit down with us, Pop.

Happy.   Sit him down, Biff!

Biff, *going to him.*   Come on, slugger, drink us under the table. To hell with it! Come on, sit down, pal.

On Biff's last insistence, Willy is about to sit.

The Woman, *now urgently.*   Willy, are you going to answer the door!

The Woman's call pulls Willy back. He starts right, befuddled.

Biff.   Hey, where are you going?

Willy.   Open the door.

Biff.   The door?

Willy.   The washroom . . . the door . . . where's the door?

Biff, *leading Willy to the left.*   Just go straight down.

Willy moves left.

The Woman.   Willy, Willy, are you going to get up, get up, get up, get up?

Willy exits left.

Letta.   I think it's sweet you bring your daddy along.

Miss Forsythe.   Oh, he isn't really your father!

Biff, *at left, turning to her resentfully.*   Miss Forsythe, you've just seen a prince walk by. A fine, troubled prince. A hard-working, unappreciated prince. A pal, you understand? A good companion. Always for his boys.

Letta.   That's so sweet.

Happy.   Well, girls, what's the program? We're wasting time. Come on, Biff. Gather round. Where would you like to go?

Biff.   Why don't you do something for him?

Happy.   Me!

Biff.   Don't you give a damn for him, Hap?

Happy.   What're you talking about? I'm the one who—

Biff.   I sense it, you don't give a good goddam about him. *He takes the rolled-up hose from his pocket and puts it on the table in front of Happy.* Look what I found in the cellar, for Christ's sake. How can you bear to let it go on?

Happy.   Me? Who goes away? Who runs off and—

Biff.   Yeah, but he doesn't mean anything to you. You could help him—I can't! Don't you understand what I'm talking about? He's going to kill himself, don't you know that?

Happy.   Don't I know it! Me!

Biff.   Hap, help him! Jesus . . . help him . . . Help me, help me, I can't bear to look at his face! *Ready to weep, he hurries out, up right.*

Happy, *starting after him.*   Where are you going?

Miss Forsythe.   What's he so mad about?

Happy.   Come on, girls, we'll catch up with him.

Miss Forsythe, *as Happy pushes her out.*   Say, I don't like that temper of his!

Happy.   He's just a little overstrung, he'll be all right!

Willy, *off left, as The Woman laughs.*   Don't answer! Don't answer!

Letta.   Don't you want to tell your father—

Happy.   No, that's not my father. He's just a guy. Come on, we'll catch Biff, and, honey, we're going to paint this town! Stanley, where's the check! Hey, Stanley!

They exit. Stanley looks toward left.

Stanley, *calling to Happy indignantly.*   Mr. Loman! Mr. Loman!

Stanley picks up a chair and follows them off. Knocking is heard off left. The Woman enters, laughing. Willy follows her. She is in a black slip; he is buttoning his shirt. Raw, sensuous music accompanies their speech.

Willy.   Will you stop laughing? Will you stop?

The Woman.   Aren't you going to answer the door? He'll wake the whole hotel.

Willy.   I'm not expecting anybody.

The Woman.   Whyn't you have another drink, honey, and stop being so damn self-centered?

Willy.   I'm so lonely.

The Woman.   You know you ruined me, Willy? From now on, whenever you come to the office, I'll see that you go right through to the buyers. No waiting at my desk any more, Willy. You ruined me.

Willy. That's nice of you to say that.

The Woman. Gee, you are self-centered! Why so sad? You are the saddest, self-centeredest soul I ever did see-saw. *She laughs. He kisses her.* Come on inside, drummer boy. It's silly to be dressing in the middle of the night. *As knocking is heard.* Aren't you going to answer the door?

Willy. They're knocking on the wrong door.

The Woman. But I felt the knocking. And he heard us talking in here. Maybe the hotel's on fire!

Willy, *his terror rising.* It's a mistake.

The Woman. Then tell him to go away!

Willy. There's nobody there.

The Woman. It's getting on my nerves, Willy. There's somebody standing out there and it's getting on my nerves!

Willy, *pushing her away from him.* All right, stay in the bathroom here, and don't come out. I think there's a law in Massachusetts about it, so don't come out. It may be that new room clerk. He looked very mean. So don't come out. It's a mistake, there's no fire.

The knocking is heard again. He takes a few steps away from her, and she vanishes into the wing. The light follows him, and now he is facing Young Biff, who carries a suitcase. Biff steps toward him. The music is gone.

Biff. Why didn't you answer?

Willy. Biff! What are you doing in Boston?

Biff. Why didn't you answer? I've been knocking for five minutes, I called you on the phone—

Willy. I just heard you. I was in the bathroom and had the door shut. Did anything happen home?

Biff. Dad—I let you down.

Willy. What do you mean?

Biff. Dad . . .

Willy. Biffo, what's this about? *Putting his arm around Biff.* Come on, let's go downstairs and get you a malted.

Biff. Dad, I flunked math.

Willy. Not for the term?

Biff. The term. I haven't got enough credits to graduate.

Willy. You mean to say Bernard wouldn't give you the answers?

Biff. He did, he tried, but I only got a sixty-one.

Willy. And they wouldn't give you four points?

Biff. Birnbaum refused absolutely. I begged him, Pop, but he won't give me those points. You gotta talk to him before they close the school. Because if he saw the kind of man you are, and you just talked to him in your way, I'm sure he'd come through for me. The class came right before practice, see, and I didn't go enough. Would you talk to him? He'd like you, Pop. You know the way you could talk.

Willy.   You're on. We'll drive right back.

Biff.   Oh, Dad, good work! I'm sure he'll change it for you!

Willy.   Go downstairs and tell the clerk I'm checkin' out. Go right down.

Biff.   Yes, sir! See, the reason he hates me, Pop—one day he was late for class so I got up at the blackboard and imitated him. I crossed my eyes and talked with a lithp.

Willy, *laughing.*   You did? The kids like it?

Biff.   They nearly died laughing!

Willy.   Yeah? What'd you do?

Biff.   The thquare root of thixthy twee is . . . *Willy bursts out laughing; Biff joins him.* And in the middle of it he walked in!

Willy laughs and The Woman joins in offstage.

Willy, *without hesitation.*   Hurry downstairs and—

Biff.   Somebody in there?

Willy.   No, that was next door.

The Woman laughs offstage.

Biff.   Somebody got in your bathroom!

Willy.   No, it's the next room, there's a party—

The Woman, *enters, laughing. She lisps this.*   Can I come in? There's something in the bathtub, Willy, and it's moving!

Willy looks at Biff, who is staring open-mouthed and horrified at The Woman.

Willy.   Ah—you better go back to your room. They must be finished painting by now. They're painting her room so I let her take a shower here. Go back, go back . . . *He pushes her.*

The Woman, *resisting.*   But I've got to get dressed, Willy, I can't—

Willy.   Get out of here! Go back, go back . . . *Suddenly striving for the ordinary.* This is Miss Francis, Biff, she's a buyer. They're painting her room. Go back, Miss Francis, go back . . .

The Woman.   But my clothes, I can't go out naked in the hall!

Willy, *pushing her offstage.*   Get outa here! Go back, go back!

Biff slowly sits down on his suitcase as the argument continues offstage.

The Woman.   Where's my stockings? You promised me stockings, Willy!

Willy.   I have no stockings here!

The Woman.   You had two boxes of size nine sheers for me, and I want them!

Willy.   Here, for God's sake, will you get outa here!

The Woman, *enters holding a box of stockings.*   I just hope there's nobody in the hall. That's all I hope. *To Biff.* Are you football or baseball?

Biff.   Football.

The Woman, *angry, humiliated.*   That's me too. G'night. *She snatches her clothes from Willy, and walks out.*

Willy, *after a pause.*   Well, better get going. I want to get to the school first thing in the morning. Get my suits out of the closet. I'll get my valise. *Biff doesn't move.* What's the matter? *Biff remains motionless, tears falling.* She's a buyer. Buys for J. H. Simmons. She lives down the hall—they're painting. You don't imagine—*He breaks off. After a pause.* Now listen, pal, she's just a buyer. She sees merchandise in her room and they have to keep it looking just so . . . *Pause. Assuming command.* All right, get my suits. *Biff doesn't move.* Now stop crying and do as I say. I gave you an order. Biff, I gave you an order! Is that what you do when I give you an order? How dare you cry! *Putting his arm around Biff.* Now look, Biff, when you grow up you'll understand about these things. You mustn't—you mustn't overemphasize a thing like this. I'll see Birnbaum first thing in the morning.

Biff.   Never mind.

Willy, *getting down beside Biff.*   Never mind! He's going to give you those points. I'll see to it.

Biff.   He wouldn't listen to you.

Willy.   He certainly will listen to me. You need those points for the U. of Virginia.

Biff.   I'm not going there.

Willy.   Heh? If I can't get him to change that mark you'll make it up in summer school. You've got all summer to—

Biff, *his weeping breaking from him.*   Dad . . .

Willy, *infected by it.*   Oh, my boy . . .

Biff.   Dad . . .

Willy.   She's nothing to me, Biff. I was lonely, I was terribly lonely.

Biff.   You—you gave her Mama's stockings! *His tears break through and he rises to go.*

Willy, *grabbing for Biff.*   I gave you an order!

Biff.   Don't touch me, you—liar!

Willy.   Apologize for that!

Biff.   You fake! You phony little fake! You fake! *Overcome, he turns quickly and weeping fully goes out with his suitcase. Willy is left on the floor on his knees.*

Willy.   I gave you an order! Biff, come back here or I'll beat you! Come back here! I'll whip you!

Stanley comes quickly in from the right and stands in front of Willy.

Willy, *shouts at Stanley.*   I gave you an order . . .

Stanley.   Hey, let's pick it up, pick it up, Mr. Loman. *He helps Willy to his feet.* Your boys left with the chippies. They said they'll see you home.

A second waiter watches some distance away.

Willy.   But we were supposed to have dinner together.

Music is heard, Willy's theme.

Stanley.   Can you make it?
Willy.   I'll—sure, I can make it. *Suddenly concerned about his clothes.* Do I— I look all right?
Stanley.   Sure, you look all right. *He flicks a speck off Willy's lapel.*
Willy.   Here—here's a dollar.
Stanley.   Oh, your son paid me. It's all right.
Willy, *putting it in Stanley's hand.*   No, take it. You're a good boy.
Stanley.   Oh, no, you don't have to . . .
Willy.   Here—here's some more, I don't need it any more. *After a slight pause.* Tell me—is there a seed store in the neighborhood?
Stanley.   Seeds? You mean like to plant?

As Willy turns, Stanley slips the money back into his jacket pocket.

Willy.   Yes. Carrots, peas . . .
Stanley.   Well, there's hardware stores on Sixth Avenue, but it may be too late now.
Willy, *anxiously.*   Oh, I'd better hurry. I've got to get some seeds. *He starts off to the right.* I've got to get some seeds, right away. Nothing's planted. I don't have a thing in the ground.

Willy hurries out as the light goes down. Stanley moves over to the right after him, watches him off. The other waiter has been staring at Willy.

Stanley, *to the waiter.*   Well, whatta you looking at?

The waiter picks up the chairs and moves off right. Stanley takes the table and follows him. The light fades on this area. There is a long pause, the sound of the flute coming over. The light gradually rises on the kitchen, which is empty. Happy appears at the door of the house, followed by Biff. Happy is carrying a large bunch of long-stemmed roses. He enters the kitchen, looks around for Linda. Not seeing her, he turns to Biff, who is just outside the house door, and makes a gesture with his hands, indicating "Not here, I guess." He looks into the living-room and freezes. Inside, Linda, unseen, is seated, Willy's coat on her lap. She rises ominously and quietly and moves toward Happy, who backs up into the kitchen, afraid.

Happy.   Hey, what're you doing up? *Linda says nothing but moves toward him implacably.* Where's Pop? *He keeps backing to the right, and now Linda is in full view in the doorway to the living-room.* Is he sleeping?

Linda.   Where were you?

Happy, *trying to laugh it off.*   We met two girls, Mom, very fine types. Here, we brought you some flowers. *Offering them to her.* Put them in your room, Ma.

She knocks them to the floor at Biff's feet. He has now come inside and closed the door behind him. She stares at Biff, silent.

Happy.   Now what'd you do that for? Mom, I want you to have some flowers—

Linda, *cutting Happy off, violently to Biff.*   Don't you care whether he lives or dies?

Happy, *going to the stairs.*   Come upstairs, Biff.

Biff, *with a flare of disgust, to Happy.*   Go away from me! *To Linda.* What do you mean, lives or dies? Nobody's dying around here, pal.

Linda.   Get out of my sight! Get out of here!

Biff.   I wanna see the boss.

Linda.   You're not going near him!

Biff.   Where is he? *He moves into the living-room and Linda follows.*

Linda, *shouting after Biff.*   You invite him for dinner. He looks forward to it all day—*Biff appears in his parents' bedroom, looks around, and exits*—and then you desert him there. There's no stranger you'd do that to!

Happy.   Why? He had a swell time with us. Listen, when I—*Linda comes back into the kitchen*—desert him I hope I don't outlive the day!

Linda.   Get out of here!

Happy.   Now look, Mom . . .

Linda.   Did you have to go to women tonight? You and your lousy rotten whores!

Biff re-enters the kitchen.

Happy.   Mom, all we did was follow Biff around trying to cheer him up! *To Biff.* Boy, what a night you gave me!

Linda.   Get out of here, both of you, and don't come back! I don't want you tormenting him any more. Go on now, get your things together! *To Biff.* You can sleep in his apartment. *She starts to pick up the flowers and stops herself.* Pick up this stuff, I'm not your maid any more. Pick it up, you bum, you!

Happy turns his back to her in refusal. Biff slowly moves over and gets down on his knees, picking up the flowers.

Linda.   You're a pair of animals! Not one, not another living soul would have had the cruelty to walk out on that man in a restaurant!

Biff, *not looking at her.*   Is that what he said?

Linda.   He didn't have to say anything. He was so humiliated he nearly limped when he came in.

Happy.   But, Mom, he had a great time with us—
Biff, *cutting him off violently.*   Shut up!

Without another word, Happy goes upstairs.

Linda.   You! You didn't even go in to see if he was all right!
Biff, *still on the floor in front of Linda, the flowers in his hand; with self-loathing.*   No. Didn't. Didn't do a damned thing. How do you like that, heh? Left him babbling in a toilet.
Linda.   You louse. You . . .
Biff.   Now you hit it on the nose! *He gets up, throws the flowers in the wastebasket.* The scum of the earth, and you're looking at him!
Linda.   Get out of here!
Biff.   I gotta talk to the boss, Mom. Where is he?
Linda.   You're not going near him. Get out of this house!
Biff, *with absolute assurance, determination.*   No. We're gonna have an abrupt conversation, him and me.
Linda.   You're not talking to him!

Hammering is heard from outside the house, off right. Biff turns toward the noise.

Linda, *suddenly pleading.*   Will you please leave him alone?
Biff.   What's he doing out there?
Linda.   He's planting the garden!
Biff, *quietly.*   Now? Oh, my God!

Biff moves outside, Linda following. The light dies down on them and comes up on the center of the apron as Willy walks into it. He is carrying a flashlight, a hoe, and a handful of seed packets. He raps the top of the hoe sharply to fix it firmly, and then moves to the left, measuring off the distance with his foot. He holds the flashlight to look at the seed packets, reading off the instructions. He is in the blue of night.

Willy.   Carrots . . . quarter-inch apart. Rows . . . one-foot rows. *He measures it off.* One foot. *He puts down a package and measures off.* Beets. *He puts down another package and measures again.* Lettuce. *He reads the package, puts it down.* One foot—*He breaks off as Ben appears at the right and moves slowly down to him.* What a proposition, ts, ts. Terrific, terrific. 'Cause she's suffered, Ben, the woman has suffered. You understand me? A man can't go out the way he came in, Ben, a man has got to add up to something. You can't, you can't—*Ben moves toward him as though to interrupt.* You gotta consider, now. Don't answer so quick. Remember, it's a guaranteed twenty-thousand-dollar proposition. Now look, Ben, I want you to go through the ins and outs of this thing with me. I've got nobody to talk to, Ben, and the woman has suffered, you hear me?
Ben, *standing still, considering.*   What's the proposition?

Willy.   It's twenty thousand dollars on the barrelhead. Guaranteed, gilt-edged, you understand?

Ben.   You don't want to make a fool of yourself. They might not honor the policy.

Willy.   How can they dare refuse? Didn't I work like a coolie to meet every premium on the nose? And now they don't pay off? Impossible!

Ben.   It's called a cowardly thing, William.

Willy.   Why? Does it take more guts to stand here the rest of my life ringing up a zero?

Ben, *yielding.*   That's a point, William. *He moves, thinking, turns.* And twenty thousand—that *is* something one can feel with the hand, it is there.

Willy, *now assured, with rising power.*   Oh, Ben, that's the whole beauty of it! I see it like a diamond, shining in the dark, hard and rough, that I can pick up and touch in my hand. Not like—like an appointment! This would not be another damned-fool appointment, Ben, and it changes all the aspects. Because he thinks I'm nothing, see, and so he spites me. But the funeral—*Straightening up.* Ben, that funeral will be massive! They'll come from Maine, Massachusetts, Vermont, New Hampshire! All the old-timers with the strange license plates—that boy will be thunder-struck, Ben, because he never realized—I am known! Rhode Island, New York, New Jersey—I am known, Ben, and he'll see it with his eyes once and for all. He'll see what I am, Ben! He's in for a shock, that boy!

Ben, *coming down to the edge of the garden.*   He'll call you a coward.

Willy, *suddenly fearful.*   No, that would be terrible.

Ben.   Yes. And a damned fool.

Willy.   No, no, he mustn't, I won't have that! *He is broken and desperate.*

Ben.   He'll hate you, William.

The gay music of the Boys is heard.

Willy.   Oh, Ben, how do we get back to all the great times? Used to be so full of light, and comradeship, the sleigh-riding in winter, and the ruddiness on his cheeks. And always some kind of good news coming up, always something nice coming up ahead. And never even let me carry the valises in the house, and simonizing, simonizing that little red car! Why, why can't I give him something and not have him hate me?

Ben.   Let me think about it. *He glances at his watch.* I still have a little time. Remarkable proposition, but you've got to be sure you're not making a fool of yourself.

Ben drifts off upstage and goes out of sight. Biff comes down from the left.

Willy, *suddenly conscious of Biff, turns and looks up at him, then begins picking up the packages of seeds in confusion.*   Where the hell is that seed? *Indignantly.* You can't see nothing out here! They boxed in the whole goddam neighborhood!

Biff. There are people all around here. Don't you realize that?

Willy. I'm busy. Don't bother me.

Biff, *taking the hoe from Willy.* I'm saying good-by to you, Pop. *Willy looks at him, silent, unable to move.* I'm not coming back any more.

Willy. You're not going to see Oliver tomorrow?

Biff. I've got no appointment, Dad.

Willy. He put his arm around you, and you've got no appointment?

Biff. Pop, get this now, will you? Everytime I've left it's been a fight that sent me out of here. Today I realized something about myself and I tried to explain it to you and I—I think I'm just not smart enough to make any sense out of it for you. To hell with whose fault it is or anything like that. *He takes Willy's arm.* Let's just wrap it up, heh? Come on in, we'll tell Mom. *He gently tries to pull Willy to left.*

Willy, *frozen, immobile, with guilt in his voice.* No, I don't want to see her.

Biff. Come on! *He pulls again, and Willy tries to pull away.*

Willy, *highly nervous.* No, no, I don't want to see her.

Biff, *tries to look into Willy's face, as if to find the answer there.* Why don't you want to see her?

Willy, *more harshly now.* Don't bother me, will you?

Biff. What do you mean, you don't want to see her? You don't want them calling you yellow, do you? This isn't your fault; it's me, I'm a bum. Now come inside! *Willy strains to get away.* Did you hear what I said to you?

Willy pulls away and quickly goes by himself into the house. Biff follows.

Linda, *to Willy.* Did you plant, dear?

Biff, *at the door, to Linda.* All right, we had it out. I'm going and I'm not writing any more.

Linda, *going to Willy in the kitchen.* I think that's the best way, dear. 'Cause there's no use drawing it out, you'll just never get along.

Willy doesn't respond.

Biff. People ask where I am and what I'm doing, you don't know, and you don't care. That way it'll be off your mind and you can start brightening up again. All right? That clears it, doesn't it? *Willy is silent, and Biff goes to him.* You gonna wish me luck, scout? *He extends his hand.* What do you say?

Linda. Shake his hand, Willy.

Willy, *turning to her, seething with hurt.* There's no necessity to mention the pen at all, y'know.

Biff, *gently.* I've got no appointment, Dad.

Willy, *erupting fiercely.* He put his arm around . . . . ?

Biff. Dad, you're never going to see what I am, so what's the use of arguing? If I strike oil I'll send you a check. Meantime forget I'm alive.

Willy, *to Linda.* Spite, see?

Biff.   Shake hands, Dad.

Willy.   Not my hand.

Biff.   I was hoping not to go this way.

Willy.   Well, this is the way you're going. Good-by.

Biff looks at him a moment, then turns sharply and goes to the stairs.

Willy, *stops him with:*   May you rot in hell if you leave this house!

Biff, *turning.*   Exactly what is it that you want from me?

Willy.   I want you to know, on the train, in the mountains, in the valleys, wherever you go, that you cut down your life for spite!

Biff.   No, no.

Willy.   Spite, spite, is the word of your undoing! And when you're down and out, remember what did it. When you're rotting somewhere beside the railroad tracks, remember, and don't you dare blame it on me!

Biff.   I'm not blaming it on you!

Willy.   I won't take the rap for this, you hear?

Happy comes down the stairs and stands on the bottom step, watching.

Biff.   That's just what I'm telling you!

Willy, *sinking into a chair at the table, with full accusation.*   You're trying to put a knife in me—don't think I don't know what you're doing!

Biff.   All right, phony! Then let's lay it on the line. *He whips the rubber tube out of his pocket and puts it on the table.*

Happy.   You crazy—

Linda.   Biff! *She moves to grab the hose, but Biff holds it down with his hand.*

Biff.   Leave it there! Don't move it!

Willy, *not looking at it.*   What is that?

Biff.   You know goddam well what that is.

Willy, *caged, wanting to escape.*   I never saw that.

Biff.   You saw it. The mice didn't bring it into the cellar! What is this supposed to do, make a hero out of you? This supposed to make me sorry for you?

Willy.   Never heard of it.

Biff.   There'll be no pity for you, you hear it? No pity!

Willy, *to Linda.*   You hear the spite!

Biff.   No, you're going to hear the truth—what you are and what I am!

Linda.   Stop it!

Willy.   Spite!

Happy, *coming down toward Biff.*   You cut it now!

Biff, *to Happy.*   The man don't know who we are! The man is gonna know! *To Willy.* We never told the truth for ten minutes in this house!

Happy.   We always told the truth!

Biff, *turning on him.*   You big blow, are you the assistant buyer? You're one of the two assistants to the assistant, aren't you?

Happy.   Well, I'm practically—

Biff.   You're practically full of it! We all are! And I'm through with it. *To Willy.* Now hear this, Willy, this is me.

Willy.   I know you!

Biff.   You know why I had no address for three months? I stole a suit in Kansas City and I was in jail. *To Linda, who is sobbing.* Stop crying. I'm through with it.

Linda turns away from them, her hands covering her face.

Willy.   I suppose that's my fault!

Biff.   I stole myself out of every good job since high school!

Willy.   And whose fault is that?

Biff.   And I never got anywhere because you blew me so full of hot air I could never stand taking orders from anybody! That's whose fault it is!

Willy.   I hear that!

Linda.   Don't, Biff!

Biff.   It's goddam time you heard that! I had to be boss big shot in two weeks, and I'm through with it!

Willy.   Then hang yourself! For spite, hang yourself!

Biff.   No! Nobody's hanging himself, Willy! I ran down eleven flights with a pen in my hand today. And suddenly I stopped, you hear me? And in the middle of that office building, do you hear this? I stopped in the middle of that building and I saw—the sky. I saw the things that I love in this world. The work and the food and time to sit and smoke. And I looked at the pen and said to myself, what the hell am I grabbing this for? Why am I trying to become what I don't want to be? What am I doing in an office, making a contemptuous, begging fool of myself, when all I want is out there, waiting for me the minute I say I know who I am! Why can't I say that, Willy? *He tries to make Willy face him, but Willy pulls away and moves to the left.*

Willy, *with hatred, threateningly.*   The door of your life is wide open!

Biff.   Pop! I'm a dime a dozen, and so are you!

Willy, *turning on him now in an uncontrolled outburst.*   I am not a dime a dozen! I am Willy Loman, and you are Biff Loman!

Biff starts for Willy, but is blocked by Happy. In his fury, Biff seems on the verge of attacking his father.

Biff.   I am not a leader of men, Willy, and neither are you. You were never anything but a hard-working drummer who landed in the ash can like all the rest of them! I'm one dollar an hour, Willy! I tried seven states and couldn't raise it. A buck an hour! Do you gather my meaning? I'm not bringing home any prizes any more, and you're going to stop waiting for me to bring them home!

Willy, *directly to Biff.*   You vengeful, spiteful mutt!

Biff breaks from Happy. Willy, in fright, starts up the stairs. Biff grabs him.

Biff, *at the peak of his fury.*   Pop, I'm nothing! I'm nothing, Pop. Can't you understand that? There's no spite in it any more. I'm just what I am, that's all.

Biff's fury has spent itself, and he breaks down, sobbing, holding on to Willy, who dumbly fumbles for Biff's face.

Willy, *astonished.*   What're you doing? What're you doing? *To Linda.* Why is he crying?

Biff, *crying, broken.*   Will you let me go, for Christ's sake? Will you take that phony dream and burn it before something happens? *Struggling to contain himself, he pulls away and moves to the stairs.* I'll go in the morning. Put him—put him to bed. *Exhausted, Biff moves up the stairs to his room.*

Willy, *after a long pause, astonished, elevated.*   Isn't that—isn't that remarkable? Biff—he likes me!

Linda.   He loves you, Willy!

Happy, *deeply moved.*   Always did, Pop.

Willy.   Oh, Biff! *Staring wildly.* He cried! Cried to me. *He is choking with his love, and now cries out his promise.* That boy—that boy is going to be magnificent!

Ben appears in the light just outside the kitchen.

Ben.   Yes, outstanding, with twenty thousand behind him.

Linda, *sensing the racing of his mind, fearfully, carefully.*   Now come to bed, Willy. It's all settled now.

Willy, *finding it difficult not to rush out of the house.*   Yes, we'll sleep. Come on. Go to sleep, Hap.

Ben.   And it does take a great kind of a man to crack the jungle.

In accents of dread, Ben's idyllic music starts up.

Happy, *his arm around Linda.*   I'm getting married, Pop, don't forget it. I'm changing everything. I'm gonna run that department before the year is up. You'll see, Mom. *He kisses her.*

Ben.   The jungle is dark but full of diamonds, Willy.

Willy turns, moves, listening to Ben.

Linda.   Be good. You're both good boys, just act that way, that's all.

Happy.   'Night, Pop. *He goes upstairs.*

Linda, *to Willy.*   Come, dear.

Ben, *with greater force.*   One must go in to fetch a diamond out.

Willy, *to Linda, as he moves slowly along the edge of the kitchen, toward the door.*   I just want to get settled down, Linda. Let me sit alone for a little.

Linda, *almost uttering her fear.*   I want you upstairs.

Willy, *taking her in his arms.*   In a few minutes, Linda. I couldn't sleep right now. Go on, you look awful tired. *He kisses her.*

Ben.   Not like an appointment at all. A diamond is rough and hard to the touch.

Willy.   Go on now. I'll be right up.

Linda.   I think this is the only way, Willy.

Willy.   Sure, it's the best thing.

Ben.   Best thing!

Willy.   The only way. Everything is gonna be—go on, kid, get to bed. You look so tired.

Linda.   Come right up.

Willy.   Two minutes.

Linda goes into the living-room, then reappears in her bedroom. Willy moves just outside the kitchen door.

Willy.   Loves me. *Wonderingly.* Always loved me. Isn't that a remarkable thing? Ben, he'll worship me for it!

Ben, *with promise.*   It's dark there, but full of diamonds.

Willy.   Can you imagine that magnificence with twenty thousand dollars in his pocket?

Linda, *calling from her room.*   Willy! Come up!

Willy, *calling into the kitchen.*   Yes! Yes. Coming! It's very smart, you realize that, don't you, sweetheart? Even Ben sees it. I gotta go, baby. 'By! 'By! *Going over to Ben, almost dancing.* Imagine? When the mail comes he'll be ahead of Bernard again!

Ben.   A perfect proposition all around.

Willy.   Did you see how he cried to me? Oh, if I could kiss him, Ben!

Ben.   Time, William, time!

Willy.   Oh, Ben, I always knew one way or another we were gonna make it, Biff and I!

Ben, *looking at his watch.*   The boat. We'll be late. *He moves slowly off into the darkness.*

Willy, *elegiacally, turning to the house.*   Now when you kick off, boy, I want a seventy-yard boot, and get right down the field under the ball, and when you hit, hit low and hit hard, because it's important, boy. *He swings around and faces the audience.* There's all kinds of important people in the stands, and the first thing you know . . . *Suddenly realizing he is alone.* Ben! Ben, where do I . . . ? *He makes a sudden movement of search.* Ben, how do I . . . ?

Linda, *calling.*   Willy, you coming up?

Willy, *uttering a gasp of fear, whirling about as if to quiet her.*   Sh! *He turns* *around as if to find his way; sounds, faces, voices, seem to be swarming in upon him and he flicks at them, crying, Sh! Sh! Suddenly music, faint and high, stops him. It rises in intensity, almost to an unbearable scream. He goes up and down on his toes, and rushes off around the house. Shhh!*

Linda.   Willy?

There is no answer. Linda waits. Biff gets up off his bed. He is still in his clothes. Happy sits up. Biff stands listening.

Linda, *with real fear.*   Willy, answer me! Willy!

There is the sound of a car starting and moving away at full speed.

Linda.   No!
Biff, *rushing down the stairs.*   Pop!

As the car speeds off, the music crashes down in a frenzy of sound, which becomes the soft pulsation of a single cello string. Biff slowly returns to his bedroom. He and Happy gravely don their jackets. Linda slowly walks out of her room. The music has developed into a dead march. The leaves of day are appearing over everything. Charley and Bernard, somberly dressed, appear and knock on the kitchen door. Biff and Happy slowly descend the stairs to the kitchen as Charley and Bernard enter. All stop a moment when Linda, in clothes of mourning, bearing a little bunch of roses, comes through the draped doorway into the kitchen. She goes to Charley and takes his arm. Now all move toward the audience, through the wall-line of the kitchen. At the limit of the apron, Linda lays down the flowers, kneels, and sits back on her heels. All stare down at the grave.

Requiem

Charley.   It's getting dark, Linda.

Linda doesn't react. She stares at the grave.

Biff.   How about it, Mom? Better get some rest, heh? They'll be closing the gate soon.

Linda makes no move. Pause.

Happy, *deeply angered.*   He had no right to do that. There was no necessity for it. We would've helped him.
Charley, *grunting.*   Hmmm.

Biff.   Come along, Mom.

Linda.   Why didn't anybody come?

Charley.   It was a very nice funeral.

Linda.   But where are all the people he knew? Maybe they blame him.

Charley.   Naa. It's a rough world, Linda. They wouldn't blame him.

Linda.   I can't understand it. At this time especially. First time in thirty-five years we were just about free and clear. He only needed a little salary. He was even finished with the dentist.

Charley.   No man only needs a little salary.

Linda.   I can't understand it.

Biff.   There were a lot of nice days. When he'd come home from a trip; or on Sundays, making the stoop; finishing the cellar; putting on the new porch; when he built the extra bathroom; and put up the garage. You know something, Charley, there's more of him in that front stoop than in all the sales he ever made.

Charley.   Yeah. He was a happy man with a batch of cement.

Linda.   He was so wonderful with his hands.

Biff.   He had the wrong dreams. All, all, wrong.

Happy, *almost ready to fight Biff.*   Don't say that!

Biff.   He never knew who he was.

Charley, *stopping Happy's movement and reply. To Biff.*   Nobody dast blame this man. You don't understand: Willy was a salesman. And for a salesman, there is no rock bottom to the life. He don't put a bolt to a nut, he don't tell you the law or give you medicine. He's a man way out there in the blue, riding on a smile and a shoeshine. And when they start not smiling back— that's an earthquake. And then you get yourself a couple of spots on your hat, and you're finished. Nobody dast blame this man. A salesman is got to dream, boy. It comes with the territory.

Biff.   Charley, the man didn't know who he was.

Happy, *infuriated.*   Don't say that!

Biff.   Why don't you come with me, Happy?

Happy.   I'm not licked that easily. I'm staying right in this city, and I'm gonna beat this racket! *He looks at Biff, his chin set.* The Loman Brothers!

Biff.   I know who I am, kid.

Happy.   All right, boy. I'm gonna show you and everybody else that Willy Loman did not die in vain. He had a good dream. It's the only dream you can have—to come out number-one man. He fought it out here, and this is where I'm gonna win it for him.

Biff, *with a hopeless glance at Happy, bends toward his mother.*   Let's go, Mom.

Linda.   I'll be with you in a minute. Go on, Charley. *He hesitates.* I want to, just for a minute. I never had a chance to say good-by.

Charley moves away, followed by Happy. Biff remains a slight distance up and left of Linda. She sits there, summoning herself. The flute begins, not far away, playing behind her speech.

Linda.   Forgive me, dear. I can't cry. I don't know what it is, but I can't cry. I don't understand it. Why did you ever do that? Help me, Willy, I can't cry. It seems to me that you're just on another trip. I keep expecting you. Willy, dear, I can't cry. Why did you do it? I search and search and I search, and I can't understand it, Willy. I made the last payment on the house today. Today, dear. And there'll be nobody home. *A sob rises in her throat.* We're free and clear. *Sobbing more fully, released.* We're free. *Biff comes slowly toward her.* We're free . . . We're free . . .

Biff lifts her to her feet and moves out up right with her in his arms. Linda sobs quietly. Bernard and Charley come together and follow them, followed by Happy. Only the music of the flute is left on the darkening stage as over the house the hard towers of the apartment buildings rise into sharp focus, and

The Curtain Falls

QUESTIONS
1.   What is Linda's role in the tragedy of Willy? Do you admire her?   **2.**   In what ways are Biff and Happy similar? In what ways different? Is Biff, as Willy asserts, a failure? Explain. Which of the brothers is most likely to become another Willy Loman?   **3.**   What does Uncle Ben represent to Willy? Are we meant to see Uncle Ben as Willy sees him? Explain.   **4.**   The play contains many references to the outdoors, the West, working with one's hands. What purpose do these references serve?

WRITING TOPICS
1.   What evidence is there that Willy is a victim of the American dream?   **2.**   Is Biff's treatment of Willy justified? Explain.

Conformity and Rebellion

QUESTIONS AND WRITING TOPICS

1. What answers do the works in this section provide to the question posed by Albert Camus in the following passage:

> The present interest of the problem of rebellion only springs from the fact that nowadays whole societies have wanted to discard the sacred. We live in an unsacrosanct moment in history. Insurrection is certainly not the sum total of human experience. But history today, with all its storm and strife, compels us to say that rebellion is one of the essential dimensions of man. It is our historic reality. Unless we choose to ignore reality, we must find our values in it. Is it possible to find a rule of conduct outside the realm of religion and its absolute values? That is the question raised by rebellion.

Writing Topic: Use this observation as the basis for an analysis of the central characters in Melville's "Bartleby the Scrivener" and Wright's "The Man Who Lived Underground."

2. What support do the works in this section offer for Emily Dickinson's assertion that "Much Madness is divinest Sense"? **Writing Topic:** The central characters in Mann's "Gladius Dei," Kafka's "A Hunger Artist" and Ellison's " 'Repent, Harlequin!' Said the Ticktockman" are viewed by society as mad. How might it be argued that they exhibit "divinest sense"?

3. Which works in this section can be criticized on the grounds that while they attack the established order, they fail to provide any alternatives? **Writing Topic:** Discuss the validity of this objection for two of the following poems: Wordsworth's "The World Is Too Much with Us," Lowell's "Patterns," Frost's "Departmental," Reed's "The Naming of Parts."

4. In a number of these works, a single individual rebels against society and suffers defeat or death. Are these works therefore pessimistic and despairing? If not, then what is the purpose of the rebellions, and why do the authors choose to bring their characters to such ends? **Writing Topic:** Compare two works from this section that offer support for the idea that a single individual can have a decisive effect on the larger society.

5. Examine some of the representatives of established order—the lawyer in "Bartleby the Scrivener," Torvald Helmer, Old Man Warner in "The Lottery," the Ticktockman—and discuss what attitudes they share and how effectively they function as spokesmen for law and order. **Writing Topic:** Compare and evaluate the kinds of order that each represents.

6. Amy Lowell's "Patterns," Karl Shapiro's "The Conscientious Objector," Lawrence Ferlinghetti's "In Goya's Greatest Scenes," and Henry Reed's "Naming of Parts" are, in different ways, antiwar poems. Which of these poems do you find the most articulate and convincing antiwar statement? **Writing Topic:** Discuss the argument that, while condemning war, none of these poems examines the specific reasons that a nation may be obliged to fight—self-defense and national self-interest, for example—and that consequently they are irresponsible.

7. Most of us live out our lives in the ordinary and humdrum world that is rejected in such poems as Wordsworth's "The World Is Too Much with Us," Auden's "The Unknown Citizen," and Lennon and McCartney's "Eleanor Rigby." Can it be said that these poems are counsels to social irresponsibility? **Writing Topic:** Consider whether "we" in Wordsworth's poem, the unknown citizen, Father McKenzie, and Eleanor Rigby are simply objects of scorn or whether they deserve sympathy and perhaps even respect.

8.   In the three plays included here, Antigonê, Nora, Uncle Ben, and Biff are rebels. Are they comparable? **Writing Topic:** Explain how the attitudes and actions of these characters constitute an attack on the *status quo*.

Love
and
Hate

Separation II, 1896 by Edvard Munch

Love and death, it is often noted, are the two great themes of literature. Much of the literary art we have placed in the sections "Innocence and Experience" and "Conformity and Rebellion" speaks of love and death as well. But in those works, other thematic interests dominate. In this section, we gather a number of works in which love and hate are thematically central.

The rosy conception of love presented in many popular and sentimental stories ill prepares us for the complicated reality we face. We know that the course of true love never runs smooth, but in those popular stories the obstacles that hinder the lovers are simple and external. If the young lover can land the high-paying job or convince the beloved's parents that he or she is worthy despite social differences, all will be well. But love in life is rarely that simple. The external obstacles may be insuperable, or the obstacles may lie deep within the personality. The major obstacle may well be an individual's difficult and painful effort to understand that he or she has been deceived by an immature and sentimental conception of love.

In this age of psychoanalytic awareness, the claims of the flesh are well recognized. But psychoanalytic theory teaches us, as well, to recognize the aggressive aspect of the human condition. The omnipresent selfishness that civilization attempts to check may be aggressively violent as well as lustful. Remarkably, many literary treatments of love envision the lovers sometimes as victims of the chaos that seems to surround them and sometimes as serene and safe in the midst of violence. D. H. Lawrence's "The Horse Dealer's Daughter" is embroidered on a fabric of violence and chaos. William Faulkner in "Dry September" recognizes the erotic sources of certain kinds of violence in stories ostensibly about hate. And Matthew Arnold in "Dover Beach" finds love the only refuge from a chaotic world in which "ignorant armies clash by night."

The cliché has it that love and hate are closely related, and much evidence supports this proposition. But why should love and hate, seeming opposites, lie so close together in the emotional lives of men and women? We are all egos,

727

separate from each other. And as separate individuals, we develop elaborate behavior mechanisms that defend us from each other. Self-esteem is terribly important, and threats to self-esteem must somehow be neutralized. But the erotic love relationship differs from other relationships in that it may be defined as a rejection of separateness. The common metaphor speaks of two lovers as joining, as merging into one. That surrender of the "me" to join in an "us" leaves the lovers uniquely vulnerable to psychic injury. In short, the defenses are down, and the self-esteem of each of the lovers depends importantly on the behavior of the other. If the lover is betrayed by the beloved, the emotional consequences are uniquely disastrous—hence the peculiarly close relationship of passionate hatred with erotic love.

Words like *love* and *hate* are so general that poets rarely use them except as one term in a metaphor designed to project sharply some aspect of emotional life. The simple sexuality in such poems as Marvell's "To His Coy Mistress," Marlowe's "The Passionate Shepherd to His Love," and Campion's "I Care Not for These Ladies" may be juxtaposed with the hatred and violence generated in Othello by sexual jealousy or with the quick reprisal of the slighted Barbara Allan. And Shakespeare's description of lust in "Th' expense of spirit in a waste of shame" notes an aspect of love quite overlooked by Edmund Waller in his song, "Go, Lovely Rose!"

Perhaps more than anything, the works in this section celebrate the elemental impulses of men and women that run counter to those rational formulations by which we govern our lives. We pursue Othello's love for Desdemona and Iago's hate for Othello and arrive at an irreducible mystery, for neither Othello's love nor Iago's hate yields satisfactorily to rational explanation. Reason does not tell us why Othello and Desdemona love one another or why Iago hates rather than honors Othello. And in Molière's *The Misanthrope*, Alceste's love for the beautiful Célimène seems to contradict everything he professes to stand for.

Love is an act of faith springing from our deep-seated need to join with another human being not only in physical nakedness but in emotional and spiritual nakedness as well. While hate is a denial of that faith and, therefore, a retreat into spiritual isolation, love is an attempt to break out of the isolation. And as Erich Fromm writes in *The Art of Loving*:

> The basic need to fuse with another person so as to transcend the prison of one's separateness is closely related to another specifically human desire, that to know the "secret of man." While life in its merely biological aspects is a miracle and a secret, man in his human aspects is an unfathomable secret to himself—and to his fellow man. We know ourselves, and yet even with all the efforts we may make, we do not know ourselves. We know our fellow man, and yet we do not know him, because we are not a thing, and our fellow man is not a thing. The further we reach into the depth of our being, or someone else's being, the more the goal of knowledge eludes us. Yet we cannot help desiring to penetrate into the secret of man's soul, into the innermost nucleus which is "he."
>
> There is one way, a desperate one, to know the secret: it is that of complete power over another person; the power which makes him do what we want, feel what we want, think what we want; which transforms him into a thing, our thing, our possession. The ultimate degree of this attempt to know lies in the extremes of sadism, the desire and ability to make a human being suffer; to torture him, to force him to betray his secret in his suffering. In this craving for penetrating man's secret, his and hence our own, lies an essential motivation for the depth and intensity of cruelty and destructiveness. . . .
>
> The other path to knowing "the secret" is love. Love is active penetration of the other person, in which my desire to know is stilled by union. In the act of fusion I know you, I know myself, I know everybody—and I "know" nothing. I know in the only way knowledge of that which is alive is possible for man—by experience of union—not by any knowledge our thought can give. Sadism is motivated by the wish to know the secret, yet I remain as ignorant as I was before. I have torn the other being apart limb from limb, yet all I have done is to destroy him. Love is the only way of knowledge, which in the act of union answers my quest. In the act of loving, of giving myself, in the act of penetrating the other person, I find myself, I discover myself, I discover us both, I discover man.

LOVE
AND
HATE

A Husband Parting from His Wife and Child, 1799 by William Blake

FICTION

The Storm   (1898)

KATE CHOPIN [1851–1904]

I

The leaves were so still that even Bibi thought it was going to rain. Bobinôt, who was accustomed to converse on terms of perfect equality with his little son, called the child's attention to certain sombre clouds that were rolling with sinister intention from the west, accompanied by a sullen, threatening roar. They were at Friedheimer's store and decided to remain there till the storm had passed. They sat within the door on two empty kegs. Bibi was four years old and looked very wise.

"Mama'll be 'fraid, yes," he suggested with blinking eyes.

"She'll shut the house. Maybe she got Sylvie helpin' her this evenin'," Bobinôt responded reassuringly.

"No; she ent got Sylvie. Sylvie was helpin' her yistiday," piped Bibi.

Bobinôt arose and going across to the counter purchased a can of shrimps, of which Calixta was very fond. Then he returned to his perch on the keg and sat stolidly holding the can of shrimps while the storm burst. It shook the wooden store and seemed to be ripping great furrows in the distant field. Bibi laid his little hand on his father's knee and was not afraid.

II

Calixta, at home, felt no uneasiness for their safety. She sat at a side window sewing furiously on a sewing machine. She was greatly occupied and did not notice the approaching storm. But she felt very warm and often stopped to mop her face on which the perspiration gathered in beads. She unfastened her white sacque at the throat. It began to grow dark, and suddenly realizing the situation she got up hurriedly and went about closing windows and doors.

Out on the small front gallery she had hung Bobinôt's Sunday clothes to air and she hastened out to gather them before the rain fell. As she stepped outside, Alcée Laballière rode in at the gate. She had not seen him very often since her marriage, and never alone. She stood there with Bobinôt's coat in her hands, and the big rain drops began to fall. Alcée rode his horse under the shelter of a side projection where the chickens had huddled and there were plows and a harrow piled up in the corner.

"May I come and wait on your gallery till the storm is over, Calixta?" he asked.

"Come 'long in, M'sieur Alcée."

His voice and her own startled her as if from a trance, and she seized Bobinôt's vest. Alcée, mounting to the porch, grabbed the trousers and snatched Bibi's braided jacket that was about to be carried away by a sudden gust of wind. He expressed an intention to remain outside, but it was soon apparent that he might as well have been out in the open: the water beat in upon the boards in driving sheets, and he went inside, closing the door after him. It was even necessary to put something beneath the door to keep the water out.

"My! what a rain! It's good two years sence it rain' like that," exclaimed Calixta as she rolled up a piece of bagging and Alcée helped her to thrust it beneath the crack.

She was a little fuller of figure than five years before when she married; but she had lost nothing of her vivacity. Her blue eyes still retained their melting quality; and her yellow hair, dishevelled by the wind and rain, kinked more stubbornly than ever about her ears and temples.

The rain beat upon the low, shingled roof with a force and clatter that threatened to break an entrance and deluge them there. They were in the dining room—the sitting room—the general utility room. Adjoining was her bed room, with Bibi's couch along side her own. The door stood open, and the room with its white, monumental bed, its closed shutters, looked dim and mysterious.

Alcée flung himself into a rocker and Calixta nervously began to gather up from the floor the lengths of a cotton sheet which she had been sewing.

"If this keeps up, *Dieu sait*[1] if the levees goin' to stan' it!" she exclaimed.

"What have you got to do with the levees?"

"I got enough to do! An' there's Bobinôt with Bibi out in that storm—if he only didn' left Friedheimer's!"

"Let us hope, Calixta, that Bobinôt's got sense enough to come in out of a cyclone."

She went and stood at the window with a greatly disturbed look on her face. She wiped the frame that was clouded with moisture. It was stiflingly hot. Alcée got up and joined her at the window, looking over her shoulder. The rain was coming down in sheets obscuring the view of far-off cabins and enveloping the distant wood in a gray mist. The playing of the lightning was incessant. A bolt struck a tall chinaberry tree at the edge of the field. It filled all visible space with a blinding glare and the crash seemed to invade the very boards they stood upon.

Calixta put her hands to her eyes, and with a cry, staggered backward. Alcée's

---

[1] God knows.

arm encircled her, and for an instant he drew her close and spasmodically to him.

"*Bonte!*"[2] she cried, releasing herself from his encircling arm and retreating from the window, "the house'll go next! If I only knew w'ere Bibi was!" She would not compose herself; she would not be seated. Alcée clasped her shoulders and looked into her face. The contact of her warm, palpitating body when he had unthinkingly drawn her into his arms, had aroused all the old-time infatuation and desire for her flesh.

"Calixta," he said, "don't be frightened. Nothing can happen. The house is too low to be struck, with so many tall trees standing about. There! aren't you going to be quiet? say, aren't you?" He pushed her hair back from her face that was warm and steaming. Her lips were as red and moist as pomegranate seed. Her white neck and a glimpse of her full, firm bosom disturbed him powerfully. As she glanced up at him the fear in her liquid blue eyes had given place to a drowsy gleam that unconsciously betrayed a sensuous desire. He looked down into her eyes and there was nothing for him to do but to gather her lips in a kiss. It reminded him of Assumption.[3]

"Do you remember—in Assumption. Calixta?" he asked in a low voice broken by passion. Oh! she remembered; for in Assumption he had kissed her and kissed and kissed her; until his senses would well nigh fail, and to save her he would resort to a desperate flight. If she was not an immaculate dove in those days, she was still inviolate; a passionate creature whose very defenselessness had made her defense, against which his honor forbade him to prevail. Now—well, now—her lips seemed in a manner free to be tasted, as well as her round, white throat and her whiter breasts.

They did not heed the crashing torrents, and the roar of the elements made her laugh as she lay in his arms. She was a revelation in that dim, mysterious chamber; as white as the couch she lay upon. Her firm, elastic flesh that was knowing for the first time its birthright, was like a creamy lily that the sun invites to contribute its breath and perfume to the undying life of the world.

The generous abundance of her passion, without guile or trickery, was like a white flame which penetrated and found response in depths of his own sensuous nature that had never yet been reached.

When he touched her breasts they gave themselves up in quivering ecstasy, inviting his lips. Her mouth was a fountain of delight. And when he possessed her, they seemed to swoon together at the very borderland of life's mystery.

He stayed cushioned upon her, breathless, dazed, enervated, with his heart beating like a hammer upon her. With one hand she clasped his head, her lips lightly touching his forehead. The other hand stroked with a soothing rhythm his muscular shoulders.

---

[2] An exclamation: Goodness!
[3] A holiday commemorating the ascent of the Virgin Mary to heaven. Assumption is also the name of a Louisiana parish (county) where Calixta and Alcée had had a rendezvous in an earlier story.

The growl of the thunder was distant and passing away. The rain beat softly upon the shingles, inviting them to drowsiness and sleep. But they dared not yield.

The rain was over; and the sun was turning the glistening green world into a palace of gems. Calixta, on the gallery, watched Alcée ride away. He turned and smiled at her with a beaming face; and she lifted her pretty chin in the air and laughed aloud.

III

Bobinôt and Bibi, trudging home, stopped without at the cistern to make themselves presentable.

"My! Bibi, w'at will yo' mama say! You ought to be ashame'. You oughtn' put on those good pants. Look at 'em! An' that mud on yo' collar! How you got that mud on yo' collar, Bibi? I never saw such a boy!" Bibi was the picture of pathetic resignation. Bobinôt was the embodiment of serious solicitude as he strove to remove from his own person and his son's the signs of their tramp over heavy roads and through wet fields. He scraped the mud off Bibi's bare legs and feet with a stick and carefully removed all traces from his heavy brogans. Then, prepared for the worst—the meeting with an over-scrupulous housewife, they entered cautiously at the back door.

Calixta was preparing supper. She had set the table and was dripping coffee at the hearth. She sprang up as they came in.

"Oh, Bobinôt! You back! My! but I was uneasy. W'ere you been during the rain? An' Bibi? he ain't wet? he ain't hurt?" She had clasped Bibi and was kissing him effusively. Bobinôt's explanations and apologies which he had been composing all along the way, died on his lips as Calixta felt him to see if he were dry, and seemed to express nothing but satisfaction at their safe return.

"I brought you some shrimps, Calixta," offered Bobinôt, hauling the can from his ample side pocket and laying it on the table.

"Shrimps! Oh, Bobinôt! you too good fo' anything!" and she gave him a smacking kiss on the cheek that resounded. "*J'vous reponds,*[4] we'll have a feas' to night! umph-umph!"

Bobinôt and Bibi began to relax and enjoy themselves, and when the three seated themselves at table they laughed much and so loud that anyone might have heard them as far away as Laballière's.

IV

Alcée Laballière wrote to his wife, Clarisse, that night. It was a loving letter, full of tender solicitude. He told her not to hurry back, but if she and the babies liked it at Biloxi, to stay a month longer. He was getting on nicely; and though

---

[4] I'm telling you.

he missed them, he was willing to bear the separation a while longer—realizing that their health and pleasure were the first things to be considered.

V

As for Clarisse, she was charmed upon receiving her husband's letter. She and the babies were doing well. The society was agreeable; many of her old friends and acquaintances were at the bay. And the first free breath since her marriage seemed to restore the pleasant liberty of her maiden days. Devoted as she was to her husband, their intimate conjugal life was something which she was more than willing to forego for a while.

So the storm passed and everyone was happy.

The Horse Dealer's Daughter   1922

D. H. LAWRENCE   [1885–1930]

"Well, Mabel, and what are you going to do with yourself?" asked Joe, with foolish flippancy. He felt quite safe himself. Without listening for an answer, he turned aside, worked a grain of tobacco to the tip of his tongue, and spat it out. He did not care about anything, since he felt safe himself.

The three brothers and the sister sat round the desolate breakfast table, attempting some sort of desultory consultation. The morning's post had given the final tap to the family fortune, and all was over. The dreary dining-room itself, with its heavy mahogany furniture, looked as if it were waiting to be done away with.

But the consultation amounted to nothing. There was a strange air of ineffectuality about the three men, as they sprawled at table, smoking and reflecting vaguely on their own condition. The girl was alone, a rather short, sullen-looking young woman of twenty-seven. She did not share the same life as her brothers. She would have been good-looking, save for the impassive fixity of her face, "bull-dog," as her brothers called it.

There was a confused tramping of horses' feet outside. The three men all sprawled round in their chairs to watch. Beyond the dark hollybushes that separated the strip of lawn from the high-road, they could see a cavalcade of shire horses swinging out of their own yard, being taken for exercise. This was the last time. These were the last horses that would go through their hands. The young men watched with critical, callous look. They were all frightened at the collapse of their lives, and the sense of disaster in which they were involved left them no inner freedom.

Yet they were three fine, well-set fellows enough. Joe, the eldest, was a man of thirty-three, broad and handsome in a hot, flushed way. His face was red, he twisted his black moustache over a thick finger, his eyes were shallow and restless. He had a sensual way of uncovering his teeth when he laughed, and his bearing was stupid. Now he watched the horses with a glazed look of helplessness in his eyes, a certain stupor of downfall.

The great draught-horses swung past. They were tied head to tail, four of them, and they heaved along to where a lane branched off from the highroad, planting their great hoofs floutingly in the fine black mud, swinging their great rounded haunches sumptuously, and trotting a few sudden steps as they were led into the lane, round the corner. Every movement showed a massive, slumbrous strength, and a stupidity which held them in subjection. The groom at the head looked back, jerking the leading rope. And the cavalcade moved out of sight up the lane, the tail of the last horse bobbed up tight and stiff, held out taut from the swinging great haunches as they rocked behind the hedges in a motion like sleep.

Joe watched with glazed hopeless eyes. The horses were almost like his own body to him. He felt he was done for now. Luckily he was engaged to a woman as old as himself, and therefore her father, who was steward of a neighbouring estate, would provide him with a job. He would marry and go into harness. His life was over, he would be a subject animal now.

He turned uneasily aside, the retreating steps of the horses echoing in his ears. Then, with foolish restlessness, he reached for the scraps of bacon-rind from the plates, and making a faint whistling sound, flung them to the terrier that lay against the fender. He watched the dog swallow them, and waited till the creature looked into his eyes. Then a faint grin came on his face, and in a high, foolish voice he said:

"You won't get much more bacon, shall you, you little bitch?"

The dog faintly and dismally wagged its tail, then lowered its haunches, circled round, and lay down again.

There was another helpless silence at the table. Joe sprawled uneasily in his seat, not willing to go till the family conclave was dissolved. Fred Henry, the second brother, was erect, clean-limbed, alert. He had watched the passing of the horses with more sangfroid. If he was an animal, like Joe, he was an animal which controls, not one which is controlled. He was master of any horse, and he carried himself with a well-tempered air of mastery. But he was not master of the situations of life. He pushed his coarse brown moustache upwards, off his lip, and glanced irritably at his sister, who sat impassive and inscrutable.

"You'll go and stop with Lucy for a bit, shan't you?" he asked. The girl did not answer.

"I don't see what else you can do," persisted Fred Henry.

"Go as a skivvy," Joe interpolated laconically.

The girl did not move a muscle.

"If I was her, I should go in for training for a nurse," said Malcolm, the youngest of them all. He was the baby of the family, a young man of twenty-two, with a fresh, jaunty *museau*.[1]

But Mabel did not take any notice of him. They had talked at her and round her for so many years, that she hardly heard them at all.

The marble clock on the mantelpiece softly chimed the half-hour, the dog rose uneasily from the hearthrug and looked at the party at the breakfast table. But still they sat on in ineffectual conclave.

"Oh, all right," said Joe suddenly, apropos of nothing. "I'll get a move on."

He pushed back his chair, straddled his knees with a downward jerk, to get them free, in horsey fashion, and went to the fire. Still he did not go out of the room; he was curious to know what the others would do or say. He began to charge his pipe, looking down at the dog and saying, in a high, affected voice:

"Going wi' me? Going wi' me are ter? Tha'rt goin' further than tha counts on just now, dost hear?"

The dog faintly wagged its tail, the man stuck out his jaw and covered his

---

[1] Face.

pipe with his hands, and puffed intently, losing himself in the tobacco, looking down all the while at the dog with an absent brown eye. The dog looked up at him in mournful distrust. Joe stood with his knees stuck out, in real horsey fashion.

"Have you had a letter from Lucy?" Fred Henry asked of his sister.

"Last week," came the neutral reply.

"And what does she say?"

There was no answer.

"Does she *ask* you to go and stop there?" persisted Fred Henry.

"She says I can if I like."

"Well, then, you'd better. Tell her you'll come on Monday."

This was received in silence.

"That's what you'll do then, is it?" said Fred Henry, in some exasperation.

But she made no answer. There was a silence of futility and irritation in the room. Malcolm grinned fatuously.

"You'll have to make up your mind between now and next Wednesday," said Joe loudly, "or else find yourself lodgings on the kerbstone."

The face of the young woman darkened, but she sat on immutable.

"Here's Jack Fergusson!" exclaimed Malcolm, who was looking aimlessly out of the window.

"Where?" exclaimed Joe, loudly.

"Just gone past."

"Coming in?"

Malcolm craned his neck to see the gate.

"Yes," he said.

There was a silence. Mabel sat on like one condemned, at the head of the table. Then a whistle was heard from the kitchen. The dog got up and barked sharply. Joe opened the door and shouted:

"Come on."

After a moment a young man entered. He was muffled up in overcoat and a purple woollen scarf, and his tweed cap, which he did not remove, was pulled down on his head. He was of medium height, his face was rather long and pale, his eyes looked tired.

"Hello, Jack! Well, Jack!" exclaimed Malcolm and Joe. Fred Henry merely said, "Jack."

"What's doing?" asked the newcomer, evidently addressing Fred Henry.

"Same. We've got to be out by Wednesday. Got a cold?"

"I have—got it bad, too."

"Why don't you stop in?"

"*Me* stop in? When I can't stand on my legs, perhaps I shall have a chance." The young man spoke huskily. He had a slight Scotch accent.

"It's a knock-out, isn't it?" said Joe, boisterously, "if a doctor goes round croaking with a cold. Looks bad for the patients, doesn't it?"

The young doctor looked at him slowly.

"Anything the matter with *you*, then?" he asked sarcastically.

"Not as I know of. Damn your eyes, I hope not. Why?"

"I thought you were very concerned about the patients, wondered if you might be one yourself."

"Damn it, no, I've never been patient to no flaming doctor, and hope I never shall be," returned Joe.

At this point Mabel rose from the table, and they all seemed to become aware of her existence. She began putting the dishes together. The young doctor looked at her, but did not address her. He had not greeted her. She went out of the room with the tray, her face impassive and unchanged.

"When are you off then, all of you?" asked the doctor.

"I'm catching the eleven-forty," replied Malcolm. "Are you goin' down wi' th' trap, Joe?"

"Yes, I've told you I am going down wi' th' trap, haven't I?"

"We'd better be getting her in then. So long, Jack, if I don't see you before I go," said Malcolm, shaking hands.

He went out, followed by Joe, who seemed to have his tail between his legs.

"Well, this is the devil's own," exclaimed the doctor, when he was left alone with Fred Henry. "Going before Wednesday, are you."

"That's the orders," replied the other.

"Where, to Northampton?"

"That's it."

"The devil!" exclaimed Fergusson, with quiet chagrin.

And there was silence between the two.

"All settled up, are you?" asked Fergusson.

"About."

There was another pause.

"Well, I shall miss yer, Freddy, boy," said the young doctor.

"And I shall miss thee, Jack," returned the other.

"Miss you like hell," mused the doctor.

Fred Henry turned aside. There was nothing to say. Mabel came in again, to finish clearing the table.

"What are *you* going to do, then, Miss Pervin?" asked Fergusson. "Going to your sister's, are you?"

Mabel looked at him with her steady, dangerous eyes, that always made him uncomfortable, unsettling his superficial ease.

"No," she said.

"Well, what in the name of fortune are *you* going to do? Say what you mean to do," cried Fred Henry, with futile intensity.

But she only averted her head, and continued her work. She folded the white table-cloth, and put on the chenille cloth.

"The sulkiest bitch that ever trod!" muttered her brother.

But she finished her task with perfectly impassive face, the young doctor watching her interestedly all the while. Then she went out.

Fred Henry stared after her, clenching his lips, his blue eyes fixing in sharp antagonism, as he made a grimace of sour exasperation.

"You could bray her into bits, and that's all you'd get out of her," he said in a small, narrowed tone.

The doctor smiled faintly.

"What's she *going* to do, then?" he asked.

"Strike me if I know!" returned the other.

There was a pause. Then the doctor stirred.

"I'll be seeing you to-night, shall I?" he said to his friend.

"Ay—where's it to be? Are we going over to Jessdale?"

"I don't know. I've got such a cold on me. I'll come round to the Moon and Stars, anyway."

"Let Lizzie and May miss their night for once, eh?"

"That's it—if I feel as I do now."

"All's one—"

The two young men went through the passage and down to the back door together. The house was large, but it was servantless now, and desolate. At the back was a small bricked house-yard, and beyond that a big square, gravelled fine and red, and having stables on two sides. Sloping, dank, winter-dark fields stretched away on the open sides.

But the stables were empty. Joseph Pervin, the father of the family, had been a man of no education, who had become a fairly large horse dealer. The stables had been full of horses, there was a great turmoil and come-and-go of horses and of dealers and grooms. Then the kitchen was full of servants. But of late things had declined. The old man had married a second time, to retrieve his fortunes. Now he was dead and everything was gone to the dogs, there was nothing but debt and threatening.

For months, Mabel had been servantless in the big house, keeping the home together in penury for her ineffectual brothers. She had kept house for ten years. But previously it was with unstinted means. Then, however brutal and coarse everything was, the sense of money had kept her proud, confident. The men might be foul-mouthed, the women in the kitchen might have bad reputations, her brothers might have illegitimate children. But so long as there was money, the girl felt herself established and brutally proud, reserved.

No company came to the house, save dealers and coarse men. Mabel had no associates of her own sex, after her sister went away. But she did not mind. She went regularly to church, she attended to her father. And she lived in the memory of her mother, who had died when she was fourteen, and whom she had loved. She had loved her father, too, in a different way, depending upon him, and feeling secure in him, until at the age of fifty-four he married again. And then she had set hard against him. Now he had died and left them all hopelessly in debt.

She had suffered badly during the period of poverty. Nothing, however, could shake the curious sullen, animal pride that dominated each member of the family. Now, for Mabel, the end had come. Still she would not cast about her. She would follow her own way just the same. She would always hold the keys of her own situation. Mindless and persistent, she endured from day to day.

What should she think? Why should she answer anybody? It was enough that this was the end and there was no way out. She need not pass any more darkly along the main street of the small town, avoiding every eye. She need not demean herself any more, going into the shops and buying the cheapest food. This was at an end. She thought of nobody, not even of herself. Mindless and persistent, she seemed in a sort of ecstasy to be coming nearer to her fulfilment, her own glorification, approaching her dead mother, who was glorified.

In the afternoon she took a little bag, with shears and sponge and a small scrubbing brush, and went out. It was a grey, wintry day, with saddened, dark green fields and an atmosphere blackened by the smoke of foundries not far off. She went quickly, darkly along the causeway, heeding nobody, through the town to the churchyard.

There she always felt secure, as if no one could see her, although as a matter of fact she was exposed to the stare of every one who passed along under the churchyard wall. Nevertheless, once under the shadow of the great looming church, among the graves, she felt immune from the world, reserved within the thick churchyard wall as in another country.

Carefully she clipped the grass from the grave, and arranged the pinky white, small chrysanthemums in the tin cross. When this was done, she took an empty jar from a neighbouring grave, brought water, and carefully, most scrupulously sponged the marble head-stone and the coping-stone.

It gave her sincere satisfaction to do this. She felt in immediate contact with the world of her mother. She took minute pains, went through the park in a state bordering on pure happiness, as if in performing this task she came into a subtle, intimate connection with her mother. For the life she followed here in the world was far less real than the world of death she inherited from her mother.

The doctor's house was just by the church. Fergusson, being a mere hired assistant, was slave to the country-side. As he hurried now to attend to the out-patients in the surgery, glancing across the graveyard with his quick eye, he saw the girl at her task at the grave. She seemed so intent and remote, it was like looking into another world. Some mystical element was touched in him. He slowed down as he walked, watching her as if spell-bound.

She lifted her eyes, feeling him looking. Their eyes met. And each looked away again at once, each feeling, in some way, found out by the other. He lifted his cap and passed on down the road. There remained distinct in his consciousness, like a vision, the memory of her face, lifted from the tombstone in the churchyard, and looking at him with slow, large, portentous eyes. It *was* portentous, her face. It seemed to mesmerize him. There was a heavy power in her eyes which laid hold of his whole being, as if he had drunk some powerful drug. He had been feeling weak and done before. Now the life came back into him, he felt delivered from his own fretted, daily self.

He finished his duties at the surgery as quickly as might be, hastily filling up the bottle of the waiting people with cheap drugs. Then, in perpetual haste, he set off again to visit several cases in another part of his round, before tea-time.

At all times he preferred to walk if he could, but particularly when he was not well. He fancied the motion restored him.

The afternoon was falling. It was grey, deadened, and wintry, with a slow, moist, heavy coldness sinking in and deadening all the faculties. But why should he think or notice? He hastily climbed the hill and turned across the dark green fields, following the black cinder-track. In the distance, across a shallow dip in the country, the small town was clustered like smouldering ash, a tower, a spire, a heap of low, raw, extinct houses. And on the nearest fringe of the town, sloping into the dip, was Oldmeadow, the Pervins' house. He could see the stables and the outbuildings distinctly, as they lay towards him on the slope. Well, he would not go there many more times! Another resource would be lost to him, another place gone: the only company he cared for in the alien, ugly little town he was losing. Nothing but work, drudgery, constant hastening from dwelling to dwelling among the colliers and the ironworkers. It wore him out, but at the same time he had a craving for it. It was a stimulant to him to be in the homes of the working people, moving as it were through the innermost body of their life. His nerves were excited and gratified. He could come so near, into the very lives of the rough, inarticulate, powerfully emotional men and women. He grumbled, he said he hated the hellish hole. But as a matter of fact it excited him, the contact with the rough, strongly-feeling people was a stimulant applied direct to his nerves.

Below Oldmeadow, in the green, shallow, soddened hollow of fields lay a square, deep pond. Roving across the landscape, the doctor's quick eye detected a figure in black passing through the gate of the field, down towards the pond. He looked again. It would be Mabel Pervin. His mind suddenly became alive and attentive.

Why was she going down there? He pulled up on the path on the slope above, and stood staring. He could just make sure of the small black figure moving in the hollow of the failing day. He seemed to see her in the midst of such obscurity, that he was like a clairvoyant, seeing rather with the mind's eye than with ordinary sight. Yet he could see her positively enough, whilst he kept his eye attentive. He felt, if he looked away from her, in the thick, ugly falling dusk, he would lose her altogether.

He followed her minutely as she moved, direct and intent, like something transmitted rather than stirring in voluntary activity, straight down the field towards the pond. There she stood on the bank for a moment. She never raised her head. Then she waded slowly into the water.

He stood motionless as the small black figure walked slowly and deliberately towards the centre of the pond, very slowly, gradually moving deeper into the motionless water, and still moving forward as the water got up to her breast. Then he could see her no more in the dusk of the dead afternoon.

"There!" he exclaimed. "Would you believe it?"

And he hastened straight down, running over the wet, soddened fields, pushing through the hedges, down into the depression of callous wintry obscurity.

It took him several minutes to come to the pond. He stood on the bank, breathing heavily. He could see nothing. His eyes seemed to penetrate the dead water. Yes, perhaps that was the dark shadow of her black clothing beneath the surface of the water.

He slowly ventured into the pond. The bottom was deep, soft clay, he sank in, and the water clasped dead cold round his legs. As he stirred he could smell the cold, rotten clay that fouled up into the water. It was objectionable in his lungs. Still, repelled and yet not heeding, he moved deeper into the pond. The cold water rose over his thighs, over his loins, upon his abdomen. The lower part of his body was all sunk in the hideous cold element. And the bottom was so deeply soft and uncertain, he was afraid of pitching with his mouth underneath. He could not swim, and was afraid.

He crouched a little, spreading his hands under the water and moving them round, trying to feel for her. The dead cold pond swayed upon his chest. He moved again, a little deeper, and again, with his hands underneath, he felt all around the water. And he touched her clothing. But it evaded his fingers. He made a desperate effort to grasp it.

And so doing he lost his balance and went under, horribly, suffocating in the foul earthy water, struggling madly for a few moments. At last, after what seemed an eternity, he got his footing, rose again into the air and looked around. He gasped, and knew he was in the world. Then he looked at the water. She had risen near him. He grasped her clothing, and drawing her nearer, turned to take his way to land again.

He went very slowly, carefully, absorbed in the slow progress. He rose higher, climbing out of the pond. The water was now only about his legs; he was thankful, full of relief to be out of the clutches of the pond. He lifted her and staggered on to the bank, out of the horror of wet, grey clay.

He laid her down on the bank. She was quite unconscious and running with water. He made the water come from her mouth, he worked to restore her. He did not have to work very long before he could feel the breathing begin again in her; she was breathing naturally. He worked a little longer. He could feel her live beneath his hands; she was coming back. He wiped her face, wrapped her in his overcoat, looked round into the dim, dark grey world, then lifted her and staggered down the bank and across the fields.

It seemed an unthinkably long way, and his burden so heavy he felt he would never get to the house. But at last he was in the stable-yard, and then in the house-yard. He opened the door and went into the house. In the kitchen he laid her down on the hearth-rug, and called. The house was empty. But the fire was burning in the grate.

Then again he kneeled to attend to her. She was breathing regularly, her eyes were wide open and as if conscious, but there seemed something missing in her look. She was conscious in herself, but unconscious of her surroundings.

He ran upstairs, took blankets from a bed, and put them before the fire to warm. Then he removed her saturated, earthy-smelling clothing, rubbed her dry with a towel, and wrapped her naked in the blankets. Then he went into the dining-room, to look for spirits. There was a little whisky. He drank a gulp himself, and put some into her mouth.

The effect was instantaneous. She looked full into his face, as if she had been seeing him for some time, and yet had only just become conscious of him.

"Dr. Fergusson?" she said.

"What?" he answered.

He was divesting himself of his coat, intending to find some dry clothing upstairs. He could not bear the smell of the dead, clayey water, and he was mortally afraid for his own health.

"What did I do?" she asked.

"Walked into the pond," he replied. He had begun to shudder like one sick, and could hardly attend to her. Her eyes remained full on him, he seemed to be going dark in his mind, looking back at her helplessly. The shuddering became quieter in him, his life came back in him, dark and unknowing, but strong again.

"Was I out of my mind?" she asked, while her eyes were fixed on him all the time.

"Maybe, for the moment," he replied. He felt quiet, because his strength had come back. The strange fretful strain had left him.

"Am I out of my mind now?" she asked.

"Are you?" he reflected a moment. "No," he answered truthfully. "I don't see that you are." He turned his face aside. He was afraid now, because he felt dazed, and felt dimly that her power was stronger than his, in this issue. And she continued to look at him fixedly all the time. "Can you tell me where I shall find some dry things to put on?" he asked.

"Did you dive into the pond for me?" she asked.

"No," he answered. "I walked in. But I went in overhead as well."

There was silence for a moment. He hesitated. He very much wanted to go upstairs to get into dry clothing. But there was another desire in him. And she seemed to hold him. His will seemed to have gone to sleep, and left him, standing there slack before her. But he felt warm inside himself. He did not shudder at all, though his clothes were sodden on him.

"Why did you?" she asked.

"Because I didn't want you to do such a foolish thing," he said.

"It wasn't foolish," she said, still gazing at him as she lay on the floor, with a sofa cushion under her head. "It was the right thing to do. I knew best, then."

"I'll go and shift these wet things," he said. But still he had not the power to move out of her presence, until she sent him. It was as if she had the life of his body in her hands, and he could not extricate himself. Or perhaps he did not want to.

Suddenly she sat up. Then she became aware of her own immediate condition. She felt the blankets about her, she knew her own limbs. For a moment it seemed as if her reason were going. She looked round, with wild eye, as if seeking something. He stood still with fear. She saw her clothing lying scattered.

"Who undressed me?" she asked, her eyes resting full and inevitable on his face.

"I did," he replied, "to bring you round."

For some moments she sat and gazed at him awfully, her lips parted.

"Do you love me, then?" she asked.

He only stood and stared at her, fascinated. His soul seemed to melt.

She shuffled forward on her knees, and put her arms around him, round his legs, as he stood there, pressing her breasts against his knees and thighs, clutching him with strange, convulsive certainty, pressing his thighs against her, drawing him to her face, her throat, as she looked up at him with flaring, humble eyes of transfiguration, triumphant in first possession.

"You love me," she murmured, in strange transport, yearning and triumphant and confident. "You love me. I know you love me, I know."

And she was passionately kissing his knees, through the wet clothing, passionately and indiscriminately kissing his knees, his legs, as if unaware of everything.

He looked down at the tangled wet hair, the wild, bare, animal shoulders. He was amazed, bewildered, and afraid. He had never thought of loving her. He had never wanted to love her. When he rescued her and restored her, he was a doctor, and she was a patient. He had had no single personal thought of her. Nay, this introduction of the personal element was very distasteful to him, a violation of his professional honour. It was horrible to have her there embracing his knees. It was horrible. He revolted from it, violently. And yet—and yet—he had not the power to break away.

She looked at him again, with the same supplication of powerful love, and that same transcendent, frightening light of triumph. In view of the delicate flame which seemed to come from her face like a light, he was powerless. And yet he had never intended to love her. He had never intended. And something stubborn in him could not give way.

"You love me," she repeated, in a murmur of deep rhapsodic assurance. "You love me."

Her hands were drawing him, drawing him down to her. He was afraid, even a little horrified. For he had, really, no intention of loving her. Yet her hands were drawing him towards her. He put out his hand quickly to steady himself, and grasped her bare shoulder. A flame seemed to burn the hand that grasped her soft shoulder. He had no intention of loving her: his whole will was against his yielding. It was horrible. And yet wonderful was the touch of her shoulders, beautiful the shining of her face. Was she perhaps mad? He had a horror of yielding to her. Yet something in him ached also.

He had been staring away at the door, away from her. But his hand remained on her shoulder. She had gone suddenly very still. He looked down at her. Her eyes were now wide with fear, with doubt, the light was dying from her face, a shadow of terrible greyness was returning. He could not bear the touch of her eyes' question upon him, and the look of death behind the question.

With an inward groan he gave way, and let his heart yield towards her. A sudden gentle smile came on his face. And her eyes, which never left his face, slowly, slowly filled with tears. He watched the strange water rise in her eyes, like some slow fountain coming up. And his heart seemed to burn and melt away in his breast.

He could not bear to look at her any more. He dropped on his knees and caught her head with his arms and pressed her face against his throat. She was very still. His heart, which seemed to have broken, was burning with a kind of agony in his breast. And he felt her slow, hot tears wetting his throat. But he could not move.

He felt the hot tears wet his neck and the hollows of his neck, and he remained motionless, suspended through one of man's eternities. Only now it had become indispensable to him to have her face pressed close to him; he could never let her go again. He could never let her head go away from the close clutch of his arm. He wanted to remain like that for ever, with his heart hurting him in a pain that was also life to him. Without knowing, he was looking down on her damp, soft brown hair.

Then, as it were suddenly, he smelt the horrid stagnant smell of that water. And at the same moment she drew away from him and looked at him. Her eyes were wistful and unfathomable. He was afraid of them, and he fell to kissing her, not knowing what he was doing. He wanted her eyes not to have that terrible, wistful, unfathomable look.

When she turned her face to him again, a faint delicate flush was glowing, and there was again dawning that terrible shining of joy in her eyes, which really terrified him, and yet which he now wanted to see, because he feared the look of doubt still more.

"You love me?" she said, rather faltering.

"Yes." The word cost him a painful effort. Not because it wasn't true. But because it was too newly true, the *saying* seemed to tear open again his newly-torn heart. And he hardly wanted it to be true, even now.

She lifted her face to him, and he bent forward and kissed her on the mouth, gently, with the one kiss that is an eternal pledge. And as he kissed her his heart strained again in his breast. He never intended to love her. But now it was over. He had crossed over the gulf to her, and all that he had left behind had shrivelled and become void.

After the kiss, her eyes again slowly filled with tears. She sat still, away from him, with her face drooped aside, and her hands folded in her lap. The tears fell very slowly. There was complete silence. He too sat there motionless and silent on the hearthrug. The strange pain of his heart that was broken seemed to consume him. That he should love her? That this was love! That he should be ripped open in this way! Him, a doctor! How they would all jeer if they knew! It was agony to him to think they might know.

In the curious naked pain of the thought he looked again to her. She was sitting there drooped into a muse. He saw a tear fall, and his heart flared hot. He saw for the first time that one of her shoulders was quite uncovered, one arm bare, he could see one of her small breasts; dimly, because it had become almost dark in the room.

"Why are you crying?" he asked, in an altered voice.

She looked up at him, and behind her tears the consciousness of her situation for the first time brought a dark look of shame to her eyes.

"I'm not crying, really," she said, watching him half frightened.

He reached his hand, and softly closed it on her bare arm.

"I love you! I love you!" he said in a soft, low vibrating voice, unlike himself.

She shrank, and dropped her head. The soft, penetrating grip of his hand on her arm distressed her. She looked up at him.

"I want to go," she said. "I want to go and get you some dry things."

"Why?" he said. "I'm all right."

"But I want to go," she said. "And I want you to change your things."

He released her arm, and she wrapped herself in the blanket, looking at him rather frightened. And still she did not rise.

"Kiss me," she said wistfully.

He kissed her, but briefly, half in anger.

Then, after a second, she rose nervously, all mixed up in the blanket. He watched her in her confusion, as she tried to extricate herself and wrap herself up so that she could walk. He watched her relentlessly, as she knew. And as she went, the blanket trailing, and as he saw a glimpse of her feet and her white leg, he tried to remember her as she was when he had wrapped her in the blanket. But then he didn't want to remember, because she had been nothing to him then, and his nature revolted from remembering her as she was when she was nothing to him.

A tumbling, muffled noise from within the dark house startled him. Then he heard her voice:—"There are clothes." He rose and went to the foot of the stairs, and gathered up the garments she had thrown down. Then he came back to the fire, to rub himself down and dress. He grinned at his own appearance when he had finished.

The fire was sinking, so he put on coal. The house was now quite dark, save for the light of a street-lamp that shone in faintly from beyond the holly trees. He lit the gas with matches he found on the mantelpiece. Then he emptied the pockets of his own clothes, and threw all his wet things in a heap into the scullery. After which he gathered up her sodden clothes, gently, and put them in a separate heap on the copper-top in the scullery.

It was six o'clock on the clock. His own watch had stopped. He ought to go back to the surgery. He waited, and still she did not come down. So he went to the foot of the stairs and called:

"I shall have to go."

Almost immediately he heard her coming down. She had on her best dress of black voile, and her hair was tidy, but still damp. She looked at him—and in spite of herself, smiled.

"I don't like you in those clothes," she said.

"Do I look a sight?" he answered.

They were shy of one another.

"I'll make you some tea," she said.

"No, I must go."

"Must you?" And she looked at him again with the wide, strained, doubtful eyes. And again, from the pain of his breast, he knew how he loved her. He went and bent to kiss her, gently, passionately, with his heart's painful kiss.

"And my hair smells so horrible," she murmured in distraction. "And I'm so awful, I'm so awful! Oh, no, I'm too awful." And she broke into bitter, heartbroken sobbing. "You can't want to love me, I'm horrible."

"Don't be silly, don't be silly," he said, trying to comfort her, kissing her, holding her in his arms. "I want you, I want to marry you, we're going to be married, quickly, quickly—tomorrow if I can."

But she only sobbed terribly, and cried:

"I feel awful. I feel awful. I feel I'm horrible to you."

"No, I want you, I want you," was all he answered, blindly, with that terrible intonation which frightened her almost more than her horror lest he should *not* want her.

QUESTIONS

1. In what way does Mabel's character change? In what way does Jack Fergusson's? **2.** Why does Fergusson resist the attraction he feels toward Mabel? Why does he finally yield? **3.** What function is served by the presence of Mabel's brothers in the first third of the story?

WRITING TOPICS

1. The central episode in the story is Mabel's attempted suicide. What symbolic qualities do the events at the pond have? **2.** Looking back at her attempted suicide, Mabel says, "It was the right thing to do." Does Lawrence's description of the event support her view?

Theater

1923

Life of nigger alleys, of pool rooms and restaurants and near-beer saloons soaks into the walls of Howard Theater and sets them throbbing jazz songs. Black-skinned, they dance and shout above the tick and trill of white-walled buildings. At night, they open doors to people who come in to stamp their feet and shout. At night, road-shows volley songs into the mass-heart of black people. Songs soak the walls and seep out to the nigger life of alleys and near-beer saloons, of the Poodle Dog and Black Bear cabarets. Afternoons, the house is dark, and the walls are sleeping singers until rehearsal begins. Or until John comes within them. Then they start throbbing to a subtle syncopation. And the space-dark air grows softly luminous.

John is the manager's brother. He is seated at the center of the theater, just before rehearsal. Light streaks down upon him from a window high above. One half his face is orange in it. One half his face is in shadow. The soft glow of the house rushes to, and compacts about, the shaft of light. John's mind coincides with the shaft of light. Thoughts rush to, and compact about it. Life of the house and of the slowly awakening stage swirls to the body of John, and thrills it. John's body is separate from the thoughts that pack his mind.

Stage-lights, soft, as if they shine through clear pink fingers. Beneath them, hid by the shadow of a set, Dorris. Other chorus girls drift in. John feels them in the mass. And as if his own body were the mass-heart of a black audience listening to them singing, he wants to stamp his feet and shout. His mind, contained above desires of his body, singles the girls out, and tries to trace origins and plot destinies.

A pianist slips into the pit and improvises jazz. The walls awake. Arms of the girls, and their limbs, which . . . jazz, jazz . . . by lifting up their tight street skirts they set free, jab the air and clog the floor in rhythm to the music. (Lift your skirts, Baby, and talk t papa!) Crude, individualized, and yet . . . monotonous. . . .

John: Soon the director will herd you, my full-lipped, distant beauties, and tame you, and blunt your sharp thrusts in loosely suggestive movements, appropriate to Broadway. (O dance!) Soon the audience will paint your dusk faces white, and call you beautiful. (O dance!) Soon I. . . . (O dance!) I'd like . . .

Girls laugh and shout. Sing discordant snatches of other jazz songs. Whirl with loose passion into the arms of passing show-men.

John: Too thick. Too easy. Too monotonous. Her whom I'd love I'd leave before she knew that I was with her. Her? Which? (O dance!) I'd like to . . .

Girls dance and sing. Men clap. The walls sing and press inward. They press the men and girls, they press John towards a center of physical ecstasy. Go to it, Baby! Fan yourself, and feed your papa! Put . . . nobody lied . . . and take

. . . when they said I cried over you. No lie! The glitter and color of stacked scenes, the gilt and brass and crimson of the house, converge towards a center of physical ecstasy. John's feet and torso and his blood press in. He wills thought to rid his mind of passion.

"All right, girls. Alaska. Miss Reynolds, please."

The director wants to get the rehearsal through with.

The girls line up. John sees the front row: dancing ponies. The rest are in shadow. The leading lady fits loosely in the front. Lack-life, monotonous. "One, two, three—" Music starts. The song is somewhere where it will not strain the leading lady's throat. The dance is somewhere where it will not strain the girls. Above the staleness, one dancer throws herself into it. Dorris. John sees her. Her hair, crisp-curled, is bobbed. Bushy, black hair bobbing about her lemon-colored face. Her lips are curiously full, and very red. Her limbs in silk purple stockings are lovely. John feels them. Desires her. Holds off.

John: Stage-door johnny; chorus-girl. No, that would be all right. Dictie,[1] educated, stuck-up; show-girl. Yep. Her suspicion would be stronger than her passion. It wouldn't work. Keep her loveliness. Let her go.

Dorris sees John and knows that he is looking at her. Her own glowing is too rich a thing to let her feel the slimness of his diluted passion.

"Who's that?" she asks her dancing partner.

"Th manager's brother. Dictie. Nothin doin, hon."

Dorris tosses her head and dances for him until she feels she has him. Then, withdrawing disdainfully, she flirts with the director.

Dorris: Nothin doin? How come? Aint I as good as him? Couldnt I have got an education if I'd wanted one? Dont I know respectable folks, lots of em, in Philadelphia and New York and Chicago? Aint I had men as good as him? Better. Doctors an lawyers. Whats a manager's brother, anyhow?

Two steps back, and two steps front.

"Say, Mame, where do you get that stuff?"

"Whatshmean, Dorris?"

"If you two girls cant listen to what I'm telling you, I know where I can get some who can. Now listen."

Mame: Go to hell, you black bastard.

Dorris: Whats eatin at him, anyway?

"Now follow me in this, you girls. Its three counts to the right, three counts to the left, and then you shimmy—"

John:—and then you shimmy. I'll bet she can. Some good cabaret, with rooms upstairs. And what in hell do you think you'd get from it? Youre going wrong. Here's right: get her to herself—(Christ, but how she'd bore you after the first five minutes)—not if you get her right she wouldnt. Touch her, I mean. To herself—in some room perhaps. Some cheap, dingy bedroom. Hell no. Cant be done. But the point is, brother John, it can be done. Get her to herself somewhere, anywhere. Go down in yourself—and she'd be calling you all sorts

---

[1] A snob.

of asses while you were in the process of going down. Hold em, bud. Cant be done. Let her go. (Dance and I'll love you!) And keep her loveliness.

"All right now, Chicken Chaser. Dorris and girls. Where's Dorris? I told you to stay on the stage, didnt I? Well? Now thats enough. All right. All right there, Professor?[2] All right. One, two, three—"

Dorris swings to the front. The line of girls, four deep, blurs within the shadow of suspended scenes. Dorris wants to dance. The director feels that and steps to one side. He smiles, and picks her for a leading lady, one of these days. Odd ends of stage-men emerge from the wings, and stare and clap. A crap game in the alley suddenly ends. Black faces crowd the rear stage doors. The girls, catching joy from Dorris, whip up within the footlights' glow. They forget set steps; they find their own. The director forgets to bawl them out. Dorris dances.

John: Her head bobs to Broadway. Dance from yourself. Dance! O just a little more.

Dorris' eyes burn across the space of seats to him.

Dorris: I bet he can love. Hell, he cant love. He's too skinny. His lips are too skinny. He wouldn't love me anyway, only for that. But I'd get a pair of silk stockings out of it. Red silk. I got purple. Cut it, kid. You cant win him to respect you that away. He wouldnt anyway. Maybe he would. Maybe he'd love. I've heard em say that men who look like him (what does he look like?) will marry if they love. O will you love me? And give me kids, and a home, and everything? (I'd like to make your nest, and honest, hon, I wouldnt run out on you.) You will if I make you. Just watch me.

Dorris dances. She forgets her tricks. She dances.

Glorious songs are the muscles of her limbs.

And her singing is of canebrake loves and mangrove feastings.

The walls press in, singing. Flesh of a throbbing body, they press close to John and Dorris. They close them in. John's heart beats tensely against her dancing body. Walls press his mind within his heart. And then, the shaft of light goes out the window high above him. John's mind sweeps up to follow it. Mind pulls him upward into dream. Dorris dances . . . John dreams:

> Dorris is dressed in a loose black gown, splashed with lemon ribbons. Her feet taper long and slim from trim ankles. She waits for him just inside the stage door. John, collar and tie colorful and flaring, walks towards the stage door. There are no trees in the alley. But his feet feel as though they step on autumn leaves whose rustle has been pressed out of them by the passing of a million satin slippers. The air is sweet with roasting chestnuts, sweet with bonfires of old leaves. John's melancholy is a deep thing that seals all senses but his eyes, and makes him whole.
>
> Dorris knows that he is coming. Just at the right moment she steps from the door, as if there were no door. Her face is tinted like the autumn alley. Of old flowers, or of a southern canefield, her perfume. "Glorious Dorris." So his eyes speak. And their sadness is too deep for sweet untruth. She barely touches his arm.

---

[2] A piano player.

They glide off with footfalls softened on the leaves, the old leaves powdered by a million satin slippers.

They are in a room. John knows nothing of it. Only, that the flesh and blood of Dorris are its walls. Singing walls. Lights, soft, as if they shine through clear pink fingers. Soft lights, and warm.

John reaches for a manuscript of his, and reads. Dorris, who has no eyes, has eyes to understand him. He comes to a dancing scene. The scene is Dorris. She dances. Dorris dances. Glorious Dorris. Dorris whirls, whirls, dances. . . .

Dorris dances. The pianist crashes a bumper chord. The whole stage claps. Dorris, flushed, looks quick at John. His whole face is in shadow. She seeks for her dance in it. She finds it a dead thing in the shadow which is his dream. She rushes from the stage. Falls down the steps into her dressing-room. Pulls her hair. Her eyes, over a floor of tears, stare at the whitewashed ceiling. (Smell of dry paste, and paint, and soiled clothing.) Her pal comes in. Dorris flings herself into the old safe arms, and cries bitterly.

"I told you nothin doing," is what Mame says to comfort her.

QUESTIONS

1. State the nature of the conflict in John.   **2.** How does Toomer achieve dramatic conflict between John and Dorris even though they do not speak to each other?   **3.** How does the opening paragraph establish the mood and the values of the story?

Dry September 1931

WILLIAM FAULKNER [1897–1962]

I

Through the bloody September twilight, aftermath of sixty-two rainless days, it had gone like a fire in a dry grass—the rumor, the story, whatever it was. Something about Miss Minnie Cooper and a Negro. Attacked, insulted, frightened: none of them, gathered in the barber shop on that Saturday evening where the ceiling fan stirred, without freshening it, the vitiated air, sending back upon them in recurrent surges of stale pomade and lotion, their own stale breath and odors, knew exactly what had happened.

"Except it wasn't Will Mayes," a barber said. He was a man of middle age; a thin, sand-colored man with a mild face, who was shaving a client. "I know Will Mayes. He's a good nigger. And I know Miss Minnie Cooper, too."

"What do you know about her?" a second barber said.

"Who is she?" the client said. "A young girl?"

"No," the barber said. "She's about forty, I reckon. She aint married. That's why I dont believe—"

"Believe, hell!" a hulking youth in a sweat-stained silk shirt said. "Wont you take a white woman's word before a nigger's?"

"I don't believe Will Mayes did it," the barber said. "I know Will Mayes."

"Maybe you know who did it, then. Maybe you already got him out of town, you damn niggerlover."

"I don't believe anybody did anything. I dont believe anything happened. I leave it to you fellows if them ladies that get old without getting married dont have notions that a man cant—"

"Then you are a hell of a white man," the client said. He moved under the cloth. The youth had sprung to his feet.

"You dont?" he said. "Do you accuse a white woman of lying?"

The barber held the razor poised above the half-risen client. He did not look around.

"It's this durn weather," another said. "It's enough to make a man do anything. Even to her."

Nobody laughed. The barber said in his mild, stubborn tone: "I aint accusing nobody of nothing. I just know and you fellows know how a woman that never—"

"You damn niggerlover!" the youth said.

"Shut up, Butch," another said. "We'll get the facts in plenty of time to act."

"Who is? Who's getting them?" the youth said. "Facts, hell! I—"

"You're a fine white man," the client said. "Aint you?" In his frothy beard he looked like a desert rat in the moving pictures. "You tell them, Jack," he

753

said to the youth. "If there aint any white men in this town, you can count on me, even if I aint only a drummer and a stranger."

"That's right, boys," the barber said. "Find out the truth first. I know Will Mayes."

"Well, by God!" the youth shouted. "To think that a white man in this town—"

"Shut up, Butch," the second speaker said. "We got plenty of time."

The client sat up. He looked at the speaker. "Do you claim that anything excuses a nigger attacking a white woman? Do you mean to tell me you are a white man and you'll stand for it? You better go back North where you came from. The South dont want your kind here."

"North what?" the second said. "I was born and raised in this town."

"Well, by God!" the youth said. He looked about with a strained, baffled gaze, as if he was trying to remember what it was he wanted to say or to do. He drew his sleeve across his sweating face. "Damn if I'm going to let a white woman—"

"You tell them, Jack," the drummer said. "By God, if they—"

The screen door crashed open. A man stood in the door, his feet apart and his heavy-set body poised easily. His white shirt was open at the throat; he wore a felt hat. His hot, bold glance swept the group. His name was McLendon. He had commanded troops at the front in France and had been decorated for valor.

"Well," he said, "are you going to sit there and let a black son rape a white woman on the streets of Jefferson?"

Butch sprang up again. The silk of his shirt clung flat to his heavy shoulders. At each armpit was a dark halfmoon. "That's what I been telling them! That's what I—"

"Did it really happen?" a third said. "This aint the first man scare she ever had, like Hawkshaw says. Wasn't there something about a man on the kitchen roof, watching her undress, about a year ago?"

"What?" the client said. "What's that?" The barber had been slowly forcing him back into the chair; he arrested himself reclining, his head lifted, the barber still pressing him down.

McLendon whirled on the third speaker. "Happen? What the hell difference does it make? Are you going to let the black sons get away with it until one really does it?"

"That's what I'm telling them!" Butch shouted. He cursed, long and steady, pointless.

"Here, here," a fourth said. "Not so loud. Dont talk so loud."

"Sure," McLendon said; "no talking necessary at all. I've done my talking. Who's with me?" He poised on the balls of his feet, roving his gaze.

The barber held the drummer's face down, the razor poised. "Find out the facts first, boys. I know Willy Mayes. It wasn't him. Let's get the sheriff and do this thing right."

McLendon whirled upon him his furious, rigid face. The barber did not look away. They looked like men of different races. The other barbers had ceased also above their prone clients. "You mean to tell me," McLendon said, "that you'd take a nigger's word before a white woman's? Why, you damn niggerloving—"

The third speaker rose and grasped McLendon's arm; he too had been a soldier, "Now, now. Let's figure this thing out. Who knows anything about what really happened?"

"Figure out hell!" McLendon jerked his arm free. "All that're with me get up from there. The ones that aint—" He roved his gaze, dragging his sleeve across his face.

Three men rose. The drummer in the chair sat up. "Here," he said, jerking at the cloth about his neck; "get this rag off me. I'm with him. I dont live here, but by God, if our mothers and wives and sisters—" He smeared the cloth over his face and flung it to the floor. McLendon stood in the floor and cursed the others. Another rose and moved toward him. The remainder sat uncomfortable, not looking at one another, then one by one they rose and joined him.

The barber picked the cloth from the floor. He began to fold it neatly. "Boys, dont do that. Will Mayes never done it. I know."

"Come on," McLendon said. He whirled. From his hip pocket protruded the butt of a heavy automatic pistol. They went out. The screen door crashed behind them reverberant in the dead air.

The barber wiped the razor carefully and swiftly, and put it away, and ran to the rear, and took his hat from the wall. "I'll be back as soon as I can," he said to the other barbers. "I cant let—" He went out, running. The two other barbers followed him to the door and caught it on the rebound, leaning out and looking up the street after him. The air was flat and dead. It had a metallic taste at the base of the tongue.

"What can he do?" the first said. The second one was saying "Jees Christ, Jees Christ" under his breath. "I'd just as lief be Will Mayes as Hawk, if he gets McLendon riled."

"Jees Christ, Jees Christ," the second whispered.

"You reckon he really done it to her?" the first said.

II

She was thirty-eight or thirty-nine. She lived in a small frame house with her invalid mother and a thin, sallow, unflagging aunt, where each morning between ten and eleven she would appear on the porch in a lace-trimmed boudoir cap, to sit swinging in the porch swing until noon. After dinner she lay down for a while, until the afternoon began to cool. Then, in one of the three or four new voile dresses which she had each summer, she would go downtown to spend the afternoon in the stores with the other ladies, where they would handle the goods and haggle over the prices in cold, immediate voices, without any intention of buying.

She was of comfortable people—not the best in Jefferson, but good people enough—and she was still on the slender side of ordinary looking, with a bright, faintly haggard manner and dress. When she was young she had had a slender, nervous body and a sort of hard vivacity which had enabled her for a time to ride upon the crest of the town's social life as exemplified by the high school party and church social period of her contemporaries while still children enough to be unclassconscious.

She was the last to realize that she was losing ground; that those among whom she had been a little brighter and louder flame than any other were beginning to learn the pleasure of snobbery—male—and retaliation—female. That was when her face began to wear that bright, haggard look. She still carried it to parties on shadowy porticoes and summer lawns, like a mask or a flag, with that bafflement of furious repudiation of truth in her eyes. One evening at a party she heard a boy and two girls, all schoolmates, talking. She never accepted another invitation.

She watched the girls with whom she had grown up as they married and got homes and children, but no man ever called on her steadily until the children of the other girls had been calling her "aunty" for several years, the while their mothers told them in bright voices about how popular Aunt Minnie had been as a girl. Then the town began to see her driving on Sunday afternoons with the cashier in the bank. He was a widower of about forty—a high-colored man, smelling always faintly of the barber shop or of whisky. He owned the first automobile in town, a red runabout; Minnie had the first motoring bonnet and veil the town ever saw. Then the town began to say: "Poor Minnie." "But she is old enough to take care of herself," others said. That was when she began to ask her old schoolmates that their children call her "cousin" instead of "aunty."

It was twelve years now since she had been relegated into adultery by public opinion, and eight years since the cashier had gone to a Memphis bank, returning for one day each Christmas, which he spent at an annual bachelors' party at a hunting club on the river. From behind their curtains the neighbors would see the party pass, and during the over-the-way Christmas day visiting they would tell her about him, about how well he looked, and how they heard that he was prospering in the city, watching with bright, secret eyes her haggard, bright face. Usually by that hour there would be the scent of whisky on her breath. It was supplied her by a youth, a clerk at the soda fountain: "Sure; I buy it for the old gal. I reckon she's entitled to a little fun."

Her mother kept to her room altogether now; the gaunt aunt ran the house. Against that background Minnie's bright dresses, her idle and empty days, had a quality of furious unreality. She went out in the evenings only with women now, neighbors, to the moving pictures. Each afternoon she dressed in one of the new dresses and went downtown alone, where her young "cousins" were already strolling in the late afternoons with their delicate, silken heads and thin, awkward arms and conscious hips, clinging to one another or shrieking and giggling with paired boys in the soda fountain when she passed and went on along the serried store fronts, in the doors of which the sitting and lounging men did not even follow her with their eyes any more.

III

The barber went swiftly up the street where the sparse lights, insect-swirled, glared in rigid and violent suspension in the lifeless air. The day had died in a pall of dust; above the darkened square, shrouded by the spent dust, the sky was as clear as the inside of a brass bell. Below the east was a rumor of the twice-waxed moon.

When he overtook them McLendon and three others were getting into a car parked in an alley. McLendon stooped his thick head, peering out beneath the top. "Changed your mind, did you?" he said. "Damn good thing; by God, tomorrow when this town hears about how you talked tonight—"

"Now, now," the other ex-soldier said. "Hawkshaw's all right. Come on, Hawk; jump in."

"Will Mayes never done it, boys," the barber said. "If anybody done it. Why, you all know well as I do there aint any town where they got better niggers than us. And you know how a lady will kind of think things about men when there aint any reason to, and Miss Minnie anyway—"

"Sure, sure," the soldier said. "We're just going to talk to him a little; that's all."

"Talk hell!" Butch said. "When we're through with the—"

"Shut up, for God's sake!" the soldier said. "Do you want everybody in town—"

"Tell them, by God!" McLendon said. "Tell every one of the sons that'll let a white woman—"

"Let's go; let's go: here's the other car." The second car slid squealing out of a cloud of dust at the alley mouth. McLendon started his car and took the lead. Dust lay like fog in the street. The street lights hung nimbused as in water. They drove on out of town.

A rutted lane turned at right angles. Dust hung above it too, and above all the land. The dark bulk of the ice plant, where the Negro Mayes was night watchman, rose against the sky. "Better stop here, hadn't we?" the soldier said. McLendon did not reply. He hurled the car up and slammed to a stop, the headlights glaring on the blank wall.

"Listen here, boys," the barber said; "if he's here, dont that prove he never done it? Dont it? If it was him, he would run. Dont you see he would?" The second car came up and stopped. McLendon got down; Butch sprang down beside him. "Listen, boys," the barber said.

"Cut the lights off!" McLendon said. The breathless dark rushed down. There was no sound in it save their lungs as they sought air in the parched dust in which for two months they had lived; then the diminishing crunch of Mc-Lendon's and Butch's feet, and a moment later McLendon's voice:

"Will! . . . Will!"

Below the east the wan hemorrhage of the moon increased. It heaved above the ridge, silvering the air, the dust, so that they seemed to breathe, live, in a bowl of molten lead. There was no sound of nightbird nor insect, no sound save their breathing and a faint ticking of contracting metal about the cars. Where their bodies touched one another they seemed to sweat dryly, for no more moisture came. "Christ!" a voice said; "let's get out of here."

But they didn't move until vague noises began to grow out of the darkness ahead; then they got out and waited tensely in the breathless dark. There was another sound: a blow, a hissing expulsion of breath and McLendon cursing in undertone. They stood a moment longer, then they ran forward. They ran in a stumbling clump, as though they were fleeing something. "Kill him, kill the son," a voice whispered. McLendon flung them back.

"Not here," he said. "Get him into the car." "Kill him, kill the black son!" the voice murmured. They dragged the Negro to the car. The barber had waited beside the car. He could feel himself sweating and he knew he was going to be sick at the stomach.

"What is it, captains?" the Negro said. "I aint done nothing. 'Fore God, Mr John." Someone produced handcuffs. They worked busily about the Negro as though he were a post, quiet, intent, getting in one another's way. He submitted to the handcuffs, looking swiftly and constantly from dim face to dim face. "Who's here, captains?" he said, leaning to peer into the faces until they could feel his breath and smell his sweaty reek. He spoke a name or two. "What you all say I done, Mr John?"

McLendon jerked the car door open. "Get in!" he said.

The Negro did not move. "What you all going to do with me, Mr John? I aint done nothing. White folks, captains, I aint done nothing: I swear 'fore God." He called another name.

"Get in!" McLendon said. He struck the Negro. The others expelled their breath in a dry hissing and struck him with random blows and he whirled and cursed them, and swept his manacled hands across their faces and slashed the barber upon the mouth, and the barber struck him also. "Get him in there," McLendon said. They pushed at him. He ceased struggling and got in and sat quietly as the others took their places. He sat between the barber and the soldier, drawing his limbs in so as not to touch them, his eyes going swiftly and constantly from face to face. Butch clung to the running board. The car moved on. The barber nursed his mouth with his handkerchief.

"What's the matter, Hawk?" the soldier said.

"Nothing," the barber said. They regained the highroad and turned away from town. The second car dropped back out of the dust. They went on, gaining speed; the final fringe of houses dropped behind.

"Goddamn, he stinks!" the soldier said.

"We'll fix that," the drummer in front beside McLendon said. On the running board Butch cursed into the hot rush of air. The barber leaned suddenly forward and touched McLendon's arm.

"Let me out, John," he said.

"Jump out, niggerlover," McLendon said without turning his head. He drove swiftly. Behind them the sourceless lights of the second car glared in the dust. Presently McLendon turned into a narrow road. It was rutted with disuse. It led back to an abandoned brick kiln—a series of reddish mounds and weed- and vine-choked vats without bottom. It had been used for pasture once, until one day the owner missed one of his mules. Although he prodded carefully in the vats with a long pole, he could not even find the bottom of them.

"John," the barber said.

"Jump out, then," McLendon said, hurling the car along the ruts. Beside the barber the Negro spoke:

"Mr. Henry."

The barber sat forward. The narrow tunnel of the road rushed up and past. Their motion was like an extinct furnace blast: cooler, but utterly dead. The car bounded from rut to rut.

"Mr. Henry," the Negro said.

The barber began to tug furiously at the door. "Look out, there!" the soldier said, but the barber had already kicked the door open and swung onto the running board. The soldier leaned across the Negro and grasped at him, but he had already jumped. The car went on without checking speed.

The impetus hurled him crashing through dust-sheathed weeds, into the ditch. Dust puffed about him, and in a thin, vicious crackling of sapless stems he lay choking and retching until the second car passed and died away. Then he rose and limped on until he reached the highroad and turned toward town, brushing at his clothes with his hands. The moon was higher, riding high and clear of the dust at last, and after a while the town began to glare beneath the dust. He went on, limping. Presently he heard cars and the glow of them grew in the dust behind him and he left the road and crouched again in the weeds until they passed. McLendon's car came last now. There were four people in it and Butch was not on the running board.

They went on; the dust swallowed them; the glare and the sound died away. The dust of them hung for a while, but soon the eternal dust absorbed it again. The barber climbed back onto the road and limped on toward town.

IV

As she dressed for supper on that Saturday evening, her own flesh felt like fever. Her hands trembled among the hooks and eyes, and her eyes had a feverish look, and her hair swirled crisp and crackling under the comb. While she was still dressing the friends called for her and sat while she donned her sheerest underthings and stockings and a new voile dress. "Do you feel strong enough to go out?" they said, their eyes bright too, with a dark glitter. "When you have had time to get over the shock, you must tell us what happened. What he said and did; everything."

In the leafed darkness, as they walked toward the square, she began to breathe deeply, something like a swimmer preparing to dive, until she ceased trembling, the four of them walking slowly because of the terrible heat and out of solicitude for her. But as they neared the square she began to tremble again, walking with her head up, her hands clenched at her sides, their voices about her murmurous, also with that feverish, glittering quality of their eyes.

They entered the square, she in the center of the group, fragile in her fresh dress. She was trembling worse. She walked slower and slower, as children eat ice cream, her head up and her eyes bright in the haggard banner of her face, passing the hotel and the coatless drummers in chairs along the curb looking around at her: "That's the one: see? The one in pink in the middle." "Is that her? What did they do with the nigger? Did they—?" "Sure.. He's all right." "All right, is he?" "Sure. He went on a little trip." Then the drug store, where even the young men lounging in the doorway tipped their hats and followed with their eyes the motion of her hips and legs when she passed.

They went on, passing the lifted hats of the gentlemen, the suddenly ceased voices, deferent, protective. "Do you see?" the friends said. Their voices sounded like long, hovering sighs of hissing exultation. "There's not a Negro on the square. Not one."

They reached the picture show. It was like a miniature fairyland with its lighted lobby and colored lithographs of life caught in its terrible and beautiful mutations. Her lips began to tingle. In the dark, when the picture began, it would be all right; she could hold back the laughing so it would not waste away so fast and so soon. So she hurried on before the turning faces, the undertones of low astonishment, and they took their accustomed places where she could see the aisle against the silver glare and the young men and girls coming in two and two against it.

The lights flicked away; the screen glowed silver, and soon life began to unfold, beautiful and passionate and sad, while still the young men and girls entered, scented and sibilant in the half dark, their paired backs in silhouette delicate and sleek, their slim, quick bodies awkward, divinely young, while beyond them the silver dream accumulated, inevitably on and on. She began to laugh. In trying to suppress it, it made more noise than ever; heads began to turn. Still laughing, her friends raised her and led her out, and she stood at the curb, laughing on a high, sustained note, until the taxi came up and they helped her in.

They removed the pink voile and the sheer underthings and the stockings, and put her to bed, and cracked ice for her temples, and sent for the doctor. He was hard to locate, so they ministered to her with hushed ejaculations, renewing the ice and fanning her. While the ice was fresh and cold she stopped laughing and lay still for a time, moaning only a little. But soon the laughing welled again and her voice rose screaming.

"Shhhhhhhhhhh! Shhhhhhhhhhhhhhh!" they said, freshening the ice-pack, smoothing her hair, examining it for gray; "poor girl!" Then to one another: "Do you suppose anything really happened?" their eyes darkly aglitter, secret and passionate. "Shhhhhhhhhh! Poor girl! Poor Minnie!"

V

It was midnight when McLendon drove up to his neat new house. It was trim and fresh as a birdcage and almost as small, with its clean, green-and-white paint. He locked the car and mounted the porch and entered. His wife rose from a chair beside the reading lamp. McLendon stopped in the floor and stared at her until she looked down.

"Look at that clock," he said, lifting his arm, pointing. She stood before him, her face lowered, a magazine in her hands. Her face was pale, strained, and weary-looking. "Haven't I told you about sitting up like this, waiting to see when I come in?"

"John," she said. She laid the magazine down. Poised on the balls of his feet, he glared at her with his hot eyes, his sweating face.

"Didn't I tell you?" He went toward her. She looked up then. He caught her shoulder. She stood passive, looking at him.

"Don't, John. I couldn't sleep . . . The heat; something. Please, John. You're hurting me."

"Didn't I tell you?" He released her and half struck, half flung her across the chair, and she lay there and watched him quietly as he left the room.

He went on through the house, ripping off his shirt, and on the dark, screened porch at the rear he stood and mopped his head and shoulders with the shirt and flung it away. He took the pistol from his hip and laid it on the table beside the bed, and sat on the bed and removed his shoes, and rose and slipped his trousers off. He was sweating again already, and he stooped and hunted furiously for the shirt. At last he found it and wiped his body again, and, with his body pressed against the dusty screen, he stood panting. There was no movement, no sound, not even an insect. The dark world seemed to lie stricken beneath the cold moon and the lidless stars.

The Chase*

ALBERTO MORAVIA [b. 1907]

I have never been a sportsman—or, rather, I have been a sportsman only once, and that was the first and last time. I was a child, and one day, for some reason or other, I found myself together with my father, who was holding a gun in his hand, behind a bush, watching a bird that had perched on a branch not very far away. It was a large, gray bird—or perhaps it was brown—with a long—or perhaps a short—beak; I don't remember. I only remember what I felt at that moment as I looked at it. It was like watching an animal whose vitality was rendered more intense by the very fact of my watching it and of the animal's not knowing that I was watching it.

At that moment, I say, the notion of wildness entered my mind, never again to leave it: everything is wild which is autonomous and unpredictable and does not depend upon us. Then all of a sudden there was an explosion; I could no longer see the bird and I thought it had flown away. But my father was leading the way, walking in front of me through the undergrowth. Finally he stooped down, picked up something and put it in my hand. I was aware of something warm and soft and I lowered my eyes: there was a bird in the palm of my hand, its dangling, shattered head crowned with a plume of already-thickening blood. I burst into tears and dropped the corpse on the ground, and that was the end of my shooting experience.

I thought again of this remote episode in my life this very day after watching my wife, for the first and also the last time, as she was walking through the streets of the city. But let us take things in order.

What had my wife been like; what was she like now? She once had been, to put it briefly, "wild"—that is, entirely autonomous and unpredictable; latterly she had become "tame"—that is, predictable and dependent. For a long time she had been like the bird that, on that far-off morning in my childhood, I had seen perching on the bough; latterly, I am sorry to say, she had become like a hen about which one knows everything in advance—how it moves, how it eats, how it lays eggs, how it sleeps, and so on.

Nevertheless I would not wish anyone to think that my wife's wildness consisted of an uncouth, rough, rebellious character. Apart from being extremely beautiful, she is the gentlest, politest, most discreet person in the world. Rather her wildness consisted of the air of charming unpredictability, of independence in her way of living, with which during the first years of our marriage she acted in my presence, both at home and abroad. Wildness signified intimacy, privacy, secrecy. Yes, my wife as she sat in front of her dressing table, her eyes fixed on the looking glass, passing the hairbrush with a repeated motion over her long,

---

* Translated by Angus Davidson.

loose hair, was just as wild as the solitary quail hopping forward along a sun-filled furrow or the furtive fox coming out into a clearing and stopping to look around before running on. She was wild because I, as I looked at her, could never manage to foresee when she would give a last stroke with the hairbrush and rise and come toward me; wild to such a degree that sometimes when I went into our bedroom the smell of her, floating in the air, would have something of the acrid quality of a wild beast's lair.

Gradually she became less wild, tamer. I had had a fox, a quail, in the house, as I have said; then one day I realized that I had a hen. What effect does a hen have on someone who watches it? It has the effect of being, so to speak, an automaton in the form of a bird; automatic are the brief, rapid steps with which it moves about; automatic its hard, terse pecking; automatic the glance of the round eyes in its head that nods and turns; automatic its ready crouching down under the cock; automatic the dropping of the egg wherever it may be and the cry with which it announces that the egg has been laid. Good-by to the fox; good-by to the quail. And her smell—this no longer brought to my mind, in any way, the innocent odor of a wild animal; rather I detected in it the chemical suavity of some ordinary French perfume.

Our flat is on the first floor of a big building in a modern quarter of the town; our windows look out on a square in which there is a small public garden, the haunt of nurses and children and dogs. One day I was standing at the window, looking in a melancholy way at the garden. My wife, shortly before, had dressed to go out; and once again, watching her, I had noticed the irrevocable and, so to speak, invisible character of her gestures and personality: something which gave one the feeling of a thing already seen and already done and which therefore evaded even the most determined observation. And now, as I stood looking at the garden and at the same time wondering why the adorable wildness of former times had so completely disappeared, suddenly my wife came into my range of vision as she walked quickly across the garden in the direction of the bus stop. I watched her and then I almost jumped for joy; in a movement she was making to pull down a fold of her narrow skirt and smooth it over her thigh with the tips of her long, sharp nails, in this movement I recognized the wildness that in the past had made me love her. It was only an instant, but in that instant I said to myself: She's become wild again because she's convinced that I am not there and am not watching her. Then I left the window and rushed out.

But I did not join her at the bus stop; I felt that I must not allow myself to be seen. Instead I hurried to my car, which was standing nearby, got in and waited. A bus came and she got in together with some other people; the bus started off again and I began following it. Then there came back to me the memory of that one shooting expedition in which I had taken part as a child, and I saw that the bus was the undergrowth with its bushes and trees, my wife the bird perching on the bough while I, unseen, watched it living before my eyes. And the whole town, during this pursuit, became, as though by magic, a fact of nature like the countryside: the houses were hills, the streets valleys, the vehicles hedges and woods, and even the passers-by on the pavements had something unpredictable and autonomous—that is, wild—about them. And in my mouth, behind my clenched teeth, there was the acrid, metallic taste of gunfire; and my eyes, usually listless and wandering, had become sharp, watchful, attentive.

These eyes were fixed intently upon the exit door when the bus came to the end of its run. A number of people got out, and then I saw my wife getting out. Once again I recognized, in the manner in which she broke free of the crowd and started off toward a neighboring street, the wildness that pleased me so much. I jumped out of the car and started following her.

She was walking in front of me, ignorant of my presence, a tall woman with an elegant figure, long-legged, narrow-hipped, broad-backed, her brown hair falling on her shoulders.

Men turned around as she went past; perhaps they were aware of what I myself was now sensing with an intensity that quickened the beating of my heart and took my breath away: the unrestricted, steadily increasing, irresistible character of her mysterious wildness.

She walked hurriedly, having evidently some purpose in view, and even the fact that she had a purpose of which I was ignorant added to her wildness; I did not know where she was going, just as on that far-off morning I had not known what the bird perching on the bough was about to do. Moreover I thought the gradual, steady increase in this quality of wildness came partly from the fact that as she drew nearer to the object of this mysterious walk there was an increase in her—how shall I express it?—of biological tension, of existential excitement, of vital effervescence. Then, unexpectedly, with the suddenness of a film, her purpose was revealed.

A fair-haired young man in a leather jacket and a pair of corduroy trousers was leaning against the wall of a house in that ancient, narrow street. He was idly smoking as he looked in front of him. But as my wife passed close to him, he threw away his cigarette with a decisive gesture, took a step forward and seized her arm. I was expecting her to rebuff him, to move away from him, but nothing happened: evidently obeying the rules of some kind of erotic ritual, she went on walking beside the young man. Then after a few steps, with a movement that confirmed her own complicity, she put her arm around her companion's waist and he put his around her.

I understood then that this unknown man who took such liberties with my wife was also attracted by wildness. And so, instead of making a conventional appointment with her, instead of meeting in a café with a handshake, a falsely friendly and respectful welcome, he had preferred, by agreement with her, to take her by surprise—or, rather, to pretend to do so—while she was apparently taking a walk on her own account. All this I perceived by intuition, noticing that at the very moment when he stepped forward and took her arm her wildness had, so to speak, given an upward bound. It was years since I had seen my wife so alive, but alas, the source of this life could not be traced to me.

They walked on thus entwined and then, without any preliminaries, just like two wild animals, they did an unexpected thing: they went into one of the dark doorways in order to kiss. I stopped and watched them from a distance, peering into the darkness of the entrance. My wife was turned away from me and was bending back with the pressure of his body, her hair hanging free. I looked at that long, thick mane of brown hair, which as she leaned back fell free of her shoulders, and I felt at that moment her vitality reached its diapason, just as happens with wild animals when they couple and their customary wildness is redoubled by the violence of love. I watched for a long time and then, since this kiss went on and on and in fact seemed to be prolonged beyond the limits of my power of endurance, I saw that I would have to intervene.

I would have to go forward, seize my wife by the arm—or actually by that hair, which hung down and conveyed so well the feeling of feminine passivity—then hurl myself with clenched fists upon the blond young man. After this encounter I would carry off my wife, weeping, mortified, ashamed, while I was raging and broken-hearted, upbraiding her and pouring scorn upon her.

But what else would this intervention amount to but the shot my father fired at that free, unknowing bird as it perched on the bough? The disorder and confusion, the mortification, the shame, that would follow would irreparably destroy the rare and precious moment of wildness that I was witnessing inside the dark doorway. It was true that this wildness was directed against me; but I had to remember that wildness, always and everywhere, is directed against everything and everybody. After the scene of my intervention it might be possible for me to regain control of my wife, but I should find her shattered and lifeless in my arms like the bird that my father placed in my hand so that I might throw it into the shooting bag.

The kiss went on and on: well, it was a kiss of passion—that could not be denied. I waited until they finished, until they came out of the doorway, until they walked on again still linked together. Then I turned back.

The Girls in Their Summer Dresses

IRWIN SHAW   [1913–1984]

1939

Fifth Avenue was shining in the sun when they left the Brevoort.[1] The sun was warm, even though it was February, and everything looked like Sunday morning—the buses and the well-dressed people walking slowly in couples and the quiet buildings with the windows closed.

Michael held Frances' arm tightly as they walked toward Washington Square[2] in the sunlight. They walked lightly, almost smiling, because they had slept late and had a good breakfast and it was Sunday. Michael unbuttoned his coat and let it flap around him in the mild wind.

"Look out," Frances said as they crossed Eighth Street. "You'll break your neck." Michael laughed and Frances laughed with him.

"She's not so pretty," Frances said. "Anyway, not pretty enough to take a chance of breaking your neck."

Michael laughed again. "How did you know I was looking at her?"

Frances cocked her head to one side and smiled at her husband under the brim of her hat. "Mike, darling," she said.

"O.K.," he said. "Excuse me."

Frances patted his arm lightly and pulled him along a little faster toward Washington Square. "Let's not see anybody all day," she said. "Let's just hang around with each other. You and me. We're always up to our neck in people, drinking their Scotch or drinking our Scotch; we only see each other in bed. I want to go out with my husband all day long. I want him to talk only to me and listen only to me."

"What's to stop us?" Michael asked.

"The Stevensons. They want us to drop by around one o'clock and they'll drive us into the country."

"The cunning Stevensons," Mike said. "Transparent. They can whistle. They can go driving in the country by themselves."

"Is it a date?"

"It's a date."

Frances leaned over and kissed him on the tip of the ear.

"Darling," Michael said, "this is Fifth Avenue."

"Let me arrange a program," Frances said. "A planned Sunday in New York for a young couple with money to throw away."

---

[1] The Brevoort was a New York hotel on lower Fifth Avenue. At the time that this story was written, the Brevoort's bar was famous as a gathering place for literary people.

[2] A park at the south end of Fifth Avenue.

"Go easy."

"First let's go to the Metropolitan Museum of Art," Frances suggested, because Michael had said during the week he wanted to go. "I haven't been there in three years and there're at least ten pictures I want to see again. Then we can take the bus down to Radio City and watch them skate. And later we'll go down to Cavanagh's and get a steak as big as a blacksmith's apron, with a bottle of wine, and after that there's a French picture at the Filmarte that everybody says—say, are you listening to me?"

"Sure," he said. He took his eyes off the hatless girl with the dark hair, cut dancer-style like a helmet, who was walking past him.

"That's the program for the day," Frances said flatly. "Or maybe you'd just rather walk up and down Fifth Avenue."

"No," Michael said. "Not at all."

"You always look at other women," Frances said. "Everywhere. Every damned place we go."

"No, darling," Michael said, "I look at everything. God gave me eyes and I look at women and men in subway excavations and moving pictures and the little flowers of the field. I casually inspect the universe."

"You ought to see the look in your eye," Frances said, "as you casually inspect the universe on Fifth Avenue."

"I'm a happily married man." Michael pressed her elbow tenderly. "Example for the whole twentieth century—Mr. and Mrs. Mike Loomis. Hey, let's have a drink," he said, stopping.

"We just had breakfast."

"Now listen, darling," Mike said, choosing his words with care, "it's a nice day and we both felt good and there's no reason why we have to break it up. Let's have a nice Sunday."

"All right. I don't know why I started this. Let's drop it. Let's have a good time."

They joined hands consciously and walked without talking among the baby carriages and the old Italian men in their Sunday clothes and the young women with Scotties in Washington Square Park.

"At least once a year everyone should go to the Metropolitan Museum of Art," Frances said after a while, her tone a good imitation of the tone she had used at breakfast and at the beginning of their walk. "And it's nice on Sunday. There're a lot of people looking at the pictures and you get the feeling maybe Art isn't on the decline in New York City, after all—"

"I want to tell you something," Michael said very seriously. "I have not touched another woman. Not once. In all the five years."

"All right," Frances said.

"You believe that, don't you?"

"All right."

They walked between the crowded benches, under the scrubby city-park trees.

"I try not to notice it," Frances said, "but I feel rotten inside, in my stomach, when we pass a woman and you look at her and I see that look in your eye and that's the way you looked at me the first time. In Alice Maxwell's house. Standing there in the living room, next to the radio, with a green hat on and all those people."

"I remember the hat," Michael said.

"The same look," Frances said. "And it makes me feel bad. It makes me feel terrible."

"Sh-h-h, please, darling, sh-h-h."

"I think I would like a drink now," Frances said.

They walked over to a bar on Eighth Street, not saying anything, Michael automatically helping her over curbstones and guiding her past automobiles. They sat near a window in the bar and the sun streamed in and there was a small, cheerful fire in the fireplace. A little Japanese waiter came over and put down some pretzels and smiled happily at them.

"What do you order after breakfast?" Michael asked.

"Brandy, I suppose," Frances said.

"Courvoisier," Michael told the waiter. "Two Courvoisiers."

The waiter came with the glasses and they sat drinking the brandy in the sunlight. Michael finished half his and drank a little water.

"I look at women," he said. "Correct. I don't say it's wrong or right. I look at them. If I pass them on the street and I don't look at them, I'm fooling you, I'm fooling myself."

"You look at them as though you want them," Frances said, playing with her brandy glass. "Every one of them."

"In a way," Michael said, speaking softly and not to his wife, "in a way that's true. I don't do anything about it, but it's true."

"I know it. That's why I feel bad."

"Another brandy," Michael called. "Waiter, two more brandies."

He sighed and closed his eyes and rubbed them gently with his fingertips. "I love the way women look. One of the things I like best about New York is the battalions of women. When I first came to New York from Ohio that was the first thing I noticed, the million wonderful women, all over the city. I walked around with my heart in my throat."

"A kid," Frances said. "That's a kid's feeling."

"Guess again," Michael said. "Guess again. I'm older now. I'm a man getting near middle age, putting on a little fat, and I still love to walk along Fifth Avenue at three o'clock on the east side of the street between Fiftieth and Fifty-seventh Streets. They're all out then, shopping, in their furs and their crazy hats, everything all concentrated from all over the world into seven blocks—the best furs, the best clothes, the handsomest women, out to spend money and feeling good about it."

The Japanese waiter put the two drinks down, smiling with great happiness.

"Everything is all right?" he asked.

"Everything is wonderful," Michael said.

"If it's just a couple of fur coats," Frances said, "and forty-five dollar hats—"

"It's not the fur coats. Or the hats. That's just the scenery for that particular kind of woman. Understand," he said, "you don't have to listen to this."

"I want to listen."

"I like the girls in the offices. Neat with their eyeglasses, smart, chipper, knowing what everything is about. I like the girls on Forty-fourth Street at lunchtime, the actresses, all dressed up on nothing a week. I like the salesgirls in the stores, paying attention to you first because you're a man, leaving the lady customers waiting. I got all this stuff accumulated in me because I've been thinking about it for ten years and now you've asked for it and here it is."

"Go ahead," Frances said.

"When I think of New York City, I think of all the girls on parade in the city. I don't know whether it's something special with me or whether every man in the city walks around with the same feeling inside him, but I feel as though I'm at a picnic in this city. I like to sit near the women in the theatres, the famous beauties who've taken six hours to get ready and look it. And the young girls at the football games, with the red cheeks, and when the warm weather comes, the girls in their summer dresses." He finished his drink. "That's the story."

Frances finished her drink and swallowed two or three times extra. "You say you love me?"

"I love you."

"I'm pretty, too," Frances said. "As pretty as any of them."

"You're beautiful," Michael said.

"I'm good for you," Frances said, pleading. "I've made a good wife, a good housekeeper, a good friend. I'd do any damn thing for you."

"I know," Michael said. He put his hand out and grasped hers.

"You'd like to be free to—" Frances said.

"Sh-h-h."

"Tell the truth." She took her hand away from under his.

Michael flicked the edge of his glass with his finger. "O.K.," he said gently. "Sometimes I feel I would like to be free."

"Well," Frances said, "any time you say."

"Don't be foolish." Michael swung his chair around to her side of the table and patted her thigh.

She began to cry silently into her handkerchief, bent over just enough so that nobody else in the bar would notice. "Someday," she said, crying, "you're going to make a move."

Michael didn't say anything. He sat watching the bartender slowly peel a lemon.

"Aren't you?" Frances asked harshly. "Come on, tell me. Talk. Aren't you?"

"Maybe," Michael said. He moved his chair back again. "How the hell do I know?"

"You know," Frances persisted. "Don't you know?"

"Yes," Michael said after a while, "I know."

Frances stopped crying then. Two or three snuffles into the handkerchief and she put it away and her face didn't tell anything to anybody. "At least do me one favor," she said.

"Sure."

"Stop talking about how pretty this woman is or that one. Nice eyes, nice breasts, a pretty figure, good voice." She mimicked his voice. "Keep it to yourself. I'm not interested."

Michael waved to the waiter. "I'll keep it to myself," he said.

Frances flicked the corners of her eyes. "Another brandy," she told the waiter.

"Two," Michael said.

"Yes, ma'am, yes, sir," said the waiter, backing away.

Frances regarded Michael coolly across the table. "Do you want me to call the Stevensons?" she asked. "It'll be nice in the country."

"Sure," Michael said. "Call them."

She got up from the table and walked across the room toward the telephone. Michael watched her walk, thinking what a pretty girl, what nice legs.

QUESTIONS
1. Is Frances's anger justified? Explain.   2.   What is the effect of the final sentence of the story?

To Room Nineteen 1963

DORIS LESSING [b. 1919]

This is a story, I suppose, about a failure in intelligence: the Rawlings' marriage was grounded in intelligence.

They were older when they married than most of their married friends: in their well-seasoned late twenties. Both had had a number of affairs, sweet rather than bitter; and when they fell in love—for they did fall in love—had known each other for some time. They joked that they had saved each other "for the real thing." That they had waited so long (but not too long) for this real thing was to them a proof of their sensible discrimination. A good many of their friends had married young, and now (they felt) probably regretted lost opportunities; while others, still unmarried, seemed to them arid, self-doubting, and likely to make desperate or romantic marriages.

Not only they, but others, felt they were well matched: their friends' delight was an additional proof of their happiness. They had played the same roles, male and female, in this group or set, if such a wide, loosely connected, constantly changing constellation of people could be called a set. They had both become, by virtue of their moderation, their humor, and their abstinence from painful experience people to whom others came for advice. They could be, and were, relied on. It was one of those cases of a man and a woman linking themselves whom no one else had ever thought of linking, probably because of their similarities. But then everyone exclaimed: Of course! How right! How was it we never thought of it before!

And so they married amid general rejoicing, and because of their foresight and their sense for what was probable, nothing was a surprise to them.

Both had well-paid jobs. Matthew was a subeditor on a large London newspaper, and Susan worked in an advertising firm. He was not the stuff of which editors or publicised journalists are made, but he was much more than "a subeditor," being one of the essential background people who in fact steady, inspire and make possible the people in the limelight. He was content with this position. Susan had a talent for commercial drawing. She was humorous about the advertisements she was responsible for, but she did not feel strongly about them one way or the other.

Both, before they married, had had pleasant flats, but they felt it unwise to base a marriage on either flat, because it might seem like a submission of personality on the part of the one whose flat it was not. They moved into a new flat in South Kensington on the clear understanding that when their marriage had settled down (a process they knew would not take long, and was in fact more a humorous concession to popular wisdom than what was due to themselves) they would buy a house and start a family.

And this is what happened. They lived in their charming flat for two years, giving parties and going to them, being a popular young married couple, and then Susan became pregnant, she gave up her job, and they bought a house in Richmond. It was typical of this couple that they had a son first, then a daughter, then twins, son and daughter. Everything right, appropriate, and what everyone would wish for, if they could choose. But people did feel these two had chosen; this balanced and sensible family was no more than what was due to them because of their infallible sense for *choosing* right.

And so they lived with their four children in their gardened house in Richmond and were happy. They had everything they had wanted and had planned for.

And yet . . .

Well, even this was expected, that there must be a certain flatness. . . .

Yes, yes, of course, it was natural they sometimes felt like this. Like what?

Their life seemed to be like a snake biting its tail. Matthew's job for the sake of Susan, children, house, and garden—which caravanserai needed a well-paid job to maintain it. And Susan's practical intelligence for the sake of Matthew, the children, the house and the garden—which unit would have collapsed in a week without her.

But there was no point about which either could say: "For the sake of *this* is all the rest." Children? But the children can't be a centre of life and a reason for being. They can be a thousand things that are delightful, interesting, satisfying, but they can't be a wellspring to live from. Or they shouldn't be. Susan and Matthew knew that well enough.

Matthew's job? Ridiculous. It was an interesting job, but scarcely a reason for living. Matthew took pride in doing it well; but he could hardly be expected to be proud of the newspaper: the newspaper he read, *his* newspaper, was not the one he worked for.

Their love for each other? Well, that was nearest it. If this wasn't a centre, what was? Yes, it was around this point, their love, that the whole extraordinary structure revolved. For extraordinary it certainly was. Both Susan and Matthew had moments of thinking so, of looking in secret disbelief at this thing they had created: marriage, four children, big house, garden, charwomen, friends, cars . . . and this *thing*, this entity, all of it had come into existence, been blown into being out of nowhere, because Susan loved Matthew and Matthew loved Susan. Extraordinary. So that was the central point, the wellspring.

And if one felt that it simply was not strong enough, important enough, to support it all, well whose fault was that? Certainly neither Susan's nor Matthew's. It was in the nature of things. And they sensibly blamed neither themselves nor each other.

On the contrary, they used their intelligence to preserve what they had created from a painful and explosive world: they looked around them, and took lessons. All around them, marriages collapsing, or breaking, or rubbing along (even worse, they felt). They must not make the same mistakes, they must not.

They had avoided the pitfall so many of their friends had fallen into—of buying a house in the country *for the sake of the children*; so that the husband became a weekend husband, a weekend father, and the wife always careful not to ask what went on in the town flat which they called (in joke) a bachelor flat. No, Matthew was a full-time husband, a full-time father, and at nights, in the big married bed in the big married bedroom (which had an attractive view of the river) they lay beside each other talking and he told her about his day, and what he had done, and whom he had met; and she told him about her day (not as interesting, but that was not her fault) for both knew of the hidden resentments and deprivations of the woman who has lived her own life—and above all, has earned her own living—and is now dependent on a husband for outside interests and money.

Nor did Susan make the mistake of taking a job for the sake of her independence, which she might very well have done, since her old firm, missing her qualities of humour, balance, and sense, invited her often to go back. Children needed their mother to a certain age, that both parents knew and agreed on; and when these four healthy wisely brought-up children were of the right age, Susan would work again, because she knew, and so did he, what happened to women of fifty at the height of their energy and ability, with grown-up children who no longer needed their full devotion.

So here was this couple, testing their marriage, looking after it, treating it like a small boat full of helpless people in a very stormy sea. Well, of course, so it was. . . . The storms of the world were bad, but not too close—which is not to say they were selfishly felt: Susan and Matthew were both well-informed and responsible people. And the inner storms and quicksands were understood and charted. So everything was all right. Everything was in order. Yes, things were under control.

So what did it matter if they felt dry, flat? People like themselves, fed on a hundred books (psychological, anthropological, sociological) could scarcely be unprepared for the dry, controlled wistfulness which is the distinguishing mark of the intelligent marriage. Two people, endowed with education, with discrimination, with judgement, linked together voluntarily from their will to be happy together and to be of use to others—one sees them everywhere, one knows them, one even is that thing oneself: sadness because so much is after all so little. These two, unsurprised, turned towards each other with even more courtesy and gentle love: this was life, that two people, no matter how carefully chosen, could not be everything to each other. In fact, even to say so, to think in such a way, was banal, they were ashamed to do it.

It was banal, too, when one night Matthew came home late and confessed he had been to a party, taken a girl home and slept with her. Susan forgave him, of course. Except that forgiveness is hardly the word. Understanding, yes. But if you understand something, you don't forgive it, you are the thing itself: forgiveness is for what you *don't* understand. Nor had he *confessed*—what sort of word is that?

The whole thing was not important. After all, years ago they had joked: Of course I'm not going to be faithful to you, no one can be faithful to one other person for a whole lifetime. (And there was the word *faithful*—stupid, all these words, stupid, belonging to a savage old world.) But the incident left both of them irritable. Strange, but they were both bad-tempered, annoyed. There was something unassimilable about it.

Making love splendidly after he had come home that night, both had felt that the idea that Myra Jenkins, a pretty girl met at a party, could be even relevant was ridiculous. They had loved each other for over a decade, would love each other for years more. Who, then, was Myra Jenkins?

Except, thought Susan, unaccountably bad-tempered, she was (is?) the first. In ten years. So either the ten years' fidelity was not important, or she isn't. (No, no, there is something wrong with this way of thinking, there must be.) But if she isn't important, presumably it wasn't important either when Matthew and I first went to bed with each other that afternoon whose delight even now (like a very long shadow at sundown) lays a long, wandlike finger over us. (Why did I say sundown?) Well, if what we felt that afternoon was not important, nothing is important, because if it hadn't been for what we felt, we wouldn't be Mr. and Mrs. Rawlings with four children, etc., etc. The whole thing is *absurd*—for him to have come home and told me was absurd. For him not to have told me was absurd. For me to care, or for that matter not to care, is absurd . . . and who is Myra Jenkins? Why, no one at all.

There was only one thing to do, and of course these sensible people did it: they put the thing behind them, and consciously, knowing what they were doing, moved forward into a different phase of their marriage, giving thanks for past good fortune as they did so.

For it was inevitable that the handsome, blond, attractive, manly man, Matthew Rawlings, should be at times tempted (oh, what a word!) by the attractive girls at parties she could not attend because of the four children; and that sometimes he would succumb (a word even more repulsive, if possible) and that she, a good-looking woman in the big well-tended garden at Richmond, would sometimes be pierced as by an arrow from the sky with bitterness. Except that bitterness was not in order, it was out of court. Did the casual girls touch the marriage? They did not. Rather it was they who knew defeat because of the handsome Matthew Rawlings' marriage body and soul to Susan Rawlings.

In that case why did Susan feel (though luckily not for longer than a few seconds at a time) as if life had become a desert, and that nothing mattered, and that her children were not her own?

Meanwhile her intelligence continued to assert that all was well. What if her Matthew did have an occasional sweet afternoon, the odd affair? For she knew quite well, except in her moments of aridity, that they were very happy, that the affairs were not important.

Perhaps that was the trouble? It was in the nature of things that the adventures and delights could no longer be hers, because of the four children and the big house that needed so much attention. But perhaps she was secretly wishing, and even knowing that she did, that the wildness and the beauty could be his. But he was married to her. She was married to him. They were married inextricably. And therefore the gods could not strike him with the real magic, not really. Well, was it Susan's fault that after he came home from an adventure he looked harassed rather than fulfilled? (In fact, that was how she knew he had been *unfaithful*, because of his sullen air, and his glances at her, similar to hers at him: What is it that I share with this person that shields all delight from me?) But none of it by anybody's fault. (But what did they feel ought to be somebody's fault?) Nobody's fault, nothing to be at fault, no one to blame, no one to offer or to take it . . . and nothing wrong, either, except that Matthew never was really struck, as he wanted to be, by joy; and that Susan was more and more often threatened by emptiness. (It was usually in the garden that she was invaded by this feeling: she was coming to avoid the garden, unless the children or Matthew were with her.) There was no need to use the dramatic words, unfaithful, forgive, and the rest: intelligence forbade them. Intelligence barred, too, quarrelling, sulking, anger, silences of withdrawal, accusations and tears. Above all, intelligence forbids tears.

A high price has to be paid for the happy marriage with the four healthy children in the large white gardened house.

And they were paying it, willingly, knowing what they were doing. When they lay side by side or breast to breast in the big civilised bedroom overlooking the wild sullied river, they laughed, often, for no particular reason; but they knew it was really because of these two small people, Susan and Matthew, supporting such an edifice on their intelligent love. The laugh comforted them; it saved them both, from what, they did not know.

They were now both fortyish. The older children, boy and girl, were ten and eight, at school. The twins, six, were still at home. Susan did not have nurses or girls to help her: childhood is short; and she did not regret the hard work. Often enough she was bored, since small children can be boring; she was often very tired; but she regretted nothing. In another decade, she would turn herself back into being a woman with a life of her own.

Soon the twins would go to school, and they would be away from home from nine until four. These hours, so Susan saw it, would be the preparation for her own slow emancipation away from the role of hub-of-the-family into woman-with-her-own-life. She was already planning for the hours of freedom when all the children would be "off her hands." That was the phrase used by Matthew and by Susan and by their friends, for the moment when the youngest child went off to school. "They'll be off your hands, darling Susan, and you'll have time to yourself." So said Matthew, the intelligent husband, who had often enough commended and consoled Susan, standing by her in spirit during the years when her soul was not her own, as she said, but her children's.

What it amounted to was that Susan saw herself as she had been at twenty-eight, unmarried; and then again somewhere about fifty, blossoming from the root of what she had been twenty years before. As if the essential Susan were in abeyance, as if she were in cold storage. Matthew said something like this to Susan one night: and she agreed that it was true—she did feel something like that. What, then, was this essential Susan? She did not know. Put like that it sounded ridiculous, and she did not really feel it. Anyway, they had a long discussion about the whole thing before going off to sleep in each other's arms.

So the twins were off to their school, two bright affectionate children who had no problems about it, since their older brother and sister had trodden this path so successfully before them. And now Susan was going to be alone in the big house, every day of the school term, except for the daily woman who came in to clean.

It was now, for the first time in this marriage, that something happened which neither of them had foreseen.

This is what happened. She returned, at nine-thirty, from taking the twins to the school by car, looking forward to seven blissful hours of freedom. On the first morning she was simply restless, worrying about the twins "naturally enough" since this was their first day away at school. She was hardly able to contain herself until they came back. Which they did happily, excited by the world of school, looking forward to the next day. And the next day Susan took them, dropped them, came back, and found herself reluctant to enter her big and beautiful home because it was as if something was waiting for her there that she did not wish to confront. Sensibly, however, she parked the car in the garage, entered the house, spoke to Mrs. Parkes the daily woman about her duties, and went up to her bedroom. She was possessed by a fever which drove her out again, downstairs, into the kitchen, where Mrs. Parkes was making cake and did not need her, and into the garden. There she sat on a bench and tried to calm herself, looking at trees, at a brown glimpse of the river. But she was filled with tension, like a panic: as if an enemy was in the garden with her. She spoke to herself severely, thus: All this is quite natural. First, I spent twelve years of my adult life working, *living my own life*. Then I married, and from the moment I became pregnant for the first time I signed myself over, so to speak, to other people. To the children. Not for one moment in twelve years have I been alone, had time to myself. So now I have to learn to be myself again. That's all.

And she went indoors to help Mrs. Parkes cook and clean, and found some sewing to do for the children. She kept herself occupied every day. At the end of the first term she understood she felt two contrary emotions. First: secret astonishment and dismay that during those weeks when the house was empty of children she had in fact been more occupied (had been careful to keep herself occupied) than ever she had been when the children were around her needing her continual attention. Second: that now she knew the house would be full of them, and for five weeks, she resented the fact she would never be alone. She was already looking back at those hours of sewing, cooking (but by herself), as at a lost freedom which would not be hers for five long weeks. And the two months of term which would succeed the five weeks stretched alluringly open to her—freedom. But what freedom—when in fact she had been so careful *not* to be free of small duties during the last weeks? She looked at herself, Susan Rawlings, sitting in a big chair by the window in the bedroom, sewing shirts or dresses, which she might just as well have bought. She saw herself making cakes for hours at a time in the big family kitchen: yet usually she bought cakes. What she saw was a woman alone, that was true, but she had not felt alone. For instance, Mrs. Parkes was always somewhere in the house. And she did not like being in the garden at all, because of the closeness there of the enemy—irritation, restlessness, emptiness, whatever it was, which keeping her hands occupied made less dangerous for some reason.

Susan did not tell Matthew of these thoughts. They were not sensible. She did not recognize herself in them. What should she say to her dear friend and husband Matthew? "When I go into the garden, that is, if the children are not there, I feel as if there is an enemy there waiting to invade me." "What enemy, Susan darling?" "Well I don't know, really. . . ." "Perhaps you should see a doctor?"

No, clearly this conversation should not take place. The holidays began and Susan welcomed them. Four children, lively, energetic, intelligent, demanding: she was never, not for a moment of her day, alone. If she was in a room, they would be in the next room, or waiting for her to do something for them; or it would soon be time for lunch or tea, or to take one of them to the dentist. Something to do: five weeks of it, thank goodness.

On the fourth day of these so welcome holidays, she found she was storming with anger at the twins, two shrinking beautiful children who (and this is what checked her) stood hand in hand looking at her with sheer dismayed disbelief. This was their calm mother, shouting at them. And for what? They had come to her with some game, some bit of nonsense. They looked at each other, moved closer for support, and went off hand in hand, leaving Susan holding on to the windowsill of the living room, breathing deep, feeling sick. She went to lie down, telling the older children, she had a headache. She heard the boy Harry telling the little ones. "It's all right, Mother's got a headache." She heard that *It's all right* with pain.

That night she said to her husband: "Today I shouted at the twins, quite unfairly." She sounded miserable, and he said gently: "Well, what of it?"

"It's more of an adjustment than I thought, their going to school."

"But Susie, Susie darling. . . ." For she was crouched weeping on the bed. He comforted her: "Susan, what is all this about? You shouted at them? What of it? If you shouted at them fifty times a day it wouldn't be more than the little devils deserve." But she wouldn't laugh. She wept. Soon he comforted her with his body. She became calm. Calm, she wondered what was wrong with her, and why she should mind so much that she might, just once, have behaved unjustly with the children. What did it matter? They had forgotten it all long ago: Mother had a headache and everything was all right.

It was a long time later that Susan understood that that night, when she had wept and Matthew had driven the misery out of her with his big solid body, was the last time, ever in their married life, that they had been—to use their mutual language—with each other. And even that was a lie, because she had not told him of her real fears at all.

The five weeks passed, and Susan was in control of herself, and good and kind, and she looked forward to the holidays with a mixture of fear and longing. She did not know what to expect. She took the twins off to school (the elder children took themselves to school) and she returned to the house determined to face the enemy wherever he was, in the house, or the garden or—where?

She was again restless, she was possessed by restlessness. She cooked and sewed and worked as before, day after day, while Mrs. Parkes remonstrated: "Mrs. Rawlings, what's the need for it? I can do that, it's what you pay me for."

And it was so irrational that she checked herself. She would put the car into the garage, go up to her bedroom, and sit, hands in her lap, forcing herself to be quiet. She listened to Mrs. Parkes moving around the house. She looked out into the garden and saw the branches shake the trees. She sat defeating the enemy, restlessness. Emptiness. She ought to be thinking about her life, about herself. But she did not. Or perhaps she could not. As soon as she forced her mind to think about Susan (for what else did she want to be alone for?) it skipped off to thoughts of butter or school clothes. Or it thought of Mrs. Parkes. She realised that she sat listening for the movements of the cleaning woman, following her every turn, bend, thought. She followed her in her mind from kitchen to bathroom, from table to oven, and it was as if the duster, the cleaning cloth, the saucepan, were in her own hand. She would hear herself saying: No, not like that, don't put that there. . . . Yet she did not give a damn what Mrs. Parkes did, or if she did it at all. Yet she could not prevent herself from being conscious of her, every minute. Yes, this was what was wrong with her: she needed, when she was alone, to be really alone, with no one near. She could not endure the knowledge that in ten minutes or in half an hour Mrs. Parkes would call up the stairs: "Mrs. Rawlings, there's no silver polish. Madam, we're out of flour."

So she left the house and went to sit in the garden where she was screened from the house by trees. She waited for the demon to appear and claim her, but he did not.

She was keeping him off, because she had not, after all, come to an end of arranging herself.

She was planning how to be somewhere where Mrs. Parkes would not come after her with a cup of tea, or a demand to be allowed to telephone (always irritating since Susan did not care who she telephoned or how often), or just a nice talk about something. Yes, she needed a place, or a state of affairs, where it would not be necessary to keep reminding herself: In ten minutes I must telephone Matthew about . . . and at half past three I must leave early for the children because the car needs cleaning. And at ten o'clock tomorrow I must remember. . . . She was possessed with resentment that the seven hours of freedom in every day (during the weekdays in the school term) were not free, that never, not for one second, ever, was she free from the pressure of time, from having to remember this or that. She could never forget herself; never really let herself go into forgetfulness.

Resentment. It was poisoning her. (She looked at this emotion and thought it was absurd. Yet she felt it.) She was a prisoner. (She looked at this thought too, and it was no good telling herself it was a ridiculous one.) She must tell Matthew—but what? She was filled with emotions that were utterly ridiculous, that she despised, yet that nevertheless she was feeling so strongly she could not shake them off.

The school holidays came round, and this time they were for nearly two months, and she behaved with a conscious controlled decency that nearly drove her crazy. She would lock herself in the bathroom, and sit on the edge of the bath, breathing deep, trying to let go into some kind of calm. Or she went up into the spare room, usually empty, where no one would expect her to be. She heard the children calling "Mother, Mother," and kept silent, feeling guilty. Or she went to the very end of the garden, by herself, and looked at the slow-moving brown river; she looked at the river and closed her eyes and breathed slow and deep, taking it into her being, into her veins.

Then she returned to the family, wife and mother, smiling and responsible, feeling as if the pressure of these people—four lively children and her husband— were a painful pressure on the surface of her skin, a hand pressing on her brain. She did not once break down into irritation during these holidays, but it was like living out a prison sentence, and when the children went back to school, she sat on a white stone seat near the flowing river, and she thought: It is not even a year since the twins went to school, since *they were off my hands* (What on earth did I think I meant when I used that stupid phrase?) and yet I'm a different person. I'm simply not myself. I don't understand it.

Yet she had to understand it. For she knew that this structure—big white house, on which the mortgage still cost four hundred a year, a husband, so good and kind and insightful, four children, all doing so nicely, and the garden where she sat, and Mrs. Parkes the cleaning woman—all this depended on her, and yet she could not understand why, or even what it was she contributed to it.

She said to Matthew in their bedroom: "I think there must be something wrong with me."

And he said: "Surely not, Susan? You look marvellous—you're as lovely as ever."

She looked at the handsome blond man, with his clear, intelligent, blue-eyed face, and thought: Why is it I can't tell him? Why not? And she said: "I need to be alone more than I am."

At which he swung his slow blue gaze at her, and she saw what she had been dreading: Incredulity. Disbelief. And fear. An incredulous blue stare from a stranger who was her husband, as close to her as her own breath.

He said: "But the children are at school and off your hands."

She said to herself: I've got to force myself to say: Yes, but do you realize that I never feel free? There's never a moment I can say to myself: There's nothing I have to remind myself about, nothing I have to do in half an hour, or an hour, or two hours. . . .

But she said: "I don't feel well."

He said: "Perhaps you need a holiday."

She said appalled: "But not without you, surely?" For she could not imagine herself going off without him. Yet that was what he meant. Seeing her face, he laughed, and opened his arms, and she went into them, thinking: Yes, yes, but why can't I say it? And what is it I have to say?

She tried to tell him, about never being free. And he listened and said: "But

Susan, what sort of freedom can you possibly want—short of being dead! Am I ever free? I go to the office, and I have to be there at ten—all right, half past ten, sometimes. And I have to do this or that, don't I? Then I've got to come home at a certain time—I don't mind it, you know I don't—but if I'm not going to be back home at six I telephone you. When can I ever say to myself: I have nothing to be responsible for in the next six hours?"

Susan, hearing this, was remorseful. Because it was true. The good marriage, the house, the children, depended just as much on his voluntary bondage as it did on hers. But why did he not feel bound? Why didn't he chafe and become restless? No, there was something really wrong with her and this proved it.

And that word *bondage*—why had she used it? She had never felt marriage, or the children, as bondage. Neither had he, or surely they wouldn't be together lying in each other's arms content after twelve years of marriage.

No, her state (whatever it was) was irrelevant, nothing to do with her real good life with her family. She had to accept the fact that after all, she was an irrational person and to live with it. Some people had to live with crippled arms, or stammers, or being deaf. She would have to live knowing she was subject to a state of mind she could not own.

Nevertheless, as a result of this conversation with her husband, there was a new regime next holidays.

The spare room at the top of the house now had a cardboard sign saying: PRIVATE! DO NOT DISTURB! on it. (This sign had been drawn in coloured chalks by the children, after a discussion between the parents in which it was decided this was psychologically the right thing.) The family and Mrs. Parkes knew this was "Mother's Room" and that she was entitled to her privacy. Many serious conversations took place between Matthew and the children about not taking Mother for granted. Susan overheard the first, between father and Harry, the older boy, and was surprised at her irritation over it. Surely she could have a room somewhere in that big house and retire into it without such a fuss being made? Without it being so solemnly discussed? Why couldn't she simply have announced: "I'm going to fit out the little top room for myself, and when I'm in it I'm not to be disturbed for anything short of fire"? Just that, and finished; instead of long earnest discussions. When she heard Harry and Matthew explaining it to the twins with Mrs. Parkes coming in—"Yes, well, a family sometimes gets on top of a woman"—she had to go right away to the bottom of the garden until the devils of exasperation had finished their dance in her blood.

But now there was a room, and she could go there when she liked, she used it seldom: she felt even more caged there than in her bedroom. One day she had gone up there after a lunch for ten children she had cooked and served because Mrs. Parkes was not there, and had sat alone for a while looking into the garden. She saw the children stream out from the kitchen and stand looking up at the window where she sat behind the curtains. They were all—her children and their friends—discussing Mother's Room. A few minutes later, the chase of children in some game came pounding up the stairs, but ended as abruptly as if they had fallen over a ravine, so sudden was the silence. They had remembered she was there, and had gone silent in a great gale of "Hush! Shhhhhh! Quiet, you'll disturb her. . . ." And they went tiptoeing downstairs like criminal conspirators. When she came down to make tea for them, they all apologised. The twins put their arms around her, from front and back, making a human cage of loving limbs, and promised it would never occur again. "We forgot, Mummy, we forgot all about it!"

What it amounted to was that Mother's Room, and her need for privacy, had become a valuable lesson in respect for other people's rights. Quite soon Susan was going up to the room only because it was a lesson it was a pity to drop. Then she took sewing up there, and the children and Mrs. Parkes came in and out: it had become another family room.

She sighed, and smiled, and resigned herself—she made jokes at her own expense with Matthew over the room. That is, she did from the self she liked, she respected. But at the same time, something inside her howled with impatience, with rage. . . . And she was frightened. One day she found herself kneeling by her bed and praying: "Dear God, keep it away from me, keep him away from me." She meant the devil, for she now thought of it, not caring if she were irrational, as some sort of demon. She imagined him, or it, as a youngish man, or perhaps a middle-aged man pretending to be young. Or a man young-looking from immaturity? At any rate, she saw the young-looking face which, when she drew close, had dry lines about mouth and eyes. He was thinnish, meagre in build. And he had a reddish complexion, and ginger hair. That was he—a gingery, energetic man, and he wore a reddish hairy jacket, unpleasant to the touch.

Well, one day she saw him. She was standing at the bottom of the garden, watching the river ebb past, when she raised her eyes and saw this person, or being, sitting on the white stone bench. He was looking at her, and grinning. In his hand was a long crooked stick, which he had picked off the ground, or broken off the tree above him. He was absent-mindedly, out of an absent-minded or freakish impulse of spite, using the stick to stir around in the coils of a blindworm or a grass snake (or some kind of snakelike creature: it was whitish and unhealthy to look at, unpleasant). The snake was twisting about, flinging its coils from side to side in a kind of dance of protest against the teasing prodding stick.

Susan looked at him thinking: Who is the stranger? What is he doing in our garden? Then she recognised the man around whom her terrors had crystallised. As she did so, he vanished. She made herself walk over to the bench. A shadow from a branch lay across thin emerald grass, moving jerkily over its roughness, and she could see why she had taken it for a snake, lashing and twisting. She went back to the house thinking: Right, then, so I've seen him with my own eyes, so I'm not crazy after all—there *is* a danger because I've seen him. He is lurking in the garden and sometimes even in the house, and he wants *to get into me and to take me over.*

She dreamed of having a room or a place, anywhere, where she could go and sit, by herself, no one knowing where she was.

Once, near Victoria, she found herself outside a news agent that had Rooms to Let advertised. She decided to rent a room, telling no one. Sometimes she could take the train in to Richmond and sit alone in it for an hour or two. Yet how could she? A room would cost three or four pounds a week, and she earned no money, and how could she explain to Matthew that she needed such a sum? What for? It did not occur to her that she was taking it for granted she wasn't going to tell him about the room.

Well, it was out of the question, having a room; yet she knew she must.

One day, when a school term was well established, and none of the children had measles or other ailments, and everything seemed in order, she did the shopping early, explained to Mrs. Parkes she was meeting an old school friend, took the train to Victoria, searched until she found a small quiet hotel, and asked for a room for the day. They did not let rooms by the day, the manageress said, looking doubtful, since Susan so obviously was not the kind of woman who needed a room for unrespectable reasons. Susan made a long explanation about not being well, being unable to shop without frequent rests for lying down. At last she was allowed to rent the room provided she paid a full night's price for it. She was taken up by the manageress and a maid, both concerned over the state of her health . . . which must be pretty bad if, living at Richmond (she had signed her name and address in the register), she needed a shelter at Victoria.

The room was ordinary and anonymous, and was just what Susan needed. She put a shilling in the gas fire, and sat, eyes shut, in a dingy armchair with her back to a dingy window. She was alone. She was alone. She was alone. She could feel pressures lifting off her. First the sounds of traffic came very loud; then they seemed to vanish; she might even have slept a little. A knock on the door; it was Miss Townsend the manageress, bringing her a cup of tea with her own hands, so concerned was she over Susan's long silence and possible illness.

Miss Townsend was a lonely woman of fifty, running this hotel with all the rectitude expected of her, and she sensed in Susan the possibility of understanding companionship. She stayed to talk. Susan found herself in the middle of a fantastic story about her illness, which got more and more improbable as she tried to make it tally with the large house at Richmond, well-off husband, and four children. Suppose she said instead: Miss Townsend, I'm here in your hotel because I need to be alone for a few hours, above all *alone and with no one knowing where I am*. She said it mentally, and saw, mentally, the look that would inevitably come on Miss Townsend's elderly maiden's face. "Miss Townsend, my four children and my husband are driving me insane, do you understand that? Yes, I can see from the gleam of hysteria in your eyes that comes from loneliness controlled but only just contained that I've got everything in the world you've ever longed for. Well, Miss Townsend, I don't want any of it. You can have it, Miss Townsend. I wish I was absolutely alone in the world, like you. Miss Townsend, I'm besieged by seven devils, Miss Townsend, Miss Townsend, let me stay here in your hotel where the devils can't get me. . . ." Instead of saying all this, she described her anaemia, agreed to try Miss Townsend's remedy for it, which was raw liver, minced, between whole-meal bread, and said yes, perhaps it would be better if she stayed at home and let a friend do shopping for her. She paid her bill and left the hotel, defeated.

At home Mrs. Parkes said she didn't really like it, no, not really, when Mrs. Rawlings was away from nine in the morning until five. The teacher had telephoned from school to say Joan's teeth were paining her, and she hadn't known what to say; and what was she to make for the children's tea, Mrs. Rawlings hadn't said.

All this was nonsense, of course. Mrs. Parkes's complaint was that Susan had withdrawn herself spiritually, leaving the burden of the big house on her.

Susan looked back at her day of "freedom" which had resulted in her becoming a friend to the lonely Miss Townsend, and in Mrs. Parkes's remonstrances. Yet she remembered the short blissful hour of being alone, really alone. She was determined to arrange her life, no matter what it cost, so that she could have that solitude more often. An absolute solitude, where no one knew her or cared about her.

But how? She thought of saying to her old employer: I want to back you up in a story with Matthew that I am doing part-time work for you. The truth is that . . . but she would have to tell him a lie too, and which lie? She could not say: I want to sit by myself three or four times a week in a rented room. And besides, he knew Matthew, and she could not really ask him to tell lies on her behalf, apart from his being bound to think it meant a lover.

Suppose she really took a part-time job, which she could get through fast and efficiently, leaving time for herself. What job? Addressing envelopes? Canvassing?

And there was Mrs. Parkes, working widow, who knew exactly what she was prepared to give to the house, who knew by instinct when her mistress withdrew in spirit from her responsibilities. Mrs. Parkes was one of the servers of this world, but she needed someone to serve. She had to have Mrs. Rawlings, her madam, at the top of the house or in the garden, so that she could come and get support from her: "Yes, the bread's not what it was when I was a girl. . . . Yes, Harry's got a wonderful appetite, I wonder where he puts it all. . . . Yes, it's lucky the twins are so much of a size, they can wear each other's shoes, that's a saving in these hard times. . . . Yes, the cherry jam from Switzerland is not a patch on the jam from Poland, and three times the price. . . ." And so on. That sort of talk Mrs. Parkes must have, every day, or she would leave, not knowing herself why she left.

Susan Rawlings, thinking these thoughts, found that she was prowling through the great thicketed garden like a wild cat: she was walking up the stairs, down the stairs, through the rooms, into the garden, along the brown running river, back, up through the house, down again. . . . It was a wonder Mrs. Parkes did not think it strange. But on the contrary, Mrs. Rawlings could do what she liked, she could stand on her head if she wanted, provided she was *there*. Susan Rawlings prowled and muttered through her house, hating Mrs. Parkes, hating poor Miss Townsend, dreaming of her hour of solitude in the dingy respectability of Miss Townsend's hotel bedroom, and she knew quite well she was mad. Yes, she was mad.

She said to Matthew that she must have a holiday. Matthew agreed with her. This was not as things had been once—how they had talked in each other's arms in the marriage bed. He had, she knew, diagnosed her finally as *unreasonable*. She had become someone outside himself that he had to manage. They were living side by side in this house like two tolerably friendly strangers.

Having told Mrs. Parkes, or rather, asked for her permission, she went off on a walking holiday in Wales. She chose the remotest place she knew of. Every morning the children telephoned her before they went off to school, to encourage and support her, just as they had over Mother's Room. Every evening she telephoned them, spoke to each child in turn, and then to Matthew. Mrs. Parkes, given permission to telephone for instructions or advice, did so every day at lunchtime. When, as happened three times, Mrs. Rawlings was out on the mountainside, Mrs. Parkes asked that she should ring back at such and such a time, for she would not be happy in what she was doing without Mrs. Rawlings' blessing.

Susan prowled over wild country with the telephone wire holding her to her duty like a leash. The next time she must telephone, or wait to be telephoned, nailed her to her cross. The mountains themselves seemed trammelled by her unfreedom. Everywhere on the mountains, where she met no one at all, from breakfast time to dusk, excepting sheep, or a shepherd, she came face to face with her own craziness which might attack her in the broadest valleys, so that they seemed too small; or on a mountaintop from which she could see a hundred other mountains and valleys, so that they seemed too low, too small, with the sky pressing down too close. She would stand gazing at a hillside brilliant with ferns and bracken, jewelled with running water, and see nothing but her devil, who lifted inhuman eyes at her from where he leaned negligently on a rock, switching at his ugly yellow boots with a leafy twig.

She returned to her home and family, with the Welsh emptiness at the back of her mind like a promise of freedom.

She told her husband she wanted to have an *au pair* girl.

They were in their bedroom, it was late at night, the children slept. He sat, shirted and slippered, in a chair by the window, looking out. She sat brushing her hair and watching him in the mirror. A time-hallowed scene in the connubial bedroom. He said nothing, while she heard the arguments coming into his mind, only to be rejected because every one was *reasonable*.

"It seems strange to get one now, after all, the children are in school most of the day. Surely the time for you to have help was when you were stuck with them day and night. Why don't you ask Mrs. Parkes to cook for you? She's even offered to—I can understand if you are tired of cooking for six people. But you know that an *au pair* girl means all kinds of problems, it's not like having an ordinary char in during the day. . . ."

Finally he said carefully: "Are you thinking of going back to work?"

"No," she said, "no, not really." She made herself sound vague, rather stupid.

She went on brushing her black hair and peering at herself so as to be oblivious of the short uneasy glances her Matthew kept giving her. "Do you think we can't afford it?" she went on vaguely, not at all the old efficient Susan who knew exactly what they could afford.

"It's not that," he said, looking out of the window at dark trees, so as not to look at her. Meanwhile she examined a round, candid, pleasant face with clear dark brows and clear grey eyes. A sensible face. She brushed thick healthy black hair and thought: Yet that's the reflection of a madwoman. How very strange! Much more to the point if what looked back at me was the gingery green-eyed demon with his dry meagre smile. . . . Why wasn't Matthew agreeing? After all, what else could he do? She was breaking her part of the bargain and there was no way of forcing her to keep it: that her spirit, her soul, should live in this house, so that the people in it could grow like plants in water, and Mrs. Parkes remain content in their service. In return for this, he would be a good loving husband, and responsible towards the children. Well, nothing like this had been true of either of them for a long time. He did his duty, perfunctorily; she did not even pretend to do hers. And he had become like other husbands, with his real life in his work and the people he met there, and very likely a serious affair. All this was her fault.

At last he drew heavy curtains, blotting out the trees, and turned to force her attention: "Susan, are you really sure we need a girl?" But she would not meet his appeal at all: She was running the brush over her hair again and again, lifting fine black clouds in a small hiss of electricity. She was peering in and smiling as if she were amused at the clinging hissing hair that followed the brush.

"Yes, I think it would be a good idea on the whole," she said, with the cunning of a madwoman evading the real point.

In the mirror she could see her Matthew lying on his back, his hands behind his head, staring upwards, his face sad and hard. She felt her heart (the old heart of Susan Rawlings) soften and call out to him. But she set it to be indifferent.

He said: "Susan, the children?" It was an appeal that *almost* reached her. He opened his arms, lifting them from where they had lain by his sides, palms up, empty. She had only to run across and fling herself into them, onto his hard, warm chest, and melt into herself, into Susan. But she could not. She would not see his lifted arms. She said vaguely: "Well, surely it'll be even better for them? We'll get a French or a German girl and they'll learn the language."

In the dark she lay beside him, feeling frozen, a stranger. She felt as if Susan had been spirited away. She disliked very much this woman who lay here, cold and indifferent beside a suffering man, but she could not change her.

Next morning she set about getting a girl, and very soon came Sophie Traub from Hamburg, a girl of twenty, laughing, healthy, blue-eyed, pretending to learn English. Indeed, she already spoke a good deal. In return for a room— "Mother's Room"—and her food, she undertook to do some light cooking, and to be with the children when Mrs. Rawlings asked. She was an intelligent girl and understood perfectly what was needed. Susan said: "I go off sometimes, for the morning or for the day—well, sometimes the children run home from school, or they ring up, or a teacher rings up. I should be here, really. And there's the daily woman. . . ." And Sophie laughed her deep fruity *Fräulein's* laugh, showed her fine white teeth and her dimples, and said: "You want some person to play mistress of the house sometimes, not so?"

"Yes, that is just so," said Susan, a bit dry, despite herself, thinking in secret fear how easy it was, how much nearer to the end she was than she thought. Healthy Fräulein Traub's instant understanding of their position proved this to be true.

The *au pair* girl, because of her own common sense, or (as Susan said to herself with her new inward shudder) because she had been *chosen* so well by Susan, was a success with everyone, the children liking her, Mrs. Parkes forgetting almost at once that she was German, and Matthew finding her "nice to have around the house." For he was now taking things as they came, from the surface of life, withdrawn both as a husband and a father from the household.

One day Susan saw how Sophie and Mrs. Parkes were talking and laughing in the kitchen, and she announced that she would be away until teatime. She knew exactly where to go and what she must look for. She took the District Line to South Kensington, changed to the Circle, got off at Paddington, and walked around looking at the smaller hotels until she was satisfied with one which had FRED'S HOTEL painted on windowpanes that needed cleaning. The façade was a faded shiny yellow, like unhealthy skin. A door at the end of a passage said she must knock; she did, and Fred appeared. He was not at all attractive, not in any way, being fattish, and run-down, and wearing a tasteless striped suit. He had small sharp eyes in a white creased face, and was quite prepared to let Mrs. Jones (she chose the farcical name deliberately, staring him out) have a room three days a week from ten until six. Provided of course that she paid in advance each time she came? Susan produced fifteen shillings (no price had been set by him) and held it out, still fixing him with a bold unblinking challenge she had not known until then she could use at will. Looking at her still, he took up a ten-shilling note from her palm between thumb and forefinger, fingered it; then shuffled up two half crowns, held out his own palm with these bits of money displayed thereon, and let his gaze lower broodingly at them. They were standing in the passage, a red-shaded light above, bare boards beneath, and a strong smell of floor polish rising about them. He shot his gaze up at her over the still-extended palm, and smiled as if to say: What do you take me for? "I shan't," said Susan, "be using this room for the purposes of making money." He still waited. She added another five shillings, at which he nodded and said: "You pay, and I ask no questions." "Good," said Susan. He now went past her to the stairs, and there waited a moment: the light from the street door being in her eyes, she lost sight of him momentarily. Then she saw a sober-suited, white-faced, white-balding little man trotting up the stairs like a waiter, and she went after him. They proceeded in utter silence up the stairs of this house where no questions were asked—Fred's Hotel, which could afford the freedom for its visitors that poor Miss Townsend's hotel could not. The room was hideous. It had a single window, with thin green brocade curtains, a three-quarter bed that had a cheap green satin bedspread on it, a fireplace with a gas fire and a shilling meter by it, a chest of drawers, and a green wicker armchair.

"Thank you," said Susan, knowing that Fred (if this was Fred, and not George, or Herbert or Charlie) was looking at her, not so much with curiosity, an emotion he would not own to, for professional reasons, but with a philosophical sense of what was appropriate. Having taken her money and shown her up and agreed to everything, he was clearly disapproving of her for coming here. She did not belong here at all, so his look said. (But she knew, already, how very much she did belong: the room had been waiting for her to join it.) "Would you have me called at five o'clock, please?" and he nodded and went downstairs.

It was twelve in the morning. She was free. She sat in the armchair, she simply sat, she closed her eyes and sat and let herself be alone. She was alone and no one knew where she was. When a knock came on the door she was annoyed, and prepared to show it: but it was Fred himself, it was five o'clock and he was calling her as ordered. He flicked his sharp little eyes over the room—bed, first. It was undisturbed. She might never have been in the room at all. She thanked him, said she would be returning the day after tomorrow, and left. She was back home in time to cook supper, to put the children to bed, to cook a second supper for her husband and herself later. And to welcome Sophie back from the pictures where she had gone with a friend. All these things she did cheerfully, willingly. But she was thinking all the time of the hotel room, she was longing for it with her whole being.

Three times a week. She arrived promptly at ten, looked Fred in the eyes, gave him twenty shillings, followed him up the stairs, went into the room, and shut the door on him with gentle firmness. For Fred, disapproving of her being here at all, was quite ready to let friendship, or at least acquaintanceship, follow his disapproval, if only she would let him. But he was content to go off on her dismissing nod, with the twenty shillings in his hand.

She sat in the armchair and shut her eyes.

What did she *do* in the room? Why, nothing at all. From the chair, when it had rested her, she went to the window, stretching her arms, smiling, treasuring her anonymity, to look out. She was no longer Susan Rawlings, mother of four, wife of Matthew, employer of Mrs. Parkes and of Sophie Traub, with these and those relations with friends, schoolteachers, tradesmen. She no longer was mistress of the big white house and garden, owning clothes suitable for this and that activity or occasion. She was Mrs. Jones, and she was alone, and she had no past and no future. Here I am, she thought, after all these years of being married and having children and playing those roles of responsibility—and I'm just the same. Yet there have been times I thought that nothing existed of me except the roles that went with being Mrs. Matthew Rawlings. Yes, here I am, and if I never saw any of my family again, here I would still be . . . how very strange that is! And she leaned on the sill, and looked into the street, loving the men and women who passed, because she did not know them. She looked at the downtrodden buildings over the street, and at the sky, wet and dingy, or sometimes blue, and she felt she had never seen buildings or sky before. And then she went back to the chair, empty, her mind a blank. Sometimes she talked aloud, saying nothing—an exclamation, meaningless, followed by a comment about the floral pattern on the thin rug, or a stain on the green satin coverlet. For the most part, she wool-gathered—what word is there for it?—brooded, wandered, simply went dark, feeling emptiness run deliciously through her veins like the movement of her blood.

This room had become more her own than the house she lived in. One morning she found Fred taking her a flight higher than usual. She stopped, refusing to go up, and demanded her usual room, Number 19. "Well, you'll have to wait half an hour then," he said. Willingly she descended to the dark disinfectant-smelling hall, and sat waiting until the two, man and woman, came down the stairs, giving her swift indifferent glances before they hurried out into the street, separating at the door. She went up to the room, *her* room, which they had just vacated. It was no less hers, though the windows were set wide open, and a maid was straightening the bed as she came in.

After these days of solitude, it was both easy to play her part as mother and wife, and difficult—because it was so easy: she felt an impostor. She felt as if her shell moved here, with her family, answering to Mummy, Mother, Susan, Mrs. Rawlings. She was surprised no one saw through her, that she wasn't turned out of doors, as a fake. On the contrary, it seemed the children loved her more; Matthew and she "got on" pleasantly, and Mrs. Parkes was happy in her work under (for the most part, it must be confessed) Sophie Traub. At night she lay beside her husband, and they made love again, apparently just as they used to, when they were really married. But she, Susan, or the being who answered so readily and improbably to the name of Susan, was not there: she was in Fred's hotel, in Paddington, waiting for the easing hours of solitude to begin.

Soon she made a new arrangement with Fred and with Sophie. It was for five days a week. As for the money, five pounds, she simply asked Matthew for it. She saw that she was not even frightened he might ask what for: he would give it to her, she knew that, and yet it was terrifying it could be so, for this close couple, these partners, had once known the destination of every shilling they must spend. He agreed to give her five pounds a week. She asked for just so much, not a penny more. He sounded indifferent about it. It was as if he were paying her, she thought: *paying her off*—yes, that was it. Terror came back for a moment, when she understood this, but she stilled it: things had gone too far for that. Now, every week, on Sunday nights, he gave her five pounds, turning away from her before their eyes could meet on the transaction. As for Sophie Traub, she was to be somewhere in or near the house until six at night, after which she was free. She was not to cook, or to clean, she was simply to be there. So she gardened or sewed, and asked friends in, being a person who was bound to have a lot of friends. If the children were sick, she nursed them.

If teachers telephoned, she answered them sensibly. For the five daytimes in the school week, she was altogether the mistress of the house.

One night in the bedroom, Matthew asked: "Susan, I don't want to interfere—don't think that, please—but are you sure you are well?"

She was brushing her hair at the mirror. She made two more strokes on either side of her head, before she replied: "Yes, dear, I am sure I am well."

He was again lying on his back, his big blond head on his hands, his elbows angled up and part-concealing his face. He said: "Then Susan, I have to ask you this question, though you must understand, I'm not putting any sort of pressure on you." (Susan heard the word pressure with dismay, because this was inevitable, of course she could not go on like this.) "Are things going to go on like this?"

"Well," she said, going vague and bright and idiotic again, so as to escape: "Well, I don't see why not."

He was jerking his elbows up and down, in annoyance or in pain, and looking at him, she saw he had got thin, even gaunt; and restless angry movements were not what she remembered of him. He said: "Do you want a divorce, is that it?"

At this, Susan only with the greatest difficulty stopped herself from laughing: she could hear the bright bubbling laughter she *would* have emitted, had she let herself. He could only mean one thing: she had a lover, and that was why she spent her days in London, as lost to him as if she had vanished to another continent.

Then the small panic set in again: she understood that he hoped she did have a lover, he was begging her to say so, because otherwise it would be too terrifying.

She thought this out, as she brushed her hair, watching the fine black stuff fly up to make its little clouds of electricity, hiss, hiss, hiss. Behind her head, across the room, was a blue wall. She realised she was absorbed in watching the black hair making shapes against the blue. She should be answering him. "Do *you* want a divorce, Matthew?"

He said: "That surely isn't the point, is it?"

"You brought it up, I didn't," she said, brightly, suppressing meaningless tinkling laughter.

Next day she asked Fred: "Have enquiries been made for me?"

He hesitated, and she said: "I've been coming here a year now. I've made no trouble, and you've been paid every day. I have a right to be told."

"As a matter of fact, Mrs. Jones, a man did come asking."

"A man from a detective agency?"

"Well, he could have been, couldn't he?"

"I was asking you . . . . well, what did you tell him?"

"I told him a Mrs. Jones came every weekday from ten until five or six and stayed in Number Nineteen by herself."

"Describing me?"

"Well Mrs. Jones, I had no alternative. Put yourself in my place."

"By rights I should deduct what that man gave you for the information."

He raised shocked eyes: she was not the sort of person to make jokes like this! Then he chose to laugh: a pinkish wet slit appeared across his white crinkled face: his eyes positively begged her to laugh, otherwise he might lose some money. She remained grave, looking at him.

He stopped laughing and said: "You want to go up now?"—returning to the familiarity, the comradeship, of the country where no questions are asked, on which (and he knew it) she depended completely.

She went up to sit in her wicker chair. But it was not the same. Her husband had searched her out. (The world had searched her out.) The pressures were on her. She was here with his connivance. He might walk in at any moment, here, into Room 19. She imagined the report from the detective agency: "A woman calling herself Mrs. Jones, fitting the description of your wife (etc., etc., etc.), stays alone all day in Room No. 19. She insists on this room, waits for it if it is engaged. As far as the proprietor knows, she receives no visitors there, male or female." A report something on these lines, Matthew must have received.

Well of course he was right: things couldn't go on like this. He had put an end to it all simply by sending the detective after her.

She tried to shrink herself back into the shelter of the room, a snail pecked out of its shell and trying to squirm back. But the peace of the room had gone. She was trying consciously to revive it, trying to let go into the dark creative trance (or whatever it was) that she had found there. It was no use, yet she craved for it, she was as ill as a suddenly deprived addict.

Several times she returned to the room, to look for herself there, but instead she found the unnamed spirit of restlessness, a prickling fevered hunger for movement, an irritable self-consciousness that made her brain feel as if it had coloured lights going on and off inside it. Instead of the soft dark that had been the room's air, were now waiting for her demons that made her dash blindly about, muttering words of hate; she was impelling herself from point to point like a moth dashing itself against a windowpane, sliding to the bottom, fluttering off on broken wings, then crashing into the invisible barrier again. And again and again. Soon she was exhausted, and she told Fred that for a while she would not be needing the room, she was going on a holiday. Home she went, to the big white house by the river. The middle of a weekday, and she felt guilty at returning to her own home when not expected. She stood unseen, looking in at the kitchen window. Mrs. Parkes, wearing a discarded floral overall of Susan's, was stooping to slide something into the oven. Sophie, arms folded, was leaning her back against a cupboard and laughing at some joke made by a girl not seen before by Susan—a dark foreign girl, Sophie's visitor. In an arm-chair Molly, one of the twins, lay curled, sucking her thumb and watching the grownups. She must have some sickness, to be kept from school. The child's listless face, the dark circles under her eyes, hurt Susan: Molly was looking at the three grownups working and talking in exactly the same way Susan looked at the four through the kitchen window: she was remote, shut off from them.

But then, just as Susan imagined herself going in, picking up the little girl, and sitting in an armchair with her, stroking her probably heated forehead, Sophie did just that: she had been standing on one leg, the other knee flexed, its foot set against the wall. Now she let her foot in its ribbon-tied red shoe slide down the wall, stood solid on two feet, clapping her hands before and behind her, and sang a couple of lines in German, so that the child lifted her heavy eyes at her and began to smile. Then she walked, or rather skipped, over to the child, swung her up, and let her fall into her lap at the same moment she sat herself. She said "Hopla! Hopla! Molly . . ." and began stroking the dark untidy young head that Molly laid on her shoulder for comfort.

Well. . . . Susan blinked the tears of farewell out of her eyes, and went quietly up the house to her bedroom. There she sat looking at the river through the trees. She felt at peace, but in a way that was new to her. She had no desire to move, to talk, to do anything at all. The devils that had haunted the house, the garden, were not there; but she knew it was because her soul was in Room 19 in Fred's Hotel; she was not really here at all. It was a sensation that should have been frightening: to sit at her own bedroom window, listening to Sophie's rich young voice sing German nursery songs to her child, listening to Mrs. Parkes clatter and move below, and to know that all this had nothing to do with her: she was already out of it.

Later, she made herself go down and say she was home: it was unfair to be here unannounced. She took lunch with Mrs. Parkes, Sophie, Sophie's Italian friend Maria, and her daughter Molly, and felt like a visitor.

A few days later, at bedtime, Matthew said: "Here's your five pounds," and pushed them over at her. Yet he must have known she had not been leaving the house at all.

She shook her head, gave it back to him, and said, in explanation, not in accusation: "As soon as you knew where I was, there was no point."

He nodded, not looking at her. He was turned away from her: thinking, she knew, how best to handle this wife who terrified him.

He said: "I wasn't trying to . . . it's just that I was worried."

"Yes, I know."

"I must confess that I was beginning to wonder . . ."

"You thought I had a lover?"

"Yes, I am afraid I did."

She knew that he wished she had. She sat wondering how to say: "For a year now I've been spending all my days in a very sordid hotel room. It's the place where I'm happy. In fact, without it I don't exist." She heard herself saying this, and understood how terrified he was that she might. So instead she said: "Well, perhaps you're not far wrong."

Probably Matthew would think the hotel proprietor lied: he would want to think so.

"Well," he said, and she could hear his voice spring up, so to speak, with relief: "in that case I must confess I've got a bit of an affair on myself."

She said, detached and interested: "Really? Who is she?" and saw Matthew's startled look because of this reaction.

"It's Phil. Phil Hunt."

She had known Phil Hunt well in the old unmarried days. She was thinking: No, she won't do, she's too neurotic and difficult. She's never been happy yet. Sophie's much better: Well Matthew will see that himself, as sensible as he is.

This line of thought went on in silence, while she said aloud: "It's no point telling you about mine, because you don't know him."

Quick, quick, invent, she thought. Remember how you invented all that nonsense for Miss Townsend.

She began slowly, careful not to contradict herself: "His name is Michael"— (*Michael What?*)—"Michael Plant." (What a silly name!) "He's rather like you—in looks, I mean." And indeed, she could imagine herself being touched by no one but Matthew himself. "He's a publisher." (Really? Why?) "He's got a wife already and two children."

She brought out this fantasy, proud of herself.

Matthew said: "Are you two thinking of marrying?"

She said, before she could stop herself: "Good God, *no!*"

She realised, if Matthew wanted to marry Phil Hunt, that this was too emphatic, but apparently it was all right, for his voice sounded relieved as he said: "It is a bit impossible to imagine oneself married to anyone else, isn't it?" With which he pulled her to him, so that her head lay on his shoulder. She turned her face into the dark of his flesh, and listened to the blood pounding through her ears saying: I am alone, I am alone, I am alone.

In the morning Susan lay in bed while he dressed.

He had been thinking things out in the night, because now he said: "Susan, why don't we make a foursome?"

Of course, she said to herself, of course he would be bound to say that. If one is sensible, if one is reasonable, if one never allows oneself a base thought or an envious emotion, naturally one says: Let's make a foursome!

"Why not?" she said.

"We could all meet for lunch. I mean, it's ridiculous, you sneaking off to filthy hotels, and me staying late at the office, and all the lies everyone has to tell."

What on earth did I say his name was?—she panicked, then said: "I think it's a good idea, but Michael is away at the moment. When he comes back though—and I'm sure you two would like each other."

"He's away, is he? So that's why you've been . . ." Her husband put his hand to the knot of his tie in a gesture of male coquetry she would not before have associated with him; and he bent to kiss her cheek with the expression that goes with the words: Oh you naughty little puss! And she felt its answering look, naughty and coy, come onto her face.

Inside she was dissolving in horror at them both, at how far they had both sunk from honesty of emotion.

So now she was saddled with a lover, and he had a mistress! How ordinary, how reassuring, how jolly! And now they would make a foursome of it, and go about to theatres and restaurants. After all, the Rawlings could well afford that sort of thing, and presumably the publisher Michael Plant could afford to do himself and his mistress quite well. No, there was nothing to stop the four of them developing the most intricate relationship of civilised tolerance, all enveloped in a charming afterglow of autumnal passion. Perhaps they would all go off on holidays together? She had known people who did. Or perhaps Matthew would draw the line there? Why should he, though, if he was capable of talking about "foursomes" at all?

She lay in the empty bedroom, listening to the car drive off with Matthew in it, off to work. Then she heard the children clattering off to school to the accompaniment of Sophie's cheerfully ringing voice. She slid down into the hollow of the bed, for shelter against her own irrelevance. And she stretched out her hand to the hollow where her husband's body had lain, but found no comfort there: he was not her husband. She curled herself up in a small tight ball under the clothes: she could stay here all day, all week, indeed, all her life.

But in a few days she must produce Michael Plant, and—but how? She must presumably find some agreeable man prepared to impersonate a publisher called Michael Plant. And in return for which she would—what? Well, for one thing they would make love. The idea made her want to cry with sheer exhaustion. Oh no, she had finished with all that—the proof of it was that the words "make love," or even imagining it, trying hard to revive no more than the pleasures of sensuality, let alone affection, or love, made her want to run away and hide from the sheer effort of the thing. . . . Good Lord, why make love at all? Why make love with anyone? Or if you are going to make love, what does it matter who with? Why shouldn't she simply walk into the street, pick up a man and have a roaring sexual affair with him? Why not? Or even with Fred? What difference did it make?

But she had let herself in for it—an interminable stretch of time with a lover, called Michael, as part of a gallant civilised foursome. Well, she could not, and she would not.

She got up, dressed, went down to find Mrs. Parkes, and asked her for the loan of a pound, since Matthew, she said, had forgotten to leave her money. She exchanged with Mrs. Parkes variations on the theme that husbands are all the same, they don't think, and without saying a word to Sophie, whose voice could be heard upstairs from the telephone, walked to the underground, travelled to South Kensington, changed to the Inner Circle, got out at Paddington, and walked to Fred's Hotel. There she told Fred that she wasn't going on holiday after all, she needed the room. She would have to wait an hour, Fred said. She went to a busy tearoom-cum-restaurant around the corner, and sat watching the people flow in and out the door that kept swinging open and shut, watched them mingle and merge and separate, felt her being flow into them, into their movement. When the hour was up she left a half crown for her pot of tea, and left the place without looking back at it, just as she had left her house, the big, beautiful white house, without another look, but silently dedicating it to Sophie.

She returned to Fred, received the key of No. 19, now free, and ascended the grimy stairs slowly, letting floor after floor fall away below her, keeping her eyes lifted, so that floor after floor descended jerkily to her level of vision, and fell away out of sight.

No. 19 was the same. She saw everything with an acute, narrow, checking glance: the cheap shine of the satin spread, which had been replaced carelessly after the two bodies had finished their convulsions under it; a trace of powder on the glass that topped the chest of drawers; an intense green shade in a fold of the curtain. She stood at the window, looking down, watching people pass and pass and pass until her mind went dark from the constant movement. Then she sat in the wicker chair, letting herself go slack. But she had to be careful, because she did not want, today, to be surprised by Fred's knock at five o'clock.

The demons were not here. They had gone forever, because she was buying her freedom from them. She was slipping already into the dark fructifying dream that seemed to caress her inwardly, like the movement of her blood . . . but she had to think about Matthew first. Should she write a letter for the coroner? But what should she say? She would like to leave him with the look on his face she had seen this morning—banal, admittedly, but at least confidently healthy. Well, that was impossible, one did not look like that with a wife dead from suicide. But how to leave him believing she was dying because of a man— because of the fascinating publisher Michael Plant? Oh, how ridiculous! How absurd! How humiliating! But she decided not to trouble about it, simply not to think about the living. If he wanted to believe she had a lover, he would believe it. And he *did* want to believe it. Even when he had found out that there was no publisher in London called Michael Plant, he would think: Oh poor Susan, she was afraid to give me his real name.

And what did it matter whether he married Phil Hunt or Sophie? Though it ought to be Sophie, who was already the mother of those children . . . and what hypocrisy to sit here worrying about the children, when she was going to leave them because she had not got the energy to stay.

She had about four hours. She spent them delightfully, darkly, sweetly, letting herself slide gently, gently, to the edge of the river. Then, with hardly a break in her consciousness, she got up, pushed the thin rug against the door, made sure the windows were tight shut, put two shillings in the meter, and turned on the gas. For the first time since she had been in the room she lay on the hard bed that smelled stale, that smelled of sweat and sex.

She lay on her back on the green satin cover, but her legs were chilly. She got up, found a blanket folded in the bottom of the chest of drawers, and carefully covered her legs with it. She was quite content lying there, listening to the faint soft hiss of the gas that poured into the room, into her lungs, into her brain, as she drifted off into the dark river.

QUESTIONS

1. In what sense is the Rawlings's marriage "grounded in intelligence"? **2.** Are

the sources of Susan's growing discontent clear? Explain.   **3.**   Why does Matthew assume that Susan is having an affair? Why does Susan encourage him in this mistaken belief?   **4.**   In what sense is Susan's suicide a "failure in intelligence"?

WRITING TOPIC
Do you believe that Susan was justified in taking her own life? Explain.

How I Met My Husband

ALICE MUNRO [b. 1931]

We heard the plane come over at noon, roaring through the radio news, and we were sure it was going to hit the house, so we all ran out into the yard. We saw it come in over the tree tops, all red and silver, the first close-up plane I ever saw. Mrs. Peebles screamed.

"Crash landing," their little boy said. Joey was his name.

"It's okay," said Dr. Peebles. "He knows what he's doing." Dr. Peebles was only an animal doctor, but had a calming way of talking, like any doctor.

This was my first job—working for Dr. and Mrs. Peebles, who had bought an old house out on the Fifth Line, about five miles out of town. It was just when the trend was starting of town people buying up old farms, not to work them but to live on them.

We watched the plane land across the road, where the fairgrounds used to be. It did make a good landing field, nice and level for the old race track, and the barns and display sheds torn down now for scrap lumber so there was nothing in the way. Even the old grandstand boys had burned.

"All right," said Mrs. Peebles, snappy as she always was when she got over her nerves. "Let's go back in the house. Let's not stand here gawking like a set of farmers."

She didn't say that to hurt my feelings. It never occurred to her.

I was just setting the dessert down when Loretta Bird arrived, out of breath, at the screen door.

"I thought it was going to crash into the house and kill youse all!"

She lived on the next place and the Peebles thought she was a country-woman, they didn't know the difference. She and her husband didn't farm, he worked on the roads and had a bad name for drinking. They had seven children and couldn't get credit at the Hi-Way Grocery. The Peebles made her welcome, not knowing any better, as I say, and offered her dessert.

Dessert was never anything to write home about, at their place. A dish of Jello or sliced bananas or fruit out of a tin. "Have a house without a pie, be ashamed until you die," my mother used to say, but Mrs. Peebles operated differently.

Loretta Bird saw me getting the can of peaches.

"Oh, never mind," she said. "I haven't got the right kind of a stomach to trust what comes out of those tins, I can only eat home canning."

I could have slapped her. I bet she never put down fruit in her life.

"I know what he's landed here for," she said. "He's got permission to use the fairgrounds and take people up for rides. It costs a dollar. It's the same fellow who was over at Palmerston last week and was up the lakeshore before that. I wouldn't go up, if you paid me."

"I'd jump at the chance," Dr. Peebles said. "I'd like to see this neighborhood from the air."

Mrs. Peebles said she would just as soon see it from the ground. Joey said he wanted to go and Heather did, too. Joey was nine and Heather was seven.

"Would you, Edie?" Heather said.

I said I didn't know. I was scared, but I never admitted that, especially in front of children I was taking care of.

"People are going to be coming out here in their cars raising dust and trampling your property, if I was you I would complain," Loretta said. She hooked her legs around the chair rung and I knew we were in for a lengthy visit. After Dr. Peebles went back to his office or out on his next call and Mrs. Peebles went for her nap, she would hang around me while I was trying to do the dishes. She would pass remarks about the Peebles in their own house.

"She wouldn't find time to lay down in the middle of the day, if she had seven kids like I got."

She asked me did they fight and did they keep things in the dresser drawer not to have babies with. She said it was a sin if they did. I pretended I didn't know what she was talking about.

I was fifteen and away from home for the first time. My parents had made the effort and sent me to high school for a year, but I didn't like it. I was shy of strangers and the work was hard, they didn't make it nice for you or explain the way they do now. At the end of the year the averages were published in the paper, and mine came out at the very bottom, 37 per cent. My father said that's enough and I didn't blame him. The last thing I wanted, anyway, was to go on and end up teaching school. It happened the very day the paper came out with my disgrace in it, Dr. Peebles was staying at our place for dinner, having just helped one of our cows have twins, and he said I looked smart to him and his wife was looking for a girl to help. He said she felt tied down, with the two children, out in the country. I guess she would, my mother said, being polite, though I could tell from her face she was wondering what on earth it would be like to have only two children and no barn work, and then to be complaining.

When I went home I would describe to them the work I had to do, and it made everybody laugh. Mrs. Peebles had an automatic washer and dryer, the first I ever saw. I have had those in my own home for such a long time now it's hard to remember how much of a miracle it was to me, not having to struggle with the wringer and hang up and haul down. Let alone not having to heat water. Then there was practically no baking. Mrs. Peebles said she couldn't make pie crust, the most amazing thing I ever heard a woman admit. I could, of course, and I could make light biscuits and a white cake and a dark cake, but they didn't want it, she said they watched their figures. The only thing I didn't like about working there, in fact, was feeling half hungry a lot of the time. I used to bring back a box of doughnuts made out at home, and hide them under my bed. The children found out, and I didn't mind sharing, but I thought I better bind them to secrecy.

The day after the plane landed Mrs. Peebles put both children in the car and drove over to Chesley, to get their hair cut. There was a good woman then at Chesley for doing hair. She got hers done at the same place, Mrs. Peebles did, and that meant they would be gone a good while. She had to pick a day Dr. Peebles wasn't going out into the country, she didn't have her own car. Cars were still in short supply then, after the war.

I loved being left in the house alone, to do my work at leisure. The kitchen was all white and bright yellow, with fluorescent lights. That was before they ever thought of making the appliances all different colors and doing the cupboards like dark old wood and hiding the lighting. I loved light. I loved the double sink. So would anybody new-come from washing dishes in a dishpan with a rag-plugged hole on an oilcloth-covered table by light of a coal-oil lamp. I kept everything shining.

The bathroom too. I had a bath in there once a week. They wouldn't have minded if I took one oftener, but to me it seemed like asking too much, or maybe risking making it less wonderful. The basin and the tub and the toilet were all pink, and there were glass doors with flamingoes painted on them, to shut off the tub. The light had a rosy cast and the mat sank under your feet like snow, except that it was warm. The mirror was three-way. With the mirror all steamed up and the air like a perfume cloud, from things I was allowed to use, I stood up on the side of the tub and admired myself naked, from three directions. Sometimes I thought about the way we lived out at home and the way we lived here and how one way was so hard to imagine when you were living the other way. But I thought it was still a lot easier, living the way we lived at home, to picture something like this, the painted flamingoes and the warmth and the soft mat, than it was for anybody knowing only things like this to picture how it was the other way. And why was that?

I was through my jobs in no time, and had the vegetables peeled for supper and sitting in cold water besides. Then I went into Mrs. Peebles' bedroom. I had been in there plenty of times, cleaning, and I always took a good look in her closet, at the clothes she had hanging there. I wouldn't have looked in her drawers, but a closet is open to anybody. That's a lie. I would have looked in drawers, but I would have felt worse doing it and been more scared she could tell.

Some clothes in her closet she wore all the time, I was quite familiar with them. Others she never put on, they were pushed to the back. I was disappointed to see no wedding dress. But there was one long dress I could just see the skirt of, and I was hungering to see the rest. Now I took note of where it hung and lifted it out. It was satin, a lovely weight on my arm, light bluish-green in color, almost silvery. It had a fitted, pointed waist and a full skirt and an off-the-shoulder fold hiding the little sleeves.

Next thing was easy. I got out of my own things and slipped it on. I was slimmer at fifteen than anybody would believe who knows me now and the fit was beautiful. I didn't, of course, have a strapless bra on, which was what it needed, I just had to slide my straps down my arms under the material. Then I tried pinning up my hair, to get the effect. One thing led to another. I put on rouge and lipstick and eyebrow pencil from her dresser. The heat of the day and the weight of the satin and all the excitement made me thirsty, and I went out to the kitchen, got-up as I was, to get a glass of ginger ale with ice cubes from the refrigerator. The Peebles drank ginger ale, or fruit drinks, all day, like water, and I was getting so I did too. Also there was no limit on ice cubes, which I was so fond of I would even put them in a glass of milk.

I turned from putting the ice tray back and saw a man watching me through the screen. It was the luckiest thing in the world I didn't spill the ginger ale down the front of me then and there.

"I never meant to scare you. I knocked but you were getting the ice out, you didn't hear me."

I couldn't see what he looked like, he was dark the way somebody is pressed up against a screen door with the bright daylight behind them. I only knew he wasn't from around here.

"I'm from the plane over there. My name is Chris Watters and what I was wondering was if I could use that pump."

There was a pump in the yard. That was the way the people used to get their water. Now I noticed he was carrying a pail.

"You're welcome," I said. "I can get it from the tap and save you pumping." I guess I wanted him to know we had piped water, didn't pump ourselves.

"I don't mind the exercise." He didn't move, though, and finally he said, "Were you going to a dance?"

Seeing a stranger there had made me entirely forget how I was dressed.

"Or is that the way ladies around here generally get dressed up in the afternoon?"

I didn't know how to joke back then. I was too embarrassed.

"You live here? Are you the lady of the house?"

"I'm the hired girl."

Some people change when they find that out, their whole way of looking at you and speaking to you changes, but his didn't.

"Well, I just wanted to tell you you look very nice. I was so surprised when I looked in the door and saw you. Just because you looked so nice and beautiful."

I wasn't even old enough then to realize how out of the common it is, for a man to say something like that to a woman, or somebody he is treating like a woman. For a man to say a word like *beautiful*. I wasn't old enough to realize or to say anything back, or in fact to do anything but wish he would go away. Not that I didn't like him, but just that it upset me so, having him look at me, and me trying to think of something to say.

He must have understood. He said good-bye, and thanked me, and went and started filling his pail from the pump. I stood behind the Venetian blinds in the dining room, watching him. When he had gone, I went into the bedroom and took the dress off and put in back in the same place. I dressed in my own clothes and took my hair down and washed my face, wiping it on Kleenex, which I threw in the wastebasket.

The Peebles asked me what kind of man he was. Young, middle-aged, short, tall? I couldn't say.

"Good-looking?" Dr. Peebles teased me.

I couldn't think a thing but that he would be coming to get his water again, he would be talking to Dr. or Mrs. Peebles, making friends with them, and he would mention seeing me that first afternoon, dressed up. Why not mention it? He would think it was funny. And no idea of the trouble it would get me into.

After supper the Peebles drove into town to go to a movie. She wanted to go somewhere with her hair fresh done. I sat in my bright kitchen wondering what to do, knowing I would never sleep. Mrs. Peebles might not fire me, when she found out, but it would give her a different feeling about me altogether. This was the first place I ever worked but I already had picked up things about the way people feel when you are working for them. They like to think you aren't curious. Not just that you aren't dishonest, that isn't enough. They like to feel you don't notice things, that you don't think or wonder about anything but what they liked to eat and how they like things ironed, and so on. I don't mean they weren't kind to me, because they were. They had me eat my meals with them (to tell the truth I expected to, I didn't know there were families who don't) and sometimes they took me along in the car. But all the same.

I went up and checked on the children being asleep and then I went out. I had to do it. I crossed the road and went in the old fairgrounds gate. The plane looked unnatural sitting there, and shining with the moon. Off at the far side of the fairgrounds, where the bush was taking over, I saw his tent.

He was sitting outside it smoking a cigarette. He saw me coming.

"Hello, were you looking for a plane ride? I don't start taking people up till tomorrow." Then he looked again and said, "Oh, it's you. I didn't know you without your long dress on."

My heart was knocking away, my tongue was dried up. I had to say something. But I couldn't. My throat was closed and I was like a deaf-and-dumb.

"Did you want a ride? Sit down. Have a cigarette."

I couldn't even shake my head to say no, so he gave me one.

"Put it in your mouth or I can't light it. It's a good thing I'm used to shy ladies."

I did. It wasn't the first time I had smoked a cigarette, actually. My girl friend out home, Muriel Lowe, used to steal them from her brother.

"Look at your hand shaking. Did you just want to have a chat, or what?"

In one burst I said, "I wisht you wouldn't say anything about that dress."

"What dress? Oh, the long dress."

"It's Mrs. Peebles'."

"Whose? Oh, the lady you work for? Is that it? She wasn't home so you got dressed up in her dress, eh? You got dressed up and played queen. I don't blame you. You're not smoking that cigarette right. Don't just puff. Draw it in. Did nobody ever show you how to inhale? Are you scared I'll tell on you? Is that it?"

I was so ashamed at having to ask him to connive this way I couldn't nod. I just looked at him and he saw *yes*.

"Well I won't. I won't in the slightest way mention it or embarrass you. I give you my word of honor."

Then he changed the subject, to help me out, seeing I couldn't even thank him.

"What do you think of this sign?"

It was a board sign lying practically at my feet.

SEE THE WORLD FROM THE SKY. ADULTS $1.00, CHILDREN 50¢. QUALIFIED PILOT.

"My old sign was getting pretty beat up, I thought I'd make a new one. That's what I've been doing with my time today."

The lettering wasn't all that handsome, I thought. I could have done a better one in half an hour.

"I'm not an expert at sign making."

"It's very good," I said.

"I don't need it for publicity, word of mouth is usually enough. I turned away two carloads tonight. I felt like taking it easy. I didn't tell them ladies were dropping in to visit me."

Now I remembered the children and I was scared again, in case one of them had waked up and called me and I wasn't there.

"Do you have to go so soon?"

I remembered some manners. "Thank you for the cigarette."

"Don't forget. You have my word of honor."

I tore off across the fairgrounds, scared I'd see the car heading home from town. My sense of time was mixed up, I didn't know how long I'd been out of the house. But it was all right, it wasn't late, the children were asleep. I got in bed myself and lay thinking what a lucky end to the day, after all, and among things to be grateful for I could be grateful Loretta Bird hadn't been the one who caught me.

The yard and borders didn't get trampled, it wasn't as bad as that. All the same it seemed very public, around the house. The sign was on the fairgrounds gate. People came mostly after supper but a good many in the afternoon, too. The Bird children all came without fifty cents between them and hung on the gate. We got used to the excitement of the plane coming in and taking off, it wasn't excitement any more. I never went over, after that one time, but would see him when he came to get his water. I would be out on the steps doing sitting-down work, like preparing vegetables, if I could.

"Why don't you come over? I'll take you up in my plane."

"I'm saving my money," I said, because I couldn't think of anything else.

"For what? For getting married?"

I shook my head.

"I'll take you up for free if you come sometime when it's slack. I thought you would come, and have another cigarette."

I made a face to hush him, because you never could tell when the children would be sneaking around the porch, or Mrs. Peebles herself listening in the house. Sometimes she came out and had a conversation with him. He told her things he hadn't bothered to tell me. But then I hadn't thought to ask. He told her he had been in the War, that was where he learned to fly a plane, and now he couldn't settle down to ordinary life, this was what he liked. She said she couldn't imagine anybody liking such a thing. Though sometimes, she said, she was almost bored enough to try anything herself, she wasn't brought up to living in the country. It's all my husband's idea, she said. This was news to me.

"Maybe you ought to give flying lessons," she said.

"Would you take them?"

She just laughed.

Sunday was a busy flying day in spite of it being preached against from two pulpits. We were all sitting out watching. Joey and Heather were over on the fence with the Bird kids. Their father had said they could go, after their mother saying all week they couldn't.

A car came down the road past the parked cars and pulled up right in the drive. It was Loretta Bird who got out, all importance, and on the driver's side another woman got out, more sedately. She was wearing sunglasses.

"This is a lady looking for the man that flies the plane," Loretta Bird said. "I heard her inquire in the hotel coffee shop where I was having a Coke and I brought her out."

"I'm sorry to bother you," the lady said. "I'm Alice Kelling, Mr. Watters' fiancée."

This Alice Kelling had on a pair of brown and white checked slacks and a yellow top. Her bust looked to me rather low and bumpy. She had a worried face. Her hair had had a permanent, but had grown out, and she wore a yellow band to keep it off her face. Nothing in the least pretty or even young-looking about her. But you could tell from how she talked she was from the city, or educated, or both.

Dr. Peebles stood up and introduced himself and his wife and me and asked her to be seated.

"He's up in the air right now, but you're welcome to sit and wait. He gets his water here and he hasn't been yet. He'll probably take his break about five."

"That is him, then?" said Alice Kelling, wrinkling and straining at the sky.

"He's not in the habit of running out on you, taking a different name?" Dr. Peebles laughed. He was the one, not his wife, to offer iced tea. Then she sent me into the kitchen to fix it. She smiled. She was wearing sunglasses too.

"He never mentioned his fiancée," she said.

I loved fixing iced tea with lots of ice and slices of lemon in tall glasses. I ought to have mentioned before, Dr. Peebles was an abstainer, at least around the house, or I wouldn't have been allowed to take the place. I had to fix a glass for Loretta Bird too, though it galled me, and when I went out she had settled in my lawn chair, leaving me the steps.

"I knew you was a nurse when I first heard you in that coffee shop."

"How would you know a thing like that?"

"I get my hunches about people. Was that how you met him, nursing?"

"Chris? Well yes. Yes, it was."

"Oh, were you overseas?" said Mrs. Peebles.

"No, it was before he went overseas. I nursed him when he was stationed at Centralia and had a ruptured appendix. We got engaged and then he went overseas. My, this is refreshing, after a long drive."

"He'll be glad to see you," Dr. Peebles said. "It's a rackety kind of life, isn't it, not staying one place long enough to really make friends."

"Youse've had a long engagement," Loretta Bird said.

Alice Kelling passed that over. "I was going to get a room at the hotel, but when I was offered directions I came on out. Do you think I could phone them?"

"No need," Dr. Peebles said. "You're five miles away from him if you stay at the hotel. Here, you're right across the road. Stay with us. We've got rooms on rooms, look at this big house."

Asking people to stay, just like that, is certainly a country thing, and maybe seemed natural to him now, but not to Mrs. Peebles, from the way she said, oh yes, we have plenty of room. Or to Alice Kelling, who kept protesting, but let herself be worn down. I got the feeling it was a temptation to her, to be that close. I was trying for a look at her ring. Her nails were painted red, her fingers were freckled and wrinkled. It was a tiny stone. Muriel Lowe's cousin had one twice as big.

Chris came to get his water, late in the afternoon just as Dr. Peebles had predicted. He must have recognized the car from a way off. He came smiling.

"Here I am chasing after you to see what you're up to," called Alice Kelling. She got up and went to meet him and they kissed, just touched, in front of us.

"You're going to spend a lot on gas that way," Chris said.

Dr. Peebles invited Chris to stay for supper, since he had already put up the sign that said: NO MORE RIDES TILL 7 P.M. Mrs. Peebles wanted it served in the yard, in spite of bugs. One thing strange to anybody from the country is this eating outside. I had made a potato salad earlier and she had made a jellied salad, that was one thing she could do, so it was just a matter of getting those out, and some sliced meat and cucumbers and fresh leaf lettuce. Loretta Bird hung around for some time saying, "Oh, well, I guess I better get home to those yappers," and, "It's so nice just sitting here, I sure hate to get up," but nobody invited her, I was relieved to see, and finally she had to go.

That night after rides were finished Alice Kelling and Chris went off somewhere in her car. I lay awake till they got back. When I saw the car lights sweep my ceiling I got up to look down on them through the slats of my blind. I don't know what I thought I was going to see. Muriel Lowe and I used to sleep on her front veranda and watch her sister and her sister's boy friend saying good night. Afterwards we couldn't get to sleep, for longing for somebody to kiss us and rub up against us and we would talk about suppose you were out in a boat with a boy and he wouldn't bring you in to shore unless you did it, or what if somebody got you trapped in a barn, you would have to, wouldn't you, it wouldn't be your fault. Muriel said two girl cousins used to try with a toilet paper roll that one of them was the boy. We wouldn't do anything like that; just lay and wondered.

All that happened was that Chris got out of the car on one side and she got out on the other and they walked off separately—him towards the fairgrounds and her towards the house. I got back in bed and imagined about me coming home with him, not like that.

Next morning Alice Kelling got up late and I fixed a grapefruit for her the way I had learned and Mrs. Peebles sat down with her to visit and have another cup of coffee. Mrs. Peebles seemed pleased enough now, having company. Alice Kelling said she guessed she better get used to putting in a day just watching Chris take off and come down, and Mrs. Peebles said she didn't know if she should suggest it because Alice Kelling was the one with the car, but the lake was only twenty-five miles away and what a good day for a picnic.

Alice Kelling took her up on the idea and by eleven o'clock they were in the car, with Joey and Heather and a sandwich lunch I had made. The only thing was that Chris hadn't come down, and she wanted to tell him where they were going.

"Edie'll go over and tell him," Mrs. Peebles said. "There's no problem."

Alice Kelling wrinkled her face and agreed.

"Be sure and tell him we'll be back by five!"

I didn't see that he would be concerned about knowing this right away, and I thought of him eating whatever he ate over there, alone, cooking on his camp stove, so I got to work and mixed up a crumb cake and baked it, in between the other work I had to do; then, when it was a bit cooled, wrapped it in a tea towel. I didn't do anything to myself but take off my apron and comb my hair. I would like to have put some make-up on, but I was too afraid it would remind him of the way he first saw me, and that would humiliate me all over again.

He had come and put another sign on the gate: NO RIDES THIS P.M. APOLOGIES. I worried that he wasn't feeling well. No sign of him outside and the tent flap was down. I knocked on the pole.

"Come in," he said, in a voice that would just as soon have said *Stay out*.

I lifted the flap.

"Oh, it's you. I'm sorry. I didn't know it was you."

He had been just sitting on the side of the bed, smoking. Why not at least sit and smoke in the fresh air?

"I brought a cake and hope you're not sick," I said.

"Why would I be sick? Oh—that sign. That's all right. I'm just tired of talking to people. I don't mean you. Have a seat." He pinned back the tent flap. "Get some fresh air in here."

I sat on the edge of the bed, there was no place else. It was one of those fold-up cots, really: I remembered and gave him his fiancée's message.

He ate some of the cake. "Good."

"Put the rest away for when you're hungry later."

"I'll tell you a secret. I won't be around here much longer."

"Are you getting married?"

"Ha ha. What time did you say they'd be back?"

"Five o'clock."

"Well, by that time this place will have seen the last of me. A plane can get further than a car." He unwrapped the cake and ate another piece of it, absentmindedly.

"Now you'll be thirsty."

"There's some water in the pail."

"It won't be very cold. I could bring some fresh. I could bring some ice from the refrigerator."

"No," he said. "I don't want you to go. I want a nice long time of saying good-bye to you."

He put the cake away carefully and sat beside me and started those little kisses, so soft, I can't ever let myself think about them, such kindness in his face and lovely kisses, all over my eyelids and neck and ears, all over, then me kissing back as well as I could (I had only kissed a boy on a dare before, and kissed my own arms for practice) and we lay back on the cot and pressed together, just gently, and he did some other things, not bad things or not in a bad way. It was lovely in the tent, that smell of grass and hot tent cloth with the sun beating down on it, and he said, "I wouldn't do you any harm for the world." Once, when he had rolled on top of me and we were sort of rocking together on the cot, he said softly, "Oh, no," and freed himself and jumped up and got the water pail. He splashed some of it on his neck and face, and the little bit left, on me lying there.

"That's to cool us off, Miss."

When we said good-bye I wasn't at all sad, because he held my face and said "I'm going to write you a letter. I'll tell you where I am and maybe you can come and see me. Would you like that? Okay then. You wait." I was really glad I think to get away from him, it was like he was piling presents on me I couldn't get the pleasure of till I considered them alone.

No consternation at first about the plane being gone. They thought he had taken somebody up, and I didn't enlighten them. Dr. Peebles had phoned he had to go to the country, so there was just us having supper, and then Loretta Bird thrusting her head in the door and saying, "I see he's took off."

"What?" said Alice Kelling, and pushed back her chair.

"The kids come and told me this afternoon he was taking down his tent. Did he think he'd run through all the business there was around here? He didn't take off without letting you know, did he?"

"He'll send me word," Alice Kelling said. "He'll probably phone tonight. He's terribly restless, since the War."

"Edie, he didn't mention to you, did he?" Mrs. Peebles said. "When you took over the message?"

"Yes," I said. So far so true.

"Well why didn't you say?" All of them were looking at me. "Did he say where he was going?"

"He said he might try Bayfield," I said. What made me tell such a lie? I didn't intend it.

"Bayfield, how far is that?" said Alice Kelling.

Mrs. Peebles said, "Thirty, thirty-five miles."

"That's not far. Oh, well, that's really not far at all. It's on the lake, isn't it?"

You'd think I'd be ashamed of myself, setting her on the wrong track. I did it to give him more time, whatever time he needed. I lied for him, and also, I have to admit, for me. Women should stick together and not do things like that. I see that now, but didn't then. I never thought of myself as being in any way like her, or coming to the same troubles, ever.

She hadn't taken her eyes off me. I thought she suspected my lie.

"When did he mention this to you?"

"Earlier."

"When you were over at the plane?"

"Yes."

"You must've stayed and had a chat." She smiled at me, not a nice smile. "You must've stayed and had a little visit with him."

"I took a cake," I said, thinking that telling some truth would spare me telling the rest.

"We didn't have a cake," said Mrs. Peebles rather sharply.

"I baked one."

Alice Kelling said, "That was very friendly of you."

"Did you get permission," said Loretta Bird. "You never know what these girls'll do next," she said. "It's not they mean harm so much, as they're ignorant."

"The cake is neither here nor there," Mrs. Peebles broke in. "Edie, I wasn't aware you knew Chris that well."

I didn't know what to say.

"I'm not surprised," Alice Kelling said in a high voice. "I knew by the look of her as soon as I saw her. We get them at the hospital all the time." She looked hard at me with her stretched smile. "Having their babies. We have to put them in a special ward because of their diseases. Little country tramps. Fourteen and fifteen years old. You should see the babies they have, too."

"There was a bad woman here in town had a baby that pus was running out of its eyes," Loretta Bird put in.

"Wait a minute," said Mrs. Peebles. "What is this talk? Edie. What about you and Mr. Watters? Were you intimate with him?"

"Yes," I said. I was thinking of us lying on the cot and kissing, wasn't that intimate? And I would never deny it.

They were all one minute quiet, even Loretta Bird.

"Well," said Mrs. Peebles. "I am surprised. I think I need a cigarette. This is the first of any such tendencies I've seen in her," she said, speaking to Alice Kelling, but Alice Kelling was looking at me.

"Loose little bitch." Tears ran down her face. "Loose little bitch, aren't you? I knew as soon as I saw you. Men despise girls like you. He just made use of you and went off, you know that, don't you? Girls like you are just nothing, they're just public conveniences, just filthy little rags!"

"Oh, now," said Mrs. Peebles.

"Filthy," Alice Kelling sobbed. "Filthy little rag!"

"Don't get yourself upset," Loretta Bird said. She was swollen up with pleasure at being in on this scene. "Men are all the same."

"Edie, I'm very surprised," Mrs. Peebles said. "I thought your parents were so strict. You don't want to have a baby, do you?"

I'm still ashamed of what happened next. I lost control, just like a six-year-old, I started howling. "You don't get a baby from just doing that!"

"You see. Some of them are that ignorant," Loretta Bird said.

But Mrs. Peebles jumped up and caught my arms and shook me.

"Calm down. Don't get hysterical. Calm down. Stop crying. Listen to me. Listen. I'm wondering, if you know what being intimate means. Now tell me. What did you think it meant?"

"Kissing," I howled.

She let go. "Oh, Edie. Stop it. Don't be silly. It's all right. It's all a misunderstanding. Being intimate means a lot more than that. Oh, I *wondered*."

"She's trying to cover up, now," said Alice Kelling. "Yes. She's not so stupid. She sees she got herself in trouble."

"I believe her," Mrs. Peebles said. "This is an awful scene."

"Well there is one way to find out," said Alice Kelling, getting up. "After all, I am a nurse."

Mrs. Peebles drew a breath and said, "No. No. Go to your room, Edie. And stop that noise. That is too disgusting."

I heard the car start in a little while. I tried to stop crying, pulling back each wave as it started over me. Finally I succeeded, and lay heaving on the bed.

Mrs. Peebles came and stood in the doorway.

"She's gone," she said. "That Bird woman too. Of course, you know you should never have gone near that man and that is the cause of all this trouble. I have a headache. As soon as you can, go and wash your face in cold water and get at the dishes and we will not say any more about this."

Nor we didn't. I didn't figure out till years later the extent of what I had been saved from. Mrs. Peebles was not very friendly to me afterwards, but she was fair. Not very friendly is the wrong way of describing what she was. She never had been very friendly. It was just that now she had to see me all the time and it got on her nerves, a little.

As for me, I put it all out of my mind like a bad dream and concentrated on waiting for my letter. The mail came every day except Sunday, between one-thirty and two in the afternoon, a good time for me because Mrs. Peebles was always having her nap. I would get the kitchen all cleaned and then go up to the mailbox and sit in the grass, waiting. I was perfectly happy, waiting, I forgot all about Alice Kelling and her misery and awful talk and Mrs. Peebles and her chilliness and the embarrassment of whether she had told Dr. Peebles and the face of Loretta Bird, getting her fill of other people's troubles. I was always smiling when the mailman got there, and continued smiling even after he gave me the mail and I saw today wasn't the day. The mailman was a Carmichael. I knew by his face because there are a lot of Carmichaels living out by us and so many of them have a sort of sticking-out top lip. So I asked his name (he was a young man, shy, but good humored, anybody could ask him anything) and then I said, "I knew by your face!" He was pleased by that and always glad to see me and got a little less shy. "You've got the smile I've been waiting on all day!" he used to holler out the car window.

It never crossed my mind for a long time a letter might not come. I believed in it coming just like I believed the sun would rise in the morning. I just put off my hope from day to day, and there was the goldenrod out around the mailbox and the children gone back to school, and the leaves turning, and I was wearing a sweater when I went to wait. One day walking back with the hydro bill stuck in my hand, that was all, looking across at the fairgrounds with the full-blown milkweed and dark teasels, so much like fall, it just struck me: *No letter was ever going to come.* It was an impossible idea to get used to. No, not impossible. If I thought about Chris's face when he said he was going to write to me, it was impossible, but if I forgot that and thought about the actual tin mailbox, empty, it was plain and true. I kept on going to meet the mail, but my heart was heavy now like a lump of lead. I only smiled because I thought of the mailman counting on it, and he didn't have an easy life, with the winter driving ahead.

Till it came to me one day there were women doing this with their lives, all over. There were women just waiting and waiting by mailboxes for one letter or another. I imagined me making this journey day after day and year after year, and my hair starting to go gray, and I thought, I was never made to go on like that. So I stopped meeting the mail. If there were women all through life waiting, and women busy and not waiting, I knew which I had to be. Even though there might be things the second kind of women have to pass up and never know about, it still is better.

I was surprised when the mailman phoned the Peebles' place in the evening and asked for me. He said he missed me. He asked if I would like to go to Goderich where some well-known movie was on, I forget now what. So I said yes, and I went out with him for two years and he asked me to marry him, and we were engaged a year more while I got my things together, and then we did marry. He always tells the children the story of how I went after him by sitting by the mailbox every day, and naturally I laugh and let him, because I like for people to think what pleases them and makes them happy.

Shiloh[1]

BOBBIE ANN MASON [b. 1940]

1982

Leroy Moffitt's wife, Norma Jean, is working on her pectorals. She lifts three-pound dumbbells to warm up, then progresses to a twenty-pound barbell. Standing with her legs apart, she reminds Leroy of Wonder Woman.

"I'd give anything if I could just get these muscles to where they're real hard," says Norma Jean. "Feel this arm. It's not as hard as the other one."

"That's 'cause you're right-handed," says Leroy, dodging as she swings the barbell in an arc.

"Do you think so?"

"Sure."

Leroy is a truckdriver. He injured his leg in a highway accident four months ago, and his physical therapy, which involves weights and a pulley, prompted Norma Jean to try building herself up. Now she is attending a body-building class. Leroy has been collecting temporary disability since his tractor-trailer jackknifed in Missouri, badly twisting his left leg in its socket. He has a steel pin in his hip. He will probably not be able to drive his rig again. It sits in the backyard, like a gigantic bird that has flown home to roost. Leroy has been home in Kentucky for three months, and his leg is almost healed, but the accident frightened him and he does not want to drive any more long hauls. He is not sure what to do next. In the meantime, he makes things from craft kits. He started by building a miniature log cabin from notched Popsicle sticks. He varnished it and placed it on the TV set, where it remains. It reminds him of a rustic Nativity scene. Then he tried string art (sailing ships on black velvet), a macramé owl kit, a snap-together B-17 Flying Fortress, and a lamp made out of a model truck, with a light fixture screwed in the top of the cab. At first the kits were diversions, something to kill time, but now he is thinking about building a full-scale log house from a kit. It would be considerably cheaper than building a regular house, and besides, Leroy has grown to appreciate how things are put together. He has begun to realize that in all the years he was on the road he never took time to examine anything. He was always flying past scenery.

"They won't let you build a log cabin in any of the new subdivisions," Norma Jean tells him.

"They will if I tell them it's for you," he says, teasing her. Ever since they were married, he has promised Norma Jean he would build her a new home one day. They have always rented, and the house they live in is small and nondescript. It does not even feel like a home, Leroy realizes now.

Norma Jean works at the Rexall drugstore, and she has acquired an amazing

---

[1] Scene in southwest Tennessee of a Union victory during the Civil War; now a national military park. Shiloh, which means "tranquillity" or "rest," is also the name of a sacred place in the Old Testament.

amount of information about cosmetics. When she explains to Leroy the three stages of complexion care, involving creams, toners, and moisturizers, he thinks happily of other petroleum products—axle grease, diesel fuel. This is a connection between him and Norma Jean. Since he has been home, he has felt unusually tender about his wife and guilty over his long absences. But he can't tell what she feels about him. Norma Jean has never complained about his traveling; she has never made hurt remarks, like calling his truck a "widow-maker." He is reasonably certain she has been faithful to him, but he wishes she would celebrate his permanent homecoming more happily. Norma Jean is often startled to find Leroy at home, and he thinks she seems a little disappointed about it. Perhaps he reminds her too much of the early days of their marriage, before he went on the road. They had a child who died as an infant, years ago. They never speak about their memories of Randy, which have almost faded, but now that Leroy is home all the time, they sometimes feel awkward around each other, and Leroy wonders if one of them should mention the child. He has the feeling that they are waking up out of a dream together— that they must create a new marriage, start afresh. They are lucky they are still married. Leroy has read that for most people losing a child destroys the marriage—or else he heard this on *Donahue*. He can't always remember where he learns things anymore.

At Christmas, Leroy bought an electric organ for Norma Jean. She used to play the piano when she was in high school. "It don't leave you," she told him once. "It's like riding a bicycle."

The new instrument had so many keys and buttons that she was bewildered by it at first. She touched the keys tentatively, pushed some buttons, then pecked out "Chopsticks." It came out in an amplified fox-trot rhythm, with marimba sounds.

"It's an orchestra!" she cried.

The organ had a pecan-look finish and eighteen preset chords, with optional flute, violin, trumpet, clarinet, and banjo accompaniments. Norma Jean mastered the organ almost immediately. At first she played Christmas songs. Then she bought *The Sixties Songbook* and learned every tune in it, adding variations to each with the rows of brightly colored buttons.

"I didn't like these old songs back then," she said. "But I have this crazy feeling I missed something."

"You didn't miss a thing," said Leroy.

Leroy likes to lie on the couch and smoke a joint and listen to Norma Jean play "Can't Take My Eyes Off You" and "I'll Be Back." He is back again. After fifteen years on the road, he is finally settling down with the woman he loves. She is still pretty. Her skin is flawless. Her frosted curls resemble pencil trimmings.

Now that Leroy has come home to stay, he notices how much the town has changed. Subdivisions are spreading across western Kentucky like an oil slick. The sign at the edge of town says "Pop: 11,500"—only seven hundred more than it said twenty years before. Leroy can't figure out who is living in all the new houses. The farmers who used to gather around the courthouse square on Saturday afternoons to play checkers and spit tobacco juice have gone. It has been years since Leroy has thought about the farmers, and they have disappeared without his noticing.

Leroy meets a kid named Stevie Hamilton in the parking lot at the new shopping center. While they pretend to be strangers meeting over a stalled car, Stevie tosses an ounce of marijuana under the front seat of Leroy's car. Stevie is wearing orange jogging shoes and a T-shirt that says CHATTAHOOCHEE SUPER-RAT. His father is a prominent doctor who lives in one of the expensive subdivisions in a new white-columned brick house that looks like a funeral parlor. In the phone book under his name there is a separate number, with the listing "Teenagers."

"Where do you get this stuff?" asks Leroy. "From your pappy?"

"That's for me to know and you to find out," Stevie says. He is slit-eyed and skinny.

"What else you got?"

"What you interested in?"

"Nothing special. Just wondered."

Leroy used to take speed on the road. Now he has to go slowly. He needs to be mellow. He leans back against the car and says, "I'm aiming to build me a log house, soon as I get time. My wife, though, I don't think she likes the idea."

"Well, let me know when you want me again," Stevie says. He has a cigarette in his cupped palm, as though sheltering it from the wind. He takes a long drag, then stomps it on the asphalt and slouches away.

Stevie's father was two years ahead of Leroy in high school. Leroy is thirty-four. He married Norma Jean when they were both eighteen, and their child Randy was born a few months later, but he died at the age of four months and three days. He would be about Stevie's age now. Norma Jean and Leroy were at the drive-in, watching a double feature (*Dr. Strangelove* and *Lover Come Back*), and the baby was sleeping in the back seat. When the first movie ended, the baby was dead. It was the sudden infant death syndrome. Leroy remembers handing Randy to a nurse at the emergency room, as though he were offering her a large doll as a present. A dead baby feels like a sack of flour. "It just happens sometimes," said the doctor, in what Leroy always recalls as a nonchalant tone. Leroy can hardly remember the child anymore, but he still sees vividly a scene from *Dr. Strangelove* in which the President of the United States was talking in a folksy voice on the hot line to the Soviet premier about the bomber accidentally headed toward Russia. He was in the War Room, and the world map was lit up. Leroy remembers Norma Jean standing catatonically beside him in the hospital and himself thinking: Who is this strange girl? He had forgotten who she was. Now scientists are saying that crib death is caused by a virus. Nobody knows anything, Leroy thinks. The answers are always changing.

When Leroy gets home from the shopping center, Norma Jean's mother, Mabel Beasley, is there. Until this year, Leroy has not realized how much time she spends with Norma Jean. When she visits, she inspects the closets and then the plants, informing Norma Jean when a plant is droopy or yellow. Mabel calls the plants "flowers," although there are never any blooms. She always notices if Norma Jean's laundry is piling up. Mabel is a short, overweight woman whose tight, brown-dyed curls look more like a wig than the actual wig she sometimes wears. Today she has brought Norma Jean an off-white dust ruffle she made for the bed; Mabel works in a custom-upholstery shop.

"This is the tenth one I made this year," Mabel says. "I got started and couldn't stop."

"It's real pretty," says Norma Jean.

"Now we can hide things under the bed," says Leroy, who gets along with his mother-in-law primarily by joking with her. Mabel has never really forgiven him for disgracing her by getting Norma Jean pregnant. When the baby died, she said that fate was mocking her.

"What's that thing?" Mabel says to Leroy in a loud voice, pointing to a tangle of yarn on a piece of canvas.

Leroy holds it up for Mabel to see. "It's my needlepoint," he explains. "This is a *Star Trek* pillow cover."

"That's what a woman would do," says Mabel. "Great day in the morning!"

"All the big football players on TV do it," he says.

"Why, Leroy, you're always trying to fool me. I don't believe you for one minute. You don't know what to do with yourself—that's the whole trouble. Sewing!"

"I'm aiming to build us a log house," says Leroy. "Soon as my plans come."

"Like *heck* you are," says Norma Jean. She takes Leroy's needlepoint and shoves it into a drawer. "You have to find a job first. Nobody can afford to build now anyway."

Mabel straightens her girdle and says, "I still think before you get tied down y'all ought to take a little run to Shiloh."

"One of these days, Mama," Norma Jean says impatiently.

Mabel is talking about Shiloh, Tennessee. For the past few years, she has been urging Leroy and Norma Jean to visit the Civil War battleground there. Mabel went there on her honeymoon—the only real trip she ever took. Her husband died of a perforated ulcer when Norma Jean was ten, but Mabel, who was accepted into the United Daughters of the Confederacy in 1975, is still preoccupied with going back to Shiloh.

"I've been to kingdom come and back in that truck out yonder," Leroy says to Mabel, "but we never yet set foot in that battleground. Ain't that something? How did I miss it?"

"It's not even that far," Mabel says.

After Mabel leaves, Norma Jean reads to Leroy from a list she has made. "Things you could do," she announces. "You could get a job as a guard at Union Carbide, where they'd let you set on a stool. You could get on at the lumberyard. You could do a little carpenter work, if you want to build so bad. You could—"

"I can't do something where I'd have to stand up all day."

"You ought to try standing up all day behind a cosmetics counter. It's amazing that I have strong feet, coming from two parents that never had strong feet at all." At the moment Norma Jean is holding on to the kitchen counter, raising her knees one at a time as she talks. She is wearing two-pound ankle weights.

"Don't worry," says Leroy. "I'll do something."

"You could truck calves to slaughter for somebody. You wouldn't have to drive any big old truck for that."

"I'm going to build you this house," says Leroy. "I want to make you a real home."

"I don't want to live in any log cabin."

"It's not a cabin. It's a house."

"I don't care. It looks like a cabin."

"You and me together could lift those logs. It's just like lifting weights."

Norma Jean doesn't answer. Under her breath, she is counting. Now she is marching through the kitchen. She is doing goose steps.

Before his accident, when Leroy came home he used to stay in the house with Norma Jean, watching TV in bed and playing cards. She would cook fried chicken, picnic ham, chocolate pie—all his favorites. Now he is home alone much of the time. In the mornings, Norma Jean disappears, leaving a cooling place in the bed. She eats a cereal called Body Buddies, and she leaves the bowl on the table, with the soggy tan balls floating in a milk puddle. He sees things about Norma Jean that he never realized before. When she chops onions, she stares off into a corner, as if she can't bear to look. She puts on her house slippers almost precisely at nine o'clock every evening and nudges her jogging shoes under the couch. She saves bread heels for the birds. Leroy watches the birds at the feeder. He notices the peculiar way goldfinches fly past the window. They close their wings, then fall, then spread their wings to catch and lift themselves. He wonders if they close their eyes when they fall. Norma Jean closes her eyes when they are in bed. She wants the lights turned out. Even then, he is sure she closes her eyes.

He goes for long drives around town. He tends to drive a car rather carelessly. Power steering and an automatic shift make a car feel so small and inconsequential that his body is hardly involved in the driving process. His injured leg stretches out comfortably. Once or twice he has almost hit something, but even the prospect of an accident seems minor in a car. He cruises the new subdivisions, feeling like a criminal rehearsing for a robbery. Norma Jean is probably right about a log house being inappropriate here in the new subdivisions. All the houses look grand and complicated. They depress him.

One day when Leroy comes home from a drive he finds Norma Jean in tears. She is in the kitchen making a potato and mushroom-soup casserole, with grated-cheese topping. She is crying because her mother caught her smoking.

"I didn't hear her coming. I was standing here puffing away pretty as you please," Norma Jean says, wiping her eyes.

"I knew it would happen sooner or later," says Leroy, putting his arm around her.

"She don't know the meaning of the word 'knock,' " says Norma Jean. "It's a wonder she hadn't caught me years ago."

"Think of it this way," Leroy says. "What if she caught me with a joint?"

"You better not let her!" Norma Jean shrieks. "I'm warning you, Leroy Moffitt!"

"I'm just kidding. Here, play me a tune. That'll help you relax."

Norma Jean puts the casserole in the oven and sets the timer. Then she plays a ragtime tune, with horns and banjo, as Leroy lights up a joint and lies on the couch, laughing to himself about Mabel's catching him at it. He thinks of Stevie Hamilton—a doctor's son pushing grass. Everything is funny. The whole town seems crazy and small. He is reminded of Virgil Mathis, a boastful policeman Leroy used to shoot pool with. Virgil recently led a drug bust in a back room at a bowling alley, where he seized ten thousand dollars' worth of marijuana. The newspaper had a picture of him holding up the bags of grass and grinning widely. Right now, Leroy can imagine Virgil breaking down the door and arresting him with a lungful of smoke. Virgil would probably have been alerted to the scene because of all the racket Norma Jean is making. Now she sounds like a hard-rock band. Norma Jean is terrific. When she switches to a Latin-rhythm version of "Sunshine Superman," Leroy hums along. Norma Jean's foot goes up and down, up and down.

"Well, what do you think?" Leroy says, when Norma Jean pauses to search through her music.

"What do I think about what?"

His mind has gone blank. Then he says, "I'll sell my rig and build us a house." That wasn't what he wanted to say. He wanted to know what she thought— what she *really* thought—about them.

"Don't start in on that again," says Norma Jean. She begins playing "Who'll Be the Next in Line?"

Leroy used to tell hitchhikers his whole life story—about his travels, his hometown, the baby. He would end with a question: "Well, what do you think?" It was just a rhetorical question. In time, he had the feeling that he'd been telling the same story over and over to the same hitchhikers. He quit talking to hitchhikers when he realized how his voice sounded—whining and self-pitying, like some teenage-tragedy song. Now Leroy has the sudden impulse to tell Norma Jean about himself, as if he had just met her. They have known each other so long they have forgotten a lot about each other. They could become reacquainted. But when the oven timer goes off and she runs to the kitchen, he forgets why he wants to do this.

The next day, Mabel drops by. It is Saturday and Norma Jean is cleaning. Leroy is studying the plans of his log house, which have finally come in the mail. He has them spread out on the table—big sheets of stiff blue paper, with diagrams and numbers printed in white. While Norma Jean runs the vacuum, Mabel drinks coffee. She sets her coffee cup on a blueprint.

"I'm just waiting for time to pass," she says to Leroy, drumming her fingers on the table.

As soon as Norma Jean switches off the vacuum, Mabel says in a loud voice, "Did you hear about the datsun dog that killed the baby?"

Norma Jean says, "The word is 'dachshund.'"

"They put the dog on trial. It chewed the baby's legs off. The mother was in the next room all the time." She raises her voice. "They thought it was neglect."

Norma Jean is holding her ears. Leroy manages to open the refrigerator and get some Diet Pepsi to offer Mabel. Mabel still has some coffee and she waves away the Pepsi.

"Datsuns are like that," Mabel says. "They're jealous dogs. They'll tear a place to pieces if you don't keep an eye on them."

"You better watch out what you're saying, Mabel," says Leroy.

"Well, facts is facts."

Leroy looks out the window at his rig. It is like a huge piece of furniture gathering dust in the backyard. Pretty soon it will be an antique. He hears the vacuum cleaner. Norma Jean seems to be cleaning the living room rug again.

Later, she says to Leroy, "She just said that about the baby because she caught me smoking. She's trying to pay me back."

"What are you talking about?" Leroy says, nervously shuffling blueprints.

"You know good and well," Norma Jean says. She is sitting in a kitchen chair with her feet up and her arms wrapped around her knees. She looks small and helpless. She says, "The very idea, her bringing up a subject like that! Saying it was neglect."

"She didn't mean that," Leroy says.

"She might not have *thought* she meant it. She always says things like that. You don't know how she goes on."

"But she didn't really mean it. She was just talking."

Leroy opens a king-sized bottle of beer and pours it into two glasses, dividing it carefully. He hands a glass to Norma Jean and she takes it from him mechanically. For a long time, they sit by the kitchen window watching the birds at the feeder.

Something is happening. Norma Jean is going to night school. She has graduated from her six-week body-building course and now she is taking an adult-education course in composition at Paducah Community College. She spends her evenings outlining paragraphs.

"First you have a topic sentence," she explains to Leroy. "Then you divide it up. Your secondary topic has to be connected to your primary topic."

To Leroy, this sounds intimidating. "I never was any good in English," he says.

"It makes a lot of sense."

"What are you doing this for, anyhow?"

She shrugs. "It's something to do." She stands up and lifts her dumbbells a few times.

"Driving a rig, nobody cared about my English."

"I'm not criticizing your English."

Norma Jean used to say, "If I lose ten minutes' sleep, I just drag all day."

Now she stays up late, writing compositions. She got a B on her first paper—a how-to theme on soup-based casseroles. Recently Norma Jean has been cooking unusual foods—tacos, lasagna, Bombay chicken. She doesn't play the organ anymore, though her second paper was called "Why Music Is Important to Me." She sits at the kitchen table, concentrating on her outlines, while Leroy plays with his log house plans, practicing with a set of Lincoln Logs. The thought of getting a truckload of notched, numbered logs scares him, and he wants to be prepared. As he and Norma Jean work together at the kitchen table, Leroy has the hopeful thought that they are sharing something, but he knows he is a fool to think this. Norma Jean is miles away. He knows he is going to lose her. Like Mabel, he is just waiting for time to pass.

One day, Mabel is there before Norma Jean gets home from work, and Leroy finds himself confiding in her. Mabel, he realizes, must know Norma Jean better than he does.

"I don't know what's got into that girl," Mabel says. "She used to go to bed with the chickens. Now you say she's up all hours. Plus her a-smoking. I like to died."

"I want to make her this beautiful home," Leroy says, indicating the Lincoln Logs. "I don't think she even wants it. Maybe she was happier with me gone."

"She don't know what to make of you, coming home like this."

"Is that it?"

Mabel takes the roof off his Lincoln Log cabin. "You couldn't get *me* in a log cabin," she says. "I was raised in one. It's no picnic, let me tell you."

"They're different now," says Leroy.

"I tell you what," Mabel says, smiling oddly at Leroy.

"What?"

"Take her on down to Shiloh. Y'all need to get out together, stir a little. Her brain's all balled up over them books."

Leroy can see traces of Norma Jean's features in her mother's face. Mabel's worn face has the texture of crinkled cotton, but suddenly she looks pretty. It occurs to Leroy that Mabel has been hinting all along that she wants them to take her with them to Shiloh.

"Let's all go to Shiloh," he says. "You and me and her. Come Sunday."

Mabel throws up her hands in protest. "Oh, no, not me. Young folks want to be by theirselves."

When Norma Jean comes in with groceries, Leroy says excitedly, "Your mama here's been dying to go to Shiloh for thirty-five years. It's about time we went, don't you think?"

"I'm not going to butt in on anybody's second honeymoon," Mabel says.

"Who's going on a honeymoon, for Christ's sake?" Norma Jean says loudly.

"I never raised no daughter of mine to talk that-a-way," Mabel says.

"You ain't seen nothing yet," says Norma Jean. She starts putting away boxes and cans, slamming cabinet doors.

"There's a log cabin at Shiloh," Mabel says. "It was there during the battle. There's bullet holes in it."

"When are you going to *shut up* about Shiloh, Mama?" asks Norma Jean.

"I always thought Shiloh was the prettiest place, so full of history," Mabel goes on. "I just hoped y'all could see it once before I die, so you could tell me about it." Later, she whispers to Leroy, "You do what I said. A little change is what she needs."

"Your name means 'the king,' " Norma Jean says to Leroy that evening. He is trying to get her to go to Shiloh, and she is reading a book about another century.

"Well, I reckon I ought to be right proud."

"I guess so."

"Am I still king around here?"

Norma Jean flexes her biceps and feels them for hardness. "I'm not fooling around with anybody, if that's what you mean," she says.

"Would you tell me if you were?"

"I don't know."

"What does *your* name mean?"

"It was Marilyn Monroe's real name."

"No kidding!"

"Norma comes from the Normans. They were invaders," she says. She closes her book and looks hard at Leroy. "I'll go to Shiloh with you if you'll stop staring at me."

On Sunday, Norma Jean packs a picnic and they go to Shiloh. To Leroy's relief, Mabel says she does not want to come with them. Norma Jean drives, and Leroy, sitting beside her, feels like some boring hitchhiker she has picked up. He tries some conversation, but she answers him in monosyllables. At Shiloh, she drives aimlessly through the park, past bluffs and trails and steep ravines. Shiloh is an immense place, and Leroy cannot see it as a battleground. It is not what he expected. He thought it would look like a golf course. Monuments are everywhere, showing through the thick clusters of trees. Norma Jean passes the log cabin Mabel mentioned. It is surrounded by tourists looking for bullet holes.

"That's not the kind of log house I've got in mind," says Leroy apologetically.

"I know *that*."

"This is a pretty place. Your mama was right."

"It's O.K.," says Norma Jean. "Well, we've seen it. I hope she's satisfied."

They burst out laughing together.

At the park museum, a movie on Shiloh is shown every half hour, but they decide that they don't want to see it. They buy a souvenir Confederate flag for Mabel, and then they find a picnic spot near the cemetery. Norma Jean has brought a picnic cooler, with pimiento sandwiches, soft drinks, and Yodels. Leroy eats a sandwich and then smokes a joint, hiding it behind the picnic cooler. Norma Jean has quit smoking altogether. She is picking cake crumbs from the cellophane wrapper, like a fussy bird.

Leroy says, "So the boys in gray ended up in Corinth. The Union soldiers zapped 'em finally. April 7, 1862."

They both know that he doesn't know any history. He is just talking about some of the historical plaques they have read. He feels awkward, like a boy on a date with an older girl. They are still just making conversation.

"Corinth is where Mama eloped to," says Norma Jean.

They sit in silence and stare at the cemetery for the Union dead and, beyond, at a tall cluster of trees. Campers are parked nearby, bumper to bumper, and small children in bright clothing are cavorting and squealing. Norma Jean wads up the cake wrapper and squeezes it tightly in her hand. Without looking at Leroy, she says, "I want to leave you."

Leroy takes a bottle of Coke out of the cooler and flips off the cap. He holds the bottle poised near his mouth but cannot remember to take a drink. Finally he says, "No, you don't."

"Yes, I do."

"I won't let you."

"You can't stop me."

"Don't do me that way."

Leroy knows Norma Jean will have her own way. "Didn't I promise to be home from now on?" he says.

"In some ways, a woman prefers a man who wanders," says Norma Jean. "That sounds crazy, I know."

"You're not crazy."

Leroy remembers to drink from his Coke. Then he says, "Yes, you *are* crazy. You and me could start all over again. Right back at the beginning."

"We *have* started all over again," says Norma Jean. "And this is how it turned out."

"What did I do wrong?"

"Nothing."

"Is this one of those women's lib things?" Leroy asks.

"Don't be funny."

The cemetery, a green slope dotted with white markers, looks like a subdivision site. Leroy is trying to comprehend that his marriage is breaking up, but for some reason he is wondering about white slabs in a graveyard.

"Everything was fine till Mama caught me smoking," says Norma Jean, standing up. "That set something off."

"What are you talking about?"

"She won't leave me alone—*you* won't leave me alone." Norma Jean seems to be crying, but she is looking away from him. "I feel eighteen again. I can't face that all over again." She starts walking away. "No, it *wasn't* fine. I don't know what I'm saying. Forget it."

Leroy takes a lungful of smoke and closes his eyes as Norma Jean's words sink in. He tries to focus on the fact that thirty-five hundred soldiers died on the grounds around him. He can only think of that war as a board game with plastic soldiers. Leroy almost smiles, as he compares the Confederates' daring attack on the Union camps and Virgil Mathis's raid on the bowling alley. General Grant, drunk and furious, shoved the Southerners back to Corinth, where Mabel and Jet Beasley were married years later, when Mabel was still thin and good-looking. The next day, Mabel and Jet visited the battleground, and then Norma Jean was born, and then she married Leroy and they had a baby, which they lost, and now Leroy and Norma Jean are here at the same battleground. Leroy knows he is leaving out a lot. He is leaving out the insides of history. History was always just names and dates to him. It occurs to him that building a house out of logs is similarly empty—too simple. And the real inner workings of a marriage, like most of history, have escaped him. Now he sees that building a log house is the dumbest idea he could have had. It was clumsy of him to think Norma Jean would want a log house. It was a crazy idea. He'll have to think of something else, quickly. He will wad the blueprints into tight balls and fling them into the lake. Then he'll get moving again. He opens his eyes. Norma Jean has moved away and is walking through the cemetery, following a serpentine brick path.

Leroy gets up to follow his wife, but his good leg is asleep and his bad leg still hurts him. Norma Jean is far away, walking rapidly toward the bluff by the river, and he tries to hobble toward her. Some children run past him, screaming noisily. Norma Jean has reached the bluff, and she is looking out over the Tennessee River. Now she turns toward Leroy and waves her arms. Is she beckoning to him? She seems to be doing an exercise for her chest muscles. The sky is unusually pale—the color of the dust ruffle Mabel made for their bed.

QUESTIONS

1. Why does Norma Jean decide to leave Leroy?   2.   Why does Norma Jean hide her smoking from her mother?   3.   What is the significance of Shiloh?

WRITING TOPIC

Do you believe that Norma Jean is justified in leaving her husband? Explain.

LOVE
AND
HATE

RAINBOW

HEART

MOON

Midsummer Wall, 1966 by Jim Dine

POETRY

Bonny Barbara Allan

ANONYMOUS

It was in and about the Martinmas[1] time,
    When the green leaves were a falling,
That Sir John Graeme, in the West Country,
    Fell in love with Barbara Allan.

He sent his man down through the town,
    To the place where she was dwelling:
"O haste and come to my master dear,
    Gin° ye be Barbara Allan."   *if*

O hooly,° hooly rose she up,   *slowly*
    To the place where he was lying,   10
And when she drew the curtain by:
    "Young man, I think you're dying."

"O it's I'm sick, and very, very sick,
    And 'tis a' for Barbara Allan."
"O the better for me ye s'° never be,   *ye shall*
    Though your heart's blood were a-spilling.

"O dinna° ye mind,° young man," said she,   *don't/remember*
    "When ye was in the tavern a drinking,
That ye made the healths gae° round and round,   *go*
    And slighted Barbara Allan?"   20

He turned his face unto the wall,
    And death was with him dealing:
"Adieu, adieu, my dear friends all,
    And be kind to Barbara Allan."

And slowly, slowly raise she up,
    And slowly, slowly left him,

Bonny Barbara Allan
  [1] November 11.

821

And sighing said, she could not stay,
    Since death of life had reft him.

She had not gane a mile but twa,
    When she heard the dead-bell ringing,   30
And every jow° that the dead-bell geid,°   *stroke/gave*
    It cried, "Woe to Barbara Allan!"

"O mother, mother, make my bed!
    O make it saft and narrow!
Since my love died for me to-day,
    I'll die for him to-morrow."

They Flee from Me   1557

SIR THOMAS WYATT [1503?–1542]

They flee from me, that sometime did me seek,[1]
With naked foot stalking in my chamber.
I have seen them, gentle, tame, and meek,
That now are wild, and do not remember
That sometime they put themselves in danger
To take bread at my hand; and now they range,
Busily seeking with a continual change.

Thanked be Fortune, it hath been otherwise
Twenty times better; but once in special,
In thin array, after a pleasant guise,   10
When her loose gown from her shoulders did fall,
And she me caught in her arms long and small,°   *slender*
And therewith all sweetly did me kiss
And softly said, "Dear heart, how like you this?"

It was no dream, I lay broad waking.
But all is turned, thorough my gentleness,
Into a strange fashion of forsaking;

They Flee from Me
   [1] I.e., formerly pursued me.

And I have leave to go, of her goodness,
And she also to use newfangleness.°   fickleness
But since that I so kindely² am served,   20
I fain would know what she hath deserved.

QUESTIONS
1. Who are "they" in line 1 and for what are they a metaphor? **2.** What sort of relationship is described in the last stanza? How does the poet feel about it? **3.** How does the first stanza serve to introduce the theme of the poem?

WRITING TOPIC
How does the poet use the extended hunting metaphor to develop his theme?

Since There's No Help, Come Let Us Kiss and Part   1619

MICHAEL DRAYTON [1563–1631]

Since there's no help, come let us kiss and part;
Nay, I have done, you get no more of me,
And I am glad, yea glad with all my heart
That thus so cleanly I myself can free;
Shake hands forever, cancel all our vows,
And when we meet at any time again,
Be it not seen in either of our brows
That we one jot of former love retain.
Now at the last gasp of love's latest breath,
When, his pulse failing, passion speechless lies,   10
When faith is kneeling by his bed of death,
And innocence is closing up his eyes,
     Now if thou wouldst, when all have given him over,
     From death to life thou mightst him yet recover.

QUESTIONS
1. Describe the scene in lines 9–12. Why is "innocence" described as closing "love's" eyes? **2.** How might the lady save love from death?

---

² I.e., served in kind. The pun on the modern meaning of *kindly* is intended.

The Passionate Shepherd to His Love[1]

1600

CHRISTOPHER MARLOWE   [1564–1593]

Come live with me and be my love,
And we will all the pleasures prove
That valleys, groves, hills, and fields,
Woods, or steepy mountain yields.

And we will sit upon the rocks,
Seeing the shepherds feed their flocks,
By shallow rivers to whose falls
Melodious birds sing madrigals.

And I will make thee beds of roses
And a thousand fragrant posies,   10
A cap of flowers, and a kirtle°   skirt
Embroidered all with leaves of myrtle;

A gown made of the finest wool
Which from our pretty lambs we pull;
Fair lined slippers for the cold,
With buckles of the purest gold;

A belt of straw and ivy buds,
With coral clasps and amber studs:
And if these pleasures may thee move,
Come live with me, and be my love.   20

The shepherds' swains shall dance and sing
For thy delight each May morning:
If these delights thy mind may move,
Then live with me and be my love.

The Passionate Shepherd . . .
    [1]This poem has elicited many responses over the centuries. Sir Walter Ralegh's early answer
follows. C. Day Lewis's twentieth-century response appears on p. 852.

The Nymph's Reply to the Shepherd

1600

SIR WALTER RALEGH   [1552?–1618]¹

If all the world and love were young,
And truth in every shepherd's tongue,
These pretty pleasures might me move
To live with thee and be thy love.

Time drives the flocks from field to fold
When rivers rage and rocks grow cold,
And Philomel° becometh dumb;   the nightingale
The rest complains of cares to come.

The flowers do fade, and wanton fields
To wayward winter reckoning yields;   10
A honey tongue, a heart of gall,
Is fancy's spring, but sorrow's fall.

Thy gowns, thy shoes, thy beds of roses,
Thy cap, thy kirtle, and thy posies
Soon break, soon wither, soon forgotten—
In folly ripe, in reason rotten.

Thy belt of straw and ivy buds,
Thy coral clasps and amber studs,
All these in me no means can move
To come to thee and be thy love.   20

But could youth last and love still breed,
Had joys no date° nor age no need,   end
Then these delights my mind might move
To live with thee and be thy love.

---

¹ Chronology has been dispensed with here to facilitate comparison with Marlowe's "Passionate Shepherd."

Sonnets   1609

WILLIAM SHAKESPEARE   [1564–1616]

18

Shall I compare thee to a summer's day?
Thou art more lovely and more temperate:
Rough winds do shake the darling buds of May,
And summer's lease hath all too short a date:
Sometime too hot the eye of heaven shines,
And often is his gold complexion dimmed;
And every fair from fair sometimes declines,
By chance or nature's changing course untrimmed;
But thy eternal summer shall not fade,
Nor lose possession of that fair thou ow'st,°   ownest
Nor shall death brag thou wander'st in his shade,   11
When in eternal lines to time thou grow'st:
    So long as men can breathe, or eyes can see,
    So long lives this, and this gives life to thee.

QUESTIONS
1. Why does the poet argue that "a summer's day" is an inappropriate metaphor for his beloved?   **2.** What is "this" in line 14?

29

When, in disgrace with fortune and men's eyes,
I all alone beweep my outcast state
And trouble deaf heaven with my bootless cries
And look upon myself and curse my fate,
Wishing me like to one more rich in hope,
Featured like him, like him with friends possessed,
Desiring this man's art and that man's scope,
With what I most enjoy contented least;
Yet in these thoughts myself almost despising,
Haply I think on thee, and then my state,   10
Like to the lark at break of day arising
From sullen earth, sings hymns at heaven's gate;
    For thy sweet love remembered such wealth brings
    That then I scorn to change my state with kings.

116

Let me not to the marriage of true minds
Admit impediments:[1] love is not love
Which alters when it alteration finds,
Or bends with the remover to remove.[2]
Oh no! it is an ever-fixed mark
That looks on tempests and is never shaken;
It is the star to every wandering bark,
Whose worth's unknown although his height be taken,[3]
Love's not Time's fool, though rosy lips and cheeks
Within his bending sickle's compass come;   10
Love alters not with his brief hours and weeks,
But bears it out![4] even to the edge of doom.
    If this be error and upon me proved,
    I never writ, nor no man ever loved.

129

Th' expense of spirit in a waste of shame
Is lust in action; and till action, lust
Is perjured, murderous, bloody, full of blame,
Savage, extreme, rude, cruel, not to trust;
Enjoyed no sooner but despisèd straight;
Past reason hunted; and no sooner had,
Past reason hated, as a swallowed bait,
On purpose laid to make the taker mad:
Mad in pursuit, and in possession so;
Had, having, and in quest to have, extreme;   10
A bliss in proof,° and proved, a very woe;   experience
Before, a joy proposed; behind, a dream.
    All this the world well knows; yet none knows well
    To shun the heaven that leads men to this hell.

Sonnet 116
   [1] An echo of the marriage service: "If any of you know cause or just impediments why these persons should not be joined together . . ."
   [2] I.e., love does not change when a rival attempts to remove its object.
   [3] The star serves the navigator who measures its height above the horizon but does not understand its value.
   [4] Endures.

QUESTIONS

1. Paraphrase "Th' expense of spirit in a waste of shame/Is lust in action."   **2.** Describe the sound patterns and metrical variations in lines 3 and 4.
What do they contribute to the "sense" of the lines?

WRITING TOPIC

How do the sound patterns, the metrical variations, and the paradox in the final
couplet contribute to the sense of this sonnet?

130

My mistress' eyes are nothing like the sun;
Coral is far more red than her lips' red;
If snow be white, why then her breasts are dun;
If hairs be wires, black wires grow on her head.
I have seen roses damasked,° red and white,   variegated
But no such roses see I in her cheeks;
And in some perfumes is there more delight
Than in the breath that from my mistress reeks.
I love to hear her speak, yet well I know
That music hath a far more pleasing sound;   10
I grant I never saw a goddess go;
My mistress, when she walks, treads on the ground.
        And yet, by heaven, I think my love as rare
        As any she belied with false compare.[1]

138

When my love swears that she is made of truth
I do believe her, though I know she lies,
That she might think me some untutored youth
Unlearnèd in the world's false subtleties.
Thus vainly thinking that she thinks me young,
Although she knows my days are past the best,
Simply I credit her false-speaking tongue:
On both sides thus is simple truth suppressed.
But wherefore says she not she is unjust?
And wherefore say not I that I am old?   10

Sonnet 130
  [1] I.e., as any woman misrepresented with false comparisons.

Oh, love's best habit[1] is in seeming trust,
And age, in love, loves not to have years told.
    Therefore I lie with her, and she with me,
    And in our faults by lies we flattered be.

I Care Not for These Ladies   1601

THOMAS CAMPION [1567–1620]

I care not for these ladies,
That must be wooed and prayed:
Give me kind Amaryllis,[1]
The wanton country maid.
Nature art disdaineth,
Her beauty is her own.
    Her when we court and kiss,
    She cries, "Forsooth, let go!"
    But when we come where comfort is,
    She never will say no.   10

If I love Amaryllis,
She gives me fruit and flowers:
But if we love these ladies,
We must give golden showers.
Give them gold, that sell love,
Give me the nut-brown lass,
    Who, when we court and kiss,
    She cries, "Forsooth, let go!"
    But when we come where comfort is,
    She never will say no.   20

These ladies must have pillows,
And beds by strangers wrought;
Give me a bower of willows,
Of moss and leaves unbought,
And fresh Amaryllis,
With milk and honey fed;

Sonnet 138
  [1] Clothing, with a pun suggesting behavior.
I Care Not for These Ladies
  [1] A conventional name for a country girl in pastoral poetry.

Who, when we court and kiss,
She cries, "Forsooth, let go!"
But when we come where comfort is,
She never will say no.   30

The Flea   1633

JOHN DONNE   [1572–1631]

Mark but this flea, and mark in this,
How little that which thou deniest me is;
It sucked me first, and now sucks thee,
And in this flea our two bloods mingled be;
Thou know'st that this cannot be said
A sin, nor shame, nor loss of maidenhead,
    Yet this enjoys before it woo,
    And pampered swells with one blood made of two,
    And this, alas, is more than we would do.

Oh stay, three lives in one flea spare,   10
Where we almost, yea more than married, are.
This flea is you and I, and this
Our marriage bed and marriage temple is;
Though parents grudge, and you, we are met,
And cloistered in these living walls of jet,
    Though use° make you apt to kill me   custom
    Let not to that, self-murder added be,
    And sacrilege, three sins in killing three.

Cruel and sudden, hast thou since
Purpled thy nail, in blood of innocence?   20
Wherein could this flea guilty be,
Except in that drop which it sucked from thee?
Yet thou triumph'st, and say'st that thou
Find'st not thy self nor me the weaker now;
    'Tis true, then learn how false fears be;
    Just so much honor, when thou yield'st to me,
    Will waste, as this flea's death took life from thee.

A Valediction: Forbidding Mourning   1633

JOHN DONNE   [1572–1631]

As virtuous men pass mildly away,
   And whisper to their souls to go,
Whilst some of their sad friends do say
   The breath goes now, and some say, No;

So let us melt, and make no noise,
   No tear-floods, nor sigh-tempests move,
'Twere profanation of our joys
   To tell the laity our love.

Moving of th' earth° brings harms and fears,   earthquake
   Men reckon what it did and meant;   10
But trepidation of the spheres,
   Though greater far, is innocent.[1]

Dull sublunary° lovers' love   under the moon
   (Whose soul is sense) cannot admit
Absence, because it doth remove
   Those things which elemented it.

But we by a love so much refined
   That our selves know not what it is,
Inter-assuréd of the mind,
   Care less, eyes, lips, and hands to miss.   20

Our two souls therefore, which are one,
   Though I must go, endure not yet
A breach, but an expansion,
   Like gold to airy thinness beat.

A Valediction: Forbidding Mourning
  [1] The movement of the heavenly spheres is harmless.

If they be two, they are two so
   As stiff twin compasses are two;
Thy soul, the fixed foot, makes no show
   To move, but doth, if th' other do.

And though it in the center sit,
   Yet when the other far doth roam,   30
It leans and harkens after it,
   And grows erect, as that comes home.

Such wilt thou be to me, who must
   Like th' other foot, obliquely run;
Thy firmness makes my circle just,
   And makes me end where I begun.

QUESTIONS

1.   Two kinds of love are described in this poem—spiritual and physical. How does the simile drawn in the first two stanzas help define the differences between them?   **2.**   How does the contrast between earthquakes and the movement of the spheres in stanza three further develop the contrast between the two types of lovers?   **3.**   Explain the comparison between a drawing compass and the lovers in the last three stanzas.

Corinna's Going A-Maying   1648

ROBERT HERRICK   [1591–1674]

Get up! get up for shame! the blooming morn
Upon her wings presents the god unshorn.
   She how Aurora[1] throws her fair
   Fresh-quilted colors through the air:
   Get up, sweet slug-a-bed, and see
   The dew bespangling herb and tree.
Each flower has wept and bowed toward the east
Above an hour since, yet you not dressed;
   Nay, not so much as out of bed?
   When all the birds have matins said,   10

Corinna's Going A-Maying
   [1] Aurora is the goddess of the morning. The god unshorn is Apollo, god of the sun.

And sung their thankful hymns, 'tis sin,
    Nay, profanation to keep in,
Whenas a thousand virgins on this day
Spring, sooner than the lark, to fetch in May.

Rise, and put on your foliage, and be seen
To come forth, like the springtime, fresh and green,
    And sweet as Flora.² Take no care
    For jewels for your gown or hair;
    Fear not; the leaves will strew
    Gems in abundance upon you;   20
Besides, the childhood of the day has kept,
Against you come, some orient pearls unwept;
    Come and receive them while the light
    Hangs on the dew-locks of the night,
    And Titan° on the eastern hill   the sun
    Retires himself, or else stands still
Till you come forth. Wash, dress, be brief in praying:
Few beads° are best when once we go a-Maying.   prayers

Come, my Corinna, come; and, coming mark
How each field turns a street, each street a park   30
    Made green and trimmed with trees; see how
    Devotion gives each house a bough
    Or branch: each porch, each door ere this,
    An ark, a tabernacle is,
Made up of whitethorn neatly interwove,
As if here were those cooler shades of love.
    Can such delights be in the street
    And open fields, and we not see 't?
    Come, we'll abroad; and let's obey
    The proclamation made for May,   40
And sin no more, as we have done, by staying;
But, my Corinna, come, let's go a-Maying.

There's not a budding boy or girl this day
But is got up and gone to bring in May;
    A deal of youth, ere this, is come
    Back, and with whitethorn laden home.
    Some have dispatched their cakes and cream
    Before that we have left to dream;
And some have wept, and wooed, and plighted troth,
And chose their priest, ere we can cast off sloth.   50

---

² Flora is the goddess of flowers.

Many a green-gown° has been given,   grass-stained gown
Many a kiss, both odd and even,
Many a glance, too, has been sent
From out the eye, love's firmament;
Many a jest told of the keys betraying
This night, and locks picked; yet we're not a-Maying.

Come, let us go while we are in our prime,
And take the harmless folly of the time.
     We shall grow old apace, and die
     Before we know our liberty.   60
     Our life is short, and our days run
     As fast away as does the sun;
And, as a vapor or a drop of rain
Once lost, can ne'er be found again;
     So when or you or I are made
     A fable, song, or fleeting shade,
     All love, all liking, all delight
     Lies drowned with us in endless night.
Then while time serves, and we are but decaying,
Come, my Corinna, come, let's go a-Maying.   70

QUESTION

1. Note that the poem alludes to pagan and to Christian elements, especially in the first three stanzas. How are these religious allusions used? Does the language introduce an ironic reversal of common Christian attitudes?

WRITING TOPIC

Mayday celebrations reflect pagan spring fertility rites designed to ensure increase in crops, herds, and population. Trace the sexual aspects of the Mayday celebration in the poem. Is the poem a frank invitation to sexual union (like Marlowe's "The Passionate Shepherd to His Love"), or does the language of the last stanza raise some questions, by implication, about the claims of the flesh?

Go, Lovely Rose!   1645

EDMUND WALLER [1606–1687]

Go, lovely rose!
Tell her that wastes her time and me
     That now she knows,

When I resemble° her to thee,   compare
How sweet and fair she seems to be.

   Tell her that's young,
And shuns to have her graces spied,
   That hadst thou sprung
In deserts, where no men abide,
Thou must have uncommended died.   10

   Small is the worth
Of beauty from the light retired;
   Bid her come forth,
Suffer herself to be desired,
And not blush so to be admired.

   Then die! that she
The common fate of all things rare
   May read in thee;
How small a part of time they share
That are so wondrous sweet and fair!   20

To His Coy Mistress   1681

ANDREW MARVELL   [1621–1678]

   Had we but world enough, and time,
This coyness, lady, were no crime.
We would sit down, and think which way
To walk, and pass our long love's day.
Thou by the Indian Ganges' side
Shouldst rubies find; I by the tide
Of Humber would complain. I would
Love you ten years before the flood,
And you should, if you please, refuse
Till the conversion of the Jews.   10
My vegetable love should grow
Vaster than empires and more slow;
An hundred years should go to praise
Thine eyes, and on thy forehead gaze;
Two hundred to adore each breast,
But thirty thousand to the rest;
An age at least to every part,
And the last age should show your heart.

For, lady, you deserve this state,
Nor would I love at lower rate.   20
   But at my back I always hear
Time's wingéd chariot hurrying near;
And yonder all before us lie
Deserts of vast eternity.
Thy beauty shall no more be found,
Nor, in thy marble vault, shall sound
My echoing song; then worms shall try
That long-preserved virginity,
And your quaint honor turn to dust,
And into ashes all my lust: 30
The grave's a fine and private place,
But none, I think, do there embrace.
   Now therefore, while the youthful hue
Sits on thy skin like morning dew,
And while thy willing soul transpires
At every pore with instant fires,
Now let us sport us while we may,
And now, like amorous birds of prey,
Rather at once our time devour   39
Than languish in his slow-chapped° power.   slow-jawed
Let us roll our strength and all
Our sweetness up into one ball,
And tear our pleasures with rough strife
Thorough the iron gates of life:
Thus, though we cannot make our sun
Stand still, yet we will make him run.

QUESTIONS

1. State the argument of the poem (see ll. 1–2, 21–22, 33–34). **2.** Compare the figures of speech in the first verse paragraph with those in the last. How do they differ? **3.** Characterize the attitude toward life recommended by the poet.

WRITING TOPIC

In what ways does the conception of love in this poem differ from that in Donne's "A Valediction: Forbidding Mourning"? In your discussion consider the imagery in both poems.

A Poison Tree   1794

WILLIAM BLAKE [1757–1827]

I was angry with my friend:
I told my wrath, my wrath did end.

I was angry with my foe:
I told it not, my wrath did grow.

And I watered it in fears,
Night & morning with my tears;
And I sunnéd it with smiles,
And with soft deceitful wiles.

And it grew both day and night,
Till it bore an apple bright.
And my foe beheld it shine,
And he knew that it was mine,

And into my garden stole,
When the night had veil'd the pole;
In the morning glad I see
My foe outstretched beneath the tree.

QUESTIONS

1. Is anything gained from the parallel readers might draw between this tree and the tree in the Garden of Eden? Explain.   **2.**   Can you articulate what the "poison" is?   **3.**   Does your own experience verify the first stanza of the poem?

A Red, Red Rose   1796

ROBERT BURNS   [1759–1796]

O My Luve's like a red, red rose,
    That's newly sprung in June;
O My Luve's like a melodie
    That's sweetly played in tune.

As fair art thou, my bonnie lass,
    So deep in luve am I;
And I will luve thee still, my dear,
    Till a' the seas gang dry.

Till a' the seas gang dry, my dear,
    And the rocks melt wi' the sun:
O I will love thee still, my dear,   10
    While the sands o' life shall run.

And fare thee weel, my only luve,
    And fare thee weel awhile!
And I will come again, my luve,
    Though it were ten thousand mile.

from

Song of Myself   1855

WALT WHITMAN [1819–1892]

11

Twenty-eight young men bathe by the shore,
Twenty-eight young men and all so friendly;
Twenty-eight years of womanly life and all so lonesome.

She owns the fine house by the rise of the bank,
She hides handsome and richly drest aft the blinds of the window.

Which of the young men does she like the best?
Ah the homeliest of them is beautiful to her.

Where are you off to, lady? for I see you,
You splash in the water there, yet stay stock still in your room.

Dancing and laughing along the beach came the twenty-ninth bather,   10
The rest did not see her, but she saw them and loved them.

The beards of the young men glisten'd with wet, it ran from their long
    hair,
Little streams pass'd all over their bodies.

An unseen hand also pass'd over their bodies,
It descended tremblingly from their temples and ribs.

The young men float on their backs, their white bellies bulge to the sun,
    they do not ask who seizes fast to them,
They do not know who puffs and declines with pendant and bending
    arch,
They do not think whom they souse with spray.

Dover Beach*   1867

MATTHEW ARNOLD   [1822–1888]

The sea is calm tonight.
The tide is full, the moon lies fair
Upon the straits; on the French coast the light
Gleams and is gone; the cliffs of England stand,
Glimmering and vast, out in the tranquil bay.
Come to the window, sweet is the night-air!
Only, from the long line of spray
Where the sea meets the moon-blanched land,
Listen! you hear the grating roar
Of pebbles which the waves draw back, and fling,   10
At their return, up the high strand,
Begin, and cease, and then again begin,
With tremulous cadence slow, and bring
The eternal note of sadness in.

Sophocles long ago
Heard it on the Aegean, and it brought
Into his mind the turbid ebb and flow
Of human misery; we
Find also in the sound a thought,
Hearing it by this distant northern sea.   20

The Sea of Faith
Was once, too, at the full, and round earth's shore
Lay like the folds of a bright girdle furled.
But now I only hear
Its melancholy, long, withdrawing roar,
Retreating, to the breath
Of the night-wind, down the vast edges drear
And naked shingles° of the world.   pebble beaches

Ah, love, let us be true
To one another! for the world, which seems   30
To lie before us like a land of dreams,
So various, so beautiful, so new,

---

*This poem is considered in detail in the appendix "Three Critical Approaches: Formalist, So-
ciological, Psychoanalytic" at the end of the book.

Hath really neither joy, nor love, nor light,
Nor certitude, nor peace, nor help for pain;
And we are here as on a darkling plain
Swept with confused alarms of struggle and flight,
Where ignorant armies clash by night.

from

Modern Love   1862

GEORGE MEREDITH   [1828–1909]

17

At dinner, she is hostess, I am host.
Went the feast ever cheerfuller? She keeps
The Topic over intellectual deeps
In buoyancy afloat. They see no ghost.
With sparkling surface-eyes we ply the ball:
It is in truth a most contagious game:
HIDING THE SKELETON, shall be its name.
Such play as this the devils might appall!
But here's the greater wonder: in that we,
Enamored of an acting naught can tire,   10
Each other, like true hypocrites, admire;
Warm-lighted looks, Love's ephemeridae,°   short-lived insects
Shoot gayly o'er the dishes and the wine.
We waken envy of our happy lot.
Fast, sweet, and golden, shows the marriage knot.
Dear guests, you now have seen Love's corpse-light[1] shine.

QUESTIONS
1. What, precisely, is "Love's corpse-light" (l. 16) a metaphor for in this poem?
2. Is the "marriage knot" really "fast, sweet, and golden" (l. 15)? Explain.

Modern Love
   [1] I.e., corpse-candle, a soft light which, when seen in churchyards, portends a funeral.

Mine Enemy Is
Growing Old   (ca. 1881)

EMILY DICKINSON   [1830–1886]

Mine Enemy is growing old—
I have at last Revenge—
The Palate of the Hate departs—
If any would avenge

Let him be quick—the Viand flits—
It is a faded Meat—
Anger as soon as fed is dead—
'Tis starving makes it fat—

QUESTION
1. Explain the paradox contained in the last two lines.

WRITING TOPIC
Compare this poem with Blake's "A Poison Tree."

The Windhover¹   1877
TO CHRIST OUR LORD

GERARD MANLEY HOPKINS   [1844–1889]

I caught this morning morning's minion,° king-   favorite
    dom of daylight's dauphin,² dapple-dawn-drawn Falcon, in his riding
    Of the rolling level underneath him steady air, and striding
High there, how he rung upon the rein of a wimpling° wing   rippling
In his ecstasy! then off, off forth on swing,

The Windhover
    ¹ A small hawk, so called because it is able to hover in the wind.
    ² Heir to kingly splendor.

As a skate's heel sweeps smooth on a bow-bend: the hurl and gliding
    Rebuffed the big wind. My heart in hiding
Stirred for a bird,—the achieve of, the mastery of the thing!

Brute beauty and valour and act, oh, air, pride, plume, here
    Buckle! AND the fire that breaks from thee then, a billion   10
Times told lovelier, more dangerous, O my chevalier!

    No wonder of it: shéer plód makes plough down sillion³
Shine, and blue-bleak embers, ah my dear,
    Fall, gall themselves, and gash gold-vermilion.

QUESTIONS

1. The poem expresses a love of God. On what is that love, or awe, of God based? **2.** Do the sound patterns of the poem convey emotional intensity? Explain. **3.** The word *Buckle* in line 10 may mean "collapse" or "join." How do you read it? Explain.

WRITING TOPIC

Although the metrical quality of this poem is unique to Hopkins, it is structured as a sonnet. How do each of its parts—that is, the octave and each of the three-line divisions of the sestet function?

Pied Beauty   1877

GERARD MANLEY HOPKINS [1844–1889]

Glory be to God for dappled things—
    For skies of couple-colour as a brinded° cow;   brindled
        For rose-moles all in stipple upon trout that swim;
Fresh-firecoal chestnut-falls,¹ finches' wings;
    Landscape plotted and pieced²—fold, fallow, and plough;
        And all trades, their gear and tackle, and trim.°   equipment
All things counter,° original, spare, strange;   contrasted
    Whatever is fickle, freckled (who knows how?)
        With swift, slow; sweet, sour; adazzle, dim;
He fathers-forth whose beauty is past change: 10
            Praise him.

---

³ The ridge between ploughed furrows.
Pied Beauty
   ¹ Fallen chestnuts, with the outer husks removed, colored like fresh fire coal.
   ² Reference to the variegated pattern of land put to different uses.

Fire and Ice   1923

ROBERT FROST   [1874–1963]

Some say the world will end in fire,
Some say in ice,
From what I've tasted of desire
I hold with those who favor fire.
But if it had to perish twice,
I think I know enough of hate
To say that for destruction ice
Is also great
And would suffice.

The Silken Tent   1942

ROBERT FROST   [1874–1963]

She is as in a field a silken tent
At midday when a sunny summer breeze
Has dried the dew and all its ropes relent,
So that in guys it gently sways at ease,
And its supporting central cedar pole,
That is its pinnacle to heavenward
And signifies the sureness of the soul,
Seems to owe naught to any single cord,
But strictly held by none, is loosely bound
By countless silken ties of love and thought   10
To everything on earth the compass round,
And only by one's going slightly taut
In the capriciousness of summer air
Is of the slightest bondage made aware.

A Virginal   1912

EZRA POUND   [1885–1972]

No, no! Go from me. I have left her lately.
I will not spoil my sheath with lesser brightness,
For my surrounding air has a new lightness;
Slight are her arms, yet they have bound me straitly
And left me cloaked as with a gauze of æther;

As with sweet leaves; as with subtle clearness.
Oh, I have picked up magic in her nearness
To sheathe me half in half the things that sheathe her.
No, no! Go from me. I have still the flavor,
Soft as spring wind that's come from birchen bowers.   10
Green come the shoots, aye April in the branches,
As winter's wound with her sleight hand she staunches,
Hath of the trees a likeness of the savor:
As white their bark, so white this lady's hours.

The Love Song
of J. Alfred Prufrock   1917

T. S. ELIOT   [1888–1965]

> S'io credessi che mia risposta fosse
> a persona che mai tornasse al mondo,
> questa fiamma staria senza più scosse.
> Ma per ciò che giammai di questo fondo
> non tornò vivo alcun, s'i'odo il vero,
> senza tema d'infamia ti rispondo. [1]

Let us go then, you and I,
When the evening is spread out against the sky
Like a patient etherized upon a table;
Let us go, through certain half-deserted streets,
The muttering retreats
Of restless nights in one-night cheap hotels
And sawdust restaurants with oyster shells:
Streets that follow like a tedious argument
Of insidious intent
To lead you to an overwhelming question . . .   10
Oh, do not ask, "What is it?"
Let us go and make our visit.

In the room the women come and go
Talking of Michelangelo.

. . . *Prufrock*
   [1] From Dante, *Inferno*, XXVII, 61–66. The speaker is Guido da Montefeltro, who is imprisoned in a flame in the level of Hell reserved for false counselors. He tells Dante and Virgil, "If I thought my answer were given to one who might return to the world, this flame would stay without further movement. But since from this depth none has ever returned alive, if what I hear is true, I answer you without fear of infamy."

The yellow fog that rubs its back upon the windowpanes,
The yellow smoke that rubs its muzzle on the windowpanes,
Licked its tongue into the corners of the evening,
Lingered upon the pools that stand in drains,
Let fall upon its back the soot that falls from chimneys,
Slipped by the terrace, made a sudden leap,   20
And seeing that it was a soft October night,
Curled once about the house, and fell asleep.

And indeed there will be time
For the yellow smoke that slides along the street,
Rubbing its back upon the windowpanes;
There will be time, there will be time
To prepare a face to meet the faces that you meet;
There will be time to murder and create,
And time for all the works and days of hands
That lift and drop a question on your plate;   30
Time for you and time for me,
And time yet for a hundred indecisions,
And for a hundred visions and revisions,
Before the taking of a toast and tea.

In the room the women come and go
Talking of Michelangelo.

And indeed there will be time
To wonder, "Do I dare?" and, "Do I dare?"
Time to turn back and descend the stair,
With a bald spot in the middle of my hair—   40
(They will say: "How his hair is growing thin!")
My morning coat, my collar mounting firmly to the chin,
My necktie rich and modest, but asserted by a simple pin—
(They will say: "But how his arms and legs are thin!")
Do I dare
Disturb the universe?
In a minute there is time
For decisions and revisions which a minute will reverse.

For I have known them all already, known them all—
Have known the evenings, mornings, afternoons,   50
I have measured out my life with coffee spoons;
I know the voices dying with a dying fall
Beneath the music from a farther room.
    So how should I presume?

And I have known the eyes already, known them all—
The eyes that fix you in a formulated phrase,
And when I am formulated, sprawling on a pin,
When I am pinned and wriggling on the wall,
Then how should I begin
To spit out all the butt-ends of my days and ways?   60
     And how should I presume?

And I have known the arms already, known them all—
Arms that are braceleted and white and bare
(But in the lamplight, downed with light brown hair!)
Is it perfume from a dress
That makes me so digress?
Arms that lie along a table, or wrap about a shawl.
     And should I then presume?
     And how should I begin?

            .   .   .   .   .   .

Shall I say, I have gone at dusk through narrow streets   70
And watched the smoke that rises from the pipes
Of lonely men in shirt-sleeves, leaning out of windows? . . . .

I should have been a pair of ragged claws
Scuttling across the floors of silent seas.

            .   .   .   .   .   .

And the afternoon, the evening, sleeps so peacefully!
Smoothed by long fingers,
Asleep . . . tired . . . or it malingers,
Stretched on the floor, here beside you and me.
Should I, after tea and cakes and ices,
Have the strength to force the moment to its crisis?   80
But though I have wept and fasted, wept and prayed,
Though I have seen my head (grown slightly bald) brought in
     upon a platter,[2]
I am no prophet—and here's no great matter;
I have seen the moment of my greatness flicker,
And I have seen the eternal Footman hold my coat, and snicker,
And in short, I was afraid.

And would it have been worth it, after all,
After the cups, the marmalade, the tea,

---

[2] Like the head of John the Baptist. See Matthew 14:3–12.

Among the porcelain, among some talk of you and me,
Would it have been worth while,   90
To have bitten off the matter with a smile,
To have squeezed the universe into a ball
To roll it toward some overwhelming question,
To say: "I am Lazarus,[3] come from the dead,
Come back to tell you all, I shall tell you all"—
If one, settling a pillow by her head,
    Should say: "That is not what I meant at all.
    That is not it, at all."

And would it have been worth it, after all,
Would it have been worth while,   100
After the sunsets and the dooryards and the sprinkled streets,
After the novels, after the teacups, after the skirts that trail along the floor—
And this, and so much more?—
It is impossible to say just what I mean!
But as if a magic lantern threw the nerves in patterns on a screen:
Would it have been worth while
If one, settling a pillow or throwing off a shawl,
And turning toward the window, should say:
    "That is not it at all,
    That is not what I meant, at all."   110

      . . . . . .

No! I am not Prince Hamlet, nor was meant to be;
Am an attendant lord, one that will do
To swell a progress,° start a scene or two,   state journey
Advise the prince; no doubt, an easy tool,
Deferential, glad to be of use,
Politic, cautious, and meticulous;
Full of high sentence,° but a bit obtuse;   sententiousness
At times, indeed, almost ridiculous—
Almost, at times, the Fool.

I grow old . . . I grow old . . .   120
I shall wear the bottoms of my trousers rolled.°   cuffed

Shall I part my hair behind? Do I dare to eat a peach?
I shall wear white flannel trousers, and walk upon the beach.
I have heard the mermaids singing, each to each.

I do not think that they will sing to me.

---

[3] See John 11:1–14 and Luke 16:19–26.

I have seen them riding seaward on the waves
Combing the white hair of the waves blown back
When the wind blows the water white and black.

We have lingered in the chambers of the sea
By sea-girls wreathed with seaweed red and brown   130
Till human voices wake us, and we drown.

QUESTIONS
1. This poem may be understood as a stream of consciousness passing through
the mind of Prufrock. The "you and I" of line 1 may be different aspects of his
personality. Or perhaps the "you and I" is parallel to Guido who speaks the epigraph and Dante to whom he tells the story that resulted in his damnation—hence,
"you" is the reader and "I" is Prufrock. Apparently, Prufrock is on his way to a tea
and is pondering his relationship with a certain woman. The poem is disjointed
because it proceeds by psychological rather than logical stages. To what social class
does Prufrock belong? How does Prufrock respond to the attitudes and values of
his class? Does he change in the course of the poem? **2.** Line 92 provides a good
example of literary allusion (see the last stanza of Marvell, "To His Coy Mistress,"
especially ll. 41–42). How does an awareness of the allusion contribute to the reader's
response to the stanza here? **3.** What might the song of the mermaids (l. 124)
signify, and why does Prufrock think they will not sing to him (l. 125)? **4.** T. S.
Eliot once said that some poetry "can communicate without being understood." Is
this such a poem?

WRITING TOPIC
What sort of man is J. Alfred Prufrock? How does the poet establish his characteristics?

Love Is Not All   1931

EDNA ST. VINCENT MILLAY [1892–1950]

Love is not all: it is not meat nor drink
Nor slumber nor a roof against the rain;
Nor yet a floating spar to men that sink
And rise and sink and rise and sink again;
Love can not fill the thickened lung with breath,
Nor clean the blood, nor set the fractured bone;
Yet many a man is making friends with death
Even as I speak, for lack of love alone.
It well may be that in a difficult hour,
Pinned down by pain and moaning for release,   10

Or nagged by want past resolution's power,
I might be driven to sell your love for peace,
Or trade the memory of this night for food.
It well may be. I do not think I would.

if everything happens
that can't be done   1944

E. E. CUMMINGS [1894–1962]

if everything happens that can't be done
(and anything's righter
than books
could plan)
the stupidest teacher will almost guess
(with a run
skip
around we go yes)
there's nothing as something as one

one hasn't a why or because or although   10
(and buds know better
than books
don't grow)
one's anything old being everything new
(with a what
which
around we come who)
one's everyanything so

so world is a leaf so tree is a bough
(and birds sing sweeter   20
than books
tell how)
so here is away and so your is a my
(with a down
up
around again fly)
forever was never till now

now i love you and you love me
(and books are shuter
than books   30

can be)
and deep in the high that does nothing but fall
(with a shout
each
around we go all)
there's somebody calling who's we

we're anything brighter than even the sun
(we're everything greater
than books
might mean)   40
we're everyanything more than believe
(with a spin
leap
alive we're alive)
we're wonderful one times one

QUESTIONS

1. What fundamental contrast is stated by the poem? **2.** Lines 2–4 and 6–8 of each stanza could be printed as single lines. Why do you think Cummings decided to print them as he does? **3.** What common attitude toward lovers is expressed by the last lines of the stanzas? **4.** Is the poem free verse or formal verse?

WRITING TOPIC

What relation do the parenthetical lines in each stanza bear to the poem as a whole?

Ballad of Love
Through the Ages*   (1983)

CARLOS DRUMMOND DE ANDRADE   [b. 1902]

From the beginning of time,
I liked you, you liked me.
I was Greek, you were Trojan—
Trojan but not Helen.
I sprang from a wooden horse[1]

Ballad of Love Through the Ages
   * Translated by Mark Strand.
   [1] According to legend, the abduction of the Spartan queen Helen by Paris, a Trojan prince, sparked a ten-year war between Greece and Troy. The Greeks fashioned a large hollow horse, filled it with soldiers, and left it at the Trojan gates. After the Trojans brought it within their walls, the hidden soldiers emerged at night and admitted the Greek army, which burned the city.

to kill your brother.
I killed, we quarrelled, we died.

I became a Roman soldier,
persecutor of Christians.
At the catacomb door   10
I met you again.
But when I saw you fall
naked in the Colosseum [2]
and the lion coming toward you,
I made a desperate leap
and the lion ate us both.

Next I was a Moorish pirate, [3]
the scourge of Tripoli. [4]
I set fire to the frigate
where you were hiding from   20
the fury of my brigantine.
But when I went to grab you
and take you as my slave,
you crossed yourself and drove
a dagger through your heart.
I killed myself as well.

Later on, in happier days,
I was a courtier at Versailles, [5]
clever and debauched.
You dreamed of being a nun . . .   30
I vaulted over the convent wall,
but difficult politics
led us to the guillotine.

These days I'm totally modern:
dancing, jogging, working out.
And I have money in the bank.
And you're a fabulous blonde:
dancing, jogging, working out.
None of it pleases your father.
But after a thousand reversals   40
I, one of Paramount's heroes, [6]
give you a hug, a kiss, and we marry.

---

[2] An amphitheater in Rome, built around 80 A.D., where Christians were persecuted by being
thrown to lions.
[3] The Moors were a Moslem people of North Africa.
[4] A port on the Mediterranean Sea.
[5] Site of the splendid palace of Louis XIV, ruler of France from 1643 to 1715.
[6] Paramount is a film studio in Hollywood.

QUESTIONS
1. Who is the speaker in this poem? What does the poem gain from having a single speaker? Does it detract from the poem that the speaker cannot be an actual human being? **2.** Examine each stanza carefully in order to describe the meaning of love during each epoch. What are the differences and similarities?

Song[1]   1935

C. DAY LEWIS [1904–1972]

Come, live with me and be my love,
And we will all the pleasures prove
Of peace and plenty, bed and board,
That chance employment may afford.

I'll handle dainties on the docks
And thou shalt read of summer frocks:
At evening by the sour canals
We'll hope to hear some madrigals.

Care on thy maiden brow shall put
A wreath of wrinkles, and thy foot
Be shod with pain: not silken dress   10
But toil shall tire thy loveliness.

Hunger shall make thy modest zone
And cheat fond death of all but bone—
If these delights thy mind may move,
Then live with me and be my love.

from

Five Songs   (1937)

W. H. AUDEN [1907–1973]

That night when joy began
Our narrowest veins to flush,
We waited for the flash
Of morning's levelled gun.

Song
[1] See Christopher Marlowe's "The Passionate Shepherd to His Love," p. 824.

But morning let us pass,
And day by day relief
Outgrew his nervous laugh,
Grows credulous of peace.

As mile by mile is seen
No trespasser's reproach,   10
And love's best glasses reach
No fields but are his own.

QUESTIONS
1. Describe the sound relationships among the last words in the lines of each
stanza. **2.** What is the controlling metaphor in the poem? Is it appropriate for a
love poem? **3.** If it were suggested that the poem describes a homosexual relationship, would your response to the poem's figurative language change?

I Knew a Woman   1958

THEODORE ROETHKE [1908–1963]

I knew a woman, lovely in her bones,
When small birds sighed, she would sigh back at them;
Ah, when she moved, she moved more ways than one:
The shapes a bright container can contain!
Of her choice virtues only gods should speak,
Or English poets who grew up on Greek
(I'd have them sing in chorus, cheek to cheek).

How well her wishes went! She stroked my chin,
She taught me Turn, and Counter-turn, and Stand;
She taught me Touch, that undulant white skin;   10
I nibbled meekly from her proffered hand;
She was the sickle; I, poor I, the rake,
Coming behind her for her pretty sake
(But what prodigious mowing we did make).

Love likes a gander, and adores a goose:
Her full lips pursed, the errant note to seize;
She played it quick, she played it light and loose;
My eyes, they dazzled at her flowing knees;
Her several parts could keep a pure repose,
Or one hip quiver with a mobile nose   20
(She moved in circles, and those circles moved).

Let seed be grass, and grass turn into hay:
I'm martyr to a motion not my own;
What's freedom for? To know eternity.
I swear she cast a shadow white as stone.
But who would count eternity in days?
These old bones live to learn her wanton ways:
(I measure time by how a body sways).

To a Child Born in Time of Small War

1966

HELEN SORRELLS   [b. 1908]

Child, you were conceived in my upstairs room,
my girlhood all around. Later I spent
nights there alone imploring the traitor moon
to keep me childless still. I never meant
to bear you in this year of discontent.
Yet you were there in your appointed place,
remnant of leaving, of a sacrament.
Child, if I loved you then, it was to trace
on a cold sheet your likeness to his absent face.

In May we were still alone. That month your life   10
stirred in my dark, as if my body's core
grew quick with wings. I turned away, more wife
than mother still, unwilling to explore
the fact of you. There was an orient shore,
a tide of hurt, that held my heart and mind.
It was as if you lived behind a door
I was afraid to open, lest you bind
my breaking. Lost in loss, I was not yours to find.

I swelled with summer. You were hard and strong,
making me know you were there. When the mail   20
brought me no letter, and the time was long
between the war's slow gains, and love seemed frail,
I fought you. You were error, judgment, jail.
Without you, there were ways I, too, could fight
a war. Trapped in your growing, I would rail
against your grotesque carriage, swollen, tight.
I would have left you, and I did in dreams of flight.

Discipline of the seasons brought me round.
Earth comes to term and so, in time, did we.
You are a living thing of sight and sound.   30
Nothing of you is his, you are all of me:
your sex, gray eye, the struggle to be free
that made your birth like death, but I awake
for that caught air, your cry. I try to see,
but cannot, the same lift his eyebrows take.
Child, if I love you now, it is for your own sake.

One Art   1976

ELIZABETH BISHOP   [1911–1979]

The art of losing isn't hard to master;
so many things seem filled with the intent
to be lost that their loss is no disaster.

Lose something every day. Accept the fluster
of lost door keys, the hour badly spent.
The art of losing isn't hard to master.

Then practice losing farther, losing faster:
places, and names, and where it was you meant
to travel. None of these will bring disaster.

I lost my mother's watch. And look! my last, or   10
next-to-last, of three loved houses went.
The art of losing isn't hard to master.

I lost two cities, lovely ones. And, vaster,
some realms I owned, two rivers, a continent.
I miss them, but it wasn't a disaster.

—Even losing you (the joking voice, a gesture
I love) I shan't have lied. It's evident
the art of losing's not too hard to master
though it may look like (*Write* it!) like disaster.

Those Winter Sundays   1975

ROBERT HAYDEN   [1913–1980]

Sundays too my father got up early
and put his clothes on in the blueblack cold,

then with cracked hands that ached
from labor in the weekday weather made
banked fires blaze. No one ever thanked him.

I'd wake and hear the cold splintering, breaking.
When the rooms were warm, he'd call,
and slowly I would rise and dress,
fearing the chronic angers of that house,

Speaking indifferently to him,   10
who had driven out the cold
and polished my good shoes as well.
What did I know, what did I know
of love's austere and lonely offices?

The Dover Bitch   1968

A CRITICISM OF LIFE

ANTHONY HECHT [b. 1922]

So there stood Matthew Arnold and this girl
With the cliffs of England crumbling away behind them,
And he said to her, "Try to be true to me,
And I'll do the same for you, for things are bad
All over, etc., etc."
Well now, I knew this girl. It's true she had read
Sophocles in a fairly good translation
And caught that bitter allusion to the sea,
But all the time he was talking she had in mind
The notion of what his whiskers would feel like   10
On the back of her neck. She told me later on
That after a while she got to looking out
At the lights across the channel, and really felt sad,
Thinking of all the wine and enormous beds
And blandishments in French and the perfumes.
And then she got really angry. To have been brought
All the way down from London, and then be addressed
As sort of a mournful cosmic last resort
Is really tough on a girl, and she was pretty.
Anyway, she watched him pace the room   20
And finger his watch-chain and seem to sweat a bit,

And then she said one or two unprintable things.
But you mustn't judge her by that. What I mean to say is,
She's really all right. I still see her once in a while
And she always treats me right. We have a drink
And I give her a good time, and perhaps it's a year
Before I see her again, but there she is,
Running to fat, but dependable as they come,
And sometimes I bring her a bottle of *Nuit d'Amour*.

QUESTIONS

1. This poem is a response to Matthew Arnold's "Dover Beach," which appears earlier in this section. Arnold's poem is often read as a pained response to the breakdown of religious tradition and social and political order in the mid-nineteenth century. Is this poem, in contrast, optimistic? Is the relationship between the speaker and the girl at the end of the poem admirable? Explain.   **2.**   Do you suppose Hecht was moved to write this poem out of admiration for "Dover Beach"? Explain.

WRITING TOPIC

What is the fundamental difference between the speaker's conception of love in Arnold's poem and the "girl's" conception of love as reported in this poem?

Love Song: I and Thou   1961

ALAN DUGAN   [b. 1923]

Nothing is plumb, level or square:
    the studs are bowed, the joists
are shaky by nature, no piece fits
    any other piece without a gap
or pinch, and bent nails
    dance all over the surfacing
like maggots. By Christ
    I am no carpenter. I built
the roof for myself, the walls
    for myself, the floors   10
for myself, and got
    hung up in it myself. I
danced with a purple thumb
    at this house-warming, drunk
with my prime whiskey: rage.
    Oh I spat rage's nails

into the frame-up of my work:
> it held. It settled plumb,
level, solid, square and true
> for that great moment. Then   20
it screamed and went on through,
> skewing as wrong the other way.
God damned it. This is hell,
> but I planned it, I sawed it,
I nailed it, and I
> will live in it until it kills me.
I can nail my left palm
> to the left-hand cross-piece but
I can't do everything myself.
> I need a hand to nail the right,   30
a help, a love, a you, a wife.

The Ache of Marriage   1964

DENISE LEVERTOV   [b. 1923]

The ache of marriage:

thigh and tongue, beloved,
are heavy with it,
it throbs in the teeth

We look for communion
and are turned away, beloved,
each and each

It is leviathan and we
in its belly
looking for joy, some joy   10
not to be known outside it

two by two in the ark of
the ache of it.

The Mutes   1967

DENISE LEVERTOV   [b. 1923]

Those groans men use
passing a woman on the street
or on the steps of the subway

to tell her she is a female
and their flesh knows it,

are they a sort of tune,
an ugly enough song, sung
by a bird with a slit tongue

but meant for music?

Or are they the muffled roaring   10
of deafmutes trapped in a building that is
slowly filling with smoke?

Perhaps both.

Such men most often
look as if groan were all they could do,
yet a woman, in spite of herself,

knows it's a tribute:
if she were lacking all grace
they'd pass her in silence:

so it's not only to say she's   20
a warm hole. It's a word

in grief-language, nothing to do with
primitive, not an ur-language[1];
language stricken, sickened, cast down

in decrepitude. She wants to
throw the tribute away, disgusted, and can't,

it goes on buzzing in her ear,
it changes the pace of her walk,
the torn posters in echoing corridors   30

spell it out, it
quakes and gnashes as the train comes in.
Her pulse sullenly

The Mutes
  [1] Primordial language.

had picked up speed,
but the cars slow down and
jar to a stop while her understanding

keeps on translating:
'Life after life after life goes by

without poetry,
without seemliness,   40
without love.'

QUESTIONS
1. Explain the title. **2.** Why does the tribute go on "buzzing in her ear" (l.
28)? **3.** Is this poem an attack on men? Explain.

Unwanted   1963

EDWARD FIELD [b. 1924]

The poster with my picture on it
Is hanging on the bulletin board in the Post Office.

I stand by it hoping to be recognized
Posing first full face and then profile

But everybody passes by and I have to admit
The photograph was taken some years ago.

I was unwanted then and I'm unwanted now
Ah guess ah'll go up echo mountain and crah.

I wish someone would find my fingerprints somewhere
Maybe on a corpse and say, You're it.   10

Description: Male, or reasonably so
White, but not lily-white and usually deep-red

Thirty-fivish, and looks it lately
Five-feet-nine and one-hundred-thirty pounds: no physique

Black hair going gray, hairline receding fast
What used to be curly, now fuzzy

Brown eyes starey under beetling brow
Mole on chin, probably will become a wen

It is perfectly obvious that he was not popular at school
No good at baseball, and wet his bed.   20

His aliases tell his history: Dumbell, Good-for-nothing,
Jewboy, Fieldinsky, Skinny, Fierce Face, Greaseball, Sissy.

Warning: This man is not dangerous, answers to any name
Responds to love, don't call him or he will come.

Regret   1963

VASSAR MILLER   [b. 1924]

Had you come to me
as I to you once
with naked asking,
I should have let you.
We should have slept,
two arrows bound together
wounding no one.
Instead, you chose to lie
set to the bow of your own darkness.

A Marriage   1962

ROBERT CREELEY   [b. 1926]

The first retainer
he gave to her
was a golden
wedding ring.

The second—late at night
he woke up,
leaned over on an elbow,
and kissed her.

The third and the last—
he died with   10
and gave up loving
and lived with her.

The Farmer's Wife

ANNE SEXTON [1928–1975]

1960

From the hodge porridge
of their country lust,
their local life in Illinois,
where all their acres look
like a sprouting broom factory,
they name just ten years now
that she has been his habit;
as again tonight he'll say
honey bunch let's go
and she will not say how there   10
must be more to living
than this brief bright bridge
of the raucous bed or even
the slow braille touch of him
like a heavy god grown light,
that old pantomime of love
that she wants although
it leaves her still alone,
built back again at last,
mind's apart from him, living   20
her own self in her own words
and hating the sweat of the house
they keep when they finally lie
each in separate dreams
and then how she watches him,
still strong in the blowzy bag
of his usual sleep while
her young years bungle past
their same marriage bed
and she wishes him cripple, or poet,   30
or even lonely, or sometimes,
better, my lover, dead.

Living in Sin

ADRIENNE RICH [b. 1929]

1955

She had thought the studio would keep itself;
no dust upon the furniture of love.

Half heresy, to wish the taps less vocal,
the panes relieved of grime. A plate of pears,
a piano with a Persian shawl, a cat
stalking the picturesque amusing mouse
had risen at his urging.
Not that at five each separate stair would writhe
under the milkman's tramp; that morning light
so coldly would delineate the scraps   10
of last night's cheese and three sepulchral bottles;
that on the kitchen shelf among the saucers
a pair of beetle-eyes would fix her own—
Envoy from some village in the moldings . . .
Meanwhile, he, with a yawn,
sounded a dozen notes upon the keyboard,
declared it out of tune, shrugged at the mirror,
rubbed at his beard, went out for cigarettes;
while she, jeered by the minor demons,
pulled back the sheets and made the bed and found   20
a towel to dust the table-top,
and let the coffee-pot boil over on the stove.
By evening she was back in love again,
though not so wholly but throughout the night
she woke sometimes to feel the daylight coming
like a relentless milkman up the stairs.

Crow's First Lesson[1]   1970

TED HUGHES   [b. 1930]

God tried to teach Crow how to talk.
"Love," said God. "Say, Love."
Crow gaped, and the white shark crashed into the sea
And went rolling downwards, discovering its own depth.

"No, no," said God, "Say Love. Now try it. LOVE."
Crow gaped, and a bluefly, a tsetse, a mosquito
Zoomed out and down
To their sundry flesh-pots.

Crow's First Lesson
   [1] In Hughes's collection of poems about him, Crow seems to be a supernatural demigod, combining human and animal traits. His exploits form a kind of creation myth.

"A final try," said God. "Now, LOVE."
Crow convulsed, gaped, retched and   10
Man's bodiless prodigious head
Bulbed out onto the earth, with swivelling eyes,
Jabbering protest—

And Crow retched again, before God could stop him.
And woman's vulva dropped over man's neck and tightened.
The two struggled together on the grass.
God struggled to part them, cursed, wept—

Crow flew guiltily off.

Daddy   1965

SYLVIA PLATH   [1932–1963]

You do not do, you do not do
Any more, black shoe
In which I have lived like a foot
For thirty years, poor and white,
Barely daring to breathe or Achoo.

Daddy, I have had to kill you,
You died before I had time—
Marble-heavy, a bag full of God,
Ghastly statue with one grey toe
Big as a Frisco seal   10

And a head in the freakish Atlantic
Where it pours bean green over blue
In the waters off beautiful Nauset.
I used to pray to recover you.
Ach, du.[1]

In the German tongue, in the Polish town
Scraped flat by the roller
Of wars, wars, wars.
But the name of the town is common.
My Polack friend   20

Daddy
  [1] German for "Ah, you."

Says there are a dozen or two.
So I never could tell where you
Put your foot, your root,
I never could talk to you.
The tongue stuck in my jaw.

It stuck in a barb wire snare.
Ich, ich, ich, ich,[2]
I could hardly speak.
I thought every German was you.
And the language obscene   30

An engine, an engine
Chuffing me off like a Jew.
A Jew to Dachau, Auschwitz, Belsen.
I began to talk like a Jew.
I think I may well be a Jew.

The snows of the Tyrol, the clear beer of Vienna
Are not very pure or true.
With my gypsy ancestress and my weird luck
And my Taroc pack and my Taroc pack
I may be a bit of a Jew.   40

I have always been scared of *you*,
With your Luftwaffe,[3] your gobbledygoo.
And your neat moustache
And your Aryan eye, bright blue.
Panzer-man,[4] panzer-man, O You—

Not God but a swastika
So black no sky could squeak through.
Every woman adores a Fascist,
The boot in the face, the brute
Brute heart of a brute like you.   50

You stand at the blackboard, daddy,
In the picture I have of you,
A cleft in your chin instead of your foot
But no less a devil for that, no not
Any less the black man who

---

[2] German for "I, I, I, I."
[3] Name of the German air force during World War II.
[4] Panzer refers to German armored divisions during World War II.

Bit my pretty red heart in two.
I was ten when they buried you.
At twenty I tried to die
And get back, back, back to you.   60
I thought even the bones would do.

But they pulled me out of the sack,
And they stuck me together with glue.
And then I knew what to do.
I made a model of you,
A man in black with a Meinkampf[5] look

And a love of the rack and the screw.
And I said I do, I do.
So daddy, I'm finally through.
The black telephone's off at the root,
The voices just can't worm through.   70

If I've killed one man, I've killed two—
The vampire who said he was you
And drank my blood for a year,
Seven years, if you want to know.
Daddy, you can lie back now.

There's a stake in your fat black heart
And the villagers never liked you.
They are dancing and stamping on you.
They always *knew* it was you.
Daddy, daddy, you bastard, I'm through.   80

QUESTIONS

1. How do the allusions to Nazism function in the poem?   **2.** Does the poem exhibit the speaker's love for her father or her hatred for him? Explain.   **3.** What sort of man does the speaker marry (see stanzas 13 and 14)?   **4.** How does the speaker characterize her husband and her father in the last two stanzas? Might the "Daddy" of the last line of the poem refer to something more than the speaker's father? Explain.

WRITING TOPIC

What is the effect of the peculiar structure, idiosyncratic rhyme, unusual words (such as *achoo, gobbledygoo*), and repetitions in the poem? What emotional associations does the title "Daddy" possess? Are those associations reinforced or contradicted by the poem?

---

[5]*My Battle*, the title of Adolf Hitler's political autobiography.

Gwen   1984

ROBERT WALLACE   [b. 1932]

You had just started sleeping
with someone when I came along—

though, as you told me,
you were only "minimally involved"

so it was okay for us (dutch-treat,
you insisted) to go out.

How angry you were! that men
have money, power, control.

Well, maybe. But no woman
ever supported me for ten years   10

while I studied and thought about
what I wanted to do with my life.

I wasted two years as a draftee,
not very patriotic, cleaning

out greasetraps for my country.
More than not, all my life,

I have been a supplicant
to women for sex and love

and have endured, over and over,
rebuff. Men have their scars.   20

(How pleasant should a pretty
lady appear in my office doorway,

and ask to take me out to dinner,
and offer herself to me!)

So we agreed to switch the roles—
thereafter you would call me

to ask me out. It would be,
you warned, the weekend after next—

next weekend you'd be out of town.
And, of course, you never called.   30

Well, men and women differ.
And so on. If such things matter,

it is because, somehow,
a man and a woman may, in love,

renounce the grievances and power
and, through Eden, hand in hand,

take their solitary way.

Brothers and Sisters   1982

KATHLEEN CUSHMAN   [b. 1950]

As if in some badly made home movie, their faces shift
and come into abrupt focus, each one
bringing its little shock of quick memories—six
faces, surrounding mine like some canny,
protective device in times of civil strife, and spliced
from *fat cheeks* to *school* to *now* in odd sequence.

Their names jumble together in the fast chant
we all knew to count after the bad day
one of us was left standing at the gas pumps, crying,
while the packed Pontiac rolled on for miles, rocking   10
in motion-sick, false assurance that it had us all:

a litter, displacing mother-and-father conflicts
by its sheer size; and, locked tight in the web of the overlapping arms
at the supper table, it's true I didn't have much
to do with the mother in the charcoal-gray maternity dress,
or with the father piling bags of groceries out of the trunk.

More my business was keeping straight the gang I led
in uniform with lunchboxes and the right coats
to the parish school, or the secrets elaborately
concealed from the oldest sister, who studied French   20
for hours before the bathroom mirror, pursing her lips
and making sounds we despised in the back of her throat,

or somehow breaking the tyranny of the stubborn
younger sister already bigger than me at nine
and passing down clothes, humiliating
me, thwarting the given order,
or squashing the one closest to me into a hiding place—
damp, electric, bursting with what we had that they didn't
and never would—being thrown on each other from the start,
mother to one another, sister, self with no boundaries guarded.   30

Big and Little, we were two camps under the same command,
jealous of privilege, rations, uniforms, but marked
by the brands we all shared: a last name, bones,
freckles, our mother's voice, the same books
dog-eared in the passages she had marked: *"Children—*
skip this." And, suddenly,

we are all the same age—all grown:
bearing the marks of each other's teeth, stretched out
into crazy patterns still branding us, our alliances
shifting, old enmities subdued and new ones born   40
to burn fiercely into the family flesh—

                              no one else
is to know all this but us; even love
will not initiate the outsiders; it is a closed club,
speaks its secret language,
the password less than a flicker of the eyelid,
knowing, impenetrable, beyond influence.

QUESTIONS

1. What is "the given order" (l. 26)?   **2.** Explain "And, suddenly, / we are all the same age" (ll. 37–38).   **3.** What does the speaker mean when she says, "even love / will not initiate the outsiders" (ll. 43–44)?   **4.** In what sense is this a poem about love? About hate?   **5.** Does the family described in this poem strike you as unique and special? Explain.

LOVE
AND
HATE

The Return of the Prodigal Son, c. 1642 by Rembrandt van Rijn

DRAMA

Othello

ca. 1604

WILLIAM SHAKESPEARE [1564–1616]

CHARACTERS

Duke of Venice
Brabantio, a Senator
Senators
Gratiano, Brother to Brabantio
Lodovico, Kinsman to Brabantio
Othello, a noble Moor; in the service of the Venetian State
Cassio, his Lieutenant
Iago, his Ancient
Roderigo, a Venetian Gentleman
Montano, Othello's predecessor in the Government of Cyprus
Clown, Servant to Othello
Desdemona, Daughter to Brabantio, and Wife to Othello
Emilia, Wife to Iago
Bianca, Mistress to Cassio
Sailor, Officers, Gentlemen, Messengers, Musicians, Heralds, Attendants

SCENE

For the first Act, in Venice; during the rest of the Play, at a Sea-port in Cyprus

Act I

SCENE 1. Venice. A Street.

(Enter Roderigo and Iago.)

Roderigo.   Tush! Never tell me; I take it much unkindly
  That thou, Iago, who hast had my purse
  As if the strings were thine, shouldst know of this.[1]

---

[1] I.e., Othello's successful courtship of Desdemona.

Iago.   'Sblood,[2] but you will not hear me:
 If ever I did dream of such a matter,
 Abhor me.
Roderigo.   Thou told'st me thou didst hold him[3] in thy hate.
Iago.   Despise me if I do not. Three great ones of the city,
 In personal suit to make me his lieutenant,
 Off-capp'd[4] to him; and, by the faith of man,   10
 I know my price, I am worth no worse a place;
 But he, as loving his own pride and purposes,
 Evades them, with a bombast circumstance[5]
 Horribly stuff'd with epithets of war;
 And, in conclusion,
 Nonsuits[6] my mediators;[7] for, 'Certes,'[8] says he,
 'I have already chosen my officer.'
 And what was he?
 Forsooth, a great arithmetician,
 One Michael Cassio, A Florentine,   20
 A fellow almost damn'd in a fair wife;[9]
 That never set a squadron in the field,
 Nor the division of a battle knows
 More than a spinster; unless[10] the bookish theoric,[11]
 Wherein the toged consuls can propose
 As masterly as he: mere prattle, without practice,
 Is all his soldiership. But he, sir, had the election;
 And I—of whom his eyes had seen the proof
 At Rhodes, at Cyprus, and on other grounds
 Christian and heathen—must be be-lee'd[12] and calm'd   30
 By debitor and creditor; this counter-caster,[13]
 He, in good time, must his lieutenant be,
 And I—God bless the mark!—his Moorship's ancient.[14]
Roderigo.   By heaven, I rather would have been his hangman.
Iago.   Why, there's no remedy: 'tis the curse of service,
 Preferment goes by letter and affection,
 Not by the old gradation,[15] where each second
 Stood heir to the first. Now, sir, be judge yourself,
 Whe'r[16] I in any just term am affin'd[17]
 To love the Moor.

---

[2] By God's blood.   [3] I.e., Othello.   [4] Took off their caps.   [5] Pompous wordiness, circumlocution.   [6] Turns down.   [7] Spokesmen.   [8] In truth.   [9] A much debated phrase. In the Italian source the Captain (i.e., Cassio) was married, and it may be that Shakespeare originally intended Bianca to be Cassio's wife but later changed his mind and failed to alter the phrase here accordingly. Or perhaps Iago simply sneers at Cassio as a notorious ladies' man.   [10] Except.   [11] Theory.   [12] Left without wind for my sails.   [13] Book-keeper (*cf.* "arithmetician" above).   [14] Ensign (but Iago's position in the play seems to be that of Othello's aide-de-camp).   [15] Seniority.   [16] Whether.   [17] Obliged.

Roderigo.   I would not follow him then.   40
Iago.   O! sir, content you;
  I follow him to serve my turn upon him;
  We cannot all be masters, nor all masters
  Cannot be truly follow'd. You shall mark
  Many a duteous and knee-crooking knave,
  That, doting on his own obsequious bondage,
  Wears out his time, much like his master's ass,
  For nought but provender, and when he's old, cashier'd;
  Whip me such honest knaves. Others there are
  Who, trimm'd in forms and visages of duty,   50
  Keep yet their hearts attending on themselves,
  And, throwing but shows of service on their lords,
  Do well thrive by them, and when they have lin'd their coats
  Do themselves homage: these fellows have some soul;
  And such a one do I profess myself. For, sir,
  It is as sure as you are Roderigo,
  Were I the Moor, I would not be Iago:
  In following him, I follow but myself;
  Heaven is my judge, not I for love and duty,
  But seeming so, for my peculiar end: 60
  For when my outward action doth demonstrate
  The native act and figure of my heart
  In compliment extern,[18] 'tis not long after
  But I will wear my heart upon my sleeve
  For daws to peck at: I am not what I am.
Roderigo.   What a full fortune does the thick-lips owe,[19]
  If he can carry 't thus!
Iago.   Call up her father;
  Rouse him, make after him, poison his delight,
  Proclaim him in the streets, incense her kinsmen,
  And, though he in a fertile climate dwell,[20]   70
  Plague him with flies; though that his joy be joy,
  Yet throw such changes of vexation on 't
  As it may lose some colour.
Roderigo.   Here is her father's house; I'll call aloud.
Iago.   Do; with like timorous[21] accent and dire yell
  As when, by night and negligence, the fire
  Is spied in populous cities.
Roderigo.   What, ho! Brabantio: Signior Brabantio, ho!
Iago.   Awake! what, ho! Brabantio! thieves! thieves! thieves!
  Look to your house, your daughter, and your bags!   80
  Thieves! thieves!

---

[18] External show.   [19] Own.   [20] I.e., is fortunate.   [21] Frightening.

(*Enter Brabantio, above, at a window.*)

Brabantio.   What is the reason of this terrible summons?
    What is the matter there?
Roderigo.   Signior, is all your family within?
Iago.   Are your doors lock'd?
Brabantio.   Why? wherefore ask you this?
Iago.   'Zounds!²² sir, you're robb'd; for shame, put on your gown;
    Your heart is burst, you have lost half your soul;
    Even now, now, very now, an old black ram
    Is tupping²³ your white ewe. Arise, arise!
    Awake the snorting²⁴ citizens with the bell,   90
    Or else the devil will make a grandsire of you.
    Arise, I say.
Brabantio.   What! have you lost your wits?
Roderigo.   Most reverend signior, do you know my voice?
Brabantio.   Not I, what are you?
Roderigo.   My name is Roderigo.
Brabantio.   The worser welcome:
    I have charg'd thee not to haunt about my doors:
    In honest plainness thou hast heard me say
    My daughter is not for thee; and now, in madness,
    Being full of supper and distempering draughts,
    Upon malicious knavery dost thou come   100
    To start my quiet.
Roderigo.   Sir, sir, sir!
Brabantio.   But thou must needs be sure
    My spirit and my place²⁵ have in them power
    To make this bitter to thee.
Roderigo.   Patience, good sir.
Brabantio.   What tell'st thou me of robbing? this is Venice;
    My house is not a grange.²⁶
Roderigo.   Most grave Brabantio,
    In simple and pure soul I come to you.
Iago.   'Zounds! sir, you are one of those that will not serve God if the devil
    bid you. Because we come to do you service and you think we are ruffians,
    you'll have your daughter covered with a Barbary horse; you'll have your
    nephews neigh to you; you'll have coursers for cousins and gennets²⁷ for
    germans.²⁸
Brabantio.   What profane wretch art thou?
Iago.   I am one, sir, that comes to tell you, your daughter and the Moor are
    now making the beast with two backs.

---

²² By God's wounds.   ²³ Copulating.   ²⁴ Snoring.   ²⁵ Position.
²⁶ Isolated farm house.   ²⁷ Spanish horses.   ²⁸ Blood relations.

Brabantio.   Thou art a villain.

Iago.   You are—a senator.

Brabantio.   This thou shalt answer; I know thee, Roderigo.

Roderigo.   Sir, I will answer any thing. But, I beseech you,   120
    If 't be your pleasure and most wise consent,—
    As partly, I find, it is,—that your fair daughter,
    At this odd-even[29] and dull watch o' the night,
    Transported with no worse nor better guard
    But with a knave of common hire, a gondolier,
    To the gross clasps of a lascivious Moor,—
    If this be known to you, and your allowance,[30]
    We then have done you bold and saucy wrongs;
    But if you know not this, my manners tell me
    We have your wrong rebuke. Do not believe   130
    That, from[31] the sense of all civility,
    I thus would play and trifle with your reverence:
    Your daughter, if you have not given her leave,
    I say again, hath made a gross revolt;
    Tying her duty, beauty, wit and fortunes
    In[32] an extravagant[33] and wheeling stranger
    Of here and every where. Straight satisfy yourself:
    If she be in her chamber or your house,
    Let loose on me the justice of the state
    For thus deluding you.

Brabantio.   Strike on the tinder, ho!   140
    Give me a taper! call up all my people!
    This accident[34] is not unlike my dream;
    Belief of it oppresses me already.
    Light, I say! light!   *(Exit, from above.)*

Iago.   Farewell, for I must leave you:
    It seems not meet nor wholesome to my place
    To be produc'd,[35] as, if I stay, I shall,
    Against the Moor; for I do know the state,
    However this may gall him with some check,[36]
    Cannot with safety cast him; for he's embark'd
    With such loud reason to the Cyprus wars,—   150
    Which even now stand in act,—that, for their souls,
    Another of his fathom[37] they have none,
    To lead their business; in which regard,
    Though I do hate him as I do hell-pains,
    Yet, for necessity of present life,

---

[29] Between night and morning.   [30] By your approval.   [31] Away from.   [32] To.
[33] Expatriate.   [34] Happening.   [35] I.e., as a witness.   [36] Restraining adversity.
[37] Caliber, ability.

I must show out a flag and sign of love,
Which is indeed but sign. That you shall surely find him,
Lead to the Sagittary[38] the raised search;
And there will I be with him. So, farewell.   *(Exit.)*

(Enter below, Brabantio, and servants with torches.)

Brabantio.   It is too true an evil: gone she is,   160
And what's to come of my despised time
Is nought but bitterness. Now, Roderigo,
Where didst thou see her? O, unhappy girl!
With the Moor, sayst thou? Who would be a father!
How didst thou know 'twas she? O, she deceives me
Past thought. What said she to you? Get more tapers!
Raise all my kindred! Are they married, think you?
Roderigo.   Truly, I think they are.
Brabantio.   O heaven! How got she out? O treason of the blood:
Fathers, from hence trust not your daughters' minds   170
By what you see them act. Are there not charms
By which the property of youth and maidhood
May be abus'd? Have you not read, Roderigo,
Of some such thing?
Roderigo.   Yes, sir, I have indeed.
Brabantio.   Call up my brother. O! that you had had her.
Some one way, some another! Do you know
Where we may apprehend her and the Moor?
Roderigo.   I think I can discover him, if you please
To get good guard and go along with me.   180
Brabantio.   Pray you, lead on. At every house I'll call;
I may command at most. Get weapons, ho!
And raise some special officers of night.
On, good Roderigo; I'll deserve[39] your pains.   *(Exeunt.)*

SCENE 2.   Another street.

(Enter Othello, Iago, and Attendants, with torches.)

Iago.   Though in the trade of war I have slain men,
Yet do I hold it very stuff o' the conscience
To do no contriv'd murder: I lack iniquity
Sometimes to do me service. Nine or ten times
I had thought to have yerk'd[40] him here under the ribs.
Othello.   'Tis better as it is.

---

[38] The name of an inn(?).   [39] I.e., reward.   [40] Stabbed.

Iago.   Nay, but he prated,
  And spoke such scurvy and provoking terms
  Against your honour
  That, with the little godliness I have,
  I did full hard forbear him. But, I pray, sir,   10
  Are you fast married? Be assur'd of this,
  That the magnifico[41] is much belov'd,
  And hath in his effect a voice potential
  As double[42] as the duke's; he will divorce you,
  Or put upon you what restraint and grievance
  The law—with all his might to enforce it on—
  Will give him cable.[43]

Othello.   Let him do his spite:
  My services which I have done the signiory[44]
  Shall out-tongue his complaints. 'Tis yet to know,[45]
  Which when I know that boasting is an honour   20
  I shall promulgate, I fetch my life and being
  From men of royal siege, and my demerits[46]
  May speak unbonneted[47] to as proud a fortune
  As this[48] that I have reach'd; for know, Iago,
  But that I love the gentle Desdemona,
  I would not my unhoused[49] free condition
  Put into circumscription and confine
  For the sea's worth. But, look! what lights come yond?

Iago.   Those are the raised[50] father and his friends:
  You were best[51] go in.

Othello.   Not I; I must be found: 30
  My parts, my title, and my perfect[52] soul
  Shall manifest me rightly. Is it they?

Iago.   By Janus,[53] I think no.

(*Enter Cassio and certain Officers, with torches.*)

Othello.   The servants of the duke, and my lieutenant.
  The goodness of the night upon you, friends!
  What is the news?

Cassio.   The duke does greet you, general,
  And he requires your haste-post-haste appearance,
  Even on the instant.

---

[41] One of the grandees, or rulers, of Venice; here, Brabantio.   [42] Iago means that Brabantio's influence equals that of the Doge's with his double vote.   [43] I.e., scope.   [44] The Venetian government.   [45] I.e., the signiory does not as yet know.   [46] Merits.   [47] I.e., as equals.   [48] I.e., that of Desdemona's family.   [49] Unconfined.   [50] Aroused.   [51] Had better.   [52] Untroubled by a bad conscience.   [53] The two-faced Roman god of portals and doors and (hence) of beginnings and ends.

Othello.   What is the matter, think you?
Cassio.   Something from Cyprus, as I may divine.
  It is a business of some heat;[54] the galleys   40
  Have sent a dozen sequent[55] messengers
  This very night at one another's heels,
  And many of the consuls,[56] rais'd and met,
  Are at the duke's already. You have been hotly call'd for;
  When, being not at your lodging to be found,
  The senate hath sent about three several[57] quests
  To search you out.
Othello.   'Tis well I am found by you.
  I will but spend a word here in the house,
  And go with you.   (*Exit.*)
Cassio.   Ancient, what makes he here?
Iago.   Faith, he to-night hath boarded a land carrack;[58]   50
  If it prove lawful prize, he's made for ever.
Cassio.   I do not understand.
Iago.   He's married.
Cassio.   To who?

(Re-enter Othello.)

Iago.   Marry,[59] to—Come, captain, will you go?
Othello.   Have with you.
Cassio.   Here comes another troop to seek for you.
Iago.   It is Brabantio. General, be advis'd;
  He comes to bad intent.

(Enter Brabantio, Roderigo, and Officers, with torches and weapons.)

Othello.   Holla! stand there!
Roderigo.   Signior, it is the Moor.
Brabantio.   Down with him, thief!

(They draw on both sides.)

Iago.   You, Roderigo! Come, sir, I am for you.[60]
Othello.   Keep up your bright swords, for the dew will rust them.
  Good signior, you shall more command with years   60
  Than with your weapons.
Brabantio.   O thou foul thief! where hast thou stow'd my daughter?
  Damn'd as thou art, thou hast enchanted her;

---

[54] Urgency.   [55] Following one another.   [56] I.e., senators.   [57] Separate.
[58] Treasure ship.   [59] By the Virgin Mary.   [60] Let you and me fight.

For I'll refer me to all things of sense,
If she in chains of magic were not bound,
Whether a maid so tender, fair, and happy,
So opposite to marriage that she shunn'd
The wealthy curled darlings of our nation,
Would ever have, to incur a general mock,
Run from her guardage to the sooty bosom   70
Of such a thing as thou; to fear, not to delight.
Judge me the world, if 'tis not gross in sense[61]
That thou hast practis'd on her with foul charms,
Abus'd her delicate youth with drugs or minerals
That weaken motion:[62] I'll have 't disputed on;
'Tis probable, and palpable to thinking.
I therefore apprehend and do attach[63] thee
For an abuser of the world, a practiser
Of arts inhibited and out of warrant.[64]
Lay hold upon him: if he do resist,   80
Subdue him at his peril.
Othello.   Hold your hands,
Both you of my inclining,[65] and the rest:
Were it my cue to fight, I should have known it
Without a prompter. Where will you that I go
To answer this your charge?
Brabantio.   To prison; till fit time
Of law and course of direct session[66]
Call thee to answer.
Othello.   What if I do obey?
How may the duke be therewith satisfied,
Whose messengers are here about my side,
Upon some present[67] business of the state   90
To bring me to him?
Officer.   'Tis true, most worthy signior;
The duke's in council, and your noble self,
I am sure, is sent for.
Brabantio.   How! the duke in council!
In this time of the night! Bring him away.
Mine's not an idle cause: the duke himself,
Or any of my brothers of the state,[68]
Cannot but feel this wrong as 'twere their own;
For if such actions may have passage free,
Bond-slaves and pagans shall our statesmen be.   *(Exeunt.)*

---

[61] Obvious.   [62] Normal reactions.   [63] Arrest.   [64] Prohibited and illegal.   [65] Party.
[66] Normal process of law.   [67] Immediate, pressing.   [68] Fellow senators.

SCENE 3. A Council Chamber.

(The Duke and Senators sitting at a table. Officers attending.)

Duke.   There is no composition[69] in these news
  That gives them credit.
First Senator.   Indeed, they are disproportion'd;
  My letters say a hundred and seven galleys.
Duke.   And mine, a hundred and forty.
Second Senator.   And mine, two hundred:
  But though they jump[70] not on a just[71] account,—
  As in these cases, where the aim[72] reports,
  'Tis oft with difference,—yet do they all confirm
  A Turkish fleet, and bearing up to Cyprus.
Duke.   Nay, it is possible enough to judgment:
  I do not so secure me in[73] the error,   10
  But the main article[74] I do approve[75]
  In fearful sense.
Sailor *(within).*   What, ho! what, ho! what, ho!
Officer.   A messenger from the galleys.

(Enter a Sailor.)

Duke.   Now, what's the business?
Sailor.   The Turkish preparation makes for Rhodes;
  So was I bid report here to the state
  By Signior Angelo.
Duke.   How say you by this change?
First Senator.   This cannot be
  By no[76] assay[77] of reason; 'tis a pageant[78]
  To keep us in false gaze.[79] When we consider
  The importancy of Cyprus to the Turk,   20
  And let ourselves again but understand,
  That as it more concerns the Turk than Rhodes,
  So may he with more facile question bear[80] it,
  For that it stands not in such warlike brace,[81]
  But altogether lacks the abilities
  That Rhodes is dress'd in: if we make thought of this,
  We must not think the Turk is so unskilful
  To leave that latest which concerns him first,

---

[69] Consistency, agreement.   [70] Coincide.   [71] Exact.   [72] Conjecture.   [73] Draw
comfort from.   [74] Substance.   [75] Believe.   [76] Any.   [77] Test.
[78] (Deceptive) show.   [79] Looking in the wrong direction.   [80] More easily capture.
[81] State of defense.

Neglecting an attempt of ease and gain,
  To wake and wage a danger profitless.   30
Duke.   Nay, in all confidence, he's not for Rhodes.
Officer.   Here is more news.

(Enter a Messenger.)

Messenger.   The Ottomites,[82] reverend and gracious,
  Steering with due course toward the isle of Rhodes,
  Have there injointed[83] them with an after fleet.[84]
First Senator.   Ay, so I thought. How many, as you guess?
Messenger.   Of thirty sail; and now they do re-stem[85]
  Their backward course, bearing with frank appearance
  Their purposes toward Cyprus. Signior Montano,
  Your trusty and most valiant servitor,   40
  With his free duty[86] recommends[87] you thus,
  And prays you to believe him.
Duke.   'Tis certain then, for Cyprus.
  Marcus Luccicos, is not he in town?
First Senator.   He's now in Florence.
Duke.   Write from us to him; post-post-haste dispatch.
First Senator.   Here comes Brabantio and the valiant Moor.

(Enter Brabantio, Othello, Iago, Roderigo, and Officers.)

Duke.   Valiant Othello, we must straight employ you
  Against the general enemy Ottoman.
  (To Brabantio) I did not see you; welcome, gentle signior;   50
  We lack'd your counsel and your help to-night.
Brabantio.   So did I yours. Good your Grace, pardon me;
  Neither my place nor aught I heard of business
  Hath rais'd me from my bed, nor doth the general care
  Take hold of me, for my particular grief
  Is of so flood-gate[88] and o'erbearing nature
  That it engluts and swallows other sorrows
  And it is still itself.
Duke.   Why, what's the matter?
Brabantio.   My daughter! O! my daughter.
Duke. ⎫
Senators. ⎭   Dead?
Brabantio.   Ay, to me;
  She is abus'd, stol'n from me, and corrupted   60

---

[82] Turks.   [83] Joined.   [84] Fleet that followed after.   [85] Steer again.   [86] Unqualified expressions of respect.   [87] Informs.   [88] Torrential.

By spells and medicines bought of mountebanks;
For nature so preposterously to err,
Being not deficient, blind, or lame of sense,
Sans[89] witchcraft could not.

Duke.   Whoe'er he be that in this foul proceeding
Hath thus beguil'd your daughter of herself
And you of her, the bloody book of law
You shall yourself read in the bitter letter
After your own sense; yea, though our proper[90] son
Stood[91] in your action.[92]

Brabantio.   Humbly I thank your Grace.   70
Here is the man, this Moor; whom now, it seems,
Your special mandate for the state affairs
Hath hither brought.

Duke. ⎫
Senators. ⎰   We are very sorry for it.

Duke (to Othello).   What, in your own part, can you say to this?
Brabantio.   Nothing, but this is so.
Othello.   Most potent, grave, and reverend signiors,
My very noble and approv'd[93] good masters,
That I have ta'en away this old man's daughter,
It is most true; true, I have married her:
The very head and front of my offending   80
Hath this extent, no more. Rude am I in my speech,
And little bless'd with the soft phrase of peace;
For since these arms of mine had seven years' pith,[94]
Till now some nine moons wasted,[95] they have us'd
Their dearest action in the tented field;
And little of this great world can I speak,
More than pertains to feats of broil and battle;
And therefore little shall I grace my cause
In speaking for myself. Yet, by your gracious patience,
I will a round[96] unvarnish'd tale deliver   90
Of my whole course of love; what drugs, what charms,
What conjuration, and what mighty magic,
For such proceeding I am charg'd withal,
I won his daughter.

Brabantio.   A maiden never bold;
Of spirit so still and quiet, that her motion
Blush'd at herself;[97] and she, in spite of nature,
Of years, of country, credit, every thing,

---

[89] Without.   [90] Own.   [91] Were accused.   [92] Suit.   [93] Tested (by past experience).   [94] Strength.   [95] Past.   [96] Blunt.   [97] I.e., (her modesty was such that) she blushed at her own emotions; or: could not move without blushing.

To fall in love with what she fear'd to look on!
It is a judgment maim'd and most imperfect
That will confess[98] perfection so could err   100
Against all rules of nature, and must be driven
To find out practices of cunning hell,
Why this should be. I therefore vouch again
That with some mixtures powerful o'er the blood,
Or with some dram conjur'd to this effect,
He wrought upon her.
Duke.   To vouch this, is no proof,
Without more certain and more overt test
Than these thin habits[99] and poor likelihoods
Of modern[100] seeming do prefer against him.
First Senator.   But, Othello, speak: 110
Did you by indirect and forced courses
Subdue and poison this young maid's affections;
Or came it by request and such fair question[101]
As soul to soul affordeth?
Othello.   I do beseech you;
Send for the lady to the Sagittary,
And let her speak of me before her father:
If you do find me foul in her report,
The trust, the office I do hold of you,
Not only take away, but let your sentence
Even fall upon my life.
Duke.   Fetch Desdemona hither.   120
Othello.   Ancient, conduct them; you best know the place.

                                  (Exeunt Iago and Attendants.)

And, till she come, as truly as to heaven
I do confess the vices of my blood,
So justly to your grave ears I'll present
How I did thrive in this fair lady's love,
And she in mine.
Duke.   Say it, Othello.
Othello.   Her father lov'd me; oft invited me;
Still[102] question'd me the story of my life
From year to year, the battles, sieges, fortunes   130
That I have pass'd.
I ran it through, even from my boyish days
To the very moment that he bade me tell it;

---

[98] Assert.   [99] Weak appearances.   [100] Commonplace.   [101] Conversation.
[102] Always, regularly.

Wherein I spake of most disastrous chances,
Of moving accidents by flood and field,
Of hair-breadth 'scapes i' the imminent deadly breach,
Of being taken by the insolent foe
And sold to slavery, of my redemption thence
And portance[103] in my travel's history;
Wherein of antres[104] vast and deserts idle,[105]   140
Rough quarries, rocks, and hills whose heads touch heaven,
It was my hint[106] to speak, such was the process;
And of the Cannibals that each other eat,
The Anthropophagi,[107] and men whose heads
Do grow beneath their shoulders. This to hear
Would Desdemona seriously incline;
But still the house-affairs would draw her thence;
Which ever as she could with haste dispatch,
She'd come again, and with a greedy ear
Devour up my discourse. Which I observing,   150
Took once a pliant[108] hour, and found good means
To draw from her a prayer of earnest heart
That I would all my pilgrimage dilate,[109]
Whereof by parcels[110] she had something heard,
But not intentively:[111] I did consent;
And often did beguile her of her tears,
When I did speak of some distressful stroke
That my youth suffer'd. My story being done,
She gave me for my pains a world of sighs:
She swore, in faith, 'twas strange, 'twas passing[112] strange;   160
'Twas pitiful, 'twas wondrous pitiful:
She wish'd she had not heard it, yet she wish'd
That heaven had made her[113] such a man; she thank'd me,
And bade me, if I had a friend that lov'd her,
I should but teach him how to tell my story,
And that would woo her. Upon this hint I spake.
She lov'd me for the dangers I had pass'd,
And I lov'd her that she did pity them.
This only is the witchcraft I have us'd:
Here comes the lady; let her witness it.   170

(Enter Desdemona, Iago, and Attendants.)

Duke.   I think this tale would win my daughter too.
    Good Brabantio,

---

[103] Behavior.   [104] Caves.   [105] Empty, sterile.   [106] Opportunity.   [107] Man-
eaters.   [108] Suitable.   [109] Relate in full.   [110] Piecemeal.   [111] In
sequence.   [112] Surpassing.   [113] Direct object; not "for her."

Take up this mangled matter at the best;
Men do their broken weapons rather use
Than their bare hands.

Brabantio.   I pray you, hear her speak:
If she confess that she was half the wooer,
Destruction on my head, if my bad blame
Light on the man! Come hither, gentle mistress:
Do you perceive in all this noble company
Where most you owe obedience?

Desdemona.   My noble father,   180
I do perceive here a divided duty:
To you I am bound for life and education;
My life and education both do learn[114] me
How to respect you; you are the lord of duty,
I am hitherto your daughter: but here's my husband;
And so much duty as my mother show'd
To you, preferring you before her father,
So much I challenge[115] that I may profess
Due to the Moor my lord.

Brabantio.   God be with you! I have done.
Please it your Grace, on to the state affairs;   190
I had rather to adopt a child than get it.
Come hither, Moor:
I here do give thee that with all my heart
Which, but thou hast[116] already, with all my heart
I would keep from thee. For your sake,[117] jewel,
I am glad at soul I have no other child;
For thy escape would teach me tyranny,
To hang clogs on them. I have done, my lord.

Duke. Let me speak like yourself and lay a sentence,[118]
Which as a grize[119] or step, may help these lovers   200
Into your favour.
When remedies are past, the griefs are ended
By seeing the worst, which[120] late on hopes depended.
To mourn a mischief that is past and gone
Is the next way to draw new mischief on.
What cannot be preserv'd when Fortune takes,
Patience her injury a mockery makes.[121]
The robb'd that smiles steals something from the thief;
He robs himself that spends a bootless grief.

Brabantio. So let the Turk of Cyprus us beguile;   210
We lose it not so long as we can smile.

---

[114] Teach.   [115] Claim as right.   [116] Didn't you have it.   [117] Because of you.
[118] Provide a maxim.   [119] Step.   [120] The antecedent is "griefs."   [121] To suffer an irreparable loss patiently is to make light of injury (i.e., to triumph over adversity).

He bears the sentence[122] well that nothing bears
But the free comfort which from thence he hears;
But he bears both the sentence and the sorrow
That, to pay grief, must of poor patience borrow.
These sentences, to sugar, or to gall,
Being strong on both sides, are equivocal:[123]
But words are words: I never yet did hear
That the bruis'd heart was pierced[124] through the ear.
I humbly beseech you, proceed to the affairs of state.   220

Duke.   The Turk with a most mighty preparation makes for Cyprus. Othello,
the fortitude[125] of the place is best known to you; and though we have there
a substitute of most allowed sufficiency,[126] yet opinion, a sovereign mistress
of effects, throws a more safer voice on you:[127] you must therefore be content
to slubber[128] the gloss of your new fortunes with this more stubborn[129] and
boisterous expedition.

Othello.   The tyrant custom, most grave senators,
Hath made the flinty and steel couch of war
My thrice-driven[130] bed of down: I do agnize[131]
A natural and prompt alacrity   230
I find in hardness, and do undertake
These present wars against the Ottomites.
Most humbly therefore bending to your state,[132]
I crave fit disposition[133] for my wife,
Due reference of place and exhibition,[134]
With such accommodation and besort[135]
As levels with[136] her breeding.

Duke.   If you please,
Be 't at her father's.

Brabantio.   I'll not have it so.

Othello.   Nor I.

Desdemona.   Nor I; I would not there reside,
To put my father in impatient thoughts   240
By being in his eye. Most gracious duke,
To my unfolding[137] lend your gracious ear;
And let me find a charter[138] in your voice
To assist my simpleness.

Duke.   What would you, Desdemona?

Desdemona.   That I did love the Moor to live with him,
My downright violence and storm of fortunes

---

[122] (1) Verdict, (2) Maxim.   [123] Sententious comfort (like the Duke's trite maxims) can hurt
as well as soothe.   [124] (1) Lanced (i.e., cured), (2) Wounded.   [125] Strength.
[126] Admitted competence.   [127] General opinion, which mainly determines action, thinks
Cyprus safer with you in command.   [128] Besmear.   [129] Rough.   [130] Made as soft
as possible.   [131] Recognize.   [132] Submitting to your authority.   [133] Disposal.
[134] Provision.   [135] Fitness.   [136] Is proper to.   [137] Explanation.   [138] Permission.

May trumpet to the world; my heart's subdu'd
Even to the very quality of my lord;[139]
I saw Othello's visage in his mind,   250
And to his honours and his valiant parts
Did I my soul and fortunes consecrate.
So that, dear lords, if I be left behind,
A moth of peace, and he go to the war,
The rites[140] for which I love him are bereft me,
And I a heavy interim shall support[141]
By his dear[142] absence. Let me go with him.

Othello.   Let her have your voices.
Vouch with me, heaven, I therefore beg it not
To please the palate of my appetite,   260
Nor to comply with heat,—the young affects[143]
In me defunct,—and proper satisfaction,
But to be free and bounteous to her mind;
And heaven defend[144] your good souls that you think
I will your serious and great business scant
For[145] she is with me. No, when light-wing'd toys
Of feather'd Cupid seel[146] with wanton dulness
My speculative and offic'd instruments,[147]
That[148] my disports corrupt and taint my business,
Let housewives make a skillet of my helm,   270
And all indign[149] and base adversities
Make head against my estimation![150]

Duke.   Be it as you shall privately determine,
Either for her stay or going. The affair cries haste,
And speed must answer it.

First Senator.   You must away to-night.

Othello.   With all my heart.

Duke.   At nine i' the morning here we'll meet again.
Othello, leave some officer behind,
And he shall our commission bring to you;
With such things else of quality and respect   280
As doth import you.[151]

Othello.   So please your Grace, my ancient;
A man he is of honesty and trust:
To his conveyance I assign my wife,
With what else needful your good grace shall think
To be sent after me.

---

[139] I.e., I have become a soldier, like Othello.   [140] I.e., of marriage, or of war, or of both.   [141] Endure.   [142] Closely concerning (i.e., Desdemona).   [143] The passions of youth (hence, here, *immoderate* sexual passion).   [144] Forbid.   [145] Because.   [146] Blind (v.) by sewing up the eyelids (a term from falconry).   [147] Reflective and executive faculties and organs.   [148] So that.   [149] Shameful.   [150] Reputation.   [151] Concern.

Duke.   Let it be so.

Good-night to every one. (*To Brabantio*) And, noble signior,

If virtue no delighted[152] beauty lack,

Your son-in-law is far more fair than black.

First Senator.   Adieu, brave Moor! use Desdemona well.

Brabantio.   Look to her, Moor, if thou hast eyes to see: 290

She has deceiv'd her father, and may thee.

(Exeunt Duke, Senators, Officers, &c.)

Othello.   My life upon her faith! Honest Iago,

My Desdemona must I leave to thee:

I prithee, let thy wife attend on her;

And bring them after in the best advantage.[153]

Come, Desdemona; I have but an hour

Of love, of worldly matters and direction,

To spend with thee: we must obey the time.

(Exeunt Othello and Desdemona.)

Roderigo.   Iago!

Iago.   What sayst thou, noble heart?   300

Roderigo.   What will I do, think'st thou?

Iago.   Why, go to bed, and sleep.

Roderigo.   I will incontinently[154] drown myself.

Iago.   Well, if thou dost, I shall never love thee after.

Why, thou silly gentleman!

Roderigo.   It is silliness to live when to live is torment; and then have we a
prescription to die when death is our physician.

Iago.   O! villanous; I have looked upon the world for four times seven years,
and since I could distinguish betwixt a benefit and an injury, I never found
man that knew how to love himself. Ere I would say, I would drown myself
for the love of a guinea-hen, I would change my humanity with a baboon.

Roderigo.   What should I do? I confess it is my shame to be so fond;[155] but
it is not in my virtue[156] to amend it.

Iago.   Virtue! a fig! 'tis in ourselves that we are thus, or thus. Our bodies are
our gardens, to the which our wills are gardeners; so that if we will plant
nettles or sow lettuce, set hyssop and weed up thyme, supply it with one
gender[157] of herbs or distract it with many, either to have it sterile with
idleness or manured with industry, why, the power and corrigible[158] authority
of this lies in our wills. If the balance of our lives had not one scale of reason

---

[152] Delightful.   [153] Opportunity.   [154] Forthwith.   [155] Infatuated.
[156] Strength.   [157] Kind.   [158] Corrective.

to poise another of sensuality, the blood and baseness of our natures would conduct us to most preposterous conclusions; but we have reason to cool our raging motions, our carnal stings, our unbitted[159] lusts, whereof I take this that you call love to be a sect or scion.[160]

Roderigo.   It cannot be.

Iago.   It is merely a lust of the blood and a permisson of the will. Come, be a man. Drown thyself! drown cats and blind puppies. I have professed me thy friend, and I confess me knit to thy deserving with cables of perdurable toughness; I could never better stead thee than now. Put money in thy purse; follow these wars; defeat thy favour[161] with a usurped[162] beard; I say, put money in thy purse. It cannot be that Desdemona should long continue her love to the Moor,—put money in thy purse,—nor he his to her. It was a violent commencement in her, and thou shalt see an answerable sequestration;[163] put but money in thy purse. These Moors are changeable in their wills;—fill thy purse with money:—the food that to him now is as luscious as locusts,[164] shall be to him shortly as bitter as coloquintida.[165] She must change for youth: when she is sated with his body, she will find the error of her choice. She must have change, she must: therefore put money in thy purse. If thou wilt needs damn thyself, do it a more delicate way than drowning. Make all the money thou canst. If sanctimony and a frail vow betwixt an erring[166] barbarian and a supersubtle[167] Venetian be not too hard for my wits and all the tribe of hell, thou shalt enjoy her; therefore make money. A pox of drowning thyself! it is clean out of the way: seek thou rather to be hanged in compassing thy joy than to be drowned and go without her.

Roderigo.   Wilt thou be fast to my hopes, if I depend on the issue?[168]

Iago.   Thou art sure of me: go, make money. I have told thee often, and I retell thee again and again, I hate the Moor; my cause is hearted; thine hath no less reason. Let us be conjunctive[169] in our revenge against him; if thou canst cuckold him, thou dost thyself a pleasure, me a sport. There are many events in the womb of time which will be delivered. Traverse;[170] go: provide thy money. We will have more of this to-morrow. Adieu.

Roderigo.   Where shall we meet i' the morning?

Iago.   At my lodging.

Roderigo.   I'll be with thee betimes.

Iago.   Go to: farewell. Do you hear, Roderigo?

Roderigo.   What say you?

Iago.   No more of drowning, do you hear?

Roderigo.   I am changed. I'll sell all my land.

Iago.   Go to; farewell! put money enough in your purse.   *(Exit Roderigo.)*

Thus do I ever make my fool my purse;

---

[159] I.e., uncontrolled.   [160] Offshoot.   [161] Change thy appearance (for the worse?). [162] Assumed.   [163] Estrangement.   [164] Sweet-tasting fruits (perhaps the carob, the edible seed-pod of an evergreen tree in the Mediterranean area).   [165] Purgative derived from a bitter apple.   [166] Vagabond.   [167] Exceedingly refined.   [168] Rely on the outcome. [169] Allied.   [170] March.

For I mine own gain'd knowledge should profane,   360
If I would time expend with such a snipe[171]
But for my sport and profit. I hate the Moor,
And it is thought abroad[172] that 'twixt my sheets
He has done my office: I know not if 't be true,
But I, for mere suspicion in that kind,
Will do as if for surety.[173] He holds me well;[174]
The better shall my purpose work on him.
Cassio's a proper[175] man; let me see now:
To get his place; and to plume up[176] my will
In double knavery; how, how? Let's see: 370
After some time to abuse Othello's ear
That he[177] is too familiar with his wife:
He hath a person and a smooth dispose[178]
To be suspected; framed[179] to make women false,
The Moor is of a free and open nature,
That thinks men honest that but seem to be so,
And will as tenderly be led by the nose
As asses are.
I have 't; it is engender'd: hell and night
Must bring this monstrous birth to the world's light.   (*Exit.*)

Act II

SCENE 1.   A Sea-port Town in Cyprus. An open place near the Quay.

(*Enter Montano and two Gentlemen.*)

Montano.   What from the cape can you discern at sea?
First Gentleman.   Nothing at all: it is a high-wrought flood;
I cannot 'twixt the heaven and the main[180]
Descry a sail.
Montano.   Methinks the wind hath spoke aloud at land;
A fuller blast ne'er shook our battlements;
If it hath ruffian'd so upon the sea,
What ribs of oak, when mountains melt on them,
Can hold the mortise?[181] What shall we hear of this?
Second Gentleman.   A segregation[182] of the Turkish fleet;   10
For do but stand upon the foaming shore,

---

[171] Dupe.   [172] People think.   [173] As if it were certain.   [174] In high regard.
[175] Handsome.   [176] Make ready.   [177] I.e., Cassio.   [178] Bearing.   [179] Designed,
apt.   [180] Ocean.   [181] Hold the joints together.   [182] Scattering.

The chidden billow seems to pelt the clouds;
The wind-shak'd surge, with high and monstrous mane,
Seems to cast water on the burning bear[183]
And quench the guards of the ever-fixed pole:[184]
I never did like[185] molestation view
On the enchafed[186] flood.
Montano.   If that[187] the Turkish fleet
Be not enshelter'd and embay'd, they are drown'd;
It is impossible they bear it out.

(Enter a Third Gentleman.)

Third Gentleman.   News, lad! our wars are done.   20
  The desperate tempest hath so bang'd the Turks
  That their designment halts;[188] a noble ship of Venice
  Hath seen a grievous wrack and suffrance[189]
  On most part of their fleet.
Montano.   How! is this true?
Third Gentleman.   The ship is here put in,
  A Veronesa;[190] Michael Cassio,
  Lieutenant to the warlike Moor Othello,
  Is come on shore: the Moor himself's at sea,
  And is in full commission here for Cyprus.
Montano.   I am glad on 't; 'tis a worthy governor.   30
Third Gentleman.   But this same Cassio, though he speak of comfort
  Touching the Turkish loss, yet he looks sadly
  And prays the Moor be safe; for they were parted
  With foul and violent tempest.
Montano.   Pray heaven he be;
  For I have serv'd him, and the man commands
  Like a full soldier. Let's to the sea-side, ho!
  As well to see the vessel that's come in
  As to throw out our eyes for brave Othello,
  Even till we make the main and the aerial blue
  An indistinct regard.[191]
Third Gentleman.   Come, let's do so;   40
  For every minute is expectancy
  Of more arrivance.

---

[183] Ursa Minor (the Little Dipper). [184] Polaris, the North Star, almost directly above the Earth's axis, is part of the constellation of the Little Bear, or Dipper. [185] Similar. [186] Agitated. [187] If. [188] Plan is stopped.   [189] Damage.   [190] Probably a *type* of ship, rather than a ship from Verona—not only because Verona is an inland city but also because of "a noble ship of Venice" above.   [191] Till our (straining) eyes can no longer distinguish sea and sky.

(Enter Cassio.)

Cassio.   Thanks, you the valiant of this warlike isle,
    That so approve the Moor. O! let the heavens
    Give him defence against the elements,
    For I have lost him on a dangerous sea.
Montano.   Is he well shipp'd?
Cassio.   His bark is stoutly timber'd, and his pilot
    Of very expert and approv'd allowance;[192]
    Therefore my hopes, not surfeited to death,[193]
    Stand in bold cure.[194]   50

(Within, 'A sail!—a sail!—a sail!' Enter a Messenger.)

Cassio.   What noise?
Messenger.   The town is empty; on the brow o' the sea
    Stand ranks of people, and they cry 'A sail!'
Cassio.   My hopes do shape him for the governor.

(Guns heard.)

Second Gentleman.   They do discharge their shot of courtesy;
    Our friends at least.
Cassio.   I pray you, sir, go forth.
    And give us truth who 'tis that is arriv'd.
Second Gentleman.   I shall.   *(Exit)*
Montano.   But, good lieutenant, is your general wiv'd?   60
Cassio.   Most fortunately: he hath achiev'd a maid
    That paragons[195] description and wild fame;
    One that excels the quirks[196] of blazoning pens,
    And in th' essential vesture of creation[197]
    Does tire the ingener.[198]

(Re-enter Second Gentleman.)

                        How now! who has put in?
Second Gentleman.   'Tis one Iago, ancient to the general.
Cassio.   He has had most favourable and happy speed:
    Tempests themselves, high seas, and howling winds,
    The gutter'd[199] rocks, and congregated sands,

---

[192] Admitted and proven to be expert. [193] Overindulged. [194] With good chance of being fulfilled.
[195] Exceeds, surpasses.   [196] Ingenuities.   [197] I.e., just as God made her; or: (even in)
the (mere) essence of human nature.   [198] Inventor (i.e., of her praises?).
[199] Jagged; or: submerged.

Traitors ensteep'd[200] to clog the guiltless keel,   70
As having sense of beauty, do omit
Their mortal[201] natures, letting go safely by
The divine Desdemona.
Montano.   What is she?
Cassio.   She that I spake of, our great captain's captain,
Left in the conduct of the bold Iago,
Whose footing[202] here anticipates our thoughts
A se'nnight's[203] speed. Great Jove, Othello guard,
And swell his sail with thine own powerful breath,
That he may bless this bay with his tall[204] ship,
Make love's quick pants in Desdemona's arms,   80
Give renew'd fire to our extinced spirits,
And bring all Cyprus comfort!

(Enter Desdemona, Emilia, Iago, Roderigo, and Attendants.)

                              O! behold,
The riches of the ship is come on shore.
Ye men of Cyprus, let her have your knees.
Hail to thee, lady! and the grace of heaven,
Before, behind thee, and on every hand,
Enwheel thee round!
Desdemona.   I thank you, valiant Cassio.
What tidings can you tell me of my lord?
Cassio.   He is not yet arriv'd; nor know I aught
But that he's well, and will be shortly here.   90
Desdemona.   O! but I fear—How lost you company?
Cassio.   The great contention of the sea and skies
Parted our fellowship. But hark! a sail.

(Cry within, 'A sail—a sail!' Guns heard.)

Second Gentleman.   They give their greeting to the citadel:
This likewise is a friend.
Cassio.   See for the news!   *(Exit Gentleman.)*
Good ancient, you are welcome:—*(To Emilia)* welcome, mistress.
Let it not gall your patience, good Iago,
That I extend my manners; 'tis my breeding
That gives me this bold show of courtesy.   *(Kissing her.)*
Iago.   Sir, would she give you so much of her lips   100
As of her tongue she oft bestows on me,
You'd have enough.

---

[200] Submerged.   [201] Deadly.   [202] Landing.   [203] Week's.   [204] Brave.

Desdemona.   Alas! she has no speech.
Iago.   In faith, too much;
   I find it still when I have list[205] to sleep:
   Marry, before your ladyship, I grant,
   She puts her tongue a little in her heart,
   And chides with thinking.[206]
Emilia.   You have little cause to say so.
Iago.   Come on, come on; you are pictures[207] out of doors,
   Bells[208] in your parlours, wild cats in your kitchens,   110
   Saints in your injuries, devils being offended,
   Players[209] in your housewifery,[210] and housewives[211] in your beds.
Desdemona.   O! fie upon thee, slanderer.
Iago.   Nay, it is true, or else I am a Turk:
   You rise to play and go to bed to work.
Emilia.   You shall not write my praise.
Iago.
                                          No, let me not.
Desdemona.   What wouldst thou write of me, if thou shouldst praise me?
Iago.   O gentle lady, do not put me to 't,
   For I am nothing if not critical.
Desdemona.   Come on; assay. There's one gone to the harbour?   120
Iago.   Ay, madam.
Desdemona *(aside).*   I am not merry, but I do beguile
   The thing I am by seeming otherwise.
   (To Iago.) Come, how wouldst thou praise me?
Iago.   I am about it; but indeed my invention
   Comes from my pate[212] as birdlime does from frize;[213]
   It plucks out brains and all: but my muse labours
   And thus she is deliver'd.
   If she be fair and wise, fairness and wit,
   The one's for use, the other useth it.   130
Desdemona.   Well prais'd! How if she be black and witty?
Iago.   If she be black,[214] and thereto have a wit,
   She'll find a white that shall her blackness fit.
Desdemona.   Worse and worse.
Emilia.   How if fair and foolish?
Iago.   She never yet was foolish that was fair,
   For even her folly[215] help'd to an heir.
Desdemona.   These are old fond[216] paradoxes to make fools laugh i' the ale-
   house. What miserable praise has thou for her that's foul and foolish?

---

[205] Wish.   [206] I.e., without words.   [207] I.e., made up, "painted."   [208] I.e.,
jangly.   [209] Triflers, wastrels.   [210] Housekeeping.   [211] (1) Hussies, (2) (unduly)
frugal with their sexual favors, (3) businesslike, serious.   [212] Head.   [213] Coarse
cloth.   [214] Brunette, dark haired.   [215] Here also, wantonness.   [216] Foolish.

Iago.   There's none so foul and foolish thereunto,   140
    But does foul pranks which fair and wise ones do.
Desdemona.   O heavy ignorance! thou praisest the worst best. But what praise
    couldst thou bestow on a deserving woman indeed, one that, in the authority
    of her merit, did justly put on the vouch[217] of very malice itself?
Iago.   She that was ever fair and never proud,
    Had tongue at will and yet was never loud,
    Never lack'd gold and yet went never gay,
    Fled from her wish and yet said 'Now I may,'
    She that being anger'd, her revenge being nigh,
    Bade her wrong stay and her displeasure fly,   150
    She that in wisdom never was so frail
    To change the cod's head for the salmon's tail,[218]
    She that could think and ne'er disclose her mind,
    See suitors following and not look behind,
    She was a wight, if ever such wight were,—
Desdemona.   To do what?
Iago.   To suckle fools and chronicle small beer.[219]
Desdemona.   O most lame and impotent conclusion! Do not learn of him,
    Emilia, though he be thy husband. How say you, Cassio? Is he not a most
    profane and liberal[220] counsellor?
Cassio.   He speaks home,[221] madam; you may relish him more in the   160
    soldier than in[222] the scholar.
Iago *(aside).*   He takes her by the palm: ay, well said, whisper; with as little a
    web as this will I ensnare as great a fly as Cassio. Ay, smile upon her, do; I
    will gyve[223] thee in thine own courtship. You say true, 'tis so, indeed. If such
    tricks as these strip you out of your lieutenantry, it had been better you had
    not kissed your three fingers so oft, which now again you are most apt to play
    the sir[224] in. Very good; well kissed! an excellent courtesy! 'tis so, indeed.
    Yet again your fingers to your lips? would they were clyster-pipes[225] for your
    sake! *(A trumpet heard.)* The Moor! I know his trumpet.[226]
Cassio.   'Tis truly so.   170
Desdemona.   Let's meet him and receive him.
Cassio.   Lo! where he comes.

(Enter Othello and Attendants.)

Othello.   O my fair warrior!
Desdemona.   My dear Othello!

---

[217] Compel the approval.   [218] To make a foolish exchange (a bawdy secondary meaning is probable).   [219] I.e., keep petty household accounts.   [220] Free-spoken, licentious.
[221] To the mark, aptly.   [222] As . . . as.   [223] Entangle.   [224] Gentleman.
[225] Syringes, enema pipes.   [226] I.e., Othello's distinctive trumpet call.

896   LOVE AND HATE

Othello.   It gives me wonder great as my content
To see you here before me. O my soul's joy!
If after every tempest come such calms,
May the winds blow till they have waken'd death!
And let the labouring bark climb hills of seas
Olympus-high, and duck again as low
As hell's from heaven! If it were now to die,
'Twere now to be most happy, for I fear   180
My soul hath her content so absolute
That not another comfort like to this
Succeeds in unknown fate.
Desdemona.   The heavens forbid
But that our loves and comforts should increase
Even as our days do grow!
Othello.   Amen to that, sweet powers!
I cannot speak enough of this content;
It stops me here; it is too much of joy:
And this, and this, the greatest discords be   *(Kissing her.)*
That e'er our hearts shall make!
Iago *(aside)*.   O! you are well tun'd now,   190
But I'll set down [227] the pegs that make this music,
As honest as I am.
Othello.   Come, let us to the castle.
News, friends; our wars are done, the Turks are drown'd.
How does my old acquaintance of this isle?
Honey, you shall be well desir'd[228] in Cyprus;
I have found great love amongst them. O my sweet,
I prattle out of fashion, and I dote
In mine own comforts. I prithee, good Iago,
Go to the bay and disembark my coffers.
Bring thou the master to the citadel;   200
He is a good one, and his worthiness
Does challenge much respect. Come, Desdemona,
Once more well met at Cyprus.

(Exeunt all except Iago and Roderigo.)

Iago.   Do thou meet me presently at the harbour. Come hither. If thou be'st
valiant, as they say base men being in love have then a nobility in their
natures more than is native to them, list[229] me. The lieutenant to-night
watches on the court of guard:[230] first, I must tell thee this, Desdemona is
directly in love with him.
Roderigo.   With him! Why, 'tis not possible.

---

[227] Loosen.   [228] Welcomed.   [229] Listen to.   [230] Guardhouse.

Iago.   Lay thy finger thus, and let thy soul be instructed. Mark me with what violence she first loved the Moor but for bragging and telling her fantastical lies; and will she love him still for prating? let not thy discreet heart think it. Her eye must be fed; and what delight shall she have to look on the devil? When the blood is made dull with the act of sport, there should be, again to inflame it, and to give satiety a fresh appetite, loveliness in favour, sympathy in years, manners, and beauties; all which the Moor is defective in. Now, for want of these required conveniences, her delicate tenderness will find itself abused, begin to heave the gorge,[231] disrelish and abhor the Moor; very nature will instruct her in it, and compel her to some second choice. Now, sir, this granted, as it is a most pregnant[232] and unforced position, who stands so eminently in the degree of this fortune as Cassio does? a knave very voluble, no further conscionable[233] than in putting on the mere form of civil and humane seeming, for the better compassing of his salt[234] and most hidden loose affection? why, none; why, none: a slipper[235] and subtle knave, a finder-out of occasions, that has an eye can stamp and counterfeit advantages, though true advantage never present itself; a devilish knave! Besides, the knave is handsome, young, and hath all those requisites in him that folly and green minds look after; a pestilent complete knave! and the woman hath found him already.

Roderigo.   I cannot believe that in her; she is full of most blessed condition.

Iago.   Blessed fig's end! the wine she drinks is made of grapes;[236] if she had been blessed she would never have loved the Moor; blessed pudding! Didst thou not see her paddle with the palm of his hand? didst not mark that?

Roderigo.   Yes, that I did; but that was but courtesy.

Iago.   Lechery, by this hand! an index[237] and obscure prologue to the history of lust and foul thoughts. They met so near with their lips, that their breaths embraced together. Villanous thoughts, Roderigo! when these mutualities so marshal the way, hard at hand comes the master and main exercise, the incorporate[238] conclusion. Pish![239] But, sir, be you ruled by me: I have brought you from Venice. Watch you to-night; for the command, I'll lay 't upon you: Cassio knows you not. I'll not be far from you: do you find some occasion to anger Cassio, either by speaking too loud, or tainting[240] his discipline; or from what other course you please, which the time shall more favourably minister.

Roderigo.   Well.

Iago.   Sir, he is rash and very sudden in choler, and haply may strike at you: provoke him, that he may; for even out of that will I cause these of Cyprus to mutiny, whose qualification[241] shall come into no true taste again but by the displanting of Cassio. So shall you have a shorter journey to your desires by the means I shall then have to prefer[242] them; and the impediment most

---

[231] Vomit.   [232] Obvious.   [233] Conscientious.   [234] Lecherous.   [235] Slippery.
[236] I.e., she is only flesh and blood.   [237] Pointer.   [238] Carnal. [239] Exclamation of disgust.   [240] Disparaging.   [241] Appeasement.   [242] Advance.

profitably removed, without the which there were no expectation of our prosperity.

Roderigo.   I will do this, if I can bring it to any opportunity.

Iago.   I warrant thee. Meet me by and by at the citadel: I must fetch his necessaries ashore. Farewell.

Roderigo.   Adieu.   (*Exit.*)

Iago.   That Cassio loves her, I do well believe it;
That she loves him, 'tis apt,[243] and of great credit:[244]
The Moor, howbeit that I endure him not,
Is of a constant, loving, noble nature;
And I dare think he'll prove to Desdemona
A most dear[245] husband. Now, I do love her too;
Not out of absolute lust,—though peradventure[246]
I stand accountant[247] for as great a sin,—
But partly led to diet my revenge,
For that I do suspect the lusty Moor
Hath leap'd into my seat; the thought whereof
Doth like a poisonous mineral gnaw my inwards;
And nothing can or shall content my soul
Till I am even'd with him, wife for wife;
Or failing so, yet that I put the Moor
At least into a jealousy so strong
That judgment cannot cure. Which thing to do,
If this poor trash[248] of Venice, whom I trash[249]
For his quick hunting, stand the putting-on,[250]
I'll have our Michael Cassio on the hip;
Abuse him to the Moor in the rank garb,[251]
For I fear Cassio with my night-cap too,
Make the Moor thank me, love me, and reward me
For making him egregiously an ass
And practising upon his peace and quiet
Even to madness. 'Tis here, but yet confus'd:
Knavery's plain face is never seen till us'd.   (*Exit.*)

SCENE 2.   A Street.

(*Enter a Herald with a proclamation; people following.*)

Herald.   It is Othello's pleasure, our noble and valiant general, that, upon certain tidings now arrived, importing the mere[252] perdition of the Turkish

---

[243] Natural, probable.   [244] Easily believable.   [245] A pun on the word in the sense of expensive.   [246] Perchance, perhaps.   [247] Accountable.   [248] I.e., Roderigo.   [249] Check, control.   [250] Inciting.   [251] Gross manner.   [252] Utter.

fleet, every man put himself into triumph; some to dance, some to make bonfires, each man to what sport and revels his addiction leads him; for, besides these beneficial news, it is the celebration of his nuptial. So much was his pleasure should be proclaimed. All offices[253] are open, and there is full liberty of feasting from this present hour of five till the bell have told eleven. Heaven bless the isle of Cyprus and our noble general Othello!

(Exeunt.)

SCENE 3.   A Hall in the Castle.

(Enter Othello, Desdemona, Cassio, and Attendants.)

Othello.   Good Michael, look you to the guard to-night:
Let's teach ourselves that honourable stop,[254]
Not to outsport discretion.
Cassio.   Iago hath direction what to do:
But, notwithstanding, with my personal[255] eye
Will I look to 't.
Othello.   Iago is most honest.
Michael, good-night; to-morrow with your earliest
Let me have speech with you. *(To Desdemona.)* Come, my dear love,
The purchase made, the fruits are to ensue;
That profit's yet to come 'twixt me and you.   10
Good-night.

(Exeunt Othello, Desdemona, and Attendants.)

(Enter Iago.)

Cassio.   Welcome, Iago; we must to the watch.
Iago.   Not this hour, lieutenant; 'tis not yet ten o' the clock. Our general casts us thus early for the love of his Desdemona, who let us not therefore blame; he hath not yet made wanton the night with her, and she is sport for Jove.
Cassio.   She's a most exquisite lady.
Iago.   And, I'll warrant her, full of game.
Cassio.   Indeed, she is a most fresh and delicate creature.
Iago.   What an eye she has! methinks it sounds a parley[256] of provocation.
Cassio.   An inviting eye: and yet methinks right modest.   20
Iago.   And when she speaks, is it not an alarum[257] to love?
Cassio.   She is indeed perfection.
Iago.   Well, happiness to their sheets! Come, lieutenant, I have a stoup of

---

[253] Kitchens and storehouses.   [254] Discipline.   [255] Own.   [256] Conference
[257] Call-to-arms.

wine, and here without are a brace[258] of Cyprus gallants that would fain have a measure to the health of black Othello.

Cassio.   Not to-night, good Iago: I have very poor and unhappy brains for drinking: I could well wish courtesy would invent some other custom of entertainment.

Iago.   O! they are our friends; but one cup: I'll drink for you.

Cassio.   I have drunk but one cup to-night, and that was craftily qualified[259] too, and, behold, what innovation[260] it makes here: I am unfortunate in the infirmity, and dare not task my weakness with any more.

Iago.   What, man! 'tis a night of revels; the gallants desire it.

Cassio.   Where are they?

Iago.   Here at the door; I pray you, call them in.

Cassio.   I'll do 't; but it dislikes me.   (*Exit.*)

Iago.   If I can fasten but one cup upon him,
With that which he hath drunk to-night already,
He'll be as full of quarrel and offence
As my young mistress' dog. Now, my sick fool Roderigo,   40
Whom love has turn'd almost the wrong side out,
To Desdemona hath to-night carous'd
Potations pottle-deep;[261] and he's to watch.
Three lads of Cyprus, noble swelling spirits,
That hold their honours in a wary distance,[262]
The very elements[263] of this warlike isle,
Have I to-night fluster'd with flowing cups,
And they watch too. Now, 'mongst this flock of drunkards,
Am I to put our Cassio in some action
That may offend the isle. But here they come.   50
If consequence[264] do but approve my dream,
My boat sails freely, both with wind and stream.

(*Re-enter Cassio, with him Montano, and Gentlemen. Servant following with wine.*)

Cassio.   'Fore God, they have given me a rouse[265] already.

Montano.   Good faith, a little one; not past a pint, as I am a soldier.

Iago.   Some wine, ho!
(*Sings.*)   And let me the canakin[266] clink, clink;
                     And let me the canakin clink:
                     A soldier's a man;
                     A life's but a span;
                     Why then let a soldier drink.   60
Some wine, boys!

---

[258] Pair.   [259] Diluted.   [260] Change, revolution.   [261] Bottoms-up.   [262] Take
offense easily.   [263] Types.   [264] Succeeding events.   [265] Drink.   [266] Small
cup.

Cassio. 'Fore God, an excellent song.

Iago. I learned it in England, where indeed they are most potent in potting; your Dane, your German, and your swag-bellied[267] Hollander,—drink ho!— are nothing to your English.

Cassio. Is your Englishman so expert in his drinking?

Iago. Why, he drinks you[268] with facility your Dane dead drunk; he sweats not to overthrow your Almain;[269] he gives your Hollander a vomit ere the next pottle can be filled.

Cassio. To the health of our general!   70

Montano. I am for it, lieutenant; and I'll do you justice.

Iago. O sweet England!

(*Sings.*)   King Stephen was a worthy peer,
      His breeches cost him but a crown;
He held them sixpence all too dear,
      With that he call'd the tailor lown.[270]
He was a wight of high renown,
      And thou art but of low degree:
'Tis pride that pulls the country down,
      Then take thine auld cloak about thee.   80

Some wine, ho!

Cassio. Why, this is a more exquisite song than the other.

Iago. Will you hear 't again?

Cassio. No; for I hold him to be unworthy of his place that does those things. Well, God's above all; and there be souls must be saved, and there be souls must not be saved.

Iago. It's true, good lieutenant.

Cassio. For mine own part,—no offence to the general, nor any man of quality,—I hope to be saved.

Iago. And so do I too, lieutenant.   90

Cassio. Ay; but, by your leave, not before me; the lieutenant is to be saved before the ancient. Let's have no more of this; let's to our affairs. God forgive us our sins! Gentlemen, let's look to our business. Do not think, gentlemen, I am drunk: this is my ancient; this is my right hand, and this is my left hand. I am not drunk now; I can stand well enough, and speak well enough.

All. Excellent well.

Cassio. Why, very well, then; you must not think then that I am drunk.

(*Exit.*)

Montano. To the platform, masters; come, let's set the watch.

Iago. You see this fellow that is gone before;
He is a soldier fit to stand by Caesar   100
And give direction; and do but see his vice;
'Tis to his virtue a just equinox,[271]

---

267 With a pendulous belly.   268 The "ethical" dative, i.e., you'll see that he drinks.
269 German.   270 Lout, rascal.   271 Equivalent.

The one as long as the other; 'tis pity of him.
I fear the trust Othello puts him in,
On some odd time of his infirmity,
Will shake this island.
Montano.   But is he often thus?
Iago.   'Tis evermore the prologue to his sleep;
He'll watch the horologe a double set,[272]
If drink rock not his cradle.
Montano.   It were well   110
The general were put in mind of it.
Perhaps he sees it not; or his good nature
Prizes the virtue that appears in Cassio,
And looks not on his evils. Is not this true?

(Enter Roderigo.)

Iago *(aside to him).*   How now, Roderigo!
I pray you, after the lieutenant; go.   *(Exit Roderigo.)*
Montano.   And 'tis great pity that the noble Moor
Should hazard such a place as his own second
With one of an ingraft[273] infirmity;
It were an honest action to say   120
So to the Moor.
Iago.   Not I, for this fair island:
I do love Cassio well, and would do much
To cure him of this evil. But hark! what noise?

(Cry within, 'Help! Help!' Re-enter Cassio, driving in Roderigo.)

Cassio.   You rogue! you rascal!
Montano.   What's the matter, lieutenant?
Cassio.   A knave teach me my duty!
I'll beat the knave into a twiggen[274] bottle.
Roderigo.   Beat me!
Cassio.   Dost thou prate, rogue?

(Striking Roderigo.)

Montano *(staying him).*   Nay, good lieutenant;
I pray you, sir, hold your hand.
Cassio.   Let me go, sir,
Or I'll knock you o'er the mazzard.[275]

---

[272] Stand watch twice twelve hours.   [273] Ingrained.   [274] Wicker.   [275] Head.

Montano.   Come, come; you're drunk.   130
Cassio.   Drunk!

(They fight.)

Iago *(aside to Roderigo).*   Away, I say! go out, and cry a mutiny.
                                                      (Exit Roderigo.)
  Nay, good lieutenant! God's will, gentlemen!
  Help, ho! Lieutenant! sir! Montano! sir!
  Help, masters! Here's a goodly watch indeed!

(Bell rings.)

  Who's that that rings the bell? Diablo, ho!
  The town will rise: God's will! lieutenant, hold!
  You will be sham'd for ever.

(Re-enter Othello and Attendants.)

Othello.   What is the matter here?
Montano.   'Zounds! I bleed still; I am hurt to the death.

(He faints.)

Othello.   Hold, for your lives!
Iago.   Hold, ho, lieutenant! Sir! Montano! gentlemen!   140
  Have you forgot all sense of place and duty?
  Hold! the general speaks to you; hold for shame!
Othello.   Why, how now, ho! from whence ariseth this?
  Are we turn'd Turks, and to ourselves do that
  Which heaven hath forbid the Ottomites?
  For Christian shame put by this barbarous brawl;
  He that stirs next to carve for his own rage
  Holds his soul light; he dies upon his motion.
  Silence that dreadful bell! it frights the isle
  From her propriety. What is the matter, masters?   150
  Honest Iago, that look'st dead with grieving,
  Speak, who began this? On thy love, I charge thee.
Iago.   I do not know; friends all but now, even now,
  In quarter[276] and in terms like bride and groom
  Devesting[277] them for bed; and then, but now,—
  As if some planet had unwitted men,—
  Swords out, and tilting one at other's breast,

---

[276] On duty.   [277] Undressing.

In opposition bloody. I cannot speak
Any beginning to this peevish odds,[278]
And would in action glorious I had lost   160
Those legs that brought me to a part of it!
Othello.   How comes it, Michael, you are thus forgot?
Cassio.   I pray you, pardon me; I cannot speak.
Othello.   Worthy Montano, you were wont be civil;
The gravity and stillness of your youth
The world hath noted, and your name is great
In mouths of wisest censure:[279] what's the matter,
That you unlace[280] your reputation thus
And spend your rich opinion[281] for the name
Of a night-brawler? give me answer to it.   170
Montano.   Worthy Othello, I am hurt to danger;
Your officer, Iago, can inform you,
While I spare speech, which something now offends[282] me,
Of all that I do know; nor know I aught
By me that 's said or done amiss this night,
Unless self-charity be sometimes a vice,
And to defend ourselves it be a sin
When violence assails us.
Othello.   Now, by heaven,
My blood begins my safer guides to rule,
And passion, having my best judgment collied,[283]   180
Assays to lead the way. If I once stir,
Or do but lift this arm, the best of you
Shall sink in my rebuke. Give me to know
How this foul rout began, who set it on;
And he that is approv'd[284] in this offence,
Though he had twinn'd with me—both at a birth—
Shall lose me. What! in a town of war,
Yet wild, the people's hearts brimful of fear,
To manage private and domestic quarrel,
In night, and on the court and guard of safety!   190
'Tis monstrous. Iago, who began 't?
Montano.   If partially affin'd,[285] or leagu'd in office,
Thou dost deliver more or less than truth,
Thou art not soldier.
Iago.   Touch me not so near;
I had rather[286] have this tongue cut from my mouth
Than it should do offence to Michael Cassio;

---

[278] Silly quarrel.   [279] Judgment.   [280] Undo.   [281] High reputation.   [282] Pains,
harms.   [283] Clouded.   [284] Proved (i.e., guilty).   [285] Favorably biased (by ties of
friendship, or as Cassio's fellow officer).   [286] More quickly.

Yet, I persuade myself, to speak the truth
Shall nothing wrong him. Thus it is, general.
Montano and myself being in speech,
There comes a fellow crying out for help,   200
And Cassio following with determin'd sword
To execute upon him. Sir, this gentleman
Steps in to Cassio, and entreats his pause;
Myself the crying fellow did pursue,
Lest by his clamour, as it so fell out,
The town might fall in fright; he, swift of foot,
Outran my purpose, and I return'd the rather
For that I heard the clink and fall of swords,
And Cassio high in oath, which till to-night
I ne'er might say before. When I came back,—   210
For this was brief,—I found them close together,
At blow and thrust, even as again they were
When you yourself did part them.
More of this matter can I not report:
But men are men; the best sometimes forget:
Though Cassio did some little wrong to him,
As men in rage strike those that wish them best,
Yet, surely Cassio, I believe, receiv'd
From him that fled some strange indignity,
Which patience could not pass.

Othello.   I know, Iago.   220
Thy honesty and love doth mince[287] this matter,
Making it light to Cassio. Cassio, I love thee;
But never more be officer of mine.

(Enter Desdemona, attended.)

Look! if my gentle love be not rais'd up;
(To Cassio.) I'll make thee an example.

Desdemona.   What's the matter?

Othello.   All's well now, sweeting; come away to bed.
Sir, for your hurts, myself will be your surgeon.
Lead him off.   *(Montano is led off.)*
Iago, look with care about the town,
And silence those whom this vile brawl distracted.   230
Come, Desdemona; 'tis the soldier's life,
To have their balmy slumbers wak'd with strife.

(Exeunt all but Iago and Cassio.)

---

[287] Tone down.

Iago.   What! are you hurt, lieutenant?

Cassio.   Ay; past all surgery.

Iago.   Marry, heaven forbid!

Cassio.   Reputation, reputation, reputation! O! I have lost my reputation. I have lost the immortal part of myself, and what remains is bestial. My reputation, Iago, my reputation!

Iago.   As I am an honest man, I thought you had received some bodily wound; there is more offence in that than in reputation. Reputation is an idle and most false imposition;[288] oft got without merit, and lost without deserving: you have lost no reputation at all, unless you repute yourself such a loser. What! man; there are ways to recover the general again; you are but now cast in his mood,[289] a punishment more in policy[290] than in malice; even so as one would beat his offenceless dog to affright an imperious lion. Sue to him again, and he is yours.

Cassio.   I will rather sue to be despised than to deceive so good a commander with so slight, so drunken and so indiscreet an officer. Drunk! and speak parrot![291] and squabble, swagger, swear, and discourse fustian[292] with one's own shadow! O thou invisible spirit of wine! if thou hast no name to be known by, let us call thee devil!

Iago.   What was he that you followed with your sword? What hath he done to you?

Cassio.   I know not.

Iago.   Is 't possible?

Cassio.   I remember a mass of things, but nothing distinctly; a quarrel, but nothing wherefore. O God! that men should put an enemy in their mouths to steal away their brains; that we should, with joy, pleasance,[293] revel, and applause, transform ourselves into beasts.

Iago.   Why, but you are now well enough; how came you thus recovered?

Cassio.   It hath pleased the devil drunkenness to give place to the devil wrath; one unperfectness shows me another, to make me frankly despise myself.

Iago.   Come, you are too severe a moraler. As the time, the place, and the condition of this country stands, I could heartily wish this had not befallen, but since it is as it is, mend it for your own good.

Cassio.   I will ask him for my place again; he shall tell me I am a drunkard! Had I as many mouths as Hydra,[294] such an answer would stop them all. To be now a sensible man, by and by a fool, and presently a beast! O strange! Every inordinate cup is unblessed and the ingredient[295] is a devil.

Iago.   Come, come; good wine is a good familiar creature if it be well used; exclaim no more against it. And, good lieutenant, I think you think I love you.

---

[288] Something external.   [289] Dismissed because he is angry.   [290] I.e., more for the sake of the example, or to show his fairness.   [291] I.e., without thinking.   [292] I.e., nonsense.   [293] Pleasure.   [294] Many-headed snake in Greek mythology.   [295] Contents.

Cassio.   I have well approved it, sir. I drunk!

Iago.   You or any man living may be drunk at some time, man. I'll tell you
what you shall do. Our general's wife is now the general; I may say so in this
respect, for that he hath devoted and given up himself to the contemplation,
mark, and denotement of her parts and graces: confess yourself freely to her;
importune her; she'll help to put you in your place again. She is of so free,
so kind, so apt, so blessed a disposition, that she holds it a vice in her goodness
not to do more than she is requested. This broken joint between you and her
husband entreat her to splinter;[296] and, my fortunes against any lay[297] worth
naming, this crack of your love shall grow stronger than it was before.

Cassio.   You advise me well.

Iago.   I protest, in the sincerity of love and honest kindness.

Cassio.   I think it freely; and betimes in the morning I will beseech the virtuous
Desdemona to undertake for me. I am desperate of my fortunes if they check
me here.

Iago.   You are in the right. Good-night, lieutenant; I must to the watch.

Cassio.   Good-night, honest Iago!   (*Exit.*)

Iago.   And what's he then that says I play the villain?   290
When this advice is free I give and honest,
Probal[298] to thinking and indeed the course
To win the Moor again? For 'tis most easy
The inclining Desdemona to subdue
In any honest suit; she's fram'd as fruitful[299]
As the free elements. And then for her
To win the Moor, were 't to renounce his baptism,
All seals and symbols of redeemed sin,
His soul is so enfetter'd to her love,
That she may make, unmake, do what she list,   300
Even as her appetite shall play the god
With his weak function.[300] How am I then a villain
To counsel Cassio to this parallel[301] course,
Directly to his good? Divinity of hell!
When devils will the blackest sins put on,
They do suggest at first with heavenly shows,
As I do now; for while this honest fool
Plies Desdemona to repair his fortunes,
And she for him pleads strongly to the Moor,
I'll pour this pestilence into his ear   310
That she repeals[302] him for her body's lust;
And, by how much she strives to do him good,
She shall undo her credit with the Moor.

---

[296] Bind up with splints.   [297] Wager.   [298] Provable.   [299] Generous.   [300] Faculties.
[301] Purposeful.   [302] I.e., seeks to recall.

So will I turn her virtue into pitch,
And out of her own goodness make the net
That shall enmesh them all.

(Re-enter Roderigo.)

                          How now, Roderigo!

Roderigo.   I do follow here in the chase, not like a hound that hunts, but one
    that fills up the cry.[303] My money is almost spent; I have been to-night
    exceedingly well cudgelled; and I think the issue will be, I shall have so much
    experience for my pains; and so, with no money at all and a little more wit,
    return again to Venice.

Iago.   How poor are they that have not patience!
    What wound did ever heal but by degrees?
    Thou know'st we work by wit and not by witchcraft,
    And wit depends on dilatory time.
    Does 't not go well? Cassio hath beaten thee,
    And thou by that small hurt hast cashiered Cassio.
    Though other things grow fair against the sun,
    Yet fruits that blossom first will first be ripe:
    Content thyself awhile. By the mass, 'tis morning;   330
    Pleasure and action make the hours seem short.
    Retire thee; go where thou art billeted:
    Away, I say; thou shalt know more hereafter:
    Nay, get thee gone. *(Exit Roderigo.)* Two things are to be done,
    My wife must move for Cassio to her mistress;
    I'll set her on;
    Myself the while to draw the Moor apart,
    And bring him jump[304] when he may Cassio find
    Soliciting his wife: ay, that's the way:
    Dull not device by coldness and delay.   *(Exit.)*

Act III

SCENE 1. Cyprus. Before the Castle.

(Enter Cassio, and some Musicians.)

Cassio.   Masters, play here, I will content your pains;[305]
    Something that's brief; and bid 'Good-morrow, general.'   *(Music.)*

(Enter Clown.)

---

[303] Pack (hunting term).   [304] At the exact moment.   [305] Reward your efforts.

Clown.   Why, masters, have your instruments been in Naples, that they speak i' the nose[306] thus?

First Musician.   How, sir, how?

Clown.   Are these, I pray you, wind-instruments?

First Musician.   Ay, marry, are they, sir.

Clown.   O! thereby hangs a tale.

First Musician.   Whereby hangs a tale, sir?

Clown.   Marry, sir, by many a wind-instrument that I know. But, masters, here's money for you; and the general so likes your music, that he desires you, for love's sake, to make no more noise with it.

First Musician.   Well, sir, we will not.

Clown.   If you have any music that may not be heard, to 't again; but, as they say, to hear music the general does not greatly care.

First Musician.   We have none such, sir.

Clown.   Then put up your pipes in your bag, for I'll away.
Go; vanish into air; away!   *(Exeunt Musicians.)*

Cassio.   Dost thou hear, mine honest friend?

Clown.   No, I hear not your honest friend; I hear you.

Cassio.   Prithee, keep up thy quillets.[307] There's a poor piece of gold for thee. If the gentlewoman that attends the general's wife be stirring, tell her there's one Cassio entreats her a little favour of speech: wilt thou do this?

Clown.   She is stirring, sir: if she will stir hither, I shall seem to notify unto her.

Cassio.   Do, good my friend.   *(Exit Clown.)*

(Enter Iago.)

In happy time, Iago.

Iago.   You have not been a-bed, then?

Cassio.   Why, no; the day had broke
Before we parted. I have made bold, Iago,
To send in to your wife; my suit to her
Is, that she will to virtuous Desdemona   30
Procure me some access.

Iago.   I'll send her to you presently;
And I'll devise a mean to draw the Moor
Out of the way, that your converse and business
May be more free.

Cassio.   I humbly thank you for 't.   *(Exit Iago.)*
                          I never knew
A Florentine more kind and honest.[308]

---

[306] Naples was notorious for venereal disease, and syphilis was believed to affect the nose. [307] Quibbles.   [308] Cassio means that not even a fellow Florentine could behave to him in a friendlier fashion than does Iago.

(Enter Emilia.)

Emilia.   Good-morrow, good lieutenant: I am sorry
  For your displeasure,[309] but all will soon be well.
  The general and his wife are talking of it,
  And she speaks for you stoutly: the Moor replies   40
  That he you hurt is of great fame in Cyprus
  And great affinity,[310] and that in wholesome wisdom
  He might not but refuse you; but he protests he loves you,
  And needs no other suitor but his likings
  To take the safest occasion by the front[311]
  To bring you in again.[312]
Cassio.   Yet, I beseech you,
  If you think fit, or that it may be done,
  Give me advantage of some brief discourse
  With Desdemona alone.
Emilia.   Pray you, come in:
  I will bestow you where you shall have time   50
  To speak your bosom[313] freely.
Cassio.   I am much bound to you.   *(Exeunt.)*

SCENE 2.   A Room in the Castle.

(Enter Othello, Iago, and Gentlemen.)

Othello.   These letters give, Iago, to the pilot,
  And by him do my duties to the senate;
  That done, I will be walking on the works;
  Repair there to me.
Iago.   Well, my good lord, I'll do 't.
Othello.   This fortification, gentlemen, shall we see 't?
Gentlemen.   We'll wait upon your lordship.   *(Exeunt.)*

SCENE 3.   Before the Castle.

(Enter Desdemona, Cassio, and Emilia.)

Desdemona.   Be thou assur'd, good Cassio, I will do
  All my abilities in thy behalf.
Emilia.   Good madam, do: I warrant it grieves my husband,
  As if the case were his.

---

[309] Disgrace.   [310] Family connection.   [311] Forelock.   [312] Restore you (to Othello's
favor).   [313] Heart, inmost thoughts.

Desdemona.   O! that's an honest fellow. Do not doubt, Cassio,
But I will have my lord and you again
As friendly as you were.

Cassio.   Bounteous madam,
Whatever shall become of Michael Cassio,
He's never any thing but your true servant.

Desdemona.   I know 't; I thank you. You do love my lord;   10
You have known him long; and be you well assur'd
He shall in strangeness[314] stand no further off
Than in a politic[315] distance.

Cassio.   Ay, but, lady,
That policy may either last so long,
Or feed upon such nice[316] and waterish diet,
Or breed itself so out of circumstance,
That, I being absent and my place supplied,
My general will forget my love and service.

Desdemona.   Do not doubt[317] that; before Emilia here
I give thee warrant of thy place. Assure thee,   20
If I do vow a friendship, I'll perform it
To the last article; my lord shall never rest;
I'll watch him tame,[318] and talk him out of patience;
His bed shall seem a school, his board a shrift;[319]
I'll intermingle every thing he does
With Cassio's suit. Therefore be merry, Cassio;
For thy solicitor shall rather die
Than give thy cause away.[320]

(Enter Othello, and Iago at a distance.)

Emilia.   Madam, here comes my lord.

Cassio.   Madam, I'll take my leave.   30

Desdemona.   Why, stay, and hear me speak.

Cassio.   Madam, not now; I am very ill at ease,
Unfit for mine own purposes.

Desdemona.   Well, do your discretion.   *(Exit Cassio.)*

Iago.   Ha! I like not that.

Othello.   What dost thou say?

Iago.   Nothing, my lord: or if—I know not what.

Othello.   Was not that Cassio parted from my wife?

Iago.   Cassio, my lord? No, sure, I cannot think it,
That he would steal away so guilty-like,
Seeing you coming.

---

[314] Aloofness.   [315] I.e., dictated by policy.   [316] Slight, trivial.   [317] Fear.
[318] Outwatch him (i.e., keep him awake) till he submits.   [319] Confessional.   [320] Abandon
your cause.

Othello.   I do believe 'twas he.   40

Desdemona.   How now, my lord!

  I have been talking with a suitor here,

  A man that languishes in your displeasure.

Othello.   Who is 't you mean?

Desdemona.   Why, your lieutenant, Cassio. Good my lord,

  If I have any grace or power to move you,

  His present[321] reconciliation take;

  For if he be not one that truly loves you,

  That errs in ignorance and not in cunning,

  I have no judgment in an honest face.   50

  I prithee[322] call him back.

Othello.   Went he hence now?

Desdemona.   Ay, sooth; so humbled,

  That he hath left part of his grief with me,

  To suffer with him. Good love, call him back.

Othello.   Not now, sweet Desdemona; some other time.

Desdemona.   But shall 't be shortly?

Othello.   The sooner, sweet, for you.

Desdemona.   Shall 't be to-night at supper?

Othello.   No, not to-night.

Desdemona.   To-morrow dinner, then?

Othello.   I shall not dine at home;

  I meet the captains at the citadel.

Desdemona.   Why, then, to-morrow night; or Tuesday morn;

  Or Tuesday noon, or night; or Wednesday morn: 60

  I prithee name the time, but let it not

  Exceed three days: in faith, he's penitent;

  And yet his trespass, in our common reason,—

  Save that they say, the wars must make examples

  Out of their best,—is not almost[323] a fault

  To incur a private check.[324] When shall he come?

  Tell me, Othello: I wonder in my soul,

  What you could ask me, that I should deny,

  Or stand so mammering[325] on. What! Michael Cassio,   70

  That came a wooing with you, and so many a time,

  When I have spoke of you dispraisingly,

  Hath ta'en your part; to have so much to do

  To bring him in! Trust me, I could do much,—

Othello.   Prithee, no more; let him come when he will;

  I deny thee nothing.

Desdemona.   Why, this is not a boon;

---

321 Immediate.   322 Pray thee.   323 Hardly.   324 (Even) a private reprimand.
325 Shilly-shallying.

'Tis as I should entreat you wear your gloves,
Or feed on nourishing dishes, or keep you warm,
Or sue to you to do a peculiar profit
To your own person: nay, when I have a suit   80
Wherein I mean to touch your love indeed,
It shall be full of poise[326] and difficult weight,
And fearful to be granted.

Othello.   I will deny thee nothing:
Whereon, I do beseech thee, grant me this,
To leave me but a little to myself.

Desdemona.   Shall I deny you? no: farewell, my lord.

Othello.   Farewell, my Desdemona: I'll come to thee straight.

Desdemona.   Emilia, come. Be as your fancies teach you;
Whate'er you be, I am obedient.   *(Exit, with Emilia.)*

Othello.   Excellent wretch![327] Perdition catch my soul,   90
But I do love thee! and when I love thee not,
Chaos is[328] come again.

Iago.   My noble lord,—

Othello.   What dost thou say, Iago?

Iago.   Did Michael Cassio, when you woo'd my lady,
Know of your love?

Othello.   He did, from first to last: why dost thou ask?

Iago.   But for a satisfaction of my thought;
No further harm.

Othello.   Why of thy thought, Iago?

Iago.   I did not think he had been acquainted with her.

Othello.   O! yes; and went between us very oft.   100

Iago.   Indeed!

Othello.   Indeed! ay, indeed; discern'st thou aught in that?
Is he not honest?

Iago.   Honest, my lord?

Othello.   Honest! ay, honest.

Iago.   My lord, for aught I know.

Othello.   What dost thou think?

Iago.   Think, my lord!

Othello.   Think, my lord!
By heaven, he echoes me,
As if there were some monster in his thought
Too hideous to be shown. Thou dost mean something:
I heard thee say but now, thou lik'dst not that,
When Cassio left my wife; what didst not like?   110
And when I told thee he was of my counsel
In my whole course of wooing, thou criedst, 'Indeed!'

---

[326] Weight.   [327] Here, a term of endearment.   [328] Will have.

And didst contract and purse thy brow together,
As if thou then hadst shut up in thy brain
Some horrible conceit.[329] If thou dost love me,
Show me thy thought.

Iago.   My lord, you know I love you.

Othello.   I think thou dost;
And, for[330] I know thou art full of love and honesty,
And weigh'st thy words before thou givest them breath,
Therefore these stops[331] of thine fright me the more;   120
For such things in a false disloyal knave
Are tricks of custom, but in a man that's just
They are close dilations,[332] working from the heart
That passion cannot rule.

Iago.   For Michael Cassio,
I dare be sworn I think that he is honest.

Othello.   I think so too.

Iago.   Men should be what they seem;
Or those that be not, would they might seem none!

Othello.   Certain men should be what they seem.

Iago.   Why then, I think Cassio's an honest man.

Othello.   Nay, yet there's more in this.   130
I pray thee, speak to me as to thy thinkings,
As thou dost ruminate, and give thy worst of thoughts
The worst of words.

Iago.   Good my lord, pardon me;
Though I am bound to every act of duty,
I am not bound to[333] that all slaves are free to.
Utter my thoughts? Why, say they are vile and false;
As where's that palace whereinto foul things
Sometimes intrude not? who has a breast so pure
But some uncleanly apprehensions[334]
Keep leets and law-days,[335] and in session sit   140
With meditations lawful?

Othello.   Thou dost conspire against thy friend, Iago,
If thou but think'st him wrong'd, and mak'st his ear
A stranger to thy thoughts.

Iago.   I do beseech you,
Though I perchance am vicious in my guess,—
As, I confess, it is my nature's plague
To spy into abuses, and oft my jealousy[336]
Shapes faults that are not,—that your wisdom yet,

---

[329] Fancy.   [330] Because.   [331] Interruptions, hesitations.   [332] Secret (i.e., involuntary, unconscious) revelations.   [333] Bound with regard to.   [334] Conceptions.
[335] Sittings of the local courts.   [336] Suspicion.

From one that so imperfectly conceits,
Would take no notice, nor build yourself a trouble   150
Out of his scattering and unsure observance.
It were not for your quiet nor your good,
Nor for my manhood, honesty, or wisdom,
To let you know my thoughts.
Othello.   What dost thou mean?
Iago.   Good name in man and woman, dear my lord,
Is the immediate jewel of[337] their souls:
Who steals my purse steals trash; 'tis something, nothing;
'Twas mine, 'tis his, and has been slave to thousands;
But he that filches from me my good name
Robs me of that which not enriches him,   160
And makes me poor indeed.
Othello.   By heaven, I'll know thy thoughts.
Iago.   You cannot, if my heart were in your hand;
Nor shall not, whilst 'tis in my custody.
Othello.   Ha!
Iago.   O! beware, my lord, of jealousy;
It is the green-ey'd monster which doth mock
The meat it feeds on: that cuckold[338] lives in bliss
Who, certain of his fate, loves not his wronger;
But, O! what damned minutes tells[339] he o'er
Who dotes, yet doubts; suspects, yet soundly loves!   170
Othello.   O misery!
Iago.   Poor and content is rich, and rich enough,
But riches fineless[340] is as poor as winter
To him that ever fears he shall be poor.
Good heaven, the souls of all my tribe defend
From jealousy!
Othello.   Why, why is this?
Think'st thou I'd make a life of jealousy,
To follow still the changes of the moon
With fresh suspicions? No; to be once in doubt
Is once to be resolved. Exchange me for a goat   180
When I shall turn the business of my soul
To such exsufflicate[341] and blown[342] surmises,
Matching thy inference. 'Tis not to make me jealous
To say my wife is fair, feeds well, loves company,
Is free of speech, sings, plays, and dances well;
Where virtue is, these are more virtuous:
Nor from mine own weak merits will I draw

---

[337] Jewel closest to.   [338] Husband of an adulterous woman.   [339] Counts.   [340] Boundless.
[341] Spat out (?).   [342] Fly-blown.

The smallest fear, or doubt of her revolt;
For she had eyes, and chose me. No, Iago;
I'll see before I doubt; when I doubt, prove;   190
And, on the proof, there is no more but this,
Away at once with love or jealousy!

Iago.   I am glad of it; for now I shall have reason
To show the love and duty that I bear you
With franker spirit; therefore, as I am bound,
Receive it from me; I speak not yet of proof.
Look to your wife; observe her well with Cassio;
Wear your eye thus, not jealous nor secure:
I would not have your free and noble nature
Out of self-bounty³⁴³ be abus'd; look to 't: 200
I know our country disposition³⁴⁴ well;
In Venice they do let heaven see the pranks
They dare not show their husbands; their best conscience
Is not to leave 't undone, but keep 't unknown.

Othello.   Dost thou say so?

Iago.   She did deceive her father, marrying you;
And when she seem'd to shake and fear your looks,
She lov'd them most.

Othello.   And so she did.

Iago.   Why, go to,³⁴⁵ then;
She that so young could give out such a seeming,
To seel her father's eyes up close as oak,   210
He thought 'twas witchcraft; but I am much to blame;
I humbly do beseech you of your pardon
For too much loving you.

Othello.   I am bound to thee for ever.

Iago.   I see, this hath a little dash'd your spirits.

Othello.   Not a jot, not a jot.

Iago.   I' faith, I fear it has.
I hope you will consider what is spoke
Comes from my love. But I do see you're mov'd;
I am to pray you not to strain my speech
To grosser issues nor to larger reach
Than to suspicion.   220

Othello.   I will not.

Iago.   Should you do so, my lord,
My speech should fall into such vile success
As my thoughts aim not at. Cassio's my worthy friend—
My lord, I see you're mov'd.

---

³⁴³ Innate generosity.   ³⁴⁴ I.e., that of Venice.   ³⁴⁵ Colloquialism; here, something like "all right."

Othello.   No, not much mov'd:
  I do not think but Desdemona's honest.[346]
Iago.   Long live she so! and long live you to think so!
Othello.   And yet, how nature erring from itself,—
Iago.   Ay, there's the point: as, to be bold with you,
  Not to affect many proposed matches
  Of her own clime,[347] complexion, and degree,[348]   230
  Whereto, we see, in all things nature tends;
  Foh! one may smell in such, a will most rank,
  Foul disproportion, thoughts unnatural.
  But pardon me; I do not in position[349]
  Distinctly[350] speak of her, though I may fear
  Her will, recoiling [351] to her better judgment,
  May fall to match you with her country forms
  And happily[352] repent.
Othello.   Farewell, farewell:
  If more thou dost perceive, let me know more;
  Set on thy wife to observe. Leave me, Iago.   240
Iago.   My lord, I take my leave.   *(Going.)*
Othello.   Why did I marry? This honest creature, doubtless,
  Sees and knows more, much more, than he unfolds.
Iago *(returning)*.   My lord, I would I might entreat your honour
  To scan this thing no further; leave it to time.
  Although 'tis fit that Cassio have his place,
  For, sure he fills it up with great ability,
  Yet, if you please to hold him off awhile,
  You shall by that perceive him and his means:
  Note if your lady strain his entertainment[353]   250
  With any strong or vehement importunity;
  Much will be seen in that. In the mean time,
  Let me be thought too busy[354] in my fears,
  As worthy cause I have to fear I am,
  And hold her free, I do beseech your honour.
Othello.   Fear not my government.
Iago.   I once more take my leave.   *(Exit.)*
Othello.   This fellow's of exceeding honesty,
  And knows all qualities, with a learned spirit,
  Of human dealings; if I do prove her haggard,[355]   260
  Though that her jesses[356] were my dear heart-strings,
  I'd whistle her off and let her down the wind,[357]

---

[346] Chaste.   [347] Country.   [348] Social rank.   [349] In definite assertion.
[350] Specifically.   [351] Reverting.   [352] Perhaps.   [353] Urge his re-welcome (i.e., to
Othello's trust and favor).   [354] Meddlesome.   [355] Wild hawk.   [356] Leather thongs
by which the hawk's legs were strapped to the trainer's wrist.   [357] I'd let her go and take care
of herself.

To prey at fortune. Haply, for I am black,
And have not those soft parts of conversation
That chamberers[358] have, or, for I am declin'd
Into the vale of years—yet that's not much—
She's gone, I am abus'd;[359] and my relief
Must be to loathe her. O curse of marriage!
That we can call these delicate creatures ours,
And not their appetites. I had rather be a toad,   270
And live upon the vapour of a dungeon,
Than keep a corner in the thing I love
For others' uses. Yet, 'tis the plague of great ones;
Prerogativ'd[360] are they less than the base;
'Tis destiny unshunnable, like death:
Even then this forked plague[361] is fated to us
When we do quicken.[362]
                    Look! where she comes.
If she be false, O! then heaven mocks itself.
I'll not believe it.

(Re-enter Desdemona and Emilia.)

Desdemona.   How now, my dear Othello!
Your dinner and the generous[363] islanders   280
By you invited, do attend your presence.
Othello.   I am to blame.
Desdemona.   Why do you speak so faintly?
Are you not well?
Othello.   I have a pain upon my forehead here.[364]
Desdemona.   Faith, that's with watching; 'twill away again:
Let me but bind it hard, within this hour
It will be well.
Othello.   Your napkin[365] is too little:

(She drops her handkerchief.)

Let it alone. Come, I'll go in with you.
Desdemona.   I am very sorry that you are not well.

                              (Exeunt Othello and Desdemona.)

Emilia.   I am glad I have found this napkin;   290
This was her first remembrance from the Moor;

---

[358] Courtiers; or (more specifically): gallants, frequenters of bed chambers.   [359] Deceived.
[360] Privileged.   [361] I.e., the cuckold's proverbial horns.   [362] Are conceived, come
alive.   [363] Noble.   [364] Othello again refers to his cuckoldom.   [365] Handkerchief.

My wayward husband hath a hundred times
Woo'd me to steal it, but she so loves the token,
For he conjur'd her she should ever keep it,
That she reserves it evermore about her
To kiss and talk to. I'll have the work ta'en out,[366]
And giv 't Iago:
What he will do with it heaven knows, not I;
I nothing but[367] to please his fantasy.[368]

(Enter Iago.)

Iago.   How now! what do you here alone?   300
Emilia.   Do not you chide; I have a thing for you.
Iago.   A thing for me? It is a common thing—
Emilia.   Ha!
Iago.   To have a foolish wife.
Emilia.   O! is that all? What will you give me now
  For that same handkerchief?
Iago.   What handkerchief?
Emilia.   What handkerchief!
  Why, that the Moor first gave to Desdemona:
  That which so often you did bid me steal.
Iago.   Hath stol'n it from her?   310
Emilia.   No, faith; she let it drop by negligence,
  And, to the advantage, I, being there, took 't up.
  Look, here it is.
Iago.   A good wench; give it me.
Emilia.   What will you do with 't, that you have been so earnest
  To have me filch it?
Iago.   Why, what's that to you?   *(Snatches it.)*
Emilia.   If it be not for some purpose of import
  Give 't me again; poor lady! she'll run mad
  When she shall lack it.
Iago.   Be not acknown on 't;[369] I have use for it.
  Go, leave me.   *(Exit Emilia.)*
  I will in Cassio's lodging lose this napkin,   321
  And let him find it; trifles light as air
  Are to the jealous confirmations strong
  As proofs of holy writ; this may do something.
  The Moor already changes with my poison:
  Dangerous conceits are in their natures poisons,
  Which at the first are scarce found to distaste,[370]

---

[366] Pattern copied.   [367] I.e., only want.   [368] Whim.   [369] You know nothing about it.   [370] Scarce can be tasted.

But with a little act upon the blood,
Burn like the mines of sulphur. I did say so:
Look! where he comes!

(Enter Othello.)

330

Not poppy,[371] nor mandragora,[372]
Nor all the drowsy syrups[373] of the world,
Shall ever medicine thee to that sweet sleep
Which thou ow'dst yesterday.
Othello.   Ha! ha! false to me?
Iago.   Why, how now, general! no more of that.
Othello.   Avaunt! be gone! thou hast set me on the rack;
I swear 'tis better to be much abus'd
Than but to know 't a little.
Iago.   How now, my lord!
Othello.   What sense had I of her stol'n hours of lust?
I saw 't not, thought it not, it harm'd not me;
I slept the next night well, was free and merry; 340
I found not Cassio's kisses on her lips;
He that is robb'd, not wanting what is stol'n,
Let him not know 't, and he's not robb'd at all.
Iago.   I am sorry to hear this.
Othello.   I had been happy, if the general camp,[374]
Pioners[375] and all, had tasted her sweet body,
So[376] I had nothing known. O! now, for ever
Farewell the tranquil mind; farewell content!
Farewell the plumed troop and the big wars
That make ambition virtue! O, farewell! 350
Farewell the neighing steed, and the shrill trump,
The spirit-stirring drum, the ear-piercing fife,
The royal banner, and all quality,
Pride, pomp, and circumstance[377] of glorious war!
And, O you mortal engines,[378] whose rude throats
The immortal Jove's dread clamours counterfeit,
Farewell! Othello's occupation's gone!
Iago.   Is it possible, my lord?
Othello.   Villain, be sure thou prove my love a whore,
Be sure of it; give me the ocular proof; 360
Or, by the worth of mine eternal soul,
Thou hadst been better have been born a dog
Than answer my wak'd wrath.
Iago.   Is 't come to this?

---

[371] Opium.   [372] A soporific.   [373] I.e., soporifics.   [374] Whole army.   [375] Lowest
rank of manual laborers in the army.   [376] As long as.   [377] Pageantry.   [378] Deadly
artillery.

Othello.   Make me to see 't; or, at the least, so prove it,
That the probation[379] bear no hinge nor loop
To hang a doubt on; or woe upon thy life!
Iago.   My noble lord—
Othello.   If thou dost slander her and torture me,
Never pray more; abandon all remorse;
On horror's head horrors accumulate;   370
Do deeds to make heaven weep, all earth amaz'd;
For nothing canst thou to damnation add
Greater than that.
Iago.   O grace! O heaven forgive me!
Are you a man! have you a soul or sense?
God be wi' you; take mine office. O wretched fool!
That liv'st to make thine honesty a vice.
O monstrous world! Take note, take note, O world!
To be direct and honest is not safe.
I thank you for this profit,[380] and, from hence
I'll love no friend, sith[381] love breeds such offence.   380
Othello.   Nay, stay; thou shouldst be honest.
Iago.   I should be wise; for honesty's a fool,
And loses that it works for.
Othello.   By the world,
I think my wife be honest and think she is not;
I think that thou art just and think thou art not.
I'll have some proof. Her name, that was as fresh
As Dian's[382] visage, is now begrim'd and black
As mine own face. If there be cords or knives,
Poison or fire or suffocating streams,
I'll not endure it. Would I were satisfied!   390
Iago.   I see, sir, you are eaten up with passion.
I do repent me that I put it to you.
You would be satisfied?
Othello.   Would! nay, I will.
Iago.   And may; but how? how satisfied, my lord?
Would you, the supervisor,[383] grossly gape on;
Behold her tupp'd?
Othello.   Death and damnation! O!
Iago.   It were a tedious[384] difficulty, I think,
To bring them to that prospect; damn them then,
If ever mortal eyes do see them bolster[385]
More[386] than their own! What then? how then?   400
What shall I say? Where's satisfaction?
It is impossible you should see this,

---

[379] Proof.   [380] Lesson.   [381] Since.   [382] Diana's, the goddess of the moon.
[383] Observer. [384] Laborious.   [385] Lie together.   [386] Other.

Were they as prime[387] as goats, as hot as monkeys,
As salt as wolves in pride,[388] and fools as gross
As ignorance made drunk; but yet, I say,
If imputation, and strong circumstances,
Which lead directly to the door of truth,
Will give you satisfaction, you may have it.

Othello.   Give me a living reason she's disloyal.

Iago.   I do not like the office;   410
But, sith I am enter'd in this cause so far,
Prick'd to 't by foolish honesty and love,
I will go on. I lay with Cassio lately;
And, being troubled with a raging tooth,
I could not sleep.
There are a kind of men so loose of soul
That in their sleeps will mutter their affairs;
One of this kind is Cassio.
In sleep I heard him say, 'Sweet Desdemona,
Let us be wary, let us hide our loves!'   420
And then, sir, would he gripe[389] and wring my hand,
Cry, 'O, sweet creature!' and then kiss me hard,
As if he pluck'd up kisses by the roots,
That grew upon my lips; then laid his leg
Over my thigh, and sigh'd, and kiss'd; and then
Cried, 'Cursed fate, that gave thee to the Moor!'

Othello.   O monstrous! monstrous!

Iago.   Nay, this was but his dream.

Othello.   But this denoted a foregone conclusion:[390]
'Tis a shrewd doubt,[391] though it be but a dream.

Iago.   And this may help to thicken other proofs   430
That do demonstrate thinly.

Othello.   I'll tear her all to pieces.

Iago.   Nay, but be wise; yet we see nothing done;
She may be honest yet. Tell me but this:
Have you not sometimes seen a handkerchief
Spotted with strawberries in your wife's hand?

Othello.   I gave her such a one; 'twas my first gift.

Iago.   I know not that; but such a handkerchief—
I am sure it was your wife's—did I to-day
See Cassio wipe his beard with.

Othello.   If it be that,—

Iago.   If it be that, or any that was hers,   440
It speaks against her with the other proofs.

Othello.   O! that the slave had forty thousand lives;

---

[387] Lustful.   [388] Heat.   [389] Seize.   [390] Previous consummation.   [391] (1) Cursed,
(2) Acute, suspicion.

One is too poor, too weak for my revenge.
Now do I see 'tis true. Look here, Iago;
All my fond love thus do I blow to heaven:
'Tis gone.
Arise, black vengeance, from the hollow hell!
Yield up, O love! thy crown and hearted throne
To tyrannous hate. Swell, bosom, with thy fraught,[392]
For 'tis of aspics'[393] tongues!

Iago.   Yet be content.[394]   450
Othello.   O! blood, blood, blood!
Iago.   Patience, I say; your mind, perhaps, may change.
Othello.   Never, Iago. Like to the Pontic sea,[395]
Whose icy current and compulsive course
Ne'er feels retiring ebb, but keeps due on
To the Propontic and the Hellespont,[396]
Even so my bloody thoughts, with violent pace,
Shall ne'er look back, ne'er ebb to humble love,
Till that a capable[397] and wide revenge
Swallow them up.   *(Kneels.)*
                    Now, by yond marble heaven,   460
In the due reverence of a sacred vow
I here engage my words.
Iago.   Do not rise yet.   *(Kneels.)*
Witness, you ever-burning lights above!
You elements that clip[398] us round about!
Witness, that here Iago doth give up
The execution of his wit, hands, heart,
To wrong'd Othello's service! Let him command,
And to obey shall be in me remorse,[399]
What bloody business ever.[400]   *(They rise.)*
Othello.   I greet thy love,
Not with vain thanks, but with acceptance bounteous,   470
And will upon the instant put thee to 't:
Within these three days let me hear thee say
That Cassio 's not alive.
Iago.   My friend is dead; 'tis done at your request:
But let her live.
Othello.   Damn her, lewd minx! O, damn her!
Come, go with me apart; I will withdraw.
To furnish me with some swift means of death
For the fair devil. Now art thou my lieutenant.
Iago.   I am your own for ever.   *(Exeunt.)*

---

[392] Burden.   [393] Poisonous snakes.   [394] Patient.   [395] The Black Sea.   [396] The
Sea of Marmara, The Dardanelles.   [397] Comprehensive.   [398] Encompass.   [399] Probably
a corrupt line; the meaning appears to be: "to obey shall be my solemn obligation."   [400] Soever.

SCENE 4.   Before the Castle.

(Enter Desdemona, Emilia, and Clown.)

Desdemona.   Do you know, sirrah,[401] where Lieutenant Cassio lies?[402]
Clown.   I dare not say he lies any where.
Desdemona.   Why, man?
Clown.   He is a soldier; and for one to say a soldier lies, is stabbing.[403]
Desdemona.   Go to;[404] where lodges he?
Clown.   To tell you where he lodges is to tell you where I lie.
Desdemona.   Can anything be made of this?
Clown.   I know not where he lodges, and for me to devise[405] a lodging, and say he lies here or he lies there, were to lie in mine own throat.
Desdemona.   Can you inquire him out, and be edified by report?
Clown.   I will catechize the world for him; that is, make questions, and by them answer.
Desdemona.   Seek him, bid him come hither; tell him I have moved my lord in his behalf, and hope all will be well.
Clown.   To do this is within the compass of man's wit, and therefore I will attempt the doing it.   *(Exit.)*
Desdemona.   Where should I lose that handkerchief, Emilia?
Emilia.   I know not, madam.
Desdemona.   Believe me, I had rather have lost my purse
Full of cruzadoes;[406] and, but my noble Moor   20
Is true of mind, and made of no such baseness
As jealous creatures are, it were enough
To put him to ill thinking.
Emilia.   Is he not jealous?
Desdemona.   Who! he? I think the sun where he was born
Drew all such humours from him.
Emilia.   Look! where he comes.
Desdemona.   I will not leave him now till Cassio
Be call'd to him.

(Enter Othello.)

                          How is 't with you, my lord?
Othello.   Well, my good lady. *(Aside)* O! hardness to dissemble.
How do you, Desdemona?
Desdemona.   Well, my good lord.
Othello.   Give me your hand. This hand is moist,[407] my lady.   30

---

[401] Common form of address to inferiors.   [402] Lives.   [403] I.e., is cause for stabbing.
[404] Here apparently: "Come on!"   [405] Invent.   [406] Portuguese gold coins.   [407] A supposed symptom of a lustful nature.

Desdemona.   It yet has felt no age nor known no sorrow.
Othello.   This argues fruitfulness and liberal[408] heart;
Hot, hot, and moist; this hand of yours requires
A sequester[409] from liberty, fasting and prayer,
Much castigation, exercise devout;
For here 's a young and sweating devil here,
That commonly rebels. 'Tis a good hand,
A frank one.
Desdemona.   You may, indeed, say so;
For 'twas that hand that gave away my heart.
Othello.   A liberal hand; the hearts of old gave hands,   40
But our new heraldry[410] is hands not hearts.
Desdemona.   I cannot speak of this. Come now, your promise.
Othello.   What promise, chuck?[411]
Desdemona.   I have sent to bid Cassio come speak with you.
Othello.   I have a salt and sorry rheum offends me.
Lend me thy handkerchief.
Desdemona.   Here, my lord.
Othello.   That which I gave you.
Desdemona.   I have it not about me.
Othello.   Not?
Desdemona.   No, indeed, my lord.
Othello.   That is a fault.
That handkerchief
Did an Egyptian[412] to my mother give;   50
She was a charmer,[413] and could almost read
The thoughts of people; she told her, while she kept it,
'Twould make her amiable[414] and subdue my father
Entirely to her love, but if she lost it
Or made a gift of it, my father's eye
Should hold her loathed, and his spirits should hunt
After new fancies.[415] She dying gave it me;
And bid me, when my fate would have me wive,
To give it her. I did so; and take heed on 't;
Make it a darling like your precious eye;   60
To lose 't or give 't away, were such perdition
As nothing else could match.
Desdemona.   Is 't possible?
Othello.   'Tis true; there 's magic in the web of it;
A sibyl,[416] that had number'd in the world

---

[408] With overtones of: too free, loose.   [409] Separation.   [410] I.e., new heraldic symbolism (Othello means that the new way is not to give the heart together with the hand).   [411] Common term of endearment.   [412] Gypsy.   [413] Sorceress.   [414] Lovable, desirable.   [415] Loves.   [416] Prophetess.

The sun to course two hundred compasses,
In her prophetic fury sew'd the work;
The worms were hallow'd that did breed the silk,
And it was dy'd in mummy[417] which the skilful
Conserv'd of maidens' hearts.
Desdemona.   Indeed! is 't true?
Othello.   Most veritable; therefore look to 't well.   70
Desdemona.   Then would to heaven that I had never seen it!
Othello.   Ha! wherefore?
Desdemona.   Why do you speak so startingly and rash?
Othello.   Is 't lost? is 't gone? speak, is it out o' the way?
Desdemona.   Heaven bless us!
Othello.   Say you?
Desdemona.   It is not lost; but what an if[418] it were?
Othello.   How!
Desdemona.   I say, it is not lost.
Othello.   Fetch 't, let me see 't!
Desdemona.   Why, so I can, sir, but I will not now.
    This is a trick to put me from my suit: 80
    Pray you let Cassio be receiv'd again.
Othello.   Fetch me the handkerchief; my mind misgives.
Desdemona.   Come, come;
    You'll never meet a more sufficient[419] man.
Othello.   The handkerchief!
Desdemona.   I pray, talk[420] me of Cassio.
Othello.   The handkerchief!
Desdemona.   A man that all his time
    Hath founded his good fortunes on your love,
    Shar'd dangers with you,—
Othello.   The handkerchief!
Desdemona.   In sooth, you are to blame.   90
Othello.   Away!   (*Exit.*)
Emilia.   Is not this man jealous?
Desdemona.   I ne'er saw this before.
    Sure, there's some wonder in this handkerchief;
    I am most unhappy in the loss of it.
Emilia.   'Tis not a year or two shows us a man;
    They are all but[421] stomachs, and we all but[421] food;
    They eat us hungerly, and when they are full
    They belch us. Look you! Cassio and my husband.

(*Enter Iago and Cassio.*)

---

[417] Drug (medicinal or magic) derived from embalmed bodies.   [418] If.
[419] Adequate.   [420] Talk to.   [421] Only . . . only.

Iago.   There is no other way; 'tis she must do 't:
And, lo! the happiness;[422] go and importune her.   100
Desdemona.   How now, good Cassio! what 's the news with you?
Cassio.   Madam, my former suit: I do beseech you
That by your virtuous means I may again
Exist, and be a member of his love
Whom I with all the office[423] of my heart
Entirely honour; I would not be delay'd.
If my offence be of such mortal kind
That nor my service past, nor present sorrows,
Nor purpos'd merit in futurity,
Can ransom me into his love again,   110
But to know so must be my benefit;
So shall I clothe me in a forc'd content,
And shut myself up in some other course
To fortune's alms.
Desdemona.   Alas! thrice-gentle Cassio!
My advocation is not now in tune;
My lord is not my lord, nor should I know him,
Were he in favour[424] as in humour alter'd.
So help me every spirit sanctified,
As I have spoken for you all my best
And stood within the blank of[425] his displeasure   120
For my free speech. You must awhile be patient;
What I can do I will, and more I will
Than for myself I dare: let that suffice you.
Iago.   Is my lord angry?
Emilia.   He went hence but now,
And certainly in strange unquietness.
Iago.   Can he be angry? I have seen the cannon,
When it hath blown his ranks[426] into the air,
And, like the devil, from his very arm
Puff'd his own brother; and can he be angry?
Something of moment[427] then; I will go meet him;   130
There's matter in 't indeed, if he be angry.
Desdemona.   I prithee, do so. (*Exit Iago.*) Something, sure, of state,[428]
Either from Venice, or some unhatch'd[429] practice
Made demonstrable here in Cyprus to him,
Hath puddled[430] his clear spirit; and, in such cases
Men's natures wrangle with inferior things,
Though great ones are their object. 'Tis even so;

---

[422] "What luck!"   [423] Duty.   [424] Appearance.   [425] As the target for.   [426] I.e.,
his soldiers.   [427] Important.   [428] Public affairs.   [429] Abortive or budding plot.
[430] Muddied.

For let our finger ache, and it indues[431]
Our other healthful members even to that sense
Of pain. Nay, we must think men are not gods,   140
Nor of them look for such observancy[432]
As fits the bridal.[433] Beshrew me much, Emilia,
I was—unhandsome warrior as I am—
Arraigning his unkindness with[434] my soul;
But now I find I had suborn'd the witness,[435]
And he's indicted falsely.

Emilia.   Pray heaven it be state matters, as you think,
And no conception,[436] nor no jealous toy[437]
Concerning you.

Desdemona.   Alas the day! I never gave him cause.   150

Emilia.   But jealous souls will not be answer'd so;
They are not ever jealous for the cause,
But jealous for they are jealous; 'tis a monster
Begot upon itself, born on itself.

Desdemona.   Heaven keep that monster from Othello's mind!

Emilia.   Lady, amen.

Desdemona.   I will go seek him. Cassio, walk hereabout;
If I do find him fit, I'll move your suit
And seek to effect it to my uttermost.

Cassio.   I humbly thank your ladyship.   160

(*Exeunt Desdemona and Emilia.*)

(*Enter Bianca.*)

Bianca.   Save you, friend Cassio!

Cassio.   What make you from home?
How is it with you, my most fair Bianca?
I' faith, sweet love, I was coming to your house.

Bianca.   And I was going to your lodging, Cassio.
What! keep a week away? seven days and nights?
Eight score eight hours? and lovers' absent hours,
More tedious than the dial eight score times?
O weary reckoning!

Cassio.   Pardon me, Bianca,
I have this while with leaden thoughts been press'd;
But I shall, in a more continuate[438] time,   170
Strike off[439] this score of absence. Sweet Bianca,

(*Giving her Desdemona's handkerchief.*)

Take me this work out.

---

[431] Brings, leads.   [432] Attention.   [433] Wedding.   [434] To.   [435] I.e., caused
my soul to bring in wrong charges.   [436] Fancy, supposition.   [437] Fancy.
[438] Uninterrupted.   [439] Cancel (i.e., make up for).

Bianca.   O Cassio! whence came this?
  This is some token from a newer friend;
  To the felt absence now I feel a cause;
  Is 't come to this? Well, well.
Cassio.   Go to, woman!
  Throw your vile guesses in the devil's teeth,
  From whence you have them. You are jealous now
  That this is from some mistress, some remembrance:
  No, in good troth, Bianca.
Bianca.   Why, whose is it?   180
Cassio.   I know not, sweet; I found it in my chamber.
  I like the work well; ere it be demanded,—[440]
  As like enough it will,—I'd have it copied;
  Take it and do 't; and leave me for this time.
Bianca.   Leave you! wherefore?
Cassio.   I do attend here on[441] the general,
  And think it no addition,[442] nor my wish,
  To have him see me woman'd.
Bianca.   Why, I pray you?
Cassio.   Not that I love you not.
Bianca.   But that you do not love me.
  I pray you, bring me on the way a little   190
  And say if I shall see you soon at night.
Cassio.   'Tis but a little way that I can bring you,
  For I attend here; but I'll see you soon.
Bianca.   'Tis very good; I must be circumstanc'd.[443]   (*Exeunt.*)

Act IV

SCENE 1.   Cyprus. Before the Castle.

(*Enter Othello and Iago.*)

Iago.   Will you think so?
Othello.   Think so, Iago!
Iago.   What!
  To kiss in private?
Othello.   An unauthoriz'd kiss.
Iago.   Or to be naked with her friend a-bed
  An hour or more, not meaning any harm?
Othello.   Naked a-bed, Iago, and not mean harm?

---

[440] Asked for.   [441] Wait for.   [442] Advantage, credit.   [443] Governed by circumstances.

It is hypocrisy against the devil:[444]
They that mean virtuously, and yet do so,
The devil their virtue tempts, and they tempt heaven.
Iago.   If they do nothing, 'tis a venial slip;
But if I give my wife a handkerchief,—   10
Othello.   What then?
Iago.   Why, then, 'tis hers, my lord; and, being hers,
She may, I think, bestow 't on any man.
Othello.   She is protectress of her honour too;
May she give that?
Iago.   Her honour is an essence that 's not seen;
They have it very oft that have it not:[445]
But for the handkerchief,—
Othello.   By heaven, I would most gladly have forgot it:—
Thou said'st,—O! it comes o'er my memory,   20
As doth the raven[446] o'er the infected house,
Boding to all,—he had my handkerchief.
Iago.   Ay, what of that?
Othello.   That's not so good now.
Iago.   What,
If I had said I had seen him do you wrong?
Or heard him say, as knaves be such abroad,[447]
Who having, by their own importunate suit,
Or voluntary dotage[448] of some mistress,
Convinced or supplied them,[449] cannot choose
But they must blab.
Othello.   Hath he said any thing?
Iago.   He hath, my lord; but be you well assur'd,   30
No more than he'll unswear.
Othello.   What hath he said?
Iago.   Faith, that he did— I know not what he did.
Othello.   What? what?
Iago.   Lie—
Othello.   With her?
Iago.   With her, on her; what you will.
Othello.   Lie with her; lie on her! We say, lie on her, when they belie her.
Lie with her! that's fulsome. Handkerchief,—confessions,—handkerchief! To
confess, and be hanged for his labour. First, to be hanged, and then to
confess: I tremble at it. Nature would not invest herself in such shadowing
passion without some instruction.[450] It is not words that shake me thus. Pish!
Noses, ears, and lips. It is possible?—Confess!—Handkerchief!—O devil!

---

[444] I.e., by not committing the sin which the situation invites.   [445] I.e., some unchaste
women are thought chaste.   [446] (1) A bad omen, (2) A carrier of the plague.   [447] As
there are some such in the world.   [448] Foolish affection.   [449] Overcome (their reluctance) or satisfied (their desires).   [450] I would not fall into such passion unless there were some
real grounds for it.

(Falls in a trance.)

Iago.   Work on,
  My medicine, work! Thus credulous fools are caught;
  And many worthy and chaste dames even thus,
  All guiltless, meet reproach. What, ho! my lord!
  My lord, I say! Othello!

(Enter Cassio.)

                              How now, Cassio!
Cassio.   What's the matter?
Iago.   My lord is fallen into an epilepsy;[451]
  This is his second fit; he had one yesterday.
Cassio.   Rub him about the temples.
Iago.   No, forbear;
  The lethargy[452] must have his quiet course,   50
  If not, he foams at mouth, and by and by
  Breaks out to savage madness. Look! he stirs;
  Do you withdraw yourself a little while,
  He will recover straight; when he is gone,
  I would on great occasion[453] speak with you.   *(Exit Cassio.)*
  How is it, general? have you not hurt your head?
Othello.   Dost thou mock me?[454]
Iago.   I mock you! no, by heaven.
  Would you would bear your fortune like a man!
Othello.   A horned man's a monster and a beast.
Iago.   There's many a beast then, in a populous city,   60
  And many a civil[455] monster.
Othello.   Did he confess it?
Iago.   Good sir, be a man;
  Think every bearded fellow that's but yok'd
  May draw[456] with you; there's millions now alive
  That nightly lie in those unproper[457] beds
  Which they dare swear peculiar;[458] your case is better.
  O! 'tis the spite of hell, the fiend's arch-mock,
  To lip[459] a wanton in a secure[460] couch,
  And to suppose her chaste. No, let me know;
  And knowing what I am, I know what she shall be.   70
Othello.   O! thou art wise; 'tis certain.

---

[451] Seizure, fit.   [452] Coma.   [453] Important matter.   [454] Another allusion to the cuckold's horns.   [455] Citizen.   [456] I.e., pull the burden of cuckoldom.   [457] Not exclusively their own.   [458] Exclusively their own.   [459] Kiss.   [460] I.e., without suspicion of having a rival.

Iago.   Stand you awhile apart;
Confine yourself but in a patient list.[461]
Whilst you were here o'erwhelmed with your grief,—
A passion most unsuiting such a man,—
Cassio came hither; I shifted him away,
And laid good 'scuse upon your ecstasy;[462]
Bade him anon return and here speak with me;
The which he promis'd. Do but encave yourself,
And mark the fleers, the gibes, and notable scorns,
That dwell in every region of his face;   80
For I will make him tell the tale anew,
Where, how, how oft, how long ago, and when
He hath, and is again to cope[463] your wife:
I say, but mark his gesture. Marry, patience;
Or I shall say you are all in all in spleen,[464]
And nothing of a man.
Othello.   Dost thou hear, Iago?
I will be found most cunning in my patience;
But—dost thou hear?—most bloody.
Iago.   That's not amiss:
But yet keep time[465] in all. Will you withdraw?   (*Othello goes apart.*)
Now will I question Cassio of Bianca,   90
A housewife[466] that by selling her desires
Buys herself bread and clothes; it is a creature
That dotes on Cassio; as 'tis the strumpet's plague
To beguile many and be beguil'd by one.
He, when he hears of her, cannot refrain
From the excess of laughter. Here he comes:

(*Re-enter Cassio.*)

As he shall smile, Othello shall go mad;
And his unbookish[467] jealousy must construe
Poor Cassio's smiles, gestures, and light behaviour
Quite in the wrong. How do you now, lieutenant?   100
Cassio.   The worser that you give me the addition[468]
Whose want[469] even kills me.
Iago.   Ply Desdemona well, and you are sure on 't.
(*Speaking lower.*) Now, if this suit lay in Bianca's power,
How quickly should you speed!
Cassio.   Alas! poor caitiff![470]
Othello.   Look! how he laughs already!

---

[461] Bounds of patience. overcome by passion. naive.   [462] Derangement, trance.   [463] Close with.   [464] Completely
[465] Maintain control.   [466] Hussy.   [467] Unpracticed,
[468] Title.   [469] The want of which.   [470] Wretch.

Iago.   I never knew woman love man so.

Cassio.   Alas! poor rogue, I think i' faith, she loves me.

Othello.   Now he denies it faintly, and laughs it out.

Iago.   Do you hear, Cassio?

Othello.   Now he importunes him   110
  To tell it o'er: go to; well said, well said.

Iago.   She gives it out that you shall marry her;
  Do you intend it?

Cassio.   Ha, ha, ha!

Othello.   Do you triumph, Roman?[471] do you triumph?

Cassio.   I marry her! what? a customer?[472] I prithee, bear some charity to my
  wit;[473] do not think it so unwholesome. Ha, ha, ha!

Othello.   So, so, so, so. They laugh that win.[474]

Iago.   Faith, the cry goes that you shall marry her.

Cassio.   Prithee, say true.   120

Iago.   I am a very villain else.

Othello.   Have you scored me?[475] Well.

Cassio.   This is the monkey's own giving out: she is persuaded I will marry
  her, out of her own love and flattery, not out of my promise.

Othello.   Iago beckons me;[476] now he begins the story.

Cassio.   She was here even now; she haunts me in every place. I was the other
  day talking on the sea-bank with certain Venetians, and thither comes this
  bauble,[477] and, by this hand, she falls me thus about my neck;—

Othello.   Crying, 'O dear Cassio!' as it were; his gesture imports it.

Cassio.   So hangs and lolls and weeps upon me; so hales[478] and pulls me; ha,
  ha, ha!

Othello.   Now he tells how she plucked him to my chamber. O! I see that
  nose of yours, but not the dog I shall throw it to.

Cassio.   Well, I must leave her company.

Iago.   Before me![479] look, where she comes.

Cassio.   'Tis such another fitchew![480] marry, a perfumed one.

(Enter Bianca.)

  What do you mean by this haunting of me?

Bianca.   Let the devil and his dam haunt you! What did you mean by that
  same handkerchief you gave me even now? I was a fine fool to take it. I must
  take out the work! A likely piece of work, that you should find it in your
  chamber, and not know who left it there! This is some minx's token, and I
  must take out the work! There, give it your hobby-horse;[481] wheresoever you
  had it I'll take out no work on 't.

---

[471] I.e., one who triumphs(?).   [472] Courtesan, prostitute.   [473] Give me credit for some
sense.   [474] "He who laughs last laughs longest"(?).   [475] Wounded, defaced(?); or: settled
my account(?).   [476] Signals.   [477] Plaything.   [478] Hauls.   [479] An exclamation
of surprise.   [480] Polecat, noted both for its strong smell and for its lechery.   [481] Harlot.

Cassio.   How now, my sweet Bianca! how now, how now!

Othello.   By heaven, that should be[482] my handkerchief!

Bianca.   An you'll come to supper to-night, you may; an you will not, come
when you are next prepared[483] for.   *(Exit.)*

Iago.   After her, after her.

Cassio.   Faith, I must; she'll rail in the street else.

Iago.   Will you sup there?

Cassio.   Faith, I intend so.

Iago.   Well, I may chance to see you, for I would very fain[484] speak with you.

Cassio.   Prithee come; will you?

Iago.   Go to; say no more.   *(Exit Cassio.)*

Othello *(advancing).*   How shall I murder him, Iago?

Iago.   Did you perceive how he laughed at his vice?

Othello.   O! Iago!

Iago.   And did you see the handkerchief?

Othello.   Was that mine?

Iago.   Yours, by this hand; and to see how he prizes the foolish woman your
wife! she gave it him, and he hath given it his whore.

Othello.   I would have him nine years a-killing. A fine woman! a fair woman!
a sweet woman!

Iago.   Nay, you must forget that.

Othello.   Ay, let her rot, and perish, and be damned to-night; for she shall not
live. No, my heart is turned to stone; I strike it, and it hurts my hand. O! the
world hath not a sweeter creature; she might lie by an emperor's side and
command him tasks.

Iago.   Nay, that's not your way.[485]

Othello.   Hang her! I do but say what she is. So delicate with her needle! An
admirable musician! O, she will sing the savageness out of a bear. Of so high
and plenteous wit and invention!

Iago.   She's the worse for all this.

Othello.   O! a thousand, a thousand times. And then, of so gentle a condition![486]

Iago.   Ay, too gentle.[487]

Othello.   Nay, that's certain;—but yet the pity of it, Iago!
O! Iago, the pity of it, Iago!

Iago.   If you are so fond over her iniquity, give her patent to offend; for, if it
touch not you, it comes near nobody.

Othello.   I will chop her into messes.[488] Cuckold me!

Iago.   O! 'tis foul in her.

Othello.   With mine officer!

Iago.   That's fouler.

---

[482] I.e., I think that is.   [483] Expected (Bianca means that if he does not come that night, she
will never want to see him again).   [484] Gladly.   [485] Proper course.   [486] So much
the high-born lady.   [487] I.e., yielding.   [488] Bits.

Othello.   Get me some poison, Iago; this night: I'll not expostulate with her,
   lest her body and beauty unprovide my mind again.[489] This night, Iago.
Iago.   Do it not with poison, strangle her in her bed, even the bed she hath
   contaminated.
Othello.   Good, good; the justice of it pleases; very good.
Iago.   And for Cassio, let me be his undertaker;[490] you shall hear more by
   midnight.
Othello.   Excellent good. (*A trumpet within.*) What trumpet is that same?
Iago.   Something from Venice, sure. 'Tis Lodovico,
   Come from the duke; and see, your wife is with him.

(*Enter Lodovico, Desdemona, and Attendants.*)

Lodovico.   God save you, worthy general!
Othello.   With all my heart, sir.
Lodovico.   The duke and senators of Venice greet you.

(*Gives him a packet.*)

Othello.   I kiss the instrument of their pleasures.

(*Opens the packet, and reads.*)

Desdemona.   And what's the news, good cousin Lodovico?
Iago.   I am very glad to see you, signior;
   Welcome to Cyprus.
Lodovico.   I thank you. How does Lieutenant Cassio?
Iago.   Lives, sir.   200
Desdemona.   Cousin, there's fall'n between him and my lord
   An unkind[491] breach; but you shall make all well.
Othello.   Are you sure of that?
Desdemona.   My lord?
Othello (*reads*).   'This fail you not to do, as you will'—
Lodovico.   He did not call; he's busy in the paper.
   Is there division[492] twixt my lord and Cassio?
Desdemona.   A most unhappy one; I would do much
   To atone[493] them, for the love I bear to Cassio.
Othello.   Fire and brimstone!
Desdemona.   My lord?
Othello.   Are you wise?   210
Desdemona.   What! is he angry?
Lodovico.   May be the letter mov'd him;

---

[489] Unsettle my intention.   [490] Dispatcher.   [491] Unnatural.   [492] Estrangement.
[493] Reconcile.

For, as I think, they do command him home,
Deputing Cassio in his government.

Desdemona. Trust me, I am glad on 't.

Othello.   Indeed!

Desdemona.   My lord?

Othello. I am glad to see you mad.

Desdemona.   Why, sweet Othello?

Othello. Devil!   (*Strikes her.*)

Desdemona. I have not deserved this.

Lodovico. My lord, this would not be believ'd in Venice,
Though I should swear I saw 't; 'tis very much;
Make her amends, she weeps.

Othello.   O devil, devil!
If that the earth could teem with woman's tears,   220
Each drop she falls[494] would prove a crocodile.[495]
Out of my sight!

Desdemona. I will not stay to offend you.   (*Going.*)

Lodovico. Truly, an obedient lady;
I do beseech your lordship, call her back.

Othello. Mistress!

Desdemona. My lord?

Othello.   What would you with her, sir?

Lodovico. Why, I, my lord?

Othello. Ay; you did wish that I would make her turn:
Sir, she can turn, and turn, and yet go on,
And turn again; and she can weep, sir, weep;
And she's obedient, as you say, obedient,   230
Very obedient. Proceed you in your tears.
Concerning this, sir—O well-painted passion!—
I am commanded home. Get you away;
I'll send for you anon. Sir, I obey the mandate,
And will return to Venice. Hence! avaunt![496]   (*Exit Desdemona.*)
Cassio shall have my place. And, sir, to-night,
I do entreat that we may sup together;
You are welcome, sir, to Cyprus. Goats and monkeys!   (*Exit.*)

Lodovico. Is this the noble Moor whom our full senate
Call all-in-all sufficient? is this the noble nature   240
Whom passion could not shake? whose solid virtue
The shot of accident nor dart of chance
Could neither graze nor pierce?

Iago.   He is much chang'd.

Lodovico. Are his wits safe? is he not light of brain?

Iago. He's that he is; I may not breathe my censure.

---

[494] Lets fall.   [495] The crocodile's tears were supposed to be hypocritical.   [496] Begone!

What he might be, if, what he might, he is not,
I would to heaven he were!⁴⁹⁷
Lodovico.   What! strike his wife!
Iago.   Faith, that was not so well; yet would I knew
That stroke would prove the worst!
Lodovico.   Is it his use?
Or did the letters work upon his blood,   250
And new-create this fault?
Iago.   Alas, alas!
It is not honesty in me to speak
What I have seen and known. You shall observe him,
And his own courses⁴⁹⁸ will denote him so
That I may save my speech. Do but go after
And mark how he continues.
Lodovico.   I am sorry that I am deceiv'd in him.   *(Exeunt.)*

SCENE 2.   A Room in the Castle.

(Enter Othello and Emilia.)

Othello.   You have seen nothing, then?
Emilia.   Nor ever heard, nor ever did suspect.
Othello.   Yes, you have seen Cassio and her together.
Emilia.   But then I saw no harm, and then I heard
Each syllable that breath made up between them.
Othello.   What! did they never whisper?
Emilia.   Never, my lord.
Othello.   Nor send you out o' the way?
Emilia.   Never.
Othello.   To fetch her fan, her gloves, her mask, nor nothing?⁴⁹⁹
Emilia.   Never, my lord.   10
Othello.   That's strange.
Emilia.   I durst, my lord, to wager she is honest,
Lay down my soul at stake: if you think other,
Remove your thought; it doth abuse your bosom.
If any wretch have put this in your head,
Let heaven requite it with the serpent's curse!
For, if she be not honest, chaste, and true,
There's no man happy; the purest of their wives
Is foul as slander.

---

⁴⁹⁷ Another of Iago's gnomic speeches; perhaps approximately: "If now he is not himself, I wish he would be what he could be!"   ⁴⁹⁸ Actions.   ⁴⁹⁹ Anything.

Othello.   Bid her come hither; go.   *(Exit Emilia.)*
   She says enough; yet she 's a simple[500] bawd   20
   That cannot say as much. This is a subtle whore,
   A closet lock and key of villanous secrets;
   And yet she 'll kneel and pray; I have seen her do 't.

(Re-enter Emilia with Desdemona.)

Desdemona.   My lord, what is your will?
Othello.   Pray, chuck, come hither.
Desdemona.   What is your pleasure?
Othello.   Let me see your eyes;
   Look in my face.
Desdemona.   What horrible fancy 's this?
Othello *(to Emilia).*   Some of your function,[501] mistress;
   Leave procreants alone and shut the door;
   Cough or cry 'hem' if any body come;
   Your mystery,[502] your mystery; nay, dispatch.   *(Exit Emilia.)*
Desdemona.   Upon my knees, what doth your speech import?   31
   I understand a fury in your words.
   But not the words.
Othello.   Why, what art thou?
Desdemona.   Your wife, my lord; your true
   And loyal wife.
Othello.   Come, swear it, damn thyself;
   Lest, being like one of heaven, the devils themselves
   Should fear to seize thee; therefore be double-damn'd;
   Swear thou art honest.
Desdemona.   Heaven doth truly know it.
Othello.   Heaven truly knows that thou art false as hell.
Desdemona.   To whom, my lord? with whom? how am I false?   40
Othello.   Ah! Desdemona; away, away, away!
Desdemona.   Alas, the heavy day!—Why do you weep?
   Am I the motive of these tears, my lord?
   If haply you my father do suspect
   An instrument of this your calling back,
   Lay not your blame on me; if you have lost him,
   Why, I have lost him too.
Othello.   Had it pleas'd heaven
   To try me with affliction, had he rain'd
   All kinds of sores and shames on my bare head,
   Steep'd me in poverty to the very lips,   50

---

[500] Simpleminded.   [501] To your duty, business.   [502] Trade.

Given to captivity me and my utmost hopes,
I should have found in some part of my soul
A drop of patience; but, alas! to make me
The fixed figure for the time of scorn[503]
To point his slow and moving finger at;
Yet could I bear that too; well, very well:
But there, where I have garner'd[504] up my heart,
Where either I must live or bear no life,
The fountain from the which my current runs
Or else dries up; to be discarded thence!   60
Or keep it as a cistern for foul toads
To knot and gender in![505] Turn thy complexion there,[506]
Patience, thou young and rose-lipp'd cherubin;
Ay, there, look grim as hell!

Desdemona.   I hope my noble lord esteems me honest.

Othello.   O! ay; as summer flies are in the shambles,[507]
That quicken even with blowing. O thou weed!
Who art so lovely fair and smell'st so sweet
That the sense aches at thee, would thou hadst ne'er been born.

Desdemona.   Alas! what ignorant sin have I commited?   70

Othello.   Was this fair paper, this most goodly book,
Made to write 'whore' upon? What committed!
Committed! O thou public commoner![508]
I should make very forges of my cheeks,
That would to cinders burn up modesty,
Did I but speak thy deeds. What committed!
Heaven stops the nose at it and the moon winks,[509]
The bawdy wind that kisses all it meets
Is hush'd within the hollow mine of earth,
And will not hear it. What committed!   80
Impudent strumpet!

Desdemona.   By heaven, you do me wrong.

Othello.   Are not you a strumpet?

Desdemona.   No, as I am a Christian.
If to preserve this vessel for my lord
From any other foul unlawful touch
Be not to be a strumpet, I am none.

Othello.   What! not a whore?

Desdemona.   No, as I shall be sav'd.

Othello.   Is it possible?

Desdemona.   O! heaven forgive us.

---

[503] I.e., the scornful world.   [504] Stored.   [505] Bunch up and procreate.   [506] I.e.,
change your color to suit the "cistern for foul toads."   [507] Slaughterhouse.   [508] Harlot.
[509] Closes her eyes.

Othello.   I cry you mercy,[510] then;
I took you for that cunning whore of Venice
That married with Othello. You, mistress,   90
That have the office opposite to Saint Peter,
And keep the gate of hell!

(Re-enter Emilia.)

                          You, you, ay, you!
We have done our course; there's money for your pains.
I pray you, turn the key and keep our counsel.   *(Exit.)*
Emilia.   Alas! what does this gentleman conceive?[511]
How do you, madam? how do you, my good lady?
Desdemona.   Faith, half asleep.
Emilia.   Good madam, what's the matter with my lord?
Desdemona.   With who?
Emilia.   Why, with my lord, madam.   100
Desdemona.   Who is thy lord?
Emilia.   He that is yours, sweet lady.
Desdemona.   I have none; do not talk to me, Emilia;
I cannot weep, nor answer have I none,
But what should go by water.[512] Prithee, to-night
Lay on my bed my wedding sheets: remember:
And call thy husband hither.
Emilia.   Here is a change indeed!   *(Exit.)*
Desdemona.   'Tis meet I should be us'd so, very meet.
How have I been behav'd, that he might stick
The small'st opinion on my least misuse?[513]

(Re-enter Emilia, with Iago.)

Iago.   What is your pleasure, madam? How is it with you?   110
Desdemona.   I cannot tell. Those that do teach young babes
Do it with gentle means and easy tasks;
He might have chid me so; for, in good faith,
I am a child to chiding.
Iago.   What's the matter, lady?
Emilia.   Alas, Iago, my lord hath so bewhor'd her,
Thrown such despite[514] and heavy terms upon her,
As true hearts cannot bear.
Desdemona.   Am I that name, Iago?
Iago.   What name, fair lady?
Desdemona.   Such as she says my lord did say I was.

---

[510] Beg your pardon.   [511] Imagine.   [512] Be conveyed by means of tears.   [513] The
least suspicion on my slightest misconduct.   [514] Abuse.

Emilia.   He call'd her whore; a beggar in his drink   120
Could not have laid such terms upon his callat.[515]
Iago.   Why did he so?
Desdemona.   I do not know; I am sure I am none such.
Iago.   Do not weep, do not weep. Alas the day!
Emilia.   Has she forsook so many noble matches,
Her father and her country and her friends,
To be call'd whore? would it not make one weep?
Desdemona.   It is my wretched fortune.
Iago.   Beshrew[516] him for it!
How comes this trick upon him?
Desdemona.   Nay, heaven doth know.
Emilia.   I will be hang'd, if some eternal villain,   130
Some busy and insinuating rogue,
Some cogging[517] cozening slave, to get some office,
Have not devis'd this slander; I 'll be hang'd else.
Iago.   Fie! there is no such man; it is impossible.
Desdemona.   If any such there be, heaven pardon him!
Emilia.   A halter pardon him, and hell gnaw his bones!
Why should he call her whore? who keeps her company?
What place? what time? what form? what likelihood?
The Moor 's abus'd by some most villanous knave,
Some base notorious knave, some scurvy fellow.   140
O heaven! that such companions[518] thou'dst unfold,
And put in every honest hand a whip
To lash the rascals naked through the world,
Even from the east to west!
Iago.   Speak within door.
Emilia.   O! fie upon them. Some such squire he was
That turn'd your wit the seamy side without,[519]
And made you to suspect me with the Moor.
Iago.   You are a fool; go to.
Desdemona.   O good Iago,
What shall I do to win my lord again?
Good friend, go to him; for, by this light of heaven,   150
I know not how I lost him. Here I kneel:
If e'er my will did trespass 'gainst his love,
Either in discourse of thought or actual deed,
Or that mine eyes, mine ears, or any sense,
Delighted them[520] in any other form;
Or that I do not yet,[521] and ever did,
And ever will, though he do shake me off
To beggarly divorcement, love him dearly,

---

[515] Slut.   [516] Curse.   [517] Cheating.   [518] Fellows   (derogatory).
[519] Outward.   [520] Found delight.   [521] Still.

Comfort forswear me! Unkindness may do much;
And his unkindness may defeat[522] my life,   160
But never taint my love. I cannot say 'whore':
It does abhor me now I speak the word;
To do the act that might the addition earn
Not the world's mass of vanity could make me.

Iago.   I pray you be content, 'tis but his humour;
The business of the state does him offence,
And he does chide with you.

Desdemona.   If 'twere no other,—

Iago.   'Tis but so, I warrant.   *(Trumpets.)*
Hark! how these instruments summon to supper;
The messengers of Venice stay the meat: 170
Go in, and weep not; all things shall be well.

                          (Exeunt Desdemona and Emilia.)

(Enter Roderigo.)

How now, Roderigo!

Roderigo.   I do not find that thou dealest justly with me.

Iago.   What in the contrary?[523]

Roderigo.   Every day thou daffest me[524] with some device, Iago; and rather, as it seems to me now, keepest from me all conveniency,[525] than suppliest me with the least advantage of hope. I will indeed no longer endure it, nor am I yet persuaded to put up[526] in peace what already I have foolishly suffered.

Iago.   Will you hear me, Roderigo?

Roderigo.   Faith, I have heard too much, for your words and performances are no kin together.

Iago.   You charge me most unjustly.

Roderigo.   With nought but truth. I have wasted myself out of my means. The jewels you have had from me to deliver to Desdemona would half have corrupted a votarist;[527] you have told me she has received them, and returned me expectations and comforts of sudden respect[528] and acquaintance, but I find none.

Iago.   Well; go to; very well.

Roderigo.   Very well! go to! I cannot go to, man; nor 'tis not very well: by this hand, I say, it is very scurvy, and begin to find myself fobbed[529] in it.

Iago.   Very well.

Roderigo.   I tell you 'tis not very well. I will make myself known to Desdemona; if she will return me my jewels, I will give over my suit and repent my unlawful solicitation; if not, assure yourself I will seek satisfaction of you.

Iago.   You have said now.[530]

---

[522] Destroy.   [523] I.e., what reason do you have for saying that.   [524] You put me off.   [525] Favorable circumstances.   [526] Put up with.   [527] Nun.   [528] Immediate consideration.   [529] Cheated.   [530] I.e, "I suppose you're through?" (?); or: "Now you're talking" (?).

Roderigo.   Ay, and said nothing, but what I protest intendment of doing.

Iago.   Why, now I see there's mettle in thee, and even from this instant do build on thee a better opinion than ever before. Give me thy hand, Roderigo; thou hast taken against me a most just exception; but yet, I protest, I have dealt most directly in thy affair.

Roderigo.   It hath not appeared.

Iago.   I grant indeed it hath not appeared, and your suspicion is not without wit and judgment. But, Roderigo, if thou hast that in thee indeed, which I have greater reason to believe now than ever, I mean purpose, courage, and valour, this night show it: if thou the next night following enjoy not Desdemona, take me from this world with treachery and devise engines for[531] my life.

Roderigo.   Well, what is it? is it within reason and compass?

Iago.   Sir, there is especial commission come from Venice to depute Cassio in Othello's place.

Roderigo.   Is that true? why, then Othello and Desdemona return again to Venice.

Iago.   O, no! he goes into Mauritania, and takes away with him the fair Desdemona, unless his abode be lingered here by some accident; wherein none can be so determinate[532] as the removing of Cassio.

Roderigo.   How do you mean, removing of him?

Iago.   Why, by making him uncapable of Othello's place; knocking out his brains.

Roderigo.   And that you would have me do?

Iago.   Ay; if you dare do yourself a profit and a right. He sups to-night with a harlotry,[533] and thither will I go to him; he knows not yet of his honourable fortune. If you will watch his going thence,—which I will fashion to fall out between twelve and one,—you may take him at your pleasure; I will be near to second your attempt, and he shall fall between us. Come, stand not amazed at it, but go along with me; I will show you such a necessity in his death that you shall think yourself bound to put it on him. It is now high supper-time, and the night grows to waste; about it.

Roderigo.   I will hear further reason for this.

Iago.   And you shall be satisfied.   *(Exeunt.)*

SCENE 3.   Another Room in the Castle.

(Enter Othello, Lodovico, Desdemona, Emilia, and Attendants.)

Lodovico.   I do beseech you, sir, trouble yourself no further.

Othello.   O! pardon me; 'twill do me good to walk.

Lodovico.   Madam, good-night; I humbly thank your ladyship.

---

[531] Devices against.   [532] Effective.   [533] Harlot.

Desdemona.   Your honour is most welcome.

Othello.   Will you walk, sir?

O! Desdemona,—

Desdemona.   My lord?

Othello.   Get you to bed on the instant; I will be returned forthwith; dismiss
your attendant there; look it be done.

Desdemona.   I will, my lord.   *(Exeunt Othello, Lodovico, and Attendants.)*

Emilia.   How goes it now? He looks gentler than he did.   240

Desdemona.   He says he will return incontinent;[534]

He hath commanded me to go to bed,

And bade me to dismiss you.

Emilia.   Dismiss me!

Desdemona.   It was his bidding; therefore, good Emilia,

Give me my nightly wearing, and adieu:

We must not now displease him.

Emilia.   I would you had never seen him.

Desdemona.   So would not I; my love doth so approve him,

That even his stubbornness,[535] his checks[536] and frowns,—

Prithee, unpin me,—have grace and favour in them.   250

Emilia.   I have laid those sheets you bade me on the bed.

Desdemona.   All's one.[537] Good faith! how foolish are our minds!

If I do die before thee, prithee, shroud me

In one of those same sheets.

Emilia.   Come, come, you talk.

Desdemona.   My mother had a maid call'd Barbara;

She was in love, and he she lov'd prov'd mad[538]

And did forsake her; she had a song of 'willow';

An old thing 'twas, but it express'd her fortune,

And she died singing it; that song to-night

Will not go from my mind; I have much to do   260

But to go hang my head all at one side,

And sing it like poor Barbara. Prithee, dispatch.

Emilia.   Shall I go fetch your night-gown?

Desdemona.   No, unpin me here.

This Lodovico is a proper man.

Emilia.   A very handsome man.

Desdemona.   He speaks well.

Emilia.   I know a lady in Venice would have walked barefoot to Palestine for
a touch of his nether lip.

Desdemona *(sings).*

The poor soul sat sighing by a sycamore tree,

Sing all a green willow;   270

---

[534] At once.   [535] Roughness.   [536] Rebukes.   [537] I.e., it doesn't matter.
[538] Wild.

Her hand on her bosom, her head on her knee,
    Sing willow, willow, willow:
The fresh streams ran by her, and murmur'd her moans;
    Sing willow, willow, willow:
Her salt tears fell from her and soften'd the stones;—

Lay by these:—
    Sing willow, willow, willow:

Prithee, hie thee;[539] he 'll come anon.—

    Sing all a green willow must be my garland.
        Let nobody blame him, his scorn I approve,—   280
    Nay, that's not next. Hark! who is it that knocks?
Emilia.   It is the wind.
Desdemona.
    I call'd my love false love; but what said he then?
        Sing willow, willow, willow:
    If I court moe[540] women, you 'll couch with moe men.

    So, get thee gone; good-night. Mine eyes do itch;
    Doth that bode weeping?
Emilia.   'Tis neither here nor there.
Desdemona.   I have heard it said so. O! these men, these men!
    Dost thou in conscience think, tell me, Emilia,
    That there be women do abuse their husbands   290
    In such gross kind?
Emilia.   There be some such, no question.
Desdemona.   Wouldst thou do such a deed for all the world?
Emilia.   Why, would not you?
Desdemona.   No, by this heavenly light!
Emilia.   Nor I neither by this heavenly light;
    I might do 't as well i' the dark.
Desdemona.   Wouldst thou do such a deed for all the world?
Emilia.   The world is a huge thing; 'tis a great price
    For a small vice.
Desdemona.   In troth, I think thou wouldst not.
Emilia.   In troth, I think I should, and undo 't when I had done. Marry, I
    would not do such a thing for a joint-ring,[541] nor measures of lawn,[542] nor
    for gowns, petticoats, nor caps, nor any petty exhibition;[543] but for the whole
    world, who would not make her husband a cuckold to make him a monarch?
    I should venture purgatory for 't.

---

[539] Hurry.   [540] More.   [541] Ring made in separable halves.   [542] Fine linen.
[543] Offer, gift.

Desdemona.   Beshrew me, if I would do such a wrong
For the whole world.

Emilia.   Why, the wrong is but a wrong i' the world; and having the world for
your labour, 'tis a wrong in your own world, and you might quickly make it
right.

Desdemona.   I do not think there is any such woman.

Emilia.   Yes, a dozen; and as many to the vantage,[544] as   310
Would store[545] the world they played for.
But I do think it is their husbands' faults
If wives do fall. Say that they slack their duties,
And pour our treasures into foreign laps,
Or else break out in peevish jealousies,
Throwing restraint upon us; or say they strike us,
Or scant[546] our former having[547] in despite;
Why, we have galls;[548] and though we have some grace,
Yet have we some revenge. Let husbands know
Their wives have sense like them; they see and smell,   320
And have their palates both for sweet and sour,
As husbands have. What is it that they do
When they change us for others? Is it sport?[549]
I think it is; and doth affection breed it?
I think it doth; is 't frailty that thus errs?
It is so too; and have not we affections,
Desires for sport, and frailty, as men have?
Then, let them use us well; else let them know,
The ills we do, their ills instruct us so.

Desdemona.   Good-night, good night; heaven me such usage[550] send,   330
Not to pick bad from bad, but by bad mend!   *(Exeunt.)*

Act V

SCENE 1.   Cyprus. A Street.

(Enter Iago and Roderigo.)

Iago.   Here, stand behind this bulk;[551] straight will he come:
Wear thy good rapier bare, and put it home.
Quick, quick; fear nothing; I 'll be at thy elbow.
It makes us, or it mars us; think on that,
And fix most firm thy resolution.

---

[544] Over and above.   [545] Populate.   [546] Reduce.   [547] Allowance.   [548] Spirits,
temper.   [549] Lust, sexual enjoyment.   [550] Habits (?), treatment (?).   [551] Jutting part
of a wall.

Roderigo.   Be near at hand; I may miscarry in 't.
Iago.   Here, at thy hand: be bold, and take thy stand.   (*Retires.*)
Roderigo.   I have no great devotion to the deed;
    And yet he has given me satisfying reasons:
    'Tis but a man gone: forth, my sword; he dies.   10
Iago.   I have rubb'd this young quat[552] almost to the sense,[553]
    And he grows angry. Now, whether he kill Cassio,
    Or Cassio him, or each do kill the other,
    Every way makes my gain: live Roderigo,
    He calls me to a restitution large
    Of gold and jewels that I bobb'd[554] from him,
    As gifts to Desdemona;
    It must not be: if Cassio do remain,
    He hath a daily beauty in his life
    That makes me ugly: and, besides, the Moor   20
    May unfold me to him; there stand I in much peril.
    No, he must die. But so;[555] I hear him coming.

(*Enter Cassio.*)

Roderigo.   I know his gait; 'tis he. Villain, thou diest!

(*Makes a pass at Cassio.*)

Cassio.   That thrust had been mine enemy indeed
    But that my coat is better than thou know'st;
    I will make proof of thine.

(*Draws, and wounds Roderigo.*)

Roderigo.   O! I am slain.

(*Iago from behind wounds Cassio in the leg, and exit.*)

Cassio.   I am maim'd for ever. Help, ho! murder! murder!   (*Falls.*)

(*Enter Othello, at a distance.*)

Othello.   The voice of Cassio: Iago keeps his word.
Roderigo.   O! villain that I am!
Othello.   It is e'en so.
Cassio.   O, help, ho! light! a surgeon!   30

---

[552] Pimple.   [553] To the quick.   [554] Swindled.   [555] I.e., that's the only way.

Othello.   'Tis he: O brave Iago, honest and just!
That hast such noble sense of thy friend's wrong;
Thou teachest me. Minion,[556] your dear lies dead,
And your unblest fate hies; strumpet, I come!
Forth of my heart those charms, thine eyes, are blotted;
Thy bed lust-stain'd shall with lust's blood be spotted.   (*Exit.*)

(Enter Lodovico and Gratiano, at a distance.)

Cassio.   What ho! no watch? no passage?[557] murder! murder!
Gratiano.   'Tis some mischance; the cry is very direful.
Cassio.   O, help!
Lodovico.   Hark!
Roderigo.   O wretched villain!   40
Lodovico.   Two or three groans: it is a heavy[558] night;
These may be counterfeits; let 's think 't unsafe
To come in to the cry[559] without more help.
Roderigo.   Nobody come? then shall I bleed to death.
Lodovico.   Hark!

(Re-enter Iago, with a light.)

Gratiano.   Here 's one comes in his shirt, with light and weapons.
Iago.   Who 's there? whose noise is this that cries on murder?
Lodovico.   We do not know.
Iago.   Did not you hear a cry?
Cassio.   Here, here! for heaven's sake, help me.
Iago.   What's the matter?   50
Gratiano.   This is Othello's ancient, as I take it.
Lodovico.   The same indeed; a very valiant fellow.
Iago.   What are you here that cry so grievously?
Cassio.   Iago? O! I am spoil'd, undone by villains!
Give me some help.
Iago.   O me, lieutenant! what villains have done this?
Cassio.   I think that one of them is hereabout,
And cannot make away.
Iago.   O treacherous villains!
(To Lodovico and Gratiano.) What are you there? come in, and
give some help.
Roderigo.   O! help me here.   60

---

[556] (Cassio's) darling, i.e., Desdemona.   [557] Passer-by.   [558] Dark.   [559] Where the
cry comes from.

Cassio.   That's one of them.
Iago.   O murderous slave! O villain!

(Stabs Roderigo.)

Roderigo.   O damn'd Iago! O inhuman dog!
Iago.   Kill men i' the dark! Where be these bloody thieves?
   How silent is this town! Ho! murder! murder!
   What may you be? are you of good or evil?
Lodovico.   As you shall prove us, praise us.
Iago.   Signior Lodovico?
Lodovico.   He, sir.
Iago.   I cry you mercy. Here 's Cassio hurt by villains.
Gratiano.   Cassio!   70
Iago.   How is it, brother?
Cassio.   My leg is cut in two.
Iago.   Marry, heaven forbid.
   Light, gentlemen; I 'll bind it with my shirt.

(Enter Bianca.)

Bianca.   What is the matter, ho? who is 't that cried?
Iago.   Who is 't that cried!
Bianca.   O my dear Cassio! my sweet Cassio!
   O Cassio, Cassio, Cassio!
Iago.   O notable strumpet! Cassio, may you suspect
   Who they should be that have thus mangled you?
Cassio.   No.   80
Gratiano.   I am sorry to find you thus; I have been to seek you.
Iago.   Lend me a garter. So. O! for a chair,
   To bear him easily hence!
Bianca.   Alas; he faints! O Cassio, Cassio, Cassio!
Iago.   Gentlemen all, I do suspect this trash[560]
   To be a party in this injury.
   Patience awhile, good Cassio. Come, come.
   Lend me a light. Know we this face, or no?
   Alas! my friend and my dear countryman,
   Roderigo? no: yes, sure, O heaven! Roderigo.   90
Gratiano.   What! of Venice?
Iago.   Even he, sir, did you know him?
Gratiano.   Know him! ay.

---

[560] I.e., Bianca.

Iago.   Signior Gratiano? I cry you gentle pardon;
These bloody accidents must excuse my manners,
That so neglected you.
Gratiano.   I am glad to see you.
Iago.   How do you, Cassio? O! a chair, a chair!
Gratiano.   Roderigo!

(A chair brought in.)

Iago.   He, he, 'tis he,—O! that 's well said; the chair:
Some good men bear him carefully from hence;
I 'll fetch the general's surgeon. *(To Bianca.)* For you, mistress,   100
Save you your labour. He that lies slain here, Cassio,
Was my dear friend. What malice was between you?
Cassio.   None in the world; nor do I know that man.
Iago *(to Bianca).*   What! look you pale? O! bear him out o' the air—

(Cassio and Roderigo are borne off.)

Stay you, good gentlemen. Look you pale, mistress?—
Do you perceive the gastness[561] of her eye?
Nay, if you stare, we shall hear more anon.
Behold her well; I pray you, look upon her.
Do you see, gentlemen? nay, guiltiness will speak
Though tongues were out of use.   110

(Enter Emilia.)

Emilia.   'Las! what 's the matter? what 's the matter, husband?
Iago.   Cassio hath here been set on in the dark
By Roderigo and fellows that are 'scaped:
He 's almost slain, and Roderigo dead.
Emilia.   Alas! good gentleman; alas! good Cassio!
Iago.   This is the fruit of whoring. Prithee, Emilia,
Go know of Cassio where he supp'd to-night.
(To Bianca.) What! do you shake at that?
Bianca.   He supp'd at my house; but I therefore shake not.
Iago.   O! did he so? I charge you, go with me.   120
Emilia.   Fie, fie, upon thee, strumpet!
Bianca.   I am no strumpet, but of life as honest
As you that thus abuse me.
Emilia.   As I! foh! fie upon thee!

---

561 Terror.

Iago.   Kind gentlemen, let 's go see poor Cassio dress'd.[562]
Come, mistress, you must tell 's another tale.
Emilia, run you to the citadel,
And tell my lord and lady what hath happ'd.
Will you go on afore? *(Aside.)* This is the night
That either makes me or fordoes[563] me quite.   *(Exeunt.)*

SCENE 2.   A Bedchamber in the Castle. Desdemona in bed asleep. A light burning.

(Enter Othello.)

Othello.   It is the cause,[564] it is the cause, my soul;
Let me not name it to you, you chaste stars!
It is the cause. Yet I 'll not shed her blood,
Nor scar that whiter skin of hers than snow,
And smooth as monumental alabaster.
Yet she must die, else she 'll betray more men.
Put out the light, and then put out the light:
If I quench thee, thou flaming minister,[565]
I can again thy former light restore,
Should I repent me; but once put out thy light,   10
Thou cunning'st[566] pattern of excelling nature,
I know not where is that Promethean[567] heat
That can thy light relume.[568] When I have pluck'd the rose,
I cannot give it vital growth again,
It needs must wither: I 'll smell it on the tree. *(Kisses her.)*
O balmy breath, that dost almost persuade
Justice to break her sword! One more, one more.
Be thus when thou art dead, and I will kill thee,
And love thee after. One more, and this the last:
So sweet was ne'er so fatal. I must weep,   20
But they are cruel tears; this sorrow 's heavenly,
It strikes where it doth love. She wakes.
Desdemona.   Who 's there? Othello?
Othello.   Ay, Desdemona.
Desdemona.   Will you come to bed, my lord?
Othello.   Have you pray'd to-night, Desdemona?
Desdemona.   Ay, my lord.

---

[562] Bandaged.   [563] Ruins.   [564] I.e., Desdemona's unchastity (Othello means that the severity of the punishment is required by the nature of her sin).   [565] I.e, the candle.
[566] Most intricately wrought.   [567] In Greek mythology the demi-god Prometheus stole fire from the gods and gave it to man.   [568] Relight.

Othello.   If you bethink yourself of any crime
    Unreconcil'd as yet to heaven and grace,
    Solicit for it straight.
Desdemona.   Alas! my lord, what may you mean by that?
Othello.   Well, do it, and be brief; I will walk by:[569]   30
    I would not kill thy unprepared spirit;
    No; heaven forfend![570] I would not kill thy soul.
Desdemona.   Talk you of killing?
Othello.   Ay, I do.
Desdemona.   Then heaven
    Have mercy on me!
Othello.   Amen! with all my heart.
Desdemona.   If you say so, I hope you will not kill me.
Othello.   Hum!
Desdemona.   And yet I fear you; for you are fatal then
    When your eyes roll so. Why I should fear I know not,
    Since guiltiness I know not; but yet I feel I fear.
Othello.   Think on thy sins.
Desdemona.   They are loves I bear to you.   40
Othello.   Ay, and for that thou diest.
Desdemona.   That death's unnatural that kills for loving.
    Alas! why gnaw you so your nether lip?
    Some bloody passion shakes your very frame;
    These are portents,[571] but yet, I hope, I hope
    They do not point on me.
Othello.   Peace, and be still!
Desdemona.   I will so. What 's the matter?
Othello.   That handkerchief which I so lov'd and gave thee
    Thou gav'st to Cassio.
Desdemona.   No, by my life and soul!
    Send for the man and ask him.
Othello.   Sweet soul, take heed,   50
    Take heed of perjury; thou 'rt on thy death-bed.
Desdemona.   Ay, but not yet to die.
Othello.   Yes, presently;[572]
    Therefore confess thee freely of thy sin;
    For to deny each article with oath
    Cannot remove nor choke the strong conception[573]
    That I do groan withal. Thou art to die.
Desdemona.   Then Lord have mercy on me!
Othello.   I say, amen.
Desdemona.   And have you mercy too! I never did
    Offend you in my life; never lov'd Cassio

---

[569] Nearby.   [570] Forbid.   [571] Omens.   [572] At once.   [573] Belief.

But with such general warranty[574] of heaven   60
As I might love; I never gave him token.

Othello.   By heaven, I saw my handkerchief in 's hand.
O perjur'd woman! thou dost stone[575] my heart,
And mak'st me call what I intend to do
A murder, which I thought a sacrifice:
I saw the handkerchief.

Desdemona.   He found it then;
I never gave it him. Send for him hither;
Let him confess a truth.

Othello.   He had confessed.

Desdemona.   What, my lord?

Othello.   That he hath us'd thee.

Desdemona.   How? Unlawfully?

Othello.   Ay.   70

Desdemona.   He will not say so.

Othello.   No; his mouth is stopp'd:
Honest Iago hath ta'en order for 't.[576]

Desdemona.   O! my fear interprets. What! is he dead?

Othello.   Had all his hairs been lives, my great revenge
Had stomach[577] for them all.

Desdemona.   Alas! he is betray'd and I undone.

Othello.   Out, strumpet! Weep'st thou for him to my face?

Desdemona.   O! banish me, my lord, but kill me not!

Othello.   Down, strumpet!

Desdemona.   Kill me to-morrow; let me live to-night!   80

Othello.   Nay, if you strive,—

Desdemona.   But half an hour!

Othello.   Being done, there is no pause.

Desdemona.   But while I say one prayer!

Othello.   It is too late.   *(He smothers her.)*

Emilia *(within)*.   My lord, my lord! what, ho! my lord, my lord!

Othello.   What noise is this? Not dead? Not yet quite dead?
I that am cruel am yet merciful;
I would have thee linger in thy pain.
So, so.

Emilia *(within)*.   What, ho! my lord, my lord!

Othello.   Who's there?

Emilia *(within)*.   O! good my lord, I would speak a word with you!   90

Othello.   Yes; 'tis Emilia: by and by.[578] She's dead.
'Tis like[579] she comes to speak of Cassio's death;
The noise was high. Ha! no more moving?

---

[574] Permission.   [575] Turn to stone.   [576] Taken steps.   [577] Appetite.   [578] I.e.,
"just a moment."   [579] Likely.

Still as the grave. Shall she come in? were 't good?[580]
I think she stirs again: no. What 's best to do?
If she come in she'll sure speak to my wife:
My wife! my wife! what wife? I have no wife;
O, insupportable! O heavy hour!
Methinks it should be now a huge eclipse
Of sun and moon, and that the affrighted globe   100
Should yawn[581] at alteration.
Emilia (*within.*)   I do beseech you
That I may speak with you, O! good my lord.
Othello.   I had forgot thee: O! come in, Emilia:
Soft, by and by: let me the curtains draw.
Where art thou?   (*Unlocks the door.*)

(*Enter Emilia*).

                What 's the matter with thee now?
Emilia.   O! my good lord, yonder 's foul murder done.
Othello.   What! now?
Emilia.   But now, my lord.
Othello.   It is the very error[582] of the moon;
She comes more near the earth than she was wont,   110
And makes men mad.
Emilia.   Cassio, my lord, has kill'd a young Venetian
Call'd Roderigo.
Othello.   Roderigo kill'd!
And Cassio kill'd?
Emilia.   No, Cassio is not kill'd.
Othello.   Not Cassio kill'd! then murder 's out of tune,
And sweet revenge grows harsh.
Desdemona.   O! falsely, falsely murder'd.
Emilia.   Alas! what cry is that?
Othello.   That! what?
Emilia.   Out, and alas! that was my lady's voice:
Help! Help, ho! help! O lady, speak again!   120
Sweet Desdemona! O! sweet mistress, speak.
Desdemona.   A guiltless death I die.
Emilia.   O! who hath done this deed?
Desdemona.   Nobody; I myself; farewell:
Commend me to my kind lord. O! farewell!   (*Dies.*)
Othello.   Why, how should she be murder'd?
Emilia.   Alas! who knows?
Othello.   You heard her say herself it was not I.

---

[580] Would that be wise.   [581] Open up (as in an earthquake).   [582] Straying.

Emilia.   She said so; I must needs report the truth.

Othello.   She 's like a liar gone to burning hell;
'Twas I that kill'd her.

Emilia.   O! the more angel she,   130
And you the blacker devil.

Othello.   She turn'd to folly, and she was a whore.

Emilia.   Thou dost belie her, and thou art a devil.

Othello.   She was false as water.

Emilia.   Thou art rash as fire to say
That she was false! O! she was heavenly true.

Othello.   Cassio did tup her; ask thy husband else.
O! I were damn'd beneath all depth in hell
But that I did proceed[583] upon just grounds
To this extremity. Thy husband knew it all.

Emilia.   My husband!   140

Othello.   Thy husband.

Emilia.   That she was false to wedlock?

Othello.   Ay, with Cassio. Nay, had she been true,
If heaven would make me such another world
Of one entire and perfect chrysolite,[584]
I'd not have sold her for it.

Emilia.   My husband!

Othello.   Ay, 'twas he that told me first:
An honest man he is, and hates the slime
That sticks on filthy deeds.

Emilia.   My husband!

Othello.   What needs this iterance,[585] woman? I say thy husband.   150

Emilia.   O mistress! villany hath made mocks with love.
My husband say that she was false!

Othello.   He, woman;
I say, thy husband: dost understand the word?
My friend, thy husband, honest, honest Iago.

Emilia.   If he say so, may his pernicious soul
Rot half a grain a day! he lies to the heart:
She was too fond of her most filthy bargain.[586]

Othello.   Ha!

Emilia.   Do thy worst:
This deed of thine is no more worthy heaven   160
Than thou wast worthy her.

Othello.   Peace! you were best.[587]

Emilia.   Thou hast not half the power to do me harm
As I have to be hurt. O gull! O dolt!

---

[583] Had I not proceeded.   [584] Topaz.   [585] Repetition.   [586] I.e., Othello.
[587] You'd better be quiet.

As ignorant as dirt! thou hast done a deed,—
I care not for thy sword; I'll make thee known,
Though I lost twenty lives. Help! help, ho! help!
The Moor has kill'd my mistress! murder! murder!

(Enter Montano, Gratiano, Iago, and others.)

Montano.   What is the matter? How now, general!
Emilia.   O! are you come, Iago? you have done well,
That men must lay their murders on your neck.   170
Gratiano.   What is the matter?
Emilia.   Disprove this villain if thou be'st a man:
He says thou told'st him that his wife was false.
I know thou didst not, thou 'rt not such a villain.
Speak, for my heart is full.
Iago.   I told him what I thought, and told no more
Than what he found himself was apt and true.
Emilia.   But did you ever tell him she was false?
Iago.   I did.
Emilia.   You told a lie, an odious damned lie;   180
Upon my soul, a lie, a wicked lie;
She false with Cassio! Did you say with Cassio?
Iago.   With Cassio, mistress. Go to, charm[588] your tongue.
Emilia.   I will not charm my tongue; I am bound to speak.
My mistress here lies murder'd in her bed.
All.   O heavens forfend!
Emilia.   And your reports have set the murder on.
Othello.   Nay, stare not, masters; it is true, indeed.
Gratiano.   'Tis a strange truth.
Montano.   O monstrous act!
Emilia.   Villany! villany! villany!   190
I think upon 't, I think, I smell 't; O villany!
I thought so then;[589] I'll kill myself for grief.
O! villany, villany!
Iago.   What! are you mad? I charge you, get you home.
Emilia.   Good gentlemen, let me have leave to speak:
'Tis proper I obey him, but not now.
Perchance, Iago, I will ne'er go home.
Othello.   O! O! O!   *(Falls on the bed.)*
Emilia.   Nay, lay thee down and roar,
For thou hast kill'd the sweetest innocent
That e'er did lift up eye.

---

[588] I.e., into silence.   [589] *Cf.* "I will be hang'd, if some eternal villain,/Some busy and insinuating rogue,/Some cogging cozening slave, to get some office,/Have not devis'd this slander . . ." (IV, ii, 130 ff.). Emilia means, not that she guessed Iago's guilt, but that she rightly guessed the slanderer's motive.

Othello.   O! she was foul.   *(Rises.)*

I scarce did know you, uncle. There lies your niece,   201

Whose breath, indeed, these hands have newly stopp'd:

I know this act shows terrible and grim.

Gratiano.   Poor Desdemona! I am glad thy father 's dead.

Thy match was mortal to him, and pure grief

Shore[590] his old thread in twain: did he live now,

This sight would make him do a desperate turn,

Yea, curse his better angel from his side,

And fall to reprobation.[591]

Othello.   'Tis pitiful; but yet Iago knows   210

That she with Cassio hath the act of shame

A thousand times committed; Cassio confess'd it:

And she did gratify[592] his amorous works

With that recognizance and pledge of love

Which I first gave her. I saw it in his hand:

It was a handkerchief, an antique token

My father gave my mother.

Emilia.   O heaven! O heavenly powers!

Iago.   Come, hold your peace.

Emilia.   'Twill out, 'twill out; I hold my peace, sir? no;

No, I will speak as liberal as the north;[593]   220

Let heaven and men and devils, let them all,

All, all, cry shame against me, yet I'll speak.

Iago.   Be wise, and get you home.

Emilia.   I will not.

(Iago threatens to stab Emilia.)

Gratiano.   Fie!

Your sword upon a woman!

Emilia.   O thou dull Moor! that handkerchief thou speak'st of

I found by fortune and did give my husband;

For often, with a solemn earnestness,

More than, indeed, belong'd to such a trifle,

He begg'd of me to steal it.

Iago.   Villainous whore!

Emilia.   She give it Cassio! no, alas! I found it,   230

And I did give 't my husband.

Iago.   Filth, thou liest!

Emilia.   By heaven, I do not, I do not, gentlemen.

O murderous coxcomb![594] what should such a fool

Do with so good a wife?

---

[590] Cut.   [591] Damnation.   [592] Reward.   [593] I.e, the north wind (?), the supposedly
free-spoken people of north England (?).   [594] Idiot.

Othello.   Are there no stones[595] in heaven
But what serve for the thunder? Precious villain!

(He runs at Iago. Iago stabs Emilia.)

Gratiano.   The woman falls; sure, he has kill'd his wife.   *(Exit Iago.)*
Emilia.   Ay, ay; O! lay me by my mistress' side.
Gratiano.   He 's gone; but his wife 's kill'd.
Montano.   'Tis a notorious[596] villain. Take you this weapon,
Which I have here recover'd from the Moor.   240
Come, guard the door without; let him not pass,
But kill him rather. I'll after that same villain,
For 'tis a damned slave.   *(Exeunt Montano and Gratiano.)*
Othello.   I am not valiant neither,
But every puny whipster[597] gets my sword.
But why should honour outlive honesty?
Let it go all.
Emilia.   What did thy song bode, lady?
Hark, canst thou hear me? I will play the swan,
And die in music:—
(Sings.)   Willow, willow, willow.
Moor, she was chaste; she lov'd thee, cruel Moor;
So come my soul to bliss as I speak true;   250
So speaking as I think, I die, I die.   *(Dies.)*
Othello.   I have another weapon in this chamber;
It is a sword of Spain, the ice-brook's temper.[598]
O! here it is. Uncle, I must come forth.
Gratiano *(within).*   If thou attempt it, it will cost thee dear:
Thou hast no weapon, and perforce must suffer.
Othello.   Look in upon me then, and speak with me,
Or, naked[599] as I am, I will assault thee.

(Re-enter Gratiano.)

Gratiano.   What is the matter?
Othello.   Behold! I have a weapon;
A better never did itself sustain   260
Upon a soldier's thigh: I have seen the day,
That with this little arm, and this good sword,
I have made my way through more impediments
Than twenty times your stop: but, O vain boast!

---

[595] I.e., thunderbolts (to strike Iago down).   [596] Notable.   [597] I.e., a small boy whipping a top.   [598] Tempered in icy water (or the reference may be to Innsbruck, famed for the quality of its steel, but this hardly fits "a sword of Spain").   [599] Unarmed.

Who can control his fate? 'tis not so now.
Be not afraid, though you do see me weapon'd;
Here is my journey's end, here is my butt,[600]
And very sea-mark of my utmost sail.[601]
Do you go back dismay'd? 'tis a lost fear;
Man but a rush[602] against Othello's breast,   270
And he retires. Where should Othello go?
Now how dost thou look now? O ill-starr'd wench!
Pale as thy smock! when we shall meet at compt,[603]
This look of thine will hurl my soul from heaven,
And fiends will snatch at it. Cold, cold, my girl!
Even like thy chastity.
O! cursed, cursed slave. Whip me, ye devils,
From the possession of this heavenly sight!
Blow me about in winds! roast me in sulphur!
Wash me in steep-down gulfs of liquid fire!   280
O Desdemona! Desdemona! dead!
Oh! Oh! Oh!

(Enter Lodovico, Montano, Cassio carried in a chair, and Officers with Iago, prisoner.)

Lodovico. Where is this rash and most unfortunate man?
Othello. That's he that was Othello; here I am.
Lodovico. Where is that viper? bring the villain forth.
Othello. I look down towards his feet;[604] but that's a fable.
  If that thou be'st a devil, I cannot kill thee. *(Wounds Iago.)*
Lodovico. Wrench his sword from him. *(Othello is disarmed.)*
Iago.   I bleed, sir; but not kill'd.
Othello. I am not sorry neither; I'd have thee live;
  For, in my sense,[605] 'tis happiness to die.   290
Lodovico. O thou Othello! that wert once so good,
  Fall'n in the practice[606] of a damned slave,[607]
  What shall be said to thee?
Othello.   Why, any thing:
  An honourable murderer, if you will;
  For nought did I in hate, but all in honour.
Lodovico. This wretch hath part confess'd his villany:
  Did you and he consent in Cassio's death?
Othello. Ay.
Cassio. Dear general, I never gave you cause.

---

[600] Goal, end, limit.   [601] Destination of my farthest journey.   [602] Wield but a reed.
[603] On the day of judgment.   [604] I.e, for the Devil's cloven hoof.   [605] The way I feel.   [606] Plot, machination.   [607] I.e., Iago.

Othello.   I do believe it, and I ask your pardon.   300
    Will you, I pray, demand that demi-devil
    Why he hath thus ensnar'd my soul and body?
Iago.   Demand me nothing: what you know, you know:
    From this time forth I never will speak word.
Lodoviro.   What! not to pray?
Gratiano.   Torments will ope[608] your lips.
Othello.   Well, thou dost best.
Lodovico.   Sir, you shall understand what hath befall'n,
    Which, as I think, you know not. Here is a letter
    Found in the pocket of the slain Roderigo,
    And here another; the one of them imports   310
    The death of Cassio to be undertook
    By Roderigo.
Othello.   O villain!
Cassio.   Most heathenish and most gross!
Lodovico.   Now here's another discontented paper,
    Found in his pocket too; and this, it seems,
    Roderigo meant to have sent this damned villain,
    But that, belike,[609] Iago in the interim[610]
    Came in and satisfied him.
Othello.   O the pernicious caitiff!
    How came you, Cassio, by that handkerchief
    That was my wife's?
Cassio.   I found it in my chamber;   320
    And he himself confess'd but even now
    That there he dropp'd it for a special purpose
    Which wrought to his desire.
Othello.   O fool! fool! fool!
Cassio.   There is besides in Roderigo's letter
    How he upbraids Iago that he made him
    Brave me upon the watch; whereon it came
    That I was cast:[611] and even but now he spake,
    After long seeming dead, Iago hurt him,
    Iago set him on.
Lodovico.   You must forsake this room and go with us;   330
    Your power and your command is taken off,
    And Cassio rules in Cyprus. For this slave,
    If there be any cunning cruelty
    That can torment him much and hold him long,
    It shall be his. You shall close prisoner rest,

---

[608] Open.   [609] Most likely.   [610] In the meantime.   [611] Dismissed.

Till that the nature of your fault be known
To the Venetian state. Come, bring him away.
Othello.   Soft you; a word or two before you go.
I have done the state some service, and they know 't;
No more of that. I pray you, in your letters,   340
When you shall these unlucky deeds relate,
Speak of me as I am; nothing extenuate,
Nor set down aught[612] in malice: then, must you speak
Of one that lov'd not wisely but too well;
Of one not easily jealous, but, being wrought,
Perplex'd[613] in the extreme; of one whose hand
Like the base Indian,[614] threw a pearl away
Richer than all his tribe; of one whose subdu'd[615] eyes
Albeit unused to the melting mood,
Drop tears as fast as the Arabian trees   350
Their med'cinable gum. Set you down this;
And say besides, that in Aleppo once,
Where a malignant and a turban'd Turk
Beat a Venetian and traduc'd the state,
I took by the throat the circumcised dog,
And smote him, thus.   *(Stabs himself.)*
Lodovico.   O bloody period![616]
Gratiano.   All that's spoke is marr'd.
Othello.   I kiss'd thee ere I killed thee; no way but this.
                                               (Falling upon Desdemona.)
                                                            (Dies.)
Killing myself to die upon a kiss.
Cassio.   This did I fear, but thought he had no weapon;
For he was great of heart.
Lodovico *(to Iago)*.   O Spartan dog!
More fell[617] than anguish, hunger, or the sea.
Look on the tragic loading of this bed;
This is thy work; the object poisons sight;
Let it be hid. Gratiano, keep the house,
And seize upon the fortunes of the Moor,
For they succeed on you. To you, lord governor,
Remains the censure of this hellish villain,
The time, the place, the torture; O! enforce it.
Myself will straight aboard, and to the state   370
This heavy act with heavy heart relate.   *(Exeunt.)*

---

[612] Anything.   [613] Distracted.   [614] The Folio reads "Iudean." Both readings denote the
foolish infidel who fails to appreciate the treasure he possesses.   [615] Overcome (by grief).
[616] Ending.   [617] Grim, cruel.

QUESTIONS
1. In what sense might it be said that Othello is responsible for his own downfall? **2.** Compare the speeches of Cassio and Iago in Act II, Scene 1. What does the difference in language and style reveal about their characters? **3.** Carefully determine how much time elapses between the arrival at Cyprus and the end of the action. Can you find narrated events that could not possibly have occurred within that time? Do the chronological inconsistencies disturb you? Explain. **4.** The first part of Act IV, Scene 2 (until Othello exits), is sometimes called the "brothel" scene. What features of Othello's language and behavior justify that designation? **5.** Discuss the relationship between love and hate in this play.

WRITING TOPICS
1. Examine the reasons Iago gives for his actions. Do you find them consistent and convincing? Explain. **2.** Discuss the functions of the minor characters, such as Roderigo, Bianca, and Emilia, in the play. **3.** Othello crumbles in Act III, Scene 3, as Iago creates the jealousy that destroys Othello's self-confidence and peace of mind. Is the rapidity of Othello's emotional collapse justified? Does his being black have anything to do with his emotional turmoil?

The Misanthrope * 1666

MOLIÈRE [1622–1673]

CHARACTERS

Alceste, *in love with Célimène*
Philinte, *Alceste's friend*
Oronte, *in love with Célimène*
Célimène, *Alceste's beloved*
Éliante, *Célimène's cousin*
Arsinoé, *a friend of Célimène's*

Acaste ⎱ *Marquesses*
Clitandre ⎰
Basque, *Célimène's servant*
A Guard *of the Marshalsea*
Dubois, *Alceste's valet*

The Scene throughout is in Célimène's house at Paris.

Act I

SCENE 1. *Philinte, Alceste*

Philinte.   Now, what's got into you?
Alceste *(seated)*.   Kindly leave me alone.
Philinte.   Come, come, what is it? This lugubrious tone . . .
Alceste.   Leave me, I said; you spoil my solitude.
Philinte.   Oh, listen to me, now, and don't be rude.
Alceste.   I choose to be rude, Sir, and to be hard of hearing.
Philinte.   These ugly moods of yours are not endearing;
   Friends though we are, I really must insist . . .
Alceste *(abruptly rising)*.   Friends? Friends, you say? Well, cross me off your list.
   I've been your friend till now, as you well know;
   But after what I saw a moment ago
   I tell you flatly that our ways must part.
   I wish no place in a dishonest heart.
Philinte.   Why, what have I done, Alceste? Is this quite just?
Alceste.   My God, you ought to die of self-disgust.
   I call your conduct inexcusable, Sir,
   And every man of honor will concur.
   I see you almost hug a man to death,
   Exclaim for joy until you're out of breath,

---

* English version by Richard Wilbur.

963

And supplement these loving demonstrations
With endless offers, vows, and protestations;
Then when I ask you "Who was that?" I find
That you can barely bring his name to mind!
Once the man's back is turned, you cease to love him,
And speak with absolute indifference of him!
By God, I say it's base and scandalous
To falsify the heart's affections thus;
If I caught myself behaving in such a way,
I'd hang myself for shame, without delay.

Philinte.   It hardly seems a hanging matter to me;
I hope that you will take it graciously
If I extend myself a slight reprieve,
And live a little longer, by your leave.

Alceste.   How dare you joke about a crime so grave?

Philinte.   What crime? How else are people to behave?

Alceste.   I'd have them be sincere, and never part
With any word that isn't from the heart.

Philinte.   When someone greets us with a show of pleasure,
It's but polite to give him equal measure,
Return his love the best that we know how,
And trade him offer for offer, vow for vow.

Alceste.   No, no, this formula you'd have me follow,
However fashionable, is false and hollow,
And I despise the frenzied operations
Of all these barterers of protestations,
These lavishers of meaningless embraces,
These utterers of obliging commonplaces,
Who court and flatter everyone on earth
And praise the fool no less than the man of worth.
Should you rejoice that someone fondles you,
Offers his love and service, swears to be true,
And fills your ears with praises of your name,
When to the first damned fop he'll say the same?
No, no: no self-respecting heart would dream
Of prizing so promiscuous an esteem;
However high the praise, there's nothing worse
Than sharing honors with the universe.
Esteem is founded on comparison:
To honor all men is to honor none.
Since you embrace this indiscriminate vice,
Your friendship comes at far too cheap a price;
I spurn the easy tribute of a heart
Which will not set the worthy man apart:
I choose, Sir, to be chosen; and in fine,
The friend of mankind is no friend of mine.

Philinte.   But in polite society, custom decrees
  That we show certain outward courtesies. . . .
Alceste.   Ah, no! we should condemn with all our force
  Such false and artificial intercourse.
  Let men behave like men; let them display
  Their inmost hearts in everything they say;
  Let the heart speak, and let our sentiments
  Not mask themselves in silly compliments.
Philinte.   In certain cases it would be uncouth
  And most absurd to speak the naked truth;
  With all respect for your exalted notions,
  It's often best to veil one's true emotions.
  Wouldn't the social fabric come undone
  If we were wholly frank with everyone?
  Suppose you met with someone you couldn't bear;
  Would you inform him of it then and there?
Alceste.   Yes.
Philinte.   Then you'd tell old Emilie it's pathetic
  The way she daubs her features with cosmetic
  And plays the gay coquette at sixty-four?
Alceste.   I would.
Philinte.   And you'd call Dorilas a bore,
  And tell him every ear at court is lame
  From hearing him brag about his noble name?
Alceste.   Precisely.
Philinte.   Ah, you're joking.
Alceste.   *Au contraire:*
  In this regard there's none I'd choose to spare.
  All are corrupt; there's nothing to be seen
  In court or town but aggravates my spleen.
  I fall into deep gloom and melancholy
  When I survey the scene of human folly,
  Finding on every hand base flattery,
  Injustice, fraud, self-interest, treachery. . . .
  Ah, it's too much; mankind has grown so base,
  I mean to break with the whole human race.
Philinte.   This philosophic rage is a bit extreme;
  You've no idea how comical you seem;
  Indeed, we're like those brothers in the play
  Called *School for Husbands*, one of whom was prey . . . .
Alceste.   Enough, now! None of your stupid similes.
Philinte.   Then let's have no more tirades, if you please.
  The world won't change, whatever you say or do;
  And since plain speaking means so much to you,
  I'll tell you plainly that by being frank
  You've earned the reputation of a crank,

And that you're thought ridiculous when you rage
And rant against the manners of the age.

Alceste. So much the better; just what I wish to hear.
No news could be more grateful to my ear.
All men are so detestable in my eyes,
I should be sorry if they thought me wise.

Philinte. Your hatred's very sweeping, is it not?

Alceste. Quite right: I hate the whole degraded lot.

Philinte. Must all poor human creatures be embraced,
Without distinction, by your vast distaste?
Even in these bad times, there are surely a few . . .

Alceste. No, I include all men in one dim view:
Some men I hate for being rogues; the others
I hate because they treat the rogues like brothers,
And, lacking a virtuous scorn for what is vile,
Receive the villain with a complaisant smile.
Notice how tolerant people choose to be
Toward that bold rascal who's at law with me.
His social polish can't conceal his nature;
One sees at once that he's a treacherous creature;
No one could possibly be taken in
By those soft speeches and that sugary grin.
The whole world knows the shady means by which
The low-brow's grown so powerful and rich,
And risen to a rank so bright and high
That virtue can but blush, and merit sigh.
Whenever his name comes up in conversation,
None will defend his wretched reputation;
Call him knave, liar, scoundrel, and all the rest,
Each head will nod, and no one will protest.
And yet his smirk is seen in every house,
He's greeted everywhere with smiles and bows,
And when there's any honor that can be got
By pulling strings, he'll get it, like as not.
My God! It chills my heart to see the ways
Men come to terms with evil nowadays;
Sometimes, I swear, I'm moved to flee and find
Some desert land unfouled by humankind.

Philinte. Come, let's forget the follies of the times
And pardon mankind for its petty crimes;
Let's have an end of rantings and of railings,
And show some leniency toward human failings.
This world requires a pliant rectitude;
Too stern a virtue makes one stiff and rude;
Good sense views all extremes with detestation,
And bids us to be noble in moderation.

The rigid virtues of the ancient days
Are not for us; they jar with all our ways
And ask of us too lofty a perfection.
Wise men accept their times without objection,
And there's no greater folly, if you ask me,
Than trying to reform society.
Like you, I see each day a hundred and one
Unhandsome deeds that might be better done,
But still, for all the faults that meet my view,
I'm never known to storm and rave like you.
I take men as they are, or let them be,
And teach my soul to bear their frailty;
And whether in court or town, whatever the scene,
My phlegm's as philosophic as your spleen.

Alceste.   This phlegm which you so eloquently commend,
Does nothing ever rile it up, my friend?
Suppose some man you trust should treacherously
Conspire to rob you of your property,
And do his best to wreck your reputation?
Wouldn't you feel a certain indignation?

Philinte.   Why, no. These faults of which you so complain
Are part of human nature, I maintain,
And it's no more a matter for disgust
That men are knavish, selfish and unjust,
Than that the vulture dines upon the dead,
And wolves are furious, and apes ill-bred.

Alceste.   Shall I see myself betrayed, robbed, torn to bits,
And not . . . Oh, let's be still and rest our wits.
Enough of reasoning, now. I've had my fill.

Philinte.   Indeed, you would do well, Sir, to be still.
Rage less at your opponent, and give some thought
To how you'll win this lawsuit that he's brought.

Alceste.   I assure you I'll do nothing of the sort.

Philinte.   Then who will plead your case before the court?

Alceste.   Reason and right and justice will plead for me.

Philinte.   Oh, Lord. What judges do you plan to see?

Alceste.   Why, none. The justice of my cause is clear.

Philinte.   Of course, man; but there's politics to fear . . . .

Alceste.   No, I refuse to lift a hand. That's flat.
I'm either right, or wrong.

Philinte.   Don't count on that.

Alceste.   No, I'll do nothing.

Philinte.   Your enemy's influence
Is great, you know . . .

Alceste.   That makes no difference.

Philinte.   It will; you'll see.

Alceste.   Must honor bow to guile?
If so, I shall be proud to lose the trial.
Philinte.   Oh, really . . .
Alceste.   I'll discover by this case
Whether or not men are sufficiently base
And impudent and villainous and perverse
To do me wrong before the universe.
Philinte.   What a man!
Alceste.   Oh, I could wish, whatever the cost,
Just for the beauty of it, that my trial were lost.
Philinte.   If people heard you talking so, Alceste,
They'd split their sides. Your name would be a jest.
Alceste.   So much the worse for jesters.
Philinte.   May I enquire
Whether this rectitude you so admire,
And these hard virtues you're enamored of
Are qualities of the lady whom you love?
It much surprises me that you, who seem
To view mankind with furious disesteem,
Have yet found something to enchant your eyes
Amidst a species which you so despise.
And what is more amazing, I'm afraid,
Is the most curious choice your heart has made.
The honest Éliante is fond of you,
Arsinoé, the prude, admires you too;
And yet your spirit's been perversely led
To choose the flighty Célimène instead,
Whose brittle malice and coquettish ways
So typify the manners of our days.
How is it that the traits you most abhor
Are bearable in this lady you adore?
Are you so blind with love that you can't find them?
Or do you contrive, in her case, not to mind them?
Alceste.   My love for that young widow's not the kind
That can't perceive defects; no, I'm not blind.
I see her faults, despite my ardent love,
And all I see I fervently reprove.
And yet I'm weak; for all her falsity,
That woman knows the art of pleasing me,
And though I never cease complaining of her,
I swear I cannot manage not to love her.
Her charm outweighs her faults; I can but aim
To cleanse her spirit in my love's pure flame.
Philinte.   That's no small task; I wish you all success.
You think then that she loves you?

Alceste. Heavens, yes!
  I wouldn't love her did she not love me.
Philinte. Well, if her taste for you is plain to see,
  Why do these rivals cause you such despair?
Alceste. True love, Sir, is possessive, and cannot bear
  To share with all the world. I'm here today
  To tell her she must send that mob away.
Philinte. If I were you, and had your choice to make,
  Éliante, her cousin, would be the one I'd take;
  That honest heart, which cares for you alone,
  Would harmonize far better with your own.
Alceste. True, true: each day my reason tells me so;
  But reason doesn't rule in love, you know.
Philinte. I fear some bitter sorrow is in store;
  This love . . .

SCENE 2.   *Oronte, Alceste, Philinte*

Oronte (*to Alceste*).   The servants told me at the door
  That Éliante and Célimène were out,
  But when I heard, dear Sir, that you were about,
  I came to say, without exaggeration,
  That I hold you in the vastest admiration,
  And that it's always been my dearest desire
  To be the friend of one I so admire.
  I hope to see my love of merit requited,
  And you and I in friendship's bond united.
  I'm sure you won't refuse—if I may be frank—
  A friend of my devotedness—and rank.

(*During this speech of Oronte's, Alceste is abstracted, and seems unaware that he is being spoken to. He only breaks off his reverie when Oronte says:*)

  It was for you, if you please, that my words were intended.
Alceste. For me, Sir?
Oronte. Yes, for you. You're not offended?
Alceste. By no means. But this much surprises me. . . .
  The honor comes most unexpectedly. . . .
Oronte. My high regard should not astonish you;
  The whole world feels the same. It is your due.
Alceste. Sir . . . .
Oronte. Why, in all the State there isn't one
  Can match your merits; they shine, Sir, like the sun.

Alceste. Sir . . .

Oronte.   You are higher in my estimation
Than all that's most illustrious in the nation.

Alceste. Sir . . .

Oronte.   If I lie, may heaven strike me dead!
To show you that I mean what I have said,
Permit me, Sir, to embrace you most sincerely,
And swear that I will prize our friendship dearly.
Give me your hand. And now, Sir, if you choose,
We'll make our vows.

Alceste.   Sir . . .

Oronte.   What! You refuse?

Alceste. Sir, it's a very great honor you extend:
But friendship is a sacred thing, my friend;
It would be profanation to bestow
The name of friend on one you hardly know.
All parts are better played when well-rehearsed;
Let's put off friendship, and get acquainted first.
We may discover it would be unwise
To try to make our natures harmonize.

Oronte. By heaven! You're sagacious to the core;
This speech has made me admire you even more.
Let time, then, bring us closer day by day;
Meanwhile, I shall be yours in every way.
If, for example, there should be anything
You wish at court, I'll mention it to the King.
I have his ear, of course; it's quite well known
That I am much in favor with the throne.
In short, I am your servant. And now, dear friend,
Since you have such fine judgment, I intend
To please you, if I can, with a small sonnet
I wrote not long ago. Please comment on it,
And tell me whether I ought to publish it.

Alceste. You must excuse me, Sir; I'm hardly fit
To judge such matters.

Oronte.   Why not?

Alceste.   I am, I fear,
Inclined to be unfashionably sincere.

Oronte. Just what I ask; I'd take no satisfaction
In anything but your sincere reaction.
I beg you not to dream of being kind.

Alceste. Since you desire it, Sir, I'll speak my mind.

Oronte. *Sonnet.* It's a sonnet. . . . *Hope* . . . The poem's addressed
To a lady who wakened hopes within my breast.
Hope . . . this is not the pompous sort of thing,
Just modest little verses, with a tender ring.

Alceste.   Well, we shall see.
Oronte.   *Hope* . . . I'm anxious to hear
   Whether the style seems properly smooth and clear,
   And whether the choice of words is good or bad.
Alceste.   We'll see, we'll see.
Oronte.   Perhaps I ought to add
   That it took me only a quarter-hour to write it.
Alceste.   The time's irrelevant, Sir: kindly recite it.
Oronte *(reading)*.

   Hope comforts us awhile, 'tis true,
   Lulling our cares with careless laughter,
   And yet such joy is full of rue,
   My Phyllis, if nothing follows after.

Philinte.   I'm charmed by this already; the style's delightful.
Alceste *(sotto voce, to Philinte)*.   How can you say that? Why, the thing is
   frightful.
Oronte.

   Your fair face smiled on me awhile,
   But was it kindness so to enchant me?
   'Twould have been fairer not to smile,
   If hope was all you meant to grant me.

Philinte.   What a clever thought! How handsomely you phrase it!
Alceste *(sotto voce, to Philinte)*.   You know the thing is trash. How dare you
   praise it?
Oronte.

   If it's to be my passion's fate
   Thus everlastingly to wait,
   Then death will come to set me free:
   For death is fairer than the fair;
   Phyllis, to hope is to despair
   When one must hope eternally.

Philinte.   The close is exquisite—full of feeling and grace.
Alceste *(sotto voce, aside)*.   Oh, blast the close; you'd better close your face
   Before you send your lying soul to hell.
Philinte.   I can't remember a poem I've liked so well.
Alceste *(sotto voce, aside)*.   Good Lord!
Oronte *(to Philinte)*.   I fear you're flattering me a bit.
Philinte.   Oh, no!
Alceste *(sotto voce, aside)*.   What else d'you call it, you hypocrite?
Oronte *(to Alceste)*.   But you, Sir, keep your promise now: don't shrink
   From telling me sincerely what you think.
Alceste.   Sir, these are delicate matters; we all desire
   To be told that we've the true poetic fire.
   But once, to one whose name I shall not mention,

I said, regarding some verse of his invention,
That gentlemen should rigorously control
That itch to write which often afflicts the soul;
That one should curb the heady inclination
To publicize one's little avocation;
And that in showing off one's works of art
One often plays a very clownish part.

Oronte.   Are you suggesting in a devious way
That I ought not . . .

Alceste.   Oh, that I do not say.
Further, I told him that no fault is worse
Than that of writing frigid, lifeless verse,
And that the merest whisper of such a shame
Suffices to destroy a man's good name.

Oronte.   D'you mean to say my sonnet's dull and trite?

Alceste.   I don't say that. But I went on to cite
Numerous cases of once-respected men
Who came to grief by taking up the pen.

Oronte.   And am I like them? Do I write so poorly?

Alceste.   I don't say that. But I told this person, "Surely
You're under no necessity to compose;
Why you should wish to publish, heaven knows.
There's no excuse for printing tedious rot
Unless one writes for bread, as you do not.
Resist temptation, then, I beg of you;
Conceal your pastimes from the public view;
And don't give up, on any provocation,
Your present high and courtly reputation,
To purchase at a greedy printer's shop
The name of silly author and scribbling fop."
These were the points I tried to make him see.

Oronte.   I sense that they are also aimed at me;
But now—about my sonnet—I'd like to be told . . .

Alceste.   Frankly, that sonnet should be pigeonholed.
You've chosen the worst models to imitate.
The style's unnatural. Let me illustrate:

> For example, *Your fair face smiled on me awhile,*
> Followed by, *'Twould have been fairer not to smile!*
> Or this: *such joy is full of rue;*
> Or this: *For death is fairer than the fair;*
> Or, *Phyllis, to hope is to despair*
>   *When one must hope eternally!*

This artificial style, that's all the fashion,
Has neither taste, nor honesty, nor passion;

It's nothing but a sort of wordy play,
And nature never spoke in such a way.
What, in this shallow age, is not debased?
Our fathers, though less refined, had better taste;
I'd barter all that men admire today
For one old love song I shall try to say:

> If the King had given me for my own
> Paris, his citadel,
> And I for that must leave alone
> Her whom I love so well,
> I'd say then to the Crown,
> Take back your glittering town;
> My darling is more fair, I swear,
> My darling is more fair.

The rhyme's not rich, the style is rough and old,
But don't you see that it's the purest gold
Beside the tinsel nonsense now preferred,
And that there's passion in its every word?

> If the King had given me for my own
> Paris, his citadel,
> And I for that must leave alone
> Her whom I love so well,
> I'd say then to the Crown,
> Take back your glittering town;
> My darling is more fair, I swear,
> My darling is more fair.

There speaks a loving heart. *(To Philinte.)* You're laughing, eh?
Laugh on, my precious wit. Whatever you say,
I hold that song's worth all the bibelots
That people hail today with ah's and oh's.

Oronte.   And I maintain my sonnet's very good.

Alceste.   It's not at all surprising that you should.
You have your reasons; permit me to have mine
For thinking that you cannot write a line.

Oronte.   Others have praised my sonnet to the skies.

Alceste.   I lack their art of telling pleasant lies.

Oronte.   You seem to think you've got no end of wit.

Alceste.   To praise your verse, I'd need still more of it.

Oronte.   I'm not in need of your approval, Sir.

Alceste.   That's good; you couldn't have it if you were.

Oronte.   Come now, I'll lend you the subject of my sonnet;
I'd like to see you try to improve upon it.

Alceste.   I might, by chance, write something just as shoddy;
But then I wouldn't show it to everybody.

Oronte.   You're most opinionated and conceited.
Alceste.   Go find your flatterers, and be better treated.
Oronte.   Look here, my little fellow, pray watch your tone.
Alceste.   My great big fellow, you'd better watch your own.
Philinte *(stepping between them)*.   Oh, please, please, gentlemen!
   This will never do.
Oronte.   The fault is mine, and I leave the field to you.
   I am your servant, Sir, in every way.
Alceste.   And I, Sir, am your most abject valet.

SCENE 3.   *Philinte, Alceste*

Philinte.   Well, as you see, sincerity in excess
   Can get you into a very pretty mess;
   Oronte was hungry for appreciation. . . .
Alceste.   Don't speak to me.
Philinte.   What?
Alceste.   No more conversation.
Philinte.   Really, now . . .
Alceste.   Leave me alone.
Philinte.   If I . . .
Alceste.   Out of my sight!
Philinte.   But what . . .
Alceste.   I won't listen.
Philinte.   But . . .
Alceste.   Silence!
Philinte.   Now, is it polite . . .
Alceste.   By heaven, I've had enough. Don't follow me.
Philinte.   Ah, you're just joking. I'll keep you company.

Act II

SCENE 1.   *Alceste, Célimène*

Alceste.   Shall I speak plainly, Madam? I confess
   Your conduct gives me infinite distress,
   And my resentment's grown too hot to smother.
   Soon, I foresee, we'll break with one another.
   If I said otherwise, I should deceive you;
   Sooner or later, I shall be forced to leave you,
   And if I swore that we shall never part,
   I should misread the omens of my heart.

Célimène. You kindly saw me home, it would appear,
   So as to pour invectives in my ear.
Alceste. I've no desire to quarrel. But I deplore
   Your inability to shut the door
   On all these suitors who beset you so.
   There's what annoys me, if you care to know.
Célimène. Is it my fault that all these men pursue me?
   Am I to blame if they're attracted to me?
   And when they gently beg an audience,
   Ought I to take a stick and drive them hence?
Alceste. Madam, there's no necessity for a stick;
   A less responsive heart would do the trick.
   Of your attractiveness I don't complain;
   But those your charms attract, you then detain
   By a most melting and receptive manner,
   And so enlist their hearts beneath your banner.
   It's the agreeable hopes which you excite
   That keep these lovers round you day and night;
   Were they less liberally smiled upon,
   That sighing troop would very soon be gone.
   But tell me, Madam, why it is that lately
   This man Clitandre interests you so greatly?
   Because of what high merits do you deem
   Him worthy of the honor of your esteem?
   Is it that your admiring glances linger
   On the splendidly long nail of his little finger?
   Or do you share the general deep respect
   For the blond wig he chooses to affect?
   Are you in love with his embroidered hose?
   Do you adore his ribbons and his bows?
   Or is it that this paragon bewitches
   Your tasteful eye with his vast German breeches?
   Perhaps his giggle, or his falsetto voice,
   Makes him the latest gallant of your choice?
Célimène. You're much mistaken to resent him so.
   Why I put up with him you surely know:
   My lawsuit's very shortly to be tried,
   And I must have his influence on my side.
Alceste. Then lose your lawsuit, Madam, or let it drop;
   Don't torture me by humoring such a fop.
Célimène. You're jealous of the whole world, Sir.
Alceste.   That's true,
   Since the whole world is well-received by you.
Célimène. That my good nature is so unconfined
   Should serve to pacify your jealous mind;

Were I to smile on one, and scorn the rest,
Then you might have some cause to be distressed.

Alceste. Well, if I mustn't be jealous, tell me, then,
Just how I'm better treated than other men.

Célimène. You know you have my love. Will that not do?

Alceste. What proof have I that what you say is true?

Célimène. I would expect, Sir, that my having said it
Might give the statement a sufficient credit.

Alceste. But how can I be sure that you don't tell
The selfsame thing to other men as well?

Célimène. What a gallant speech! How flattering to me!
What a sweet creature you make me out to be!
Well then, to save you from the pangs of doubt,
All that I've said I hereby cancel out;
Now, none but yourself shall make a monkey of you:
Are you content?

Alceste.   Why, why am I doomed to love you?
I swear that I shall bless the blissful hour
When this poor heart's no longer in your power!
I make no secret of it: I've done my best
To exorcise this passion from my breast;
But thus far all in vain; it will not go;
It's for my sins that I must love you so.

Célimène. Your love for me is matchless, Sir; that's clear.

Alceste. Indeed, in all the world it has no peer;
Words can't describe the nature of my passion,
And no man ever loved in such a fashion.

Célimène. Yes, it's a brand-new fashion, I agree:
You show your love by castigating me,
And all your speeches are enraged and rude.
I've never been so furiously wooed.

Alceste. Yet you could calm that fury, if you chose.
Come, shall we bring our quarrels to a close?
Let's speak with open hearts, then, and begin . . .

SCENE 2. *Célimène, Alceste, Basque*

Célimène.   What is it?

Basque.   Acaste is here.

Célimène.   Well, send him in.

SCENE 3. *Célimène, Alceste*

Alceste. What! Shall we never be alone at all?
You're always ready to receive a call,

And you can't bear, for ten ticks of the clock,
Not to keep open house for all who knock.
Célimène.   I couldn't refuse him: he'd be most put out.
Alceste.   Surely that's not worth worrying about.
Célimène.   Acaste would never forgive me if he guessed
That I consider him a dreadful pest.
Alceste.   If he's a pest, why bother with him then?
Célimène.   Heavens! One can't antagonize such men;
Why, they're the chartered gossips of the court,
And have a say in things of every sort.
One must receive them, and be full of charm;
They're no great help, but they can do you harm,
And though your influence be ever so great,
They're hardly the best people to alienate.
Alceste.   I see, dear lady, that you could make a case
For putting up with the whole human race;
These friendships that you calculate so nicely . . .

SCENE 4.   *Alceste, Célimène, Basque*

Basque.   Madam, Clitandre is here as well.
Alceste.   Precisely.
Célimène.   Where are you going?
Alceste.   Elsewhere.
Célimène.   Stay.
Alceste.   No, no.
Célimène.   Stay, Sir.
Alceste.   I can't.
Célimène.   I wish it.
Alceste.   No, I must go.
I beg you, Madam, not to press the matter;
You know I have no taste for idle chatter.
Célimène.   Stay: I command you.
Alceste.   No, I cannot stay.
Célimène.   Very well; you have my leave to go away.

SCENE 5.   *Éliante, Philinte, Acaste, Clitandre, Alceste, Célimène, Basque*

Éliante *(to Célimène)*.   The Marquesses have kindly come to call.
Were they announced?
Célimène.   Yes. Basque, bring chairs for all.

(Basque provides the chairs, and exits.)

(To Alceste.) You haven't gone?

Alceste.   No; and I shan't depart
Till you decide who's foremost in your heart.
Célimène.   Oh, hush.
Alceste.   It's time to choose; take them, or me.
Célimène.   You're mad.
Alceste.   I'm not, as you shall shortly see.
Célimène.   Oh?
Alceste.   You'll decide.
Célimène.   You're joking now, dear friend.
Alceste.   No, no; you'll choose; my patience is at an end.
Clitandre.   Madam, I come from court, where poor Cléonte
Behaved like a perfect fool, as is his wont.
Has he no friend to counsel him, I wonder,
And teach him less unerringly to blunder?
Célimène.   It's true, the man's a most accomplished dunce;
His gauche behavior charms the eye at once;
And every time one sees him, on my word,
His manner's grown a trifle more absurd.
Acaste.   Speaking of dunces, I've just now conversed
With old Damon, who's one of the very worst;
I stood a lifetime in the broiling sun
Before his dreary monologue was done.
Célimène.   Oh, he's a wondrous talker, and has the power
To tell you nothing hour after hour:
If, by mistake, he ever came to the point,
The shock would put his jawbone out of joint.
Éliante (*to Philinte*).   The conversation takes its usual turn,
And all our dear friends' ears will shortly burn.
Clitandre.   Timante's a character, Madam.
Célimène.   Isn't he, though?
A man of mystery from top to toe,
Who moves about in a romantic mist
On secret missions which do not exist.
His talk is full of eyebrows and grimaces;
How tired one gets of his momentous faces;
He's always whispering something confidential
Which turns out to be quite inconsequential;
Nothing's too slight for him to mystify;
He even whispers when he says "good-by."
Acaste.   Tell us about Géralde.
Célimène.   That tiresome ass.
He mixes only with the titled class,
And fawns on dukes and princes, and is bored
With anyone who's not at least a lord.
The man's obsessed with rank, and his discourses

Are all of hounds and carriages and horses;
He uses Christian names with all the great,
And the word Milord, with him, is out of date.
Clitandre.   He's very taken with Bélise, I hear.
Célimène.   She is the dreariest company, poor dear.
　Whenever she comes to call, I grope about
　To find some topic which will draw her out,
　But, owing to her dry and faint replies,
　The conversation wilts, and droops, and dies.
　In vain one hopes to animate her face
　By mentioning the ultimate commonplace;
　But sun or shower, even hail or frost
　Are matters she can instantly exhaust.
　Meanwhile her visit, painful though it is,
　Drags on and on through mute eternities,
　And though you ask the time, and yawn, and yawn,
　She sits there like a stone and won't be gone.
Acaste.   Now for Adraste.
Célimène.   Oh, that conceited elf
　Has a gigantic passion for himself;
　He rails against the court, and cannot bear it
　That none will recognize his hidden merit;
　All honors given to others give offense
　To his imaginary excellence.
Clitandre.   What about young Cléon? His house, they say,
　Is full of the best society, night and day.
Célimène.   His cook has made him popular, not he:
　It's Cléon's table that people come to see.
Éliante.   He gives a splendid dinner, you must admit.
Célimène.   But must he serve himself along with it?
　For my taste, he's a most insipid dish
　Whose presence sours the wine and spoils the fish.
Philinte.   Damis, his uncle, is admired no end.
　What's your opinion, Madam?
Célimène.   Why, he's my friend.
Philinte.   He seems a decent fellow, and rather clever.
Célimène.   He works too hard at cleverness, however.
　I hate to see him sweat and struggle so
　To fill his conversation with bons mots.
　Since he's decided to become a wit
　His taste's so pure that nothing pleases it;
　He scolds at all the latest books and plays,
　Thinking that wit must never stoop to praise,
　That finding fault's a sign of intellect,
　That all appreciation is abject,

And that by damning everything in sight
One shows oneself in a distinguished light.
He's scornful even of our conversations:
Their trivial nature sorely tries his patience;
He folds his arms, and stands above the battle,
And listens sadly to our childish prattle.

Acaste. Wonderful, Madam! You've hit him off precisely.

Clitandre. No one can sketch a character so nicely.

Alceste. How bravely, Sirs, you cut and thrust at all
These absent fools, till one by one they fall:
But let one come in sight, and you'll at once
Embrace the man you lately called a dunce,
Telling him in a tone sincere and fervent
How proud you are to be his humble servant.

Clitandre. Why pick on us? *Madame's* been speaking, Sir,
And you should quarrel, if you must, with her.

Alceste. No, no, by God, the fault is yours, because
You lead her on with laughter and applause,
And make her think that she's the more delightful
The more her talk is scandalous and spiteful.
Oh, she would stoop to malice far, far less
If no such claque approved her cleverness.
It's flatterers like you whose foolish praise
Nourishes all the vices of these days.

Philinte. But why protest when someone ridicules
Those you'd condemn, yourself, as knaves or fools?

Célimène. Why, Sir? Because he loves to make a fuss.
You don't expect him to agree with us,
When there's an opportunity to express
His heaven-sent spirit of contrariness?
What other people think, he can't abide;
Whatever they say, he's on the other side;
He lives in deadly terror of agreeing;
'Twould make him seem an ordinary being.
Indeed, he's so in love with contradiction,
He'll turn against his most profound conviction
And with a furious eloquence deplore it,
If only someone else is speaking for it.

Alceste. Go on, dear lady, mock me as you please;
You have your audience in ecstasies.

Philinte. But what she says is true: you have a way
Of bridling at whatever people say;
Whether they praise or blame, your angry spirit
Is equally unsatisfied to hear it.

Alceste. Men, Sir, are always wrong, and that's the reason

That righteous anger's never out of season;
All that I hear in all their conversation
Is flattering praise or reckless condemnation.

Célimène.   But . . .

Alceste.   No, no, Madam, I am forced to state
That you have pleasures which I deprecate,
And that these others, here, are much to blame
For nourishing the faults which are your shame.

Clitandre.   I shan't defend myself, Sir; but I vow
I'd thought this lady faultless until now.

Acaste.   I see her charms and graces, which are many;
But as for faults, I've never noticed any.

Alceste.   I see them, Sir; and rather than ignore them,
I strenuously criticize her for them.
The more one loves, the more one should object
To every blemish, every least defect.
Were I this lady, I would soon get rid
Of lovers who approved of all I did,
And by their slack indulgence and applause
Endorsed my follies and excused my flaws.

Célimène.   If all hearts beat according to your measure,
The dawn of love would be the end of pleasure;
And love would find its perfect consummation
In ecstasies of rage and reprobation.

Éliante.   Love, as a rule, affects men otherwise,
And lovers rarely love to criticize.
They see their lady as a charming blur,
And find all things commendable in her.
If she has any blemish, fault, or shame,
They will redeem it by a pleasing name.
The pale-faced lady's lily-white, perforce;
The swarthy one's a sweet brunette, of course;
The spindly lady has a slender grace;
The fat one has a most majestic pace;
The plain one, with her dress in disarray,
They classify as *beauté négligée*;
The hulking one's a goddess in their eyes,
The dwarf, a concentrate of Paradise;
The haughty lady has a noble mind;
The mean one's witty, and the dull one's kind;
The chatterbox has liveliness and verve,
The mute one has a virtuous reserve.
So lovers manage, in their passion's cause,
To love their ladies even for their flaws.

Alceste.   But I still say . . .

Célimène. I think it would be nice
To stroll around the gallery once or twice.
What! You're not going, Sirs?
Clitandre and Acaste. No, Madam, no.
Alceste. You seem to be in terror lest they go.
Do what you will, Sirs; leave, or linger on,
But I shan't go till after you are gone.
Acaste. I'm free to linger, unless I should perceive
Madame is tired, and wishes me to leave.
Clitandre. And as for me, I needn't go today
Until the hour of the King's *coucher*.
Célimène (*to Alceste*). You're joking, surely?
Alceste. Not in the least; we'll see
Whether you'd ràther part with them, or me.

SCENE 6. *Alceste, Célimène, Éliante, Acaste, Philinte, Clitandre, Basque*

Basque (*to Alceste*). Sir, there's a fellow here who bids me state
That he must see you, and that it can't wait.
Alceste. Tell him that I have no such pressing affairs.
Basque. It's a long tailcoat that this fellow wears,
With gold all over.
Célimène (*to Alceste*). You'd best go down and see.
Or—have him enter.

SCENE 7. *Alceste, Célimène, Éliante, Acaste, Philinte, Clitandre, Guard*

Alceste (*confronting the Guard*). Well, what do you want with me?
Come in, Sir.
Guard. I've a word, Sir, for your ear.
Alceste. Speak it aloud, Sir; I shall strive to hear.
Guard. The Marshals have instructed me to say
You must report to them without delay.
Alceste. Who? Me, Sir?
Guard. Yes, Sir; you.
Alceste. But what do they want?
Philinte (*to Alceste*). To scotch your silly quarrel with Oronte.
Célimène (*to Philinte*). What quarrel?
Philinte. Oronte and he have fallen out
Over some verse he spoke his mind about;
The Marshals wish to arbitrate the matter.

Alceste.   Never shall I equivocate or flatter!
Philinte.   You'd best obey their summons; come, let's go.
Alceste.   How can they mend our quarrel, I'd like to know?
  Am I to make a cowardly retraction,
  And praise those jingles to his satisfaction?
  I'll not recant; I've judged that sonnet rightly.
  It's bad.
Philinte.   But you might say so more politely. . . .
Alceste.   I'll not back down; his verses make me sick.
Philinte.   If only you could be more politic!
  But come, let's go.
Alceste.   I'll go, but I won't unsay
  A single word.
Philinte.   Well, let's be on our way.
Alceste.   Till I am ordered by my lord the King
  To praise that poem, I shall say the thing
  Is scandalous, by God, and that the poet
  Ought to be hanged for having the nerve to show it.

(To Clitandre *and* Acaste, *who are laughing.)*

  By heaven, Sirs, I really didn't know
  That I was being humorous.
Célimène.   Go, Sir, go;
  Settle your business.
Alceste.   I shall, and when I'm through,
  I shall return to settle things with you.

Act III

SCENE 1. *Clitandre, Acaste*

Clitandre.   Dear Marquess, how contented you appear;
  All things delight you, nothing mars your cheer.
  Can you, in perfect honesty, declare
  That you've a right to be so debonair?
Acaste.   By Jove, when I survey myself, I find
  No cause whatever for distress of mind.
  I'm young and rich; I can in modesty
  Lay claim to an exalted pedigree;
  And owing to my name and my condition

I shall not want for honors and position.
Then as to courage, that most precious trait,
I seem to have it, as was proved of late
Upon the field of honor, where my bearing,
They say, was very cool and rather daring.
I've wit, of course; and taste in such perfection
That I can judge without the least reflection,
And at the theater, which is my delight,
Can make or break a play on opening night,
And lead the crowd in hisses or bravos,
And generally be known as one who knows.
I'm clever, handsome, gracefully polite;
My waist is small, my teeth are strong and white;
As for my dress, the world's astonished eyes
Assure me that I bear away the prize.
I find myself in favor everywhere,
Honored by men, and worshiped by the fair;
And since these things are so, it seems to me
I'm justified in my complacency.

Clitandre.   Well, if so many ladies hold you dear,
Why do you press a hopeless courtship here?

Acaste.   Hopeless, you say? I'm not the sort of fool
That likes his ladies difficult and cool.
Men who are awkward, shy, and peasantish
May pine for heartless beauties, if they wish,
Grovel before them, bear their cruelties,
Woo them with tears and sighs and bended knees,
And hope by dogged faithfulness to gain
What their poor merits never could obtain.
For men like me, however, it makes no sense
To love on trust, and foot the whole expense.
Whatever any lady's merits be,
I think, thank God, that I'm as choice as she;
That if my heart is kind enough to burn
For her, she owes me something in return;
And that in any proper love affair
The partners must invest an equal share.

Clitandre.   You think, then, that our hostess favors you?

Acaste.   I've reason to believe that that is true.

Clitandre.   How did you come to such a mad conclusion?
You're blind, dear fellow. This is sheer delusion.

Acaste.   All right, then: I'm deluded and I'm blind.

Clitandre.   Whatever put the notion in your mind?

Acaste.   Delusion.

Clitandre.   What persuades you that you're right?

Acaste.   I'm blind.

Clitandre.   But have you any proofs to cite?

Acaste.   I tell you I'm deluded.

Clitandre.   Have you, then,
   Received some secret pledge from Célimène?

Acaste.   Oh, no: she scorns me.

Clitandre.   Tell me the truth, I beg.

Acaste.   She just can't bear me.

Clitandre.   Ah, don't pull my leg.
   Tell me what hope she's given you, I pray.

Acaste.   I'm hopeless, and it's you who win the day.
   She hates me thoroughly, and I'm so vexed
   I mean to hang myself on Tuesday next.

Clitandre.   Dear Marquess, let us have an armistice
   And make a treaty. What do you say to this?
   If ever one of us can plainly prove
   That Célimène encourages his love,
   The other must abandon hope, and yield,
   And leave him in possession of the field.

Acaste.   Now, there's a bargain that appeals to me;
   With all my heart, dear Marquess, I agree.
   But hush.

SCENE 2.   *Célimène, Acaste, Clitandre*

Célimène.   Still here?

Clitandre.   'Twas love that stayed our feet.

Célimène.   I think I heard a carriage in the street.
   Whose is it? D'you know?

SCENE 3.   *Célimène, Acaste, Clitandre, Basque*

Basque.   Arsinoé is here,
   Madame.

Célimène.   Arsinoé, you say? Oh, dear.

Basque.   Éliante is entertaining her below.

Célimène.   What brings the creature here, I'd like to know?

Acaste.   They say she's dreadfully prudish, but in fact
   I think her piety . . .

Célimène.   It's all an act.
   At heart she's worldly, and her poor success

In snaring men explains her prudishness.
It breaks her heart to see the beaux and gallants
Engrossed by other women's charms and talents,
And so she's always in a jealous rage
Against the faulty standards of the age.
She lets the world believe that she's a prude
To justify her loveless solitude,
And strives to put a brand of moral shame
On all the graces that she cannot claim.
But still she'd love a lover; and Alceste
Appears to be the one she'd love the best.
His visits here are poison to her pride;
She seems to think I've lured him from her side;
And everywhere, at court or in the town,
The spiteful, envious woman runs me down.
In short, she's just as stupid as can be,
Vicious and arrogant in the last degree,
And . . .

SCENE 4.   *Arsinoé, Célimène, Clitandre, Acaste*

Célimène.   Ah! What happy chance has brought you here?
I've thought about you ever so much, my dear.
Arsinoé.   I've come to tell you something you should know.
Célimène.   How good of you to think of doing so!

(Clitandre and Acaste go out, laughing.)

SCENE 5.   *Arsinoé, Célimène*

Arsinoé.   It's just as well those gentlemen didn't tarry.
Célimène.   Shall we sit down?
Arsinoé.   That won't be necessary.
Madam, the flame of friendship ought to burn
Brightest in matters of the most concern,
And as there's nothing which concerns us more
Than honor, I have hastened to your door
To bring you, as your friend, some information
About the status of your reputation.
I visited, last night, some virtuous folk,
And, quite by chance, it was of you they spoke;

There was, I fear, no tendency to praise
Your light behavior and your dashing ways.
The quantity of gentlemen you see
And your by now notorious coquetry
Were both so vehemently criticized
By everyone, that I was much surprised.
Of course, I needn't tell you where I stood;
I came to your defense as best I could,
Assured them you were harmless, and declared
Your soul was absolutely unimpaired.
But there are some things, you must realize,
One can't excuse, however hard one tries,
And I was forced at last into conceding
That your behavior, Madam, is misleading,
That it makes a bad impression, giving rise
To ugly gossip and obscene surmise,
And that if you were more *overtly* good,
You wouldn't be so much misunderstood.
Not that I think you've been unchaste—no! no!
The saints preserve me from a thought so low!
But mere good conscience never did suffice:
One must avoid the outward show of vice.
Madam, you're too intelligent, I'm sure,
To think my motives anything but pure
In offering you this counsel—which I do
Out of a zealous interest in you.

Célimène.   Madam, I haven't taken you amiss;
    I'm very much obliged to you for this;
    And I'll at once discharge the obligation
    By telling you about *your* reputation.
    You've been so friendly as to let me know
    What certain people say of me, and so
    I mean to follow your benign example
    By offering you a somewhat similar sample.
    The other day, I went to an affair
    And found some most distinguished people there
    Discussing piety, both false and true.
    The conversation soon came round to you.
    Alas! Your prudery and bustling zeal
    Appeared to have a very slight appeal.
    Your affectation of a grave demeanor,
    Your endless talk of virtue and of honor,
    The aptitude of your suspicious mind
    For finding sin where there is none to find,
    Your towering self-esteem, that pitying face

With which you contemplate the human race,
Your sermonizings and your sharp aspersions
On people's pure and innocent diversions—
All these were mentioned, Madam, and, in fact,
Were roundly and concertedly attacked.
"What good," they said, "are all these outward shows,
When everything belies her pious pose?
She prays incessantly; but then, they say,
She beats her maids and cheats them of their pay;
She shows her zeal in every holy place,
But still she's vain enough to paint her face;
She holds that naked statues are immoral,
But with a naked *man* she'd have no quarrel."
Of course, I said to everybody there
That they were being viciously unfair;
But still they were disposed to criticize you,
And all agreed that someone should advise you
To leave the morals of the world alone,
And worry rather more about your own.
They felt that one's self-knowledge should be great
Before one thinks of setting others straight;
That one should learn the art of living well
Before one threatens other men with hell,
And that the Church is best equipped, no doubt,
To guide our souls and root our vices out.
Madam, you're too intelligent, I'm sure,
To think my motives anything but pure
In offering you this counsel—which I do
Out of a zealous interest in you.

Arsinoé.   I dared not hope for gratitude, but I
Did not expect so acid a reply;
I judge, since you've been so extremely tart,
That my good counsel pierced you to the heart.

Célimène.   Far from it, Madam. Indeed, it seems to me
We ought to trade advice more frequently.
One's vision of oneself is so defective
That it would be an excellent corrective.
If you are willing, Madam, let's arrange
Shortly to have another frank exchange
In which we'll tell each other, *entre nous,*
What you've heard tell of me, and I of you.

Arsinoé.   Oh, people never censure you, my dear;
It's me they criticize. Or so I hear.

Célimène.   Madam, I think we either blame or praise
According to our taste and length of days.

There is a time of life for coquetry,
And there's a season, too, for prudery.
When all one's charms are gone, it is, I'm sure,
Good strategy to be devout and pure:
It makes one seem a little less forsaken.
Some day, perhaps, I'll take the road you've taken:
Time brings all things. But I have time aplenty,
And see no cause to be a prude at twenty.

Arsinoé.   You give your age in such a gloating tone
That one would think I was an ancient crone;
We're not so far apart, in sober truth,
That you can mock me with a boast of youth!
Madam, you baffle me. I wish I knew
What moves you to provoke me as you do.

Célimène.   For my part, Madam, I should like to know
Why you abuse me everywhere you go.
Is it my fault, dear lady, that your hand
Is not, alas, in very great demand?
If men admire me, if they pay me court
And daily make me offers of the sort
You'd dearly love to have them make to you,
How can I help it? What would you have me do?
If what you want is lovers, please feel free
To take as many as you can from me.

Arsinoé.   Oh, come. D'you think the world is losing sleep
Over that flock of lovers which you keep,
Or that we find it difficult to guess
What price you pay for their devotedness?
Surely you don't expect us to suppose
Mere merit could attract so many beaux?
It's not your virtue that they're dazzled by;
Nor is it virtuous love for which they sigh.
You're fooling no one, Madam; the world's not blind;
There's many a lady heaven has designed
To call men's noblest, tenderest feelings out,
Who has no lovers dogging her about;
From which it's plain that lovers nowadays
Must be acquired in bold and shameless ways,
And only pay one court for such reward
As modesty and virtue can't afford.
Then don't be quite so puffed up, if you please,
About your tawdry little victories;
Try, if you can, to be a shade less vain,
And treat the world with somewhat less disdain.
If one were envious of your amours,

> One soon could have a following like yours;
> Lovers are no great trouble to collect
> If one prefers them to one's self-respect.

Célimène.   Collect them then, my dear; I'd love to see
> You demonstrate that charming theory;
> Who knows, you might . . .

Arsinoé.   Now, Madam, that will do;
> It's time to end this trying interview,
> My coach is late in coming to your door,
> Or I'd have taken leave of you before.

Célimène.   Oh, please don't feel that you must rush away;
> I'd be delighted, Madam, if you'd stay.
> However, lest my conversation bore you,
> Let me provide some better company for you;
> This gentleman, who comes most apropos,
> Will please you more than I could do, I know.

SCENE 6.   *Alceste, Célimène, Arsinoé*

Célimène.   Alceste, I have a little note to write
> Which simply must go out before tonight;
> Please entertain *Madame*; I'm sure that she
> Will overlook my incivility.

SCENE 7.   *Alceste, Arsinoé*

Arsinoé.   Well, Sir, our hostess graciously contrives
> For us to chat until my coach arrives;
> And I shall be forever in her debt
> For granting me this little tête-a-tête.
> We women very rightly give our hearts
> To men of noble character and parts,
> And your especial merits, dear Alceste,
> Have roused the deepest sympathy in my breast.
> Oh, how I wish they had sufficient sense
> At court, to recognize your excellence!
> They wrong you greatly, Sir. How it must hurt you
> Never to be rewarded for your virtue!

Alceste.   Why, Madam, what cause have I to feel aggrieved?
> What great and brilliant thing have I achieved?

What service have I rendered to the King
That I should look to him for anything?
Arsinoé.   Not everyone who's honored by the State
Has done great services. A man must wait
Till time and fortune offer him the chance.
Your merit, Sir, is obvious at a glance,
And . . .
Alceste.   Ah, forget my merit; I am not neglected.
The court, I think, can hardly be expected
To mine men's souls for merit, and unearth
Our hidden virtues and our secret worth.
Arsinoé.   *Some* virtues, though, are far too bright to hide;
Yours are acknowledged, Sir, on every side.
Indeed, I've heard you warmly praised of late
By persons of considerable weight.
Alceste.   This fawning age has praise for everyone,
And all distinctions, Madam, are undone.
All things have equal honor nowadays,
And no one should be gratified by praise.
To be admired, one only need exist,
And every lackey's on the honors list.
Arsinoé.   I only wish, Sir, that you had your eye
On some position at court, however high;
You'd only have to hint at such a notion
For me to set the proper wheels in motion;
I've certain friendships I'd be glad to use
To get you any office you might choose.
Alceste.   Madam, I fear that any such ambition
Is wholly foreign to my disposition.
The soul God gave me isn't of the sort
That prospers in the weather of a court.
It's all too obvious that I don't possess
The virtues necessary for success.
My one great talent is for speaking plain;
I've never learned to flatter or to feign;
And anyone so stupidly sincere
Had best not seek a courtier's career.
Outside the court, I know, one must dispense
With honors, privilege, and influence;
But still one gains the right, foregoing these,
Not to be tortured by the wish to please.
One needn't live in dread of snubs and slights,
Nor praise the verse that every idiot writes,
Nor humor silly Marquesses, nor bestow
Politic sighs on Madam So-and-So.
Arsinoé.   Forget the court, then; let the matter rest.

But I've another cause to be distressed
About your present situation, Sir.
It's to your love affair that I refer.
She whom you love, and who pretends to love you,
Is, I regret to say, unworthy of you.

Alceste. Why, Madam? Can you seriously intend
To make so grave a charge against your friend?

Arsinoé. Alas, I must. I've stood aside too long
And let that lady do you grievous wrong;
But now my debt to conscience shall be paid:
I tell you that your love has been betrayed.

Alceste. I thank you, Madam; you're extremely kind.
Such words are soothing to a lover's mind.

Arsinoé. Yes, though she *is* my friend, I say again
You're very much too good for Célimène.
She's wantonly misled you from the start.

Alceste. You may be right; who knows another's heart?
But ask yourself if it's the part of charity
To shake my soul with doubts of her sincerity.

Arsinoé. Well, if you'd rather be a dupe than doubt her,
That's your affair. I'll say no more about her.

Alceste. Madam, you know that doubt and vague suspicion
Are painful to a man in my position;
It's most unkind to worry me this way
Unless you've some real proof of what you say.

Arsinoé. Sir, say no more: all doubts shall be removed,
And all that I've been saying shall be proved.
You've only to escort me home, and there
We'll look into the heart of this affair.
I've ocular evidence which will persuade you
Beyond a doubt, that Célimène's betrayed you.
Then, if you're saddened by that revelation,
Perhaps I can provide some consolation.

Act IV

SCENE 1. *Éliante, Philinte*

Philinte. Madam, he acted like a stubborn child;
I thought they never would be reconciled;
In vain we reasoned, threatened, and appealed;

He stood his ground and simply would not yield.
The Marshals, I feel sure, have never heard
An argument so splendidly absurd.
"No, gentlemen," said he, "I'll not retract.
His verse is bad: extremely bad, in fact.
Surely it does the man no harm to know it.
Does it disgrace him, not to be a poet?
A gentleman may be respected still,
Whether he writes a sonnet well or ill.
That I dislike his verse should not offend him;
In all that touches honor, I commend him;
He's noble, brave, and virtuous—but I fear
He can't in truth be called a sonneteer.
I'll gladly praise his wardrobe; I'll endorse
His dancing, or the way he sits a horse;
But, gentlemen, I cannot praise his rhyme.
In fact, it ought to be a capital crime
For anyone so sadly unendowed
To write a sonnet, and read the thing aloud."
At length he fell into a gentler mood
And, striking a concessive attitude,
He paid Oronte the following courtesies:
"Sir, I regret that I'm so hard to please,
And I'm profoundly sorry that your lyric
Failed to provoke me to a panegyric."
After these curious words, the two embraced,
And then the hearing was adjourned—in haste.

Éliante. His conduct has been very singular lately;
Still, I confess that I respect him greatly.
The honesty in which he takes such pride
Has—to my mind—its noble, heroic side.
In this false age, such candor seems outrageous;
But I could wish that it were more contagious.

Philinte. What most intrigues me in our friend Alceste
Is the grand passion that rages in his breast.
The sullen humors he's compounded of
Should not, I think, dispose his heart to love;
But since they do, it puzzles me still more
That he should choose your cousin to adore.

Éliante. It does, indeed, belie the theory
That love is born of gentle sympathy,
And that the tender passion must be based
On sweet accords of temper and of taste.

Philinte. Does she return his love, do you suppose?

Éliante. Ah, that's a difficult question, Sir. Who knows?

How can we judge the truth of her devotion?
Her heart's a stranger to its own emotion.
Sometimes it thinks it loves, when no love's there;
At other times it loves quite unaware.

Philinte.   I rather think Alceste is in for more
Distress and sorrow than he's bargained for;
Were he of my mind, Madam, his affection
Would turn in quite a different direction,
And we would see him more responsive to
The kind regard which he receives from you.

Éliante.   Sir, I believe in frankness, and I'm inclined,
In matters of the heart, to speak my mind.
I don't oppose his love for her; indeed,
I hope with all my heart that he'll succeed,
And were it in my power, I'd rejoice
In giving him the lady of his choice.
But if, as happens frequently enough
In love affairs, he meets with a rebuff—
If Célimène should grant some rival's suit—
I'd gladly play the role of substitute;
Nor would his tender speeches please me less
Because they'd once been made without success.

Philinte.   Well, Madam, as for me, I don't oppose
Your hopes in this affair; and heaven knows
That in my conversations with the man
I plead your cause as often as I can.
But if those two should marry, and so remove
All chance that he will offer you his love,
Then I'll declare my own, and hope to see
Your gracious favor pass from him to me.
In short, should you be cheated of Alceste,
I'd be most happy to be second best.

Éliante.   Philinte, you're teasing.

Philinte.   Ah, Madam, never fear;
No words of mine were ever so sincere,
And I shall live in fretful expectation
Till I can make a fuller declaration.

SCENE 2.   *Alceste, Éliante, Philinte*

Alceste.   Avenge me, Madam! I must have satisfaction,
Or this great wrong will drive me to distraction!

Éliante.   Why, what's the matter? What's upset you so?

Alceste.   Madam, I've had a mortal, mortal blow.
   If Chaos repossessed the universe,
   I swear I'd not be shaken any worse,
   I'm ruined. . . . I can say no more. . . . My soul . . .
Éliante.   Do try, Sir, to regain your self-control.
Alceste.   Just heaven! Why were so much beauty and grace
   Bestowed on one so vicious and so base?
Éliante.   Once more, Sir, tell us. . . .
                          My world has gone to wrack;
Alceste.
   I'm—I'm betrayed; she's stabbed me in the back:
   Yes, Célimène (who would have thought it of her?)
   Is false to me, and has another lover.
Éliante.   Are you quite certain? Can you prove these things?
Philinte.   Lovers are prey to wild imaginings
   And jealous fancies. No doubt there's some mistake. . . .
Alceste.   Mind your own business, Sir, for heaven's sake.

(To Éliante.)

   Madam, I have the proof that you demand
   Here in my pocket, penned by her own hand.
   Yes, all the shameful evidence one could want
   Lies in this letter written to Oronte—
   Oronte! whom I felt sure she couldn't love,
   And hardly bothered to be jealous of.
Philinte.   Still, in a letter, appearances may deceive;
   This may not be so bad as you believe.
Alceste.   Once more I beg you, Sir, to let me be;
   Tend to your own affairs; leave mine to me.
Éliante.   Compose yourself; this anguish that you feel . . .
Alceste.   Is something, Madam, you alone can heal.
   My outraged heart, beside itself with grief,
   Appeals to you for comfort and relief.
   Avenge me on your cousin, whose unjust
   And faithless nature has deceived my trust;
   Avenge a crime your pure soul must detest.
Éliante.   But how, Sir?
Alceste.   Madam, this heart within my breast
   Is yours; pray take it; redeem my heart from her,
   And so avenge me on my torturer.
   Let her be punished by the fond emotion,
   The ardent love, the bottomless devotion,
   The faithful worship which this heart of mine
   Will offer up to yours as to a shrine.
Éliante.   You have my sympathy, Sir, in all you suffer;

Nor do I scorn the noble heart you offer;
But I suspect you'll soon be mollified,
And this desire for vengeance will subside.
When some belovèd hand has done us wrong
We thirst for retribution—but not for long;
However dark the deed that she's committed,
A lovely culprit's very soon acquitted.
Nothing's so stormy as an injured lover,
And yet no storm so quickly passes over.

Alceste.   No, Madam, no—this is no lovers' spat;
I'll not forgive her; it's gone too far for that;
My mind's made up; I'll kill myself before
I waste my hopes upon her any more.
Ah, here she is. My wrath intensifies.
I shall confront her with her tricks and lies,
And crush her utterly, and bring you then
A heart no longer slave to Célimène.

SCENE 3.   *Célimène, Alceste*

Alceste *(aside).*   Sweet heaven, help me to control my passion.
Célimène *(aside).*   Oh, Lord.

(To Alceste)

                    Why stand there staring in that fashion?
And what d'you mean by those dramatic sighs,
And that malignant glitter in your eyes?

Alceste.   I mean that sins which cause the blood to freeze
Look innocent beside your treacheries;
That nothing Hell's or Heaven's wrath could do
Ever produced so bad a thing as you.

Célimène.   Your compliments were always sweet and pretty.

Alceste.   Madam, it's not the moment to be witty.
No, blush and hang your head; you've ample reason,
Since I've the fullest evidence of your treason.
Ah, this is what my sad heart prophesied;
Now all my anxious fears are verified;
My dark suspicion and my gloomy doubt
Divined the truth, and now the truth is out.
For all your trickery, I was not deceived;
It was my bitter stars that I believed.
But don't imagine that you'll go scot-free;

You shan't misuse me with impunity.
I know that love's irrational and blind;
I know the heart's not subject to the mind,
And can't be reasoned into beating faster;
I know each soul is free to choose its master;
Therefore had you but spoken from the heart,
Rejecting my attentions from the start,
I'd have no grievance, or at any rate
I could complain of nothing but my fate.
Ah, but so falsely to encourage me—
That was a treason and a treachery
For which you cannot suffer too severely,
And you shall pay for that behavior dearly.
Yes, now I have no pity, not a shred;
My temper's out of hand; I've lost my head;
Shocked by the knowledge of your double-dealings,
My reason can't restrain my savage feelings;
A righteous wrath deprives me of my senses,
And I won't answer for the consequences.

Célimène. What does this outburst mean? Will you please explain?
Have you, by any chance, gone quite insane?

Alceste. Yes, yes, I went insane the day I fell
A victim to your black and fatal spell,
Thinking to meet with some sincerity
Among the treacherous charms that beckoned me.

Célimène. Pooh. Of what treachery can you complain?

Alceste. How sly you are, how cleverly you feign!
But you'll not victimize me any more.
Look: here's a document you've seen before.
This evidence, which I acquired today,
Leaves you, I think, without a thing to say.

Célimène. Is this what sent you into such a fit?

Alceste. You should be blushing at the sight of it.

Célimène. Ought I to blush? I truly don't see why.

Alceste. Ah, now you're being bold as well as sly;
Since there's no signature, perhaps you'll claim . . . .

Célimène. I wrote it, whether or not it bears my name.

Alceste. And you can view with equanimity
This proof of your disloyalty to me!

Célimène. Oh, don't be so outrageous and extreme.

Alceste. You take this matter lightly, it would seem.
Was it no wrong to me, no shame to you,
That you should send Oronte this billet-doux?

Célimène. Oronte! Who said it was for him?

Alceste.   Why, those

Who brought me this example of your prose.
But what's the difference? If you wrote the letter
To someone else, it pleases me no better.
My grievance and your guilt remain the same.
Célimène.   But need you rage, and need I blush for shame,
   If this was written to a *woman* friend?
Alceste.   Ah! Most ingenious. I'm impressed no end;
   And after that incredible evasion
   Your guilt is clear. I need no more persuasion.
   How dare you try so clumsy a deception?
   D'you think I'm wholly wanting in perception?
   Come, come, let's see how brazenly you'll try
   To bolster up so palpable a lie:
   Kindly construe this ardent closing section
   As nothing more than sisterly affection!
   Here, let me read it. Tell me, if you dare to,
   That this is for a woman . . .
Célimène.   I don't care to.
   What right have you to badger and berate me,
   And so highhandedly interrogate me?
Alceste.   Now, don't be angry; all I ask of you
   Is that you justify a phrase or two . . .
Célimène.   No, I shall not. I utterly refuse,
   And you may take those phrases as you choose.
Alceste.   Just show me how this letter could be meant
   For a woman's eyes, and I shall be content.
Célimène.   No, no, it's for Oronte; you're perfectly right.
   I welcome his attentions with delight,
   I prize his character and his intellect,
   And everything is just as you suspect.
   Come, do your worst now; give your rage free rein;
   But kindly cease to bicker and complain.
Alceste (*aside*).   Good God! Could anything be more inhuman?
   Was ever a heart so mangled by a woman?
   When I complain of how she has betrayed me,
   She bridles, and commences to upbraid me!
   She tries my tortured patience to the limit;
   She won't deny her guilt; she glories in it!
   And yet my heart's too faint and cowardly
   To break these chains of passion, and be free,
   To scorn her as it should, and rise above
   This unrewarded, mad, and bitter love.

(*To Célimène.*)

Ah, traitress, in how confident a fashion
You take advantage of my helpless passion,
And use my weakness for your faithless charms
To make me once again throw down my arms!
But do at least deny this black transgression;
Take back that mocking and perverse confession;
Defend this letter and your innocence,
And I, poor fool, will aid in your defense.
Pretend, pretend, that you are just and true,
And I shall make myself believe in you.

Célimène.   Oh, stop it. Don't be such a jealous dunce,
Or I shall leave off loving you at once.
Just why should I *pretend?* What could impel me
To stoop so low as that? And kindly tell me
Why, if I loved another, I shouldn't merely
Inform you of it, simply and sincerely!
I've told you where you stand, and that admission
Should altogether clear me of suspicion;
After so generous a guarantee,
What right have you to harbor doubts of me?
Since women are (from natural reticence)
Reluctant to declare their sentiments,
And since the honor of our sex requires
That we conceal our amorous desires,
Ought any man for whom such laws are broken
To question what the oracle has spoken?
Should he not rather feel an obligation
To trust that most obliging declaration?
Enough, now. Your suspicions quite disgust me;
Why should I love a man who doesn't trust me?
I cannot understand why I continue,
Fool that I am, to take an interest in you.
I ought to choose a man less prone to doubt,
And give you something to be vexed about.

Alceste.   Ah, what a poor enchanted fool I am;
These gentle words, no doubt, were all a sham,
But destiny requires me to entrust
My happiness to you, and so I must.
I'll love you to the bitter end, and see
How false and treacherous you dare to be.

Célimène.   No, you don't really love me as you ought.

Alceste.   I love you more than can be said or thought;
Indeed, I wish you were in such distress
That I might show my deep devotedness.

Yes, I could wish that you were wretchedly poor,
Unloved, uncherished, utterly obscure;
That fate had set you down upon the earth
Without possessions, rank, or gentle birth;
Then, by the offer of my heart, I might
Repair the great injustice of your plight;
I'd raise you from the dust, and proudly prove
The purity and vastness of my love.

Célimène.   This is a strange benevolence indeed!
God grant that I may never be in need. . . .
Ah, here's Monsieur Dubois, in quaint disguise.

SCENE 4.   *Célimène, Alceste, Dubois*

Alceste.   Well, why this costume? Why those frightened eyes?
What ails you?
Dubois.   Well, Sir, things are most mysterious.
Alceste.   What do you mean?
Dubois.   I fear they're very serious.
Alceste.   What?
Dubois.   Shall I speak more loudly?
Alceste.   Yes; speak out.
Dubois.   Isn't there someone here, Sir?
Alceste.   Speak, you lout!
Stop wasting time.
Dubois.   Sir, we must slip away.
Alceste.   How's that?
Dubois.   We must decamp without delay.
Alceste.   Explain yourself.
Dubois.   I tell you we must fly.
Alceste.   What for?
Dubois.   We mustn't pause to say good-by.
Alceste.   Now what d'you mean by all of this, you clown?
Dubois.   I mean, Sir, that we've got to leave this town.
Alceste.   I'll tear you limb from limb and joint from joint
If you don't come more quickly to the point.
Dubois.   Well, Sir, today a man in a black suit,
Who wore a black and ugly scowl to boot,
Left us a document scrawled in such a hand
As even Satan couldn't understand.
It bears upon your lawsuit, I don't doubt;
But all hell's devils couldn't make it out.
Alceste.   Well, well, go on. What then? I fail to see
How this event obliges us to flee.

Dubois.   Well, Sir: an hour later, hardly more,
A gentleman who's often called before
Came looking for you in an anxious way.
Not finding you, he asked me to convey
(Knowing I could be trusted with the same)
The following message. . . . Now, what *was* his name?

Alceste.   Forget his name, you idiot. What did he say?

Dubois.   Well, it was one of your friends, Sir, anyway.
He warned you to begone, and he suggested
That if you stay, you may well be arrested.

Alceste.   What? Nothing more specific? Think, man, think!

Dubois.   No, Sir. He had me bring him pen and ink,
And dashed you off a letter which, I'm sure,
Will render things distinctly less obscure.

Alceste.   Well—let me have it!

Célimène.   What *is* this all about?

Alceste.   God knows; but I have hopes of finding out.
How long am I to wait, you blitherer?

Dubois (*after a protracted search for the letter*).   I must have left it on your
table, Sir.

Alceste.   I ought to . . .

Célimène.   No, no, keep your self-control;
Go find out what's behind his rigmarole.

Alceste.   It seems that fate, no matter what I do,
Has sworn that I may not converse with you;
But, Madam, pray permit your faithful lover
To try once more before the day is over.

Act V

SCENE 1.   *Alceste, Philinte*

Alceste.   No, it's too much. My mind's made up, I tell you.

Philinte.   Why should this blow, however hard, compel you . . .

Alceste.   No, no, don't waste your breath in argument;
Nothing you say will alter my intent;
This age is vile, and I've made up my mind
To have no further commerce with mankind.
Did not truth, honor, decency, and the laws
Oppose my enemy and approve my cause?
My claims were justified in all men's sight;
I put my trust in equity and right;

Yet, to my horror and the world's disgrace,
Justice is mocked, and I have lost my case!
A scoundrel whose dishonesty is notorious
Emerges from another lie victorious!
Honor and right condone his brazen fraud,
While rectitude and decency applaud!
Before his smirking face, the truth stands charmed,
And virtue conquered, and the law disarmed!
His crime is sanctioned by a court decree!
And not content with what he's done to me,
The dog now seeks to ruin me by stating
That I composed a book now circulating,
A book so wholly criminal and vicious
That even to speak its title is seditious!
Meanwhile Oronte, my rival, lends his credit
To the same libelous tale, and helps to spread it!
Oronte! a man of honor and of rank,
With whom I've been entirely fair and frank;
Who sought me out and forced me, willy-nilly,
To judge some verse I found extremely silly;
And who, because I properly refused
To flatter him, or see the truth abused,
Abets my enemy in a rotten slander!
There's the reward of honesty and candor!
The man will hate me to the end of time
For failing to commend his wretched rhyme!
And not this man alone, but all humanity
Do what they do from interest and vanity;
They prate of honor, truth, and righteousness,
But lie, betray, and swindle nonetheless.
Come then: man's villainy is too much to bear;
Let's leave this jungle and this jackal's lair.
Yes! treacherous and savage race of men,
You shall not look upon my face again.
Philinte.   Oh, don't rush into exile prematurely;
Things aren't as dreadful as you make them, surely.
It's rather obvious, since you're still at large,
That people don't believe your enemy's charge.
Indeed, his tale's so patently untrue
That it may do more harm to him than you.
Alceste.   Nothing could do that scoundrel any harm:
His frank corruption is his greatest charm,
And, far from hurting him, a further shame
Would only serve to magnify his name.
Philinte.   In any case, his bald prevarication

Has done no injury to your reputation,
And you may feel secure in that regard.
As for your lawsuit, it should not be hard
To have the case reopened, and contest
This judgment . . .

Alceste.   No, no, let the verdict rest.
Whatever cruel penalty it may bring,
I wouldn't have it changed for anything.
It shows the times' injustice with such clarity
That I shall pass it down to our posterity
As a great proof and signal demonstration
Of the black wickedness of this generation.
It may cost twenty thousand francs; but I
Shall pay their twenty thousand, and gain thereby
The right to storm and rage at human evil,
And send the race of mankind to the devil.

Philinte.   Listen to me. . . .

Alceste.   Why? What can you possibly say?
Don't argue, Sir; your labor's thrown away.
Do you propose to offer lame excuses
For men's behavior and the times' abuses?

Philinte.   No, all you say I'll readily concede:
This is a low, conniving age indeed;
Nothing but trickery prospers nowadays,
And people ought to mend their shabby ways.
Yes, man's a beastly creature; but must we then
Abandon the society of men?
Here in the world, each human frailty
Provides occasion for philosophy,
And that is virtue's noblest exercise;
If honesty shone forth from all men's eyes,
If every heart were frank and kind and just,
What could our virtues do but gather dust
(Since their employment is to help us bear
The villainies of men without despair)?
A heart well-armed with virtue can endure. . . .

Alceste.   Sir, you're a matchless reasoner, to be sure;
Your words are fine and full of cogency;
But don't waste time and eloquence on me.
My reason bids me go, for my own good.
My tongue won't lie and flatter as it should;
God knows what frankness it might next commit,
And what I'd suffer on account of it.
Pray let me wait for Célimène's return
In peace and quiet. I shall shortly learn,

By her response to what I have in view,
Whether her love for me is feigned or true.
Philinte. Till then, let's visit Éliante upstairs.
Alceste. No, I am too weighed down with somber cares.
Go to her, do; and leave me with my gloom
Here in the darkened corner of this room.
Philinte. Why, that's no sort of company, my friend;
I'll see if Éliante will not descend.

SCENE 2. *Célimène, Oronte, Alceste*

Oronte. Yes, Madam, if you wish me to remain
Your true and ardent lover, you must deign
To give me some more positive assurance.
All this suspense is quite beyond endurance.
If your heart shares the sweet desires of mine,
Show me as much by some convincing sign;
And here's the sign I urgently suggest:
That you no longer tolerate Alceste,
But sacrifice him to my love, and sever
All your relations with the man forever.
Célimène. Why do you suddenly dislike him so?
You praised him to the skies not long ago.
Oronte. Madam, that's not the point. I'm here to find
Which way your tender feelings are inclined.
Choose, if you please, between Alceste and me,
And I shall stay or go accordingly.
Alceste (*emerging from the corner*). Yes, Madam, choose; this gentleman's demand
Is wholly just, and I support his stand.
I too am true and ardent; I too am here
To ask you that you make your feelings clear.
No more delays, now; no equivocation;
The time has come to make your declaration.
Oronte. Sir, I've no wish in any way to be
An obstacle to your felicity.
Alceste. Sir, I've no wish to share her heart with you;
That may sound jealous, but at least it's true.
Oronte. If, weighing us, she leans in your direction . . .
Alceste. If she regards you with the least affection . . .
Oronte. I swear I'll yield her to you there and then.
Alceste. I swear I'll never see her face again.

Oronte.   Now Madam, tell us what we've come to hear.
Alceste.   Madam, speak openly and have no fear.
Oronte.   Just say which one is to remain your lover.
Alceste.   Just name one name, and it will all be over.
Oronte.   What! Is it possible that you're undecided?
Alceste.   What! Can your feelings possibly be divided?
Célimène.   Enough: this inquisition's gone too far:
   How utterly unreasonable you are!
   Not that I couldn't make the choice with ease;
   My heart has no conflicting sympathies;
   I know full well which one of you I favor,
   And you'd not see me hesitate or waver.
   But how can you expect me to reveal
   So cruelly and bluntly what I feel?
   I think it altogether too unpleasant
   To choose between two men when both are present;
   One's heart has means more subtle and more kind
   Of letting its affections be divined,
   Nor need one be uncharitably plain
   To let a lover know he loves in vain.
Oronte.   No, no, speak plainly; I for one can stand it.
   I beg you to be frank.
Alceste.   And I demand it.
   The simple truth is what I wish to know,
   And there's no need for softening the blow.
   You've made an art of pleasing everyone,
   But now your days of coquetry are done:
   You have no choice now, Madam, but to choose,
   For I'll know what to think if you refuse;
   I'll take your silence for a clear admission
   That I'm entitled to my worst suspicion.
Oronte.   I thank you for this ultimatum, Sir,
   And I may say I heartily concur.
Célimène.   Really, this foolishness is very wearing:
   Must you be so unjust and overbearing?
   Haven't I told you why I must demur?
   Ah, here's Éliante; I'll put the case to her.

SCENE 3.   *Éliante, Philinte, Célimène, Oronte, Alceste*

Célimène.   Cousin, I'm being persecuted here
   By these two persons, who, it would appear,
   Will not be satisfied till I confess

Which one I love the more, and which the less,
And tell the latter to his face that he
Is henceforth banished from my company.
Tell me, has ever such a thing been done?

Éliante.   You'd best not turn to me; I'm not the one
To back you in a matter of this kind:
I'm all for those who frankly speak their mind.

Oronte.   Madam, you'll search in vain for a defender.

Alceste.   You're beaten, Madam, and may as well surrender.

Oronte.   Speak, speak, you must; and end this awful strain.

Alceste.   Or don't, and your position will be plain.

Oronte.   A single word will close this painful scene.

Alceste.   But if you're silent, I'll know what you mean.

> **SCENE 4.**   *Arsinoé, Célimène, Éliante, Alceste, Philinte, Acaste, Clitandre, Oronte*

Acaste *(to Célimène)*.   Madam, with all due deference, we two
Have come to pick a little bone with you.

Clitandre *(to Oronte and Alceste)*.   I'm glad you're present, Sirs; as you'll soon learn,
Our business here is also your concern.

Arsinoé *(to Célimène)*.   Madam, I visit you so soon again
Only because of these two gentlemen,
Who came to me indignant and aggrieved
About a crime too base to be believed.
Knowing your virtue, having such confidence in it,
I couldn't think you guilty for a minute,
In spite of all their telling evidence;
And, rising above our little difference,
I've hastened here in friendship's name to see
You clear yourself of this great calumny.

Acaste.   Yes, Madam, let us see with what composure
You'll manage to respond to this disclosure.
You lately sent Clitandre this tender note.

Clitandre.   And this one, for Acaste, you also wrote.

Acaste *(to Oronte and Alceste)*.   You'll recognize this writing, Sirs, I think;
The lady is so free with pen and ink
That you must know it all too well, I fear.
But listen: this is something you should hear.

"How absurd you are to condemn my lightheartedness in society, and to accuse me of being happiest in the company of others. Nothing could be more unjust; and if you do not come to me instantly and beg pardon for saying such a thing, I shall never forgive you as long as I live. Our big bumbling friend the Viscount . . . ."

What a shame that he's not here.

"Our big bumbling friend the Viscount, whose name stands first in your complaint, is hardly a man to my taste; and ever since the day I watched him spend three-quarters of an hour spitting into a well, so as to make circles in the water, I have been unable to think highly of him. As for the little Marquess . . ."

In all modesty, gentlemen, that is I.

"As for the little Marquess, who sat squeezing my hand for such a long while yesterday, I find him in all respects the most trifling creature alive; and the only things of value about him are his cape and his sword. As for the man with the green ribbons . . ."

(To Alceste.)   It's your turn now, Sir.

"As for the man with the green ribbons, he amuses me now and then with his bluntness and his bearish ill-humor; but there are many times indeed when I think him the greatest bore in the world. And as for the sonneteer . . . ."

(To Oronte.)   Here's your helping.

"And as for the sonneteer, who has taken it into his head to be witty, and insists on being an author in the teeth of opinion, I simply cannot be bothered to listen to him, and his prose wearies me quite as much as his poetry. Be assured that I am not always so well-entertained as you suppose; that I long for your company, more than I dare to say, at all these entertainments to which people drag me, and that the presence of those one loves is the true and perfect seasoning to all one's pleasures."

Clitandre.   And now for me.

"Clitandre, whom you mention, and who so pesters me with his saccharine speeches, is the last man on earth for whom I could feel any affection. He is quite mad to suppose that I love him, and so are you, to doubt that you are loved. Do come to your senses; exchange your suppositions for his; and visit me as often as possible, to help me bear the annoyance of his unwelcome attentions."

It's a sweet character that these letters show,
And what to call it, Madam, you well know.

Enough. We're off to make the world acquainted
With this sublime self-portrait that you've painted.
Acaste.   Madam, I'll make you no farewell oration;
No, you're not worthy of my indignation.
Far choicer hearts than yours, as you'll discover,
Would like this little Marquess for a lover.

SCENE 5.   *Célimène, Éliante, Arsinoé, Alceste, Oronte, Philinte*

Oronte.   So! After all those loving letters you wrote,
You turn on me like this, and cut my throat!
And your dissembling, faithless heart, I find,
Has pledged itself by turns to all mankind!
How blind I've been! But now I clearly see;
I thank you, Madam, for enlightening me.
My heart is mine once more, and I'm content;
The loss of it shall be your punishment.

(To Alceste.)

Sir, she is yours; I'll seek no more to stand
Between your wishes and this lady's hand.

SCENE 6.   *Célimène, Éliante, Arsinoé, Alceste, Philinte*

Arsinoé *(to Célimène).*   Madam, I'm forced to speak. I'm far too stirred
To keep my counsel, after what I've heard.
I'm shocked and staggered by your want of morals.
It's not my way to mix in others' quarrels;
But really, when this fine and noble spirit,
This man of honor and surpassing merit,
Laid down the offering of his heart before you,
How *could* you . . .
Alceste.   Madam, permit me, I implore you,
To represent myself in this debate.
Don't bother, please, to be my advocate.
My heart, in any case, could not afford
To give your services their due reward;
And if I chose, for consolation's sake,
Some other lady, 'twould not be you I'd take.

Arsinoé.   What makes you think you could, Sir? And how dare you
  Imply that I've been trying to ensnare you?
  If you can for a moment entertain
  Such flattering fancies, you're extremely vain.
  I'm not so interested as you suppose
  In Célimène's discarded gigolos.
  Get rid of that absurd illusion, do.
  Women like me are not for such as you.
  Stay with this creature, to whom you're so attached;
  I've never seen two people better matched.

SCENE 7.   *Célimène, Éliante, Alceste, Philinte*

Alceste *(to Célimène).*   Well, I've been still throughout this exposé,
  Till everyone but me has said his say.
  Come, have I shown sufficient self-restraint?
  And may I now . . .
Célimène.   Yes, make your just complaint.
  Reproach me freely, call me what you will;
  You've every right to say I've used you ill.
  I've wronged you, I confess it; and in my shame
  I'll make no effort to escape the blame.
  The anger of those others I could despise;
  My guilt toward you I sadly recognize.
  Your wrath is wholly justified, I fear;
  I know how culpable I must appear,
  I know all things bespeak my treachery,
  And that, in short, you've grounds for hating me.
  Do so; I give you leave.
Alceste.   Ah, traitress—how,
  How should I cease to love you, even now?
  Though mind and will were passionately bent
  On hating you, my heart would not consent.

(To Éliante and Philinte.)

  Be witness to my madness, both of you;
  See what infatuation drives one to;
  But wait; my folly's only just begun,
  And I shall prove to you before I'm done
  How strange the human heart is, and how far
  From rational we sorry creatures are.

(*To Célimène.*)

Woman, I'm willing to forget your shame,
And clothe your treacheries in a sweeter name;
I'll call them youthful errors, instead of crimes,
And lay the blame on these corrupting times.
My one condition is that you agree
To share my chosen fate, and fly with me
To that wild, trackless, solitary place
In which I shall forget the human race.
Only by such a course can you atone
For those atrocious letters; by that alone
Can you remove my present horror of you,
And make it possible for me to love you.

Célimène.   What! *I* renounce the world at my young age,
And die of boredom in some hermitage?

Alceste.   Ah, if you really loved me as you ought,
You wouldn't give the world a moment's thought;
Must you have me, and all the world beside?

Célimène.   Alas, at twenty one is terrified
Of solitude. I fear I lack the force
And depth of soul to take so stern a course.
But if my hand in marriage will content you,
Why, there's a plan which I might well consent to,
And . . .

Alceste.   No, I detest you now. I could excuse
Everything else, but since you thus refuse
To love me wholly, as a wife should do,
And see the world in me, as I in you,
Go! I reject your hand, and disenthrall
My heart from your enchantments, once for all.

SCENE 8.   *Éliante, Alceste, Philinte*

Alceste *(to Éliante)*.   Madam, your virtuous beauty has no peer;
Of all this world, you only are sincere;
I've long esteemed you highly, as you know;
Permit me ever to esteem you so,
And if I do not now request your hand,
Forgive me, Madam, and try to understand.
I feel unworthy of it; I sense that fate
Does not intend me for the married state,
That I should do you wrong by offering you

My shattered heart's unhappy residue,
And that in short . . .

Éliante.   Your argument's well taken:
Nor need you fear that I shall feel forsaken.
Were I to offer him this hand of mine,
Your friend Philinte, I think, would not decline.

Philinte.   Ah, Madam, that's my heart's most cherished goal,
For which I'd gladly give my life and soul.

Alceste *(to Éliante and Philinte).*   May you be true to all you now profess,
And so deserve unending happiness.
Meanwhile, betrayed and wronged in everything,
I'll flee this bitter world where vice is king,
And seek some spot unpeopled and apart
Where I'll be free to have an honest heart.

Philinte.   Come, Madam, let's do everything we can
To change the mind of this unhappy man.

QUESTIONS

1.   Contrast Philinte's attitudes with those of Alceste. Why, despite their differences, does Philinte remain loyal to Alceste?   **2.**   What bearing does the exchange between Célimène and Arsinoé at the end of Act III have on the theme of the play?   **3.**   What does Alceste's jealous love for Célimène tell us about his character and principles?   **4.**   Considering Alceste's own attitudes and the kind of society he is a part of, what explanation is there for his assertion (in Act I, Scene 1), regarding his lawsuit, that "Reason and right and justice will plead for me"?   **5.**   What is Éliante's function in the play?

WRITING TOPICS

1.   Does the final scene of the play present a clear resolution of the issues? Explain   **2.**   Is the reader meant to admire Alceste for his principled refusal to abide by the rules of a complacent and superficial aristocratic society, or does Molière want us to laugh at Alceste's rigidity, his insistence on turning everything into a challenge? Explain.

The Stronger*   1889

AUGUST STRINDBERG   [1849–1912]

CHARACTERS

Mrs. X., an actress, married
Miss Y., an actress, unmarried
A Waitress

SCENE

The corner of a ladies' café. Two little iron tables, a red velvet sofa, several chairs. Enter **Mrs. X.,** *dressed in winter clothes, carrying a Japanese basket on her arm.*

Miss Y.   *sits with a half-empty beer bottle before her, reading an illustrated paper, which she changes later for another.*

Mrs. X.   Good afternoon, Amelia. You're sitting here alone on Christmas eve like a poor bachelor!

Miss Y.   *(Looks up, nods, and resumes her reading.)*

Mrs. X.   Do you know it really hurts me to see you like this, alone, in a café, and on Christmas eve, too. It makes me feel as I did one time when I saw a bridal party in a Paris restaurant, and the bride sat reading a comic paper, while the groom played billiards with the witnesses. Huh, thought I, with such a beginning, what will follow, and what will be the end? He played billiards on his wedding eve!   *(Miss Y. starts to speak)*   And she read a comic paper, you mean? Well, they are not altogether the same thing.

(A Waitress enters, places a cup of chocolate before Mrs. X. and goes out.)

Mrs. X.   You know what, Amelia! I believe you would have done better to have kept him! Do you remember, I was the first to say "Forgive him?" Do you remember that? You would be married now and have a home. Remember that Christmas when you went out to visit your fiancé's parents in the country? How you gloried in the happiness of home life and really longed to quit the theater forever? Yes, Amelia dear, home is the best of all—next to the theater—and as for children—well, you don't understand that.

Miss Y. *(Looks up scornfully.)*

---

*Translated by Edith and Warner Oland.

(Mrs. X. sips a few spoonfuls out of the cup, then opens her basket and shows Christmas presents.)

Mrs. X.   Now you shall see what I bought for my piggywigs. *(Takes up a doll.)* Look at this! This is for Lisa, ha! Do you see how she can roll her eyes and turn her head, eh? And here is Maja's popgun.

(Loads it and shoots at Miss Y.)

Miss Y. *(Makes a startled gesture.)*
Mrs. X.   Did I frighten you? Do you think I would like to shoot you, eh? On my soul, if I don't think you did! If you wanted to shoot *me* it wouldn't be so surprising, because I stood in your way—and I know you can never forget that—although I was absolutely innocent. You still believe I intrigued and got you out of the Stora theater, but I didn't. I didn't do that, although you think so. Well, it doesn't make any difference what I say to you. You still believe I did it. *(Takes up a pair of embroidered slippers.)* And these are for my better half. I embroidered them myself—I can't bear tulips, but he wants tulips on everything.
Miss Y. *(Looks up ironically and curiously.)*
Mrs. X. *(putting a hand in each slipper).*   See what little feet Bob has! What? And you should see what a splendid stride he has! You've never seen him in slippers! *(Miss Y. laughs aloud.)* Look! *(She makes the slippers walk on the table. Miss Y. laughs loudly.)* And when he is grumpy he stamps like this with his foot. "What! damn those servants who can never learn to make coffee. Oh, now those creatures haven't trimmed the lamp wick properly!" And then there are drafts on the floor and his feet are cold. "Ugh, how cold it is; the stupid idiots can never keep the fire going." *(She rubs the slippers together, one sole over the other.)*
Miss Y. *(Shrieks with laughter.)*
Mrs. X.   And then he comes home and has to hunt for his slippers which Marie has stuck under the chiffonier—oh, but it's sinful to sit here and make fun of one's husband this way when he is kind and a good little man. You ought to have had such a husband, Amelia. What are you laughing at? What? What? And you see he's true to me. Yes, I'm sure of that, because he told me himself—what are you laughing at?—that when I was touring in Norway that brazen Frederika came and wanted to seduce him! Can you fancy anything so infamous? *(pause)* I'd have torn her eyes out if she had come to see him when I was at home. *(pause)* It was lucky that Bob told me about it himself and that it didn't reach me through gossip. *(pause)* But would you believe it, Frederika wasn't the only one! I don't know why, but the women

are crazy about my husband. They must think he has influence about getting them theatrical engagements, because he is connected with the government. Perhaps you were after him yourself. I didn't use to trust you any too much. But now I know he never bothered his head about you, and you always seemed to have a grudge against him someway.

(Pause. They look at each other in a puzzled way.)

Mrs. X.   Come and see us this evening, Amelia, and show us that you're not put out with us—not put out with me at any rate. I don't know, but I think it would be uncomfortable to have you for an enemy. Perhaps it's because I stood in your way *(more slowly)* or—I really—don't know why—in particular.

(Pause. Miss Y. stares at Mrs. X. curiously.)

Mrs. X.   *(thoughtfully)*.   Our acquaintance has been so queer. When I saw you for the first time I was afraid of you, so afraid that I didn't dare let you out of my sight; no matter when or where, I always found myself near you— I didn't dare have you for an enemy, so I became your friend. But there was always discord when you came to our house, because I saw that my husband couldn't endure you, and the whole thing seemed as awry to me as an ill-fitting gown—and I did all I could to make him friendly toward you, but with no success until you became engaged. Then came a violent friendship between you, so that it looked all at once as though you both dared show your real feelings only when you were secure—and then—how was it later? I didn't get jealous—strange to say! And I remember at the christening, when you acted as godmother, I made him kiss you—he did so, and you became so confused—as it were; I didn't notice it then—didn't think about it later, either—have never thought about it until—now! *(Rises suddenly.)* Why are you silent? You haven't said a word this whole time, but you have let me go on talking! You have sat there, and your eyes have reeled out of me all these thoughts which lay like raw silk in its cocoon—thoughts—suspicious thoughts, perhaps. Let me see—why did you break your engagement? Why do you never come to our house any more? Why won't you come to see us tonight?

(Miss Y. appears as if about to speak.)

Mrs. X.   Hush, you needn't speak—I understand it all! It was because—and because—and because! Yes, yes! Now all the accounts balance. That's it. Fie, I won't sit at the same table with you. *(Moves her things to another table.)* That's the reason I had to embroider tulips—which I hate— on his slippers, because you are fond of tulips; that's why *(throws slippers on the floor)* we go to Lake Mälarn in the summer, because you don't like salt water; that's why my boy is named Eskil—because it's your father's name; that's why I wear your colors, read your authors, eat your favorite dishes, drink your drinks—chocolate, for instance; that's why—oh—my God—it's terrible, when I think about it; it's terrible. Everything, everything came from you to me, even your passions. Your soul crept into mine, like a worm into an apple, ate and ate, bored and bored, until nothing was left but the rind and a little black dust within. I wanted to get away from you, but I couldn't; you lay like a snake and charmed me with your black eyes; I felt that when I lifted my wings they only dragged me down; I lay in the water with bound feet, and the stronger I strove to keep up the deeper I worked myself down, down, until I sank to the bottom, where you lay like a giant crab to clutch me in your claws—and there I am lying now.

I hate you, hate you, hate you! And you only sit there silent—silent and indifferent; indifferent whether it's new moon or waning moon, Christmas or New Year's, whether others are happy or unhappy; without power to hate or to love; as quiet as a stork by a rat hole—you couldn't scent your prey and capture it, but you could lie in wait for it! You sit here in your corner of the café—did you know it's called "The Rat Trap" for you?—and read the papers to see if misfortune hasn't befallen someone, to see if someone hasn't been given notice at the theater, perhaps; you sit here and calculate about your next victim and reckon on your chances of recompense like a pilot in a shipwreck. Poor Amelia, I pity you, nevertheless, because I know you are unhappy, unhappy like one who has been wounded, and angry because you are wounded. I can't be angry with you, no matter how much I want to be— because you come out the weaker one. Yes, all that with Bob doesn't trouble me. What is that to me, after all? And what difference does it make whether I learned to drink chocolate from you or some one else. *(Sips a spoonful from her cup)* Besides, chocolate is very healthful. And if you taught me how to dress—*tant mieux!*[1]—that has only made me more attractive to my husband; so you lost and I won there. Well, judging by certain signs, I believe you have already lost him; and you certainly intended that I should leave him—do as you did with your fiancé and regret as you now regret; but, you see, I don't do that—we mustn't be too exacting. And why should I take only what no one else wants?

Perhaps, take it all in all, I am at this moment the stronger one. You received nothing from me, but you gave me much. And now I seem like a thief since you have awakened and find I possess what is your loss. How could

---

[1]So much the better!

it be otherwise when everything is worthless and sterile in your hands? You can never keep a man's love with your tulips and your passions—but I can keep it. You can't learn how to live from your authors, as I have learned. You have no little Eskil to cherish, even if your father's name was Eskil. And why are you always silent, silent, silent? I thought that was strength, but perhaps it is because you have nothing to say! Because you never think about anything! *(Rises and picks up slippers.)* Now I'm going home—and take the tulips with me—*your* tulips! You are unable to learn from another; you can't bend—therefore, you broke like a dry stalk. But I won't break! Thank you, Amelia, for all your good lessons. Thanks for teaching my husband how to love. Now I'm going home to love him. *(Goes.)*

QUESTIONS

1.   What has been the relationship among Mrs. X, her husband, and Miss Y? Why is Mrs. X hostile to Miss Y?   **2.**   Are we meant to accept Mrs. X's account of the past as accurate, or is there the possibility that she is lying about certain things? Explain.   **3.**   What does Mrs. X discover about the past that she had not known before?   **4.**   Based on what Mrs. X says, how would you characterize Miss Y?   **5.**   To whom does the title refer?

Love and Hate

QUESTIONS AND WRITING TOPICS

1. Every story in this section incorporates some sexual element. Distinguish among the functions served by the sexual aspects of the stories. **Writing Topic:** Contrast the function of sexuality in Lawrence's "The Horse Dealer's Daughter" and Faulkner's "Dry September."

2. Examine the works in this section in terms of the support they provide for the contention that love and hate are closely related emotions. **Writing Topic:** Discuss the relationship between love and hate in Molière's *The Misanthrope* and Shakespeare's *Othello*.

3. What images are characteristically associated with love in the prose and poetry of this section? What images are associated with hate? What insight, if any, does this use of figurative language provide into our cultural evaluations of nature? **Writing Topic:** Compare the image patterns in Shakespeare's sonnets 18 and 130 or the image patterns in Donne's "A Valediction: Forbidding Mourning" and Herrick's "Corinna's Going A-Maying."

4. The Greeks have three words that can be translated by the English word *love: eros, agape,* and *philia*. Discover the differences among these three manifestations of love. **Writing Topic:** For each of these three types of human love, find a story or poem that you think is representative. In analyzing each work, discuss the extent to which the primary notion of love being addressed or celebrated is tempered by the other two types.

5. Blake's "A Poison Tree," Dickinson's "Mine Enemy Is Growing Old," Dugan's "Love Song: I and Thou," and Plath's "Daddy" all seem to describe aspects of hate. How can one distinguish the different varieties of hatred being expressed? **Writing Topic:** Compare and contrast the source of the speaker's hatred in two of these poems.

6. Chopin's "The Storm" and Lessing's "To Room Nineteen" deal with infidelity. Distinguish between the attitudes toward infidelity developed by these stories. **Writing Topic:** Describe the effects of marital infidelity on the lives of the major characters in each story.

7. Mason's "Shiloh" and Lessing's "To Room Nineteen" deal with failed marriages. Why do they fail? **Writing Topic:** Compare and contrast the sources of the marital conflict in these stories.

8. Moravia's "The Chase" and Shaw's "The Girls in Their Summer Dresses" deal with jealousy. Contrast both the sources of the jealousy and the resolution of the problems caused by jealousy in the stories. **Writing Topic:** Who in your opinion has the better reason for being jealous, the husband in "The Chase" or the wife in "The Girls in Their Summer Dresses"? Explain.

9. Which works in this section treat love or hate in a way that corresponds with your own experience or conception of those emotional states? Which contradict your experience? **Writing Topic:** Isolate, in each case, the elements in the work that provoke your response and discuss them in terms of their "truth" or "falsity."

The Presence of Death

The Death Chamber, 1896 by Edvard Munch

The inevitability of death is not implied in the Biblical story of creation; it required an act of disobedience before an angry God passed sentence of hard labor and mortality on humankind: "In the sweat of your face you shall eat bread till you return to the ground, for out of it you were taken; you are dust and to dust you shall return." These words, written down some 2,800 years ago, preserve an ancient explanation for a condition of life that yet remains persistently enigmatic—the dissolution of the flesh and the personality as accident or age culminates in death, the "undiscovered country, from whose bourn / No traveller returns." Though we cannot know what death is like, from earliest times men and women have attempted to characterize death, to cultivate beliefs about it. The mystery of it and the certainty of it make death, in every age, an important theme for literary art.

Beliefs about the nature of death vary widely. The ancient Jews of the Pentateuch reveal no conception of immortality. Ancient Buddhist writings describe death as a mere translation from one painful life to another in an ongoing expiation that only the purest can avoid. The Christians came to conceive of a soul, separate from the body, which at the body's death is freed for a better (or worse) disembodied eternal life. More recently in the western world, the history of the attitudes about death reflects the great ideological revolutions that affected all thought—the Copernican revolution, which displaced the earth from the center of the solar system; the Darwinian revolution, which exchanged for humans, the greatest glory of God's creation, an upright primate with an opposable thumb whose days, like the dinosaur's, are likely to be numbered by the flux between the fire and ice of geological history; and the Freudian revolution, which robbed men and women of their proudest certainty, the conviction that they possessed a dependable and controlling rational mind. All these ideological changes serve to diminish us, to mock our self-importance, and, inevitably, to alter our conception of death.

But despite the impact of intellectual history, death remains invested with a special awe—perhaps because it infallibly mediates between all human differences. For the churchly, death, like birth and marriage, is the occasion for solemn ritual that reaffirms for the congregation its own communal life and the promise of a better life hereafter—though the belief in immortality does not eliminate sadness and regret. For those for whom there is no immortality, death is nonetheless a ceremonial affair, full of awe, for nothing human is so purely defined, so utterly important, as a life ended. Furthermore, both the religious and the secular see death in moral terms. For both, the killer is hateful. For both, there are some deaths that are deserved, some deaths that human weakness makes inevitable, some deaths that are outrageously unfair. For both, there are courageous deaths, which exalt the community, and cowardly deaths too embarrassing to recognize.

For the knight of *The Seventh Seal* and his strange band of followers, death comes, one feels, as a release from a dark and menacing world. And this conception of *release* from the prison of life animates much of the essentially optimistic religious poetry of death—John Donne's sonnet "Death, Be Not Proud" is an outstanding example. Another view that establishes death as the great leveler, bringing kings and emperors to that selfsame dust, reassures the impoverished when they contrast their misery with the wealth of the mighty.

That leveling aspect of death, apparent in such poems as Nashe's "A Litany in Time of Plague" and Shakespeare's "Fear No More the Heat o' the Sun," leads easily and logically to the tradition wherein life itself is made absurd by the fact of death. You may remember that Macbeth finally declares that life is "a tale / Told by an idiot, full of sound and fury, / Signifying nothing." And the contemplation of suicide, which the pain and absurdity of life would seem to commend, provokes such diverse responses as Mishima's macabre story "Patriotism," Arna Bontemp's "A Summer Tragedy," and Edward Arlington Robinson's ironic "Richard Cory." Some rage against death—Dylan Thomas in "Do Not Go Gentle into That Good Night"; others caution a quiet resignation—Frost in "After Apple-Picking" and Catherine Davis in her answer to Thomas, "After a Time." Much fine poetry on death is elegiac; it speaks the melancholy response of the living to the fact of death in such poems as Gray's "Elegy Written in a Country Churchyard," Housman's "To an Athlete Dying Young," Ransom's "Bells for John Whiteside's Daughter," and Roethke's "Elegy for Jane."

In short, literary treatments of death display immense diversity. In Tolstoy's *The Death of Iván Ilých*, dying leads to a redemptive awareness. In Malamud's tragicomic "Idiots First," the protagonist insists upon and wins fair treatment from death, and in Cummings's "nobody loses all the time" and in Woody Allen's "Death Knocks," the comic lightens the weight of death. The circumstances of death and the way one confronts it paradoxically lend to life its meaning and its value.

THE PRESENCE OF DEATH

Sacred to Washington, 1822 by Margarett Smith

FICTION

The Death of Iván Ilých*   1886

LEO TOLSTOY   [1828–1910]

CHAPTER I

During an interval in the Melvínski trial in the large building of the Law Courts the members and public prosecutor met in Iván Egorovich Shébek's private room, where the conversation turned on the celebrated Krasóvski case. Fëdor Vasílievich warmly maintained that it was not subject to their jurisdiction, Iván Egórovich maintained the contrary, while Peter Ivánovich, not having entered into the discussion at the start, took no part in it but looked through the *Gazette* which had just been handed in.

"Gentlemen," he said, "Iván Ilých has died!"

"You don't say so!"

"Here, read it yourself," replied Peter Ivánovich, handing Fëdor Vasílievich the paper still damp from the press. Surrounded by a black border were the words: "Praskóvya Fëdorovna Golovíná, with profound sorrow, informs relatives and friends of the demise of her beloved husband Iván Ilých Golovín, Member of the Court of Justice, which occurred on February the 4th of this year 1882. The funeral will take place on Friday at one o'clock in the afternoon."

Iván Ilých had been a colleague of the gentlemen present and was liked by them all. He had been ill for some weeks with an illness said to be incurable. His post had been kept open for him, but there had been conjectures that in case of his death Alexéev might receive his appointment, and that either Vínnikov or Shtábel would succeed Alexéev. So on receiving the news of Iván Ilých's death the first thought of each of the gentlemen in that private room was of the changes and promotions it might occasion among themselves or their acquaintances.

"I shall be sure to get Shtábel's place or Vínnikov's," thought Fëdor Vasílievich. "I was promised that long ago, and the promotion means an extra eight hundred rubles a year for me besides the allowance."

"Now I must apply for my brother-in-law's transfer from Kalúga," thought

---

* Translated by Aylmer Maude.

Peter Ivánovich. "My wife will be very glad, and then she won't be able to say that I never do anything for her relations."

"I thought he would never leave his bed again," said Peter Ivánovich aloud. "It's very sad."

"But what really was the matter with him?"

"The doctors couldn't say—at least they could, but each of them said something different. When last I saw him I thought he was getting better."

"And I haven't been to see him since the holidays. I always meant to go."

"Had he any property?"

"I think his wife had a little—but something quite trifling."

"We shall have to go to see her, but they live so terribly far away."

"Far away from you, you mean. Everything's far away from your place."

"You see, he never can forgive my living on the other side of the river," said Peter Ivánovich, smiling at Shébek. Then, still talking of the distances between different parts of the city, they returned to the Court.

Besides considerations as to the possible transfers and promotions likely to result from Iván Ilých's death, the mere fact of the death of a near acquaintance aroused, as usual, in all who heard of it the complacent feeling that "it is he who is dead and not I."

Each one thought or felt, "Well, he's dead but I'm alive!" But the more intimate of Iván Ilých's acquaintances, his so-called friends, could not help thinking also that they would now have to fulfill the very tiresome demands of propriety by attending the funeral service and paying a visit of condolence to the widow.

Fëdor Vasílievich and Peter Ivánovich had been his nearest acquaintances. Peter Ivánovich had studied law with Iván Ilých and had considered himself to be under obligations to him.

Having told his wife at dinner-time of Iván Ilých's death, and of his conjecture that it might be possible to get her brother transferred to their circuit, Peter Ivánovich sacrificed his usual nap, put on his evening clothes, and drove to Iván Ilých's house.

At the entrance stood a carriage and two cabs. Leaning against the wall in the hall downstairs near the cloak-stand was a coffin-lid covered with cloth of gold, ornamented with gold cord and tassels, that had been polished up with metal powder. Two ladies in black were taking off their fur cloaks. Peter Ivánovich recognized one of them as Iván Ilých's sister, but the other was a stranger to him. His colleague Schwartz was just coming downstairs, but on seeing Peter Ivánovich enter he stopped and winked at him, as if to say: "Iván Ilých has made a mess of things—not like you and me."

Schwartz's face with his Piccadilly whiskers, and his slim figure in evening dress, had as usual an air of elegant solemnity which contrasted with the playfulness of his character and had a special piquancy here, or so it seemed to Peter Ivánovich.

Peter Ivánovich allowed the ladies to precede him and slowly followed them upstairs. Schwartz did not come down but remained where he was, and Peter

Ivánovich understood that he wanted to arrange where they should play bridge that evening. The ladies went upstairs to the widow's room, and Schwartz with seriously compressed lips but a playful look in his eyes, indicated by a twist of his eye-brows the room to the right where the body lay.

Peter Ivánovich, like everyone else on such occasions, entered feeling uncertain what he would have to do. All he knew was that at such times it is always safe to cross oneself. But he was not quite sure whether one should make obeisances while doing so. He therefore adopted a middle course. On entering the room he began crossing himself and made a slight movement resembling a bow. At the same time, as far as the motion of his head and arm allowed, he surveyed the room. Two young men—apparently nephews, one of whom was a high school pupil—were leaving the room, crossing themselves as they did so. An old woman was standing motionless, and a lady with strangely arched eyebrows was saying something to her in a whisper. A vigorous, resolute Church Reader, in a frock-coat, was reading something in a loud voice with an expression that precluded any contradiction. The butler's assistant, Gerásim, stepping lightly in front of Peter Ivánovich, was strewing something on the floor. Noticing this, Peter Ivánovich was immediately aware of a faint odour of a decomposing body.

The last time he had called on Iván Ilých, Peter Ivánovich had seen Gerásim in the study. Iván Ilých had been particularly fond of him and he was performing the duty of a sick nurse.

Peter Ivánovich continued to make the sign of the cross slightly inclining his head in an intermediate direction between the coffin, the Reader, and the icons on the table in a corner of the room. Afterwards, when it seemed to him that this movement of his arm in crossing himself had gone on too long, he stopped and began to look at the corpse.

The dead man lay, as dead men always lie, in a specially heavy way, his rigid limbs sunk in the soft cushions of the coffin, with the head forever bowed on the pillow. His yellow waxen brow with bald patches over his sunken temples was thrust up in the way peculiar to the dead, the protruding nose seeming to press on the upper lip. He was much changed and had grown even thinner since Peter Ivánovich had last seen him, but, as is always the case with the dead, his face was handsomer and above all more dignified than when he was alive. The expression on the face said that what was necessary had been accomplished, and accomplished rightly. Besides this there was in that expression a reproach and a warning to the living. This warning seemed to Peter Ivánovich out of place, or at least not applicable to him. He felt a certain discomfort and so he hurriedly crossed himself once more and turned and went out of the door—too hurriedly and too regardless of propriety, as he himself was aware.

Schwartz was waiting for him in the adjoining room with legs spread wide apart and both hands toying with his top-hat behind his back. The mere sight of that playful, well-groomed, and elegant figure refreshed Peter Ivánovich. He felt that Schwartz was above all these happenings and would not surrender to any depressing influences. His very look said that this incident of a church service for Iván Ilých could not be a sufficient reason for infringing the order of the session—in other words, that it would certainly not prevent his unwrapping a new pack of cards and shuffling them that evening while a footman placed four fresh candles on the table: in fact, there was no reason for supposing that this incident would hinder their spending the evening agreeably. Indeed he said this in a whisper as Peter Ivánovich passed him, proposing that they should meet for a game at Fëdor Vasílievich's. But apparently Peter Ivánovich was not destined to play bridge that evening. Praskóvya Fëdorovna (a short, fat woman who despite all efforts to the contrary had continued to broaden steadily from her shoulders downwards and who had the same extraordinarily arched eyebrows as the lady who had been standing by the coffin), dressed all in black, her head covered with lace, came out of her own room with some other ladies, conducted them to the room where the dead body lay, and said: "The service will begin immediately. Please go in."

Schwartz, making an indefinite bow, stood still, evidently neither accepting nor declining this invitation. Praskóvya Fëdorovna recognizing Peter Ivánovich, sighed, went close up to him, took his hand, and said: "I know you were a true friend to Iván Ilých . . . " and looked at him awaiting some suitable response. And Peter Ivánovich knew that, just as it had been the right thing to cross himself in that room, so what he had to do here was to press her hand, sigh, and say, "Believe me . . . " So he did all this and as he did it felt that the desired result had been achieved: that both he and she were touched.

"Come with me. I want to speak to you before it begins," said the widow. "Give me your arm."

Peter Ivánovich gave her his arm and they went to the inner rooms, passing Schwartz who winked at Peter Ivánovich compassionately.

"That does for our bridge! Don't object if we find another player. Perhaps you can cut in when you do escape," said his playful look.

Peter Ivánovich sighed still more deeply and despondently, and Praskóvya Fëdorovna pressed his arm gratefully. When they reached the drawing-room, upholstered in pink cretonne and lighted by a dim lamp, they sat down at the table—she on a sofa and Peter Ivánovich on a low pouffe, the springs of which yielded spasmodically under his weight. Praskóvya Fëdorovna had been on the point of warning him to take another seat, but felt that such a warning was out of keeping with her present condition and so changed her mind. As he sat down on the pouffe Peter Ivánovich recalled how Iván Ilých had arranged this room and had consulted him regarding this pink cretonne with green leaves. The whole room was full of furniture and knick-knacks, and on her way to the sofa the lace of the widow's black shawl caught on the carved edge of the table. Peter Ivánovich rose to detach it, and the springs of the pouffe, relieved of his weight, rose also and gave him a push. The widow began detaching her shawl herself, and Peter Ivánovich again sat down, suppressing the rebellious springs of the pouffe under him. But the widow had not quite freed herself and Peter Ivánovich got up again, and again the pouffe rebelled and even creaked. When this was all over she took out a clean cambric handkerchief and began to weep. The

episode with the shawl and the struggle with the pouffe had cooled Peter Ivánovich's emotions and he sat there with a sullen look on his face. This awkward
situation was interrupted by Sokolóv, Iván Ilých's butler, who came to report
that the plot in the cemetery that Praskóvya Fëdorovna had chosen would cost
two hundred rubles. She stopped weeping and, looking at Peter Ivánovich with
the air of a victim, remarked in French that it was very hard for her. Peter
Ivánovich made a silent gesture signifying his full conviction that it must indeed
be so.

"Please smoke," she said in a magnanimous yet crushed voice, and turned
to discuss with Sokolóv the price of the plot for the grave.

Peter Ivánovich while lighting his cigarette heard her inquiring very circum-
stantially into the price of different plots in the cemetery and finally decide
which she would take. When that was done she gave instructions about engaging
the choir. Sokólov then left the room.

"I look after everything myself," she told Peter Ivánovich, shifting the albums
that lay on the table; and noticing that the table was endangered by his cigarette-
ash, she immediately passed him an ashtray, saying as she did so: "I consider
it an affectation to say that my grief prevents my attending to practical affairs.
On the contrary, if anything can—I won't say console me, but—distract me,
it is seeing to everything concerning him." She again took out her handkerchief
as if preparing to cry, but suddenly, as if mastering her feeling, she shook herself
and began to speak calmly. "But there is something I want to talk to you about."

Peter Ivánovich bowed, keeping control of the springs of the pouffe, which
immediately began quivering under him.

"He suffered terribly the last few days."

"Did he?" said Peter Ivánovich.

"Oh, terribly! He screamed unceasingly, not for minutes but for hours. For
the last three days he screamed incessantly. It was unendurable. I cannot understand how I bore it; you could hear him three rooms off. Oh, what I have
suffered!"

"Is it possible that he was conscious all that time?" asked Peter Ivánovich.

"Yes," she whispered. "To the last moment. He took leave of us a quarter of
an hour before he died, and asked us to take Volódya away."

The thought of the sufferings of this man he had known so intimately, first
as a merry little boy, then as a school-mate, and later as a grown-up colleague,
suddenly struck Peter Ivánovich with horror, despite an unpleasant consciousness of his own and this woman's dissimulation. He again saw that brow, and
that nose pressing down on the lip, and felt afraid for himself.

"Three days of frightful suffering and then death! Why, that might suddenly,
at any time, happen to me," he thought, and for a moment felt terrified. But—
he did not himself know how—the customary reflection at once occurred to
him that this had happened to Iván Ilých and not to him, and that it should
not and could not happen to him, and that to think that it could would be
yielding to depression which he ought not to do, as Schwartz's expression plainly
showed. After which reflection Peter Ivánovich felt reassured, and began to ask

with interest about the details of Iván Ilých's death, as though death was an accident natural to Iván Ilých but certainly not to himself.

After many details of the really dreadful physical sufferings Iván Ilých had endured (which details he learnt only from the effect those sufferings had produced on Praskóvya Fëdorovna's nerves) the widow apparently found it necessary to get to business.

"Oh, Peter Ivánovich, how hard it is! How terribly, terribly hard!" and she again began to weep.

Peter Ivánovich sighed and waited for her to finish blowing her nose. When she had done so he said, "Believe me . . ." and she again began talking and brought out what was evidently her chief concern with him—namely, to question him as to how she could obtain a grant of money from the government on the occasion of her husband's death. She made it appear that she was asking Peter Ivánovich's advice about her pension, but he soon saw that she already knew about that to the minutest detail, more even than he did himself. She knew how much could be got out of the government in consequence of her husband's death, but wanted to find out whether she could not possibly extract something more. Peter Ivánovich tried to think of some means of doing so, but after reflecting for a while and, out of propriety, condemning the government for its niggardliness, he said he thought that nothing more could be got. Then she sighed and evidently began to devise means of getting rid of her visitor. Noticing this, he put out his cigarette, rose, pressed her hand, and went out into the anteroom.

In the dining-room where the clock stood that Iván Ilých had liked so much and had bought at an antique shop, Peter Ivánovich met a priest and a few acquaintances who had come to attend the service, and he recognized Iván Ilých's daughter, a handsome young woman. She was in black and her slim figure appeared slimmer than ever. She had a gloomy, determined, almost angry expression, and bowed to Peter Ivánovich as though he were in some way to blame. Behind her, with the same offended look, stood a wealthy young man, an examining magistrate, whom Peter Ivánovich also knew and who was her fiancé, as he had heard. He bowed mournfully to them and was about to pass into the death-chamber, when from under the stairs appeared the figure of Iván Ilých's schoolboy son, who was extremely like his father. He seemed a little Iván Ilých, such as Peter Ivánovich remembered when they studied law together. His tear-stained eyes had in them the look that is seen in the eyes of boys of thirteen or fourteen who are not pure-minded. When he saw Peter Ivánovich he scowled morosely and shame-facedly. Peter Ivánovich nodded to him and entered the death-chamber. The service began: candles, groans, incense, tears, and sobs. Peter Ivánovich stood looking gloomily down at his feet. He did not look once at the dead man, did not yield to any depressing influence, and was one of the first to leave the room. There was no one in the anteroom, but Gerásim darted out of the dead man's room, rummaged with his strong hands among the fur coats to find Peter Ivánovich's and helped him on with it.

"Well, friend Gerásim," said Peter Ivánovich, so as to say something. "It's a sad affair, isn't it?"

"It's God's will. We shall all come to it some day," said Gerásim, displaying his teeth—the even, white teeth of a healthy peasant—and, like a man in the thick of urgent work, he briskly opened the front door, called the coachman, helped Peter Ivánovich into the sledge, and sprang back to the porch as if in readiness for what he had to do next.

Peter Ivánovich found the fresh air particularly pleasant after the smell of incense, the dead body, and carbolic acid.

"Where to, sir?" asked the coachman.

"It's not too late even now. . . . I'll call around on Fëdor Vasílievich."

He accordingly drove there and found them just finishing the first rubber, so that it was quite convenient for him to cut in.

CHAPTER II

Iván Ilých's life had been most simple and most ordinary and therefore most terrible.

He had been a member of the Court of Justice, and died at the age of forty-five. His father had been an official who after serving in various ministries and departments of Petersburg had made the sort of career which brings men to positions from which by reason of their long service they cannot be dismissed, though they are obviously unfit to hold any responsible position, and for whom therefore posts are specially created, which though fictitious carry salaries of from six to ten thousand rubles that are not fictitious, and in receipt of which they live on to a great age.

Such was the Privy Councillor and superfluous member of various superfluous institutions, Ilyá Epímovich Golovín.

He had three sons, of whom Iván Ilých was the second. The eldest son was following in his father's footsteps only in another department, and was already approaching that stage in the service at which a similar sinecure would be reached. The third son was a failure. He had ruined his prospects in a number of positions and was now serving in the railway department. His father and brothers, and still more their wives, not merely disliked meeting him, but avoided remembering his existence unless compelled to do so. His sister had married Baron Greff, a Petersburg official of her father's type. Iván Ilých was *le phénix de la famille*[1] as people said. He was neither as cold and formal as his elder brother nor as wild as the younger, but was a happy mean between them— an intelligent, polished, lively and agreeable man. He had studied with his younger brother at the School of Law, but the latter had failed to complete the course and was expelled when he was in the fifth class. Iván Ilých finished the course well. Even when he was at the School of Law he was just what he remained for the rest of his life: a capable, cheerful, good-natured, and sociable man, though strict in the fulfilment of what he considered to be his duty: and

---

[1] The phoenix of the family, here meaning "rare bird" or "prodigy."

he considered his duty to be what was so considered by those in authority. Neither as a boy nor as a man was he a toady, but from early youth was by nature attracted to people of high station as a fly is drawn to the light, assimilating their ways and views of life and establishing friendly relations with them. All the enthusiasms of childhood and youth passed without leaving much trace on him; he succumbed to sensuality, to vanity, and latterly among the highest classes to liberalism, but always within limits which his instinct unfailingly indicated to him as correct.

At school he had done things which had formerly seemed to him very horrid and made him feel disgusted with himself when he did them; but when later on he saw that such actions were done by people of good position and that they did not regard them as wrong, he was able not exactly to regard them as right, but to forget about them entirely or not be at all troubled at remembering them.

Having graduated from the School of Law and qualified for the tenth rank of the civil service, and having received money from his father for his equipment, Iván Ilých ordered himself clothes at Scharmer's, the fashionable tailor, hung a medallion inscribed *respice finen*[2] on his watch-chain, took leave of his professor and the prince who was patron of the school, had a farewell dinner with his comrades at Donon's first-class restaurant, and with his new and fashionable portmanteau, linen, clothes, shaving and other toilet appliances, and a travelling rug, all purchased at the best shops, he set off for one of the provinces where, through his father's influence, he had been attached to the Governor as an official for special service.

In the province Iván Ilých soon arranged as easy and agreeable a position for himself as he had had at the School of Law. He performed his official tasks, made his career, and at the same time amused himself pleasantly and decorously. Occasionally he paid official visits to country districts, where he behaved with dignity both to his superiors and inferiors, and performed the duties entrusted to him, which related chiefly to the sectarians,[3] with an exactness and incorruptible honesty of which he could not but feel proud.

In official matters, despite his youth and taste for frivolous gaiety, he was exceedingly reserved, punctilious, and even severe; but in society he was often amusing and witty, and always good-natured, correct in his manner, and *bon enfant*, as the governor and his wife—with whom he was like one of the family—used to say of him.

In the provinces he had an affair with a lady who made advances to the elegant young lawyer, and there was also a milliner; and there were carousals with aides-de-camp who visited the district, and after-supper visits to a certain outlying street of doubtful reputation; and there was too some obsequiousness to his chief and even to his chief's wife, but all this was done with such a tone of good breeding that no hard names could be applied to it. It all came under

---

[2] Regard the end.
[3] A large sect, whose members were placed under many legal restrictions, which broke away from the Orthodox Church in the seventeenth century.

the heading of the French saying: "Il faut que jeunesse se passe."[4] It was all done with clean hands, in clean linen, with French phrases, and above all among people of the best society and consequently with the approval of people of rank.

So Iván Ilých served for five years and then came a change in his official life. The new and reformed judicial institutions were introduced, and new men were needed. Iván Ilých became such a new man. He was offered the post of Examining Magistrate, and he accepted it though the post was in another province and obliged him to give up the connexions he had formed and to make new ones. His friends met to give him a send-off; they had a group-photograph taken and presented him with a silver cigarette-case, and he set off to his new post.

As examining magistrate Iván Ilých was just as *comme il faut*[5] and decorous a man, inspiring general respect and capable of separating his official duties from his private life, as he had been when acting as an official on special service. His duties now as examining magistrate were far more interesting and attractive than before. In his former position it had been pleasant to wear an undress uniform made by Scharmer, and to pass through the crowd of petitioners and officials who were timorously awaiting an audience with the governor, and who envied him as with free and easy gait he went straight into his chief's private room to have a cup of tea and a cigarette with him. But not many people had then been directly dependent on him—only police officials and the sectarians when he went on special missions—and he liked to treat them politely, almost as comrades, as if he were letting them feel that he who had the power to crush them was treating them in this simple, friendly way. There were then but few such people. But now, as an examining magistrate, Iván Ilých felt that everyone without exception, even the most important and self-satisfied, was in his power, and that he need only write a few words on a sheet of paper with a certain heading, and this or that important, self-satisfied person would be brought before him in the role of an accused person or a witness, and if he did not choose to allow him to sit down, would have to stand before him and answer his questions. Iván Ilých never abused his power; he tried on the contrary to soften its expression, but the consciousness of it and of the possibility of softening its effect, supplied the chief interest and attraction of his office. In his work itself, especially in his examinations, he very soon acquired a method of eliminating all considerations irrelevant to the legal aspect of the case, and reducing even the most complicated case to a form in which it would be presented on paper only in its externals, completely excluding his personal opinion of the matter, while above all observing every prescribed formality. The work was new and Iván Ilých was one of the first men to apply the new Code of 1864.[6]

On taking up the post of examining magistrate in a new town, he made new acquaintances and connexions, placed himself on a new footing, and assumed

---

[4] Youth must have its fling.
[5] Proper.
[6] Judicial procedures were thoroughly reformed after the emancipation of the serfs in 1861.

a somewhat different tone. He took up an attitude of rather dignified aloofness towards the provincial authorities, but picked out the best circle of legal gentlemen and wealthy gentry living in the town and assumed a tone of slight dissatisfaction with the government, of moderate liberalism, and of enlightened citizenship. At the same time, without at all altering the elegance of his toilet, he ceased shaving his chin and allowed his beard to grow as it pleased.

Iván Ilých settled down very pleasantly in this new town. The society there, which inclined towards opposition to the Governor, was friendly, his salary was larger, and he began to play *vint*,[7] which he found added not a little to the pleasure of life, for he had a capacity for cards, played good-humouredly, and calculated rapidly and astutely, so that he usually won.

After living there for two years he met his future wife, Praskóvya Fëdorovna Míkhel, who was the most attractive, clever, and brilliant girl of the set in which he moved, and among other amusements and relaxations from his labours as examining magistrate, Iván Ilých established light and playful relations with her.

While he had been an official on special service he had been accustomed to dance, but now as an examining magistrate it was exceptional for him to do so. If he danced now, he did it as if to show that though he served under the reformed order of things, and had reached the fifth official rank, yet when it came to dancing he could do it better than most people. So at the end of an evening he sometimes danced with Praskóvya Fëdorovna, and it was chiefly during these dances that he captivated her. She fell in love with him. Iván Ilých had at first no definite intention of marrying, but when the girl fell in love with him he said to himself: "Really, why shouldn't I marry?"

Praskóvya Fëdorovna came of a good family, was not bad looking and had some little property. Iván Ilých might have aspired to a more brilliant match, but even this was good. He had his salary, and she, he hoped, would have an equal income. She was well connected, and was a sweet, pretty, and thoroughly correct young woman. To say that Iván Ilých married because he fell in love with Praskóvya Fëdorovna and found that she sympathized with his views of life would be as incorrect as to say that he married because his social circle approved of the match. He was swayed by both these considerations: the marriage gave him personal satisfaction, and at the same time it was considered the right thing by the most highly placed of his associates.

So Iván Ilých got married.

The preparations for marriage and the beginning of married life, with its conjugal caresses, the new furniture, new crockery, and new linen, were very pleasant until his wife became pregnant—so that Iván Ilých had begun to think that marriage would not impair the easy, agreeable, gay and always decorous character of his life, approved of by society and regarded by himself as natural, but would even improve it. But from the first months of his wife's pregnancy, something new, unpleasant, depressing, and unseemly, and from which there was no way of escape, unexpectedly showed itself.

---

[7] A card game similar to bridge.

His wife, without any reason—*de gaieté de coeur* as Iván Ilých expressed it to himself—began to disturb the pleasure and propriety of their life. She began to be jealous without any cause, expected him to devote his whole attention to her, found fault with everything, and made coarse and ill-mannered scenes.

At first Iván Ilých hoped to escape from the unpleasantness of this state of affairs by the same easy and decorous relation to life that had served him heretofore: he tried to ignore his wife's disagreeable moods, continued to live in his usual easy and pleasant way, invited friends to his house for a game of cards, and also tried going out to his club or spending his evenings with friends. But one day his wife began upbraiding him so vigorously, using such coarse words, and continued to abuse him every time he did not fulfil her demands, so resolutely and with such evident determination not to give way till he submitted—that is, till he stayed at home and was bored just as she was—that he became alarmed. He now realized that matrimony—at any rate with Praskóvya Fëdorovna—was not always conducive to the pleasures and amenities of life but on the contrary often infringed both comfort and propriety, and that he must therefore entrench himself against such infringement. And Iván Ilých began to seek for means of doing so. His official duties were the one thing that imposed upon Praskóvya Fëdorovna, and by means of his official work and the duties attached to it he began struggling with his wife to secure his own independence.

With the birth of their child, the attempts to feed it and the various failures in doing so, and with the real and imaginary illnesses of mother and child, in which Iván Ilých's sympathy was demanded but about which he understood nothing, the need of securing for himself an existence outside his family life became still more imperative.

As his wife grew more irritable and exacting and Iván Ilých transferred the centre of gravity of his life more and more to his official work, so did he grow to like his work better and became more ambitious than before.

Very soon, within a year of his wedding, Iván Ilých had realized that marriage, though it may add some comforts to life, is in fact a very intricate and difficult affair towards which in order to perform one's duty, that is, to lead a decorous life approved of by society, one must adopt a definite attitude just as towards one's official duties.

And Iván Ilých evolved such an attitude towards married life. He only required of it those conveniences—dinner at home, housewife, and bed—which it could give him, and above all that propriety of external forms required by public opinion. For the rest he looked for light-hearted pleasure and propriety, and was very thankful when he found them, but if he met with antagonism and querulousness he at once retired into his separate fenced-off world of official duties, where he found satisfaction.

Iván Ilých was esteemed a good official, and after three years was made Assistant Public Prosecutor. His new duties, their importance, the possibility of indicting and imprisoning anyone he chose, the publicity his speeches received, and the success he had in all these things, made his work still more attractive.

More children came. His wife became more and more querulous and ill-tempered, but the attitude Iván Ilých had adopted towards his home life rendered him almost impervious to her grumbling.

After seven years' service in that town he was transferred to another province as Public Prosecutor. They moved, but were short of money and his wife did not like the place they moved to. Though the salary was higher the cost of living was greater, besides which two of their children died and family life became still more unpleasant for him.

Praskóvya Fëdorovna blamed her husband for every inconvenience they encountered in their new home. Most of the conversations between husband and wife, especially as to the children's education, led to topics which recalled former disputes, and those disputes were apt to flare up again at any moment. There remained only those rare periods of amorousness which still came to them at times but did not last long. These were islets at which they anchored for a while and then again set out upon that ocean of veiled hostility which showed itself in their aloofness from one another. This aloofness might have grieved Iván Ilých had he considered that it ought not to exist, but he now regarded the position as normal, and even made it the goal at which he aimed in family life. His aim was to free himself more and more from those unpleasantnesses and to give them a semblance of harmlessness and propriety. He attained this by spending less and less time with his family, and when obliged to be at home he tried to safeguard his position by the presence of outsiders. The chief thing however was that he had his official duties. The whole interest of his life now centered in the official world and that interest absorbed him. The consciousness of his power, being able to ruin anybody he wished to ruin, the importance, even the external dignity of his entry into court, or meetings with his subordinates, his success with superiors and inferiors, and above all his masterly handling of cases, of which he was conscious—all this gave him pleasure and filled his life, together with chats with his colleagues, dinners, and bridge. So that on the whole Iván Ilých's life continued to flow as he considered it should do—pleasantly and properly.

So things continued for another seven years. His eldest daughter was already sixteen, another child had died, and only one son was left, a schoolboy and a subject of dissension. Iván Ilých wanted to put him in the School of Law, but to spite him Praskóvya Fëdorovna entered him at the High School. The daughter had been educated at home and had turned out well: the boy did not learn badly either.

CHAPTER III

So Iván Ilých lived for seventeen years after his marriage. He was already a Public Prosecutor of long standing, and had declined several proposed transfers while awaiting a more desirable post, when an unanticipated and unpleasant occurrence quite upset the peaceful course of his life. He was expecting to be offered the post of presiding judge in a University town, but Happe somehow came to the front and obtained the appointment instead. Iván Ilých became irritable, reproached Happe, and quarrelled both with him and with his immediate superiors—who became colder to him and again passed him over when other appointments were made.

This was in 1880, the hardest year of Iván Ilých's life. It was then that it became evident on the one hand that his salary was insufficient for them to live on, and on the other that he had been forgotten, and not only this, but that what was for him the greatest and most cruel injustice appeared to others a quite ordinary occurrence. Even his father did not consider it his duty to help him. Iván Ilých felt himself abandoned by everyone, and that they regarded his position with a salary of 3,500 rubles as quite normal and even fortunate. He alone knew that with the consciousness of the injustices done him, with his wife's incessant nagging, and with the debts he had contracted by living beyond his means, his position was far from normal.

In order to save money that summer he obtained leave of absence and went with his wife to live in the country at her brother's place.

In the country, without his work, he experienced *ennui* for the first time in his life, and not only *ennui* but intolerable depression, and he decided that it was impossible to go on living like that, and that it was necessary to take energetic measures.

Having passed a sleepless night pacing up and down the veranda, he decided to go to Petersburg and bestir himself, in order to punish those who had failed to appreciate him and to get transferred to another ministry.

Next day, despite many protests from his wife and her brother, he started for Petersburg with the sole object of obtaining a post with a salary of five thousand rubles a year. He was no longer bent on any particular department, or tendency, or kind of activity. All he now wanted was an appointment to another post with a salary of five thousand rubles, either in the administration, in the banks, with the railways, in one of the Empress Márya's Institutions,[8] or even in the customs—but it had to carry with it a salary of five thousand rubles and be in a ministry other than that in which they had failed to appreciate him.

And this quest of Iván Ilých's was crowned with remarkable and unexpected success. At Kursk an acquaintance of his, F. I. Ilyín, got into the first-class carriage, sat down beside Iván Ilých, and told him of a telegram just received by the Governor of Kursk announcing that a change was about to take place in the ministry: Peter Ivánovich was to be superseded by Iván Semënovich.

The proposed change, apart from its significance for Russia, had a special significance for Iván Ilých, because by bringing forward a new man, Peter Petróvich, and consequently his friend Zachár Ivánovich, it was highly favourable for Iván Ilých, since Zachár Ivánovich was a friend and colleague of his.

In Moscow this news was confirmed, and on reaching Petersburg Iván Ilých found Zachár Ivánovich and received a definite promise of an appointment in his former Department of Justice.

---

[8] A charitable organization founded in the late eighteenth century by the Empress Márya.

A week later he telegraphed to his wife: "Zachár in Miller's place. I shall receive appointment on presentation of report."

Thanks to this change of personnel, Iván Ilých had unexpectedly obtained an appointment in his former ministry which placed him two stages above his former colleagues besides giving him five thousand rubles salary and three thousand five hundred rubles for expenses connected with his removal. All his ill humour towards his former enemies and the whole department vanished, and Iván Ilých was completely happy.

He returned to the country more cheerful and contented than he had been for a long time. Praskóvya Fëdorovna also cheered up and a truce was arranged between them. Iván Ilých told of how he had been fêted by everybody in Petersburg, how all those who had been his enemies were put to shame and now fawned on him, how envious they were of his appointment, and how much everybody in Petersburg had liked him.

Praskóvya Fëdorovna listened to all this and appeared to believe it. She did not contradict anything, but only made plans for their life in the town to which they were going. Iván Ilých saw with delight that these plans were his plans, that he and his wife agreed, and that, after a stumble, his life was regaining its due and natural character of pleasant lightheartedness and decorum.

Iván Ilých had come back for a short time only, for he had to take up his new duties on the 10th of September. Moreover, he needed time to settle into the new place, to move all his belongings from the province, and to buy and order many additional things: in a word, to make such arrangements as he had resolved on, which were almost exactly what Praskóvya Fëdorovna too had decided on.

Now that everything had happened so fortunately, and that he and his wife were at one in their aims and moreover saw so little of one another, they got on together better than they had done since the first years of marriage. Iván Ilých had thought of taking his family away with him at once, but the insistence of his wife's brother and her sister-in-law, who had suddenly become particularly amiable and friendly to him and his family, induced him to depart alone.

So he departed, and the cheerful state of mind induced by his success and by the harmony between his wife and himself, the one intensifying the other, did not leave him. He found a delightful house, just the thing both he and his wife had dreamt of. Spacious, lofty reception rooms in the old style, a convenient and dignified study, rooms for his wife and daughter, a study for his son— it might have been specially built for them. Iván Ilých himself superintended the arrangements, chose the wall-papers, supplemented the furniture (preferably with antiques which he considered particularly *comme il faut*), and supervised the upholstering. Everything progressed and progressed and approached the ideal he had set himself: even when things were only half completed they exceeded his expectations. He saw what a refined and elegant character, free from vulgarity, it would all have when it was ready. On falling asleep he pictured to himself how the reception-room would look. Looking at the yet unfinished drawing-room he could see the fireplace, the screen, the what-not, the little chairs dotted here and there, the dishes and plates on the walls, and the bronzes, as they would be when everything was in place. He was pleased by the thought of how his wife and daughter, who shared his taste in this matter, would be impressed by it. They were certainly not expecting as much. He had been particularly successful in finding, and buying cheaply, antiques which gave a particularly aristocratic character to the whole place. But in his letters he intentionally understated everything in order to be able to surprise them. All this so absorbed him that his new duties—though he liked his official work—interested him less than he had expected. Sometimes he even had moments of absent-mindedness during the Court Sessions, and would consider whether he should have straight or curved cornices for his curtains. He was so interested in it all that he often did things himself, rearranging the furniture, or rehanging the curtains. Once when mounting a step-ladder to show the upholsterer, who did not understand, how he wanted the hangings draped, he made a false step and slipped, but being a strong and agile man he clung on and only knocked his side against the knob of the window frame. The bruised place was painful but the pain soon passed, and he felt particularly bright and well just then. He wrote: "I feel fifteen years younger." He thought he would have everything ready by September, but it dragged on till mid-October. But the result was charming not only in his eyes but to everyone who saw it.

In reality it was just what is usually seen in the houses of people of moderate means who want to appear rich, and therefore succeed only in resembling others like themselves: there were damasks, dark wood, plants, rugs, and dull and polished bronzes—all the things people of a certain class have in order to resemble other people of that class. His house was so like the others that it would never have been noticed, but to him it all seemed to be quite exceptional. He was very happy when he met his family at the station and brought them to the newly furnished house all lit up, where a footman in a white tie opened the door into the hall decorated with plants, and when they went on into the drawing-room and the study uttering exclamations of delight. He conducted them everywhere, drank in their praises eagerly, and beamed with pleasure. At tea that evening, when Praskóvya Fëdorovna among other things asked him about his fall, he laughed, and showed them how he had gone flying and had frightened the upholsterer.

"It's a good thing I'm a bit of an athlete. Another man might have been killed, but I merely knocked myself, just here; it hurts when it's touched, but it's passing off already—it's only a bruise."

So they began living in their new home—in which, as always happens, when they got thoroughly settled in they found they were just one room short—and with the increased income, which as always was just a little (some five hundred rubles) too little, but it was all very nice.

Things went particularly well at first, before everything was finally arranged and while something had still to be done: this thing bought, that thing ordered, another thing moved, and something else adjusted. Though there were some disputes between husband and wife, they were both so well satisfied and had so much to do that it all passed off without any serious quarrels. When nothing was left to arrange it became rather dull and something seemed to be lacking, but they were then making acquaintances, forming habits, and life was growing fuller.

Iván Ilých spent his mornings at the law court and came home to dinner, and at first he was generally in a good humour, though he occasionally became irritable just on account of his house. (Every spot on the tablecloth or the upholstery, and every broken window-blind string, irritated him. He had devoted so much trouble to arranging it all that every disturbance of it distressed him.) But on the whole his life ran its course as he believed life should do: easily, pleasantly, and decorously.

He got up at nine, drank his coffee, read the paper, and then put on his undress uniform and went to the law courts. There the harness in which he worked had already been stretched to fit him and he donned it without a hitch: petitioners, inquiries at the chancery, the chancery itself, and the sittings public and administrative. In all this the thing was to exclude everything fresh and vital, which always disturbs the regular course of official business, and to admit only official relations with people, and then only on official grounds. A man would come, for instance, wanting some information. Iván Ilých, as one in whose sphere the matter did not lie, would have nothing to do with him: but if the man had some business with him in his official capacity, something that could be expressed on officially stamped paper, he would do everything, positively everything he could within the limits of such relations, and in doing so would maintain the semblance of friendly human relations, that is, would observe the courtesies of life. As soon as the official relations ended, so did everything else. Iván Ilých possessed this capacity to separate his real life from the official side of affairs and not mix the two, in the highest degree, and by long practice and natural aptitude had brought it to such a pitch that sometimes, in the manner of a virtuoso, he would even allow himself to let the human and official relations mingle. He let himself do this just because he felt that he could at any time he chose resume the strictly official attitude again and drop the human relation. And he did it all easily, pleasantly, correctly, and even artistically. In the intervals between the sessions he smoked, drank tea, chatted a little about politics, a little about general topics, a little about cards, but most of all about official appointments. Tired, but with the feelings of a virtuoso— one of the first violins who has played his part in an orchestra with precision— he would return home to find that his wife and daughter had been out paying calls, or had a visitor, and that his son had been to school, had done his homework with his tutor, and was duly learning what is taught at High Schools. Everything was as it should be. After dinner, if they had no visitors, Iván Ilých sometimes read a book that was being much discussed at the time, and in the evening settled down to work, that is, read official papers, compared the depositions of witnesses, and noted paragraphs of the Code applying to them. This was neither dull nor amusing. It was dull when he might have been playing bridge, but if no bridge was available it was at any rate better than doing nothing or sitting with his wife. Iván Ilých's chief pleasure was giving little dinners to which he invited men and women of good social position, and just as his drawing-room resembled all other drawing-rooms so did his enjoyable little parties resemble all other such parties.

Once they even gave a dance. Iván Ilých enjoyed it and everything went off well, except that it led to a violent quarrel with his wife about the cakes and sweets. Praskóvya Fëdorovna had made her own plans, but Iván Ilých insisted on getting everything from an expensive confectioner and ordered too many cakes, and the quarrel occurred because some of those cakes were left over and the confectioner's bill came to forty-five rubles. It was a great and disagreeable quarrel. Praskóvya Fëdorovna called him "a fool and an imbecile," and he clutched at his head and made angry allusions to divorce.

But the dance itself had been enjoyable. The best people were there, and Iván Ilých had danced with Princess Trúfonova, a sister of the distinguished founder of the Society "Bear my Burden."

The pleasures connected with his work were pleasures of ambition; his social pleasures were those of vanity; but Iván Ilých's greatest pleasure was playing bridge. He acknowledged that whatever disagreeable incident happened in his life, the pleasure that beamed like a ray of light above everything else was to sit down to bridge with good players, not noisy partners, and of course to four-handed bridge (with five players it was annoying to have to stand out, though one pretended not to mind), to play a clever and serious game (when the cards allowed it) and then to have supper and drink a glass of wine. After a game of bridge, especially if he had won a little (to win a large sum was unpleasant), Iván Ilých went to bed in specially good humour.

So they lived. They formed a circle of acquaintances among the best people and were visited by people of importance and by young folk. In their views as to their acquaintances, husband, wife and daughter were entirely agreed, and tacitly and unanimously kept at arm's length and shook off the various shabby friends and relations who, with much show of affection, gushed into the draw-ing-room with its Japanese plates on the walls. Soon these shabby friends ceased to obtrude themselves and only the best people remained in the Golovíns' set.

Young men made up to Lisa, and Petríshchev, an examining magistrate and Dmítri Ivanovich Petríshchev's son and sole heir, began to be so attentive to her that Iván Ilých had already spoken to Praskóvya Fëdorovna about it, and considered whether they should not arrange a party for them or get up some private theatricals.

So they lived, and all went well, without change, and life flowed pleasantly.

CHAPTER IV

They were all in good health. It could not be called ill health if Iván Ilých sometimes said that he had a queer taste in his mouth and felt some discomfort in his left side.

But this discomfort increased and, though not exactly painful, grew into a sense of pressure in his side accompanied by ill humour. And his irritability became worse and worse and began to mar the agreeable, easy, and correct life that had established itself in the Golovín family. Quarrels between husband and wife became more and more frequent, and soon the ease and amenity disappeared and even the decorum was barely maintained. Scenes again became frequent, and very few of those islets remained on which husband and wife could meet without an explosion. Praskóvya Fëdorovna now had good reason to say that her husband's temper was trying. With characteristic exaggeration she said he had always had a dreadful temper, and that it had needed all her good nature to put up with it for twenty years. It was true that now the quarrels were started by him. His bursts of temper always came just before dinner, often just as he began to eat his soup. Sometimes he noticed that a plate or dish was chipped, or the food was not right, or his son put his elbow on the table, or his daughter's hair was not done as he liked it, and for all this he blamed Praskóvya Fëdorovna. At first she retorted and said disagreeable things to him, but once or twice he fell into such a rage at the beginning of dinner that she realized it was due to some physical derangement brought on by taking food, and so she restrained herself and did not answer, but only hurried to get the dinner over. She regarded this self-restraint as highly praiseworthy. Having come to the conclusion that her husband had a dreadful temper and made her life miserable, she began to feel sorry for herself, and the more she pitied herself the more she hated her husband. She began to wish he would die; yet she did not want him to die because then his salary would cease. And this irritated her against him still more. She considered herself dreadfully unhappy just because not even his death could save her, and though she concealed her exasperation, that hidden exasperation of hers increased his irritation also.

After one scene in which Iván Ilých had been particularly unfair and after which he had said in explanation that he certainly was irritable but that it was due to his not being well, she said that if he was ill it should be attended to, and insisted on his going to see a celebrated doctor.

He went. Everything took place as he had expected and as it always does. There was the usual waiting and the important air assumed by the doctor, with which he was so familiar (resembling that which he himself assumed in court), and the sounding and listening, and the questions which called for answers that were forgone conclusions and were evidently unnecessary, and the look of importance which implied that "if only you put yourself in our hands we will arrange everything—we know indubitably how it has to be done, always in the same way for everybody alike." It was all just as it was in the law courts. The doctor put on just the same air towards him as he himself put on towards an accused person.

The doctor said that so-and-so indicated that there was so-and-so inside the patient, but if the investigation of so-and-so did not confirm this, then he must assume that and that. If he assumed that and that, then . . . and so on. To Iván Ilých only one question was important: was his case serious or not? But the doctor ignored that inappropriate question. From his point of view it was not the one under consideration, the real question was to decide between a floating kidney, chronic catarrh, or appendicitis. It was not a question of Iván Ilých's life or death, but one between a floating kidney and appendicitis. And that question the doctor solved brilliantly, as it seemed to Iván Ilých, in favour of the appendix, with the reservation that should an examination of the urine give fresh indications the matter would be reconsidered. All this was just what Iván Ilých had himself brilliantly accomplished a thousand times in dealing with men on trial. The doctor summed up just as brilliantly, looking over his spectacles triumphantly and even gaily at the accused. From the doctor's summing up Iván Ilých concluded that things were bad, but that for the doctor, and perhaps for everybody else, it was a matter of indifference, though for him it was bad. And this conclusion struck him painfully, arousing in him a great feeling of pity for himself and of bitterness towards the doctor's indifference to a matter of such importance.

He said nothing of this, but rose, placed the doctor's fee on the table, and remarked with a sigh: "We sick people probably often put inappropriate questions. But tell me, in general, is this complaint dangerous, or not? . . ."

The doctor looked at him sternly over his spectacles with one eye, as if to say: "Prisoner, if you will not keep to the questions put to you, I shall be obliged to have you removed from the court."

"I have already told you what I consider necessary and proper. The analysis may show something more." And the doctor bowed.

Iván Ilých went out slowly, seated himself disconsolately in his sledge, and drove home. All the way home he was going over what the doctor had said, trying to translate those complicated, obscure, scientific phrases into plain language and find in them an answer to the question: "Is my condition bad? Is it very bad? Or is there as yet nothing much wrong?" And it seemed to him that the meaning of what the doctor had said was that it was very bad. Everything in the streets seemed depressing. The cabmen, the houses, the passers-by, and the shops, were dismal. His ache, this dull gnawing ache that never ceased for a moment, seemed to have acquired a new and more serious significance from the doctor's dubious remarks. Iván Ilých now watched it with a new and oppressive feeling.

He reached home and began to tell his wife about it. She listened, but in the middle of his account his daughter came in with her hat on, ready to go out with her mother. She sat down reluctantly to listen to this tedious story, but could not stand it long, and her mother too did not hear him to the end.

"Well, I am very glad," she said. "Mind now to take your medicine regularly. Give me the prescription and I'll send Gerásim to the chemist's." And she went to get ready to go out.

While she was in the room Iván Ilých had hardly taken time to breathe, but he sighed deeply when she left it.

"Well," he thought, "perhaps it isn't so bad after all."

He began taking his medicine and following the doctor's directions, which had been altered after the examination of the urine. But then it happened that there was a contradiction between the indications drawn from the examination of the urine and the symptoms that showed themselves. It turned out that what was happening differed from what the doctor had told him, and that he had either forgotten, or blundered, or hidden something from him. He could not, however, be blamed for that, and Iván Ilých still obeyed his orders implicitly and at first derived some comfort from doing so.

From the time of his visit to the doctor, Iván Ilých's chief occupation was the exact fulfilment of the doctor's instructions regarding hygiene and the taking of medicine, and the observation of his pain and his excretions. His chief interests came to be people's ailments and people's health. When sickness, deaths, or recoveries, were mentioned in his presence, especially when the illness resembled his own, he listened with agitation which he tried to hide, asked questions, and applied what he heard to his own case.

The pain did not grow less, but Iván Ilých made efforts to force himself to think that he was better. And he could do this so long as nothing agitated him. But as soon as he had any unpleasantness with his wife, any lack of success in his official work, or held bad cards at bridge, he was at once acutely sensible of his disease. He had formerly borne such mischances, hoping soon to adjust what was wrong, to master it and attain success, or make a grand slam. But now every mischance upset him and plunged him into despair. He would say to himself: "There now, just as I was beginning to get better and the medicine had begun to take effect, comes this accursed misfortune, or unpleasantness . . . " And he was furious with the mishap, or with the people who were causing the unpleasantness and killing him, for he felt that this fury was killing him but could not restrain it. One would have thought that it should have been clear to him that this exasperation with circumstances and people aggravated his illness, and that he ought therefore to ignore unpleasant occurrences. But he drew the very opposite conclusion: he said that he needed peace, and he watched for everything that might disturb it and became irritable at the slightest infringement of it. His condition was rendered worse by the fact that he read medical books and consulted doctors. The progress of his disease was so gradual that he could deceive himself when comparing one day with another—the difference was so slight. But when he consulted the doctors it seemed to him that he was getting worse, and even very rapidly. Yet despite this he was continually consulting them.

That month he went to see another celebrity, who told him almost the same as the first had done but put his questions rather differently, and the interview with this celebrity only increased Iván Ilých's doubts and fears. A friend of a friend of his, a very good doctor, diagnosed his illness again quite differently from the others, and though he predicted recovery, his questions and suppositions bewildered Iván Ilých still more and increased his doubts. A homoeopathist diagnosed the disease in yet another way, and prescribed medicine which Iván Ilých took secretly for a week. But after a week, not feeling any improvement and having lost confidence both in the former doctor's treatment and in this one's, he became still more despondent. One day a lady acquaintance mentioned a cure effected by a wonder-working icon. Iván Ilých caught himself listening attentively and beginning to believe that it had occurred. This incident alarmed him. "Has my mind really weakened to such an extent?" he asked himself. "Nonsense! It's all rubbish. I mustn't give way to nervous fears but having chosen a doctor must keep strictly to his treatment. That is what I will do. Now it's all settled. I won't think about it, but will follow the treatment seriously till summer, and then we shall see. From now there must be no more of this wavering!" This was easy to say but impossible to carry out. The pain in his side oppressed him and seemed to grow worse and more incessant, while the taste in his mouth grew stranger and stranger. It seemed to him that his breath had a disgusting smell, and he was conscious of a loss of appetite and strength. There was no deceiving himself: something terrible, new, and more important than anything before in his life, was taking place within him of which he alone was aware. Those about him did not understand or would not understand it, but thought everything in the world was going on as usual. That tormented Iván Ilých more than anything. He saw that his household, especially his wife and daughter who were in a perfect whirl of visiting, did not understand anything of it and were annoyed that he was so depressed and so exacting, as if he were to blame for it. Though they tried to disguise it he saw that he was an obstacle in their path, and that his wife had adopted a definite line in regard to his illness and kept to it regardless of anything he said or did. Her attitude was this: "You know," she would say to her friends, "Iván Ilých can't do as other people do, and keep to the treatment prescribed for him. One day he'll take his drops and keep strictly to his diet and go to bed in good time, but the next day unless I watch him he'll suddenly forget his medicine, eat sturgeon— which is forbidden—and sit up playing cards till one o'clock in the morning."

"Oh, come, when was that?" Iván Ilých would ask in vexation. "Only once at Peter Ivánovich's."

"And yesterday with Shébek."

"Well, even if I hadn't stayed up, this pain would have kept me awake."

"Be that as it may you'll never get well like that, but will always make us wretched."

Praskóvya Fëdorovna's attitude to Iván Ilých's illness, as she expressed it both to others and to him, was that it was his own fault and was another of the annoyances he caused her. Iván Ilých felt that this opinion escaped her involuntarily—but that did not make it easier for him.

At the law courts too, Iván Ilých noticed, or thought he noticed, a strange attitude towards himself. It sometimes seemed to him that people were watching him inquisitively as a man whose place might soon be vacant. Then again, his friends would suddenly begin to chaff him in a friendly way about his low spirits, as if the awful, horrible, and unheard-of thing that was going on within him, incessantly gnawing at him and irresistibly drawing him away, was a very agreeable subject for jests. Schwartz in particular irritated him by his jocularity, vivacity, and *savoir-faire*, which reminded him of what he himself had been ten years ago.

Friends came to make up a set and they sat down to cards. They dealt,

bending the new cards to soften them, and he sorted the diamonds in his hand
and found he had seven. His partner said "No trumps" and supported him with
two diamonds. What more could be wished for? It ought to be jolly and lively.
They would make a grand slam. But suddenly Iván Ilých was conscious of that
gnawing pain, that taste in his mouth, and it seemed ridiculous that in such
circumstances he should be pleased to make a grand slam.

He looked at his partner Mikháil Mikháylovich, who rapped the table with
his strong hand and instead of snatching up the tricks pushed the cards courteously and indulgently towards Iván Ilých that he might have the pleasure of
gathering them up without the trouble of stretching out his hand for them.
"Does he think I am too weak to stretch out my arm?" thought Iván Ilých, and
forgetting what he was doing he over-trumped his partner, missing the grand
slam by three tricks. And what was most awful of all was that he saw how upset
Mikháil Mikháylovich was about it but did not himself care. And it was dreadful
to realize why he did not care.

They all saw that he was suffering, and said: "We can stop if you are tired.
Take a rest." Lie down? No, he was not at all tired, and he finished the rubber.
All were gloomy and silent. Iván Ilých felt that he diffused this gloom over them
and could not dispel it. They had supper and went away, and Iván Ilých was
left alone with the consciousness that his life was poisoned and was poisoning
the lives of others, and that this poison did not weaken but penetrated more and
more deeply into his whole being.

With this consciousness, and with physical pain besides the terror, he must
go to bed, often to lie awake the greater part of the night. Next morning he had
to get up again, dress, go to the law courts, speak, and write; or if he did not
go out, spend at home those twenty-four hours a day each of which was a
torture. And he had to live thus all alone on the brink of an abyss, with no one
who understood or pitied him.

CHAPTER V

So one month passed and then another. Just before the New Year his brother-
in-law came to town and stayed at their house. Iván Ilých was at the law courts
and Praskóvya Fëdorovna had gone shopping. When Iván Ilých came home
and entered his study he found his brother-in-law there—a healthy, florid
man—unpacking his portmanteau himself. He raised his head on hearing Iván
Ilých's footsteps and looked up at him for a moment without a word. That stare
told Iván Ilých everything. His brother-in-law opened his mouth to utter an
exclamation of surprise but checked himself, and that action confirmed it all.

"I have changed, eh?"

"Yes, there is a change."

And after that, try as he would to get his brother-in-law to return to the
subject of his looks, the latter would say nothing about it. Praskóvya Fëdorovna
came home and her brother went out to her. Iván Ilých locked the door and
began to examine himself in the glass, first full face, then in profile. He took

up a portrait of himself taken with his wife, and compared it with what he saw in the glass. The change in him was immense. Then he bared his arms to the elbow, looked at them, drew the sleeves down again, sat down on an ottoman, and grew blacker than night.

"No, no, this won't do!" he said to himself, and jumped up, went to the table, took up some law papers and began to read them, but could not continue. He unlocked the door and went into the reception-room. The door leading to the drawing-room was shut. He approached it on tiptoe and listened.

"No, you are exaggerating!" Praskóvya Fëdorovna was saying.

"Exaggerating! Don't you see it? Why, he's a dead man! Look at his eyes—there's no light in them. But what is it that is wrong with him?"

"No one knows. Nikoláevich (that was another doctor) said something, but I don't know what. And Leshchetítsky (this was the celebrated specialist) said quite the contrary . . ."

Iván Ilých walked away, went to his own room, lay down, and began musing: "The kidney, a floating kidney." He recalled all the doctors had told him of how it detached itself and swayed about. And by an effort of imagination he tried to catch that kidney and arrest it and support it. So little was needed for this, it seemed to him. "No, I'll go to see Peter Ivánovich again." (That was the friend whose friend was a doctor.) He rang, ordered the carriage, and got ready to go.

"Where are you going, Jean?" asked his wife, with a specially sad and exceptionally kind look.

This exceptionally kind look irritated him. He looked morosely at her.

"I must go to see Peter Ivánovich."

He went to see Peter Ivánovich, and together they went to see his friend, the doctor. He was in, and Iván Ilých had a long talk with him.

Reviewing the anatomical and physiological details of what in the doctor's opinion was going on inside him, he understood it all.

There was something, a small thing, in the vermiform appendix. It might all come right. Only stimulate the energy of one organ and check the activity of another, then absorption would take place and everything would come right. He got home rather late for dinner, ate his dinner, and conversed cheerfully, but could not for a long time bring himself to go back to work in his room. At last, however, he went to his study and did what was necessary, but the consciousness that he had put something aside—an important, intimate matter which he would revert to when his work was done—never left him. When he had finished his work he remembered that this intimate matter was the thought of his vermiform appendix. But he did not give himself up to it, and went to the drawing-room for tea. There were callers there, including the examining magistrate who was a desirable match for his daughter, and they were conversing, playing the piano and singing. Iván Ilých, as Praskóvya Fëdorovna remarked, spent that evening more cheerfully than usual, but he never for a moment forgot that he had postponed the important matter of the appendix. At eleven o'clock he said good-night and went to his bedroom. Since his illness he had slept alone in a small room next to his study. He undressed and took up a novel by Zola, but instead of reading it he fell into thought, and in his imagination that desired improvement in the vermiform appendix occurred. There was the absorption and evacuation and the reestablishment of normal activity. "Yes, that's it!" he said to himself. "One need only assist nature, that's all." He remembered his medicine, rose, took it, and lay down on his back watching for the beneficent action of the medicine and for it to lessen the pain. "I need only take it regularly and avoid all injurious influences. I am already feeling better, much better." He began touching his side: it was not painful to the touch. "There, I really don't feel it. It's much better already." He put out the light and turned on his side . . . "The appendix is getting better, absorption is occurring." Suddenly he felt the old, familiar, dull, gnawing pain, stubborn and serious. There was the same familiar loathsome taste in his mouth. His heart sank and he felt dazed. "My God! My God!" he muttered. "Again, again! And it will never cease." And suddenly the matter presented itself in a quite different aspect. "Vermiform appendix! Kidney!" he said to himself. "It's not a question of appendix or kidney, but of life and . . . death. Yes, life was there and now it is going, going and I cannot stop it. Yes. Why deceive myself? Isn't it obvious to everyone but me that I'm dying, and that it's only a question of weeks, days . . . it may happen this moment. There was light and now there is darkness. I was here and now I'm going there! Where?" A chill came over him, his breathing ceased, and he felt only the throbbing of his heart.

"When I am not, what will there be? There will be nothing. Then where shall I be when I am no more? Can this be dying? No, I don't want to!" He jumped up and tried to light the candle, felt for it with trembling hands, dropped candle and candlestick on the floor, and fell back on his pillow.

"What's the use? It makes no difference," he said to himself, staring with wide-open eyes into the darkness. "Death. Yes, death. And none of them know or wish to know it, and they have no pity for me. Now they are playing." (He heard through the door the distant sound of a song and its accompaniment.) "It's all the same to them, but they will die too! Fools! I first, and they later, but it will be the same for them. And now they are merry . . . the beasts!"

Anger choked him and he was agonizingly, unbearably miserable. "It is impossible that all men have been doomed to suffer this awful horror!" He raised himself.

"Something must be wrong. I must calm myself—must think it all over from the beginning." And he again began thinking. "Yes, the beginning of my illness: I knocked my side, but I was still quite well that day and the next. It hurt a little, then rather more. I saw the doctors, then followed despondency and anguish, more doctors, and I drew nearer to the abyss. My strength grew less and I kept coming nearer and nearer, and now I have wasted away and there is no light in my eyes. I think of the appendix—but this is death! I think of mending the appendix, and all the while here is death! Can it really be death?" Again terror seized him and he gasped for breath. He leant down and began feeling for the matches, pressing with his elbow on the stand beside the bed. It was in his way and hurt him, he grew furious with it, pressed on it still harder, and upset it. Breathless and in despair he fell on his back, expecting death to come immediately.

Meanwhile the visitors were leaving. Praskóvya Fëdorovna was seeing them off. She heard something fall and came in.

"What has happened?"

"Nothing. I knocked it over accidentally."

She went out and returned with a candle. He lay there panting heavily, like a man who has run a thousand yards, and stared upwards at her with a fixed look.

"What is it, Jean?"

"No . . . o . . . thing. I upset it." ("Why speak of it? She won't understand," he thought.)

And in truth she did not understand. She picked up the stand, lit his candle, and hurried away to see another visitor off. When she came back he still lay on his back, looking upwards.

"What is it? Do you feel worse?"

"Yes."

She shook her head and sat down.

"Do you know, Jean, I think we must ask Leshchetítsky to come and see you here."

This meant calling in the famous specialist, regardless of expense. He smiled malignantly and said "No." She remained a little longer and then went up to him and kissed his forehead.

While she was kissing him he hated her from the bottom of his soul and with difficulty refrained from pushing her away.

"Good-night. Please God you'll sleep."

"Yes."

CHAPTER VI

Iván Ilých saw that he was dying, and he was in continual despair.

In the depth of his heart he knew he was dying, but not only was he not accustomed to the thought, he simply did not and could not grasp it.

The syllogism he had learnt from Kiezewetter's Logic:[9] "Caius is a man, men are mortal, therefore Caius is mortal," had always seemed to him correct as applied to Caius, but certainly not as applied to himself. That Caius—man in the abstract—was mortal, was perfectly correct, but he was not Caius, not an abstract man, but a creature quite, quite separate from all others. He had been little Ványa, with a mamma and a papa; with Mitya and Volódya, and the toys, a coachman and a nurse, afterwards with Kátenka and with all the joys, griefs, and delights of childhood, boyhood, and youth. What did Caius know of the

---

[9] Karl Kiezewetter (1766–1819), author of an outline of logic widely used in Russian schools at the time.

smell of that striped leather ball Ványa had been so fond of? Had Caius kissed his mother's hand like that, and did the silk of her dress rustle so for Caius? Had he rioted like that at school when the pastry was bad? Had Caius been in love like that? Could Caius preside at a session as he did? "Caius really was mortal, and it was right for him to die; but for me, little Ványa, Iván Ilých, with all my thoughts and emotions, it's altogether a different matter. It cannot be that I ought to die. That would be too terrible."

Such was his feeling.

"If I had to die like Caius I should have known it was so. An inner voice would have told me so, but there was nothing of the sort in me and I and all my friends felt that our case was quite different from that of Caius. And now here it is!" he said to himself. "It can't be. It's impossible! But here it is. How is this? How is one to understand it?"

He could not understand it, and tried to drive this false, incorrect, morbid thought away and to replace it by other proper and healthy thoughts. But that thought and not the thought only but the reality itself, seemed to come and confront him.

And to replace that thought he called up a succession of others, hoping to find in them some support. He tried to get back into the former current of thoughts that had once screened the thought of death from him. But strange to say, all that had formerly shut off, hidden, and destroyed, his consciousness of death, no longer had that effect. Iván Ilých now spent most of his time in attempting to re-establish that old current. He would say to himself: "I will take up my duties again—after all I used to live by them." And banishing all doubts he would go to the law courts, enter into conversation with his colleagues, and sit carelessly as was his wont, scanning the crowd with a thoughtful look and leaning both his emaciated arms on the arms of his oak chair; bending over as usual to a colleague and drawing his papers nearer he would interchange whispers with him, and then suddenly raising his eyes and sitting erect would pronounce certain words and open the proceedings. But suddenly in the midst of those proceedings the pain in his side, regardless of the stage the proceedings had reached, would begin its own gnawing work. Iván Ilých would turn his attention to it and try to drive the thought of it away, but without success. *It* would come and stand before him and look at him, and he would be petrified and the light would die out of his eyes, and he would again begin asking himself whether *It* alone was true. And his colleagues and subordinates would see with surprise and distress that he, the brilliant and subtle judge, was becoming confused and making mistakes. He would shake himself, try to pull himself together, manage somehow to bring the sitting to a close, and return home with the sorrowful consciousness that his judicial labours could not as formerly hide from him what he wanted them to hide, and could not deliver him from *It*. And what was worst of all was that *It* drew his attention to itself not in order to make him take some action but only that he should look at *It*, look it straight in the face: look at it and without doing anything, suffer inexpressibly.

And to save himself from this condition Iván Ilých looked for consolations—new screens—and new screens were found and for a while seemed to save him, but then they immediately fell to pieces or rather became transparent, as if *It* penetrated them and nothing could veil *It*.

In these latter days he would go into the drawing-room he had arranged—that drawing-room where he had fallen and for the sake of which (how bitterly ridiculous it seemed) he had sacrificed his life—for he knew that his illness originated with that knock. He would enter and see that something had scratched the polished table. He would look for the cause of this and find that it was the bronze ornamentation of an album, that had got bent. He would take up the expensive album which he had lovingly arranged, and feel vexed with his daughter and her friends for their untidiness—for the album was torn here and there and some of the photographs turned upside down. He would put it carefully in order and bend the ornamentation back into position. Then it would occur to him to place all those things in another corner of the room, near the plants. He could call the footman, but his daughter or wife would come to help him. They would not agree, and his wife would contradict him, and he would dispute and grow angry. But that was all right, for then he did not think about *It*. *It* was invisible.

But then, when he was moving something himself, his wife would say: "Let the servants do it. You will hurt yourself again." And suddenly *It* would flash through the screen and he would see it. It was just a flash, and he hoped it would disappear, but he would involuntarily pay attention to his side. "It sits there as before, gnawing just the same!" And he could no longer forget *It*, but could distinctly see it looking at him from behind the flowers. "What is it all for?"

"It really is so! I lost my life over that curtain as I might have done when storming a fort. Is that possible? How terrible and how stupid. It can't be true! It can't, but it is!"

He would go to his study, lie down, and again be alone with *It*: face to face with *It*. And nothing could be done with *It* except to look at it and shudder.

CHAPTER VII

How it happened it is impossible to say because it came about step by step, unnoticed, but in the third month of Iván Ilých's illness, his wife, his daughter, his son, his acquaintances, the doctors, the servants, and above all he himself, were aware that the whole interest he had for other people was whether he would soon vacate his place, and at last release the living from the discomfort caused by his presence and be himself released from his sufferings.

He slept less and less. He was given opium and hypodermic injections of morphine, but this did not relieve him. The dull depression he experienced in a somnolent condition at first gave him a little relief, but only as something new, afterwards it became as distressing as the pain itself or even more so.

Special foods were prepared for him by the doctors' orders, but all those foods became increasingly distasteful and disgusting to him.

For his excretions also special arrangements had to be made, and this was a torment to him every time—a torment from the uncleanliness, the unseemliness, and the smell, and from knowing that another person had to take part in it.

But just through this most unpleasant matter Iván Ilých obtained comfort. Gerásim, the butler's young assistant, always came in to carry the things out. Gerásim was a clean, fresh peasant lad, grown stout on town food and always cheerful and bright. At first the sight of him, in his clean Russian peasant costume, engaged on that disgusting task embarrassed Iván Ilých.

Once when he got up from the commode too weak to draw up his trousers, he dropped into a soft armchair and looked with horror at his bare, enfeebled thighs with the muscles so sharply marked on them.

Gerásim with a firm light tread, his heavy boots emitting a pleasant smell of tar and fresh winter air, came in wearing a clean Hessian apron, the sleeves of his print shirt tucked up over his strong bare young arms; and refraining from looking at his sick master out of consideration for his feelings, and restraining the joy of life that beamed from his face, went up to the commode.

"Gerásim!" said Iván Ilých in a weak voice.

Gerásim started, evidently afraid he might have committed some blunder, and with a rapid movement turned his fresh, kind, simple young face which just showed the first downy signs of a beard.

"Yes, sir?"

"That must be very unpleasant for you. You must forgive me. I am helpless."

"Oh, why, sir," and Gerásim's eyes beamed and he showed his glistening white teeth, "what's a little trouble? It's a case of illness with you, sir."

And his deft strong hands did their accustomed task, and he went out of the room stepping lightly. Five minutes later he as lightly returned.

Iván Ilých was still sitting in the same position in the armchair.

"Gerásim," he said when the latter had replaced the freshly-washed utensil. "Please come here and help me." Gerásim went up to him. "Lift me up. It is hard for me to get up, and I have sent Dmítri away."

Gerásim went up to him, grasped his master with his strong arms deftly but gently, in the same way that he stepped—lifted him, supported him with one hand, and with the other drew up his trousers and would have set him down again, but Iván Ilých asked to be led to the sofa. Gerásim, without an effort and without apparent pressure, led him, almost lifting him, to the sofa and placed him on it.

"Thank you. How easily and well you do it all!"

Gerásim smiled again and turned to leave the room. But Iván Ilých felt his presence such a comfort that he did not want to let him go.

"One thing more, please move up that chair. No, the other one—under my feet. It is easier for me when my feet are raised."

Gerásim brought the chair, set it down gently in place, and raised Iván Ilých's legs on to it. It seemed to Iván Ilých that he felt better while Gerásim was holding up his legs.

"It's better when my legs are higher," he said. "Place that cushion under them."

Gerásim did so. He again lifted the legs and placed them, and again Iván Ilých felt better while Gerásim held his legs. When he set them down Iván Ilých fancied he felt worse.

"Gerásim," he said. "Are you busy now?"

"Not at all, sir," said Gerásim, who had learnt from the townsfolk how to speak to gentlefolk.

"What have you still to do?"

"What have I to do? I've done everything except chopping the logs for to-morrow."

"Then hold my legs up a bit higher, can you?"

"Of course I can. Why not?" And Gerásim raised his master's legs higher and Iván Ilých thought that in that position he did not feel any pain at all.

"And how about the logs?"

"Don't trouble about that, sir. There's plenty of time."

Iván Ilých told Gerásim to sit down and hold his legs, and began to talk to him. And strange to say it seemed to him that he felt better while Gerásim held his legs up.

After that Iván Ilých would sometimes call Gerásim and get him to hold his legs on his shoulders, and he liked talking to him. Gerásim did it all easily, willingly, simply, and with a good nature that touched Iván Ilých. Health, strength, and vitality in other people were offensive to him, but Gerásim's strength and vitality did not mortify but soothed him.

What tormented Iván Ilých most was the deception, the lie, which for some reason they all accepted, that he was not dying but was simply ill, and that he only need keep quiet and undergo a treatment and then something very good would result. He however knew that do what they would nothing would come of it, only still more agonizing suffering and death. This deception tortured him—their not wishing to admit what they all knew and what he knew, but wanting to lie to him concerning his terrible condition, and wishing and forcing him to participate in that lie. Those lies—lies enacted over him on the eve of his death and destined to degrade this awful, solemn act to the level of their visitings, their curtains, their sturgeon for dinner—were a terrible agony for Iván Ilých. And strangely enough, many times when they were going through their antics over him he had been within a hairbreadth of calling out to them: "Stop lying! You know and I know that I am dying. Then at least stop lying about it!" But he had never had the spirit to do it. The awful, terrible act of his dying was, he could see, reduced by those about him to the level of a casual, un-pleasant, and almost indecorous incident (as if someone entered a drawing-room diffusing an unpleasant odour) and this was done by that very decorum which he had served all his life long. He saw that no one felt for him, because no one even wished to grasp his position. Only Gerásim recognized it and pitied him.

And so Iván Ilých felt at ease only with him. He felt comforted when Gerásim supported his legs (sometimes all night long) and refused to go to bed, saying: "Don't you worry, Iván Ilých. I'll get sleep enough later on," or when he suddenly became familiar and exclaimed: "If you weren't sick it would be another matter, but as it is, why should I grudge a little trouble?" Gerásim alone did not lie; everything showed that he alone understood the facts of the case and did not consider it necessary to disguise them, but simply felt sorry for his emaciated and enfeebled master. Once when Iván Ilých was sending him away he even said straight out: "We shall all of us die, so why should I grudge a little trouble?"—expressing the fact that he did not think his work burdensome, because he was doing it for a dying man and hoped someone would do the same for him when his time came.

Apart from this lying, or because of it, what most tormented Iván Ilých was that no one pitied him as he wished to be pitied. At certain moments after prolonged suffering he wished most of all (though he would have been ashamed to confess it) for someone to pity him as a sick child is pitied. He longed to be petted and comforted. He knew he was an important functionary, that he had a beard turning grey, and that therefore what he longed for was impossible, but still he longed for it. And in Gerásim's attitude towards him there was something akin to what he wished for, and so that attitude comforted him. Iván Ilých wanted to weep, wanted to be petted and cried over, and then his colleague Shébek would come, and instead of weeping and being petted, Iván Ilých would assume a serious, severe, and profound air, and by force of habit would express his opinion on a decision of the Court of Cassation and would stubbornly insist on that view. This falsity around him and within him did more than anything else to poison his last days.

CHAPTER VIII

It was morning. He knew it was morning because Gerásim had gone, and Peter the footman had come and put out the candles, drawn back one of the curtains, and begun quietly to tidy up. Whether it was morning or evening, Friday or Sunday, made no difference, it was all just the same: the gnawing, unmitigated, agonizing pain, never ceasing for an instant, the consciousness of life inexorably waning but not yet extinguished, that approach of that ever dreaded and hateful Death which was the only reality, and always the same falsity. What were days, weeks, hours, in such a case?

"Will you have some tea, sir?"

"He wants things to be regular, and wishes the gentlefolk to drink tea in the morning," thought Iván Ilých, and only said "No."

"Wouldn't you like to move onto the sofa, sir?"

"He wants to tidy up the room, and I'm in the way. I am uncleanliness and disorder," he thought, and said only:

"No, leave me alone."

The man went on bustling about. Iván Ilých stretched out his hand. Peter came up, ready to help.

"What is it, sir?"

"My watch."

Peter took the watch which was close at hand and gave it to his master.

"Half-past eight. Are they up?"

"No sir, except Vladímir Ivánich" (the son) "who has gone to school. Praskóvya Fëdorovna ordered me to wake her if you asked for her. Shall I do so?"

"No, there's no need to." "Perhaps I'd better have some tea," he thought, and added aloud: "Yes, bring me some tea."

Peter went to the door but Iván Ilých dreaded being left alone. "How can I keep him here? Oh yes, my medicine." "Peter, give me my medicine." "Why not? Perhaps it may still do me some good." He took a spoonful and swallowed it. "No, it won't help. It's all tomfoolery, all deception," he decided as soon as he became aware of the familiar, sickly, hopeless taste. "No, I can't believe in it any longer. But the pain, why this pain? If it would only cease just for a moment!" And he moaned. Peter turned towards him. "It's all right. Go and fetch me some tea."

Peter went out. Left alone Iván Ilých groaned not so much with pain, terrible though that was, as from mental anguish. Always and for ever the same, always these endless days and nights. If only it would come quicker! If only *what* would come quicker? Death, darkness? . . . No, no! Anything rather than death!

When Peter returned with the tea on a tray, Iván Ilých stared at him for a time in perplexity, not realizing who and what he was. Peter was disconcerted by that look and his embarrassment brought Iván Ilých to himself.

"Oh, tea! All right, put it down. Only help me to wash and put on a clean shirt."

And Iván Ilých began to wash. With pauses for rest, he washed his hands and then his face, cleaned his teeth, brushed his hair, and looked in the glass. He was terrified by what he saw, especially by the limp way in which his hair clung to his pallid forehead.

While his shirt was being changed he knew that he would be still more frightened at the sight of his body, so he avoided looking at it. Finally he was ready. He drew on a dressing-gown, wrapped himself in a plaid, and sat down in the armchair to take his tea. For a moment he felt refreshed, but as soon as he began to drink the tea he was again aware of the same taste, and the pain also returned. He finished it with an effort, and then lay down stretching out his legs, and dismissed Peter.

Always the same. Now a spark of hope flashes up, then a sea of despair rages, and always pain; always pain, always despair, and always the same. When alone he had a dreadful and distressing desire to call someone, but he knew beforehand that with others present it would be still worse. "Another dose of morphine—to lose consciousness. I will tell him, the doctor, that he must think of something else. It's impossible, impossible, to go on like this."

An hour and another pass like that. But now there is a ring at the door bell. Perhaps it's the doctor? It is. He comes in fresh, hearty, plump, and cheerful, with that look on his face that seems to say: "There now, you're in a panic about something, but we'll arrange it all for you directly!" The doctor knows this expression is out of place here, but he has put it on once for all and can't take it off—like a man who has put on a frock-coat in the morning to pay a round of calls.

The doctor rubs his hands vigorously and reassuringly.

"Brr! How cold it is! There's such a sharp frost; just let me warm myself!" he says, as if it were only a matter of waiting till he was warm, and then he would put everything right.

"Well now, how are you?"

Iván Ilých feels that the doctor would like to say: "Well, how are our affairs?" but that even he feels that this would not do, and says instead: "What sort of a night have you had?"

Iván Ilých looks at him as much as to say: "Are you really never ashamed of lying?" But the doctor does not wish to understand this question, and Iván Ilých says: "Just as terrible as ever. The pain never leaves me and never subsides. If only something . . . ."

"Yes, you sick people are always like that. . . . There, now I think I am warm enough. Even Praskóvya Fëdorovna, who is so particular, could find no fault with my temperature. Well, now I can say good-morning," and the doctor presses his patient's hand.

Then, dropping his former playfulness, he begins with a most serious face to examine the patient, feeling his pulse and taking his temperature, and then begins the sounding and auscultation.

Ivan Ilých knows quite well and definitely that all this is nonsense and pure deception, but when the doctor, getting down on his knee, leans over him, putting his ear first higher then lower, and performs various gymnastic movements over him with a significant expression on his face, Iván Ilých submits to it all as he used to submit to the speeches of the lawyers, though he knew very well that they were all lying and why they were lying.

The doctor, kneeling on the sofa, is still sounding him when Praskóvya Fëdorovna's silk dress rustles at the door and she is heard scolding Peter for not having let her know of the doctor's arrival.

She comes in, kisses her husband, and at once proceeds to prove that she has been up a long time already, and only owing to a misunderstanding failed to be there when the doctor arrived.

Iván Ilých looks at her, scans her all over, sets against her the whiteness and plumpness and cleanness of her hands and neck, the gloss of her hair, and the sparkle of her vivacious eyes. He hates her with his whole soul. And the thrill of hatred he feels for her makes him suffer from her touch.

Her attitude towards him and his disease is still the same. Just as the doctor had adopted a certain relation to his patient which he could not abandon, so had she formed one towards him—that he was not doing something he ought to do and was himself to blame, and that she reproached him lovingly for this— and she could not now change that attitude.

"You see he doesn't listen to me and doesn't take his medicine at the proper time. And above all he lies in a position that is no doubt bad for him—with his legs up."

She described how he made Gerásim hold his legs up.

The doctor smiled with a contemptuous affability that said: "What's to be done? These sick people do have foolish fancies of that kind, but we must forgive them."

When the examination was over the doctor looked at his watch, and then Praskóvya Fëdorovna announced to Iván Ilých that it was of course as he pleased, but she had sent to-day for a celebrated specialist who would examine him and have a consultation with Michael Danílovich (their regular doctor).

"Please don't raise any objections. I am doing this for my own sake," she said ironically, letting it be felt that she was doing it all for his sake and only said that to leave him no right to refuse. He remained silent, knitting his brows. He felt that he was so surrounded and involved in a mesh of falsity that it was hard to unravel anything.

Everything she did for him was entirely for her own sake, and she told him she was doing for herself what she actually was doing for herself, as if that was so incredible that he must understand the opposite.

At half-past eleven the celebrated specialist arrived. Again the sounding began and the significant conversations in his presence and in another room, about the kidneys and the appendix, and the questions and answers, with such an air of importance that again, instead of the real question of life and death which now alone confronted him, the question arose of the kidney and appendix which were not behaving as they ought to and would now be attacked by Michael Danílovich and the specialist and forced to amend their ways.

The celebrated specialist took leave of him with a serious though not hopeless look, and in reply to the timid question Iván Ilých, with eyes glistening with fear and hope, put to him as to whether there was a chance of recovery, said that he could not vouch for it but there was a possibility. The look of hope with which Iván Ilých watched the doctor out was so pathetic that Praskóvya Fëdorovna, seeing it, even wept as she left the room to hand the doctor his fee.

The gleam of hope kindled by the doctor's encouragement did not last long. The same room, the same pictures, curtains, wall-paper, medicine bottles, were all there, and the same aching suffering body, and Iván Ilých began to moan. They gave him a subcutaneous injection and he sank into oblivion.

It was twilight when he came to. They brought him his dinner and he swallowed some beef tea with difficulty, and then everything was the same again and night was coming on.

After dinner, at seven o'clock, Praskóvya Fëdorovna came into the room in evening dress, her full bosom pushed up by her corset, and with traces of powder on her face. She had reminded him in the morning that they were going to the theatre. Sarah Bernhardt was visiting the town and they had a box, which he had insisted on their taking. Now he had forgotten about it and her toilet offended him, but he concealed his vexation when he remembered that he had himself insisted on their securing a box and going because it would be an instructive and aesthetic pleasure for the children.

Praskóvya Fëdorovna came in, self-satisfied but yet with a rather guilty air. She sat down and asked how he was but, as he saw, only for the sake of asking and not in order to learn about it, knowing that there was nothing to learn— and then went on to what she really wanted to say: that she would not on any account have gone but that the box had been taken and Helen and their daughter were going, as well as Petríshchev (the examining magistrate, their daughter's fiancé) and that it was out of the question to let them go alone; but that she would have much preferred to sit with him for a while; and he must be sure to follow the doctor's orders while she was away.

"Oh, and Fëdor Petróvich" (the fiancé) "would like to come in. May he? And Lisa?"

"All right."

Their daughter came in in full evening dress, her fresh young flesh exposed (making a show of that very flesh which in his own case caused so much suffering), strong, healthy, evidently in love, and impatient with illness, suffering, and death, because they interfered with her happiness.

Fëdor Petróvich came in too, in evening dress, his hair curled á la Capoul, a tight stiff collar round his long sinewy neck, an enormous white shirt-front and narrow black trousers tightly stretched over his strong thighs. He had one white glove tightly drawn on, and was holding his opera hat in his hand.

Following him the schoolboy crept in unnoticed, in a new uniform, poor little fellow, and wearing gloves. Terribly dark shadows showed under his eyes, the meaning of which Iván Ilých knew well.

His son had always seemed pathetic to him, and now it was dreadful to see the boy's frightened look of pity. It seemed to Iván Ilých that Vásya was the only one besides Gerásim who understood and pitied him.

They all sat down and again asked how he was. A silence followed. Lisa asked her mother about the opera-glasses, and there was an altercation between mother and daughter as to who had taken them and where they had been put. This occasioned some unpleasantness.

Fëdor Petróvich inquired of Iván Ilých whether he had ever seen Sarah Bernhardt. Iván Ilých did not at first catch the question, but then replied: "No, have you seen her before?"

"Yes, In *Adrienne Lecouvreur*." [10]

Praskóvya Fëdorovna mentioned some roles in which Sarah Bernhardt was particularly good. Her daughter disagreed. Conversation sprang up as to the elegance and realism of her acting—the sort of conversation that is always repeated and is always the same.

---

[10] A play by the French dramatist Eugène Scribe (1791–1861).

In the midst of the conversation Fëdor Petróvich glanced at Iván Ilých and became silent. The others also looked at him and grew silent. Iván Ilých was staring with glittering eyes straight before him, evidently indignant with them. This had to be rectified, but it was impossible to do so. The silence had to be broken, but for a time no one dared to break it and they all became afraid that the conventional deception would suddenly become obvious and the truth become plain to all. Lisa was the first to pluck up courage and break that silence, but by trying to hide what everybody was feeling, she betrayed it.

"Well, if we are going it's time to start," she said, looking at her watch, a present from her father, and with a faint and significant smile at Fëdor Petróvich relating to something known only to them. She got up with a rustle of her dress.

They all rose, said good-night, and went away.

When they had gone it seemed to Iván Ilých that he felt better; the falsity had gone with them. But the pain remained—that same pain and that same fear that made everything monotonously alike, nothing harder and nothing easier. Everything was worse.

Again minute followed minute and hour followed hour. Everything remained the same and there was no cessation. And the inevitable end of it all became more and more terrible.

"Yes, send Gerásim here," he replied to a question Peter asked.

CHAPTER IX

His wife returned late at night. She came in on tiptoe, but he heard her, opened his eyes, and made haste to close them again. She wished to send Gerásim away and to sit with him herself, but he opened his eyes and said: "No, go away."

"Are you in great pain?"

"Always the same."

"Take some opium."

He agreed and took some. She went away.

Till about three in the morning he was in a state of stupefied misery. It seemed to him that he and his pain were being thrust into a narrow, deep black sack, but though they were pushed further and further in they could not be pushed to the bottom. And this, terrible enough in itself, was accompanied by suffering. He was frightened yet wanted to fall through the sack, he struggled but yet co-operated. And suddenly he broke through, fell, and regained consciousness. Gerásim was sitting at the foot of the bed dozing quietly and patiently, while he himself lay with his emaciated stockinged legs resting on Gerásim's shoulders; the same shaded candle was there and the same unceasing pain.

"Go away, Gerásim," he whispered.

"It's all right, sir. I'll stay a while."

"No. Go away."

He removed his legs from Gerásim's shoulders, turned sideways onto his arm, and felt sorry for himself. He only waited till Gerásim had gone into the next room and then restrained himself no longer but wept like a child. He wept on account of his helplessness, his terrible loneliness, the cruelty of man, the cruelty of God, and the absence of God.

"Why hast Thou done all this? Why hast Thou brought me here? Why, why dost Thou torment me so terribly?"

He did not expect an answer and yet wept because there was no answer and could be none. The pain again grew more acute, but he did not stir and did not call. He said to himself: "Go on! Strike me! But what is it for? What have I done to Thee? What is it for?"

Then he grew quiet and not only ceased weeping but even held his breath and became all attention. It was as though he were listening not to an audible voice but to the voice of his soul, to the current of thoughts arising within him.

"What is it you want?" was the first clear conception capable of expression in words, that he heard.

"What do you want? What do you want?" he repeated to himself.

"What do I want? To live and not to suffer," he answered.

And again he listened with such concentrated attention that even his pain did not distract him.

"To live? How?" asked his inner voice.

"Why, to live as I used to—well and pleasantly."

"As you lived before, well and pleasantly?" the voice repeated.

And in imagination he began to recall the best moments of his pleasant life. But strange to say none of these best moments of his pleasant life now seemed at all what they had then seemed—none of them except the first recollections of childhood. There, in childhood, there had been something really pleasant with which it would be possible to live if it could return. But the child who had experienced that happiness existed no longer, it was like a reminiscence of somebody else.

As soon as the period began which had produced the present Iván Ilých, all that had then seemed joys now melted before his sight and turned into something trivial and often nasty.

And the further he departed from childhood and the nearer he came to the present the more worthless and doubtful were the joys. This began with the School of Law. A little that was really good was still found there—there was light-heartedness, friendship, and hope. But in the upper classes there had already been fewer of such good moments. Then during the first years of his official career, when he was in the service of the Governor, some pleasant moments again occurred: they were the memories of love for a woman. Then all became confused and there was still less of what was good; later on again there was still less that was good, and the further he went the less there was. His marriage, a mere accident, then the disenchantment that followed it, his wife's bad breath and the sensuality and hypocrisy: then that deadly official life and those preoccupations about money, a year of it, and two, and ten, and twenty, and always the same thing. And the longer it lasted the more deadly it became. "It is as if I had been going downhill while I imagined I was going up.

And that is really what it was. I was going up in public opinion, but to the same extent life was ebbing away from me. And now it is all done and there is only death."

"Then what does it mean? Why? It can't be that life is so senseless and horrible. But if it really has been so horrible and senseless, why must I die and die in agony? There is something wrong!"

"Maybe I did not live as I ought to have done," it suddenly occurred to him. "But how could that be, when I did everything properly?" he replied, and immediately dismissed from his mind this, the sole solution of all the riddles of life and death, as something quite impossible.

"Then what do you want now? To live? Live how? Live as you lived in the law courts when the usher proclaimed 'The judge is coming!' " "The judge is coming, the judge!" he repeated to himself. "Here he is, the judge. But I am not guilty!" he exclaimed angrily. "What is it for?" And he ceased crying, but turning his face to the wall continued to ponder on the same question: Why, and for what purpose, is there all this horror? But however much he pondered he found no answer. And whenever the thought occurred to him, as it often did, that it all resulted from his not having lived as he ought to have done, he at once recalled the correctness of his whole life and dismissed so strange an idea.

CHAPTER X

Another fortnight passed. Iván Ilých now no longer left his sofa. He would not lie in bed but lay on the sofa, facing the wall nearly all the time. He suffered ever the same unceasing agonies and in his loneliness pondered always on the same insoluble question: "What is this? Can it be that it is Death?" And the inner voice answered: "Yes, it is Death."

"Why these sufferings?" And the voice answered, "For no reason—they just are so." Beyond and besides this there was nothing.

From the very beginning of his illness, ever since he had first been to see the doctor, Iván Ilých's life had been divided between two contrary and alternating moods: now it was despair and the expectation of this uncomprehended and terrible death, and now hope and an intently interested observation of the functioning of his organs. Now before his eyes there was only a kidney or an intestine that temporarily evaded its duty, and now only that incomprehensible and dreadful death from which it was impossible to escape.

These two states of mind had alternated from the very beginning of his illness, but the further it progressed the more doubtful and fantastic became the conception of the kidney, and the more real the sense of impending death.

He had but to call to mind what he had been three months before and what he was now, to call to mind with what regularity he had been going downhill, for every possibility of hope to be shattered.

Latterly during that loneliness in which he found himself as he lay facing the back of the sofa, a loneliness in the midst of a populous town and surrounded by numerous acquaintances and relations but that yet could not have been more complete anywhere—either at the bottom of the sea or under the earth—during that terrible loneliness Iván Ilých had lived only in memories of the past. Pictures of his past rose before him one after another. They always began with what was nearest in time and then went back to what was most remote—to his childhood—and rested there. If he thought of the stewed prunes that had been offered him that day, his mind went back to the raw shrivelled French plums of his childhood, their peculiar flavour and the flow of saliva when he sucked their stones, and along with the memory of that taste came a whole series of memories of those days: his nurse, his brother, and their toys. "No, I mustn't think of that. . . . It is too painful," Iván Ilých said to himself, and brought himself back to the present—to the button on the back of the sofa and the creases in its morocco. "Morocco is expensive, but it does not wear well: There had been a quarrel about it. It was a different kind of quarrel and a different kind of morocco that time when we tore father's portfolio and were punished, and mamma brought us some tarts. . . ." And again his thoughts dwelt on his childhood, and again it was painful and he tried to banish them and fix his mind on something else.

Then again together with that chain of memories another series passed through his mind—of how his illness had progressed and grown worse. There also the further back he looked the more life there had been. There had been more of what was good in life and more of life itself. The two merged together. "Just as the pain went on getting worse and worse so my life grew worse and worse," he thought. "There is one bright spot there at the back, at the beginning of life, and afterwards all becomes blacker and blacker and proceeds more and more rapidly—in inverse ratio to the square of the distance from death," thought Iván Ilých. And the example of a stone falling downwards with increasing velocity entered his mind. Life, a series of increasing sufferings, flies, further and further towards its end—the most terrible suffering. "I am flying. . . ." He shuddered, shifted himself, and tried to resist, but was already aware that resistance was impossible, and again with eyes weary of gazing but unable to cease seeing what was before them, he stared at the back of the sofa and waited—awaiting that dreadful fall and shock and destruction.

"Resistance is impossible!" he said to himself. "If I could only understand what it is all for! But that too is impossible. An explanation would be possible if it could be said that I have not lived as I ought to. But it is impossible to say that," and he remembered all the legality, correctitude, and propriety of his life. "That at any rate can certainly not be admitted," he thought, and his lips smiled ironically as if someone could see that smile and be taken in by it. "There is no explanation! Agony, death. . . . What for?"

CHAPTER XI

Another two weeks went by in this way and during that fortnight an event occurred that Iván Ilých and his wife had desired. Petríshchev formally proposed. It happened in the evening. The next day Praskóvya Fëdorovna came into her husband's room considering how best to inform him of it, but that very night there had been a fresh change for the worse in his condition. She found him still lying on the sofa but in a different position. He lay on his back, groaning and staring fixedly straight in front of him.

She began to remind him of his medicines, but he turned his eyes towards her with such a look that she did not finish what she was saying; so great an animosity, to her in particular, did that look express.

"For Christ's sake, let me die in peace!" he said.

She would have gone away, but just then their daughter came in and went up to say good morning. He looked at her as he had done at his wife, and in reply to her inquiry about his health said dryly that he would soon free them all of himself. They were both silent and after sitting with him for a while went away.

"Is it our fault?" Lisa said to her mother. "It's as if we were to blame! I am sorry for papa, but why should we be tortured?"

The doctor came at his usual time. Iván Ilých answered "Yes" and "No," never taking his angry eyes from him, and at last said: "You know you can do nothing for me, so leave me alone."

"We can ease your sufferings."

"You can't even do that. Let me be."

The doctor went into the drawing-room and told Praskóvya Fëdorovna that the case was very serious and that the only resource left was opium to allay her husband's sufferings, which must be terrible.

It was true, as the doctor said, that Iván Ilých's physical sufferings were terrible, but worse than the physical sufferings were his mental sufferings which were his chief torture.

His mental sufferings were due to the fact that that night, as he looked at Gerásim's sleepy, good-natured face with its prominent cheek-bones, the question suddenly occurred to him: "What if my whole life has really been wrong?"

It occurred to him that what had appeared perfectly impossible before, namely that he had not spent his life as he should have done, might after all be true. It occurred to him that his scarcely perceptible attempts to struggle against what was considered good by the most highly placed people, those scarcely noticeable impulses which he had immediately suppressed, might have been the real thing, and all the rest false. And his professional duties and the whole arrangement of his life and of his family, and all his social and official interests, might all have been false. He tried to defend all those things to himself and suddenly felt the weakness of what he was defending. There was nothing to defend.

"But if that is so," he said to himself, "and I am leaving this life with the consciousness that I have lost all that was given me and it is impossible to rectify it—what then?"

He lay on his back and began to pass his life in review in quite a new way. In the morning when he saw first his footman, then his wife, then his daughter, and then the doctor, their every word and movement confirmed to him the awful truth that had been revealed to him during the night. In them he saw himself—all that for which he had lived—and saw clearly that it was not real at all, but a terrible and huge deception which had hidden both life and death. This consciousness intensified his physical suffering tenfold. He groaned and tossed about, and pulled at his clothing which choked and stifled him. And he hated them on that account.

He was given a large dose of opium and became unconscious, but at noon his sufferings began again. He drove everybody away and tossed from side to side.

His wife came to him and said:

"Jean my dear, do this for me. It can't do any harm and often helps. Healthy people often do it."

He opened his eyes wide.

"What? Take communion? Why? It's unnecessary! However. . . ."

She began to cry.

"Yes, do, my dear. I'll send for our priest. He is such a nice man."

"All right. Very well," he muttered.

When the priest came and heard his confession, Iván Ilých was softened and seemed to feel a relief from his doubts and consequently from his sufferings, and for a moment there came a ray of hope. He again began to think of the vermiform appendix and the possibility of correcting it. He received the sacrament with tears in his eyes.

When they laid him down again afterwards he felt a moment's ease, and the hope that he might live awoke in him again. He began to think of the operation that had been suggested to him. "To live! I want to live!" he said to himself.

His wife came in to congratulate him after his communion, and when uttering the usual conventional words she added:

"You feel better, don't you?"

Without looking at her he said "Yes."

Her dress, her figure, the expression of her face, the tone of her voice, all revealed the same thing. "This is wrong, it is not as it should be. All you have lived for and still live for is falsehood and deception, hiding life and death from you." And as soon as he admitted that thought, his hatred and his agonizing physical suffering again sprang up, and with that suffering a consciousness of the unavoidable, approaching end. And to this was added a new sensation of grinding shooting pain and a feeling of suffocation.

The expression of his face when he uttered that "yes" was dreadful. Having uttered it, he looked her straight in the eyes, turned on his face with a rapidity extraordinary in his weak state and shouted:

"Go away! Go away and leave me alone!"

CHAPTER XII

From that moment the screaming began that continued for three days, and was so terrible that one could not hear it through two closed doors without horror. At the moment he answered his wife he realized that he was lost, that there was no return, that the end had come, the very end, and his doubts were still unsolved and remained doubts.

"Oh! Oh! Oh!" he cried in various intonations. He had begun by screaming "I won't!" and continued screaming on the letter "o."

For three whole days, during which time did not exist for him, he struggled in that black sack into which he was being thrust by an invisible, resistless force. He struggled as a man condemned to death struggles in the hands of the executioner, knowing that he cannot save himself. And every moment he felt that despite all his efforts he was drawing nearer and nearer to what terrified him. He felt that his agony was due to his being thrust into that black hole and still more to his not being able to get right into it. He was hindered from getting into it by his conviction that his life had been a good one. That very justification of his life held him fast and prevented his moving forward, and it caused him most torment of all.

Suddenly some force struck him in the chest and side, making it still harder to breathe, and he fell through the hole and there at the bottom was a light. What had happened to him was like the sensation one sometimes experiences in a railway carriage when one thinks one is going backwards while one is really going forwards and suddenly becomes aware of the real direction.

"Yes, it was all not the right thing," he said to himself, "but that's no matter. It can be done. But what *is* the right thing?" he asked himself, and suddenly grew quiet.

This occurred at the end of the third day, two hours before his death. Just then his schoolboy son had crept softly in and gone up to the bedside. The dying man was still screaming desperately and waving his arms. His hand fell on the boy's head, and the boy caught it, pressed it to his lips, and began to cry.

At that very moment Iván Ilých fell through and caught sight of the light, and it was revealed to him that though his life had not been what it should have been, this could still be rectified. He asked himself, "What *is* the right thing?" and grew still, listening. Then he felt that someone was kissing his hand. He opened his eyes, looked at his son, and felt sorry for him. His wife came up to him and he glanced at her. She was gazing at him open-mouthed, with undried tears on her nose and cheek and a despairing look on her face. He felt sorry for her too.

"Yes, I am making them wretched," he thought. "They are sorry, but it will be better for them when I die." He wished to say this but had not the strength to utter it. "Besides, why speak? I must act," he thought. With a look at his wife he indicated his son and said: "Take him away . . . sorry for him . . . sorry for you too. . . ." He tried to add, "forgive me," but said "forego" and waved his hand, knowing that He whose understanding mattered would understand.

And suddenly it grew clear to him that what had been oppressing him and would not leave him was all dropping away at once from two sides, from ten sides, and from all sides. He was sorry for them, he must act so as not to hurt them: release them and free himself from these sufferings. "How good and how simple!" he thought. "And the pain?" he asked himself. "What has become of it? Where are you, pain?"

He turned his attention to it.

"Yes, here it is. Well, what of it? Let the pain be."

"And death . . . where is it?"

He sought his former accustomed fear of death and did not find it. "Where is it? What death?" There was no fear because there was no death.

In place of death there was light.

"So that's what it is!" he suddenly exclaimed aloud. "What joy!"

To him all this happened in a single instant, and the meaning of that instant did not change. For those present his agony continued for another two hours. Something rattled in his throat, his emaciated body twitched, then the gasping and rattle became less and less frequent.

"It is finished!" said someone near him.

He heard these words and repeated them in his soul.

"Death is finished," he said to himself. "It is no more!"

He drew in a breath, stopped in the midst of a sigh, stretched out, and died.

QUESTIONS

1. Why does Tolstoy begin the story immediately after Ilých's death and then move back to recount his life? **2.** Is there any evidence that Ilých's death is a moral judgment—that is, a punishment for his life? Explain. **3.** Why is Gerásim, Ilých's peasant servant, most sympathetic to his plight?

WRITING TOPIC

At the very end, Ilých achieves peace and understanding, and the questions that have been torturing him are resolved. He realizes that "though his life had not been what it should have been, this could still be rectified." What does this mean?

An Occurrence at Owl Creek Bridge (1891)

AMBROSE BIERCE [1842–1914?]

I

A man stood upon a railroad bridge in northern Alabama, looking down into the swift water twenty feet below. The man's hands were behind his back, the wrists bound with a cord. A rope closely encircled his neck. It was attached to a stout cross-timber above his head and the slack fell to the level of his knees. Some loose boards laid upon the sleepers supporting the metals of the railway supplied a footing for him and his executioners—two private soldiers of the Federal army, directed by a sergeant who in civil life may have been a deputy sheriff. At a short remove upon the same temporary platform was an officer in the uniform of his rank, armed. He was a captain. A sentinel at each end of the bridge stood with his rifle in the position known as "support," that is to say, vertical in front of the left shoulder, the hammer resting on the forearm thrown straight across the chest—a formal and unnatural position, enforcing an erect carriage of the body. It did not appear to be the duty of these two men to know what was occurring at the centre of the bridge; they merely blockaded the two ends of the foot planking that traversed it.

Beyond one of the sentinels nobody was in sight; the railroad ran straight away into a forest for a hundred yards, then, curving, was lost to view. Doubtless there was an outpost farther along. The other bank of the stream was open ground—a gentle acclivity topped with a stockade of vertical tree trunks, loop-holed for rifles, with a single embrasure through which protruded the muzzle of a brass cannon commanding the bridge. Midway of the slope between bridge and fort were the spectators—a single company of infantry in line, at "parade rest," the butts of the rifles on the ground, the barrels inclining slightly backward against the right shoulder, the hands crossed upon the stock. A lieutenant stood at the right of the line, the point of his sword upon the ground, his left hand resting upon his right. Excepting the group of four at the centre of the bridge, not a man moved. The company faced the bridge, staring stonily, motionless. The sentinels, facing the banks of the stream, might have been statues to adorn the bridge. The captain stood with folded arms, silent, observing the work of his subordinates, but making no sign. Death is a dignitary who when he comes announced is to be received with formal manifestations of respect, even by those most familiar with him. In the code of military etiquette silence and fixity are forms of deference.

The man who was engaged in being hanged was apparently about thirty-five years of age. He was a civilian, if one might judge from his habit, which was that of a planter. His features were good—a straight nose, firm mouth, broad forehead, from which his long, dark hair was combed straight back, falling behind his ears to the collar of his well-fitting frock-coat. He wore a mustache and pointed beard, but no whiskers; his eyes were large and dark gray, and had a kindly expression which one would hardly have expected in one whose neck was in the hemp. Evidently this was no vulgar assassin. The liberal military code makes provision for hanging many kinds of persons, and gentlemen are not excluded.

The preparations being complete, the two private soldiers stepped aside and each drew away the plank upon which he had been standing. The sergeant turned to the captain, saluted and placed himself immediately behind that officer, who in turn moved apart one pace. These movements left the condemned man and the sergeant standing on the two ends of the same plank, which spanned three of the cross-ties of the bridge. The end upon which the civilian stood almost, but not quite, reached a fourth. This plank had been held in place by the weight of the captain; it was now held by that of the sergeant. At a signal from the former the latter would step aside, the plank would tilt and the condemned man go down between two ties. The arrangement commended itself to his judgment as simple and effective. His face had not been covered nor his eyes bandaged. He looked a moment at his "unsteadfast footing," then let his gaze wander to the swirling water of the stream racing madly beneath his feet. A piece of dancing driftwood caught his attention and his eyes followed it down the current. How slowly it appeared to move! What a sluggish stream!

He closed his eyes in order to fix his last thoughts upon his wife and children. The water, touched to gold by the early sun, the brooding mists under the banks at some distance down the stream, the fort, the soldiers, the piece of drift—all had distracted him. And now he became conscious of a new disturbance. Striking through the thought of his dear ones was a sound which he could neither ignore nor understand, a sharp, distinct, metallic percussion like the stroke of a blacksmith's hammer upon the anvil; it had the same ringing quality. He wondered what it was, and whether immeasurably distant or near by—it seemed both. Its recurrence was regular, but as slow as the tolling of a death knell. He awaited each stroke with impatience and—he knew not why—apprehension. The intervals of silence grew progressively longer; the delays became maddening. With their greater infrequency the sounds increased in strength and sharpness. They hurt his ear like the thrust of a knife; he feared he would shriek. What he heard was the ticking of his watch.

He unclosed his eyes and saw again the water below him. "If I could free my hands," he thought, "I might throw off the noose and spring into the stream. By diving I could evade the bullets and, swimming vigorously, reach the bank, take to the woods and get away home. My home, thank God, is as yet outside their lines; my wife and little ones are still beyond the invader's farthest advance."

As these thoughts, which have here to be set down in words, were flashed into the doomed man's brain rather than evolved from it the captain nodded to the sergeant. The sergeant stepped aside.

II

Peyton Farquhar was a well-to-do planter, of an old and highly respected Alabama family. Being a slave owner and like other slave owners a politician he was naturally an original secessionist and ardently devoted to the Southern cause. Circumstances of an imperious nature, which it is unnecessary to relate here, had prevented him from taking service with the gallant army that had fought the disastrous campaigns ending with the fall of Corinth, and he chafed under the inglorious restraint, longing for the release of his energies, the larger life of the soldier, the opportunity for distinction. That opportunity, he felt, would come, as it comes to all in war time. Meanwhile he did what he could. No service was too humble for him to perform in aid of the South, no adventure too perilous for him to undertake if consistent with the character of a civilian who was at heart a soldier, and who in good faith and without too much qualification assented to at least a part of the frankly villainous dictum that all is fair in love and war.

One evening while Farquhar and his wife were sitting on a rustic bench near the entrance to his grounds, a gray-clad soldier rode up to the gate and asked for a drink of water. Mrs. Farquhar was only too happy to serve him with her own white hands. While she was fetching the water her husband approached the dusty horseman and inquired eagerly for news from the front.

"The Yanks are repairing the railroads," said the man, "and are getting ready for another advance. They have reached the Owl Creek bridge, put it in order and built a stockade on the north bank. The commandant has issued an order, which is posted everywhere, declaring that any civilian caught interfering with the railroad, its bridges, tunnels or trains will be summarily hanged. I saw the order."

"How far is it to the Owl Creek bridge?" Farquhar asked.

"About thirty miles."

"Is there no force on this side of the creek?"

"Only a picket post half a mile out, on the railroad, and a single sentinel at this end of the bridge."

"Suppose a man—a civilian and student of hanging—should elude the picket post and perhaps get the better of the sentinel," said Farquhar, smiling, "what could he accomplish?"

The soldier reflected. "I was there a month ago," he replied. "I observed that the flood of last winter had lodged a great quantity of driftwood against the wooden pier at this end of the bridge. It is now dry and would burn like tow."

The lady had now brought the water, which the soldier drank. He thanked her ceremoniously, bowed to her husband and rode away. An hour later, after nightfall, he repassed the plantation, going northward in the direction from which he had come. He was a Federal scout.

III

As Peyton Farquhar fell straight downward through the bridge he lost consciousness and was as one already dead. From this state he was awakened—ages later, it seemed to him—by the pain of a sharp pressure upon his throat, followed by a sense of suffocation. Keen, poignant agonies seemed to shoot from his neck downward through every fibre of his body and limbs. These pains appeared to flash along well-defined lines of ramification and to beat with an inconceivably rapid periodicity. They seemed like streams of pulsating fire heating him to an intolerable temperature. As to his head, he was conscious of nothing but a feeling of fulness—of congestion. These sensations were unaccompanied by thought. The intellectual part of his nature was already effaced; he had power only to feel, and feeling was torment. He was conscious of motion. Encompassed in a luminous cloud, of which he was now merely the fiery heart, without material substance, he swung through unthinkable arcs of oscillation, like a vast pendulum. Then all at once, with terrible suddenness, the light about him shot upward with the noise of a loud plash; a frightful roaring was in his ears, and all was cold and dark. The power of thought was restored; he knew that the rope had broken and he had fallen into the stream. There was no additional strangulation; the noose about his neck was already suffocating him and kept the water from his lungs. To die of hanging at the bottom of a river!—the idea seemed to him ludicrous. He opened his eyes in the darkness and saw above him a gleam of light, but how distant, how inaccessible! He was still sinking, for the light became fainter and fainter until it was a mere glimmer. Then it began to grow and brighten, and he knew that he was rising toward the surface—knew it with reluctance, for he was now very comfortable. "To be hanged and drowned," he thought, "that is not so bad; but I do not wish to be shot. No; I will not be shot; that is not fair."

He was not conscious of an effort, but a sharp pain in his wrist apprised him that he was trying to free his hands. He gave the struggle his attention, as an idler might observe the feat of a juggler, without interest in the outcome. What splendid effort!—what magnificent, what superhuman strength! Ah, that was a fine endeavor! Bravo! The cord fell away; his arms parted and floated upward, the hands dimly seen on each side in the growing light. He watched them with a new interest as first one and then the other pounced upon the noose at his neck. They tore it away and thrust it fiercely aside, its undulations resembling those of a water-snake. "Put it back, put it back!" He thought he shouted these words to his hands, for the undoing of the noose had been succeeded by the direst pang that he had yet experienced. His neck ached horribly, his brain was on fire; his heart, which had been fluttering faintly, gave a great leap, trying to force itself out at his mouth. His whole body was racked and wrenched with an insupportable anguish! But his disobedient hands gave no need to the command. They beat the water vigorously with quick, downward strokes, forcing him to the surface. He felt his head emerge; his eyes were blinded by the sunlight; his chest expanded convulsively, and with a supreme and crowning agony his lungs engulfed a great draught of air, which instantly he expelled in a shriek!

He was now in full possession of his physical senses. They were, indeed, preternaturally keen and alert. Something in the awful disturbance of his organic system had so exalted and refined them that they made record of things never before perceived. He felt the ripples upon his face and heard their separate sounds as they struck. He looked at the forest on the bank of the stream, saw the individual trees, the leaves and the veining of each leaf—saw the very insects upon them: the locusts, the brilliant-bodied flies, the gray spiders stretching their webs from twig to twig. He noted the prismatic colors in all the dewdrops upon a million blades of grass. The humming of the gnats that danced above the eddies of the stream, the beating of the dragon-flies' wings, the strokes of the water-spiders' legs, like oars which had lifted their boat—all these made audible music. A fish slid along beneath his eyes and he heard the rush of its body parting the water.

He had come to the surface facing down the stream; in a moment the visible world seemed to wheel slowly round, himself the pivotal point, and he saw the bridge, the fort, the soldiers upon the bridge, the captain, the sergeant, the two privates, his executioners. They were in silhouette against the blue sky. They shouted and gesticulated, pointing at him. The captain had drawn his pistol, but did not fire; the others were unarmed. Their movements were grotesque and horrible, their forms gigantic.

Suddenly he heard a sharp report and something struck the water smartly within a few inches of his head, spattering his face with spray. He heard a second report, and saw one of the sentinels with his rifle at his shoulder, a light cloud of blue smoke rising from the muzzle. The man in the water saw the eye of the man on the bridge gazing into his own through the sights of the rifle. He observed that it was a gray eye and remembered having read that gray eyes were keenest, and that all famous marksmen had them. Nevertheless, this one had missed.

A counter-swirl had caught Farquhar and turned him half round; he was again looking into the forest on the bank opposite the fort. The sound of a clear, high voice in a monotonous singsong now rang out behind him and came across the water with a distinctness that pierced and subdued all other sounds, even the beating of the ripples in his ears. Although no soldier, he had frequented camps enough to know the dread significance of that deliberate, drawling, as- pirated chant; the lieutenant on shore was taking a part in the morning's work. How coldly and pitilessly—with what an even, calm intonation, presaging, and enforcing tranquility in the men—with what accurately measured intervals fell those cruel words:

"Attention, company! . . . Shoulder arms! . . . Ready! . . . Aim! . . . Fire!"

Farquhar dived—dived as deeply as he could. The water roared in his ears like the voice of Niagara, yet he heard the dulled thunder of the volley and, rising again toward the surface, met shining bits of metal, singularly flattened, oscillating slowly downward. Some of them touched him on the face and hands, then fell away, continuing their descent. One lodged between his collar and neck; it was uncomfortably warm and he snatched it out.

As he rose to the surface, gasping for breath, he saw that he had been a long time under water; he was perceptibly farther down stream—nearer to safety. The soldiers had almost finished reloading; the metal ramrods flashed all at once in the sunshine as they were drawn from the barrels, turned in the air, and thrust into their sockets. The two sentinels fired again, independently and ineffectually.

The hunted man saw all this over his shoulder; he was now swimming vigorously with the current. His brain was as energetic as his arms and legs; he thought with the rapidity of lightning.

"The officer," he reasoned, "will not make that martinet's error a second time. It is as easy to dodge a volley as a single shot. He has probably already given the command to fire at will. God help me, I cannot dodge them all!"

An appalling plash within two yards of him was followed by a loud, rushing sound, *diminuendo*, which seemed to travel back through the air to the fort and died in an explosion which stirred the very river to its deeps! A rising sheet of water curved over him, fell down upon him, blinded him, strangled him! The cannon had taken a hand in the game. As he shook his head free from the commotion of the smitten water he heard the deflected shot humming through the air ahead, and in an instant it was cracking and smashing the branches in the forest beyond.

"They will not do that again," he thought; "the next time they will use a charge of grape. I must keep my eye upon the gun; the smoke will apprise me— the report arrives too late; it lags behind the missile. That is a good gun."

Suddenly he felt himself whirled round and round—spinning like a top. The water, the banks, the forests, the now distant bridge, fort and men—all were commingled and blurred. Objects were represented by their colors only; circular horizontal streaks of color—that was all he saw. He had been caught in a vortex and was being whirled on with a velocity of advance and gyration that made him giddy and sick. In a few moments he was flung upon the gravel at the foot of the left bank of the stream—the southern bank—and behind a projecting point which concealed him from his enemies. The sudden arrest of his motion, the abrasion of one of his hands on the gravel, restored him, and he wept with delight. He dug his fingers into the sand, threw it over himself in handfuls and audibly blessed it. It looked like diamonds, rubies, emeralds; he could think of nothing beautiful which it did not resemble. The trees upon the bank were giant garden plants; he noted a definite order in their arrangement, inhaled the fragrance of their blooms. A strange, roseate light shone through the spaces among their trunks and the wind made in their branches the music of aeolian harps. He had no wish to perfect his escape—was content to remain in that enchanting spot until retaken.

A whiz and rattle of grapeshot among the branches high above his head roused him from his dream. The baffled cannoneer had fired him a random farewell. He sprang to his feet, rushed up the sloping bank, and plunged into the forest.

All that day he traveled, laying his course by the rounding sun. The forest seemed interminable; nowhere did he discover a break in it, not even a wood-man's road. He had not known that he lived in so wild a region. There was something uncanny in the revelation.

By night fall he was fatigued, footsore, famishing. The thought of his wife and children urged him on. At last he found a road which led him in what he knew to be the right direction. It was as wide and straight as a city street, yet it seemed untraveled. No fields bordered it, no dwelling anywhere. Not so much as the barking of a dog suggested human habitation. The black bodies of the trees formed a straight wall on both sides, terminating on the horizon in a point, like a diagram in a lesson in perspective. Overhead, as he looked up through this rift in the wood, shone great golden stars looking unfamiliar and grouped in strange constellations. He was sure they were arranged in some order which had a secret and malign significance. The wood on either side was full of singular noises, among which—once, twice, and again, he distinctly heard whispers in an unknown tongue.

His neck was in pain and lifting his hand to it he found it horribly swollen. He knew that it had a circle of black where the rope had bruised it. His eyes felt congested; he could no longer close them. His tongue was swollen with thirst; he relieved its fever by thrusting it forward from between his teeth into the cold air. How softly the turf had carpeted the untraveled avenue—he could no longer feel the roadway beneath his feet!

Doubtless, despite his suffering, he had fallen asleep while walking, for now he sees another scene—perhaps he has merely recovered from a delirium. He stands at the gate of his own home. All is as he left it, and all bright and beautiful in the morning sunshine. He must have traveled the entire night. As he pushes open the gate and passes up the wide white walk, he sees a flutter of female garments; his wife, looking fresh and cool and sweet, steps down from the veranda to meet him. At the bottom of the steps she stands waiting, with a smile of ineffable joy, an attitude of matchless grace and dignity. Ah, how beautiful she is! He springs forward with extended arms. As he is about to clasp her he feels a stunning blow upon the back of the neck; a blinding white light blazes all about him with a sound like the shock of a cannon—then all is darkness and silence!

Peyton Farquhar was dead; his body, with a broken neck, swung gently from side to side beneath the timbers of the Owl Creek bridge.

The Jilting
of Granny Weatherall

1930

KATHERINE ANNE PORTER [1890–1980]

She flicked her wrist neatly out of Doctor Harry's pudgy careful fingers and pulled the sheet up to her chin. The brat ought to be in knee breeches. Doctoring around the country with spectacles on his nose! "Get along now, take your schoolbooks and go. There's nothing wrong with me."

Doctor Harry spread a warm paw like a cushion on her forehead where the forked green vein danced and made her eyelids twitch. "Now, now, be a good girl, and we'll have you up in no time."

"That's no way to speak to a woman nearly eighty years old just because she's down. I'd have you respect your elders, young man."

"Well, Missy, excuse me." Doctor Harry patted her cheek. "But I've got to warn you, haven't I? You're a marvel, but you must be careful or you're going to be good and sorry."

"Don't tell me what I'm going to be. I'm on my feet now, morally speaking. It's Cornelia. I had to go to bed to get rid of her."

Her bones felt loose, and floated around in her skin, and Doctor Harry floated like a balloon around the foot of the bed. He floated and pulled down his waistcoat and swung his glasses on a cord. "Well, stay where you are, it certainly can't hurt you."

"Get along and doctor your sick," said Granny Weatherall. "Leave a well woman alone. I'll call for you when I want you. . . . Where were you forty years ago when I pulled through milk-leg and double pneumonia? You weren't even born. Don't let Cornelia lead you on," she shouted, because Doctor Harry appeared to float up to the ceiling and out. "I pay my own bills, and I don't throw my money away on nonsense!"

She meant to wave good-by, but it was too much trouble. Her eyes closed of themselves, it was like a dark curtain drawn around the bed. The pillow rose and floated under her, pleasant as a hammock in a light wind. She listened to the leaves rustling outside the window. No, somebody was swishing newspapers: no, Cornelia and Doctor Harry were whispering together. She leaped broad awake, thinking they whispered in her ear.

"She was never like this, *never* like this!" "Well, what can we expect?" "Yes, eighty years old. . . ."

Well, and what if she was? She still had ears. It was like Cornelia to whisper around doors. She always kept things secret in such a public way. She was always being tactful and kind. Cornelia was dutiful; that was the trouble with her. Dutiful and good: "So good and dutiful," said Granny, "that I'd like to spank her." She saw herself spanking Cornelia and making a fine job of it.

"What'd you say, Mother?"

1072

Granny felt her face tying up in hard knots.

"Can't a body think, I'd like to know?"

"I thought you might want something."

"I do. I want a lot of things. First off, go away and don't whisper."

She lay and drowsed, hoping in her sleep that the children would keep out and let her rest a minute. It had been a long day. Not that she was tired. It was always pleasant to snatch a minute now and then. There was always so much to be done, let me see: tomorrow.

Tomorrow was far away and there was nothing to trouble about. Things were finished somehow when the time came; thank God there was always a little margin over for peace: then a person could spread out the plan of life and tuck in the edges orderly. It was good to have everything clean and folded away, with the hair brushes and tonic bottles sitting straight on the white embroidered linen: the day started without fuss and the pantry shelves laid out with rows of jelly glasses and brown jugs and white stone-china jars with blue whirligigs and words painted on them: coffee, tea, sugar, ginger, cinnamon, allspice: and the bronze clock with the lion on top nicely dusted off. The dust that lion could collect in twenty-four hours! The box in the attic with all those letters tied up, well she'd have to go through that tomorrow. All those letters—George's letters and John's letters and her letters to them both—lying around for the children to find afterwards made her uneasy. Yes, that would be tomorrow's business. No use to let them know how silly she had been once.

While she was rummaging around she found death in her mind and it felt clammy and unfamiliar. She had spent so much time preparing for death there was no need for bringing it up again. Let it take care of itself now. When she was sixty she had felt very old, finished, and went around making farewell trips to see her children and grandchildren, with a secret in her mind: This is the very last of your mother, children! Then she made her will and came down with a long fever. That was all just a notion like a lot of other things, but it was lucky too, for she had once for all got over the idea of dying for a long time. Now she couldn't be worried. She hoped she had better sense now. Her father had lived to be one hundred and two years old and had drunk a noggin of strong hot toddy on his last birthday. He told the reporters it was his daily habit, and he owed his long life to that. He had made quite a scandal and was very pleased about it. She believed she'd just plague Cornelia a little.

"Cornelia! Cornelia!" No footsteps, but a sudden hand on her cheek. "Bless you, where have you been?"

"Here, mother."

"Well, Cornelia, I want a noggin of hot toddy."

"Are you cold, darling?"

"I'm chilly, Cornelia. Lying in bed stops the circulation. I must have told you that a thousand times."

Well, she could just hear Cornelia telling her husband that Mother was getting childish and they'd have to humor her. The thing that most annoyed her was that Cornelia thought she was deaf, dumb, and blind. Little hasty glances and tiny gestures tossed around her and over her head saying, "Don't cross her, let her have her way, she's eighty years old," and she sitting there as if she lived in a thin glass cage. Sometimes Granny almost made up her mind to pack up and move back to her own house where nobody could remind her every minute that she was old. Wait, wait, Cornelia, till your own children whisper behind your back!

In her day she had kept a better house and had got more work done. She wasn't too old yet for Lydia to be driving eighty miles for advice when one of the children jumped the track, and Jimmy still dropped in and talked things over: "Now, Mammy, you've a good business head, I want to know what you think of this? . . ." Old Cornelia couldn't change the furniture around without asking. Little things, little things! They had been so sweet when they were little. Granny wished the old days were back again with the children young and everything to be done over. It had been a hard pull, but not too much for her. When she thought of all the food she had cooked, and all the clothes she had cut and sewed, and all the gardens she had made—well, the children showed it. There they were, made out of her, and they couldn't get away from that. Sometimes she wanted to see John again and point to them and say, Well, I didn't do so badly, did I? But that would have to wait. That was for tomorrow. She used to think of him as a man, but now all the children were older than their father, and he would be a child beside her if she saw him now. It seemed strange and there was something wrong in the idea. Why, he couldn't possibly recognize her. She had fenced in a hundred acres once, digging the post holes herself and clamping the wires with just a negro boy to help. That changed a woman. John would be looking for a young woman with the peaked Spanish comb in her hair and the painted fan. Digging post holes changed a woman. Riding country roads in the winter when women had their babies was another thing: sitting up nights with sick horses and sick negroes and sick children and hardly ever losing one. John, I hardly ever lost one of them! John would see that in a minute, that would be something he could understand, she wouldn't have to explain anything!

It made her feel like rolling up her sleeves and putting the whole place to rights again. No matter if Cornelia was determined to be everywhere at once, there were a great many things left undone on this place. She would start tomorrow and do them. It was good to be strong enough for everything, even if all you made melted and changed and slipped under your hands, so that by the time you finished you almost forgot what you were working for. What was it I set out to do? she asked herself intently, but she could not remember. A fog rose over the valley, she saw it marching across the creek swallowing the trees and moving up the hill like an army of ghosts. Soon it would be at the near edge of the orchard, and then it was time to go in and light the lamps. Come in, children, don't stay out in the night air.

Lighting the lamps had been beautiful. The children huddled up to her and breathed like little calves waiting at the bars in the twilight. Their eyes followed the match and watched the flame rise and settle in a blue curve, then they moved away from her. The lamp was lit, they didn't have to be scared and hang on to mother any more. Never, never, never more. God, for all my life I thank Thee. Without Thee, my God, I could never have done it. Hail, Mary, full of grace.

I want you to pick all the fruit this year and see that nothing is wasted. There's always someone who can use it. Don't let good things rot for want of using. You waste life when you waste good food. Don't let things get lost. It's bitter to lose things. Now, don't let me get to thinking, not when I am tired and taking a little nap before supper. . . .

The pillow rose about her shoulders and pressed against her heart and the memory was being squeezed out of it: oh, push down the pillow, somebody: it would smother her if she tried to hold it. Such a fresh breeze blowing and such a green day with no threats in it. But he had not come, just the same. What does a woman do when she has put on the white veil and set out the white cake for a man and he doesn't come? She tried to remember. No, I swear he never harmed me but in that. He never harmed me but in that . . . and what if he did? There was the day, the day, but a whirl of dark smoke rose and covered it, crept up and over into the bright field where everything was planted so carefully in orderly rows. That was hell, she knew hell when she saw it. For sixty years she had prayed against remembering him and against losing her soul in the deep pit of hell, and now the two things were mingled in one and the thought of him was a smoky cloud from hell that moved and crept in her head when she had just got rid of Doctor Harry and was trying to rest a minute. Wounded vanity, Ellen, said a sharp voice in the top of her mind. Don't let your wounded vanity get the upper hand of you. Plenty of girls get jilted. You were jilted, weren't you? Then stand up to it. Her eyelids wavered and let in streamers of blue-gray light like tissue paper over her eyes. She must get up and pull the shades down or she'd never sleep. She was in bed again and the shades were not down. How could that happen? Better turn over, hide from the light, sleeping in the light gave you nightmares. "Mother, how do you feel now?" and a stinging wetness on her forehead. But I don't like having my face washed in cold water!

Hapsy? George? Lydia? Jimmy? No, Cornelia, and her features were swollen and full of little puddles. "They're coming, darling, they'll all be here soon." Go wash your face, child, you look funny.

Instead of obeying, Cornelia knelt down and put her head on the pillow. She seemed to be talking but there was no sound. "Well, are you tongue-tied? Whose birthday is it? Are you going to give a party?"

Cornelia's mouth moved urgently in strange shapes. "Don't do that, you bother me, daughter."

"Oh, no, Mother, Oh, no. . . ."

Nonsense. It was strange about children. They disputed your every word. "No what, Cornelia?"

"Here's Doctor Harry."

"I won't see that boy again. He just left five minutes ago."

"That was this morning, Mother. It's night now. Here's the nurse."

"This is Doctor Harry, Mrs. Weatherall. I never saw you look so young and happy!"

"Ah, I'll never be young again—but I'd be happy if they'd let me lie in peace and get rested."

She thought she spoke up loudly, but no one answered. A warm weight on her forehead, a warm bracelet on her wrist, and a breeze went on whispering, trying to tell her something. A shuffle of leaves in the everlasting hand of God. He blew on them and they danced and rattled. "Mother, don't mind, we're going to give you a little hypodermic." "Look here, daughter, how do ants get in this bed? I saw sugar ants yesterday." Did you send for Hapsy too?

It was Hapsy she really wanted. She had to go a long way back through a great many rooms to find Hapsy standing with a baby on her arm. She seemed to herself to be Hapsy also, and the baby on Hapsy's arm was Hapsy and himself and herself, all at once, and there was no surprise in the meeting. Then Hapsy melted from within and turned flimsy as gray gauze and the baby was a gauzy shadow, and Hapsy came up close and said, "I thought you'd never come," and looked at her very searchingly and said, "You haven't changed a bit!" They leaned forward to kiss, when Cornelia began whispering from a long way off, "Oh, is there anything you want to tell me? Is there anything I can do for you?"

Yes, she had changed her mind after sixty years and she would like to see George. I want you to find George. Find him and be sure to tell him I forgot him. I want him to know I had my husband just the same and my children and my house like any other woman. A good house too and a good husband that I loved and fine children out of him. Better than I hoped for even. Tell him I was given back everything he took away and more. Oh, no, oh, God, no, there was something else besides the house and the man and the children. Oh, surely they were not all? What was it? Something not given back. . . . Her breath crowded down under her ribs and grew into a monstrous frightening shape with cutting edges; it bored up into her head, and the agony was unbelievable: Yes, John, get the doctor now, no more talk, my time has come.

When this one was born it should be the last. The last. It should have been born first, for it was the one she had truly wanted. Everything came in good time. Nothing left out, left over. She was strong, in three days she would be as well as ever. Better. A woman needed milk in her to have her full health.

"Mother, do you hear me?"

"I've been telling you—"

"Mother, Father Connolly's here."

"I went to Holy Communion only last week. Tell him I'm not so sinful as all that."

"Father just wants to speak to you."

He could speak as much as he pleased. It was like him to drop in and inquire about her soul as if it were a teething baby, and then stay on for a cup of tea and a round of cards and gossip. He always had a funny story of some sort, usually about an Irishman who made his little mistakes and confessed them, and the point lay in some absurd thing he would blurt out in the confessional showing his struggles between native piety and original sin. Granny felt easy about her soul. Cornelia, where are your manners? Give Father Connolly a chair. She had her secret comfortable understanding with a few favorite saints who cleared a straight road to God for her. All as surely signed and sealed as the papers for the new Forty Acres. Forever . . . heirs and assigns forever. Since the day the wedding cake was not cut, but thrown out and wasted. The whole bottom dropped out of the world, and there she was blind and sweating with nothing under her feet and the walls falling away. His hand had caught her under the breast, she had not fallen, there was the freshly polished floor with the green rug on it, just as before. He had cursed like a sailor's parrot and said, "I'll kill him for you." Don't lay a hand on him, for my sake leave something to God. "Now, Ellen, you must believe what I tell you. . . ."

So there was nothing, nothing to worry about any more, except sometimes in the night one of the children screamed in a nightmare, and they both hustled out shaking and hunting for the matches and calling, "There, wait a minute, here we are!" John, get the doctor now, Hapsy's time has come. But there was Hapsy standing by the bed in a white cap. "Cornelia, tell Hapsy to take off her cap. I can't see her plain."

Her eyes opened very wide and the room stood out like a picture she had seen somewhere. Dark colors with the shadows rising towards the ceiling in long angles. The tall black dresser gleamed with nothing on it but John's picture, enlarged from a little one, with John's eyes very black when they should have been blue. You never saw him, so how do you know how he looked? But the man insisted the copy was perfect, it was very rich and handsome. For a picture, yes, but it's not my husband. The table by the bed had a linen cover and a candle and a crucifix. The light was blue from Cornelia's silk lampshades. No sort of light at all, just frippery. You had to live forty years with kerosene lamps to appreciate honest electricity. She felt very strong and she saw Doctor Harry with a rosy nimbus around him.

"You look like a saint, Doctor Harry, and I vow that's as near as you'll ever come to it."

"She's saying something."

"I heard you, Cornelia. What's all this carrying-on?"

"Father Connolly's saying—"

Cornelia's voice staggered and bumped like a cart in a bad road. It rounded corners and turned back again and arrived nowhere. Granny stepped up in the cart very lightly and reached for the reins, but a man sat beside her and she knew him by his hands, driving the cart. She did not look in his face, for she knew without seeing, but looked instead down the road where the trees leaned over and bowed to each other and a thousand birds were singing a Mass. She felt like singing too, but she put her hand in the bosom of her dress and pulled out a rosary, and Father Connolly murmured Latin in a very solemn voice and tickled her feet. My God, will you stop that nonsense? I'm a married woman. What if he did run away and leave me to face the priest by myself? I found another a whole world better. I wouldn't have exchanged my husband for anybody except St. Michael himself, and you may tell him that for me with a thank you in the bargain.

Light flashed on her closed eyelids, and a deep roaring shook her. Cornelia, is that lightning? I hear thunder. There's going to be a storm. Close all the windows. Call the children in. . . . "Mother, here we are, all of us." "Is that you, Hapsy?" "Oh, no, I'm Lydia. We drove as fast as we could." Their faces drifted above her, drifted away. The rosary fell out of her hands and Lydia put it back. Jimmy tried to help, their hands fumbled together, and Granny closed two fingers around Jimmy's thumb. Beads wouldn't do, it must be something alive. She was so amazed her thoughts ran round and round. So, my dear Lord, this is my death and I wasn't even thinking about it. My children have come to see me die. But I can't, it's not time. Oh, I always hated surprises. I wanted to give Cornelia the amethyst set—Cornelia, you're to have the amethyst set, but Hapsy's to wear it when she wants, and, Doctor Harry, do shut up. Nobody sent for you. Oh, my dear Lord, do wait a minute. I meant to do something about the Forty Acres, Jimmy doesn't need it and Lydia will later on, with that worthless husband of hers. I meant to finish the altar cloth and send six bottles of wine to Sister Borgia for her dyspepsia. I want to send six bottles of wine to Sister Borgia, Father Connolly, now don't let me forget.

Cornelia's voice made short turns and tilted over and crashed. "Oh, Mother, oh, Mother, oh, Mother. . . ."

"I'm not going, Cornelia. I'm taken by surprise. I can't go."

You'll see Hapsy again. What about her? "I thought you'd never come." Granny made a long journey outward, looking for Hapsy. What if I don't find her? What then? Her heart sank down and down, there was no bottom to death, she couldn't come to the end of it. The blue light from Cornelia's lampshade drew into a tiny point in the center of her brain, it flickered and winked like an eye, quietly it fluttered and dwindled. Granny lay curled down within herself, amazed and watchful, staring at the point of light that was herself; her body was now only a deeper mass of shadow in an endless darkness and this darkness would curl around the light and swallow it up. God, give a sign!

For the second time there was no sign. Again no bridegroom and the priest in the house. She could not remember any other sorrow because this grief wiped them all away. Oh, no, there's nothing more cruel than this—I'll never forgive it. She stretched herself with a deep breath and blew out the light.

QUESTIONS

1. Characterize Granny. What facts do we know about her life? **2.** Why, after sixty full years, does the jilting by George loom so large in Granny's mind? Are we to accept her own strong statements that the pain of the jilting was more than compensated for by the happiness she ultimately found with her husband John, her children, and her grandchildren? Explain.   **3.**   Why does the author not present us with Granny's final thoughts in an orderly and sequential pattern? **4.**   Granny is revealed to us not only through her direct thoughts but also through the many images that float through her mind—the fog, the blowing breeze, "a whirl of dark smoke," and others. What do these images reveal about Granny?

WRITING TOPIC
The final paragraph echoes Christ's parable of the bridegroom (Matthew 25:1–13). Why does Granny connect this final, deep religious grief with the grief she felt when George jilted her?

A Summer Tragedy

ARNA BONTEMPS [1902–1973]

Old Jeff Patton, the black share farmer, fumbled with his bow tie. His fingers trembled and the high, stiff collar pinched his throat. A fellow loses his hand for such vanities after thirty or forty years of simple life. Once a year, or maybe twice if there's a wedding among his kinfolks, he may spruce up, but generally fancy clothes do nothing but adorn the wall of the big room and feed the moths. That had been Jeff Patton's experience. He had not worn his stiff-bosomed shirt more than a dozen times in all his married life. His swallow-tailed coat lay on the bed beside him, freshly brushed and pressed, but it was as full of holes as the overalls in which he worked on weekdays. The moths had used it badly. Jeff twisted his mouth into a hideous toothless grimace as he contended with the obstinate bow. He stamped his good foot and decided to give up the struggle.

"Jennie," he called.

"What's that, Jeff?" His wife's shrunken voice came out of the adjoining room like an echo. It was hardly bigger than a whisper.

"I reckon you'll have to he'p me wid this heah bow tie, baby," he said meekly. "Dog if I can hitch it up."

Her answer was not strong enough to reach him, but presently the old woman came to the door, feeling her way with a stick. She had a wasted, dead-leaf appearance. Her body, as scrawny and gnarled as a string bean, seemed less than nothing in the ocean of frayed and faded petticoats that surrounded her. These hung an inch or two above the tops of her heavy unlaced shoes and showed little grotesque piles where the stockings had fallen down from her negligible legs.

"You oughta could do a heap mo' wid a thing like that'n me—beingst as you got yo' good sight."

"Looks like I oughta could," he admitted. "But my fingers is gone democrat on me. I get all mixed up in the looking glass an' can't tell wicha way to twist the devilish thing."

Jennie sat on the side of the bed, and old Jeff Patton got down on one knee while she tied the bow knot. It was a slow and painful ordeal for each of them in this position. Jeff's bones cracked, his knee ached, and it was only after a half dozen attempts that Jennie worked a semblance of a bow into the tie.

"I got to dress maself now," the old woman whispered. "These is ma old shoes an' stockings, and I ain't so much as unwrapped ma dress."

"Well, don't worry 'bout me no mo', baby," Jeff said. "That 'bout finishes me. All I gotta do now is slip on that old coat 'n ves' an' I'll be fixed to leave."

Jennie disappeared again through the dim passage into the shed room. Being blind was no handicap to her in that black hole. Jeff heard the cane placed against the wall beside the door and knew that his wife was on easy ground. He put on his coat, took a battered top hat from the bed post, and hobbled to the front door. He was ready to travel. As soon as Jennie could get on her Sunday shoes and her old black silk dress, they would start.

Outside the tiny log house, the day was warm and mellow with sunshine. A host of wasps were humming with busy excitement in the trunk of a dead sycamore. Gray squirrels were searching through the grass for hickory nuts, and blue jays were in the trees, hopping from branch to branch. Pine woods stretched away to the left like a black sea. Among them were scattered scores of log houses like Jeff's, houses of black share farmers. Cows and pigs wandered freely among the trees. There was no danger of loss. Each farmer knew his own stock and knew his neighbor's as well as he knew his neighbor's children.

Down the slope to the right were the cultivated acres on which the colored folks worked. They extended to the river, more than two miles away, and they were today green with the unmade cotton crop. A tiny thread of a road, which passed directly in front of Jeff's place, ran through these green fields like a pencil mark.

Jeff, standing outside the door, with his absurd hat in his left hand, surveyed the wide scene tenderly. He had been forty-five years on these acres. He loved them with the unexplained affection that others have for the countries to which they belong.

The sun was hot on his head, his collar still pinched his throat, and the Sunday clothes were intolerably hot. Jeff transferred the hat to his right hand and began fanning with it. Suddenly the whisper that was Jennie's voice came out of the shed room.

"You can bring the car round front whilst you's waitin'," it said feebly. There was a tired pause; then it added, "I'll soon be fixed to go."

"A'right, baby," Jeff answered. "I'll get it in a minute."

But he didn't move. A thought struck him that made his mouth fall open. The mention of the car brought to his mind with new intensity, the trip he and Jennie were about to take. Fear came into his eyes; excitement took his breath. Lord, Jesus!

"Jeff. . . . O Jeff," the old woman's whisper called.

He awakened with a jolt. "Hunh, baby?"

"What you doin'?"

"Nuthin. Jes studyin'. I jes been turnin' things round 'n round in ma mind."

"You could be gettin' the car," she said.

"Oh yes, right away, baby."

He started round to the shed, limping heavily on his bad leg. There were three frizzly chickens in the yard. All his other chickens had been killed or stolen recently. But the frizzly chickens had been saved somehow. That was fortunate indeed, for these curious creatures had a way of devouring "poison" from the yard and in that way protecting against conjure and black luck and spells. But even the frizzly chickens seemed now to be in a stupor. Jeff thought they had some ailment; he expected all three of them to die shortly.

The shed in which the old T-model Ford stood was only a grass roof held up by four corner poles. It had been built by tremulous hands at a time when the little rattletrap car had been regarded as a peculiar treasure. And, miraculously, despite wind and downpour, it still stood.

Jeff adjusted the crank and put his weight upon it. The engine came to life with a sputter and bang that rattled the old car from radiator to tail light. Jeff hopped into the seat and put his foot on the accelerator. The sputtering and banging increased. The rattling became more violent. That was good. It was good banging, good sputtering and rattling, and it meant that the aged car was still in running condition. She could be depended on for this trip.

Again Jeff's thought halted as if paralyzed. The suggestion of the trip fell into the machinery of his mind like a wrench. He felt dazed and weak. He swung the car out into the yard, made a half turn, and drove around to the front door. When he took his hands off the wheel, he noticed that he was trembling violently. He cut off the motor and climbed to the ground to wait for Jennie.

A few minutes later she was at the window, her voice rattling against the pane like a broken shutter.

"I'm ready, Jeff."

He did not answer, but limped into the house and took her by the arm. He led her slowly through the big room, down the step, and across the yard.

"You reckon I'd oughta lock the do'?" he asked softly.

They stopped and Jennie weighed the question. Finally she shook her head. "Ne' mind the door," she said. "I don't see no cause to lock up things."

"You right," Jeff agreed. "No cause to lock up."

Jeff opened the door and helped his wife into the car. A quick shudder passed over him. Jesus! Again he trembled.

"How come you shaking so?" Jennie whispered.

"I don't know," he said.

"You mus' be scairt, Jeff."

"No, baby, I ain't scairt."

He slammed the door after her and went around to crank up again. The motor started easily. Jeff wished that it had not been so responsive. He would have liked a few more minutes in which to turn things around in his head. As it was, with Jennie chiding him about being afraid, he had to keep going. He swung the car into the little pencil-mark road and started off toward the river, driving very slowly, very cautiously.

Chugging across the green countryside, the small battered Ford seemed tiny indeed. Jeff felt a familiar excitement, a thrill, as they came down the first slope to the immense levels on which the cotton was growing. He could not help reflecting that the crops were good. He knew what that meant, too; he had made forty-five of them with his own hands. It was true that he had worn out nearly a dozen mules, but that was the fault of old man Stevenson, the owner of the land. Major Stevenson had the old notion that one mule was all a share farmer needed to work a thirty-acre plot. It was an expensive notion, the way it killed mules from overwork but the old man held to it. Jeff thought it killed a good many share farmers as well as mules, but he had no sympathy for them. He had always been strong, and he had been taught to have no patience with weakness in men. Women or children might be tolerated if they were puny, but a weak man was a curse. Of course, his own children—

Jeff's thought halted there. He and Jennie never mentioned their dead children any more. And naturally, he did not wish to dwell upon them in his mind. Before he knew it, some remark would slip out of his mouth and that would make Jennie feel blue. Perhaps she would cry. A woman like Jennie could not easily throw off the grief that comes from losing five grown children within two years. Even Jeff was still staggered by the blow. His memory had not been much good recently. He frequently talked to himself. And, although he had kept it a secret, he knew that his courage had left him. He was terrified by the least unfamiliar sound at night. He was reluctant to venture far from home in the daytime. Sometimes he became afraid and trembled without knowing what had frightened him. The feeling would just come over him like a chill.

The car rattled slowly over the dusty road. Jennie sat erect and silent with a little absurd hat pinned to her hair. Her useless eyes seemed very large, very white in their deep sockets. Suddenly Jeff heard her voice, and he inclined his head to catch the words.

"Is we passed Delia Moore's house yet?" she asked.

"Not yet," he said.

"You must be drivin' mighty slow, Jeff."

"We just as well take our time, baby."

There was a pause. A little puff of steam was coming out of the radiator of the car. Heat wavered above the hood. Delia Moore's house was nearly half a mile away. After a moment Jennie spoke again.

"You ain't really scairt, is you, Jeff?"

"Nah, baby, I ain't scairt."

"You know how we agreed—we gotta keep on goin'."

Jewels of perspiration appeared on Jeff's forehead. His eyes rounded, blinked, became fixed on the road.

"I don't know," he said with a shiver, "I reckon it's the only thing to do."

"Hm."

A flock of guinea fowls, pecking in the road, were scattered by the passing car. Some of them took to their wings; others hid under bushes. A blue jay, swaying on a leafy twig, was annoying a roadside squirrel. Jeff held an even speed till he came near Delia's place. Then he slowed down noticeably.

Delia's house was really no house at all, but an abandoned stone building converted into a dwelling. It sat near a crossroads, beneath a single black cedar tree. There Delia, a cattish old creature of Jennie's age, lived alone. She had been there more years than anybody could remember, and long ago had won the disfavor of such women as Jennie. For in her young days Delia had been gayer, yellower, and saucier than seemed proper in those parts. Her ways with menfolks had been dark and suspicious. And the fact that she had had as many husbands as children did not help her reputation.

"Yonder's old Delia," Jeff said as they passed.

"What she doin'?"

"Jes sittin' in the do'," he said.

"She see us?"

"Hm," Jeff said. "Musta did."

That relieved Jennie. It strengthened her to know that her old enemy had seen her pass in her best clothes. That would give the old she-devil something to chew her gums and fret about, Jennie thought. Wouldn't she have a fit if she didn't find out? Old evil Delia! This would be just the thing for her. It would pay her back for being so evil. It would also pay her, Jennie thought, for the way she used to grin at Jeff—long ago, when her teeth were good.

The road became smooth and red, and Jeff could tell by the smell of the air that they were nearing the river. He could see the rise where the road turned and ran along parallel to the stream. The car chugged on monotonously. After a long silent spell, Jennie leaned against Jeff and spoke.

"How many bale o' cotton you think we got standin'?" she said.

Jeff wrinkled his forehead as he calculated.

"'Bout twenty-five, I reckon."

"How many you make las' year?"

"Twenty-eight," he said. "How come you ask that?"

"I's jes thinkin'," Jennie said quietly.

"It don't make a speck o' difference though," Jeff reflected. "If we get much or if we get little, we still gonna be in debt to old man Stevenson when he gets through counting up agin us. It's took us a long time to learn that."

Jennie was not listening to these words. She had fallen into a trancelike meditation. Her lips twitched. She chewed her gums and rubbed her gnarled hands nervously. Suddenly, she leaned forward, buried her face in the nervous hands, and burst into tears. She cried aloud in a dry, cracked voice that suggested the rattle of fodder on dead stalks. She cried aloud like a child, for she had never learned to suppress a genuine sob. Her slight old frame shook heavily and seemed hardly able to sustain such violent grief.

"What's the matter, baby?" Jeff asked awkwardly. "Why you cryin' like all that?"

"I's jes thinkin'," she said.

"So you the one what's scairt now, hunh?"

"I ain't scairt, Jeff. I's jes thinkin' 'bout leavin' eve'thing like this—eve'thing we been used to. It's right sad-like."

Jeff did not answer, and presently Jennie buried her face again and cried.

The sun was almost overhead. It beat down furiously on the dusty wagon-path road, on the parched roadside grass and the tiny battered car. Jeff's hands, gripping the wheel, became wet with perspiration; his forehead sparkled. Jeff's lips parted. His mouth shaped a hideous grimace. His face suggested the face of a man being burned. But the torture passed and his expression softened again.

"You mustn't cry, baby," he said to his wife. "We gotta be strong. We can't break down."

Jennie waited a few seconds, then said, "You reckon we oughta do it, Jeff? You reckon we oughta go 'head an' do it, really?"

Jeff's voice choked; his eyes blurred. He was terrified to hear Jennie say the thing that had been in his mind all morning. She had egged him on when he had wanted more than anything in the world to wait, to reconsider, to think things over a little longer. Now she was getting cold feet. Actually, there was no need of thinking the question through again. It would only end in making the same painful decision once more. Jeff knew that. There was no need of fooling around longer.

"We jes as well to do like we planned," he said. "They ain't nothin' else for us now—it's the bes' thing."

Jeff thought of the handicaps, the near impossibility, of making another crop with his leg bothering him more and more each week. Then there was always the chance that he would have another stroke, like the one that had made him lame. Another one might kill him. The least it could do would be to leave him helpless. Jeff gasped—Lord Jesus! He could not bear to think of being helpless, like a baby, on Jennie's hands. Frail, blind Jennie.

The little pounding motor of the car worked harder and harder. The puff of steam from the cracked radiator became larger. Jeff realized that they were climbing a little rise. A moment later the road turned abruptly, and he looked upon the face of the river.

"Jeff."

"Hunh?"

"Is that the water I hear?"

"Hm. Tha's it."

"Well, which way you goin' now?"

"Down this-a way," he said. "The road runs 'long 'side o' the water a lil piece."

She waited a while calmly. Then she said, "Drive faster."

"A'right, baby," Jeff said.

The water roared in the bed of the river. It was fifty or sixty feet below the level of the road. Between the road and the water there was a long smooth slope, sharply inclined. The slope was dry, the clay hardened by prolonged summer heat. The water below, roaring in a narrow channel, was noisy and wild.

"Jeff."

"Hunh?"

"How far you goin'?"

"Jes a lil piece down the road."

"You ain't scairt, is you, Jeff?"

"Nah, baby," he said trembling. "I ain't scairt."

"Remember how we planned it, Jeff. We gotta do it like we said. Brave-like."

"Hm."

Jeff's brain darkened. Things suddenly seemed unreal, like figures in a dream. Thoughts swam in his mind foolishly, hysterically, like little blind fish in a pool within a dense cave. They rushed again. Jeff soon became dizzy. He shuddered violently and turned to his wife.

"Jennie, I can't do it. I can't." His voice broke pitifully.

She did not appear to be listening. All the grief had gone from her face. She sat erect, her unseeing eyes wide open, strained and frightful. Her glossy black skin had become dull. She seemed as thin, as sharp and bony, as a starved bird. Now, having suffered and endured the sadness of tearing herself away from beloved things, she showed no anguish. She was absorbed with her own thoughts, and she didn't even hear Jeff's voice shouting in her ear.

Jeff said nothing more. For an instant there was light in his cavernous brain. The great chamber was, for less than a second, peopled by characters he knew and loved. They were simple, healthy creatures, and they behaved in a manner that he could understand. They had quality. But since he had already taken leave of them long ago, the remembrance did not break his heart again. Young Jeff Patton was among them, the Jeff Patton of fifty years ago who went down to New Orleans with a crowd of country boys to the Mardi Gras doings. The gay young crowd, boys with candy-striped shirts and rouged brown girls in noisy silks, was like a picture in his head. Yet it did not make him sad. On that very trip Slim Burns had killed Joe Beasley—the crowd had been broken up. Since then Jeff Patton's world had been the Greenbriar Plantation. If there had been other Mardi Gras carnivals, he had not heard of them. Since then there had been no time; the years had fallen on him like waves. Now he was old, worn out. Another paralytic stroke (like the one he had already suffered) would put him on his back for keeps. In that condition, with a frail blind woman to look after him, he would be worse off than if he were dead.

Suddenly Jeff's hands became steady. He actually felt brave. He slowed down the motor of the car and carefully pulled off the road. Below, the water of the stream boomed, a soft thunder in the deep channel. Jeff ran the car onto the clay slope, pointed it directly toward the stream, and put his foot heavily on the accelerator. The little car leaped furiously down the steep incline toward the water. The movement was nearly as swift and direct as a fall. The two old black folks, sitting quietly side by side, showed no excitement. In another instant the car hit the water and dropped immediately out of sight.

A little later it lodged in the mud of a shallow place. One wheel of the crushed and upturned little Ford became visible above the rushing water.

Idiots First

BERNARD MALAMUD [b. 1914]

The thick ticking of the tin clock stopped. Mendel, dozing in the dark, awoke in fright. The pain returned as he listened. He drew on his cold embittered clothing, and wasted minutes sitting at the edge of the bed.

"Isaac," he ultimately sighed.

In the kitchen, Isaac, his astonished mouth open, held six peanuts in his palm. He placed each on the table. "One . . . two . . . nine."

He gathered each peanut and appeared in the doorway. Mendel, in loose hat and long overcoat, still sat on the bed. Isaac watched with small eyes and ears, thick hair graying the sides of his head.

"Schlaf," he nasally said.

"No," muttered Mendel. As if stifling he rose. "Come, Isaac."

He wound his old watch though the sight of the stopped clock nauseated him.

Isaac wanted to hold it to his ear.

"No, it's late." Mendel put the watch carefully away. In the drawer he found the little paper bag of crumpled ones and fives and slipped it into his overcoat pocket. He helped Isaac on with his coat.

Isaac looked at one dark window, then at the other. Mendel stared at both blank windows.

They went slowly down the darkly lit stairs, Mendel first, Isaac watching the moving shadows on the wall. To one long shadow he offered a peanut.

"Hungrig."

In the vestibule the old man gazed through the thin glass. The November night was cold and bleak. Opening the door he cautiously thrust his head out. Though he saw nothing he quickly shut the door.

"Ginzburg, that he came to see me yesterday," he whispered in Isaac's ear.

Isaac sucked air.

"You know who I mean?"

Isaac combed his chin with his fingers.

"That's the one, with the black whiskers. Don't talk to him or go with him if he asks you."

Isaac moaned.

"Young people he don't bother so much," Mendel said in afterthought.

It was suppertime and the street was empty but the store windows dimly lit their way to the corner. They crossed the deserted street and went on. Isaac, with a happy cry, pointed to the three golden balls. Mendel smiled but was exhausted when they got to the pawnshop.

The pawnbroker, a red-bearded man with black horn-rimmed glasses, was eating a whitefish at the rear of the store. He craned his head, saw them, and settled back to sip his tea.

In five minutes he came forward, patting his shapeless lips with a large white handkerchief.

Mendel, breathing heavily, handed him the worn gold watch. The pawnbroker, raising his glasses, screwed in his eyepiece. He turned the watch over
once. "Eight dollars."

The dying man wet his cracked lips. "I must have thirty-five."

"So go to Rothschild."

"Cost me myself sixty."

"In 1905." The pawnbroker handed back the watch. It had stopped ticking.
Mendel wound it slowly. It ticked hollowly.

"Isaac must go to my uncle that he lives in California."

"It's a free country," said the pawnbroker.

Isaac, watching a banjo, snickered.

"What's the matter with him?" the pawnbroker asked.

"So let be eight dollars," muttered Mendel, "but where will I get the rest till
tonight?"

"How much for my hat and coat?" he asked.

"No sale." The pawnbroker went behind the cage and wrote out a ticket. He
locked the watch in a small drawer but Mendel still heard it ticking.

In the street he slipped the eight dollars into the paper bag, then searched in
his pockets for a scrap of writing. Finding it, he strained to read the address by
the light of the street lamp.

As they trudged to the subway, Mendel pointed to the sprinkled sky.

"Isaac, look how many stars are tonight."

"Eggs," said Isaac.

"First we will go to Mr. Fishbein, after we will eat."

They got off the train in upper Manhattan and had to walk several blocks
before they located Fishbein's house.

"A regular palace," Mendel murmured, looking forward to a moment's
warmth.

Isaac stared uneasily at the heavy door of the house.

Mendel rang. The servant, a man with long sideburns, came to the door and
said Mr. and Mrs. Fishbein were dining and could see no one.

"He should eat in peace but we will wait till he finishes."

"Come back tomorrow morning. Tomorrow morning Mr. Fishbein will talk
to you. He don't do business or charity at this time of the night."

"Charity I am not interested—"

"Come back tomorrow."

"Tell him it's life or death—"

"Whose life or death?"

"So if not his, then mine."

"Don't be such a big smart aleck."

"Look me in my face," said Mendel, "and tell me if I got time till tomorrow
morning?"

The servant stared at him, then at Isaac, and reluctantly let them in.

The foyer was a vast high-ceilinged room with many oil paintings on the
walls, voluminous silken draperies, a thick flowered rug at foot, and a marble
staircase.

Mr. Fishbein, a paunchy bald-headed man with hairy nostrils and small patent leather feet, ran lightly down the stairs, a large napkin tucked under a tuxedo coat button. He stopped on the fifth step from the bottom and examined his visitors.

"Who comes on Friday night to a man that he has guests, to spoil him his supper?"

"Excuse me that I bother you, Mr. Fishbein," Mendel said. "If I didn't come now I couldn't come tomorrow."

"Without more preliminaries, please state your business. I'm a hungry man."

"Hungrig," wailed Isaac.

Fishbein adjusted his pince-nez. "What's the matter with him?"

"This is my son Isaac. He is like this all his life."

Isaac mewled.

"I am sending him to California."

"Mr. Fishbein don't contribute to personal pleasure trips."

"I am a sick man and he must go tonight on the train to my Uncle Leo."

"I never give to unorganized charity," Fishbein said, "but if you are hungry I will invite you downstairs in my kitchen. We having tonight chicken with stuffed derma."

"All I ask is thirty-five dollars for the train ticket to my uncle in California. I have already the rest."

"Who is your uncle? How old a man?"

"Eighty-one years, a long life to him."

Fishbein burst into laughter. "Eighty-one years and you are sending him this halfwit."

Mendel, flailing both arms, cried, "Please, without names."

Fishbein politely conceded.

"Where is open the door there we go in the house," the sick man said. "If you will kindly give me thirty-five dollars, God will bless you. What is thirty-five dollars to Mr. Fishbein? Nothing. To me, for my boy, is everything."

Fishbein drew himself up to his tallest height.

"Private contributions I don't make—only to institutions. This is my fixed policy."

Mendel sank to his creaking knees on the rug.

"Please, Mr. Fishbein, if not thirty-five, give maybe twenty."

"Levinson!" Fishbein angrily called.

The servant with the long sideburns appeared at the top of the stairs.

"Show this party where is the door—unless he wishes to partake food before leaving the premises."

"For what I got chicken won't cure it," Mendel said.

"This way if you please," said Levinson, descending.

Isaac assisted his father up.

"Take him to an institution," Fishbein advised over the marble balustrade. He ran quickly up the stairs and they were at once outside, buffeted by winds.

The walk to the subway was tedious. The wind blew mournfully. Mendel, breathless, glanced furtively at shadows. Isaac, clutching his peanuts in his frozen fist, clung to his father's side. They entered a small park to rest for a minute on a stone bench under a leafless two-branched tree. The thick right branch was raised, the thin left one hung down. A very pale moon rose slowly. So did a stranger as they approached the bench.

"Gut yuntif" [Happy holiday], he said hoarsely.

Mendel, drained of blood, waved his wasted arms. Isaac yowled sickly. Then a bell chimed and it was only ten. Mendel let out a piercing anguished cry as the bearded stranger disappeared into the bushes. A policeman came running, and though he beat the bushes with his nightstick, could turn up nothing. Mendel and Isaac hurried out of the little park. When Mendel glanced back the dead tree had its thin arm raised, the thick one down. He moaned.

They boarded a trolley, stopping at the home of a former friend, but he had died years ago. On the same block they went into a cafeteria and ordered two fried eggs for Isaac. The tables were crowded except where a heavy-set man sat eating soup with kasha. After one look at him they left in haste, although Isaac wept.

Mendel had another address on a slip of paper but the house was too far away, in Queens, so they stood in a doorway shivering.

What can I do, he frantically thought, in one short hour?

He remembered the furniture in the house. It was junk but might bring a few dollars. "Come, Isaac." They went once more to the pawnbroker's to talk to him, but the shop was dark and an iron gate—rings and gold watches glinting through it—was drawn tight across his place of business.

They huddled behind a telephone pole, both freezing. Isaac whimpered.

"See the big moon, Isaac. The whole sky is white."

He pointed but Isaac wouldn't look.

Mendel dreamed for a minute of the sky lit up, long sheets of light in all directions. Under the sky, in California, sat Uncle Leo drinking tea with lemon. Mendel felt warm but woke up cold.

Across the street stood an ancient brick synagogue.

He pounded on the huge door but no one appeared. He waited till he had breath and desperately knocked again. At last there were footsteps within, and the synagogue door creaked open on its massive brass hinges.

A darkly dressed sexton, holding a dripping candle, glared at them.

"Who knocks this time of night with so much noise on the synagogue door?"

Mendel told the sexton his troubles. "Please, I would like to speak to the rabbi."

"The rabbi is an old man. He sleeps now. His wife won't let you see him. Go home and come back tomorrow."

"To tomorrow I said goodbye already. I am a dying man."

Though the sexton seemed doubtful he pointed to an old wooden house next door. "In there he lives." He disappeared into the synagogue with his lit candle casting shadows around him.

Mendel, with Isaac clutching his sleeve, went up the wooden steps and rang the bell. After five minutes a big-faced, gray-haired bulky woman came out on the porch with a torn robe thrown over her nightdress. She emphatically said the rabbi was sleeping and could not be waked.

But as she was insisting, the rabbi himself tottered to the door. He listened a minute and said, "Who wants to see me let them come in."

They entered a cluttered room. The rabbi was an old skinny man with bent shoulders and a wisp of white beard. He wore a flannel nightgown and black skullcap; his feet were bare.

"Vey is mir" [Woe is me], his wife muttered. "Put on shoes or tomorrow comes sure pneumonia." She was a woman with a big belly, years younger than her husband. Staring at Isaac, she turned away.

Mendel apologetically related his errand. "All I need more is thirty-five dollars."

"Thirty-five?" said the rabbi's wife. "Why not thirty-five thousand? Who has so much money? My husband is a poor rabbi. The doctors take away every penny."

"Dear friend," said the rabbi, "if I had I would give you."

"I got already seventy," Mendel said, heavy-hearted. "All I need more is thirty-five."

"God will give you," said the rabbi.

"In the grave," said Mendel. "I need tonight. Come, Isaac."

"Wait," called the rabbi.

He hurried inside, came out with a fur-lined caftan, and handed it to Mendel.

"Yascha," shrieked his wife, "not your new coat!"

"I got my old one. Who needs two coats for one body?"

"Yascha, I am screaming—"

"Who can go among poor people, tell me, in a new coat?"

"Yascha," she cried, "what can this man do with your coat? He needs tonight the money. The pawnbrokers are asleep."

"So let him wake them up."

"No." She grabbed the coat from Mendel.

He held on to a sleeve, wrestling her for the coat. Her I know, Mendel thought. "Shylock," he muttered. Her eyes glittered.

The rabbi groaned and tottered dizzily. His wife cried out as Mendel yanked the coat from her hands.

"Run," cried the rabbi.

"Run, Isaac."

They ran out of the house and down the steps.

"Stop, you thief," called the rabbi's wife.

The rabbi pressed both hands to his temples and fell to the floor.

"Help!" his wife wept. "Heart attack! Help!"

But Mendel and Isaac ran through the streets with the rabbi's new fur-lined caftan. After them noiselessly ran Ginzburg.

It was very late when Mendel bought the train ticket in the only booth open.

There was no time to stop for a sandwich so Isaac ate his peanuts and they hurried to the train in the vast deserted station.

"So in the morning," Mendel gasped as they ran, "there comes a man that he sells sandwiches and coffee. Eat but get change. When reaches California the train, will be waiting for you on the station Uncle Leo. If you don't recognize him he will recognize you. Tell him I send best regards."

But when they arrived at the gate to the platform it was shut, the light out. Mendel, groaning, beat on the gate with his fists.

"Too late," said the uniformed ticket collector, a bulky, bearded man with hairy nostrils and a fishy smell.

He pointed to the station clock. "Already past twelve."

"But I see standing there still the train," Mendel said, hopping in his grief.

"It just left—in one more minute."

"A minute is enough. Just open the gate."

"Too late I told you."

Mendel socked his bony chest with both hands. "With my whole heart I beg you this little favor."

"Favors you had enough already. For you the train is gone. You shoulda been dead already at midnight. I told you that yesterday. This is the best I can do."

"Ginzburg!" Mendel shrank from him.

"Who else?" The voice was metallic, eyes glittered, the expression amused.

"For myself," the old man begged, "I don't ask a thing. But what will happen to my boy?"

Ginzburg shrugged slightly. "What will happen happens. This isn't my responsibility. I got enough to think about without worrying about somebody on one cylinder."

"What then is your responsibility?"

"To create conditions. To make happen what happens. I ain't in the anthropomorphic business."

"Whatever business you in, where is your pity?"

"This ain't my commodity. The law is the law."

"Which law is this?"

"The cosmic universal law, goddamit, the one I got to follow myself."

"What kind of a law is it?" cried Mendel. "For God's sake, don't you understand what I went through in my life with this poor boy? Look at him. For thirty-nine years, since the day he was born, I wait for him to grow up, but he don't. Do you understand what this means in a father's heart? Why don't you let him go to his uncle?" His voice had risen and he was shouting.

Isaac mewled loudly.

"Better calm down or you'll hurt somebody's feelings," Ginzburg said with a wink toward Isaac.

"All my life," Mendel cried, his body trembling, "what did I have? I was poor. I suffered from my health. When I worked I worked too hard. When I didn't work was worse. My wife died a young woman. But I didn't ask from anybody nothing. Now I ask a small favor. Be so kind, Mr. Ginzburg."

The ticket collector was picking his teeth with a match stick.

"You ain't the only one, my friend, some got it worse than you. That's how it goes in this country."

"You dog you." Mendel lunged at Ginzburg's throat and began to choke. "You bastard, don't you understand what it means human?"

They struggled nose to nose, Ginzburg, though his astonished eyes bulged, began to laugh. "You pipsqueak nothing. I'll freeze you to pieces."

His eyes lit in rage and Mendel felt an unbearable cold like an icy dagger invading his body, all of his parts shriveling.

Now I die without helping Isaac.

A crowd gathered. Isaac yelped in fright.

Clinging to Ginzburg in his last agony, Mendel saw reflected in the ticket collector's eyes the depth of his terror. But he saw that Ginzburg, staring at himself in Mendel's eyes, saw mirrored in them the extent of his own awful wrath. He beheld a shimmering, starry, blinding light that produced darkness.

Ginzburg looked astounded. "Who me?"

His grip on the squirming old man slowly loosened, and Mendel, his heart barely beating, slumped to the ground.

"Go." Ginzburg muttered, "take him to the train."

"Let pass," he commanded a guard.

The crowd parted. Isaac helped his father up and they tottered down the steps to the platform where the train waited, lit and ready to go.

Mendel found Isaac a coach seat and hastily embraced him. "Help Uncle Leo, Isaakil. Also remember your father and mother."

"Be nice to him," he said to the conductor. "Show him where everything is."

He waited on the platform until the train began slowly to move. Isaac sat at the edge of his seat, his face strained in the direction of his journey. When the train was gone, Mendel ascended the stairs to see what had become of Ginzburg.

QUESTIONS

1. Can this story be read as a religious drama? In this connection, consider the rabbi, the only person who helps Mendel. His compassion and his indifference to material things reveal him as a man of God. What does the supernatural Ginzburg represent? **2.** What is the significance of the fact that Isaac, for whom Mendel is determined to provide before death claims him, is an idiot? **3.** Mendel wins his battle with Ginzburg. What does that victory signify?

WRITING TOPIC

How do the various episodes in this story establish Mendel's character and prepare the reader for the final, climactic confrontation between Mendel and Ginzburg?

Patriotism*

YUKIO MISHIMA [1925–1970]

In the twenty-eighth of February, 1936 (on the third day, that is, of the February Incident[1]), Lieutenant Shinji Takeyama of the Konoe Transport Battalion—profoundly disturbed by the knowledge that his closest colleagues had been with the mutineers from the beginning, and indignant at the imminent prospect of Imperial troops attacking Imperial troops—took his officer's sword and ceremonially disemboweled himself in the eight-mat room of his private residence in the sixth block of Aoba-chō, in Yotsuya Ward. His wife, Reiko, followed him, stabbing herself to death. The lieutenant's farewell note consisted of one sentence: "Long live the Imperial Forces." His wife's, after apologies for her unfilial conduct in thus preceding her parents to the grave, concluded: "The day which, for a soldier's wife, had to come, has come. . . ." The last moments of this heroic and dedicated couple were such as to make the gods themselves weep. The lieutenant's age, it should be noted, was thirty-one, his wife's twenty-three; and it was not half a year since the celebration of their marriage.

2

Those who saw the bride and bridegroom in the commemorative photograph—perhaps no less than those actually present at the lieutenant's wedding—had exclaimed in wonder at the bearing of this handsome couple. The lieutenant, majestic in military uniform, stood protectively beside his bride, his right hand resting upon his sword, his officer's cap held at his left side. His expression was severe, and his dark brows and wide-gazing eyes well conveyed the clear integrity of youth. For the beauty of the bride in her white over-robe no comparisons were adequate. In the eyes, round beneath soft brows, in the slender, finely shaped nose, and in the full lips, there was both sensuousness and refinement. One hand, emerging shyly from a sleeve of the over-robe, held a fan, and the tips of the fingers, clustering delicately, were like the bud of a moonflower.

After the suicide, people would take out this photograph and examine it, and sadly reflect that too often there was a curse on these seemingly flawless unions. Perhaps it was no more than imagination, but looking at the picture after the tragedy it almost seemed as if the two young people before the gold-lacquered screen were gazing, each with equal clarity, at the deaths which lay before them.

Thanks to the good offices of their go-between, Lieutenant General Ozeki, they had been able to set themselves up in a new home at Aoba-chō in Yotsuya.

---

* Translated by Geoffrey W. Sargeant.
[1] On February 26, 1936, a long period of political turmoil culminated in an attempted coup led by young officers. Units commanded by the rebels seized and held central Tokyo for a number of days, and numerous high-ranking government officials, including Lord Privy Seal Saitō, were assassinated. The mutiny was crushed by loyal troops, and the leaders were executed.

"New home" is perhaps misleading. It was an old three-room rented house backing onto a small garden. As neither the six- nor the four-and-a-half-mat room downstairs was favored by the sun, they used the upstairs eight-mat room as both bedroom and guest room. There was no maid, so Reiko was left alone to guard the house in her husband's absence.

The honeymoon trip was dispensed with on the grounds that these were times of national emergency. The two of them had spent the first night of their marriage at this house. Before going to bed, Shinji, sitting erect on the floor with his sword laid before him, had bestowed upon his wife a soldierly lecture. A woman who had become the wife of a soldier should know and resolutely accept that her husband's death might come at any moment. It could be tomorrow. It could be the day after. But, no matter when it came—he asked—was she steadfast in her resolve to accept it? Reiko rose to her feet, pulled open a drawer of the cabinet, and took out what was the most prized of her new possessions, the dagger her mother had given her. Returning to her place, she laid the dagger without a word on the mat before her, just as her husband had laid his sword. A silent understanding was achieved at once and the lieutenant never again sought to test his wife's resolve.

In the first few months of her marriage Reiko's beauty grew daily more radiant, shining serene like the moon after rain.

As both were possessed of young, vigorous bodies, their relationship was passionate. Nor was this merely a matter of the night. On more than one occasion, returning home straight from maneuvers, and begrudging even the time it took to remove his mud-splashed uniform, the lieutenant had pushed his wife to the floor almost as soon as he had entered the house. Reiko was equally ardent in her response. For a little more or a little less than a month, from the first night of their marriage Reiko knew happiness, and the lieutenant, seeing this, was happy too.

Reiko's body was white and pure, and her swelling breasts conveyed a firm and chaste refusal; but, upon consent, those breasts were lavish with their intimate, welcoming warmth. Even in bed these two were frighteningly and awesomely serious. In the very midst of wild, intoxicating passions, their hearts were sober and serious.

By day the lieutenant would think of his wife in the brief rest periods between training; and all day long, at home, Reiko would recall the image of her husband. Even when apart, however, they had only to look at the wedding photograph for their happiness to be once more confirmed. Reiko felt not the slightest surprise that a man who had been a complete stranger until a few months ago should now have become the sun about which her whole world revolved.

All these things had a moral basis, and were in accordance with the Education Rescript's[2] injunction that "husband and wife should be harmonious." Not once

---

[2] The Education Rescript was a code promulgated during the Meiji, the reign of Emperor Mutsuhito which lasted from 1867 to 1912. The period is regarded as an historic era in the development of Modern Japan.

did Reiko contradict her husband, nor did the lieutenant ever find reason to scold his wife. On the god shelf below the stairway, alongside the tablet from the Great Ise Shrine,[3] were set photographs of their Imperial Majesties, and regularly every morning, before leaving for duty, the lieutenant would stand with his wife at this hallowed place and together they would bow their heads low. The offering water was renewed each morning, and the sacred sprig of *sasaki* was always green and fresh. Their lives were lived beneath the solemn protection of the gods and were filled with an intense happiness which set every fiber in their bodies trembling.

3

Although Lord Privy Seal Saitō's house was in their neighborhood, neither of them heard any noise of gunfire on the morning of February 26. It was a bugle, sounding muster in the dim, snowy dawn, when the ten-minute tragedy had already ended, which first disrupted the lieutenant's slumbers. Leaping at once from his bed, and without speaking a word, the lieutenant donned his uniform, buckled on the sword held ready for him by his wife, and hurried swiftly out into the snow-covered streets of the still darkened morning. He did not return until the evening of the twenty-eighth.

Later, from the radio news, Reiko learned the full extent of this sudden eruption of violence. Her life throughout the subsequent two days was lived alone, in complete tranquility, and behind locked doors.

In the lieutenant's face, as he hurried silently out into the snowy morning, Reiko had read the determination to die. If her husband did not return, her own decision was made: she too would die. Quietly she attended to the disposition of her personal possessions. She chose her sets of visiting kimonos as keepsakes for friends of her schooldays, and she wrote a name and address on the stiff paper wrapping in which each was folded. Constantly admonished by her husband never to think of the morrow, Reiko had not even kept a diary and was now denied the pleasure of assiduously rereading her record of the happiness of the past few months and consigning each page to the fire as she did so. Ranged across the top of the radio were a small china dog, a rabbit, a squirrel, a bear, and a fox. There were also a small vase and a water pitcher. These comprised Reiko's one and only collection. But it would hardly do, she imagined, to give such things as keepsakes. Nor again would it be quite proper to ask specifically for them to be included in the coffin. It seemed to Reiko, as these thoughts passed through her mind, that the expressions on the small animals' faces grew even more lost and forlorn.

Reiko took the squirrel in her hand and looked at it. And then, her thoughts turning to a realm far beyond these childlike affections, she gazed up into the distance at the great sunlike principle which her husband embodied. She was ready, and happy, to be hurtled along to her destruction in that gleaming sun

---

[3] The Great Ise Shrine is the highest ranking shrine in Japan. The emperor's ancestors were buried there.

chariot—but now, for these few moments of solitude, she allowed herself to luxuriate in this innocent attachment to trifles. The time when she had genuinely loved these things, however, was long past. Now she merely loved the memory of having once loved them, and their place in her heart had been filled by more intense passions, by a more frenzied happiness. . . . For Reiko had never, even to herself, thought of those soaring joys of the flesh as a mere pleasure. The February cold, and the icy touch of the china squirrel, had numbed Reiko's slender fingers; yet, even so, in her lower limbs, beneath the ordered repetition of the pattern which crossed the skirt of her trim *meisen* kimono, she could feel now, as she thought of the lieutenant's powerful arms reaching out toward her, a hot moistness of the flesh which defied the snows.

She was not in the least afraid of the death hovering in her mind. Waiting alone at home, Reiko firmly believed that everything her husband was feeling or thinking now, his anguish and distress, was leading her—just as surely as the power in his flesh—to a welcome death. She felt as if her body could melt away with ease and be transformed to the merest fraction of her husband's thought.

Listening to the frequent announcements on the radio, she heard the names of several of her husband's colleagues mentioned among those of the insurgents. This was news of death. She followed the developments closely, wondering anxiously, as the situation became daily more irrevocable, why no Imperial ordinance was sent down, and watching what had at first been taken as a movement to restore the nation's honor come gradually to be branded with the infamous name of mutiny. There was no communication from the regiment. At any moment, it seemed, fighting might commence in the city streets where the remains of the snow still lay.

Toward sundown on the twenty-eighth Reiko was startled by a furious pounding on the front door. She hurried downstairs. As she pulled with fumbling fingers at the bolt, the shape dimly outlined beyond the frosted-glass panel made no sound, but she knew it was her husband. Reiko had never known the bolt on the sliding door to be so stiff. Still it resisted. The door just would not open.

In a moment, almost before she knew she had succeeded, the lieutenant was standing before her on the cement floor inside the porch, muffled in a khaki greatcoat, his top boots heavy with slush from the street. Closing the door behind him, he returned the bolt once more to its socket. With what significance, Reiko did not understand.

"Welcome home."

Reiko bowed deeply, but her husband made no response. As he had already unfastened his sword and was about to remove his greatcoat, Reiko moved around behind to assist. The coat, which was cold and damp and had lost the odor of horse dung it normally exuded when exposed to the sun, weighed heavily upon her arm. Draping it across a hanger, and cradling the sword and leather belt in her sleeves, she waited while her husband removed his top boots and then followed behind him into the "living room." This was the six-mat room downstairs.

Seen in the clear light from the lamp, her husband's face, covered with a heavy growth of bristle, was almost unrecognizably wasted and thin. The cheeks were hollow, their luster and resilience gone. In his normal good spirits he would have changed into old clothes as soon as he was home and have pressed her to get supper at once, but now he sat before the table still in his uniform, his head dropping dejectedly. Reiko refrained from asking whether she should prepare the supper.

After an interval the lieutenant spoke.

"I knew nothing. They hadn't asked me to join. Perhaps out of consideration, because I was newly married. Kanō, and Homma too, and Yamaguchi."

Reiko recalled momentarily the faces of high-spirited young officers, friends of her husband, who had come to the house occasionally as guests.

"There may be an Imperial ordinance sent down tomorrow. They'll be posted as rebels, I imagine. I shall be in command of a unit with orders to attack them. . . . I can't do it. It's impossible to do a thing like that."

He spoke again.

"They've taken me off guard duty, and I have permission to return home for one night. Tomorrow morning, without question, I must leave to join the attack. I can't do it, Reiko."

Reiko sat erect with lowered eyes. She understood clearly that her husband had spoken of his death. The lieutenant was resolved. Each word, being rooted in death, emerged sharply and with powerful significance against this dark, unmovable background. Although the lieutenant was speaking of his dilemma, already there was no room in his mind for vacillation.

However, there was a clarity, like the clarity of a stream fed from melting snows, in the silence which rested between them. Sitting in his own home after the long two-day ordeal, and looking across at the face of his beautiful wife, the lieutenant was for the first time experiencing true peace of mind. For he had at once known, though she said nothing, that his wife divined the resolve which lay beneath his words.

"Well, then . . ." The lieutenant's eyes opened wide. Despite his exhaustion they were strong and clear, and now for the first time they looked straight into the eyes of his wife. "Tonight I shall cut my stomach."

Reiko did not flinch.

Her round eyes showed tension, as taut as the clang of a bell.

"I am ready," she said. "I ask permission to accompany you."

The lieutenant felt almost mesmerized by the strength in those eyes. His words flowed swiftly and easily, like the utterances of a man in delirium, and it was beyond his understanding how permission in a matter of such weight could be expressed so casually.

"Good. We'll go together. But I want you as a witness, first, for my own suicide. Agreed?"

When this was said a sudden release of abundant happiness welled up in both their hearts. Reiko was deeply affected by the greatness of her husband's trust in her. It was vital for the lieutenant, whatever else might happen, that there should be no irregularity in his death. For that reason there had to be a witness.

The fact that he had chosen his wife for this was the first mark of his trust. The second, and even greater mark, was that though he had pledged that they should die together he did not intend to kill his wife first—he had deferred her death to a time when he would no longer be there to verify it. If the lieutenant had been a suspicious husband, he would doubtless, as in the usual suicide pact, have chosen to kill his wife first.

When Reiko said, "I ask permission to accompany you," the lieutenant felt these words to be the final fruit of the education which he had himself given his wife, starting on the first night of their marriage, and which had schooled her, when the moment came, to say what had to be said without a shadow of hesitation. This flattered the lieutenant's opinion of himself as a self-reliant man. He was not so romantic or conceited as to imagine that the words were spoken spontaneously, out of love for her husband.

With happiness welling almost too abundantly in their hearts, they could not help smiling at each other. Reiko felt as if she had returned to her wedding night.

Before her eyes was neither pain nor death. She seemed to see only a free and limitless expanse opening out into vast distances.

"The water is hot. Will you take your bath now?"

"Ah yes, of course."

"And supper . . . ?"

The words were delivered in such level, domestic tones that the lieutenant came near to thinking, for the fraction of a second, that everything had been a hallucination.

"I don't think we'll need supper. But perhaps you could warm some sake?"

"As you wish."

As Reiko rose and took a *tanzen* gown from the cabinet for after the bath, she purposely directed her husband's attention to the opened drawer. The lieutenant rose, crossed to the cabinet, and looked inside. From the ordered array of paper wrappings he read, one by one, the addresses of the keepsakes. There was no grief in the lieutenant's response to this demonstration of heroic resolve. His heart was filled with tenderness. Like a husband who is proudly shown the childish purchases of a young wife, the lieutenant, overwhelmed by affection, lovingly embraced his wife from behind and implanted a kiss upon her neck.

Reiko felt the roughness of the lieutenant's unshaven skin against her neck. This sensation, more than being just a thing of this world, was for Reiko almost the world itself, but now—with the feeling that it was soon to be lost forever— it had freshness beyond all her experience. Each moment had its own vital strength, and the senses in every corner of her body were reawakened. Accepting her husband's caresses from behind, Reiko raised herself on the tips of her toes, letting the vitality seep through her entire body.

"First the bath, and then, after some sake . . . lay out the bedding upstairs, will you?"

The lieutenant whispered the words into his wife's ear. Reiko silently nodded.

Flinging off his uniform, the lieutenant went to the bath. To faint background noises of slopping water Reiko tended the charcoal brazier in the living room and began the preparations for warming the sake.

Taking the *tanzen*, a sash, and some underclothes, she went to the bathroom to ask how the water was. In the midst of a coiling cloud of steam the lieutenant was sitting cross-legged on the floor, shaving, and she could dimly discern the rippling movements of the muscles on his damp, powerful back as they responded to the movement of his arms.

There was nothing to suggest a time of any special significance. Reiko, going busily about her tasks, was preparing side dishes from odds and ends in stock. Her hands did not tremble. If anything, she managed even more efficiently and smoothly than usual. From time to time, it is true, there was a strange throbbing deep within her breast. Like distant lightning, it had a moment of sharp intensity and then vanished without trace. Apart from that, nothing was in any way out of the ordinary.

The lieutenant, shaving in the bathroom, felt his warmed body miraculously healed at last of the desperate tiredness of the days of indecision and filled—in spite of the death which lay ahead—with pleasurable anticipation. The sound of his wife going about her work came to him faintly. A healthy physical craving, submerged for two days, reasserted itself.

The lieutenant was confident there had been no impurity in that joy they had experienced when resolving upon death. They had both sensed at that moment—though not, of course, in any clear and conscious way—that those permissible pleasures which they shared in private were once more beneath the protection of Righteousness and Divine Power, and of a complete and unassailable morality. On looking into each other's eyes and discovering there an honorable death, they had felt themselves safe once more behind steel walls which none could destroy, encased in an impenetrable armor of Beauty and Truth. Thus, so far from seeing any inconsistency or conflict between the urges of his flesh and the sincerity of his patriotism, the lieutenant was even able to regard the two as parts of the same thing.

Thrusting his face close to the dark, cracked, misted wall mirror, the lieutenant shaved himself with great care. This would be his death face. There must be no unsightly blemishes. The clean-shaven face gleamed once more with a youthful luster, seeming to brighten the darkness of the mirror. There was a certain elegance, he even felt, in the association of death with this radiantly healthy face.

Just as it looked now, this would become his death face! Already, in fact, it had half departed from the lieutenant's personal possession and had become the bust above a dead soldier's memorial. As an experiment he closed his eyes tight. Everything was wrapped in blackness, and he was no longer a living, seeing creature.

Returning from the bath, the traces of the shave glowing faintly blue beneath his smooth cheeks, he seated himself beside the now well-kindled charcoal brazier. Busy though Reiko was, he noticed, she had found time lightly to touch up her face. Her cheeks were gay and her lips moist. There was no shadow of sadness to be seen. Truly, the lieutenant felt, as he saw this mark of his young wife's passionate nature, he had chosen the wife he ought to have chosen.

As soon as the lieutenant had drained his sake cup he offered it to Reiko. Reiko had never before tasted sake, but she accepted without hesitation and sipped timidly.

"Come here," the lieutenant said.

Reiko moved to her husband's side and was embraced as she leaned backward across his lap. Her breast was in violent commotion, as if sadness, joy, and the potent sake were mingling and reacting within her. The lieutenant looked down into his wife's face. It was the last face he would see in this world, the last face he would see of his wife. The lieutenant scrutinized the face minutely, with the eyes of a traveler bidding farewell to splendid vistas which he will never revisit. It was a face he could not tire of looking at—the features regular yet not cold, the lips lightly closed with a soft strength. The lieutenant kissed those lips, unthinkingly. And suddenly, though there was not the slightest distortion of the face into the unsightliness of sobbing, he noticed that tears were welling slowly from beneath the long lashes of the closed eyes and brimming over into a glistening stream.

When, a little later, the lieutenant urged that they should move to the upstairs bedroom, his wife replied that she would follow after taking a bath. Climbing the stairs alone to the bedroom, where the air was already warmed by the gas heater, the lieutenant lay down on the bedding with arms outstretched and legs apart. Even the time at which he lay waiting for his wife to join him was no later and no earlier than usual.

He folded his hands beneath his head and gazed at the dark boards of the ceiling in the dimness beyond the range of the standard lamp. Was it death he was now waiting for? Or a wild ecstasy of the senses? The two seemed to overlap, almost as if the object of this bodily desire was death itself. But, however that might be, it was certain that never before had the lieutenant tasted such total freedom.

There was the sound of a car outside the window. He could hear the screech of its tires skidding in the snow piled at the side of the street. The sound of its horn re-echoed from near-by walls. . . . Listening to these noises he had the feeling that this house rose like a solitary island in the ocean of a society going as restlessly about its business as ever. All around, vastly and untidily, stretched the country for which he grieved. He was to give his life for it. But would that great country, with which he was prepared to remonstrate to the extent of destroying himself, take the slightest heed of his death? He did not know; and it did not matter. His was a battlefield without glory, a battlefield where none could display deeds of valor: it was the front line of the spirit.

Reiko's footsteps sounded on the stairway. The steep stairs in this old house creaked badly. There were fond memories in that creaking, and many a time, while waiting in bed, the lieutenant had listened to its welcome sound. At the thought that he would hear it no more he listened with intense concentration, striving for every corner of every moment of this precious time to be filled with the sound of those soft footfalls on the creaking stairway. The moments seemed transformed to jewels, sparkling with inner light.

Reiko wore a Nagoya sash about the waist of her *yukata*, but as the lieutenant reached toward it, its redness sobered by the dimness of the light, Reiko's hand moved to his assistance and the sash fell away, slithering swiftly to the floor. As she stood before him, still in her *yukata*, the lieutenant inserted his hands through the side slits beneath each sleeve, intending to embrace her as she was; but at the touch of his finger tips upon the warm naked flesh, and as the armpits closed gently about his hands, his whole body was suddenly aflame.

In a few moments the two lay naked before the glowing gas heater.

Neither spoke the thought, but their hearts, their bodies, and their pounding breasts blazed with the knowledge that this was the very last time. It was as if the words "The Last Time" were spelled out, in invisible brushstrokes, across every inch of their bodies.

The lieutenant drew his wife close and kissed her vehemently. As their tongues explored each other's mouths, reaching out into the smooth, moist interior, they felt as if the still unknown agonies of death had tempered their senses to the keenness of red-hot steel. The agonies they could not yet feel, the distant pains of death, had refined their awareness of pleasure.

"This is the last time I shall see your body," said the lieutenant. "Let me look at it closely." And, tilting the shade on the lampstand to one side, he directed the rays along the full length of Reiko's outstretched form.

Reiko lay still with her eyes closed. The light from the low lamp clearly revealed the majestic sweep of her white flesh. The lieutenant, not without a touch of egocentricity, rejoiced that he would never see this beauty crumble in death.

At his leisure, the lieutenant allowed the unforgettable spectacle to engrave itself upon his mind. With one hand he fondled the hair, with the other he softly stroked the magnificent face, implanting kisses here and there where his eyes lingered. The quiet coldness of the high, tapering forehead, the closed eyes with their long lashes beneath faintly etched brows, the set of the finely shaped nose, the gleam of teeth glimpsed between full, regular lips, the soft cheeks and the small, wise chin . . . these things conjured up in the lieutenant's mind the vision of a truly radiant death face, and again and again he pressed his lips tight against the white throat—where Reiko's own hand was soon to strike—and the throat reddened faintly beneath his kisses. Returning to the mouth he laid his lips against it with the gentlest of pressures, and moved them rhythmically over Reiko's with the light rolling motion of a small boat. If he closed his eyes, the world became a rocking cradle.

Wherever the lieutenant's eyes moved his lips faithfully followed. The high, swelling breasts, surmounted by nipples like the buds of a wild cherry, hardened as the lieutenant's lips closed about them. The arms flowed smoothly downward from each side of the breast, tapering toward the wrists, yet losing nothing of their roundness or symmetry, and at their tips were those delicate fingers which had held the fan at the wedding ceremony. One by one, as the lieutenant kissed them, the fingers withdrew behind their neighbor as if in shame. . . . The natural hollow curving between the bosom and the stomach carried in its lines a suggestion not only of softness but of resilient strength, and while it gave forewarning of the rich curves spreading outward from here to the hips it had, in itself, an appearance only of restraint and proper discipline. The whiteness and richness of the stomach and hips was like milk brimming in a great bowl, and the sharply shadowed dip of the navel could have been the fresh impress of a raindrop, fallen there that very moment. Where the shadows gathered more thickly, hair clustered, gentle and sensitive, and as the agitation mounted in the now no longer passive body there hung over this region a scent like the smoldering of fragrant blossoms, growing steadily more pervasive.

At length, in a tremulous voice, Reiko spoke.

"Show me. . . . Let me look too, for the last time."

Never before had he heard from his wife's lips so strong and unequivocal a request. It was as if something which her modesty had wished to keep hidden to the end had suddenly burst its bonds of constraint. The lieutenant obediently lay back and surrendered himself to his wife. Lithely she raised her white, trembling body, and—burning with an innocent desire to return to her husband what he had done for her—placed two white fingers on the lieutenant's eyes, which gazed fixedly up at her, and gently stroked them shut.

Suddenly overwhelmed by tenderness, her cheeks flushed by a dizzying uprush of emotion, Reiko threw her arms about the lieutenant's close-cropped head. The bristly hairs rubbed painfully against her breast, the prominent nose was cold as it dug into her flesh, and his breath was hot. Relaxing her embrace, she gazed down at her husband's masculine face. The severe brows, the closed eyes, the splendid bridge of the nose, the shapely lips drawn firmly together . . . the blue, cleanshaven cheeks reflecting the light and gleaming smoothly. Reiko kissed each of these. She kissed the broad nape of the neck, the strong, erect shoulders, the powerful chest with its twin circles like shields and its russet nipples. In the armpits, deeply shadowed by the ample flesh of the shoulders and chest, a sweet and melancholy odor emanated from the growth of hair, and in the sweetness of this odor was contained, somehow, the essence of young death. The lieutenant's naked skin glowed like a field of barley, and everywhere the muscles showed in sharp relief, converging on the lower abdomen about the small, unassuming navel. Gazing at the youthful, firm stomach, modestly covered by a vigorous growth of hair, Reiko thought of it as it was soon to be, cruelly cut by the sword, and she laid her head upon it, sobbing in pity, and bathed it with kisses.

At the touch of his wife's tears upon his stomach the lieutenant felt ready to endure with courage the cruelest agonies of his suicide.

What ecstasies they experienced after these tender exchanges may well be imagined. The lieutenant raised himself and enfolded his wife in a powerful embrace, her body now limp with exhaustion after her grief and tears. Passionately they held their faces close, rubbing cheek against cheek. Reiko's body was trembling. Their breasts, moist with sweat, were tightly joined, and every inch of the young and beautiful bodies had become so much one with the other that it seemed impossible there should ever again be a separation. Reiko cried out. From the heights they plunged into the abyss, and from the abyss they took wing and soared once more to dizzying heights. The lieutenant panted like the regimental standard-bearer on a route march. . . . As one cycle ended, almost immediately a new wave of passion would be generated, and together—with no trace of fatigue—they would climb again in a single breathless movement to the very summit.

4

When the lieutenant at last turned away, it was not from weariness. For one thing, he was anxious not to undermine the considerable strength he would need in carrying out his suicide. For another, he would have been sorry to mar the sweetness of these last memories by overindulgence.

Since the lieutenant had clearly desisted, Reiko too, with her usual compliance, followed his example. The two lay naked on their backs, with fingers interlaced, staring fixedly at the dark ceiling. The room was warm from the heater, and even when the sweat had ceased to pour from their bodies they felt no cold. Outside, in the hushed night, the sounds of passing traffic had ceased. Even the noises of the trains and streetcars around Yotsuya station did not penetrate this far. After echoing through the region bounded by the moat, they were lost in the heavily wooded park fronting the broad driveway before Akasaka Palace. It was hard to believe in the tension gripping this whole quarter, where the two factions of the bitterly divided Imperial Army now confronted each other, poised for battle.

Savoring the warmth glowing within themselves, they lay still and recalled the ecstasies they had just known. Each moment of the experience was relived. They remembered the taste of kisses which had never wearied, the touch of naked flesh, episode after episode of dizzying bliss. But already, from the dark boards of the ceiling, the face of death was peering down. These joys had been final, and their bodies would never know them again. Not that joy of this intensity—and the same thought had occurred to them both—was ever likely to be reexperienced, even if they should live on to old age.

The feel of their fingers intertwined—this too would soon be lost. Even the wood-grain patterns they now gazed at on the dark ceiling boards would be taken from them. They could feel death edging in, nearer and nearer. There could be no hesitation now. They must have the courage to reach out to death themselves, and to seize it.

"Well, let's make our preparations," said the lieutenant. The note of determination in the words was unmistakable, but at the same time Reiko had never heard her husband's voice so warm and tender.

After they had risen, a variety of tasks awaited them.

The lieutenant, who had never once before helped with the bedding, now cheerfully slid back the door of the closet, lifted the mattress across the room by himself, and stowed it away inside.

Reiko turned off the gas heater and put away the lamp standard. During the lieutenant's absence she had arranged this room carefully, sweeping and dusting it to a fresh cleanness, and now—if one overlooked the rosewood table drawn into one corner—the eight-mat room gave all the appearance of a reception room ready to welcome an important guest.

"We've seen some drinking here, haven't we? With Kanō and Homma and Noguchi. . . ."

"Yes, they were great drinkers, all of them."

"We'll be meeting them before long, in the other world. They'll tease us, I imagine, when they find I've brought you with me."

Descending the stairs, the lieutenant turned to look back into this calm clean room, now brightly illuminated by the ceiling lamp. There floated across his mind the faces of the young officers who had drunk there, and laughed, and innocently bragged. He had never dreamed then that he would one day cut open his stomach in this room.

In the two rooms downstairs husband and wife busied themselves smoothly and serenely with their respective preparations. The lieutenant went to the toilet, and then to the bathroom to wash. Meanwhile Reiko folded away her husband's padded robe, placed his uniform tunic, his trousers, and a newly cut bleached loincloth in the bathroom, and set out sheets of paper on the living-room table for the farewell notes. Then she removed the lid from the writing box and began rubbing ink from the ink tablet. She had already decided upon the wording of her own note.

Reiko's fingers pressed hard upon the cold gilt letters of the ink tablet, and the water in the shallow well at once darkened, as if a black cloud had spread across it. She stopped thinking that this repeated action, this pressure from her fingers, this rise and fall of faint sound, was all and solely for death. It was a routine domestic task, a simple paring away of time until death should finally stand before her. But somehow, in the increasingly smooth motion of the tablet rubbing on the stone, and in the scent from the thickening ink, there was unspeakable darkness.

Neat in his uniform, which he now wore next to his skin, the lieutenant emerged from the bathroom. Without a word he seated himself at the table, bolt upright, took a brush in his hand, and stared undecidedly at the paper before him.

Reiko took a white silk kimono with her and entered the bathroom. When she reappeared in the living room, clad in the white kimono and with her face lightly made up, the farewell note lay completed on the table beneath the lamp. The thick black brushstrokes said simply:

"Long Live the Imperial Forces—Army Lieutenant Takeyama Shinji."

While Reiko sat opposite him writing her own note, the lieutenant gazed in silence, intensely serious, at the controlled movement of his wife's pale fingers as they manipulated the brush.

With their respective notes in their hands—the lieutenant's sword strapped to his side, Reiko's small dagger thrust into the sash of her white kimono—the two of them stood before the god shelf and silently prayed. Then they put out all the downstairs lights. As he mounted the stairs the lieutenant turned his head and gazed back at the striking, white-clad figure of his wife, climbing behind him, with lowered eyes, from the darkness beneath.

The farewell notes were laid side by side in the alcove of the upstairs room. They wondered whether they ought not to remove the hanging scroll, but since it had been written by their go-between, Lieutenant General Ozeki, and consisted, moreover, of two Chinese characters signifying "Sincerity," they left it where it was. Even if it were to become stained with splashes of blood, they felt that the lieutenant general would understand.

The lieutenant sitting erect with his back to the alcove, laid his sword on the floor before him.

Reiko sat facing him, a mat's width away. With the rest of her so severely white the touch of rouge on her lips seemed remarkably seductive.

Across the dividing mat they gazed intently into each other's eyes. The lieutenant's sword lay before his knees. Seeing it, Reiko recalled their first night and was overwhelmed with sadness. The lieutenant spoke, in a hoarse voice:

"As I have no second to help me I shall cut deep. It may look unpleasant, but please do not panic. Death of any sort is a fearful thing to watch. You must not be discouraged by what you see. Is that all right?"

"Yes."

Reiko nodded deeply.

Looking at the slender white figure of his wife the lieutenant experienced a bizarre excitement. What he was about to perform was an act in his public capacity as a soldier, something he had never previously shown his wife. It called for a resolution equal to the courage to enter battle; it was a death of no less degree and quality than death in the front line. It was his conduct on the battlefield that he was now to display.

Momentarily the thought led the lieutenant to a strange fantasy. A lonely death on the battlefield, a death beneath the eyes of his beautiful wife . . . in the sensation that he was now to die in these two dimensions, realizing an impossible union of them both, there was sweetness beyond words. This must be the very pinnacle of good fortune, he thought. To have every moment of his death observed by those beautiful eyes—it was like being borne to death on a gentle, fragrant breeze. There was some special favor here. He did not understand precisely what it was, but it was a domain unknown to others: a dispensation granted to no one else had been permitted to himself. In the radiant, bridelike figure of his white-robed wife the lieutenant seemed to see a vision of all those things he had loved and for which he was to lay down his life—the Imperial Household, the Nation, the Army Flag. All these, no less than the wife who sat before him, were presences observing him closely with clear and never-faltering eyes.

Reiko too was gazing intently at her husband, so soon to die, and she thought that never in this world had she seen anything so beautiful. The lieutenant always looked well in uniform, but now, as he contemplated death with severe brows and firmly closed lips, he revealed what was perhaps masculine beauty as its most superb.

"It's time to go," the lieutenant said at last.

Reiko bent her body low to the mat in a deep bow. She could not raise her face. She did not wish to spoil her make-up with tears, but the tears could not be held back.

When at length she looked up she saw hazily through the tears that her husband had wound a white bandage around the blade of his now unsheathed sword, leaving five or six inches of naked steel showing at the point.

Resting the sword in its cloth wrapping on the mat before him, the lieutenant rose from his knees, resettled himself cross-legged, and unfastened the hooks of his uniform collar. His eyes no longer saw his wife. Slowly, one by one, he undid the flat brass buttons. The dusky brown chest was revealed, and then the stomach. He unclasped his belt and undid the buttons of his trousers. The pure whiteness of the thickly coiled loincloth showed itself. The lieutenant pushed the cloth down with both hands, further to ease his stomach, and then reached for the white-bandaged blade of his sword. With his left hand he massaged his abdomen, glancing downward as he did so.

To reassure himself on the sharpness of his sword's cutting edge the lieutenant folded back the left trouser flap, exposing a little of his thigh, and lightly drew the blade across the skin. Blood welled up in the wound at once, and several streaks of red trickled downward, glistening in the strong light.

It was the first time Reiko had ever seen her husband's blood, and she felt a violent throbbing in her chest. She looked at her husband's face. The lieutenant was looking at the blood with calm appraisal. For a moment—though thinking at the same time that it was hollow comfort—Reiko experienced a sense of relief.

The lieutenant's eyes fixed his wife with an intense, hawk-like stare. Moving the sword around to his front, he raised himself slightly on his hips and let the upper half of his body lean over the sword point. That he was mustering his whole strength was apparent from the angry tension of the uniform at his shoulders. The lieutenant aimed to strike deep into the left of his stomach. His sharp cry pierced the silence of the room.

Despite the effort he had himself put into the blow, the lieutenant had the impression that someone else had struck the side of his stomach agonizingly with a thick rod of iron. For a second or so his head reeled and he had no idea what had happened. The five or six inches of naked point had vanished completely into his flesh, and the white bandage, gripped in his clenched fist, pressed directly against his stomach.

He returned to consciousness. The blade had certainly pierced the wall of the stomach, he thought. His breathing was difficult, his chest thumped violently, and in some far deep region, which he could hardly believe was a part of himself, a fearful and excruciating pain came welling up as if the ground had split open to disgorge a boiling stream of molten rock. The pain came suddenly nearer, with terrifying speed. The lieutenant bit his lower lip and stifled an instinctive moan.

Was this *seppuku?*—he was thinking. It was a sensation of utter chaos, as if the sky had fallen on his head and the world was reeling drunkenly. His will power and courage, which had seemed so robust before he made the incision, had now dwindled to something like a single hairlike thread of steel, and he was assailed by the uneasy feeling that he must advance along this thread, clinging to it with desperation. His clenched fist had grown moist. Looking down, he saw that both his hand and the cloth were drenched in blood. His loincloth too was dyed a deep red. It struck him as incredible that, amidst this terrible agony, things which could be seen could still be seen, and existing things existed still.

The moment the lieutenant thrust the sword into his left side and she saw the deathly pallor fall across his face, like an abruptly lowered curtain, Reiko had to struggle to prevent herself from rushing to his side. Whatever happened, she must watch. She must be a witness. That was the duty her husband had lain upon her. Opposite her, a mat's space away, she could clearly see her husband biting his lip to stifle the pain. The pain was there, with absolute certainty, before her eyes. And Reiko had no means of rescuing him from it.

The sweat glistened on her husband's forehead. The lieutenant closed his eyes, and then opened them again, as if experimenting. The eyes had lost their luster, and seemed innocent and empty like the eyes of a small animal.

The agony before Reiko's eyes burned as strong as the summer sun, utterly remote from the grief which seemed to be tearing herself apart within. The pain grew steadily in stature, stretching upward. Reiko felt that her husband had already become a man in a separate world, a man whose whole being had been resolved into pain, a prisoner in a cage of pain where no hand could reach out to him. But Reiko felt no pain at all. Her grief was not pain. As she thought about this, Reiko began to feel as if someone had raised a cruel wall of glass high between herself and her husband.

Ever since her marriage her husband's existence had been her own existence, and every breath of his had been a breath drawn by herself. But now, while her husband's existence in pain was a vivid reality, Reiko could find in this grief of hers no certain proof at all of her own existence.

With only his right hand on the sword the lieutenant began to cut sideways across his stomach. But as the blade became entangled with the entrails it was pushed constantly outward by their soft resilience; and the lieutenant realized that it would be necessary, as he cut, to use both hands to keep the point pressed deep into his stomach. He pulled the blade across. It did not cut as easily as he had expected. He directed the strength of his whole body into his right hand and pulled again. There was a cut of three or four inches.

The pain spread slowly outward from the inner depths until the whole stomach reverberated. It was like the wild clanging of a bell. Or like a thousand bells which jangled simultaneously at every breath he breathed and every throb of his pulse, rocking his whole being. The lieutenant could no longer stop himself from moaning. But by now the blade had cut its way through to below the navel, and when he noticed this he felt a sense of satisfaction, and a renewal of courage.

The volume of blood had steadily increased, and now it spurted from the wound as if propelled by the beat of the pulse. The mat before the lieutenant was drenched red with splattered blood, and more blood overflowed onto it from pools which gathered in folds of the lieutenant's khaki trousers. A spot, like a bird, came flying across to Reiko and settled on the lap of her white silk kimono.

By the time the lieutenant had at last drawn the sword across to the right side of his stomach, the blade was already cutting shallow and had revealed its naked tip, slippery with blood and grease. But, suddenly stricken by a fit of vomiting, the lieutenant cried out hoarsely. The vomiting made the fierce pain fiercer still, and the stomach, which had thus far remained firm and compact, now abruptly heaved, opening wide its wound, and the entrails burst through, as if the wound too were vomiting. Seemingly ignorant of their master's suffering, the entrails gave an impression of robust health and almost disagreeable vitality as they slipped smoothly out and spilled over into the crotch. The lieutenant's head dropped, his shoulders heaved, his eyes opened to narrow slits, and a thin trickle of saliva dribbled from his mouth. The gold markings on his epaulettes caught the light and glinted.

Blood was scattered everywhere. The lieutenant was soaked in it to his knees, and he sat now in a crumpled and listless posture, one hand on the floor. A raw smell filled the room. The lieutenant, his head drooping, retched repeatedly, and the movement showed vividly in his shoulders. The blade of the sword, now pushed back by the entrails and exposed to its tip, was still in the lieutenant's right hand.

It would be difficult to imagine a more heroic sight than that of the lieutenant at this moment, as he mustered his strength and flung back his head. The movement was performed with sudden violence, and the back of his head struck with a sharp crack against the alcove pillar. Reiko had been sitting until now with her face lowered, gazing in fascination at the tide of blood advancing toward her knees, but the sound took her by surprise and she looked up.

The lieutenant's face was not the face of a living man. The eyes were hollow, the skin parched, the once so lustrous cheeks and lips the color of dried mud. The right hand alone was moving. Laboriously gripping the sword, it hovered shakily in the air like the hand of a marionette and strove to direct the point at the base of the lieutenant's throat. Reiko watched her husband make this last, most heart-rending, futile exertion. Glistening with blood and grease, the point was thrust at the throat again and again. And each time it missed its aim. The strength to guide it was no longer there. The straying point struck the collar and the collar badges. Although its hooks had been unfastened, the stiff military collar had closed together again and was protecting the throat.

Reiko could bear the sight no longer. She tried to go to her husband's help, but she could not stand. She moved through the blood on her knees, and her white skirts grew deep red. Moving to the rear of her husband, she helped no more than by loosening the collar. The quivering blade at last contacted the naked flesh of the throat. At that moment Reiko's impression was that she herself had propelled her husband forward; but that was not the case. It was a movement planned by the lieutenant himself, his last exertion of strength. Abruptly he threw his body at the blade, and the blade pierced his neck, emerging at the nape. There was a tremendous spurt of blood and the lieutenant lay still, cold blue-tinged steel protruding from his neck at the back.

5

Slowly, her socks slippery with blood, Reiko descended the stairway. The up-stairs room was now completely still.

Switching on the ground-floor lights, she checked the gas jet and the main gas plug and poured water over the smoldering, half-buried charcoal in the brazier. She stood before the upright mirror in the four-and-a-half-mat room and held up her skirts. The bloodstains made it seem as if a bold, vivid pattern was printed across the lower half of her white kimono. When she sat down before the mirror, she was conscious of the dampness and coldness of her husband's blood in the region of her thighs, and she shivered. Then, for a long while, she lingered over her toilet preparations. She applied the rouge generously to her cheeks, and her lips too she painted heavily. This was no longer make-up to please her husband. It was make-up for the world which she would leave behind, and there was a touch of the magnificent and the spectacular in her brushwork. When she rose, the mat before the mirror was wet with blood. Reiko was not concerned about this.

Returning from the toilet, Reiko stood finally on the cement floor of the porchway. When her husband had bolted the door here last night it had been in preparation for death. For a while she stood immersed in the consideration of a simple problem. Should she now leave the bolt drawn? If she were to lock the door, it could be that the neighbors might not notice their suicide for several days. Reiko did not relish the thought of their two corpses putrifying before discovery. After all, it seemed, it would be best to leave it open. . . . . She released the bolt, and also drew open the frosted-glass door a fraction. . . . . At once a chill wind blew in. There was no sign of anyone in the midnight streets and stars glittered ice-cold through the trees in the large house opposite.

Leaving the door as it was, Reiko mounted the stairs. She had walked here and there for some time and her socks were no longer slippery. About halfway up, her nostrils were already assailed by a peculiar smell.

The lieutenant was lying on his face in a sea of blood. The point protruding from his neck seemed to have grown even more prominent than before. Reiko walked heedlessly across the blood. Sitting beside the lieutenant's corpse, she stared intently at the face, which lay on one cheek on the mat. The eyes were opened wide, as if the lieutenant's attention had been attracted by something. She raised the head, folding it in her sleeve, wiped the blood from the lips, and bestowed a last kiss.

Then she rose and took from the closet a new white blanket and a waist cord. To prevent any derangement of her skirts, she wrapped the blanket about her waist and bound it firmly with the cord.

Reiko sat herself on a spot about one foot distant from the lieutenant's body.

Drawing the dagger from her sash, she examined its dully gleaming blade intently, and held it to her tongue. The taste of the polished steel was slightly sweet.

Reiko did not linger. When she thought how the pain which had previously opened such a gulf between herself and her dying husband was now to become a part of her own experience, she saw before her only the joy of herself entering a realm her husband had already made his own. In her husband's agonized face there had been something inexplicable which she was seeing for the first time. Now she would solve that riddle. Reiko sensed that at last she too would be able to taste the true bitterness and sweetness of that great moral principle in which her husband believed. What had until now been tasted only faintly through her husband's example she was about to savor directly with her own tongue.

Reiko rested the point of the blade against the base of her throat. She thrust hard. The wound was only shallow. Her head blazed, and her hands shook uncontrollably. She gave the blade a strong pull sideways. A warm substance flooded into her mouth, and everything before her eyes reddened, in a vision of spouting blood. She gathered her strength and plunged the point of the blade deep into her throat.

QUESTIONS

1. Despite the title and the political event that sets the plot in motion, this story focuses almost exclusively on the relationship between the hero and heroine, their lovemaking, and their ritual suicides. In what ways do the intensely psychological explorations of the story define and clarify the meaning of patriotism for Lieutenant Takeyama? **2.** In the West, we tend to view the family—the relationship between husband and wife—as a private and personal matter that has little to do with public, political life. How do Lieutenant Takeyama and his wife view their relationship? **3.** Lieutenant Takeyama views "the urges of his flesh and the sincerity of his patriotism" as "two parts of the same thing." What does he mean by this? **4.** What does Mishima achieve by the opening paragraph? Why does he sacrifice suspense by recounting at the outset the major events and the story's outcome? **5.** What is the significance of Reiko's deliberations as to whether or not she should leave the door bolt drawn?

WRITING TOPIC

What connections does the story establish between love, marriage, and death?

THE
PRESENCE
OF DEATH

Orderly Retreat, 1943 by Philip Evergood

POETRY

Edward

ANONYMOUS

1

"Why does your brand° sae° drap wi' bluid,   sword/so
      Edward, Edward,
Why does your brand sae drap wi' bluid,
   And why sae sad gang° ye, O?"   go
"O I ha'e killed my hawk sae guid,
      Mither, mither,
O I ha'e killed my hawk sae guid,
   And I had nae mair but he, O."

2

"Your hawke's bluid was never sae reid,°   red
      Edward, Edward,   10
Your hawke's bluid was never sae reid,
   My dear son I tell thee, O."
"O I ha'e killed my reid-roan steed,
      Mither, mither,
O I ha'e killed my reid-roan steed,
   That erst was sae fair and free, O."

3

"Your steed was auld, and ye ha'e gat mair,
      Edward, Edward,
Your steed was auld, and ye ha'e gat mair,
   Some other dule° ye drie,° O."   grief/suffer
"O I ha'e killed my fader dear,   21
      Mither, mither,
O I ha'e killed my fader dear,
   Alas, and wae° is me, O!"   woe

4

"And whatten penance wul ye drie for that,
       Edward, Edward?
And whatten penance wul ye drie for that,
  My dear son, now tell me O?"
"I'll set my feet in yonder boat,
       Mither, mither,   30
I'll set my feet in yonder boat,
  And I'll fare over the sea, O."

5

"And what wul ye do wi' your towers and your ha',
       Edward, Edward?
And what wul ye do wi' your towers and your ha',
  That were sae fair to see, O?"
"I'll let them stand tul they down fa',
       Mither, mither,
I'll let them stand tul they down fa',   39
  For here never mair maun° I be, O."   must

6

"And what wul ye leave to your bairns° and your wife,   children
       Edward, Edward?
And what wul ye leave to your bairns and your wife,
  Whan ye gang over the sea, O?"
"The warlde's° room, let them beg thrae° life,   world's/through
       Mither, mither,
The warlde's room, let them beg thrae life,
  For them never mair wul I see, O."

7

"And what wul ye leave to your ain mither dear,
       Edward, Edward?   50
And what wul ye leave to your ain mither dear,
  My dear son, now tell me, O?"
"The curse of hell frae° me sall° ye bear,   from/shall
       Mither, mither,
The curse of hell frae me sall ye bear,
  Sic° counsels ye gave to me, O."   such

QUESTIONS
1. Why does the mother reject Edward's answers to her first two questions? **2.** Does the poem provide any clues as to the motive of the murder? **3.** Edward has murdered his father and then bitterly turns away from his mother, wife, and children. What basis is there in the poem for nevertheless sympathizing with Edward?

WRITING TOPIC
What effects are achieved through the question-and-answer technique and the repetition of lines?

Sonnet   1609

WILLIAM SHAKESPEARE   [1564–1616]

73

That time of year thou mayst in me behold
When yellow leaves, or none, or few, do hang
Upon those boughs which shake against the cold,
Bare ruined choirs, where late the sweet birds sang.
In me thou see'st the twilight of such day
As after sunset fadeth in the west;
Which by and by black night doth take away,
Death's second self, that seals up all in rest.
In me thou see'st the glowing of such fire,
That on the ashes of his youth doth lie,   10
As the deathbed whereon it must expire,
Consumed with that which it was nourished by.
This thou perceiv'st, which makes thy love more strong,
To love that well which thou must leave ere long.

Fear No More
the Heat o' the Sun   1623

WILLIAM SHAKESPEARE   [1564–1616]

Fear no more the heat o' the sun,[1]
  Nor the furious winter's rages;

Fear No More the Heat o' the Sun
  [1] From *Cymbeline*, Act IV, Scene 2.

Thou thy worldly task hast done,
   Home art gone, and ta'en thy wages:
Golden lads and girls all must,
As chimney-sweepers, come to dust.

Fear no more the frown o' the great;
   Thou art past the tyrant's stroke;
Care no more to clothe and eat;
   To thee the reed is as the oak:
The scepter, learning, physic°, must²   medicine
All follow this, and come to dust.   10

Fear no more the lightning flash,
   Nor the all-dreaded thunder stone;³
Fear not slander, censure rash;
   Thou hast finished joy and moan:
All lovers young, all lovers must
Consign to° thee, and come to dust.   agree with

No exorciser harm thee!
Nor no witchcraft charm thee!   20
Ghost unlaid forbear thee!
Nothing ill come near thee!
Quiet consummation have;
And renownéd be thy grave!

A Litany in Time of Plague   1600

THOMAS NASHE   [1567–1601]

Adieu, farewell, earth's bliss;
This world uncertain is;
Fond° are life's lustful joys;   foolish
Death proves them all but toys;
None from his darts can fly;
I am sick, I must die.
   Lord, have mercy on us!

Rich men, trust not in wealth,
Gold cannot buy you health;

---

² I.e., kings, scholars, and physicians.
³ It was believed that thunder was caused by falling meteorites.

Physic himself must fade.   10
All things to end are made,
The plague full swift goes by;
I am sick, I must die.
   Lord, have mercy on us!

Beauty is but a flower
Which wrinkles will devour;
Brightness falls from the air;
Queens have died young and fair;
Dust hath closed Helen's[1] eye.
I am sick, I must die.   20
   Lord, have mercy on us!

Strength stoops unto the grave,
Worms feed on Hector[2] brave;
Swords may not fight with fate,
Earth still holds ope her gate.
"Come, come!" the bells do cry.
I am sick, I must die.
   Lord, have mercy on us.

Wit with his wantonness
Tasteth death's bitterness;
Hell's executioner   30
Hath no ears for to hear
What vain art can reply.
I am sick, I must die.
   Lord, have mercy on us.

Haste, therefore, each degree,
To welcome destiny;
Heaven is our heritage,
Earth but a player's stage;
Mount we unto the sky.   40
I am sick, I must die.
   Lord, have mercy on us.

A Litany in Time of Plague
  [1] Helen of Troy, a fabled beauty.
  [2] Commander of the Trojan forces in the Trojan War.

Death, Be Not Proud   1633

JOHN DONNE   [1572–1631]

Death, be not proud, though some have calléd thee
Mighty and dreadful, for thou art not so;
For those whom thou think'st thou dost overthrow
Die not, poor Death, nor yet canst thou kill me.
From rest and sleep, which but thy pictures be,
Much pleasure; then from thee much more must flow,
And soonest our best men with thee do go,
Rest of their bones, and soul's delivery.
Thou art slave to fate, chance, kings, and desperate men,
And dost with poison, war, and sickness dwell,   10
And poppy or charms can make us sleep as well
And better than thy stroke; why swell'st thou then?
One short sleep past, we wake eternally
And death shall be no more; Death, thou shalt die.

Elegy Written in a
Country Churchyard   1753

THOMAS GRAY   [1716–1771]

The curfew tolls the knell of parting day,
   The lowing herd wind slowly o'er the lea,
The plowman homeward plods his weary way,
   And leaves the world to darkness and to me.

Now fades the glimmering landscape on the sight,
   And all the air a solemn stillness holds,
Save where the beetle wheels his droning flight,
   And drowsy tinklings lull the distant folds;

Save that from yonder ivy-mantled tower
   The moping owl does to the moon complain   10
Of such, as wandering near her secret bower,
   Molest her ancient solitary reign.

Beneath those rugged elms, that yew tree's shade,
   Where heaves the turf in many a moldering heap,

Each in his narrow cell forever laid,
    The rude° forefathers of the hamlet sleep.   *untaught*

The breezy call of incense-breathing Morn,
    The swallow twittering from the straw-built shed,
The cock's shrill clarion, or the echoing horn,°   *hunter's horn*
    No more shall rouse them from their lowly bed.   20

For them no more the blazing hearth shall burn,
    Or busy housewife ply her evening care;
No children run to lisp their sire's return,
    Or climb his knees the envied kiss to share.

Oft did the harvest to their sickle yield,
    Their furrow oft the stubborn glebe° has broke;   *field*
How jocund did they drive their team afield!
    How bowed the woods beneath their sturdy stroke!

Let not Ambition mock their useful toil,
    Their homely joys, and destiny obscure;   30
Nor Grandeur hear with a disdainful smile
    The short and simple annals of the poor.

The boast of heraldry,° the pomp of power,   *noble birth*
    And all that beauty, all that wealth e'er gave,
Awaits alike the inevitable hour.
    The paths of glory lead but to the grave.

Nor you, ye proud, impute to these the fault,
    If Memory o'er their tomb no trophies° raise,   *memorial*
Where through the long-drawn aisle and fretted° vault   *decorated*
    The pealing anthem swells the note of praise.   40

Can storied° urn or animated bust   *inscribed*
    Back to its mansion call the fleeting breath?
Can Honor's voice provoke the silent dust,
    Or Flattery soothe the full cold ear of Death?

Perhaps in this neglected spot is laid
    Some heart once pregnant with celestial fire;
Hands that the rod of empire might have swayed,
    Or waked to ecstasy the living lyre.

But Knowledge to their eyes her ample page
    Rich with the spoils of time did ne'er unroll;   50

Chill Penury repressed their noble rage,
   And froze the genial current of the soul.

Full many a gem of purest ray serene,
   The dark unfathomed caves of ocean bear:
Full many a flower is born to blush unseen,
   And waste its sweetness on the desert air.

Some village Hampden,[1] that with dauntless breast
   The little tyrant of his fields withstood;
Some mute inglorious Milton here may rest,
   Some Cromwell guiltless of his country's blood.   60

The applause of listening senates to command,
   The threats of pain and ruin to despise,
To scatter plenty o'er a smiling land,
   And read their history in a nation's eyes,

Their lot forbade: nor circumscribed alone
   Their growing virtues, but their crimes confined;
Forbade to wade through slaughter to a throne,
   And shut the gates of mercy on mankind,

The struggling pangs of conscious truth to hide,
   To quench the blushes of ingenuous shame,   70
Or heap the shrine of Luxury and Pride
   With incense kindled at the Muse's flame.

Far from the madding crowd's ignoble strife,
   Their sober wishes never learned to stray;
Along the cool sequestered vale of life
   They kept the noiseless tenor of their way.

Yet even these bones from insult to protect
   Some frail memorial still erected nigh,
With uncouth rhymes and shapeless sculpture decked,
   Implores the passing tribute of a sigh.   80

Their name, their years, spelt by the unlettered Muse,
   The place of fame and elegy supply:
And many a holy text around she strews,
   That teach the rustic moralist to die.

Elegy Written in a Country Churchyard
 [1] John Hampden (1594–1643) championed the people against the autocratic policies of
Charles I.

For who to dumb Forgetfulness a prey,
   This pleasing anxious being e'er resigned,
Left the warm precincts of the cheerful day,
   Nor cast one longing lingering look behind?

On some fond breast the parting soul relies,
   Some pious drops the closing eye requires;
Even from the tomb the voice of Nature cries,   90
   Even in our ashes live their wonted fires.

For thee, who mindful of the unhonored dead
   Dost in these lines their artless tale relate;
If chance, by lonely contemplation led,
   Some kindred spirit shall inquire thy fate,

Haply some hoary-headed swain may say,
   "Oft have we seen him at the peep of dawn
Brushing with hasty steps the dews away
   To meet the sun upon the upland lawn.   100

"There at the foot of yonder nodding beech
   That wreathes its old fantastic roots so high,
His listless length at noontide would he stretch,
   And pore upon the brook that babbles by.

"Hard by yon wood, now smiling as in scorn,
   Muttering his wayward fancies he would rove,
Now drooping, woeful wan, like one forlorn,
   Or crazed with care, or crossed in hopeless love.

"One morn I missed him on the customed hill,
   Along the heath and near his favorite tree;   110
Another came; nor yet beside the rill,
   Nor up the lawn, nor at the wood was he;

"The next with dirges due in sad array
   Slow through the churchway path we saw him borne.
Approach and read (for thou canst read) the lay,
   Graved on the stone beneath yon aged thorn."

THE EPITAPH

Here rests his head upon the lap of Earth
   A youth to Fortune and to Fame unknown

Fair Science° frowned not on his humble birth,   learning
  And Melancholy marked him for her own.   120

Large was his bounty, and his soul sincere,
  Heaven did a recompense as largely send:
He gave to Misery all he had, a tear,
  He gained from Heaven ('twas all he wished) a friend.

No farther seek his merits to disclose,
  Or draw his frailties from their dread abode
(There they alike in trembling hope repose),
  The bosom of his Father and his God.

QUESTIONS
1. Why have the people Gray honors in this poem lived and died in obscurity? Does the poet offer any suggestions for change? Explain. **2.** Why would "Ambition mock their useful toil" (l. 29)?

WRITING TOPIC
Does this poem celebrate the advantages of obscurity and ignorance over fame, wealth, and knowledge?

Lines Inscribed Upon a Cup Formed from a Skull   1814

GEORGE GORDON, LORD BYRON   [1788–1824]

Start not—nor deem my spirit fled;
  In me behold the only skull,
From which, unlike a living head,
  Whatever flows is never dull.

I lived, I loved, I quaff'd, like thee:
  I died: let earth my bones resign;
Fill up—thou canst not injure me;
  The worm hath fouler lips than thine.

Better to hold the sparkling grape,
  Than nurse the earth-worm's slimy brood;
And circle in the goblet's shape   10
  The drink of gods, than reptile's food.

Where once my wit, perchance, hath shone,
  In aid of others' let me shine;
And when, alas! our brains are gone,
  What nobler substitute than wine?

Quaff while thou canst: another race,
  When thou and thine, like me, are sped,
May rescue thee from earth's embrace,
  And rhyme and revel with the dead.   20

Why not? since through life's little day
  Our heads such sad effects produce;
Redeem'd from worms and wasting clay,
  This chance is theirs, to be of use.

The Destruction
of Sennacherib[1]   1815

GEORGE GORDON, LORD BYRON   [1788–1824]

The Assyrian came down like the wolf on the fold,
And his cohorts were gleaming in purple and gold;
And the sheen of their spears was like stars on the sea,
When the blue wave rolls nightly on deep Galilee.

Like the leaves of the forest when summer is green,
That host with their banners at sunset were seen:
Like the leaves of the forest when autumn hath blown,
That host on the morrow lay withered and strown.

For the Angel of Death spread his wings on the blast,
And breathed in the face of the foe as he passed;   10
And the eyes of the sleepers waxed deadly and chill,
And their hearts but once heaved—and for ever grew still!

And there lay the steed with his nostril all wide,
But through it there rolled not the breath of his pride;
And the foam of his gasping lay white on the turf,
And cold as the spray of the rock-beating surf.

The Destruction of Sennacherib
  [1] Byron retells the account of the Assyrian siege of Jerusalem, found in II Kings 19, which culminates in the death of 185,000 Assyrian troops at the hand of the angel of the Lord.

And there lay the rider distorted and pale,
With the dew on his brow, and the rust on his mail;
And the tents were all silent, the banners alone,
The lances unlifted, the trumpet unblown.   20

And the widows of Ashur[2] are loud in their wail,
And the idols are broke in the temple of Baal;[3]
And the might of the Gentile,[4] unsmote by the sword,
Hath melted like snow in the glance of the Lord!

Ozymandias[1]   1818

PERCY BYSSHE SHELLEY [1792–1822]

I met a traveller from an antique land
Who said: Two vast and trunkless legs of stone
Stand in the desert . . . Near them, on the sand,
Half sunk, a shattered visage lies, whose frown,
And wrinkled lip, and sneer of cold command,
Tell that its sculptor well those passions read
Which yet survive, stamped on these lifeless things,
The hand that mocked them, and the heart that fed:
And on the pedestal these words appear:
"My name is Ozymandias, king of kings: 10
Look on my works, ye Mighty, and despair!"
Nothing beside remains. Round the decay
Of that colossal wreck, boundless and bare
The lone and level sands stretch far away.

Ode to a Nightingale   1819

JOHN KEATS [1795–1821]

1

My heart aches, and a drowsy numbness pains
    My sense, as though of hemlock I had drunk,

---

  [2] Another name for Assyria.
  [3] A Canaanite deity.
  [4] A non-Hebrew, in this case Sennacherib, the King of Assyria.

Ozymandias
  [1] Egyptian monarch of the thirteenth century B.C., said to have erected a huge statue of himself.

Or emptied some dull opiate to the drains
    One minute past, and Lethe-wards[1] had sunk:
'Tis not through envy of thy happy lot,
    But being too happy in thine happiness—
        That thou, light-wingéd Dryad of the trees,
            In some melodious plot
    Of beechen green, and shadows numberless,
        Singest of summer in full-throated ease.   10

2

O, for a draught of vintage! that hath been
    Cooled a long age in the deep-delvéd earth,
Tasting of Flora[2] and the country green,
    Dance, and Provencal song,[3] and sunburnt mirth!
O for a beaker full of the warm South,
    Full of the true, the blushful Hippocrene,[4]
        With beaded bubbles winking at the brim,
            And purple-stainéd mouth;
    That I might drink, and leave the world unseen,
    And with thee fade away into the forest dim: 20

3

Fade far away, dissolve, and quite forget
    What thou among the leaves hast never known,
The weariness, the fever, and the fret
    Here, where men sit and hear each other groan;
Where palsy shakes a few, sad, last gray hairs,
    Where youth grows pale, and specter-thin, and dies;
        Where but to think is to be full of sorrow
            And leaden-eyed despairs,
    Where Beauty cannot keep her lustrous eyes,
        Or new Love pine at them beyond tomorrow.   30

4

Away! away! for I will fly to thee,
    Not charioted by Bacchus[5] and his pards,

Ode to a Nightingale
  [1] Towards Lethe, in Greek mythology the river in Hades which caused forgetfulness.
  [2] Roman goddess of flowers.
  [3] Provence, in southern France, renowned for its medieval troubadors.
  [4] In Greek mythology, the fountain of the Muses whose waters gave poetic inspiration.
  [5] The god of wine, often represented in a chariot drawn by leopards ("pards").

But on the viewless wings of Poesy,
 Though the dull brain perplexes and retards:
Already with thee! tender is the night,
 And haply the Queen-Moon is on her throne,
  Clustered around by all her starry Fays;°   fairies
   But here there is no light,
 Save what from heaven is with the breezes blown
  Through verdurous glooms and winding mossy ways.   40

5

I cannot see what flowers are at my feet,
 Nor what soft incense hangs upon the boughs,
But, in embalmèd darkness, guess each sweet
 Wherewith the seasonable month endows
The grass, the thicket, and the fruit tree wild;
 White hawthorn, and the pastoral eglantine;
  Fast fading violets covered up in leaves;
   And mid-May's eldest child,
 The coming musk-rose, full of dewy wine,
  The murmurous haunt of flies on summer eves.   50

6

Darkling° I listen; and for many a time   in darkness
 I have been half in love with easeful Death,
Called him soft names in many a musèd rhyme,
 To take into the air my quiet breath;
Now more than ever seems it rich to die,
 To cease upon the midnight with no pain,
  While thou art pouring forth thy soul abroad
   In such an ecstasy!
 Still wouldst thou sing, and I have ears in vain—
  To thy high requiem become a sod.   60

7

Thou wast not born for death, immortal Bird!
 No hungry generations tread thee down;
The voice I hear this passing night was heard
 In ancient days by emperor and clown:
Perhaps the selfsame song that found a path
 Through the sad heart of Ruth,[6] when, sick for home,

---

[6] The young widow in the Old Testament (Ruth, 2) who left her own people to live in a strange land, where she gleaned in the barley fields ("alien corn").

She stood in tears amid the alien corn;
   The same that ofttimes hath
Charmed magic casements, opening on the foam
   Of perilous seas, in faery lands forlorn.   70

8

Forlorn! the very word is like a bell
   To toll me back from thee to my sole self!
Adieu! the fancy cannot cheat so well
   As she is famed to do, deceiving elf.
Adieu! adieu! thy plaintive anthem fades
   Past the near meadows, over the still stream,
      Up the hill side; and now 'tis buried deep
      In the next valley-glades:
Was it a vision, or a waking dream?
   Fled is that music:—Do I wake or sleep?   80

QUESTIONS

1. What does the nightingale represent? **2.** In stanza 6, Keats declares that the very moment at which the nightingale's song is most ecstatic would be the right moment to die; yet the realization that the nightingale's song would continue after his death jars him. Why? **3.** In what sense is the nightingale "not born for death" (l. 61)? Does this line imply that all men are born for death? Explain.

WRITING TOPIC

In stanza 4, Keats says that he will reach the nightingale "on the viewless wings of Poesy." Why are the wings of poetry "viewless," and what is the connection between the nightingale and poetry?

Ode on a Grecian Urn   1820

JOHN KEATS [1795–1821]

I

Thou still unravished bride of quietness,
   Thou foster child of silence and slow time,
Sylvan historian, who canst thus express
   A flowery tale more sweetly than our rhyme:

What leaf-fringed legend haunts about thy shape
 Of deities or mortals, or of both,
  In Tempe or the dales of Arcady?[1]
What men or gods are these? What maidens loath?
What mad pursuit? What struggle to escape?
  What pipes and timbrels? What wild ecstasy?   10

II

Heard melodies are sweet, but those unheard
 Are sweeter; therefore, ye soft pipes, play on;
Not to the sensual ear, but, more endeared,
 Pipe to the spirit ditties of no tone:
Fair youth, beneath the trees, thou canst not leave
 Thy song, nor ever can those trees be bare;
  Bold Lover, never, never canst thou kiss,
Though winning near the goal—yet, do not grieve;
  She cannot fade, though thou hast not thy bliss,
Forever wilt thou love, and she be fair!   20

III

Ah, happy, happy boughs! that cannot shed
 Your leaves, nor ever bid the Spring adieu;
And, happy melodist, unwearièd,
 Forever piping songs forever new;
More happy love! more happy, happy love!
 Forever warm and still to be enjoyed,
  Forever panting, and forever young;
All breathing human passion far above,[2]
  That leaves a heart high-sorrowful and cloyed,
  A burning forehead, and a parching tongue.   30

IV

Who are these coming to the sacrifice?
 To what green altar, O mysterious priest,
Lead'st thou that heifer lowing at the skies,
 And all her silken flanks with garlands dressed?

Ode on a Grecian Urn
 [1] Tempe and Arcady are valleys in Greece famous for their beauty. In ancient times, Tempe was regarded as sacred to Apollo.

 [2] I.e., far above all breathing human passion.

What little town by river or sea shore,
   Or mountain-built with peaceful citadel,
      Is emptied of this folk, this pious morn?
And, little town, thy streets forevermore
   Will silent be; and not a soul to tell
      Why thou art desolate, can e'er return.   40

      V

O Attic³ shape! Fair attitude! with brede
   Of marble men and maidens overwrought,
With forest branches and the trodden weed;
   Thou, silent form, dost tease us out of thought
As doth eternity: Cold Pastoral!
   When old age shall this generation waste,
      Thou shalt remain, in midst of other woe
   Than ours, a friend to man, to whom thou say'st,
"Beauty is truth, truth beauty,—that is all
      Ye know on earth, and all ye need to know."   50

QUESTIONS

1. Describe the scene the poet sees depicted on the urn. Describe the scene the poet imagines as a consequence of the scene on the urn. **2.** Why are the boughs, the piper, and the lovers happy in stanza 3? **3.** Explain the assertion of stanza 2 that "Heard melodies are sweet, but those unheard/Are sweeter." **4.** Does the poem support the assertion of the last two lines? What does that assertion mean?

WRITING TOPIC

In what sense might it be argued that this poem is about mortality and immortality? In this connection, consider the meaning of the phrase "Cold Pastoral!" (l. 45).

When I Have Fears   1848

JOHN KEATS [1795–1821]

When I have fears that I may cease to be
   Before my pen has gleaned my teeming brain,
Before high-piléd books, in charact'ry,°   written symbols

---

³ Athenian, thus simple and graceful.

Hold like rich garners the full-ripened grain;
When I behold, upon the night's starred face,
   Huge cloudy symbols of a high romance,
And think that I may never live to trace
   Their shadows, with the magic hand of chance;
And when I feel, fair creature of an hour,
   That I shall never look upon thee more,   10
Never have relish in the faery° power   *magical*
   Of unreflecting love!—then on the shore
Of the wide world I stand alone, and think
Till Love and Fame to nothingness do sink.

QUESTIONS

1. What consequences of death does the poet fear in each of the three quatrains? **2.** What value have "Love and Fame" in the face of death?

The Conqueror Worm   (1838)

EDGAR ALLAN POE   [1809–1849]

Lo! 'tis a gala night
   Within the lonesome latter years!
An angel throng, bewinged, bedight
   In veils, and drowned in tears,
Sit in a theatre, to see
   A play of hopes and fears,
While the orchestra breathes fitfully
   The music of the spheres.

Mimes, in the form of God on high,
   Mutter and mumble low,   10
And hither and thither fly—
   Mere puppets they, who come and go
At bidding of vast formless things
   That shift the scenery to and fro,
Flapping from out their Condor wings
   Invisible Woe!

That motley drama!—oh, be sure
   It shall not be forgot!
With its Phantom chased forever more,
   By a crowd that seize it not,   20

Through a circle that ever returneth in
    To the self-same spot,
And much of Madness and more of Sin
    And Horror the soul of the plot.

But see, amid the mimic rout,
    A crawling shape intrude!
A blood-red thing that writhes from out
    The scenic solitude!
It writhes!—it writhes!—with mortal pangs
    The mimes become its food,
And the seraphs sob at vermin fangs   30
    In human gore imbued.

Out—out are the lights—out all!
    And over each quivering form,
The curtain, a funeral pall,
    Comes down with the rush of a storm,
And the angels, all pallid and wan,
    Uprising, unveiling, affirm
That the play is the tragedy, "Man,"
    And its hero the Conqueror Worm.   40

from

In Memoriam A. H. H.   1850

ALFRED, LORD TENNYSON [1809–1892]

54

O, yet we trust that somehow good
    Will be the final goal of ill,
    To pangs of nature, sins of will,
Defects of doubt, and taints of blood;

That nothing walks with aimless feet;
    That not one life shall be destroyed,
    Or cast as rubbish to the void,
When God hath made the pile complete;

That not a worm is cloven in vain;
    That not a moth with vain desire   10

Is shriveled in a fruitless fire,
Or but subserves another's gain.

Behold, we know not anything;
   I can but trust that good shall fall
   At last—far off—at last, to all,
And every winter change to spring.

So runs my dream; but what am I?
   An infant crying in the night;
   An infant crying for the light,
And with no language but a cry.   20

55

The wish, that of the living whole
   No life may fail beyond the grave,
   Derives it not from what we have
The likest God within the soul?

Are God and Nature then at strife,
   That Nature lends such evil dreams?
   So careful of the type° she seems,   species
So careless of the single life,

That I, considering everywhere
   Her secret meaning in her deeds,   10
   And finding that of fifty seeds
She often brings but one to bear,

I falter where I firmly trod,
   And falling with my weight of cares
   Upon the great world's altar-stairs
That slope through darkness up to God,

I stretch lame hands of faith, and grope,
   And gather dust and chaff, and call
   To what I feel is Lord of all,
And faintly trust the larger hope.[1]   20

56

"So careful of the type?" but no.
   From scarpéd[2] cliff and quarried stone

In Memoriam A. H. H.
  [1] The hope expressed in the first two lines of this section.
  [2] Cut away (so that fossil remains can be seen).

She[3] cries, "A thousand types are gone;
I care for nothing, all shall go.

"Thou makest thine appeal to me:
   I bring to life, I bring to death;
   The spirit does but mean the breath:
I know no more." And he, shall he,

Man; her last work, who seemed so fair,
   Such splendid purpose in his eyes,   10
   Who rolled the psalm to wintry skies,
Who built him fanes° of fruitless prayer,   *temples*

Who trusted God was love indeed
   And love Creation's final law—
   Though Nature, red in tooth and claw
With ravine, shrieked against his creed—

Who loved, who suffered countless ills,
   Who battled for the True, the Just,
   Be blown about the desert dust,
Or sealed within the iron hills?[4]   20

No more? A monster then, a dream,
   A discord. Dragons of the prime,
   That tare° each other in their slime,   *tore*
Were mellow music matched with him.

O life as futile, then, as frail!
   O for thy voice to soothe and bless!
   What hope of answer, or redress?
Behind the veil, behind the veil.

QUESTIONS

1. In these self-contained sections from Tennyson's long elegy to a friend who died at 22, the poet raises some anguished questions about God, humanity, and nature. What conviction is embodied in the first verses of sections 54 and 55? What issues does the poet raise that threaten that conviction? **2.** How is nature characterized in section 55? In section 56? **3.** In section 56, how does the poet characterize humanity's notions about God? Are those notions justified by the remainder of the section?

WRITING TOPIC

Do these verses culminate in positive affirmation of the human condition and the relationship of individuals to God and nature? Explain.

---

[3] Nature.

Growing Old

1867

MATTHEW ARNOLD [1822–1888]

What is it to grow old?
Is it to lose the glory of the form,
The luster of the eye?
Is it for beauty to forego her wreath?
—Yes, but not this alone.

Is it to feel our strength—
Not our bloom only, but our strength—decay?
Is it to feel each limb
Grow stiffer, every function less exact,
Each nerve more loosely strung?   10

Yes, this, and more; but not
Ah, 'tis not what in youth we dreamed 'twould be!
'Tis not to have our life
Mellowed and softened as with sunset glow,
A golden day's decline.

'Tis not to see the world
As from a height, with rapt prophetic eyes,
And heart profoundly stirred;
And weep, and feel the fullness of the past,
The years that are no more.   20

It is to spend long days
And not once feel that we were ever young;
It is to add, immured
In the hot prison of the present, month
To month with weary pain.

It is to suffer this,
And feel but half, and feebly, what we feel.
Deep in our hidden heart
Festers the dull remembrance of a change,
But no emotion—none.   30

It is—last stage of all—
When we are frozen up within, and quite
The phantom of ourselves,
To hear the world applaud the hollow ghost
Which blamed the living man.

After Great Pain, a Formal Feeling Comes   (ca. 1862)

EMILY DICKINSON   [1830–1886]

After great pain, a formal feeling comes—
The Nerves sit ceremonious, like Tombs—
The stiff Heart questions was it He, that bore,
And Yesterday, or Centuries before?

The Feet, mechanical, go round—
Of Ground, or Air, or Ought—
A Wooden way
Regardless grown,
A Quartz contentment, like a stone—

This is the Hour of Lead—   10
Remembered, if outlived,
As Freezing persons, recollect the Snow—
First—Chill—then Stupor—then the letting go—

QUESTION
1. Is this poem about physical or psychic pain? Explain.

WRITING TOPIC
What is the meaning of "stiff Heart" (l. 3) and "Quartz contentment" (l. 9)? What part do they play in the larger pattern of images?

I Heard a Fly Buzz— When I Died   (ca. 1862)

EMILY DICKINSON   [1830–1886]

I heard a Fly buzz—when I died—
The Stillness in the Room
Was like the Stillness in the Air—
Between the Heaves of Storm—

The Eyes around—had wrung them dry—
And Breaths were gathering firm

For that last Onset—when the King
Be witnessed—in the Room—

I willed my Keepsakes—Signed away
What portion of me be   10
Assignable—and then it was
There interposed a Fly—

With Blue—uncertain stumbling Buzz—
Between the light—and me—
And then the Windows failed—and then
I could not see to see—

How the Waters
Closed Above Him   (ca. 1864)

EMILY DICKINSON   [1830–1886]

How the Waters closed above Him
We shall never know—
How He stretched His Anguish to us
That—is covered too—

Spreads the Pond Her Base of Lilies
Bold above the Boy
Whose unclaimed Hat and Jacket
Sum the History—

Apparently with No Surprise (ca. 1884)

EMILY DICKINSON   [1830–1886]

Apparently with no surprise
To any happy flower,
The frost beheads it at its play
In accidental power.
The blond assassin passes on,
The sun proceeds unmoved
To measure off another day
For an approving God.

To an Athlete Dying Young   1896

A. E. HOUSMAN   [1859–1936]

The time you won your town the race
We chaired you through the market place;
Man and boy stood cheering by,
And home we brought you shoulder-high.

Today, the road all runners come,
Shoulder-high we bring you home,
And set you at your threshold down,
Townsman of a stiller town.

Smart lad, to slip betimes away
From fields where glory does not stay   10
And early though the laurel grows
It withers quicker than the rose.

Eyes the shady night has shut
Cannot see the record cut,
And silence sounds no worse than cheers
After earth has stopped the ears:

Now you will not swell the rout
Of lads that wore their honors out,
Runners whom renown outran
And the name died before the man.   20

So set, before its echoes fade,
The fleet foot on the sill of shade,
And hold to the low lintel up
The still defended challenge cup.

And round that early laureled head
Will flock to gaze the strengthless dead
And find unwithered on its curls
The garland briefer than a girl's.

Sailing to Byzantium[1]   1927

WILLIAM BUTLER YEATS   [1865–1939]

1

That is no country for old men. The young
In one another's arms, birds in the trees
—Those dying generations—at their song,
The salmon-falls, the mackerel-crowded seas,
Fish, flesh, or fowl, commend all summer long
Whatever is begotten, born, and dies.
Caught in that sensual music all neglect
Monuments of unaging intellect.

2

An aged man is but a paltry thing,
A tattered coat upon a stick, unless   10
Soul clap its hands and sing, and louder sing
For every tatter in its mortal dress,
Nor is there singing school but studying
Monuments of its own magnificence;
And therefore I have sailed the seas and come
To the holy city of Byzantium.

3

O sages standing in God's holy fire
As in the gold mosaic of a wall,
Come from the holy fire, perne in a gyre,[2]
And be the singing-masters of my soul.   20
Consume my heart away; sick with desire
And fastened to a dying animal
It knows not what it is; and gather me
Into the artifice of eternity.

Sailing to Byzantium
[1] Capital of the ancient Eastern Roman Empire, Byzantium (modern Istanbul) is celebrated for its great art, including mosaics (in ll. 17–18, Yeats addresses the figures in one of these mosaics). In *A Vision*, Yeats cites Byzantium as possibly the only civilization which had achieved what he called "Unity of Being," a state where "religious, aesthetic and practical life were one. . . ."
[2] I.e., whirl in a spiral motion. Yeats associated this motion with the cycles of history and the fate of the individual. Here he entreats the sages represented in the mosaic to take him out of the natural world described in the first stanza and into the eternal world of art.

4

Once out of nature I shall never take
My bodily form from any natural thing,
But such a form as Grecian goldsmiths make
Of hammered gold and gold enameling
To keep a drowsy Emperor awake;[3]
Or set upon a golden bough to sing   30
To lords and ladies of Byzantium
Of what is past, or passing, or to come.

QUESTIONS

1. This poem incorporates a series of contrasts, among them "That" country and Byzantium, the real birds of the first stanza and the artificial bird of the final stanza. What others do you find? **2.** What are the meanings of "generations" (l. 3)? **3.** For what is the poet "sick with desire" (l. 21): **4.** In what sense is eternity an "artifice" (l. 24)?

WRITING TOPIC

In what ways are the images of bird and song used throughout this poem?

Richard Cory   1897

EDWIN ARLINGTON ROBINSON [1869–1935]

Whenever Richard Cory went down town,
We people on the pavement looked at him:
He was a gentleman from sole to crown,
Clean favored, and imperially slim.

And he was always quietly arrayed,
And he was always human when he talked;
But still he fluttered pulses when he said,
"Good-morning," and he glittered when he walked.

And he was rich—yes, richer than a king—
And admirably schooled in every grace: 10
In fine, we thought that he was everything
To make us wish that we were in his place.

---

[3] "I have read somewhere," Yeats wrote, "that in the Emperor's palace at Byzantium was a tree made of gold and silver, and artificial birds that sang." The poet wishes to become an artificial bird (a work of art) in contrast to the real birds of the first stanza.

So on we worked, and waited for the light,
And went without the meat, and cursed the bread;
And Richard Cory, one calm summer night,
Went home and put a bullet through his head.

Mr. Flood's Party   1921

EDWIN ARLINGTON ROBINSON   [1869–1935]

Old Eben Flood, climbing alone one night
Over the hill between the town below
And the forsaken upland hermitage
That held as much as he should ever know
On earth again of home, paused warily.
The road was his with not a native near;
And Eben, having leisure, said aloud,
For no man else in Tilbury Town to hear:

"Well, Mr. Flood, we have the harvest moon
Again, and we may not have many more;   10
The bird is on the wing, the poet says,
And you and I have said it here before.
Drink to the bird." He raised up to the light
The jug that he had gone so far to fill,
And answered huskily: "Well, Mr. Flood,
Since you propose it, I believe I will."

Alone, as if enduring to the end
A valiant armor of scarred hopes outworn,
He stood there in the middle of the road
Like Roland's ghost winding a silent horn.   20
Below him, in the town among the trees,
Where friends of other days had honored him,
A phantom salutation of the dead
Rang thinly till old Eben's eyes were dim.

Then, as a mother lays her sleeping child
Down tenderly, fearing it may awake,
He set the jug down slowly at his feet
With trembling care, knowing that most things break;
And only when assured that on firm earth
It stood, as the uncertain lives of men   30
Assuredly did not, he paced away,
And with his hand extended paused again:

"Well, Mr. Flood, we have not met like this
In a long time; and many a change has come
To both of us, I fear, since last it was
We had a drop together. Welcome home!"
Convivially returning with himself,
Again he raised the jug up to the light;
And with an acquiescent quaver said:
"Well, Mr. Flood, if you insist, I might.   40

"Only a very little, Mr. Flood—
For auld lang syne. No more, sir; that will do."
So, for the time, apparently it did,
And Eben evidently thought so too;
For soon amid the silver loneliness
Of night he lifted up his voice and sang,
Secure, with only two moons listening,
Until the whole harmonious landscape rang—

"For auld lang syne." The weary throat gave out,
The last word wavered; and the song being done,   50
He raised again the jug regretfully
And shook his head, and was again alone.
There was not much that was ahead of him,
And there was nothing in the town below—
Where strangers would have shut the many doors
That many friends had opened long ago.

On the Vanity of Earthly Greatness   1936

ARTHUR GUITERMAN   [1871–1943]

The tusks that clashed in mighty brawls
Of mastodons, are billiard balls.

The sword of Charlemagne the Just
Is ferric oxide, known as rust.

The grizzly bear whose potent hug
Was feared by all, is now a rug.

Great Caesar's bust is on the shelf,
And I don't feel so well myself.

After Apple-Picking   1914

ROBERT FROST   [1874–1963]

My long two-pointed ladder's sticking through a tree
Toward heaven still,
And there's a barrel that I didn't fill
Beside it, and there may be two or three
Apples I didn't pick upon some bough.
But I am done with apple-picking now.
Essence of winter sleep is on the night,
The scent of apples: I am drowsing off.
I cannot rub the strangeness from my sight
I got from looking through a pane of glass   10
I skimmed this morning from the drinking trough
And held against the world of hoary grass.
It melted, and I let it fall and break.
But I was well
Upon my way to sleep before it fell,
And I could tell
What form my dreaming was about to take.
Magnified apples appear and disappear,
Stem end and blossom end,
And every fleck of russet showing clear.   20
My instep arch not only keeps the ache,
It keeps the pressure of a ladder-round.
I feel the ladder sway as the boughs bend.
And I keep hearing from the cellar bin
The rumbling sound
Of load on load of apples coming in.
For I have had too much
Of apple-picking: I am overtired
Of the great harvest I myself desired.
There were ten thousand thousand fruit to touch,   30
Cherish in hand, lift down, and not let fall.
For all
That struck the earth,
No matter if not bruised or spiked with stubble,
Went surely to the cider-apple heap
As of no worth.
One can see what will trouble
This sleep of mine, whatever sleep it is.
Were he not gone,
The woodchuck could say whether it's like his   40
Long sleep, as I describe its coming on,
Or just some human sleep.

QUESTIONS
1. What does apple-picking symbolize? **2.** At the end of the poem, why is the speaker uncertain about what kind of sleep is coming on him?

Nothing Gold Can Stay   1923

ROBERT FROST [1874-1963]

Nature's first green is gold,
Her hardest hue to hold.
Her early leaf's a flower;
But only so an hour.
Then leaf subsides to leaf.
So Eden sank to grief,
So dawn goes down to day.
Nothing gold can stay.

QUESTIONS
1. Does this poem protest or accept the transitoriness of things? **2.** Why does Frost use the word "subsides" in line 5 rather than a word like "expands" or "grows"? **3.** How are "Nature's first green" (l. 1), "Eden" (l. 6), and "dawn" (l. 7) linked together?

'Out, Out—'[1]   1916

ROBERT FROST [1874–1963]

The buzz-saw snarled and rattled in the yard
And made dust and dropped stove-length sticks of wood,
Sweet-scented stuff when the breeze drew across it.
And from there those that lifted eyes could count
Five mountain ranges one behind the other
Under the sunset far into Vermont.
And the saw snarled and rattled, snarled and rattled,
As it ran light, or had to bear a load.
And nothing happened: day was all but done.
Call it a day, I wish they might have said   10
To please the boy by giving him the half hour
That a boy counts so much when saved from work.

'*Out, Out*'
     [1] The title is taken from the famous speech of Macbeth upon hearing that his wife has died (*Macbeth*, Act V, Scene 5).

His sister stood beside them in her apron
To tell them 'Supper.' At the word, the saw,
As if to prove saws knew what supper meant,
Leaped out at the boy's hand, or seemed to leap—
He must have given the hand. However it was,
Neither refused the meeting. But the hand!
The boy's first outcry was a rueful laugh,
As he swung toward them holding up the hand   20
Half in appeal, but half as if to keep
The life from spilling. Then the boy saw all—
Since he was old enough to know, big boy
Doing a man's work, though a child at heart—
He saw all spoiled. 'Don't let him cut my hand off—
The doctor, when he comes. Don't let him, sister!'
So. But the hand was gone already.
The doctor put him in the dark of ether.
He lay and puffed his lips out with his breath.
And then—the watcher at his pulse took fright.   30
No one believed. They listened at his heart.
Little—less—nothing!—and that ended it.
No more to build on there. And they, since they
Were not the one dead, turned to their affairs.

WRITING TOPIC
Compare this poem with Emily Dickinson's "Apparently with No Surprise."

Design   1936

ROBERT FROST   [1874–1963]

I found a dimpled spider, fat and white,
On a white heal-all, holding up a moth
Like a white piece of rigid satin cloth—
Assorted characters of death and blight
Mixed ready to begin the morning right,
Like the ingredients of a witches' broth—
A snow-drop spider, a flower like a froth,
And dead wings carried like a paper kite.

What had that flower to do with being white,
The wayside blue and innocent heal-all?   10
What brought the kindred spider to that height,
Then steered the white moth thither in the night?

What but design of darkness to appall?—
If design govern in a thing so small.

Rain

1916

EDWARD THOMAS [1878–1917]

Rain, midnight rain, nothing but the wild rain
On this bleak hut, and solitude, and me
Remembering again that I shall die
And neither hear the rain nor give it thanks
For washing me cleaner than I have been
Since I was born into this solitude.
Blessed are the dead that the rain rains upon:
But here I pray that none whom once I loved
Is dying to-night or lying still awake
Solitary, listening to the rain,   10
Either in pain or thus in sympathy
Helpless among the living and the dead,
Like a cold water among broken reeds,
Myriads of broken reeds all still and stiff,
Like me who have no love which this wild rain
Has not dissolved except the love of death,
If love it be for what is perfect and
Cannot, the tempest tells me, disappoint.

QUESTIONS

1. What does the rain symbolize? **2.** How would you characterize the tone of this poem? Does the speaker make clear why he feels alone and helpless? **3.** What do the "broken reeds" of lines 13–14 suggest? **4.** In what sense is death "perfect" (l. 17)?

Tract

1917

WILLIAM CARLOS WILLIAMS [1883–1963]

I will teach you my townspeople
how to perform a funeral—
for you have it over a troop
of artists—
unless one should scour the world—
you have the ground sense necessary.

See! the hearse leads.
I begin with a design for a hearse.
For Christ's sake not black—
nor white either—and not polished!   10
Let it be weathered—like a farm wagon—
with gilt wheels (this could be
applied fresh at small expense)
or no wheels at all:
a rough dray to drag over the ground.

Knock the glass out!
My God—glass, my townspeople!
For what purpose? Is it for the dead
to look out or for us to see
how well he is housed or to see   20
the flowers or the lack of them—
or what?
To keep the rain and snow from him?
He will have a heavier rain soon:
pebbles and dirt and what not.
Let there be no glass—
and no upholstery! phew!
and no little brass rollers
and small easy wheels on the bottom—
my townspeople what are you thinking of!   30

A rough plain hearse then
with gilt wheels and no top at all.
On this the coffin lies
by its own weight.
                    No wreaths please—
especially no hot-house flowers.
Some common memento is better,
something he prized and is known by:
his old clothes—a few books perhaps—
God knows what! You realize   40
how we are about these things,
my townspeople—
something will be found—anything—
even flowers if he had come to that.
So much for the hearse.

For heaven's sake though see to the driver!
Take off the silk hat! In fact
that's no place at all for him
up there unceremoniously

dragging our friend out of his own dignity!   50
Bring him down—bring him down!
Low and inconspicuous! I'd not have him ride
on the wagon at all—damn him—
the undertaker's understrapper!
Let him hold the reins
and walk at the side
and inconspicuously too!

Then briefly as to yourselves:
Walk behind—as they do in France,
seventh class, or if you ride   60
Hell take curtains! Go with some show
of inconvenience; sit openly—
to the weather as to grief.
Or do you think you can shut grief in?
What—from us? We who have perhaps
nothing to lose? Share with us
share with us—it will be money
in your pockets.
                Go now
I think you are ready.   70

Hurt Hawks   1928

ROBINSON JEFFERS   [1887–1962]

1

The broken pillar of the wing jags from the clotted shoulder,
The wing trails like a banner in defeat,
No more to use the sky forever but live with famine
And pain a few days: cat nor coyote
Will shorten the week of waiting for death, there is game without talons.
He stands under the oak-bush and waits
The lame feet of salvation; at night he remembers freedom
And flies in a dream, the dawns ruin it.
He is strong and pain is worse to the strong, incapacity is worse.
The curs of the day come and torment him   10
At distance, no one but death the redeemer will humble that head,
The intrepid readiness, the terrible eyes.
The wild God of the world is sometimes merciful to those
That ask mercy, not often to the arrogant.
You do not know him, you communal people, or you have forgotten him;

Intemperate and savage, the hawk remembers him;
Beautiful and wild, the hawks, and men that are dying, remember him.

2

I'd sooner, except the penalties, kill a man than a hawk; but the great
    redtail[1]
Had nothing left but unable misery
From the bone too shattered for mending, the wing that trailed under his
    talons when he moved.   20
We had fed him six weeks, I gave him freedom,
He wandered over the foreland hill and returned in the evening, asking
    for death,
Not like a beggar, still eyed with the old
Implacable arrogance. I gave him the lead gift in the twilight. What fell
    was relaxed,
Owl-downy, soft feminine feathers; but what
Soared: the fierce rush: the night-herons by the flooded river cried fear at
    its rising
Before it was quite unsheathed from reality.

Bells for John Whiteside's Daughter

1924

JOHN CROWE RANSOM [1888–1974]

There was such speed in her little body,
And such lightness in her footfall,
It is no wonder that her brown study°   reverie
Astonishes us all.

Her wars were bruited in our high window.
We looked among orchard trees and beyond,
Where she took arms against her shadow,
Or harried unto the pond

The lazy geese, like a snow cloud
Dripping their snow on the green grass,   10
Tricking and stopping, sleepy and proud,
Who cried in goose, Alas,

Hurt Hawks
[1] I. e., red-tailed hawk.

For the tireless heart within the little
Lady with rod that made them rise
From their noon apple-dreams, and scuttle
Goose-fashion under the skies!

But now go the bells, and we are ready;
In one house we are sternly stopped
To say we are vexed at her brown study,
Lying so primly propped.   20

Dulce et Decorum Est   1920

WILFRED OWEN   [1893–1918]

Bent double, like old beggars under sacks,
Knock-kneed, coughing like hags, we cursed through sludge,
Till on the haunting flares we turned our backs,
And towards our distant rest began to trudge.
Men marched asleep. Many had lost their boots,
But limped on, blood-shod. All went lame, all blind;
Drunk with fatigue; deaf even to the hoots
Of gas-shells dropping softly behind.

Gas! GAS! Quick, boys!—An ecstasy of fumbling,
Fitting the clumsy helmets just in time,   10
But someone still was yelling out and stumbling
And flound'ring like a man in fire or lime.—
Dim through the misty panes and thick green light,
As under a green sea, I saw him drowning.
In all my dreams before my helpless sight
He plunges at me, guttering, choking, drowning.

If in some smothering dreams, you too could pace
Behind the wagon that we flung him in,
And watch the white eyes writhing in his face,
His hanging face, like a devil's sick of sin,   20
If you could hear, at every jolt, the blood
Come gargling from the froth-corrupted lungs
Bitter as the cud
Of vile, incurable sores on innocent tongues,—
My friend, you would not tell with such high zest
To children ardent for some desperate glory,
The old lie: *Dulce et decorum est*
Pro patria mori.[1]

Dulce et Decorum Est
   [1] A quotation from the Latin poet Horace, "It is sweet and fitting to die for one's country."

nobody loses all the time   1926

E. E. CUMMINGS   [1894–1962]

nobody loses all the time

i had an uncle named
Sol who was a born failure and
nearly everybody said he should have gone
into vaudeville perhaps because my Uncle Sol could
sing McCann He Was A Diver on Xmas Eve like Hell Itself which
may or may not account for the fact that my Uncle

Sol indulged in that possibly most inexcusable
of all to use a highfalootin phrase
luxuries that is or to   10
wit farming and be
it needlessly
added

my Uncle Sol's farm
failed because the chickens
ate the vegetables so
my Uncle Sol had a
chicken farm till the
skunks ate the chickens when

my Uncle Sol   20
had a skunk farm but
the skunks caught cold and
died and so
my Uncle Sol imitated the
skunks in a subtle manner

or by drowning himself in the watertank
but somebody who'd given my Uncle Sol a Victor
Victrola and records while he lived presented to
him upon the auspicious occasion of his decease a
scrumptious not to mention splendiferous funeral with   30
tall boys in black gloves and flowers and everything and

i remember we all cried like the Missouri
when my Uncle Sol's coffin lurched because
somebody pressed a button
(and down went
my Uncle
Sol

and started a worm farm)

QUESTIONS
1. Explain the title. 2. What is the speaker's attitude toward Uncle Sol?

O Sweet Spontaneous   1923

E. E. CUMMINGS [1894–1962]

O sweet spontaneous
earth how often have
the
doting

      fingers of
prurient philosophers pinched
and
poked

thee
, has the naughty thumb   10
of science prodded
thy

      beauty   .how
often have religions taken
thee upon their scraggy knees
squeezing and

buffeting thee that thou mightest conceive
gods
    (but
true   20

to the incomparable
couch of death thy
rhythmic
lover

      thou answerest

them only with

      spring)

QUESTIONS
1. Analyze the erotic imagery in this poem. What does it tell us about the speaker's attitude toward philosophy, science, and religion? **2.** What does the speaker mean by calling death earth's "lover" (l. 24)? And why "rhythmic" lover (l. 23)? **3.** In what sense is "spring" (l. 27) an answer?

On a Squirrel Crossing the Road in Autumn, in New England 1957

RICHARD EBERHART [b. 1904]

It is what he does not know,
Crossing the road under the elm trees,
About the mechanism of my car,
About the Commonwealth of Massachusetts,
About Mozart, India, Arcturus,

That wins my praise. I engage
At once in whirling squirrel-praise.

He obeys the orders of nature
Without knowing them.
It is what he does not know   10
That makes him beautiful.
Such a knot of little purposeful nature!

I who can see him as he cannot see himself
Repose in the ignorance that is his blessing.

It is what man does not know of God
Composes the visible poem of the world.
                    . . . Just missed him!

In Memory of W. B. Yeats 1940
(D. JAN. 1939)

W. H. AUDEN [1907–1973]

1

He disappeared in the dead of winter:
The brooks were frozen, the airports almost deserted,

And snow disfigured the public statues;
The mercury sank in the mouth of the dying day.
O all the instruments agree
The day of his death was a dark cold day.

Far from his illness
The wolves ran on through the evergreen forests,
The peasant river was untempted by the fashionable quays;
By mourning tongues   10
The death of the poet was kept from his poems.

But for him it was his last afternoon as himself,
An afternoon of nurses and rumors;
The provinces of his body revolted,
The squares of his mind were empty,
Silence invaded the suburbs,
The current of his feeling failed: he became his admirers.

Now he is scattered among a hundred cities
And wholly given over to unfamiliar affections;
To find his happiness in another kind of wood   20
And be punished under a foreign code of conscience.
The words of a dead man
Are modified in the guts of the living.

But in the importance and noise of tomorrow
When the brokers are roaring like beasts on the floor of the Bourse,[1]
And the poor have the sufferings to which they are fairly accustomed,
And each in the cell of himself is almost convinced of his freedom;
A few thousand will think of this day
As one thinks of a day when one did something slightly unusual.
O all the instruments agree   30
The day of his death was a dark cold day.

2

You were silly like us: your gift survived it all;
The parish of rich women, physical decay,
Yourself; mad Ireland hurt you into poetry.
Now Ireland has her madness and her weather still,
For poetry makes nothing happen: it survives
In the valley of its saying where executives

In Memory of W. B. Yeats
   [1] A European stock exchange, especially that in Paris.

Would never want to tamper; it flows south
From ranches of isolation and the busy griefs,
Raw towns that we believe and die in; it survives,   40
A way of happening, a mouth.

3

Earth, receive an honored guest;
William Yeats is laid to rest:
Let the Irish vessel lie
Emptied of its poetry.

In the nightmare of the dark
All the dogs of Europe bark,
And the living nations wait,
Each sequestered in its hate;

Intellectual disgrace   50
Stares from every human face,
And the seas of pity lie
Locked and frozen in each eye.

Follow, poet, follow right
To the bottom of the night,
With your unconstraining voice
Still persuade us to rejoice;

With the farming of a verse
Make a vineyard of the curse,
Sing of human unsuccess   60
In a rapture of distress;

In the deserts of the heart
Let the healing fountain start,
In the prison of his days
Teach the free man how to praise.

QUESTIONS
1. In what sense does a dead poet become "his admirers" (l. 17)? **2.** Is Auden's statement that "poetry makes nothing happen" (l. 36) consistent with the attitudes expressed in the final three stanzas?

WRITING TOPIC
Why does Auden view the death of Yeats as a significant event?

Landscape with the Fall of Icarus, c. 1560 by Pieter Brueghel the Elder

Musée des Beaux Arts   1940

W. H. AUDEN [1907–1973]

About suffering they were never wrong,
The Old Masters: how well they understood
Its human position; how it takes place
While someone else is eating or opening a window or just walking dully
  along;
How, when the aged are reverently, passionately waiting
For the miraculous birth, there always must be
Children who did not specially want it to happen, skating
On a pond at the edge of the wood:
They never forgot
That even the dreadful martyrdom must run its course   10
Anyhow in a corner, some untidy spot
Where the dogs go on with their doggy life and the torturer's horse
Scratches its innocent behind on a tree.

In Brueghel's *Icarus*,[1] for instance: how everything turns away
Quite leisurely from the disaster; the ploughman may
Have heard the splash, the forsaken cry,
But for him it was not an important failure; the sun shone
As it had to on the white legs disappearing into the green
Water; and the expensive delicate ship that must have seen
Something amazing, a boy falling out of the sky,   20
Had somewhere to get to and sailed calmly on.

Elegy for Jane   1958
MY STUDENT, THROWN BY A HORSE

THEODORE ROETHKE   [1908–1963]

I remember the neckcurls, limp and damp as tendrils;
And her quick look, a sidelong pickerel smile;
And how, once startled into talk, the light syllables leaped for her,
And she balanced in the delight of her thought,
A wren, happy, tail into the wind,
Her song trembling the twigs and small branches.
The shade sang with her;
The leaves, their whispers turned to kissing;
And the mold sang in the bleached valleys under the rose.

Oh, when she was sad, she cast herself down into such a pure depth,   10
Even a father could not find her:
Scraping her cheek against straw;
Stirring the clearest water.

My sparrow, you are not here,
Waiting like a fern, making a spiny shadow.
The sides of wet stones cannot console me,
Nor the moss, wound with the last light.

If only I could nudge you from this sleep,
My maimed darling, my skittery pigeon.

Musée des Beaux Arts
[1]This poem describes and comments on Pieter Breughel's painting *Landscape with the Fall of Icarus.* (See p. 1155.) According to myth, Daedalus and his son Icarus made wings, whose feathers they attached with wax, to escape Crete. Icarus flew so near the sun that the wax melted and he fell.

Over this damp grave I speak the words of my love: 20
I, with no rights in this matter,
Neither father nor lover.

Between the World and Me   1935

RICHARD WRIGHT   [1908–1960]

And one morning while in the woods I stumbled suddenly upon the
    thing,
Stumbled upon it in a grassy clearing guarded by scaly oaks and elms.
And the sooty details of the scene rose, thrusting themselves between the
    world and me. . . .
There was a design of white bones slumbering forgottenly upon a cushion
    of ashes.
There was a charred stump of a sapling pointing a blunt finger accusingly
    at the sky.
There were torn tree limbs, tiny veins of burnt leaves, and a scorched coil
    of greasy hemp;
A vacant shoe, an empty tie, a ripped shirt, a lonely hat, and a pair of
    trousers stiff with black blood.
And upon the trampled grass were buttons, dead matches, butt-ends of
    cigars and cigarettes, peanut shells, a drained gin-flask, and a whore's
    lipstick;
Scattered traces of tar, restless arrays of feathers, and the lingering smell of
    gasoline.
And through the morning air the sun poured yellow surprise into the eye
    sockets of a stony skull. . . .   10
And while I stood my mind was frozen with a cold pity for the life that
    was gone.
The ground gripped my feet and my heart was circled by icy walls of
    fear—
The sun died in the sky; a night wind muttered in the grass and fumbled
    the leaves in the trees; the woods poured forth the hungry yelping of
    hounds; the darkness screamed with thirsty voices; and the witnesses
    rose and lived: The dry bones stirred, rattled, lifted, melting themselves
    into my bones.
The grey ashes formed flesh firm and black, entering into my flesh.
The gin-flask passed from mouth to mouth; cigars and cigarettes glowed,
    the whore smeared the lipstick red upon her lips,
And a thousand faces swirled around me, clamoring that my life be
    burned. . . .

And then they had me, stripped me, battering my teeth into my throat till
    I swallowed my own blood.
My voice was drowned in the roar of their voices, and my black wet body
    slipped and rolled in their hands as they bound me to the sapling.
And my skin clung to the bubbling hot tar, falling from me in limp
    patches.   20
And the down and quills of the white feathers sank into my raw flesh, and
    I moaned in my agony.
Then my blood was cooled mercifully, cooled by a baptism of gasoline.
And in a blaze of red I leaped to the sky as pain rose like water, boiling
    my limbs.
Panting, begging I clutched childlike, clutched to the hot sides of death.
Now I am dry bones and my face a stony skull staring in my yellow
    surprise at the sun. . . .

Do Not Go Gentle
into That Good Night   1952

DYLAN THOMAS   [1914–1953]

Do not go gentle into that good night,
Old age should burn and rave at close of day;
Rage, rage against the dying of the light.

Though wise men at their end know dark is right,
Because their words had forked no lightning they
Do not go gentle into that good night.

Good men, the last wave by, crying how bright
Their frail deeds might have danced in a green bay,
Rage, rage against the dying of the light.

Wild men who caught and sang the sun in flight,   10
And learn, too late, they grieved it on its way,
Do not go gentle into that good night.

Grave men, near death, who see with blinding sight
Blind eyes could blaze like meteors and be gay,
Rage, rage against the dying of the light.

And you, my father, there on the sad height,
Curse, bless, me now with your fierce tears, I pray.

Do not go gentle into that good night.
Rage, rage against the dying of the light.

QUESTIONS

1. What do wise, good, wild, and grave men have in common?   **2.** Why does the poet use the adjective "gentle" rather than the adverb "gently"?   **3.** What is the "sad height" (l.16)?

The Death of the
Ball Turret Gunner   1945

RANDALL JARRELL   [1914–1965]

From my mother's sleep I fell into the State,
And I hunched in its belly till my wet fur froze.
Six miles from earth, loosed from its dream of life,
I woke to black flak and the nightmare fighters.
When I died they washed me out of the turret with a hose.

QUESTIONS

1. To what do "its" (ll. 2 and 3) and "they" (l. 5) refer?   **2.** Why is the mother described as asleep?

Losses   1945

RANDALL JARRELL   [1914–1965]

It was not dying: everybody died.
It was not dying: we had died before
In the routine crashes—and our fields
Called up the papers, wrote home to our folks,
And the rates rose, all because of us.
We died on the wrong page of the almanac,
Scattered on mountains fifty miles away;
Diving on haystacks, fighting with a friend,
We blazed up on the lines we never saw.
We died like aunts or pets or foreigners.   10
(When we left high school nothing else had died
For us to figure we had died like.)

In our new planes, with our new crews, we bombed
The ranges by the desert or the shore,
Fired at towed targets, waited for our scores—
And turned into replacements and woke up
One morning, over England, operational.
It wasn't different: but if we died
It was not an accident but a mistake
(But an easy one for anyone to make).   20
We read our mail and counted up our missions—
In bombers named for girls, we burned
The cities we had learned about in school—
Till our lives wore out; our bodies lay among
The people we had killed and never seen.
When we lasted long enough they gave us medals;
When we died they said, "Our casualties were low."
They said, "Here are the maps"; we burned the cities.

It was not dying—no, not ever dying;
But the night I died I dreamed that I was dead,   30
And the cities said to me: "Why are you dying?
We are satisfied, if you are; but why did I die?"

QUESTIONS
1. Who is the speaker in this poem?   **2.**   Why are the deaths described as "not
an accident but a mistake" (l. 19)?   **3.**   Explain the final stanza.

The Pardon   1950

RICHARD WILBUR   [b. 1921]

My dog lay dead five days without a grave
In the thick of summer, hid in a clump of pine
And a jungle of grass and honeysuckle-vine.
I who had loved him while he kept alive

Went only close enough to where he was
To sniff the heavy honeysuckle-smell
Twined with another odor heavier still
And hear the flies' intolerable buzz.

Well, I was ten and very much afraid.
In my kind world the dead were out of range   10

And I could not forgive the sad or strange
In beast or man. My father took the spade

And buried him. Last night I saw the grass
Slowly divide (it was the same scene
But now it glowed a fierce and mortal green)
And saw the dog emerging. I confess

I felt afraid again, but still he came
In the carnal sun, clothed in a hymn of flies,
And death was breeding in his lively eyes.
I started in to cry and call his name,   20

Asking forgiveness of his tongueless head.
. . . I dreamt the past was never past redeeming:
But whether this was false or honest dreaming
I beg death's pardon now. And mourn the dead.

Aubade [1]   1977

PHILIP LARKIN   [1922–1985]

I work all day, and get half drunk at night.
Waking at four to soundless dark, I stare.
In time the curtain-edges will grow light.
Till then I see what's really always there:
Unresting death, a whole day nearer now,
Making all thought impossible but how
And where and when I shall myself die.
Arid interrogation: yet the dread
Of dying, and being dead,
Flashes afresh to hold and horrify.   10

The mind blanks at the glare. Not in remorse
—The good not done, the love not given, time
Torn off unused—nor wretchedly because
An only life can take so long to climb
Clear of its wrong beginnings, and may never;
But at the total emptiness for ever,
The sure extinction that we travel to

Aubade.
  [1] Morning song.

And shall be lost in always. Not to be here,
Not to be anywhere,
And soon; nothing more terrible, nothing more true.   20

This is a special way of being afraid
No trick dispels. Religion used to try,
That vast moth-eaten musical brocade
Created to pretend we never die,
And specious stuff that says *No rational being
Can fear a thing it will not feel*, not seeing
That this is what we fear—no sight, no sound.
No touch or taste to smell, nothing to think with.
Nothing to love or link with,
The anaesthetic from which none come round.   30

And so it stays just on the edge of vision,
A small unfocused blur, a standing chill
That slows each impulse down to indecision.
Most things may never happen: this one will.
And realisation of it rages out
In furnace-fear when we are caught without
People or drink. Courage is no good:
It means not scaring others. Being brave
Lets no one off the grave.
Death is no different whined at than withstood.   40

Slowly light strengthens, and the room takes shape.
It stands plain as a wardrobe, what we know,
Have always known, know that we can't escape,
Yet can't accept. One side will have to go.
Meanwhile telephones crouch, getting ready to ring
In locked-up offices, and all the uncaring
Intricate rented world begins to rouse.
The sky is white as clay, with no sun.
Work has to be done.
Postmen like doctors go from house to house.   50

After a Time   (1961?)

CATHERINE DAVIS [b. 1924]

After a time, all losses are the same.
One more thing lost is one thing less to lose;
And we go stripped at last the way we came.

Though we shall probe, time and again, our shame,
Who lack the wit to keep or to refuse,
After a time, all losses are the same.

No wit, no luck can beat a losing game;
Good fortune is a reassuring ruse:
And we go stripped at last the way we came.

Rage as we will for what we think to claim,   10
Nothing so much as this bare thought subdues:
After a time, all losses are the same.

The sense of treachery—the want, the blame—
Goes in the end, whether or not we choose,
And we go stripped at last the way we came.

So we, who would go raging, will go tame
When what we have we can no longer use:
After a time, all losses are the same;
And we go stripped at last the way we came.

QUESTIONS
1. What difference in effect would occur if the refrain "After a time" were changed to "When life is done"? **2.** What are the various meanings of "stripped" in line 3 and line 19? **3.** Explain the meaning of "The sense of treachery" (l. 13). **4.** Does this poem say that life is meaningless? Explain.

WRITING TOPIC
Compare this poem with Dylan Thomas's "Do Not Go Gentle into That Good Night."

Woodchucks   1972

MAXINE KUMIN [b. 1925]

Gassing the woodchucks didn't turn out right.
The knockout bomb from the Feed and Grain Exchange
was featured as merciful, quick at the bone
and the case we had against them was airtight
both exits shoehorned shut with puddingstone,
but they had a sub-sub-basement out of range.

Next morning they turned up again, no worse
for the cyanide than we for our cigarettes

and state-store Scotch, all of us up to scratch.
They brought down the marigolds as a matter of course   10
and then took over the vegetable patch
nipping the broccoli shoots, beheading the carrots.

The food from our mouths, I said, righteously thrilling
to the feel of the .22, the bullets' neat noses.
I, a lapsed pacifist fallen from grace
puffed with Darwinian pieties for killing,
now drew a bead on the littlest woodchuck's face.
He died down in the everbearing roses.

Ten minutes later I dropped the mother. She
flipflopped in the air and fell, her needle teeth   20
still hooked in a leaf of early Swiss chard.
Another baby next. O one-two-three
the murderer inside me rose up hard,
the hawkeye killer came on stage forthwith.

There's one chuck left. Old wily fellow, he keeps
me cocked and ready day after day after day.
All night I hunt his humped-up form. I dream
I sight along the barrel in my sleep.
If only they'd all consented to die unseen
gassed underground the quiet Nazi way.   30

To Aunt Rose   1961

ALLEN GINSBERG   [b. 1926]

Aunt Rose—now—might I see you
with your thin face and buck tooth smile and pain
                of rheumatism—and a long black heavy shoe
                        for your bony left leg
        limping down the long hall in Newark on the running carpet
                past the black grand piano
                        in the day room
                                where the parties were
        and I sang Spanish loyalist songs[1]

To Aunt Rose
   [1] Between 1936 and 1939, a civil war occurred in Spain in which rebel forces under General
Francisco Franco defeated the Loyalist forces supporting the politically liberal monarchy. In some
ways a foreshadowing of World War II, the Spanish Civil War attracted the attention of the great
powers, with Russia supporting the Loyalist forces and Germany and Italy supporting the rebel
forces. Many American writers and intellectuals saw the war as a struggle between fascism and

in a high squeaky voice   10
        (hysterical) the committee listening
    while you limped around the room
    collected the money—
Aunt Honey, Uncle Sam, a stranger with a cloth arm
      in his pocket
        and huge young bald head
          of Abraham Lincoln Brigade

—your long sad face
      your tears of sexual frustration
        (what smothered sobs and bony hips   20
          under the pillows of Osborne Terrace)
—the time I stood on the toilet seat naked
    and you powdered my thighs with Calomine
      against the poison ivy—my tender
        and shamed first black curled hairs
what were you thinking in secret heart then
      knowing me a man already—
and I an ignorant girl of family silence on the thin pedestal
    of my legs in the bathroom—Museum of Newark.

          Aunt Rose   30
Hitler is dead, Hitler is in Eternity; Hitler is with
    Tamburlane and Emily Brontë[2]

Though I see you walking still, a ghost on Osborne Terrace
      down the long dark hall to the front door
    limping a little with a pinched smile
      in what must have been a silken
        flower dress
welcoming my father, the Poet, on his visit to Newark
      —see you arriving in the living room
        dancing on your crippled leg   40
        and clapping hands his book
          had been accepted by Liveright[3]

Hitler is dead and Liveright's gone out of business
The Attic of the Past and *Everlasting Minute* are out of print
      Uncle Harry sold his last silk stocking
      Claire quit interpretive dancing school
      Buba sits a wrinkled monument in Old
        Ladies Home blinking at new babies

---

democracy and supported the Loyalist cause energetically; the Abraham Lincoln Brigade (line 17) was a volunteer unit of Americans that went to Spain to fight on the Loyalist side.
  [2] Tamburlane (1336?–1405) Mongol conqueror; Emily Brontë (1818–1848) English novelist.
  [3] A publishing firm.

> last time I saw you was the hospital
> > pale skull protruding under ashen skin   50
> > > blue veined unconscious girl
> > > > in an oxygen tent
> > > the war in Spain has ended long ago
> > > > Aunt Rose

Five Ways to Kill a Man   1963

EDWIN BROCK   [b. 1927]

There are many cumbersome ways to kill a man:
you can make him carry a plank of wood
to the top of a hill and nail him to it. To do this
properly you require a crowd of people
wearing sandals, a cock that crows, a cloak
to dissect, a sponge, some vinegar and one
man to hammer the nails home.

Or you can take a length of steel,
shaped and chased° in a traditional way,   ornamented
and attempt to pierce the metal cage he wears.   10
But for this you need white horses,
English trees, men with bows and arrows,
at least two flags, a prince and a
castle to hold your banquet in.

Dispensing with nobility, you may, if the wind
allows, blow gas at him. But then you need
a mile of mud sliced through with ditches,
not to mention black boots, bomb craters,
more mud, a plague of rats, a dozen songs
and some round hats made of steel.   20

In an age of aeroplanes, you may fly
miles above your victim and dispose of him by
pressing one small switch. All you then
require is an ocean to separate you, two
systems of government, a nation's scientists,

several factories, a psychopath and
land that no one needs for several years.

These are, as I began, cumbersome ways
to kill a man. Simpler, direct, and much more neat
is to see that he is living somewhere in the middle   30
of the twentieth century, and leave him there.

Seaman, 1941   1971

MOLLY HOLDEN   [1927–1981]

This was not to be expected.

Waves, wind, and tide brought him again
to Barra.[1] Clinging to driftwood many hours
the night before, he had not recognized
the current far offshore his own nor
known he drifted home. He gave up, anyway,
some time before the smell of land reached out
or dawn outlined the morning gulls.

                                           They found him
on the white sand southward of the ness,[2]   10
not long enough in the sea to be
disfigured, cheek sideways as in sleep;
old men who had fished with his father
and grandfather knew him at once,
before they even turned him on his back, by the set
of the dead shoulders, and were shocked.

This was not to be expected.

His mother, with hot eyes, preparing the parlor
for his corpse, would have preferred, she thought,
to have been told by telegram rather
than so to know that convoy, ship, and son
had only been a hundred miles northwest

Seaman, 1941
  [1] An island in the Hebrides off the western coast of Scotland.
  [2] Promontory.

of home when the torpedoes struck.
She could have gone on thinking that
he'd had no chance; but to die offshore,
in Hebridean tides, as if he'd stayed
a fisherman for life and never gone to war
was not to be expected.

For the Anniversary of My Death   1967

W. S. MERWIN   [b. 1927]

Every year without knowing it I have passed the day
When the last fires will wave to me
And the silence will set out
Tireless traveller
Like the beam of a lightless star

Then I will no longer
Find myself in life as in a strange garment
Surprised at the earth
And the love of a woman
And the shamelessness of men   10
As today writing after three days of rain
Hearing the wren sing and the falling cease
And bowing not knowing to what

Relic   1960

TED HUGHES   [b. 1930]

I found this jawbone at the sea's edge:
There, crabs, dogfish, broken by the breakers or tossed
To flap for half an hour and turn to a crust
Continue the beginning. The deeps are cold:
In that darkness camaraderie does not hold:
Nothing touches but, clutching, devours. And the jaws,
Before they are satisfied or their stretched purpose
Slacken, go down jaws; go gnawn bare. Jaws
Eat and are finished and the jawbone comes to the beach:

This is the sea's achievement; with shells,   10
Vertebrae, claws, carapaces, skulls.

Time in the sea eats its tail, thrives, casts these
Indigestibles, the spars of purposes
That failed far from the surface. None grow rich
In the sea. This curved jawbone did not laugh
But gripped, gripped and is now a cenotaph.°   empty tomb

QUESTIONS
1. What is the "relic" of the title? What characteristic of nature does it symbolize? **2.** What does "Continue the beginning" (l. 4) signify? **3.** This poem is
metrically quite irregular and thus difficult to scan. Further, there are only two pair
of perfect rhymes (ll. 4-5 and 15-16). Yet the poem is richly musical. Identify the
poetic devices that generate the music.

People*   (trans. 1962)

YEVGENY YEVTUSHENKO   [b. 1933]

No people are uninteresting.
Their fate is like the chronicle of planets.

Nothing in them is not particular,
and planet is dissimilar from planet.

And if a man lived in obscurity
making his friends in that obscurity
obscurity is not uninteresting.

To each his world is private,
and in that world one excellent minute.

And in that world one tragic minute.   10
These are private.

In any man who dies there dies with him
his first snow and kiss and fight.
It goes with him.

People
  * Translated by Robin Milner-Gulland and Peter Levi.

They are left books and bridges
and painted canvas and machinery.

Whose fate is to survive.
But what has gone is also not nothing:

by the rule of the game something has gone.   20
Not people die but worlds die in them.

Whom we knew as faulty, the earth's creatures.
Of whom, essentially, what did we know?

Brother of a brother? Friend of friends?
Lover of lover?

We who knew our fathers
in everything, in nothing.

They perish. They cannot be brought back.
The secret worlds are not regenerated.

And every time again and again
I make my lament against destruction.   30

The Dead Ladies   1973

FOR MAUREEN SUGDEN

MARY GORDON   [b. 1949]

> We can sit down and weep;
>   we can go shopping
>   *Elizabeth Bishop*

What's to be done with death,
My friend?
          We sit
Cross legged, hating men.

Virginia[1] filled her English skirt
With stones.
Always well bred she left behind

Her sensible shoes, her stick,
Her hat, her last note
(An apology)   10
And walked in water
'Til it didn't matter.

We speak of Sylvia[2]
Who could not live
For babies or for poetry.

You switch on Joplin's[3] blues
The room looms black
With what we know
But are afraid to think.

Too scared to say: "and us?"   20
We leave for work.
Hearts in our mouths.
In love with the wrong men.

QUESTIONS

1. What is the implied difference between the three women mentioned in the poem "and us" (l. 20)? **2.** What do you suppose the poet means by the assertion in line 4 that she and her friend hate men? How can that assertion be reconciled with the last line of the poem? **3.** What is the point of mentioning three famous women, all of whom died what might be called tragic and untimely deaths?

The Dead Ladies
[1] Virginia Woolf (1882-1941), British novelist, committed suicide by weighting herself with stones and walking into the Ouse River.
[2] Sylvia Plath (1932–1963), American poet, committed suicide by asphyxiating herself with cooking gas.
[3] Janice Joplin (1943–1970), popular American singer, apparently died of an overdose of drugs.

THE
PRESENCE
OF DEATH

from *The Seventh Seal*, 1956 by Ingmar Bergman

DRAMA

The Seventh Seal* 1956

INGMAR BERGMAN [b. 1918]

THE CAST

The squire	Raval
Death	The monk
Jof	The smith
The knight	The church painter
Mia	Skat
Lisa	The merchant
The witch	Woman at the inn
The knight's wife	Leader of the soldiers
The girl	The young monk

The night had brought little relief from the heat, and at dawn, a hot gust of wind blows across the colorless sea.

The knight, Antonius Block, lies prostrate on some spruce branches spread over the fine sand. His eyes are wide-open and bloodshot from lack of sleep.

Nearby his squire Jöns is snoring loudly. He has fallen asleep where he collapsed, at the edge of the forest among the wind-gnarled fir trees. His open mouth gapes toward the dawn, and unearthly sounds come from his throat.

At the sudden gust of wind the horses stir, stretching their parched muzzles toward the sea. They are as thin and worn as their masters.

The knight has risen and waded into the shallow water, where he rinses his sunburned face and blistered lips.

Jöns rolls over to face the forest and the darkness. He moans in his sleep and vigorously scratches the stubbled hair on his head. A scar stretches diagonally across his scalp, as white as lightning against the grime.

The knight returns to the beach and falls on his knees. With his eyes closed and brow furrowed, he says his morning prayers. His hands are clenched together and his lips form the words silently. His face is sad and bitter. He opens his eyes and stares directly into the morning sun which wallows up from the misty sea

---

* Translated by Lars Malmstrom and David Kushner.

like some bloated, dying fish. The sky is gray and immobile, a dome of lead. A cloud hangs mute and dark over the western horizon. High up, barely visible, a sea gull floats on motionless wings. Its cry is weird and restless.

The knight's large gray horse lifts its head and whinnies. Antonius Block turns around.

Behind him stands a man in black. His face is very pale and he keeps his hands hidden in the wide folds of his cloak.

Knight   Who are you?
Death.   I am Death.
Knight.   Have you come for me?
Death.   I have been walking by your side for a long time.
Knight.   That I know.
Death.   Are you prepared?
Knight.   My body is frightened, but I am not.
Death.   Well, there is no shame in that.

The knight has risen to his feet. He shivers. Death opens his cloak to place it around the knight's shoulders.

Knight.   Wait a moment.
Death.   That's what they all say. I grant no reprieves.
Knight.   You play chess, don't you?

A gleam of interest kindles in Death's eyes.

Death.   How did you know that?
Knight.   I have seen it in paintings and heard it sung in ballads.
Death.   Yes, in fact I'm quite a good chess player.
Knight.   But you can't be better than I am.

The knight rummages in the big black bag which he keeps beside him and takes out a small chessboard. He places it carefully on the ground and begins setting up the pieces.

Death.   Why do you want to play chess with me?
Knight.   I have my reasons.
Death.   That is your privilege.
Knight.   The condition is that I may live as long as I hold out against you. If I win, you will release me. Is it agreed?

The knight holds out his two fists to Death, who smiles at him suddenly. Death points to one of the knight's hands; it contains a black pawn.

Knight.   You drew black!
Death.   Very appropriate. Don't you think so?

The knight and Death bend over the chessboard. After a moment of hesitation, Antonius Block opens with his king's pawn. Death moves, also using his king's pawn.

The morning breeze has died down. The restless movement of the sea has ceased, the water is silent. The sun rises from the haze and its glow whitens. The sea gull floats under the dark cloud, frozen in space. The day is already scorchingly hot.

The squire Jöns is awakened by a kick in the rear. Opening his eyes, he grunts like a pig and yawns broadly. He scrambles to his feet, saddles his horse and picks up the heavy pack.

The knight slowly rides away from the sea, into the forest near the beach and up toward the road. He pretends not to hear the morning prayers of his squire. Jöns soon overtakes him.

Jöns *(sings).*   Between a strumpet's legs to lie
                        Is the life for which I sigh.

He stops and looks at his master, but the knight hasn't heard Jöns' song, or he pretends that he hasn't. To give further vent to his irritation, the squire sings even louder.

Jöns *(sings).*   Up above is God Almighty
                        So very far away,
                        But your brother the Devil
                        You will meet on every level.

Jöns finally gets the knight's attention. He stops singing. The knight, his horse, Jöns' own horse and Jöns himself know all the songs by heart. The long, dusty journey from the Holy Land hasn't made them any cleaner.

They ride across a mossy heath which stretches toward the horizon. Beyond it, the sea lies shimmering in the white glitter of the sun.

Jöns.   In Farjestad everyone was talking about evil omens and other horrible
             things. Two horses had eaten each other in the night, and, in the churchyard,
             graves had been opened and the remains of corpses scattered all over the
             place. Yesterday afternoon there were as many as four suns in the heavens.

The knight doesn't answer. Close by a scrawny dog is whining, crawling toward its master, who is sleeping in a sitting position in the blazing hot sun. A black cloud of flies clusters around his head and shoulders. The miserable-looking dog whines incessantly as it lies flat on its stomach, wagging its tail.

Jöns dismounts and approaches the sleeping man. Jöns addresses him politely. When he doesn't receive an answer, he walks up to the man in order to shake him awake. He bends over the sleeping man's shoulder, but quickly pulls back his hand. The man falls backward on the heath, his face turned toward Jöns. It is a corpse, staring at Jöns with empty eye sockets and white teeth.

The squire remounts and overtakes his master. He takes a drink from his waterskin and hands the bag to the knight.

Knight.   Well, did he show you the way?

Jöns.   Not exactly.

Knight.   What did he say?

Jöns.   Nothing.

Knight.   Was he a mute?

Jöns.   No, sir, I wouldn't say that. As a matter of fact, he was quite eloquent.

Knight.   Oh?

Jöns.   He was eloquent, all right. The trouble is that what he had to say was most depressing. *(Sings)*

> One moment you're bright and lively,
> The next you're crawling with worms.
> Fate is a terrible villain
> And you, my friend, its poor victim.

Knight.   Must you sing?

Jöns.   No.

The knight hands his squire a piece of bread, which keeps him quiet for a while. The sun burns down on them cruelly, and beads of perspiration trickle down their faces. There is a cloud of dust around the horses' hoofs.

They ride past an inlet and along verdant groves. In the shade of some large trees stands a bulging wagon covered with a mottled canvas. A horse whinnies nearby and is answered by the knight's horse. The two travelers do not stop to rest under the shade of the trees but continue riding until they disappear at the bend of the road.

In his sleep, Jof the juggler hears the neighing of his horse and the answer from a distance. He tries to go on sleeping, but it is stifling inside the wagon. The rays of the sun filtering through the canvas cast streaks of light across the face of Jof's wife, Mia, and their one-year-old son, Mikael, who are sleeping deeply and peacefully. Near them, Jonas Skat, an older man, snores loudly.

Jof crawls out of the wagon. There is still a spot of shade under the big trees. He takes a drink of water, gargles, stretches and talks to his scrawny old horse.

Jof.   Good morning. Have you had breakfast? I can't eat grass, worse luck. Can't you teach me how? We're a little hard up. People aren't very interested in juggling in this part of the country.

He has picked up the juggling balls and slowly begins to toss them. Then he stands on his head and cackles like a hen. Suddenly he stops and sits down with a look of utter astonishment on his face. The wind causes the trees to sway

*slightly. The leaves stir and there is a soft murmur. The flowers and the grass
bend gracefully, and somewhere a bird raises its voice in a long warble.*

*Jof's face breaks into a smile and his eyes fill with tears. With a dazed expression he sits flat on his behind while the grass rustles softly, and bees and butterflies
hum around his head. The unseen bird continues to sing.*

*Suddenly the breeze stops blowing, the birds stop singing, Jof's smile fades,
the flowers and grass wilt in the heat. The old horse is still walking around
grazing and swishing its tail to ward off the flies.*

Jof comes to life. He rushes into the wagon and shakes Mia awake.

Jof.   Mia, wake up, Wake up! Mia, I've just seen something. I've got to tell
  you about it!

Mia *(sits-up, terrified)*.   What is it? What's happened?

Jof.   Listen, I've had a vision. No, it wasn't a vision. It was real, absolutely
  real.

Mia.   Oh, so you've had a vision again!

*Mia's voice is filled with gentle irony. Jof shakes his head and grabs her by the
shoulders.*

Jof.   But I did see her!

Mia.   Whom did you see?

Jof.   The Virgin Mary.

Mia can't help being impressed by her husband's fervor. She lowers her voice.

Mia.   Did you really see her?

Jof.   She was so close to me that I could have touched her. She had a golden
  crown on her head and wore a blue gown with flowers of gold. She was
  barefoot and had small brown hands with which she was holding the Child
  and teaching Him to walk. And then she saw me watching her and she smiled
  at me. My eyes filled with tears and when I wiped them away, she had
  disappeared. And everything became so still in the sky and on the earth. Can
  you understand . . .

Mia.   What an imagination you have.

Jof.   You don't believe me! But it was real, I tell you, not the kind of reality
  you see everyday, but a different kind.

Mia.   Perhaps it was the kind of reality you told us about when you saw the
  Devil paint your wagon wheels red, using his tail as a brush.

Jof *(embarrassed)*.   Why must you keep bringing that up?

Mia.   And then you discovered that you had red paint under your nails.

Jof.   Well, perhaps that time I made it up. *(Eagerly)* I did it just so that you
  would believe in my other visions. The real ones. The ones that I didn't make
  up.

Mia *(severely)*.   You have to keep your visions under control. Otherwise people
  will think that you're a half-wit, which you're not. At least not yet—as far as
  I know. But, come to think of it, I'm not so sure about that.

Jof *(angry).*   I didn't ask to have visions. I can't help it if voices speak to me, if the Holy Virgin appears before me and angels and devils like my company.

Skat *(sits up).*   Haven't I told you once and for all that I need my morning's sleep! I have asked you politely, pleaded with you, but nothing works. So now I'm telling you to *shut up!*

His eyes are popping with rage. He turns over and continues snoring where he left off. Mia and Jof decide that it would be wisest to leave the wagon. They sit down on a crate. Mia has Mikael on her knees. He is naked and squirms vigorously. Jof sits close to his wife. Slumped over, he still looks dazed and astonished. A dry, hot wind blows from the sea.

Mia.   If we would only get some rain. Everything is burned to cinders. We won't have anything to eat this winter.

Jof *(yawning).*   We'll get by.

He says this smilingly, with a casual air. He stretches and laughs contentedly.

Mia.   I want Mikael to have a better life than ours.

Jof.   Mikael will grow up to be a great acrobat—or a juggler who can do the one impossible trick.

Mia.   What's that?

Jof.   To make one of the balls stand absolutely still in the air.

Mia.   But that's impossible.

Jof.   Impossible for us—but not for him.

Mia.   You're dreaming again.

She yawns. The sun has made her a bit drowsy and she lies down on the grass. Jof does likewise and puts one arm around his wife's shoulders.

Jof.   I've composed a song. I made it up during the night when I couldn't sleep. Do you want to hear it?

Mia.   Sing it. I'm very curious.

Jof.   I have to sit up first.

He sits with his legs crossed, makes a dramatic gesture with his arms and sings in a loud voice.

Jof.   On a lily branch a dove is perched
            Against the summer sky,
            She sings a wondrous song of Christ
            And there's great joy on high.

He interrupts his singing in order to be complimented by his wife.

Jof.   Mia! Are you asleep?

Mia.   It's a lovely song.

Jof.   I haven't finished yet.

Mia.   I heard it, but I think I'll sleep a little longer. You can sing the rest to me afterward.

Jof.   All you do is sleep.

Jof is a bit offended and glances over at his son, Mikael, but he is also sleeping soundly in the high grass. Jonas Skat comes out from the wagon. He yawns; he is very tired and in a bad humor. In his hands he holds a crudely made death mask.

Skat.   Is this supposed to be a mask for an actor? If the priests didn't pay us so well, I'd say no thank you.

Jof.   Are you going to play Death?

Skat.   Just think, scaring decent folk out of their wits with this kind of nonsense.

Jof.   When are we supposed to do this play?

Skat.   At the saints' feast in Elsinore. We're going to perform right on the church steps, believe it or not.

Jof.   Wouldn't it be better to play something bawdy? People like it better, and, besides, it's more fun.

Skat.   Idiot. There's a rumor going around that there's a terrible pestilence in the land, and now the priests are prophesying sudden death and all sorts of spiritual agonies.

Mia is awake now and lies contentedly on her back, sucking on a blade of grass and looking smilingly at her husband.

Jof.   And what part am I to play?

Skat.   You're such a damn fool, so you're going to be the Soul of Man.

Jof.   That's a bad part, of course.

Skat.   Who makes the decisions around here? Who is the director of this company anyhow?

Skat, grinning, holds the mask in front of his face and recites dramatically.

Skat.   Bear this in mind, you fool. Your life hangs by a thread. Your time is short. *(In his usual voice)* Are the women going to like me in this getup? Will I make a hit? No! I feel as if I were dead already.

He stumbles into the wagon muttering furiously. Jof sits, leaning forward. Mia lies beside him on the grass.

Mia.   Jof!

Jof.   What is it?

Mia.   Sit still. Don't move.
Jof.   What do you mean?
Mia.   Don't say anything.
Jof.   I'm as silent as a grave.
Mia.   Shh! I love you.

Waves of heat envelop the gray stone church in a strange white mist. The knight dismounts and enters. After tying up the horses, Jöns slowly follows him in. When he comes onto the church porch he stops in surprise. To the right of the entrance there is a large fresco on the wall, not quite finished. Perched on a crude scaffolding is a painter wearing a red cap and paint-stained clothes. He has one brush in his mouth, while with another in his hand he outlines a small, terrified human face amidst a sea of other faces.

Jöns.   What is this supposed to represent?
Painter.   The Dance of Death.
Jöns.   And that one is Death?
Painter.   Yes, he dances off with all of them.
Jöns.   Why do you paint such nonsense?
Painter.   I thought it would serve to remind people that they must die.
Jöns.   Well, it's not going to make them feel any happier.
Painter.   Why should one always make people happy? It might not be a bad idea to scare them a little once in a while.
Jöns.   Then they'll close their eyes and refuse to look at your painting.
Painter.   Oh, they'll look. A skull is almost more interesting than a naked woman.
Jöns.   If you do scare them . . .
Painter.   They'll think.
Jöns.   And if they think . . .
Painter.   They'll become still more scared.
Jöns.   And then they'll run right into the arms of the priests.
Painter.   That's not my business.
Jöns.   You're only painting your Dance of Death.
Painter.   I'm only painting things as they are. Everyone else can do as he likes.
Jöns.   Just think how some people will curse you.
Painter.   Maybe. But then I'll paint something amusing for them to look at. I have to make a living—at least until the plague takes me.
Jöns.   The plague. That sounds horrible.
Painter.   You should see the boils on a diseased man's throat. You should see how his body shrivels up so that his legs look like knotted strings—like the man I've painted over there.

The painter points with his brush. Jöns sees a small human form writhing in the grass, its eyes turned upward in a frenzied look of horror and pain.

Jöns.   That looks terrible.

Painter.   It certainly does. He tries to rip out the boil, he bites his hands, tears his veins open with his fingernails and his screams can be heard everywhere. Does that scare you?

Jöns.   Scare? Me? You don't know me. What are the horrors you've painted over there?

Painter.   The remarkable thing is that the poor creatures think the pestilence is the Lord's punishment. Mobs of people who call themselves Slaves of Sin are swarming over the country, flagellating themselves and others, all for the glory of God.

Jöns.   Do they really whip themselves?

Painter.   Yes, it's a terrible sight. I crawl into a ditch and hide when they pass by.

Jöns.   Do you have any brandy? I've been drinking water all day and it's made me as thirsty as a camel in the desert.

Painter.   I think I frightened you after all.

Jöns sits down with the painter, who produces a jug of brandy.

The knight is kneeling before a small altar. It is dark and quiet around him. The air is cool and musty. Pictures of saints look down on him with stony eyes. Christ's face is turned upward, His mouth open as if in a cry of anguish. On the ceiling beam there is a representation of a hideous devil spying on a miserable human being. The knight hears a sound from the confession booth and approaches it. The face of Death appears behind the grill for an instant, but the knight doesn't see him.

Knight.   I want to talk to you as openly as I can, but my heart is empty.

Death doesn't answer.

Knight.   The emptiness is a mirror turned toward my own face. I see myself in it, and I am filled with fear and disgust.

Death doesn't answer.

Knight.   Through my indifference to my fellow men, I have isolated myself from their company. Now I live in a world of phantoms. I am imprisoned in my dreams and fantasies.

Death.   And yet you don't want to die.

Knight.   Yes, I do.

Death.   What are you waiting for?

Knight.   I want knowledge.

Death.   You want guarantees?

Knight.   Call it whatever you like. Is it so cruelly inconceivable to grasp God with the senses? Why should he hide himself in a mist of half-spoken promises and unseen miracles?

Death doesn't answer.

Knight.   How can we have faith in those who believe when we can't have faith in ourselves? What is going to happen to those of us who want to believe but aren't able to? And what is to become of those who neither want to nor are capable of believing?

The knight stops and waits for a reply, but no one speaks or answers him. There is complete silence.

Knight.   Why can't I kill God within me? Why does he live on in this painful and humiliating way even though I curse Him and want to tear Him out of my heart? Why, in spite of everything, is He a baffling reality that I can't shake off? Do you hear me?

Death.   Yes, I hear you.

Knight.   I want knowledge, not faith, not suppositions, but knowledge. I want God to stretch out his hand toward me, reveal Himself and speak to me.

Death.   But he remains silent.

Knight.   I call out to him in the dark but no one seems to be there.

Death.   Perhaps no one is there.

Knight.   Then life is an outrageous horror. No one can live in the face of death, knowing that all is nothingness.

Death.   Most people never reflect about either death or the futility of life.

Knight.   But one day they will have to stand at that last moment of life and look toward the darkness.

Death.   When *that* day comes . . .

Knight.   In our fear, we make an image, and that image we call God.

Death.   You are worrying . . . .

Knight.   Death visited me this morning. We are playing chess together. This reprieve gives me the chance to arrange an urgent matter.

Death.   What matter is that?

Knight.   My life has been a futile pursuit, a wandering, a great deal of talk without meaning. I feel no bitterness or self-reproach because the lives of most people are very much like this. But I will use my reprieve for one meaningful deed.

Death.   Is that why you are playing chess with Death?

Knight.   He is a clever opponent, but up to now I haven't lost a single man.

Death.   How will you outwit Death in your game?

Knight.   I use a combination of the bishop and the knight which he hasn't yet discovered. In the next move I'll shatter one of his flanks.

Death.   I'll remember that.

Death shows his face at the grill of the confession booth for a moment but disappears instantly.

Knight.   You've tricked and cheated me! But we'll meet again, and I'll find a way.

Death *(invisible).*   We'll meet at the inn, and there we'll continue playing.

The knight raises his hand and looks at it in the sunlight which comes through the tiny window.

Knight.   This is my hand. I can move it, feel the blood pulsing through it. The sun is still high in the sky and I, Antonius Block, am playing chess with Death.

He makes a fist of his hand and lifts it to his temple.
   Meanwhile, Jöns and the painter have gotten drunk and are talking animatedly together.

Jöns.   Me and my master have been abroad and have just come home. Do you understand, you little pictor?

Painter.   The Crusade.

Jöns *(drunk).*   Precisely. For ten years we sat in the Holy Land and let snakes bite us, flies sting us, wild animals eat us, heathens butcher us, the wine poison us, the women give us lice, the lice devour us, the fevers rot us, all for the Glory of God. Our crusade was such madness that only a real idealist could have thought it up. But what you said about the plague was horrible.

Painter.   It's worse than that.

Jöns.   Ah me. No matter which way you turn, you have your rump behind you. That's the truth.

Painter.   The rump behind you, the rump behind you—there's a profound truth.

Jöns paints a small figure which is supposed to represent himself.

Jöns.   This is squire Jöns. He grins at Death, mocks the Lord, laughs at himself and leers at the girls. His world is a Jöns-world, believable only to himself, ridiculous to all including himself, meaningless to Heaven and of no interest to Hell.

The knight walks by, calls to his squire and goes out into the bright sunshine. Jöns manages to get himself down from the scaffolding.
   Outside the church, four soldiers and a monk are in the process of putting a woman in the stocks. Her face is pale and child-like, her head has been shaved, and her knuckles are bloody and broken. Her eyes are wide open, yet she doesn't appear to be fully conscious.

Jöns and the knight stop and watch in silence. The soldiers are working quickly and skillfully, but they seem frightened and dejected. The monk mumbles from a small book. One of the soldiers picks up a wooden bucket and with his hand begins to smear a bloody paste on the wall of the church and around the woman. Jöns holds his nose.

Jöns.   That soup of yours has a hell of a stink. What is it good for?
Soldier.   She has had carnal intercourse with the Evil One.

He whispers this with a horrified face and continues to splash the sticky mess on the wall.

Jöns.   And now she's in the stocks.
Soldier.   She will be burned tomorrow morning at the parish boundary. But we have to keep the Devil away from the rest of us.
Jöns *(holding his nose).*   And you do that with this stinking mess?
Soldier.   It's the best remedy: blood mixed with the bile of a big black dog. The Devil can't stand the smell.
Jöns.   Neither can I.

Jöns walks over toward the horses. The knight stands for a few moments looking at the young girl. She is almost a child. Slowly she turns her eyes toward him.

Knight.   Have you seen the Devil?

The monk stops reading and raises his head.

Monk.   You must not talk to her.
Knight.   Can that be so dangerous?
Monk.   I don't know, but she is believed to have caused the pestilence with which we are afflicted.
Knight.   I understand.

He nods resignedly and walks away. The young woman starts to moan as though she were having a horrible nightmare. The sound of her cries follows the two riders for a considerable distance down the road.

The sun stands high in the sky, like a red ball of fire. The waterskin is empty and Jöns looks for a well where he can fill it.
　　They approach a group of peasant cottages at the edge of the forest. Jöns ties up the horses, slings the skin over his shoulder and walks along the path toward the nearest cottage. As always, his movements are light and almost soundless. The door to the cottage is open. He stops outside, but when no one appears he enters. It is very dark inside and his foot touches a soft object. He looks down. Beside the whitewashed fireplace, a woman is lying with her face to the ground.

At the sound of approaching steps, Jöns quickly hides behind the door. A man comes down a ladder from the loft. He is broad and thick-set. His eyes are black and his face is pale and puffy. His clothes are well cut but dirty and in rags. He carries a cloth sack. Looking around, he goes into the inner room, bends over the bed, tucks something into the bag, slinks along the walls, looking on the shelves, finds something else which he tucks in his bag.

Slowly he re-enters the outer room, bends over the dead woman and carefully slips a ring from her finger. At that moment a young woman comes through the door. She stops and stares at the stranger.

Raval. Why do you look so surprised? I steal from the dead. These days it's quite a lucrative enterprise.

The girl makes a movement as if to run away.

Raval. You're thinking of running to the village and telling. That wouldn't serve any purpose. Each of us has to save his own skin. It's as simple as that.
Girl. Don't touch me.
Raval. Don't try to scream. There's no one around to hear you, neither God nor man.

Slowly he closes the door behind the girl. The stuffy room is now in almost total darkness. But Jöns becomes clearly visible.

Jöns. I recognize you, although it's a long time since we met. Your name is Raval, from the theological college at Roskilde. You are Dr. Mirabilis, Coelestis et Diabilis.

Raval smiles uneasily and looks around.

Jöns. Am I not right?

The girl stands immobile.

Jöns. You were the one who, ten years ago, convinced my master of the necessity to join a better-class crusade to the Holy Land.

Raval looks around.

Jöns. You look uncomfortable. Do you have a stomach-ache?

Raval smiles anxiously.

Jöns. When I see you, I suddenly understand the meaning of these ten years, which previously seemed to me such a waste. Our life was too good and we were too satisfied with ourselves. The Lord wanted to punish us for our complacency. That is why He sent you to spew out your holy venom and poison the knight.

Raval. I acted in good faith.

Jöns. But now you know better, don't you. Because now you have turned into a thief. A more fitting and rewarding occupation for scoundrels. Isn't that so?

With a quick movement he knocks the knife out of Raval's hand, gives him a kick so that he falls on the floor and is about to finish him off. Suddenly the girl screams. Jöns stops and makes a gesture of generosity with his hand.

Jöns. By all means. I'm not bloodthirsty. *(He bends over Raval)*

Raval. Don't beat me.

Jöns. I don't have the heart to touch you, Doctor. But remember this: The next time we meet, I'll brand your face the way one does with thieves. *(He rises)* What I really came for is to get my waterskin filled.

Girl. We have a deep well with cool, fresh water. Come, I'll show you.

They walk out of the house. Raval lies still for a few moments, then he rises slowly and looks around. When no one is in sight, he takes his bag and steals away.

Jöns quenches his thirst and fills his bag with water. The girl helps him.

Jöns. Jöns is my name. I am a pleasant and talkative young man who has never had anything but kind thoughts and has only done beautiful and noble deeds. I'm kindest of all to young women. With them, there is no limit to my kindness.

He embraces her and tries to kiss her, but she holds herself back. Almost immediately he loses interest, hoists the waterbag on his shoulder and pats the girl on the cheek.

Jöns. Goodbye, my girl. I could very well have raped you, but between you and me, I'm tired of that kind of love. It runs a little dry in the end.

He laughs kindly and walks away from her. When he has walked a short distance he turns; the girl is still there.

Jöns. Now that I think of it, I will need a housekeeper. Can you prepare good food? *(The girl nods)* As far as I know, I'm still a married man, but I have high hopes that my wife is dead by now. That's why I need a housekeeper. *(The girl doesn't answer but gets up)* The devil with it! Come along and don't stand there staring. I've saved your life, so you owe me a great deal.

She begins walking toward him, her head bent. He doesn't wait for her but walks toward the knight, who patiently awaits his squire.

The Embarrassment Inn lies in the eastern section of the province. The plague has not yet reached this area on its way along the coast.

The actors have placed their wagon under a tree in the yard of the inn. Dressed in colorful costumes, they perform a farce.

The spectators watch the performance, commenting on it noisily. There are merchants with fat, beer-sweaty faces, apprentices and journeymen, farmhands and milkmaids. A whole flock of children perch in the trees around the wagon.

The knight and his squire have sat down in the shadow of a wall. They drink beer and doze in the midday heat. The girl from the deserted village sleeps at Jöns' side.

Skat beats the drums, Jof blows the flute, Mia performs a gay and lively dance. They perspire under the hot white sun. When they have finished Skat comes forward and bows.

Skat.   Noble ladies and gentlemen, I thank you for your interest. Please remain standing a little longer, or sit on the ground, because we are now going to perform a tragedia about an unfaithful wife, her jealous husband, and the handsome lover—that's me.

Mia and Jof have quickly changed costumes and again step out on the stage. They bow to the public.

Skat.   Here is the husband. Here is the wife. If you'll shut up over there, you'll see something splendid. As I said, I play the lover and I haven't entered yet. That's why I'm going to hide behind the curtain for the time being. (*He wipes the sweat from his forehead*) It's damned hot. I think we'll have a thunderstorm.

He places his leg in front of Jof as if to trip him, raises Mia's skirt, makes a face as if he could see all the wonders of the world underneath it, and disappears behind the gaudily patched curtains.

Skat is very handsome, now that he can see himself in the reflection of a tin washbowl. His hair is tightly curled, his eyebrows are beautifully bushy, glittering earrings vie for equal attention with his teeth, and his cheeks are flushed rose red.

He sits out in back on the tailboard of the wagon, dangling his legs and whistling to himself.

In the meantime Jof and Mia play their tragedy; it is not, however, received with great acclaim.

Skat suddenly discovers that someone is watching him as he gazes contentedly into the tin bowl. A woman stands there, stately in both height and volume.

Skat frowns, toys with his small dagger and occasionally throws a roguish but fiery glance at the beautiful visitor.

She suddenly discovers that one of her shoes doesn't quite fit. She leans down to fix it and in doing so allows her generous bosom to burst out of its prison—no more than honor and chastity allow, but still enough so that the actor with his experienced eye immediately sees that there are ample rewards to be had here.

Now she comes a little closer, kneels down and opens a bundle containing several dainty morsels and a skin filled with red wine. Jonas Skat manages not to fall off the wagon in his excitement. Standing on the steps of the wagon, he supports himself against a nearby tree, crosses his legs and bows.

The woman quietly bites into a chicken leg dripping with fat. At this moment the actor is stricken by a radiant glance full of lustful appetites.

When he sees this look, Skat makes an instantaneous decision, jumps down from the wagon and kneels in front of the blushing damsel.

She becomes weak and faint from his nearness, looks at him with a glassy glance and breathes heavily. Skat doesn't neglect to press kisses on her small, chubby hands. The sun shines brightly and small birds make noises in the bushes.

Now she is forced to sit back; her legs seem unwilling to support her any longer. Bewildered, she singles out another chicken leg from the large sack of food and holds it up in front of Skat with an appealing and triumphant expression, as if it were her maidenhood being offered as a prize.

Skat hesitates momentarily, but he is still the strategist. He lets the chicken leg fall to the grass, and murmurs in the woman's rosy ear.

His words seem to please her. She puts her arms around the actor's neck and pulls him to her with such fierceness that both of them lose their balance and tumble down on the soft grass. The small birds take to their wings with frightened shrieks.

Jof stands in the hot sun with a flickering lantern in his hand. Mia pretends to be asleep on a bench which has been pulled forward on the stage.

Jof.   Night and moonlight now prevail
              Here sleeps my wife so frail . . .

Voice from the Public.   Does she snore?
Jof.   May I point out that this is a tragedy, and in tragedies one doesn't snore.
Voice from the Public.   I think she should snore anyhow.

This opinion causes mirth in the audience. Jof becomes slightly confused and goes out of character, but Mia keeps her head and begins snoring.

Jof.   Night and moonlight now prevail.
              There snores—I mean sleeps—my wife so frail.
              Jealous I am, as never before,
              I hide myself behind this door.
              Faithful is she
              To her lover—not me.
              He soon comes a-stealing
              To awaken her lusty feeling.
              I shall now kill him dead
              For cuckolding me in my bed.
              There he comes in the moonlight,

His white legs shining bright.
Quiet as a mouse, here I'll lie,
Tell him not that he's about to die.

Jof hides himself. Mia immediately ends her snoring and sits up, looking to the left.

Mia.   Look, there he comes in the night
My lover, my heart's delight.

She becomes silent and looks wide-eyed in front of her.

The mood in the yard in front of the inn has, up to now, been rather light-hearted despite the heat.

Now a rapid change occurs. People who had been laughing and chattering fall silent. Their faces seem to pale under their sunbrowned skins, the children stop their games and stand with gaping mouths and frightened eyes. Jof steps out in front of the curtain. His painted face bears an expression of horror. Mia has risen with Mikael in her arms. Some of the women in the yard have fallen on their knees, others hide their faces, many begin to mutter half-forgotten prayers.

All have turned their faces toward the white road. Now a shrill song is heard. It is frenzied, almost a scream.

A crucified Christ sways above the hilltop.

The cross-bearers come into sight. They are Dominican monks, their hoods pulled down over their faces. More and more of them follow, carrying litters with heavy coffins or clutching holy relics, their hands stretched out spasmodically. The dust wells up around their black hoods; the censers sway and emit a thick, ashen smoke which smells of rancid herbs.

After the line of monks comes another procession. It is a column of men, boys, old men, women, girls, children. All of them have steel-edged scourges in their hands with which they whip themselves and each other, howling ecstatically. They twist in pain; their eyes bulge wildly; their lips are gnawed to shreds and dripping with foam. They have been seized by madness. They bite their own hands and arms, whip each other in violent, almost rhythmic outbursts. Throughout it all the shrill song howls from their bursting throats. Many sway and fall, lift themselves up again, support each other and help each other to intensify the scourging.

Now the procession pauses at the crossroads in front of the inn. The monks fall on their knees, hiding their faces with clenched hands, arms pressed tightly together. Their song never stops. The Christ figure on its timbered cross is raised above the heads of the crowd. It is not Christ triumphant, but the suffering Jesus with the sores, the blood, the hammered nails and the face in convulsive pain. The Son of God, nailed on the wood of the cross, suffering scorn and shame.

The penitents have now sunk down in the dirt of the road. They collapse where they stood like slaughtered cattle. Their screams rise with the song of the monks, through misty clouds of incense, toward the white fire of the sun.

A large square monk rises from his knees and reveals his face, which is red-brown in the sun. His eyes glitter; his voice is thick with impotent scorn.

Monk.   God has sentenced us to punishment. We shall all perish in the black death. You, standing there like gaping cattle, you who sit there in your glutted complacency, do you know that this may be your last hour? Death stands right behind you. I can see how his crown gleams in the sun. His scythe flashes as he raises it above your heads. Which one of you shall he strike first? You there, who stand staring like a goat, will your mouth be twisted into the last unfinished gasp before nightfall? And you, woman, who bloom with life and self-satisfaction, will you pale and become extinguished before the morning dawns? You back there, with your swollen nose and stupid grin, do you have another year left to dirty the earth with your refuse? Do you know, you insensible fools, that you shall die today or tomorrow, or the next day, because all of you have been sentenced? Do you hear what I say? Do you hear the word? You have been sentenced, sentenced!

The monk falls silent, looking around with a bitter face and a cold scornful glance. Now he clenches his hands, straddles the ground and turns his face upward.

Monk.   Lord have mercy on us in our humiliation! Don't turn your face from us in loathing and contempt, but be merciful to us for the sake of your son, Jesus Christ.

He makes the sign of the cross over the crowd and then begins a new song in a strong voice. The monks rise and join in the song. As if driven by some super-human force, the penitents begin to whip themselves again, still wailing and moaning.

The procession continues. New members have joined the rear of the column; others who were unable to go on lie weeping in the dust of the road.

Jöns the squire drinks his beer.

Jöns.   This damned ranting about doom. Is that food for the minds of modern people? Do they really expect us to take them seriously?

The knight grins tiredly.

Jöns.   Yes, now you grin at me, my lord. But allow me to point out that I've either read, heard or experienced most of the tales which we people tell each other.

Knight *(yawns).*   Yes, yes.

Jöns.   Even the ghost stories about God the Father, the angels, Jesus Christ and the Holy Ghost—all these I've accepted without too much emotion.

He leans down over the girl as she crouches at his feet and pats her on the head. The knight drinks his beer silently.

Jöns *(contentedly)*.   My little stomach is my world, my head is my eternity, and my hands, two wonderful suns. My legs are time's damned pendulums, and my dirty feet are two splendid starting points for my philosophy. Everything is worth precisely as much as a belch, the only difference being that a belch is more satisfying.

The beer mug is empty. Sighing, Jöns gets to his feet. The girl follows him like a shadow.
    In the yard he meets a large man with a sooty face and a dark expression. He stops Jöns with a roar.

Jöns.   What are you screaming about?
Plog.   I am Plog, the smith, and you are the squire Jöns.
Jöns.   That's possible.
Plog.   Have you seen my wife?
Jöns.   No, I haven't. But if I had seen her and she looked like you, I'd quickly forget that I'd seen her.
Plog.   Well, in that case you haven't seen her.
Jöns.   Maybe she's run off.
Plog.   Do you know anything?
Jöns.   I know quite a lot, but not about your wife. Go to the inn. Maybe they can help you.

The smith sighs sadly and goes inside.

The inn is very small and full of people eating and drinking to forget their newly aroused fear of eternity. In the open fireplace a roasting pig turns on an iron spit. The sun shines outside the casement window, its sharp rays piercing the darkness of the room, which is thick with fumes and perspiration.

Merchant.   Yes, it's true! The plague is spreading along the west coast. People are dying like flies. Usually business would be good at this time of year, but, damn it, I've still got my whole stock unsold.
Woman.   They speak of the judgment day. And all these omens are terrible. Worms, chopped-off hands and other monstrosities began pouring out of an old woman, and down in the village another woman gave birth to a calf's head.
Old Man.   The day of judgment. Imagine.
Farmer.   It hasn't rained here for a month. We'll surely lose our crops.
Merchant.   And people are acting crazy, I'd say. They flee the country and carry the plague with them wherever they go.
Old Man.   The day of judgment. Just think, just think!

Farmer.   If it's as they say, I suppose a person should look after his house and try to enjoy life as long as he can.

Woman.   But there have been other things too, such things that can't even be spoken of. *(Whispers)* Things that mustn't be named—but the priests say that the woman carries it between her legs and that's why she must cleanse herself.

Old Man.   Judgment day. And the Riders of the Apocalypse stand at the bend in the village road. I imagine they'll come on judgment night, at sundown.

Woman.   There are many who have purged themselves with fire and died from it, but the priests say that it's better to die pure than to live for hell.

Merchant.   This is the end, yes, it is. No one says it out loud, but all of us know that it's the end. And people are going mad from fear.

Farmer.   So you're afraid too.

Merchant.   Of course I'm afraid.

Old Man.   The judgment day becomes night, and the angels descend and the graves open. It will be terrible to see.

They whisper in low tones and sit close to each other. Plog, the smith, shoves his way into a place next to Jof, who is still dressed in his costume. Opposite him sits Raval, leaning slightly forward, his face perspiring heavily. Raval rolls an armlet out on the table.

Raval.   Do you want this armlet? You can have it cheap.

Jof.   I can't afford it.

Raval.   It's real silver.

Jof.   It's nice. But it's surely too expensive for me.

Plog.   Excuse me, but has anyone here seen my wife?

Jof.   Has she disappeared?

Plog.   They say she's run away.

Jof.   Has she deserted you?

Plog.   With an actor.

Jof.   An actor! If she's got such bad taste, then I think you should let her go.

Plog.   You're right. My first thought, of course, was to kill her.

Jof.   Oh. But to murder her, that's a terrible thing to do.

Plog.   I'm also going to kill the actor.

Jof.   The actor?

Plog.   Of course, the one she eloped with.

Jof.   What has he done to deserve that?

Plog.   Are you stupid?

Jof.   The actor! Now I understand. There are too many of them, so even if he hasn't done anything in particular you ought to kill him merely because he's an actor.

Plog.   You see, my wife has always been interested in the tricks of the theater.

Jof.   And that turned out to be her misfortune.

Plog.   Her misfortune, but not mine, because a person who's born unfortunate can hardly suffer from any further misfortune. Isn't that true?

Now Raval enters the discussion. He is slightly drunk and his voice is shrill and evil.

Raval. Listen, you! You sit there and lie to the smith.
Jof. I! A liar!
Raval. You're an actor too and it's probably your partner who's run off with Plog's old lady.
Plog. Are you an actor too?
Jof. An actor! Me! I wouldn't quite call myself that!
Raval. We ought to kill you; it's only logical.
Jof *(laughs).* You're really funny.
Raval. How strange—you've turned pale. Have you anything on your conscience?
Jof. You're funny. Don't you think he's funny? *(To Plog)* Oh, you don't.
Raval. Maybe we should mark you up a little with a knife, like they do petty scoundrels of your kind.

Plog bangs his hands down on the table so that the dishes jump. He gets up.

Plog *(shouting).* What have you done with my wife?

The room becomes silent. Jof looks around, but there is no exit, no way to escape. He puts his hands on the table. Suddenly a knife flashes through the air and sinks into the table top between his fingers.

Jof snatches away his hands and raises his head. He looks half surprised, as if the truth had just become apparent to him.

Jof. Do you want to hurt me? Why? Have I provoked someone, or got in the way? I'll leave right now and never come back.

Jof looks from one face to another, but no one seems ready to help him or come to his defense.

Raval. Get up so everyone can hear you. Talk louder.

Trembling, Jof rises. He opens his mouth as if to say something, but not a word comes out.

Raval. Stand on your head so that we can see how good an actor you are.

Jof gets up on the table and stands on his head. A hand pushes him forward so that he collapses on the floor. Plog rises, pulls him to his feet with one hand.

Plog *(shouts).* What have you done with my wife?

The smith beats him so furiously that Jof flies across the table. Raval leans over him.

Raval. Don't lie there moaning. Get up and dance.
Jof. I don't want to. I can't.
Raval. Show us how you imitate a bear.
Jof. I can't play a bear.
Raval. Let's see if you can't after all.

Raval prods Jof lightly with the knife point. Jof gets up with cold sweat on his cheeks and forehead, frightened half to death. He begins to jump and hop on top of the tables, swinging his arms and legs and making grotesque faces. Some laugh, but most of the people sit silently. Jof gasps as if his lungs were about to burst. He sinks to his knees, and someone pours beer over him.

Raval. Up again! Be a good bear.
Jof. I haven't done any harm. I haven't got the strength to play a bear any more.

At that moment the door opens and Jöns enters. Jof sees his chance and steals out. Raval intends to follow him, but suddenly stops. Jöns and Raval look at each other.

Jöns. Do you remember what I was going to do to you if we met again?

Raval steps back without speaking.

Jöns. I'm a man who keeps his word.

Jön raises his knife and cuts Raval from forehead to cheek. Raval staggers toward the wall.

The hot day has become night. Singing and howling can be heard from the inn. In a hollow near the forest, the light still lingers. Hidden in the grass and the shrubbery, nightingales sing and their voices echo through the stillness.
The players' wagon stands in a small ravine, and not far away the horse grazes on the dry grass. Mia has sat down in front of the wagon with her son in her arms. They play together and laugh happily.
Now a soft gleam of light strokes the hilltops, a last reflection from the red clouds over the sea.
Not far from the wagon, the knight sits crouched over his chess game. He lifts his head.
The evening light moves across the heavy wagon wheels, across the woman and the child.
The knight gets up.

Mia sees him and smiles. She holds up her struggling son, as if to amuse the knight.

Knight.   What's his name?
Mia.   Mikael.
Knight.   How old is he?
Mia.   Oh, he'll soon be two.
Knight.   He's big for his age.
Mia.   Do you think so? Yes, I guess he's rather big.

She puts the child down on the ground and half rises to shake out her red skirt. When she sits down again, the knight steps closer.

Knight.   You played some kind of show this afternoon.
Mia.   Did you think it was bad?
Knight.   You are more beautiful now without your face painted, and this gown is more becoming.
Mia.   You see, Jonas Skat has run off and left us, so we're in real trouble now.
Knight.   Is that your husband?
Mia *(laughs).*   Jonas! The other man is my husband. His name is Jof.
Knight.   Oh, that one.
Mia.   And now there's only him and me. We'll have to start doing tricks again and that's more trouble than it's worth.
Knight.   Do you do tricks also?
Mia.   We certainly do. And Jof is a very skillful juggler.
Knight.   Is Mikael going to be an acrobat?
Mia.   Jof wants him to be.
Knight.   But you don't.
Mia.   I don't know. *(Smiling)* Perhaps he'll become a knight.
Knight.   Let me assure you, that's no pleasure either.
Mia.   No, you don't look so happy.
Knight.   No.
Mia.   Are you tired?
Knight.   Yes.
Mia.   Why?
Knight.   I have dull company.
Mia.   Do you mean your squire?
Knight.   No, not him.
Mia.   Who do you mean, then?
Knight.   Myself.
Mia.   I understand.
Knight.   Do you really?
Mia.   Yes, I understand rather well. I have often wondered why people torture themselves as often as they can. Isn't that so?

She nods energetically and the knight smiles seriously.

Now the shrieks and the noise from the inn become louder. Black figures flicker across the grass mound. Someone collapses, gets up and runs. It is Jof. Mia stretches out her arms and receives him. He holds his hands in front of his face, moaning like a child, and his body sways. He kneels. Mia holds him close to her and sprinkles him with small, anxious questions: What have you done? How are you? What is it? Does it hurt? What can I do? Have they been cruel to you? She runs for a rag, which she dips in water, and carefully bathes her husband's dirty, bloody face.

Eventually a rather sorrowful visage emerges. Blood runs from a bruise on his forehead and his nose, and a tooth has been loosened, but otherwise Jof seems unhurt.*

Jof.   Ouch, it hurts.
Mia.   Why did you have to go there? And of course you drank.

Mia's anxiety has been replaced by mild anger. She pats him a little harder than necessary.

Jof.   Ouch! I didn't drink anything.
Mia.   Then I suppose you were boasting about the angels and devils you consort with. People don't like someone who has too many ideas and fantasies.
Jof.   I swear to you that I didn't say a word about angels.
Mia.   You were, of course, busy singing and dancing. You can never stop being an actor. People also become angry at that, and you know it.

Jof doesn't answer but searches for the armlet. He holds it up in front of Mia with an injured expression.

Jof.   Look what I bought for you.
Mia.   You couldn't afford it.
Jof (*angry*).   But I got it anyhow.

The armlet glitters faintly in the twilight. Mia now pulls it across her wrist. They look at it in silence, and their faces soften. They look at each other, touch each other's hands. Jof puts his head against Mia's shoulder and sighs.

Jof.   Oh, how they beat me.
Mia.   Why didn't you beat them back?
Jof.   I only become frightened and angry. I never get a chance to hit back. I can get angry, you know that. I roared like a lion.
Mia.   Were they frightened?
Jof.   No, they just laughed.

Their son Mikael crawls over to them. Jof lies down on the ground and pulls his son on top of him. Mia gets down on her hands and knees and playfully sniffs at Mikael.

Mia.   Do you notice how good he smells?
Jof.   And he is so compact to hold. You're a sturdy one. A real acrobat's body.

He lifts Mikael up and holds him by the legs. Mia looks up suddenly, remembering the knight's presence.

Mia.   Yes, this is my husband, Jof.
Jof.   Good evening.
Knight.   Good evening.

Jof becomes a little embarrassed and rises. All three of them look at one another silently.

Knight.   I have just told your wife that you have a splendid son. He'll bring
  great joy to you.
Jof.   Yes, he's fine.

They become silent again.

Jof.   Have we nothing to offer the knight, Mia?
Knight.   Thank you, I don't want anything.
Mia *(housewifely)*.   I picked a basket of wild strawberries this afternoon. And
  we have a drop of milk fresh from a cow . . .
Jof.   . . . that we were *allowed* to milk. So, if you would like to partake of this
  humble fare, it would be a great honor.
Mia.   Please be seated and I'll bring the food.

They sit down. Mia disappears with Mikael.

Knight.   Where are you going next?
Jof.   Up to the saints' feast at Elsinore.
Knight.   I wouldn't advise you to go there.
Jof.   Why not, if I may ask?
Knight.   The plague has spread in that direction, following the coast line south.
  It's said that people are dying by the tens of thousands.
Jof.   Really! Well, sometimes life is a little hard.
Knight.   May I suggest . . . *(Jof looks at him, surprised)* . . . that you follow
  me through the forest tonight and stay at my home if you like. Or go along
  the east coast. You'll probably be safer there.

*Mia has returned with a bowl of wild strawberries and the milk, places it between
them and gives each of them a spoon.*

Jof.   I wish you good appetite.
Knight.   I humbly thank you.

Mia.   These are wild strawberries from the forest. I have never seen such large ones. They grow up there on the hillside. Notice how they smell!

She points with a spoon and smiles. The knight nods, as if he were pondering some profound thought. Jof eats heartily.

Jof.   Your suggestion is good, but I must think it over.

Mia.   It might be wise to have company going through the forest. It's said to be full of trolls and ghosts and bandits. That's what I've heard.

Jof *(staunchly).*   Yes, I'd say that it's not a bad idea, but I have to think about it. Now that Skat has left, I am responsible for the troupe. After all, I have become director of the whole company.

Mia *(mimics).*   After all, I have become director of the whole company.

Jöns comes walking slowly down the hill, closely followed by the girl. Mia points with her spoon.

Mia.   Do you want some strawberries?

Jof.   This man saved my life. Sit down, my friend, and let us be together.

Mia *(stretches herself).*   Oh, how nice this is.

Knight.   For a short while.

Mia.   Nearly always. One day is like another. There is nothing strange about that. The summer, of course, is better than the winter, because in summer you don't have to be cold. But spring is best of all.

Jof.   I have written a poem about the spring. Perhaps you'd like to hear it. I'll run and get my lyre. *(He sprints toward the wagon)*

Mia.   Not now, Jof. Our guests may not be amused by your songs.

Jöns *(politely).*   By all means. I write little songs myself. For example, I know a very funny song about a wanton fish which I doubt that you've heard yet.

The knight looks at him.

Jöns.   You'll not get to hear it either. There are persons here who don't appreciate my art and I don't want to upset anyone. I'm a sensitive soul.

Jof has come out with his lyre, sits on a small, gaudy box and plucks at the instrument, humming quietly, searching for his melody. Jöns yawns and lies down.

Knight.   People are troubled by so much.

Mia.   It's always better when one is two. Have you no one of your own?

Knight.   Yes, I think I had someone.

Mia.   And what is she doing now?

Knight.   I don't know.

Mia.   You look so solemn. Was she your beloved?

Knight.   We were newly married and we played together. We laughed a great deal. I wrote songs to her eyes, to her nose, to her beautiful little ears. We went hunting together and at night we danced. The house was full of life . . .

Mia.   Do you want some more strawberries?

Knight *(shakes his head)*.   Faith is a torment, did you know that? It is like loving someone who is out there in the darkness but never appears, no matter how loudly you call.

Mia.   I don't understand what you mean.

Knight.   Everything I've said seems meaningless and unreal while I sit here with you and your husband. How unimportant it all becomes suddenly.

He takes the bowl of milk in his hand and drinks deeply from it several times. Then he carefully puts it down and looks up, smiling.

Mia.   Now you don't look so solemn.

Knight.   I shall remember this moment. The silence, the twilight, the bowls of strawberries and milk, your faces in the evening light. Mikael sleeping, Jof with his lyre. I'll try to remember what we have talked about. I'll carry this memory between my hands as carefully as if it were a bowl filled to the brim with fresh milk. *(He turns his face away and looks out toward the sea and the colorless gray sky)* And it will be an adequate sign—it will be enough for me.

He rises, nods to the others and walks down toward the forest. Jof continues to play on his lyre. Mia stretches out on the grass.

The knight picks up his chess game and carries it toward the beach. It is quiet and deserted; the sea is still.

Death.   I have been waiting for you.

Knight.   Pardon me. I was detained for a few moments. Because I revealed my tactics to you, I'm in retreat. It's your move.

Death.   Why do you look so satisfied?

Knight.   That's my secret.

Death.   Of course. Now I take your knight.

Knight.   You did the right thing.

Death.   Have you tricked me?

Knight.   Of course. You fell right in the trap. Check!

Death.   What are you laughing at?

Knight.   Don't worry about my laughter; save your king instead.

Death.   You're rather arrogant.

Knight.   Our game amuses me.

Death.   It's your move. Hurry up. I'm a little pressed for time.

Knight.   I understand that you've a lot to do, but you can't get out of our game. It takes time.

Death is about to answer him but stops and leans over the board. The knight smiles.

Death.   Are you going to escort the juggler and his wife through the forest? Those whose names are Jof and Mia and who have a small son.

Knight.   Why do you ask?

Death.   Oh, no reason at all.

The knight suddenly stops smiling. Death looks at him scornfully.

Immediately after sundown, the little company gathers in the yard of the inn. There is the knight, Jöns and the girl, Jof and Mia in their wagon. Their son, Mikael, is already asleep. Jonas Skat is still missing.

Jöns goes into the inn to get provisions for the night journey and to have a last mug of beer. The inn is now empty and quiet except for a few farmhands and maidens who are eating their evening meal in a corner.

At one of the small windows sits a lonely, hunched-over fellow, with a jug of brandy in his hands. His expression is very sad. Once in a while he is shaken by a gigantic sob. It is Plog, the smith, who sits there and whimpers.

Jöns.   God in heaven, isn't this Plog, the smith?

Plog.   Good evening.

Jöns.   Are you sitting here sniveling in loneliness?

Plog.   Yes, yes, look at the smith. He moans like a rabbit.

Jöns.   If I were in your boots, I'd be happy to get rid of a wife in such an easy way.

Jöns pats the smith on the back, quenches his thirst with beer, and sits down by his side.

Plog.   Are *you* married?

Jöns.   *I!* A hundred times and more. I can't keep count of all my wives any longer. But it's often that way when you're a traveling man.

Plog.   I can assure you that *one* wife is worse than a hundred, or else I've had worse luck than any poor wretch in this miserable world, which isn't impossible.

Jöns.   Yes, it's hell *with* women and hell *without* them. So, however you look at it, it's still best to kill them off while it's most amusing.

Plog.   Women's nagging, the shrieking of children and wet diapers, sharp nails and sharp words, blows and pokes, and the devil's aunt for a mother-in-law. And then, when one wants to sleep after a long day, there's a new song— tears, whining and moans loud enough to wake the dead.

Jöns nods delightedly. He has drunk deeply and talks with an old woman's voice.

Jöns.   Why don't you kiss me good night?

Plog *(in the same way).*   Why don't you sing a song for me?

Jöns.   Why don't you love me the way you did when we first met?

Plog. Why don't you look at my new shift?

Jöns. You only turn your back and snore.

Plog. Oh hell!

Jöns. Oh hell. And now she's gone. Rejoice!

Plog *(furious)*. I'll snip their noses with pliers, I'll bash in their chests with a small hammer, I'll tap their heads ever so lightly with a sledge.

Plog begins to cry loudly and his whole body sways in an enormous attack of sorrow. Jöns looks at him with interest.

Jöns. Look how he howls again.

Plog. Maybe I love her.

Jöns. So, maybe you love her! Then, you poor misguided ham shank, I'll tell you that love is another word for lust, plus lust, plus lust and a damn lot of cheating, falseness, lies and all kinds of other fooling around.

Plog. Yes, but it hurts anyway.

Jöns. Of course. Love is the blackest of all plagues, and if one could die of it, there would be some pleasure in love. But you almost always get over it.

Plog. No, no, not me.

Jöns. Yes, you too. There are only a couple of poor wretches who die of love once in a while. Love is as contagious as a cold in the nose. It eats away at your strength, your independence, your morale, if you have any. If everything is imperfect in this imperfect world, love is most perfect in its perfect imperfection.

Plog. You're happy, you with your oily words, and, besides, you believe your own drivel.

Jöns. Believe! Who said that I believed it? But I love to give good advice. If you ask me for advice you'll get two pieces for the price of one, because after all I really am an educated man.

Jöns gets up from the table and strokes his face with his hands. The smith becomes very unhappy and grabs his belt.

Plog. Listen, Jöns. May I go with you through the forest? I'm so lonely and don't want to go home because everyone will laugh at me.

Jöns. Only if you don't whimper all the time, because in that case we'll all have to avoid you.

The smith gets up and embraces Jöns. Slightly drunk, the two new friends walk toward the door.

When they come out in the yard, Jof immediately catches sight of them, becomes angry and yells a warning to Jöns.

Jof. Jöns! Watch out. That one wants to fight all the time. He's not quite sane.

Jöns. Yes, but now he's just sniveling.

The smith steps up to Jof, who blanches with fear. Plog offers his hand.

Plog.   I'm really sorry if I hurt you. But I have such a hell of a temper, you know. Shake hands.

Jof gingerly proffers a frightened hand and gets it thoroughly shaken and squeezed. While Jof tries to straighten out his fingers, Plog is seized by great good will and opens his arms.

Plog.   Come in my arms, little brother.
Jof.   Thank you, thank you, perhaps later. But now we're really in a hurry.

Jof climbs up on the wagon seat quickly and clucks at the horse.
   The small company is on its way toward the forest and the night.
   It is dark in the forest.
   First comes the knight on his large horse. Then Jof and Mia follow, sitting close to each other in the juggler's wagon. Mia holds her son in her arms. Jöns follows them with his heavily laden horse. He has the smith in tow. The girl sits on top of the load on the horse's back, hunched over as if asleep.
   The footsteps, the horses' heavy tramp on the soft path, the human breathing— yet it is quiet.
   Then the moon sails out of the clouds. The forest suddenly becomes alive with the night's unreality. The dazzling light pours through the thick foliage of the beech trees, a moving, quivering world of light and shadow.
   The wanderers stop. Their eyes are dark with anxiety and foreboding. Their faces are pale and unreal in the floating light. It is very quiet.

Plog.   Now the moon has come out of the clouds.
Jöns.   That's good. Now we can see the road better.
Mia.   I don't like the moon tonight.
Jof.   The trees stand so still.
Jöns.   That's because there's no wind.
Plog.   I guess he means that they stand *very* still.
Jof.   It's completely quiet.
Jöns.   If one could hear a fox at least.
Jof.   Or an owl.
Jöns.   Or a human voice besides one's own.
Girl.   They say it's dangerous to remain standing in moonlight.

Suddenly, out of the silence and the dim light falling across the forest road, a ghostlike cart emerges.
   It is the witch being taken to the place where she will be burned. Next to her eight soldiers shuffle along tiredly, carrying their lances on their backs. The girl sits in the cart, bound with iron chains around her throat and arms. She stares fixedly into the moonlight.

A black figure sits next to her, a monk with his hood pulled down over his head.

Jöns.   Where are you going?

Soldier.   To the place of execution.

Jöns.   Yes, now I can see. It's the girl who has done it with the Black One. The witch?

The soldier nods sourly. Hesitantly, the travelers follow. The knight guides his horse over to the side of the cart. The witch seems to be half conscious, but her eyes are wide open.

Knight.   I see that they have hurt your hands.

The witch's pale, childish face turns toward the knight and she shakes her head.

Knight.   I have a potion that will stop your pain.

She shakes her head again.

Jöns.   Why do you burn her at this time of night? People have so few diversions these days.

Soldier.   Saints preserve us, be quiet! It's said that she brings the Devil with her wherever she goes.

Jöns.   You are eight brave men, then.

Soldier.   Well, we've been paid. And this is a volunteer job.

The soldier speaks in whispers while glancing anxiously at the witch.

Knight *(to witch)*.   What's your name?

Tyan.   My name is Tyan, my lord.

Knight.   How old are you?

Tyan.   Fourteen, my lord.

Knight.   And is it true that you have been in league with the Devil?

Tyan nods quietly and looks away. Now they arrive at the parish border. At the foot of the nearby hills lies a crossroads. The pyre has already been stacked in the center of the forest clearing. The travelers remain there, hesitant and curious.

The soldiers have tied up the cart horse and bring out two long wooden beams. They nail rungs across the beams so that it looks like a ladder. Tyan will be bound to this like an eelskin stretched out to dry.

The sound of the hammering echoes through the forest. The knight has dismounted and walks closer to the cart. Again he tries to catch Tyan's eyes, touches her very lightly as if to waken her.

Slowly she turns her face toward him.

Knight.   They say that you have been in league with the Devil.

Tyan.   Why do you ask?

Knight.   Not out of curiosity, but for very personal reasons. I too want to meet him.

Tyan.   Why?

Knight.   I want to ask him about God. He, if anyone, must know.

Tyan.   You can see him anytime.

Knight.   How?

Tyan.   You must do as I tell you.

The knight grips the wooden rail of the cart so tightly that his knuckles whiten. Tyan leans forward and joins her gaze with his.

Tyan.   Look into my eyes.

The knight meets her gaze. They stare at each other for a long time.

Tyan.   What do you see? Do you see *him*?

Knight.   I see fear in your eyes, an empty, numb fear. But nothing else.

He falls silent. The soldiers work at the stacks; their hammering echoes in the forest.

Tyan.   No one, nothing, no one?

Knight (*shakes his head*).   No.

Tyan.   Can't you see him behind your back?

Knight (*looks around*).   No, there is no one there.

Tyan.   But he is with me everywhere. I only have to stretch out my hand and I can feel his hand. He is with me now too. The fire won't hurt me. He will protect me from everything evil.

Knight.   Has he told you this?

Tyan.   I know it.

Knight.   Has he said it?

Tyan.   I know it, I know it. You must see him somewhere, you must. The priests had no difficulty seeing him, nor did the soldiers. They are so afraid of him that they don't even dare touch me.

The sound of the hammers stops. The soldiers stand like black shadows rooted in the moss. They fumble with the chains and pull at the neck iron. Tyan moans weakly, as if she were far away.

Knight.   Why have you crushed her hands?

Soldier (*surly*).   We didn't do it.

Knight.   Who did?

Soldier.   Ask the monk.

The soldiers pull the iron and chains. Tyan's shaven head sways, gleaming in the moonlight. Her blackened mouth opens as if to scream, but no sound emerges.

They take her down from the cart and lead her toward the ladder and the stake. The knight turns to the monk, who remains seated in the cart.

Knight.   What have you done with the child?

Death turns around and looks at him.

Death.   Don't you ever stop asking questions?
Knight.   No, I'll never stop.

The soldiers chain Tyan to the rungs of the ladder. She submits resignedly, moans weakly like an animal and tries to ease her body into position.

When they have fastened her, they walk over to light the pyre. The knight steps up and leans over her.

Jöns.   For a moment I thought of killing the soldiers, but it would do no good. She's nearly dead already.

One of the soldiers approaches. Thick smoke wells down from the pyre and sweeps over the quiet shadows near the crossroads and the hill.

Soldier.   I've told you to be careful. Don't go too close to her.

The knight doesn't heed this warning. He cups his hand, fills it with water from the skin and gives it to Tyan. Then he gives her a potion.

Knight.   Take this and it will stop the pain.

Smoke billows down over them and they begin to cough. The soldiers step forward and raise the ladder against a nearby fir tree. Tyan hangs there motionlessly, her eyes wide open.

The knight straightens up and stands immobile. Jöns is behind him, his voice nearly choked with rage.

Jöns.   What does she see? Can you tell me?
Knight *(shakes his head)*.   She feels no more pain.
Jöns.   You don't answer my question. Who watches over that child? Is it the angels, or God, or the Devil, or only the emptiness? Emptiness, my lord!
Knight.   This cannot be.
Jöns.   Look at her eyes, my lord. Her poor brain has just made a discovery. Emptiness under the moon.
Knight.   No.
Jöns.   We stand powerless, our arms hanging at our sides, because we see what

she sees, and our terror and hers are the same. (*An outburst*) That poor little child. I can't stand it, I can't stand it . . .

His voice sticks in his throat and he suddenly walks away. The knight mounts his horse. The travelers depart from the crossroads. Tyan finally closes her eyes.

The forest is now very dark. The road winds between the trees. The wagon squeaks and rattles over stones and roots. A bird suddenly shrieks.

Jof lifts his head and wakes up. He has been asleep with his arms around Mia's shoulders. The knight is sharply silhouetted against the tree trunks.

His silence makes him seem almost unreal.

Jöns and the smith are slightly drunk and support each other. Suddenly Plog has to sit down. He puts his hands over his face and howls piteously.

Plog.   Oh, now it came over me again!
Jöns.   Don't scream. What came over you?
Plog.   My wife, damn it. She is so beautiful. She is so beautiful that she can't be described without the accompaniment of a lyre.
Jöns.   Now it starts again.
Plog.   Her smile is like brandy. Her eyes like blackberries . . .

Plog searches for beautiful words. He gestures gropingly with his large hands.

Jöns (*sighs*).   Get up, you tear-drenched pig. We'll lose the others.
Plog.   Yes, of course, of course. Her nose is like a little pink potato; her behind is like a juicy pear—yes, the whole woman is like a strawberry patch. I can see her in front of me, with arms like wonderful cucumbers.
Jöns.   Saints almighty, stop! You're a very bad poet, despite the fact that you're drunk. And your vegetable garden bores me.

They walk across an open meadow. Here it is a little brighter and the moon shimmers behind a thin sky. Suddenly the smith points a large finger toward the edge of the forest.

Plog.   Look there.
Jöns.   Do you see something?
Plog.   There, over there!
Jöns.   I don't see anything.
Plog.   Hang on to something, my friends. The hour is near! Who is that at the edge of the forest if not my own dearly beloved, with actor attached?

The two lovers discover the smith and it's too late. They cannot retreat. Skat immediately takes to his heels. Plog chases him, swinging his sledge and bellowing like a wild boar.

For a few confusing moments the two rivals stumble among the stones and bushes in the gray gloom of the forest. The duel begins to look senseless, because both of them are equally frightened.

The travelers silently observe this confused performance. Lisa screams once in a while, more out of duty than out of impulse.

Skat *(panting).*   You miserable stubbleheaded bastard of seven scurvy bitches, if I were in your lousy rags I would be stricken with such eternal shame about my breath, my voice, my arms and legs—in short, about my whole body— that I would immediately rid nature of my own embarrassing self.

Plog *(angry).*   Watch out, you perfumed slob, that I don't fart on you and immediately blow you down to the actor's own red-hot hell, where you can sit and recite monologues to each other until the dust comes out of the Devil's ears.

Then Lisa throws herself around her husband's neck.

Lisa.   Forgive me, dear little husband. I'll never do it again. I am so sorry and you can't imagine how terribly that man over there betrayed me.

Plog.   I'll kill him anyway.

Lisa.   Yes, do that, just kill him. He isn't even a human being.

Jöns.   Hell, he's an actor.

Lisa.   He is only a false beard, false teeth, false smiles, rehearsed lines, and he's as empty as a jug. Just kill him.

Lisa sobs with excitement and sorrow. The smith looks around, a little confused. The actor uses this opportunity. He pulls out a dagger and places the point against his breast.

Skat.   She's right. Just kill me. If you thought that I was going to apologize for being what I am, you are mistaken.

Lisa.   Look how sickening he is. How he makes a fool of himself, how he puts on an act. Dear Plog, kill him!

Skat.   My friends, you have only to push, and my unreality will soon be transformed into a new solid reality. An absolutely tangible corpse.

Lisa.   Do something then. Kill him.

Plog *(embarrassed).*   He has to fight me, otherwise I can't kill him.

Skat.   Your life's thread now hangs by a very ragged shred. Idiot, your day is short.

Plog.   You'll have to irritate me a little more to get me as angry as before.

Skat looks at the travelers with a pained expression and then lifts his eyes toward the night sky.

Skat.   I forgive all of you. Pray for me sometimes.

Skat sinks the dagger into his breast and slowly falls to the ground. The travelers stand confused. The smith rushes forward and begins to pull at the actor's hands.

Plog.   Oh dear, dear, I didn't mean it that way! Look, there's no life left in him. I was beginning to like him, and in my opinion Lisa was much too spiteful.

Jof leans over his colleague.

Jof.   He's dead, totally, enormously dead. In fact, I've never seen such a dead actor.

Lisa.   Come on, let's go. This is nothing to mourn over. He has only himself to blame.

Plog.   And I have to be married to *her*.

Jöns.   We must go on.

Skat lies in the grass and keeps the dagger pressed tightly to his breast. The travelers depart and soon they have disappeared into the dark forest on the other side of the meadow. When Skat is sure that no one can see him, he sits up and lifts the dagger from his breast. It is a stage dagger with a blade that pushes into the handle. Skat laughs to himself.

Skat.   Now that was a good scene. I'm really a good actor. After all, why shouldn't I be a little pleased with myself? But where shall I go? I'll wait until it becomes light and then I'll find the easiest way out of the forest. I'll climb up a tree for the time being so that no bears, wolves or ghosts can get at me.

He soons finds a likely tree and climbs up into its thick foliage. He sits down as comfortably as possible and reaches for his food pouch.

Skat (*yawns*).   Tomorrow I'll find Jof and Mia and then we'll go to the saints' feast in Elsinore. We'll make lots of money there. (*Yawns*) Now, I'll sing a little song to myself:

> I am a little bird
> Who sings whate'er he will,
> And when I am in danger
> I fling out a pissing trill
> As in the carnal thrill.

(*Speaks*) It's boring to be alone in the forest tonight. (*Sings*) The terrible night doesn't frighten me . . .

He interrupts himself and listens. The sound of industrious sawing is heard through the silence.

Skat.   Workmen in the forest. Oh, well! *(Sings)* The terrible night doesn't frighten me . . . Hey, what the devil . . . it's *my* tree they're cutting down.

He peers through the foliage. Below him stands a dark figure diligently sawing away at the base of the tree. Skat becomes frightened and angry.

Skat.   Hey, you! Do you hear me, you tricky bastard? What are you doing with my tree?

The sawing continues without a pause. Skat becomes more frightened.

Skat.   Can't you at least answer me? Politeness costs so little. Who are you?

Death straightens his back and squints up at him. Skat cries out in terror.

Death.   I'm sawing down your tree because your time is up.
Skat.   It won't do. I haven't got time.
Death.   So you haven't got time.
Skat.   No, I have my performance.
Death.   Then it's been canceled because of death.
Skat.   My contract.
Death.   Your contract is terminated.
Skat.   My children, my family.
Death.   Shame on you, Skat!
Skat.   Yes, I'm ashamed.

Death begins to saw again. The tree creaks.

Skat.   Isn't there any way to get off? Aren't there any special rules for actors?
Death.   No, not in this case.
Skat.   No loopholes, no exceptions?

Death saws.

Skat.   Perhaps you'll take a bribe.

Death saws.

Skat.   Help!

Death saws.

Skat.   Help! Help!

The tree falls. The forest becomes silent again.

Night and then dawn.

The travelers have come to a sort of clearing and have collapsed on the moss. They lie quietly and listen to their own breathing, their heartbeats, and the wind in the tree tops. Here the forest is wild and impenetrable. Huge boulders stick up out of the ground like the heads of black giants. A fallen tree lies like a mighty barrier between light and shadow.

Mia, Jof and their child have sat down apart from the others. They look at the light of the moon, which is no longer full and dead but mysterious and unstable.

The knight sits bent over his chess game. Lisa cries quietly behind the smith's back. Jöns lies on the ground and looks up at the heavens.

Jöns.   Soon dawn will come, but the heat continues to hang over us like a smothering blanket.

Lisa.   I'm so frightened.

Plog.   We feel that something is going to happen to us, but we don't know what.

Jöns.   Maybe it's the day of judgment.

Plog.   The day of judgment . . .

Now something moves behind the fallen tree. There is a rustling sound and a moaning cry that seems to come from a wounded animal. Everyone listens intently, all faces turned toward the sound.

A voice comes out of the darkness.

Raval.   Do you have some water?

Raval's perspiring face soon becomes visible. He disappears in the darkness but his voice is heard again.

Raval.   Can't you give me a little water? (*Pause*) I have the plague.

Jöns.   Don't come here. If you do I'll slit your throat. Keep to the other side of the tree.

Raval.   I'm afraid of death.

No one answers. There is complete silence. Raval gasps heavily for air. The dry leaves rustle with his movements.

Raval.   I don't want to die! I don't want to!

No one answers. Raval's face appears suddenly at the base of the tree. His eyes bulge wildly and his mouth is ringed with foam.

Raval.   Can't you have pity on me? Help me! At least talk to me.

No one answers. The trees sigh. Raval begins to cry.

Raval.   I am going to die. I. I. *I!* What will happen to me! Can no one console me? Haven't you any compassion? Can't you see that I . . .

His words are choked off by a gurgling sound. He disappears in the darkness behind the fallen tree. It becomes quiet for a few moments.

Raval (*Whispers*).   Can't anyone . . . only a little water.

Suddenly the girl gets up with a quick movement, snatches Jöns' water bag and runs a few steps. Jöns grabs her and holds her fast.

Jöns.   It's no use. It's no use. I know that it's no use. It's meaningless. It's totally meaningless. I tell you that it's meaningless. Can't you hear that I'm consoling you?
Raval.   Help me, help me!

No one answers, no one moves. Raval's sobs are dry and convulsive, like a frightened child's. His sudden scream is cut off in the middle.
    Then it becomes quiet.
    The girl sinks down and hides her face in her hands. Jöns places his hand on her shoulder.

The knight is no longer alone. Death has come to him and he raises his hand.

Death.   Shall we play our game to the end?
Knight.   Your move!

Death raises his hand and strikes the knight's queen. Antonius Block looks at Death.

Death.   Now I take your queen.
Knight.   I didn't notice that.

The knight leans over the game. The moonlight moves over the chess pieces, which seem to have a life of their own.
    Jof has dozed off for a few moments, but suddenly he wakens. Then he sees the knight and Death together.
    He becomes very frightened and awakens Mia.

Jof.   Mia!
Mia.   Yes, what is it?
Jof.   I see something terrible. Something I almost can't talk about.
Mia.   What do you see?
Jof.   The knight is sitting over there playing chess.

Mia.   Yes, I can see that too and I don't think it's so terrible.

Jof.   But do you see who he's playing with?

Mia.   He is alone. You *mustn't* frighten me this way.

Jof.   No, no, he isn't alone.

Mia.   Who is it, then?

Jof.   Death. He is sitting there playing chess with Death himself.

Mia.   You mustn't say that.

Jof.   We must try to escape.

Mia.   One can't do that.

Jof.   We must try. They are so occupied with their game that if we move very quietly, they won't notice us.

Jof gets up carefully and disappears into the darkness behind the trees. Mia remains standing, as if paralyzed by fear. She stares fixedly at the knight and the chess game. She holds her son in her arms.
        Now Jof returns.

Jof.   I have harnessed the horse. The wagon is standing near the big tree. You go first and I'll follow you with the packs. See that Mikael doesn't wake up.

Mia does what Jof has told her. At the same moment, the knight looks up from his game.

Death.   It is your move, Antonius Block.

The knight remains silent. He sees Mia go through the moonlight toward the wagon. Jof bends down to pick up the pack and follows at a distance.

Death.   Have you lost interest in our game?

The knight's eyes become alarmed. Death looks at him intently.

Knight.   Lost interest? On the contrary.

Death.   You seem anxious. Are you hiding anything?

Knight.   Nothing escapes you—or does it?

Death.   Nothing escapes me. No one escapes from me.

Knight.   It's true that I'm worried.

He pretends to be clumsy and knocks the chess pieces over with the hem of his coat. He looks up at Death.

Knight.   I've forgotten how the pieces stood.

Death *(laughs contentedly)*.   But I have not forgotten. You can't get away that easily.

Death leans over the board and rearranges the pieces. The knight looks past him toward the road. Mia has just climbed up on the wagon. Jof takes the horse by the bridle and leads it down to the road. Death notices nothing; he is completely occupied with reconstructing the game.

Death.   Now I see something interesting.
Knight.   What do you see?
Death.   You are mated on the next move, Antonius Block.
Knight.   That's true.
Death.   Did you enjoy your reprieve?
Knight.   Yes, I did.
Death.   I'm happy to hear that. Now I'll be leaving you. When we meet again, you and your companions' time will be up.
Knight.   And you will divulge your secrets.
Death.   I have no secrets.
Knight.   So you know nothing.
Death.   I have nothing to tell.

The knight wants to answer, but Death is already gone.

A murmur is heard in the tree tops. Dawn comes, a flickering light without life, making the forest seem threatening and evil. Jof drives over the twisting road. Mia sits beside him.

Mia.   What a strange light.
Jof.   I guess it's the thunderstorm which comes with dawn.
Mia.   No, it's something else. Something terrible. Do you hear the roar in the forest?
Jof.   It's probably rain.
Mia.   No, it isn't rain. He has seen us and he's following us. He has overtaken us; he's coming toward us.
Jof.   Not yet, Mia. In any case, not yet.
Mia.   I'm so afraid. I'm so afraid.

The wagon rattles over roots and stones; it sways and creaks. Now the horse stops with his ears flat against his head. The forest sighs and stirs ponderously.

Jof.   Get into the wagon, Mia. Crawl in quickly. We'll lie down, Mia, with Mikael between us.

They crawl into the wagon and crouch around the sleeping child.

Jof.   It is the Angel of Death that's passing over us, Mia. It's the Angel of Death. *The Angel of Death, and he's very big.*
Mia.   Do you feel how cold it is? I'm freezing. I'm terribly cold.

She shivers as if she had a fever. They pull the blankets over them and lie closely together. The wagon canvas flutters and beats in the wind. The roar outside is like a giant bellowing.

The castle is silhouetted like a black boulder against the heavy dawn. Now the storm moves there, throwing itself powerfully against walls and abutments. The sky darkens; it is almost like night.

Antonius Block has brought his companions with him to the castle. But it seems deserted. They walk from room to room. There is only emptiness and quiet echoes. Outside, the rain is heard roaring noisily.

Suddenly the knight stands face to face with his wife. They look at each other quietly.

Karin.   I heard from people who came from the crusade that you were on your way home. I've been waiting for you here. All the others have fled from the plague.

The knight is silent. He looks at her.

Karin.   Don't you recognize me any more?

The knight nods, silent.

Karin.   You also have changed.

She walks closer and looks searchingly into his face. The smile lingers in her eyes and she touches his hand lightly.

Karin.   Now I can see that it's you. Somewhere in your eyes, somewhere in your face, but hidden and frightened, is that boy who went away so many years ago.
Knight.   It's over now and I'm a little tired.
Karin.   I see that you're tired.
Knight.   Over there stand my friends.
Karin.   Ask them in. They will break the fast with us.

They all sit down at the table in the room, which is lit by torches on the walls. Silently they eat the hard bread and the salt-darkened meat. Karin sits at the head of the table and reads aloud from a thick book.

Karin.   "And when the Lamb broke the seventh seal, there was silence in heaven for about the space of half an hour. And I saw the seven angels which stood before God; and to them were given seven trumpets. And another . . ."

Three mighty knocks sound on the large portal. Karin interrupts her reading and looks up from the book. Jöns rises quickly and goes to open the door.

Karin. "The first angel sounded, and there followed hail and fire mingled with blood, and they were cast upon the earth; and the third part of the trees were burnt up and all the green grass was burnt up."

Now the rain becomes quiet. There is suddenly an immense, frightening silence in the large, murky room where the burning torches throw uneasy shadows over the ceiling and the walls. Everyone listens tensely to the stillness.

Karin. "And the second angel sounded, and as it were a great mountain burning with fire was cast into the sea; and a third part of the sea became blood . . ."

Steps are heard on the stairs. Jöns returns and sits down silently at his place but does not continue to eat.

Knight. Was someone there?
Jöns. No, my lord. I saw no one.

Karin lifts her head for a moment but once again leans over the large book.

Karin. "And the third angel sounded, and there fell a great star from heaven, burning as it were a torch, and it fell upon the third part of the rivers and upon the fountains of waters; and the name of the star is called Wormwood . . ."

They all lift their heads, and when they see who is coming toward them through the twilight of the large room, they rise from the table and stand close together.

Knight. Good morning, noble lord.
Karin. I am Karin, the knight's wife, and welcome you courteously to my house.
Plog. I am a smith by profession and rather good at my trade, if I say so myself. My wife Lisa—curtsy for the great lord, Lisa. She's a little difficult to handle once in a while and we had a little spat, so to say, but no worse than most people.

The knight hides his face in his hands.

Knight. From our darkness, we call out to Thee, Lord. Have mercy on us because we are small and frightened and ignorant.
Jöns *(bitterly):* In the darkness where You are supposed to be, where all of us probably are . . . In the darkness You will find no one to listen to Your cries or be touched by Your sufferings. Wash Your tears and mirror Yourself in Your indifference.

Knight.   God, You who are somewhere, who *must* be somewhere, have mercy upon us.

Jöns.   I could have given you an herb to purge you of your worries about eternity. Now it seems to be too late. But in any case, feel the immense triumph of this last minute when you can still roll your eyes and move your toes.

Karin.   Quiet, quiet.

Jöns.   I shall be silent, but under protest.

Girl *(on her knees).*   It is the end.

Jof and Mia lie close together and listen to the rain tapping lightly on the wagon canvas, a sound which diminishes until finally there are only single drops.

They crawl out of their hiding place. The wagon stands on a height above a slope, protected by an enormous tree. They look across ridges, forests, the wide plains, and the sea, which glistens in the sunlight breaking through the clouds.

Jof stretches his arms and legs. Mia dries the wagon seat and sits down next to her husband. Mikael crawls between Jof's knees.

A lone bird tests its voice after the storm. The trees and bushes drip. From the sea comes a strong and fragrant wind.

Jof points to the dark, retreating sky where summer lightning glitters like silver needles over the horizon.

Jof.   I see them, Mia! I see them! Over there against the dark, stormy sky. They are all there. The smith and Lisa and the knight and Raval and Jöns and Skat. And Death, the severe master, invites them to dance. He tells them to hold each other's hands and then they must tread the dance in a long row. And first goes the master with his scythe and hourglass, but Skat dangles at the end with his lyre. They dance away from the dawn and it's a solemn dance toward the dark lands, while the rain washes their faces and cleans the salt of the tears from their cheeks.

He is silent. He lowers his hand.

His son, Mikael, has listened to his words. Now he crawls up to Mia and sits down in her lap.

Mia *(smiling).*   You with your visions and dreams.

QUESTIONS

1. What is the nature of the knight's quest? Do you admire him for the serious- ness and single-mindedness of his quest? What is the knight's own judgment on the result of his lifelong pursuit? **2.** How does the comic subplot of Skat, Plog the blacksmith, and his faithless wife relate to the theme? **3.** Why do Jof, Mia, and their child survive? Has Bergman prepared us for this ending, or does it come as a surprise?   **4.**   Can you suggest why Bergman, a twentieth-century artist concerned with modern man, set his drama in the Middle Ages?

WRITING TOPICS
1.   How does the milk-and-wild-strawberries scene help define the theme of this play?   **2.**   In contrast to the knight, his squire Jons is an agnostic and hedonist who believes that the meaning of life is to be found in living. Does a comparison of the actions of the two men suggest which one is more humane?

Death Knocks

WOODY ALLEN [b. 1935]

The play takes place in the bedroom of the Nat Ackermans' two-story house, somewhere in Kew Gardens. The carpeting is wall-to-wall. There is a big double bed and a large vanity. The room is elaborately furnished and curtained, and on the walls there are several paintings and a not really attractive barometer. Soft theme music as the curtain rises. Nat Ackerman, a bald, paunchy fifty-seven-year-old dress manufacturer is lying on the bed finishing off tomorrow's Daily News. He wears a bathrobe and slippers, and reads by a bed light clipped to the white headboard of the bed. The time is near midnight. Suddenly we hear a noise, and Nat sits up and looks at the window.

Nat.   What the hell is that?

(Climbing awkwardly through the window is a sombre, caped figure. The intruder wears a black hood and skintight black clothes. The hood covers his head but not his face, which is middle-aged and stark white. He is something like Nat in appearance. He huffs audibly and then trips over the windowsill and falls into the room.)

Death *(for it is no one else).*   Jesus Christ. I nearly broke my neck.
Nat *(watching with bewilderment).*   Who are you?
Death.   Death.
Nat.   Who?
Death.   Death. Listen—can I sit down? I nearly broke my neck. I'm shaking like a leaf.
Nat.   Who *are* you?
Death.   *Death.* You got a glass of water?
Nat.   Death? What do you mean, Death?
Death.   What is wrong with you? You see the black costume and the whitened face?
Nat.   Yeah.
Death.   Is it Halloween?
Nat.   No.
Death.   Then I'm Death. Now can I get a glass of water—or a Fresca?
Nat.   If this is some joke—
Death.   What kind of joke? You're fifty-seven? Nat Ackerman? One eighteen Pacific Street? Unless I blew it—where's that call sheet? *(He fumbles through pocket, finally producing a card with an address on it. It seems to check.)*
Nat.   What do you want with me?
Death.   What do I want? What do you think I want?
Nat.   You must be kidding. I'm in perfect health.

Death *(unimpressed)*.   Uh-huh. *(Looking around)* This is a nice place. You do it yourself?

Nat.   We had a decorator, but we worked with her.

Death *(looking at picture on the wall)*.   I love those kids with the big eyes.

Nat.   I don't want to go yet.

Death.   *You* don't want to go? Please don't start in. As it is, I'm nauseous from the climb.

Nat.   What climb?

Death.   I climbed up the drainpipe. I was trying to make a dramatic entrance. I see the big windows and you're awake reading. I figure it's worth a shot. I'll climb up and enter with a little—you know . . . *(Snaps fingers)* Meanwhile, I get my heel caught on some vines, the drainpipe breaks, and I'm hanging by a thread. Then my cape begins to tear. Look, let's just go. It's been a rough night.

Nat.   You broke my drainpipe?

Death.   Broke. It didn't break. It's a little bent. Didn't you hear anything? I slammed into the ground.

Nat.   I was reading.

Death.   You must have really been engrossed. *(Lifting newspaper Nat was reading)* "NAB COEDS IN POT ORGY." Can I borrow this?

Nat.   I'm not finished.

Death.   Er—I don't know how to put this to you, pal. . . .

Nat.   Why didn't you just ring downstairs?

Death.   I'm telling you, I could have, but how does it look? This way I get a little drama going. Something. Did you read "Faust"?

Nat.   What?

Death.   And what if you had company? You're sitting there with important people. I'm Death—I should ring the bell and traipse right in the front? Where's your thinking?

Nat.   Listen, Mister, it's very late.

Death.   Yeah. Well, you want to go?

Nat.   Go where?

Death.   Death. It. The Thing. The Happy Hunting Grounds. *(Looking at his own knee)* Y'know, that's a pretty bad cut. My first job, I'm liable to get gangrene yet.

Nat.   Now, wait a minute. I need time. I'm not ready to go.

Death.   I'm sorry. I can't help you. I'd like to, but it's the moment.

Nat.   How can it be the moment? I just merged with Modiste Originals.

Death.   What's the difference, a couple of bucks more or less.

Nat.   Sure, what do you care? You guys probably have all your expenses paid.

Death.   You want to come along now?

Nat *(studying him)*.   I'm sorry, but I cannot believe you're Death.

Death.   Why? What'd you expect—Rock Hudson?

Nat.   No, it's not that.

Death.   I'm sorry if I disappointed you.

Nat.   Don't get upset. I don't know, I always thought you'd be . . . uh . . . taller.

Death.   I'm five seven. It's average for my weight.

Nat.   You look a little like me.

Death.   Who should I look like? I'm your death.

Nat.   Give me some time. Another day.

Death.   I can't. What do you want me to say?

Nat.   One more day. Twenty-four hours.

Death.   What do you need it for? The radio said rain tomorrow.

Nat.   Can't we work out something?

Death.   Like what?

Nat.   You play chess?

Death.   No, I don't.

Nat.   I once saw a picture of you playing chess.

Death.   Couldn't be me, because I don't play chess. Gin rummy, maybe.

Nat.   You play gin rummy?

Death.   Do I play gin rummy? Is Paris a city?

Nat.   You're good, huh?

Death.   Very good.

Nat.   I'll tell you what I'll do—

Death.   Don't make any deals with me.

Nat.   I'll play you gin rummy. If you win, I'll go immediately. If I win, give me some more time. A little bit—one more day.

Death.   Who's got time to play gin rummy?

Nat.   Come on. If you're so good.

Death.   Although I feel like a game . . .

Nat.   Come on. Be a sport. We'll shoot for a half hour.

Death.   I really shouldn't.

Nat.   I got the cards right here. Don't make a production.

Death.   All right, come on. We'll play a little. It'll relax me.

Nat (*getting cards, pad, and pencil*). You won't regret this.

Death.   Don't give me a sales talk. Get the cards and give me a Fresca and put out something. For God's sake, a stranger drops in, you don't have potato chips or pretzels.

Nat.   There's M&M's downstairs in a dish.

Death.   M&M's. What if the President came? He'd get M&M's, too?

Nat.   You're not the President.

Death.   Deal.

(*Nat deals, turns up a five.*)

Nat.   You want to play a tenth of a cent a point to make it interesting?

Death.   It's not interesting enough for you?

Nat.   I play better when money's at stake.

Death.   Whatever you say, Newt.

Nat.   Nat. Nat Ackerman. You don't know my name?

Death.   Newt, Nat—I got such a headache.

Nat.   You want that five?

Death.   No.

Nat.   So pick.

Death *(surveying his hand as he picks).*   Jesus, I got nothing here.

Nat.   What's it like?

Death.   What's what like?

(Throughout the following, they pick and discard.)

Nat.   Death.

Death.   What should it be like? You lay there.

Nat.   Is there anything after?

Death.   Aha, you're saving twos.

Nat.   I'm asking. Is there anything after?

Death *(absently).*   You'll see.

Nat.   Oh, then I will actually see something?

Death.   Well, maybe I shouldn't have put it that way. Throw.

Nat.   To get an answer from you is a big deal.

Death.   I'm playing cards.

Nat.   All right, play, play.

Death.   Meanwhile, I'm giving you one card after another.

Nat.   Don't look through the discards.

Death.   I'm not looking. I'm straightening them up. What was the knock card?

Nat.   Four. You ready to knock already?

Death.   Who said I'm ready to knock. All I asked was what was the knock card.

Nat.   And all I asked was is there anything for me to look forward to.

Death.   Play.

Nat.   Can't you tell me anything? Where do we go?

Death.   We? To tell you the truth, *you* fall in a crumpled heap on the floor.

Nat.   Oh, I can't wait for that! Is it going to hurt?

Death.   Be over in a second.

Nat.   Terrific. *(Sighs)* I needed this. A man merges with Modiste Originals
. . .

Death.   How's four points?

Nat.   You're knocking?

Death.   Four points is good?

Nat.   No, I got two.

Death.   You're kidding.

Nat.   No, you lose.

Death.   Holy Christ, and I thought you were saving sixes.

Nat.   No. Your deal. Twenty points and two boxes. Shoot. *(Death deals.)* I
   must fall on the floor, eh? I can't be standing over the sofa when it happens?

Death.   No. Play.

Nat.   Why not?

Death.   Because you fall on the floor! Leave me alone. I'm trying to concentrate.

Nat.   Why must it be on the floor? That's all I'm saying! Why can't the whole thing happen and I'll stand next to the sofa?

Death.   I'll try my best. Now can we play?

Nat.   That's all I'm saying. You remind me of Moe Lefkowitz. He's also stubborn.

Death.   I remind him of Moe Lefkowitz. I'm one of the most terrifying figures you could possibly imagine, and him I remind of Moe Lefkowitz. What is he, a furrier?

Nat.   You should be such a furrier. He's good for eighty thousand a year. Passementeries. He's got his own factory. Two points.

Death.   What?

Nat.   Two points. I'm knocking. What have you got?

Death.   My hand is like a basketball score.

Nat.   And it's spades.

Death.   If you didn't talk so much.

(They redeal and play on.)

Nat.   What'd you mean before when you said this was your first job?

Death.   What does it sound like?

Nat.   What are you telling me—that nobody ever went before?

Death.   Sure they went. But I didn't take them.

Nat.   So who did?

Death.   Others.

Nat.   There's others?

Death.   Sure. Each one has his own personal way of going.

Nat.   I never knew that.

Death.   Why should you know? Who are you?

Nat.   What do you mean who am I? Why—I'm nothing?

Death.   Not nothing. You're a dress manufacturer. Where do you come to knowledge of the eternal mysteries?

Nat.   What are you talking about? I make a beautiful dollar. I sent two kids through college. One is in advertising, the other's married. I got my own home. I drive a Chrysler. My wife has whatever she wants. Maids, mink coat, vacations. Right now she's at the Eden Roc. Fifty dollars a day because she wants to be near her sister. I'm supposed to join her next week, so what do you think I am—some guy off the street?

Death.   All right. Don't be so touchy.

Nat.   Who's touchy?

Death.   How would you like it if I got insulted quickly?

Nat.   Did I insult you?

Death.   You didn't say you were disappointed in me?

Nat.   What do you expect? You want me to throw you a block party?

Death.   I'm not talking about that. I mean me personally. I'm too short, I'm this, I'm that.

Nat.   I said you looked like me. It's like a reflection.

Death.   All right, deal, deal.

(They continue to play as music steals in and the lights dim until all is in total darkness. The lights slowly come up again, and now it is later and their game is over. Nat tallies.)

Nat.   Sixty-eight . . . one-fifty . . . Well, you lose.

Death *(dejectedly looking through the deck)*.   I knew I shouldn't have thrown that nine. Damn it.

Nat.   So I'll see you tomorrow.

Death.   What do you mean you'll see me tomorrow?

Nat.   I won the extra day. Leave me alone.

Death.   You were serious?

Nat.   We made a deal.

Death.   Yeah, but—

Nat.   Don't "but" me. I won twenty-four hours. Come back tomorrow.

Death.   I didn't know we were actually playing for time.

Nat.   That's too bad about you. You should pay attention.

Death.   Where am I going to go for twenty-four hours?

Nat.   What's the difference? The main thing is I won an extra day.

Death.   What do you want me to do—walk the streets?

Nat.   Check into a hotel and go to a movie. Take a *schvitz.*[1] Don't make a federal case.

Death.   Add the score again.

Nat.   Plus you owe me twenty-eight dollars.

Death.   *What?*

Nat.   That's right, Buster. Here it is—read it.

Death *(going through pockets)*.   I have a few singles—not twenty-eight dollars.

Nat.   I'll take a check.

Death.   From what account?

Nat.   Look who I'm dealing with.

Death.   Sue me. Where do I keep my checking account?

Nat.   All right, gimme what you got and we'll call it square.

Death.   Listen, I need that money.

Nat.   Why should you need money?

Death.   What are you talking about? You're going to the Beyond.

Nat.   So?

Death.   So—you know how far that is?

---

[1] Steam bath.

Nat.   So?

Death.   So where's gas? Where's tolls?

Nat.   We're going by car!

Death.   You'll find out. *(Agitatedly)* Look—I'll be back tomorrow, and you'll give me a chance to win the money back. Otherwise I'm in definite trouble.

Nat.   Anything you want. Double or nothing we'll play. I'm liable to win an extra week or a month. The way you play, maybe years.

Death.   Meantime I'm stranded.

Nat.   See you tomorrow.

Death *(being edged to the doorway).*   Where's a good hotel? What am I talking about hotel, I got no money. I'll go sit in Bickford's.² *(He picks up the* News.*)*

Nat.   Out. Out. That's my paper. *(He takes it back.)*

Death *(exiting).*   I couldn't just take him and go. I had to get involved in rummy.

Nat *(calling after him).*   And be careful going downstairs. On one of the steps the rug is loose.

(And, on cue, we hear a terrific crash. Nat sighs, then crosses to the bedside table and makes a phone call.)

Nat.   Hello, Moe? Me. Listen, I don't know if somebody's playing a joke, or what, but Death was just here. We played a little gin. . . . No, *Death.* In person. Or somebody who claims to be Death. But, Moe, he's such a *schlep!*³

Curtain

QUESTIONS

1.   Upon what allusions does this play depend for its humor?   **2.**   Characterize the speech patterns of the characters. How do they contribute to the play's effect?

---

² Bickford's was a chain of inexpensive all-night cafeterias in New York City.
³ Boring jerk.

End of the World * 1984

ARTHUR KOPIT [b. 1937]

Act One: The Commission

Music: *lazy, bluesy music for a hard-boiled detective. It is "Trent's Theme."*
Curtain up.

Spotlight *up on* **Michael Trent,** *downstage, in a trench coat. Stage dark around*
him. He puffs on a cigarette. The music continues under.

Trent.   I have now, at most, two hours left—two hours to solve a mystery which
  so far seems to yield no solution. If I fail, it is highly possible that I and all
  of you will die sooner than we'd hoped. Do I exaggerate? Of course. That is
  my method. I am a playwright. My name is Trent, Michael Trent. I work
  out of Stamford, Connecticut—that's where my office is, that's where this
  case began, when Philip Stone came to see me with a notion for a play.
  Generally I don't take commissions. This time I did.

Lights up on **Philip Stone,** *a man in his sixties, large, elegant, powerful.*

Stone.   I can only tell you it is a matter of great urgency, and I would be most
  appreciative if I could see you tonight!

Blackout on **Stone.**

Trent.   I'd never met the man, though I knew of course who he was—who
  didn't? He told me what he wanted, which was a play, but gave no details.
  He assured me he'd pay well—a man as rich as Stone ought to pay well; I
  told him to come right out. To put it mildly, I was in great need of money

*Author's Note: This play derives from real events. In the spring of 1981 I was approached by
Leonard Davis, who wished to commission me to write a play about nuclear proliferation, based
on a scenario he had written. Between that day and August 1983 I worked on the project—although
not on his scenario—which turned out to be very different from his scenario. The events that unfold in my play mirror, almost exactly, the experiences I had when I embarked on the commission.
   Much of the play—in particular the section entitled "The Investigation"—is based on personal
interviews. Though some of those interviewed asked that they not be named, those who can be
named include Walter Slocum, Fritz Ermath, Joel Resnick, Douglas Olin, Ambassador Edward
Rowny, and Kurt Guthe. I would like to thank all of them for their patience, time, and generosity.
   Those whose written work proved especially valuable in the creation of this play and in my un-
derstanding of the issues involved include Herman Kahn, Freeman Dyson, Colin Gray, Keith Payne,
Jack Geiger, Jonathan Schell, George Kennan, Richard Pipes, and Edward Teller.
   In particular I wish to thank Roger Molander for his extraordinary help and encouragement dur-
ing the writing of this play, and Robert Scheer for allowing me to use an extensive section of his*

at the time. Most playwrights need money *all* the time. It's not one of your top-paying professions. Besides, I had a wife, a kid, and two golden retrievers to support. As things now stand, you won't see any one of them. I want to keep them out of this!

Lights up on Trent's office in Stamford, Connecticut. It looks like the sort of office Philip Marlowe[1] *might use. On the glass door, reversed, are the following words:*

MICHAEL TRENT, PLAYWRIGHT
—No Domestic Comedies—

This is my office. At least, as it looked ten months ago, on the night Stone came by and changed my life irrevocably. Actually, in *real* life, where these events occurred, it doesn't look like this at all. Neither do the characters who were, and still are, involved. I have altered these details, not so much to protect the innocent, as to heighten interest. That's how playwrights work. We've got limited time. You don't want to stay here all night any more than I do. (*A buzzer sounds on Trent's cluttered desk*) Yah!

Stella (*Voice only*).   Mike, there's a guy out here says his name is, get this— Philip Stone! (*Sound of Stella giggling*)

Trent.   Hey, dollface, this guy *is* Philip Stone. Tell him I'll be with him in a minute. (*To audience*) It was important that Stone think I was in the middle of a project. If he didn't, he might figure he could get me cheap. My pulse was going wild; I'd been hoping to sell out for years. This could be it. (*Into the intercom*) Send Stone in. (*Back to audience*) Actually, I didn't even have a secretary. And that's all I'm going to tell you. From here on, you're going to have to figure out what I'm making up, and what I'm not, on your own. Be warned: the roads are very slippery, the ones we're going on tonight.

Trent starts typing. The office door opens and Philip Stone walks in. Black greatcoat. Sense of mystery and menace.

---

book *With Enough Shovels*, published by Random House, as the basis for Philip Stone's final speech. I would also like to thank Physicians for Social Responsibility for their continued support.

A word about Audrey Wood. Audrey Wood was my agent from 1960, when my play *Oh Dad, Poor Dad, Mamma's Hung You in the Closet and I'm Feelin' So Sad* was produced at Harvard, until 1981, when she suffered a devastating massive stroke. She was a crucial, integral, and loving part of my life. When I came to the writing of this play and found I needed to write in an agent for Michael Trent, my playwright/detective, I instinctively used Audrey's name, never intending to keep her name in the play. But I have done so.

I kept it in while writing it in the belief that her presence, as I went along, would force me to delve into the material and into myself as deeply as I could—for to do any less would be to belittle her.

And I kept it in in the hope that what I wrote might, in some small way, measure up to the measure of her—A. K.

[1] Hard-boiled private eye in a number of Raymond Chandler (1888–1959) novels.

Stone.   Trent?

Trent *(Typing wildly).*   Just a second, be right with you, finishing touches here. Yes . . . Yes-yes, good, hah-hah, amazing, what a scene, never *seen* a scene like this!

Stone.   Perhaps the moment is inopportune.

Trent.   NO! No-no, almost finished! Last few lines. Real bitch, this play; been working on it for a year—commission from the RSC.[2] There! Yes! Got it! Beginning to think I'd *never* get it right! *(Rips the page from the typewriter, rises, and goes over to Stone, hand extended)* Mr. Stone, Michael Trent. Great honor to meet you. *(Into the intercom)* Stella, hold my calls. *(To Stone)* Can I offer you a drink?

Stone.   Thank you. Yes. A Scotch would be welcome, most welcome indeed.

Trent.   All I've got is beer.

Stone.   I'll stay like this . . . Mr. Trent, I am not a man who wastes words or time; words take time to say, time is precious. I have conceived an outline for a play. I wish to see this play produced, and quickly. I will provide the capital, you will write it. How much do you want, when can you begin?

Stunned pause. Then Trent rushes to the door.

Trent.   Stella!

Enter Stella, a real dish.

Stella.   Yes, boss!

Trent.   Be an angel. Run down to B.J.'s and get a bottle of Scotch.

Stella.   Right, boss!

Exit Stella.

Trent *(To audience).*   If you're going to invent a secretary, might as well go with it all the way! *(To Stone, trying to control his euphoria)* Well, this is just very . . . very flattering. Let me check my appointment book here, see what sort of commissions I've got lined up. *(Rummages through the mess on his desk; he finds the appointment book)* Here it is. Let's see now . . . *(Flips the pages)* And you say you want this play written . . . ?

Stone.   Right away!

Trent.   Right away, I see . . . Well, I could shuffle this, I guess. Delay this commission here . . . Might have to give up some work over here, that's something I really wanted too, *damn!* What, uh, kind of dollars exactly are we, uh, talking about?

Stone.   As I said before, sir, tell me what you want.

---

[2] The RSC (Royal Shakespeare Company) is an outstanding repertory theater company based in Stratford-on-Avon in Great Britain.

Trent. (*So I* did *hear him right!*) *What I* WANT! Well, that's not so . . . . easy to say. It depends very much on how long this will take to *write*. Then to *rewrite*! . . . . Then to rewrite *that* revision! I do very careful work, I'm sure you've heard. Then of course we have to factor in the research. If this project, I don't know it yet, takes research of some sort—

Stone. It will.

Trent. There you are! So *that* must be factored in. Plus of course transportation, limousine, mind you now I don't absolutely *need* a limousine—

Stone. I use a limousine. No reason you should not.

Trent. My God, the theater needs men like you!

Stone. Don't you want to hear the idea?

Trent. No. No-no, I'll just begin. Obviously, if it matters all this much to you, it's got to be worth *something*! I'll need a day or two to figure out the terms, of course. Where can you be reached? You seem to have appeared a bit out of thin air.

Stone (*Handing him a card*).   My business card.

Trent. Good. Thank you. Well! I don't see that we need to discuss this any further—you've got yourself a playwright! I've got myself a producer! (*Stone holds out a manila envelope*) This the idea?

Stone. Yes.

Trent. Well, I can't wait to read it!

Stone. Why not read it now?

Trent. Well, because right now I just can't give it my complete attention. We'll talk tomorrow. Sir, a great, *great* pleasure meeting you! (*Trent ushers him out*) Till tomorrow.

Stone. Till tomorrow.

Exit Stone.

Trent (*To audience*).   I didn't want to look at his idea while he was here in case I hated it.

The door opens. Stone pops back in.

Stone. Sir. Forgive me. But in my excitement I forgot to give you this . . . (*Hands Trent an envelope*) . . . retainer. As a token of good faith. (*Leaves*)

Trent tears open the envelope. He pulls out five bills.

Trent. *Five thousand dollars!* (*Opens the door*) SIR, YOU ARE TOO GENEROUS!

Stone (*Offstage*).   What?

Trent. *That* was the wrong thing to say. I meant to say, MAYBE WE CAN DO SOME *MORE* PLAYS! YOU KNOW—AFTER THIS! (*To the audi-*

ence) Five thousand dollars! . . . Well, it may not seem like a lot to you. But to a playwright, as an advance, it's enough to save his life. It really is.

Enter Stone, somber-faced.

Stone.   Sir, you do not understand. I have no interest in producing plays. I am interested in producing one play only. *This is it!*

Exit Stone.

Trent clearly taken aback by this. Nervously, he opens the manila envelope and peeks inside. Cautiously, he slides the pages out. He stares down at the title page. Then he stares out with a look of alarm.

Blackout.

Lights up on Audrey Wood, Trent's agent. She is a woman in her sixties. Very short. She wears a tiny pillbox hat. She is hardly visible above her desk. At the moment, she is talking on the phone with Trent.

Audrey.   Dear, I checked him out. He's legitimate, he has the money. So I'd say you've got a deal.
Trent.   Audrey, his idea is terrible!
Audrey.   Then don't take it.
Trent.   How can I not take a deal like this? This is a definitional sweetheart deal, this is the deal of a lifetime!
Audrey.   Dear, what do you want me to do?
Trent.   ADVISE me!
Audrey.   Take the deal.
Trent.   Audrey, you don't understand. You haven't read this man's scenario. There is no way anyone, ANYONE! can write a play based on this. Do you know why? Because the characters are completely cardboard, and the plot preposterous.
Audrey.   Dear, listen, calm down, brush your hair, make yourself presentable, come in and show me this notorious scenario. I'm sure it's not half as bad as you think. Really, dear, you're still young, you've got a lovely wife, a lovely child, this is no time to panic.
Trent.   I've used up the advance.

Pause.

Audrey.   *What?*
Trent.   *I've used up the advance.*
Audrey.   Darling, I'm sorry, I must have misunderstood. I thought you got this advance last night.

Trent.   I did.

She checks her watch.

Audrey.   Dear, it is ten-thirty in the morning. What do you *do* up there in Connecticut?

Trent.   Audrey, I used it to pay our mortgage. We owed three months—I'm sorry, that's the way it is—we're going through a rough time here.

Audrey.   Maybe you should go out to the Coast.

Trent.   I DON'T WANT TO GO TO THE COAST! I'LL START TAKING MORE DRUGS THAN I'M TAKING NOW!

Audrey.   Darling, you mustn't take drugs. It's bad for your health.

Trent.   I'll see you this afternoon.

Audrey.   Dear, I'm afraid you may have to take this deal.

Trent.   I'll see you this after— *(But Audrey has already clicked off)*—noon. *(Lights off on Audrey. Trent turns to audience)* Okay, I know exactly what you're thinking: Where is the problem? You take the money, you write what you can, the play's no good, no one does the play, you've got your money, basta![3] end of deal. If I could actually count on that, you're right, no problem. Here's the hitch: this guy is so rich he's liable to produce this play no matter *how* bad it is! Why should this matter?

Audrey's Assistant *(Voice only).*   Miss Wood will see you now!

Trent.   One second! I'll be right with her. *(To audience)* People who write plays are a little crazy, okay? For one thing, no one writes plays to make money. I mean you *do*, of course. But you don't go into it, as a profession, because that's where you figure the big bucks lie. You do it . . . and you spend your life doing it, because it *matters*. And you have a kind of pact with yourself. And it says you don't screw around with what matters or else it's gone.

Audrey's Assistant *(Voice only).*   Miss Wood will see you now!

Trent.   Yes, yes. Coming!

Lights back up on Audrey. Trent walks over, manila envelope in hand.

Audrey.   Dear, if you want to get out of this, I'll loan you the money.

Trent.   No, I can't do that.

Audrey.   Of course you can, don't be a fool.

Trent.   Look, here's his scenario. Four pages. Actually, only three. The first page is taken by the title.

Audrey.   What's the title?

Trent.   *The End of the World.*

Audrey.   Ohhhh, dear.

Trent.   You know what it deals with?

Audrey.   I was afraid to ask.

---

[3] *Basta* is Italian for "enough."

Trent.   Nuclear proliferation.

Audrey.   Oh dear, oh dear, oh dear.

Trent.   I mean, is that an exciting subject or isn't it?

Audrey.   Why does he want to *do* this play?

Trent.   No idea.

Audrey.   Well, let's call him up! *(Buzzing her intercom)* Get me Philip Stone. Bob Montgomery has his number. *(Back to Trent)* Montgomery's his lawyer. He called after you did. Stone will agree to whatever terms you want.

Trent.   The man is mad!

Audrey.   That's no reason not to work with him. *(The intercom buzzes)* Yes?

Audrey's Assistant *(Voice only).*   Philip Stone on the line.

Audrey *(Into phone).*   Philip Stone? Audrey Wood—I am Michael Trent's agent. I gather you met with my client last night. Mr. Trent is sitting here with me in my office now. *(To Trent)* Say hello, dear.

Trent *(Picking up a second phone).*   Hello!

Lights up on Stone, on the phone.

Stone.   Hello!

Audrey *(Into phone).*   Dear, we would like to know why you're so anxious to produce this particular play.

Stone.   I want to produce it because I believe the earth is doomed.

Audrey.   I'm sorry . . . *What?*

Stone.   Doomed! I believe the earth is doomed!

Audrey stares at Trent.

Audrey.   He *is* mad! *(Into phone)* Mr. Stone, I'm sorry, are you suggesting that a production of your play could prevent this doom?

Stone.   Yes, I think perhaps it could.

Trent *(Sotto voce).*   Ask him if he's planning on road companies.

She waves him off.

Audrey.   Well, dear, I must say this is certainly one of the *worthiest* projects I've come across in a very long time.

Stone.   Possibly ever.

Audrey.   . . . Yes. Possibly ever. *(To Trent, sotto voce)* You've got to get out of this! *(Back to Stone)* Darling, you still there?

Stone.   Still here!

Audrey.   How long would you say we have till doom strikes?

Stone.   My statistics suggest it could be almost any time.

Audrey.   So then you'll be anxious to get it on this season.

Stone.   I was hoping for this spring.

Audrey *(To Trent).*   I've never heard of anything like this. *(Back into phone)* I take it you've never produced before.

Stone.   No.

Audrey.   Well, you have to be prepared for this play closing. *Rapidly.*

Stone.   Why?

Audrey.   Well, I think there's a good chance audiences may not like it. Just by definition. Frankly, unless I'm missing some essential elements, it sounds rather *downbeat* to me.

Stone.   I'm sorry, I don't understand. If audiences don't like it, do I *have* to close the play?

Audrey *(Stunned)*.   Well . . . no, of course not.

Stone.   Then I won't.

Audrey.   But what if no one comes?

Stone.   No one at *all?*

Audrey.   Dear, it's been known to happen!

Stone.   I find it hard to believe someone would not come in *eventually.* *(Audrey and Trent stare at each other in astonishment)* In the winter, for example. It's *warm* inside a theater. People are bound to come in . . . No, I'm going to keep this thing running. The earth's future is at stake! One doesn't close a play when the earth's future is at stake.

Audrey *(To Trent, sotto voce).*   *We've got to keep this man to ourselves!* *(Back to Stone)* Dear, I think this is one of the most unusual and worthwhile projects I've ever come across. Hold on a sec. *(Cups her hand over the mouthpiece)* What if he really *knows* something here?

Trent.   What do you mean?

Audrey.   About the earth! About its doom!

Trent.   Oh, my God.

Audrey.   Dear, listen, why take a chance? *Talk* with the man. If a play of yours could in some way help prevent global doom, well!

Trent.   Oh, my God!

Audrey *(Into the phone).*   If you like, my client will meet with you this afternoon.

Blackout on Audrey and Stone.

Trent. *(To audience).*   I was, of course, an innocent . . . As I soon found out.

Lights up on Stone.

Stone.   To put it mildly, sir, I am thrilled by your stopping by. Already I feel hope rising in my breast. Charles! Some drinks! Scotch, if you like; we have it.

Trent *(To audience).*   I told him I wanted nothing.

Stone.   Good. All business. For me, then, nothing either.

Trent *(To audience).*   Stone had requested that the meeting be at his place.

Now I was in his apartment. *(Stone's sumptuous Fifth Avenue apartment glides into view)* If I'd ever wanted booze this was it, but something warned me. I sensed a need for clearheadedness: the height had already made me dizzy enough. As a rule, I dislike elevators. For some reason, I cannot rid my mind of the image of what lies underneath as I ascend. Because of this, whenever possible, I walk upstairs. Stone lived in a penthouse forty floors up. There is a limit to any neurosis; forty floors was mine. Now the world was reeling. Looking down through the half-opened window of Stone's library, which I desperately did not *want* to do but felt myself *compelled* to do, I saw the people on the streets below wobbling like rubber. Like dolls made of rubber. The buildings were also like rubber. And, in the hot summer sun, seemed to be *melting!*

Stone *(Coming up behind him).*   Extraordinary perspective from up here.

Trent.   . . . Yes.

Stone.   Why don't you sit down?

Trent.   Thank you. *(Stone leads him to a seat. To audience)* And I missed the seat!

Trent, *in sitting, indeed misses the seat. He lands on the floor like a clown. Stunned expression. Beat.*

Blackout.

Lights up on Audrey.

Audrey *(To audience).*   What does an agent do? *(Pause)* This is a question I am asked all the time . . . In *theory,* an agent is supposed to find her client *work* . . . Now, while this has certainly been *known* to happen, fortunately, for all concerned, we do much, much more. Take this instance here. Michael Trent had been my client now for nearly fifteen years, and, relatively speaking, we'd done well together; though he wasn't rich, neither was he starving. Comfortable, I would say, is what he was—till recently . . . Now, all writers go through down periods; this was something more. What worried me about Michael was his growing eccentricity. He imagined himself as a kind of *detective!* Even on the hottest, brightest summer day he would wear a trench coat, collar up; slouch hat, brim down! Frankly, he looked ridiculous. Well, I'm very fond of him. And consider it my job to protect him from harm . . . Anyway, when this Stone project came along, though financially the deal was incredible, unprecedented, something just said to me, *Audrey, watch out!* I decided I needed help . . . So I called a meeting: Merv Rosenblatt—he's the president of our agency, and Paul Cowan, Agent to the Stars! Paul refused to come downstairs to *my* office, I refused to go up to *his,* so we agreed to meet for lunch at the Russian Tea Room. *(A booth from the Russian Tea Room glides on)* Paul was the first to arrive— *(Enter* **Paul Cowan,** *in sweat suit)*—dressed in his normal dapper style.

Paul *(Sullenly).* Hi, Audrey. *(Slides in next to her and starts chewing on a napkin.)*

Audrey. Merv Rosenblatt came next. *(Enter **Merv Rosenblatt**, in sharp, pin-striped suit with carnation in lapel. He is suntanned)* He'd canceled a lunch with Frank Perdue,[4] that's how important this meeting was!

Merv. Okay, what's this about global doom?

Paul. I'm sure it's an exaggeration.

Merv. Hi, Paul. Hope that's not a contract you're chewing on.

Paul. No-no. Napkin. Listen, why don't we get started. I've got a screening in twenty minutes. *(To someone unseen by us)* Hey! I'll be in till seven, gimme a call! *(To someone else)* Hi! *(Back to Audrey)* Sorry, Audrey. Go ahead.

Audrey. Gentlemen. At this very instant, not ten blocks from here, my client is meeting with Philip Stone.

Paul. Who's he?

Audrey. Paul, I sent you a memo on *all* of this!

Paul. Well, I can't remember! What are we, playing games?

Audrey. Philip Stone is the man who's vowed to keep my client's play running no matter what.

Paul. Right. Now I remember! This is the kind of producer our theater NEEDS! Mervin, what would you like?

Merv. Campari and soda.

Paul. CAMPARI AND SODA AND A BLOODY MARY! Now, when can I meet this guy?

Audrey. Well—

Headwaiter. PHONE CALL FOR MR. COWAN!

Paul. Bring it here!

Merv. Isn't Stone the guy who says we're doomed?

Audrey. He's the one.

Merv. Well, that's *not* the kind of producer our theater needs! What the hell's Paul talking about?

Headwaiter *(Arriving with plug-in phone).* Here you are, Mr. Cowan.

Paul. You think I'm gonna plug it in? Plug it in.

The Waiter climbs over Merv.

Merv *(From beneath the Waiter).* Paul, is this really necessary?

Paul. How do I know? *(The Waiter climbs back out. Paul picks up the phone. To the others)* Keep talking; I can listen. *(Starts scribbling on the tablecloth)*

Audrey. Stone says he's willing to pay anything my client wants.

Paul *(Still on phone).* Maybe it's a project Paramount would like.

Audrey. I've read Stone's scenario and it's terrible.

---

[4]Frank Perdue is an entrepreneur in the poultry business who performs in his company's commercials.

Paul. Why don't we let Paramount decide.

Audrey. It's about nuclear war.

Paul *(Into phone).* Hold on. *(To Audrey)* Paramount will only consider projects about nuclear war if there's an upbeat ending.

Audrey. This has no ending whatsoever.

Paul. Well, that, I would say, is a problem. *(Back into phone)* Yeah. Go ahead. *(Continues scribbling on the tablecloth)*

Audrey. My instinct is to turn the project down.

Paul. Are you mad?

Audrey. Paul, I will not stand for rudeness! I am seeking advice, all right? *Seeking.* And I've brought you in on this as a courtesy.

Paul. Mervin, talk to her.

Merv. Audrey, if your client turns this project down, how will we find out if the earth is doomed?

Paul. Right! At least have him stay with this till we find out *that.* I've got deals pending here.

Audrey. My client feels it is unethical to—

Merv. *What?*

Audrey. *Unethical—*

Paul *(Into phone).* Hold on. *(To Audrey)* WHAT?

Audrey. My client feels it is unethical to accept a deal knowing from the outset that there's no way it can be done.

Paul *(Into phone).* Did you hear that? Can you believe what you're hearing here? *(To Audrey)* So you're advising him to turn this *down?*

Audrey. I'm not advising him to do *anything.*

Paul. WELL, WHAT KIND OF GODDAMN ADVICE IS *THAT?*

Merv. Paul!

Paul. Where the hell are our drinks? WOULD YOU PLEASE BRING OUR GODDAMN DRINKS! *(Into phone)* I better call you back. *(Hangs up. To Audrey)* Audrey, look, far be it from me to butt into your affairs, but how much did your client earn last year?

Audrey. Not a lot.

Paul. I will personally guarantee him twice what he made just to keep this project alive. Mervin, are you in on this?

Merv. Well—

Paul. Mervin's in. Audrey, all your client has to do is string this guy along. Meanwhile, we interest him in *other* worthy projects—I've got I'd say ten— and, simultaneously, find out if the earth is doomed. If it is, we make plans.

Audrey. What sort of plans?

Paul. How do I know? You just gave me this today!

Merv. When he says doomed, does he mean the West Coast, too?

Audrey. I believe that's included, yes.

Paul. You know I have to tell you, from the little I am gleaning here, this doesn't sound like what I'd call a box-office smash.

Merv. Well now, *Earthquake* did quite well.

Paul.   As a FILM? Hey, this could be sensational. But I understand he's talking drama, right?

Audrey.   Drama.

Paul *(To Merv)*.   We could take the Winter Garden after *Cats*[5] is gone, blow the whole place up. I mean, it's halfway there already, right? *(To Audrey)* What about this as a musical?

Merv.   Paul!

Paul.   Don't reject things out of hand. *(To Audrey)* Who are the main characters?

Audrey.   Well, the main one I would say is the President.

Paul *(To Merv)*.   Who could we get?

Merv ponders. Paul ponders. The same inspired casting idea hits them simultaneously.

Audrey.   Gentlemen, Ron is President, right now!

Paul.   Well, when he LEAVES!

Audrey.   The man wants to do the play this spring.

Merv.   Name the other characters, we can always cast the President.

Audrey.   There's only one other major character: the Soviet premier.

Merv ponders. Paul ponders.

Paul.   Ann-Margret's looking for something.

Audrey.   Paul, the premier is a *man!*

Paul.   It's written that it cannot be a woman? Where? In what Russian document? I don't speak Russian; do you speak Russian? The British have a woman; why can't the Russians?

Merv.   Audrey, Ann-Margret's a good idea.

Paul.   No, great idea, *great* idea! Look, the important thing is this: cast it right, I don't care what the thing's about, it runs! You want my advice? Your client *doesn't* take this deal. He *grabs* this deal! GRABS this deal!

Merv.   And, meanwhile, finds out if the earth is doomed.

Paul.   Right. CHECK!

Blackout.

Lights up on Trent, still on the floor. Charles helps him to a chair.

Trent *(To Stone)*.   I don't know why . . . I suddenly felt quite dizzy.

Stone *(Warm and helpful)*.   Perhaps it was the open window . . . Many people—perfectly *normal* people, people of a *sunny disposition*—confronted

---

[5]The Winter Garden is a Broadway theatre. *Cats*, a successful, long-running musical, opened at the Winter Garden in October 1982.

suddenly by an open window, all at once find themselves wondering if they shouldn't jump. The notion takes their breath away. And they faint. Charles, bring our guest some water. *(Exit Charles)* Now obviously I'm not saying this was you.

Trent.   It certainly sounds that way.

Stone.   Well, I'm only speculating. Anyway, I don't think you were literally about to jump. I think you were just *thinking* about jumping!

Trent.   I'm the most self-protective person you have ever *met!*

Stone.   That's why you fainted. Trent, look, why shilly-shally? You're a man of imagination. How can you *look* at a window and NOT think about jumping?

Trent.   I didn't realize that's what imagination led to.

Stone.   For God's sake, man, the window was *open!* What do you want, a written invitation?

Trent.   I think I'd like something stronger than water.

Stone.   CHARLES!

Charles *(Reentering instantly).*   You shouted?

Stone.   Our guest would like something stronger than water.

Charles.   I'm not surprised.

Exit Charles.

Stone.   Now listen, Trent. If you're not going to be honest with me, *or* yourself, what's the point of our going on? In front of you is an open window; beyond, forty exhilarating floors below, *oblivion!* Now. How can you, as a normal human being, not at least *contemplate* jumping out?

Trent.   I don't contemplate jumping out because I'm not in *despair!*

Stone.   What's despair got to do with this?

Trent.   I'd have thought everything.

Stone.   I'm beginning to think you're some kind of ninny. Trent, listen to me. We are on the verge of beating a dead horse. I did *not* expect you to jump out the window, all right? In fact, to be perfectly fair, I'd have been astounded had you even stood on the LEDGE! The point is this. *(Enter Charles, rolling a cart filled with booze)* Ah, thank you, Charles. The point is this. *(Trent hurries toward the cart)* Trent, are you listening?

Trent *(Grabbing a bottle).*   Avidly.

Stone.   THE POINT IS THIS! *(Trent starts to open it)* The urge to leap out of windows does not derive from despair. It derives from *curiosity.*

Trent.   . . . Curiosity?

Stone.   Yes sir, curiosity, rampant curiosity! I myself feel the urge *all the time.* Fortunately, I resist . . . Fortunate for me. Fortunate for those down below. *(Grins)* Enough! On to business. Your agent informs me you have certain reservations about my scenario. If you'd be so kind, I'd like to hear what these reservations are; please speak freely, our relationship will founder if it isn't based on absolute, unwavering trust.

Trent.   Right. Uhhh, thank you. Well! I would say, offhand, that the single biggest problem with your scenario is that it's basically *implausible*.

Stone.   It's *supposed* to be implausible.

Trent.   I see . . . Well, I didn't catch that.

Stone.   Do you honestly think the next world war is going to start in some *plausible* way?

Trent.   No, I see what you mean.

Stone.   In fact, *I* think this basic implausibility is the most plausible thing *in* my scenario . . . And I worked very hard to achieve it.

Trent.   Yes, well, you've succeeded.

Stone.   So when can I expect a script? *(Trent looks about as if for a way to escape)* You understand, I don't mean to rush you now, but time is clearly of the essence here, I'm sure you can see why.

Trent.   Doom, you mean.

Stone.   Yes, sir, doom. Could be any moment now.

Trent.   Look, Stone, I've got to tell you something. The truth is, I just don't see doom in your scenario. I mean, I see *theatrical* doom. That's written all over the place. But historic doom? global doom? Can't seem to catch sight of it.

Stone.   That's because it's not in.

Trent.   Not *in?*

Stone.   My scenario.

Trent.   The global doom you are so concerned about is not IN your scenario?

Stone.   That's correct.

Trent.   Well, don't you want to *put* it in?

Stone.   No, sir!

Trent.   Why?

Stone.   Because if I put in everything I know, no one will BELIEVE me, sir!

Trent.   But NO ONE WILL BELIEVE WHAT YOU'VE GOT!

Stone.   By gad, we're at an impasse here!

Trent.   Maybe what we need is a new approach.

Stone.   Good idea! What do you suggest?

Trent.   That you tell me what you know. And let *me* figure out how to dramatize it—how's that sound?

Stone.   No, sir, I cannot.

Trent.   I thought our relationship was based on TRUST!

Stone.   And so it is. And you're just going to have to trust me when I tell you doom approaches.

Trent.   Stone, listen. Let me explain something about basic dramatic construction: I cannot go out on the stage during my play and say to my audience, "Hey! Trust me! Doom approaches!" I have got to *convince* them that doom approaches. And how'm I going to do that if you can't convince ME?

Stone.   It's a stickler.

Trent.   It's a stickler, absolutely right. Now, what I'm going to do—*(Downs his drink)*—is go home. *(Puts down his glass)* And let you think this whole thing over. It's been a fascinating afternoon. No need to show me to the door.

Stone. Trent! For God's sake, don't you understand? If I could just TELL you how I *know* doom is approaching, why, what's to stop me from telling *everyone?* You see? And then why would I need a play? I wouldn't!

Trent. Stone. As I see it, there are only two possibilities here. Either you are certifiable. Or you're certifiable. In the first instance, you are certifiable because you've made all this up; in the second, you are certifiable because you *haven't* made it up but won't TALK! To this, I have but two possible responses. Out the door. And out the door. Farewell. Farewell.

Stone. No! Please, sir, you mustn't! Look, sir, I am on my knees! Future generations are on their knees!

Trent. All I see is you.

Stone. That's because you are shortsighted, sir. You see only the immediate!

Trent. No. I see a door, that's what I see. And I'm going through it!

Stone. Trent! *(Grabs Trent's legs)* The fate of the world lies in your hands.

Trent. Really? You know what? Fuck it! Let it blow!

Stone. It's attitudes like this, sir, that will do us in, attitudes like this!

Trent. Hey! Hold on . . . I've just figured out the problem. You know the problem? I'm the wrong writer for this project! With the right writer, this project could just go ZOOM! What you must do, right away, is call my agent: she will send you another writer!

Stone. But you, sir, are the writer that I want.

Trent. Wonderful! Why?

Stone. I can't tell you that.

Trent. Stone, listen to me: if you don't let me out this door this instant, I am going to create, before your eyes, in his room, a doom such as you have never dreamed! *(Stone takes out a gun)* Oh, my God.

Stone. Now I suggest you sit down over there.

Trent. HELP!

Stone. I am the only tenant on this floor.

Trent. CHARLES!

Stone. Charles works for me; he's used to my behavior. Sir, please sit down. This is no frivolous enterprise! My life is in jeopardy. And, like it or not, so is yours. *(Trent decides to sit)* Now. When I am done, if you still wish to leave my employ, you may do so. Furthermore, you may keep the money I have paid so far. How does that strike you, sir? Is that fairness or not?

Trent. That . . . seems quite fair. Yes.

Stone. Good. So, with your permission, then, I will put this morbid instrument away.

Trent. Oh. Yes. Please.

Stone. I find guns tend to have a will of their own! Fascinating creatures. I call this particular gun Fred.

Trent. Fred! That's a *nice* name for a gun.

Stone. Yes, it is. It's strong. Guns *need* good strong names. You can get into all *kinds* of trouble if your gun doesn't have a good strong name. Donald, for example. That's a dreadful name for a gun!

Trent.   Yes. Yes, I can see that. Gun wouldn't *respect* you if you called it Donald.

Stone.   Exactly! Gun like that could turn on you and *kill* you! Any moment! Have *you* ever had a gun?

Trent.   No. *(Pause)* Well. Actually, I once had a BB gun.

Stone.   And what did you call it?

Trent.   Uhhhhhhh, Jim.

Stone.   Jim! Yes, that's a *good* name for a gun.

Trent *(Heading for the phone).*   You know, I wonder, would you mind very much if I asked my agent to come over here?

Stone.   No need, sir! We'll be through in a trice!

Trent.   Good.

Stone.   Next time, though. Now, on to doom.

Trent.   Global doom!

Stone.   Clear this whole thing up!

Trent.   Good.

Stone.   Tell me, sir, what these ten countries have in common: India, Egypt, Iraq, Argentina, Israel, Japan, Korea, South Africa, Libya, Brazil.

Trent.   No idea.

Stone.   Within ten years, sir, each of these countries will possess the bomb.

Trent.   Really!

Stone.   Yes, sir.

Trent.   And to you this means we're doomed.

Stone.   No, sir! No, not in and of itself. This is but the *clay* from which our doom will be shaped! Sculpted! Formed!

Trent.   You see doom as a work of *art?*

Stone.   Yes sir. Exactly! And, to me, this is part of its *horror* . . . and *allure.* *(Stone smiles at Trent. Trent leans back and studies Stone with a new intensity. Sotto voce)* Now, the reason I believe doom approaches rapidly has to do with certain . . . *information* I stumbled upon quite by accident about a year ago, I shan't tell you how, not now at least . . . This information is at first blush so incredible that were I to simply tell you what it is, you would be bound not to believe it, just as I at first did not and in some ways still do not, *cannot!* though I know full well all of it is true. You see my dilemma here. If I tell you what I know, you will say Stone is mad, and leave. End of project, end of hope. On the other hand, if somehow you believe what I reveal, then I can only conclude that you are the one who's mad. So what am I to do? The answer's obvious. What I have come to know, on my own, you must somehow come to know on your own, as well . . . How? . . . By proceeding systematically . . . and *following your nose.*

Trent.   My nose tells me to get out of here.

Stone.   Of course! To save yourself from a terror such as you have never known! Why do your eyes dart toward the window, sir? That's no way out.

Trent. *Why a play?*

Stone. Why, indeed! . . . Because the theater, sir, alone among the arts, engages, in equal measure, the emotion and the intellect. And both must be touched here, if we are to survive.

Silence.

Trent. Why me?

Stone. As I said, sir: I cannot tell you that.

Trent. *Why?*

Stone. Because at this moment, sir, your greatest strength is your innocence.

Pause.

Trent. Well, I can't work like that, I'm sorry. *(Stone turns away)* All right. Look. I *will* work on this, okay? . . . BUT *only* if you tell me what it is about *my* plays that makes you think I am right for this job.

Stone. Well, sir, the truth is, and I hope you take this in the proper spirit— I've never actually *seen* a play of yours.

Trent. WHAT?

Stone. But I've been assured they're very good.

Trent. Stone, you are out of your goddamn mind!

Stone. No sir. Would that I were.

Trent. Well, something's cuckoo here. And I think I'll leave before it's me! *(Starts out)*

Stone *(Drawing his gun).* Sorry, sir, I object. *(Trent sees the gun and stops)* Sir, I am a desperate man! . . . But I am also a *gambling* man. I will gamble. I will tell you this: . . . *we have met before.*

Trent *(Amazed).* Where?

Stone. I cannot tell you that.

Trent. STONE, I CANNOT TAKE THESE GAMES ANYMORE! NOW, IF YOU WANT TO SHOOT ME, SHOOT ME, BUT THAT'S IT, GOODBYE!

Stone. SIR!

Trent. *I don't recall meeting you, all right?*

Stone. I am aware.

Trent. So how important could this meeting have been?

Stone. To me, crucial.

Trent. When did this meeting take place?

Stone. I can't tell you that.

Trent. How many were there?

Stone. I can't tell you that, either!

Trent. I see! And yet, at this meeting, something happened which has convinced you I could save the world from doom!

Stone. Yes, sir. Absolutely!

Trent.   Aren't you a bit surprised I don't remember?

Stone.   No, sir. I *thought* you might blot it out.

Trent.   BLOT IT OUT?

Stone.   Yes, sir.

Trent.   If the incident was anything like this, of COURSE I've blotted it out! People must be blotting you from their lives all the time! I AM LEAVING!

Stone.   All right, sir! All right! *(Trent stops and turns back)* I will tell you this . . . but *only* this . . . More than this and my cause is lost. *(Pause)* This . . . particular incident . . . *convinced* me . . . that you, sir, had a thorough understanding of *evil*.

Trent.   . . . I?

Stone.   Yes, sir. You. *(Trent stares at him in astonishment)* And now, sir, it is *my* turn to leave. I hope you take this job. *(Warm smile)* Good day.

Trent turns to the audience. As he does, the light in the room fades almost to black. However, the sky beyond the open window does not dim at all. In this darkened room, Stone, unmoving, is a shadowy presence.

Trent.   I had, of course, no idea what he meant. *(Pause)* I would say I took the job . . . because of *two* factors . . . *(Music: "Trent's Theme")* One, of course, was the money. How could I turn down a deal like that? *(Takes out a cigarette)* And the other, of course, was curiosity.

Lights the cigarette. Puffs.

The light through the window has been growing brighter. Now, blazing white, it seems to beckon.

Act Two: The Investigation

Music: "Trent's Theme." It continues as lights come up on a seedy hotel room. It is night. Through the one window in this room, a red neon hotel sign is visible across the street; the sign says "Sunset Motel." Except for this light, the only other light in the room comes from a lamp. Trent, in his trench coat, looks out at the audience.

Trent.   To be precise, ten months, five days, twelve hours, and . . . *(Checks his watch)* . . . twenty-three minutes have passed now since Philip Stone came into my life wielding a four-page scenario of dubious merit. Frankly, I've still no idea what he meant when he said I understood evil. As far as I know, I'm a pussycat, a sweetheart, aces—what the hell was he talking about?

(Puffs on a cigarette) Not that I haven't uncovered some rather peculiar goings-on, you understand! No-no, quite the contrary, this case has been a real eye-opener! There's funny business going on out there, and I had no idea of it. Can't remember when I've been so depressed by a case. *(Pours a shot of bourbon)* And I've never made so much money, either. Tells you something about money, doesn't it. You know what it tells you? Tells you, without all this money I'd be even *more* depressed. By the way, this is Washington. The Pentagon's back that way. I was there early this morning. *(There is a soft rap on the door. He tenses)* I know it isn't Stella; Stella has a key. *(Sets his glass down quietly)* She came down on the six o'clock shuttle. About an hour ago, I sent her across the street to case the lobby of a two-bit fleabag called the Sunset Motel—*(Starts moving cautiously toward the window)*—where I'm supposed to meet with a man who claims he can clear up everything. A man who calls himself The Shadow—really, I'm not kidding, that's what the message said. Is Stone behind all this? If so, I've been set up. Why? *(Another rap. Trent peers out through the half-opened slats of the Venetian blinds)* I can see the lobby from here. No sign of Stella.

Muffled Voice *(Softly, from other side of door).*   Mr. Trent? *(Trent turns off the lamp. The room is now dark except for the flickering neon sign of the Sunset Motel. Another knock)* Mr. Trent?

Trent.   The door's open.

The door opens. A **Man** *stands silhouetted in the bright hallway.*

Man In Hallway.   Mr. Trent?

Trent.   Stay where you are.

Man in Hallway.   Mr. Trent! Apparently, you have not understood the conditions of this meeting . . . The man you are about to see is not supposed to talk to outsiders. By agreeing to do just this for *you*, he places into jeopardy not only his job but his life. For this reason, you were specifically instructed to come alone. Instead, you sent an emissary to check out our hotel. Naturally, the meeting place must now be changed. One more violation and the meeting will be off. We will come for you when we're ready. Your friend has been sent back to New York. *(Leaves)*

Trent visible only in the eerie red glow of the neon light.

Trent.   Poor Stella. And she hates flying, too! *(Music: "Trent's Theme")* I'll tell you, this whole thing, it's not been easy on her . . . Right from the start.

Lights up on Stella. The hotel room disappears.

Stella *(To audience).*   Mike's instructions were simple. He said, "Dollface, I want you to get me every book and article published last year that deals with nuclear weapons." Wow, I thought! Within a week, his desktop looked like the Adirondacks.

Trent.   That's when the trouble began.

Lights up on Audrey.

Audrey *(To audience).*   About a month after he'd started his research, Stella gave me a call at home. She asked if she could come by. She said it was urgent. I told her to come right over. *(To Stella)* And he's been working?

Stella.   'Round the clock!

Audrey.   So what's the problem, dear?

Stella.   Well, it's his . . . . moaning.

Audrey.   . . . *Moaning?*

Stella nods. She holds out a small cassette player. She pushes the Play button. A terrible loud moan is heard. Audrey is aghast.

Trent *(To audience).*   Actually, I was not aware I was *making* this dreadful noise. I thought I was just reading quietly to myself. I did *hear* the noise, and thought it came from next door. I was in fact about to complain to the landlord, telling him it was hurting my concentration.

Audrey.   Well, this is not right, dear, not right at all. I'll call him in the morning.

Trent *(To audience).*   Which she did. Gave me a real chewing out!

Audrey.   I told him that, in my book, professionals, real professionals, do not sit around moaning. They knuckle down and DO THEIR JOB! No one had *asked* him to be a writer. He agreed.

Trent.   I told her not to worry, I'd figure out the problem. I asked her to arrange a meeting with Stone, and asked if she could be there, too. Frankly, I didn't want to be alone with this guy when I gave him the bad news.

Lights up on Stone in Audrey's office. He is staring at Trent in cold fury.

Stone.   Well, sir, all I can say is, obviously I've misjudged you! A grave mistake, indeed.

Audrey *(To Stone).*   Now, let's not panic. I'm sure we can work this out. *(To Trent)* Dear, Mr. Stone has been very generous to you. Don't you think you owe him a little more *time?*

Trent.   I cannot write a play from this material. NO one can write a play from this material! This stuff is INDESCRIBABLE!

Audrey.   Dear, we know the project's difficult. *(To Stone)* I think the research may be getting him down. *(Taking her client aside)* Dear, if you don't deliver a draft to this nice gentleman—doesn't have to be a *good* draft, you understand, just a *draft*—I think this man may not only destroy you financially but possibly have you killed, that's just a feeling I have. Now, what exactly is the problem, please spell it out; perhaps in the *talking*, things will seem easier. *(To Stone)* We're getting there!

Trent *(With obvious pain).*   I have been finding things . . . I did not *expect!*

Audrey.   Dear, that's what research is *about!*

Stone.   This is a waste of time. Clearly, Mr. Trent does not have the temperament for serious material.

Trent.   Look, there are certain things playwrights *know!* One of those is what makes a play. This material does not!

Audrey.   Dear, that is the silliest thing you've ever said—*anything* can make a play. You just have to figure out how to *handle* it! I've never seen you like this, really! *(To Stone)* And yet something tells me we're not that far apart.

Stone.   If this is not far apart, I am a rabbit!

Trent *(To Stone).*   Look! In every play there is a central character and this central character does not just *want* something; he NEEDS something, needs it so badly if he doesn't *get this thing* he will die . . . not necessarily physically, could be emotionally, spiritually, all right? In fact, dramatically, the worse his potential fate, the better. But! BUT! only up to a point. And that's the problem in this instance. Here, the consequences of failure are so far beyond our imagination, so far beyond anything we have ever experienced, or even *DREAMED*, an audience could not believe, fully believe, what it was watching . . . It will all seem like a lie.

Audrey.   Dear, maybe if you just gave it more *time.*

Trent.   I cannot READ this stuff anymore! I DON'T WANT TO *READ* ABOUT THIS STUFF ANYMORE! "The Prompt and Delayed Effects of Thermonuclear Explosions" is not what I wish to read at night! I am scaring the shit out of my family! My son runs from me in HORROR when he sees me coming. You know why? Because I have become a sentimental goddamn dishrag! I see him walking toward me and I start to weep. I see him playing on the lawn with his dogs and I start to weep. I DON'T WANT TO HAVE TO THINK ABOUT THIS STUFF EVERY DAY! WHAT SORT OF PEOPLE CAN *THINK ABOUT THIS STUFF EVERY DAY?* *(A sudden look of amazement comes over Trent's face)* . . . I'll work on it.

Audrey.   *What?*

Trent.   I know what to do . . . I'll work on it, I can work on it! I KNOW WHAT TO DO! *(Audrey stares at him in astonishment, then looks at Stone triumphantly. Lights to black on everyone but Trent. To audience)* Through Stone, I arranged to meet with some of the people who think about this stuff every day . . . The ones I asked to meet held opinions that seemed to me to go against all common sense. Anyhow, it was a way in. When there's a mystery, there's at least the possibility of a play. Whatever—it was all I had to go on. Stone said he thought I was doing the right thing. *(Pause)* The first man I talked to, I will call . . . General Wilmer. *(The library of **General Wilmer's** sumptuous Virginia estate starts to glide in)* He was one of the President's chief advisers on nuclear policy. He had a Ph.D. in physics. *(The*

· *General is seated behind an elegant Empire desk. There is an intercom on the desk. He wears casual country-squire clothes)* His house was in Virginia, about an hour's drive from Washington. Usually, he worked at the Pentagon. But this was a Saturday afternoon . . . *(The General lights a pipe)* A lovely autumn day.

General Wilmer.   So you want to make a play out of this.

Trent.   Well, that's what I'm hoping.

General Wilmer.   Some kind of Strangelove thing?

Trent.   No, I wouldn't think so.

General Wilmer.   Good. Because the Strangelove scenario only works if you postulate a Doomsday weapon, and no one contemplates that. To save ourselves by threatening to annihilate ourselves is surely the height of preposterousness!

Trent.   I would think so, yes.

Silence.

General Wilmer.   So have you got a plot?

Trent.   Well, no, I'm afraid I don't.

General Wilmer.   Don't plays *need* plots?

Trent.   Well, I'm hoping to find one. That's one of the reasons I've come down to Washington.

General Wilmer *(Merrily)*.   Not plot in the sense of conspiracy, I trust!

Trent *(Laughing)*.   No-no! Plot in the sense of narrative thrust. The thing that makes you ask what happens next. That kind of thing. *(The General smiles and tamps down the tobacco)* So how long have you known Philip Stone?

General Wilmer.   I've never met the man. *(Relights the pipe)*

Trent.   Well, then how did he arrange this meeting?

General Wilmer.   Someone else set it up. *(Puffs as an **Aide-de-Camp** in military uniform enters. He carries a folder. The General gestures to his desk. The Aide puts the folder on the desk and leaves)* So. You don't understand why we need more nuclear weapons.

Trent.   Right. It's probably 'cause I'm new at this.

Pause.

General Wilmer.   I gave a talk last month at Princeton, and it was on this very issue. And a number of the students started shouting, "Why don't we just *stop* this madness?" And I said, "You know, it's easy to avoid a nuclear war. All you have to do is surrender." *(Grins)* The problem is to find a way to *avoid* nuclear war while preserving the values that we cherish . . . Okay. Don't we have enough to accomplish this right now? Of course we do. Right *now*. But we don't need to deter the Russians now; why would they attack? They'd gain nothing . . . Deterrence comes into play during *crisis*. During crisis, people tend to think in peculiar ways. A successful deterrent says to the Russians, "No matter what, your best case scenario is just no good."

Trent. But that's where we are right now.

General Wilmer. Of course! But what makes you think we're going to stay where we are? . . . And things may turn better for us, or for them. Either way, it's dangerous. That's because any imbalance at all is dangerous, even if the imbalance is only *imagined*. In this business, it's how you're *perceived* that counts! *(The Aide enters with a note, which he gives to the General, then leaves. The General glances at the note. Crumples it. Puts it in a pocket)* For example, the weaker side starts thinking: Maybe we'd better hit these guys before they get even *stronger*. The stonger side, knowing what the weaker side's thinking, says: Maybe we'd better do what they *think* we're gonna do, even though we don't want to, 'cause otherwise they *might*. In which case, we're done for. So they do. You see? And all this comes about because of one simple, fundamental truth, and it governs everything we do: the guy who goes first goes best.

Trent. You want more so you can go *first*?

General Wilmer. In a crisis? Absolutely.

Trent. Well, that is a piece of encouraging news!

General Wilmer. Well, what's the alternative? We say we'd never, under any conditions, go first. And the Russians actually believe us. So *they* go first.

Trent. Why would they go first if they believe us? I thought you just said they'd go first because they're afraid *we'd* go first!

General Wilmer. Either way.

Trent. EITHER WAY?

General Wilmer. Well, you certainly can't expect them to believe us *completely*.

Trent. . . . So it doesn't matter *what* we say.

General Wilmer. In a way, that's true.

Trent. Maybe we should back up a bit. I think I may have started at too high a level! Why do we need nuclear weapons in the first place?

General Wilmer. To prevent their use.

Trent. Good. Just what I thought. YET if we suddenly realize we *can't* prevent their use, we'd better hurry up and use them.

General Wilmer. Right.

Trent. Isn't there some kind of basic contradiction here?

General Wilmer. Absolutely! It's what makes the problem so difficult to solve.

Trent. Do you enjoy this job?

General Wilmer. Someone's got to do it. *(The intercom buzzes)* Yes?

Man's Voice. The turtle is in Zurich.

General Wilmer *(Stunned)*. . . . Zurich? What's it doing in Zurich?

Man's Voice. No one knows. *Should we feed it?*

General Wilmer. . . . Not till we find out what it's doing there. *(Clicks off)*

Trent. So the turtle is in Zurich! *(Wilmer relights his pipe)* Well, I'm GLAD the turtle is in Zurich.

Wilmer smiles at him.

General Wilmer.   No, you're not. *(Pause)* Look. The sole purpose of possessing nuclear weapons . . .

Trent.   . . . is not to win wars but to *prevent* them. I've *got* that. Solid.

General Wilmer.   Good. Now. In order to *prevent* a nuclear war, you have
to be able to *fight* a nuclear war at *all levels*, even though they're probably
unwinnable and unfightable. You understand, this doesn't mean you want
to. Doesn't even mean you *will*. That's because, for the purpose of deterrence, a bluff taken seriously is far more helpful than a serious threat taken
as a bluff. What we're talking about now is credibility. Okay? . . . To this
end, what your opponent *thinks* you'll do is much more important than what
you *actually* will do. *(Buzzer sounds. He flicks the intercom)* I'm sorry, not
now. *(Clicks off)* For example, for the purpose of deterrence, it's a good idea
to tell the Russians that if they move into Western Europe—*(Buzzer sounds.
He flicks the intercom)* What?

Little Boy's Voice.   Dad?

General Wilmer.   Dear. Not now. All right? *(Clicks off)*—that if they move
into Western Europe we will use nuclear weapons to stop their advance. No
ambiguity there: you make *this* move, we make *this* move. However! Should
deterrence fail, it would seem wiser not to use our nuclear weapons at all,
the reason being that once we've gone nuclear, the likelihood of Soviet nuclear retaliation is overwhelming. *(Enter Aide with note. He hands it to Wilmer. Wilmer keeps talking)* What's more, the probability is that it would es-
calate. What this means is that instead of Western Europe being overrun by
the Soviets—*(He glances at the note)*—a thing we certainly don't want! *(To
the Aide)* Have his mother take care of it. *(Exit the Aide)*—Western Europe,
and the United States, AND the Soviet Union would quickly and effectively
cease to exist. In fact, according to our latest figures, so probably would the
entire world. *(Buzzer sounds. He flicks it. With annoyance)* Yes?

Woman's Voice.   This is for *you* to handle, dear.

General Wilmer.   I'll take care of it later. *(Clicks off)* Okay, so here we are,
then, with two policies, one overt—you move here and we will strike; the
second, *covert*—we may choose not to do any such thing. The Soviets, who
know it makes no *sense* for us to strike with nuclear weapons if they move
in, nonetheless are deterred from moving in because it's *just possible* we might
be *crazy* enough to do it. Now. What this means is that, for every level of
engagement, we must possess a credible response, even if this response is quite
incredible on its surface. This is one of the reasons it's important for our
President, whoever he is, to every so often say something that sounds a bit
insane. *(Pause)* Fear, you see. That's the great deterrent . . . Don't want to
do too much to reduce the fear. By the way, that's the problem with a nuclear freeze: to the extent that it makes people feel safer, it raises the chances
of war. You look shocked. I'll tell you something shocking—I think things

are going just fine. And you should relax. We really *do* know what we're doing. Take a look. In the past forty years, have we had a nuclear war? No. Why? . . . Nuclear weapons. The fact is, nuclear weapons not only prevent *nuclear* war, they prevent *all* war . . . And I think they just may be the best damned thing that's ever happened to us. Really do!

Beat. Blackout on everything but Trent.

Music.   "Trent's Theme." Trent walks downstage to the audience.

Trent *(To audience).*   My conversation with General Wilmer had left me in a quandary: I didn't know whether to laugh or cry. I was on the verge of doing both when the general gave me a call.

Lights up on Wilmer.

General Wilmer.   I've been thinking. Maybe you should meet a man named Stanley Berent. If you like, I can set it up.

Lights off on Wilmer.

Trent *(To audience).*   I'd come across Berent's name in my research. He was a Russian scholar, connected to Georgetown University, and a real hard-liner, particularly where the Soviet Union was concerned. *(Japanese koto music heard)* We met at a small Japanese restaurant I assume he frequented out of war guilt. We sat on tatami mats, cross-legged, which made the experience even more excruciating. An inescapable feeling of unreality began to hang over all of this.

The restaurant has slid into view during the above.

Berent *(Eastern European accent).*   No, I agree with you completely—our present nuclear policy does not make sense, not at all!
Trent *(To audience).*   Why had the general sent me to *this* man?
Berent.   What we must do—very simple: we must stop regarding nuclear war as some kind of goddamn inevitable holocaust . . . and start looking at it as a goddamn WAR!
Trent.   . . . What?
Berent.   We have to learn how to wage nuclear war *rationally.*
Trent.   *What?*
Berent.   Rationally. We have got to learn how to wage nuclear war *rationally.* I'm sorry—*sake?*
Trent.   Uhhhhh, thank you.
Berent.   You see, even though a strong case can be made for the fact that

nuclear war is essentially an act of insane desperation, and therefore fundamentally irrational, this doesn't mean that once you're in the thing you shouldn't do it *right!*

Trent.   I see. *(Pause)* Of course, this would seem to suggest you think it's possible to *win* a nuclear war.

Berent.   No-no! *Limited* nuclear war. No one can win an all-out nuclear war. Unless, of course, the other side decides not to hit back, and one could never count on that, ALTHOUGH, I must say—*(Gives a brief, sharp command to a Waitress in fluent Japanese)*—although, I must say, in all the scenarios I've seen, the side that hits first definitely comes out best. So if push comes to shove, you do go first, no question of it, particularly if you employ what we call a controlled counterforce strike with restraint. In effect, you hit everything but your opponent's cities.

Trent.   That's the restraint part.

Berent.   Right. His cities are held hostage. And what you—I'm sorry! Chopsticks?

Trent.   Yes, chopsticks.

Berent.   And what you do is, you tell him you'll demolish them if he doesn't capitulate. Now, this is actually quite reasonable *if*, big if, *big* if, IF you have an adequate civil-defense system. That way, even if the Russians strike back, you should be able to absorb the blow and still have enough left to strike back at *them*. And this time just wipe them out. This is what I mean when I talk about credibility. What I have just described to you is a CREDIBLE offensive and defensive nuclear strategy. What we have now, forgive my French, is diddly-shit. *(To the Waitress, a short command in Japanese, at which she nods and leaves. To Trent)* You don't speak Japanese, I take it.

Trent.   No. Why? Are you passing secrets?

Berent *(Laughing)*.   Secrets? I'm not privy to any secrets. Ah, thank you. *(A Waiter delivers a noodle dish)* Now. Do I *really* know how to fight a limited nuclear war? Not at all. No one does. No one's *fought* one. And yet if we're not prepared, we're in the soup. Okay. What do I propose?

Trent.   You're not eating.

Berent.   I'm not hungry. What do I propose. I propose we send a clear signal to the Russians, and this signal says: You fuck around with us, we're gonna fuck around with you! This is the sort of talk the Russians understand. How do we do this? First, we build the MX, the Trident 2, the Pershing II, and the Cruise. Why do I want these things? Because they have the ability to take out hardened targets. If we get into a major crisis with these people, I want the ability to disarm them to the greatest extent possible.

Trent.   *Disarm?*

Berent.   Remove. Surgically remove. As much of their military capability as is possible.

Trent.   That's called a first strike, I believe.

Berent.   Oh, no.

Trent.   It's *not?*

Berent.   No.

Pause.

Trent.   Why?

Berent.   Because the connotation is *aggressive*. This is a *defensive* act.

Trent.   I see . . . . Out of curiosity, what do you call it?

Berent.   Anticipatory retaliation.

Trent.   Ah!

Berent.   Some prefer "preemptive strike," but that can get cumbersome. Because, if you sense they're about to preempt *you*, then what you have to do is *pre*-preempt them.

Trent (*Getting into the spirit now*).   And of course if they should somehow become *aware* that you've discovered their *plans* to preempt, and are about to *pre*-preempt, they'll have to start discussing a *pre*-pre-preemptive strike. And one can obviously just get lost in this kind of talk.

Berent.   That's right. Anticipatory retaliation simply covers everything! Unfortunately, we can't even begin to consider this if we don't have the proper weapons.

Trent.   And we don't have them now?

Berent.   No, sir, we do not.

Trent.   I realize you're going to lose all respect for me. But isn't it possible we'd be better off *not* getting these things?

Berent.   Of course! . . . . If the Russians didn't have them.

Trent.   They *have* them?

Berent.   They're *getting* them.

Trent.   WHERE DOES THIS ALL END?

Berent.   When each of us is secure.

Trent.   Well, that's fair enough.

Berent.   Unfortunately, we're not even close . . . . To be secure, the United States must possess a credible nuclear-war fighting policy. Now, what might such a policy be?

Trent.   Got me.

Berent.   In a war, what do you think the Russian command would least like to lose?

Trent.   I would say, offhand, Russia.

Berent.   Short of that.

Trent.   Half of Russia?

Berent.   Short of *that*.

Trent.   A third of Russia.

Berent.   Wrong approach. The point is to avoid killing civilians needlessly. Now, come on, think. In a war, outside of its population, what can the Soviet leaders least afford to lose?

Trent.   . . . I don't know.

Berent.   Oh, come on!

Trent.   No, really, I don't know.

Berent. ThemSELVES!

Trent. Themselves?

Berent. Of course! Without a Kremlin, without leadership—you know what Russia's got? It's got shit, that's what it's got!

Trent. So how do we get rid of their leaders?

Berent. Well, we know where they are. And we bomb them.

Trent. . . . Surely they're not just going to sit there and *wait!*

Berent. No-no! They're going to hide. That's expected.

Trent. I would think Russia has a lot of hiding places.

Berent. Of course. And we know where they are. And we target them.

Trent. Sounds to me like you're about to wipe out all of Russia.

Berent. Well, that's certainly not what we *intend*.

Trent. It's just a side effect, you mean.

Berent. Correct.

Trent. And this wouldn't piss them off?

Berent. Piss *who* off?

Trent. The Russians who are left. I see! They're all *gone*.

Berent. That's right.

Trent. Listen. Question. Let's say we've successfully wiped out their leaders, somehow some of their population still exist, and we decide we want to stop this thing. With *whom* do we negotiate?

Berent. Well, that is a genuine problem.

Trent. Listen, this is just off the top of my head. Don't you think it might be a good idea to try really very seriously to *negotiate* something with these fellas *now?*

Berent. Of course! That would be *wonderful!* And yet, if history shows anything, it shows that the Soviet Union cannot be trusted to keep the terms of a treaty!

Trent. Hold it! Hold it, hold it! Are you trying to tell me we shouldn't enter into treaties with these guys till we're convinced they can be TRUSTED?

Berent. That's correct.

Trent. If we knew they could be trusted, why would we need TREATIES? SAYONARA! *(Berent stares at him in astonishment. To audience)* I could barely contain my excitement! *(Rises as Berent and the restaurant fade from view)* I called Stone at the first pay phone I could find. *(Lights up on Stone. He is in a room next to a wing chair, its back to us)* Okay, I've got it!

Stone *(Trace of nervousness in his voice)*. Got what, sir?

Trent. The answer. The mystery is solved. I've discovered why we're doomed.

Stone. Really. And why is that?

Trent. We're in the hands of assholes! *(Silence)* . . . Hello?

Stone *(Sotto voce)*. I'm afraid I cannot speak right now.

Trent. Why?

The lights have come up enough to reveal that there is a man sitting in the wing chair—we see only his legs. The man appears to be smoking, for smoke curls upward from the chair.

Stone.   Sir, I can only tell you, if you persist in believing these men you've met are not smart, or not . . . *(In a whisper) dangerous* . . . *(Back to his normal voice)* . . . you are gravely mistaken. I can say no more, not now.

Stone hangs up. Turns back to his mysterious companion. Lights to black on them both.

Trent *(To audience).*   There are times you want to chuck it all. This wasn't one. I was on to something here, no question. I decided to check out the guys they call war-gamers, the guys who *play* with these war scenarios. I called General Wilmer and asked if he could arrange it—things had gone so well with the last meeting he'd set up! He said he would. Gladly. And he did. *(Lights up on Jim and Pete)* I will call them Jim and Pete. *(We are in Jim's kitchen)* Both were connected with the Harley Corporation, a government think tank in nearby Virginia. *(Pete and Jim are preparing a meal—tiny birds stuffed, seasoned, wrapped in gauze, to be cooked in a microwave)* But the place was off-limits to plain ol' folk like me, so they very graciously invited me to Jim's house, though perhaps it was Pete's, I was never altogether sure— *one* of theirs. For a meal in my honor. Why had they gone to all this trouble for me? Something was very odd.

Jim *(While working at the meal).*   So you talked with Stanley Berent!

Pete *(Also while working at the meal).*   Bet *that* was fun!

Trent.   He poked a lot of holes in our deterrence strategy.

Jim.   I'm sure he was right, it's not hard to do.

They work in tandem on the meal; lots of coordinated teamwork.

Pete.   There's a curious paradox built into deterrence strategy, and no one has a *clue* how to get around it. The paradox is this: Deterrence is dependent upon strength—well, that's obvious; the stronger your nuclear arsenal, the more the other side's deterred. *However,* should deterrence *fail* for any reason, your strength *instantly* becomes your greatest liability, *inviting* attack *instead* of preventing it.

Jim.   HOIST on your own petard!

Pete.   And *that* is where all these crazy scenarios come in in which war breaks out PRECISELY because *no one* WANTS it to! Really! I'm not kidding. This business is *filled* with paradox! Here, I'll run one by you.

Jim.   I think, before you do, we should point out it isn't *easy* starting a nuclear war.

Pete.   Right! Sorry. Getting carried away.

Jim.   In fact, we can run scenario after scenario—the Persian Gulf is the most popular.

Pete.   That's the hot spot!

Jim.   People just will not go nuclear.

Pete.   Right! And at first it absolutely drove us up the wall! Here we had all these tests designed to see what happens when people go nuclear?

Jim.   And no one would do it!

Pete.   To the man, they just refused to believe there wasn't some other way to resolve the crisis!

Jim.   Well, the military started freaking out. They figured all those guys down in the silos?—maybe they won't push the button when they're told.

Pete.   Real freak-out scene.

Jim.   The whole Pentagon—

Pete.   They just went bananas! *Total* banana scene.

Jim.   Some general called me up. He said, "You incompetent jackass, what the hell kind of scenario are you *giving* these guys?" I said, "We're giving 'em every scenario we can think of, SIR! No one'll push the button, SIR!" You know what he said?

Pete.   Get this!—"Don't tell 'em it's the button!"

Jim.   "Really!" we said. "Then what good's the test?"

Pete.   Anyway, happy ending.

Jim.   Finally we solved it.

Pete.   *You* solved it.

Jim.   *I* solved it, *you* solved it, what's it matter? We *solved* the thing!

Pete.   What a bitch!

Jim.   People think it's *easy* starting a nuclear war?

Pete.   Hey! Let 'em try!

Trent.   Okay, I'll bite: how *do* you start a nuclear war?

Jim.   Well, *first* you have to assume that a nuclear war is the *last* thing either side wants.

Pete.   Right! That's the key! Who would've thought it! Jim?

Jim.   Okay. Let's say we're in a confrontation situation where we and the Soviets are facing down in the Middle East: let's say, Iran. Big Soviet pour-down. Let's further say we're losing conventionally on the ground—

Pete.   Not hard to believe—

Jim.   —and the President decides he wants the option of using nuclear weapons in the area, so he moves them in.

Pete.   Mind you, he doesn't want to *use* them now.

Jim.   Right! Absolutely not! Last thing he wants!

Pete.   He's just hoping, by showing strength, the Soviets will rethink their position and pull back.

Jim.   In other works, it's a *bluff*.

Pete.   Right, good ol' poker bluff!

Jim.   And, by the way, probably the proper move to make.

Pete.   Now, at the *same* time we ask our NATO allies to join us in raising the military alert level in Europe. Why? We want to tie the Soviet forces down that are in Eastern Europe.

Jim.   Again, absolutely the right move.

Pete.   So far, the President's batting a thousand. No appeasement here. Yet not too strong, nothing precipitous.

Jim.   Okay. The Soviets now go to a higher level of readiness themselves. Why? They want to tie *our* forces down so *we* don't shift 'em to the Middle East.

Pete.   Now we start to move nuclear weapons out of storage! *(Mimics the sound of a trumpet)*

Jim.   Okay, now let's suppose the Soviets, in the heat of this crisis, *misinterpret* the moves we've made, and believe that in fact we're about to *launch* these weapons! Not a farfetched supposition!

Pete.   Particularly, given their tendency to paranoia!

Jim.   Right!

Pete.   Okay. Now, at *this* point the issue for them is *not* do they want to be *in* a war.

Jim.   They're already *in* a war in the Middle East!

Pete.   Right. The issue isn't even do they want to launch a nuclear attack against the West.

Jim.   That's because they know they'll HAVE to if the West attacks *them!*

Pete.   You see?

Jim.   *The only issue—*

Pete.   Absolutely ONLY issue—

Jim.   —is do they want to go *first* and *preempt* this attack?

Pete.   Or wait it out—

Jim.   —and go second.

Pete.   Now, they recognize, just as much as we . . . .

Jim.   . . . . that going *first*—

Pete.   —is going *best.*

Jim.   Right!

Pete.   And by a shocking margin, too. No scenario *ever* shows ANYTHING else! I mean, these notions of our riding out a nuclear attack and then launching again, without substantial loss of capability—well, it's nonsense.

Jim.   By the way, you have to posit here that events are moving rapidly. A short time frame is crucial to this scenario. No time to sit back and say, "Hey! wait, why would he want to shoot at me? I know he's in trouble, but he isn't crazy!" No. He doesn't have *time* to think things out. He's got to make a move! Okay, What's he do? *(Pete makes the gesture and sound of a missile taking off).* He shoots. Now, are we saying it's a likely thing? No. But, from the Soviet perspective, they HAVE to shoot. Under these conditions, holding back is clearly wrong, politically and militarily.

Pete.   And *that*—

Jim.   —is how a nuclear war begins.

Pete.   Not out of anger.

Jim.   Or greed.

Pete.   But *fear!*

Jim.   With neither side *wanting* to.

Pete.   Yet each side *having* to.

Jim.   'Cause the other guy thinks they're *going* to.

Pete.   So they'd better.

Pete and Jim *(Together, à la W. C. Fields).*   HOIST ON OUR OWN PETARD!

Jim.   By the way, where *is* the petard?

Pete *(Tossing a jar of mustard)*.   Petard!

Jim   *(Catching it)*. Petard!

Pete and Jim *(Together, à la W. C. Fields)*.   Ahhhh, yes!

Trent.   You guys are a scream.

Jim.   Actually—should we tell him?

Pete.   Sure.

Jim.   Actually, over at the center, we all try to scream at least once a day.

Pete.   Usually it happens in the cafeteria.

Jim.   Someone on the staff will stand up and shout "SCREAMIN' TIME!" And everyone just, you know . . . *(Gives a choked comic scream)*

Pete.   It's a ritual we only do when no one from the Pentagon's around.

Jim.   We did it once when some honcho military brass were there.

Pete.   *Freaked them out!*

Jim.   Within minutes we had lost I don't know *how* many grants! *(Laughs)*

Pete.   So, anyway, now we're pretty choosy 'bout who we scream in front of.

Jim.   I'll tell you . . . I sometimes think, if it really happens, and we all, you know . . . *(Makes the sound and gesture of a giant explosion)* . . . and by the way, the whole thing *could* be over! No matter what anybody says, no one knows *what* happens to the ozone layer in a nuclear war. Really! No idea! *(Laughs)* Okay, so I sometimes think, now it's all over, and we're all up there in the big debriefing space in the sky, and the Good Lord decides to hold a symposium 'cause he's curious: how did this thing happen? And everybody says, "Hey, don't look at me, I didn't wanna do it!" The end result being that everyone realizes *no* one wanted to do it! But there was suddenly no choice. Or no choice they could *see*. And the symposium gets nowhere.

Trent.   How do we get out of this?

Pete.   Well, you try like hell to not get *into* these kinds of conflicts!

Jim.   Obviously, sometimes it can't be helped.

Trent.   This is not pleasant news.

Pete *(Putting the birds into the microwave)*.   On the other hand, let's not exaggerate. Things are not that bad, maybe we *shouldn't* get out of it. *(With a laugh, to Jim)* Would you not love to have a snapshot of this man's expression?

Jim mimes taking a snapshot of Trent.

Trent.   So you mean we're just supposed to sit around, twiddle our thumbs, and WAIT?

Pete.   Well . . .

Jim.   Sometimes . . . there's really not an awful lot you *can* do.

Pete.   Except *hold on.*

Jim.   And hope for some kind of discontinuity.

Pete.   Right.

Trent.   Ah! Discontinuity! What the hell is that?

Pete.   It's an event . . . by definition unpredictable, which causes a sudden and radical shift in the general mode of thinking.

Jim.   Sadat's going to Jerusalem is the prime example.

Pete.   Sadat looked down the road and saw nuclear weapons in Cairo and Alexandria in maybe five, ten years, and he just didn't like what he saw.

Jim.   So he decided he was gonna do something about it.

Pete.   And what he decided to do no one, I mean *no* one, anticipated.

Jim.   And it changed the whole ball game.

Pete.   *Just like that!*

Jim.   And THAT—

Pete.   —is a discontinuity.

Trent.   Okay! all right! . . . any candidates?

Pete.   Well, I'd say the best we've come up with so *far* is . . . *(Looks to Jim for help)*

Jim *(To Pete)*.   Extraterrestrial?

Pete.   Yah. *(To Trent)* Extraterrestrial.

Trent *(Stunned)*.   You mean, like E.T. comes down?

Pete.   You got it!

Trent.   Jesus Christ!

Jim.   That's another!

Trent.   You guys are a riot!

Jim.   Hey! In this business? Important to keep smiling.

Trent.   No, I can see that. Listen, have you guys given any real thought to, you know, touring the country? Nightclubs, things like that?

Pete.   Oh, sure, it's occurred to us.

Trent.   I'm sure it has.

Jim.   People are very interested in this nuclear issue.

Pete.   And we're right there at the dirty heart of it!

Trent.   Good. Listen, while we're on the subject of humor, what's your attitude toward doom?

Pete.   . . . *Doom?*

Pete looks at Jim. Jim looks at Pete.

Jim.   It's just no solution.

Pete.   No. No solution.

Trent.   I'm being serious!

Pete and Jim *(Together)*.   So are we! *(They smile at Trent)*

Blackout on Jim and Pete. Trent turns to the audience. Music: "Trent's Theme."

Trent.   Okay. Even with *my* lousy sinuses, I could tell something wasn't smelling right. I figured it was *my* fault. What've I missed? I decided to retrace my steps. *(Trent's office has begun to reappear)* The next day I was back in my office in Stamford, going through all my notes, when Stella came in with a rather large package.

Enter Stella pushing a huge flat object wrapped in plain brown paper.

Stella.   Boy, is this big!

On the wrapper, crayoned in enormous black letters, are these words:

MICHAEL TRENT—PLAYWRIGHT
and
DETECTIVE

Trent.   Hey, dollface, what gives?
Stella.   I dunno. I found it in the hallway. Someone left it outside your door.
   I had t' bring it in, 'cause otherwise I couldn't get out. *(Starts to unwrap it)*
Trent.   *(To audience).*   It had no return address.

Inside the package is an oversized, framed photograph. This is the photograph:

Crazy Crate, photograph by Dr. Cochran

Trent and Stella stare at it in silence.

Stella.   Hey, Mike, how do ya *build* a box like that?

Trent.   I dunno.

Stella.   Hey! Maybe there's instructions in the back. *(Checks in back)* Mikey! Look! . . . A card.

Stella hands the small white card to Trent. Trent, not needing to read, moves toward the audience. As he does, Stella, the box, and the office disappear into the dark.

Trent *(To audience)*.   The card said, "If you want help with your quest, be in Washington tomorrow night, ten o'clock." And it was signed "The Shadow." *(There is the sound of a knock from the darkness behind him. Trent turns toward the sound)* It's open!

The door of his hotel room has appeared. It opens. The Man who appeared earlier is seen, silhouetted against a dazzlingly bright white hallway light.

Man in Hallway.   We're ready, Mr. Trent.

Trent.   Right! *(Blackout except for a pin-spot of light on Trent)* I am led down the backstairs to a car—an old Ford wagon. In the rear seat are two men. I get in. No one says a word to me. And the car pulls out . . . Fog moves in off the Potomac . . . We are heading toward the center of the capital, that much I can tell. We move at a crawl. Even the road is scarcely visible. *(Pause)* And then . . . the sky begins to *glow*. A dazzling milky phosphorescence! I have never seen anything like this in my life! And then I hear *music*. *(Music dimly heard)* . . . Band music. *(So it is)* And then I see the *source* of this strange light! *(Music louder)* We approach the Jefferson Memorial. On the grounds surrounding it are rows upon rows of giant klieg lights! The lawn— what I can see of it—is packed. Obviously, it's a concert of some sort. We pass near a clearing in the fog, and I see that in the crowd are many men in military uniforms! . . . The car stops. I can see a sign but can't make out what it says. The people who have brought me here tell me to get out. "But how will I recognize The Shadow?" I say. "Don't worry," they say. "But where should I walk?" "Wherever you wish." So I get out and the car drives off. *(Pause)* I head for the sign. The sign says: U.S. Marine Corps Band. *(Music louder)* Well, I don't like crowds in the best of times, and this is terrible! So I decide to go toward the Memorial, which looms through the fog like a spectral white mushroom. *(The interior of the Jefferson Memorial begins to form around him)* The rotunda is empty. I look down through the fog and can see . . . almost no one. *(Jefferson's statue can be discerned only in shape. The same for the surrounding columns)* And then I hear . . .

Footsteps suddenly moving toward him. Then they stop on the far side of a shimmering shaft of light caused by the klieg lights' piercing the fog. All we can see of this Man are the bottoms of his legs.

Man's Voice. Mr. Trent?
Trent. And I recognize the voice!

The Man walks toward Trent, through the eerie light. The first feature we see is that he is in uniform. But we can't yet make out his face. And then he moves forward, into a better light. It is General Wilmer. He smiles.

General Wilmer *(Warmly).* Shall we talk?

Beat. Blackout.

Act Three: The Discovery

Lights up on Trent in his trench coat.

Trent. Okay. I have proceeded systematically, I have followed my nose and have found the piece of the puzzle I was looking for. Unfortunately, instead of the puzzle being solved, the puzzle has expanded . . . I am a man who knows too much . . . and not enough. *Why me? Why has Stone picked me? (The cozy living room of Trent's house in Connecticut slides into view. Through rear windows, open, with curtains fluttering in a gentle spring breeze, we can see trees and a meadow)* By the way, this is my house in Connecticut—my beloved retreat to which I have retreated. Fat chance! About an hour ago, Stone called to say he was coming out to see how I'm doing. *How I'm doing!* . . . All right, the truth: I have told him the meeting with The Shadow was canceled. Actually, I didn't have the nerve to tell him this directly, I left a message. I've told the same thing to my agent and my wife. I need time to think things through! It's not an easy racket, writing plays; stay out of it!
Alex *(Offstage).* DAD!
Trent. That's my son. He's eleven.
Boy's Voice. I think your producer's here!
Trent. Great. Here it goes.
Boy's Voice. Should I tell Mom to let him in?
Trent. No-no! Let him find his own way in! *(To audience)* My wife is on the patio, in a chaise, reading Yeats. That's what life's like here in the country. Now, if things go well today—and at this point I've no idea just how that's possible—you won't be meeting either my wife *or* my son; as I said earlier, I don't want them involved in this!
Stone. TRENT!
Trent. The Call of the Wild! *(To Stone)* I'M IN THE LIVING ROOM, PHIL! *(To audience)* What you are about to see is scrambling of the highest order! *(Trent removes his trench coat. Enter Stone)* Phil! *(Stone stops and turns his*

gaze on Trent. He stares at Trent closely. Then, after a moment, Stone grins)
Well, I'm glad to see you're happy!

Stone walks slowly over to Trent and rests his hands on Trent's shoulders. Trent stares back, terrified. Stone continues to grin.

Stone.   I haven't seen you in such a long time!
Trent.   That's right! About . . . a month, I guess—maybe . . . more.
Stone.   Why was the meeting canceled?
Trent.   Oh! With, uhh, The Shadow? I don't know, they didn't say. Security, I suspect. I'm waiting now to see when it will be rescheduled.
Stone.   What makes you think it will be rescheduled?
Trent.   Well, that's what they said.
Stone.   And yet, for some reason, they neglected to tell you why it was canceled.
Trent.   No-no, uh, *security!* . . . I mean they, you know, *said* that. Said it. "Too risky for him to meet with you tonight"—that's what they said.

Enter Ann, Trent's wife. She is in her sixth month of pregnancy.

Ann.   Dear, Audrey has arrived.
Trent.   What?
Ann *(Going toward Stone).*   Hi! I'm Ann Trent.
Trent.   Ann! Out! Get out!
Ann.   *What?*

He rushes toward her.

Trent *(Sotto voce).*   Get out of here! Go! I'll tell you about it later. I don't want you involved in this! Out, get out! *(Leads/pushes/coaxes her out of the room as Audrey enters)* Audrey!
Stone.   I was not aware you were joining us today!
Audrey.   No. Nor was my client. Dear, I need to speak to you alone.
Trent *(Startled).*   Of course.
Audrey.   Mr. Stone, would you mind very much if my client and I went into—
Stone.   No, please, dear lady, you stay here, I can use the time to look around the house. I *love* country houses! And this is such a charming one. *(Exits)*

Trent stares after him, perplexed.

Trent.   Well, he's the weirdest man I've ever met!
Audrey.   Dear, I'm afraid I have some extremely bad news for you.
Trent.   Oh!
Audrey.   Could I have a drink?
Trent.   Uhhhh, right. Ummmm—

Audrey. *Martini.*

Trent. With an *olive!*

Audrey. No, dear. Lemon twist.

Trent. Right, of course. *(Heading for the bar)* So what's the, uh, bad news?

Audrey. Well. It seems, dear, that your producer has instituted legal action against you.

Trent. *What?*

Audrey. He is bringing suit against you, dear. For fraud and breach of contract.

Trent. WHAT?

Audrey. Sssh. Dear. Please.

Trent. *Why?*

Audrey. I'm not sure.

Trent. Well, how much is he suing me for? I mean, is it the retainer, the advance?

Audrey. I'm afraid it's a bit more than that.

Trent. How can it be for more, that's all I made!

Audrey. The suit is for fifteen million dollars.

Trent. Fifteen million DOLLARS?

Audrey. Yes, dear, dollars.

Trent. But that makes no SENSE!

Audrey. I know.

Trent. Maybe it's not dollars! Maybe it's zlotys!

Audrey. No, dear, dollars, Yankee dollars.

Trent. WHAT'S HE THINK I'VE GOT?

Audrey. Well . . . it's not worth a *great* deal . . . but you've got this house.

Trent *(Staring in direction that Stone went).* Oh, my God!

Audrey. Perhaps if you turned in your *script!*

Trent. Oh, come on, Audrey! No one sues a playwright for fifteen million dollars because he's a few weeks late delivering a script! I mean, what's he hope to gain? A house? He doesn't need another house!

Stone *(Who has entered, unnoticed).* It's not the house that interests me . . . It's your *ruination. (They turn to him, astonished)* And I expect your legal fees alone should accomplish that. You look surprised; that surprises me. Did you really think I'd allow your treachery to go unchallenged?

Trent. What are you talking about?

Stone. Sir, please, the time for innocence is past.

Audrey. *What* treachery?

Stone. Evidence suggests, madam, that your client has in fact found what he set *out* to find.

Trent. That's not TRUE!

Stone. And I believe otherwise.

Audrey. Michael, have you lied to Mr. Stone?

Trent. Not at all.

Audrey. You owe my client an apology.

Stone.   Tell this lady what you've done.

Trent.   *I don't know WHAT you are TALKING about.*

Stone.   Does the name "The Shadow" ring a bell?

Trent.   The meeting was called OFF!

Stone.   AND THAT, SIR, IS A LIE!

Audrey.   Mr. Stone, forgive me. If my client says the meeting was called off, the meeting was called off.

Stone.   I disagree.

Audrey.   Michael?

Trent.   It was called off.

Audrey.   The matter's closed.

Stone.   THIS MAN HAS VIOLATED THE TERMS OF OUR AGREE-MENT!

Audrey.   Mr. Stone!

Trent.   Audrey.

Audrey.   Dear, let me handle this! *(To Stone)* I believe the time has come, sir, for you to leave.

Stone *(To Trent)*.   Tell her what you've done.

Audrey.   Is there something wrong, sir, with your ears?

Trent.   Audrey.

Audrey.   I SAID STAY OUT OF THIS! I CAN HANDLE THIS! *(To Stone)* Mr. Stone, if my client says the meeting was called off, it was called off. My clients do not lie to me.

Trent *(Weakly)*.   Audrey, please.

Audrey.   DEAR, STAY OUT OF THIS! *(To Stone)* The matter's therefore closed. Except, sir, for your appalling lack of manners. Where, may I ask, were you brought up?

Trent.   I LIED!!!! *(She turns to him as if struck)* I lied, I lied! I'm sorry! *(He holds his head in his hands and fights tears. She does not know what to do, where to turn. She turns to Stone)*

Audrey *(To Stone)*.   Would you . . . be so kind . . .

Stone.   A drink?

Audrey.   Yes, please, some . . . water would be nice, I think. *(To Trent)* Why? Don't you trust me?

Trent.   Of course I trust you! This has nothing to do with trust! I just had no idea what to say. I haven't even told Ann! I've told no one!

Audrey *(Taking the glass from Stone)*.   I owe you an apology.

Stone.   Not at all.

Audrey *(To Trent)*.   I don't understand what's happening.

Trent *(To Stone, angrily)*.   Did you set the meeting up? *(Stone shakes his head no)* Then how do you know it happened?

Stone.   I've had you followed, sir. Ever since you accepted this job.

Trent.   Great!

Stone.   I should add, in all this time my emissaries have never actually seen you *writing*.

Trent.   What do you think, I write in the *street?* I write in my OFFICE!

Stone.   Good! Then you can show me some pages.

Trent.   *Pages?*

Stone.   Sir, doom approaches, I need pages.

Trent.   ANYONE CAN WRITE PAGES!

Stone.   I ask only to see yours.

Trent.   Well, I never show pages till I'm done. Audrey can confirm this. Audrey, are you all right? *(She nods)* Anyhow, the important thing isn't pages, the important thing is *concept!* CONCEPT is what we should be talking about! Without a concept, a play is nothing.

Stone.   Sir, a play may be nothing without a concept—without pages, it is even less.

Trent.   Who said that? Aristotle, I believe.

Audrey *(Sotto voce).*   Dear, this man is *suing* you!

Trent.   Okay, fine, you want pages? I'll give you pages! I've got pages *here*— *(Runs to a drawer, opens it)*—and in here—*(Opens another drawer)*—pages everywhere! You want pages? Here! Pages! *(Starts flinging the pages into the air. Stone looks down at them)*

Stone.   These are not pages from a play!

Trent.   Right! For that, you need a CONCEPT!

Audrey.   *Michael.*

Trent *(To Audrey, sotto voce).*   I'm okay, I know what I'm doing. Really. *(To Stone)* Now, do you want to hear what my concept is? Because I will tell you. Gladly. Because this is a concept I am wild about! And it took a long time finding. In fact, I only found it today. But well worth the waiting, because this concept means this play will be *fun.*

Stone.   *What?*

Trent.   Fun! Fun to write, fun to look at.

Audrey.   Dear, are we talking about the same play?

Trent.   Of course! The play that deals with doom! Going to be fun! So you want to hear what this concept is? Okay, here it is . . . *(Very long pause, during which time he takes out a cigarette and hopes that a concept will come. The lighting of the cigarette, in a kind of Philip Marlowe way, seems to do the trick. A look of astonishment comes over his face, which he masks from the others)* The playwright . . . is conceived . . . as being very much like a *detective. (To Audrey)* Wha'd'ya think?

Stone.   *What* playwright?

Trent.   The playwright who's at the CENTER of this play!

Stone.   What's a playwright doing in this play?

Trent.   He's in this play because he is the only reality I can hang on to here! And this playwright is sent on a *strannnnge* mission by a man, I would say quite like *you,* a kindly man, a man who would surely never, for example, sue anyone. And this playwright *respects* this man because this playwright is without doubt the very salt of the earth! Though possibly with some knowledge of evil—I still haven't figured that one out, I may have to come back

to you for that, I'm nowhere on that so far, that's the truth, I just can't remember where we met. *(Silence)* Okay, so this playwright, down he goes to
Washington, figuring if this mystery can be solved anywhere, there's the spot.

Audrey.   Dear, what happened down in Washington?

Trent.   The case took a turn for the worse, all right? I didn't think it possible.

Audrey.   Michael, *please!*

Trent.   I DO NOT BELIEVE WHAT THE SHADOW TOLD ME, OKAY?
And there you are. Now, what am I to do with that?

Enter Ann Trent, carrying a tea tray.

Ann.   Tea time!

Trent *(Angry, sotto voce)*.   Ann, I asked you specifically—

Ann.   Dear, I am not coming to sit in on your meeting, this is *your* meeting,
not mine. *(To Audrey and Stone)* I just thought you might all like some iced
tea. The mint is from the garden. *(To Trent, sotto voce)* I was being *nice*. You
might try the same. *(She sets the tray down and leaves. Silence)*

Stone.   When is your wife due?

Trent.   Uh, due where? . . . Oh! Uhhh, she's, let's see, in her sixth month,
so in four, I mean three. Unless doom strikes first, of course. I'm sorry, I'm
just very edgy today.

*Ann comes back in, holding the sugar bowl. She comes face to face with a glow-
ering Trent. She puts the bowl down on the floor.*

Ann.   The sugar.

She tiptoes back out.

Stone.   She's very graceful, your wife.

Trent.   Yes. *(Silence)* Look, you want to know what happened down in Washington? You show me what to do with it, I'll tell you what happened. Is that
fair? Fair enough? Terrific. This guy, The Shadow, he says, "Okay, tell me
what you *think* you know." So I started in. I told him I thought the notion
of using nuclear weapons to prevent the use of nuclear weapons—*(To Audrey)*—which is the system we depend upon—*(To them both)*—simply doesn't
work, not in the *long* run, too many places where the system just plain breaks
down! Breakdown, in fact, I said, seems built in. What we've got, I said, is
a fail-safe built-in breakdown machine. He said: "So how can I help you?"
I said I want to know where I've gone wrong. He said: "You're not wrong.
You've *got it!*"*(Audrey stares at him, stunned. To Stone, with a gesture toward Audrey)* I would think my expression probably looked a bit like that!
(To them both) I said, "Wait, hold on, you're telling me the system doesn't
work?" He said: "Why are you surprised? That's what you told me." I said:
"But I didn't think I was right!" He said: "Well, you are." I said: "Well then,

how come you and I are the only two who seem to know it?" You know what he said? Hold on to your seats, folks. He said actually *everybody* knew. It was common knowledge.

Audrey.   . . . Dear, that makes no sense.

Trent *(Excitedly)*.   That's right! Of COURSE it makes no sense! But WHY does it make no sense?

Audrey.   Well . . . *(Pause)* Well, because if everyone knows . . . that what they're working on doesn't *work* . . .

Trent.   . . . Yes?

Audrey   . . . Why would they keep working?

Trent.   EXACTLY!

Audrey.   I assume these are people who can find other jobs.

Alex *(Offstage)*.   DAD, CAN I ASK YOU A QUESTION?

Trent.   No! And stay out of here. Go to your room. *(Back to Audrey and Stone)* All right. So I asked what you asked: If they know it doesn't work, why do they keep working? . . . *"Because they don't believe what they know!"* *(Audrey stares at him blankly)* Look, look, they know it doesn't work, okay? I mean, they've run the charts, the projections, intellectually they are fine, they understand, *but* they just can't BELIEVE it! Why? Because it SEEEEEEMS as if it should work. It's worked so far, right? So why not forever? You see? Logic! Worst thing that's ever *happened* to man! Oh, my God!

Audrey.   What?

Trent.   Down in Washington? Where I went to interview all these guys? There was something on their walls. I mean, each one had it. And I remember thinking: I wonder if these guys belong to some kind of club. Anyway, I didn't give it too much thought . . . Other guys, they put up posters of Bo Derek. These guys—they had Escher prints! *(Pause)* The Shadow! Let me show you how he got in touch with me! *(Looks up)* DOWN!

The photograph of the "crazy crate" descends on wires.

Audrey *(To audience)*.   Aren't playwrights' houses *wonderful!*

Trent.   Look. You see? It doesn't work! And yet it *does*. It's not possible! And yet it *is*.

Audrey.   How does one *construct* an object like this?

Trent.   Not quite sure.

Audrey.   I'd love one in my office.

Trent.   So would I. Here's the Escher print they all had. DOWN!

Another hugely oversized print descends on wires, this one larger even than the first. Audrey stares up, puzzled.

Audrey.   Dear, what's happened to your second floor? *(Now she sees the picture)* . . . Well, there's something very wrong with this.

They stare at the picture.

This is the picture that descends:

Waterfall, 1961 by M. C. Escher

Audrey.   I'm afraid I'm quite confused. How does one get the water to flow both up and down?

Trent.   It's a puzzler. (*Snaps his fingers, and the Escher print disappears*)

Audrey.   Thank you, dear.

Trent.   Okay, what he said so far, that the system doesn't work, that I can accept. But I said, "Surely, not *everyone* is like this. *Some* must believe what they know. You, for instance." "Absolutely," he said. "So, then, why are *you* working on it?" And he grinned . . . and said, *"Guess."* *(Silence)* Well, I was stumped. So I went back to the very first question I'd asked him, weeks before: "If the system doesn't work, why do we need more weapons?" His answer remained the same: we need more so we can strike first.

Audrey.   What!

Trent.   It's a defensive act.

Audrey.   Hitting someone first is a *defensive* act?

Trent.   If you know he's planning to hit you.

Audrey.   Why would he be planning to hit you?

Trent.   Because he thinks you're planning to hit him.

Audrey.   Well . . . he's *right.*

Trent.   There you are.

Audrey.   Dear, by this scheme, nobody does anything *offensive.*

Trent.   Exactly. Every act of aggression is defensive here. It's a completely moral system!

Audrey.   Well, something's wrong with it!

Trent.   I know.

Audrey.   Not quite sure what.

Trent.   It's a puzzler! *(To Stone)* So I said to him, "This is crazy, this is suicidal! If we strike first, they'll just retaliate, and wipe us out in return!"

Audrey.   THAT'S what's wrong with it!

Trent.   That's just one of them.

Audrey.   With one like that, you don't *need* any more.

Trent.   Exactly! And he agreed! *"That's why we've abandoned deterrence."* *(Looks to Audrey for her response)*

Audrey.   . . . What?

Trent.   Exactly! WHAT? I mean, even if deterrence *doesn't* work, it works a *bit.* You don't just chuck it out, not without a substitute! Not a substitute, he said. An *improvement!* . . . And he grinned and said: "It seems, at least in theory, that a better mousetrap has been designed!" . . . Look, he said, an attack by us right now is suicidal because the enemy can always retaliate and wipe us out. However—what if we could *prevent* retaliation? "Well, in the future," he said, "which is what we're working toward, we think it may be possible, technologically, to do just this. And if we *can*, even if for the briefest time, a week, a month, create some kind of invulnerable window shade allowing our missiles out but nothing in, a kind of 'ion curtain'—incoming missiles hit it, bam! they disintegrate; then, in that brief moment of invulnerability, we can just . . . *take care of things."*

Audrey.   That's barbaric!

Trent.   Ahhhh! Watch! No! Not at all! It's *defensive!* It's defensive because the Russians are working on the very same plan!

Audrey.   How do we know?

Trent.   Well, if *we* are, they *have* to be. Just in case *we* are. Which means *they* are—you see? Defensive! Again, a completely moral system. *(To Stone)*

I *told* you this was fun! *(To Audrey)* BUT! *(To Stone)* Here's the best part. *(To Audrey)* Here's the *twist!* Even *this* doesn't work. *(To them both)* Watch! Let's say this ion curtain has been built and Sears has it, we call up and order one. Two weeks for delivery, they say. Well, that's not so bad, so we say send it on. PROBLEM: Surely the Soviets know somebody who works for Sears. "Psst! Guess what the Americans have just ordered!" Well! The Soviets know what's in store for them if we get this thing. Which means they have got to preempt. Whch means we must PRE—preempt! We're right back where we started! You cannot beat the system, not from within; it simply doesn't work, *cannot* work, not in ANY permutation! It's that goddamn Escher print. "Right!" he said. And I could see his eyes—they were on FIRE! I mean, this man was *excited!* I thought, Am I dreaming this? This makes no sense! *(Pause)* And a moment later he was gone, in the fog, by the bandstand.

Long silence.

Audrey.   Dear, there's something very *wrong* here, something . . . you have *missed*, I think, I couldn't . . . say, of course, just *what*, I'm not an expert, dear, but clearly somewhere in your research you've gone wrong, that's just obvious, because this just makes no sense, as you yourself have even pointed out. *(Pause)* I mean, the world you are describing, dear, this is not a world I know. Furthermore, it's not a world I *care* to know, that's the truth, dear, I don't want to know any more. I think I need some air . . . Perhaps a stroll across the field! It's such a lovely day. Not the sort of day one wants to spend inside! *(She smiles and goes to get her purse. She stops near Stone. Pause)* Mr. Stone, if you would be so kind as to help him. Show him where he's wrong. I don't think I can be much more help to him on this . . . Not right now. I need to think this through. *(She stares at Trent. Pause)* Keep with it, dear. *(She walks out. Long pause)*
Trent.   Is this what you mean by doom? That no one will believe?
Stone.   Not quite. *(He smiles ever so faintly. Then he rises and pours himself a glass of iced tea)*
Trent.   Look, Stone, I am stumped, all right? I am at the end! What the hell was The Shadow up to? And why have you picked me for this?

Stone stares at him. Pause.

Stone.   Have you ever been to the South Pacific?
Trent *(Puzzled)*.   No.
Stone.   Remarkable place! Beautiful beyond imagining! The imagination belittles its beauty. *(Pause)* Anyway, I was there in the early fifties. A close friend of mine was involved in our nuclear tests and asked if I'd like to go along on the viewing ship. It was not inappropriate for me to be there, for among my many financial interests at that time was a laboratory and development center. It was in Utah.

Trent. . . . You make weapons?

Stone *(Slight smile).*   I used to. *(Pause)* In any event, there we were on this ship, this battleship, not too far from where the detonation was to take place, which was near an island known, interestingly enough, as Christmas Island. *(Smiles. Pause)* We'd been told the bomb was to be a small one, and so none of us was particularly worried. Even though I'd never seen one go off, I figured, well, these people must know what they are doing! *(Pause)* Actually, the truth is I was in a kind of funk! That's because I hadn't come all this way just to see a *little* bomb! This one was ten kilotons, smaller even than the bomb at Hiroshima! These bombs were classified as *tactical* weapons. These are weapons you would use in combat. And, quite frankly, I was disappointed. I wanted some BIG-time stuff, and I'm not ashamed to say it, either. There's a glitter to nuclear weapons. I had sensed it in others and *felt it in myself.* If you come to these things as a scientist, it is irresistible, to feel it's there in your hands, so to speak, the ability to release this energy that fuels the stars! . . . to make it do your bidding! to make it perform these miracles! to lift a million tons of rock into the sky. And all from a thimbleful of stuff. *Irresistible! (Pause)* Well, we were standing by the railing when the countdown came on, we could hear it over the P-A. We'd all been adequately briefed, and we were in suits, some kind of lead, tinted visors on our helmets. And then I saw these . . . *birds.* Albatrosses! Phenomenal creatures, truly! They'd been flying beside the ship for days, accompanying us to the site, so to speak. Watching them was a wonder! *(Pause. Then in a tone of great amazement)* And suddenly I could see that they were smoking. Their feathers were on fire! And they were doing cartwheels . . . The light persisted for some time. It was instantaneously bright, and lingered, long enough for me to see the birds crash into the water. *(Alex has come in unobserved by the others, and stands to the side, listening)* They were sizzling. Smoking! They were not vaporized, it's just that they were absorbing such intense radiation that they were being consumed by the heat! And so far there'd been no shock, none of the blast damage we talk about when we discuss the effects of these bombs. Instead, there were just these smoking, twisting, fantastically contorted birds crashing into things . . . And I could see vapor rising from the inner lagoon as the surface of the water was heated by the intense flash. *(Pause)* Well, I'd never seen anything like this in my life! . . . And I thought: *This is what it will be like at the end of time. (Pause)* And we all felt . . . the *thrill* of that idea. *(Long pause. Stone stares at Trent, who stares back at him in horror)* This is your son, I believe. *(Trent turns toward his son in horror. Alex looks frightened)* I've never met the lad, though of course I heard you speak of him many years ago. I guess he must be . . . eleven now. *(Trent turns toward Stone. Trent seems stunned by this last remark. To Alex)* I met your father shortly after you were born.

Trent is reeling now. He stares from one to the other.

Alex.   Was that a movie you saw?

Stone. Just now? Describing? *(Alex nods)* Yes. A movie. *(Alex nods and leaves. Trent stares out, stunned. The lights start to fade on everything but Trent)* I think I'm going to have some more iced tea! *(He crosses to the pitcher and pours himself a glass of tea. Soon Stone is but a shape in the dark)*

Light on Trent.

Trent. Now I know where we met! . . . It was at *our* place, our apartment! We were living in the city then, and some friends came by to see our child, he'd just been born; obviously, one of them brought Stone—who? doesn't matter, Stone was there, I can see him, in a corner, *listening*, as I . . . tell. *(Pause)* But *evil*? *(Long pause)* Our son had just been born. We'd brought him home. He was what, five days old, I guess. *(Pause)* And then one day my wife went out . . . And I was left alone with him. And I was very excited. Because it was the first time I was alone with him. And I picked him up, this tiny thing, and started walking around the living room. We lived on a high floor, overlooking the river, the Hudson. Light was streaming in; it was a lovely, lilting autumn day, cool, beautiful. And I looked down at this tiny creature, this tiny thing, and I realized . . . *(Pause)* I realized I had never had anyone completely in my power before! . . . And I'd never known what that *meant*! Never felt anything remotely like that before! And I saw I was standing near a window. And it was open. It was but a few feet away. And I thought: I could . . . *drop him out*! And I went *toward* the window, because I couldn't believe this thought had come into my head—*where had it come from?* Not one part of me felt anything for this boy but love, not one part! My wife and I had planned, we were both in love, there was no anger, no resentment, nothing dark in me toward him at all, no one could ever have been more in love with his child than I, as much yes, but not more, not more, and I was thinking: I can throw him out of here! . . . and then he will be falling ten, twelve, fifteen, twenty stories down, and as he's falling, I will be *unable to get him back*! . . . And I felt a *thrill*! I FELT A THRILL! IT WAS THERE! . . . And, of course, I resisted this. It wasn't hard to do, resisting wasn't hard . . . BUT I DIDN'T STAY BY THE WINDOW! . . . AND I CLOSED IT! I resisted by moving away; back into the room . . . And I sat down with him. *(Pause)* Well, there's not a chance I would have done it, not a chance! *(Pause)* But I couldn't *take* a chance, it was very, very . . . seductive. *(Pause. He looks at Stone. The lights come back a bit. Stone is sipping his tea, his eyes on Trent)* If doom comes . . . it will come in *that* way.
Stone. I would think.

Pause.

Trent. You want it to come, don't you!
Stone. What?
Trent. Doom. You'd like to see it come!

Stone.   No-no, of course not, that's ridiculous. *(He sips)* I just know that if it did, it would not be altogether without interest. I mean, it has its appeal, that's all I mean. It arouses my *curiosity*. *(Smiles)* But then, many things arouse my curiosity. Mustn't make too much of it. This is really good iced tea! My compliments to your wife. I think the secret is fresh mint, nothing like fresh mint; if you don't mind, I shall pick some from your garden when I leave. *(Pause)* I'm glad you've taken this job.

Trent.   Don't you understand, I can't write this play! Really, that's the truth, it is totally beyond me!

Stone puts his hands on Trent's shoulders.

Stone *(Warmly)*.   Work on it.

He turns and starts out. At the rear of the room, by the window, he stops and looks out. Then he looks back at Trent.

The lights go nearly to black on everything but Trent and the field outside the house. In this darkened room, Stone is but a shadowy presence. The curtains on the rear window flutter. Trent stares out, lost in thought. Through the rear window, Ann can be seen strolling out across the bright field, hand in hand with Alex.

QUESTIONS

1.   Presenting the playwright Michael Trent as a private eye adds a comic dimension to the play. But can you think of any serious reasons for this style of characterization? Why do you suppose Kopit made his central character a playwright?
2.   Toward the end of Act One, Trent and Stone discuss the fascinating temptation provided by the open window forty stories above the street. What is the relationship of that exchange to the play as a whole?   **3.**   What causes Trent to moan loudly as he pursues his research? Why does he not wish to read such stuff as "The Prompt and Delayed Effects of Thermonuclear Explosions"? How would you answer Trent's thematically central question: "WHAT SORT OF PEOPLE CAN *THINK ABOUT THAT STUFF EVERY DAY?*" Why does Trent differ from such people?   **4.**   What is the significance of the photograph of the Crazy Crate and the Escher print that appear in Act Two and Act Three, respectively?

WRITING TOPICS

1.   How does Stone's description in Act Three of an atomic bomb explosion relate to Trent's subsequent account of the temptation to drop his infant son from a high window? How does the word *thrill* figure in these speeches? What conclusion about the "end of the world" can one draw from them? Explain.   **2.**   Characters in the play, particularly Trent, frequently speak directly to the audience, sometimes even interrupting conversations with other characters. Is this violation of dramatic illusion distracting? Can it be justified? Analyze the cumulative effect of such interruptions and the play's insistence on including the audience.

The Presence of Death

QUESTIONS AND WRITING TOPICS

1. Although Gray's "Elegy Written in a Country Churchyard," Housman's "To an Athlete Dying Young," Ransom's "Bells for John Whiteside's Daughter," Auden's "In Memory of W. B. Yeats," and Roethke's "Elegy for Jane" employ different poetic forms, they all embody a poetic mode called *elegy*. Define *elegy* in terms of the characteristic tone of these poems. Compare the elegiac tone of these poems. **Writing Topic:** Compare the elegiac tone of one of these poems with the tone of Poe's "The Conqueror Worm" or Owen's "Dulce et Decorum Est" or Thomas's "Do Not Go Gentle into That Good Night."

2. What figurative language in the prose and poetry of this section is commonly associated with death itself? With dying? Contrast the characteristic imagery of this section with the characteristic imagery of love poetry. **Writing Topic:** Compare the imagery in Shakespeare's sonnet 18 with the imagery in sonnet 73.

3. In Tolstoy's "The Death of Iván Ilých," Bergman's *The Seventh Seal,* and Donne's sonnet "Death, Be Not Proud," death and dying are considered from a religious viewpoint. **Writing Topic:** Discuss whether these works develop a similar attitude toward death, or whether the attitudes they develop differ crucially.

4. State the argument against resignation to death made in Thomas's "Do Not Go Gentle into That Good Night." State the argument of Catherine Davis's reply, "After a Time." **Writing Topic:** Using these positions as the basis of your discussion, select for analysis two works that support Thomas's argument and two works that support Davis's.

5. Read chapters 8–10 in The Revelation of St. John the Divine in the New Testament. The opening of the "seventh seal" is described there, along with the consequences of that event. **Writing Topic:** Discuss whether the allusive title of Bergman's screenplay enhances or detracts from the story line and whether the knight and his friends are "saved" or "damned" at the end.

6. Yevtushenko, in his poem "People," writes, "Not people die but worlds die in them." **Writing Topic:** Illustrate the meaning of this line with a discussion of Bierce's "An Occurrence at Owl Creek Bridge" or Katherine Anne Porter's "The Jilting of Granny Weatherall" or Arna Bontemps's "A Summer Tragedy."

7. Discuss the attitude toward death developed in Mishima's "Patriotism." **Writing Topic:** Contrast the treatment of death in Mishima's "Patriotism" with the treatment of death developed in any other story in this section.

8. Although Bergman's *The Seventh Seal* and Kopit's *End of the World* both present a grim picture of the human condition, they are often funny. What function does humor serve in each play? **Writing Topic:** Which play embodies a more hopeful vision of the human condition? Discuss both plays in your response.

9. Which works in this section treat death and dying in a way that corresponds most closely with your own attitudes toward mortality? Which contradict your attitudes? **Writing Topic:** Isolate, in each case, the elements in the work responsible for your response and discuss them in terms of their "truth" or "falsity."

APPENDICES

The Vanity of the Artist's Dream, 1830 by Charles Bird King

APPENDICES

Poems About Poetry

Most of us would probably define poetry as a form of writing that employs rhyme and metrical regularity and deals with serious and "heavy" subjects (unless, of course, it's light verse). But you don't have to go further than the poems in this anthology to see that many poems do not use rhyme, have no metrical regularity, and deal with ordinary subjects in prosaic language. Maybe we can best define poetry (someone once did) as the kind of writing where the lines don't end at the same place on the right-hand side of the page. Here are a few poems about poetry, in which poets attempt to describe what it is, how it works, what it does, and why it does it.

Poetry   1921

MARIANNE MOORE   [1887–1972]

I, too, dislike it: there are things that are important beyond all
            this fiddle.
   Reading it, however, with a perfect contempt for it, one
            discovers in
it after all, a place for the genuine.
      Hands that can grasp, eyes
      that can dilate, hair that can rise
         if it must, these things are important not because a

high-sounding interpretation can be put upon them but because
            they are   10
   useful. When they become so derivative as to become
            unintelligible,
the same thing may be said for all of us, that we
      do not admire what
      we cannot understand: the bat
         holding on upside down or in quest of something to

eat, elephants pushing, a wild horse taking a roll, a tireless wolf
            under
   a tree, the immovable critic twitching his skin like a horse
            that feels a flea, the base-   20
      ball fan, the statistician—

> nor is it valid
>> to discriminate against 'business documents and
>
> school-books';[1] all these phenomena are important. One must
>> make a distinction
>> however: when dragged into prominence by half poets, the
>>> result is not poetry,
>> nor till the poets among us can be
>>> 'literalists of
>>> the imagination'—[2] above   30
>>>> insolence and triviality and can present
>
> for inspection, imaginary gardens with real toads in them, shall
>> we have
>> it. In the meantime, if you demand on the one hand,
>> the raw material of poetry in
>>> all its rawness and
>>> that which is on the other hand
>>>> genuine, then you are interested in poetry.

Pitcher   1960

ROBERT FRANCIS   [b. 1901]

His art is eccentricity, his aim
How not to hit the mark he seems to aim at,

His passion how to avoid the obvious,
His technique how to vary the avoidance.

The others throw to be comprehended. He
Throws to be a moment misunderstood.

Yet not too much. Not errant, arrant, wild,
But every seeming aberration willed.

Poetry
 [1] "Diary of Tolstoy (Dutton), p. 84. 'Where the boundary between prose and poetry lies, I shall never be able to understand. The question is raised in manuals of style, yet the answer to it lies beyond me. Poetry is verse; prose is not verse. Or else poetry is everything with the exception of business documents and school books' " [Moore's note].
 [2] "Yeats: *Ideas of Good and Evil* (A. H. Bullen), p. 182: 'The limitation of his view was from the very intensity of his vision; he was a too literal realist of imagination, as others are of nature; and because he believed that the figures seen by the mind's eye, when exalted by inspiration, were "eternal existences," symbols of divine essences, he hated every grace of style that might obscure their lineaments' " [Moore's note].

Not to, yet still, still to communicate
Making the batter understand too late.   10

QUESTIONS
1. The poem describes the art of the baseball pitcher. But the description is an extended metaphor for the art of the poet. Is the pitcher described accurately? **2.** Is the analogy between pitcher and poet apt? Explain.

Very Like a Whale   1945

OGDEN NASH [1902–1971]

One thing that literature would be greatly the better for
Would be a more restricted employment by authors of simile and metaphor.
Authors of all races, be they Greeks, Romans, Teutons or Celts,
Can't seem just to say that anything is the thing it is but have to go out of
    their way to say that it is like something else.
What does it mean when we are told
That the Assyrian came down like a wolf on the fold?[1]
In the first place, George Gordon Byron had had enough experience
To know that it probably wasn't just one Assyrian, it was a lot of Assyr-
    ians.
However, as too many arguments are apt to induce apoplexy and thus
    hinder longevity,
We'll let it pass as one Assyrian for the sake of brevity.   10
Now then, this particular Assyrian, the one whose cohorts were gleam-
    ing in purple and gold,
Just what does the poet mean when he says he came down like a wolf on
    the fold?
In heaven and earth more than is dreamed of in our philosophy there are
    a great many things,
But I don't imagine that among them there is a wolf with purple and gold
    cohorts or purple and gold anythings.

No, no, Lord Byron, before I'll believe that this Assyrian was actually
    like a wolf I must have some kind of proof;
Did he run on all fours and did he have a hairy tail and a big red mouth
    and big white teeth and did he say Woof woof?
Frankly I think it very unlikely, and all you were entitled to say, at the
    very most,

Very Like a Whale
    [1]Nash is responding to Lord Byron's "The Destruction of Sennacherib," a poetic account of the events in 2 Kings 19. Byron's poem appears on p. 1123.

Was that the Assyrian cohorts came down like a lot of Assyrian cohorts
    about to destroy the Hebrew host.
But that wasn't fancy enough for Lord Byron, oh dear me no, he had to
    invent a lot of figures of speech and then interpolate them,
With the result that whenever you mention Old Testament soldiers to
    people they say Oh yes, they're the ones that a lot of wolves dressed
    up in gold and purple ate them.   20
That's the kind of thing that's being done all the time by poets, from
    Homer to Tennyson;
They're always comparing ladies to lilies and veal to venison,
And they always say things like that the snow is a white blanket after a
    winter storm.
Oh it is, is it, all right then, you sleep under a six-inch blanket of snow
    and I'll sleep under a half-inch blanket of unpoetical blanket material
    and we'll see which one keeps warm,
And after that maybe you'll begin to comprehend dimly
What I mean by too much metaphor and simile.

In My Craft or Sullen Art   1946

DYLAN THOMAS [1914–1953]

In my craft or sullen art
Exercised in the still night
When only the moon rages
And the lovers lie abed
With all their griefs in their arms,
I labor by singing light
Not for ambition or bread
Or the strut and trade of charms
On the ivory stages
But for the common wages   10
Of their most secret heart.
Not for the proud man apart
From the raging moon I write
On these spindrift pages
Nor for the towering dead
With their nightingales and psalms
But for the lovers, their arms
Round the griefs of the ages,
Who pay no praise or wages
Nor heed my craft or art.   20

A Poem about a Poem about a Poem

1961

ROBERT CONQUEST [b. 1917]

". . . *often writes not about life but poetry*"—[a critic]

To gallop horses (or eat buns)
  Is Life, and may be Song,
(To sink drains or interpret dreams
Or listen to a Baby's screams)
But not to write a poem, it seems.
    That isn't Life, it's wrong.

And yet—at least I thought so once
  The time I wrote those lines—
To ride a verse is quite a thing,
(Sinking a rhyme, interpreting   10
The wordless cry, the concept's ring.
  The field of sensuous signs.)

But let the bays, the greys, the duns
  Go pounding round the course.
Stallions may sometimes turn vicious.
But art gets so damned meretricious.
Yes, horses are better than wishes:
  I wish I had a horse.

Constantly Risking Absurdity   1958

LAWRENCE FERLINGHETTI [b. 1919]

    Constantly risking absurdity
                    and death
            whenever he performs
                    above the heads
                            of his audience
        the poet like an acrobat
                climbs on rime
                    to a high wire of his own making
    and balancing on eyebeams
                    above a sea of faces   10
        paces his way

to the other side of day
performing entrechats
and sleight-of-foot tricks
and other high theatrics
and all without mistaking
any thing
for what it may not be

For he's the super realist
who must perforce perceive   20
taut truth
before the taking of each stance or step
in his supposed advance
toward that still higher perch
where Beauty stands and waits
with gravity
to start her death-defying leap

And he
a little charleychaplin man
who may or may not catch   30
her fair eternal form
spreadeagled in the empty air
of existence

The Writer   1976

RICHARD WILBUR   [b. 1921]

In her room at the prow of the house
Where light breaks, and the windows are tossed with linden,
My daughter is writing a story.

I pause in the stairwell, hearing
From her shut door a commotion of typewriter-keys
Like a chain hauled over a gunwale.

Young as she is, the stuff
Of her life is a great cargo, and some of it heavy:
I wish her a lucky passage.

But now it is she who pauses,   10
As if to reject my thought and its easy figure.
A stillness greatens, in which

The whole house seems to be thinking.
And then she is at it again with a bunched clamor
Of strokes, and again is silent.

I remember the dazed starling
Which was trapped in that very room, two years ago;
How we stole in, lifted a sash

And retreated, not to affright it;
And how for a helpless hour, through the crack of the door,   20
We watched the sleek, wild, dark

And iridescent creature
Batter against the brilliance, drop like a glove
To the hard floor, or the desk-top,

And wait then, humped and bloody,
For the wits to try it again; and how our spirits
Rose when, suddenly sure,

It lifted off from a chair-back,
Beating a smooth course for the right window
And clearing the sill of the world.
                                                                30
It is always a matter, my darling,
Of life or death, as I had forgotten. I wish
What I wished you before, but harder.

QUESTIONS
1. What is the relationship between the "dazed starling" and the young writer? **2.** What is the significance of the alternate clamor of the typewriter and silence? **3.** What does the speaker wish for his daughter?

WRITING TOPIC
How do the central metaphors of the poem, the ship (stanzas 1–3) and the bird (6–10), convey the theme?

A Poet's Progress   1950

MICHAEL HAMBURGER   [b. 1924]

Like snooker balls thrown on the table's faded green,
Rare ivory and weighted with his best ambitions,
At first his words are launched: not certain what they mean,

He loves to see them roll, rebound, assume positions
Which—since not he—some power beyond him has assigned.

But now the game begins: dead players, living critics
Are watching him—and suddenly one eye goes blind,
The hand that holds the cue shakes like a paralytic's,
Till every thudding, every clinking sound portends
New failure, new defeat. Amazed, he finds that still   10
It is not he who guides his missiles to their ends
But an unkind geometry that mocks his will.

If he persists, for years he'll practise patiently,
Lock all the doors, learn all the tricks, keep noises out,
Though he may pick a ghost or two for company
Or pierce the room's inhuman silence with a shout.
More often silence wins; then soon the green felt seems
An evil playground, lawless, lost to time, forsaken,
And he a fool caught in the water weeds of dreams
Whom only death or frantic effort can awaken.   20

At last, a master player, he can face applause,
Looks for a fit opponent, former friends, emerges;
But no one knows him now. He questions his own cause,
And has forgotten why he yielded to those urges,
Took up a wooden cue to strike a coloured ball.
Wise now, he goes on playing; both his house and heart
Unguarded solitudes, hospitable to all
Who can endure the cold intensity of art.

For Saundra   1968

NIKKI GIOVANNI   [b. 1943]

i wanted to write
a poem
that rhymes
but revolution doesn't lend
itself to be-bopping

then my neighbor
who thinks i hate
asked—do you ever write
tree poems—i like trees
so i thought   10

i'll write a beautiful green tree poem
peeked from my window
to check the image
noticed the school yard was covered
with asphalt
no green—no trees grow
in manhattan

then, well, i thought the sky
i'll do a big blue sky poem

but all the clouds have winged   20
low since no-Dick[1] was elected

so i thought again
and it occurred to me
maybe i shouldn't write
at all
but clean my gun
and check my kerosene supply

perhaps these are not poetic
times
at all   30

Today Is a Day of Great Joy   1968

VICTOR HERNANDEZ CRUZ   [b. 1949]

when they stop poems
in the mail & clap
their hands & dance to
them
when women become pregnant
by the side of poems
the strongest sounds making
the river go along

it is a great day

as poems fall down to   10

For Saundra
[1] A derogatory reference to Richard Nixon.

movie crowds in restaurants
in bars

when poems start to
knock down walls to
choke politicians
when poems scream &
begin to break the air

that is the time of
true poets that is
the time of greatness   20

a true poet aiming
poems & watching things
fall to the ground

it is a great day.

The Poet's Craft

One of the discoveries a student of poetry quickly makes is that a good poem grows in richness and subtlety with rereading and close scrutiny. We grasp the theme of the poem perhaps on first reading, but on further reading and analysis, we discover that a particular word is charged with more meaning than we had thought or that an image relates to other parts of the poem in ways the first reading did not reveal. The excitement that comes from discovering something new and enriching in a poem is one of the great pleasures of studying poetry. Soon, however, the excitement is dampened for many readers as they inevitably begin to ask themselves, "Did the poet really intend to put this or that into the poem, or are we just demonstrating a cleverness and supersubtlety that would surprise the poet as much as it disquiets us?"

The question cannot be answered with direct evidence because most poets do not give us statements about their intentions in writing a particular poem. But many poets have left records, in the form of notebooks and journals, of early versions of their poems. An examination of these early versions shows very clearly that most finished poems are the result of painstaking and often protracted revision as the poet searches for the right word, the right phrase, the right sequence of image and idea to embody his theme. That poets work with such care and calculation suggests a general answer to our question: What we find in a good poem is more likely than not the result of the poet's skill, assuming that we are attending to the whole poem and not just free associating from some part of it.

A comparison of the drafts with the final versions of the three poems below provides a fascinating glimpse into the process of poetic creation. A careful consideration of why particular changes were made will probably make for a fuller understanding of the final version. But more important for our purposes here, your analysis will be an exercise in close and subtle reading firmly grounded in different versions. While the reasons you offer for changes will be speculative and not subject to any kind of definitive proof, the poet did make these changes for *some* reason. Thus, although we can rarely, if ever, know what the poet intended, our detailed knowledge of how poems are written makes equally clear that what we find in a poem is probably the result of the poet's skill, not chance or our clever imaginings.

In the drafts, variants and deletions are indicated by brackets. Line numbers in the questions refer to the final version.

LONDON (WILLIAM BLAKE, 1757–1827)

I wander through each chartered[1] street,
Near where the chartered Thames does flow
And mark in every face I meet
Marks of weakness, marks of woe.

In every cry of every man,
In every infant's cry of fear,
In every voice; in every ban,
The mind-forged manacles I hear:

How the chimney-sweeper's cry
Every blackening church appalls,   10
And the hapless soldier's sigh
Runs in blood down palace-walls.

But most, through midnight streets I hear
How the youthful harlot's curse
Blasts the new-born infant's tear,
And blights with plagues the marriage-hearse.

LONDON (notebook version, 1793)

I wander thro' each dirty street,
Near where the dirty Thames does flow,
And [see] mark in every face I meet
Marks of weakness, marks of woe.

In every cry of every man
In [every voice of every child]
   every infant's cry of fear
In every voice, in every ban
The [german] mind forg'd [links I hear] manacles I hear.

London
  [1] Preempted by the state and leased out under royal patent.

[But most] How the chimney sweeper's cry
[Blackens o'er the churches' walls]   10
Every black'ning church appalls,
And the hapless soldier's sigh·
Runs in blood down palace walls.

[But most the midnight harlot's curse
From every dismal street I hear,
Weaves around the marriage hearse
And blasts the new born infant's tear.]

But most [from every] thro' wintry streets I hear
How the midnight harlot's curse   20
Blasts the new born infant's tear,
And [hangs] smites with plagues the marriage hearse.

But most the shrieks of youth I hear
But most thro' midnight & . . . .
How the youthful . . .

QUESTIONS

1. How does the change from "dirty" to "chartered" (ll. 1–2) help establish the theme of the poem?   **2.** Suggest why Blake changed "see" to "mark" in line 3. **3.** Would it have made any significant difference if Blake had retained "In every voice of every child" as line 6? Explain.   **4.** Look up the meaning and derivation of "appalls" and then consider what Blake achieves by the revision of line 10.

THE LAST LAUGH (WILFRED OWEN, 1893–1918)

'O Jesus Christ! I'm hit,' he said; and died.
Whether he vainly cursed, or prayed indeed,
The Bullets chirped—In vain! vain! vain!
Machine-guns chuckled,—Tut-tut! Tut-tut!
And the Big Gun guffawed.

Another sighed,—'O Mother, mother! Dad!'
Then smiled, at nothing, childlike, being dead.
   And the lofty Shrapnel-cloud

Leisurely gestured,—Fool!
And the falling splinters tittered.   10

'My Love!' one moaned. Love-languid seemed his mood,
Till, slowly lowered, his whole face kissed the mud.
   And the Bayonets' long teeth grinned;
   Rabbles of Shells hooted and groaned;
   And the Gas hissed.

LAST WORDS (early version of THE LAST LAUGH)

"O Jesus Christ!" one fellow sighed.
And kneeled, and bowed, tho' not in prayer, and died.
   And the Bullets sang "In Vain,"
   Machine Guns chuckled "Vain,"
   Big Guns guffawed "In Vain."

"Father and mother!" one boy said.
Then smiled—at nothing, like a small child; being dead.
   And the Shrapnel Cloud
   Slowly gestured "Vain,"   10
   The falling splinters muttered "Vain."

"My love!" another cried, "My love, my bud!"
Then, gently lowered, his whole face kissed the mud.
   And the Flares gesticulated, "Vain."
   The Shells hooted, "In Vain,"
   And the Gas hissed, "In Vain."

QUESTIONS
1. What does Owen achieve in dramatic effect by the revision of the first two lines? **2.** How does Owen's changing the exact rhymes of the first version to the off rhymes of the final version affect the meaning of the poem? **3.** What insights into the revision of line 7 are provided by scanning the poem? **4.** Suggest why Owen abandoned the "In Vain" motif in the final version. **5.** Examine the changes in verbs. What effect do the changes have on the tone of the poem?

THE SECOND COMING (WILLIAM BUTLER YEATS, 1865–1939)

Turning and turning in the widening gyre°   spiral
The falcon cannot hear the falconer;
Things fall apart; the center cannot hold;
Mere anarchy is loosed upon the world,
The blood-dimmed tide is loosed, and everywhere
The ceremony of innocence is drowned;
The best lack all conviction, while the worst
Are full of passionate intensity.

Surely some revelation is at hand;
Surely the Second Coming is at hand;   10
The Second Coming! Hardly are those words out
When a vast image out of *Spiritus Mundi* [1]
Troubles my sight: somewhere in sands of the desert
A shape with lion body and the head of a man,
A gaze blank and pitiless as the sun,
Is moving its slow thighs, while all about it
Reel shadows of the indignant desert birds.
The darkness drops again; but now I know
That twenty centuries of stony sleep   20
Were vexed to nightmare by a rocking cradle,
And what rough beast, its hour come round at last,
Slouches towards Bethlehem to be born?

THE SECOND COMING (first full draft)

Turning and turning in the wide gyre [widening gyre]
The falcon cannot hear the falconer
[Things fall apart, the centre has lost]
Things fall apart—the centre cannot hold
[Vile] Mere anarchy is loose there on the world
The blood stained flood [dim tide] is loose and anarchy
[The good are wavering and intensity]
The best [lose] lack all conviction while the worst
Are full of passionate intensity.

The Second Coming
    [1] The Soul or Spirit of the Universe, which Yeats believed constituted a fund of racial images
and memories.

Surely some revelation is at hand   10
[The cradle at Bethlehem has rocked must leap anew]
[Surely the great falcon must come]
[Surely the hour of the second birth is here]
[Surely the hour of the second birth has struck]
[The second Birth! Scarce have those] words been spoken
The second [Birth] coming. [Scarce have the words been spoken]
[Before the dark was cut as with a knife]
And new intensity rent as it were cloth
And a [stark] lost image out of spiritus mundi
Troubles my sight. [Waste of sand]—A waste of desert sand   20
A shape with lion's body & with and the head [breast and head] of a
    man
[An eye] A gaze blank and pitiless as the sun
[Move with a slow slouching step]
Moves its slow [feet] thighs while all about its head
[An angry crowd of desert]
[Fall] [Run] shadows of the [desert birds they] indignant desert birds
The darkness drops again but now I know
[For] That twenty centuries of [its] stony sleep
[Were vexed & all but broken by the second]   30
Were vexed to nightmare by a rocking cradle
[And now at last]
[And now at last knowing its hour come round]
And what [at last] [wild thing] rough beast its hour come round at last
    knowing the hour [come round]
[It slouches towards Bethlehem to be born]
It has set out for Bethlehem to be born
It has set out for Bethlehem to be born
[Is slouching] towards Bethlehem to be born
Slouches towards Bethlehem to be born

QUESTIONS
1. Can you suggest why "Reel" (l. 17) is a better word than "Fall" or "Run"?
2. After many trials, Yeats decided on "The Second Coming" rather than "The
Second Birth" for line 10. Can you suggest why (aside from number of syllables)
Yeats decided as he did? **3.** Examine the changes Yeats made in the description
of the sphinx (ll. 14–16). Does the description in the final version represent an
improvement over that of the draft version? Why? **4.** In the draft version of line
19, Yeats used the pronoun "its" to modify "stony sleep," making clear that these
words refer to the sphinx. Does the deletion of the pronoun in the final version
weaken the poem by making "stony sleep" ambiguous? Explain.

Reading Fiction

An author is a god, creator of the world he describes. That world has a limited and very special landscape. It is peopled with men and women of a particular complexion, of particular gifts and failings. Its history, almost always, is determined by the tight interaction of its people within its narrow geography. Everything that occurs in a work of fiction—every figure, every tree, every furnished room and crescent moon and dreary fog—has been *purposely* put there by its creator. When a story pleases, when it moves its reader, he has responded to that carefully created world. The pleasure, the emotional commitment, the human response are not results of analysis. The reader has not registered in some mental adding machine the several details that establish character, the particular appropriateness of the weather to the events in the story, the marvelous rightness of the furnishings, the manipulation of the point of view, the plot, the theme, the style. He has recognized and accepted the world of the author and has been delighted (or saddened or made angry) by what happens in it.

But how does it come about that readers recognize the artificial worlds, often quite different from their own, that authors create? And why is it that readers who recognize some fictional worlds effortlessly are bewildered and lost in other fictional worlds? Is it possible to extend the boundaries of readers' recognition? Can more and more of the landscapes and societies of fiction be made available to that onlooking audience?

The answer to the first of these questions is easy. Readers are comfortable in literary worlds that, however exotic the landscapes and the personalities that people them, incorporate moral imperatives which reflect the value system in the readers' world. Put another way, much fiction ends with its virtuous characters rewarded and its villains punished. This we speak of as poetic justice. Comedies, and most motion pictures of the recent past, end this way. But such endings are illustrations of poetic justice, and *poetic* seems to suggest that somehow such endings are ideal rather than "real." Not much experience of life is required to recognize that injustice, pain, frustration, and downright villainy often prevail, that the beautiful young girl and the strong, handsome hero do not always overcome all obstacles, marry, and live happily ever after, that not every man is strong and handsome nor every woman beautiful. But readers, knowing that, respond to tragic fiction as well—where virtue is defeated, where obstacles prove too much for the men and women, where ponderous forces result in defeat, even death. Unhappy outcomes are painful to contemplate, but it is not difficult to recognize the world in which they occur. That world is much like our own. And unhappy outcomes serve to emphasize the very ideals which we have established in this world as the aims and goals of human activity. Consequently, both the "romantic" comedies that gladden with justice and success and the "realistic" stories that end in defeat provide readers with recognizable and available emotional worlds, however exotic the settings and the characters in those stories might be.

If we look at fiction this way, the answer to the question "Why is it that some readers are bewildered and lost in some fictional worlds?" is clearly implied. Some fictional worlds *seem* to incorporate a strange set of moral imperatives. Readers are not altogether certain who are the virtuous characters and who are the villains or even what constitutes virtue and evil. Sometimes tragic oppositions in a fictional world that brooks no compromise puzzle readers who live in a world where compromise has become almost a virtue. Sometimes, particularly in more recent fiction that reflects the ever-widening influence of psychoanalytic theory, the landscape and the behavior of characters is designed to represent deep interiors, the less-than-rational hearts and minds of characters. Those weird interiors are not part of the common awareness of readers; the moral questions raised there are not the same moral questions that occupy most of our waking hours. Such fictional worlds (those of Franz Kafka, for example) are difficult to map, and bewildered readers may well reject these underworlds for the sunshine of the surfaces they know more immediately.

Studying Literature

It might be useful to distinguish here between overlapping kinds of discussion that seek to explain the effectiveness of a piece of writing. *Literary history* deals with literature as the product of a particular time and place. Certain genres that were popular and universally accessible in medieval times—religious allegory, for instance—are remote today unless they are read in historical perspective. Also, many authors have been influenced measurably by their predecessors, and an understanding of a derivative work's literary antecedents can contribute to a reader's appreciation of it. Features of Elizabethan culture and theatrical conventions established by early Renaissance drama, for example, illuminate many obscure passages in Shakespeare's plays. (Most of the glosses and footnotes in this book provide readers with historical information—the meaning of an archaic word, the attributes of a mythological character, or the significance of an allusion to an earlier literary work.) For modern readers, such information can often revive a "dead" work. Nonetheless, interpreting obscure clues, however important they may be for textual explication, is not *literary criticism*.

Although he may rely on the work of the literary historian (and may well be a literary historian), the critic's role is to evaluate literature. Criticism divides into two major branches—theory and practice. The basic question that *theoretical criticism* asks is "What constitutes literary merit?", and the theoretical critic attempts to define a set of *criteria* by which any literary work may be judged.

Practical criticism, on the other hand, asks of specific works "Are they saying well what they wish to say?" The practical critic adopts the criteria of a theoretical position and measures particular pieces of literature against these standards to determine, primarily, whether the works in question are good or bad, major or minor. In the section "Three Critical Approaches" that follows (pp. 1322–1343), six examples of critical practice illustrate the application of three critical theories to two works—Hawthorne's "My Kinsman, Major Molineux" and Arnold's "Dover Beach."

Theories, of course, change, and the history of criticism reflects shifting tastes and cultural values. These changes may themselves influence the direction of creative art. Nonetheless, regardless of the practical critic's theoretical criteria, to determine the quality of a literary work he must examine the *craft* that an author has brought to it; he must determine how an author manipulates language and theme to create something that affects the reader. Often this determination is presented in terms that have evolved over the long history of criticism to identify recurrent techniques, uses of language, and formal conventions. Both literary history and criticism make particular use of this technical vocabulary in discussing form and the features that shape it.

Literary criticism frequently trespasses into nonliterary disciplines—notably psychology and sociology—for theory and subsequent practice. Although any reader, however unconsciously, responds to the effect of an author's craft, for the critic to assert that certain combinations of ideas will invariably generate the same response in the sensitive reader is a dangerous business. What are we to make of the spectacle of two critics, or two teachers, testifying that the same story affects them quite differently? Is one of them wrong? Are both of them wrong, perhaps? Perhaps, but we do the best we can, and we use all the varieties of human experience that authors and critics and theoreticians share in an attempt to respond significantly to significant literature.

Fiction and Reality

Why do people read fiction (or go to movies)? The question is not so easy to answer as one might suppose. The first response is likely to have something to do with "amusement" or "entertainment." But you have doubtless read stories and novels (or seen movies) that end tragically. Is it accurate to say that they were amusing or entertaining? Is it entertaining to be sad or to be made angry by the defeat of "good" people? Or does the emotional impact of such stories somehow enlarge our own humanity? Fiction teaches its readers by providing them a vast range of experience that they could not acquire otherwise. Especially for the relatively young, conceptions of love, of success in life, of war, of malignant evil and cleansing virtue are learned from fiction—not from life. And herein lies a great danger, for literary artists are notorious liars, and their lies frequently become the source of people's convictions about human nature and human society.

To illustrate, a huge number of television series based on the exploits of the FBI, or the Hawaiian police force, or the dedicated surgeons at the general hospital, or the young lawyers always end with a capture, with a successful (though dangerous) operation, with justice triumphant. But, in the real world, police are able to resolve only about 10 percent of reported crime, disease ravages, and economic and political power often extends into the courtroom. The very existence of such television drama bespeaks a yearning that things should be different; their heroes are heroic in that they regularly overcome those obstacles that we all experience but that, alas, we do not overcome.

Some writers, beginning about the middle of the nineteenth century, were particularly incensed at the real damage which a lying literature promotes, and they devoted their energies to exposing and counteracting the lies of the novelists, particularly those lies that formed attitudes about what constituted human success and happiness. Yet that popular fiction, loosely called *escapist*, is still most widely read for reasons that would probably fill several studies in social psychology. It needs no advocate. The fiction in this book, on the other hand, has been chosen largely because it does not lie about life—at least it does not lie about life in the ordinary way. And the various authors employ a large variety of literary methods and modes in an effort to illuminate the deepest wells of human experience. Consequently, many of these stories do not retail high adventure (though some do), since an adventurous inner life does not depend on an incident-filled outer life. Some stories, like Toomer's "Theater" and Porter's "The Jilting of Granny Weatherall," might almost be said to be about what does *not* happen rather than what does—not-happening being as much incident, after all, as happening.

All fiction attempts to be interesting, to involve the reader in situations, to force some aesthetic response from him—most simply put, in the widest sense of the word, to entertain. Some fiction aspires to nothing more. Other fiction seeks, as well, to establish some truth about the nature of man—Kafka's "A Hunger Artist," Hemingway's "A Clean, Well-Lighted Place," and Lessing's "To Room Nineteen" ask the reader to perceive the inner life of central figures. Some fiction seeks to explore the relationships among people—Faulkner's "Dry September," Toomer's "Theater," and Lawrence's "The Horse Dealer's Daughter" depend for their force on the powerful interaction of one character with another. Still other fiction seeks to explore the connection between people and society—Ellison's " 'Repent, Harlequin!' Said the Ticktockman" and Wright's "The Man Who Lived Underground" acquire their force from the implied struggle between men seeking a free and rich emotional life and the tyrannically ordering society that would sacrifice their humanity to some ideal of social efficiency.

We have been talking about that aspect of fiction which literary theorists identify as *theme*. Theorists also talk about plot, characterization, setting, point of view, and conflict—all terms naming aspects of fiction that generally have to do with the author's technique. Let us here deal with one story—James Joyce's "Araby." Read it. Then compare your private responses to the story with what we hope will be helpful and suggestive remarks about the methods of fiction.

The Methods of Fiction

One can perceive only a few things simultaneously and can hardly respond to everything contained in a well-wrought story all at once. When he has finished the story, the reader likely thinks back, makes adjustments, and reflects on the significance of things before he reaches that set of emotional and intellectual experiences that we have been calling *response*. Most readers of short stories respond first to what may be called the *tone* of the opening lines. Now tone is an aspect of literature about which it is particularly difficult to talk, because it is an aura—a shimmering and shifting atmosphere that depends for its substance on rather delicate emotional responses to language and situation. Surely, before the reader knows anything at all about the plot of "Araby," he has experienced a tone.

> North Richmond Street, being blind, was a quiet street except at the hour when the Christian Brothers' School set the boys free. An uninhabited house of two storeys stood at the blind end, detached from its neighbors in a square ground. The other houses of the street, conscious of decent lives within them, gazed at one another with brown imperturbable faces.

Is the scene gay? Vital and active? Is this opening appropriate for a story that goes on to celebrate joyous affirmations about life and living? You should answer these questions negatively. Why? Because the dead end street is described as "blind," because the Christian Brothers' School sounds much like a prison (it sets the boys free), because a vacant house fronts the dead end, because the other houses, personified, are conscious of decent lives within (a mildly ironic description—*decent* suggesting ordinary, thin-lipped respectability rather than passion or heroism), because those houses gaze at one another with "brown imperturbable faces"—*brown* being nondescript, as opposed, say, to scarlet, gold, bright blue, and *imperturbable faces* reinforcing the priggish decency within.

Compare this opening from Faulkner's "Dry September":

> Through the bloody September twilight, aftermath of sixty-two rainless days, it had gone like fire in a dry grass—the rumor, the story, whatever it was. Something about Miss Minnie Cooper and a Negro.

The tone generated by "bloody twilight," "rainless days," "fire in a dry grass" is quite different from the blind, brown apathy of "Araby." And unsurprisingly, Faulkner's story involves movement to a horrifying violence. "Araby," on the other hand, is a story about the dawning of awareness in the mind and heart of the child of one of those decent families in brown and blind North Richmond Street. Tone, of course, permeates all fiction, and it may change as the narrative develops. Since short stories generally reveal change, the manipulation of tone is just one more tool used in the working of design.

Short stories, of course, are short, but this fact implies some serious considerations. In some ways, a large class of good short fiction deals with events that may be compared to the tip of the proverbial iceberg. The events animating the story represent only a tiny fraction of the characters' lives and experiences; yet, that fraction is terribly important and provides the basis for wide understanding both to the characters within the story and to its readers. In "Araby," the plot, the connected sequence of events, may be simply stated. A young boy who lives in a rather drab, respectable neighborhood develops a crush on the sister of one of his playmates. She asks him if he intends to go to a charity fair that she cannot attend. He resolves to go and purchase a gift for her. He is tormented by the late and drunken arrival of his uncle who has promised him the money he needs. When the boy finally arrives at the bazaar, he is disappointed by the difference between his expectation and the actuality of the almost deserted fair. He perceives some minor events, overhears some minor conversation, and finally sees himself "as a creature driven and derided by vanity." Yet this tiny stretch of experience out of the life of the boy introduces him to an awareness about the differences between imagination and reality, between his romantic infatuation and the vulgar reality all about him. We are talking now about what is called the *theme* of the story. Emerging from the workaday events that constitute its plot is a general statement about intensely idealized childish "love," the shattering recognition of the false sentimentality that occasions it, and the enveloping vulgarity of adult life. The few pages of the story, by detailing a few events out of a short period of the protagonist's life, illuminate one aspect of the loss of innocence that we all endure and that is always painful. In much of the literature in the section on innocence and experience, the protagonists learn painfully the moral complexities of a world that had once seemed uncomplicated and predictable. That education does not always occur, as in "Araby," at an early age, either in literature or life.

Certainly theme is a centrally important aspect of prose fiction, but "good" themes do not neccessarily ensure good stories. One may write a wretched story with the same theme as "Araby." What, then, independent of theme, is the difference between good stories and bad stories? Instinctively you know how to answer this question. Good stories, to begin with, are interesting; they present characters you care about; however fantastic, they are yet somehow plausible; they project a moral world you recognize. One of the obvious differences between short stories and novels requires that story writers develop character rapidly and limit the number of developed characters. Many stories have only one fleshed character; the other characters are frequently two-dimensional projections or even stereotypes. We see their surface only, not their souls. Rarely does a short story have more than three developed characters. Again, unlike novels, short stories usually work themselves out in restricted geographical setting, in a single place, and within a rather short period of time.

We often speak of character, setting, plot, theme, and style as separate aspects of a story in order to break down a complex narrative into more manageable parts. But it is important to understand that this analytic process of separating various elements is something we have done to the story—the story (if it is a good one) is an integrated whole. The closer we examine the separate elements, the clearer it becomes that each is integrally related to the others.

It is part of the boy's character that he lives in a brown imperturbable house in North Richmond Street, that he does the things he does (which is, after all, the plot), that he learns what he does (which is the theme), and that all of this characterization emerges from Joyce's rich and suggestive style. Consider this paragraph:

> Her image accompanied me even in places the most hostile to romance. On Saturday evenings when my aunt went marketing I had to go to carry some of the parcels. We walked through the flaring streets, jostled by drunken men and bargaining women, amid the curses of labourers, the shrill litanies of shop-boys who stood on guard by the barrels of pigs' cheeks, the nasal chanting of street-singers, who sang a *come-all-you* about O'Donovan Rossa, or a ballad about the troubles in our native land. These noises converged in a single sensation of life for me: I imagined that I bore my chalice safely through a throng of foes. Her name sprang to my lips at moments in strange prayers and praises which I myself did not understand. My eyes were often full of tears (I could not tell why) and at times a flood from my heart seemed to pour itself out into my bosom. I thought little of the future. I did not know whether I would ever speak to her or not or, if I spoke to her, how I could tell her of my confused adoration. But my body was like a harp and her words and gestures were like fingers running upon the wires.

This paragraph furthers the plot. But it suggests much more. The boy thinks of his friend's sister even when he carries parcels for his aunt during the shopping trips through a crowded and coarse part of town. In those coarse market streets the shop-boys cry shrill "litanies," the girl's name springs to his lips in strange "prayers and praises," and the boy confesses a confused "adoration." Further, he bears "his chalice safely through a throng of foes." Now the words *litanies*, *prayers*, *praises*, *adoration* all come from a special vocabulary that is easy to identify. It is the vocabulary of the church. The *chalice* and the *throng of foes* come from the vocabulary of chivalric romance, which is alluded to in the first line of the quoted paragraph. Joyce's diction evokes a sort of holy chivalry that characterizes the boy on this otherwise altogether ordinary shopping trip. This paragraph suggests to the careful reader that the boy has cast his awakening sexuality in a mold that mixes the disparate shapes of the heroic knight, winning his lady by force of arms, and the ascetic penitent, adoring the holy virgin, mother of god.

Playing the word game, of course, can be dangerous. But from the beginning of this story to its end, a certain religious quality shimmers. That now-dead priest of the story's second paragraph had three books (at least). One is a romantic chivalric novel by Sir Walter Scott; one is a sensational account of the adventures of a famous criminal-turned-detective; one is what a priest might be expected to have at hand—an Easter week devotional guide. That priest who read Scott novels might have understood the boy's response—that mixture of religious devotion and romance. Shortly after the shopping trip, the boy finally speaks to the girl, and it is instructive to see her as he does. He stands at the *railings* and looks up (presumbably) at her, she bowing her head towards him. "The light from the lamp opposite our door caught the white curve of her neck, lit up her hair that rested there and, falling, lit up the hand upon the railing. It fell over one side of her dress and caught the white border of a petticoat, just visible as she stood at ease." Skip the petticoat, for a moment. Might the description of Mangan's sister remind the careful reader of quite common sculptured representations of the Virgin Mary? But the petticoat! And the white curve of her neck! This erotic overlay characterizes the boy's response. The sexuality is his own; the chivalry, the religious adoration, comes from the culture in which he is immersed—comes from Scott, the ballads sung in the market place, the "Arab's Farewell to his Steed" that the boy's uncle threatens to recite. And it is the culture that so romanticizes and elevates the boy's yearning.

He finally gets to Araby—"the syllables of the word . . . were called to [him] through the silence in which [his] soul luxuriated and cast an Eastern enchantment over [him]." His purpose is to serve his lady—to bring her something from that exotic place. What he finds is a weary-looking man guarding a turnstile, the silence that pervades a church after a service, and two men counting money on a salver (that tray is called a *salver* by design). And in this setting he overhears a young lady flirting with two gentlemen:

> "O, I never said such a thing!"
> "O, but you did!"
> "O, but I didn't!"
> "Didn't she say that?"
> "Yes, I heard her."
> "O, there's a . . . . fib!"

This is Araby, this is love in a darkened hall where money is counted. Is it any wonder that the boy, in the moment of personal illumination that Joyce calls an epiphany, sees himself as a creature driven and derided by vanity?

"Araby" is a careful, even a delicate story. Nothing much happens—what does occurs largely in the boy's perception and imagination. The story focuses on the boy's confusion of sexual attraction with the lofty sentiments of chivalry and religion. The climax occurs when he confronts the darkened, money-grubbing fair and the banal expression of the sexual attraction between the gentlemen and the young lady. The result is a sudden deflation of the boy's ego, his sense of self, as he recognizes his own delusions about the nature of love and the relationship between men, women, heroism, God, and money.

We would like to conclude with a discussion of one feature of fiction that sometimes proves troublesome to developing readers. Often the events of a story, upon which much depends, puzzle or annoy readers. Why does that fool do that? Why doesn't X simply tell Y the way he feels and then the tragedy would be averted? In a sense, such responses reflect the intrusion of a reader into the world of the story. The reader, a sensible and sensitive person, understands some things about life after all and is oppressed by the characters' inability to understand at least as much. Characters choose to die when they might with a slight adjustment live. They risk danger when with a slight adjustment they might proceed safely. They suffer the pain of an unfortunate marriage when with a little trouble they might be free to live joyously. If the "whys" issuing from the reader are too insistent, too sensible, then the story must fail, at least for that reader. But many "whys" are not legitimate. Many are intrusions of the reader's hindsight, the reader's altogether different cultural and emotional fix. Henry James urged that the author must be allowed his *donnée*, his "given." He creates the society and the rules by which it operates within his own fictional world. Sometimes his creation is so close to the reader's own world that it is hardly possible to object. Black readers will recognize the inner life of Wright's man who lived underground even if the events are bizarre. Those who have grown up in a small southern town will recognize the atmosphere of Faulkner's "Dry September." But few readers of this book know 1895 Dublin and Irish middle-class society, which plays a brooding role in "Araby" (as it does in almost all of Joyce's work). None know the futuristic world of Harlan Ellison's Harlequin. In every case, we must finally imagine those worlds, even where setting is familiar. If we cannot, the events that take place in them will be of no consequence. If those worlds are unimaginable, then the stories must fail. If they too much strain belief or remain too foreign to the reader's heart, they must likewise fail. But all response to fiction depends on the reader's acquiescence to the world of the author and his perceptions of the moral consequences of acts and attitudes in that world. At best, that acquiescence will provide much pleasure as well as emotional insight into his own existence.

Reading Poetry

For many people, the question "What is poetry?" is irrelevant if not irreverent. The attempt to answer such a question leads to abstract intellectual analysis, the very opposite of the emotional pleasure one seeks in a good poem. Why does it matter what poetry is so long as readers enjoy poems? Doesn't the attempt to define the nature of poetry lead to technical analysis of poetic devices so that study, finally, destroys pleasure?

These are valid issues that touch on very real dangers. If the study of poetry bogs down in theoretical or historical issues and the study of a poem becomes a mere exercise in the identification and discussion of poetic devices, the reader may well find that reading a poem is more effort than pleasure. He may begin to feel like the many nineteenth-century poets who complained that science, in laying bare the laws of nature, robbed the universe of its ancient awe and mystery. Walt Whitman, for example, describes such a feeling in his poem "When I Heard The Learn'd Astronomer."

> When I heard the learn'd astronomer,
> When the proofs, the figures, were ranged in columns before me,
> When I was shown the charts and diagrams, to add, divide, and measure them,
> When I sitting heard the astronomer where he lectured with much applause in the
> lecture-room,
> How soon unaccountable I became tired and sick,
> Till rising and gliding out I wander'd off by myself,
> In the mystical moist night-air, and from time to time,
> Look'd up in perfect silence at the stars.

The distinction implicit in Whitman's poem between the mind (intellectual knowledge) and the heart (emotion and feelings) is very old, but still a useful one. All of us have no doubt felt at some time that the overexercise of the mind interfered with our capacity to feel. Compelled to analyze, dissect, categorize, and classify, we finally yearn for the simple and "mindless" pleasure of unanalytical enjoyment, the pleasure of sensuous experience. But man derives pleasure in a variety of ways, and while we needn't assert a *necessary* connection between understanding and pleasure, understanding can enhance pleasure. The distinction between the mind and the heart is, after all, a fiction or metaphor that cannot be pushed too far before it breaks down. Readers may very well enjoy Dylan Thomas's "Fern Hill" without understanding Thomas's use of symbolism or color or religious imagery. But understanding that symbolism and imagery will certainly deepen the pleasure derived from the poem.

We don't mean to suggest by all this that every poem needs to be studied in detail or that it is possible to say in the abstract what kind and amount of study will be rewarding. Some poems are straightforward, requiring little by way of analysis; others, dense and complex, seem to yield little without some study. But study of even the simplest poems can be rewarding. (Consider the effect of the special vocabulary implied by such words as "arrayed," "imperially," "crown," and "glittered" in Edwin Arlington Robinson's "Richard Cory.") On the other hand, it is possible to be moved on first reading by the tone and quality of such complex poems as Wallace Stevens's "Sunday Morning" and T. S. Eliot's "The Love Song of J. Alfred Prufrock" even though they are difficult to understand immediately.

As to our original question—What is poetry?—we cannot offer anything like a definitive and comprehensive answer. Poetry is a form of writing that often employs rhyme, a regular rhythm, unusual word order, and an intense or heightened language. This formal definition will serve about as well as any although it is by no means comprehensive, as any collection of poems will readily demonstrate. Up to about a century ago, poetry was governed by rather precise and often elaborate rules and conventions; if a poem did not use rhyme, it certainly was characterized by rhythmic regularity, or meter. Further, there existed a long tradition of poetic types (epic, elegiac, odic, etc.), each with quite specific rules and characteristics. While these traditions still retain some force, the old notion that these forms are part of the natural scheme of things has been largely abandoned. No one insists that the form of writing we call poetry must exhibit a combination of fixed characteristics.

Consider poetry from a different angle and ask not what poetry is but rather what functions it serves. Poetry fulfills some deep and abiding need of man, for no culture we know of has been without it. We know also that in ancient societies, before the advent of science and technology in the modern sense, the arts were not divided by types or differentiated from science. In ancient tribal societies, poetry, dance, sculpture, and painting might all be parts of a tribal ceremony designed to propitiate the gods and thereby ensure a full harvest or a successful hunt. Poetry, then, was part of a primitive (we would now label it "superstitious") science that defined and helped control the external world. Though one can only guess in these matters, it is probably safe to assume that in such a primitive society the inner emotional world of the individual was not sharply distinguished from the outer world of nature. Nature and the gods who controlled it might be harsh and unpredictable, and the function of ritual was to control and appease these gods (to ensure rain, for example). But ritual also nurtured and strengthened the individual's communal spirit and conditioned his feelings about the arduous work that the life of the tribe required.

The conditions of our lives are, of course, vastly different. We operate within an enormous industrialized society that developed over centuries as men abandoned primitive explanations of the universe and sought others. One result of that development was a continuing differentiation and specialization of human endeavors, as science broke away from art and both divided into separate if related disciplines. Science became astronomy, biology, physics, and the like, while art branched into various types of aesthetic creation. And it was modern science, not poetry or the other arts, that produced profound and measurable changes in man's life. Poetry might movingly and memorably remind us of the sorrow of unrequited love or the ravages of growing old, but science created a technology that produced undreamed of material wealth and power.

Is the very persistence of poetry evidence that it serves some important function, however obscure? On the other hand, maybe poetry is merely a vestigial organ of evolution that, like the appendix, continues to exist even though it has outlived its usefulness. Certainly, the historical process we have sketched here seems to involve a gradual diminution in the importance men attach to poetry.

It would be misleading, of course, to suggest that the scientist and the poet exist in separate worlds. But the differences between them are important. The truth that science seeks is the truth of physical reality. Social sciences such as psychology, sociology, and economics have attempted to demonstrate that human behavior can be understood in terms of a set of definite and quantifiable mechanisms. And, though no one would assert that science has achieved final answers, it is clear that the spectacular discoveries of science have left many, Walt Whitman among them, with the feeling that man's importance in the universe has diminished. Further, modern physical science has uncovered a disturbing indeterminateness and asymmetry in the universe that have far-reaching philosophical implications not only for science but for society as a whole. As the old scientific verities crumble, so, too, do the old social verities.

Science may describe and educate us about the outer world and its inexorable laws with as rigorous an objectivity and neutrality as it can achieve. It may explain to us that in a naturalistic world death comes to all living creatures or that sunsets result from certain physical phenomena; but it is silent on the terror of death and its human or emotional meaning or on the beauty of a sunset. To understand those emotions, to give them form and meaning, we turn to poetry—we read it and, perhaps, even write it. For poetry, so to speak, educates our emotions and our feelings, allows us to learn who we are and to articulate what we feel.

We might wonder whether such an assertion makes sense. What we feel, we feel. We don't need a poem to tell us that. Not so. Often we don't know what we feel except in a vague and inarticulate way. A powerful poem articulates and thereby clarifies. Further, a poem may even deepen feelings. Although the literary historian might correctly observe that it is an academic exercise in wit, Andrew Marvell's poem "To His Coy Mistress" may well help the reader understand his own feelings about physical love and mortality. The outrageous absurdity of death cutting down a person whose life has barely begun is articulated in Robert Frost's " 'Out, Out—' " and John Crowe Ransom's "Bells for John Whiteside's Daughter." The confusion that often attends the powerful emotion generated by love and death is arrested by the poet who provides order.

Poetry at its highest and most general level is a form of communication, a means of defining, affirming, and deepening its reader's humanity. This is not to say that one should approach poetry solemnly, expecting always to be loftily enlightened. Poetry is a complex form of communication that provides pleasure in various ways. One may, for instance, look upon a poem as a kind of game in which the poet skillfully works within a set of self-imposed rules—rhyme, meter, and stanzaic pattern—and delights in clever rhymes, as when Lord Byron rhymes "intellectual" with "henpecked you all" or "maxim" with "tax 'em." Anyone familiar with Plato's theory that everything in our world is an imperfect replica of an ideal heavenly form will appreciate the beauty and condensed brilliance of William Butler Yeats's lines from "Among School Children":

> Plato thought nature but a spume that plays
> Upon a ghostly paradigm of things.

Some will discover in poetry, as children often do in nursery rhymes, the pleasure of rhythm, meter, and sound—the musical aspects of poetry. The pleasures of poetry range from the loftiest insights and discoveries to memorable lines and clever rhymes.

   A discussion of the major techniques and devices of poetry will provide some suggestions about how to approach poems and also furnish tools and a vocabulary for analyzing and discussing them. Keep in mind that a tool is not an end in itself but the means to an end. The end is fuller understanding and, thereby, deeper enjoyment of poetry.

The Words of Poetry

It is not unusual to hear some great and original philosopher, sociologist, or economist referred to as a mediocre writer. Yet, while one may judge the writing poor, he may at the same time recognize and honor the originality and significance of the idea conveyed. Such a distinction cannot be made in poetry. If a poem is written poorly, it is a poor poem. "In reading prose," Ralph Waldo Emerson said, "I am sensitive as soon as a sentence drags; but in poetry, as soon as one word drags." *Where* a poem arrives is inseparable from *how* it arrives. Everything must be right in a poem, every word. "The correction of prose," said Yeats, "is endless, a poem comes right with a click like a closing box."

   "Poetry is heightened language" means, among other things, that the poet strives for precision and richness in the words he uses, and "precision" and "richness" are not contradictory for the poet. Words have dictionary or denotative meanings as well as associative or connotative meanings; they also have histories and relationships with other words. The English language is rich in synonyms, groups of words whose denotative meanings are roughly the same but whose connotations vary widely (portly, stout, fat; horse, steed, courser; official, statesman, politician). Many words are identical in sound and often in spelling but different in meaning (forepaws, four paws; lie [recline] lie [fib]). The meanings of words have changed in the course of time, and the poet may consciously select a word whose older meaning adds a dimension to his poem. There are, of course, no rules that can be given to a reader for judging a poet's effectiveness and skill in the handling of words (or anything else, for that matter). All we can do is look at particular works for examples of how a good poet manipulates words.

In a moving and passionate poem on his dying father, "Do Not Go Gentle into That Good Night," Dylan Thomas pleads with his father not to accept death passively but rather to "Rage, rage against the dying of the light." He then declares in the following stanzas that neither "wise men" nor "good men" nor "wild men" accept death quietly. And neither, Thomas says, do "grave men," punning on *grave* in its meaning of both "serious" and "burial place." William Blake's poem about the inhumane jobs children were forced into in eighteenth-century England, "The Chimney Sweeper" begins:

When my mother died I was very young,
And my Father sold me while yet my tongue
Could scarcely cry " 'weep! 'weep! 'weep! 'weep!"
So your chimneys I sweep, and in soot I sleep.

" 'Weep," a clipped form of "sweep," is what the boy cries as he walks a street looking for work, but *weep* clearly evokes the tears and sorrow of the mother's death and the sadness of the small boy's cruel life. And this is only part of Blake's skillful handling of words. "Cry" is also an effective pun, the precise word to describe how the boy seeks work while simultaneously reinforcing the emotional meaning of *weep*.

Henry Reed's "Naming of Parts" develops a contrast between the instructions a group of soldiers are receiving on how to operate a rifle (in order to cause death) and the lovely world of nature (which represents life and beauty). In the fourth stanza, bees are described as "assaulting and fumbling the flowers." "Fumbling," with its meaning of awkwardness and nervous uncertainy, may strike us as an arresting and perhaps puzzling word at first. Yet anyone who has watched a bee pollinating a flower will find the word extremely effective. In addition, of course, *fumbling* is a word often used to describe the actions of human beings caught up in sexual passion—a connotation precisely appropriate to the poet's purposes, since pollination is, in a sense, a sexual process. Furthermore, these various interpretations of *fumbling* contrast powerfully with the cold, mechanical precision of the death-dealing instruments the recruits are learning how to use. The next line of Reed's poem exhibits yet another resource of words: "They call it easing the Spring." The line is an exact repetition of a phrase used two lines earlier except *Spring* is now capitalized. While *Spring* retains its first meaning as part of the bolt action of the rifle, the capitalization makes it the season of the year when flowers are pollinated and the world of nature is reborn. With a mere typographical device, Reed has charged a single word with the theme of his poem. These few illustrations will suggest how sensitive the poet is to words and how much more pleasure the reader will find in poems if he develops the same sensitivity.

Sometimes meanings are not inherent in the isolated words but created in the poet's use of the word. A tree is a tree and a rose is a rose. A tree is also the apple tree in Frost's "After Apple-Picking" and something quite different in William Blake's "A Poison Tree"; a rose is specially defined in Robert Burns's 'A Red, Red Rose" and Edmund Waller's "Go, Lovely Rose!" In these poems, because *tree* and *rose* are given such rich and varied meaning and are so central to the poems' development and meaning, they exceed mere connotation and become images that, finally, are symbolic.

Imagery

The world is revealed to us through our senses—sight, sound, taste, touch, and smell. And while some philosophers and pyschologists might challenge the statement, it seems pretty clear that much, if not all, of our knowledge is linked to sensory experience. *Imagery* is the representation in poetry of sensory experience, one of the means by which the poet creates a world that we all know and share. Or, put another way, imagery allows the poet to create a recognizable world by drawing upon a fund of common experiences. Bad poetry is often bad because the imagery is stale ("golden sunset," "the smiling sun," "the rolling sea") or so skimpy that the poem dissolves into vague and shadowy and meaningless abstractions.

A good poet never loses touch with the sensory world. The invisible, the intangible, the abstract, are anchored to the visible, the tangible, the concrete. Andrew Marvell begins his poem "To His Coy Mistress" with an elaborate statement of how he would court his beloved if their lives were measured in centuries rather than years. In the second stanza, he describes the reality:

> But at my back I always hear
> Time's wingéd chariot hurrying near;
> And yonder all before us lie
> Deserts of vast eternity.
> Thy beauty shall no more be found,
> Nor, in thy marble vault, shall sound
> My echoing song; then worms shall try
> That long-preserved virginity,
> And your quaint honor turn to dust,
> And into ashes all my lust:
> The grave's a fine and private place,
> But none, I think, do there embrace.

Time, eternity, honor, and *lust* are all abstractions, but Marvell joins each to a sensuous image that gives to the abstraction an extraordinary sharpness and power. Time is a winged *chariot,* eternity a sequence of *deserts,* honor turns to *dust* and lust to *ashes.* Time has long been associated with the chariot of Apollo and eternity, for the damned, with a desert. "Ashes" and "dust" echo the funeral service. Nonetheless, Marvell gives life to these stock images by renewing their appeal to the senses.

Any analysis of the imagery of a poem will soon reveal that our definition of imagery as the representation of sensory experience needs to be qualified. One of the primary functions of language is to bring meaning and order into our lives, and poetry is the most intense use of language. We will find, therefore, that the images in poetry tend to be charged with meanings. A rose may be only a rose, but it becomes much more in Burns's and Waller's poems. Imagery, then, is closely related to, perhaps inseparable from, *figurative* language, the language which *says* one thing and *means* another.

The difference between good and bad poetry often turns on the skill with which imagery (or figurative language) is used. When Robert Frost in his poem "Birches" compares life to "a pathless wood," the image strikes us as natural and appropriate (the comparison of life to a path or road is a common one, as is a wood or forest to a state of moral bewilderment). We are accustomed to the imagery of birds, flowers, and sunsets in love poems, but when John Donne in "A Valediction: Forbidding Mourning" describes the relationship between himself and his beloved in terms of a drawing compass, the image may seem jarring or even ludicrous. Such a bold and daring comparison is a kind of challenge. The poet intends not only to surmount the reader's feeling that the image is strange but to develop it with such skill that the reader will accept it as natural and appropriate. And as Donne elaborates the comparison through various stages and concludes it (and the poem) with the brilliantly appropriate image of the completed circle, we recognize that he has successfully met the challenge.

Figurative Language

Figurative language is the general phrase we use to describe the many devices of language that allow us to speak nonliterally, to say one thing and mean another. Any attempt to communicate an emotion will very quickly utilize figurative language. When Robert Burns compares his love to a red rose, he does so not because he is unable to find the literal language he needs but because what he wants to say can only be expressed in figurative language. (Literal language might be used by a scientist to describe the physiological state of someone in love, but that is not what interests Burns.) The world of emotions, feelings, attitudes remains shadowy and insubstantial until figurative language gives it form and substance.

Consider, for example, these familiar old sayings: "The grass is always greener on the other side of the fence"; "A rolling stone gathers no moss"; "A bird in the hand is worth two in the bush"; "The early bird catches the worm." While these sayings unquestionably make sense in literal terms (the grass you see from a distance looks greener than the grass under your feet), the meaning of these phrases to a native speaker of English is clearly nonliteral. When we use them we are not speaking about grass or rolling stones or birds; we are making general and highly abstract observations about human attitudes and behavior. Yet strangely these generalizations and abstractions are embodied in concrete and sensuous imagery. Try to explain what any one of these expressions means and you will quickly discover that you are using many more words and much vaguer language than the expression itself. Indeed, this is precisely what happens when you attempt to paraphrase—that is, put into your own words—the meaning of a poem. Like poetry, these sayings rely on the figurative use of language.

Since poetry is an intense and heightened use of language that explores the world of feeling, it uses more varied figurative devices than does ordinary language. One of the most common figurative devices, *metaphor*, where one thing is called something else, occurs frequently in ordinary speech. "School is a rat race," we say, or "She's a bundle of nerves," and the meaning is perfectly clear—too clear, perhaps, because these metaphors are by now so common and unoriginal they have lost whatever vividness they may once have had. But when Thomas Nashe declares that "Beauty is but a flower/Which wrinkles will devour" or W. H. Auden, commenting on the death of William Butler Yeats, says, "Let the Irish vessel lie/Emptied of its poetry," we have metaphors that compel readers to confront certain painful aspects of life.

Simile is closely related to metaphor. But where metaphor says that one thing *is* another, simile says that one thing is *like* another, as in Burns's "O My Luve's like a red, red rose" and Frost's "life is too much like a pathless wood." The distinction between simile and metaphor, while easy enough to make technically, is often difficult to distinguish in terms of effects. Frost establishes a comparison between life and a pathless wood and keeps the two even more fully separated by adding the qualifiers, "too much." Burns's simile maintains the same separation and, in addition, because it occurs in the opening line of the poem, eliminates any possible confusion the reader might momentarily experience about the subject of the poem if the line read, "O My Love is a red, red rose." The reader can test the difference in effect between simile and metaphor by changing a metaphor into a simile or a simile into a metaphor to see if the meaning of the poem is thereby altered.

The critical vocabulary useful in discussions of poetry includes several additional terms, all of which name particular figures of speech: *metonymy, synecdoche, personification, hyperbole, understatement, paradox.* These terms are defined and illustrated in the Glossary of Literary Terms. But, though there may be a certain academic pleasure in recognizing the figures a poet uses, naming a figure of speech will never explain its effectiveness. The reader must, finally, perceive the usefulness of figures and respond emotionally to the construction of language that the poet creates in order to touch his reader's nerves.

Symbol

A *symbol* is anything that stands for or suggests something else. In this sense, most words are symbolic: the word *tree* stands for an object in the real world. When we speak of a symbol in poetry, however, we usually mean something more precise. In poetry, a symbol is an object or event that suggests more than itself. It is one of the most common and most powerful devices available to the poet, for it allows him to convey economically and simply a wide range of meanings.

It is useful to distinguish between two kinds of symbols, *public symbols* and *contextual symbols*. Public symbols are those objects or events that history has invested with rich meanings and associations. In a sense, then, a public symbol is a ready-made symbol. Yeats utilizes such a symbol in his poem "Leda and the Swan," assuming that his readers will be familiar with the myths that tell of the erotic affairs of Zeus and the consequences of those affairs—in this case, the birth of Clytemnestra, the wife of Agamemnon, and Helen, the most beautiful woman of antiquity, whose abduction precipitated the Trojan War. In "The Conscientious Objector," Karl Shapiro uses Noah's Ark and the Mayflower as symbols of a political prison whose inmates refuse to conform.

When a poet uses a public symbol, he is drawing from what he assumes is a common and shared fund of knowledge and tradition. If Yeats's reader is unaware of the symbolic meaning with which history has invested the Trojan War, it is doubtful that the poem will have much meaning for him. Nor will Shapiro's poem be clear unless we understand that Noah's Ark and the Mayflower evoke unique virtue and daring and heroic nonconformity.

In contrast to public symbols, contextual symbols are objects or events that are symbolic by virtue of the poet's handling of them in a particular poem— that is, by virtue of the context. Consider for example, the opening lines of Robert Frost's "After Apple-Picking":

> My long two-pointed ladder's sticking through a tree
> Toward heaven still,
> And there's a barrel that I didn't fill
> Beside it, and there may be two or three
> Apples I didn't pick upon some bough.

The apple tree is a literal tree, but as one reads through the poem, it becomes clear that the apple tree also symbolizes the speaker's life with a wide range of possible meanings (do the few apples he hasn't picked symbolize the hopes, dreams, aspirations that even the fullest life cannot satisfy?).

Amy Lowell's "Patterns" is rich in symbols. The speaker is an aristocratic lady whose life and most vital emotions are kept in rigid control by a series of patterns that the society she lives in has imposed on her. She describes herself as walking in her elegant gown down the garden paths laid out in precise patterns. Her gown is real; the path is a real path. But it very quickly becomes apparent that the patterned paths and her elegant gown are symbolic of the narrowly restricted and oppressive life her deepest feelings are at war with. They are the visible manifestation, the symbols, of the trap in which she is caught. She weeps when she notices "The daffodils and squills/Flutter in the breeze/As they please" because the flowers symbolize a freedom she knows she will never have.

The paths and flowers in Amy Lowell's poem are clear and easily recognizable examples of contextual symbols. However, contextual symbols by their very nature tend to present more difficulties than public symbols, because recognizing them depends on a sensitivity to everything else in the poem. In T. S. Eliot's dense and difficult poem "The Love Song of J. Alfred Prufrock," the speaker twice says, "In the room the women come and go/Talking of Michelangelo," a couplet that is baffling at first because it seems to have no clear relationship to what precedes and follows it. But as one reads through the poem, he begins to see that Prufrock is a man, like the young woman in Amy Lowell's poem, trapped in a life of upper-class superficialities and meaninglessness. The women discussing Michelangelo symbolize this dilettantish and arid life from which Prufrock desperately wishes to escape. Prufrock reminds himself that he will have time "To prepare a face to meet the faces that you meet," and Eleanor Rigby, in John Lennon and Paul McCartney's song, is described as "wearing the face that she keeps in a jar by the door." In both poems, that face is a symbol of a lonely existence in a society where people play elaborate games in order to conceal from others their real emotions and feelings.

A final word on symbols. If a reader fails to recognize a symbol, he has missed an important part of the poem's meaning. On the other hand, one of the pitfalls of reading poetry is that some readers become so intent on finding symbols they tend to forget that an object must first have a literal meaning before it can function as a symbol. Or, put in terms of our earlier definition, an object or event is itself before it is something else.

The setting of "After Apple-Picking" is an orchard, and the setting of "Patterns" the paths of a manorial garden. As we begin to understand the theme of each poem, we come to recognize the symbolic meanings these objects gradually take on. But there are rules that will allow a reader to identify symbols. If you do not know what Troy symbolizes and have never heard of Helen of Troy, you will not discover the meanings of these public symbols by repeated and intensive readings of the poem; like unfamiliar words, you must look up (or be told of) their significance. On the other hand, the recognition of contextual symbols often depends on careful and sensitive reading. Readers may very well disagree on whether or not something should be taken as a symbol. When this occurs, one can only consider whether the symbolic reading adds meanings that are consistent with other elements in the poem. Is the fly in Emily Dickinson's "I Heard a Fly Buzz—When I Died" a symbol or merely an insect? Your answer will depend on what you see as the theme of the poem.

Archibald MacLeish renders the modern critical attitude toward symbolism in poetry and, at the same time, argues for the view that poems do not "mean" in the ordinary sense of that word. The various elements of a poem—imagery, figurative language, symbol—coalesce to form an *object*, something characterized not by its truth but by its objective correlation to some human experience. And most remarkably, MacLeish renders these rather complex critical positions in a poem rich in contextual symbols:

ARS POETICA

A poem should be palpable and mute
As a globed fruit,

Dumb
As old medallions to the thumb,

Silent as the sleeve-worn stone
Of casement ledges where the moss has grown—

A poem should be wordless
As the flight of birds.

A poem should be motionless in time
As the moon climbs,

Leaving, as the moon releases
Twig by twig the night-entangled trees,

Leaving, as the moon behind the winter leaves,
Memory by memory the mind—

A poem should be motionless in time
As the moon climbs.

A poem should be equal to:
Not true.

For all the history of grief
An empty doorway and a maple leaf.

For love
The leaning grasses and two lights above the sea—

A poem should not mean
But be.

Music

The *music* of poetry, by which we mean the poetic use of all the devices of
sound and rhythm inherent in language, is at once central to the poetic effect
and yet the most difficult to account for. We can discuss the ways in which
figurative language works with some clarity because we are using words to explain words. Anyone who has ever tried to explain the effect a piece of music
had on him (or who has read music criticism) will be familiar with the problem
of describing a nonverbal medium with words.

The possible musical effects of language are complex. The terms we have to
describe various musical devices deal only with the most obvious and easily
recognizable patterns. *Alliteration, assonance, consonance, caesura, meter, onomatopoeia, rhythm,* and *rhyme* (all of them defined in the Glossary) are the
key traditional terms for discussing the music of poetry. Along with the other
terms already introduced, they are an indispensable part of the vocabulary one
needs to discuss poetry. But the relationship between sound and sense can be
perceived nicely in a celebrated passage from Alexander Pope's poem "An Essay
on Criticism," in which the meaning of each line, first a condemnation of

mechanical bad verse, then an illustration of well-managed verse, is ingeniously supported by the musical devices:

> These[1] equal syllables alone require,
> Though oft the ear the open vowels tire;
> While expletives their feeble aid do join;
> And ten low words oft creep in one dull line:
> While they ring round the same unvaried chimes,
> With sure returns of still expected rhymes;
> Where 'er you find "the cooling western breeze,"
> In the next line, it "whispers through the trees";
> If crystal streams "with pleasing murmurs creep,"
> The reader's threatened (not in vain) with "sleep";
> Then, at the last and only couplet fraught
> With some unmeaning thing they call a thought,
> A needless Alexandrine[2] ends the song
> That, like a wounded snake, drags its slow length along.
>
> . . . . .
>
> True ease in writing comes from art, not chance,
> As those move easiest who have learned to dance.
> 'Tis not enough no harshness gives offense,
> The sound must seem an echo to the sense:
> Soft is the strain when Zephyr gently blows,
> And the smooth stream in smoother numbers flows;
> But when loud surges lash the sounding shore,
> The hoarse, rough verse should like the torrent roar:
> When Ajax[3] strives some rock's vast weight to throw,
> The line too labors, and the words move slow;
> Not so, when swift Camilla[4] scours the plain,
> Flies o'er the unbending corn, and skims along the main.

When Pope speaks of open vowels, the line is loaded with open vowels. When Pope condemns the use of ten monosyllables, the line contains ten monosyllables. When Pope urges that the sound should echo the sense and speaks of the wind, the line is rich in sibilants that hiss, like the wind. When he speaks of Ajax striving, the combination of final consonants and initial sounds slow the line; when he speaks of Camilla's swiftness, the final consonants and initial sounds form liaisons that are swiftly pronounceable.

Or, consider the opening lines of Wilfred Owen's poem "Dulce et Decorum Est," describing a company of battle-weary soldiers trudging toward their camp and rest:

> Bent double, like old beggars under sacks,
> Knock-kneed, coughing like hags, we cursed through sludge.

---

[1] Bad poets.
[2] Twelve-syllable line.
[3] A Greek warrior celebrated for his strength.
[4] A swift-footed queen in Virgil's *Aeneid*.

These lines are dominated by a series of harsh, explosive consonant sounds (*b*, *d*, *k*, *g*) that reinforce the meaning of the lines (a description of tired World War I soldiers). More specifically, the first two syllables of each line are heavily stressed, which serves to slow the reading. And, finally, while the poem ultimately develops a prevailing meter, the meter is only faintly suggested in these opening lines, through the irregular rhythms used to describe a weary stumbling march.

Let us remember, then, that analysis of musical (or for that matter any other) devices can illuminate and enrich our understanding of poetry. But let us also remember that analysis has its limitations. Dylan Thomas once remarked:

> You can tear a poem apart to see what makes it technically tick and say to yourself when the works are laid out before you—the vowels, the consonants, the rhymes, and rhythms—"Yes, this is it. This is why the poem moves me so. It is because of the craftsmanship." But you're back where you began. The best craftsmanship always leaves holes and gaps in the works of the poem so that something that is not in the poem can creep, crawl, flash, or thunder in.

Another writer, X. J. Kennedy, doubtless with MacLeish's poetic critical observations in mind, puts the same idea with less reverence:

ARS POETICA

The goose that laid the golden egg
Died looking up its crotch
To find out how its sphincter worked.
Would you lay well? Don't watch.

Reading Drama

Plays are fundamentally different from other literary forms. Unlike stories and poems, almost all plays are designed to be performed, not to be read. Consequently, the aural and the visual aspects of the drama, which should be at least as important as its dialogue, are left altogether to the imagination of the reader (with the aid of some meager stage directions). Great effort is invested in such matters as costuming, set design, lighting effects, and stage movement by the director and his staff; all of that effort is lost to the reader who must somehow contrive to supply imaginatively some of those dramatic features not contained on the printed page.

As much as possible, the way to read a play is to imagine that you are its director. Hence you will concern yourself with creating the set and the lighting. You will see people dressed so that their clothes give support to their words. You will think about timing—how long between events and speeches—and blocking—how the characters move as they interact on stage. Perhaps the best way to confront the literature of the stage, to respond most fully to what is there, is to attempt to produce some scenes in class or after class. If possible, attend the rehearsals of plays in production on the campus. Nothing will provide better insight into the complexities of the theater than attending a rehearsal where the problems are encountered and solved.

As an exercise, read the opening speeches of any of the plays here and make decisions. How should the lines be spoken (quietly, angrily, haltingly)? What should the characters do as they speak (remain stationary, look in some direction, traverse the stage)? How should the stage be lit (partially, brightly, in some color that contributes to the mood of the dialogue and action)? What should the characters who are not speaking do? What possibilities exist for conveying appropriate signals solely through gesture and facial expression—signals not contained in the words you read?

Staging

Since plays are written to be staged, the particular kind of theater available to the dramatist is often crucial to the structure of the play. The Greek theater of Dionysius in Athens, for which Sophocles wrote, was an open-air amphitheater seating about 14,000 people. The skene, or stage house, from which actors entered, was fixed, though it might have had painted panels to suggest the scene. Consequently, there is no scene shifting in *Antigone*. All the dialogue and action take place in the same location before the skene building, which represents the Palace of Creon. Important things happen elsewhere, but the audience is informed of these events by messenger. Three deaths occur, but none in sight of the audience, partly as a matter of taste and partly because the conditions of the Greek stage prevented the playwright from moving the action inside the palace or to that terrifying mausoleum where both Antigone and her betrothed chose death before submission. Later dramatists, writing for a more flexible stage and a more intimate theater, were able to profit from the intensely dramatic nature of murder and suicide, but the Greeks, almost invariably, chose to tell, rather than show, the most gripping physical events in their stories.

Further, an outdoor theater of vast dimensions implies obvious restrictions on acting style. Facial expression can play no important role in such a theater, and, in fact, the actors of Sophoclean tragedy wore masks, larger than life and probably equipped with some sort of megaphone device to aid in voice projection. Those voices were denied the possibility of subtle variety in tone and expression, and the speeches were probably delivered in rather formal declamatory style. The characters wore special built-up footwear which made them larger than life. In addition to these limitations, Sophocles had as well to write within the formal limitations imposed by the Athenian government, which made available only three principal actors, all male, as the cast (exclusive of the chorus) for each play. Consequently, there are never more than three players on stage at once, and the roles are designed so that each actor takes several parts—signified by different masks. Yet, despite the austerity of production values, the unavoidable clumsiness of fortuitous messengers appearing at all the right moments, and the sharply restricted dramatis personae, among the few Greek plays that have survived are some still universally regarded as superlatively fine dramatic representations of tragic humanity.

Until recently we thought we had a clear conception of what Shakespeare's stage looked like. Scholarship has raised some doubts about this conception, but we still have a good enough understanding of the shape of the playing area to recreate roughly the staging of a Shakespearean play. That staging was altogether different from the Greek. Though both theaters were open air, the enclosure around the Elizabethan stage was much smaller and the audience capacity limited to something between 2,000 and 3,000. As in classical drama, men played all the roles, but they no longer wore masks, and a stage that protruded into the audience made for great intimacy. Hence the actors' art expanded to matters of facial expression, and the style of speech and movement was certainly closer than was Greek style to what we might loosely call realism. Shakespeare has Hamlet caution the actors: "Suit the action to the word, the word to the action, with this special observance, that you o'erstep not the modesty of nature: for anything so overdone is from the purpose of playing, whose end, both at first and now, was and is, to hold as 't were, the mirror up to nature. . . ." But the characteristic matter of Shakespearean tragedy certainly did not lend itself to a modern realistic style. Those great speeches are written in verse; they frequently are meant to augment the rather meager set design by providing verbal pictures to set the stage; they are much denser in texture, image, and import than is ordinary speech. These characteristics all serve to distinguish the Shakespearean stage from the familiar realism of most recent theater and film.

The Elizabethan stage made possible a tremendous versatility for the dramatist and the acting company. Most of the important action was played out on the uncurtained main platform, jutting into the audience and surrounded on three sides by spectators. The swiftly moving scenes followed each other without interruption, doubtless using different areas of the stage to signify different locations. There was some sort of terrace or balcony one story above the main stage, and there was an area at the back of the main protruding stage that could be curtained off when not in use. Although Shakespeare's plays are usually divided into five separate acts in printed versions, they were played straight through, without intermission, much like a modern motion picture.

Though more versatile and intimate than the Greek stage, the Elizabethan stage had limitations which clearly influenced the playwright. Those critical imperatives of time, place, and action (i.e., the time represented should not exceed one day, the location should be fixed in one place, and the action should be limited to one cohesive story line—one plot), the so-called unities that Aristotle discovered in the drama of Sophocles, may well reflect the physical conditions of the Greek theater. Elizabethan dramatists largely ignored them, and in *Othello* we move from Venice to Cyprus, from the fortifications of the island to the city streets to Desdemona's bedchamber. Certainly some props were used to suggest these locations, but nothing comparable to the furniture of Ibsen's stage. Instead, the playwright often wove a sort of literary scenery into the speeches of the characters. For example, in *Othello*, Roderigo has occasion to say to Iago, "Here is her father's house; I'll call aloud." The second act of *Othello* opens with some gentlemen at "an open place near the Quay." Notice the dialogue:

> **Montano.**   What from the cape can you discern at sea?
> **First Gentleman.**   Nothing at all: it is a high-wrought flood;
>   I cannot 'twixt the heaven and the main
>   Descry a sail.
> **Montano.**   Methinks the wind hath spoke aloud at land;
>   A fuller blast ne'er shook our battlements;
>   If it hath ruffian'd so upon the sea,
>   What ribs of oak, when mountains melt on them,
>   Can hold the mortise?

There is no sea, of course, and Elizabethan technology was not up to a wind machine. The men are, doubtless, looking off stage and creating the stormy setting through language. An open-air theater which played in daylight had few techniques for controlling lighting, and speeches had to be written to supply the effect:

> But look, the morn, in russet mantle clad,
> Walks o'er the dew of yon high eastern hill.

Further, the company had not the resources to place armies on the stage; hence, a speaker in *King Henry* V boldly invites the audience to profit from imagination:

> Piece out our imperfections with your thoughts;
> Into a thousand parts divide one man,
> And make imaginary puissance;
> Think, when we talk of horses, that you see them
> Printing their proud hoofs i' the receiving earth.
> For 'tis your thoughts that now must deck our kings.

The theater in the Petit-Bourbon Palace, built about twenty-five years after Shakespeare's death, was a forerunner of the common "box stage" on which so much recent drama is acted. Essentially, this stage is a box with one wall removed so that the audience can see into the playing area. Such a stage lends itself to realistic settings. Since the stage is essentially a room, it can easily be furnished to look like one. If street scenes are required, painted backdrops provide perspective and an accompanying sense of distance. Sets at an angle to the edge of the stage might be constructed. The possibilities for scenic design allowed by such a stage soon produced great set designers, and the structure of such a stage led to the development of increasingly sophisticated stage machinery, which in turn freed the dramatist from the physical limitations imposed by earlier stages. By Ibsen's time the versatility of the box stage enabled him to write elaborately detailed stage settings for the various locations in which the drama unfolds. Further, the furnishing of the stage in Ibsen's plays sometimes functions symbolically to convey visually the choking quality of certain bourgeois life-styles.

None of the historical stages has passed into mere history. The modern theater still uses Greek amphitheaters such as that at Epidaurus, constructs approximations of the Elizabethan stage for Shakespeare festivals, and employs the box stage with ever-increasing inventiveness. Early in the twentieth century, some plays were produced in the "round," the action taking place on a stage in the center of the theater with the audience on all sides. A number of theaters were built that incorporated a permanent in-the-round arrangement. But versatility has become so important to the modern production designer that some feel the very best theater is simply a large empty room (with provisions for technical flexibility in the matter of lighting) that can be rearranged to suit the requirements of specific productions. This ideal of a "theater space" that can be freely manipulated has become increasingly attractive—some have been constructed— since it frees the dramatist and the performance from limitations built into permanent stage design.

Drama and Society

The history of dramatic literature (like the history of literature in general) provides evidence for another kind of history as well—the history of changing attitudes, changing values, and even changing taste. In ancient Greece, in Elizabethan England when Shakespeare wrote his enduring tragedies, right up to the end of the eighteenth century, certain expectations controlled the nature of tragedy. Those expectations were discussed by Aristotle as early as 335 B.C.;

they involved the fall of a noble figure from a high place. Such tragedy reflects important cultural attitudes. It flourished in conjunction with a certain sort of politics and certain notions about human nature. The largest part of an audience of several thousand Athenians in the fifth century B.C. was certainly not itself noble. Neither was Shakespeare's audience at the Globe Theatre in London. That audience, much as a modern audience, was composed of tradesmen, artisans, and petty officials. In Greece, even slaves attended the tragedy festivals. Why then were there no tragedies in which the central figure was a storekeeper, a baker, or a butcher?

There have been many attempts to answer this difficult question, and those answers tend to make assumptions about the way individuals see themselves and their society. If the butcher down the street dies, well, that is sad, but after all rather unimportant to society. If the king falls, however, society itself is touched, and a general grief prevails that makes possible sweeping observations about the chancy conditions of life. A culture always elevates some of its members to the status of heroes—often by virtue of the office they hold. Even now, societies are collectively moved, and moved profoundly, by the death of a president, a prime minister—a Kennedy, a de Gaulle, a Churchill—when they are not nearly so moved by immense disasters such as killing storms or earthquakes or civil wars. But things have changed, and most rapidly within the last 150 years or so.

Simply stated, new cultural values—new attitudes about human nature—have developed, especially since the advent of industrialism and since Freud began publishing his systematic observations about the way men's minds interact with their bodies. The result has been an increasing humanization of those who used to be heroes and an increasing realization of the capacity for heroism in those who are merely bakers and butchers. Thus Henrik Ibsen, frequently referred to as "the father of modern drama," can compel a serious emotional response from his audience over the tribulations of a middle-class lawyer's wife in A *Doll's House*. And Arthur Miller can write an immensely successful tragedy on the life and death of a loud-mouthed traveling salesman named Willie Loman (and that last name may not be altogether accidental). These plays succeed in spite of their commonplace heroes because, as a society, we can now accept the experiences of ordinary people as emblems of our own. Perhaps we can because political institutions in the modern republics and in the socialist countries have, at least theoretically, exalted the common man and rejected political aristocracy. Certainly the reasons for the change are complex. But it remains true that neither Sophocles nor Shakespeare could have written A *Doll's House*.

Dramatic Irony

Dramatic irony allows the audience to know more than the characters do about their own circumstances. Consequently, that audience *hears more* (the ironic component) than do the characters who speak. Shakespeare's *Othello* provides an excellent illustration of the uses of dramatic irony. At the end of Act II,

Cassio, who has lost his position as Othello's lieutenant, asks Iago for advice on how to regain favor. Iago, who, unknown to Cassio, had engineered Cassio's disgrace, advises him to ask Desdemona, Othello's adored wife, to intervene. Actually this is good advice; ordinarily the tactic would succeed, so much does Othello love his wife and wish to please her. But Iago explains, in a soliloquy to the audience, that he is laying groundwork for the ruin of all the objects of his envy and hatred—Cassio, Desdemona, and Othello:

> . . . for while this honest fool
> Plies Desdemona to repair his fortunes,
> And she for him pleads strongly to the Moor,
> I'll pour this pestilence into his ear
> That she repeals him for her body's lust;
> And, by how much she strives to do him good,
> She shall undo her credit with the Moor.
> So will I turn her virtue into pitch,
> And out of her own goodness make the net
> That shall enmesh them all.

Of course Desdemona, Cassio, and Othello are ignorant of Iago's enmity. Worse, all of them consider Iago a loyal friend. But the audience knows Iago's design, and that knowledge provides the chilling dramatic irony of Act III, scene 3.

When Cassio asks for Desdemona's help, she immediately consents, declaring, "I'll intermingle every thing he does/With Cassio's suit." At this, the audience, knowing what it does, grows a little uneasy—that audience, after all, rather likes Desdemona and doesn't want her injured. As Iago and Othello come on stage, Cassio, understandably ill at ease, leaves at the approach of the commander who has stripped him of his rank, thus providing Iago with a magnificent tactical advantage. And as Cassio leaves, Iago utters an exclamation and four simple words that may rank among the most electrifying in all of English drama:

> Ha! I like not that.

They are certainly not very poetic words; they do not conjure up any telling images; they do not mean much either to Othello or Desdemona. But they are for the audience the intensely anticipated first drop of poison. Othello hasn't heard clearly:

> What dost thou say?

Maybe it all will pass, and Iago's clever design will fail. But what a hiss of held breath the audience expels when Iago replies:

> Nothing, my lord: or if—I know not what.

And Othello is hooked:

> Was not that Cassio parted from my wife?

The bait taken, Iago begins to play his line:

> Cassio, my lord? No, sure, I cannot think it,
> That he would steal away so guilty-like,
> Seeing you coming.

And from this point on in the scene, Iago cleverly and cautiously leads Othello. He assumes the role of Cassio's great friend—reluctant to say anything that might cast suspicion on him. But he is also the "friend" of Othello and cannot keep silent his suspicions. So honest Iago (he is often called "honest" by the others in the play), apparently full of sympathy and kindness, skillfully brings the trusting Othello to emotional chaos. And every word they exchange is doubly meaningful to the audience, which perceives Othello led on the descent into a horrible jealousy by his "friend." The scene ends with Othello visibly shaken and convinced of Desdemona's faithlessness and Cassio's perfidy:

> Damn her, lewd minx! O, damn her!
> Come, go with me apart; I will withdraw,
> To furnish me with some swift means of death
> For the fair devil. Now art thou my lieutenant.

To which Iago replies:

> I am your own for ever.

Now, all of Iago's speeches in this scene operate on the audience through dramatic irony. The tension, the horror, the urge to cry out, to save Cassio, Desdemona, and Othello from the devilish Iago—all the emotional tautness in the audience results from irony, from knowing what the victims do not know. The play would have much less force if the audience did not know Iago's intentions from the outset and did not anticipate as he bends so many innocent events to his own increasingly evil ends. Note that dramatic irony is not limited to the drama; poetry, sometimes (as in William Blake's "The Chimney Sweeper"), and fiction, often (as in Joseph Conrad's "The Secret Sharer"), make use of this technique. But dramatic irony is the special tool of the dramatist, well suited to produce an electric tension in a live audience that overhears the interaction of people on stage.

Drama and Belief

Scholarly ordering that identifies the parts of drama and discusses the perceptive distinctions made by Aristotle among its parts can help you confront a play and understand how your responses were triggered by the playwright, the designers of the play, and the performers. But such analysis cannot substitute for the emotional experience produced by successful drama—your deepest responses have to do with states of mind, not with the three dramatic unities. Plays, no less than other art forms, address themselves to that incredibly complex melange of belief, attitude, intellect, and awareness that constitutes a human psyche. As in *Antigone*, sometimes the play torments its audience by imposing on a courageous central character a duty that must be performed and must end in tragic death. Sometimes, as in George Bernard Shaw's *Pygmalion*, the play mocks widely held cultural values—the link between social position and speech patterns—and compels the audience to reexamine some of its fundamental values. If, as humans, we did not share the capacity for possessive love as well as jealousy, with all its terror, all its threat to self-esteem, then the tragedy of *Othello* would be incomprehensible.

While plays operate from within elaborate social and cultural constructions, response to dramatic art depends to a large extent on the condition of the responder's psyche, the state of mind he brings to the performance (or the reading). And that state of mind almost certainly changes with experience and, perhaps, with mood or preoccupation. A confirmed atheist, indifferent to religious dogma, may find himself engrossed by the powerful dramatic values in Ingmar Bergman's modern morality play *The Seventh Seal*. Though atheist, our hypothetical viewer is steeped in the tradition emanating from the Book of Revelations in the New Testament. He has frequently seen or read of death personified—that grim reaper. He discovers in Bergman's squire a character who puts forward his own skeptical view with wit and vigor. If he sees the film, he must be struck with the effect of what Aristotle called spectacle—those lowering leaden skies, the black and whiteness of things, the flagellants attempting to scourge themselves free of some God-sent plague, the burning of a beautiful young witch in the name of God, the relentless pursuit by Death, a figure of some strength, understanding, and wit himself. So, despite disbelief in God, in personifications of death, or in the validity of the Christian experience, the audience is nonetheless moved by the drama that is believable within its own well-known context.

Film

For all the versatility modern technology has given the modern dramatist in lighting, sound effects, scenery, and the like, a play, finally, is fundamentally static—locked in place upon a narrow stage, seen from a vantage point that never changes, dependent on dialogue and stage business for all its effects. If motion pictures were made by filming a performance with a stationary camera, then films would be no more than plays permanently recorded. But films are not made that way. While the film bears some obvious relationships to plays, the differences in technique and range are so significant that one must recognize that film is truly an art form itself, as distinguishable from plays as plays are from novels.

Consider some of the distinctive features of the film. It can take its audience anywhere and provide constantly changing vantage points (thus sharing something of the omniscient point of view available to the novelist). It can look up or look down. It can move in, focus on a single sinister eye, or move out to watch the whole earth circle slowly below. It will, characteristically, in the time consumed by a typical scene in a play, combine scores of different shots lasting from one to fifteen seconds—long shots of characters in a room, middle shots of one character listening to another talk, close-ups of a head alone grimacing expressively. Through the use of fade technique, the film can change time and place instantly. Perhaps most significantly, the film can, somewhat like the novel, provide with comparative ease a great deal of descriptive material—a long shot of the whole village in which the hero's house lies or a raging, ominous sea. The dramatist most often cannot. Again, through the use of close-up, the film can comment, like the novelist. But the effect of a single watching, malevolent eye occupying almost the entire screen has no counterpart in the dramatist's or novelist's art.

These distinguishing techniques of the film point to the unique and crucial characteristic that distinguishes it from novel and play: the film is overwhelmingly and flexibly visual. For this reason film scripts are almost always very difficult to read. Not only is a shooting script distractingly cluttered with camera directions, but, more significantly, the narrative development and meaning conveyed through visual imagery is lost in print. While we would not want to suggest that there are not important differences between reading a play and seeing it performed (plays *are* written to be produced), it is nonetheless true that plays have always enjoyed wide success as literary pieces for reading, because they can be understood and enjoyed as a purely verbal art form. If the dramatist feels that the printed version of his play loses significant meanings or coherence, he can make up for the loss by adding or expanding stage directions (note the elaborate and novelistic stage directions of Bernard Shaw's *Pygmalion*).

This is the remedy employed by Ingmar Bergman for his screenplay *The Seventh Seal*. The very first clause, "The night had brought very little relief from the heat," establishes a fact novelistically. Indeed, much of the power of *The Seventh Seal* as a literary document is attributable to Bergman's skill as a writer. The entire opening passage is a skillful evocation in words of the scene evoked visually in the film with equal power. But Bergman clearly knows that the writer's art differs from the filmmaker's, and so he tells us, as he cannot in the film, that "the morning sun . . . wallows up from the misty sea like some bloated, dying fish." Bergman employs this kind of purely verbal technique throughout the descriptive prose passages, but only sparingly. For the most part, the prose passages *describe* what the film *shows*.

As successful as the printed screenplay is in describing what the film shows, we must recognize that we are ultimately dealing with a translation, with all the loss of power that translations usually involve. The dialogue, set down on paper and strung together and fleshed out by descriptive passages, captures everything except the overwhelmingly visual quality that is unique to the film, with its almost infinite possibilities for varying movement, point of view, clarity, time, and place. While the screenplay of *The Seventh Seal*, then, is a powerful work in its own right, the film is even more powerful. And comparison of the two will teach the reader much about the film as art.

Three Critical Approaches: Formalist, Sociological, Psychoanalytic

Literary criticism has to do with the *value* of literature, its goodness or badness, not with the history of literature. Because value judgments tend to be highly subjective, lively, and sometimes even acrimonious, debates among literary critics accompany their diverse responses to and judgments of the same work. The judgment a literary critic makes about a story or poem is bound to reflect his own cherished values. The truth of a work of art is, obviously, very different from the truth of a mathematical formula. Certainly one's attitudes toward war, religion, sex, and politics are irrelevant to the truth of a formula but quite relevant to one's judgment of a literary work.

Yet, any examination of the broad range of literary criticism reveals that groups of critics (and all readers, ultimately, are critics) share certain assumptions about literature. These shared assumptions govern the way the critic approaches a work, the elements he tends to look for and emphasize, the details he finds significant or insignificant, and, finally, his overall judgment of the value of the work. In order to illustrate diverse critical methodologies, we have examined two of the works in this anthology—Matthew Arnold's poem, "Dover Beach" (p. 839), and Nathaniel Hawthorne's short story, "My Kinsman, Major Molineux" (p. 7)—from three different critical positions: the formalist, the sociological, and the psychoanalytic. We have selected these three critical positions not because they are the only ones (there are others), but because they represent three major and distinctive approaches of literary criticism that may help readers formulate their own responses to a work of literature.

We do not suggest that one approach is more valid than the others or that the lines dividing the approaches are always clear and distinct. Readers will, perhaps, discover one approach more congenial to their temperament, more "true" to their sense of the world, than another. Again, they may find that some works seem to lend themselves to one approach, other works to a different approach. More likely, they will find themselves utilizing more than one approach in dealing with a single work. What the reader will discover in reading the three analyses of the Arnold poem and the Hawthorne story is not that they contradict one another, but that, taken together, they complement and enrich his understanding and enjoyment of these works.

Formalist Criticism

While the formalist critic would not deny the relevance of sociological, bio-graphical, and historical information to a work of art, he insists that the function of criticism is to focus on the work itself as a verbal structure and to discover the ways in which the work achieves (or does not achieve) unity. The job of criticism is to show how the various parts of the work are wedded together into an organic whole. That is to say, we must examine the *form* of the work, for it is the form that is its meaning. Put somewhat oversimply, the formalist critic views a work as a timeless aesthetic object; we may find whatever we wish in the work as long as what we find is demonstrably in the work itself.

DOVER BEACH

From the perspective of the formalist critic, the fact that Matthew Arnold was deeply concerned with how man could live a civilized and enjoyable life under the pressures of modern industrialization or that Arnold appears to have suffered in his youth an intense conflict between sexual and spiritual love may be in-teresting but ought not to be the focal point in an analysis of his poetry. After all, the historian is best equipped to reconstruct and illuminate Matthew Ar-nold's Victorian England, and it is the biographer's and psychologist's job to tell us about his personal life. A critic of "Dover Beach" who speculates on these matters is doing many things, perhaps quite interesting things, but he is not giving us a description of the work itself.

"Dover Beach" is a dramatic monologue, a poem in which a speaker addresses another person at a particular time and place. In the opening lines, Arnold skillfully sets the scene, introduces the image of the sea that is to dominate the poem, and establishes a moment of tranquility and moon-bathed loveliness appropriate to a poem in which a man addresses his beloved. The beauty of the scene is established through visual images that give way, beginning with line 9, to a series of auditory images that undermine or bring into serious question the atmosphere established by the opening eight lines. In this contrast between visual and auditory imagery, a contrast that is developed through the entire poem, Arnold embodies one of the poem's major themes: appearance differs from reality.

In the second stanza, the "eternal note of sadness" struck in the final line of the first stanza is given an historical dimension and universalized by the allusion to Sophocles, the great Greek tragedian of fifth-century B.C. Athens. We be-come aware that the sadness and misery the speaker refers to are not the con-sequences of some momentary despair or particular historical event but are rather perennial, universal conditions of man's mortal life. Indeed, the allusion to Sophocles and the Aegean extends the feeling not only over centuries of time but over an immense geographical area, from the Aegean to the English Chan-nel.

The third stanza develops further the dominant sea imagery. But the real, literal seas of the earlier stanzas now become a metaphor for faith, perhaps religious faith, which once gave unity and meaning to man's life but now has ebbed away and left man stranded, helpless, bereft of virtually any defenses against sadness and misery. The "bright girdle furled," suggesting a happy and universal state, turns into a "roar" down the "naked shingles [i.e., pebble beaches] of the world."

The poet, therefore, turns, in the final stanza, to his beloved, to their love for each other as the only possible hope, meaning, and happiness in such a world. And his words to her echo the imagery of the opening lines with the important difference that the controlling verb *is* of the opening lines, denoting the actual and the real, is now replaced by the verb *seems*. The beautiful world is an illusion that conceals the bleak truth that the world provides no relief for man's misery. This grim realization leads to the powerful final image which compares man's life to a battle of armies at night. We have moved from the calm, serene, moon-bathed loveliness of the opening scene to an image of violence in a dark world where it is impossible to distinguish friend from foe or indeed even to understand what is happening.

"Dover Beach," then, is a meditation upon the irremediable pain and anguish of human existence, in the face of which the only possibility for joy and love and beauty is to be found in an intimate relationship between two human beings. The depth of the speaker's sadness is emphasized by his powerful evocation in the opening lines of the beauty of the scene. The first eight lines move with a quiet ease and flow with liquids and nasals, a movement enhanced by the balancing effect of the caesuras. In lines 9 to 14, the sounds also echo the sense, for now the sounds are much harsher as the plosive *b*s intrude and most of the lines are broken irregularly by more than one caesura.

We have already noted that the dominant image of the poem, the key to the poem's structure, is the sea. It is the real sea the speaker describes in the opening stanza, but when it sounds the "eternal note of sadness," the sea becomes symbolic. In the second stanza, the speaker is reminded of another real sea, the Aegean, which he associates with Sophocles, and the developing unity is achieved, not only at the literal level (Sophocles listening to the Aegean parallels the speaker's listening to the northern sea) but at the symbolic level (Sophocles perceived the ebb and flow of human misery as the speaker perceives the eternal note of sadness). The third stanza further develops the sea image but presents something of a problem, for it is not altogether clear what the speaker means by "Faith." If he means religious faith, and that seems most likely, we face the problem of determining what period of history Arnold is alluding to. "Dover Beach" establishes two reference points in time—the present and fifth-century B.C. Athens—that are related to each other by negative auditory images. Since the function of the lines about the Sea of Faith is to provide a sharp contrast to the present and fifth-century Athens (the visual image of "a bright girdle furled" associates the Sea of Faith with the opening eight lines), the time when the Sea of Faith was full must lie somewhere between these two points or earlier than the fifth century. Since a formalist critic deals only with the work *itself* and since there appears to be nothing elsewhere in the poem that will allow us to make a choice, we might conclude that these lines weaken the poem.

For the formalist critic, however, the final stanza presents the most serious problem. Most critics of whatever persuasion agree that they are moving and memorable lines, poignant in the speaker's desperate turning to his beloved in the face of a world whose beauty is a deception, and powerful in their description of that world, especially in the final image of ignorant armies clashing by night. But what, the formalist critic will ask, has become of the sea image? Is it not strange that the image which had dominated the poem throughout, has given it its unity, is in the climactic stanza simply dropped? On the face of it, at least, we, as formalist critics, would have to conclude that the abandonment of the unifying image in the concluding stanza is a serious structural weakness, lessened perhaps by the power of the images that replace it, but a structural weakness nonetheless. On the other hand, a formalist critic might commend the poet for his effective alternation of visual and auditory imagery throughout the poem. The first four lines of the final stanza return to visual images of an illusory "good" world (controlled by *seems,* as we have already noted) and concludes with a simile that fuses a sombre vision of darkness and night, with the harsh auditory images of *alarms* and *clashes.*

MY KINSMAN, MAJOR MOLINEUX

This rather strange story by Hawthorne may be summarized easily. After an opening paragraph in which Hawthorne comments on the harsh treatment of colonial governors appointed by the British crown at the hands of the people of the Massachusetts Bay Colony, we meet an eighteen-year-old boy named Robin who crosses the ferry one night into an unnamed town. He is the second son of a country minister and has been sent to town to seek out his powerful kinsman, Major Molineux, who, presumably, will use his influence to help the boy make his way in the world. Strangely, the boy is unsuccessful in locating the residence of his kinsman. Worse, he is mocked and threatened by the several people he accosts and is almost seduced by a pretty harlot. Finally, he is told to wait in a certain spot, and shortly a boisterous procession, led by a man with a face painted half red and half black, passes. The procession conducts an open cart in which his kinsman, Major Molineux, tarred and feathered, is being led out of the town and into exile. The boy joins in the laughter at the plight of his once powerful relative but soon decides (his prospects blasted) to return home. A kindly bystander urges him to stay and make his way in the world without the help of his kinsman.

The formalist critic would note that the story is about a young man's initiation into the rude adult world where he must make his own way unprotected by a sheltering family. That world is at best morally ambiguous and at worst menacingly hostile. The transformation in Robin from a self-confident but ignorant grown child to a self-doubting but aware young adult is conveyed through a series of events culminating in a violent climax. Those events, and the atmosphere surrounding them, make for a story that creates, through irony, a mounting suspense released for Robin and the reader with explosive suddenness. Hawthorne's considerable skill in creating that suspense and his method for releasing it are fundamental to the successful embodiment of the *theme*. Naive Robin, a "good child," becomes experienced Robin, more sober and more aware of the evil aspect of the human condition.

The story opens with an apparently superfluous preface in which Hawthorne tells his readers that royal governors in Massachusetts Bay (that is, governors appointed by the English crown rather than elected by the people) were treated roughly, even if they were fair and lenient. The discussion is to serve as "a preface to the following adventures, which chanced upon a summer night, not far from a hundred years ago [approximately 1732]." Hawthorne concludes that opening paragraph: "The reader, in order to avoid a long and dry detail of colonial affairs, is requested to dispense with an account of the train of circumstances that had caused much temporary inflammation of the popular mind." Now it is an article of faith for the formalist critic that no part of a literary work is superfluous. Art is *organic*. All its parts are essential to the whole. The reader may remain ignorant of some particular events that caused some particular social inflammation, but he cannot go on to the adventures of that summer night without some expectation that they will have something to do with the politics of colonial Massachusetts. If this prefatory paragraph is really superfluous, then it constitutes a flaw in the work. If it is not, we shall have, finally, to understand its function in the story.

The narrative begins with an account of the arrival of an eighteen-year-old country-bred youth on his first visit to town, at nine o'clock of a moonlit evening. All of the details provided in this second paragraph are significant and repay close reading. The young man from the country, on his first visit to town, dressed humbly but serviceably, with brown curly hair, well-shaped features, and bright cheerful eyes, presents an agreeable character. His physical description is pleasing. He is doubtless rather innocent (being country-bred and on his first visit to town). But he arrives at night and remains hidden in darkness until illuminated by some light-giving source. The moonlight alone doesn't suffice, and we require the help of the boatman's lantern to see him.

The manipulation of the light and the darkness in the story is crucial. As Robin walks about the town looking for the lodging of his kinsman, Major Molineux, he encounters six different people. The first, a rather dignified old man, is stopped by Robin "just when the light from the open door and windows of a barber's shop fell upon both their figures." The second encounter is within the inn, where there is light. The third encounter is with the harlot who is discerned by Robin as "a strip of scarlet petticoat, and the occasional sparkle of an eye, as if the moonbeams were trembling on some bright thing." We will see those moonbeams trembling on something altogether different later on. The fourth encounter, like the first two, ends with a threat from the sleepy watchman who carried a lantern. The fifth encounter is with the demonic man with the parti-colored face who "stepped back into the moonlight" when he unmuffled to Robin.

Now for all the local illumination that surrounds the threats, the temptation, and the final promise to Robin that his kinsman would soon be by, Robin remains in the dark. He does not understand why his questions generate such fierce threats from the elderly gentleman, the innkeeper, the watchman, and the demonic man. He sees the harlot in her parlor but doubts (quite rightly) her words and, finally, frightened a bit by the watchman, resists her seduction. The sixth encounter differs from the rest. The kindly stranger dimly sees Robin in the darkness—a literal and metaphorical darkness—and joins him. What of all this?

When the climactic moment occurs, when the procession arrives, it is lit by a dense multitude of torches "concealing, by their glare, whatever object they illuminated." This is rather a strange statement. When there is at last adequate light, the very glare conceals—and conceals what Robin must discover. Yet again, when the demonic leader of the procession fixes his eyes on Robin, "the unsteady brightness of the [torches] formed a veil which he could not penetrate. Finally, as the cart stops before Robin, "the torches blazed the brightest, there the moon shone out like day, and there, in tar-and-feathery dignity, sat his kinsman, Major Molineux!"

The orchestration of the light and darkness in the story becomes a metaphor for Robin's condition. Throughout, he is blind, despite the light. Rebuffs and laughter repeatedly greet his reiterated simple question, and in every case Robin—being, as he says, a "shrewd" youth—rationalizes the responses so that he can accept them without loss of self-esteem. The old man who threatens him is a "country representative" who simply doesn't know how powerful his kinsman is. The innkeeper who expels him is responding to Robin's poverty. The grinning demonic man with face painted half red, half black generates the ejaculation "Strange things we travellers see!" And Robin engages in some philosophical speculations upon the weird sight, which "settled this point shrewdly, rationally, and satisfactorily." In every case, however, Robin's rationalizations are wrong. As "shrewd" as he is, he constantly misunderstands because he is optimistic and self-confident. The reality would shatter both his optimism and his confidence. Despite the lighted places in the darkness, the places where the fate of his kinsman is hinted, he remains in the dark. At the climax, as the light becomes brighter and brighter, it does not illuminate but rather conceals by glare, forming an impenetrable veil through which he cannot see. Finally, when the torches blaze the brightest and the moon shines out like day, Robin sees! Presumably, now, he understands correctly the events of that long night.

But what is it that Robin understands? The question might be put another way. What is it that from the outset Robin doesn't understand? A good-looking, "shrewd" lad with a powerful relative, he expects the people he meets to behave with kindness and civility. A country youth, a minister's son, his experience of the world is limited. As the night wears on, the reader perceives Robin doggedly refusing to recognize that some sinister, evil action is afoot. Robin doesn't accept the existence of evil—everything can be explained in some rational way. With the temptation by the lovely harlot, Robin discovers within himself a sinfulness he might indignantly deny—and he does, after all, resist the temptation. But his weakness might be the beginning of wisdom, because Robin must discover that the human condition is not simple—it is complex. As he waits by the church, he peers into the window and notices the "awful radiance" within; he notices that a solitary ray of moonlight dares to rest upon the open page of the Bible. He wonders whether "that heavenly light" was "visible because no earthly and impure feet were within the walls?" And the thought makes him shiver with a strong loneliness. The implication that humans are inevitably impure grows strong.

This notion is driven home by the cryptic exchange between Robin and the kindly stranger when a great shout comes up from the still distant crowd. Robin is astonished by the numerous voices which constitute that one shout, and the stranger replies, "May not a man have several voices, Robin, as well as two complexions?" The notion that a man may have several voices has never occurred to Robin. In his attempt to deal with the strange sight of the man with two complexions, Robin rationalizes. But he does not learn from the evidence of his senses that man is complex, has different, even conflicting aspects. The stranger tries to teach him this truth—a man has many voices. Robin responds rather fatuously, thinking of the pretty harlot, "Perhaps a man may; but Heaven forbid that a woman should!" What does he mean? Doubtless he wishes to believe that the harlot was indeed the major's housekeeper, that she told the truth, spoke with one voice, and was not the embodiment of a sort of satanic evil attempting to entrap him. All in all, Robin's view of the world from the outset is simplistic. And that view encourages him in his optimistic confidence. The stranger tells him that the world is not simple—that each man speaks with many voices, that the human condition comprises many aspects. The heavenly radiance enters only into an empty church, unsoiled by impure human feet. But Robin still does not understand.

The procession approaches. Grotesque sounds—"tuneless bray," the "antipodes of music," "din"—announce the rout. Laughter dominates, and the light grows brighter and brighter. But still Robin does not understand. There sits his kinsman in tar-and feathery dignity. Their eyes meet in an anguished and humiliating recognition. And Robin laughs.

That laughter is the outward symbol of his understanding. He has learned of human complexity. He has learned that he too contains a satanic aspect. His innocent optimism, based on an unrealistic conception of man, is altered to experienced doubt by his new understanding of the complexity and universality of that evil aspect of humanity that is symbolized by the behavior of the mob and the wild abiding laughter that infects even Robin.

The story is based on colonial history. The opening paragraph serves to remind us of the literal level on which the story operates. Mobs did roam the streets of Boston, did disguise themselves as Indians, did tar and feather and expel crown officers. But our attention is directed to a young, inexperienced boy. Finally, we must ask what has happened. How is Robin changed by his experiences? The images of darkness and light, the temptation scene, the moon-lit church, the mob, and Robin's response to it all weave together into a single cord, the strands of which guide him to a new awareness both of himself and of his world.

Sociological Criticism

In contrast to the formalistic critic, who maintains that the proper job of criticism is to approach each work of art as a self-contained aesthetic object and to attempt to illuminate its inherent structure and unity, the sociological critic asserts that since all men are the products of a particular time and place, we can never fully understand a work without some understanding of the social forces that molded the author and all that he did and thought. The sociological critic feels that the formalistic critic's attempt to view a work as timeless denies the fundamental and self-evident fact that authors do not (and cannot) divest themselves of all the shaping forces of their history and environment. Consequently, the critic must look to those forces if he is to understand a man's works.

DOVER BEACH

To understand "Dover Beach," we must, according to the sociological critic, know something about the major intellectual and social currents of Victorian England and the way in which Arnold responded to them. By the time Arnold was born in 1822, the rapid advances in technology that had begun with the Industrial Revolution of the eighteenth century were producing severe strains on the social and intellectual fabric. An agrarian economy was giving way to an industrial economy, and the transition was long and painful. The new economy was creating a new merchant middle class whose growing wealth and power made it increasingly difficult for the upper classes to maintain exclusive political power. The passage of the celebrated Reform Bill of 1832, extending suffrage to any man who owned property worth at least ten pounds in annual rent, shifted political power to the middle class and gave cities a greater political voice. It was not until 1867 that the franchise was extended to the lower classes. The intervening years were marked by severe social crises: depression, unemployment, rioting. Indeed, during these critical years when England was attempting to cope with the new problems of urban industrialism, the agitation and rioting of the lower classes created genuine fears of revolution (Englishmen remembered very clearly the French Revolution of 1789).

The ferment was no less intense and disruptive in the more rarefied world of intellectual and theoretical debate. While it would be erroneous to assume that pre-industrial England was a world of idyllic stability, there can be little doubt that the pace of change was much slower than during the nineteenth century. Despite sectarian strife, perhaps the greatest stabilizing force in pre-industrial

England was religion. It offered answers to the ultimate questions of human existence and, on the basis of those answers, justification and authority for the temporal order—kingship (or political control by a small aristocracy), sharp class distinctions, and the like. The technology that made industrialism possible grew out of the scientific discoveries and methodologies that challenged some of man's fundamental assumptions and faith. Specific scientific discoveries seemed to undermine the old religious faith (for example, Darwin's *Origin of Species*, published in 1859); the scientific approach of skepticism and empirical investigation, in addition to critical scholarship, led to numerous studies of the Bible not as a sacred text of infallible truth but as a historical text that arose out of a particular time and place in the history of man. Close examination of the Bible itself resulted in discoveries of inconsistencies and contradictions as well as demonstrable evidence of its temporal rather than supernatural origin.

Matthew Arnold, born into a substantial middle-class family and educated at England's finest schools, established himself early as an important poet and as one of the leading social critics of the period. In much of his poetry and his voluminous prose writings, Arnold addressed critical questions of his time. The old values, particularly religious, were crumbling under the onslaught of new ideas; Arnold recognized that a simple reactionary defense of the old values was not possible (even if one still believed in them). Unless some new system of values could be formulated, society was likely to, at worst, fall into anarchy or, at best, offer the prospect of an arid and narrow life to individuals. And since the destiny of the nation was clearly devolving into the hands of the middle class, Arnold spent much of his career attempting to show the middle class the way to a richer and fuller life.

For an understanding of "Dover Beach," however, Arnold's attempt to define and advance cultural values is less important than his confrontation with the pain and dilemma of his age. Caught in what he called in one of his poems "this strange disease of modern life," Arnold found that modern discoveries made religious faith impossible, and yet he yearned for the security and certainty of his childhood faith. In his darker and more despairing moments, it seemed to him that with the destruction of old values the world was dissolving into chaos and meaninglessness. In these moments, he saw himself as "wandering between two worlds, one dead, / The other powerless to be born."

"Dover Beach" expresses one of those dark moments in Arnold's life—a moment shared by many of Arnold's contemporaries and modern readers as well, who, in many ways, instinctively understand the mood and meaning of the poem because the realities to which it responds are still very much with us. Simply stated, it is a poem in which the speaker declares that even in a setting of the utmost loveliness and tranquility (a sociological critic might very well here discuss the opening lines in much the same way a formalistic critic does) the uncertainty and chaos of modern life cannot for long be forgotten or ignored. For uncertainty and chaos so permeate the life and consciousness of the speaker that everything he sees, everything he meditates upon, is infected. The scene of silent loveliness described in the opening lines turns into a grating roar that sounds the eternal note of sadness.

In the second stanza, the speaker turns to ancient Greece and its greatest tragic playwright in an effort to generalize and thereby lessen and defend against the overwhelming despair he feels. If the confusion and chaos of modern life are part of the eternal human condition, then perhaps it can be borne with resignation. Yet the third stanza seems to deny this possibility, for it suggests that at some other time in man's history Christian faith gave meaning and direction to life but now that faith is no longer available.

Trapped in a world where faith is no longer possible, the speaker turns in the final stanza—turns with a kind of desperation because no other possibilities seem to exist—to his beloved and their relationship as the only chance of securing from a meaningless and grim life some fragment of meaning and joy. Everything else, he tells her, everything positive in which man might place his faith, is a mere "seeming." The real world, he concludes, in a powerful and strikingly modern image, is like two armies battling in darkness. Whether or not the final image is an allusion to a particular historical battle (as many critics have suggested), it is a graphic image to describe what modern life seemed to a sensitive Victorian who could see no way out of the dilemma.

For the sociological critic, then, an understanding of "Dover Beach" requires some knowledge of the major stresses and intellectual issues of Victorian England, because the poem is a response to and comment upon those issues by one of the great Victorian poets and social critics. Our description of those issues and Arnold's ideas is extremely sketchy and selective; it merely illustrates the approach a sociological critic might take in dealing with the poem. Nevertheless, the sketchiness of the presentation raises important questions about sociological criticism: Where does the sociological critic stop? How deep and detailed an understanding of the times and the writer's relationship to the period is necessary to understand the work? The formalistic critic might charge that the sociological critic is in constant danger of becoming so immersed in sociological matters (and even biography) that he loses sight of the work he set out to investigate. The danger, of course, is a real one, and the sociological critic must be mindful, always, that his primary focus is art, not sociology, history, or biography; the extent of his sociological investigations will be controlled and limited by the work he is attempting to illuminate. To this charge, the sociological critic might very well respond (perhaps in pique) that the formalistic critic becomes so preoccupied with matters of structure and unity that his criticism becomes arid and apparently divorced from all the human concerns that make people want to read poems in the first place. The sociological critic would agree with the comment made by Leon Trotsky, the Russian Marxist revolutionary, in his book *Literature and Revolution*:

> The methods of formal analysis are necessary, but insufficient. You may count up the alliterations in popular proverbs, classify metaphors, count up the number of vowels and consonants in a wedding song. It will undoubtedly enrich our knowledge of folk art, in one way or another; but if you don't know the peasant system of sowing, and the life that is based on it, if you don't know the part the scythe plays, and if you have not mastered the meaning of the church calendar to the peasant, of the time when the peasant marries, or when the peasant women give birth, you

will have only understood the outer shell of folk art, but the kernel will not have been reached.

As a final note, a few remarks need to be made on a special form of sociological criticism, namely, ideological (i.e., Marxist, Christian, etc.) criticism. While the sociological critic differs from the formalistic critic in his approach to literature, the sociological critic tends to share with the formalistic critic the view that works of art are important in their own right and do not need to be justified in terms of any other human activity or interest. The Marxist critic, on the other hand, while sharing many of the assumptions and the approaches of the sociological critic, carries the approach an important step further. The Marxist critic sees literature as one activity among many that are to be studied and judged in terms of a larger and all-encompassing ideology. He holds that one cannot understand the literature of the past unless he understands how it reflects the relationship between economic production and social class. And since the Marxist sees his duty—indeed, the duty of all responsible and humane people— as not merely to describe the world but to change it in such a way as to free the oppressed masses of the world, he will not be content merely to illuminate a work, as does the sociological critic, or to demonstrate its aesthetic unity and beauty, as does the formalist critic. The Marxist critic will judge contemporary litarature by the contribution it makes to bringing about revolution or in some way making the masses of workers (the proletariat) more conscious of their oppression and, therefore, more equipped to struggle against the oppressors.

The Marxist critic might describe "Dover Beach" very much as the socological critic, but he would go on to point out that the emotion Arnold expresses in the poem is predictable, the inevitable end product of a dehumanizing, capitalistic economy in which a small class of oligarchs is willing, at whatever cost, to protect and increase its wealth and power. Moreover, the Marxist critic, as a materialist who believes that man makes his own history, would find Arnold's reference to "the eternal note of sadness" a mystic evasion of the real sources of his alienation and pain; Arnold's misery can be clearly and unmystically explained by the socioeconomic conditions of his time. It is Arnold's refusal to face this fact which leads him to the conclusion typical of a bourgeois artist-intellectual who refuses to face the truth; the cure for Arnold's pain cannot be found in a love relationship, because relationships between people, like everything else, are determined by socioeconomic conditions. The cure for the pain which he describes so well will be found in the world of action, in the struggle to create a socioeconomic system that is just and humane. "Dover Beach," then, is both a brilliant evocation of the alienation and misery caused by a capitalistic economy and a testimony to the inability of a bourgeois intellectual to understand what is responsible for his feelings.

MY KINSMAN, MAJOR MOLINEUX

"My Kinsman, Major Molineux" presents a nocturnal world, viewed largely from the point of view of its young hero, where nothing makes sense to him.

It appears to be an allegoric or symbolic world, a dreamlike world where everything seems to mean something else. Robin searches for the meaning to the strange behavior of townsmen he accosts, for some key which will unlock the mystery. The sociological critic also searches for the key, and he finds it in the opening paragraph of the story, the paragraph that in any short story is crucial in setting the stage for the action about to unfold.

That paragraph, the sociological critic would note, is not a part of the narrative itself but is rather a straightforward summary of the historical situation in the American colonies prior to the Revolutionary War. We are given this summary, Hawthorne tells us, "as a preface to the following adventures." No critic, of whatever persuasion, can ignore that paragraph. In contrast to the actual story, the opening paragraph is clear and straightforward: on the eve of the Revolution, the bitterness and hostility of the colonists toward the mother country had become so intense that no colonial administrators, even those who were kindest in exercising their power, were safe from the wrath of the people. It is in the context of this moment of American history, when there occurred a "temporary inflammation of the popular mind," that the story of Robin's search for his kinsman must be read and interpreted. For "My Kinsman, Major Molineux" is an examination of and comment upon the American colonies as they prepared to achieve, by violence if necessary, independence from the increasingly intolerable domination of England.

We are introduced to Robin as he arrives in town, an energetic, likable, and innocent young man who has left the secure comfort of his rural family to commence a career. He is on the verge of manhood and independence, filled with anticipation and promise, as well as apprehension, as he confronts an uncertain future. But Robin, unlike most young men in his position, has the advantage of a wealthy cousin who has offered to help the young man establish himself. The story narrates Robin's polite and reasonable inquiries as to where Major Molineux resides and the bafflingly rude and hostile responses of the townspeople.

The mystery is Major Molineux, or, rather, the hostility his name evokes. For the reader, at least, the mystery begins to dispel when he learns that the major, an aristocratic and commanding figure, represents inherited wealth and civil and military rank—in short, the authority and values of the mother country. To Robin, fresh from the simple and nonpolitical world of his pastoral home, Major Molineux is a real person, his cousin, whose aid he seeks. To the townsman, on the other hand, Molineux is a symbol of the hated mother country in a political struggle that is turning increasingly ugly.

This difference between what Major Molineux means to Robin and what he means to the townspeople is prepared for at the very outset of the narrative. Robin has left the morally simplistic and nonpolitical world of his country home and come to a town that is seething with revolutionary fervor. The country is the past, America's past; the town is the present, the place where America's future will be decided. As Robin wends his way through the metropolis vainly searching for his kinsman, Hawthorne skillfully weaves into the narrative details suggestive of the political theme. Robin, we are told, enters the town "with as eager an eye as if he were entering London city." Before entering the tavern, "he beheld the broad countenance of a British hero swinging before the door." Once in the tavern, he observes a group of men who look like sailors drinking punch, which, Hawthorne tells us, "the West India trade had long since made a familiar drink in the colony." More significantly, this episode ends when the innkeeper, in response to Robin's inquiry about his cousin, merely points to a poster offering a reward for a runaway "bounden servant" and ominously advises Robin to leave. The suggestion is clear—anyone seeking Major Molineux must be a willing bond servant (bond servitude being a form of limited slavery used by England to help populate the American colonies) and, therefore, an enemy of the revolutionaries.

Robin continues his wanderings, his confusion deepening, until a stranger he accosts tells him that Major Molineux will soon pass by the very spot where they are standing. As Robin waits, his thoughts drift to his country home and family. In a dreamlike state, he dwells upon the warmth and security of the life he has left, the sturdy simplicity of a happy family bound together by a gentle and loving clergyman father. The dream ends abruptly, however, when Robin, attempting to follow his family into their home, finds the door locked. After an evening of "ambiguity and weariness," it is natural that Robin's thoughts should turn back to his home. It is just as natural that his dream should end as it does, for Robin has begun the journey to manhood and independence from which there is no turning back. Although he is not fully aware of the fact, he shares a good deal with the townsmen who have so baffled and angered him. The world of manhood and independence is the complex and ambiguous world where political battles are fought out, and Robin, like America itself, is set upon a course of action from which there is no turning back. The simplicities of an older, rural America, where authority is vested in a gentle father and the Scriptures or figures of authority like Major Molineux, must inevitably yield to the ambiguities of the metropolis, where the future will be decided.

That future, Robin's and the nation's, is dramatically embodied in the climactic episode, when Robin finally finds his kinsman. Tarred and feathered, Major Molineux sits in the midst of a garish and riotous procession, led by a man whose face is half red and half black. This man, Hawthorne tells us, is the personification of war and its consequences:

> The single horseman, clad in a military dress, and bearing a drawn sword, rode onward as the leader, and, by his fierce and variegated countenance, appeared like war personified; the red of one cheek an emblem of fire and sword; the blackness of the other betokened the mourning that attends them.

The strange Indian masquerade of those in the procession is a clear allusion to the disguise of the rebellious participants in the Boston tea party. The incomprehensible words addressed to Robin earlier by various townspeople are clearly passwords arranged to identify the conspirators against established authority.

The meaning of the night's events begins to dawn on Robin as he joins in the laughter of the throng as it wildly celebrates the demise of Major Molineux, whom Hawthorne compares to "some dead potentate, mighty no more, but majestic still in his agony." The entire scene, the entire story which this scene brings to a climax, gives Robin's laughter a crucial meaning. In joining in the laughter of the throng, Robin identifies himself with the political goals of the revolutionaries. But more than that, in so doing he begins, finally, to see that his personal relationship, to both his home and his cousin, is parallel with and inseparable from the relationship of the colonies to its past and the mother country. Robin's joy in seeing his dignified and powerful cousin a scorned captive of the townsmen is intensely personal, the joy a young man feels, ambivalent though it may be, when he is released from the bonds of an authority figure. But the meaning of that authority figure, as the story makes clear, cannot be separated from the political theme, as Robin himself now recognizes.

Such a reading is not meant to imply that "My Kinsman, Major Molineux" is a simple story, a kind of allegory, which embodies in dramatic action a straightforward set of abstract ideas. It is, rather, a story revealing how complex a particular historical event is. That Hawthorne himself had equivocal feelings about the event is made clear by his description of the major, whose dignity and majestic bearing the utmost humiliation cannot altogether extinguish. This fact, together with the unflattering way the townspeople are presented throughout, suggests that Hawthorne viewed the event itself, as least in part, as the victory of mob rule over dignified and settled authority.

At any rate, the procession past, the tension released, Robin turns to the friendly citizen and asks directions back to the ferry. Defeated in his purpose, shaken by and perhaps not yet fully comprehending the extraordinary events of the evening, he decides to return to his family. But the kindly stranger urges Robin to stay. "Perhaps," he says, "as you are a shrewd youth, you may rise in the world without the help of your kinsman, Major Molineux." The stranger's comment is an appropriate conclusion to the story, for it appeals to Robin as a man, as an American man who must achieve independence through his own efforts, however difficult and ambiguous the struggle. Robin must make his way without the aid of his wealthy and powerful kinsman, just as America must make its way without the aid of the mother country. However problematical that freedom is, however dangerous and frightening, it is the inescapable price that real independence exacts.

Psychoanalytic Criticism

Psychoanalytic criticism always proceeds from a set of principles which describe the inner life of *all* men and women. Though there is now a great diversity of conviction about the nature of inner life and how to deal with it, certainly all analysts, and all psychoanalytic critics, assume that the development of the psyche in humans is analagous to the development of physique. Doctors can provide charts indicating physical growth stages, and analysts can supply similar charts, based on generations of case history, indicating stages in the growth of the psyche. Obviously the best psychoanalytic critic is a trained analyst, but few analysts engage in literary criticism. Most of that criticism is performed by more or less knowledgeable amateurs, and much of that criticism is based on a relatively few universal principles set down by Sigmund Freud which describe the dominating human drives and the confusions they produce. We must examine those principles.

First among them is the universality of the Oedipus complex. Freud contends that everyone moves through a psychic history which at one point, in early childhood, involves an erotic attachment to the parent of the opposite sex and an accompanying hostility and aggression against the parent of the same sex, who is seen as a rival in the jealous struggle. Such feelings, part of the natural biography of the psyche, pass or are effectively controlled in most cases. But sometimes, the child grown to adulthood is still strongly gripped by that Oedipal mode, which then may result in neurotic or even psychotic behavior. A famous lengthy analysis of Shakespeare's *Hamlet* argues that Hamlet is best understood as gripped by Oedipal feelings which account for his difficulties and his inability to act decisively, and the Laurence Olivier film of *Hamlet* presents such an interpretation. But how could Shakespeare create an Oedipal Hamlet when Freud was not to be born for some two and a half centuries? Freud did not invent the Oedipus complex—he simply described it. It was always there, especially noticeable in the work of great literary artists who in every era demonstrate a special insight into the human condition. At one point in Sophocles's *Oedipus Rex*, written about 429 B.C., Iocastê the queen says to her son-husband, "Have no more fear of sleeping with your mother: /How many men, in dreams, have lain with their mothers / No reasonable man is troubled by such things." And the situation of Oedipus, and the awareness of Iocastê, provide for Freud the very name for the psychic phase he detects.

Paralleling the Oedipal phase in the natural history of the psyche is the aggressive phase. This psychic feature urges physical and destructive attacks on those who exercise authority, that is, those in a position to control and to deny the primal desires of each of us. For the young, the authority figure is frequently the father. For the more mature, that authority figure may be the policeman, the government official, the office manager. As far back as the Hebrew Bible story of the Tower of Babel and the old Greek myths in which the giant Titans, led by Cronus, overthrow their father Uranus, and Zeus and the Olympians subsequently overthrow Cronus, there appears evidence of the rebellion against the father-authority figure. Freud views that aggressive hostility as another ever present component of the developing psyche. But, in the interest of civilization and the advantages which organized society provides, that aggressiveness must be controlled. The mechanisms of control are various. Early on comes the command to honor one's father and mother. The culture demands of its members that they love and revere their parents. What, then, of the frequent hostility which children feel toward those parents who punish them and deny them the freedom they seek? That hostility often results in guilt—one is supposed to love not hate his parents—and the guilt can be severe as the child (or adult) detects the variance between his desires and his "duty." Such guilt feelings sometimes generate behavior that effectively punishes. The punishment may be internal—may take the form of psychotic withdrawal or psychosomatic illness. Or the guilt may generate external behavior that requires punishment at the hands of society. In any case, the psychoanalytic critic is constantly aware that the author and/or his characters suffer and resuffer a primal tension that results from the conflict between psychic aggressions and social obligations.

DOVER BEACH

"Dover Beach" is richly suggestive of the fundamental psychic dilemma of man in civilization. And since man in civilization is, by definition, discontent because his social duties require him to repress his primal urges, it is not surprising that the opening visual images of the poem which create a lovely and tranquil scene—calm sea, glimmering cliffs, a tranquil bay, sweet night air—are quickly modified by the ominous "only" that begins the seventh line of the poem. That *only*, in the sense of "in contrast," is addressed to a lady who has been called to the window to see the quiet and reassuring scene. No reassurance, finally, remains, as the images shift to an auditory mode:

> Listen! you hear the grating roar
> Of pebbles which the waves draw back, and fling

The tone is strangely changed, the emotional impact of "roar" suggesting something quite different from the serenity of the opening image, and the second stanza closes with the sounds of the surf bringing "the eternal note of sadness in."

Why should sadness be an *eternal* note? And why is the visual imagery largely pleasing while the auditory imagery is largely ominous? The answers to these two questions provide the focus for a psychoanalytic reading of the poem.

The "eternal note of sadness" (an auditory image) represents Arnold's recognition that, however sweet the night air and calm the sea, the central human experience is sadness. At the point in the poem where that sadness is recognized, the poet recalls the great Greek tragedian Sophocles who heard that same note of sadness over 2,000 years ago. (It is, after all, an eternal sadness.) For Sophocles, the sadness brings to mind the "turbid ebb and flow of human misery." Now Sophocles's greatest and best known tragedy, *Oedipus Rex*, ends with the chorus pointing out that no man should count himself happy until at the moment of his death he can look back over a life without pain. Fate, as it afflicted Oedipus, afflicts us all. And the fate of Oedipus provided Freud with the name of that psychic mode through which we all pass. We would all be guilty of parental murder and incest were it not for the necessity to repress those urges in order to construct a viable society. The unacceptable passions are controlled by guilt. We may not commit murder or incest on pain of punishment. We may not even desire to commit murder or incest on pain of possible psychic punishment. The dilemma, the guarantee of guilt or the guarantee of discontent, defines that eternal note of sadness which the poet hears.

We might go further. There is agreement that in infancy and very early childhood the tactile and the visual senses are most important. Somewhat later the auditory sense increases in importance. Consequently, the child recognizes security—certitude, peace, help for pain—tactilely and visually, in the warmth and the form of the omnipresent and succoring mother. Later, through his ears comes the angry "no!" When discipline and painful interaction with others begin, he experiences the auditory admonition which frustrates his desires. It is immensely interesting to the psychoanalytic critic that in "Dover Beach" the tranquilities are visual but the ominous sadness is auditory—the "roar" which brings in the "note" of sadness, the "roar" of the sea of faith retreating to the breath of the night-wind, the "alarms," and the "clash" of ignorant armies by night.

We need to look at the opening lines of the final stanza. Certainly the principal agency developed by society to enforce the morality it required was religion. Ancient religious teaching recognized those very primal urges that Freud systematically described and made them offenses against God. Faith, then, became the condition that made society possible; religious injunction and religious duty served as a sort of cultural superego, a mass conscience, that not only controlled human aggression but substituted for it a set of ideal behavior patterns that could guarantee a set of gratifying rewards for humanity. Hence the poet recalls:

> The Sea of Faith
> Was once, too, at the full, and round earth's shore
> Lay like the folds of a bright girdle furled.

This is a strange image. Surely the emotional tone of "the folds of a bright girdle furled" is positive—that bright girdle is a "good" thing, not an ominous thing. Yet, that girdle (i.e., a sash or belt worn round the waist) is restrictive. It is furled (i.e., rolled up, bound) around the land. In short, the Sea of Faith contains, limits, strictly controls the land. In the context of the poem, that containment is a good thing, for without the restricting Sea of Faith the world, despite appearances,

> Hath really neither joy, nor love, nor light,
> Nor certitude, nor peace, nor help for pain.

Without strong religious faith, acting as a cultural superego, the primal aspects of men are released—aggression comes to dominate human activity:

> And we are here as on a darkling plain
> Swept with confused alarms of struggle and flight,
> Where ignorant armies clash by night.

A certain confusion persists. On the one hand, the Sea of Faith serves a useful function as an emblem of the superego (loosely, the conscience), the name Freud gives to the guilt-inducing mechanism that incessantly "watches" the ego to punish it for certain kinds of behavior. When it is at the full, ignorant armies, presumably, do not clash by night. On the other hand, the superego as associated with auditory imagery is ominous. It reverberates with the painful experience of frustration. Finally, however, the usefulness of the Sea of Faith is illusory. The note of sadness is eternal. Sophocles, long before the foundation of Christianity, heard it. What emerges from the poem's images, understood psychoanalytically, is a progression from a mild note of sadness (frustrated desires) to alarms and clashes (threatening uncontrolled aggressive desires). The calm sea and the fair moon suggest a land of dreams—illusory and without substance. Sadness, struggle, and flight are real.

We need to deal with the girl to whom the poet speaks; we need to understand his relationship to her. The quest for that understanding involves another psychoanalytic principle, another set of images, and a reconsideration of the image of the Sea of Faith.

In earliest infancy, the ego, the sense of self, is not yet formed. The infant child considers the mother, particularly the mother's breast, as part of himself. A gradual and a painful recognition must occur in which the child is dissociated from the mother. The process begins with the birth trauma. In the womb, the child is utterly safe, never hungry, never cold. After birth, there are discomforts. But for a time the mother and her nourishing breast are so much present that the infant does not distinguish where he ends and the other, the mother, begins. But this state of affairs does not continue, and the infant becomes increasingly dissociated. Slowly he learns what is "him" and what is not, what he can control by will (moving his arm, say) and what he cannot (his mother's availability). In short, he learns the borders of his being, the edges of his existence.

Images of borders and edges constantly recur in the poem. Such images may be taken as emblems of dissociation—that is, symbols of the separation between the warm, nourishing mother and the child. Consequently, they are symbols of painful dissatisfaction. The Sea of Faith that

> . . . round earth's shore
> Lay like the folds of a bright girdle furled

seems, on the other hand, much like that warm, encompassing mother who, to the infant, was a part of himself. But dissociation occurs, and the distressed poet perceives that comforting entity withdrawing, retreating "down the vast edges drear / And naked shingles of the world." He has an edge and can no longer reside safely in close association with the source of comfort and security.

Instantly the poet turns to the girl and says

> Ah, love, let us be true
> To one another!

He perceives his companion not erotically but as the source of security, as a replacement for the withdrawing emblematic mother. He offers his "love" a mutual fidelity not to reassure her of his commitment but to assure himself of hers. He wishes to dissolve the edges of his ego and associate, as in infancy, with his "mother." Such an association will protect him from a world in which "ignorant armies clash by night."

MY KINSMAN, MAJOR MOLINEUX

The story opens with Robin crossing a river into an unnamed town after dark. If one takes a psychoanalytic stance, the mysterious opening nicely symbolizes a sort of spiritual journey into mysterious realms. More specifically, the opening suggests an inward journey into the dark recesses of the human spirit. Robin has to confront the psychic confusion resulting from the conflict between the civilized and the psychological response to paternal authority. Robin takes his journey to discover and deal with the paternal figure that is identified in his mind with safety and security, his powerful kinsman, Major Molineux. From a psychoanalytic point of view, it is reasonable to point out that Robin has at least two fathers, since his kinsman, if Robin ever finds him, will serve a paternal function. Some critics suggest that every male Robin encounters serves as a surrogate father. Note that the men Robin meets, with one exception, all act threateningly, all offer to punish him, all assume a position of authority, and, hence, all in some respect are paternalistic. The one exception, the kindly stranger who joins Robin in his watch and who urges him to make his own way without the aid of a paternalistic power is in some ways himself a kind of unreal, idealized father figure, who, though kindly and helpful, requires no price for his help.

From the psychoanalytic point of view, the story is precisely about the price required of young men by their fathers. The price, of course, is not coin. It is behavior. Robin must behave as authority wishes, not as Robin wishes. In return, he will be secure—but almost certainly discontent. Perhaps, deeper than consciousness, Robin feels the pinch of such an economy and unwittingly seeks to avoid payment. After all, the story runs its course as Robin seeks directions to the house of his kinsman. But a kind of haunting inefficiency constantly disrupts his search. Early he realizes that he should have asked the ferryman to take him to Major Molineux. But he didn't. He stops an old gentleman by seizing hold of his coat—rather curious behavior to an elderly stranger. And the stranger's response to the youth's behavior is an angry threat. That threat provokes the first round of recurrent laughter from the loungers in the barber shop. And the threat frightens Robin. Next he becomes "entangled in a succession of crooked and narrow streets," a set of literal streets near the waterfront (but also a lovely metaphor for the human psyche), where he is attracted to an inn. There he receives his second rebuff from the innkeeper, another threat, and is followed out into the street by more laughter.

Robin responds to this rebuff with considerable anger, thinks violent thoughts, but continues to pursue his quest in a most curious way. He walks up and down the main street of the town hoping to run into his kinsman. Actually he is thrilled by the rich and exotic shopwindows and strollers. It is reasonable to assert that at this point, regardless of his rationalization, Robin is not at all seeking his kinsman. He is, for once, doing what he wishes to do. He is enjoying himself, free from any paternal interference. Remarkably, as he gawks along the exotic street, he hears the distinctive cough of the old gentleman he first encountered, the gentleman who threatened him with the stocks, the gentleman who proclaimed, "I have—hem, hem—authority." Robin responds by declaring "Mercy on us!" and ducking around a corner to avoid meeting him and therefore escape authority. Strange as this evasion of authority might seem, stranger still is the half-opened door through which around that corner Robin discerns "a strip of scarlet petticoat, and the occasional sparkle of an eye."

This encounter is quite different from the others which occur both before and after. That red petticoat and sparkling eye belong to a vivacious and devastatingly attractive lady. A harlot, to be sure, but awfully attractive. She tells Robin, in response to his standard question, that Major Molineux is asleep within (an outrageous lie which Robin can't help but doubt), and she takes him by the hand "and the touch was light, and the force was gentleness, and though Robin read in her eyes what he did not hear in her words, yet the slender-waisted woman in the scarlet petticoat proved stronger than the athletic country youth. She had drawn his half-willing footsteps nearly to the threshold" when the watchman appeared. The girl hastily withdraws, and Robin is once again warned by authority of punishment for bad behavior.

The frightened youth does not realize until the watchman has turned the corner that *he* would certainly know the whereabouts of his kinsman, Major Molineux, but his tardy shouted request to the vanished watchman is answered only by more vague laughter. Why didn't Robin ask for directions immediately? Well, he was about to sin against the paternal authority which generally represses and most particularly represses the sexual instincts of sons. The psychoanalytic critic might go even further here in explaining the sources of Robin's guilty demeanor before the watchman whose appearance is fantastically coincidental. (Is he the ever present psychic "watchman" who cries "guilty" at even our ego-gratifying *thoughts* when they violate the "law"?) The desirable girl in the scarlet petticoat says that Major Molineux cohabits with her. Her eyes and her behavior invite Robin to a sexual encounter which he, however nervously, welcomes. If Major Molineux is a surrogate father for Robin, is not the lovely scarlet lady a surrogate mother? And is not an Oedipal situation developed? For students not familiar with principles of psychoanalytic criticism, this will seem a rather wild reading. But reserve judgment. Consider how the story ends. Then, perhaps, the Oedipal feature will not seem bizarre.

Now events move rapidly. Robin, brought to his "senses" by the intrusion of the watchman, remembers that he is a "good" boy and rejects the lovely beckoning arm. But he is upset and feeling violent. He intends to succeed in his quest, even if it means clubbing someone with his stout oak cudgel. The next man he meets, mysteriously muffled, is forced to answer—and answer he does. The muffling, dropped, reveals a hideous, satanic face painted half red and half black. Certainly that painting is a disguise. But this man, we later discover, is the leader of the mob which destroys Major Molineux's power and dignity and, as such, represents a certain aspect first of the community but also of each man in it, particularly of Robin. An old-fashioned Freudian would have no trouble identifying him as Robin's embodied *id*, the name given by Freud to the insistent selfish, lustful, and aggressive aspect of man's psyche, just as he would have no trouble earlier identifying the intrusive watchman as Robin's *superego*. Our awful demonic parti-colored citizen tells Robin to wait where he is and within an hour he will surely meet his kinsman, Major Molineux.

Robin waits and experiences some dreams which are almost hallucinations. He is standing by a church and notices the graves. Perhaps the major is already dead and will appear to haunt him. Wouldn't it be nice to be at home, safe in his family circle? And he is there, but when he seeks to follow his family into the house, the door is closed and locked in his face. It is a normal dream for a frightened young man the first time away from home. But in the context of the story, this dream acts as a metaphor for Robin's expulsion from the safety of home. Even if he would submit again to the "father" in return for security, the opportunity is denied. One father only remains for him—his kinsman, Major Molineux (who may be dead). It is his home that Robin must seek for shelter from all the perils of independence. But the price is the same—submission and repression. The rioters draw near, the tumult grows loud, the torches cast a great light into the darkness—some revelation is at hand. And the light reveals the demonic man on horseback with a drawn sword leading a riotous procession around a cart in which the powerful, gray, dignified, upright, fatherly Major Molineux sits trembling and humiliated. All the figures Robin encountered during the story return—old "hem-hem," the laughing innkeeper, the saucy harlot. And all laugh. But Robin's laugh is louder than all the rest! For the psychoanalytic critic, that laugh cannot be interpreted other than as the laugh of exultant release from the tyranny of the father, of established authority, and the prospect of independent activity free of stifling inner guilt.

The psychoanalytic critic might go further. He might call attention to the drawn sword held by the embodied id and remark on the relationship between that phallic symbol and the thwarted desire of Robin in the encounter with the harlot. Certain figures which recur throughout the history of literature (and in dreams and psychiatric case histories) are accepted by Freudian critics as symbols of the sexual and aggressive aspects of the human condition. Such deep reading, like all deep reading, is perilous. Yet to the reader well versed in the premises of psychoanalysis and the universal symbols behind which the mind conceals its primal nature, the bold analysis enriches the literary art.

Did Hawthorne deliberately design the psychoanalytic structure of "My Kinsman, Major Molineux"? A difficult question. He certainly did not incorporate an embodied superego and id. He never heard of those psychic abstractions. He certainly did not incorporate by design a phallic sword suggesting that Robin's sexual freedom is obtained through Major Molineux's exile. But, the psychoanalytic critic responds, Hawthorne, as a sensitive artist, perceives the deep struggle between desire and duty, between primal urge and social restraint. And that struggle he incorporates. As for the drawn sword, he had no idea of its psychic significance. He would be appalled by the modern psychoanalytic response. But, for the analyst, that does not in the least contradict the modern conviction that universal symbols, however unconscious, struggle to the surface in all art. That psychoanalytic critic would admire Hawthorne's "My Kinsman, Major Molineux" for effectively and accurately portraying the rite of passage of young Robin from innocence to experience, from repressed childhood to independent manhood.

Writing About Literature*

Writing about literature compels the student to discover and come to terms with, his or her own often complex response to an author's work. Every element in a literary work has been deliberately incorporated by the author—the description of the setting, the events that constitute the plot, the particular speeches of characters, the imagery. A rather mysterious intellectual and emotional event occurs within the reader as a result of the writer's purposeful manipulation of language. An essay about literature inevitably attempts some description of the author's purposes and techniques and some discussion of the reader's response.

As an illustration of the relationship between author's purpose and reader's response, consider these opening lines of a poem by W. H. Auden (the poem appears on p. 852):

> That night when joy began
> Our narrowest veins to flush,
> We waited for the flash
> Of morning's levelled gun.

The stanza tells of a new joy, probably erotic, that the speaker and his companion experience one night. But the reader must see that the speaker is apprehensive about that joy. The writer has created that mood of apprehension by using a violent image—the flash of morning's gun—to characterize the speaker's fears about the consequences of possible discovery. The images in the subsequent stanzas of the poem suggest that the lovers are trespassers and that the leveled gun they fear belongs to the keeper of the forbidden fields they enjoyed. Thus the reader responds to the poem with an awareness that the lovers have risked danger for the sake of joy.

Though the correspondence between "writer's purpose" and "reader's response" is by no means exact, any attempt to write about literature is, in one way or another, an attempt to discover and describe that correspondence. In other words, whatever the assignment, your fundamental task is to provide the answers to two questions: How do I respond to this piece? How has the author brought about my response?

---

*See, as well, the appendices "Reading Fiction," "Reading Poetry," "Reading Drama," and "Three Critical Approaches." Those discussions may well suggest useful approaches to writing assignments.

The Journal

Many instructors will require you to keep a journal, a day-by-day account of your reactions to and reflections about what you've been reading. Even if a journal is not required, you might want to keep one for a variety of reasons. From a purely practical perspective, a journal provides valuable mental exercise: forcing yourself to write in a journal regularly is an excellent way to limber up your writing abilities and overcome the fear of facing a blank page. Because journals are like diaries in the sense that they are not meant to be seen by anyone else, you need not worry about whether you are constructing grammatical sentences, whether you are writing cohesive paragraphs and developing your ideas, or even whether you are always making sense. You are free to comment on some aspect of a work or set down a highly personal recollection that something in the work triggered. What is important is that you are recording your reactions, ideas, feelings, questions. If you are conscientious about keeping your journal, you may come to find the act of writing a challenging and—who knows?—even a pleasant activity.

A journal's usefulness extends beyond personal pleasure. When the time comes to write a formal essay for your class, the journal can provide you with a large range of possible topics. Suppose while you were reading Alastair Reid's poem "Curiosity" you confided to your journal your own curiosity about the reasons the poet selected cats and dogs to carry the theme. You might write an interesting essay on this topic, based on the thesis that, although both are domestic animals, the cat is a far wilder creature than the more docile and domestic dog.

You can also use a journal to record unfamiliar words that you encounter in your reading and plan to look up later. In reading Stevie Smith's "To Carry the Child," for example, you might wonder what *carapace* means. You enter the word in your journal, and, when you look it up, you find that *carapace* means a bony shell, such as a turtle's. With this knowledge you can return to the poem and appreciate the image, which might suggest the topic for an essay.

Some of your journal entries will probably be confessions of bafflement and confusion. Why does Tolstoy begin "The Death of Iván Ilých" at the end? Why does Crane in "The Bride Comes to Yellow Sky" open part III with a reference to a character's shirt and the place where it was made as well as the ethnic origin of the people who made it? Why does Fred Daniels, the protagonist in Richard Wright's "The Man Who Lived Underground," use the money and precious stones he's acquired to decorate his hideout rather than try to reenter the upper world and live as a rich man? Is he crazy? What is the point of reading a story about a crazy man? Working out an answer to any of these questions could lead to an interesting essay.

Anything you want to enter in your journal is relevant, including the most personal feelings and recollections triggered by a work. Adrienne Rich's "The Middle-aged" might remind you of the feelings you had as a child when you visited the homes of relatives. Exploring your own childhood feelings and comparing them with those expressed in Rich's poem could lead in any number of ways to a fascinating essay (for example, how poets give memorable and vivid expression to experiences we've all had). Or you might jot down, after reading Kate Chopin's "The Storm," your moral disapproval of the story's central event— marital infidelity. You might then reread the story to discover whether it seems to disapprove of infidelity or whether you have imposed on it your own personal moral values. Sorting out such feelings could result in an essay on the interaction between the moral values of a reader and those embodied in a particular work.

Finally, remember that (unless your instructor has specific guidelines for your journal keeping) your journal will be the one place where you can write as much or as little as you please, as often or infrequently as you wish, with care and deliberation or careless speed. Its only purpose is to serve your needs. But if you write fairly regularly, you will probably be surprised not only at how much easier the act of writing becomes but also at how many ideas suddenly pop into your head in the act of writing. Henry Adams was surely right when he observed, "The habit of expression leads to the search for something to express."

The Summary Report

Another form of writing, more structured than the journal, is the summary report. In a summary report, you answer, in order, a series of basic questions about a literary work. Your instructor may assign such a report, but even if he or she does not, you might want to try one occasionally as a way of coming to terms with the essential elements of a work. Instructors usually ask that a summary report be limited to a page (or at most two pages) of looseleaf notebook paper or to both sides of a five-by-eight-inch note card. If you are doing one for your own satisfaction only, you might want to allow yourself a little more space than these limits specify. Summary reports not only are good exercise but also give you a valuable resource when, at the end of the semester, you sit down to review the term's reading assignments.

The general format for a summary report is similar for all genres, but the details in each genre, of course, vary. For example, the essential elements of both a play and a story will include plot, whereas plot will be irrelevant for most (though not all) poems. Listed below are the essential elements for summary reports in each of the three genres. Following the lists are two sample summary reports. If the listed elements do not apply to the particular work you are trying to cover in a summary report, don't hesitate to make appropriate deletions and changes in the elements.

Short Story

1. Author and title; date of publication
2. Name (if any) of central character and character's important traits

3. Point of view
4. Setting of action; significance, if any, of setting
5. Summary of plot
6. Nature of conflict
7. Tone
8. Style
9. Central event(s)
10. Theme
11. Evaluation

Poem

1. Author and title; date of publication
2. Speaker
3. Occasion of the poem
4. Setting
5. Formal Structure
6. Image patterns
7. Symbols
8. Theme
9. Other noteworthy elements
10. Evaluation

Play

1. Author and title; date of publication
2. Name of central character and character's important traits
3. Other important characters
4. Setting, place and time
5. Summary of plot
6. Nature of conflict
7. Style
8. Central event(s)
9. Theme
10. Evaluation

> (Student's name)
>
> Frank O'Connor, "My Oedipus Complex," 1950
>
> Central character: Larry, an adult male
>
> Point of view: First-person narration of events that occurred during Larry's early childhood.
>
> Setting: Larry's childhood home.
>
> Summary of plot: Until Larry was five, his father, Mick, was

away in the army most of the time. Larry's comfortable life
with his mother abruptly ends when the war ends and his
father returns home. Larry no longer has his mother to himself, and he begins to see his father as an enemy. Larry's
constant struggle to regain the dominant place in his mother's affections ends when his brother is born. The new baby
absorbs all the mother's time, so now the father, too, is excluded from the mother's attention. One night, Larry awakens
to find his father in bed with him. He had been driven from
his own bed by the mother's attention to the crying infant.
Now the child and his father become friends, bound together
by the experience of rejection.

Nature of conflict: The competition between the narrator and
his father for the mother's attention.

Tone: Humorous and ironic because we understand the reason
for Larry's puzzlement and pain, though he didn't at the
time.

Style: The language, except when dialogue is reproduced, is
ironic, civilized, and precise, but nonetheless relaxed. One
hears an educated adult, not a small boy.

Central events: The first is the permanent return of the
father when Larry realizes that things are going to be different (and worse) for him. The second occurs when Larry discovers his father in bed with him, and they, both rejected,
become friends.

Theme: Depends on Freud's theory that young male children
love their mothers possessively and see their fathers as rivals for their mothers' love. The idea of sibling rivalry is
also important to the story. Tension and antagonism are replaced by friendship when the authority figure, the father,
suffers the same rejection as the child.

Evaluation: A clever story because it depends for much of its
effect on what the reader knows and the young boy doesn't.
The poetic justice of the ending delighted me, as did the
ironic line that set the tone for the story: "The war was the
most peaceful period of my life."

(Student's name)
William Shakespeare, Sonnet 73, 1609
Speaker: Lyric voice.
Occasion of the poem: Speaker's realization that he is grow-
ing old and will soon die.

Setting: None.

Formal structure: A sonnet in iambic pentameter rhyming ababcdcdefefgg.

Image patterns: As the rhyme scheme shows, the sonnet divides into three quatrains and a concluding couplet. The image in the first quatrain evokes autumn, in the second, twilight, and in the third, a dying fire. Together, they make up a pattern of endings.

Symbols: Because the speaker associates himself with the approaching end of a year, of a day, and of a fire, it is clear that these images symbolize the speaker's keen sense of his (everyone's?) mortality.

Theme: The poet calls upon his friend to cherish him (the poet) and life, because our stay on earth is brief and death inevitable.

Other noteworthy elements: The ordering of the symbols is very effective. They go from wide (year) to narrow (day) to specific and concrete (fire). The progression is also effective because the first image describes the bare boughs of winter, the second refers to sleep ("Death's second self"), and the third refers to "ashes" and "the deathbed," each one making the reality of death more immediate and vivid.

Evaluation: I found this a very hard poem to understand. I was confused by line 4 until I recognized that "choirs" were "choir stalls" and not "birds." The image in the third quatrain was also hard, but once I realized that "his" in line 10 meant "its," the image became clear. In fact, I was, finally, impressed with how much meaning Shakespeare packed into 14 lines.

Essays

Your journal will allow you to struggle with your reading privately. It may produce wonders of understanding; it should, as well, reveal to you lapses in understanding. The summary report, although a useful tool for identifying the substance of a work, remains, after all, a set of notes. It asks little of your wits. Most instructors will demand some demonstration of those wits—they will ask you to write formal essays that provide evidence of your talent for critical response. Formal essays in introduction-to-literature courses characteristically fall into one of three modes: explication, analysis, and comparison and contrast.

Explication

In explication, you examine a work in as much detail as possible, line by line, stanza by stanza, scene by scene, explaining each part as fully as you can and showing how the author's techniques produce the reader's response. An explication is essentially a demonstration of your thorough understanding of the poem, the story, or the play.

Here is a sample essay that explicates a relatively difficult poem, Dylan Thomas's "Do Not Go Gentle into That Good Night." (The poem appears on p. 1158.)

Dylan Thomas's villanelle "Do Not Go Gentle into That Good Night" is addressed to his aged father. The poem is remarkable in a number of ways, most notably in that contrary to the most common poetic treatments of the inevitability of death which argue for serenity or celebrate the peace that death provides, this poem urges resistance and rage in the face of death. It justifies that unusual attitude by describing the rage and resistance to death of four kinds of men, all of whom can summon up the image of a complete and satisfying life that is denied to them by death.

The first tercet of the intricately rhymed villanelle opens with an arresting line. The adjective "gentle" appears where we would expect the adverb "gently." The strange diction suggests that "gentle" may describe both the going (i.e., gently dying) and the person (i.e., gentleman) who confronts death. Further, the speaker characterizes "night," here clearly a figure for death, as "good." Yet in the next line, the speaker urges that the aged should violently resist death, characterized as the "close of day" and "the dying of the light." In effect, the first three lines argue that however good death may be, the aged should refuse to die gently, should passionately rave and rage against death.

In the second tercet, the speaker turns to a description of the way the first of four types of men confronts inevitable death (which is figuratively defined throughout the poem as "that good night" and "the dying of the light"). These are the "wise men," the scholars, the philosophers, those who understand the nature and even the necessity of death, men who "know dark is right." But they do not acquiesce in death "because their words had forked no lightning," because their

published wisdom failed to bring them to that sense of completeness and fulfillment that can accept death. Therefore,
wise as they are, they reject the theoretical "rightness" of
death and refuse to "go gentle."

The second sort of men—"good men," the moralists, the social reformers, those who attempt to better the world through
action as the wise men attempt to better it through "words"—
also rage against death. Their deeds are, after all, "frail."
With sea imagery, the speaker suggests that these men might
have accomplished fine and fertile things—their deeds "might
have danced in a green bay." But, with the "last wave" gone,
they see only the frailty, the impermanence of their acts,
and so they, too, rage against the death that deprives them
of the opportunity to leave a meaningful legacy.

So, too, the "wild men," the poets who "sang" the loveliness and vitality of nature, learn, as they approach death,
that the sensuous joys of human existence wane. As the life-
giving sun moves toward dusk, as death approaches, their
singing turns to grieving, and they refuse to surrender
gently, to leave willingly the warmth and pleasure and beauty
that life may entail.

And finally, with a pun suggestive of death, the "grave
men," those who go through life with such high seriousness as
never to experience gaiety and pleasure, see, as death approaches, all the joyous possibilities that they were blind
to in life. And they, too, rage against the dying of a light
that they had never properly seen before.

The speaker then calls upon his aged father to join these
men raging against death. It is only in this final stanza
that we discover that the entire poem is addressed to the
speaker's father and that, despite the generalized statements
about old age and the focus upon types of men, the poem is a
personal lyric. The edge of death becomes a "sad height,"
that summit of wisdom and experience old age attains that includes the sad knowledge of life's failure to satisfy the vision we all pursue. The depth and complexity of the speaker's
sadness is startlingly given in the second line when he calls
upon his father to both curse and bless him. These opposites
richly suggest several related possibilities. Curse me for
not living up to your expectations. Curse me for remaining
alive as you die. Bless me with forgiveness for my failings.

```
Bless me for teaching you to rage against death. And the
curses and blessings are contained in the "fierce tears"--
fierce because you will burn and rave and rage against death.
As the poem closes by bringing together the two powerful re-
frains, we may reasonably feel that the speaker himself,
while not facing imminent death, rages because his father's
death will cut off a relationship that is incomplete.
```

The explication, as you can see, deals with the entire poem by coming to grips with each element in it. This same mode can be used to write about the drama as well, but the length of plays will probably require that you focus on a single segment—a scene, for example—rather than the entire play.

You can learn a great deal about the technique of drama by selecting a short self-contained scene and writing a careful description of it. This method, a variety of explication, will force you to confront every speech and stage direction and to come to some conclusion regarding its function. Why is the set furnished as it is? Why does a character speak the words he does or hold his peace? What do we learn of characters from the interchanges among them? Assume that everything that occurs in the play, whether on the printed page or on the stage, is put there for a purpose. Seek to discover the purpose, and you will, at the same time, discover the peculiar nature of dramatic art.

Suppose you are asked to explicate the short first act of Bernard Shaw's *Pygmalion*. You will be mindful that most plays begin with exposition. The playwright must quickly convey a great deal of information before the audience can begin to respond to the issues developed in the play. Conveying that information is a difficult task, and quite often the opening scenes of even great plays are rather static and talky. But good playwrights sometimes meet the challenge with amazing skill. The short first act of *Pygmalion* is a *tour de force* of dramatic craft, because Shaw is able to convey so much information through action and dialogue. A short paper discussing the anatomy of that scene might proceed like this.

```
    In Bernard Shaw's Pygmalion, the curtain goes up on a rainy
night, in a rather seedy part of London, the Covent Garden
vegetable market district. An audience will quickly conclude
that some of the characters, particularly the two women in
evening dress, have been to some formal entertainment--their
clothes suggest that they are of high social standing. A mys-
terious gentleman, unbothered by the rain, stands with his
back to the audience and writes from time to time in his
```

notebook—a peculiar pastime under the circumstances. The first two speeches of the play inform us that a man named Freddy has been sent to search for a taxicab to carry the two women home.

Shaw conveys for a reader of the play the same uncertainty that a performance audience would feel—he does not identify the characters by name. Instead the speeches are assigned to The Daughter, The Mother, The Gentleman, The Flower Girl, The Note Taker. Freddy's name is assigned to his speeches because The Mother mentions his name in her first remarks. The others, except for the bystanders, will be introduced to us in due course.

Though we do not know the names of most of the characters that open the play, we quickly learn something about them and their relationships to one another. The Mother (Mrs. Eynsford Hill, we will later discover) is timid and long-suffering. The Daughter (Clara Eynsford Hill) is generally angry and impatient and a hopeless snob. These qualities are established with just a few brief speeches from each. The Mother, worrying about Freddy (who is later identified as her son), says, "What could he have done, poor boy?" To which the hot-headed Daughter replies, "Other people got cabs. Why couldn't he?" When poor Freddy does return, without a cab, both women attack him unmercifully—The Daughter with particular venom. When Freddy complains about getting soaked for no good reason, she blurts, "What about us? Are we to stay here all night in this draught, with next to nothing on? You selfish pig—." Those hard words reveal not only that The Daughter is selfish herself, but that poor Freddy does not rate very high in the opinion of what turns out to be his own family. He does seem, as The Mother declares, to be "very helpless."

Through this exchange between the two women and Freddy, Shaw establishes in less than one page the nature of the Eynsford Hill family before we even know their names. And with one moment of action, highlighted with "a blinding flash of lightning, followed instantly by a rattling peal of thunder," Shaw causes Freddy to collide with The Flower Girl. We will not be surprised, later in the play, to discover that Freddy is hopelessly in love with her. Surely the lightning and thunder mean something has happened. Meanwhile, the vio-

lent collision provides the new character the opportunity to
reveal all the vulgar manners of a street person. We are told
in the stage directions that she is shabbily dressed--an audience would, of course, see that. And her horrible dialect,
together with her raggedy clothes, defines her place in the
world.

The Flower Girl has innocently called Freddy by his name--
it's just a name. She will later call the taxi driver Charlie; he will call her Judy. But The Mother is obviously horrified that her son Freddy might know this creature socially.
By pumping The Flower Girl, Mrs. Eynsford Hill reveals her
fear that her son has made an improper connection, revealing
that, like her daughter, she is a snob.

Now we meet two more major characters in a bit of exposition managed with great skill. While The Flower Girl begs The
Gentleman (whom we soon discover is Colonel Pickering) to buy
a flower, the mysterious Note Taker becomes interested enough
to be noticed by some bystanders. In this seedy neighborhood,
they immediately assume that The Note Taker is a cop--and The
Flower Girl, clearly feeling uncertain about her position,
practically goes into hysterics. But all is made well. The
Note Taker (later identified as Henry Higgins) is not a cop,
but a linguist, as is Colonel Pickering. And the extraordinary talent of The Note Taker to identify the origins of the
various people by their speech patterns is dramatically established. As well, the central theme of the play is fore-
shadowed when Higgins says, "You see this creature with her
kerbstone English: the English that will keep her in the gutter to the end of her days. Well, sir, in three months I
could pass that girl off as a duchess at an ambassador's garden party."

By the time the scene has ended, we have met and had a
chance to judge the Eynsford Hills--a timid, socially conscious mother; a hard, hot-tempered, and snobbish daughter;
and an inept, but anxious-to-please son. We have met the un-
believably uncouth and dirty Liza, who insists on her dignity
as a human being and shows a curious vanity by not wanting to
give her slum address until Freddy cannot hear her. Furthermore, though she is poor, she is not miserly--she takes the
cab and pretends that she often does. She, as we are told in
the stage directions, has tacked up some prints of fashion-

```
able clothing clipped from a newspaper. All this suggests
that there is a spark in her that has not been put out by her
miserable poverty.
   All of these characterizations are dramatically presented
through action and dialogue. Only in the revelation that The
Note Taker is Higgins and The Gentleman is Colonel Pickering
can the author be accused of a bit of clumsiness. What a pe-
culiar coincidence that they should meet as they do. And they
simply introduce themselves to each other. But, even so,
Pickering has shown himself in his conversation with Liza to
be a sympathetic and generous man--quite different from the
snobbish Clara Eynsford Hill. That is, Pickering is a true
gentleman--Clara is not a true lady. Pickering also differs
from the arrogant Higgins, who reveals himself with the first
words he speaks as an excitable and irritating man. Of all
the characters here introduced, none will change very much
except, of course, Liza, whose possibilities are hinted at in
her behavior with the taxi driver and the cheap prints she
has tacked to her walls.
```

Fiction, too, can be treated effectively in a formal explication. As with drama, it will be necessary to limit the text—you will not be able to explicate a 10-page story in a 1,000-word essay. Choose a key passage—a half page that reflects the form and content of the overall story, if possible. Often the first half page of a story, where the author, like the playwright, must supply information to the reader, will make a fine text for an explication. Although the explication will deal principally with only an excerpt, feel free to range across the story and show how the introductory material foreshadows what is to come. Or, perhaps, you can explicate the climax of the story—the half page that most pointedly establishes the story's theme—and subject it to a close line-by-line reading that illuminates the whole story.

Analysis

Analyzing literature is not the same kind of exercise as analyzing a chemical compound: breaking a literary work down into its elements is only the first step in literary analysis. When you are assigned an analysis essay, you are expected to focus on one of the elements that contribute to the complex compound that is the substance of any work of literary merit. This process requires that you extricate the element you plan to explore from the other elements that you can identify, study this element—not only in isolation but also in relation to the other elements and the work as a whole—and, using the insights you have gained from your special perspective, make an informed statement about it.

This process may sound complicated, but if you approach it methodically, each stage follows naturally from the stage that precedes it. If, for example, an instructor assigns an analysis essay on some aspect of characterization in *Othello*, you would begin by thinking about each character in the play. You would then select the character whose development you would like to explore and reread carefully those speeches that help to establish his or her substance. Exploring a character's development in this way involves a good deal of explication: in order to identify the "building blocks" that Shakespeare uses to create a three-dimensional role, you must comb very carefully through that character's speeches and actions. You must also be sensitive to the ways in which other characters respond to these speeches and actions. When you have completed this investigation, you will probably have a good understanding of why you intuitively responded to the character as you did when you first read the play. You will also probably be prepared to make a statement about the character's development: "From a realistic perspective, it is hard to believe that a man of Othello's position could be so gullible; however, Shakespeare develops the role with such craft that we accept the Moor as flesh and blood." At this point, you have moved from the broad *subject* "characterization in *Othello*" to a *thesis*, a statement that you must prove. As you formulate your thesis, think of it as a position that you intend to *argue* for with a reader who is not easy to persuade. This approach is useful in any essay that requires a thesis—in other words, in any essay in which you move beyond simple explication and commit yourself to a stand. Note that "From a realistic perspective, it is hard to believe that a man of Othello's position could be so gullible; however, Shakespeare develops the role with such craft that we accept him as flesh and blood" is *argumentative* on two counts. "Characterization in *Othello*" is not remotely argumentative. Further, you have more than enough material to write a well-documented essay of 1,000 words supporting your proposition; you cannot write a well-documented 1,000-word essay on the general subject of characterization in *Othello* without being superficial.

You may be one among the many students who find it difficult to find a starting point. For example, you have been assigned an analysis essay on a very broad subject, such as "imagery in love poetry." A few poems come to mind, but you don't know where to begin. You read these poems and underline all the images that you can find. You look at these images over and over, finding no relation among them. You read some more poems, again underlining the images, but you still do not have even the germ of a thesis.

The technique of free writing might help to overcome your block. You have read and reread the works you intend to write about. Now, put the assignment temporarily out of your mind and start writing about one or two of the poems without organizing your ideas, without trying to reach a point. Write down what you like about a poem, what you dislike about it, what sort of person the speaker is, which images seemed striking to you—write anything at all about the work. If you do this for some minutes, you will probably discover that you are voicing opinions. Pick one that interests you or seems the most promising to explore.

Now go back over the poems and seek to discover how specific images might have elicited your responses.

There are a few variations on the basic form of the analysis assignment. Occasionally, an instructor will narrow the subject to a specific assignment: "Analyze the development of Othello's character in Act I." This sort of assignment saves you the trouble of selecting a character on whom to focus and also limits the amount of text that you will have to study. However, the process from this point on is no different from the process that you would employ addressing a broader subject. Sometimes instructors will supply you with a thesis, and you will have to work backward from the thesis to find supporting material. Again, careful analysis of the text is required.

The problem you will have to deal with when writing an analytical essay remains the same regardless of the literary genre you are asked to discuss. You still must find an arguable thesis that deals with the literary sources of your response to the work. For instance, an analysis of a poem might show how a particular pattern of imagery contributes to the meaning of the poem. Or it might argue, from clues within the poem, that the speaker of the poem is a certain kind of character. Or it might demonstrate how the connotations of certain words the poet has chosen to use help to create a particular mood. An analysis may also go outside the poem to throw light on it (see the discussion of sociological criticism, page 1329). For instance, a poem might be analyzed as an embodiment of (or departure from) a particular religious, social, political, or scientific doctrine; as an example of traditional poetic form such as the ballad or the pastoral elegy; or as a new expression of an ancient myth. These are but a few examples; the possibilities are almost endless.

Though plays can be analyzed, like stories and poems, in terms of theme, image patterns, and the like, the playwright must solve problems that are unique to drama as a literary form meant to be acted on a stage before an audience. For example, the mechanics of staging a play limit the extent to which the playwright can shift the locations and times of the action, whereas the writer of fiction can make such shifts very readily with a few words of narration. Similarly, the writer of fiction can, if he wishes, tell the story through a narrator who not only can comment on the meaning of events but can describe the thoughts and motives of some or even all of the characters. In a play, on the other hand, the curtain rises and the characters must convey information through their own words or behavior. The audience does not know what the characters think unless they speak their thoughts aloud. As *readers* of a play we may read the stage directions and any other information the author has provided for the director and actors (and perhaps for readers). We must bear in mind that the audience viewing the play can only know such things as the time of year, the location of the setting, the relationships among characters, or the events that have led up to the action with which the play begins if they are stated in the program or if someone or something on the stage conveys that information.

Playwrights have developed many techniques for solving their special problems, and you may wish to focus on one of these in your analysis of some aspect of a play. For example, you might explain the role of the Chorus or the dramatic function of the messenger in Sophocles's *Oedipus Rex*. Or you might argue that the passage of time is distorted for dramatic purposes in Shakespeare's *Othello*. All of these subjects would involve the consideration of problems that are peculiar to the drama as a literary form that is meant to be acted on a stage.

When you confront the assignment to write about a play, ask yourself some fundamental questions. For instance, what sort of person is the protagonist? Is he admirable? If so, in what respects? Generous? Wise? Courageous? Fairminded? What evidence do you find to support your judgment? Does it come from his own speeches and behavior or from what other characters say about him? If the latter, are we meant to take the opinions of those characters as the truth? Is the tragic conclusion of the play brought about by some flaw or weakness in the character or merely by the malice of others?

Of course, these questions represent only a very few of those you might ask as you think about a play and search for a thesis. If you do choose to deal with some aspect of characterization, you may find that a minor character interests you more as a subject than a major one. And, as we have suggested, you can also ask questions about imagery, about theme, or about various formal or structural aspects of a play. If you ask yourself enough questions, you will discover some thesis you can argue for.

Suppose that your instructor has made the following assignment: Write an analysis of Harlan Ellison's story, " 'Repent Harlequin!' Said the Ticktockman," in which you discuss the theme of the story in terms of the characters and the setting. Now consider the following opening (taken from a student paper):

```
" 'Repent, Harlequin!' Said the Ticktockman" is a story de-
picting a society in which time governs one's life. The set-
ting is America, the time approximately A.D. 2400 somewhere
in the heart of the country. Business deals, work shifts, and
school lessons are started and finished with exacting preci-
sion. Tardiness is intolerable as this would hinder the sys-
tem. In a society of order, precision, and punctuality, there
is no room for likes, dislikes, scruples, or morals. Thus,
personalities in people no longer exist. As these "person-
less" people know no good or bad, they very happily follow in
the course of activities which their society has dictated.
```

At the outset, can you locate a thesis statement? The only sentences that would seem to qualify are the last three in the paragraph. But notice that, although those sentences are not unreasonable responses to the story, they do not establish a thesis that is *responsive to the assignment*. Because the assignment calls for a discussion of theme in terms of character and setting, there should be a

thesis statement about the way in which character and setting embody the theme. Here is another opening paragraph on the same assignment (also taken from a student paper):

> Harlan Ellison's " 'Repent, Harlequin!' Said the Ticktock-
> man" opens with a quotation from Thoreau's essay "Civil Dis-
> obedience," which establishes the story's theme. Thoreau's
> observations about three varieties of men, those who serve
> the state as machines, those who serve it with their heads,
> and those who serve it with their consciences, are dramatized
> in Ellison's story, which takes place about 400 years in the
> future in a setting characterized by machinelike order. The
> interaction among the three characters, each of whom repre-
> sents one of Thoreau's types, results in a telling restate-
> ment of his observation that "heroes, patriots, martyrs, re-
> formers in the great sense, and *men* . . . necessarily resist
> [the state] and . . . are commonly treated as enemies by it."

Compare the two opening paragraphs sentence by sentence for their responsiveness to the assignment. The first sentence of the first opening does not refer to the theme of the story (or to its setting or characterization). In the second sentence, the discussion of the setting ignores the most important aspect—that the story is set in a machine- and time-dominated future. The last three sentences deal rather obliquely with character, but they are imprecise and do not establish a thesis. The second opening, on the other hand, immediately alludes to the theme of the story. It goes on to emphasize the relevant aspects of the futuristic setting and then moves to a discussion of the three characters that animate the story in terms of their reactions to the setting. The last sentence addresses the assignment directly and also serves as a thesis statement for the paper. It states the proposition or argument that will be supported by the information and evidence in the rest of the paper. The reader of the second opening will expect the next paragraph of the paper to discuss the setting of the story and subsequent paragraphs to discuss the response to the setting of the three principal characters.

The middles of essays are largely determined by their opening paragraphs. However long the middle of any essay may be, each of its paragraphs ought to be responsive to some explicit statement made at the beginning of the essay. Note that it is practically impossible to predict what the paragraph following the first opening will deal with. Here is the first half of that next paragraph as the student wrote it:

> The Harlequin is a man in the society with no sense of
> time. His having a personality enables him to have a sense of

> moral values and a mind of his own. The Harlequin thinks that
> it is obscene and wrong to let time totally govern the lives
> of people. So he sets out to disrupt the time schedule with
> ridiculous antics such as showering people with jelly beans
> in order to try to break up the military fashion in which
> they are used to doing things.

The paragraph then goes on to discuss the Ticktockman, the capture and brainwashing of the Harlequin, and the resulting lateness of the Ticktockman.

Note that nothing in the opening of this student's paper prepared for the introduction of the Harlequin. In fact, the opening concluded rather inaccurately that the people within the story "happily follow in the course of activities which their society has dictated." Hence, the introduction of the Harlequin in the second paragraph represents a wholly new and unanticipated element of the story. Further, because the student has not dealt with the theme of the story (remember the assignment explicitly asked for a discussion of *theme* in terms of character and setting), the student's comments about the Harlequin's antics remain disconnected from any clear purpose. They are essentially devoted to what teachers constantly warn against: a mere plot summary. The student has obviously begun to write before he or she has analyzed the story sufficiently to understand its theme. With further thought, the student would have perceived that the central thematic issue is resistance to an oppressive state—the issue stated in the epigraph from Thoreau. The second opening, on the other hand, makes that thematic point clearly and ought to be followed by a discussion of the environment (that is, the setting) in which the action occurs. Here is such a paragraph taken from the second student's paper:

> Ellison creates a society that reflects one possible future
> development of the modern American passion for productivity
> and efficiency. The setting is in perfect keeping with the
> time-conscious people who inhabit the city. It is pictured as
> a neat, colorless, and mechanized city. No mention is made of
> nature: grass, flowers, trees, and birds do not appear. The
> buildings are in a "Mondrian arrangement," stark and geomet-
> rical. The cold steel slidewalks, slowstrips, and expresstrips
> move with precision. Like a chorus line, people move in uni-
> son to board the movers without a wasted motion. Doors close
> silently and lock themselves automatically. An ideal effi-
> ciency so dominates the social system that any "wasted time"
> is deducted from the life of an inefficient citizen.

Once the setting has been established, as in the paragraph just quoted, writers attentive to the assignment will turn to the characters. But they will insis-

tently link those characters to thematic considerations. It might be well to proceed with a short transitional paragraph that shapes the remainder of the middle of the essay:

> Into this smoothly functioning but coldly mechanized society, Ellison introduces three characters: pretty Alice, one of Thoreau's machinelike creatures; the Ticktockman, one of those who "serve the state chiefly with their heads, and, as they rarely make any moral distinctions, they are as likely to serve the Devil without intending it, as God"; and Everett C. Marm, the Harlequin, whose conscience forces him to resist the oppressive state.

The reader will now expect a paragraph devoted to each of the three characters:

> Pretty Alice is, probably, very pretty. (Everett didn't fall in love with her brains.) In the brief section in which we meet her, we find her hopelessly ordinary in her attitudes. She is upset that Marm finds it necessary to go about "annoying people." She finds him ridiculous and wishes only that he would stay home, as other people do. Clearly, she has no understanding of what Everett is struggling against. Though her anger finally leads her to betray him, Everett himself can't believe that she has done so. His own loyal and understanding nature colors his view of her so thoroughly that he cannot imagine the treachery that must have been so simple and satisfying for Alice, whose only desire is to be like everybody else.
>
> The Ticktockman is more complex. He sees himself as a servant of the state, and he performs his duties with resolution and competence. He skillfully supports a system he has never questioned. The system exists; it must be good. His conscience is simply not involved in the performance of his duty. He is one of those who follow orders and expect others to follow orders. As a result, the behavior of the Harlequin is more than just an irritant or a rebellion against authority. It is unnerving. The Ticktockman wishes to understand that behavior, and with Everett's time-card in his hand, he muses that he has the name of "<u>what</u> he is . . . not <u>who</u> he is. . . . Before I can exercise proper revocation, I have to know who this what is." And when he confronts Everett, he does not just liquidate him. He insists that Everett repent.

He tries to convince Everett that the system is sound, and
when he cannot win the argument, he dutifully reconditions
Everett, since he is, after all, more interested in justify-
ing the system than in destroying its enemies. It is easy to
see this man as a competent servant of the Devil who thinks
he is serving God.

But only Everett C. Marm truly serves the state because his
conscience requires him to resist. He is certainly not physically heroic. His very name suggests weak conformity. Though
he loves his Pretty Alice, he cannot resign from the rebellious campaign his conscience insists upon. So, without violence, and mainly with the weapon of laughter, he attacks the
mechanical precision of the system and succeeds in breaking
it down simply by making people late. He is himself, as Alice
points out, always late, and the delays that his antics produce seriously threaten the well-being of the smooth but
mindless system he hates. He is, of course, captured. He refuses, even then, to submit and has his personality destroyed
by the authorities that fear him. The Ticktockman is too
strong for him.

An appropriate ending emerges naturally from this student's treatment of the
assignment. Having established that the story presents characters who deal in
different ways with the oppressive quality of life in a time- and machine-ob-
sessed society, the student concludes with a view of the author's explicit and
implicit criticisms of such a society:

Harlequin is defeated, but Ellison, finally, leaves us with
an optimistic note. The idea of rebellion against the system
will linger in the minds of others. There will be more Harle-
quins and more disruption of this system. Many rebels will be
defeated, but any system that suppresses individualism will
give birth to resistance. And Harlequin's defeat is by no
means total. The story ends with the Ticktockman himself arriving three minutes late for work.

Comparison and Contrast

An essay in comparison and contrast, showing how two works are similar to
and different from one another, almost always starts with a recognition of similarities, most likely similarities of subject matter. While it is possible to compare *any* two works, the best comparison and contrast essays emerge from the

analysis of two works similar enough to illuminate each other (most comparison and contrast assignments will involve two works of the same genre). Two works about love, or death, or conformity, or innocence, or discovery give you something to begin with. But these are very large categories; two random poems about the same subject may be so dissimilar that a comparison and contrast essay about them would be very difficult. Both Shelley's "Ozymandias" and Randall Jarrell's "The Death of the Ball Turret Gunner" are about death; but they deal with the subject so differently that they would probably not yield a very interesting essay. On the other hand, not only are Dickinson's "Apparently with No Surprise" and Frost's "Design" both about death, but they both use remarkably similar events as the occasion for the poem. And starting with these similarities, you would soon find yourself noting the contrasts (in tone, for example, and theme) between nineteenth-century and twentieth-century views of the nature of God.

Before you begin writing your paper, you ought to have clearly in mind the points of comparison and contrast you wish to discuss and the order in which you can most effectively discuss them. You will need to give careful thought to the best way to organize your paper. As a general rule, it is best to avoid dividing the paper into separate discussions of each work. That method tends to produce two separate, loosely joined analysis essays. The successful comparison and contrast essay treats some point of similarity or contrast between the two works, then moves on to succeeding points, and ends with an evaluation of the comparative merits of the works.

Like analysis essays—indeed like any essay that goes beyond simple explication—comparison and contrast essays require theses. However, a comparison and contrast thesis is generally not difficult to formulate: you must identify the works under consideration and summarize briefly your reasons for making the comparison.

Here is a student paper that compares and contrasts a Dylan Thomas poem ("Do Not Go Gentle into That Good Night," explicated earlier in this discussion) with the poetic response it triggered from a poet with different views.

> Dylan Thomas's "Do Not Go Gentle into That Good Night" and Catherine Davis's "After a Time" demand comparison: Davis's poem was written in deliberate response to Thomas's. Davis assumes the reader's familiarity with "Do Not Go Gentle," which she uses to articulate her contrasting ideas. "After a Time," although it is a literary work in its own right, might even be thought of as serious parody—perhaps the greatest compliment one writer can pay another.
>
> "Do Not Go Gentle into That Good Night" was written by a young man of thirty-eight who addresses it to his old and ailing father. It's interesting to note that the author himself had very little of his own self-destructive life left as

he was composing this piece. Perhaps that's why he seems to have more insight into the subject of death than most men of his age. He advocates raging and fighting against it, not giving in and accepting it.

"After a Time" was written by a woman of about the same age and is addressed to no one in particular. Davis has a different philosophy about death. She "answers" Thomas's poem and presents her differing views, using the same poetic form—a villanelle. Evidently, she felt it necessary to present a contrasting point of view eight years after Thomas's death.

While "Do Not Go Gentle" protests and rages against death, Davis's poem suggests a quiet resignation and acquiescence. She seems to feel that raging against death is useless and profitless. She argues that we'll eventually become tame, anyway, after the raging is done. At the risk of sounding sexist, I think it interesting that the man rages and the woman submits, as if the traditionally perceived differences between the behavior of men and women are reflected in the poems.

Thomas talks about different types of men and why they rage against death. "Wise men" desire immortality. They rage against death occurring before they've made their mark on history. "Good men" lament the frailty of their deeds. Given more time, they might have accomplished great things. "Wild men" regret their constant hedonistic pursuits. With more time they could prove their worth. "Grave men" are quite the opposite and regret they never took time for the pleasures in life. Now it's too late. They rage against death because they're not ready for it.

His father's death is painful to Thomas because he sees himself lying in that bed; his dying father reminds him of his own inevitable death. The passion of the last stanza, in which the poet asks his father to bless and curse him, suggests that he has doubts about his relationship with his father. He may feel that he has not been enough of a son. He put off doing things with and for his father because he always felt there would be time later. Now time has run out and he feels cheated. He's raging for his father now. He'll rage for himself later.

Catherine Davis advocates a calm submission, a peaceful acquiescence. She feels raging is useless and says that those of us who rage will finally "go tame/When what we have we can no longer use." When she says "One more thing lost is one thing less to lose," the reader can understand and come to terms with the loss of different aspects of the mind and body, such as strength, eyesight, hearing, and intellect. Once we've lost one of these, it's one thing less to worry about losing. After a time, everything will be lost, and we'll accept that, too, because we'll be ready for it.

In a contest of imagery, Thomas would certainly win the day. His various men not only rage and rave, they <u>burn</u>. Their words "forked no lightning," their deeds might have "danced in a green bay," they "sang the sun in flight," and they see that "blind eyes could blaze like meteors." Davis's images are quiet—generally abstract and without much sensory suggestiveness. She gives us "things lost," a "reassuring ruse," and "all losses are the same." Her most powerful image—"And we go stripped at last the way we came"—makes its point with none of the excitement of Thomas's rage. And yet, I prefer the quiet intelligence of Davis to the high energy of Thomas.

"And we go stripped at last the way we came" can give strange comfort and solace to those of us who always envied those in high places. Death is a great leveller. Men are not all created equal at birth, not by a long shot. But we will bloody well all be equal when we make our final exit. Kings, popes, and heads of state will go just as "stripped" as the rest of us. They won't get to take anything with them. All wealth, power, and trappings will be left behind. We will all finally and ultimately be equal. So why rage? It won't do us any good.

Writing the Essay

If you have thought about an assignment sufficiently and reread the work you intend to write about with enough care to formulate a thesis, then you have already accomplished a major part of the task. You have, however loosely, constructed an argument and marshaled some of the evidence to support it. Now you must begin to be rigorous. Take notes. The most efficient method is to use three-by-five-inch index cards. Take one note per card, and use some key words at the top to identify the subject of the note. This procedure allows you to arrange your note cards in the most workable order when you are drafting your paper.

As you take your notes and then arrange the cards, you will begin to get some sense of the number of paragraphs you will need to support the thesis you have announced in the opening paragraph. Generally, each paragraph will focus on one major point (perhaps with its own mini-thesis), and bring together the evidence necessary to support that point.

As you write and rewrite, you should make sure that the progression of ideas from paragraph to paragraph is clear. To accomplish this, link each paragraph to the preceding one with a transitional word or phrase. Even the most carefully organized essay may seem abrupt or disjointed to the reader if you neglect to provide bridges between the paragraphs. A simple "However," "Nevertheless," "Furthermore," or "On the other hand" will often be adequate. Sometimes the entire opening sentence of a paragraph may provide the transition (and avoid the monotony of the standard words and phrases). Let us assume, for example, that you are writing an essay in which you argue that in Dylan Thomas's poem "Fern Hill" the mature speaker, now keenly aware of mortality, perceives the innocence of his childhood as a state of religious grace. In one or more paragraphs, you have analyzed the religious imagery of the poem, and you now begin a new paragraph with the sentence, "While the religious imagery dominates the poem, it is supported by a well-developed pattern of color imagery." Such a transitional sentence signals the reader that you will now consider another pattern of imagery that provides further evidence to support the thesis, since, as you will show, the color imagery is in fact a subpattern of the religious imagery.

Simply stated, in a tightly organized essay there ought to be a reason why one paragraph follows rather than precedes another. In fact, you may test the organization of your essay by asking yourself whether the paragraphs can be rearranged without significant effect. If they can be, chances are that your organization is weak, your ideas unclarified.

Having worked out an opening paragraph with a thesis and worked through the body of your essay to support the thesis, you now must confront the problem of how to conclude. Your conclusion should be brief, rarely more than three or four sentences. Ideally, it should leave the reader with a sense of both completeness and significance. For a short paper, it is unnecessary to restate or summarize your main points, because your reader will not have trouble remembering them. If your essay has been primarily appreciative and impressionistic, a general statement about the value of the work to you might bring the essay nicely to rest. Or you might conclude with a statement about the relevance of the work to the world we live in. When you have said all you have to say, you have finished. Avoid the common error of turning the conclusion into a beginning by taking up new evidence or ideas in the final paragraph.

Exploring Fiction, Poetry, and Drama

Here are a number of pertinent questions you might ask yourself when you are faced with the task of writing about literature. To a large extent, they are

elaborations of the questions that you answer for a summary report. Your answers to these questions can help you overcome the awful whiteness of the empty
page.

Fiction

1. From what point of view is the story told? Can you speculate on the appropriateness of that point of view? If a story is told from the point of view of a
   first-person narrator who participates in the action, what significant changes
   would occur if it were told from the point of view of an omniscient author?
   And, of course, *vice versa*. Note that first-person narrators do not know what
   other characters think. On the other hand, omniscient narrators know
   everything about the lives of the characters. How would the story you are
   writing about be changed if the viewpoint were changed?

2. What is the tone of the story? The first several paragraphs will establish that
   tone. Does the tone change with events, or remain fixed? How does the
   tone contribute to the effect of the story?

3. Who are the principal characters in the story (there will rarely be more than
   two in a short story—the other characters will often be portrayed sketchily;
   sometimes they are even stereotypes)? What functions do the minor characters serve? Do any of the characters change during the course of the story?
   How, and why?

4. What is the plot of the story? Do the events that constitute the plot emerge
   logically from the nature of the characters and circumstances, or are the
   plot elements coincidental and arbitrary?

5. What is the setting of the story? Does the setting play an important role in
   the story, or is it simply the place where things happen? You might ask yourself
   what the consequences of some other setting might be for the effectiveness
   of the story.

6. What is the theme of the story? This, finally, is the most significant question to answer. All of the elements of fiction—point of view, tone, character, plot, setting—have been marshaled to project a theme—the moral proposition the author wishes to advance. Although themeless stories exist, they
   are rare. When you write about fiction, or any literary form, you must resist
   the tendency to do the easiest thing—retell the plot, incident by incident.
   You must, instead, come to understand the artful devices the author uses to
   convey his theme, and, in your paper, reveal that understanding.

Poetry

1. Who is the speaker? What does the poem reveal about the speaker's character? In some poems the speaker may be nothing more than a voice meditating on a theme, while in others the speaker takes on a specific person-

ality. For example, the speaker in Shelley's "Ozymandias" is a voice meditating on the transitoriness of all things; except for the views he expresses in the poem, we know nothing about his character. The same might be said of the speaker in Hopkins's "Spring and Fall" but with this important exception: we know that he is older than Margaret and therefore has a wisdom she does not.

2. Is the speaker addressing a particular person? If so, who is that person, and why is the speaker interested in him or her? Many poems, like "Ozymandias," are addressed to no one in particular and therefore to anyone, any reader. Others, such as Donne's "A Valediction: Forbidding Mourning," while addressed to a specific person, reveal nothing about that person because the focus of the poem is on the speaker's feelings and attitudes. In a dramatic monologue (see "Glossary of Literary Terms"), the speaker usually addresses a silent auditor. The identity of the auditor will be important to the poem.

3. Does the poem have a setting? Is the poem occasioned by a particular event? The answer to these questions will often be "no" for lyric poems, such as Frost's "Fire and Ice." It will always be "yes" if the poem is a dramatic monologue or a poem that tells or implies a story, such as Tennyson's "Ulysses" and Lowell's "Patterns."

4. Is the theme of the poem stated directly or indirectly? Some poems, such as Frost's "Provide, Provide" and Owen's "Dulce et Decorum Est," use language in a fairly straightforward and literal way and state the theme, often in the final lines. Others, relying more heavily on figurative language and symbollism, may conclude with a statement of the theme that is more difficult to apprehend because it is made with figurative language and symbols. This difference will be readily apparent if you compare the final lines of the Frost and Owen poems mentioned above with, say, the final stanzas of Stevens's "Sunday Morning."

5. If the speaker is describing specific events, from what perspective (roughly similar to point of view in fiction) is he or she doing so? Is the speaker recounting events of the past or events that are occurring in the present? If past events are being recalled, what present meaning do they have for the speaker? These questions are particularly appropriate to the works in the section "Innocence and Experience," many of which contrast an early innocence with adult experience.

6. Does a close examination of the figurative language (see "Glossary of Literary Terms") of the poem reveal any patterns? Yeats's "Sailing to Byzantium" may begin to open up to you once you recognize the pattern of bird imagery. Likewise, Thomas's attitude toward his childhood in "Fern Hill" will be clearer if you detect the pattern of Biblical imagery that associates childhood with Adam and Eve before the fall.

7. What is the structure of the poem? Since narrative poems, those that tell stories, reveal a high degree of selectivity, it is useful to ask why the poet

has focused on particular details and left out others. Analyzing the structure of a nonnarrative or lyric poem can be more difficult because it does not contain an obvious series of chronologically related events. The structure of Thomas's "Fern Hill," for example, is based in part on a description of perhaps a day and a half in the speaker's life as a child. But more significant in terms of its structure is the speaker's present realization that the immortality he felt as a child was merely a stage in the inexorable movement of life toward death. The structure of the poem, therefore, will be revealed through an analysis of patterns of images (Biblical, color, day and night, dark and light) that embody the theme. To take another example, Marvell's "To His Coy Mistress" is divided into three verse paragraphs, the opening words of each ("Had we . . . ," "But . . . ," "Now therefore . . . ,") suggesting a logically constructed argument.

8. What do sound and meter (see "Glossary of Literary Terms") contribute to the poem? Alexander Pope said that in good poetry "the sound must seem an echo to the sense," a statement that is sometimes easier to agree with than to demonstrate. For sample analyses of the music of poetry, see the section on music in the appendix "Reading Poetry" (p. 1310) and the discussion of "Dover Beach" under formalist criticism (p. 1323) in "Three Critical Approaches."

9. What was your response to the poem on first reading? Did your response change after rereadings and study of the poem?

Drama

1. How does the play begin? Is the exposition presented dramatically through the interaction among characters, or novelistically through long, unrealistic, and unwieldy speeches that convey a lot of information, or through some trickery such as the reading of long letters or lengthy reports delivered by a messenger?

2. How does the information conveyed in exposition (which may occur at various moments throughout the play) establish the basis for dramatic irony— that is, the ironic response generated in an audience when it knows more than do the characters. For example, because we know that Iago is a villain in Shakespeare's *Othello*, we hear an ironic dimension in his speeches that the characters do not hear, and that irony is the source of much tension in the audience. An assessment of dramatic irony in a play makes an interesting and instructive writing assignment.

3. Who are the principal characters, and how are the distinctive qualities of each dramatically conveyed? Inevitably, there will be minor characters in a play. What function do they serve? A paper that thoughtfully assesses the role of minor characters can often succeed better than the attempt to ana-

lyze the major figures who may embody too much complexity to deal with in 1,000 words.

4. Where is the play set? Does it matter that it is set there? Why? Does the setting play some significant role in the drama, or is it merely a place, anyplace?

5. What is the central conflict in the play? How is it resolved? Do you need to know something of the historical circumstances out of which the play emerged, or something of the life of the author in order fully to appreciate the play? If so, how does that information enhance your understanding?

6. Since plays are usually written to be performed rather than read, what visual and auditory elements of the play are significant to your response? Obviously, if you are writing from a reading text, you will have to place yourself in the position of the director and the actors in order to respond to this aspect of drama.

7. What is the play's theme? How does the dramatic action embody that theme?

Note that any one of these questions might provoke an effective paper—one could do a thousand words on the settings of *Othello*, or the minor characters of *A Doll's House*, or the methods of exposition in *Oedipus Rex*. But each of those papers, to be successful, needs to relate the issues it deals with to the thematic force of the play. Plot summaries (except as a variety of note-taking) are unsatisfactory.

A Final Word

Many questions may be asked about literature. Your assignment may require you to compare and contrast literary works, to analyze the language of a work, to discuss the interaction of parts of a work, to discuss the theme of a work. Sometimes the instructor may give you free choice and ask simply that you write an essay on one of the pieces you read. This liberty will require that you create your own feasible boundaries—you will have to find a specific focus that suits the piece you choose and is manageable within a paper of the assigned length. But be sure that you do create boundaries—that, as we urged at the outset, you have a clear thesis.

Give yourself time. If you attempt to write your paper the night before it is due, you are unlikely to write a paper that is worth reading. Even professional writers rarely accomplish serious and thoughtful writing overnight. You must give yourself time to think before you write a draft. Let the draft age a bit before rewriting a final draft. If you do not allow yourself a reasonable time period, you will convert an assignment that has the potential to enlarge your understanding and to produce real pleasure into an obstacle that you will surely trip over.

Consider also that finally you have to feel something, know something, bring something of yourself to the assignment. We can discuss formal methods for dealing with the problem of writing essays—but if you bring neither awareness, nor information, nor genuine interest to the task, the essay will remain an empty form.

Suggestions For Writing

Fiction

1. Explicate the opening paragraph or page of a story in order to demonstrate how it sets the tone and anticipates what is to follow.

2. Select a story that uses a central symbol or symbolic event and analyze its function. Some suggestions:
   A. The tree in White's "The Second Tree from the Corner."
   B. The pond episode in Lawrence's "The Horse Dealer's Daughter."
   C. Iván's fall from the ladder in Tolstoy's "The Death of Iván Ilých."
   D. The panther at the end of Kafka's "A Hunger Artist."
   E. The underground in Wright's "The Man Who Lived Underground."
   F. The mysterious stranger in Lessing's "To Room Nineteen."

3. Select a story in which the narrative does not unfold chronologically and explain why.

4. Here are some suggestions for essays in comparison and contrast:
   A. Compare and contrast the nature and function of the dream sequences in Hawthorne's "My Kinsman, Major Molineux" and Wright's "The Man Who Lived Underground."
   B. Compare and contrast the function of art as revealed in Mann's "*Gladius Dei*" and Paley's "A Conversation with My Father."
   C. Compare and contrast the idea of "the hero" in Crane's "The Bride Comes to Yellow Sky" and Thurber's "The Greatest Man In the World."
   D. Compare and contrast the significance of the religious experience of the central characters in the final paragraphs of Tolstoy's "The Death of Iván Ilých" and Porter's "The Jilting of Granny Weatherall."
   E. Compare and contrast the attitude toward sexuality in Chopin's "The Storm" and Shaw's "The Girls in Their Summer Dresses."
   F. Compare and contrast the marriages in Shaw's "The Girls in Their Summer Dresses" and Mason's "Shiloh."

5. Write an essay on an especially interesting story title.

6. Did the ending of any story you read violate your expectations? What led you to those expectations? Do you find the author's ending more satisfactory than the one you had anticipated?

7. Select a story you feel is weak, and explain why you feel so. You might consider the credibility of the plot or of a character's behavior.

Poetry

1. Select a short lyric poem you found difficult, and explicate it line by line. Conclude with a paragraph or two describing how the process of explication helped you to clarify the meaning of the poem.

2. Here is a list of poems about poets and poetry. Select two and compare and contrast their treatment of the subject.
   Auden, "In Memory of W. B. Yeats"
   Conquest, "A Poem about a Poem about a Poem"
   Housman, "Terence, This Is Stupid Stuff"
   Moore, "Poetry"
   MacLeish, "Ars Poetica"
   Kennedy, "Ars Poetica"
   Francis, "Pitcher"
   Hamburger, "A Poet's Progress"
   Wallace, "In a Spring Still Not Written Of"
   Giovanni, "For Saundra"
   Cruz, "Today Is a Day of Great Joy"

3. The poems listed below tell or imply a story. Select one, and write out the story in your own words. Use your imagination to fill in details.
   Anonymous, "Bonny Barbara Allen"
   Anonymous, "Edward"
   Tennyson, "Ulysses"
   Browning, "My Last Duchess"
   Hardy, "The Ruined Maid"
   Lowell, "Patterns"
   Eliot, "The Love Song of J. Alfred Prufrock"
   Owen, "Dulce et Decorum Est"
   Wright, "Between the World and Me"
   Wallace, "Gwen"

4. Analyze a poem in which the author uses a particular kind of diction. Identify the pattern, and explain how it functions in the poem. Some suggestions:
   A. The language of bureaucracy in Auden's "The Unknown Citizen" or Frost's "Departmental."
   B. Contrasting patterns of diction in Reed's "Naming of Parts."
   C. Colloquial and formal diction in Hughes's "Same in Blues."
   D. Formal diction in Brooks's "The Sundays of Satin-Legs Smith."
   E. Colloquial diction in Jordan's "A Poem About Intelligence for My Brothers and Sisters."
   F. Prosaic diction in Forché's "The Colonel" or Kirby's "The Last Song on the Jukebox."

5. As an exercise to illuminate the importance of connotation, select a poem that you like, identify some of its key words, and then consult a dictionary

or thesaurus for synonyms of those key words. Reread the poem, substituting the synonyms for the words the poet used (for purposes of this exercise, ignore the fact that the synonyms may have more or fewer syllables and thus alter the rhythm). Write an essay analyzing the effects of your substitutions. Provide a sample of the rewritten poem.

6. Select one of the following titles for an essay in comparison and contrast.
   A. The Cost of Conformity: Dickinson's "What Soft—Cherubic Creatures" and Cummings's "the Cambridge ladies who live in furnished souls."
   B. The Psychology of Hate: Blake's "A Poison Tree" and Dickinson's "Mine Enemy Is Growing Old."
   C. The Meaning of Love: Marvell's "To His Coy Mistress" and Donne's "A Valediction: Forbidding Mourning."
   D. The Logic of Love: Donne's "The Flea" and Marvell's "To His Coy Mistress."
   E. The Images of Love: Shakespeare's Sonnet 130 and Millay's "Love Is Not All."
   F. In Praise of a Beloved: Frost's "The Silken Tent" and Roethke's "I Knew a Woman."
   G. The Death of Love: Sexton's "The Farmer's Wife" and Wallace's "Gwen."
   H. Remembering Childhood: Frost's "Birches" and Thomas's "Fern Hill."
   I. What the Young Can Never Understand: Rich's "The Middle-aged" and Wallace's "In a Spring Still Not Written Of."
   J. The Woman's Role: Swenson's "Women" and Sexton's "Cinderella."
   K. The Meaning of Nature: Dickinson's "Apparently with No Surprise" and Frost's "Design."
   L. The Meaning of Old Age: Arnold's "Growing Old" and Yeats's "Sailing to Byzantium."
   M. Untimely Death: Frost's " 'Out, Out—' " and Housman's "To an Athlete Dying Young" or Ransom's "Bells for John Whiteside's Daughter" and Roethke's "Elegy for Jane."

7. Analyze the allusions in a poem. Include in your discussion an explanation of the allusion and what it contributes to the poem. Some suggestions:
   Eliot's "The Love Song of J. Alfred Prufrock."
   Auden's "The Unknown Citizen."
   Frost's "Provide, Provide."
   Reid's "Curiosity."
   Milton's Sonnet XVII.
   Wordsworth's "The World Is Too Much with Us."
   Cummings's "the Cambridge ladies who live in furnished souls."
   Arnold's "Dover Beach."
   Plath's "Daddy."
   Yeats's "Sailing to Byzantium."

Frost's " 'Out, Out—'."
Brooks's "The Sundays of Satin-Legs Smith."
de Andrade's "Ballad of Love Through the Ages."

8. Analyze the use of irony in a poem. Some suggestions:
Blake's "The Chimney Sweeper."
Browning's "My Last Duchess."
Arnold's "Growing Old."
Hardy's "The Ruined Maid."
Robinson's "Richard Cory."
Frost's " 'Out, Out—'."
Swenson's "Women."
Bishop's "One Art."
Holden's "Seaman, 1941."

9. Analyze the use of one form of figurative language in a poem. Some sug-
gestions:
   A. Hyperbole in Burns's "A Red, Red Rose" or Marvell's "To His Coy
   Mistress."
   B. Simile and metaphor in Donne's "A Valediction: Forbidding Mourn-
   ing," Marvell's "To His Coy Mistress," Frost's "The Silken Tent,"
   Burns's "A Red, Red Rose," Keats's "On First Looking into Chap-
   man's Homer," Shakespeare's sonnets 18 and 130, MacLeish's "Ars
   Poetica," or Cummings's "o sweet spontaneous."
   C. Symbols in Waller's "Go Lovely Rose!" Blake's "The Tyger," Yeats's
   "The Second Coming," Frost's "Fire and Ice," Lowell's "Patterns,"
   Reid's "Curiosity," or Meinke's "Advice to My Son."
   D. Paradox in Wallace's "In a Spring Still Not Written Of," Shake-
   speare's sonnet 138, Meinke's "Advice to My Son," Yeats's "Easter
   1916," Blake's "The Tyger," Stevens's "Peter Quince at the Clavier,"
   Stevens's "Sunday Morning," or Donne's "Death, Be Not Proud."

10. Look carefully at the reproduction of Breughel's painting *The Fall of Icarus*
(p. 1155), and jot down your impressions of it. Include a sentence or two
on the "statement" you think Breughel is making. Now read Auden's poem
"Musée des Beaux Arts." In an essay, compare your impressions of the
painting with those of the poet. If the poem taught you something about
the painting, include that in your essay.

Drama

1. Explicate the opening scene of a play in order to demonstrate how the dramatist lays the groundwork for what is to follow. Some questions you might
consider: What information necessary to understanding the action are we

given? What do we learn about the characters and their relationships? Do settings and costumes contribute to the exposition?

2. Analyze a play in order to show how nonverbal elements, such as costumes and stage sets, contribute to the theme.

3. Select a minor character in a play, and analyze that character's function. Some possibilities: Roderigo in *Othello*; Dr. Rank in *A Doll's House*; Mrs. Higgins in *Pygmalion*; Uncle Ben in *Death of a Salesman*; Jim and Pete in *End of the World*.

4. Analyze the language of a play for patterns of imagery that contribute to the development of character, mood, or the theme. Some suggestions: images of bestial sexuality in Shakespeare's *Othello*; images of blindness and seeing in Sophocles's *Oedipus Rex*; images of the natural world associated with the Knight on the one hand, and Jof and Mia on the other in Bergman's *The Seventh Seal*.

5. Assume you are the director of one of the plays in this anthology. For one of the major characters, write a set of director's notes intended for the actor playing the role, in which you describe your conception of how the role should be played.

6. In an essay, describe the playwright's method for achieving dramatic irony in one of the plays you have read.

7. When you attend a performance of a play, you are usually given a program indicating, among other things, the number of acts, the elapsed time between acts, the time and place of the action. It will not include the stage directions of the printed version of the play. Examine the stage directions of a play, and suggest how a director might convey in a performance what the dramatist describes in the stage directions.

8. If you have the opportunity to see the film version of any of the works in this anthology, write an essay evaluating the success or failure of the film adaptation. Some suggestions:
   A. What did the film adaptation omit? Can you suggest why?
   B. What did the film adaptation add? Can you suggest why?
   C. Melville's "Bartleby the Scrivener" is a first-person narration. How does the film director deal with the problem of the narrative voice?
   D. Write an essay on the general problems of transposing a story into a film.

And one final general question: One of the commonly accepted notions of art is that it helps us to clarify our own feelings, to give us in vivid and memorable form what we had perhaps felt or thought only vaguely. Select a work (one that you found especially relevant to your own life), and describe how it clarified your own feelings.

Some Matters of Form

Titles

The first word and all main words of titles have their first letters capitalized. Ordinarily (unless, of course, they are the first or last word), articles (*a*, *an*, and *the*), prepositions (*in*, *on*, *of*, *with*, *about*, etc.), and conjunctions (*and*, *but*, *or*, etc.) do not have their first letters capitalized.

The titles of parts of larger collections, short stories, poems, articles, essays, and songs are enclosed in quotation marks.

The titles of plays, books, movies, periodicals, operas, paintings, and newspapers are italicized. In typed and handwritten manuscripts, italics are represented by underlining.

The title you give your own essay is neither placed in quotation marks nor underlined. However, a quotation used as a part of your title would be enclosed in quotation marks (see the following section on quotations). Similarly, the title of a literary work used as a part of your title would be either placed in quotation marks or underlined depending on the type of work it is.

Quotations

Quotation marks indicate you are transcribing someone else's words; those words must, therefore, be *exactly* as they appear in your source.

As a general rule, quotations of not more than four lines of prose or two lines of poetry are placed between quotation marks and incorporated in your own text:

> At the climactic moment, Robin observes "an uncovered cart.
> There the torches blazed the brightest, there the moon shone
> out like day, and there, in tar-and-feathery dignity, sat his
> kinsman, Major Molineux!"

If you are quoting two lines of verse in your text, indicate the division between lines with a slash:

> Prufrock hears the dilletantish talk in a room where "the
> women come and go/Talking of Michelangelo."

Longer quotations are indented five typewriter spaces and can be single-spaced. They are not enclosed in quotation marks, since the indentation signals a quotation.

As noted above, anything quoted, whether enclosed in quotation marks or indented, must be reproduced exactly. If you insert anything—even a word— the inserted material must be placed within brackets. If you wish to omit some material from a passage in quotation marks, the omission (ellipsis) must be indicated by three spaced periods: . . . (an ellipsis mark). When an ellipsis occurs between complete sentences or at the end of a sentence, a fourth period, indicating the end of the sentence, should be inserted.

Full quotation from original:

> "Richard Wright, like Dostoevsky before him, sends his hero underground to discover the truth about the upper world, a world that has forced him to confess to a crime he has not committed."

With insertion and omissions:

> "Richard Wright . . . sends his hero [Fred Daniels] under-ground to discover the truth about the upper world . . . ."

Use a full line of spaced periods to indicate the omission of a line or more of poetry (or of a whole paragraph or more of prose):

> For I have known them all already, known them all——
> Have known the evenings, mornings, afternoons,
> I have measured out my life with coffee spoons;
>
> . . . .
>
> And I have known the eyes already, known them all——
> The eyes that fix you in a formulated phrase.

Periods and commas are placed *inside* quotation marks:

> In "My Oedipus Complex," the narrator says, "The war was the most peaceful period of my life."

Other punctuation marks go outside the quotation marks unless they are part of the material being quoted.

For poetry quotations, provide the line number or numbers in parentheses immediately following the quotation:

> With ironic detachment, Prufrock declares that he is "no prophet" (line 83).

Documentation

You must acknowledge the source of ideas you paraphrase and material you quote. Such acknowledgments are extremely important, for even an unintentional failure to give formal credit to others for their words or ideas can leave you open to an accusation of plagiarism—that is, the presentation of someone else's ideas as your own.

If you use published works as you prepare your paper, you should list those sources as the last page of your essay. Then, in the body of your essay, you will use parenthetical citations that refer to the works you quote or paraphrase. Here is a sample bibliography that illustrates the mechanical form for a list of citations. These samples will probably satisfy your needs, but if you use different kinds of source material, you should consult Joseph Gibaldi and Walter S. Achtert, *MLA Handbook for Writers of Research Papers*, 2nd ed. (New York: The Modern Language Association of America, 1984). That *Handbook* provides sample entries for every imaginable source.

Works Cited

Abcarian, Richard, and Marvin Klotz, eds. Literature: The Human Experience. 4th ed. New York: St. Martin's, 1986.

Cooper, Wendy. Hair, Sex, Society, Symbolism. New York: Stein, 1971.

Fiedler, Leslie. "Come Back to the Raft Ag'in, Huck Honey." Partisan Review 15 (1948): 664—671.

Joyce, James. "Araby." Literature: The Human Experience. 3rd ed. Eds. Richard Abcarian and Marvin Klotz. New York: St. Martin's, 1982. 67—71.

———. Dubliners. Eds. Robert Scholes and A. Walton Litz. New York: Penguin, 1976.

The first of these citations is this book. You would use it if you used materials from the editors' introduction or critical appendices. The entry illustrates the form for citing a book with two editors. Note that the first editor's name is presented surname first, but the second is presented with the surname last.

The second entry illustrates the form for citing a book with one author. The third gives the form for an article published in a periodical (note that the title of the article is in quotes and the title of the journal is underlined). The fourth entry shows how to cite a work included in an anthology. The fifth citation, because it is by the same author as the fourth, begins with three hyphens in place of the author's name.

The following paragraph demonstrates the use of parenthetical citations.

Leslie Fiedler's controversial view of the relationship between Jim and Huck (669—670) uses a method often discussed by other critics (Abcarian and Klotz 1207—1208). Cooper's 1971 study (180) raises similar issues, but such methods are not useful when one deals with such a line as "North Richmond

```
Street, being blind, was a quiet street except at the hour
when the Christian Brothers' School set the boys free"
(Joyce, "Araby" 67). But when Joyce refers to the weather
(Dubliners 224), the issue becomes clouded.
```

This rather whimsical paragraph illustrates the form your parenthetical citations should take. The first citation gives only the page reference, which is all that is necessary, because the author's name is given in the text and only one work by that author appears in the list of works cited.

The second citation gives the editors' names and thus identifies the work being cited. It then indicates the appropriate pages.

The third citation, because the author's name is mentioned in the text, gives only a page reference.

The fourth citation must provide the author's name *and* the work cited, because two works by the same author appear in the bibliography.

The last citation, because it refers to an author with two works in the list of works cited, gives the name of the work and the page where the reference can be found.

In short, your parenthetical acknowledgement should contain (1) the *minimum* information required to lead the reader to the appropriate work in the list of works cited and (2) the location within the work to which you refer.

Rather than parenthetical references, some instructors may prefer footnotes (or endnotes). Here is the same paragraph documented with footnotes.

```
    Leslie Fiedler's controversial view of the relationship
between Jim and Huck[1] uses a method often discussed by other
critics.[2] Cooper's 1971 study[3] raises similar issues, but
such methods are not useful when one deals with such a line
as "North Richmond Street, being blind, was a quiet street
except at the hour when the Christian Brothers' School set
the boys free."[4] But when Joyce refers to the weather,[5] the
issue becomes clouded.
    [1]"Come back to the Raft Ag'in, Huck Honey," Partisan Re-
view 15 (1948): 664–671.
    [2]Richard Abcarian and Marvin Klotz, eds., Literature: The
Human Experience (New York: St. Martin's, 1982) 1207–1208.
    [3]Hair, Sex, Society, Symbolism (New York: Stein, 1971)
180.
    [4]James Joyce, "Araby," Literature: The Human Experience,
eds. Richard Abcarian and Marvin Klotz (New York: St. Mar-
tin's, 1982) 67.
    [5]Dubliners, eds. Robert Scholes and A. Walton Litz (New
York: Penguin, 1976) 224.
```

Note that when the author's name is given in the text, you do not have to repeat it in the footnote. Subsequent references to a work generally require only the surname of the author (or authors, editor, or editors) and the page number; thus:

⁴Cooper 175.

If you need to find a model for a different kind of source, don't despair. Simply refer to the MLA Handbook (1984).

The main thing to remember about footnoting, and about citations in general, is that the object is to give credit to others wherever it is due and to enable your reader to go directly to your sources, if he or she wishes to do so, as quickly and easily as possible.

Summing Up: A Checklist

1. Start early. You're going to need time for thinking, time for reading and taking notes, time for writing, and (very important) time for breaks between steps.

2. Read the work carefully, and more than once.

3. If you are allowed to choose a topic, choose one that interests you and that you can explore in some depth in a paper of the assigned length. If you have trouble finding a topic, ask yourself as many questions as you can about the work: *What* is it about? *Who* is it about? *Why* do I respond to it as I do? And so forth. Many kinds of questions have been suggested in the preceding pages, and there are numerous questions following the selections and at the ends of the five main sections in this anthology.

4. Convert your topic into a clearly defined thesis: a proposition you intend to argue for and support with evidence from the work. If you have trouble shaping a thesis, try the technique of free writing—forget about form and just scribble down all your thoughts and opinions: what you like, what you don't like, anything at all. Then ask yourself what made you think or feel as you do.

5. Once you have a thesis, reread the work and take careful notes on three-by-five-inch cards, one note to a card, with a page (or, for poetry, line) reference and a short descriptive heading to remind you of the note's significance. Then arrange the cards in the order that seems appropriate to follow in your essay.

6. Start writing, and keep going. This is a rough draft—essentially a blueprint—and is for your eyes only, so don't worry about formalities and polishing. The point is to get your ideas down on paper in approximately the

right order. If making a rough outline first will help you, do it. If spontaneous writing works better, do that. But do get a clear statement of your thesis into your first paragraph; it will guide you as you write, since everything you write will (or should) be related to it.

7. Take a break. Let the rough draft cool for at least a few hours, preferably overnight. When you come back to it, you'll be refreshed and you'll think more clearly. You may find that you want to do some reorganizing or add or delete material. You may also want to go back and reread or at least take another look at the work you're writing about.

8. Now, more carefully, working from your rough draft, write a second draft. This will be fuller, clearer, more polished. You'll have a chance to revise (assuming you followed step 1, above), so don't get unnecessarily bogged down; but write this version *as if* it were the version your reader will see. This version, when finished, should be logically and clearly organized. The point of each paragraph should be clear—well expressed and well supported by details or examples—and its relationship to the thesis should be apparent. Transitions between paragraphs should be supplied wherever necessary to make the argument progress smoothly. Quotations should be in place and accurately transcribed.

9. Take a break. This time allow the draft to age for two or three days. At the moment, you're too close to the draft to read it objectively.

10. Pick up the draft as if you were the reader and had never seen it before. Now you will make your final revisions. More than polishing is involved here. This is the time to cut out, mercilessly, things that are not pertinent to your discussion, no matter how interesting or well written they may be. Putting yourself in your reader's place, clarify anything that is vague or ambiguous. Make sure each word is the most precise one you could have chosen for your purpose. Watch, too, for overkill—points that are driven into the ground by too much discussion or detail. Finally, no matter how careful you think you have been, check all your quotations and citations for accuracy. Instructors—rightly—take these things seriously.

11. Type or neatly write out in ink the final copy for submission to your instructor, taking care to follow any special instructions about format that you have been given. Don't rush; be meticulous. When you have finished, proofread the final copy very carefully, keeping an eye out for errors in spelling or punctuation, omitted words, disagreement between subjects and verbs or between pronouns and antecedents, and other flaws (such as typographical errors) that will detract from what you have worked so hard to write.

Glossary of Literary Terms

Alexandrine   See Meter.

Allegory   A form of symbolism in which ideas or abstract qualities are represented as characters in a narrative and dramatic situation, resulting in a moral or philosophic statement.

    Ingmar Bergman, *The Seventh Seal*, p. 1173

Alliteration   The repetition within a line or phrase of the same initial consonant sound.

    Death, thou shalt die.—John Donne, "Death, Be Not Proud," l. 14, p. 1118
    And mouth with myriad subtleties—Paul Laurence Dunbar, "We Wear the Mask," l. 5, p. 528

Allusion   A reference, explicit or indirect, to something outside the work itself. The reference is usually to some famous person, event, or other literary work.

    No! I am not Prince Hamlet, nor was meant to be—T. S. Eliot, "The Love Song of J. Alfred Prufrock," l. 111, p. 844
    W. H. Auden, title of "The Unknown Citizen," p. 539

Ambiguity   A phrase, statement, or situation that may be understood in two or more ways. As a literary device, it is used to enrich meaning or achieve irony.

    my Uncle Sol imitated the
    skunks in a subtle manner

    or by drowning himself in the watertank—E. E. Cummings, "nobody loses all the time," ll. 24–26, p. 1150

Anapest   See Meter.

Antistrophe   See Strophe.

Apostrophe   A direct address to a person who is absent or to an abstract or inanimate entity.

    How oft, in spirit, have I turned thee,
    O sylvan Wye! thou wanderer through the woods—William Wordsworth, "Lines Composed a Few Miles Above Tintern Abbey," ll. 55–56, p. 118
    John Donne, "Death, Be Not Proud," p. 1118

Archetype   Themes, images, and narrative patterns that are universal and thus embody some enduring aspects of human experience. Some of these themes are the death and rebirth of the hero, the underground journey, and the search for the father.

Assonance   The repetition of vowel sounds in a line, stanza, or sentence.

    His lesions are legion—Gwendolyn Brooks, "The Children of the Poor," Stanza II, l. 17, p. 548
    W. H. Auden, *from* "Five Songs," p. 852

Ballad   A narrative poem, originally of folk origin, usually focusing upon a climactic episode and told without comment. The most common form is a quatrain of alternating four- and three-stress iambic lines, with the second and fourth lines rhyming. Often the ballad will employ a *refrain*—that is, the last line of each stanza will be identical or similar.

"Edward," p. 1113

"Bonny Barbara Allan," p. 821

Blank Verse   Lines of unrhymed iambic pentameter.

William Wordsworth, "Lines Composed a Few Miles Above Tintern Abbey," p.
117

Cacophony   Harsh and discordant language. *Compare* Euphony.

Is perjured, murderous, bloody, full of blame,

Savage, extreme, rude, cruel, not to trust—William Shakespeare, Sonnet 129,
ll. 3–4, p. 827

Caesura   A strong phrasal pause within a line of verse.

There is a loveliness exists.

Preserves us.//Not for specialists.—W. D. Snodgrass, "April Inventory," ll. 59–
60, p. 152

Carpe Diem   Latin, meaning "seize the day." A work, generally a lyric poem, in which
the speaker calls the attention of his auditor (often a young girl) to the shortness of
life and youth and then urges her to enjoy life while there is time.

Andrew Marvell, "To His Coy Mistress," p. 835

Robert Herrick, "Corinna's Going A-Maying," p. 832

Catharsis   One of the key concepts in *The Poetics* of Aristotle by which he attempts to
account for the fact that representations of suffering and death in drama paradoxically
leave the audience feeling relieved rather than depressed. According to Aristotle, a
tragic hero arouses in the viewer feelings of "pity and fear," pity because the hero is
an individual of great moral worth, and fear because the viewer sees himself or herself
in the hero.

Central Intelligence   *See* Point of View.

Comedy   In drama, situations that are designed to delight and amuse rather than concern or sadden. Comedy usually is concerned with social values and ends happily.
Compare Tragedy.

Conceit   A figure of speech that establishes an elaborate parallel between unlike things.

John Donne, "A Valediction: Forbidding Mourning," ll. 25–36, p. 831

Conflict   The struggle of a protagonist, or main character, with forces that threaten to
destroy him or her. The struggle creates suspense and is usually resolved at the end
of the story. The force opposing the main character may be either another person—
the antagonist—(as in O'Connor's "My Oedipus Complex"), or society (as in Ellison's
" 'Repent, Harlequin!' Said the Ticktockman"), or natural forces (as in Malamud's
"Idiots First"), or an internal conflict within the main character (as in Conrad's "The
Secret Sharer")

Connotation   The associative and suggestive meanings of a word in contrast to its literal meaning. *Compare* Denotation.

Consonance   Repetition of the final consonant sounds in stressed syllables.

That night when joy began

Our narrowest veins to flush,

We waited for the flash

Of morning's levelled gun—W. H. Auden, *from* "Five Songs," ll. 1–4, 852

Couplet   A pair of rhymed lines.

Cease then, nor ORDER imperfection name:

Our proper bliss depends on what we blame.—Alexander Pope, *from* "An Essay
on Man," ll. 1–2, p. 518

Dactyl   *See* Meter.

Denotation   The literal, dictionary definition of a word. *Compare* Connotation.

Denouement   The final outcome or unraveling of the main conflict; literally, the "untying" of the plot following the climax.

Diction   The choice of words in a work of literature, generally applied to indicate such distinctions as abstract or concrete, formal or colloquial, literal or figurative.

Didactic   A term applied to works whose primary and avowed purpose is to teach or to persuade the reader of the truth of some philosophical, religious, or moral statement or doctrine.

Dimeter   *See* Meter.

Dramatic Distance   In fiction, the point of view that enables the reader to know more than the narrator of the story.

Dramatic Irony   *See* Irony.

Dramatic Monologue   A type of poem in which the speaker, who is not the poet, addresses another person (or persons) whose presence is known only from the speaker's words. Such poems are dramatic because the speaker interacts with another character at a specific time and place; they are monologues because the entire poem is uttered by the speaker.

> Robert Browning, "My Last Duchess," p. 122
> Matthew Arnold, "Dover Beach," p. 839
> T. S. Eliot, "The Love Song of J. Alfred Prufrock," p. 844

Elegy   Usually a poem lamenting the death of a particular person, but often used to describe meditative poems on the subject of human mortality.

> W. H. Auden, "In Memory of W. B. Yeats," p. 1152
> Thomas Gray, "Elegy Written in a Country Churchyard," p. 1118

End-rhyme   *See* Rhyme.

End-stopped Line   A line of verse that constitutes a complete logical and grammatical unit. A line of verse that does not constitute a complete syntactic unit is designated *run-on*. Thus, in the opening lines of Browning's "My Last Duchess":

> That's my last Duchess painted on the wall,
> Looking as if she were alive. I call
> That piece a wonder, now: . . . .

The opening line is end-stopped, while the second line is run-on, because the direct object of *call* "runs on" to the third line.

English Sonnet   *See* Sonnet.

Epode   *See* Strophe.

Euphony   Sounds that are pleasing to the ear. *Compare* Cacophony.

> Wallace Stevens, "Peter Quince at the Clavier," ll. 1–9, p. 139

Farce   A type of comedy, usually satiric, that relies on exaggerated character types, ridiculous situations, and, often, horseplay.

Figurative Language   A general term covering the many ways in which language is used nonliterally. *See* Hyperbole, Irony, Metaphor, Metonymy, Paradox, Simile, Symbol, Synecdoche, Understatement.

First-person Narrator   *See* Point of View.

Foot   *See* Meter.

Free Verse   Poetry, usually unrhymed, that does not adhere to the metric regularity of traditional verse.

> Walt Whitman, "Out of the Cradle Endlessly Rocking," p. 124

Hexameter   *See* Meter.

Hubris   In Greek tragedy, overweening pride usually exhibited in a character's defiance of the gods. Oedipus, in Sophocles's *Oedipus Rex*, is guilty of hubris.

Hyperbole   Exaggeration; overstatement. *Compare* Understatement.

>   on freeways fifty lanes wide—Lawrence Ferlinghetti, "In Goya's Greatest Scenes,"
>   l. 28, p. 549
>   Robert Burns, "A Red, Red Rose," p. 837

Iamb   *See* Meter.

Imagery   Narrowly, language that embodies an appeal to the senses, particularly sight.

>   William Shakespeare, Sonnet 18, p. 826
>   William Shakespeare, Sonnet 130, p. 828
>   Robert Frost, "Birches," p. 136
>   Wallace Stevens, "Peter Quince at the Clavier," p. 139

The term is often applied to all figurative language.

Internal Rhyme   *See* Rhyme.

Irony   Language in which the intended meaning is different from or opposite to the literal meaning. Verbal irony includes overstatement (hyperbole), understatement, and opposite statement.

>   As fair art thou, my bonnie lass,
>   So deep in luve am I;
>   And I will luve thee still, my dear,
>   Till a' the sea gang dry.—Robert Burns, "A Red, Red Rose," p. 837

>   The grave's a fine and private place,
>   But none, I think, do there embrace—Andrew Marvell, "To His Coy Mistress,"
>   ll. 31–32, p. 835

>   Was he free? Was he happy? The question is absurd:
>   Had anything been wrong, we should certainly have heard.—W. H. Auden, "The
>   Unknown Citizen," ll. 28–29, p. 539

Dramatic irony occurs when a reader knows things a character is ignorant of or when the speech and action of a character reveal the character to be different from what he or she believes himself or herself to be.

>   William Blake, "The Chimney Sweeper," p. 113
>   Robert Browning, "My Last Duchess," p. 122
>   William Shakespeare, *Othello*, Act III, Scene 3, p. 871

Italian Sonnet   *See* Sonnet.

Lyric   Originally, a song accompanied by lyre music. Now, a relatively short poem expressing the thought or feeling of a single speaker. Almost all of the nondramatic poetry in this anthology is lyric poetry.

Metaphor   A figurative expression consisting of two elements in which one element is provided with special attributes by being equated with a second unlike element.

>   If only I could nudge you from this sleep,
>   My maimed darling, my skittery pigeon—Theodore Roethke, "Elegy for Jane,"
>   ll. 18–19, p. 1156

Meter   Refers to recurrent patterns of accented and unaccented syllables in verse. A metrical unit is called a *foot*, and there are four basic accented patterns. An *iamb*, or *iambic foot*, consists of an unaccented syllable followed by an accented syllable (bĕfóre, tŏdáy.) A *trochee*, or *trochaic foot*, consists of an accented syllable followed by an unaccented syllable (fúnny, phántŏm). An *anapest,* or *anapestic foot*, consists of two unaccented syllables followed by an accented syllable (in the line "Ĭf evé | ĕry-thĭng háp | pĕns thăt cán't | bĕ dóne," the second and third metrical feet are anapests). A *dactyl*, or *dactyllic foot*, consists of a stressed syllable followed by two unstressed syllables (sýllăblĕ, métrĭcăl). One common variant, consisting of two stressed syllables, is called a *spondee*, or *spondaic foot* (dáybf̌eak, moónshíne).

Lines are classified according to the number of metrical feet they contain.

one foot	monometer
two feet	dimeter
three feet	trimeter
four feet	tetrameter
five feet	pentameter
six feet	hexameter (An iambic hexameter line is an *Alexandrine*.)

Here are some examples of various metrical patterns:

| Tŏ eách | hĭs súff | erĭngs: áll | arĕ mén, | *iambic tetrameter* |
| Cŏndemńed | ălíké | tŏ groán; | | *iambic trimeter* |

| Ońce ŭp | oń ă | mídnĭght | dréary̆, | whíle Ĭ | pónderĕd | | |
| wéak ănd | wéary̆ | | *trochaic octameter* |

| Ĭs thís | thĕ rég | ĭŏn, thís | thĕ soíl, | thĕ clíme, | *iambic pentmeter* |

| Fóllŏw ĭt | úttĕrly̆, | *dactyllic dimeter* |

| Hópe bĕ | yońd hópe: | *dimeter line—trochee and spondee* |

Metonymy   A figure of speech in which a word stands for a closely related idea. In the expression "The pen is mightier than the sword," *pen* and *sword* are metonyms for written ideas and military force respectively.

> Free hearts, free foreheads—you and I are old—Alfred, Lord Tennyson, "Ulysses," l. 49, p. 521

> . . . if you survive
> the shattered windshield and the bursting shell—Peter Meinke, "Advice to My Son," ll. 6–7, p. 157

Monometer   *See* Meter.

Near Rhyme   *See* Rhyme.

Octave   *See* Sonnet.

Ode   Usually a long, serious poem on exalted subjects, often in the form of an address.
> John Keats, "Ode to a Nightingale," p. 1124

Off Rhyme   *See* Rhyme.

Omniscient Narrator   *See* Point of View.

Onomatopoeia   Language that sounds like what it means. Words like *buzz*, *bark*, and *hiss* are onomatopoetic. Also, sound patterns that reinforce the meaning over one or more lines may be designated onomatopoetic.

> Is lust in action; and till action, lust
> Is perjured, murderous, bloody, full of blame—William Shakespeare, Sonnet 129, ll. 2–4, p. 827

> Wallace Stevens, "Peter Quince at the Clavier," stanza one, p. 139

Opposite Statement *See* Irony.
Overstatement *See* Hyperbole.

Paradox A statement that seems self-contradictory or absurd but is, somehow, valid.
> And death shall be no more; Death, thou shalt die—John Donne, "Death, Be Not Proud," l. 14, p. 1118

Pentameter *See* Meter.
Persona Literally "mask." The term is applied to a narrator in fiction (Sherwood Anderson's "I Want to Know Why") or speaker in a poem (Robert Browning's "My Last Duchess"). The persona's views may be different from the author's views.
Personification The attribution of human qualities to nature, animals, or things.
> Edmund Waller, "Go, Lovely Rose!" p. 834
> John Donne, "Death, Be Not Proud," p. 1118

Petrarchan Sonnet *See* Sonnet.
Plot A series of actions in a story or drama that bear a significant relationship to each other. E. M. Forster illuminates the definition: " 'The King died, and then the Queen died,' is a story. 'The King died and then the Queen died of grief,' is a plot."
Point of View The person or intelligence a writer of fiction creates to tell the story to the reader. The major techniques are:
> *First person*, where the story is told by someone, often, though not necessarily, the principal character, who identifies himself as "I."
>> Sherwood Anderson, "I Want to Know Why," p. 60
>
> *Third person*, where the story is told by someone (not identified as "I") who is not a participant in the action and who refers to the characters by name or as "he," "she," and "they."
>> Harlan Ellison, " 'Repent, Harlequin!' Said the Ticktockman," p. 499
>
> *Omniscient*, a variation on the third person, where the narrator knows everything about the characters and events, can move about in time and place as well as from character to character at will, and can, whenever he or she wishes, enter the mind of any character.
>> Leo Tolstoy, "The Death of Iván Ilých," p. 1023
>
> *Central intelligence*, another variation on the third person, where narrative elements are limited to what a single character sees, thinks, and hears.
>> Richard Wright, "The Man Who Lived Underground," p. 444

Quatrain A four-line stanza that may incorporate various metrical patterns.
> "Bonny Barbara Allan," p. 821
> Thomas Gray, "Elegy Written in a Country Churchyard," p. 1118

Refrain *See* Ballad.
Rhyme The repetition of the final stressed vowel sound and any sounds following (debate, relate; pelican, belly can) produces perfect rhyme. When rhyming words appear at the end of lines, the poem is *end-rhymed*. When rhyming words appear within one line, the line contains *internal rhyme*. When the correspondence in sounds is imperfect (heaven, given; began, gun), *off rhyme*, or *near rhyme*, is produced.
> Off rhyme: W. H. Auden, *from* "Five Songs," p. 852

Rhythm The alternation of accented and unaccented syllables in language. A regular pattern of alternation produces *meter*. Irregular alternation of stressed and unstressed syllables produces *free verse*.

Run-on Line   *See* End-stopped Line.

Satire   Writing in a comic mode that holds a subject up to scorn and ridicule, often with the purpose of correcting human vice and folly.

> E. E. Cummings, "the Cambridge ladies who live in furnished souls," p. 536
> W. H. Auden, "The Unknown Citizen," p. 539
> Robert Frost, "Departmental," p. 531
> Harlan Ellison, " 'Repent, Harlequin!' Said the Ticktockman," p. 499

Scansion   The analysis of the metrical or rhythmical pattern of a poem. *See* Meter.

Sestet   *See* Sonnet.

Setting   The place where the story occurs. Often the setting contributes significantly to the story; for example, the dank world of the sewers that Fred Daniels inhabits in "The Man Who Lived Underground" enables him to understand his relationship with the upper world.

Shakespearean Sonnet   *See* Sonnet.

Simile   A figurative expression in which an element is provided with special attributes through a comparison with something quite different. The words *like* or *as* create the comparison, e.g., "O My Luve's like a red, red rose."

> Robert Burns, "A Red, Red Rose," p. 837

Soliloquy   A dramatic convention in which an actor, alone on the stage, speaks his or her thoughts aloud.

> William Shakespeare, *Othello*, Iago's speech, Act I, Scene 3, p. 889

Sonnet   A lyric poem of fourteen lines, usually of iambic pentameter. The two major types are the Petrarchan (or Italian) and Shakespearean (or English). The *Petrarchan sonnet* is divided into an octave (the first eight lines, rhymed abbaabba) and a sestet (the final six lines, usually rhymed cdecde or cdcdcd). The *Shakespearean sonnet* consists of three quatrains and a concluding couplet, rhymed abab cdcd efef gg.

> William Shakespeare, Sonnets, pp. 826–828, 1115
> Robert Frost, "Design," p. 1144

Spondee   *See* Meter.

Stanza   The grouping of the lines of a poem in a recurring pattern of meter, rhyme, and number of lines. Among the most common are the *couplet* and the *quatrain*.

Stream of Consciousness   The narrative technique of some modern fiction which attempts to reproduce the full and uninterrupted flow of a character's mental process, in which ideas, memories, and sense impressions may intermingle without logical transitions. A characteristic of this technique is the abandonment of conventional rules of syntax and punctuation.

> Katherine Anne Porter, "The Jilting of Granny Weatherall," p. 1072

Strophe   In Greek tragedy, the unit of verse the chorus chanted as it moved to the left in a dance rhythm. The chorus sang the *antistrophe* as it moved to the right and the *epode* while standing still.

Symbol   A thing or an action that embodies more than its literal, concrete meaning.

> Alastair Reid, "Curiosity," p. 149
> Peter Meinke, "Advice to My Son," p. 157

Synecdoche   A figure of speech in which a part is used to signify the whole.

> Perhaps in this neglected spot is laid
>   Some heart once pregnant with celestial fire;

Hands that the rod of empire might have swayed,
> Or waked to ecstacy the living lyre.—Thomas Gray, "Elegy Written in a Country
> Churchyard," ll. 45–48, p. 1118

Synesthesia   In literature, the description of one kind of sensory experience in terms of another. Taste might be described as a color or a song.
> John Keats, "Ode to a Nightingale," stanza two, p. 1125

Tetrameter   *See* Meter.

Theme   The moral proposition that a literary work is designed to advance. The theme of Milton's *Paradise Lost* is to "justify the ways of God to men." The theme of Joseph Conrad's "The Secret Sharer" might be briefly stated: The recognition of complex moral ambiguities is essential to maturity.

Third-person Narrator   *See* Point of View.

Tone   The attitude embodied in the language a writer chooses. The tone of a work might be sad, joyful, ironic, solemn, playful.
> Compare: Matthew Arnold, "Dover Beach," p. 839, with Anthony Hecht, "The
> Dover Bitch," p. 856

Tragedy   The dramatic representation of serious and important actions that bring misfortune to the chief character. Aristsotle saw tragedy as the fall of a noble figure from a high position as the result of a flaw in his character. *Compare* Comedy.

Trimeter   *See* Meter.

Trochee   *See* Meter

Understatement   A figure of speech that represents something as less important than it really is. *Compare* Hyperbole.
> . . . This grew; I gave commands;
> Then all smiles stopped together. . . .—Robert Browning, "My Last Duchess,"
> ll. 45–46, p. 123

Villanelle   A French verse form of nineteen lines (of any length) divided into six stanzas—five triplets and a final quatrain—employing two rhymes and two refrains. The refrains consist of lines one (repeated as lines six, twelve, and eighteen) and three (repeated as lines nine, fifteen, and nineteen).
> Dylan Thomas "Do Not Go Gentle into That Good Night," p. 1158
> Catherine Davis, "After a Time," p. 1162

Acknowledgments (continued from page iv)

"The Last Laugh" and "Dulce et Decorum Est" from *The Collected Poems of Wilfred Owen* edited by C. Day Lewis, together with the early version of "Last Words" by Wilfred Owen. Reprinted by permission of the Owen Estate and Chatto and Windus Ltd.

JONATHAN CLOWES LIMITED: "To Room Nineteen" from *A Man and Two Women* by Doris Lessing. Copyright © 1963 Doris Lessing. Reprinted by permission of Jonathan Clowes Ltd., London, on behalf of Doris Lessing.

TOBY COLE: "War" from *The Medal & Other Stories* by Luigi Pirandello. Reprinted by permission of the Pirandello Estate and Toby Cole, agent. © E. P. Dutton, N.Y.

CATHERINE DAVIS: "After a Time" by Catherine Davis. Reprinted by permission of the author.

DODD, MEAD & COMPANY: "A Summer Tragedy" by Arna Bontemps. Reprinted by permission of Dodd, Mead & Company, Inc. from *The Old South* by Arna Bontemps. Copyright 1933 by Arna Bontemps. Copyright renewed 1961 by Arna Bontemps. Copyright © 1973 by Alberta Bontemps, Executrix.

"We Wear the Mask" by Paul Laurence Dunbar. Reprinted by permission of Dodd, Mead & Company, Inc. from *The Complete Poems of Paul Laurence Dunbar*.

Pygmalion by Bernard Shaw. Copyright 1913, 1914, 1916, 1930, 1941, 1944 George Bernard Shaw. Copyright 1957, The Public Trustee as Executor of the Estate of George Bernard Shaw. Copyright © 1972, The Trustees of the British Museum, The Governors and Guardians of the National Gallery of Ireland and Royal Academy of Dramatic Art. Reprinted by permission of Dodd, Mead & Company, Inc. and The Society of Authors for the Estate of George Bernard Shaw.

DOUBLEDAY: "Dolor" by Theodore Roethke. Copyright 1943 by Modern Poetry Association, Inc. from the book *The Collected Poems of Theodore Roethke* by Theodore Roethke. Reprinted by permission of Doubleday & Company, Inc.

"Elegy for Jane" by Theodore Roethke. Copyright 1950 by Theodore Roethke from the book *The Collected Poems of Theodore Roethke* by Theodore Roethke. Reprinted by permission of Doubleday & Company, Inc.

"I Knew a Woman" by Theodore Roethke. Copyright 1954 by Theodore Roethke from the book *The Collected Poems of Theodore Roethke*. Reprinted by permission of Doubleday & Company, Inc.

ALAN DUGAN: "Love Song: I and Thou" by Alan Dugan. Copyright © 1961 by Alan Dugan. Originally published in *Poems, 1961* by Yale University Press. Reprinted by permission of the author.

"Relic" by Ted Hughes. Reprinted by permission of Faber and Faber Ltd. from *Lupercal* by Ted Hughes.

"Rain" by Edward Thomas. Reprinted by permission of Faber & Faber Ltd., publishers of *Collected Poems* by Edward Thomas, and Myfanwy Thomas.

FARRAR, STRAUS & GIROUX, INC.: "The Sandman" from *Sadness* by Donald Barthelme. Copyright © 1972 by Donald Barthelme. Reprinted by permission of Farrar, Straus & Giroux, Inc.

"One Art" by Elizabeth Bishop reprinted by permission of Farrar, Straus & Giroux, Inc. "One Art" from *Geography III* by Elizabeth Bishop. Copyright © 1976 by Elizabeth Bishop. This poem originally appeared in *The New Yorker*.

"The Lottery" from *The Lottery* by Shirley Jackson. Copyright 1948 by Shirley Jackson. Copyright renewed © 1976 by Laurence Hyman, Barry Hyman, Mrs. Sarah Webster & Mrs. Joanne Schnurer. Reprinted by permission of Farrar, Straus & Giroux, Inc.

"Losses" and "The Death of the Ball Turret Gunner" from *The Complete Poems* by Randall Jarrell. Copyright 1945, 1948, 1969 by Mrs. Randall Jarrell. Copyright renewed © 1972, 1975 by Mrs. Randall Jarrell. Reprinted by permission of Farrar, Straus and Giroux, Inc.

End of the World by Arthur Kopit. Copyright © 1984 by Arthur Kopit. All rights reserved. Reprinted by permission of Hill and Wang, a division of Farrar, Straus & Giroux, Inc. CAUTION: Professionals and amateurs are hereby warned that *End of the World*, being fully protected under the copyright laws of the United States, the British Empire including the Dominion of Canada, and all other countries of the Copyright Union, is subject to royalty. All rights, including professional, amateur, motion picture, recitation, lecturing, public reading,

ica, the British Empire, including the Dominion of Canada, and all other countries which are signatories to the Universal Copyright Convention and the International Copyright Union, is subject to royalty. All rights, including professional, amateur, motion picture, recitation, lecturing, public reading, radio broadcasting, and television, are strictly reserved. Particular emphasis is laid on the question of readings, permission for which must be secured from the author's agent in writing. Inquiries on professional rights (except for amateur rights) should be addressed to Mr. Gilbert Parker, Curtis Brown, Ltd., 575 Madison Avenue, New York, New York 10022; inquiries on translation rights should be addressed to Harcourt Brace Jovanovich, Inc., Orlando, Florida 32887. The amateur acting rights of *The Misanthrope* are controlled exclusively by the Dramatists Play Service, Inc., 440 Park Avenue South, New York, New York. No amateur performance of the play may be given without obtaining in advance the written permission of the Dramatists Play Service, Inc., and paying the requisite fee.

HARPER & ROW: Selections from *The Children of the Poor* by Gwendolyn Brooks. Copyright 1949 by Gwendolyn Brooks Blakely. Reprinted by permission of Harper & Row, Publishers, Inc.

"The Sundays of Satin-Legs Smith" from *The World of Gwendolyn Brooks* by Gwendolyn Brooks. Copyright 1945 by Gwendolyn Brooks Blakely. Reprinted by permission of Harper & Row, Publishers, Inc.

"Incident" from *On These I Stand* by Countee Cullen. Copyright 1925 by Harper & Row, Publishers, Inc. Renewed 1953 by Ida M. Cullen. Reprinted by permission of Harper & Row, Publishers, Inc.

"The Colonel" from *The Country Between Us* by Carolyn Forché. Copyright © 1980 by Carolyn Forché. Reprinted by permission of Harper & Row, Publishers, Inc.

"To Aunt Rose" from *Collected Poems 1947–1980* by Allen Ginsberg. Copyright © 1958 by Allen Ginsberg. Reprinted by permission of Harper & Row, Publishers, Inc.

"Crow's First Lesson" from *New Selected Poems* by Ted Hughes. Copyright © 1971 by Ted Hughes. Reprinted by permission of Harper & Row, Publishers, Inc.

"Daddy" from *The Collected Poems of Sylvia Plath* edited by Ted Hughes. Copyright © 1963 by Ted Hughes. Reprinted by permission of Harper & Row, Publishers, Inc.

"Shiloh" (originally appeared in *The New Yorker*) from *Shiloh and Other Stories* by Bobbie Ann Mason. Copyright © 1982 by Bobbie Ann Mason. Reprinted by permission of Harper & Row, Publishers, Inc.

"The Second Tree From the Corner" from *The Second Tree From the Corner* by E. B. White. Copyright 1947 by E. B. White. Reprinted by permission of Harper & Row, Publishers, Inc.

HARVARD UNIVERSITY PRESS: Poems #465, "I Heard a Fly Buzz"; #1509," Mine Enemy Is Growing Old"; #341, "After Great Pain"; #435, "Much Madness"; #280, "I Felt a Funeral"; #923, "How the Waters Closed"; #288, "I'm Nobody"; #401, "What Soft—Cherubic Creatures"; #162, "Apparently with No Surprise," by Emily Dickinson. Reprinted by permission of the publishers and the Trustees of Amherst College from *The Poems of Emily Dickinson*, edited by Thomas H. Johnson, Cambridge, Mass.: The Belknap Press of Harvard University Press, Copyright 1951, © 1955, 1979, 1983 by the President and Fellows of Harvard College.

JOHN HAWKINS AND ASSOCIATES: "Between the World and Me" by Richard Wright. Copyright 1935 by *Partisan Review*. Reprinted by permission of John Hawkins & Associates, Inc., 71 West 23rd Street, New York, NY 10010. "The Man Who Lived Underground" from *Eight Men* by Richard Wright. Copyright © 1961 by Richard Wright, from *Eight Men* by Richard Wright, copyright © 1940 (T. Y. Crowell). Reprinted by permission of John Hawkins & Associates, Inc.

DAVID HIGHAM ASSOCIATES LIMITED: "Fern Hill" and "Do Not Go Gentle into That Good Night" by Dylan Thomas from *Collected Poems*, published by Dent. Reprinted by permission of David Higham Associates Limited.

ALAN HOLDEN: "Seaman, 1941" by Molly Holden. Sole copyright, Alan Holden.

HOLT, RINEHART AND WINSTON, PUBLISHERS: "After Apple-Picking"; "Birches"; "Provide, Provide"; "Out, Out—"; "The Silken Tent"; "Fire and Ice"; "Departmental"; "Design"; "Nothing Gold Can Stay," by Robert Frost. From *The Poetry of Robert Frost* edited by Edward Connery Lathem. Copyright 1916, 1923, 1930, 1939, © 1969 by Holt, Rinehart and Winston. Copyright 1936, 1942, 1944, 1951, © 1958 by Robert Frost. Copyright © 1964, 1967, 1970 by Lesley Frost Ballantine. Reprinted by permission of Holt, Rinehart and Winston, Publishers.

"When I Was One-and-Twenty," "To an Athlete Dying Young," and "Terence, This Is Stupid Stuff" by A. E. Housman. From "A Shropshire Lad"—authorized edition—from *The Collected Poems of* A. E. Housman. Copyright 1939, 1940, © 1965 by Holt, Rinehart and Winston. Copyright © 1967, 1968 by Robert E. Symons. Reprinted by permission of Holt, Rinehart and Winston, Publishers.

HOUGHTON MIFFLIN COMPANY: "Ars Poetica" from *New and Collected Poems 1917–1976* by Archibald MacLeish. Copyright © 1976 by Archibald MacLeish. Reprinted by permission of Houghton Mifflin Company.

"The Farmer's Wife" from *To Bedlam and Part Way Back* by Anne Sexton. Copyright © 1960 by Anne Sexton. Reprinted by permission of Houghton Mifflin Company.

"Cinderella" from *Transformations* by Anne Sexton. Copyright © 1971 by Anne Sexton. Reprinted by permission of Houghton Mifflin Company.

OLWYN HUGHES: "Daddy" from *Ariel* by Sylvia Plath, published by Faber and Faber, London. Copyright Ted Hughes, 1965.

INTERNATIONAL CREATIVE MANAGEMENT, INC.: "Myth" from *Breaking Open* by Muriel Rukeyser. Reprinted by permission of International Creative Management. Copyright © 1973.

VIRGINIA KIDD: "The Ones Who Walk Away from Omelas" by Ursula K. Le Guin. Copyright © 1973, 1975 by Ursula K. Le Guin; reprinted by permission of the author's agent, Virginia Kidd.

THE KILIMANJARO CORPORATION: " 'Repent, Halequin!' Said the Ticktockman" by Harlan Ellison. Copyright © 1966 by Harlan Ellison. Reprinted by arrangement with, and permission of, the Author and the Author's agent, Richard Curtis Associates, Inc., New York. All rights reserved.

DAVID KIRBY: "The Last Song on the Jukebox" from *Sarah Bernhardt's Leg* © David Kirby 1983.

ETHERIDGE KNIGHT: "Hard Rock Returns to Prison from the Hospital for the Criminal Insane" from *Poems From Prison* by Etheridge Knight. Reprinted by permission of the author.

ALFRED A. KNOPF, INC.: "Harlem" by Langston Hughes. Copyright 1951 by Langston Hughes. Reprinted from *Selected Poems of Langston Hughes*, by permission of Alfred A. Knopf, Inc.

"Gladius Dei" pages 181–193 by Thomas Mann. Copyright 1936 and renewed 1964 by Alfred A. Knopf, Inc. Reprinted from *Stories of Three Decades*, by Thomas Mann, by permission of Alfred A. Knopf, Inc.

"My Oedipus Complex" pages 282–292 by Frank O'Connor. Copyright 1950 by Frank O'Connor. Reprinted from *Collected Stories* by Frank O'Connor, by permission of Alfred A. Knopf, Inc. and John Daves.

"Bells for John Whiteside's Daughter" by John Crowe Ransom. Copyright 1924 by Alfred A. Knopf, Inc. and renewed 1952 by John Crowe Ransom. Reprinted from *Selected Poems, Third Edition, Revised and Enlarged*, by John Crowe Ransom, by permission of Alfred A. Knopf, Inc.

"April Inventory" by W. D. Snodgrass. Copyright 1957 by W. D. Snodgrass. Reprinted from *Heart's Needle*, by W. D. Snodgrass, by permission of Alfred A. Knopf, Inc.

"Sunday Morning" and "Peter Quince at the Clavier" by Wallace Stevens. Copyright 1923 and renewed 1951 by Wallace Stevens. Reprinted from *The Collected Poems of Wallace Stevens*, by permission of Alfred A. Knopf, Inc.

PHILIP LARKIN: "Aubade" by Philip Larkin, © Philip Larkin 1977.

THE ADELE LEONE AGENCY, INC.: "The Dead Ladies" by Mary Gordon, from *New American Poetry*, ed. Richard Monaco (1973).

LITTLE, BROWN AND COMPANY: "Very Like a Whale" from *Verses from 1929 On* by Ogden Nash. Copyright 1934 by The Curtis Publishing Company. By permission of Little, Brown and Company.

A *Doll's House* by Henrik Ibsen, translated by Otto Reinert. Copyright © 1977 by Otto Reinert. Reprinted from *Twenty-Three Plays: An Introductory Anthology*, edited by Otto Reinert and Peter Arnott, by permission of Little, Brown and Company (Inc.).

"Women" from *New and Selected Things Taking Place* by Mary Swenson. Copyright © 1968 by May Swenson. By permission of Little, Brown and Company in association with the Atlantic Monthly Press.

LIVERIGHT PUBLISHING CORPORATION: "the Cambridge ladies who live in furnished souls" and "O sweet spontaneous" by E. E. Cummings. Reprinted from *Tulips & Chimneys* by E. E. Cummings by permission of Liveright Publishing Corporation. Copyright 1923, 1925 and renewed 1951, 1953 by E. E. Cummings. Copyright © 1973, 1976 by the Trustees for the E. E. Cummings Trust. Copyright © 1973, 1976 by George James Firmage.

"nobody loses all the time" is reprinted from *IS 5 poems* by E. E. Cummings by permission of Liveright Publishing Corporation. Copyright 1926 by Horace Liveright. Copyright © 1954 by E. E. Cummings. Copyright © by the E. E. Cummings Trust. Copyright © 1985 by George James Firmage.

"Those Winter Sundays" is reprinted from *Angle of Ascent, New and Selected Poems* by Robert Hayden, with the permission of Liveright Publishing Corporation. Copyright © 1975, 1972, 1970, 1966 by Robert Hayden.

"Theater" is reprinted from *Cane* by Jean Toomer, with the permission of Liveright Publishing Corporation. Copyright 1923 by Boni & Liveright. Copyright renewed 1951 by Jean Toomer.

LOUISIANA STATE UNIVERSITY PRESS: "The Storm" by Kate Chopin. Reprinted by permission of Louisiana State University Press from *The Complete Works of Kate Chopin*, Volume II, edited by Per Seyersted, copyright 1969.

THE MACMILLAN COMPANY: "The Ruined Maid" and "Hap" by Thomas Hardy from *Collected Poems of Thomas Hardy*. Copyright 1925 by The Macmillan Company. Reprinted by permission of the Trustees of the Hardy Estate, Macmillan London & Basingstoke, and The Macmillan Company of Canada Limited, and by permission of The Macmillan Company of New York.

The Shadow of a Gunman taken from *The Complete Plays of Sean O'Casey, Volume 1.* Reproduced by permission of Macmillan, London and Basingstoke. Copyright in all countries signatory to the Berne Convention.

MACMILLAN PUBLISHING COMPANY, INC.: "The Ruined Maid" from *The Complete Poems of Thomas Hardy* edited by James Gibson (New York: Macmillan, 1978).

"Poetry" by Marianne Moore from *Collected Poems* by James Stepens. Reprinted with permission of Macmillan Publishing Company from *Collected Poems* by Marianne Moore. Copyright 1935 by Marianne Moore, renewed 1963 by Marianne Moore and T. S. Eliot.

"Mr. Flood's Party" by Edwin Arlington Robinson. Reprinted with permission of Macmillan Publishing Company from *Collected Poems* by Edwin Arlington Robinson. Copyright 1921 by Edwin Arlington Robinson, renewed 1949 by Ruth Nivison.

"Adam's Curse," "Leda and the Swan," and "Sailing to Byzantium" by William Butler Yeats. Reprinted with permission of Macmillan Publishing Co., Inc., from *Collected Poems* by William Butler Yeats. Copyright 1928 by Macmillan Publishing Company, renewed 1956 by Georgie Yeats. "Easter 1916" and "The Second Coming" reprinted with permission of Macmillan Publishing Company from *Collected Poems* by William Butler Yeats. Copyright 1924 by Macmillan Publishing Company, renewed 1952 by Bertha Georgie Yeats.

THE MARVELL PRESS: "Poetry of Departures" by Philip Larkin is reprinted from *The Less Deceived* by permission of The Marvell Press, England.

PETER MEINKE: "Advice to My Son" by Peter Meinke, from *Trying to Surprise God*, University of Pittsburgh Press 1981, © Peter Meinke.

ROBERT MEZEY: "My Mother" by Robert Mezey. From *The Door Standing Open* published by Houghton Mifflin Company and *White Blossoms* published by Cummington Press. Reprinted by permission of the author.

WILLIAM MORROW & COMPANY, INC.: "For Saundra" from *Black Feeling, Black Talk, Black Judgement* by Nikki Giovanni. Copyright © 1968, 1970 by Nikki Giovanni. By permission of William Morrow & Company.

"Revolutionary Dreams" from *The Women and The Men* by Nikki Giovanni. Copyright © 1970, 1974, 1975 by Nikki Giovanni. By permission of William Morrow & Company.

UNIVERSITY OF NEBRASKA PRESS: "For My Daughter" by Weldon Kees. Reprinted from *The Collected Poems of Weldon Kees*, by permission of University of Nebraska Press. Copyright © 1975 by the University of Nebraska Press.

newed 1968 by W. H. Auden. "Musée des Beaux Arts" Copyright 1940 and renewed 1968 by W. H. Auden. Reprinted from *W. H. Auden: Collected Poems*, edited by Edward Mendelson, by permission of Random House, Inc.

"The Lesson" from *Gorilla, My Love*, by Toni Cade Bambara. Copyright © 1972 by Toni Cade Bambara. Reprinted by permission of Random House, Inc.

"Today Is a Day of Great Joy" from *Snaps*, by Victor Hernandez Cruz. Copyright © 1969 by Victor Hernandez Cruz. Reprinted by permission of Random House, Inc.

"Dry September," pages 169–183. Copyright 1930 and renewed 1958 by William Faulkner. Reprinted from *The Collected Stories of William Faulkner*, by permission of Random House, Inc.

"Hurt Hawks" by Robinson Jeffers. Copyright 1928 and renewed 1956 by Robinson Jeffers. Reprinted from *The Selected Poetry of Robinson Jeffers*, by permission Random House, Inc.

"The Conscientious Objector" by Karl Shapiro. Copyright 1947 and renewed 1975 by Karl Shapiro. Reprinted from *Collected Poems, 1940–1978* by Karl Shapiro, by permission of Random House, Inc.

"Confession to Settle a Curse" from *The Aggressive Ways of the Casual Stranger* by Rosmarie Waldrop. Copyright © 1972 by Rosmarie Waldrop. Reprinted by permission of Random House, Inc.

The Glass Menagerie, by Tennessee Williams. Copyright 1945 by Tennessee Williams and Edwina D. Williams and renewed 1973 by Tennessee Williams. Reprinted by permission of Random House, Inc. CAUTION: Professionals and amateurs are hereby warned *The Glass Menagerie*, being fully protected under the copyright laws of the United States of America, the British Empire, including the Dominion of Canada, and all other countries of the Copyright Union, is subject to royalty. All rights, including professional, amateur, motion picture, recitation, lecturing, public reading, radio-broadcasting and the rights of translation into foreign languages, are strictly reserved. Particular emphasis is laid on the question of readings, permission for which must be secured from the author's agent in writing.

OTTO REINERT: *Othello* notes by Otto Reinert. Copyright 1964. Reprinted by permission of the author.

SATURDAY REVIEW: "Formal Application" by Donald Baker. © 1963 Saturday Review magazine. Reprinted by permission.

SHOCKEN BOOKS INC.: "The Penal Colony" by Franz Kafka, translated by Willa and Edwin Muir. Copyright © 1948, 1976 by Schocken Books Inc. Reprinted by permission of Schocken Books Inc.

LOUISE SCLOVE: "On the Vanity of Earthly Greatness" by Arthur Guiterman from *Gaily the Troubadour* (1936). Reprinted by permission of Louise H. Sclove.

CHARLES SCRIBNER'S SONS: "A Marriage" from *For Love: Poems 1950–1960* by Robert Creeley. Copyright © 1962 Robert Creeley. Reprinted with the permission of Charles Scribner's Sons.

"A Clean, Well-Lighted Place" from *The Short Stories of Ernest Hemingway* by Ernest Hemingway. Copyright 1933 Ernest Hemingway; copyright renewed © 1961 Mary Hemingway. Reprinted with the permission of Charles Scribner's Sons.

IRWIN SHAW: "The Girls in Their Summer Dresses" by Irwin Shaw. Reprinted by permission of the author.

SIMON & SCHUSTER, INC.: *The Seventh Seal* from *Four Screen Plays of Ingmar Bergman*. Copyright © 1960 by Ingmar Bergman. Reprinted by permission of Simon & Schuster, Inc.

"To Room Nineteen" from *A Man and Two Women* by Doris Lessing. Copyright © 1958, 1962, 1963 by Doris Lessing. Reprinted by permission of Simon & Schuster, Inc.

THE SOCIETY OF AUTHORS: "When I Was One-and-Twenty," "Terence, This is Stupid Stuff," and "To an Athlete Dying Young" by A. E. Houseman, from *Collected Poems*. Reprinted by permission of The Society of Authors as the literary representative of the Estate of A. E. Housman, and Jonathan Cape Ltd., publishers of A. E. Houseman's *Collected Poems*.

MRS. JAMES THURBER: "The Greatest Man in the World" by James Thurber. Copyright © 1935 James Thurber. Copyright © 1963 Helen W. Thurber and Rosemary Thurber Sauers. From *The Middle Aged Man on the Flying Trapeze*, published by Harper & Row. Originally printed in *The New Yorker*.

PICTURE CREDITS

Innocence and Experience

Conformity and Rebellion

Fiction, p. 384: Epoch, 1950 by Ben Shahn. Tempera on board, 52 × 31″. '51-31-5, Philadelphia Museum of Art: Purchased: Bloomfield Moore Fund.

Poetry, p. 516: Au Moulin Rouge. Le Depart du Quadrille, 1892, after a painting by Henri de Toulouse-Lautrec. Photograph, The Bettmann Archive.

Drama, p. 558: The Accused, 1886 by Odilon Redon. Charcoal, sheet: 21 × 14-⅝″. Collection, The Museum of Modern Art, New York. Acquired through the Lillie P. Bliss Bequest.

Love and Hate

Part opener, p. 724: Separation II, 1896 by Edvard Munch. Lithograph, 41 × 62.5 cm. Copyright Oslo Kommunes Kunstsamlinger. Munch Museet (OKK G/1 210-12).

Fiction, p. 730: A Husband Parting From His Wife and Child, 1799 by William Blake. Pen and watercolor on paper, 11-⅞ × 8-⅞″. '64-110-3, Philadelphia Museum of Art: Given by Mrs. William T. Tonner.

Poetry, p. 820: Midsummer Wall, 1966 by Jim Dine. Color lithograph on paper, 41-½ × 29-11⁄16″ (sheet). Collection of Whitney Museum of American Art. Gift of Mr. and Mrs. Herbert C. Lee. Acq. No. 66.103.

Drama, p. 870: The Return of the Prodigal Son, c. 1642 by Rembrandt van Rijn. Pen and wash in bistre with white gouache. Teylers Museum, Haarlem, Holland.

The Presence of Death

Part opener, p. 1018: The Death Chamber, 1896 by Edvard Munch. Lithograph, printed in black, 15-¼ × 21-⅝″. Collection, The Museum of Modern Art, New York. Gift of Abby Aldrich Rockefeller.

Fiction, p. 1022: Sacred to Washington, 1822 by Margarett Smith. Watercolor, 20-¼ × 16-½″. The Baltimore Museum of Art. Gift of Edgar William and Bernice Chrysler Garbisch, New York. BMA 1967.76.6.

Poetry, p. 1112: Orderly Retreat, 1943 by Philip Evergood. Oil, 40 × 25″. From the Carleton College Collections. Gift of the Encyclopedia Britannica.

p. 1155: Landscape with the Fall of Icarus, c. 1560 by Pieter Brueghel the Elder. Museum of Fine Arts, Brussels. Photograph, Art Resource, New York.

Drama, p. 1172: "The Dance of Death" from *The Seventh Seal*, directed by Ingmar Bergman. Film Still from The Museum of Modern Art/Film Stills Archive, New York.

p. 1258: Crazy Crate, photograph by Dr. Cochran.

p. 1267: Waterfall, 1961 by M. C. Escher. Lithograph, 38 × 30 cm. Haags Gemeentemuseum, 's Gravenhage, Holland. © M. C. Escher Heirs, c/o Cordon Art, Baarn, Holland.

Appendices

Opening, p. 1274: The Vanity of the Artist's Dream, 1830 by Charles Bird King. Oil on canvas, 36 × 30″. Courtesy of the Fogg Art Museum, Harvard University. Gift of Grenville L. Winthrop.

Cover: The False Mirror (Le Faux Miroir), 1928 by René Magritte. Oil on canvas, 21-¼″ × 31-⅞″. Collection, The Museum of Modern Art, New York. Purchase.

INDEX OF AUTHORS AND TITLES